THE WEST IN THE WORLD

A History of Western Civilization

CONNECT
by experiencing history

Students will experience history in a variety of ways:

- With *Connect History*, students are no longer simply reading—they can also interact online with text activities, engaging in a visual, auditory, and hands-on experience.

- Through its narrative approach and its features, *The West in the World* emphasizes that history is not just a collection of facts but is created from the ongoing detective work of historians examining evidence from the past.

- "Thinking About" boxes—exploring primary source documents, geography, art, and (new to this edition) science and technology—involve students actively and analytically in the learning process, guiding them to approach documentary and material evidence in the ways that working historians do.

- *Connect History* helps students confirm what they know and learn what they don't know through interactive exercises and review questions.

- *Connect History* builds critical thinking skills by placing students in a "critical mission" and asking them to examine, evaluate, and analyze the data in order to support a point of view.

- *Connect History* includes tools for understanding maps and geography, exploring primary source documents, and writing a research paper (including how to document sources and avoid plagiarism).

THE WEST IN THE WORLD
A History of Western Civilization

FOURTH EDITION

Dennis Sherman
John Jay College
City University of New York

Joyce Salisbury
University of Wisconsin–Green Bay

McGraw Hill

Connect
Learn
Succeed™

Published by McGraw-Hill, an imprint of The McGraw-Hill Companies, Inc., 1221 Avenue of the Americas, New York, NY 10020. Copyright © 2011, 2008, 2006, 2004, 2001. All rights reserved. No part of this publication may be reproduced or distributed in any form or by any means, or stored in a database or retrieval system, without the prior written consent of The McGraw-Hill Companies, Inc., including, but not limited to, in any network or other electronic storage or transmission, or broadcast for distance learning.

This book is printed on acid-free paper.

3 4 5 6 7 8 9 0 DOW/DOW 9 8 7 6 5 4 3 2

ISBN: 978-0-07338565-5
MHID: 0-07-338565-4

Vice President Editorial: *Michael Ryan*
Editorial Director: *William R. Glass*
Publisher: *Christopher Freitag*
Sponsoring Editor: *Matthew Busbridge*
Marketing Manager: *Stacy Best Ruel*
Director of Development: *Rhona Robbin*
Developmental Editors: *Arthur Pomponio, Sylvia Mallory*
Editorial Coordinators: *Briana Porco, Jaclyn Mautone*
Senior Production Editor: *Carey Eisner*
Art Editor: *Robin Mouat*
Illustrator: *Patti Isaacs*
Design Manager: *Laurie Entringer*
Interior Designer: *Maureen McCutcheon*
Cover Designers: *Laurie Entringer and David Carlson, Gearbox*
Lead Photo Research Coordinator: *Alexandra Ambrose*
Photo Researcher: *Judy Mason*
Buyer II: *Sherry L. Kane*
Composition: *10.5/12 Goudy Old Style by Laserwords Private Limited*
Printing: *45# New Era Matte Thin, R.R. Donnelley & Sons*

Cover: Top: © Mike Agliolo/Corbis; Middle: Detail from the Bayeux Tapestry, before 1082 (wool embroidery on linen), / Musee de la Tapisserie, Bayeux, France / The Bridgeman Art Library; Bottom: © Digital Vision/ Getty Images

Library of Congress Cataloging-in-Publication Data

Sherman, Dennis.
    The West in the world : a history of western civilization / Dennis Sherman, Joyce Salisbury. —4th ed.
        p. cm.
    Includes index.
    ISBN-13: 978-0-07-338565-5 (softcover : alk. paper)
    ISBN-10: 0-07-338565-4 (softcover : alk. paper)
    I. Salisbury, Joyce E. II. Title.
CB245.S465 2011b
909'.09821—dc22

                                                                    2010037320

The Internet addresses listed in the text were accurate at the time of publication. The inclusion of a Web site does not indicate an endorsement by the authors or McGraw-Hill, and McGraw-Hill does not guarantee the accuracy of the information presented at these sites.

www.mhhe.com

Dennis Sherman

DENNIS SHERMAN is Professor of History at John Jay College, the City University of New York. He received his B.A. (1962) and J.D. (1965) degrees from the University of California at Berkeley and his Ph.D. (1970) from the University of Michigan. He was Visiting Professor at the University of Paris (1978–1979, 1985). He received the Ford Foundation Prize Fellowship (1968–1969, 1969–1970), a fellowship from the Council for Research on Economic History (1971–1972), and fellowships from the National Endowment for the Humanities (1973–1976). His publications include *A Short History of Western Civilization*, Eighth Edition (coauthor), *Western Civilization: Sources, Images, and Interpretations*, Seventh Edition, *World History: Sources, Images, and Interpretations*, Fourth Edition, a series of introductions in the Garland Library of War and Peace, several articles and reviews on nineteenth-century French economic and social history in American and European journals, and several short stories in literary reviews. He is the recipient of John Jay College's *"Outstanding Teacher of the Year"* award.

Joyce Salisbury

JOYCE SALISBURY is Professor Emerita of History at the University of Wisconsin–Green Bay, where she taught history to undergraduates for more than twenty years. She received a Ph.D. in medieval history from Rutgers University in New Jersey. She is a respected historian who has published many articles and has written or edited more than ten books, including the critically acclaimed *Perpetua's Passion: Death and Memory of a Young Roman Woman, The Blood of Martyrs: Unintended Consequences of Ancient Violence, The Encyclopedia of Women in the Ancient World*, and *The Greenwood Encyclopedia of Daily Life*, which won many awards for its creative organization and timely presentation of the material. In 2010, Salisbury published a second edition of her classic work on the history of attitudes toward animals: *The Beast Within: Humans and Animals in the Middle Ages*. Salisbury is an award-winning teacher who was named *"Professor of the Year for Wisconsin in 1991"* by CASE (Council for Advancement and Support of Education), a prestigious national organization. Since retiring from the University of Wisconsin–Green Bay, Salisbury has taught twice on Semester at Sea, a program sponsored by the University of Virginia that teaches students as they circumnavigate the world. Salisbury brought a global perspective to the history of Western civilization while teaching abroad, and this edition of the book has benefited from her interaction with students as they make sense of our twenty-first-century global civilization.

ABOUT THE AUTHORS

What's the best way to write an interesting, accessible, and accurate account of the West's complex history? This question confronts everyone who approaches this huge and important task. On the one hand, we believed strongly that different authors' perspectives would give readers a sense of the richness of the past. On the other hand, we wanted a seamless narrative that read like a good story. We decided that a careful, two-author collaboration would best enable us to achieve both goals. We brought our different backgrounds, research interests, and teaching experiences to the table. We talked over our ideas and read and struggled with one another's words. Throughout, we never lost sight of our goal: to bring the compelling history of the West in the world to students of the twenty-first century.

A NOTE FROM THE AUTHORS

Dennis Sherman

I was in the twelfth grade in west Los Angeles when I first realized I had a flair for history. Our teacher wisely gave us much latitude in selecting topics for two lengthy papers. I chose ancient Egypt (I liked the National Geographic visuals) as my first topic and Tasmania as the second. (I was the only one who seemed to know that Tasmania was an island below Australia.) Assembling the material and writing the papers just came easily to me, as did any questions our history teacher posed in class (though I was an otherwise fading-into-the-background student). I more or less blundered into different majors in college and then slid through law school (which taught me how to be succinct) before returning to history. At the beginning of my first semester of graduate school, I met my advisor, who asked me what courses I wanted to take. I ticked off four selections: History of South Asia; Nineteenth-Century Europe; Twentieth-Century America; and European Intellectual History. "You're a generalist," he said. Indeed I was. He wisely counseled me to narrow my focus. However, throughout my studies and professional career I have found the big picture—the forest rather than the trees—the most interesting aspect of history.

A few years later I moved to the front of the classroom and, never forgetting what it was like to be a student, found my heart in teaching. Teaching and writing about the sweep of Western civilization within the broadest possible context has remained my greatest interest over the years. That is why I have written this book with Joyce.

Dennis Sherman

Joyce Salisbury

I grew up in Latin America (ten years in Brazil and five in Mexico). Through those years, I attended American schools filled with expatriates. There I studied a curriculum of Western culture, which in those days was equated with European history. But even as a young girl, I knew I wasn't getting the whole story. After all, we celebrated Mardi Gras (a Christian holiday) to an African drumbeat, and the national museum of Mexico was bursting with Napoleonic artifacts. I knew that the history and culture of the West was intimately tied to that of the rest of the world.

In the more than twenty years that I've been teaching Western civilization, I've brought this global perspective to the classroom, and now Dennis and I have brought it to this book. It is very satisfying to me to work with my students as we trace the unfolding history of the West and to see that all my students—with their own rich and varied cultural backgrounds—recognize their stories within the larger narrative. In Spring 2007 and Spring 2009, I had the opportunity to implement intensively my commitment to the integration of Western and global history: I signed on to the University of Virginia's Semester at Sea and had the wonderful experience of teaching Western civilization (as well as other courses) to students as we cruised around the world. This was indeed the opportunity to teach the West in the world!

Joyce Salisbury

BRIEF CONTENTS

CONTENTS

CHAPTER 6

A WORLD DIVIDED: WESTERN KINGDOMS, BYZANTIUM, AND THE ISLAMIC WORLD, ca. 376–1000   177

CHAPTER 7

THE STRUGGLE TO BRING ORDER: THE EARLY MIDDLE AGES, ca. 750–1000   213

CHAPTER 23

DARKENING DECADES: RECOVERY, DICTATORS, AND DEPRESSION, 1920–1939 721

CHAPTER 24

INTO THE FIRE AGAIN: WORLD WAR II, 1939–1945 747

CHAPTER 25

SUPERPOWER STRUGGLES AND GLOBAL TRANSFORMATIONS: THE COLD WAR, 1945–1980s   775

THINKING ABOUT DOCUMENTS

LIST OF PRIMARY SOURCE DOCUMENTS

THINKING ABOUT GEOGRAPHY

LIST OF MAPS

Connect your students to history. Connect your students to the dramatic story of Western civilization. Connect your students to your course.

With *The West in the World*, Fourth Edition, students take an active, analytical approach to understanding history and historical change. They come to appreciate that history does not happen in isolation but rather is the consequence of a complex set of intersecting events, forces, and human actions among which there are cause-and-effect links that extend into the present day. As it compellingly tells the story of Western civilization, *The West in the World* encourages a critical examination and analysis of major events and themes, to promote student understanding and to uncover students' personal connections to the past.

HOW DOES *THE WEST IN THE WORLD*, FOURTH EDITION, ACHIEVE ITS PEDAGOGICAL GOALS?

The West in the World offers students broad and deep pedagogical support, including chapter previews, timelines, key dates boxes, margin notes, and critical thinking questions. In addition, the chapters feature a series of "Thinking About" selections with accompanying questions, focused on primary source documents, geography, science and technology, and works of art. The "Thinking About" examples encourage analytical thinking and active learning, as students read about, reflect on, and connect the events and themes of Western civilization to build an understanding of the past and an appreciation of history's influence on the present. In addition, new "Connect to Today" questions at the end of each chapter ask students to apply lessons from the past to today's issues.

With this edition, *The West in the World* also immerses students in *Connect History*, a new web-based assignment and assessment platform that includes a fully integrated e-book plus interactive quizzes and activities that make learning and studying both engaging and efficient.

HOW CAN *CONNECT HISTORY* HELP ENSURE THAT STUDENTS WILL COME TO CLASS PREPARED TO LEARN AND PREPARED FOR EXAMINATIONS?

A recent survey of professors by the *Chronicle of Higher Education* showed that 84 percent believe that their students are "unprepared" or only "somewhat prepared" to pursue a college degree. Through pre-tests and post-tests, map labeling, primary source activities, and a variety of question types, *Connect History* helps students determine what they know and do not yet know, guiding them to concentrate on their particular needs and to better prepare for class discussions, writing assignments, and examinations.

****

GOALS OF *THE WEST IN THE WORLD*, FOURTH EDITION

We have written the story of the West in a way that vividly reveals the complicated interactions and connections that distinguish it. Our primary goals have been to:

• *Tell the dramatic, diverse, and personal stories of Western Civilization*.

We showcase both the "art" and the "science" of history, as *The West and the World*'s engaging narrative of Western civilization (the "art") probes the events, individuals, ideas, and developments (the "science"). Students are drawn into the drama as they follow the evolution of Western culture from its earliest roots to the present day.

Building on a political framework, we integrate social history throughout the narrative. Our approach illuminates how individuals from *all* walks of life have shaped history—not just generals and political leaders or artistic and scientific geniuses.

• *Demonstrate the relationship between the West and the wider world.*

Historians use the term "Western civilization" to identify societies that seemed to share certain historical traditions and cultural traits. We present Western civilization as an ever-changing pattern of culture that originated in the ancient Middle East and spread westward through the Mediterranean lands, northward to Europe, and, in the sixteenth century, across the Atlantic.

To emphasize that the West did not progress in isolation, and to help students appreciate how the evolving West interacted with the rest of the world, we include **The World & the West** and **Global Connections** essays. What's more, throughout the narrative, we emphasize the importance of all interactions—economic, social, and cultural, as well as political—that have shaped Western civilization.

• *Create an accessible text of manageable length.*

The medium length of *The West in the World* is unusual for a history of Western civilization. Long accounts can overwhelm students in their level of detail and can make the assignment of supplementary readings difficult. Brief texts, while allowing time for additional reading, typically lack essential coverage and detail and make it a challenge for the authors to achieve the braided, nuanced narrative that history deserves. *The West in the World* is long enough to present a comprehensive, rich narrative but concise enough to give instructors the flexibility to use other sources and books as supplements.

A Note About the Dating System

The various civilizations across the world do not all use the same dating system. For example, the Hebrew calendar counts the Western year 3760 B.C.E. as year 1—which some consider to be when the world was created. Muslims use the date 622, the year that the Prophet fled from Mecca to Medina, as year 1 in their history. Furthermore, all cultures do not measure months on a solar calendar, which marks days based on the earth's revolution of the sun. Muslims, for instance, use a purely lunar calendar consisting of twelve lunar months in a year of 354 or 355 days. This tradition makes it particularly complicated to translate a date from the Islamic system to the Christian system.

Before the seventh century, people in the West (and in many other parts of the world) used dating systems based on rulers. That is, they might say "in the third year of the reign of Emperor Vespasian." Beginning in about the seventh century, many people in the West began to use a dating system that counts backward and forward from the birth of Christ, which Westerners consider year 1. Events that took place "Before Christ," designated as B.C., were counted backward from year 1. Thus something that happened 300 years before Christ's birth was dated 300 B.C. Events that took place after the birth of Christ were also dated from the hypothetical year 1 and were labeled A.D., which stands for the Latin *anno Domini*, meaning "in the year of our Lord."

In the twentieth century, many historians, scholars, and others who recognized that the West was not solely Christian wanted a dating designation that would apply more easily to non-Christians and that could be used more universally in a global context. They kept the same numerical system—counting backward and forward using the hypothetical date of Jesus' birth—but changed the designations. Now the common usage is "B.C.E.," which means "Before the Common Era," and "C.E.," meaning the "Common Era." We first adopted this system in the third edition of *The West in the World*, and we continue this practice in the fourth edition. The events described in the first four chapters all took place B.C.E. In Chapter 5, we have marked all dates with C.E., but because everything after that time is C.E., we then drop the designation.

We have revised the narrative and the features throughout this fourth edition so as to keep the account up-to-date and in pace with the latest scholarly work. We have also made revisions in response to adopters' and reviewers' comments.

In all chapters, we have:

- Redesigned the maps and fine-tuned their content for enhanced clarity and pedagogical value.
- Rewritten and reformatted the critical thinking questions for the maps, biographies, and art to facilitate their use in the classroom and in individual study.
- Expanded and enriched the photo captions to increase their value as learning tools.
- Added a new section at the end of each chapter—"Connect to Today"—asking questions that help students connect what they have learned to current Western and world issues.
- Updated the suggested readings in the "Beyond the Classroom" section.

On a chapter-by-chapter basis, the significant changes include the following:

CHAPTER 1 THE ROOTS OF WESTERN CIVILIZATION: THE ANCIENT MIDDLE EAST TO THE SIXTH CENTURY B.C.E.

- New treatment of the lives and livelihoods of Paleolithic peoples
- New discussion of Paleolithic peoples' expression of symbolic thought through art, featuring a recent excavation of the earliest-known work of figurative sculpture
- New material on the Phoenicians' trade and industry and their impact on regional growth
- Expanded treatment of the Hittites' introduction of a new technology of warfare

CHAPTER 2 THE CONTEST FOR EXCELLENCE: GREECE, 2000–338 B.C.E.

- Extensive new material on the Greek architectural orders
- Expanded discussion of city-states beyond Athens and Sparta
- New information on Delos, shedding light on the growth of Athenian imperial ambitions

CHAPTER 3 THE POLEIS BECOME COSMOPOLITAN: THE HELLENISTIC WORLD, 336–150 B.C.E.

- Fresh discussion of the Greeks' achievements in applying theoretical science to practical applications

- New "Thinking About Science & Technology" feature on the invention of latitude and longitude

CHAPTER 4 PRIDE IN FAMILY AND CITY: ROME FROM ITS ORIGINS TO THE REPUBLIC, 753–44 B.C.E

- New material on the Etruscans, including a look at recent DNA studies of their origin
- Expanded examination of the government structure and social classes of the Roman Republic
- New account of Roman engineering genius as applied to the building of aqueducts across the Mediterranean world

CHAPTER 5 TERRITORIAL AND CHRISTIAN EMPIRES: THE ROMAN EMPIRE, 31 B.C.E–410 C.E.

- New, extended treatment of the praetorian guard
- New information on the Roman imperial government's finances and its considerable reliance on philanthropy
- Extended treatment of the fall of the Roman Empire, including new discussion of the invasions of the Goths and Visigoths
- More on the Wailing Wall and its symbolic significance
- Expanded examination of Constantine and his support of Christians

CHAPTER 6 A WORLD DIVIDED: WESTERN KINGDOMS, BYZANTIUM, AND THE ISLAMIC WORLD, ca. 376–1000

- New information on the discovery of a hoard of Anglo-Saxon gold and silver objects, ca. 675, excavated in 2009 in Staffordshire, England, and its confirmation of the accuracy of the accounts in *Beowulf*
- Expanded narrative on Muslim science, featuring a look at the invention of the mariner's astrolabe

CHAPTER 8 ORDER RESTORED: THE HIGH MIDDLE AGES, 1000–1300

- Revised section on medieval European peasants' use of windmills, incorporating details on recent excavations of tidal mills
- New "Thinking About Science & Technology" feature on windmills
- Substantial new discussion of Byzantium's external threats and disintegration on the eve of the crusades
- Expanded coverage of the Fourth Crusade

CHAPTER 9 THE WEST STRUGGLES AND EASTERN EMPIRES FLOURISH: THE LATE MIDDLE AGES, ca. 1300–1500

- New information on the Black Death, taking into account recent DNA studies
- Extended treatment of the Ottoman Turks' expansion, including a new look at their military structure
- Additional material on eastern Europe and the fall of the Byzantine Empire
- Expanded analysis of Russia and the impact of the Mongol legacy

CHAPTER 10 A NEW SPIRIT IN THE WEST: THE RENAISSANCE, ca. 1300–1640

- Revised introduction establishing the chapter's key theme of the transformative ideas of the Renaissance
- Extended treatment of the aftermath of the Great Schism and the influence of Pope Martin V, including his development of Rome as a seat of papal power
- New information on the expansion of the popes' territorial power
- Substantial new discussion and analysis of Renaissance music and the popularization of music in this era

CHAPTER 11 "ALONE BEFORE GOD": RELIGIOUS REFORM AND WARFARE, 1500–1648

- Increased coverage of John Calvin and his influence
- New analysis of Scotland's adherence to the firm Calvinism preached by John Knox and of the Scots Confession of 1560
- Expanded discussion of warfare in the Thirty Years' War
- New "Thinking About Science & Technology" feature on the invention of gunpowder

CHAPTER 12 FAITH, FORTUNE, AND FAME: EUROPEAN EXPANSION, 1450–1700

- Continued discussion of the impact of gunpowder and cannons, focused on explorations in the New World
- In-depth new treatment of Native Americans in North America, with examination of the cultures and livelihoods of southwestern, Mississippi Valley, and eastern tribes
- New account of the first European contacts with North America and their impact on native peoples in the form of rampant disease and devastating depopulation

CHAPTER 13 THE STRUGGLE FOR SURVIVAL AND SOVEREIGNTY: EUROPE'S SOCIAL AND POLITICAL ORDER, 1600–1715

- New material on the Ottomans' military defeat at the hands of Leopold and Sobieski and the subsequent stagnation and deterioration of the once-powerful Ottoman Empire

CHAPTER 15 COMPETING FOR POWER AND WEALTH: THE OLD REGIME, 1715–1789

- New narrative and analysis on the Ottoman Empire and the Middle East, including an examination of the empire's continuing decline
- New material on the institution of the monarchy, focusing on the emergence of a public sphere where individuals and groups exchanged information and ideas
- New analysis of France's celebration of the American Revolution as a triumph in France's own competition with its British rivals

CHAPTER 16 OVERTURNING THE POLITICAL AND SOCIAL ORDER: THE FRENCH REVOLUTION AND NAPOLEON, 1789–1815

- Increased coverage of Napoleon's invasion of Egypt and the consequences

CHAPTER 17 FACTORIES, CITIES, AND FAMILIES IN THE INDUSTRIAL AGE: THE INDUSTRIAL REVOLUTION, 1780–1850

- Updated material on England's Industrial Revolution

CHAPTER 19 NATIONALISM AND STATEBUILDING: UNIFYING NATIONS, 1850–1870

- Expanded treatment of the Ottoman Empire's struggles with the divisive forces of nationalism, highlighting the Ottomans' troubles with their North African and Balkan provinces as well as with their Russian neighbors

CHAPTER 20 MASS POLITICS AND IMPERIAL DOMINATION: DEMOCRACY AND THE NEW IMPERIALISM, 1870–1914

- Revised account of Western imperialism in Asia and Africa, emphasizing the advantages conferred by new ships, weapons, and finances
- New information on the Russian expansion that influenced Britain's imperialist strategy and of tensions between Russia and Britain in the 1880s.
- Extensive new narrative on the opening of Japan to trade and foreign presences and on the subsequent collapse of the Tokugawa shogunate

- Concise analysis of Japan's transformation from a feudal society with a preindustrial economy to a modern industrialized nation

CHAPTER 21 MODERN LIFE AND THE CULTURE OF PROGRESS: WESTERN SOCIETY, 1850–1914

- New "Thinking About Science & Technology" feature on universities and the professionalism of science

CHAPTER 22 DESCENDING INTO THE TWENTIETH CENTURY: WORLD WAR AND REVOLUTION, 1914–1920

- Extended coverage of the Ottoman Empire's attempts to reverse its decline
- New information on the 1918 flu pandemic and its ravages
- New account of the events leading up to the establishment of the republic of Turkey
- New material on Arab outrage in areas of North Africa and the Middle East owing to decisions of the Allied powers.
- Revised treatment of the course and consequences of World War I
- New "Thinking About Science & Technology" feature on the invention of the tank

CHAPTER 23 DARKENING DECADES: RECOVERY, DICTATORS, AND DEPRESSION, 1920–1939

- New material on Turkey focusing on Atatürk and his reforms and dictatorship
- Revised analysis of the appeal of Nazism and Nazi doctrine

CHAPTER 24 INTO THE FIRE AGAIN: WORLD WAR II, 1939–1945

- Revised treatment of the Holocaust
- New material on German society during World War II and citizens' knowledge of Hitler's Final Solution
- New analysis of developments in Eastern Europe

CHAPTER 26 INTO THE TWENTY-FIRST CENTURY: THE PRESENT IN PERSPECTIVE

- New text on Europeans' concerns about welcoming Turkey into the European Union and on the 2009 ratification of the Lisbon Treaty
- New material updating developments in the Middle East
- Revised, updated account of the political situation in Afghanistan and Pakistan
- New material on the recent U.S. financial crisis and economic recession and their global impacts
- Updated look at Russia's leadership and its internal and external political status
- New material on Barack Obama's election as president of the United States and its potential wider political impact
- New information on economic growth in Asia and worldwide
- New "Thinking About Science & Technology" feature on CERN—the European Organization for Nuclear Research
- All-new documents looking respectively at the end of the Cold War, the war in Afghanistan, and the Copenhagen Accord on climate change

Teaching the Art and Science

The powerful pedagogy of *The West in the World* features easy-to-use critical thinking tools that involve students actively in the quest for understanding the Western past—and that forge vital connections to the present and future.

The Thinking About series of boxes focuses on four key areas: primary source documents, geography, art, and, new to this edition, science and technology. All include critical thinking questions to help students connect with, understand, and apply the material.

thinking about DOCUMENTS

DOCUMENT 4.2

Hannibal Triumphs at the Battle of Cannae

The Battle of Cannae, 216 B.C.E.

Rome
→ Advance ■ Infantry
→ Retreat ■ Cavalry

Carthage
→ Advance ■ Infantry
→ Retreat ■ Cavalry

The Carthaginians, led by Hannibal, were able to inflict the single greatest defeat of the Romans in the history of their empire. By feigning retreat and convincing the Romans that they were abandoning Cannae, the Carthaginian army was able to surround the Romans and defeat them without mercy. This defeat caused great alarm to the citizens of Rome, as it left them nearly defenseless.

FIGURE 4.9 The Battle of Cannae, 216 B.C.E.

The Roman historian Florus (ca. 70–ca. 140 C.E.) wrote History of the Romans, in which he recounted the long-remembered Battle of Cannae (216 B.C.E.), a turning point during the Second Punic War between Rome and Carthage. Military thinkers today still study Hannibal's winning battle strategy, but Florus notes Hannibal's mistake. Study Figure 4.9 to understand Hannibal's winning strategy.

The fourth and almost mortal wound of the Roman Empire was at Cannæ, an obscure village of Apulia; which, however, became famous by the greatness of the defeat, its celebrity being acquired by the slaughter of forty thousand men. Here the general, the ground, the face of heaven, the day, indeed, all nature conspired together for the destruction of the unfortunate army. For Hannibal, the most artful of generals, not content with sending pretended deserters among the Romans, who fell upon their rear as they were fighting, but having also noted the nature of the ground in those open plains, where the heat of the sun is extremely violent, the dust very great, and the wind blows constantly, and as it were stately, from the east, drew up his army in such a position that, while the Romans were exposed to all these inconveniences, he himself, having heaven, as it were, on his side, fought with wind, dust, and sun in his favor. Two vast armies, in consequence, were slaughtered till the enemy were satiated, and till Hannibal said to his soldiers, "Put up your swords." Of the two commanders, one escaped, the other was slain; which of them showed the greater spirit is doubtful. Paulus was ashamed to survive; Varro did not despair. Of the greatness of the slaughter the following proofs may be noticed: that the Aufidus was for some time red with blood; that a bridge was made of dead bodies, by order of Hannibal, over the torrent of Vergellus, and that two *modii* of rings were sent to Carthage, and the equestrian dignity estimated by measure.

It was afterward not doubted but that Rome might have seen its last day, and that Hannibal, within five days, might have feasted in the Capitol, if—as they say that Adherbal, the Carthaginian, the son of Bomilcar, observed—"he had known as well how to use his victory as how to gain it." But at that crisis, as is generally said, either the fate of the city that was to be empress of the world, or his own want of judgment, and the influence of deities unfavorable to Carthage, carried him in a different direction. When he might have taken advantage of his victory, he chose rather to seek enjoyment from it, and, leaving Rome, to march into Campania and to Tarentum, where both he and his army soon lost their vigor, so that it was justly remarked that "Capua proved a Cannæ to Hannibal"; since the sunshine of Campania and the warm springs of Baiæ subdued—who could have believed it?—him who had been unconquered by the Alps and unshaken in the field.

SOURCE: Florus, History of the Romans, in The Great Events by Famous Historians, vol. II, ed. Rossiter Johnson (The National Alumni, 1905), pp. 186–187.

Analyze the Document

1. What are the tactics of ancient battles, and in what ways is Hannibal particularly skilled?

🔺 Thinking About Documents

thinking about GEOGRAPHY

Legend:
■ Habsburg Lands
■ Valois Lands
■ Ottoman Lands
→ Ottoman Attacks
□ Boundary of the Holy Roman Empire
⚔ Battle Sites

MAP 11.1

Europe in 1526— Habsburg-Valois Wars

This map illustrates the political division of Europe in 1526 and highlights the Habsburg lands inherited by Charles V. It also shows the Ottoman Empire on Charles's borders.

Explore the Map

1. Why did the French king feel threatened by his powerful neighbor?

2. Why was Charles so concerned about the proximity of the Ottoman Empire?

3. Notice all the battles Charles fought. What might have been the impact of this warfare both on the people and on the emperor's ability to rule?

Thinking About Geography ▶

Thinking About Art ▶

thinking about
ART

FIGURE 10.12
Raphael, *School of Athens*, 1510–1511

Pope Julius II commissioned the painter Raphael to create a fresco for his library. The artist portrayed famous ancient philosophers, such as Euclid, Pythagoras, and Socrates, along with Plato and Aristotle in the center. Plato (looking remarkably like Leonardo da [Vinci] is on the left, with his hand pointing in the air to [...] is speaking to [...], reminding [...] knowledge. [...] the right (in the black hat) and a depiction of a brooding Michelangelo sitting in the center foreground, leaning his head on his hand.

Connecting Art & Society

1. Identify the following characteristics of the Renaissance in this image: individualism, appreciation of the classics, and perspective.

2. Why would the pope find the content of this fresco suitable subject matter for the papal library?

3. Why do you think Raphael included portraits of his artist contemporaries in the company of the philosophers?

---

thinking about
SCIENCE & TECHNOLOGY

Destruction and Amusement: The Development and Uses of Gunpowder

By the tenth century, Chinese alchemists—recall that alchemy was the early practice of chemistry—were experimenting with mixing various substances for medicinal purposes. In the process, they invented an effective gunpowder. The formula was 75 percent saltpeter (potassium nitrate), which released chemically bound oxygen to support combustion; 15 percent charcoal to supply carbon to fuel the fire; and 10 percent sulfur to lower the temperature of ignition and speed up combustion.

Europeans adopted this recipe and began to use gunpowder on

FIGURE 11.1 Experimenting with gunpowder.

the battlefield in the fourteenth century. Then, in the fifteenth century, Western powder engineers developed a technique of binding the powder into small clumps called corned powder, which was easy to transport, to keep dry, and to load efficiently into guns and cannons. Importantly, the corned powder also was more stable; the corning technology prevented accidental dust explosions and detonation from static electricity and provided a more controlled burn rate. With the enhanced stability and transportability of the improved powder, large, mobile cannons could be brought into the battlefields, whereas previously they could only be mounted on ships and forts. From this moment on, battlefield violence increased dramatically, and foot soldiers faced devastating explosions as they charged. Gunpowder's impact would become starkly evident in the violence of the early modern wars and in the sea battles that would bring Europeans to power across the world.

People throughout history have found ways to adapt technological innovations for entertainment purposes, and this ingenuity was true for gunpowder. As early as the late fifteenth century in the West, gunpowder moved from wartime to peacetime uses as people set off gunpowder-powered fireworks to light up European night skies on special occasions. These displays were potentially hazardous, however; for example, the pyrotechnics that were lit during one of Shakespeare's productions ignited the fire that burned down the playwright's Globe Theatre in 1613. Even firemasters, individuals who made gunpowder, did not know exactly how gunpowder worked, and **Figure 11.1** shows the explosive results that often accompanied their experiments. This mystery stimulated scientific investigation for years to come, helping to move science from alchemy to chemistry as researchers finally identified the oxygen hidden in the saltpeter that fed the fires of what had long been believed to be a magic powder.

Remember the struggle for mastery of the chemistry of gunpowder so that when you learn about the Scientific Revolution in Chapter 14, you might consider again the relationship between practical utility and scientific theory.

Connecting Science & Society

1. Trace how the scientific experimentation behind the development and improvement of gunpowder led to the application of gunpowder technology for various purposes.

2. How did advances in the stability and transportability of gunpowder transform warfare?

3. Cite some instances in your lifetime where inventions of practical items or techniques have been later adapted for entertainment purposes.

◀ Thinking About Science & Technology

The **Biography** feature spotlights the lives of men and women who embody major themes. Accompanying **Connecting People & Society** questions draw students into each individual's life and help them to link this personal experience to larger developments.

Biography ▶

The text demonstrates the complex relationship between Western and world history through **The World & the West** and **Global Connections** essays.

◀ Four essays titled **The World & the West** investigate what historians have considered the "West" and how the West related to the wider world in various periods. Featuring an accompanying map, each essay ends with **Thinking Globally** questions.

Global Connections essays reinforce the key idea that the West has always developed within a world context. Analytical **Making Connections** questions ask students to see the links between the events in the West and those in the wider world.

The West in the World *ensures student success through* **preview** *and* **review** *features and an exciting digital program,* **Connect History.**

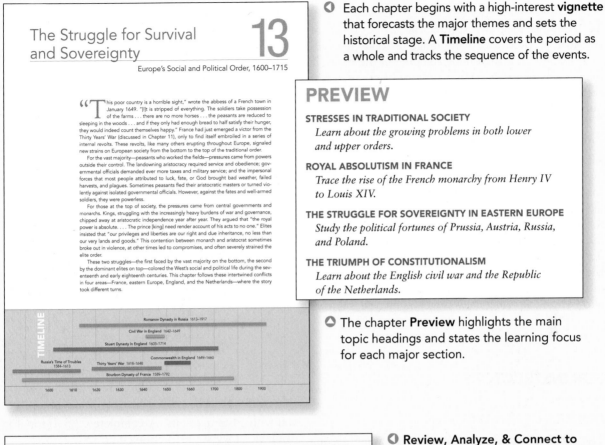

Each chapter begins with a high-interest **vignette** that forecasts the major themes and sets the historical stage. A **Timeline** covers the period as a whole and tracks the sequence of the events.

The Struggle for Survival and Sovereignty

13

Europe's Social and Political Order, 1600–1715

"This poor country is a horrible sight," wrote the abbess of a French town in January 1649. "[I]t is stripped of everything. The soldiers take possession of the farms . . . there are no more horses . . . the peasants are reduced to sleeping in the woods . . . and if they only had enough bread to half satisfy their hunger, they would indeed count themselves happy." France had just emerged a victor from the Thirty Years' War (discussed in Chapter 11), only to find itself embroiled in a series of internal revolts. These revolts, like many others erupting throughout Europe, signaled new strains on European society from the bottom to the top of the traditional order.

For the vast majority—peasants who worked the fields—pressures came from powers outside their control. The landowning aristocracy required service and obedience; governmental officials demanded ever more taxes and military service; and the impersonal forces that most people attributed to luck, fate, or God brought bad weather, failed harvests, and plagues. Sometimes peasants fled their aristocratic masters or turned violently against isolated governmental officials. However, against the fates and well-armed soldiers, they were powerless.

For those at the top of society, the pressures came from central governments and monarchs. Kings, struggling with the increasingly heavy burdens of war and governance, chipped away at aristocratic independence year after year. They argued that "the royal power is absolute. . . . The prince [king] need render account of his acts to no one." Elites insisted that "our privileges and liberties are our right and due inheritance, no less than our very lands and goods." This contention between monarch and aristocrat sometimes broke out in violence, at other times led to compromises, and often severely strained the elite order.

These two struggles—the first faced by the vast majority on the bottom, the second by the dominant elites on top—colored the West's social and political life during the seventeenth and early eighteenth centuries. This chapter follows these intertwined conflicts in four areas—France, eastern Europe, England, and the Netherlands—where the story took different turns.

PREVIEW

STRESSES IN TRADITIONAL SOCIETY
Learn about the growing problems in both lower and upper orders.

ROYAL ABSOLUTISM IN FRANCE
Trace the rise of the French monarchy from Henry IV to Louis XIV.

THE STRUGGLE FOR SOVEREIGNTY IN EASTERN EUROPE
Study the political fortunes of Prussia, Austria, Russia, and Poland.

THE TRIUMPH OF CONSTITUTIONALISM
Learn about the English civil war and the Republic of the Netherlands.

The chapter **Preview** highlights the main topic headings and states the learning focus for each major section.

TIMELINE

Romanov Dynasty in Russia 1613–1917
Civil War in England 1642–1649
Stuart Dynasty in England 1603–1714
Russia's Time of Troubles 1584–1613
Thirty Years' War 1618–1648
Commonwealth in England 1649–1660
Bourbon Dynasty of France 1589–1792

1600 1610 1620 1630 1640 1650 1660 1700 1800 1900

Review, Analyze, & Connect to Today questions at the end of each chapter ask students first to review the preceding chapters and to place the present chapter's history in the context of what has come before; second, to analyze developments in the current chapter; and third, to connect the ideas and developments discussed in the chapter at hand to present-day issues

REVIEW, ANALYZE, & CONNECT TO TODAY

REVIEW THE PREVIOUS CHAPTERS

Chapter 12—"Faith, Fortune, and Fame"—told how several European powers expanded overseas during the fifteenth, sixteenth, and seventeenth centuries and grew rich from the commerce. Chapter 13—"The Struggle for Survival and Sovereignty"—focused on how kings and nobles battled for power, the resolutions of those struggles, and their impact on the millions of people outside the elite.

1. Analyze how the expansion of Europe might have stimulated scientific research.

2. In what ways did the effort of monarchs to increase their power and create stability relate to the promotion of science and the desire for greater intellectual certainty?

ANALYZE THIS CHAPTER

Chapter 14—"A New World of Reason and Reform"—examines the changing intellectual foundations of the West.

1. List and analyze the differences between the new scientific views of the world and traditional medieval views.

How did standards for ascertaining the "truth" differ between these two perspectives?

2. Analyze the beliefs and motives of three central figures in the Scientific Revolution. What barriers did they have to overcome to present their views?

3. Do you think the Enlightenment merely popularized the Scientific Revolution, or did it accomplish something more?

4. In what ways did the Enlightenment threaten traditional views and authorities?

CONNECT TO TODAY

Think about the meaning of the Scientific Revolution and the values underlying the Enlightenment.

1. In what ways are our present-day assumptions about the physical universe and the workings of nature based on the ideas and discoveries of the Scientific Revolution?

2. What aspects of world politics today reflect Enlightenment values? What aspects of global politics seem to be oppo[sed?]

Connect History provides students with a fully integrated e-book with highlighting and note-taking features, plus interactive quizzes and activities that make learning and studying engaging and efficient.

CH-13 LO-08:Analyze the English Civil War, the Commonwealth, and the restoratio

Question #4 (of 6)

4.
10 points
Drag and drop the location names to the appropriate places on the map.

Marston Moor
Lichfield
Naseby
Newbury
Philiphaugh

Controlled by the Parliamentarians, Beginning of 1645
Controlled by the Royalists, Beginning of 1645
Conquered by the Parliamentarians, in 1645
Battle Site

Marston Moor
Naseby

Reset Help

Check My Work

FOR STUDENTS

ONLINE LEARNING CENTER

The Online Learning Center, at www.mhhe.com /sherman4e, provides a wide range of tools that will help students test their understanding of the book. It includes chapter summaries, learning objectives, interactive maps and glossary, and multiple choice and essay quizzes, as well as matching and identifying games.

PRIMARY SOURCE INVESTIGATOR ONLINE

McGraw-Hill's Primary Source Investigator (PSI), available online at www.mhhe.com/psi, is designed to support and enrich the text discussion in *The West in the World*, 4e. PSI gives instructors and students access to more than 650 primary and secondary sources including documents, images, maps, and videos. Students can use these resources to formulate and defend their arguments as well as further their understanding of the topics discussed in each chapter. All assets are also indexed alphabetically as well as by type, subject, place, and time period, allowing students and instructors to locate resources quickly and easily.

INVESTIGATIONS

The Investigation activities give students an opportunity to try their hand at historical analysis. Based on sources found in PSI, the modules ask students to evaluate multiple sources and formulate their own interpretation of an historical event, providing valuable skills for their own research.

RESEARCH AND WRITING CENTER

The online Research and Writing Center offers a guide to college success, plus general assistance for writing college papers, as well as specific tips for history papers. Topics include research, paragraph and argument creation, a comparison of style guides, information on plagiarism and source citation, and much more.

FOR INSTRUCTORS

ONLINE LEARNING CENTER

The Online Learning Center, at www.mhhe.com /sherman4e, contains several instructor tools including a link to the faculty guide on Primary Source Investigator (www.mhhe.com/psi), PowerPoint presentations for each chapter, and the computerized test bank. The instructor side of the OLC is password protected to prevent tampering. Please contact your local McGraw-Hill representative for details.

CLASSROOM PERFORMANCE SYSTEM (CPS)

The Classroom Performance System brings ultimate interactivity to *The West in the World*. CPS is a wireless response system that gives you immediate feedback from every student in the class. With CPS you can ask subjective and objective questions during your lecture, prompting every student to respond with his or her individual, wireless response pad, and providing you with instant results. A complete CPS Tutorial is available at www.einstruction.com.

VIDEOS

Created and narrated by Joyce Salisbury, this three-video collection illuminates the author's lectures on the Middle Ages with the sculpture and fine art of the times. Available to adopters through your local McGraw-Hill representative, this unique series contains a video on each of the following topics: medieval women, medieval Judaism, and medieval life. A wide range of videos on classic and contemporary topics in history is available through the Films for the Humanities and Sciences collection. Instructors can illustrate classroom discussion and enhance lectures by selecting from a series of videos that are correlated to complement *The West in the World*. Contact your local McGraw-Hill sales representative for further information.

PRIMARY SOURCE INVESTIGATOR ONLINE FACULTY GUIDE

The annotated Faculty Guide provides easy reference to all learning assets, both in the text and on PSI, available to instructors and students. Each chapter is accompanied by a rich list of resources, including PowerPoint slides, image bank, outline maps, book maps, and test bank questions, all keyed to the chapter. Resources are organized within chapters by A-heads to streamline lecture and assignment preparation. Icons allow users to quickly differentiate between text and PSI sources. Each asset is listed by title and includes a brief annotation.

In addition to assets, the Faculty Guide also includes a chapter overview, a list of themes, lecture strategies, teaching suggestions, suggestions for further reading, and chapter-specific film recommendations. These, too, are organized by chapter and A-head to make classroom implementation simple.

ACKNOWLEDGMENTS

We have nurtured this book through many drafts, and every page has benefited from the advice of numerous reviewers, some of whom we have gone back to several times. For their thoughtful comments and generous contribution of time and expertise, we would like to thank the following reviewers:

For the Fourth Edition

Karen A. Bartley, *University of Dayton*; Carl Boening, *Shelton State Community College*; Fred Boettcher, *Otero Junior College*; Robert Brennan, *Cape Fear Community College*; Robert J. Brown, *SUNY Finger Lakes Community College*; Tracy Nichols Busch, *Ferris State University*; Marie Therese Champagne, *University of West Florida*; Margaret Crowe, *Bridgewater State College*; Salvador Diaz, *Santa Rosa Junior College*; Martin F. Ederer, *Buffalo State College*; Natalie Kimbrough, *Community College of Baltimore County*; Janilyn Kocher, *Richland Community College*; Pamela Koenig, *Seminole State College*; Ilana Krug, *York College of Pennsylvania*; Mike Kugler, *Northwestern College*; Margaret H. Mahoney, *Bellarmine University*; Thomas Martin, *Sinclair Community College*; Ronald Palmer, *SUNY Jefferson Community College*; Elizabeth Propes, *Mesa State College*; Mark Edward Ruff, *Saint Louis University*; Steven Soper, *University of Georgia*; John F. Weinzierl, *Lyon College*; Steven Jay White, *Bluegrass Community and Technical College*; Julianna Wilson, *Pima Community College*; Sergei I. Zhuk, *Ball State University*

For the Third Edition

April Brooks, *South Dakota State University*; Daniel Patrick Brown, *Moorpark College*; Kathleen Carter, *High Point University*; Laura Cruz, *Western Carolina University*; Philip Daileader, *College of William and Mary*; Cassie Farrelly, *Fordham University*; Beth Fickling, *Coastal Carolina Community College*; Ginger Guardiola, *Colorado State University*; Jennifer Hedda, *Simpson College*; Barry Jackisch, *Gannon University*; Molly Johnson, *University of Alabama–Huntsville*; William Kinsella, *Northern Virginia Community College*; Todd Larson, *Xavier University*; Elizabeth Lehfeldt, *Cleveland State University*; William Lipkin, *Union County College*; Nancy Locklin, *Maryville College*; Karl Loewenstein, *University of Wisconsin–Oshkosh*; Michael Loughlin, *Ohio Northern University*; Jack Pesda, *Camden County College*; Penne Prigge, *Rockingham Community College*; Dana Sample, *University of Virginia's College at Wise*

For the Second Edition

Joseph Appiah, *Virginia Community College*; Douglas C. Baxter, *Ohio University*; Jonathan Bone, *William Paterson University*; Suzanne Bowles, *William Paterson University*; April Brooks, *South Dakota State University*; Katherine Clark, *University of Kansas*; Sandi Cooper, *City University of New York*; Florin Curta, *University of Florida*; Norman C. Delany, *Del Mar College*; David D. Flaten, *Plymouth State College*; Marsha L. Frey, *Kansas State University*; Bruce Garver, *University of Nebraska at Omaha*; Carla Hay, *Marquette University*; Holly Hurlburt, *Southern Illinois University*; Andrew Keitt, *University of Alabama at Birmingham*; Dave Kelly, *Colorado State University*; Jason Knirck, *Humboldt State University*; Mark W. McLeod, *University of Delaware*; Carol Menning, *University of Toledo*; Jeffrey Lee Meriwether, *Roger Williams University*; Zachary Morgan, *William Paterson University*; Michael Myers, *University of Illinois*; Max Okenfuss, *Washington University*; Jack Pesda, *Camden County College*; Dolores Davison Peterson, *Foothill College*; Paul Rempe, *Carroll College*; Harry Rosenberg, *Colorado State University*; Shawn Ross, *William Paterson University*; Glenn Sanders, *Oklahoma Baptist University*; Marc Schwarz, *University of New Hampshire*; David Stefanic, *Saint Mary's College*; Aliza Wong, *Texas Technical University*; Michael A. Zaccaria, *Cumberland County College*

For the First Edition

Edward Anson, *University of Arkansas*; William S. Arnett, *West Virginia University*; Richard Berthold, *University of New Mexico*; Robert Blackey, *California State University–San Bernardino*; Hugh Boyer, *Michigan Technical University*; Carol Bresnahan-Menning, *University of Toledo*; April Brooks, *South Dakota State University*; Nathan Brooks, *New Mexico State University*; Blaine T. Browne, *Broward Community College*; Donald Butts, *Gordon College*; Frederick Corney, *University of Florida*; Jeffrey Cox, *University of Iowa*; Florin Curta, *University of Florida*; Norman Delaney, *Del Mar College*; Robert Dise, *University of Northern Iowa*; Chris Drake, *Houston Community College–Northwest*; Lawrence G. Duggan, *University of Delaware*; Laird Easton, *California State University–Chico*; Gregory Elder, *Riverside Community College*; Nancy Erickson, *Erskine College*; Chiarella Esposito, *University of Mississippi*; Gary Ferngren, *Oregon State University*; Nancy Fitch, *California State University–Fullerton*; Elizabeth Lane Furdell, *University of North Florida*; Frank Garosi, *California State University–Sacramento*; Don Gawronski, *Mesa Community College*; Paul Goodwin, *University of Connecticut*; Anita Guerrini, *University of California–Santa Barbara*; Louis Haas, *Duquesne University*; Alice Henderson, *University of South Carolina–Spartanburg*; Jennifer Hevelone-Harper, *Gordon College*; Steven Hill, *Wake Technical Community College*; Laura J. Hilton, *Ohio State University*; Karen Holland, *Providence College*; David Hudson,

California State University–Fresno; Gary Johnson, *University of Southern Maine;* Jonathan G. Katz, *Oregon State University;* Andrew Keitt, *University of Alabama–Birmingham;* Charles Killinger, *Valencia Community College;* Lisa Lane, *Mira Costa College;* John Livingston, *University of Denver;* David Longfellow, *Baylor University;* Donna Maier, *University of Northern Iowa;* James I. Martin Sr., *Campbell University;* Carol Miller, *Tallahassee Community College;* Eileen Moore, *University of Alabama–Birmingham;* Frederick I. Murphy, *Western Kentucky University;* Max J. Okenfuss, *Washington University;* Michael Osborne, *University of California–Santa Barbara;* Jack Pesda, *Camden County College;* Russell Quinlan, *Northern Arizona University;* Patricia Ranft, *Central Michigan University;* Roger Reese, *Texas A&M University;* Harry Rosenberg, *Colorado State University;* Constance M. Rousseau, *Providence College;* Jay Rubenstein, *University of New Mexico;* Claire Sanders, *Texas Christian College;* Alan Schaffer, *Clemson University;* Daryl Schuster, *University of Central Florida;* Marc Schwarz, *University of New Hampshire;* David Shearer, *University of Delaware;* Arlene Sindelar, *University of Central Arkansas;* James Sisson, *Central Texas College;* Ronald D. Smith, *Arizona State University;* Saulius Suziedelis, *Millersville University of Pennsylvania;* Hunt Tooley, *Austin College;* Kevin Uhalde, *Northern Illinois University;* David Ulbrich, *Kansas State University;* Bruce Venarde, *University of Pittsburgh;* Charlotte Wells, *University of Northern Iowa;* Michael Wilson, *University of Texas–Dallas;* Robert Wise, *University of Northern Iowa;* Bill Wrightson, *American River College*

In addition to our reviewers and focus group participants, we would like to thank Matthew Busbridge, sponsoring editor; Rhona Robbin, director of development; Arthur Pomponio and Sylvia Mallory, developmental editors; Briana Porco, Carey Eisner, Robin Mouat, Laurie Entringer, Alexandra Ambrose, and the rest of the Fourth Edition team, whose efforts have made this a better book. Last, but certainly not least, we would like to thank the many professors who choose to use this text in their classrooms. It is they who will fulfill our hope for this text—that it will bring the past to life for many undergraduates and will perhaps awaken in them a love for history and an awareness that understanding the past is the key to our future.

TUTANKHAMEN'S GOLDEN THRONE, ca. 1322 B.C.E.

In this image from the burial of the boy-king Tutankhamen, the king sits on his throne as his wife, Akhsenamun, anoints him with scented unguent. Both bask in the rays of the holy sun-disk that they worshiped as a god. This colorful scene vividly captures the essential character of ancient Egypt and its people: the wealth and power of the god-kings; the importance of marriage and family ties; and the deep connection of the institutions of marriage and family with religion and longing for immortality. This image also reveals the power of written words—in this case, the hieroglyphs in the background—which allow us, millennia later, to read firsthand about the past and trace the developing story of the West.

The Roots of Western Civilization

The Ancient Middle East to the Sixth Century B.C.E.

"Since time immemorial, since the seedcorn first sprouted forth . . . [powerful men] have been in charge for their own benefit. The workingman was forced to beg for his bread; the youth was forced to work for others." In 2400 B.C.E., the Sumerian ruler Uruinimgina wrote these words as he took power in a Mesopotamian city. He claimed that his reforms freed citizens from usury, burdensome controls, hunger, theft, and murder—troubles that, in varying forms, have periodically plagued civilization since it first arose in cities. With his thoughtful policies and passionate sense of justice, Uruinimgina embodied another important characteristic of Western civilization: the occasional rise to power of people who strive to correct social injustice.

In the growing cities of Mesopotamia, Egypt, and the coast of the eastern Mediterranean Sea, other ideas developed that would also form the basis of civilization in the West. Societies practicing social stratification, sophisticated religious ideas, and concepts of law emerged in the same environment that spawned the social ills Uruinimgina briefly corrected. Perhaps most important, these early peoples invented writing, which preserved their cultures in the tablets and scrolls that reveal their world to us as we explore ancient cultures. The culture of the West was born in the Fertile Crescent of what we now know as the Middle East.

By the tenth century B.C.E., some states in the Fertile Crescent were able to create large, multinational empires, introducing a new political structure in the early history of the West. The Egyptians, Assyrians, Babylonians, and finally Persians established their rule over extensive areas and developed new ways of governing, as the concept of empire entered the Western consciousness.

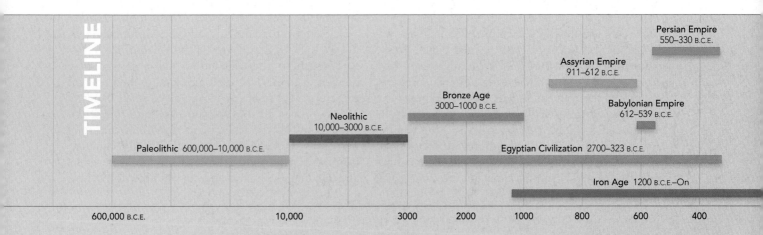

TIMELINE

Persian Empire 550–330 B.C.E.

Assyrian Empire 911–612 B.C.E.

Bronze Age 3000–1000 B.C.E.

Babylonian Empire 612–539 B.C.E.

Neolithic 10,000–3000 B.C.E.

Paleolithic 600,000–10,000 B.C.E.

Egyptian Civilization 2700–323 B.C.E.

Iron Age 1200 B.C.E.–On

600,000 B.C.E. 10,000 3000 2000 1000 800 600 400

PREVIEW

BEFORE WESTERN CIVILIZATION

In 2500 B.C.E., a Sumerian schoolboy wrote an essay about his struggles to learn reading and writing. He claimed in his essay that he practiced these skills in school all day, and he took his writing tablet home to his father, who praised the boy's progress. That night, the boy ate his dinner, washed his feet, and went to bed. The next day, however, he had a difficult time in school. He arrived late and was beaten for his tardiness and several other offenses, including poor handwriting. In despair, the boy invited the schoolmaster home to dinner. The father gave the teacher gifts, and the boy began having fewer problems in school.

This narrative, dating from 4,500 years ago, is perhaps most remarkable for its timeless themes. Tardy students, schools, and concerned parents are all a part of life for most of us today. Here, in the village of this young boy, we can find the roots of what we have come to call Western civilization (or "the West"). This term does not define one location but instead refers to a series of cultures that slowly evolved and spread to impact societies all over the world. Even 4,500 years ago, in the village of this Sumerian, we can identify certain characteristics that define Western civilization and that gave it an advantage—for better or worse—over competing cultures. Western civilization began in the Middle East, which enjoyed the striking advantage of having plants for agriculture and animals for domestication native to the region. Then large cities arose with attendant division of labor and social stratification based on relationships other than family. Another dramatic advantage was the development of writing, which gave schoolboys so much difficulty but allowed the preservation and transmission of advantageous developments.

Finally, one of the hallmarks of Western civilization was that it never developed in isolation. Throughout its recorded history, the peoples of the Mediterranean basin traded with other societies, and the resulting cultural diffusion strengthened all the cultures involved. For example, crops from the ancient Middle East spread westward as far as Britain as early as about 4000 B.C.E., and by the second millennium B.C.E., wheat, barley, and horses from the Middle East reached as far east as China. In fact, the trade routes from the Middle East to India and China, and west and south to Africa and Europe, have a permanence that dwarfs the accomplishments of conquerors and empire builders. These constant and fruitful interactions with other cultures perhaps gave Western civilization its greatest advantage.

Yet, recorded history represents less than 1 percent of the time that humans have lived on the earth. Hundreds of thousands of years before this day in the life of a young, urban Sumerian, life for human beings was completely different. Before we begin the story of the development of Western civilization, we must explore the life of the first humans in the lush lands of sub-Saharan Africa.

Out of Africa: The Paleolithic Period, 600,000–10,000 B.C.E.

Human beings first appeared in sub-Saharan Africa hundreds of thousands of years ago. Archaeologists have classified the remains of these early humans into various species and subspecies, most of which were evolutionary dead ends. Modern humans belong to *Homo sapiens sapiens* ("thinking, thinking man"), a subspecies that migrated north and northeast from Africa. These earliest ancestors first appeared some 40,000 years ago and ultimately colonized the world. The first humans used tools made from materials at hand, including wood and bone, but the most useful tools were those made of stone. Initial stone tools were sharpened only roughly, but later humans crafted stones into finely finished flakes ideal for spearheads, arrowheads, and other blades. These tools have led archaeologists to name this long period of human prehistory the Old Stone Age, or the **Paleolithic.**

Throughout the Paleolithic, our ancestors were nomadic peoples living off the land as hunters and gatherers. This nomadic life involved small bands of people—about 30 to 40—who moved to follow the animals and the cycles of plant growth. A culture of hunters and gatherers prevents people from accumulating property, for whatever one owns must be portable, and that includes infants and small children. Anything extra is a burden, not a benefit. Paleolithic cultures also enjoyed a good deal of leisure time—indeed, estimates suggest that working four hours a day would usually generate enough food for a group. Of course, the ancient hunters and gatherers also faced famine if they exhausted the resources of a local area.

Our earliest human ancestors were also distinguished by their ability to use symbols to represent not only reality but also their hopes and fears. That is, the earliest humans created and appreciated what we call art. **Figure 1.1** shows a wonderful, tiny carving on mammoth tusk that was discovered in 2008 in Germany. Carbon dating places this figure between 35,000 and 40,000 years ago, making it the oldest piece of figurative sculpture in the world and demonstrating that art was one of the defining characteristics of humans. The 2.4-inch-tall carving shows a female figure that looks pregnant, and its creator seems to have designed it to be worn as a pendant. It was most likely intended as a sympathetic magic figurine to ensure fertility and perhaps safety in childbirth. This diminutive yet striking figure from the dawn of human history marks the beginning of symbolic thought expressed in sculpture, painting, and ultimately writing. These products of the human imagination serve to give us remarkably revealing windows on the past.

Paleolithic peoples developed their artistic skills over millennia, and the greatest expression of this ancient art survives in cave paintings from about 17,000 years ago. People returned seasonally to the same caves and painted new figures near, and sometimes over, earlier images. Some caves show evidence of repeated painting across an astonishing span of 10,000 years, revealing the preservation of traditions over lengths of time that are almost unimaginable today. These paintings probably coincided with the gathering of the small tribes of hunter-gatherers, and the movement of peoples and their goods shows that commerce joined art as a defining quality of early human societies.

Evidence from the late Paleolithic Age tells us that groups of humans returned seasonally to the same regions instead of wandering endlessly to new areas. As they traveled, kin groups | Trade networks | encountered other clans and traded goods as well as stories. Archaeological evidence indicates that shells and especially stone tools were often traded in places far from their

FIGURE 1.1 The World's Oldest Sculpture, ca. 33,000 B.C.E. This carving on mammoth tusk is the oldest figurative sculpture found to date. Showing a pregnant woman, it probably was a magic talisman for fertility.

original sites. For example, late Stone Age people living in what is now Scotland rowed small boats to an offshore island to bring back precious bloodstone that flaked accurately into strong tools. This bloodstone spread widely across northern Europe through trade with the original sailors. Commerce thus became established as an early human enterprise.

By the end of the Paleolithic Age (about 10,000 B.C.E.), the human population of Europe stood at about 20,000. These numbers may seem sparse by today's standards, but | Stone monuments | they suggest that *Homo sapiens sapiens* had gained a sturdy foothold on the European continent. By the late Stone Age, these early Europeans practiced agriculture and copper metallurgy, but their most enduring remains are huge stone monuments (called *megaliths*), of which Stonehenge in western England (shown in **Figure 1.2**) is probably the most famous. Stonehenge was built in stages over millennia beginning in about 7000 B.C.E., although most of the stones were erected about 3000 B.C.E. In its present form, it consists of about 160 massive rocks, some weighing up to 50 tons, which are arranged in concentric circles and semicircles. People moved the heavy stones long distances without using wheels, which were unknown in Europe at this time, and shaped many of them with only stone tools. Most scholars believe that the stones were carefully aligned to show the movements of the sun and moon. If this is so, the astonishing structure shows both a long tradition of studying the heavens and humans' impressive curiosity. Whatever the purpose of these stone structures that dot Europe, they all suggest highly organized societies that were able to marshal the labor

FIGURE 1.2 Stone Age Monuments from Stonehenge, Southern England, ca. 7000–1500 B.C.E. These huge structures of stone, carefully shaped and moved long distances, testify to early human technical skill. The alignment of the stones suggests knowledge of the heavens gained from many years of observations.

needed for such complex building projects. (**Map 1.1** shows the range of the megaliths.)

However, although these early Europeans displayed some characteristics that would mark Western civilization—agriculture, a curiosity about nature, and a highly developed political structure—these great builders in stone lacked a critical component: writing. Although wisdom transmitted solely through memory can be impressive, it is also fragile, and thus engineering skills and astronomical knowledge of the earliest Europeans were lost. The real origins of Western civilization lay in the Middle East, where an agricultural revolution occurred that changed the course of human history, and where writing preserved the story of the developing West.

The Neolithic Period: The First Stirrings of Agriculture, 10,000–3000 B.C.E.

Sometime around 10,000 B.C.E., people living in what we call the Middle East learned how to plant and cultivate the grains that they and their ancestors had gathered for millennia. With this skill, humankind entered the **Neolithic** era, or the New Stone Age. Agriculture did not bring complete improvement in people's lives compared to hunting and gathering. Diets were often worse (with a reliance on fewer foods), sewage and animal wastes brought more health problems, and farming was a lot of work. People adopted this way of life because the environment changed, but once people learned how to plant crops instead of simply gathering what grew naturally, human society changed dramatically.

Just as people discovered how to control crops, they also began to domesticate animals instead of hunting them. Dogs had been domesticated as hunting partners during the Paleolithic, but around 8500 B.C.E., people first domesticated sheep as a source of food. Throughout the Middle East, some people lived off their herds as they traveled about looking for pasturage. Others lived as agriculturalists, keeping their herds near stationary villages.

Domestic animals

These two related developments—agriculture and animal domestication—fostered larger populations than hunting and gathering cultures, and gradually agricultural societies prevailed. In large part, the success of the Western civilization in eventually spreading throughout the world lay in its agricultural beginnings in the Middle East. Why were people in this region able to embrace agriculture so successfully? The main answer is luck—the Middle East was equipped with the necessary resources.

Of the wealth of plant species in the world—over 200,000 different varieties—humans eat only a few thousand. Of these, only a few hundred have been more or less domesticated, but almost 80 percent of the world's human diet is made up of about a dozen species (primarily cereals). The Middle East was home to the highest number of the world's prized grains, such as wheat and barley, which are easy to grow and contain the highest levels of protein. By contrast, people who independently domesticated local crops in other regions did not enjoy the same abundance.

Middle East plants and animals

The Middle East maintained the same advantage when it came to animals for domestication. Very few species yield to domestication; beyond the most common—dogs, sheep, goats, cows, pigs, and horses—there are only a few others—from camels to reindeer to water buffalo. Because domesticated animals provide so many benefits to humans—from food to labor—the distribution of animals fit for domestication helped determine which societies would flourish. Most of these animals were confined to Europe and Asia, and seven—including goats, sheep, and cattle—were native specifically to the Middle East. With these resources, the people of the Middle East created civilization, which quickly spread east and west (along with valuable crops and animals).

With the rise of agriculture, some small kin groups stopped wandering and instead slowly settled in permanent villages to cultivate the surrounding land. As early as 8000 B.C.E., Jericho (see **Map 1.1**) boasted about 2,000

Population growth

MAP 1.1

Mesopotamia and Egypt, ca. 2000 B.C.E.

This map illustrates the cradles of Western civilization in Mesopotamia (the Fertile Crescent), along the coast of the Mediterranean Sea, and in Egypt. It also identifies this region's major Neolithic sites, which may be contrasted with the locations of the European stone monuments (megaliths) in western Europe shown on the inset.

Explore the Map

1. What advantages did the locations of the rivers provide to the growing cultures?

2. How do the distances between the European megaliths (stone monuments) and Mesopotamia support the view that these cultures developed independently?

3. How did Nubia serve geographically to connect the Mediterranean world with sub-Saharan Africa?

people who lived in round huts scattered over about 12 acres. Human social forms broadened from small kin groups to include relative strangers. The schoolboy whom we met earlier had to make a point of introducing his teacher to his father. This effort would have been unheard of in the small hunting clans of the Paleolithic.

Agriculture also sparked a major change in values. Since people no longer had to carry everything they owned as they traveled, farming, animal husbandry, and fixed settlement led to the accumulation of goods, including domesticated animals. Consequently, a new social differentiation arose in agricultural villages as some people acquired more belongings than others.

The social stratification that arose in the earliest cities included slavery as part of what people thought of as the natural order of things. | Slavery | There were various ways to become a slave in ancient Middle Eastern society. Sometimes economic catastrophe caused parents to sell their children or even themselves into slavery to repay their debts, and children born to slaves were automatically enslaved. Although slavery was part of ancient societies, it was a slavery that could be fairly fluid—unlike the slavery of the early modern world, it was not a racial issue. Slaves could save money to purchase their freedom, and children born of a freewoman and a slave were free. Ancient slavery, while taken for granted, was based on an individual's bad luck or unfortunate birth, so a servile status did not hold the severe stigma it later would acquire.

The accumulation of goods also changed the nature of warfare. Although hunter-gatherers fought over territory at times, the skirmishes tended to be short-lived and small scale because the individuals involved were too valuable to waste through this sort of conflict. The agricultural revolution pushed warfare to a larger scale. With the population increase that the revolution fueled, there were more people to engage in conflict and more rewards for the winners, who could gain more goods and enslave the losers. Excavations have shown that the early settlement of Jericho was surrounded by a great stone wall about three yards thick—one of the earliest human-made defensive structures. Indeed, people must have greatly feared their neighbors to invest the labor needed to build such a wall with only stone hand tools. Settlements arose throughout the Neolithic in Europe and in Asia Minor (as well as in many regions in Asia), but the mainstream in the story of the West arose farther east in a river valley where writing preserved the details of the development of even larger and more sophisticated cities.

STRUGGLING WITH THE FORCES OF NATURE: MESOPOTAMIA, 3000–ca. 1000 B.C.E.

Between 3000 and 1000 B.C.E., people began to cultivate a broad curve of land that stretched from the Persian Gulf to the shores of the Mediterranean (**Map 1.1**). This arc, the Fertile Crescent, has been called the cradle or birthplace of Western civilization. It earned this appellation in part because of its lucky possession of essential plants and animals and its central location, which placed it at a crossroads, for mingling of ideas and peoples. The | Bronze Age | ancient Greeks called this region Mesopotamia, or "land between the rivers," emphasizing the importance of the great Tigris and Euphrates rivers to the life of the area. The earliest cities in which civilization took root were located in the southern part of Mesopotamia. During the late Neolithic period, people living in this region used agriculture; sometime after 3000 B.C.E., they learned to smelt metals to make tools and weapons. By smelting, they developed a process to combine copper and tin to make a much stronger metal, bronze. At last, there was a substance that improved on stone, and archaeologists note this innovation by calling this period the Bronze Age.

Life in southern Mesopotamia was harsh but manageable. Summer temperatures reached a sweltering 120 degrees Fahrenheit, and the region received a meager average rainfall of less than 10 inches a year. Yet the slow-running Euphrates created vast marshlands that stayed muddy and wet even during the dry season. Villagers living along the slightly higher ground near the marshes poled their boats through the shallow waters as they netted abundant river fish and shot waterfowl with their bows and arrows. Domesticated cattle and sheep grazed on the rich marsh grass while agriculturalists farmed the fertile high ground, which was actually made up of islands in the marshland. The villagers used the marsh reeds as fuel and as material to make sturdy baskets, and they fashioned the swamp mud into bricks and pottery.

The Origins of Western Civilization

In about 3000 B.C.E., a climate change occurred that forced the southern Mesopotamians to alter their way of life. As they did so, they created a more complex society that we call Sumerian—the earliest civilization. Starting around 3200 B.C.E., the region became drier. The rivers no longer flooded as much of the land as before, and more and more of the marshes evaporated. When the rivers flooded, they still deposited fertile soil in the former marshlands, but the floods came at the wrong times of the year for easy agriculture. Fed by the melting snows in the Zagros Mountains (see **Map 1.1**), the Tigris flooded between April and June—a time highly inconvenient for agriculture in a region where the growing season runs from autumn to early summer. Furthermore, the floods were unpredictable; they could wash away crops still ripening in the fields or come too early to leave residual moisture in the soil for planting. Men and women had to learn how to use the river water efficiently to maintain the population that had established itself during centuries of simpler marsh life. Now people began to dig channels to irrigate the dry land and save the water for when they needed it, but these efforts were never certain because the floods were unpredictable. Mesopotamians developed an intense pessimism that was shaped by the difficult natural environment of the land between the rivers, which could bring seemingly random abundance or disaster.

FIGURE 1.3 Ziggurat at Ur, ca. 2100 B.C.E. The great mud-brick temples known as ziggurats rose from the flat landscapes of Mesopotamia. The builder wrote that he was ordered to erect this ziggurat by his god Marduk. The structure shows both the power of religion and the skill of builders in this cradle of Western civilization.

To manage the complex irrigation projects and planning required to survive in this unpredictable environment, the Sumerians developed a highly organized society—they worked hard to bring order to the chaos that seemed to surround them. Their resourcefulness paid off; by 3000 B.C.E., the valley had become a rich food-producing area. The population of Uruk, shown on **Map 1.1**, had expanded to nearly 10,000 by about 2900 B.C.E. Neighbors no longer knew each other, and everyone looked to a centralized administration to organize daily life.

| Administration |

Priests and priestesses provided the needed organization. In exchange, these religious leaders claimed a percentage of the land's produce. With their new wealth, they built imposing temples that dominated the skylines of cities like Uruk and Ur. **Figure 1.3** is a modern-day photograph of one of those temples, which was built about 2100 B.C.E. The temple shown here consists of levels of steps that were designed to lead the faithful up toward heaven. Known as a **ziggurat,** the structure was intended to bridge the gap between gods and humans. These huge structures were located in a temple complex that spanned several acres. A statue of a god or goddess was placed in a sacred room at the top, and after priests and priestesses conducted a ritual dedication of the statue, people believed the deity dwelled symbolically within the temple, bringing blessings to the whole community. The scale and wealth committed to the ziggurat revealed the dominant role that religion played in the Sumerians' lives.

Ziggurats also served as administrative and economic centers of cities, with storehouses and administrative rooms housed in the lower levels. They were bustling places as people came to bring goods and socialize with neighbors. Just as religion was at the center of the Sumerian world, these buildings, rising like mountains out of the mud plains, served as the center of city life.

| Economic functions |

The labor and goods of the local men and women belonged to the deity who lived in the inner room at the top of the temple. In one temple dedicated to a goddess, attendants washed, clothed, and perfumed the statue every day, and servants burned incense and played music for the statue's pleasure. Meanwhile, temple administrators organized irrigation projects and tax collection in the cities to foster the abundance that allowed the great cities to flourish and serve their patron deities. Through these centralized religious organizations, ancient loyalties to family and clan were slowly replaced by political and religious ties that linked devoted followers to the city guarded by their favored deity. This was a crucial step in creating the large political units that were to become a hallmark of Western civilization.

Life in a Sumerian City

In the shadow of the ziggurats, people lived in mud-brick houses with thick walls that insulated them from heat, cold, and noise. Women and slaves prepared the family meals, which consisted mostly of barley (in the south) or wheat (in the north). Vegetables, cheese, fish, figs, and dates supplemented the Sumerian diet. A large portion of the calories people consumed came from ale. Forty percent of all the grain grown in the region was brewed for ale by women in their homes, not only for their family's consumption but also for sale.

Although Mesopotamia offered early settlements the significant advantage of indigenous plants and animals, the area had some severe

Trade

shortages. The river valleys lacked metal and stone, which were essential for tools and weapons. The earliest settlements depended on long-distance trade for these essential items, and soon the wheel was invented to move cartloads of goods more easily. Materials came from Syria, the Arabian peninsula, and even India, and Mesopotamian traders produced goods for trade. The most lucrative products were textiles. Traders transported woven wool great distances in their quest for stone, metal, and, later, luxury goods. Mesopotamian goods, animals, and even plants moved slowly as far as China as the ancient cultures of the Eurasian land embarked on mass trade. The essential trade routes that marked the whole history of Western civilization appeared at the dawn of its inception.

In the bustling urban centers, families remained the central social tie. Parents arranged marriages for their sons and daughters and bound the contract with an exchange of goods that women brought to the marriage as their dowry. The earliest

Families

written laws regulated married life in an attempt to preserve public peace through private ties. Adultery was a serious crime punished by death, but divorce was permitted. If a woman who was above reproach as a wife wished a divorce, she could keep her dowry. If, however, a wife neglected her home and acted foolishly in public, she would lose her dowry. Her husband could then insist that she remain as a servant in his house even when he remarried. The laws also recognized that men kept concubines in addition to their legal wives and provided ways for children of such informal unions to be considered legitimate. All these laws attempted to preserve the family as an economic unit and as the central social unit in a complex, changing society.

Sumerian women worked in many shops in the cities—as wine sellers, tavern keepers, and merchants. Some women were prosti-

Women's work

tutes, although in time Sumerians came to view this profession as a threat to more traditional ties. Late in Mesopotamian history, laws arose that insisted on special clothing to distinguish "respectable" women from prostitutes. Ordinary women were expected to veil their heads in public, whereas prostitutes and slaves were forced to go about their day with bare heads. At the end of Mesopotamian ascendancy, these laws were made extremely strict—any slave woman who dared to wear a veil was punished by having her ears cut off. In this society, in which people did not know one another, city residents strove mightily to distinguish social ranks. City life came with increasing emphasis on social stratification as the cornerstone of urban order.

Gods and Goddesses of the River Valley

The men and women of the Tigris-Euphrates river valley believed that all parts of the natural world were invested with will. For example, if a river flooded, the event was interpreted as an act of the gods. People also viewed intercity warfare as a battle between each city's gods. On a broader level, the Sumerians saw themselves and their deities as combatants locked in a struggle against a mysterious chaos that could destroy the world at any moment—just as sometimes the unpredictable rivers flooded and brought destruction. People viewed themselves as slaves of the gods and provided the deities with everything they needed—from sacrifices to incense to music—to try to keep order in their uncertain world. In spite of their appeasements, however, when disorder appeared in the form of natural disasters or disease, the pessimistic Sumerians were not surprised.

In addition to venerating their city's patron, Sumerians in time invested their universe with a bewildering number of demons who needed placating. Demons caused illness, and magicians or priests—rather than physicians—were called on for cures. To understand the world, priests tried to read the future in the entrails of animals (a practice known as **augury**). Magic, omens, and amulets rounded out the Mesopotamian religious world, as people struggled to try to control what seemed to be a world in which people owed everything to capricious deities.

An anonymous Sumerian poem of despair expresses the anxiety that came with this view of religious responsibility. In this

Sumerian pessimism

poem, a once-prosperous man suffers a reversal of fortune. He laments:

My ill luck has increased, and I do not find the right.
I called to my god, but he did not show his face,
I prayed to my goddess, but she did not raise her head.

The man seeks out diviners and dream priests, but no one can tell him the omission that brought about his downfall. In his despair, he can only hope that continued devotion to the gods will restore his prosperity, but his tone is not optimistic.

Neither the Sumerians nor their eventual conquerors envisioned an attractive afterlife. They believed that the spirits of the dead went to a shadowy, disagreeable place from where they might occasionally affect the living, usually for ill. Sumerians' only hope for happiness lay in the present life, and that happiness hinged on capricious deities who cared little for humans.

These beliefs prevailed in the Fertile Crescent from the fourth millennium B.C.E. up to the middle of the first millennium B.C.E., even as conquests changed the prevailing rulers.

Sargon

During that time, conquerors made a conscious effort to appease the local deities, and this

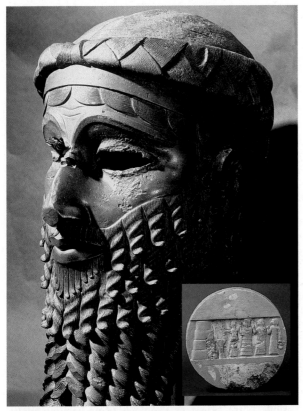

FIGURE 1.4 King Sargon and His Daughter, Enheduanna, ca. 2350 B.C.E. Sargon used religion to unite the people of his empire, and his daughter served as high priestess of both the Akkadian and the Sumerian goddesses. She is shown in the inset (second figure from the left) worshiping at an altar.

administration, sky gods became more crucial in the heavenly hierarchy. Fearsome war gods like Marduk sometimes demanded human sacrifices in exchange for victory over invading tribes. The heavenly hierarchy grew more elaborate and demanding.

By the third millennium B.C.E., earthly society in the ancient Middle East mirrored the hierarchical heavenly one. Kingship was universally accepted as the correct political order, and castes of nobles and priests were also deemed natural. Inequality among people was seen as normal and theologically justified, and people accepted their place in this highly ordered world with kings on top and slaves on the bottom. Individuals' longings for social justice and hopes for improving their situations all took place within a frame of reality that was very different from ours— one that assumed inequality was natural.

Sometime during the second millennium B.C.E., the Sumerians began to reflect on individuals' relationships with the gods. Instead of being content with a corporate association between a city and its guardian, some men and women looked to a more personal alliance, just as the despairing poet we met earlier cried out for a divine explanation of his plight. This longing led individuals to ponder the concept of immortality, wondering whether death was avoidable. In the celebrated poem *The Epic of Gilgamesh,* the poet articulates this search for meaning in death while telling an engaging story of a Sumerian hero and his fortunes. This is an early example of an important literary genre called the epic of quest. Gilgamesh (shown in **Figure 1.5**) was a king who ruled Uruk (see **Map 1.1**) in about 2700 B.C.E. Sometime after 2000 B.C.E., stories about the by-then semimythical king were collected and written down in the epic. In one version of Gilgamesh's adventures, his best friend, Enkidu, is killed and the reality of death strikes home. Gilgamesh refuses to bury Enkidu; in his grief he is unwilling to give up his friend. When the reality of decomposition confronts the king, he travels to find the secret of immortality. At the bottom of the sea he finds a plant that will give eternal life, only to see the magic herb stolen by a snake before he can bring it back to Enkidu. Gilgamesh is left facing the reality of death and the equally important reality of the value of finding joy in the present. This pessimistic epic once again reveals the Sumerian assumption that humans are doomed to struggle endlessly in a difficult universe.

The carving of Gilgamesh shown in **Figure 1.5** was made in the eighth century B.C.E. and shows the enduring popularity of the Sumerian legend. Here Gilgamesh is shown with the long curled beard of a king—which looks remarkably like Sargon's in **Figure 1.4.** The captured lion illustrates his hunting prowess. These characteristics of kings—power and strength—persist through the ancient world.

Individual longings

accommodation serves as a model for the continuing interchange of ideas that was one of the strengths of Western culture. For example, when the Akkadian ruler Sargon invaded Sumer in about 2350 B.C.E., he had to facilitate peace among the Akkadian northerners and the Sumerian southerners. The bronze head probably depicting Sargon shown in **Figure 1.4** was designed to show the power of this great king. His long beard, carefully curled, was a symbol of masculine strength, and he wears a band around his head showing his royal office.

Sargon chose religion as the key to uniting the people and appointed his daughter Enheduanna as high priestess of both the Akkadian and Sumerian goddesses. In the inset in **Figure 1.4,** the priestess (the second figure from the left) is shown wearing the elaborate clothing appropriate to her rank, surrounded by her attendants as she moves to the altar to worship. Enheduanna wrote beautiful hymns (which have survived to the present) in which she identified the Sumerian goddess Inanna with her Akkadian counterpart, Ishtar. She proved so successful in reconciling goddesses in this way that Sargon's successors continued the practice of making their daughters high priestesses, thus forging a link between the cultures of the region. As kings began to handle earthly

FIGURE 1.5. Gilgamesh, eighth century B.C.E. *The Epic of Gilgamesh,* preserved on cuneiform tablets, is the oldest surviving epic poem, ca. 2000 B.C.E. This image of Gilgamesh holding a conquered lion reveals how visual illustrations served to remind people of their treasured literature.

The Development of Writing

Although religion dominated Mesopotamian thought, the Sumerians' real impact on the future of Western civilization derived from their more practical inventions. As Mesopotamian cities expanded and grew wealthy, the need arose for a system of keeping records that would prove more enduring and accurate than the spoken word. In response, the Sumerians developed a system of writing. Some scholars believe that writing first emerged from a system of trade tokens. For example, if a merchant wanted to verify the number of sheep someone else was supposed to deliver, he would count out tokens to represent the sheep and

seal them in a clay envelope that would be broken open upon delivery. The tokens left an imprint in the clay, and in time people realized that they could omit the tokens entirely and simply mark the clay.

At first, Sumerian writing consisted of stylized pictures of the objects represented—birds, sheep, or bowls to signify food. Soon the characters became more abstract and indicated sounds as well as objects. By 2800 B.C.E., the Sumerians had developed a sophisticated writing system called **cuneiform** (named from the Latin word that means "wedge"). Scribes imprinted wedge-shaped characters into wet clay tablets, which became highly durable when dried. **Figure 1.6** shows a tablet of cuneiform script made in about 2600 B.C.E., which lists quantities of various commodities.

Cuneiform

Scribes labored for many years to memorize the thousands of characters of cuneiform script. By 2500 B.C.E., scribal schools had been established to train the numerous clerks needed to serve the palaces and temples. Some surviving cuneiform tablets reveal that these students also studied mathematics and geometry. At first, girls attended these scribal schools, and records testify to a number of successful female scribes. Later, however, the occupation became exclusively male, but the reasons for this change have been lost. The schoolboy described at the beginning of this chapter was one of the lucky few who were trained to read and write. Anyone possessing these skills was assured a prosperous future.

Most of the Sumerian tablets that have been excavated refer to inventories, wills, contracts, payrolls, property transfers, and correspondence between monarchs. Such content reflects both the complexity of this civilization and the everyday necessity of tracking economic transactions. However, writing also let people record more abstract subject matter. *The Epic of Gilgamesh* and other myths preserved the dreams and hopes of these early civilizations, and the hymns of the priestess-poet Enheduanna attest to their spiritual longings and aesthetic sensibilities. However, beyond providing us a glimpse of this long-lost civilization, the invention of writing gave Western culture a distinct advantage over societies that depended only on human memory to recall their achievements. Writing enabled the transfer and dissemination of knowledge, which allowed people to build on previously acquired advancements instead of continually rediscovering and relearning the same material.

Written records

Laws and Justice

Writing also fostered the emergence of another element that would remain an essential component of Western civilization: a written law code. Recording laws in writing was an attempt to establish order in the land between the rivers that seemed so susceptible to chaos. But these laws also tried to express principles of justice that outlasted the ruler who issued them. As early as 2500 B.C.E., Uruinimgina tried to reform his society by passing laws that protected the powerless while preserving the socially stratified society that all took for granted. This tradition continued throughout Mesopotamian history and formed a powerful precedent for subsequent civilizations. In about 2100 B.C.E., Ur-Nammu, king of Ur, wrote laws to preserve "the principles of truth and equity."

The most famous and complete of the ancient law codes was that of the Babylonian king Hammurabi (ca. 1792–1750 B.C.E.), who ruled the southern Mesopotamian valley. In the prologue to his law code, which is preserved in cuneiform script on a stone column, the king expressed the highest principles of justice: "I established law and justice in the language of the land and promoted the welfare of the people." Studying Hammurabi's code, which was a compilation of existing laws, opens a window into the lives of these ancient urban dwellers. It regulated everything from family life to physicians' fees to building requirements. The king seemed determined to order his society, for he introduced harsh penalties that had been absent from earlier laws. His code literally demanded an "eye for an eye"—one law stipulated that "should a man destroy another's eye, he shall lose his own." Another stated that a son who strikes his father shall have his hand cut off.

Hammurabi's code clearly expressed the strict social hierarchy that Mesopotamian society counted as natural. The laws specified different penalties for the three social orders: elites, freemen, and slaves. The elites included everyone from officials to priests and warriors. Beneath them were freemen, including artisans, merchants, professionals, and some farmers. Slaves occupied the bottom stratum, but they, too, had some rights under Hammurabi's laws—for example, they might own land and marry free persons. Many of the laws sought to protect the powerless so, as the prologue says, "that the strong may not oppress the weak."

Many laws tried to protect women and children from unfair treatment and limited the authority of husbands over their households. For example, women could practice various trades and hold public positions. Husbands could not accuse their wives of adultery without proof, for the penalty for proven adultery was harsh—the adulterous wife and her lover would be drowned. However, a woman could obtain a divorce from her husband. In spite of

Code of Hammurabi

Women and children

FIGURE 1.6 Cuneiform Script, ca. 2600 B.C.E. Sumerian writing, made with wedge-shaped indentations in wet clay, revolutionized record keeping, allowing texts to long outlast memory. This tablet records lists of trade commodities.

these protections, women still remained largely the property of their husbands. For example, a woman could be put to death for entering—without her husband—a facility that served alcoholic beverages. Furthermore, a wife's fortunes were so dependent upon her husband that he could even sell her into slavery to pay his debts.

Perhaps one of the most significant things about Hammurabi's code was that the king intended his laws to outlast his own rule. On the tablet, he inscribed: "For all future time, may the king who is in the land observe the words of justice which I have written upon my monument!" Writing, and written law in particular, gave kings and reformers like Hammurabi hope for the establishment of timeless justice and a chance for a kind of personal immortality for the king.

Indo-Europeans: New Contributions in the Story of the West

While the people in the Fertile Crescent developed many of the elements that contributed to the formation of Western civilization—agriculture, writing, and law—the emerging culture remained subject to transformation. As we have seen, one of the advantages of the ancient Middle East was its location, which permitted it to benefit from influences from the far reaches of Asia. Of course, this geographic openness also contributed to instability—ideas often came with invaders and destruction. The region north of the Black Sea and the Caucasus Mountains (see **Map 1.4**) produced peoples living on the steppes who waged war on the peoples of the Fertile Crescent and developed a culture that eventually had a profound influence on the West.

Linguists, who analyze similarities in languages, have labeled these people Indo-European because their language served as the basis for virtually all subsequent European languages (except Finnish, Hungarian, and Basque). This language family sepa-

| Indo-European languages |

rates the Indo-Europeans from most of the original inhabitants of the Fertile Crescent, who spoke "Semitic" languages. The steady influx of Indo-European invaders (later called Celts, Latins, Greeks, or Germans) formed the dominant population of Europe. Other Indo-Europeans moved east and settled in India or traveled south into modern-day Turkey and Iran.

The Indo-Europeans were led by a warrior elite, who were buried in elaborate graves. Excavations of these graves have allowed scholars to analyze the prized possessions and weapons that were buried with these rulers, yielding many insights into this society. Some archaeologists refer to the Indo-Europeans as "battle-ax people" because of the many axes found in their burial sites. They also rode

| Mounted warriors |

horses, which they first domesticated for riding in about 2000 B.C.E. Riding on horseback gave Indo-European warriors the deadly advantages of speed, mobility, and reach over the Stone and Bronze Age archers they encountered in their travels.

The warrior elite of the Indo-Europeans excelled in battle and moved their families with them as they journeyed and fought. They carried their belongings in heavy carts outfitted with four solid, wooden wheels. The carts were a significant departure from the Sumerian two-wheeled chariots, which proved too unstable over long distances.

| Contributions |

The heavy carts traveled best over flat surfaces, and evidence indicates that as early as 2000 B.C.E. wooden roadways were built across boglands in northern Europe to accommodate the movement of people and their goods.

When the Indo-Europeans moved into the Fertile Crescent, they were not literate, but they preserved their values in oral traditions. Later, influenced by the literary traditions of those they conquered, Indo-Europeans developed their own written languages, and many of these tales were written down and preserved. Ideals of a warrior elite and worship of gods who lived in the sky instead of on the earth continued, as did the Indo-European language. These elements were among the Indo-European contributions

to Western civilization. In turn, early in the history of the Indo-Europeans (long before they acquired a written language), they adopted some things from the Mesopotamian cradle of civilization. They acquired many of the grains and other foods that were native to Mesopotamia and spread them widely. The successful culture of the Fertile Crescent was making its impact known far outside the river valleys that spawned it.

Hittites Establish Their Empire

In about 1650 B.C.E., an Indo-European people called the Hittites established a kingdom in Asia Minor (modern Turkey) and set up their capital at Hattusas (see **Map 1.2**). For the next three hundred years, the Hittite people planted crops on the fertile lands north of their capital, irrigated their fruit groves, and mined the ore-rich mountains. Throughout this time, they interacted with their neighbors in Mesopotamia and integrated much of Mesopotamian language, literature, law, and religion into their own Indo-European heritage. The interactions were often violent as the Hittites entered into the stormy politics of the ancient world.

The Hittites introduced a new technology of warfare into the West in the form of powerful—and deadly—war chariots. The oldest reference to chariot warfare in the ancient Near East comes from about the eighteenth century B.C.E., in a text that mentions

FIGURE 1.7. War Chariot, ca. 1299 B.C.E. The Hittites' war chariot was a fearsome military innovation that launched an arms race in the ancient world. The light wheels allowed rapid deployment that overwhelmed slower infantry.

forty teams of horses at one battle. The wheels of the Hittite chariots, lighter than those for any previous vehicle, made the chariots highly maneuverable, and the axle was set forward for stability. **Figure 1.7** shows a Hittite chariot with an archer trampling a fallen enemy. The Hittites' chariot-building prowess led to an arms race of sorts, culminating in the Battle of Kadesh in 1299 B.C.E., when some five thousand chariots participated in the struggle between Egyptians and Hittites.

Fortunately for historians, the Hittites learned the art of writing from the Mesopotamians. At Hattusas archaeologists have excavated about 10,000 cuneiform tablets, which shed much light on this culture that stood at the crossroads of the Middle East for such a long time.

A king whose military and administrative skill significantly changed the Hittite fortunes came to power in about 1380 B.C.E. Suppiluliuma I (r. ca. 1380–ca. 1345) thought of himself as both avenger and conqueror, and he launched the Hittites into building an empire. Within a century, he and his successors had built the most powerful state in the region. Suppiluliuma placed his sons in control of Syrian states and gained control of the lucrative trade along the Euphrates. Inevitably, Hittite armies clashed with the culture arising to the south and west—along the river valley of the magnificent Nile River.

RULE OF THE GOD-KING: ANCIENT EGYPT,
ca. 3100–1000 B.C.E.

The food crops that proved so successful in Mesopotamia spread to Egypt, stimulating another ancient civilization that arose on the banks of a great river—the roots of Western civilization moved farther west. The Nile River in Egypt flows more than 4,000 miles, from central Africa north to the Mediterranean Sea. Just as in Mesopotamia, a climate change forced dependence on the great river. In about 6000 B.C.E. the prevailing Atlantic rains shifted, changing great grassy plains into desert and forcing people to move closer to the Nile to use its waters.

Nile Valley

Unlike the Tigris and Euphrates, the Nile reliably overflowed its banks every year at a time convenient for planting—flooding in June and receding by October. During this flood, the river deposited a layer of fertile black earth in time for a winter planting of cereal crops. In ancient times, the Nile also provided the Egyptians with an excellent communication and transportation system. The river flowed north, encouraging traffic in that direction, but the prevailing winds blew from north to south, helping ships to sail against the current.

Egypt was more isolated than the ancient civilizations to the northeast. The deserts to the Nile's east and west stymied most would-be invaders, and in the southern Sudan a vast marsh protected the area from encroachers. Potential invaders from the Mediterranean Sea confronted shallows that prevented ships from easily approaching the Egyptian coast. As a result, Egyptian civilization developed without the fear of conquest or the resultant blending and conflict among cultures that marked the Mesopotamian cities. By about 3100 B.C.E., a king from Upper Egypt (in the south), who according to tradition was named Menes, had consolidated his rule over the entire Egyptian land.

Prosperity and Order: The Old Kingdom, ca. 2700–2181 B.C.E.

Ancient Egyptians believed that the power of the gods was visible in the natural world—in the Nile and in the people and animals that benefited from its bounty. Consequently, they worshiped the divine spirit that was expressed through heavenly bodies, animals, and even insects. Over time, some gods were exalted over others, and deities were combined and blurred. However, through most of Egypt's history the most important deities were the sun god Re (or Amon) and the Nile spirits Isis, her husband-consort, Osiris, and their son, the falcon-god Horus. Unlike the Mesopotamians, the Egyptians were optimistic about their fortunes. They believed they were blessed by the gods, who brought such a regular and fertile flooding of the Nile, not cursed by their chaotic whims. This optimism infused Egyptian culture with extraordinary continuity—why change something that brought such blessings?

At the heart of their prosperity was the king, whom Egyptians considered the living embodiment of the deity, and this linking of political power with religion reinforced the stability of the Old Kingdom. While

Preserving order

Mesopotamians believed their kings served as priests to their gods, Egyptians believed their rulers *were* gods, who had come to earth to bring truth, justice, and order—all summarized in the word **ma'at**. In return, the populace was obligated to observe a code of correct behavior that was included in the concept of *ma'at*. In about 2450 B.C.E., a high palace official named Ptah-hotep left a series of instructions for his son, in which he urged the boy to follow the precepts of *ma'at*: "He who departs from its laws is punished. . . . Evil may win riches, but it is the strength of *ma'at* that endures long." For millennia, kings and advisors like Ptah-hotep believed strongly that the importance of proper behavior brought prosperity to the land, and such beliefs contributed to a stable society. (The funeral inscription in Document 1.1 shows

DOCUMENTS

An Egyptian Nobleman Writes His Obituary

This document from second-millennium B.C.E. Egypt records the obituary inscribed on the tomb of an Egyptian nobleman named Ameni (or Amenemhet). This excerpt reveals what he counted as his greatest deeds in his years of service during Egypt's Middle Kingdom.

First Expedition

I followed my lord when he sailed southward to overthrow his enemies among the four barbarians. I sailed southward, as the son of a count, wearer of the royal seal, and commander in chief of the troops of the Oryx nome, as a man represents his old father, according to [his] favor in the palace and his love in the court. I passed Kush, sailing southward, I advanced the boundary of the land, I brought all gifts; my praise, it reached heaven. Then his majesty returned in safety, having overthrown his enemies in Kush the vile. I returned, following him, with ready face. There was no loss among my soldiers.

Second Expedition

I sailed southward, to bring gold ore for the majesty of the King of Upper and Lower Egypt, Kheperkere (Sesostris I), living forever and ever. I sailed southward together with the hereditary prince, count, oldest son of the king, of his body, Ameni. I sailed southward, with a number, 400 of all the choicest of my troops, who returned in safety, having suffered no loss. I brought the gold exacted of me; I was praised for it in the palace, the king's-son praised god for me.

Ameni's Able Administration

I was amiable, and greatly loved, a ruler beloved of his city. Now, I passed years as ruler in the Oryx nome. All the imposts of the king's house passed through my hand. The gang-overseers of the crown possessions of the shepherds of the Oryx nome gave to me 3,000 bulls in their yokes. I was praised on account of it in the palace each year of the loan-herds. I carried all their dues to the king's house; there were no arrears against me in any office of his. The entire Oryx nome labored for me.

Ameni's Impartiality and Benevolence

There was no citizen's daughter whom I misused, there was no widow whom I oppressed, there was no [peasant] whom I repulsed, there was no shepherd whom I repelled, there was no overseer of serf-laborers whose people I took for (unpaid) imposts, there was none wretched in my community, there was none hungry in my time. When years of famine came I plowed all the fields of the Oryx nome, as far as its southern and northern boundary, preserving its people alive and furnishing its food so that there was none hungry therein. I gave to the widow as (to) her who had a husband; I did not exalt the great above the small in all that I gave. Then came great Niles, possessors of grain and all things, [but] I did not collect the arrears of the field.

SOURCE: James Henry Breasted, *Ancient Records of Egypt*, vol. 1 (Chicago: University of Chicago Press, 1906), pp. 251–253.

Analyze the Document

1. Where did the nobleman travel in the course of his service, and what does this tell you about the global connections of the ancient world?

2. What kinds of accomplishments did he most want readers of this inscription to remember about him?

3. What does this inscription reveal about the values of ancient Egypt?

---

these enduring values.) This ordered society was ruled by a god-king later called **pharaoh** (great house), a term that referred to the general institution of the monarchy as well as the ruler.

The Old Kingdom period (ca. 2700–2181 B.C.E.) saw astonishing prosperity and peace, as farming and irrigation methods provided an abundance of crops and wealth to many. Unlike the Mesopotamian valley, Egypt had ready access to mineral resources, most importantly copper, which was in great demand for tools. Egyptians refined copper ore at the site of the surface mines, and ingots of copper were transported by caravans of donkeys overland to the Nile. From there, the precious ores were manufactured or used to trade abroad. Egypt was also happily situated to capitalize on trade with Nubia, which gave access to the resources of sub-Saharan Africa. (See Global Connections on page 17.) From Nubia, Egyptians gained gold, ivory, ebony, gems, and aromatics in exchange for Egyptian cloth and manufactured goods. With the surpluses of metals and grains, Egyptians could import goods from the Middle East and beyond. In addition to textiles, Egyptians desperately needed wood to make large seagoing vessels for their trade and navy. All this industry generated prosperity for many people, and in the Old Kingdom, people used these resources to support close families.

Ptah-hotep advised his son to start a family as soon as he could afford to: "If you are prosperous you should establish a household and love your wife as is fitting. . . . Make her heart glad as long as you live." The artwork of the time suggests that many Egyptians took Ptah-hotep's advice and established

Trade

Family life

Nubia: The Passage from the Mediterranean to the Heart of Africa

From the dawn of civilization, the history of the West and the history of Africa developed together through cultural interactions that unfolded along the Nubian corridor. And throughout history, diverse groups—who spoke languages different from Egyptian—mingled in ancient Nubia. At times these groups even managed to unite into large kingdoms—one of which would conquer Egypt itself. Late in ancient Egyptian history, Nubian kings even became Egyptian pharaohs.

Lush and flat, the northern Nile valley stimulated the ancient Egyptians' agriculture and settlement. But near Aswan, in the south, the land changed. Here sandstone cliffs dropped directly from the desert plateau to the riverbank, and the river churned as it descended through a succession of swift rapids. These rapids are the first of six cataracts that impeded navigation south along the great river. Early rulers of Egypt marked the First Cataract as a natural southern border of their kingdom. However, later Egyptians pushed south beyond the First Cataract into Nubia. Egyptians had strong motivation to do so: Nubia provided the only reliable route around the Sahara desert to the riches that lay deep within the interior of the African continent.

In Nubia, goods moved north to the Mediterranean and south from Egypt and Mesopotamia. From the beginning, both Nubians and northerners recognized the benefits of this trade. See **Figure 1.11** for an artistic portrayal of Nubian trade. As early as 3000 B.C.E., domestic goats and sheep that had originated in Mesopotamia showed up in Nubia. Sometime after that, Nubians began to cultivate the domestic grains from Mesopotamia along the valley of the southern Nile beyond the First Cataract.

As early as the Old Kingdom in Egypt, kings valued the goods that came through Nubia, and even the sparse records from this ancient time reveal the importance of the trade with the south. For example, the Egyptian princes who governed Aswan bore the title "Keeper of the Door of the South," and sometime around 2250 B.C.E., the pharaohs sent a prince of Aswan named Herkhuf (or Harkhuf) on three journeys into Nubia to trade and to recruit mercenary troops to fight in Egypt's armies. Herkhuf headed south on the Nile, his ships propelled against the current by the prevailing north winds. The skilled navigators he employed negotiated the roiling rapids. The proud records carved on Herkhuf's tomb do not indicate how far beyond the Second Cataract he traveled, for we cannot identify the names of the various tribes he encountered. Yet most scholars think he made it to the Third Cataract. Seven months later, Herkhuf returned from one journey with 300 donkeys laden with incense, ebony, oil, leopard skins, elephant tusks, boomerangs, and other goods. His bounty revealed that Nubia served as a trading hub for luxuries and staples far beyond the Nile. The lure of Nubia was only increased when rich gold mines were discovered there in about 1980 B.C.E.

During the Middle Kingdom under the reign of Senwosret I (ca. 1980 B.C.E.), Egyptians began to mine for gold in Nubia, and the rich mines brought Nubia into the politics as well as the trade of the north. (Indeed, "Nubia" means "gold" in Egyptian.) Egyptians began to fortify the Nile, and Nubia engaged in the wars of the north. The fall of the ancient Egyptian kingdom did not end the importance of Nubia, which remained the major passage to the heart of Africa.

Making Connections

1. What aspect of its geographic location made Nubia so important to the ancient world? What role did Nubia play in trade?

2. How did the presence of domestic animals in sub-Saharan Africa demonstrate ancient connections between this region and Mesopotamia?

3. What trade items stimulated the connections between Africa and the Mediterranean?

loving families during this prosperous era. **Figure 1.8** shows a limestone carving of one such family. Seneb, the man depicted in the portrait, was a dwarf who had made a successful career in the court. He headed the court's weaving mill and then became the priest of the dead for two kings. His success was acknowledged when he married a member of the royal house. Husband and wife are shown side by side, perhaps suggesting the woman's high status. In this sculpture, the couple embrace affectionately and smile with seeming self-satisfaction while they tower protectively over the children below. The two figures at the lower left are each placing a finger over their lips, the Egyptian sign for "child." Stylized portraits like these suggest the success, contentment, and prosperity of many Old Kingdom families—at least those with enough wealth to commission portraits.

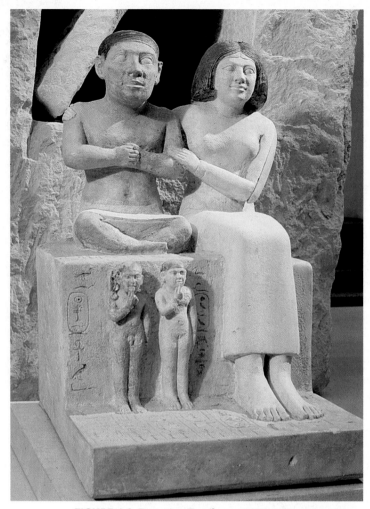

FIGURE 1.8 Egyptian Family, ca. 2320–2250 B.C.E. This is the family portrait of Seneb, head of the royal weaving mill, who married a woman of the royal family. The two are shown with their children in this idealized view of Egyptian family life.

Hieroglyphs: Sacred Writing

Sometime around 3000 B.C.E., Egyptians developed a system of writing. Egyptian writing was not cuneiform, nor was it used primarily for accounting purposes. While Egyptian administrators surely had as much need for clear records as the Sumerians, they primarily used writing to forward religious and magical power. Every sign in their writing system represented a real or mythical object and was designed to express that object's power. The ancient Greeks saw these images on temples and named Egyptian script **hieroglyph,** meaning "sacred writing."

Hieroglyphs were more than a series of simple pictures. Each symbol could express one of three things: the object it portrayed, an abstract idea associated with the object, or one or more sounds of speech from the spoken Egyptian word for the object. (The technical terms for these three uses are *pictogram*, *ideogram*, and *phonogram*.) Because this writing had ceremonial religious use, it changed little over the centuries as

scribes carved it into stone monuments. An example of hieroglyphic writing can be seen in the background of **Figure 1.10** (p. 20).

However, hieroglyphs were too cumbersome for everyday use, so scribes learned two other simplified scripts—called Hieratic and Demotic—to keep records or write literature. Whereas many of the hieroglyphs were carved into stone, everyday records were more often written on papyrus, a kind of paper made from the Nile's abundant papyrus reeds. This versatile, sturdy reed could be reused—much like recycled paper today—and in the dry desert air was very durable. Often in Egypt's history, the lucrative export of papyrus increased the royal treasury.

Scribes studied for many years to master the complicated, varied Egyptian scripts. As in Mesopotamia, there are early records of women scribes, but the occupation later became restricted to men. On one surviving papyrus fragment, a scribe praised his occupation: "Writing for him who knows it is better than all other professions. It pleases more than bread and beer, more than clothing and ointment. It is worth more than an inheritance in Egypt, than a tomb in the west."

Scribes

Pyramids and the Afterlife

Scribes furthered the prosperity of the god-kings by carefully tracking the rulers' finances as they grew rich from state monopolies and taxes on all the products created in the fertile land. Whenever they had excess income, the kings proved their greatness by building pyramids, monuments to their glory that in some cases survive today. Imhotep, the chief advisor to the Egyptian king Djoser in about 2650 B.C.E., designed and built the first pyramid at Sakkara (near Memphis, shown on **Map 1.2,** on page 21). This early pyramid, depicted in **Figure 1.9a,** is called a step pyramid. It was intended to join heaven and earth. An inscription on one pyramid explains: "A staircase to heaven is laid for [the king] so that he may mount up to heaven thereby." Unlike the ziggurats, which were made of dried clay bricks, these pyramids were built of cut stone—a remarkable building innovation.

The Old Kingdom rulers made the pyramids the great symbol of Egyptian power and longevity. An anonymous architect refined the early pyramid design and built the Great Pyramid as a burial tomb for the Fourth Dynasty ruler, Khufu (also known as Kheops), in about 2590 B.C.E. This pyramid became the model for the later Old Kingdom tombs that were built in Giza, which continue to dominate the skyline there. **Figure 1.9b** shows the pyramids at Giza, with the Great Pyramid of Khufu on the left. The pyramid of Khufu's son is in the back; it appears taller because it is on

Pyramids

higher ground. Khufu's pyramid covers about 13 acres and is made of more than two million stone blocks. Peasants labored on these pyramids before planting season during the months when the Nile was in flood. Ancient Greek historians later claimed that the Great Pyramid of Giza took twenty years to build and required the labor of 100,000 workers. Modern estimates tend to agree with these calculations. The pyramids—so visible in the ancient skyline—proclaimed the god-king's immortality and the permanence of the order he brought to the land along the Nile.

Pyramids—and later mortuary temples—were built as tombs for the god-kings or, more precisely, as houses for their departed spirits. The departed's soul was sustained in the tomb by the same food and goods that had sustained the living body.

Afterlife

The Egyptian notion of immortality marked an important contribution to the world of ideas, for the afterlife Egyptians conceived of was dramatically different from the dark world of the Mesopotamian dead. We do not have an exact idea of how the Egyptians visualized the afterlife, but it seems to have been an improved version of this world—a heavenly Nile valley. Some poets even wrote of death as a pleasant release:

Death is before me today
Like a man's longing to see his home
When he has spent many years in captivity.

Upon the death of a king, or in later years a nobleman who could afford a burial, the body was embalmed. Embalmers removed the internal organs through an incision in the abdomen and placed them in a vessel filled with a salty preserving solution. The body cavity was then probably dried in a pile of natron crystals. Later in Egypt's history, embalmers used resin-soaked linen to pack the body cavity. Finally the embalmers wrapped the body in more linen with resin. The wrapped, embalmed body—the mummy—along with a box containing the internal organs, was then placed in a chamber deep within the pyramid. Stocking the tomb with an array of food, household goods, and precious jewels for the pharaoh to enjoy in the afterlife completed the burial process.

Burial rituals

Pyramids from the Old Kingdom contained no images, but later artists painted the interior walls of tombs with scenes of activities that the deceased could expect to enjoy in the afterlife, and these scenes offer us a glimpse of how Egyptians viewed the next world. **Figure 1.10** shows a happy scene that was painted on the walls of a New Kingdom tomb. In this picture, the noble family frolics on a bird-hunting trip that yields far more abundance than any real-life trip ever could. Under their boat

FIGURE 1.9 Pyramids, ca. 2590 B.C.E. These burial places for the royal dead had a long history in the Old Kingdom. Figure 1.9a is the earliest such structure (ca. 2680 B.C.E.), a "step pyramid" intended to join heaven and earth. Figure 1.9b shows the later, most famous pyramids at Giza, with the Great Pyramid of Khufu on the left.

swims a fish so fat it belongs in a fisherman's paradise. A child grips her father's leg while he catches birds with the help of his hunting falcon. His well-dressed wife stands in the background. Even the family cat enjoys an abundant afterlife, catching three

ANCIENT EGYPT CIVILIZATION

ca. 2700–2181 B.C.E.	Old Kingdom
2181–2140 B.C.E.	First Intermediate Period
ca. 2060–1785 B.C.E.	Middle Kingdom
ca. 1785–1575 B.C.E.	Second Intermediate Period
1570–1085 B.C.E.	New Kingdom
ca. 1504–1482 B.C.E.	Pharaoh Hatshepsut
ca. 1377–1360 B.C.E.	Pharaoh Akhenaten
ca. 1279–1213 B.C.E.	Pharaoh Ramses II

KEY DATES

FIGURE 1.10 Egyptian Paradise, ca. 1400 B.C.E.   In this tomb painting of the New Kingdom, the deceased, a court official named Nebamun, is shown with his wife and daughter on a hunting trip in the afterlife. The depiction of scenes of daily life reveals the Egyptians' joy in earthly life, as well as their expectations of a pleasant existence beyond death.

birds at once. This illustration reveals how much the Egyptian "heaven" had changed from the dark Mesopotamian netherworld.

Changing Political Fortunes, ca. 2200–1570 B.C.E.

The order and prosperity promised by the pyramids proved less enduring than the Egyptians expected. At the end of the Old Kingdom period, the climate turned against the god-kings. As drought in southern Nubia led to a series of low floods in Egypt, crops failed, and people pillaged the countryside in a desperate search for food. There was even one account of cannibalism. Under such pressure, Egypt needed a strong ruler to preserve *ma'at*, but one was not forthcoming. Near the end of the Old Kingdom, one king—Pepi II (ca. 2270–2180 B.C.E.)—reputedly ruled for more than 90 years,

> Famine

which was an extraordinary feat in an age when a decade or two was considered a substantial rule and when 40 years of age was the normal life expectancy. However, the old king was unable to keep a strong rule; during his reign, authority broke down, and he outlived his heirs. After his death a succession of little-known kings with very short reigns followed—a clear indication that all was not well within Egypt. Sources indicate that one of these ephemeral rulers was a woman—Nitocris—who ruled for about two years. During these times of weak central authority, local nobles exerted power, and Egypt suffered a period of social and political instability called the First Intermediate Period (2181–2140 B.C.E.).

A text from the time articulated poignantly the widespread misery experienced during these hard years: "Everything is filthy: there is no such thing as clean linen these days. The dead are thrown into the river. . . . The ladies of the nobility exclaim: 'If only

MAP 1.2

The Ancient Near East, ca. 1450 B.C.E.

This map shows the growth of the Egyptian Empire along with the territories of its neighbors, the Hittite Empire and the Mesopotamian kingdoms.

Explore the Map

1. Compare this map with **Map 1.1.** What new territories has Egypt conquered?

2. How was Egyptian culture affected by the conquest of territories populated by peoples of different cultures?

3. How do you think the Egyptian presence in Palestine drew Egypt into the many wars of the Middle East?

we had something to eat!' They are forced to prostitute their daughters. They are reduced to sleeping with men who were once too badly off to take a woman."

During these difficult times, people began to hope for a more pleasant afterlife, which many began to believe was possible for more than just the royal family. In the First Intermediate Period, anyone who could afford the appropriate burial rituals and magic spells could expect to achieve immortality. Still, prosperity continued to elude the Nile valley.

In about 2060 B.C.E., Amenemhat I of Thebes finally restored peace to the crippled valley and introduced what has come to be called the Middle King-

Middle Kingdom

dom period (ca. 2060–1785 B.C.E.). Egypt prospered once again, and one pharaoh wrote: "None was hungry in my years, none thirsted then; men dwelled in peace." During these years, the kings conquered Nubia and grew rich on the gold of that kingdom. This conquest also brought sub-Saharan Africa into closer contact with the Mediterranean world, and continued trade with Nubia integrated African goods and elements of their culture into Egypt's and into the developing Western culture in general. The funeral

inscription in Document 1.1 testifies to the increased trade. Egypt's rulers also introduced impressive engineering projects that expanded Egypt's amount of irrigated land by more than 17,000 acres. The Egyptians also began engaging in lucrative trade with the peoples of the Fertile Crescent. This practice had a price, however: It drew Egypt into the volatile politics of the ancient Middle East.

In the eighteenth century B.C.E., trouble struck again. The kings at the end of the twelfth dynasty were weak, and local magnates began to claim autonomy. Without a strong central authority,

Egypt conquered

the Nubians in the south revolted and broke away from Egyptian control, taking their gold with them. In 1650 B.C.E., the Hyksos who had settled in the lowland where the Nile poured into the Mediterranean (the Delta) rose to power (see **Map 1.1**). The Hyksos brought with them a new technology of warfare. They fought with bronze weapons, chariots, and body armor against the nearly nude Egyptians, who used only javelins and light copper weapons. The Hyksos established a kingdom in the Delta and this uneasy time, the Second Intermediate Period, extended from about 1785 to 1575 B.C.E.

FIGURE 1.11

Egyptian Fresco, ca. 1295–1186 B.C.E.

A fresco is a kind of mural painted on plaster. This **fresco** from Thebes shows Nubians bearing gifts (tribute) of an exotic giraffe, an animal skin draped over a man's arm, a mound of ostrich eggs, and most valuable of all, highly bred cattle, valued for their coloring. All these were brought to the Egyptian pharaoh. Egyptian artists created this fresco to show the power of their ruler, and in the process they portrayed sub-Saharan Africans realistically, with dark skin, particular hairstyles, and woven clothing that we can use as historical evidence for Nubian society.

Connecting Art & Society

1. What does the fresco suggest about the value of Nubian trade to Egypt?

2. Which of the trade items that are depicted continue to be valued today? What makes them valuable?

3. How might this image, with its accurate portrayal of Nubians, be used as historical evidence for the imperial aspirations of the Egyptians?

Political Expansion: The New Kingdom, 1570–1085 B.C.E.

In about 1570 B.C.E., the Egyptians adopted the new technology of warfare. With bronze weapons and chariots of their own, they liberated themselves from the hated Hyksos and established a new dynasty that introduced what historians call the New Kingdom (1570–1085 B.C.E.). While these kings—now officially called pharaohs—intended to restore the conservative glory of the Old Kingdom, they nevertheless remembered the lesson of the invasion from the north and no longer relied on Egypt's geographic isolation to protect their way of life. Instead, the newly militant god-kings embarked on a series of foreign wars to build an empire that would erect a territorial barrier between Egypt and any potential invaders. **Map 1.2** shows the extent of the Egyptian Empire by 1450 B.C.E.

As the Egyptian Empire expanded, it was in turn shaped by Fertile Crescent politics and culture. For example, the riches that poured into the Nile valley from foreign conquests often ended up in the hands of temple priests, who began rivaling the pharaohs in power. Slaves, captured abroad and brought to Egypt, introduced new languages, views, and religions to the valley. Not surprisingly, the lives of Egyptian soldiers, battling in foreign wars, changed for the worse. The scribe we met earlier, who praised his own occupation above all others, wrote about the grim life of a soldier of the New Kingdom: "He is called up for Syria. He may not rest. There are no clothes, no sandals. He drinks water every third day; it is smelly and tastes of salt. His body is ravaged by illness. He does not know what he is about. His body is weak, his legs fail him." As **Map 1.2** shows, the imperial expansion of Egypt encroached on the borders of the strong Hittite Empire, which soon threatened the restored New Kingdom.

Despite the challenges, the imperial pharaohs successfully built their empire and made Egypt prosperous again. However, such expansion always came with a cost. Rulers had to weigh placing resources into military expansion or into local projects. Hatshepsut's (ca. 1504–1482 B.C.E.) endeavors demonstrated this tension as she ruled the extended Egypt (see the Biography on pages 24–25). While protecting her borders, Hatshepsut concentrated her resources on domestic developments and commercial enterprises. Her inscriptions claim that she restored temples that had lain in ruins since the Second Intermediate Period, and she engaged in numerous public works, all achievements that made her popular among her people.

Hatshepsut's accomplishments were all the more remarkable since it was highly unusual for a woman to rule alone. Women in a pharaoh's family had always held the important position of consort to their brother-husbands. They joined them in being descended from gods, but the king had always been the incarnation of the principal deity. Hatshepsut used artistic representations to overcome this problem, ordering that all statues of her portray her as a man. In **Figure 1.13,** on page 25, a formal portrait, she is dressed in the traditional male royal style—bare-chested and wearing a short, stiff skirt. She even wears an artificial, ceremonial beard.

Hatshepsut's successors reversed her traditional politics and revived Egypt's imperial ambitions. The New Kingdom reached its apogee in expansion and prosperity under the reign of Amenhotep III (r. ca. 1412–ca. 1375 B.C.E.). This confident pharaoh built huge statues of himself and a spacious new temple. His luxurious lifestyle, however, took its toll on him. He died at age 38, and his mummified remains reveal a balding, overweight man with rotted teeth.

Empire building

The Religious Experiment of Akhenaten, ca. 1377–1360 B.C.E.

During the New Kingdom, the traditional relationship between the god-king and his priests began to change. Priests of Amon became almost as powerful as the pharaohs in administering the kingdom. The priests of Osiris grew popular with wealthy people, to whom they offered the possibility of immortal life in return for money. Within this increasingly tense environment arose a reformer who tried to create a religious revolution.

Amenhotep IV (r. ca. 1377–1360 B.C.E.), the son of Amenhotep III, tried to renounce the many divine principles worshiped in all the temples of Egypt and institute worship of a single god whom he called Aten, the sun-disk. The god-king changed his name from Amenhotep (Amon is satisfied) to Akhenaten (useful to Aten, the sun-disk). Then he withdrew his support from the old temples and tried to dissolve the powerful priesthoods. Akhenaten also departed from tradition by introducing a new naturalism in art, in which he allowed himself to be portrayed realistically, protruding belly and all (see **Figure 1.12**). However, the artwork in Aten's new temples often featured portraits of Akhenaten's beautiful wife, Nefertiti, without the pharaoh, suggesting that the queen may have played a large role in planning the new cult.

Akhenaten's religion

FIGURE 1.12 Pharaoh Akhenaten and Family, ca. 1340 B.C.E. This limestone carving shows Akhenaten, his wife, Nefertiti, and three of their daughters relaxing in a family pose that departed from the usual formal depictions of the pharaoh. They bask in the rays of Aten, the sun-disk, the new deity they worshiped.

BIOGRAPHY

Hatshepsut & Thutmose
(r. 1473–1458 B.C.E.)   (ca. 1482–1450 B.C.E.)

The Egyptian pharaoh Thutmose I had three children by his chief wife—two sons who died in their youths, and a daughter, Hatshepsut. In the complex households of the pharaohs, the succession to the throne was never clear; Thutmose I also had a son by a lesser wife. This son, Thutmose II, married his half-sister Hatshepsut and succeeded his father as pharaoh.

Thutmose II apparently was sickly and died in 1504 B.C.E. after he and Hatshepsut had a daughter, Neferure. The succession again went to a son by a concubine. However, this next son, Thutmose III, was younger than 10 years old when his father died. The logical regent was his aunt/stepmother, Hatshepsut. Although it was customary for a man to rule,

Powerful

Queen and

Vengeful

Son-in-Law

Hatshepsut wanted to be pharaoh, not regent. To this end, she cultivated the support of the powerful priests of Amon, and of the army, and had herself declared pharaoh. Thutmose III had to accept a position of titular co-ruler with no actual authority. Hatshepsut seems to have treated her young charge well. Contemporaries praised his extraordinary skills in reading and writing and his study of military arts. He was also healthy and a strong athlete. His remains show that he escaped even the severe dental decay that appears in many royal mummies. Thutmose III was probably married to his aunt's daughter, Neferure, to guarantee his succession.

Hatshepsut grappled with two major challenges during her reign: how to forward her political vision for Egypt and how to ensure her

credibility. She approached both tasks shrewdly, ever aware of the importance of appearances as well as policy. In her political vision, she focused attention on trade and peaceful pursuits, and she turned to art and building to validate her rule. Hatshepsut commissioned portraits that showed her dressed as a male king, and she built a magnificent funerary temple intended to stand forever and proclaim her passage into the land of the gods.

While Hatshepsut focused on internal building projects, she kept the army strong, because Egypt's neighbors did not feel powerful enough to threaten the borders. The accomplishments she seemed proudest of, however, were in trade. She commissioned a great carving that recounted her successful trade mission to "Punt," an African kingdom that we can no longer exactly identify, although some historians suggest it may be near modern-day Somalia (see **Map 1.2**). In any case, this wealthy sub-Saharan kingdom had been the destination of several trade

---

Figure 1.12 shows a casual family portrait of Akhenaten, Nefertiti, and three of their daughters. Husband and wife are shown the same size. Both wear regal headdresses that suggest an unusual equality, and Akhenaten affectionately kisses one of his daughters in a remarkably informal portrayal. The sun-disk is above and shines down on both, indicating not only that the family is blessed by the sun deity, but also that they can serve to bring the blessings of the sun to their people.

A beautiful hymn to Aten has survived, perhaps written by Akhenaten himself. In the hymn, the pharaoh praises Aten as the only god: "O sole god, like whom there is no other! Thou didst create the world according to thy desire." In a development remarkable for the ancient world, Akhenaten declares this god to be universal, belonging to all peoples: "Their tongues are separate in speech, and their natures as well; Their skins are distinguished, As thou distinguishest the foreign peoples. . . . The lord of all of them, . . . The lord of every land." In the ancient world, gods were associated with individual peoples and cities, so Akhenaten's praise of a universal god is extraordinary.

Many scholars have speculated about the motives behind this dramatic religious innovation. Had

Akhenaten been influenced by Israelites living in Egypt? Was his declaration of a single god a political move to reduce the power of the priests of Amon? Or was the king a sickly dreamer who merely had a strange spiritual vision? We will never know Akhenaten's motives, but his reign caused turmoil in Egypt.

The Twilight of the Egyptian Empire, 1360–ca. 1000 B.C.E.

Akhenaten was succeeded by Tutankhaton (r. 1347–1338 B.C.E.), who was only 9 years old at the time of his succession. He is shown with his wife in the chapter opener on page 2. Compare the chapter opener with **Figure 1.12**. Notice that both feature the comfortable family grouping that marked the artwork of Akhenaten's reign and that both show the sun-disk—Aten—bestowing blessings. However, the young Tutankhaton was unable to carry on the unpopular religious reforms of his father-in-law. The priests of the old cults had grown increasingly resentful of Akhenaten—whom they called "the criminal"—and within three years the young king changed his name to Tutankh*amen* as he renounced the old pharaoh's

FIGURE 1.13 Hatshepsut, ca. 1460 B.C.E.

missions during the Middle Kingdom, and all knew of the wealth that was available. The carving depicts the pharaoh meeting with the Queen of Punt—an obese and powerful woman—and bringing back many luxury items of trade. Hatshepsut's ships were filled with incense, ebony, gold, ivory, animal skins, and even live baboons, sacred to Egyptian gods. The pharaoh brought these great luxuries back to Egypt and used much of the wealth in her monumental building projects.

When Thutmose III grew to manhood, he gained control of the army and seemed ready to rule without Hatshepsut's guidance. The early death of his wife, Neferure, weakened his ties to Hatshepsut, and sources hint that the woman pharaoh was murdered (or simply deposed) in 1458 B.C.E. Late in his reign, the pharaoh Thutmose III tried to eradicate all memory of Hatshepsut. He had her temples and most of her statues destroyed and her name scraped off stone monuments. Was he angry about his long regency? Did he object to Hatshepsut's gender? Did he disapprove of her popular political agenda, or was he trying to ensure a smooth succession for his son? We can never know the answers to these questions. Fortunately for students of history, Thutmose was unable to erase all the evidence that tells of his remarkable predecessor.

Thutmose III was a great leader, although his political vision for Egypt differed markedly from that of his aunt. Specifically, he believed that Egypt should be an imperial power. During his 54-year reign, he led military expeditions and established the empire that defined Egypt during the New Kingdom. In the story of Hatshepsut and Thutmose, we see two accomplished pharaohs with conflicting visions of Egypt—one looking backward to its Old Kingdom greatness, the other looking forward to the empire building of the future. Both rules embodied major, dramatic themes in Egyptian history.

Connecting People & Society

1. In what ways does the queen's life reveal the tensions between the New Kingdom's involvement with other regions and its desire for isolation?

2. How does the queen work to rule within the constraints of her gender? How successful is this strategy?

religious convictions. Tutankhamen died at just 18 years of age, and the general who succeeded him as pharaoh—Harmhab—destroyed Akhenaten's temples and restored the worship of the old gods.

Egypt showed a hint of its former greatness during the reign of Ramses II (1279–1213 B.C.E.), who reestablished the imperial frontiers in Syria and restored peace under Egypt's traditional gods. After the hard-fought battle at Kadesh in 1274 B.C.E., Ramses negotiated a treaty with the Hittites that is believed to be the first recorded nonaggression pact. Ramses' success in bringing peace allowed him to free resources for huge building projects, most notably a great temple carved out of the rocky cliffs along the Nile. The tribute portrayed in **Figure 1.11** testifies to the prosperity restored during the New Kingdom.

Subsequent pharaohs, through the end of the New Kingdom in 1085 B.C.E., tried to maintain the fragile empire. However, major challengers arose to confront the god-kings. Libyans to the west and Nubians from the south invaded the Nile valley and took power for a while. Eventually, greater empires to the east and north would conquer Egypt permanently, and the center of Western civilization would move to other lands. However, the advanced culture, ordered life, and intense spirituality of the rich land of the Nile would again exert a profound impact on the early peoples of the West, as we will see in Chapter 3.

PEOPLES OF THE MEDITERRANEAN COAST,
ca. 1300–500 B.C.E.

Along the eastern coast of the Mediterranean Sea, various civilizations arose and became part of the power struggles plaguing the Middle East. Most of these Mediterranean cultures eventually were absorbed by their neighbors and disappeared. However, two of them—the Phoenicians and the Hebrews—made a lasting impact as they vigorously expanded their fortunes and furthered the worship of their gods.

The Phoenicians: Traders on the Sea

The Phoenicians were successful traders whose culture was based in the coastal cities of Sidon, Tyre, and Byblos (see **Map 1.2**). These seagoing merchants made the most of their location by engaging in prosperous trade with Egypt and the lands in the Fertile Crescent. The Phoenicians controlled forests of cedar trees that were highly prized in both Mesopotamia and Egypt. They also had an even more lucrative monopoly on purple dye made from coastal shellfish. Purple dyes were so rare that cloth of this color was expensive, so it soon became identified with royalty. Phoenician weavers dyed cloth purple and sold it throughout the Middle East and western Mediterranean for huge profits. Throughout the ancient world, nobility was demonstrated by wearing purple clothing.

Explorers from the Phoenician cities traveled widely throughout the Mediterranean Sea. By 950 B.C.E., these remarkable sailors traded as far west as Spain, and even into the Atlantic down the west coast of Africa. Like all ancient sailors, they hugged the coast as they traveled so that they could stop each night to beach the ships and sleep. To guarantee safe harbors, Phoenician traders established merchant colonies all along the north coast of Africa; by some estimates there was a colony about every 30 miles. The most important colony was Carthage, which was founded about 800 B.C.E. and would become a significant power in the Mediterranean (see Chapter 4). Through these colonies, the Phoenicians spread the culture of the ancient Middle East—from their trading expertise to their gods and goddesses—around the Mediterranean all the way to Spain.

| Trading colonies |

The enterprising Phoenician sailors left their mark on the Mediterranean world long after neighboring empires conquered the Phoenicians' home cities on the eastern coast. They began their early voyages in search of metals: tin, copper, iron for tools and weapons, and silver and gold for luxury items. This quest even led these intrepid sailors through the Strait of Gibraltar into the Atlantic, where they traded as far as the African coast and Britain. They were skilled at smelting metals—including the difficult-to-forge iron—and their metallurgy talents, along with the trade they fostered, stimulated growth throughout the region.

The Phoenicians' most important contribution to Western culture was their remarkable alphabet. In developing a writing system, the Phoenicians improved on the Sumerian script by creating a purely phonetic alphabet of only twenty-two letters. This system was simpler than the unwieldy cuneiform and hieroglyph that dominated the rest of the Middle East. The Phoenician alphabet spread rapidly and allowed later cultures to write without the long apprenticeships that characterized the proud scribes like the one shown at the beginning of this chapter. Through adopting a Phoenician-style alphabet, cultures of the West achieved a significant advantage over cultures whose written languages remained the exclusive province of the elite.

| Phoenician alphabet |

The People of the One God: Early Hebrew History, 1500–900 B.C.E.

Phoenician society in the Near East ultimately disappeared as an independent state, but not before it had performed an immense service as a transmitter of culture throughout the Mediterranean. The Phoenicians' neighbors, the Hebrews, followed an entirely different course. The Hebrews resiliently withstood both time and conquest and emerged from a difficult journey with their culture intact.

While the Sumerians and their successors in Mesopotamia developed complex civilizations based on irrigation and built ziggurats to their many deities, the seminomadic Hebrews moved their flocks from Mesopotamia into the land of Canaan, comprising much of the modern states of Israel, Lebanon, and western Syria. As they traveled, they shared many of the ancient stories of Mesopotamia, such as the tale of a great flood that destroyed the land (present in *The Epic of Gilgamesh*, described earlier) and a lost Garden of Eden. The Hebrews, perhaps seeing the Mesopotamian ziggurats from a distance, also viewed their neighbors as overly proud. The Hebrew story of the ill-fated Tower of Babel captures this theme of overweening pride.

Sometime before about 1700 B.C.E., the early leaders of the Hebrews, the patriarchs—Abraham, Isaac, and Jacob—led these seminomadic tribes that roamed the eastern Mediterranean and beyond. Jacob changed his name to Israel ("he who prevails with God"), and this name marked Jacob's followers as having a special relationship with one God. Consequently, historians refer to these tribes as the Israelites. Several clans traveled to Egypt, where Israelite texts claim they were enslaved by the Egyptians, although their status is not clear. They might simply have been employed in the labor-intensive Egyptian work projects, and their position may have changed over time to a more restrictive relationship. Some historians identify the Israelites with a group who helped build the huge projects of the Egyptian pharaoh Ramses II (r. ca. 1279–1213 B.C.E.). According to the Bible, Moses led this same group from Egypt. This Exodus (which means "journey out" in Greek) transformed them into a nation with a specific religious calling.

| Patriarchs |

The details of the history of the Israelites are found in the Hebrew Scriptures (later called the Old Testament by Christians). Made up of writings from oral and written traditions and dating from about 1250 to 150 B.C.E., these Scriptures record laws, wisdom, legends, literature, and the history of the ancient Israelites. The first five books (known as the Pentateuch) constitute the **Torah**, or law code, which governed the people's lives. The Bible contains some information that is historically accurate and can be generally confirmed by archaeological evidence. For example, as early as 1208 B.C.E. the pharaoh Marneptah, the son of Ramses II, erected a victory stone recording his triumphs, including the conquest of Israel: "Israel is laid waste, his seed is no more. . . ." The Egyptian god-king would not have bothered to brag about the conquest of the Israelites if this accomplishment had not been fairly substantial, so we know that the Bible's descriptions of a strong Israelite kingdom in Palestine during the second millennium B.C.E. are well founded.

Hebrew Scriptures

Historians must be cautious when using the Bible as a source, because it is basically a religious book that reveals faith, not science. Archaeology and history can illuminate the events of the ancient Israelites, but these sciences can shed no light on the faith that underlies the text. Used carefully, though, the Bible is an important source of information on these early Israelites, for they made a point to record and remember their own history—they wove teachings and morality into a historical narrative. Thus, Hebrew religion was rooted in history rather than myth, and from this text we can begin to re-create the early history of this profoundly influential people.

According to the Bible, the Hebrews from Egypt eventually returned to ancient Palestine and slowly reconquered the land, uniting the other nearby Hebrew tribes in the process. During this period of settlement, between about 1200 and 1050 B.C.E., Israelites experienced a change in leadership. Instead of relying solely on tribal leaders, people turned to "judges"—charismatic leaders who helped unite the people against the threats of their neighbors. In time, the elders of the tribes felt they needed a king to lead the people, declaring, "then we shall be like other nations, with a king to govern us, to lead us out to war and fight our battles" (1 Sam. 8:20). The people insisted that Samuel, the last of the judges, anoint their first king, Saul (r. ca. 1024–ca. 1000 B.C.E.).

Establishing a kingdom

Saul's successor, David (r. ca. 1000–ca. 961 B.C.E.), began encouraging the tribes to settle in a fixed location, with their capital at Jerusalem. David's successor, Solomon (r. ca. 961–ca. 922 B.C.E.), brought Phoenician craftsmen to Jerusalem to build a great temple there. Now a territorial power like others in the Fertile Crescent, the Hebrews worshiped their God in the temple overlooking a majestic city. But the costs of the temple were exorbitant, causing increased taxes and the growth of an administrative structure to collect them.

Solomon was a king in the Mesopotamian style. If the biblical account is to be believed, he used marriage to forge political alliances, accumulating hundreds of wives and many hundreds more concubines, including the daughter of an Egyptian pharaoh. The biblical excerpts in Document 1.2 show Solomon's fame, long-distance trade, and the difficulties accompanying his many marriages. However, the unified kingdom of tribes barely outlasted Solomon's reign. After his death, the northern tribes—particularly angry about Solomon's taxation and administrative innovations—broke away to form the separate kingdom of Israel (**Map 1.3**). The southern state was called Judah, with its capital at Jerusalem, and at this time the southern Israelites began to be called Jews. Israel was the more prosperous of the two kingdoms and was tied more closely to Phoenicia by trade and other contacts. Judah adhered more rigorously to the old Hebrew laws. The two kingdoms often fought each other as they participated in the shifting alliances of their neighbors. Dominating all politics, however, was their commitment to their one God.

Dividing a kingdom

The authors of the Scriptures developed an overriding theme in Jewish history: the intimate relationship between obedience to God's laws and the unfolding of the history of the Jewish people. As these authors recorded their recollection of events, they told of periodic violations of the uncompromising covenant with God and the resulting punishments that God imposed.

A Jealous God, 1300–587 B.C.E.

When Moses led his people out of Egypt, they reportedly wandered for forty years in the wilderness of the Sinai Peninsula before returning to the land of Canaan (see **Map 1.3**). During that time, Moses bound his people to God in a special covenant, or agreement, through which the Jews would be God's "chosen people" in return for their undivided worship. The ancient Hebrews were not strictly monotheistic, for they believed in the existence of the many deities of their neighbors. For Moses' people, however, there was only one God, and this God demanded their exclusive worship. As the historian of the sixth century B.C.E. wrote in the Bible's Book of Deuteronomy, "He is the faithful God, keeping his covenant of love to a thousand generations of those who love him and keep his commands." This promise was a conditional one: God would care for his people only if they practiced his laws, and there were many laws.

The covenant

The core of the Hebrew legal tradition lay in the Ten Commandments that the Bible claims God gave to Moses during his exodus from Egypt, and these were supplemented by other requirements listed in the Scriptures. Adhering to these laws defined one as a Jew. While the laws bound the Jewish people together—to "love thy neighbor as thyself"—they also set the Jews apart from their neighbors. For

Hebrew laws

thinking about
DOCUMENTS

DOCUMENT 1.2

King Solomon Secures His Realm's Fortune

These passages from the Book of Kings in the Bible show that King Solomon, like other ancient leaders, tried to secure the fortunes of his kingdom through marriages with neighboring peoples. They tell of King Solomon's fame and his relationship with women. The first passage describes the wealthy queen of Sheba (modern Yemen), and the second passage describes Solomon's many marriages.

Now when the queen of Sheba heard of the fame of Solomon concerning the name of the Lord, she came to test him with hard questions. She came to Jerusalem with a very great retinue, with camels bearing spices, and very much gold, and precious stones; and when she came to Solomon, she told him all that was on her mind. And Solomon answered all her questions; there was nothing hidden from the king which he could not explain to her. And when the queen of Sheba had seen all the wisdom of Solomon, the house that he had built, the food of his table, the seating of his officials, and the attendance of his servants, their clothing, his cupbearers, and his burnt offerings which he offered at the house of the Lord, there was no more spirit in her.

And she said to the king, "The report was true which I heard in my own land of your affairs and of your wisdom, but I did not believe the reports until I came and my own eyes had seen it; and behold, the half was not told me; your wisdom and prosperity surpass the report which I heard . . . then she gave the king a hundred and twenty talents of gold, and a very great quantity of spices, and precious stones; never again came such an abundance of spices as these which the queen of Sheba gave to King Solomon (1 Kings 10:1–7, 10).

Now King Solomon loved many foreign women: the daughter of Pharaoh, and Moabite, Ammomite, Edomite, Sidonian, and Hittite women, from the nations concerning which the Lord had said to the people of Israel, "You shall not enter into marriage with them, neither shall they with you, for surely they will turn away your heart after their gods"; Solomon clung to these in love. He had seven hundred wives, princesses, and three hundred concubines; and his wives turned away his heart. For when Solomon was old his wives turned away his heart after other gods; and his heart was not wholly true to the Lord his God, as was the heart of David his father. For Solomon went after Ashtoreth the goddess of the Sidonians and after Milcom the abomination of the Ammonites. So Solomon did what was evil in the sight of the Lord, and did not wholly follow the Lord as David his father had done. Then Solomon built a high place for Chemosh the abomination of Moab, and for Molech the abomination of the Ammonites, on the mountain east of Jerusalem. And so he did for all his foreign wives, who burned incense and sacrificed to their gods. And the Lord was angry with Solomon . . . (1 Kings 11:1–9).

SOURCE: Bible. 1 Kings 10:1–13; 1 Kings 11:1–13 *(New Oxford Annotated Bible with the Apocrypha.* New York: Oxford University Press, 1973).

Analyze the Document

1. How do the two passages, in different ways, reveal the importance of women during Solomon's reign?

2. What goods does the queen bring from Arabia? How does her gift of these materials illustrate the importance of long-distance trade to the Hebrew state?

3. What particular challenges do monotheistic Jews face in dealing with their neighbors?

KEY DATES

HEBREWS

2000–1700 B.C.E.	Patriarchs
ca. 1250 B.C.E.	Moses exodus from Egypt
ca. 1200–1050 B.C.E.	Judges
ca. 1024–ca. 1000 B.C.E.	King Saul
ca. 1000–ca. 961 B.C.E.	King David
ca. 961–ca. 922 B.C.E.	King Solomon
ca. 800 B.C.E.	Prophets
587 B.C.E.	Babylonian Captivity
515 B.C.E.	Second Temple built

example, boys were circumcised as a mark of the covenant between God and his people. In addition, Jews observed strict dietary laws that separated them from others—for example, they could eat no pork nor any animal that had been improperly slaughtered. But the fundamental commandment that allowed for no compromise with non-Jews was the injunction against worshiping the idols, or deities, of their neighbors.

Around the eighth century B.C.E., Jews were called to even higher ethical standards by a remarkable series of charismatic men—the prophets. These men, such as Amos, Micah, Hosea, Jeremiah, and Isaiah, were | Prophets | neither kings nor priests nor soldiers. Instead, they were common people—shepherds or tradesmen—who cared nothing for power or glory. They were brave men

Mediterranean Coast in the First Millennium B.C.E.

This map shows the major kingdoms of the Mediterranean coast, together called the Land of Canaan in the Bible. The kingdoms include those of the Philistines, Hebrews, and Phoenicians.

Explore the Map

1. Look at the scale of the map. How close were these kingdoms? How might that proximity have contributed to increased warfare in the region?

2. Based on the map, why do you think there were so many battles between the Philistines and the Hebrews?

who urged their people to return to the covenant and traditional Hebrew law. In times of social distress, they became the conscience of Israel, and in turn they helped shape the social conscience that was to become part of Western civilization. The prophets reminded the Jews to care for the poor: "Seek justice, relieve the oppressed, Judge the fatherless, plead for the widow" (Isa. 1:17). In doing so, they emphasized the direct ethical responsibility of every individual. Unlike the other religions of the ancient Middle East, Judaism called individuals to follow their consciences to create a more ethical world. Religion was no longer a matter of rituals of the temple, but a matter of people's hearts and minds. The prophets preached a religion that would be able to withstand turmoil and political destruction, and it is fortunate that they did so, for the Hebrews would suffer much adversity, which they believed was a form of testing by their God.

According to the Bible, King Solomon had a weakness that stemmed from his polygamy. (See Document 1.2.) Not only did he violate the biblical command not to take foreign wives, but to please them he allowed the worship of other deities (especially the fertility goddess Astarte), even in the holy city of Jerusalem. Prophets claimed that it was his impiety that had divided the kingdom against itself. Later events showed a similar theme. Ahab (r. 869–850 B.C.E.), king of the northern kingdom of Israel, married a Phoenician princess, Jezebel, and erected an altar to her god Baal in order to please her. When Israel was conquered in 721 B.C.E. by the Assyrians, prophets who had predicted its downfall pointed to Ahab's breach of the covenant as the cause of the misfortune. The southern kingdom of Judah fared little better than Israel in trying to escape the aggressions of its neighbors. In 587 B.C.E., the Babylonians captured Jerusalem and destroyed Solomon's magnificent temple. Many Jews were exiled and enslaved in Babylon, and the "chosen people" were once more without a country or a religious center. From then on, there would be substantial numbers of Jews who lived outside Israel or Judah, and they later would be collectively known

"God's punishments"

as the **Diaspora.** Instead of renouncing their God, however, the Jews reaffirmed their covenant in a different way.

Judaism in Exile

Hebrew priests in exile worried that Diaspora Jews living among non-Jews would forget the old traditions and be assimilated into the cultures of their neighbors. Therefore, they carefully compiled and edited the Scriptures to preserve their unique view of religion and history. These written accounts helped Judaism survive without a geographic center. The authors of the Scriptures arranged the history of the Jews to show that, despite hardships, God had always cared for his people. The priests believed that the destruction of the two Hebrew kingdoms had come because people either did not know the laws or had failed to obey them. As a result, Hebrew teachers emphasized the study of and strict adherence to the purity laws to keep their people separate from others even when they lived in close proximity as neighbors.

Without the temple in Jerusalem to serve as the center of worship, Jewish worship began to convene in more local establishments—synagogues and the home itself. This movement had an important impact on the status of women in Jewish culture. The emphasis on details of purity law to keep the chosen people separate reduced women's roles in formal prayer because the law stressed that anyone worshiping God had to be "clean." Women, seen as sometimes unclean because of menstrual blood or childbirth, were excluded from participating in the formal worship rituals. On the other hand, the experience of exile strengthened the family as a social and religious unit, a change that improved women's lives in other ways. For example, concubinage disappeared and women presided over the household, upholding the dietary laws and household rituals that preserved the Jewish culture wherever they lived.

In time, however, the Hebrews were able to reestablish their religious center in Jerusalem. After ruling Judah for forty-eight years, the Babylonians were, in turn, conquered by new peoples, the **"Second Temple" period** Persians. The Persians proved much more tolerant than the Babylonians of the varied beliefs of their subject peoples. In 538 B.C.E., the Persian king Cyrus let the Jewish exiles return to Jerusalem. The Jews built a new temple in 515 B.C.E., an event that introduced the "Second Temple" period. Again, the Jews had a temple and center of worship like other Mesopotamian peoples. However, all Jews did not return to Israel, and the question of the relationship between Diaspora Jews and the cultures in which they lived would reemerge periodically throughout history as followers of this old covenant interacted with their neighbors.

The ancient Hebrews made a tremendous impact on the future of Western civilization. They believed that God created the world at a specific point in time, and this notion set them apart dramatically from their neighbors, such as the Egyptians, who believed in the eternity of the world. The Hebrews' view of history as a series of purposeful, morally significant events was unprecedented in the ancient world. Their concept of ethical monotheism, in which a single God of justice interacted with humans in a personal and spiritual way, offered a vision of religion that eventually dominated in the West. The many deities and demons that ruled the Mesopotamian and Egyptian worlds would in time be rendered insignificant by the God of the Hebrews, who transcended nature. The Hebrews believed that there was a profound distance between people and God, and thus individuals took more responsibility for the events of this world even as they worshiped and held in awe the deity who had made a deep and abiding covenant with the Jewish people.

Hebrew contributions

TERROR AND BENEVOLENCE: THE GROWTH OF EMPIRES, 1200–500 B.C.E.

By the second millennium B.C.E., many people could see the value of centralized control over larger territories. The Egyptians were establishing an empire, and the Hebrews had united into a kingdom. Not only did size offer the potential for larger armies, but expansion westward also secured access to valuable seaborne trade (which was making the Phoenicians wealthy) and would secure the strategically important region of Syria and Palestine. Perhaps most important, people wanted to expand their territories to acquire the metals so necessary for military and economic success. These impulses led to the growth of a new political form in the West—huge empires based on a new technology, iron.

The Age of Iron

Before the eleventh century B.C.E., ancient civilizations depended on bronze, an alloy of copper and tin. All across Europe and the Middle East, people used bronze plows to cultivate the land and employed bronze-tipped weapons to make war. While agriculture remained the most important enterprise, the economies of these civilizations were fueled by trade in copper and tin. Initially, these essential metals came largely from Asia Minor (see **Map 1.2**), Arabia, and India. Later, sources of these metals were also found in the western Mediterranean.

In about 1200 B.C.E., warfare disrupted the usual trade routes, making tin scarce. Pure copper is a soft

MAP 1.4

The Assyrian Empire, ca. 662 B.C.E.

This map shows the homeland of the Assyrians and their expansion as they conquered the older centers of Western civilization. Compare this map with **Maps 1.1, 1.2,** and **1.3.**

Explore the Map

1. How many cultures were included in this large empire?

2. What problems would you expect to arise in the governance of such a diverse empire?

3. How might the location of the Assyrians' homeland have facilitated their expansion?

metal, and without the tin needed to make bronze, smiths could not produce effective tools and weapons.

Iron Age To overcome the tin shortage, Hittite metalworkers in Asia Minor first began to employ iron, an abundant mineral in that region. Unforged iron is not much stronger than copper. However, when it is repeatedly heated in a hot charcoal furnace, carbon molecules combine with iron molecules to form a very reliable metal known as carbon steel. Even low-carbon steel is stronger than bronze, and when it is cold hammered, the strength more than doubles. People—and particularly soldiers—gained a huge advantage by using the new metal.

The technology used to create the superior forged iron spread rapidly throughout the Mediterranean world, and from about 1000 B.C.E. on it was used in tools, cookware, and weapons. The use of iron spread to sub-Saharan Africa through Nubia, and ironworking became prominent throughout much of that continent, which was rich in iron ore. Soldiers wielding iron weapons easily vanquished those armed with bronze. The Age of Iron had dawned, and it dominated the world until the late nineteenth century when metalsmiths developed new ways to make iron into steel without the carbon method (Bessemer steel). Iron Age kings in Mesopotamia forged enough weapons and fielded armies so large, their extensive conquests introduced multiethnic empires that dwarfed all that had gone before.

Rule by Terror: The Assyrians, 911–612 B.C.E.

The Assyrians, a people living originally in the northern Tigris-Euphrates valley, had traded profitably with their neighbors for centuries. In the early tenth century B.C.E., they began arming themselves with iron weapons and following the one command of their god Assur: Expand the frontiers of Assyria so that Assur finally rules over all. **Map 1.4** shows the striking success of the Assyrians as they cut a swath through the civilizations of the ancient Near East.

The Assyrians' success stemmed from the skill of their armies and their willingness to engage in almost constant warfare to follow the command of Assur. Assyrian histories recounting their military campaigns were written as propaganda pieces to instill fear in their enemies. The historians accomplished their goal, and the cold-blooded details cemented the Assyrians' reputation for ruthlessness. King Sargon II's (r. 722–706 B.C.E.) description of his conquest of Babylon is one chilling example of these accounts: "I blew like the onrush of a hurricane and enveloped the city like a fog. . . . I did not spare his mighty warriors, young or old, but filled the city square with their corpses."

Beyond sheer brutality, the Assyrians relied on some of the most advanced military techniques that the ancient world had seen. They employed a corps of military engineers to build bridges, tunnels, and efficient siege weapons capable of penetrating strongly

FIGURE 1.14 Escaping a Battle   The Assyrians were fearsome warriors. Their art frequently memorialized their accomplishments, as in the case of this image of fugitives escaping from Assyrian archers. This depiction shows an ancient technique of swimming underwater with air-filled pigskins.

fortified cities. Furthermore, they had a highly trained and well-rewarded officer corps who became the elite in Assyrian society.

The Assyrians portrayed their military achievements in their art as well as in their writings. But along with interminable portrayals of destruction and carnage, Assyrian art occasionally reveals unusual details of experience during the ninth century B.C.E. The carving shown in **Figure 1.14** depicts three men fleeing Assyrian archers as they swim the river toward the fortified town on the right. Two of the swimmers hold pigskins filled with air to breathe underwater, offering a surprising glimpse of an underwater swimming technique. This carving captures an incident that may have been particularly memorable due to the fugitives' creative escape. However, although the fugitives eluded the archers, the Assyrians conquered the town.

The Assyrians were first both to acquire such a large territory and to try to govern it cohesively. In many ways, they proved to be skilled administrators. For example, they built roads to unify their holdings, and kings appointed governors and tax collectors to serve as their representatives in the more distant territories. One of the elements that facilitated governing and trade over large areas was the Assyrians' use of Aramaic as a common language. This was a Semitic language originally spoken by the Aramaeans, successful merchants who lived in Mesopotamia in about 1100 B.C.E. Aramaic remained the official language of subsequent empires—it was even spoken by Jesus. In spite of the Assyrians' reputation for violence, the Greek historian Herodotus (ca. 484–ca. 424 B.C.E.) recalled the peaceful accomplishments of Queen Semiramis, who built "magnificent embankments to retain the river [Euphrates], which till then used to overflow and flood the whole country around Babylon."

> Governing an empire

Many Assyrian rulers also appreciated the wealth of knowledge and culture that had accumulated in these lands for centuries. The great Assyrian king Ashurbanipal (669–627 B.C.E.) collected a huge library from which 20,000 clay tablets have survived. Within this collection, the king preserved the best of Mesopotamian literature, including *The Epic of Gilgamesh*. The highly educated Ashurbanipal took pride in his accomplishments: "I acquired the hidden treasure of all scribal knowledge, the signs of the heaven and the earth. . . . I have solved the laborious problems of division and multiplication. . . . I have read the artistic script of Sumer and the obscure Akkadian." This quotation offers an excellent example of how a written language served to preserve and disseminate the culture developing in the ancient Middle East.

> Preserving learning

Although the Assyrians were skilled in making both war and peace, they still faced the problem that confronted all empire builders: how to keep the empire together when subject peoples resisted. The Assyrians used terror to control their far-flung territories. When individuals dissented, they were publicly tortured; when cities revolted, they were razed to serve as examples to others. To break up local loyalties, Assyrian commanders uprooted and moved entire populations. These methods worked for a while; eventually, however, they catalyzed effective opposition.

> Fall of Assyrians

Ashurbanipal ruled from his capital in Nineveh—reputedly so well fortified that three chariots could ride abreast along the top of the walls surrounding the city. However, even those great walls could not save the king's successors. A coalition including Babylonians from southern Mesopotamia; Medes, an Indo-European tribe from western Iran; and Egyptians gathered against the Assyrian domination. Because the empire was so large it overextended the Assyrians' resources, and the provinces gave way quickly. Nineveh itself finally collapsed in 612 B.C.E. after a brutal two-year siege. In an ironic turn of events, the great city was defeated by the very river that had sustained it for so long—the Tigris flooded higher than normal and eroded Nineveh's defensive wall. Assyrian rule came to an ignominious end. However, the Assyrians left an enduring legacy for Western civilization: centralized empires that ruled over extended lands and different peoples.

Babylonian Rule, 612–539 B.C.E.

After vanquishing the Assyrians, the Medes left Mesopotamia and returned to their homeland near the Zagros Mountains (see **Map 1.4**). The Babylonians (also called Chaldeans, or Neo-Babylonians, to distinguish them from the earlier kingdom of Hammurabi) remained and ruled the lands of the former Assyrian Empire. The new rulers emulated the Assyrian use of terror to enforce their will on subject peoples. King Nebuchadrezzar (r. 605–561 B.C.E.) kept penalties similar to those in the Code of Hammurabi for civil crimes, but introduced extreme punishments for enemy rulers and their followers. When captured, these people were often flayed or burned alive. It was this severity that led Nebuchadrezzar to destroy Jerusalem in 587 B.C.E. and lead the Jews into captivity. This incident was the formative "Babylonian Captivity" discussed earlier that shaped much of subsequent Jewish history.

The Babylonians also continued the Assyrian passion for art and education. The king rebuilt his capital city of Babylon in such splendor that it was admired throughout the ancient world. His architects constructed huge ziggurats in praise of the Babylonian god Marduk and fortified the structures with walls more impressive than even Nineveh's had been. Under Nebuchadrezzar, Babylon blossomed into an impressive city graced by gardens, palaces, and temples.

Culture and commerce

The magnificent architecture that marked Babylon cost a fortune, and the Babylonian kings obtained these funds largely through fostering the commerce that often guided their military policies. One king, for example, besieged Tyre for thirteen years, hoping to win control over the Phoenicians' far-reaching trade. Another king established himself in Arabia in an attempt to control a new trade—in incense—that came from southern Arabia to the Mediterranean Sea.

Kings used their new wealth not only to decorate their cities, but also to foster learning. Within the cosmopolitan city, Babylonian priests excelled in astronomy and mathematics. They observed the heavens in an effort to understand the will of the gods, and in the process they charted the skies with impressive accuracy; they could predict solstices, equinoxes, and other heavenly phenomena. Their passion for predictions led them to develop another innovation with which they sought to foretell the future for individuals: astrology. By the fifth century B.C.E., Babylonian astrologers had divided the heavens into twelve signs—including the familiar Gemini, Scorpio, Virgo, and others—and began to cast horoscopes to predict people's futures based on their birth dates. The earliest surviving example of a horoscope was for a child born in 410 B.C.E. and marks the beginning of a long-standing practice.

Astronomy and mathematics

As part of their astronomical calculations, Babylonians developed advanced mathematics. Their tablets show that they regularly used multiplication, division, calculations of square and cube roots, algebra, and other operations. In addition, they based their numerical system on the number 60, working out an elaborate method of keeping time that led to the division of hours and minutes that we use today. The benefits of the Babylonians' impressive intellectual achievements were not spread widely through society. More subjects resented Babylonian rule than benefited from its accomplishments.

Rule by Tolerance: The Persian Empire, ca. 550–330 B.C.E.

In 553 B.C.E., the fortunes of the Babylonian Empire changed. The Persians, a people from east of the Zagros Mountains, overran the land of their Indo-European relatives, the Medes. Under their wise king, Cyrus the Great (r. 559–530 B.C.E.), the Persians expanded westward to establish an empire even larger than that of the Assyrians (**Map 1.5**). They quickly conquered the kingdom of Lydia in Asia Minor and then turned southeast to the Babylonian Empire. The Babylonian rulers found few supporters against the invaders even among their own people, and in 539 B.C.E. Babylon fell to the Persians virtually without a struggle.

Cyrus rejected the Assyrian policies of terror and sought to hold his vast empire together by tolerating differences among his many subject peoples. As mentioned earlier, in 538 B.C.E. he allowed the Jewish captives in Babylon to return to Jerusalem and rebuild their temple. At the same time, he appeased Babylonians by claiming he was "friend and companion" to their god Marduk. In the conquered provinces—or satrapies—Cyrus retained local officials but installed Persian governors called **satraps.** He controlled the satraps' power by appointing additional officials who were directly responsible to the king. The Persians required subject peoples to pay

Persian administration

MAP 1.5

The Persian Empire, ca. 500 B.C.E.

This map illustrates the Persian Empire that replaced and greatly expanded the previous Assyrian domain and highlights the Royal Road, which spanned a large portion of the territory. It also shows the capital of the empire, Persepolis. Compare the extent of this empire with that of the Assyrians shown in **Map 1.4.**

Explore the Map

1. What problems do you think the Persians encountered due to the empire's vast expanse and diverse cultures?

2. How might the Royal Road have helped the Persian rulers to deal with the challenges of administering such a large empire?

3. Given that the Persian homeland and capital were so far east, what might the impact have been on Western culture?

---

reasonable taxes and serve in their armies, but Cyrus's system prevented local officials from abusing their power excessively. Conquered peoples could worship their own gods and follow their own customs, and under Cyrus's reign, the ancient civilizations enjoyed a long period of peace. The great king (as his subjects called him) was seen as a semidivine figure who ruled benignly from his golden throne.

After Cyrus's death in 530 B.C.E., his son Cambyses II (r. 529–522 B.C.E.) inherited the throne and continued the expansion his father had begun so effectively. The new king extended Persian control to the eastern Mediterranean by conquering Egypt and the Phoenician port cities. (See Document 1.3 for a description of Cambyses' military expansion.)

Cambyses was succeeded by Darius (r. 521–486 B.C.E.), a brilliant ruler who was able to consolidate and further organize what Cyrus and Cambyses had hastily conquered. Darius built a new capital city at Persepolis (see **Map 1.5**), moving the center of his empire east, but he also realized how important it was to facilitate travel throughout his empire. To accomplish this, he built and carefully maintained a complex system of roads, and the most famous was the Royal Road, between Susa in the east (in modern Iran) and Sardis (in modern Turkey) in the west. This impressive road, almost 1,700 miles long, fostered the economic life of the empire.

A unified empire allowed the Persians to adopt ideas that had proven successful in the civilizations

thinking about

DOCUMENT 1.3

Cambyses Conquers Egypt

This passage from the fifth-century B.C.E. Greek historian Herodotus describes the Persian king Cambyses' conquest of Egypt in 525 B.C.E. and his treatment of the pharaoh who had opposed his conquest. Cambyses was a controversial king, known for his "madness" (perhaps caused by alcoholism), yet even his reign was marked by policies that helped make the Persian Empire so successful.

After their defeat, the Egyptians fled in disorder and shut themselves up in Memphis. Cambyses called upon them to come to terms, sending a Persian herald up the river to the town in a Mytilenean vessel; but directly they saw the ship coming into the town, they rushed out from the walls in a body, smashed up the ship, tore everyone on board limb from limb, and carried the bits back inside the walls. They then stood a siege, but after a time surrendered. The neighbouring Libyans were alarmed by the fate of Egypt and gave themselves up without a battle, agreeing to pay tribute and sending presents. . . . Ten days passed, and Cambyses, wishing to see what stuff the Egyptian king Psammenitus was made of—he had been but six months on the throne—forced him with other Egyptians, to witness from a seat in the city outskirts a spectacle deliberately devised to humiliate him. . . .

[Cambyses was pleased at the young king's reactions.] They brought Psammenitus to Cambyses, at whose court he lived from that time onward. Here he was well treated; and indeed, if he had only had the sense to keep out of mischief, he might have recovered Egypt and ruled it as governor; for the Persians are in the habit of treating the sons of kings with honour, and even of restoring to their sons the thrones of those who have rebelled against them. There are many instances from which one may infer that this sort of generosity is usual in Persia. . . . Psammenitus, however, did not refrain from stirring up trouble, and paid for it. He was caught trying to raise a revolt amongst the Egyptians, and as soon as his guilt was known by Cambyses, he drank bull's blood and died on the spot. And that was the end of Psammenitus.

SOURCE: Herodotus, *The Histories*, trans. Aubrey de Sélincourt (New York: Penguin, 1996), pp. 159–160.

Analyze the Document

1. Why do you think the document emphasizes the treatment of Cambyses' enemies?

2. What persuades the Libyans to surrender? Is this strategy effective? Explain.

3. How does Herodotus expect Cambyses to treat the defeated Egyptian king? What actually happens to the king?

---

that preceded them. For example, Persians retained Aramaic as the common language of commerce, making communication easier across many cultures, and they fostered the trade routes that had brought so much wealth to the Babylonians. Persian astrologers learned from their Babylonian predecessors as well. These wise men, or magi, became celebrated for their knowledge of the heavens.

Of all the conventions the Persians borrowed from the inhabitants of their diverse empire, the adoption of coinage had the greatest long-term impact. The Lydians seem to have invented the use of coins in the seventh century B.C.E. Before this time, traders either bartered or used cumbersome bars of precious metals to purchase goods. For example, in Egypt in 1170 B.C.E., a burial vault that was priced at 5 pounds of copper might have been bought with 2½ pounds of copper, one hog, two goats, and two trees. By minting coins with precise, identifiable values, kingdoms greatly facilitated trade. The kings of Lydia were said to have grown fabulously rich after their invention, and the Persians rapidly spread the use of coins throughout their far-flung lands.

While the Persians adopted many novelties of their predecessors, they also made a unique contribution of their own: a new movement in religious thought initiated by the talented prophet Zoroaster (ca. 628–551 B.C.E.). One of the most important religious reformers of the ancient world, Zoroaster founded a new religion (later called **Zoroastrianism**) that contained the seeds of many modern belief systems. Zoroaster experienced a revelation given to him by the one god, Ahura Mazda, the Lord of Light. In this revelation, recorded in a holy book called the Avesta, Zoroaster was called to reform Persian religion by eliminating polytheism and animal sacrifice. In the tradition of Uruinimgina, Hebrew prophets, and others throughout the early history of Western civilization who called for social justice, Zoroaster also urged people to live ethical lives and to show care for others. Finally, the prophet believed that the history of the world was one of ongoing conflict between Ahura Mazda and the forces of the evil god Ahriman. Zoroaster also felt confident that Ahura Mazda would ultimately prevail over evil and that eventually the dead would be resurrected. Believers would go to paradise, while evildoers would fall into a hell of perpetual torture.

Beginning with the pious Zoroastrian Darius, the Persian kings claimed to rule the earth as Ahura Mazda's viceroys, but slowly the old nature worship returned and became incorporated into Zoroastrian beliefs. For example, people began to venerate Mithra, the ancient sun god, as an assistant to Ahura Mazda. Zoroaster's ideas had an influence that far outlasted the Persian rulers. During the Roman Empire, the worship of Mithra would be an important cult (see Chapter 5). Furthermore, followers of Zoroastrianism still exist today, and even in the ancient world many of the prophet's ideas influenced other religions as well. Over time, some believers transformed Zoroaster's monotheism into a dualistic belief in two gods, one good and one evil. Judaism—and, later, Christianity—seem to have been influenced by his vision, for Jewish texts began to write of the power of a devil and of a final struggle between good and evil. Zoroaster was the first prophet whose ideas would spread throughout a large political empire, but he would not be the last.

LOOKING BACK & MOVING FORWARD

Summary   In the 3,000 years that make up the history of the ancient Middle East, many elements that characterize Western civilization emerged. Great cities sprang up, introducing commerce, excitement, diversity, and extremes of wealth and poverty that the West both values and struggles with even today. Tyranny and oppression arose, as did the laws and principles designed to hold them in check. Sophisticated religions provided vehicles for metaphysical reflection, and artists expressed those hopes and dreams in beautiful forms. Perhaps most important, writing systems evolved to let people preserve their accumulated knowledge for future generations, including ours. Finally, these early centuries established a pattern of interaction and cross-fertilization of goods and ideas that would mark Western civilization from its beginnings through today.

The great civilizations of the Nile and Tigris-Euphrates valleys—the Egyptians, Sumerians, Akkadians, Babylonians, and others—were ultimately absorbed by larger empires. Yet their contributions endured as a result of the mutual influence that always occurs when cultures mingle. The Hebrews, too, contributed much to the growing body of Western ideas and values. By 500 B.C.E., the Persian kings had united the region, creating an empire rich with the diversity of many peoples and thousands of years of history. The Persian Empire marks a culmination of the first stirrings of Western civilization in the ancient Middle East. The next developments in the story of the West would come from different peoples: the Greeks.

KEY TERMS

Paleolithic, *p. 4*

Neolithic, *p. 6*

ziggurat, *p. 9*

augury, *p. 10*

cuneiform, *p. 12*

ma'at, *p. 15*

pharaoh, *p. 16*

hieroglyph, *p. 18*

fresco, *p. 22*

Torah, *p. 26*

Diaspora, *p. 30*

satraps, *p. 33*

Zoroastrianism, *p. 35*

REVIEW, ANALYZE, & CONNECT TO TODAY

REVIEW AND ANALYZE THIS CHAPTER

Chapter 1 traces the development of Western civilization from its earliest beginnings in the cities of the ancient Middle East through the establishment of great empires. One of the significant themes throughout this chapter is the interaction among the various cultures that allowed each to assimilate and build on the innovations of the others.

1. What environmental advantages did the ancient Middle East have that permitted the growth of agriculture and cities? What disadvantages did the Middle East have? How did environmental conditions affect the various cultures?

2. Review the long-standing contributions of the Sumerians, Egyptians, Nubians, Phoenicians, and Hebrews.

3. How were the Jews able to maintain their integrity while being part of the Diaspora?

4. Review the empires—Assyrian, Babylonian, Persian—that arose in the ancient Middle East, and note the strengths and weaknesses of each.

CONNECT TO TODAY

Think about the changes in agriculture and animal husbandry discussed in this chapter.

1. How did the development of agriculture affect ancient societies? In what ways might advances in agriculture in more recent times have stimulated changes similar to those that occurred in the ancient world? Consider modern innovations such as the development of

drought-resistant grains and genetically modified foods. What other modern agricultural advances can you think of?

2. Ancient diseases moved from domesticated animals to humans, creating waves of pandemics followed by the development of immunities. What related situations do we face in our own times?

BEYOND THE CLASSROOM

BEFORE WESTERN CIVILIZATION

Diamond, Jared. *Guns, Germs, and Steel.* New York: W.W. Norton, 1997. A brilliant Pulitzer Prize–winning global analysis of the natural advantages that gave Western civilization its head start.

STRUGGLING WITH THE FORCES OF NATURE: MESOPOTAMIA, 3000–ca. 1000 B.C.E.

Binford, Lewis R. *In Pursuit of the Past.* New York: Thames & Hudson, 1988. An archaeological study of the transformation of human society.

Bryce, Trevor. *The Kingdom of the Hittites.* New York: Oxford University Press, 2006. A work that describes the rise and fall of the Hittites and includes the latest archaeology and translations of primary sources.

Crawford, Harriet. *Sumer and the Sumerians.* New York: Cambridge University Press, 1991. A summary of the historical and archaeological evidence that offers a solid survey of the field.

Hawkes, Jacquetta. *The Atlas of Early Man.* New York: St. Martin's Press, 1993. An accessible study of human thought.

Hooker, Jeremy T. *Reading the Past: Ancient Writing from Cuneiform to the Alphabet.* Berkeley: University of California Press, 1991. An exploration of the stages of the ancient scripts of past civilizations.

Postgate, Nicholas. *Early Mesopotamia: Society and Economy at the Dawn of History.* New York: Routledge, Chapman and Hall, 1992. A narrative depiction of the life of the peoples of early Mesopotamia.

Roux, Georges. *Ancient Iraq.* New York: Penguin, 1993. An excellent overview of the ancient world—from Mesopotamia to the Hellenistic conquests—that incorporates archaeological finds through 1992.

RULE OF THE GOD-KING: ANCIENT EGYPT, ca. 3100–1000 B.C.E.

Capel, A.X., and G.E. Markoe. *Mistress of the House, Mistress of Heaven: Women in Ancient Egypt.* New York: Hudson Hills Press, 1996. A beautifully illustrated study of the roles of women in ancient Egypt.

Grimal, N. *A History of Ancient Egypt.* Oxford: Oxford University Press, 1994. An insight into the essence of Egyptian culture and its relations with outsiders throughout its history.

Hornung, Erik. *History of Ancient Egypt: An Introduction.* Translated by David Lorton. Ithaca, NY: Cornell University Press, 1999. A concise and accessible summary of history that incorporates an excellent discussion of daily life in ancient times.

Tyldesley, Joyce. *Daughters of Isis: Women of Ancient Egypt.* New York: Penguin, 1995. A highly readable, illustrated account of women in Egypt.

PEOPLES OF THE MEDITERRANEAN COAST, ca. 1300–500 B.C.E.

Smith, Mark K. *Early History of God: Yahweh and the Other Deities in Ancient Israel.* San Francisco: Harper, 1990. A controversial look at the convergence and differentiation of deities toward monotheism in Israel.

Walton, John. *Ancient Near Eastern Thought and the Old Testament: Introducing the Conceptual World of the Hebrew Bible.* Grand Rapids, MI: Baker Academic, 2006. Balanced introductory look at the ideas in the Hebrew Bible, with excellent comparative dimensions.

TERROR AND BENEVOLENCE: THE GROWTH OF EMPIRES, 1200–500 B.C.E.

Curtis, J.E., and N. Tallis, eds. *Forgotten Empire: The World of Ancient Persia.* Berkeley: University of California Press, 2005. Comprehensive and scholarly view of the Persian Empire, beautifully illustrated with new archaeological finds.

Holland, Tom. *Persian Fire: The First World Empire and the Battle for the West.* New York: Anchor, 2007. Bold and engaging retelling of the Greek-Persian conflict, with a new emphasis on the Persian background.

Kuhrt, Amelie. *The Ancient Near East, ca. 3000–330 B.C.* New York: Routledge, 1997. A definitive account of ancient history, including the Israelites, that incorporates current scholarship and bibliography.

GLOBAL CONNECTIONS

Adams, William Y. *Nubia: Corridor to Africa.* Princeton, NJ: Princeton University Press, 1977. A comprehensive history of Nubia from prehistory through the nineteenth century.

The Ancient World, 700 B.C.E.–400 C.E.

By 700 B.C.E., the roots of Western civilization had been firmly planted in the great civilizations that arose in the Fertile Crescent from Mesopotamia to Egypt. Skilled farmers cultivated diverse crops and domesticated animals. A bustling commerce connected traders from far Asia with merchants operating around the Mediterranean basin, through Egypt, and into sub-Saharan Africa. A developing sense of law and a new tradition of writing fostered growing communities, even as leaders regularly launched armies at one another in hopes of expanding their power.

Although the peoples of the Eurasian landmass did not know it, successful cultures were also developing in the extensive lands far to the west across the Atlantic ocean. While scholars are still thinking about how the Americas were settled, it is clear that humans arrived at least 20,000 years ago. Studies of blood type, teeth, and language suggest a direct link between humans in the Americas and those in northern China and northeastern Siberia. Therefore, most scholars still argue that people walked across a land bridge from Siberia to Alaska before it disappeared about 14,000 years ago under floods caused by melting glaciers. Other scholars argue that people may have migrated by boats along the coasts from Siberia down the Pacific coasts of the Americas. Whatever their origin, groups of successful hunters began to spread through this vast north-south landmass.

By 5000 B.C.E., many of the peoples of the Americas had developed maize (corn) as a domesticated crop that cannot grow on its own without human intervention. The abundance of this kind of agriculture allowed agricultural societies to spread throughout Mesoamerica. Toward the end of the second millennium B.C.E., large ceremonial centers began to appear, similar to the great centers of Egypt. Recent studies even suggest that indigenous peoples in the Amazon basin successfully began to build thriving populations in the rainforests. Certainly, there were flourishing communities from Alaska to Chile while Europe was still virtually unpopulated.

Advanced civilizations in the great river valleys of Asia—the Yellow River in China and the Indus and Ganges valleys in India—had characteristics in common with the agricultural societies in the West. They, too, cultivated crops, raised animals, and valued a bustling trade. Western civilization took a different course as Greece, and later Rome, rose to prominence and the civilization's center moved farther west.

If the agricultural roots of the West lay in the Fertile Crescent, its philosophical roots lay in Greece. This society planted the seeds for many of the West's values—from its praise of democracy and rational inquiry and its aesthetic tastes to its appreciation for individual human accomplishment. These ideas spread all the way to India with the conquests of Alexander the Great, the Macedonian military genius, in the fourth century B.C.E. However, the ideas also changed as they spread. For example, after Alexander's conquests, Greek artists began to infuse more emotion into their works, and philosophers thought less about abstract concepts of truth and justice, and more about how an individual might live a tranquil life. Indeed, when East and West met in the kingdoms that arose after Alexander's death, each transformed the other.

By the first century B.C.E., the center of Western civilization had shifted still farther west as the Romans built a powerful empire that endured for centuries. In this thriving realm, Westerners solidified their love of law, duty, and engineering (among other things). As we will see, the Roman Empire was counted among the most diverse empires of the ancient world, rivaling even the Persian Empire in its ability to bring together people from many cultures. As just one example, Roman soldiers hailing from sub-Saharan Africa helped guard Hadrian's Wall in Scotland, the northern reaches of the empire.

Of course, as these centuries unfolded, the rest of the world did not sit idle. In China, successive dynasties of rulers unified the centers of civilization along the Yellow River. Later dynasties then spread Chinese unification well beyond the Yellow River—into central Asia and south to the South China Sea. The Qin dynasty (221–207 B.C.E.) began joining culturally distinct regions into a larger Chinese society, a process that continued during the Han dynasty (206 B.C.E.–220 C.E.). Han China then spread its cultural accomplishments to neighbors in Korea, Vietnam, and central Asia and fostered the prosperous Silk Road, by which merchants in the East traded with the Roman Empire in the West.

In India, a complex society grew up in the valley of the great Indus River. Archaeologists call this culture Harappan, named after Harappa, one of its two chief cities. Scholars have not yet deciphered Harappan written records, so the details of this culture remain obscure. But thanks to archaeological remains, we do know that people living in this early society conducted long-distance trade with Mesopotamians and Egyptians.

During the second millennium B.C.E., roving bands of peoples from the north swept into India, replacing a declining Harappan society. Scholars have determined that these new arrivals, who later established the Mauryan dynasty, had connections with the West because the invaders spoke an Indo-European language similar to those that later appeared in western lands. Linguists have identified similarities between words in English, German, Greek, Latin, and Indian Sanskrit, and these commonalities testify to ancient cross-cultural contacts throughout the Eurasian landmass.

Inspired by the imperial successes of Alexander the Great in the West,

Ancient Empires and the Spread of Religion

leaders of the Mauryan dynasty unified diverse Indian peoples under one ruler in the fourth century B.C.E. When the Mauryan dynasty broke apart in the second century B.C.E., later rulers who remembered its accomplishments tried to re-create a single India. In the fourth century C.E., a new leader once again unified the northern Indian lands and established the Gupta dynasty, which endured until the end of the fifth century C.E. The idea of one India may have come initially from the West. But with the establishment of the successful Gupta dynasty, the new India served as a conduit by which goods and ideas flowed from east to west.

Thanks to such interactions, civilizations around the world flourished. The empires that expanded during the ancient world embraced and fostered profitable trade, even as rulers changed. The famous Silk Road, stretching from China to the Mediterranean, conveyed goods and peoples from realm to realm. Meanwhile, trade in India stretched northwest through the Hindu Kush mountains to Persia, east along the Silk Road, and overseas in the Indian Ocean basin, where sailors learned to predict the prevailing

winds. Archaeologists working in southern India have unearthed hoards of Roman coins that offer silent testimony to the dynamic trade between east and west in the ancient world.

As always, movements of goods and peoples spurred exchanges of ideas both within and across civilizations. For example, during the ancient era, civilizations all over the Eurasian landmass experienced striking revolutions in religious thought. In China, the great philosopher Confucius (551–479 B.C.E.) urged Chinese leaders to adopt new moral and ethical principles and implored ordinary people to be kind and humane. At roughly the same time, a prince in India, Siddhartha Gautama (563–483 B.C.E.), struggled to understand and solve the problem of human suffering. Once he became "enlightened," he was called Buddha, and he initiated a movement that spread out from India during the Mauryan dynasty and influenced societies all over the world.

Westerners, too, experienced a wave of religious innovation during approximately the same time. In about the eighth century B.C.E., the ancient Hebrews were called to a higher ethical

standard by prophets who maintained that worship of God belonged as much in people's hearts as in Temple rituals. Four centuries later, Socrates and his student Plato argued for a philosophy that recognized and sought transcendent moral truths.

The most influential religious transformation in the ancient West came with the life of Jesus, a Jew born in the Roman Empire. Christian apostles and missionaries traveling through the empire slowly spread Jesus' teachings even as far as India. Eventually the Roman Empire adopted Christianity as its official faith. This transformation gave the West the last attribute it acquired from the ancient world over the next millennium and beyond: The West would be equated with Judeo-Christian beliefs.

Thinking Globally

1. What empires had begun to dominate the Eurasian landmass in this period?

2. How would these empires foster global interactions?

3. What examples of the spread of cultures do you notice on the map?

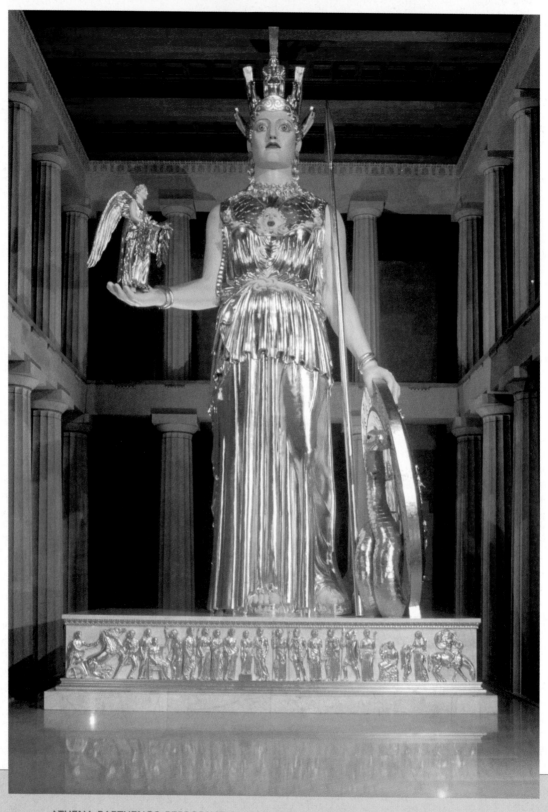

ATHENA *PARTHENOS*, REPRODUCTION IN NASHVILLE, TN, 2002

Athena *Parthenos*, a magnificent cult statue of the Greek goddess Athena, was unveiled in the temple known as the Parthenon, in Athens, in about 438 B.C.E. Built by the famous sculptor Phideas, the 41-foot-tall statue was made with skin of ivory and dressed in more than a ton of gold. In Phideas's interpretation, Athena held a 6-foot-high *Nike* (victory) statue in her hand. As Athenians looked with pride and awe at their patron goddess, who splendidly portrayed wisdom, wealth, and victory, they recognized their city at the height of its power. The original statue was destroyed after a millennium but was long remembered as a paragon of beauty. This carefully researched reproduction, completed in Nashville, Tennessee, in 2002, is the largest indoor statue in the West. The re-creation reveals our debt to the glory that was Greece.

The Contest for Excellence

Greece, 2000–338 B.C.E.

"It is the greatest good every day to discuss virtue . . . for life without enquiry is not worth living for a man. . . ." The Greek philosopher Socrates reputedly spoke these words, and they have become a famous articulation of the value of the spirit of inquiry. But the society that produced Socrates was also one that spawned an often-violent competition among men and among cities. Violence even swept up Socrates' voice of rationalism, for his memorable words were spoken at his trial as his neighbors accused him of undermining their way of life. Yet the philosopher/stonemason claimed he would rather die than give up challenging his neighbors to think about everything from truth and beauty to life and death. Because he refused to be silent, he was condemned to die. Fortunately his call for rational inquiry did not die with him but flourished in the contentious city-states of Greece, ultimately to become a fundamental characteristic of Western civilization.

The Greeks grappled with other challenges in addition to new philosophical approaches. Two brilliant Aegean civilizations, the Minoans and the Mycenaeans, rose and fell. In city-states such as Athens and Sparta, Greek citizens battled powerful neighbors such as the Persians, fought over spheres of influence, and invented unprecedented forms of participatory government. The individualistic Greeks also created magnificent works of art that set the standard of beauty for millennia and literature that inspires readers even in modern times. Ancient Greeks believed that in a heroic search for excellence, a man could accomplish anything. In some cases, they were almost right. However, in their quest for excellence—whether in war or peace—they also planted the seeds of their own downfall by valuing competition over cooperation.

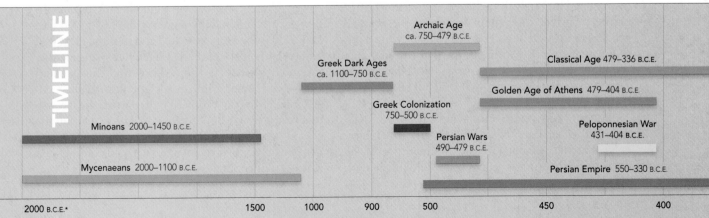

TIMELINE

Minoans 2000–1450 B.C.E.

Mycenaeans 2000–1100 B.C.E.

Greek Dark Ages ca. 1100–750 B.C.E.

Archaic Age ca. 750–479 B.C.E.

Greek Colonization 750–500 B.C.E.

Persian Wars 490–479 B.C.E.

Classical Age 479–336 B.C.E.

Golden Age of Athens 479–404 B.C.E.

Peloponnesian War 431–404 B.C.E.

Persian Empire 550–330 B.C.E.

2000 B.C.E.*   1500   1000   900   500   450   400

* For clarity, the dates in this line are not drawn to scale.

THE RISE AND FALL OF ANCIENT HEROES,
2000–800 B.C.E.

Ancient Greek men and boys gathered in the household hall in the evenings to enjoy songs of heroic deeds recited by skilled performers. (Literary texts also show that women and girls listened from the seclusion of their own rooms.) For centuries, poets recited accounts that later were gathered together to form the epic poem the *Iliad*. This work, by the eighth-century poet Homer, told of 50 days in the 10-year war between the Greeks and the Trojans, a people living on the coast of Asia Minor. The *Iliad* was also a story of the Greek mythic hero Achilles, whose prowess in battle overcame great odds. Despite his successes, Achilles was subject to outbursts of monumental anger—a trait that, as Homer wrote, "brought the Greeks so much suffering." The leader of the Greeks, King Agamemnon, provoked a quarrel with Achilles. When exerting his right to take the booty seized in war, he took Briseis, a woman who first had been allotted to Achilles. In protest, the wrathful warrior sat in his tent and refused to fight while many of his compatriots died under the Trojan onslaught. As one Greek leader in the story said, "Now look at Achilles. He is a brave man, yet who but he will profit by that bravery?"

Modern historians understandably have questioned the accuracy of certain details in Homer's epics, but the ancient Greeks saw these poems differently. For centuries, people believed that the epics portrayed Achilles' actions accurately. Indeed, many aspiring heroes strove to emulate the mythical soldier whose mere presence or absence on the battlefield could change the course of the war. By reading or listening to these accounts of a lost age, young men learned about heroism and about the destructiveness of human weakness. The tension between heroic aspirations and dangerous individual pride became a prominent theme throughout the history of the ancient Greeks as they built their civilization on a rocky peninsula in the Aegean Sea.

The Greek Peninsula

The Greek peninsula is dominated by striking mountain ranges. Lacking large rivers that would have provided natural communication links, the ancient Greek civilization consisted of separate communities scattered throughout the peninsula and the numerous Aegean islands. The mountain ranges protected the Greeks from large-scale invasions, but the rocky soil made agriculture difficult. The Greeks had to grow their wheat and barley on the scarce lowland, and in time they came to depend on imports for the grain they needed. The Greek historian Herodotus summed up the difficulties of agriculture when he wrote, "Greece has always poverty as her companion." As **Map 2.1** indicates, most places in Greece enjoyed a close proximity to the sea, which allowed overseas trade to become an essential part of ancient Greek society. This orientation toward the sea stimulated the many cultural contacts that marked the development of Western civilization (as discussed in Chapter 1). In fact, the earliest advanced civilization that arose in this region originated on an island that lay at the heart of the eastern Mediterranean.

The Minoans,
2000–1450 B.C.E.

By 2000 B.C.E., the islanders living on Crete boasted the wealthiest, most advanced civilization in the Mediterranean. They were not Greek—nor Indo-European—but were probably a Semitic people related to those living in the eastern and southern Mediterranean. At the height of its economic and political power, Crete consisted of a number of principalities, each dominated by a great palace. Knossos (see **Map 2.1**) is the best excavated and thus the most well known of the palaces. Early Greek historians identify the ruler of Crete as King Minos, and thus modern excavators named Minoan society after this legendary king. Minoan prosperity permitted the growth of a relatively large, peaceful population. During the golden age of this culture, the population of Crete reached an impressive 250,000, with 40,000 living in Knossos alone.

MAP 2.1

The World of the Greeks

This map shows the Greek peninsula with the surrounding seas. Notice the locations of Asia Minor and the islands of Crete and the Cyclades. Locate the important cities of Troy (in Asia Minor), Athens, and Sparta.

Explore the Map

1. How would sea travelers best proceed from the Greek mainland to Asia Minor and back? What does this route suggest about the importance of the islands in the Aegean Sea?

2. Where is Troy? What does its location at the entrance of the Hellespont (the narrow strait that allows access to the Black Sea and the interior of Asia) indicate about its strategic importance?

3. How did the location of Crete allow the island's people to control the trade in the region?

By trading with the peoples of the Fertile Crescent, the Minoans learned much of the best of early Western civilization. They learned to make bronze from the Sumerians, and their foundries produced a steady stream of valuable bronze tools and weapons. Minoan ships were the best made in the region. With their heavy construction and high front prows, these vessels cut effortlessly through rough seas and proved reliable in conditions that the islanders' shore-hugging contemporaries deemed impossible.

Economic power

Centers of economic as well as political power, Minoan palaces comprised vast mazes of storerooms, workrooms, and living quarters. These structures were markedly different from the huge buildings in Sumeria and Egypt, where architects of pyramids and ziggurats valued symmetry. Minoan architects preferred to build palace rooms of different sizes that wandered without any apparent design. The Greeks later called these palaces labyrinths. Kings controlling the trade through which wealth poured into Crete stashed goods away in the huge palace storerooms. One room in the palace at Knossos contained clay jars for olive oil that totaled a remarkable capacity of 60,000 gallons.

Like many maritime civilizations, the Minoans learned much from their encounters with other peoples. For example, their artwork reveals the influence of Egyptian colors and styles. The Minoans also learned writing from the Sumerians, and their script (called Linear A) was also a pictographic script written on clay tablets. As in Sumer, archaeologists have excavated clay tablets in Crete that seem to have been used for accounting and for tracking the movement of merchandise. So far, the symbols of Linear A have not been translated, so to learn about Minoan society, we must rely on archaeological remains, including their riveting artwork.

The Minoans decorated their palaces with magnificent frescoes, created by mixing paint with plaster and crafting the image as part of the wall. These paintings portrayed many of the everyday objects and activities that Minoans held dear, including religious rituals. Many statuettes from Crete showing goddesses holding snakes suggest that the predominant Minoan deity was a fertility goddess. The fresco in **Figure 2.1** shows a ritual in which men and women performed gymnastic activities with a wild bull. In this painting, one woman grabs the bull's horns to prepare to vault over it, while a man is already at the apex of his leap. Another woman waits to guide the jumper's descent. Some scholars suggest that this dangerous event may have been a religious ritual that culminated with the sacrifice of the bull and an opulent banquet at which men and women feasted on the meat and celebrated the goddess's generosity in bringing abundance to the society.

In the centuries after the Minoans, the ancient Greeks often told their history in the form of myths that recounted heroic acts from the Greek past. Some of these myths recalled the eventual destruction of Minoan society. In their myths, Greeks remembered a time when Greece owed tribute to Crete, including young people to be sacrificed to the Minotaur—a

Religious ritual

Minoan destruction

FIGURE 2.1 Minoan Acrobats, ca. 1500 B.C.E. This fresco from Knossos, Crete, depicts what was probably a religious ritual in which women (shown with pale skin) and a man leap over a charging bull.

creature that was half human and half bull. The king of Knossos may have worn the head of a bull on ceremonial occasions, and perhaps it was this tradition that gave rise to the legend of the Minotaur. One mythical Greek hero, Theseus, joined the sacrificial group, killed the Minotaur, and escaped the palace labyrinth by following a thread he had unraveled as he entered. (See Document 2.1, page 56, for more on the myth of Theseus.) This myth may hold a core of truth, for archaeological evidence shows that Minoan society was toppled by invaders. The great Minoan palaces apparently were burned by invaders who destroyed the unfortified cities. A man named Theseus may not have killed a minotaur, but it seems that Greeks killed the king of Crete.

Historians have looked further for the cause of the Minoans' downfall. Some suggest that a natural disaster contributed to their decline. In about 1450 B.C.E., a volcanic explosion on the nearby island of Thera (today known as Santorini) caused a tidal wave that may have destroyed the Minoans' protective fleet. However, this explanation is uncertain because other scholars question the date of the eruption, placing it two centuries earlier than the burning of Crete. Whatever the cause, the center of Aegean civilization passed to the earliest Greeks, whom we call the Mycenaeans.

Mycenaean Civilization: The First Greeks, 2000–1100 B.C.E.

Sometime after 2000 B.C.E., Indo-European Greek-speaking people settled on the mountainous Greek peninsula. By 1600 B.C.E., they were increasingly influenced by the Minoans and had developed a wealthy, hierarchic society centered in the city of Mycenae (see **Map 2.1**). Excavations of their shaft graves have yielded golden crowns and masks and, as with other Indo-European burials, many weapons, perhaps confirming ancient writers' characterizations of these people as the "war-mad Greeks." Yet, these early Greeks were also traders, and much of their wealth came from the growing commerce in the Aegean. As the Mycenaeans traded with wealthy Minoans, they learned much from them, evidenced by the strong Minoan influences in Mycenaean artwork. Mycenaean Greeks even learned to write from the Minoans, and their script is called Linear B for its similarity to the Minoan script. Because Linear B recorded an early form of the spoken Greek language, linguists have been able to translate Mycenaean tablets.

After Minoan society was destroyed in about 1450 B.C.E., the Mycenaeans took over as the commercial masters of the Mediterranean. As their wealth increased, so did the complexity of their governing system, which had a hierarchy of kings, nobles, and slaves. Powerful kings built palaces of stone so large that later Greeks thought they must have been constructed by giants. Unlike Minoan palaces, these structures were walled, indicating to archaeologists that there was a great deal of warfare, necessitating defensive fortifications. This conclusion is reinforced by written sources claiming that the kings surrounded themselves with soldiers.

Mycenaean states were not self-sufficient. Like the civilizations of the ancient Middle East, they depended on trade for many essentials. For example, there was little **Trade** copper and no tin on the peninsula, so they had to trade for ore to make bronze weapons and tools. The vast expanse of Mycenaean trade is clear. Mycenaean pottery has been found on the coast of Italy, and after the destruction of Crete, Mycenaean pottery replaced Minoan pottery in Egypt, Syria, Palestine, and Cyprus. These pottery remnants testify to the beginnings of the trade that linked the fortunes of the ancient Greeks intimately with those of their neighbors.

In about 1200 B.C.E., violence and a wide-ranging movement of peoples disrupted the eastern Mediterranean. A scarcity of sources does not allow historians to detail the exact causes of the upheaval, but we can see the effects **Violence and disruption** on kingdoms and individuals. The Egyptian Empire was besieged and lost territory as Syria and cities all along the coast confronted invaders. A letter from the king of the island of Cyprus urged the king of a city in Syria to hold firm against invaders: "You have written to me: enemy ships have been seen at sea. . . . Where are your troops and chariots? . . . Await the enemy steadfastly." Archaeological evidence shows towns sacked and burned throughout the region during these times of trouble. The important trade in copper from Cyprus was interrupted, and as we saw in Chapter 1, this violent era stimulated the dawning of the Iron Age.

The Mycenaeans were surely involved in these invasions that disrupted the ancient civilizations. According to later Greek myths, part of this violence included the Mycenaean invasion of Troy (see **Map 2.1**) in about 1250 B.C.E. The Trojan War became the basis of Homer's influential epics. Greek mythology attributes the conflict to a rivalry over a beautiful Greek woman, Helen, who was seduced by the Trojan prince Paris. Less-romantic historians believe the war stemmed primarily from the intensifying economic competition and growing violence in the eastern Mediterranean. Either way, the fighting was relentless and devastating—Homer claimed that the Greeks besieged Troy for ten years. At the end of this ordeal, Troy was destroyed (demonstrated by evidence from archaeological excavations).

Sometime after 1200 B.C.E., Mycenaean civilization itself dissolved. Later Greeks attributed this downfall to the Trojan War, which supposedly kept the Mycenaean leaders and soldiers away from home for so long. Archaeological evidence, however, shows that during and shortly after the Trojan War, the highly structured life on the Greek mainland broke down. Amid crop failures due to drought and internal instability, more Greek invaders from the north (later called Dorian Greeks) moved into the peninsula, especially the southern part, the Peloponnese. Population dropped dramatically. Excavations in one region reveal thirteen villages during the Mycenaean period; by 1100 B.C.E. only three remained. We do not know exactly what happened, but the flourishing Bronze Age Mycenaean society came to such a complete end that even the valuable art of writing was lost. All the great Mycenaean centers except Athens were destroyed. Life on the Greek mainland now consisted of a smattering of small villages, where people survived largely through subsistence farming.

From Dark Ages to Colonies

The period after the fall of Mycenae is called the Dark Ages (which extend from about 1100 B.C.E. to about 750 B.C.E.), because with the loss of writing, we have no texts that illuminate life during this time. For three centuries, life went on in the small villages, and people told tales that preserved their values. At the end of the Dark Ages, in about 800 B.C.E., Homer brilliantly recast some of these oral tales. The details he included offer glimpses into life during the previous three centuries. For example, Homer's descriptions of the cremation of the dead, which had not been practiced in Mycenaean civilization, suggest that cremation was developed after the fall of the early Greeks. As tantalizing as these bits of literary evidence are, most of our information for this period nevertheless must come from archaeology.

Excavations show that during these years, bronze gave way to iron as the primary metal used in weapons and tools. Archaeological findings also reveal that near the end of the Dark Ages, trade of wine, olive oil, and other goods began to flourish again all over the Mediterranean. By tracing the movement of Greek goods through the remnants of pottery and other artifacts excavated around the Mediterranean, archaeologists have discovered that Greek culture spread through the many colonies Greeks established in the region. At first, Greeks fled the disasters on the peninsula by settling on the numerous islands of the Aegean and the coast of Asia Minor (called Ionia) (see Global Connections on page 50). Later, colonists may have left the peninsula to escape overpopulation and seek new land and prosperity. Some aristocrats in Greek cities used the founding of

Founding colonies

new colonies as a way to diffuse social unrest by sending the dissatisfied elsewhere. **Map 2.2** shows the extent of the Greek colonies along the coast of the Mediterranean Sea. They were rivaled in number only by the Phoenicians, the master colonists we met in Chapter 1. Greek colonies were very different from modern colonial efforts because Greeks in the new settlements arranged themselves in cities that were just as independent as the mother city. The ties to the original cities were ones of emotion, not of colonial control.

For a time, Greeks in the new colonies remained independent from the other civilizations around them—the neighboring Phoenicians and the Babylonian and Persian Empires. However, while trading with their neighbors, the Greeks participated in the growth of Western civilization by adopting much that had gone before. For example, they derived their systems of weight from Babylonia and Phoenicia and adopted the practice of making coins from the Lydians (see Chapter 1). Societies transform acquired innovations, and the Greeks were no exception. For their coins, they minted silver (instead of the Lydian white gold) and usually placed secular images on them—sometimes illustrating their exports, like grapes or fish, and sometimes using emblems of civic pride. However, when describing Greek use of others' inventions, the Greek philosopher Plato (428–348 B.C.E.) characteristically gave the Greeks undue praise, boasting, "Whatever the Greeks have acquired from foreigners, they have in the end turned into something finer."

EMERGING FROM THE DARK: HEROIC BELIEFS AND VALUES

Through their trade with the Phoenicians, the Greeks acquired and adapted the Phoenician alphabet, and writing reemerged among the Greeks around 800 B.C.E. Once more Greek society was illuminated for historians. The Greeks did not use writing only for trade and contractual agreements—the Phoenician alphabet was simpler than other scripts, so it lent itself to a wider use. Talented Greeks used writing to record and transmit powerful and inspiring poetry that had been preserved for centuries only through human memory, and the ideas of the ancient Greeks once more came to light; the Dark Ages were over.

Heroic Values Preserved

The earliest of this Greek literature preserved a series of values that define what historians call a heroic society, in which individuals seek fame through great deeds and advocate values such as honor, reputation, and prowess.

MAP 2.2

The Greek Colonies in About 500 B.C.E.

This map shows the locations of the Greek and Phoenician colonies. Because ancient ships could not navigate at night, these colonies provided essential stopping points for long-distance trade.

Explore the Map

1. What spheres of influence are implied by the locations for the respective colonies?

2. Based on the map, in what regions would the Greeks most likely come in conflict with other powers?

3. How did the fall of Troy allow for Greek colonization around the Black Sea?

As we saw in the opening account of Achilles, the most influential Greek poet was Homer, who historians believe lived in the early eighth century B.C.E. Homer's two greatest epics were the *Iliad*, the tale of Achilles' heroic wrath, and the *Odyssey*, the story of the Greek warrior Odysseus's ten-year travels to return home from Troy. The *Iliad* became a seminal text for later ancient Greeks—schoolchildren and adults never tired of this tale of heroic deeds that captured details from Homer's times and preserved many Mycenaean values.

The highest virtue for Homer (and subsequent Greeks) was *arête*—manliness, courage, and excellence. *Arête* was best revealed in a "contest," whether

> Homer

sporting, warfare, or activities extending into many other areas of life and recreation. The ancient Greeks believed that striving for individual supremacy enhanced one's family honor, and the hero's name would live in poetic memory. Such beliefs and values helped fuel the greatness of ancient Greece. However, this striving for excellence—for heroism—was not always beneficial. At times it created a self-centered competitiveness that caused much suffering—just as Achilles' heroic-scale rage was said to have caused his companions' deaths. Harboring such intense competitive spirit, Greeks also held a deep disregard for all cultures other than their own (and they even had disdain for neighboring Greeks from different cities). Greeks distinguished themselves from "barbarians"

In literature, too, poets praised human accomplishments. Hesiod, an early Greek poet who wrote around 750 B.C.E., left almost as important a mark as Homer. His *Works and Days* describes farm life, wisdom, and values near the end of the Greek Dark Ages. Like social critics who had come before him, Hesiod complained of the powerful who cheat and exploit the poor and strive only for riches. Deploring the selfish "age of iron" in which he lived, Hesiod lamented the loss of what he believed were more virtuous heroic ages of "gold" and "bronze." He was no doubt wrong in assuming that the leaders of the Mycenaean age were less corrupt than those in his time, but his vision reveals the desire to imagine better times.

Hesiod

Hesiod lived in poverty—cheated out of his inheritance by a greedy brother and corrupt officials—yet he still articulated the ideals of heroic individualism. However, he clearly saw that the pursuit of excellence was a two-sided coin. At the end of *Works and Days*, he wrote of two kinds of "strife." One was good—a healthy spirit of competitiveness that Hesiod believed made people work and achieve their best. The other kind of strife, however, was bad and led to some people exploiting others, as happened in Hesiod's own life. This tension within heroic values marked Greek life and values and even their gods and goddesses.

The Family of the Gods

The ancient Greek historian Herodotus (482–425 B.C.E.) claimed that Homer and Hesiod powerfully shaped subsequent Greek religious beliefs. As Herodotus observed, these early poets "gave the gods their epithets, divided out offices and functions among them and described their appearance." The poems of Homer's and Hesiod's day were indeed populated by an extended family of gods and goddesses, loosely ruled by Zeus and his wife, Hera. This family included ten other main deities, among them Aphrodite, goddess of love; Athena, goddess of wisdom and war; Poseidon, god of the sea; Apollo, god of music, divination, and healing; and Demeter, goddess of fertility. These gods lived on Mount Olympus and periodically interfered in human affairs.

The Greek gods and goddesses resembled humans so much that one Greek critic from the sixth century B.C.E. observed that "Homer and Hesiod ascribed to the gods everything that among men is a shame and disgrace: theft, adultery, and deceiving one another." It is true that the gods shared human flaws, but they also shared admirable human qualities. Like the Greeks themselves, they loved beauty, banquets, processions, athletic competitions, music, and theater. The Greeks therefore infused all these activities with a feeling of worship. Religious rituals, for example, had an intensely festive air, and ancient Greek

FIGURE 2.2 Perfecting the Human Form, ca. 530 B.C.E. Greek artists glorified humanity by carving monumental, realistic life-size statues. Sculptors revealed their interest in the human form by depicting the males—called *kouros* (pl. *kouroi*), a word that is Greek for "boy"—without clothing. The females—called *kore* (pl. *korai*), the Greek word for "girl"—are always portrayed modestly clothed. Yet the female humanity is indicated by a smile on the female's face, referred to as the *archaic smile*.

who "spoke other languages" and felt it demeaned them to work alongside such foreigners. Individuals adhering to "heroic" values brought a combination of good and bad results, and the best of the Greeks from Homer on recognized this ambiguity.

Visual artists in the archaic age also glorified humanity in their increasingly realistic portrayal of the human figure. **Figures 2.2a** and **b** show two typical sculptures from the sixth century B.C.E. Both portray adolescent youths, called **kouros** (male) and **kore** (female). Such figures begin an aesthetic that will dominate ancient Greece—the male body is portrayed nude as the ideal of human perfection and beauty; the female is modestly clothed.

writings characterize religious activities as "sacrificing and having a good time."

As with the ancient religions of the Middle East, proper worship for the Greeks involved sacrificing a portion of human production to the gods. In contrast to the Mesopotamians, Greeks sacrificed things of relatively little value—the fat-wrapped thigh bones or internal organs of sacrificial animals—while keeping the best parts for themselves. Families, magistrates, and citizen assemblies were primarily responsible for observing proper respect for the gods. As a result, unlike in Egypt and Mesopotamia, powerful religious institutions never developed in ancient Greek society. Each temple had a priest or priestess, but their duties were usually part-time activities requiring little training.

The real religious professionals were oracles—people who interpreted divine will. Among these, the Delphic oracle, a woman who reputedly could enter into a trance and receive cryptic | **Oracles** | messages from Apollo, was the most famous. **Figure 2.3** shows the Delphic oracle sitting on a tripod under which vapors emerge from the earth, sending her into a trance. The latest scientific speculation suggests that the vapors were ethane, a gas that can be used as an anesthetic. The oracle consults a bowl in which float herbs or animal entrails to help stimulate her vision so that she might advise the man (here, Theseus's father) seeking advice.

Oracle messages were received in the form of ambiguous riddles and had to be interpreted by humans, so a central role for human agency remained in Greek religion. Perhaps the most famous inquiry at Delphi was made by King Croesus of Lydia in about 546 B.C.E. Croesus was worried about the Persian king Cyrus, who was threatening his kingdom (see Chapter 1), and asked the oracle whether he should wage war against Persia. The priests of Delphi returned with the answer: If Croesus were to make war on the Persians, he would destroy a mighty empire. Croesus was elated, but he had misinterpreted the oracle: The mighty empire that fell was that of Croesus as Cyrus defeated the Lydians. Messages from oracles needed to be interpreted very carefully, indeed.

Just as they envisioned their gods with all the qualities and foibles of humans, the Greeks embraced all facets of human behavior, even the irrational. To Homer's list of Olympians, subsequent Greeks added the worship of Dionysus, the god of wine and fertility. | **Worship of Dionysus** | Men worshiped this god during lavish banquets, but the cult had special appeal to women. During worship of Dionysus, women temporarily escaped their domestic confinement and engaged in drinking, ecstatic dancing, and sometimes sexual license as part of the ritual.

FIGURE 2.3 Foretelling the Future, ca. fifth century B.C.E. This pottery depicts the famous Delphic oracle sitting on a tripod where vapors from the earth sent her into a trance. Here she is shown recovered from her trance and reading the future in the bowl she holds.

Greek religious thought marked a significant departure from the forms of worship of the ancient Middle East. In Greece, the gods were so much like humans that worshiping them encouraged people to aspire to the greatest in human accomplishments and to acknowledge the worst in human frailties. It | **Impact of religious ideas** | was this view, for instance, that caused them to count Achilles as a flawed, yet powerful, hero. The Greeks did add a cautionary warning in their praise of humanity. If people exhibited excessive pride or arrogance as they tried to become godlike (called **hubris**), the gods would destroy them. Yet they still had a great deal of room to celebrate human accomplishments. As Greek thinkers placed humans rather than gods at the center of their understanding of the world, and as they studied reality from a human perspective, they began to transform the Mesopotamian view that had contributed so much to Western civilization. Humans were no longer impotent before a chaotic world ruled by arbitrary deities; instead, they were encouraged to understand and master their world.

Studying the Material World

The Greeks had great confidence in their ability to learn everything about the world. They rejected many earlier explanations and began an objective, almost scientific, approach to comprehending nature. This special search for knowledge was termed

Transforming Science in Asia Minor

In 585 B.C.E., Asia Minor—the turbulent crossroads where Eastern empires met Western Greeks—once again became embroiled in warfare. Lydians (in Asia Minor) and Medes (Persians) had skirmished over land and power for five years, when suddenly, amid a battle, the sun darkened. Frightened by this apparent message from the gods, the two armies laid down their weapons and negotiated peace. Not far away, the Ionian Greeks interpreted the darkening sun differently. One of their own, the esteemed teacher Thales of Miletus (ca. 642–ca. 548 B.C.E.), had predicted this solar eclipse well in advance of that day. Based on his studies of the heavens, he knew eclipses were natural occurrences, not messages of divine anger. This kind of thinking gave birth to a new, rational approach to understanding previously mysterious events.

How did this new view of natural occurrences appear in Ionia on the coast of Asia Minor? (See **Map 2.1** for the locations of Lydia and Ionia.) Miletus was a cosmopolitan city on the coast of the Aegean Sea (see **Maps 2.1** and **2.2**). In this bustling urban center, travelers from the New Babylonian Empire, Egypt, and Greece mingled and shared ideas. By the seventh century B.C.E., these Ionian Greeks had already learned much from their Asian neighbors. For example, they were using the Phoenician alphabet, a Babylonian system of weights, and Phrygian structures of music, called modes. Soon they would also begin using coins invented by the Lydians. But as Thales' knowledge of eclipses demonstrated, these practical tools were only a few of the important ideas that spread from the East to Greece.

Thales himself probably came from a distinguished family of mixed Greek and Phoenician background. He took an interest in everything from Greek myths to Babylonian science, and his unconventional, cross-cultural background proved fertile soil for sprouting new ideas. Fortunately for him, he had access to the sophisticated learning of the Babylonians.

The Babylonian king Nebuchadrezzar (r. 605–561 B.C.E.), though he destroyed Jerusalem in 587 B.C.E. and led the Jews into the Babylonian Captivity, was also a builder. He made Babylon the greatest city in the world. Covering 2,100 acres—far more than the 135 acres of the typical Sumerian city—Babylon amazed the Ionian Greeks who visited the city to trade or simply tour. They returned home with captivating stories of grand palaces and temples aglow with brightly colored glazed bricks. These architectural wonders only underscored the considerable skill of the Babylonian engineers.

The greatest Babylonian accomplishments, however, came in the fields of astronomy and mathematics. For thousands of years, Mesopotamians had studied the night sky, and Babylonians perfected this art. Starting in 747 B.C.E., Babylonian court astronomers kept monthly tables on which they recorded all planetary movements together with reports of earthly affairs. These efforts gave birth to the pseudoscience of astrology, through which Babylonians tried to understand the effect of heavenly objects on earthly events. Their observations set the stage for astronomical science in the Greek world and beyond.

The Babylonians also made great strides in mathematics. Using their base-60 number system, Babylonian mathematicians pioneered detailed calculations such as square and cube roots, as well as many other impressive reckonings. To demonstrate the complexity of solving mathematical problems using a base-60 system, **Figure 2.4** shows a calculation to obtain the square of 147 (or 147 times 147). Using our number system, multiplying 147 by itself is fairly simple and yields the result of 21,609. In the cuneiform calculation shown in the figure, the number 147 is indicated as 2,27, and squaring gives the answer of 6,0,9. The location of these digits refers to a position of a number on a complex chart containing six columns, each of which had ten numbers. Only specialists had access to such charts.

The difficulties of these early mathematics makes Thales' ability to apply their principles even more impressive. He purportedly mastered mathematics and geometry so thoroughly that he could determine the height of a pyramid by measuring the length of its shadow at the time of day when the length of a person's shadow equaled his or her height. Thales' skill made him a much-sought-after teacher who could explain the Babylonians' arcane mathematical wisdom to ordinary people and extend that learning to a new generation.

In 539 B.C.E., the Persians finally conquered Asia Minor. One of Thales' students, Pythagoras, fled the violence in Ionia to settle in Croton in southern Italy. There he continued his studies of mathematics and geometry, spreading the mix of Asian and Greek science farther west. His work would leave a lasting influence on Western science.

Making Connections

1. Why was Ionia well placed to serve as a crossroads between East and West?

2. How did Thales help make mathematics and astronomy relevant to the Greeks?

3. How difficult would it have been to use Babylonian mathematics? Can *you* figure the system out?

4. How did this fruitful combination of Eastern and Western science influence our science today?

FIGURE 2.4 147 squared = 21,609. Babylonian: 2,27 squared is 6,0,9.

philosophy (love of wisdom) and would become the Greeks' most important intellectual invention. The earliest known scholar of this kind was Thales of Miletus (ca. 624–ca. 548 B.C.E.). The location of Miletus on the Ionian coast (see **Map 2.2,** on page 47) shows how Greek culture and its tremendous influence had moved beyond the Greek mainland itself.

Thales reputedly studied Egyptian and Babylonian astronomy and geometry and brought this knowledge to practical use by measuring pyramids, based on the length of their shadows, and predicting a solar eclipse. (See Global Connections on page 50.) Departing from most of his Egyptian and Mesopotamian predecessors, Thales believed in an orderly cosmos that was accessible to human reason. This formed the heart of much subsequent Greek (and Western) inquiry. He sought a single primal element that would explain a cosmic unity and believed that element was water. Although Thales' conclusion was wrong, his assumption of an orderly universe accessible to human inquiry was pivotal to the future of Western thought.

Thales and Democritus

Thales was followed by others who continued the rational approach to the natural world. Democritus (ca. 460–ca. 370 B.C.E.), for example, posited an infinite universe of tiny atoms with spaces between them. Although his ideas were not widely supported in ancient Greece, they were proven by early-twentieth-century physicists.

Pythagoras (ca. 582–507 B.C.E.), who fled from Ionia to Italy, made even greater discoveries in the fields of mathematics and astronomy. He believed that order in the universe was based on numbers (not water), and that mathematics was the key to understanding reality. Pythagoras is credited with being the first to suggest that the number 13 is unlucky, but his mathematics extended far beyond such attempts to quantify fortune. He developed the Pythagorean Theorem, the geometrical statement that the square of the hypotenuse of a right triangle is equal to the sum of the squares of the other two sides. He went on to explore additional theories of proportion that have contributed to much modern mathematics. Pythagoras was also among the first to claim that the earth and other heavenly bodies were spherical and that they rotated on their axes. The mathematician was so respected that his followers later developed a religious cult in his name.

Pythagoras

These philosophers, in a dramatic way, changed the direction of thinking about the world. They rejected the mythopoeic approach to understanding the world and made the first attempts to understand and explain the world in a scientific and philosophical way. Because they had little experimental equipment and no prior knowledge to draw upon, their ideas were not necessarily accurate by our standards, but we would not be who we are without them.

Men like Thales, Democritus, and Pythagoras operated on an abstract level of almost pure science. Yet the Greeks also practiced an applied technology, with results that continue to astound us. The sixth-century B.C.E. engineer Eupalinus, for example, constructed a 3,000-foot-long tunnel through a mountain in order to bring water from a spring into a city. To accomplish this feat, he used only hand tools, and he had to work in the dark because he lacked a light source. Most extraordinary, he dug from both sides of the mountain—and the two parts of the tunnel met in the middle with only a slight adjustment needed. Pythagoras was on Eupalinus's island of Samos at about the time the tunnel was dug, so some scholars speculate that the mathematician helped in the process. Others have suggested that Eupalinus used a system of mirrors to line up the halves of the tunnel and illuminate the interior as he excavated. However he managed this feat, he counts among the most accomplished Greeks who applied reason to practical matters.

Practical applications

While modern scholars admire these early Greek thinkers, many contemporaries looked with suspicion on those who studied the world while seemingly ignoring the gods. Even though the Greeks worshiped humanlike gods and goddesses, they still revered them, and accusations of impiety always hovered on the borders of scientific inquiry. In 432 B.C.E., the democratic assembly of Athens made it a crime to "deny the gods, or disseminate teachings about the things that take place in the heavens." This law was precipitated by the teachings of Anaxagoras (ca. 500–ca. 428 B.C.E.), who claimed that the sun was a white-hot stone instead of a god. Even in the field of rational inquiry, in which the Greeks made such impressive strides, the ambiguities that marked this dynamic society are evident. The same culture that produced impressive thinkers like Anaxagoras and Socrates (whom we met at the beginning of this chapter) sometimes recoiled from the results of their studies. Nevertheless, Greek intellectual accomplishments formed one of their central contributions to Western civilization.

Fears of "impiety"

LIFE IN THE GREEK POLEIS

As we saw in Chapter 1, ancient societies had taken for granted a natural order of society that placed kings and priests in charge, and the Mycenaean Greeks had shared this view. With the brisk trade that comes so naturally to sea peoples, however, a new prosperity based on commercial expansion emerged, creating

thinking about

ART

FIGURE 2.5

Ezekias, Suicide of Ajax, Athenian Vase, ca. 450 B.C.E.

The famous vase painter Ezekias has portrayed a significant moment in the Trojan War. After the death of Achilles, the hero Ajax expected to be named to lead the army. Instead, the Greeks chose Odysseus. In his humiliation, Ajax commits suicide. The artist shows him preparing for his death, burying the hilt of his sword in the earth so that he can fall on his sword. On the right, the artist shows the all-important hoplite weaponry: the great shield with the head of the mythological monster Gorgon emblazoned on the front, the helmet, and the long spear. Yet, in this contest for excellence the pride of the individual was more important than the strength of the army, and the artist shows this in the vase.

Connecting Art & Society

1. Would the Greeks have considered this act heroic or cowardly?

2. Is Ajax showing the same kind of individualistic pride as Achilles did in the incident described at the beginning of this chapter, when he refused to fight?

3. What would our society think of this act?

long thrusting spears formed a **phalanx**—a tight formation about eight men deep and as wide as the number of troops available. As long as these soldiers stayed tightly pressed together, they were virtually impenetrable. Elite warriors once could rely on their own heroism and on their monopoly of horses and cavalry to ensure victory on the battlefield. Now that a hoplite phalanx could withstand cavalry charges, the aristocracy no longer maintained a privileged position; they needed the support of citizen armies. This dependence further weakened aristocratic rule. **Figure 2.5** shows the tension between the traditional values of heroic pride on the one hand and the needs of the phalanx-dependent hoplite army on the other hand. Even as the artist immortalized the hero's prideful suicide, he also highlighted the hoplite weaponry that made the phalanx invincible.

The Invention of Politics

Between 650 and 550 B.C.E., civil war broke out in many cities as the lower classes rose to overthrow the aristocracy. This violence led to the rule of men who became rulers by physical force. Although kingship | Tyrants | had a long-standing tradition in the West, this was a new form of authority—based on power, not hereditary right. The Greeks called such rulers *tyrants* to distinguish them from more traditional kings. At first the term had no pejorative connotation—one could easily be a kind tyrant, and indeed some were sincere reformers seeking to end aristocratic exploitation. For example, some tyrants gained popular support by such reforms as freeing slaves, eliminating debts, redistributing land. Later, however, as these rulers relied on force to hold power, the term *tyrant* acquired the negative meaning it holds today. Tyrants often favored the commercial classes to try to hold on to power, but such alliances proved insubstantial. In some city-states, tyrants were replaced by various forms of participatory governments.

Greek citizens—especially those who controlled the lucrative trade and fought in the successful phalanxes—thus began to take charge of the political life of their cities. A Greek city-state was called a **polis** (pl. *poleis*). It was a small but autonomous political unit that generated intense loyalty from its citizens, who conducted their political, social, and religious activities in | City-states | its heart. The poleis frequently included a fortified high ground—called an *acropolis*, the most famous of which is in Athens. They also had a central place of assembly and market, called the **agora** (pl. *agorae*). Surrounding villages began to consolidate and share a political identity, and the word *polis* came to mean the city-state itself and its surrounding countryside. Each city-state was an independent

an urban middle class of merchants and artisans who owed no loyalty to aristocratic landowners.

By 700 B.C.E., changes in warfare brought about in part by the growth of Greek trade also made aristocratic warriors less important. First, the growing commercial classes became wealthier, | Hoplite armies | and at the same time the increased trade brought down the price of metals. Now more men could afford to arm themselves and go to war. New armies of infantrymen (called **hoplites**) dominated the art of making war. Common citizens armed with swords, shields, and governing entity, but in the view of its residents, a polis was also a state of mind. Unlike in Mesopotamia, Egypt, and Mycenae, polis inhabitants did not think of themselves as subjects of a king or as owing obedience to a priesthood. Instead, they were "citizens" who were actively responsible for guiding their poleis. Aristotle (384–322 B.C.E.) even characterized humans by their participation in politics (the word *politics* is derived from the word *polis*), arguing that "man is a political animal" (although a more accurate translation is "man is an animal of the polis").

Although Greece's rocky terrain separated the land into many small city-states, they shared certain characteristics. They all developed self-government by male citizens, with variations as to the exact form. For example, Corinth and many other small poleis had an **oligarchy** (rule by a few), whereas Athens developed an early form of democracy that was strikingly new in the West and in the world. All the states relied on hoplite armies, and all used slavery to run their small-scale industries and farming. In all the city-states as well, Greek men who fought together in the hoplite armies gathered daily in the agorae to discuss matters of life and politics.

The Heart of the Polis

The heart of the polis was the household, which consisted of a male citizen, his wife and children, and their slaves. This configuration formed the basis for both the rural and urban economies. In the villages outside the walls of the city itself, household members herded sheep and goats, worked in the vineyards and olive groves, and struggled to plant crops in the rocky ground. Olive trees yielded abundant fruit, but harvesting required a good deal of labor.

Olive harvesting was well worth the effort, however, for the olives and their precious oil brought much wealth into some of the city-states. Athens's economy in particular depended upon its olive oil exports. A well-known story about the philosopher Thales illustrates the economic importance of olives to the Greeks. His neighbors mocked him, saying, "If you are smart, why aren't you rich?" In response, he purchased the use of all the local olive presses cheaply during the off season. Then, when everyone was trying to press their olives after the harvest, they had to buy the use of the presses from Thales. He made a fortune and silenced his neighbors. As his final retort, Thales pointed out that philosophers could easily become rich, but they loved the life of the mind more than money.

In addition to olive harvesting, craftsmanship and trade completed the polis economy. Artisans in the polis labored at their crafts or sold their merchandise in the open market during the mornings. After a large afternoon meal, they napped and then either returned to their shops or (more likely) went to the gymnasium to exercise and talk with other citizens. The gymnasium grew in part out of the Greek belief in cultivating perfection in all things; thus a skilled artisan or philosopher also needed to cultivate his physical prowess as part of his pursuit of excellence. The gymnasium proved an enduring feature of life in the Mediterranean city-states. This was a highly public life for male citizens; work, exercise, and talk were all central activities of the masculine life.

Men's and women's roles

In most city-states, women's lives were more restricted than men's—at least in the ideal. Wealthy, upper-class women were married at puberty and were supposed to stay indoors. A text from the early fourth century B.C.E. describes how a husband educated his 15-year-old wife on domestic responsibilities. He told her that men belonged outdoors: "For a man to remain indoors . . . is a thing discreditable." Women, on the other hand, should stay inside, teaching female slaves necessary skills, managing the goods brought into the household, and presiding over the spinning and weaving. When men entertained their peers at dinner parties or visited, "respectable" women stayed home and out of sight along with their female slaves and children. (As we will see, life for women in Sparta marked an exception to this pattern.)

Of course, real life seldom measures up to the extremes of the ideal. Even in Athens, many women were visible in the marketplace: Slaves went to the fountains to carry water, prostitutes offered their services, and priestesses served in more than forty religious cults of the city. Between these extremes, there were many women of the poorer classes who sold their wares—cloth or garden produce—in market stalls as they worked hard to supplement the family income.

In addition to having defined gender roles, Greek society depended heavily on slave labor; virtually every household had a few slaves. In the earliest years of the poleis, just as elsewhere in the ancient Middle East, slaves were either captives of war or debtors. By the sixth century B.C.E., debt slavery had been virtually banned throughout the Greek world, but slavery itself remained a central institution. However, in many ways slaves' lives resembled those of their owners. Numerous slaves worked alongside free men and women in almost every occupation. (There were even slave policemen in Athens.) Slaves frequently lived in their own residences, worked in a trade, and earned their own money. Sometimes called "pay-bringers," they owed their owners a portion of their income but could retain some of the money they earned. With this revenue, some slaves in turn bought slaves for themselves or purchased their own freedom. Many Greek cities even had benefit clubs that lent slaves

Slave labor

enough money to buy their freedom and repay the loan later. Numerous bright, ambitious slaves gained their freedom and became quite prosperous.

All slaves did not enjoy this relatively easy life. Some slaves had brutal masters and suffered all forms of abuse; in Athens, some slaves who tried to flee their condition bore the brand of a runaway on their foreheads. Slaves who lived under the worst conditions were those who had the misfortune to work in the silver mines, an essential source of income for Athens. In these mines, they were fed just enough to stay strong and were beaten regularly to keep them working in the mines that produced immense wealth for free Greeks. For the most part, however, slavery was treated as a simple fact of life—an essential tool for getting necessary work done.

Fears and Attachments in Greek Emotional Life

The extreme separation of men and women seems to have contributed to a wide range of insecurities and emotional attachments in Greek society. Many Greek writers expressed a great suspicion of women. As one poet, Semonides of Amorgos, wrote: "God made the mind of women a thing apart." The strict segregation of men and women through their lives may have contributed to misunderstandings. Men with little experience with women believed that virtuous women were scarce. Many husbands feared that their wives would escape their seclusion and take lovers, and thereby raise questions about the paternity of their children. These fears permeate many writings by Greek men.

Perhaps as part of their overall praise of masculinity, many ancient Greeks accepted bisexuality, at least among wealthy urban dwellers. The ideal of such a relationship took the form of a mentoring arrangement between a well-connected older man and a "beardless youth" (although school-aged, free-born boys were protected from such liaisons). As the pair matured, the elder man would marry and take up his family responsibilities, and the younger would serve as a mentor to a new youth. Such relationships were seen as a natural part of a world in which men often feared female sexuality, spent all their time together, exercised nude in the gymnasia, and praised the male body as the ideal of beauty. Indeed, many Greeks believed that the male-male relationship offered the highest possibility for love and that such ties usually brought out the best in each partner, making both braver and nobler.

Bisexual relations

We have fewer examples of women engaging in homosexual behavior, probably because their lives were conducted in privacy and were not recorded in as many historical documents. However, one sixth-century B.C.E. poet, Sappho from the island of Lesbos, expressed passionate love for the young women in her social circle. Her poetry has since been both highly respected for its beauty and severely criticized for its content. The philosopher Plato admired Sappho so much that he referred to her as a goddess of poetry, but some Greek playwrights dismissed and ridiculed her as an ugly woman who could not attract a man. Nevertheless, Sappho's poetry was so influential that the word *Lesbian*, meaning a resident of Sappho's island of Lesbos, has become synonymous with female homosexuality.

Sappho of Lesbos

Not all women were confined to the home. While respectable women stayed carefully indoors, some women—slaves or foreigners—who had no economic resources or family ties became prostitutes and courtesans who shared men's public lives at dinners and drinking parties. Prostitutes were even registered and taxed in many Greek city-states and thereby became a legitimate part of social and economic life. Men and prostitutes drank freely together from the wine bowls abundantly filled at banquets. These bowls were decorated inside and out with appropriate themes. **Figure 2.6** shows a prostitute dressed in loose, seductive clothing who holds a wine bowl in each hand as she plays a Greek drinking game in which the participant twirls the drinking vessel until the dregs go flying. Such exuberant images not only portrayed scenes from the parties but also were intended to spur people on to greater abandon. Women in ancient Greece, particularly Athens, were thus placed in the peculiar situation of being invisible if they were "respectable," and mingling with and influencing powerful men only if they were not.

Courtesans

All the city-states shared many of these elements of urban life, from work to pleasure. However, each polis had its own distinctive character, as citizens structured their political lives to suit themselves. The two best-documented Greek cities were Athens and Sparta, and yet most of the cities did not match the extremes in art and austerity that marked these two influential states.

Athens: City of Democracy

Theseus, whose father was portrayed consulting the Delphic oracle in **Figure 2.3,** founded Athens. Document 2.1 relates the city's founding myth and suggests that participatory democracy was at the heart of its origins. The reality of a developing democratic form of government was more complicated. By 700 B.C.E., Athenian aristocrats had established a form of government that allowed them to run and control the growing city. Three (and later nine) administrators—called *archons*—were elected by an assembly of male

Oligarchy

FIGURE 2.6 A Drinking Game, ca. fifth century B.C.E. This pottery cup shows a courtesan swirling a wine bowl until the dregs fly out. It reminds us that although respectable women stayed home, prostitutes were a regular part of Athenian social life.

economic heart of the problem. He ordered that no agricultural product could be exported except olive oil, thus stimulating the cultivation of the valuable olives that would become the basis of Athens's prosperity. He also standardized the weights used by the Athenians, making it easier for them to trade with other poleis. With the economic reforms in place, Solon turned to the political structures that had proved inadequate to prevent civil strife.

Solon did not try to eliminate the old families from power; instead, he paved the way for men growing wealthy from the export trade to participate in government. He first divided up all citizens into four groups based on wealth (instead of birth), and only members of the top two groups were eligible to become archons (and subsequently members of the Areopagus). While this preserved some privilege of rank, it nevertheless appeased the newly wealthy, who were now permitted to aspire to the highest offices. Solon then revitalized the assembly of citizens, and to further weaken the power of the Areopagus, he created a Council of 400 to set the agenda for the Ecclesia. To round out the reforms, Solon tried to ensure justice for everyone by establishing a special people's court of appeal intended to offer protection against the abuse of power by archons.

> Increased democracy

Solon's reforms were balanced and attempted to provide a compromise among the contentious social groups in Athens. However, his attempts to placate the various factions were unsuccessful because each party tried to gain more privileges. During the resulting civil strife, Athens turned to tyranny, bringing Peisistratus to power in 560 B.C.E. He ruled (between periods of exile) until 527 B.C.E., when his son Hippias tried to continue the rule. He was to be the last of Athens's tyrants. He fell to a coalition of aristocrats and Greeks from other city-states hoping to gain some political advantage for themselves. The period of tyranny broke the power of the aristocrats and paved the way for full democracy.

> Tyranny

The people rallied to Cleisthenes, a nobleman who stood for popular interests. In 508 B.C.E., Athens adopted the Constitution of Cleisthenes, which refined Solon's reforms and brought a remarkable degree of direct democracy to the city. Cleisthenes kept Solon's basic structure, but his major innovation (which has earned him the credit for establishing democracy in Athens) was to redistrict the city in a way that old alliances of geography and clan were broken and could no longer control the city offices. Everyone was divided up into ten tribal units, and this was how they were represented in the Assembly. Furthermore, Solon's old Council of 400 was increased to 500—each tribal unit could select 50 members by lot. By breaking the old alliance system, Cleisthenes

citizens (the *Ecclesia*) and ran the business of the city. They served for only one year, and after their tenure they permanently entered a council called the Areopagus (eventually numbering 300 men), which held the real power because it was composed of senior men who could not be removed from office. This government, in which the wealthy effectively controlled power, proved unable to respond to changing economic fortunes, which had profound political consequences.

By about 600 B.C.E., the weaknesses in the Athenian economy had become apparent. Small farmers could not produce enough to feed the growing population, and many fell into debt and even slavery by offering themselves as security in exchange for food. At about the same time, the hoplite armies caused the aristocracy to lose its monopoly over the military. A social crisis was in the making, but it was resolved by a far-sighted Athenian aristocrat, Solon, who was elected as sole archon in 594 B.C.E. Like so many men in the West who periodically tried to alleviate social ills, Solon introduced reforms intended to appease these lower classes while keeping aristocrats in power.

> Solon's reforms

Solon first addressed the alarming debt crisis by introducing reforms—called the Shaking Off of Burdens—that canceled (or limited) existing debts and banned debt slavery altogether. Solon also introduced some agricultural reforms, striking at the

thinking about
DOCUMENTS

DOCUMENT 2.1

Theseus Founds the City of Athens

The famous ancient biographer Plutarch (46–120 C.E.) related Athens's founding myth, in which the hero Theseus defeated the Minotaur of Crete and returned to establish a city that would be unlike any that had gone before.

After the death of Ægeus, Theseus conceived a great and important design. He gathered together all the inhabitants of Attica and made them citizens of one city, whereas before they had lived dispersed, so as to be hard to assemble together for the common weal, and at times even fighting with one another.

He visited all the villages and tribes, and won their consent, the poor and lower classes gladly accepting his proposals, while he gained over the more powerful by promising that the new constitution should not include a king, but that it should be a pure commonwealth, with himself merely acting as general of its army and guardian of its laws, while in other respects it would allow perfect freedom and equality to every one. By these arguments he convinced some of them, and the rest knowing his power and courage chose rather to be persuaded than forced into compliance.

He therefore destroyed the prytanea, the senate house, and the magistracy of each individual township, built one common prytaneum and senate house for them all on the site of the present acropolis, called the city Athens, and instituted the Panathenaic festival common to all of them. He also instituted a festival for the resident aliens, on the sixteenth of the month, Hecatombaion, which is still kept up. And having, according to his promise, laid down his sovereign power, he arranged the new constitution under the auspices of the gods. . . .

Wishing still further to increase the number of his citizens, he invited all strangers to come and share equal privileges, and they say that the worlds now used, "Come hither all ye peoples," was the proclamation then used by Theseus, establishing as it were a commonwealth of all nations. But he did not permit his state to fall into the disorder which this influx of all kinds of people would probably have produced, but divided the people into three classes, of Eupatridæ or nobles, Geomori or farmers, Demiurgi or artisans.

To the Eupatridæ he assigned the care of religious rites, the supply of magistrates for the city, and the interpretation of the laws and customs sacred or profane; yet he placed them on an equality with the other citizens, thinking that the nobles would always excel in dignity, the farmers in usefulness, and the artisans in numbers. Aristotle tells us that he was the first who inclined to democracy, and gave up the title of king; and Homer seems to confirm this view by speaking of the people of the Athenians alone of all the states mentioned in his catalogue of ships.

SOURCE: Plutarch, "Life of Theseus," in *The Great Events by Famous Historians*, vol. I, ed. Rossiter Johnson (The National Alumni, 1905), pp. 50–51.

Analyze the Document

1. What was unusual about Theseus's vision for the city?

2. How might this myth have influenced the development of Athenian democracy?

3. Might the myth have been created after Athens had adopted a democratic constitution?

---

secured a remarkable form of direct democracy for Athens with provisions to curb the power of any group that might become too strong.

Although the Ecclesia offered a new level of participation to the men of the ancient world and a model of representation that has been praised since, it was not a perfect democracy. It still represented only about 20 percent of the population of Athens, for it excluded women and slaves. 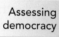 Also excluded were the *metics*, resident foreigners who lived and worked in Athens in manufacturing and commerce and who represented nearly one-third of the free population of Athens. Furthermore, recent scholarship shows that only a minority of the qualified citizens could attend the assembly at any given time—only about 6,000 can fit into the meeting place, a small sloping hillside. It seems that when the meeting place was full, no one else could enter and a quorum was declared. Thus, probably many of the same people (those living nearby) attended the Ecclesia regularly.

However, other parts of the Athenian government made sure the principle of egalitarian democracy prevailed. The Council of 500 was chosen annually by lot from male citizens over age 30, and citizens could not repeat tenure. Choosing representatives by lot (instead of by election or other device) removed much of the influence of wealth and personal power from the political process. The Council set the agenda for the Ecclesia, preparing forms of legislation for the assembly's action. Its influence was enormous, but the full governing power remained in the direct democracy of the Ecclesia. These practices assumed that all citizens could fulfill the duties of government, and this egalitarian assumption is astonishing for the ancient world (and perhaps for the modern one as well). The great leader of Athens Pericles, in a famous funeral oration preserved (or paraphrased) by the historian Thucydides, rightly observed: "Our constitution is called a democracy because it is in the hands not of the few but of the many."

The people did recognize that sometimes individuals could threaten the rule of the many, and to protect the democracy, Cleisthenes instituted an unusual procedure early in the sixth century B.C.E.: ostracism. Once a year, Athenians could vote for the man they considered most dangerous to the state by inscribing his name on a scrap of pottery (called an *ostracon*). If a man received 6,000 votes, he was sent into exile for ten years. **Figure 2.7** shows examples of these pottery shards. The scrap on the lower left votes to exile a man named Hippocrates, while the other three cast votes for "Themistocles, son of Neocles." It appears that Themistocles was well on his way to exile! Although Athenian democracy was not perfect, it was an extraordinary new chapter in the history of the West, and one that has held long-standing appeal.

| Ostracism |

Sparta: Model Military State

Sparta's development led to the emergence of a state thoroughly different from Athens, with a markedly different set of values. Whereas Athenians were creative, artistic, and eloquent, Spartans were militaristic, strict, and sparing of words (our word *laconic* comes from the Greek word for "Spartans" or the region they inhabited). The nature of their state was shaped by an early solution to their land hunger.

FIGURE 2.7 Pottery Voting Ballots Once a year, Athenians were able to vote for someone whom they believed should be exiled for ten years. They inscribed his name on pottery scraps called *ostraca*, such as the ones shown here. That Greek word is the source of the English word *ostracize*, meaning "to ban from the group."

Instead of sending out colonists or negotiating partnerships with the peoples in their vicinity (as the Athenians had done), the Spartans conquered their neighboring districts and enslaved the local populations. The slaves, called **helots,** were treated harshly. As one Spartan poet observed, they were like "donkeys worn down by intolerable labor." Sparta's helots greatly outnumbered free citizens and always seemed to threaten rebellion. To keep the helots in slavery, the Spartans virtually enslaved themselves in a military state of perpetual watchfulness. They consoled themselves by observing that at least they had chosen their harsh life, whereas their helots had not.

The Spartan constitution—reputedly introduced by the semilegendary Lycurgus in about 600 B.C.E.—reflected their deep conservatism and made a minimal concession to democracy. Authority was carefully kept in the hands of the elders. In this oligarchy, citizen representation was firmly guided by age and experience, and many outsiders admired Sparta's "mixed constitution," which seemed to balance democracy with oligarchy.

Life in Sparta was harsh, although it was much admired by many Greeks who appreciated the Spartans' powers of self-denial. At birth, each child was examined by elders, and if deemed physically deficient, the child would be exposed—left outdoors to die. At the age of 7, boys were turned over to the state

| Spartan life |

and spent the next thirteen years in training to learn military skills, endurance, and loyalty to the polis. At 20, young men entered the army and lived the next ten years in barracks. They could marry but could visit their wives only by eluding the barracks guards. At 30, men became full citizens and could live at home. Nevertheless, they were expected to take all meals in the military dining hall, where food was sparse and plain.

While their men lived isolated in the barracks, Spartan women had far more freedom than Greek women of other city-states. Because men concentrated on their military activities, women handled most of the household arrangements and had wide economic powers. They attended contests to cheer the brave and mock the losers, but they were not simply spectators. Women, too, trained in athletic endurance, and the fierceness of Spartan women was said to match that of their men. The Greek biographer Plutarch (46?–120? C.E.) recorded a series of quotations that were supposedly the words of Spartan women. The most famous is from a woman who tells her son to come back from war either with his shield (victorious) or on it (dead). Such resolve made the armies of Sparta the best in Greece, and though the Spartans created no works of art, they probably would have said that their own lives were masterpiece enough.

The Love of the Contest: Olympic Games

Athens and Sparta were only two examples of the many varieties of city-states that developed with fierce independence on the Greek mainland and in the colonies throughout the Mediterranean. But, although there was much rivalry among the poleis, they still shared a certain sense of identity. They spoke the same language, worshiped the same gods, cherished Homer's poetry, and had a passionate love for individual competition. They recognized these affinities, calling themselves *Hellenes* (the Romans later called them "Greek" after a Greek colony), and they considered all Hellenes to be better than other peoples. Their love of contest caused Hellenes to gather at many local competitions that included drama as well as sport. The largest and most famous of these events was a religious festival dedicated to Zeus, and Hellenes even stopped their almost interminable warfare to come together and compete.

The first pan-Hellenic Olympic Games were held in 776 B.C.E. At first, the event consisted only of a footrace, but soon the games

| Olympic Games |

expanded to include boxing, wrestling, chariot racing, and the grueling pentathlon, which consisted of long jumping, discus and javelin throwing, wrestling, and the 200-meter sprint. Olympic victors brought glory to their home cities and were richly rewarded there with honor and free meals.

The Olympics were so popular that they served as an inspiration to many artists. The athletes shown in **Figure 2.8** demonstrate the perfection that people expected from their athletic heroes. The scene portrays several of the contests: the footrace, the javelin throw, and, in the center of the relief, the most difficult event, wrestling. The athletes tense all their muscles as they begin the contest that virtually defined Greek life. Critics, such as the playwright Euripides (485–406 B.C.E.), chided Greeks for their adulation of athletes. "We ought rather to crown the good man and the wise man," he scolded. Nevertheless, spectators flocked to the games.

Olympic planners prohibited women from attending the contest, although they could purchase a chariot and horses with which men would compete in their names. One woman defied the convention and dressed as a trainer so that she could watch her son compete. After he won, she jumped over a fence in her excitement and accidentally revealed her gender. Olympic officials promptly passed a law requiring all future trainers to attend the games in the nude to prevent further disguises.

| Women at Olympics |

Some women conducted games of their own separately from the men's. These games, dedicated to Zeus's wife, Hera, involved footraces run by unmarried women of various ages. Women judged and sponsored the games and awarded the fastest competitors crowns of olive branches. However, these winners did not receive the high level of acclaim or wealth accorded to male victors, who brought prestige to their cities and fame for themselves through their athletic prowess. Although the Olympic Games offered a safe outlet for the Greeks' love of competition, Greek history was shaped by more devastating strife in which city-states tried to outdo each other on the battlefields.

The Persian Wars, 490–479 B.C.E.

Greek colonists who settled in Asia Minor built their city-states in lands that the Persian Empire had claimed by 500 B.C.E. As we saw in Chapter 1, the

FIGURE 2.8 The Olympic Games, late sixth century B.C.E.   As part of their ongoing contest for excellence, the Greeks developed the Olympic Games in honor of Zeus. Here, athletes participate in the footrace, wrestling, and the javelin throw.

thinking about
GEOGRAPHY

(map of the Persian Wars, 490–479 B.C.E., showing the Aegean region with labels including: Black Sea, Bosporus, Propontis, THRACE, Persian invasion 480, MACEDONIA, Xerxes' Canal, Mount Athos, Hellespont, Pontoon Bridge, Marathon 490, Athens, ATTICA, THESSALY, Thermopylae 480, Aegean Sea, Sardis, PERSIAN EMPIRE, Plataea 479, Athens, ATTICA, Salamis 480, Gulf of Corinth, PELOPONNESE, CYCLADES, Miletus, Ionian Sea, Mediterranean Sea, MELOS, RHODES, Sea of Crete. Legend: Greeks, Persians, Major battle)

2.3(a) The first
invasion—490 B.C.E.

2.3(b) The second
invasion—480 B.C.E.

MAP 2.3A & B

The Persian Wars, 490–479 B.C.E.

This map shows the routes of invasions and the major battles of the wars between Persia and the Greek poleis. Map 2.3a traces the first invasion by sea in 490 B.C.E., and Map 2.3b illustrates the routes of the second invasion, during which armies marched by land, supported by accompanying ships.

Explore the Map

1. What might have been the particular advantages and disadvantages posed by the land and sea routes?

2. How did the topography of Greece, with its narrow passes, serve as a disadvantage to the more numerous Persian forces?

3. Why did the Persian land route require engineering marvels such as the Pontoon Bridge and Xerxes' canal? How might these have served as models for future military expeditions?

Persians were tolerant of the various subject peoples within their territories, so they did not object to the growing spirit of independence that accompanied the prosperity of these successful commercial cities. However, open revolt was another matter.

In 499 B.C.E., the Greek tyrant ruling in the city of Miletus (**Map 2.3**) offended the Persian rulers. Hoping to avoid retribution, he staged a revolt against Persian rule and asked for help from his compatriots on the Greek mainland. Sparta refused, but Athens sent twenty ships—enough only to anger the Persians

Causes of war

but not to save Miletus. The Greek city was sacked, and the Persians turned their attention to the Greek peninsula. They planned an invasion in part to punish Athens for its involvement in the Miletus uprising.

Any forces seeking to invade the Greek mainland had to negotiate the mountainous terrain and the narrow passes that afforded the only access to the interior. Furthermore, an invading land army had to be supplied by a shore-hugging fleet that backed up the infantry while navigating the narrow straits of the Aegean shoreline. In 490 B.C.E., the Persian king

Darius I (r. 522–486 B.C.E.), therefore, sailed across the Aegean and landed near Athens. **Map 2.3a** depicts the route of the invading Persian army and the battle site located on the plain of Marathon.

At the Battle of Marathon, the Athenians and their allies were far outmatched by the numerous Persians. The worried Athenians asked their Spartan compatriots for reinforcements, but the Spartans replied that they had to complete their religious festival first—then it would be too late to repel the Persians. Athens and its allies had to stand alone. In spite of being outnumbered, the Athenians decided to march from Athens to meet the Persians near their landing site on the plain of Marathon. Confident of an easy victory, the Persians launched their attack. Things did not go as expected for the Persians, however. The Athenian general, Miltiades, developed a clever strategy that helped the Greeks outwit the lightly armed Persians. Weakening the center of their line and strengthening the two wings, the Athenians outflanked the advancing Persian force and inflicted severe damage. The Greeks also made a running advance, a novelty that surprised and confused their enemy. Athenian innovation and energy won the day, bringing a decisive and stunning victory to the Greeks. According to the texts, 6,400 Persians perished in the battle, compared with only 192 Athenians. This unexpected victory of the polis over the huge empire of Persia earned Athens great prestige, and the Athenian victory also inspired confidence in the newly emerging democracy itself.

One of the heroes of Marathon was a fast runner, Philippides, who ran approximately 150 miles in two days to request the help of the Spartans. However, he is more remembered for a probably untrue story that claims he ran to Athens to deliver the news of victory to the polis and then died on the spot from his exertions. Modern-day races are called *marathons* in commemoration of Philippides' legendary 26-mile run from the plain of Marathon to Athens.

Athens had fended off the invaders, but the humiliated Persians were determined to try again. Ten years after the disaster at Marathon, Darius's successor, Xerxes (r. 486–465 B.C.E.), plotted a full-scale invasion of the Greek mainland. Xerxes brought the best of ancient engineering to the invasion to try to avoid the disaster of the first war. To move a large infantry force, he built a pontoon bridge across the Hellespont and marched 180,000 soldiers to Greece. Even more impressive, he ordered his men to build a canal a mile and a quarter long through a peninsula in northern Greece so that his fleet could supply the ground force. Historians have debated for decades about whether the canal existed, but recently, scientists from Britain and Greece proved conclusively that the canal was built. It spanned about 100 feet at the surface, just wide enough for two war galleys to pass. It was an astonishing engineering feat and showed Xerxes' determination. (Both the bridge and the canal are shown on **Map 2.3b**.)

As the Persians invaded, several Greek city-states in the north surrendered quickly to the Persian Great King. Meanwhile, Athens had readied its own fleet, assuming that the best way to withstand the Persians was to control the Aegean and therefore the supply routes to troops on the march. Athens also secured the participation of Sparta and its allies to aid in the battle.

For the Persian army, the gateway to the south lay through the pass at Thermopylae (see **Map 2.3b**). Yet the narrow pass, held by a small coalition of Greeks led by Spartans, turned the Persians' greater numbers into a liability. The Greeks held the pass for days against repeated assaults by the best Persian forces. In the end, however, they were betrayed by a Greek who expected to enrich himself by aiding the attackers. The traitor led the Persians around the defended pass, where they could fight the Greeks from the rear. Only the Spartans stayed to fight to the death. Defending themselves from front and back, the Spartans fought fiercely in a long-remembered feat of bravery, and all died with sword in hand. An inscription placed on their graves immortalized their heroic stand: "Tell them the news in Sparta, passer by. That here, obedient to their words, we lie."

The Persians' success at Thermopylae opened a route for them to march south to Athens itself. The outmatched Athenians consulted the Delphic oracle (shown in **Figure 2.3**), who told them to trust in wooden walls. The Athenian leader, Themistocles, persuaded the people that the oracle meant the wooden "walls" of their ships, not the walls of Athens, so the Athenians scattered, taking refuge in their fleet and abandoning the polis for nearby islands. Many horrified Greeks were close enough to watch as the Persians plundered Athens and burned the temples on the Acropolis as an act of revenge for their previous losses. Yet, as in Marathon, the tide again turned against the mighty Persians, this time in the bay of Salamis (see **Map 2.3b**).

Artemisia, queen of Caria in Persia and commander of a squadron of Xerxes' fleet, immediately saw that the Persians would lose their advantage in numbers fighting in a narrow bay and strongly advised the Persian king against it. Her military wisdom proved well founded; the swift Greek vessels rallied and crushed almost the entire Persian fleet. Artemisia managed to escape through her remarkable strategy and bravery. Xerxes withdrew from the melee after sending his children home to safety on Artemisia's ship. The despondent emperor, watching Artemesia's

> Battle of Marathon

> A second invasion

> Thermopylae

> Greek naval victory

success and the destruction of the rest of his fleet, lamented: "My men have become women, and my women men." The next year, the Spartans led a coalition that defeated the remnants of the Persian army at Plataea (see **Map 2.3b**). The individualistic, dispersed Greeks had triumphed once more over the vast, unified Persian Empire.

Herodotus: The Father of History

In a famous work called simply *The History*, the Greek historian Herodotus recorded the great deeds of the Persian Wars with a combination of a broad perspective and an attention to detail. This monumental work—some 600 pages long—was so pathbreaking that he is universally considered the father of Western history. With his first sentence, Herodotus placed himself within the Greek heroic tradition, claiming to have written in order "that the deeds of men may not be forgotten, and that the great and noble actions of the Greeks and Asiatics may not lose their fame." While immortalizing these warriors, Herodotus did not take the traditional approach of converting heroic deeds into godlike myths. Instead, he drew from oral traditions acquired during his extensive travels—the things he had "seen and been told"—and wrote what he intended to be a total picture of the known world. This was an account not simply of a war but of a heroic-scale conflict between two types of societies, the poleis and the Asian empire—or, for Herodotus, between freedom and despotism.

Herodotus did much for the discipline of history by striving to record historical events as accurately as possible and separating fact from fable, but his efforts marked only a beginning in the quest for historical objectivity. He clearly shared the Greeks' belief that their culture was far superior to that of the "barbarians," and these preconceptions biased his conclusions.

Although Herodotus wrote a lively, fascinating history, as we will see, he was wrong in identifying the Persians as the Greeks' worst enemies. Just as a Greek had betrayed the Spartans at Thermopylae, the Greeks themselves would one day bring about their own downfall. But for the time being, they gloried in their astounding victory over Persia, the great power of Asia.

GREECE ENTERS ITS CLASSICAL AGE,
479–336 B.C.E.

Victory over the mighty Persian Empire launched the Greeks into a vigorous, creative period that later historians and art critics admired so much they named it the classical age. This period was marked by stunning accomplishments in art, architecture, literature, philosophy, and representative democracy in Athens. This same age that saw such impressive artistic innovations ended as the contest for excellence among the city-states plunged them into devastating wars. At the beginning of the period, however, Athens, which took the lead in guarding Greece from Persian incursions, began to flex its muscles.

Athens Builds an Empire, 477–431 B.C.E.

The Greeks' defeat of the Persians, though sweet, presented the fiercely independent poleis with a new dilemma. The Persian Empire was still powerful. How would the Greek city-states work together to remain vigilant in the face of this threat, and who would lead them? The most effective defense of Greece lay in controlling the Aegean, and the Athenians possessed the strongest fleet.

In 477 B.C.E., most maritime poleis on the coasts and the islands of the Aegean finally decided to form a defensive league. Each member of the league contributed money to maintain a large fleet for the defense of them all. The island of Delos (near modern Mykonos) is small and rocky, only about 2 miles | Delian League | long and less than a mile wide, but its importance was disproportionate to its size (see **Map 2.1,** on page 43). Its location was perfect; as the halfway point between mainland Greece and Ionia, it capitalized on the trade through the Aegean. Furthermore, it was reputed to be the birthplace of Apollo, so its sanctuary to that god brought pilgrims (and wealth) from all over the Greek world. Even Homer mentioned Delos as a religious center for Ionian Greeks. Because people thought the sanctuary was sacred and protected by the god, the alliance decided to establish their treasury on Delos. The coalition was thus called the Delian League. Theoretically, all league members were entitled to an equal voice in decision making, but Athens was the strongest member and began to dominate league policy.

As early as the 470s B.C.E., some members took offense at Athens's prominent role and sought to withdraw from the arrangement. But the Athenians swiftly made the situation clear: This was not a league of independent states after all, but an Athenian empire with subject cities. In 454 B.C.E., the Athenians dropped any pretense of the member states' autonomy and moved the league's treasury from Delos to Athens. It is hard to imagine how deeply the Athenian actions horrified the Greek world, but consider that it was a sacrilege to raid the shrine that had been safe under Apollo's protection for centuries. It is also hard to grasp how vast were the stores of money on Delos. The Athenians would use this wealth to rebuild the Acropolis and to fund Athens's Golden Age, which included dressing the cult statue of Athena in astonishing amounts of gold (see the chapter-opening photo on page 40).

One critic of Athenian policy complained that, because the smaller Aegean states depended on sea-borne imports and exports for their survival, they did not dare to defy the Athenian "rulers of the sea." Nevertheless, the Athenian Empire did succeed in protecting the mainland from further Persian assaults and conferred other benefits: The poleis of the Aegean and Asia Minor were free to trade safely under the protection of the Greek ships. They received peace in exchange for autonomy.

During the Persian Wars, the Athenian military commanders had understandably acquired a good deal of power. Officials called **strategoi** (sing. *strategos*) were elected as commanders of the tribal army units, and during Athens's imperial age, a particularly strong strategos came to wield considerable power for a time. The political architect of Athens's Golden Age was the statesman Pericles (495–429 B.C.E.), who was elected strategos every year from 443 B.C.E. to his death in 429 B.C.E. He so dominated Athenian affairs that many compared him to a tyrant, yet this powerful aristocrat eloquently championed democracy in the assembly of Athens and encouraged democratic principles within the states of the league. However, he did not permit independent action by subject states. Thus, Pericles supported Athens's removal of the league treasury. As he pointed out, it was only right that Athenians enjoy the money, given that they had led the victory over Persia in the first place and their city had been burned in the process. Pericles followed up this argument by playing an instrumental role in plans for spending the money.

| Pericles |

Pericles' closest companion and most influential advisor was the talented courtesan Aspasia, who headed an establishment that boasted the most cultured young courtesans in Athens, and in the mid-440s B.C.E., she became Pericles' mistress. Despite her status with Pericles, Aspasia drew intense criticism for her "undue" influence over Athens's great leader. For example, the Athenians suspected her of persuading Pericles to involve Athens in military alliances advantageous to her native city of Miletus. Rumors also circulated that she helped write the orator's speeches. The ever-loyal Pericles ignored all these complaints, however, and maintained his close relationship with Aspasia until his death.

Pericles forwarded democracy within Athens by trying to ensure that even poor citizens could participate fully in Athenian politics and culture. His most significant contribution was to pay the people who served as jurors or on the Council of 500. Now all male citizens—not just the rich—could

| Pericles' democracy |

participate in the democracy. Equally important, he used much of the treasury to employ citizens on a project designed to beautify the public spaces of Athens. He organized armies of talented artists and artisans and paid thousands of workers to participate in the project. Finally, he put about 20,000 Athenians on the municipal payroll, a move that stimulated widespread involvement in the democratic proceedings of the city.

Artistic Athens

Pericles' leadership made Athens the political and cultural jewel of Greece. At the heart of the reconstruction program lay a plan to rebuild the Acropolis, which the Persians had destroyed. The restored Acropolis consisted of several temples and related buildings. As they designed the buildings, architects drew from the best of Greek tradition to make a political as well as an artistic statement. Design came first: Greek temples had always been constructed of *post and lintel* form, in which columns supported the roof. By 600 B.C.E., Greeks had developed "orders" of architecture to describe the various designs of the columns (and buildings), and these orders have influenced architecture down to the modern day. There were three orders of classic Greek buildings—Doric, Ionic, and Corinthian. **Doric,** the oldest order, developed on the Greek mainline, has a simple capital on top of a fluted column. The **Ionic** order, developed in Ionia on the eastern Mediterranean (see **Map 2.2**), features taller, more slender columns topped with elegant scroll shapes. The **Corinthian** order was a later development (probably from the fifth century B.C.E.) and was not used on the Acropolis, but its columns, topped with an acanthus-leaf capital, were extremely popular in later architecture. **Figure 2.9** shows a sketch of the major elements of these three

Greek Doric   Greek Ionic   Greek Corinthian

FIGURE 2.9 Architectural Orders The magnificent Greek architects developed *orders*, conventional architectural styles most readily identified by the tops of the columns. The Doric, Ionic, and Corinthian orders are shown here. The Greeks' orders have influenced architecture into modern times.

FIGURE 2.10 Acropolis of Athens, 448–432 B.C.E.   After raiding the treasury of Delos, Athenians rebuilt their Acropolis with temples to the deities. The greatest temple was the Parthenon, featured here, which continues to be a model of architectural perfection.

orders that make them recognizable. The architects of the buildings on the Acropolis used both Doric and Ionic columns in the temples, as you can see in **Figure 2.10.** Specifically, the Doric style was featured on the magnificent Parthenon, and the Ionic on the Temple of Athena Nike.

In effect, these structures were nothing less than a political statement. Indeed, visitors to the Acropolis could see the empire's might in the majestic columns, which proclaimed Athenian control over the mainland to the Ionian coast. Although people would forget that political statement over time, the architectural elements would constantly be duplicated.

Builders designed all the temples with extraordinary care, constructing them according to principles of mathematical proportion, which the Greeks (following in the footsteps of Pythagoras) believed underlay the beauty of the universe. At the same time, the architects knew that human beings cannot visually perceive absolute, mathematical perfection, so they compensated by creating an optical illusion, curving some of the temples' lines to make them appear straight to the human eye. In other words, Greek architects used practical means to strive for abstract perfection. In this longing, the buildings of the Acropolis mirrored the Greeks' pursuit of excellence.

The largest temple in the Acropolis was the Parthenon (shown in the center in **Figure 2.10**), located on the highest point and dedicated to Athena, the patron goddess of the city. The temple had a magnificent statue of the goddess (now lost) created by Phidias, the greatest sculptor of the day, whose reputation for excellence continues today. The reproduction of this statue is on page 40.

The Athenians adorned the Parthenon with many sculptures and statues of both gods and humans. (Today, few statues remain in Athens—most are in museums elsewhere.) These statues, which all bear a strong resemblance to one another, echo the Greek belief that gods and humans had much in common.

Figures 2.11 and **2.12**, photos of sculptures from the Parthenon, depict both gods and ordinary Athenians. The gods and goddess in **Figure 2.11** are seated, waiting for the procession of the Athenians to begin. They are shown posed and dressed as Athenian citizens. At the same time, the Athenian youths in **Figure 2.12** who ride in the procession are as beautifully formed and as serenely confident as gods. By blurring humanity and divinity in their visual arts in this way, the Greeks explored the highest potential of humanity in their artwork. Their sculpture represented an idealized humanity, not real people.

FIGURE 2.11 Gods on the Parthenon, ca. 440 B.C.E. Every four years, Athenians staged a major festival, the Panathenaic procession. The frieze along the Parthenon's inner colonnade memorializes the event. In this detail, the humanlike gods are shown reclining and enjoying their tribute.

FIGURE 2.12 Athenians on the Parthenon, ca. 440 B.C.E. The human riders in this detail from the frieze along the Parthenon's inner colonnade look godlike as they take part in the Panathenaic procession. The artist, Phidias, carved the horses' legs in deeper relief to cast shadows on the lower part of the frieze and thereby to increase the optical illusion of movement.

Greek Theater: Exploring Complex Moral Problems

In addition to their architecture and sculpture, the Athenians' theatrical achievements set new standards for Greek culture. Greek theater grew as part of the religious celebration of Dionysus, held in the late spring. Every year, Athens's leaders chose eight playwrights to present serious and comic plays at the festival in a competition as fierce as the Olympics. The plays were performed in open-air theaters with simple staging. Men played both male and female parts, and all actors wore stylized masks. The themes of these plays centered on weighty matters such as religion, politics, and the deep dilemmas that arose as people grappled with their fates. During Athens's Golden Age, playwrights reminded the Athenians that, even at the height of their power, they faced complex moral problems.

One of Athens's most accomplished playwrights was Aeschylus (ca. 525–456 B.C.E.), who had fought at the Battle of Marathon. His earliest play, *The Persians*, added thoughtful nuance to the celebrations that the Athenians had enjoyed after their victory. Instead of simply praising Athenian success, Aeschylus studied Persian loss, attributing it to Xerxes' hubris at trying to upset the established international order. This also subtly warned the Athenians not to let their own arrogant pride bring about their own destruction.

Aeschylus and Sophocles

The most revered playwright of this period, however, was Sophocles (ca. 496–406 B.C.E.), who is best known for *The Theban Plays*, a great series about the mythological figure Oedipus and his family. All Athenians would have known the story of Oedipus, an ill-fated man whose family was told by a soothsayer at his birth that he was doomed to kill his father and marry his mother. The family exposed the baby to die, but he was rescued by a shepherd and raised as a prince in a faraway land. When he was grown, a soothsayer in his new land repeated the prediction, and when Oedipus fled to avoid killing the man he believed was his father, he returned to his original home, where he unintentionally fulfilled the prophecy. In Sophocles' hands, the play became a study in the range of human emotions measured by how man responds to tragic fates. As Document 2.2 shows, Oedipus moves from pride in his own position as king to deep agony and humility as he discovers the horrifying truth of his life. The play concludes with a reminder to all spectators not to feel complacent in their own lives.

DESTRUCTION, DISILLUSION, AND A SEARCH FOR MEANING

Sadly for the Athenians, they failed to heed Sophocles' warnings about pride and impiety. Their era of prosperity came to a violent end with the onset of the Peloponnesian War, a long, destructive conflict between Athens and Sparta and their respective allies. Like the Persian Wars, this new contest generated its own historian. Thucydides (460–400 B.C.E.), an even more objective historian than Herodotus, wrote: "I began my history at the very outbreak of the war, in

Thucydides

DOCUMENT 2.2

A Playwright Reflects on the Meaning of Life

The tragic playwright Sophocles wrote Oedipus the King *in about 429* B.C.E. *at the beginning of the Peloponnesian War and at the height of Athenian power. The two passages included here express two Greek views of life. In the first, Oedipus has just learned of his adoptive father, Polybus's, death, which seemed to make a lie of the prophecy that Oedipus would kill his father and marry his mother. Oedipus's wife, Jocasta, urges him to the heroic values of fearlessness and boldness. The final speech, given by the chorus, reminds all of Athens never to be prideful and complacent. Notice the contrast between these two speeches.*

Oedipus: It was sickness, then [that killed Polybus]?

Messenger: Yes, and his many years.

Oedipus: Ah! Why should a man respect the Pythian hearth, or give heed to the birds that jangle above his head? They prophesied that I should kill Polybus, kill my own father; but he is dead and buried, and I am here— I never touched him, never, unless he died of grief for my departure, and thus, in a sense, through me. No. Polybus has packed the oracles off with him underground. They are empty words.

Jocasta: Had I not told you so?

Oedipus: You had; it was my faint heart that betrayed me.

Jocasta: From now on never think of those things again.

Oedipus: And yet—must I not fear my mother's bed?

Jocasta: Why should anyone in this world be afraid? Since Fate rules us and nothing can be foreseen? A man should live only for the present day. Have no more fear of sleeping with your mother: How many men, in dreams, have lain with their mothers! No reasonable man is troubled by such things.

. . . .

Chorus: Men of Thebes: look upon Oedipus. This is the king who solved the famous riddle and towered up, most powerful of men. No mortal eyes but looked on him with envy. Yet in the end ruin swept over him. Let every man in mankind's frailty consider his last day; and let none presume on his good fortune until he find life, at his death, a memory without pain.

SOURCE: Dudley Fitts and Robert Fitzgerald, *The Oedipus Rex of Sophocles: An English Version* (New York: Harcourt Brace, 1977) in Lamm, *The Humanities in Western Culture* (New York: McGraw-Hill, 2003), p. 13.

Analyze the Document

1. Which of the two speeches—by Jocasta or the chorus—better represents the Greek heroic ideal? Why?

2. What are Jocasta's and Oedipus's views on prophecies and auguries? Why do you think the playwright included these skeptical opinions?

3. How do you think the Athenian audience would have reacted to Sophocles' warning against pride just as Athens was beginning a war against Sparta?

---

the belief that it was going to be a great war. . . . My belief was based on the fact that the two sides were at the very height of their power and preparedness. . . ." Historians today share his desire for intellectual analysis of the facts but might come to different conclusions about the results. In any case, as a result of Thucydides' *History of the Peloponnesian War*, we now have the earliest, most carefully detailed record of a war—and of the destruction of a way of life.

The Peloponnesian War, 431–404 B.C.E.

To counter growing Athenian power, Sparta gathered together allies—the Peloponnesian League—to challenge the power of the Athenian Empire. While the flash point of the conflict was a dispute between two poleis, Thucydides recorded the Spartan viewpoint: "What made war inevitable was the growth of Athenian power and the fear which this caused in Sparta." At its core, this was a war to preserve the independence of each city-state and the unique brand of competitiveness among all the poleis. Athens had grown too strong, and the contest too uneven. Sparta felt compelled to take action when Athens increased its imperial ambitions.

The actual fighting proved awkward and difficult, for Athens and Sparta each had differing strengths and military styles. Athens was surrounded by long walls that extended to the shore (see inset in **Map 2.4**). Therefore, as long as the Athenian navy controlled the sea, Athens could not be successfully besieged. Thus Athens preferred to conduct battle with its navy and harried Spartan and allied territories from the sea. Sparta, on the other hand, put its trust in its formidable infantry. Bolstering their individual strengths, Athens's allies surrounded the Aegean Sea, while Sparta's allies were largely land based, as **Map 2.4** shows. As the Spartans marched across the isthmus near Megara to burn Athens's crops and fields, Athenians watched safely from behind their walls and supplied their needs with their massive fleet. However, there were bloody clashes as young Athenians tried to stop the Spartans, who were ravaging

MAP 2.4

The Peloponnesian War, 431–404 B.C.E.

This map shows Athens and Sparta and their allies during the Peloponnesian War. The inset illustrates the "long walls" that joined Athens to the sea at its port of Piraeus.

Explore the Map

1. What evidence for the importance of Athens's fleet can you draw from the map?

2. Which city-state's allies were closest to Persia? Given the proximity of these allies, which side might Persia be disposed to support in this war? Why?

the countryside, and Athenians suffered inside the city, which was overcrowded with refugees. Under these conditions, plague struck the city in 430–429 B.C.E. Even Pericles succumbed, along with about one-quarter of the population. Athenian leadership fell to lesser men, whom contemporaries denounced as selfish and impulsive (such as Alcibiades, featured in the Biography on page 67).

The realities of war caused Athenian ethics to deteriorate further with the city-state's shameful

BIOGRAPHY

Alcibiades

(ca. 450–404 B.C.E.)

Alcibiades was born to a well-placed family in Athens, but his father died when the boy was only about three. The child was then raised in the house of Pericles, the talented leader of Athens, who was his mother's cousin. Tall, handsome, wealthy, charming, and a skilled orator (in spite of a lisp), Alcibiades had all the advantages of a privileged Athenian youth. The philosopher Socrates took a personal interest in the promising young man and spent a great deal of time teaching him. Alcibiades was perfectly positioned to succeed Pericles as a leader in Athens. However, he lacked his foster father's integrity and his teacher's sense of virtue. Instead, he seems to have been overly proud and impulsive and placed his own interests above those of his polis.

The outbreak of the Peloponnesian War in 431 B.C.E. gave the young man the opportunity to win the admiration of his countrymen. At one point in the war, Alcibiades shared a tent with Socrates, who saved his life during a skirmish but allowed the youth to take credit for heroism. Alcibiades' political career was launched on the battlefield, where Athenian men traditionally proved their manhood.

Alcibiades married a well-born woman, Hipparete, with whom he had a son. Hipparete quickly learned of Alcibiades' character flaws and licentiousness and tried to divorce him. Family ties and political expedience were against her, however, and she was forced to remain a dutiful wife. She chose to ignore her husband's philandering, while he built his reputation in public life.

When the war against Sparta subsided temporarily after 421 B.C.E.,

Alcibiades turned to other means to buttress his fame. In 416 B.C.E., he entered seven four-horse teams in the chariot races of the Olympics and won the top prizes. Except for one Greek king, no one had ever before spent so much money on the races, and no one had won so much. Yet Alcibiades saw war as the real path to glory. He maneuvered to revive the conflict with Sparta and urged Athens to request a deputation from Sicily, which wanted Athens's assistance against Syracuse. Alcibiades saw in this alliance an opportunity to win riches and land, and he persuaded the Athenians to send a large expedition to Sicily.

Before the expedition could depart, however, the Athenians were shocked by a display of impiety that seemed to bring a bad omen. The statues of Hermes that adorned the city had been smashed and mutilated. During an investigation into this desecration, which struck at the very heart of Athenian pride, the citizens heard testimony that implicated Alcibiades himself. In addition, one of his own slaves accused Alcibiades of ridiculing the sacred "mysteries" of Demeter by drunkenly mocking the goddess's religious rituals at a dinner party. The charge seems to have been true and shows the tension between those Athenians who had little fear of the gods and those who found impiety terrifying.

As the proceedings against Alcibiades dragged on, the summer sailing season began to wane. The Athenian expedition left for Sicily with Alcibiades in the lead. However, the fleet had not even reached Sicily when Alcibiades was recalled to answer the mounting charges against him.

The Sicilian expedition ended in disaster, but Alcibiades was not there to see it.

Instead of returning to Athens, Alcibiades fled to Sparta, offering advice and leadership to his traditional enemy. He impressed the Spartans with his obvious talents and with his seeming ability to live with no luxuries. He stayed in Sparta for two years, helping his newfound allies plot against Athens.

Alcibiades' luck evaporated when he reputedly seduced the Spartan king's wife. To escape the king's ire, he fled to Persia, the enemy of both Sparta and Athens. The Persians, too, were impressed with Alcibiades' talents. He negotiated an alliance with the Persians that would prove damaging to Sparta and then returned triumphant to Athens. When war broke out again between Sparta and Athens, Alcibiades was given command of the Athenian fleet and the opportunity to assume the kind of power that Pericles had held. However, the Spartan commander Lysander won a spectacular victory. The loss was not Alcibiades' fault, but the Athenians blamed him and he was again forced to flee. In 404 B.C.E., the Spartans and Persians arranged the assassination of Alcibiades. In an ironic twist, the heroic opportunist who chose personal glory over allegiance to his polis died at the hands of his former partners in treachery.

Hero,

Military

Genius, and

Traitor

Connecting People & Society

1. How did Alcibiades' life illustrate the concept of the drive for excellence and personal greatness at any expense?

2. How might Alcibiades' relationship to Socrates have contributed to the philosopher's condemnation?

treatment of Melos, an island that sought neutrality in 416 B.C.E. in the conflict between Athens and Sparta. Athens argued that its superior strength gave it the right to force Melos into serving as its ally.

Melos destroyed

Maintaining that they had the right to make their own choices, the Melians held their ground. The furious Athenians struck back, killing every last man on Melos and enslaving the women and children. Dismayed by this atrocity, Thucydides observed that the ravages of war had reduced "men's characters to a level with their fortunes." By this he meant that, under the relentless pressure of war, the Athenians had sacrificed their ideals of justice in favor of expediency.

A significant event in the war came when Alcibiades, one of the new leaders of Athens, persuaded residents of the polis to meddle in a dispute between two Greek city-states in Sicily.

Athens loses

Alcibiades saw this involvement as a way to gain glory for himself, and perhaps as a ploy by which Athens could extend its control outside the Aegean Sea. It may have worked, for if Athens could control the sea trade between Greece and Italy (the Ionian Sea), Sparta's commercial allies would have been ruined. However, the venture ended in disaster: Athens lost as many as 200 ships and 40,000 men. Its fleet severely weakened, Athens could no longer rule the Aegean, and its reluctant "allies" began to fall away. Although eight years would elapse between the Sicilian disaster and Athens's final defeat, the city-state could not recover enough to prevail. The Peloponnesian League's fleet, partially financed by a Persia eager to help weaken Athens, destroyed the remnants of the Athenian fleet. Cut off from the trade that would have let them survive a siege, the Athenians were forced to surrender in 404 B.C.E. Their defeat would have profound political and philosophic ramifications.

Philosophical Musings: Athens Contemplates Defeat

During the devastating war, some Athenians started asking themselves sobering questions about justice and the meaning of life. The answers they came up with led them down new pathways of thought—pathways that would permanently alter the direction of Western philosophy. Athenian politicians like Alcibiades and the architects of the Melos atrocity had promulgated the principle of moral relativism—whatever was good for them was right. At the time, some philosophers in Athens shared this belief. These Sophists (or "wise ones") doubted the existence of universal truths and, instead, taught their followers how to influence public opinion and how to forward their own fortunes. Rather than seeking truth, the Sophists argued that "man is the measure of all things" and that people should therefore act in accordance with their own needs and desires—exactly what Alcibiades had done during the Peloponnesian conflict.

Socrates (ca. 470–399 B.C.E.), the first great philosopher of the West, developed his ideas as a reaction against the Sophists' moral relativism. Supposedly, the Delphic oracle had reported that there was "no man wiser than Socrates." After this revelation, the philosopher spent the rest of his life roaming the streets of Athens, questioning his fellow citizens in an effort to find someone wiser than he.

Socrates

His questions took the form of dialogues that forced people to examine their beliefs critically and confront the logical consequences of their ideas. Socrates came to the conclusion that, indeed, he was the wisest man because he alone understood that he knew nothing, and that wisdom lies in the endless search for knowledge. Athenians came to know the rather homely man, whose father worked as a stonemason and whose mother was a midwife. Socrates, who saw himself as giving birth to ideas, claimed to have followed his mother's occupation more closely than his father's.

Socrates left no writings, so we know of his ideas only from the words of one of his students, Plato. According to these texts, Socrates expressed the idea that there were absolutes of truth and justice and excellence, and that a dormant knowledge of these absolutes rested within all people. In these inquiries, Socrates departed not only from the Sophists but from the early philosophers like Thales who wanted to know the nature of the world—Socrates wanted to explore the nature of right action. The method he employed was that of questioning and refuting students' answers, and with this method—now called the **Socratic method**—he brought students to see the truth.

Socrates called himself a gadfly for his efforts to goad other Athenians into examining their opinions—but gadflies that sting painfully are seldom appreciated. Socrates began his inquiries in the dynamic period before the Peloponnesian War, but in the times of disillusionment after the war, Athenian jurors were suspicious of anyone who seemed to oppose the democracy—even by pointing out humankind's inadequacies. Socrates was brought to trial and accused of impiety and corruption of the young. The latter charge was no doubt forwarded by the reprehensible behavior of Alcibiades, who had been Socrates' student, but the former charge had no basis. Socrates was found guilty, even though he shrewdly refuted the charges during his trial. His friends urged him to stop questioning others and to simply flee, to which he replied with the famous words that began this chapter: "Life without enquiry is not worth living." He received the death penalty and drank a cup of the deadly poison hemlock.

Socrates' ideas, however, did not die with him but lived on in his students. Plato, his best-known

Plato

follower, wrote many dialogues in which he seems to have preserved his teacher's ideas, although historians are uncertain where Socrates' teachings end and Plato's begin. Plato believed that truth and justice existed only as ideal models, or forms, but that humans could apprehend those realities only to a limited degree. Real people, he argued, lived in the imperfect world of the senses, a world that revealed only shadows of reality. This was his answer to the relativist Sophists, who saw the imperfect world as the true measure of right and wrong. For Plato, the goal of philosophical inquiry was to find the abstract and perfect "right" that was so elusive in this world. He established a school in Athens called the Academy to educate young Greek men in the tenets of virtue, for he believed that only through long training in philosophy could one learn to understand the ideal forms that exist outside the human world.

Plato was disillusioned with the democracy that had killed his teacher, Socrates, and admired Sparta's rigorous way of life. This political affinity shaped what is perhaps Plato's best-known work, *The Republic*, in which he outlined the ideal form of government. Instead of encouraging democracy, he explained, states should be ruled autocratically by philosopher-kings. In this way, the world might exhibit almost perfect justice. In some respects, this work expresses an articulate disillusionment with the failure of Athenian democracy to conduct a long war with honor or to tolerate a decent man pointing out citizens' shortcomings.

Plato's perfect state was never founded, but his ideas nevertheless had an enduring impact on Western civilization. Subsequent philosophers would confront his theory of ideal forms as they created other philosophic systems. His call for introspection and an awareness of self as the way to true knowledge would also have profound intellectual and religious implications.

Plato's ideas were not accepted universally in the Greek world. The career of his student Aristotle is one example. The son of a physi-

Aristotle

cian, Aristotle studied at Plato's Academy and then spent another twenty years refining his thinking, debating his ideas, and writing. As much as Aristotle valued his teacher, he departed from Plato's theory of "perfect forms"

and declared that ideas cannot exist outside their physical manifestations. Therefore, he concluded, to study anything—from plants to poetics to politics—one had to observe and study actual entities. Through his practical observations, Aristotle divided knowledge into categories, which remained the organizing principle of learning for over a thousand years. He said there were three categories of knowledge: ethics, or the principles of social life; natural history, the study of nature; and metaphysics, the study of the primary laws of the universe. He approached these studies through logic, which, in his hands, became a primary tool of philosophy and science. Aristotle's approach represented a major departure from the perspective of Plato, who argued that one should think about ideals instead of studying the imperfect nature of this world.

Aristotle also departed from his teacher on the subject of politics. As was his custom, the philosopher studied the different kinds of governments—monarchies, aristocracies, and republics—and discussed how each style could degenerate into corruption. He thought the ideal state was a small polis with a mixed constitution and a powerful middle class to prevent extremes. Aristotle recoiled from extremes in all aspects of life and argued for a balance—in his famous phrase, a "golden mean"—that would bring happiness. The philosopher extended his idea of moderation to the realm of ethics, arguing that the lack of excess would yield virtue.

Tragedy and Comedy: Innovations in Greek Theater

Athens's disillusioning war with Sparta had prompted philosophers to explore challenging questions of justice and virtue. Athenian theater, too, underwent change during the conflict. The playwright Euripides (485–406 B.C.E.) wrote tragedies in which people grappled with anguish

Euripides

on a heroic scale. In these plays, he expressed an intense pessimism and the lack of a divine moral order that marked Athens after the Peloponnesian War. In *Women of Troy*, written in the year of Alcibiades' expedition against Sicily, Euripides explored the pain of a small group of captured Trojan women. Though set in the era of the war immortalized by Homer, *Women of Troy* also had a strong contemporary message. In part, it represented a criticism of Athens's treatment of Melos and of the enslavement of Greek women and children. When a character in *Women of Troy* mused, "Strange how intolerable the indignity of slavery is to those born free," Euripides was really asking the Athenians to reflect on their own actions. In foretelling destruction to the Greeks who abused the women of Troy, Euripides predicted the eventual downfall of Athens.

Tragedy was not the only way to challenge contemporary society; talented playwrights also used comedy. As Greeks laughed at the crudest of sexual jokes and bathroom humor, they criticized public figures and conquered their own anxieties. These plays appeal less to modern audiences than do the Greek tragedies, for in their intense fascination with human nature, Greeks embraced even our basest inclinations. The comedies of this era also reveal much about Greek perceptions of the human body; just as their character flaws became the subject of tragedies, their bodies were often the focus of comedies.

The vase in **Figure 2.13** portrays a typical scene from Greek comedy. In this rendering, each actor sports a long, artificial phallus hanging well below his tunic, and padded buttocks to increase the comic effect. The actors also wear highly stylized masks. In the window is a man wearing a woman's mask. The scene portrays Zeus trying to seduce the woman in the window, and the extreme costuming highlights the bawdy and disrespectful subject matter. Although we often find such graphic portrayals tasteless at best, Greek society was surrounded with them, and we cannot fully understand the Greeks without recognizing the way they accepted their humanity in its fullest sense.

While people laughed at these comic portrayals, the greatest of the comic playwrights also used humor for serious purposes. Aristophanes (455–385 B.C.E.), for example, used costumes and crude humor to deliver biting political satire. This esteemed Athenian playwright delivered a ruthless criticism of contemporary

Aristophanes

FIGURE 2.13 Greek Comedy, fourth century B.C.E. This urn depicts a scene from a comedy with all the typical features: artificial phallus, stylized masks, and simple staging. Bawdy comedies reveal the Greeks' love of everything human, even tasteless jokes.

Athens. Like many citizens, Aristophanes longed for peace. In 411 B.C.E.—at the height of the Peloponnesian War—he wrote *Lysistrata*, a hilarious antiwar play in which the women of Athens force their men to make peace by refusing to have sexual intercourse with them until they comply. With *Lysistrata*, Aristophanes reminded people that life and sex are more important than death and war.

Hippocrates and Medicine

While philosophers and playwrights mulled over abstract notions of life and human nature, Greek physicians turned to a practical study of the human body, influencing subsequent opinions of medicine. Previous ancient societies had made a number of strides in medical knowledge—the Babylonians and Assyrians kept catalogs of healing herbs, and the Egyptians were famed for medical treatments such as setting fractures, amputating limbs, and even opening skulls to relieve pressure on head injuries. However, most of the medical knowledge that influenced the West for centuries came from the Greeks, whose systematic treatises really began to separate medicine from the supernatural. Hippocrates (ca. 460–ca. 377 B.C.E.), considered the father of modern Western medicine, supposedly claimed that "every disease has a natural cause, and without natural causes nothing ever happens." With this statement Hippocrates rejected the ancient belief that spirits were responsible for human ailments.

KEY DATES

GREEK HISTORY AND CULTURE

ca. 1250 B.C.E.	Trojan War
ca. 750 B.C.E.	Homer composes *Iliad* and *Odyssey*
490 B.C.E.	First Persian invasion repelled
495–429 B.C.E.	Pericles leads Athens, builds Acropolis temples
480–479 B.C.E.	Second Persian invasion repelled
431–404 B.C.E.	Peloponnesian War—Athens vs. Sparta
399 B.C.E.	Death of Socrates
399–347 B.C.E.	Plato flourishes
322 B.C.E.	Death of Aristotle

Hippocrates was a highly respected physician and gave his name to a body of medical writing known as the *Hippocratic Collection*, compiled between the fifth and third centuries B.C.E. The *Collection* established medicine on a rational basis devoid of supernatural explanations of disease—a major innovation in Western culture. Consistent with other Greek thinkers from Thucydides to Aristotle, Hippocrates also emphasized careful observation. This body of writings contains more than four hundred short observations about health and disease—for example, "People who are excessively overweight are far more apt to die suddenly than those of average weight," or "Extremes in diet must be avoided." Overall, this new approach to medicine put human beings, rather than the gods, at the center of study. The human-centered outlook of Greek medicine culminated in a long-standing idea expressed in the Hippocratic Oath. Modern physicians still take this oath, in which they vow first to do no harm to their patients.

Though Athens suffered some dark days of war and disillusionment, this difficult era also witnessed the rise of geniuses who used the hard times as a backdrop for exploring the complex nature of humanity. Greek philosophers, playwrights, and physicians created brilliant works and conceived of ideas that transcended their time despite the turmoil of the age.

The Aftermath of War, 404–338 B.C.E.

As a condition of its surrender at the end of the Peloponnesian War, Athens agreed to break down its defensive walls and reduce its fleet to only twelve ships. These harsh measures not only ended the Athenian Empire but also erased any possibility for a politically united Greece. The Spartans left a garrison in Athens and sent the rest of their troops home to their barrack state to guard their slaves. Sparta's subsequent attempts to assemble a political coalition foundered on its high-handed and inept foreign policy. Sparta's major allies, especially Corinth, opposed the Peloponnesian peace treaty, accusing Sparta of grabbing all the tribute and objecting to what they saw as lenience toward Athens. The generous treaty also stipulated that the Greek states in Asia Minor be given to Persia as the price for Persia's aid to Sparta, further eroding Greek unity.

All these postwar developments heightened competition among the poleis in the years after Athens's loss. For example, Corinth and Thebes fought wars to earn control of other Greek city-states, while Sparta ineptly struggled to preserve some leadership. Persia remained involved in Greek affairs, shrewdly offering money to one side and then another so that the Greeks would continue to fight one another. In this way, Persia kept the poleis from marshaling their strength against their longtime imperial enemy.

Power struggles

These wars among the poleis only aggravated serious weaknesses within each city. Democracy in Athens as a political form, for example, had been deeply threatened by the long, devastating war, especially since decisions made by the citizens led to failure. Antidemocratic feelings expressed in the works of Plato erupted as Athens fell. As Thucydides had noted, democracy was not safe during turbulent times. As the war came to an end in 404 B.C.E., Sparta imposed an oligarchy of 30 men over Athens, a brutal tyranny that tried to stamp out the vestiges of democracy. Fifteen hundred democratic leaders were killed in the coup, and 5,000 more were exiled. This oligarchy lasted only eight months before democracy was restored, but the revived government had only a shadow of its former vigor. Fed by an involved citizenry, democracy had flourished in Athens. Now, without its empire and large fleet, fewer citizens became wealthy, and political involvement waned.

Traditional participatory government in all the poleis unraveled further with innovations in military tactics. Under skillful generals, lightly armed javelin throwers, slingers, and archers began to defeat the heavily armed citizen hoplite armies that had once been the glory of Greece. Moreover, in the century following the Peloponnesian War, more and more Greeks served as mercenaries. See Document 2.3 for a famous account of Greek mercenaries fighting in Persia. These paid soldiers, owing allegiance to no city, added further disruption to an already unstable time, finally breaking the link between the poleis and the citizen-soldiers who defended them. In this period of growing unrest, every major Greek polis endured at least one war or revolution every ten years.

The nascent collective power of the Greek city-states also deteriorated during the postwar era. None of the poleis had succeeded in forging a lasting Hellenic coalition. The sovereignty of each city remained the defining idea in Greek politics. With this principle as a backdrop, individualism and loyalty to one's own city overrode any notions of a larger civic discipline. This competitive attitude had fueled the greatest of the Greeks' accomplishments in the arts, athletics, and politics, but it also gave rise to men like Alcibiades, who could not see beyond their own self-interests. In the midst of the troubled fourth century B.C.E., many Greeks feared that Persia would return to conquer a weakened Greece. As we will see in the next chapter, they should have worried about the "backward" people to the north instead.

DOCUMENT 2.3

Ten Thousand Greek Mercenaries Return Home

After the Peloponnesian War ended (404 B.C.E.), many Greek soldiers served as mercenaries in the Persian armies. This account written by the Greek historian Xenophon (ca. 434–ca. 355 B.C.E.), who traveled with the expedition, tells of a famous incident in which some mercenaries struggled to return home to Greece.

It was thought necessary to march away as fast as possible, before the enemy's force should be reassembled, and get possession of the pass.

Collecting their baggage at once, therefore, they set forward through a deep snow, taking with them several guides, and, having the same day passed the height on which Tiribazus had intended to attack them, they encamped. Hence they proceeded three days' journey through a desert tract of country, a distance of fifteen parasangs, to the river Euphrates, and passed it without being wet higher than the middle. The sources of the river were said not to be far off. From hence they advanced three days' march, through much snow and a level plain, a distance of fifteen parasang; the third day's march was extremely troublesome, as the north wind blew full in their faces, completely parching up everything and benumbing the men. One of the augurs, in consequence, advised that they should sacrifice to the wind, and a sacrifice was accordingly offered, when the vehemence of the wind appeared to everyone manifestly to abate. The depth of the snow was a fathom, so that many of the baggage cattle and slaves perished, with about a third of the soldiers.

They continued to burn fires through the whole night, for there was plenty of wood at the place of encampment. But those who came up late could get no wood; those, therefore, who had arrived before and had kindled fires would not admit the late comers to the fire unless they gave them a share of the corn or other provisions that they had brought. Thus they shared with each other what they respectively had. In the places where the fires were made, as the snow melted, there were formed large pits that reached down to the ground, and here there was accordingly opportunity to measure the depth of the snow.

From hence they marched through snow the whole of the following day, and many of the men contracted the *bulimia*. Xenophon, who commanded in the rear, finding in his way such of the men as had fallen down with it, knew not what disease it was. But as one of these acquainted with it told him that they were evidently affected with bulimia, and that they would get up if they had something to eat, he went round among the baggage and wherever he saw anything eatable he gave it out, and sent such as were able to run to distribute it among those diseased, who, as soon as they had eaten, rose up and continued their march. . . . Some of the enemy too, who had collected themselves into a body, pursued our rear, and seized any of the baggage-cattle that were unable to proceed, fighting with one another for the possession of them. Such of the soldiers also as had lost their sight from the effects of the snow, or had their toes mortified by the cold, were left behind. It was found to be a relief to the eyes against the snow, if the soldiers kept something black before them on the march, and to the feet, if they kept constantly in motion, and allowed themselves no rest, and if they took off their shoes in the night. But as to such as slept with their shoes on, the straps worked into their feet, and the soles were frozen about them, for when their old shoes had failed them, shoes of raw hides had been made by the men themselves from the newly skinned oxen.

From such unavoidable sufferings some of the soldiers were left behind, who, seeing a piece of ground of a black appearance, from the snow having disappeared there, conjectured that it must have melted, and it had in fact melted in the spot from the effect of a fountain, which was sending up vapor in a wooded hollow close at hand. Turning aside thither, they sat down and refused to proceed farther. Xenophon, who was with the rear-guard, as soon as he heard this tried to prevail on them by every art and means not to be left behind, telling them, at the same time, that the enemy were collected and pursuing them in great numbers. At last he grew angry, and they told him to kill them, as they were quite unable to go forward. He then thought it the best course to strike a terror, if possible, into the enemy that were behind, lest they should fall upon the exhausted soldiers [so he urged the tired Greeks to rise and make noise to frighten the Persians following them].

SOURCE: *The Great Events by Famous Historians,* vol. II, ed. Rossiter Johnson (The National Alumni, 1905), pp. 70–71.

Analyze the Document

1. What kinds of hardships do the Greeks face, and what do we learn about ancient travel?

2. What is the Greek view of augurs and sacrifices? How does this perspective contrast with the ideas of Jocasta in Document 2.2?

3. Why do you think this account became so inspiring and influential to future Greek armies?

LOOKING BACK & MOVING FORWARD

Summary Small city-states nestled in the mountains of the Greek peninsula rerouted the course of Western civilization. These fiercely independent cities developed participatory forms of government that encouraged men to take active roles in all aspects of their cities. Through their vigorous involvement in the life of their poleis, the men of ancient Greece created magnificent works of art, theater, and architecture that came to define Western aesthetics. These men also developed a rational approach to inquiry that has enriched Westerners' understanding of life, history, philosophy, and medicine even in modern times.

But the pride in individual accomplishment that catalyzed such extraordinary accomplishments also contained the seeds of Greece's own political destruction. The future leadership of the eastern Mediterranean would come from a people who could set aside their heroic individualism to support a larger unity. However, this influx of new ideas did not erase the legacy of Greek achievement. The newcomers would ultimately spread the accomplishments of this complex culture as far east as India as they forged a new empire.

REVIEW, ANALYZE, & CONNECT TO TODAY

REVIEW THE PREVIOUS CHAPTER

Chapter 1—"The Roots of Western Civilization"—described the growth and development of the civilizations of Mesopotamia, Egypt, and the eastern Mediterranean coast, highlighting their contributions to the future of Western civilization. It also described the growth of empires in that region.

1. Review the growth of empires in the ancient Middle East and contrast that process with the political development of Greece.

2. Review the characteristics of Phoenician society discussed in Chapter 1. Consider what qualities the Phoenicians had in common with the early Greeks that might have led both peoples to be such successful colonizers.

ANALYZE THIS CHAPTER

Chapter 2—"The Contest for Excellence"—looks at the rise and fall of the civilizations in the Aegean region culminating in the growth of classic Greek civilization. It describes life in ancient Greece, the political fortunes of the city-states, and the dramatic accomplishments in culture and science that influenced the future.

1. Review the causes of the decline of the Minoans, the Mycenaeans, and the Athenian Empire.

2. Review the economic life of the Greek city-states, and consider the impact of geography on their economic choices. Also consider how the Greek economy influenced political decisions.

3. Compare and contrast Athens and Sparta and their political and social systems. Why did Spartan women play a more meaningful role in society than did Athenian women?

4. Consider the Greeks' views on religion and review how these views influenced their approach to other aspects of their lives, like science and medicine.

5. Review Greek accomplishments in the arts, sciences, and political life, and consider why they would be so influential on future societies.

CONNECT TO TODAY

Think about the tensions in the ancient Greek world between individualism and society, as discussed in this chapter.

1. In what ways do societies today have to struggle with the same issues? Give some examples.

2. The trial of Socrates has remained a reference point for discussions of freedom of speech and thought. How do you think his trial might apply to contemporary issues such as hate speech and political postings on Internet sites such as Facebook and YouTube? For what other present-day issues is Socrates' trial relevant?

Morris, Ian, and B.B. Powell. *The Greeks: History, Culture, and Society.* Upper Saddle River, NJ: Prentice Hall, 2005. A comprehensive and up-to-date work that integrates art, architecture, literature, and political history.

THE RISE AND FALL OF ANCIENT HEROES, 2000–800 B.C.E.

Burkert, Walter. *Greek Religion.* Cambridge, MA: Harvard University Press, 1985. A masterful reconstruction of Greek festival activities that addresses the problem of rituals of animal sacrifice.

Fitton, J. Lesley. *The Discovery of the Greek Bronze Age.* Cambridge, MA: Harvard University Press, 1996. An informed and elegantly written account of the history of archaeological investigations.

Graves, Robert. *The Greek Myths: Complete Edition.* New York: Viking Penguin, 1993. An in-depth study of the major Greek myths.

Larson, Jennifer. *Greek Heroine Cults.* Madison: University of Wisconsin Press, 1995. A solid study of an unusual and little explored phenomenon: women venerated as heroes.

LIFE IN THE GREEK POLEIS

Cartledge, Paul. *The Spartans: The World of Warrior Heroes of Ancient Greece.* New York: Vintage, 2004. A detailed description of Spartan life, arguing that the Spartans contributed discipline and self-sacrifice to the ideals of Western civilization.

Dodds, Eric R. *The Greeks and the Irrational.* Berkeley: University of California Press, 1968. A classic study of human experience through the Greek mind.

Dover, Kenneth J. *Greek Homosexuality.* Cambridge, MA: Harvard University Press, 1978. A description of homosexual behavior and sentiment in Greek art and literature between the eighth and second centuries B.C.E.

Fantham, E., H.P. Foley, N.B. Hampen, S.B. Pomeroy, and H.A. Shapiro. *Women in the Classical World.* New York: Oxford University Press, 1995. A readable, illustrated, chronological survey of Greek and Roman women's lives, focusing on vivid cultural and social history.

Garland, Robert. *Daily Life of the Ancient Greeks.* Westport, CT: Greenwood Press, 2008. An exploration of the daily lives of ordinary people, illuminating every aspect of ancient Greece life.

Miller, Stephen G. *Arete: Greek Sports from Ancient Sources,* enl. ed. Berkeley: University of California Press, 2004. A study of all aspects of ancient sports, including male and female athletes and athletic festivals.

Sealey, R. *Athenian Democracy.* University Park: Pennsylvania State University Press, 1987. An interpretation of Athenian constitutional history.

GREECE ENTERS ITS CLASSICAL AGE, 479–336 B.C.E.

Herodotus. *The History of Herodotus,* trans. D. Grene. Chicago: University of Chicago Press, 1987. The primary source for the Persian Wars by the acknowledged father of history.

McGregor, Malcolm F. *The Athenians and Their Empire.* Vancouver: University of British Columbia Press, 1987. The standard brief history of the Athenian Empire.

Pedley, John Griffiths. *Greek Art and Archaeology.* New York: H.N. Abrams, 1993. A study of the architecture, sculpture, pottery, and wall paintings of ancient Greece.

Wood, Ellen M. *Peasant-Citizen and Slave: The Foundations of Athenian Democracy.* New York: Routledge, Chapman and Hall, 1988. Controversial piece disputing two modern myths—that of the idle mob and that of slavery—as the basis of Athenian democracy.

DESTRUCTION, DISILLUSION, AND A SEARCH FOR MEANING

Lindberg, David C. *The Beginnings of Western Science: The European Scientific Tradition in Philosophical, Religious, and Institutional Context, 600 B.C. to A.D. 1450.* Chicago: University of Chicago Press, 1992. An accessible and comprehensive study showing scientific advances and offering the benefits of a broad historical view.

Roochnik, David. *Retrieving the Ancients: An Introduction to Greek Philosophy.* Oxford: Wiley-Blackwell, 2004. Highly accessible narrative surveying Greek thought—a perfect introduction to the subject.

Sutton, D. *Self and Society in Aristophanes.* Washington, DC: University Press of America, 1980. A sophisticated analysis of the portrayal of Greek society in the plays of Aristophanes.

Thucydides. *The Peloponnesian War,* trans. J.H. Finley. New York: The Modern Library, 1951. The great primary source on the Peloponnesian War, which forms the starting point for any study.

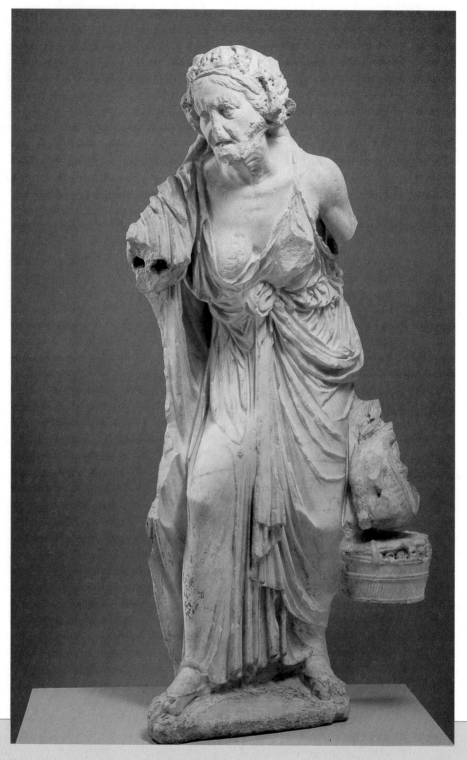

OLD MARKET WOMAN, third or second century B.C.E.

In the great cosmopolitan cities of the Hellenistic world, many people lived in poverty and struggled all their lives just to survive. Artists began to portray these people in realistic images that were much less heroic than those favored by earlier Greek artists. Change was afoot in the Greek world.

The Poleis Become Cosmopolitan 3

The Hellenistic World, 336–150 B.C.E.

Alexander "conducted himself as he did out of a desire to subject all the races in the world to one rule and one form of government making all mankind a single people." The Greek biographer Plutarch (46–119 C.E.) wrote these words four hundred years after the death of the Macedonian king Alexander the Great (356–323 B.C.E.). In his description of Alexander, Plutarch attributed high ideals to the young conqueror that Alexander himself may not have held. However, the biographer's glowing portrayal captured the reality of Alexander's conquests, whereby he joined the great civilizations of the ancient Middle East and classical Greece in a way that transformed them both.

This new world that began in 336 B.C.E. with Alexander's conquest of Persia was described as "Hellenistic" (meaning "Greek-like") by nineteenth-century historians. During this time, the ideal Greek poleis changed from scattered, independent city-states into large, multiethnic urban centers—what the Greeks called "world cities," or cosmopolitan sites—firmly anchored within substantial kingdoms. Greek colonists achieved high status in the new cities springing up far from the Greek mainland, making the Greek language and culture the ruling ideal from Egypt to India. In this Hellenistic age, classical Greek culture was in turn altered through the influences of the subject peoples, and the new world left the old world of the Greek mainland behind. Society, economy, and politics all played out on a larger scale, and kings, rather than citizens, now ruled. Royal patronage stimulated intellectual and cultural achievement among the privileged classes, while ordinary people struggled to find their place in a new world.

The Hellenistic culture continued even as these kingdoms were conquered by Rome, the next power to rise in the West. In this chapter, we will see the origins and characteristics of this cosmopolitan culture that endured for so long.

TIMELINE

Alexander the Great
337–323 B.C.E.

Philip II
359–336 B.C.E.

Hellenistic Kingdoms 337–31 B.C.E.

Decline of the Poleis
400–323 B.C.E.

Seleucid Kingdom 305–64 B.C.E.

• Philip conquers Greece
338 B.C.E.

Persian Empire 550–330 B.C.E.

Ptolemaic Egypt 305–30 B.C.E.

500 B.C.E.   380   300   180   100

THE CONQUEST OF THE POLEIS

In 220 B.C.E., an Egyptian father appealed to the Greek king to help him resolve a domestic dispute. He claimed that his daughter, Nice, had abandoned him in his old age. According to the father, Nice had promised to get a job and pay him a pension out of her wages every month. To his dismay, she instead became involved with a comic actor and neglected her filial duties. The father implored the king, Ptolemy IV, to force Nice to care for him, pleading, "I beg you O king, not to suffer me to be wronged by my daughter and Dionysus the comedian who has corrupted her."

This request—one of many sent to the king during this period—reveals several interesting points about Mediterranean life in the Hellenistic era. For example, it suggests that women worked and earned money instead of staying carefully guarded within the home. It also shows a loosening of the tight family ties that had marked the Greek poleis and the ancient Middle East civilizations—a father could no longer exert authority over his rebellious daughter and could no longer count on his children to care for him in his old age. Finally, it indicates people's view of their king as the highest authority in redressing personal problems. These were dramatic changes, and to trace their origins, we must look to Macedonia, a province on the northeast border of Greece. There, in a land traditionally ruled by strong monarchs, a king arose who would redefine life in the ancient world.

Tribal Macedonia

Although Macedonia was inhabited by Greek-speaking people, it had not developed the poleis that marked Greek civilization on the peninsula. Instead, it had retained a tribal structure in which aristocrats selected a king and served in his army bound by ties of loyalty and kinship. The southern Greek poleis—populated by self-described "civilized" Greeks—had disdain for the Macedonians, whom they saw as backward because they did not embrace the political life of the city-states.

The Macedonian territory consisted of two distinct parts: the coastal plain to the south and east, and the mountainous interior. The plain offered fertile land for farming and lush pastures in which fine warhorses grazed along | Geography | with sheep and oxen. The level land of the coastline bordered two bays that afforded access to the Aegean Sea. The Macedonian interior, by contrast, was mountainous and remote and posed the same problems for rulers that the Greek landscape presented. Kings struggled to exert even a little authority over the fierce tribes in the hills. Yet, concealed within the mountains were precious reserves of timber and metals, including abundant veins of gold and silver in the more remote locations.

For centuries, the weak Macedonian kings failed to take full advantage of such treasures, in large part because they could not control the remote tribes. Repeated invasions of Macedonia by its neighbors to the north only | Uniting the tribes | added to the problem. Throughout this turbulent period, the southern Greeks thought of Macedonia only as an area to exploit for its natural resources. The Greeks neither helped nor feared their beleaguered relatives to the north and instead focused on keeping their old enemy, Persia, at bay. Nevertheless, eventually a Macedonian king arose who not only succeeded in marshaling the resources of his land but also rerouted the direction of Greek history.

This great king, Philip II (r. 359–336 B.C.E.), had participated in some of the many wars that disrupted Greece during the fourth century B.C.E. (see Chapter 2) and, as a result, had been held hostage as a young man in the Greek city-state of Thebes for three years. During his captivity, he learned much about the strengths and weaknesses of Greek politics and warfare. When he returned to Macedonia, he used his new knowledge to educate his people. As his son Alexander later reminded the Macedonians: "Philip took you over when you were helpless vagabonds mostly clothed in skins, feeding a few animals on the mountains. . . . He gave you cloaks to wear instead of skins, he brought you down from the mountains to the plains. . . . He made you city dwellers and established the order that comes from good laws and customs."

Philip II: Military Genius

The pride of the Macedonian army was the cavalry, led by the king himself and made up of his nobles, known as "companions." Yet Philip showed his military genius in the way he reorganized the supporting forces. The shrewd monarch changed the traditional Greek phalanx, already threatened by a new fighting style that favored lightly armed—and therefore more mobile—foot soldiers. Philip strengthened the phalanx by arming his soldiers with pikes 13 feet long or longer instead of the standard 9-foot weapons. Then he instructed the infantry to arrange themselves in a more open formation, which let them take full advantage of the longer pikes. Philip also hired lightly armed, mobile mercenaries who could augment the Macedonian phalanx with arrows, javelins, and slings.

In battle, the long Macedonian pikes kept opponents at a distance, while the cavalry made the decisive difference in almost every battle. The mounted warriors surrounded the enemy and struck at their flank, leaving the lightly armed mercenaries to move in to deliver the final blow. This strategy, which combined traditional heavily armed foot soldiers with the mobility of cavalry and light troops, would prove virtually invincible.

Military innovations

Philip also developed weapons for besieging walled cities. During the Peloponnesian War, even mighty Sparta's only strategy against the sturdy walls of Athens had been to starve the inhabitants to death—a slow and uncertain method. Philip is credited with using a torsion catapult that twisted launching ropes to gain more force than the older models that used counterweights could exert. With this new device, his forces could fire rocks at city walls with deadly force. Although Philip is credited with developing these siege weapons, his son would be the one to successfully use them against many fortified cities.

With his forces reorganized and equipped with the latest weapons, Philip readied himself to expand his kingdom. First, he consolidated his own highlands and the lands to the north and east. These conquests allowed him to exploit the gold and silver mines in the hills, which yielded the riches he needed to finance his campaigns. With his northern flank secure and his treasury full, the conqueror then turned his attention to the warring Greek cities to the south.

Philip dreamed of uniting the Greek city-states under his leadership. Some southern Greeks shared this dream, looking to the Macedonian king to save them from their own intercity violence. Isocrates (436–338 B.C.E.), an Athenian orator and educator, made eloquent speeches in which he supported Philip's expansionist aims. Expressing a prevalent disillusionment with democracy, Isocrates argued that the Greeks were incapable of forming a cohesive union without a leader like Philip. In his view, this form of participatory governance had become so corrupt that "violence is regarded as democracy, lawlessness as

Greek responses

liberty, impudence of speech as equality." Isocrates believed that only Philip could unify the Greeks and empower them to face Asia as one people finally to vanquish their ancient enemy, Persia.

Isocrates' words were compelling. But Athens had another great orator who opposed Philip and who proved more convincing than Isocrates. Demosthenes (384–322 B.C.E.) argued brilliantly for a position that rejected union under a tyrant like Philip in order to preserve Athens's traditional freedom and the self-government of the polis. As we saw in Chapter 2, the classic polis had eroded in the aftermath of the Peloponnesian War, but the orator was looking backward to a more golden age of democracy. Historians have characterized Demosthenes as everything from a stubborn, old-fashioned orator to the last champion of the lost cause of Athenian freedom. Ultimately, however, the spirited debate about Philip became moot. The question of freedom was answered not in the marketplace of Athens but on the battlefield.

In 338 B.C.E., Philip and his armies marched south toward the peninsula, where they confronted a Greek coalition led by Athens and Thebes, longtime rivals who at last joined in cooperation. The belated cooperation among the Greeks came too late. At the Battle of Chaeronea near Thebes, the powerful left wing of Philip's phalanx enveloped the approaching Greeks. The Macedonian cavalry, led by Philip's talented son, Alexander, slaughtered the surrounded Greeks. The victory paved the way for Philip to take control of the Greek city-states (except Sparta).

Greece conquered

Philip proved a lenient conqueror; he charged the Greeks no tribute, but instead united them in a league under his command, so they were technically allies with Macedonia. No longer allowed to wage war against one another, the poleis joined the combined army of Greeks and Macedonians. Isocrates' hope was fulfilled, and the Greeks reluctantly renounced internal warfare. Now they prepared to follow Philip to attack the Persian Empire, which extended far beyond the borders of the Persian homeland into Asia.

Death of the King

Philip's brilliance on the battlefield exceeded his judgment in domestic matters. In the tradition of Macedonian kings, Philip had taken at least six wives. The most important was Olympias, daughter of the king of Epirus (which was southwest of Macedonia and bordered the Greek city-states) and mother of Alexander. According to Plutarch, who drew from earlier sources, Olympias and Alexander were highly insulted when Philip, in his forties, took a young bride, Cleopatra. At the wedding, Cleopatra's uncle made a toast implying that he hoped Philip would disinherit Alexander.

Political and personal resentments came to a head in 336 B.C.E. at the wedding of Alexander's sister, also named Cleopatra. On the morning of the festivities, members of the court attended the theater. Philip was escorted by his son, the bridegroom, and his bodyguards. As the little group separated to enter the theater, Pausanias, one of Philip's jilted companions, saw his opportunity. He stepped in and mortally stabbed the king. Pursued by the guards, Pausanias ran outside but tripped and fell. A guard drew his sword and killed him on the spot.

Philip murdered

Alexander, suspecting a conspiracy behind the assassination, vigorously investigated the murder. He tried and executed the diviner who had predicted good omens for the day, and he put to death anyone who he thought had even a remote claim to the Macedonian throne. Later, even Philip's wife Cleopatra and their infant child were killed, an act that finally eliminated Alexander's rivals. Because of insufficient evidence, historians have never ascertained the full reasons for Philip's assassination. Some ancient sources accused Olympias of organizing the murder; others blame a conspiracy of nobles; still others consider the killing the solitary act of a jealous courtier. Whatever the cause, Alexander was now king.

Alexander's Conquests

The brilliant king was dead, but Philip's son, Alexander, would make an even greater mark on the world than his father had. Alexander (r. 337–323 B.C.E.) was born in 356 B.C.E. and raised by his parents expressly to rule. Philip diligently taught the young boy the arts of Macedonian warfare, including horsemanship, an essential skill for service in the cavalry. Philip and Olympias also encouraged Alexander's intellectual development. They appreciated the accomplishments of the classical Greeks and hired the revered philosopher Aristotle (384–322 B.C.E.) to tutor their

promising heir. We cannot know the exact influence of the philosopher on his young student, but Aristotle certainly imparted a love of Greek culture and literature to Alexander. Moreover, he may well have cultivated Alexander's curiosity about the world, which would fuel the young man's later urge to explore. However, Alexander seems to have rejected Aristotle's prejudice against non-Greek "barbarians." Philip's son imagined a world much wider than that of Aristotle's ideal, small city-state.

As soon as Alexander ascended the Macedonian throne, he needed to be recognized as the legitimate king, so he consolidated his rule in the region with a decisive ruthlessness that marked all his subsequent campaigns. For example, when the Greeks revolted after hearing false rumors of Alexander's death, the king promptly marched south, sacked the city of Thebes, and slaughtered or enslaved the inhabitants. With the Greeks subdued, he then turned to implementing Philip's planned war against the Persian Empire. In 334 B.C.E., Alexander advanced into Asia Minor with a large army of hoplites and cavalry. He was joined by Callisthenes, Aristotle's nephew, who later wrote the history of Alexander's campaigns. Although this text has been lost, it served as a pro-Macedonian, but carefully detailed source for Alexander's early campaigns, and subsequent chroniclers who had access to the work have passed elements of it on to us.

Military exploits

After several decisive victories in Asia Minor, Alexander engaged the full power of Persia at the Battle of Issus (**Map 3.1**), where he matched with Persian forces and Greek mercenaries led by the Persian Great King Darius III. Through skillful deployment and swift action, Alexander's armies defeated a force more than twice as large as their own. Darius fled the battle, leaving his mother, wife, and children. The young king captured Darius's family but treated them with respect and courtesy. In this way, he showed his belief that savagery should be reserved for the battlefield.

Before driving deeper into Asia, Alexander turned south along the Phoenician coast, shrewdly recognizing the problem of the superior Persian fleet, which was reinforced by Phoenician vessels. He captured the great coastal cities of Sidon, Tyre, and finally Gaza, thus rendering the fleet useless without ever engaging it. The brilliant young strategist also perfected the art of siege warfare, improving on Philip's catapults and adding siege towers erected next to the defensive walls that allowed attackers to penetrate the fortresses. As the proud cities fell one by one, Alexander gained a reputation for brutal warfare but generosity to subject peoples. Subsequent cities surrendered quickly and joined the rapidly growing Macedonian Empire.

KEY DATES

POLITICAL EVENTS

359–336 B.C.E.	Philip II rules Macedonia
338 B.C.E.	Philip conquers Greece
337–323 B.C.E.	Alexander rules
333 B.C.E.	Battle of Issus
332 B.C.E.	Alexander conquers Egypt
331 B.C.E.	Battle of Gaugamela
330 B.C.E.	Alexander destroys Persepolis
323 B.C.E.	Successor kingdoms established
ca. 166–164 B.C.E.	Maccabean Revolt

MAP 3.1

Alexander's Empire

This map shows the vast territory Alexander conquered, the route he took, and the major battle sites. Using the scale on the map, calculate the distance Alexander traveled. Consider the difficulties of supplying an army over this distance.

Explore the Map

1. Compare this map with **Map 1.5,** of the Persian Empire. What additional lands did Alexander conquer?

2. Based on the map and what you have learned from the text, what effects might Alexander's expansion have on the old Persian Empire?

3. What effects might his conquests have on Egypt?

After conquering Gaza, Alexander swept into Egypt virtually unopposed in 332 B.C.E. The Egyptian priests declared Alexander the incarnation of their god Amon, treating him as pharaoh. Now the god-king of Egypt, the young Macedonian founded a new city, Alexandria, on the Delta. This development brought Egypt more fully into Mediterranean economy and culture than it had ever been before, as the new northern, coastal capital encouraged trade and attracted colonists from elsewhere—a cosmopolitan center was founded in Egypt. With his western flank thus secured, Alexander once again headed for Asia to revive his pursuit of the Persian Great King, Darius.

After crossing the Euphrates and Tigris rivers, Alexander encountered Darius at Gaugamela in 331 B.C.E. The Persian ruler had fitted chariots with sharp scythes to cut down the Macedonian infantry, and his forces far outnumbered Alexander's army—by about 250,000 to 47,000 (although these figures are certainly exaggerated). Despite the Persian strength, Alexander's superior strategy vanquished the Persian warriors yet again. He forced the Persians to turn to confront his wheeling formation and thus opened fatal gaps in the long Persian line. His cavalry set upon the trapped Persian infantry. In the ensuing slaughter, a reputed 50,000 Persians died. Alexander entered Babylon and was welcomed as a liberator. He then turned southeast to Persepolis, the Persian capital. Despite fierce resistance, in 330 B.C.E. Alexander captured the city and plundered it ruthlessly, acquiring enough wealth to fund his future military ambitions. Then he burned it to the ground. Alexander never met Darius on the battlefield again, for the Persian king was assassinated by one of his own guards. After this, no one could doubt that the mighty Persian Empire had a new master—Alexander, who was crowned Great King.

Alexander thought of himself as a powerful, semi-divine Greek hero; he claimed descent from Achilles through his mother and from Heracles (whom we remember by the Roman name Hercules) through his father. The shrewd conqueror was also a skilled propagandist, and his identification with ancient heroes helped consolidate his authority in the minds of Greeks raised on the stories of Homer. **Figure 3.1** shows a portion of a beautifully carved sarcophagus from the city of Sidon, on the Phoenician coast of the Mediterranean. The local royalty buried here had commissioned a scene of Alexander's victory over Darius to grace the side of the coffin, recognizing the moment that the Sidonian king changed his allegiance from Persia to Macedonia. Alexander sits

| The Greek hero |

astride a rearing horse at the left, while the defeated Persians fall before him. The conqueror wears a lion skin on his head, in a typical portrayal of Heracles. It is highly unlikely that Alexander fought in anything other than the traditional Macedonian armor, but the artistic license reveals the popular view of Alexander as a true Greek hero.

Alexander himself identified most strongly with the hero Achilles. According to Plutarch, Alexander slept with a copy of Homer's *Iliad*, edited by Aristotle, under his pillow and "esteemed it a perfect portable treasure of all military virtue and knowledge." Through Alexander, then, the heroic values of the Greek world endured and spread, and as Plutarch maintained, "thanks to Alexander, Homer was read in Asia. . . ."

The war against Persia had finally ended, but the young conqueror was still not satisfied. Having studied world geography as documented by the ancient Greeks, Alexander yearned to push his conquests to the edge of the known world. He mistakenly believed that this enticing frontier lay just beyond the Indus River in India. A last major battle against an Indian king eliminated opposition in northern India, and Alexander made plans to press farther into the subcontinent. However, his Macedonian troops had had enough and refused to go on. Alexander wept in his tent for days at the mutiny of his beloved troops, but he finally conceded and turned back. However, instead of returning along the northern route, he led his troops south to explore the barren lands at the edge of the Arabian Sea (see **Map 3.1**). His exhausted, parched army finally reached the prosperous lands of Mesopotamia. Yet their relief was marred by an ironic tragedy: Alexander, seriously weakened by ever-growing alcohol abuse, caught a fever and died in Babylon in 323 B.C.E. He was just 32 years old. Others would have to rule the lands conquered by Alexander the Great.

| India |

A Young Ruler's Legacy

Was Plutarch right in thinking that Alexander wanted to make "all mankind a single people"? This ideal, which marked a radical departure from traditional Greek attitudes, has provoked intense historical debate virtually from the time of Alexander's life to the present. The Macedonian conqueror implemented several policies that some have interpreted as his desire to rule over a unified rather than a conquered people. One such policy, and certainly the most influential, was his founding of cities. In all his conquered territories, Alexander established an array of new cities. He intended these urban centers in part to recreate the Greek city life that he and his father had so admired. To this end, the conqueror helped settle numerous Greek and Macedonian

FIGURE 3.1 Alexander in Battle, fourth century B.C.E
This magnificent marble sarcophagus (burial casket) found in Sidon (present-day Lebanon) shows a victorious Alexander defeating the Persians at the Battle of Issus. Originally painted in brilliant colors, the coffin reveals the tremendous influence of classic Greek art.

DOCUMENT 3.1

Alexander Restores Greek Exiles

In 324 B.C.E., Alexander issued a proclamation that all Greek exiles should be allowed to return to their homes, even though many had been gone for generations. This policy pleased the exiles, but it also offended many residents who resented Alexander's high-handed interference in their affairs—in stark contrast to Philip's promise to give the Greeks a measure of autonomy. The Sicilian historian Diodorus describes the decree and its reception. Alexander died less than a year after this decree, and his successors rescinded it.

A short time before his death, Alexander decided to restore all the exiles in the Greek cities, partly for the sake of gaining fame and partly wishing to secure many devoted personal followers in each city to counter the revolutionary movements and seditions of the Greeks. Therefore, the Olympic games being at hand, he sent Nicanor of Strageira to Greece, giving him a decree about the restoration, which he ordered him to have proclaimed by the victorious herald to the crowds at the festival. Nicanor carried out his instructions, and the herald received and read the following message: "King Alexander to the exiles from the Greek cities. We have not been the cause of your exile, but, save for those of you who are under a curse, we shall be the cause of your return to your own native cities. We have written to Antipater about this to the end that if any cities are not willing to restore you, he may constrain them." When the herald had announced this, the crowd showed its approval with loud applause; for those at the festival welcomed the favour of the king with cries of joy, and repaid his good deed with praises. All the exiles had come together at the festival, being more than twenty thousand in number.

Now people in general welcomed the restoration of the exiles as a good thing, but the Aetolians and the Athenians took offence at the action and were angry. The reason for this was that the Aetolians had exiled the Oeniadae from their native city and expected the punishment appropriate to their wrongdoing; for the king himself had threatened that no sons of the Oeniadae, but he himself would punish them. Likewise, the Athenians who had distributed [the island of] Samos in allotments to their citizens, were by no means willing to abandon that island.

SOURCE: R.M. Greer, trans., *Diodorus of Sicily* 18.8, vol. 8 of Loeb Classical Library (Cambridge, MA: Harvard University Press, 1969).

Analyze the Document

1. Why was the problem of displaced Greeks so significant during this period? (Consider this in the light of Document 2.3.)

2. Why do you think Alexander made the announcement at the Olympic Games?

3. What were Alexander's motives according to Diodorus?

4. Who supported and opposed the decree?

5. Why do you think the decree was rescinded?

---

colonists in the new cities. Hundreds of thousands of Greeks emigrated to the newly claimed lands in Asia, taking privileged positions. We will see that as they introduced their culture into Asia, these colonists inevitably influenced and were changed by the subject peoples. These culturally rich cities rank among Alexander's most enduring legacies.

The movement of Greeks to cities far into Asia raised questions about exiles' continued ties with their cities of origin, and Alexander's royal power raised questions about the traditional autonomy of the Greek poleis. Document 3.1 reproduces an edict issued by Alexander near the end of his life that intended to address these lingering issues.

Meanwhile, in Asia, Alexander strongly supported the intermarriage of Greeks and Macedonians with Asians. He himself married the daughter of Darius and Roxane, the daughter of an Asian tribal king who ruled near modern-day Afghanistan. Alexander also presided over the weddings of hundreds of his generals to highborn Persian women. As Plutarch said, he "joined together the greatest and most powerful peoples into one community by wedlock." Ten thousand more of Alexander's soldiers also married Asian women. Alexander might well have imagined that the offspring of these marriages would help seal the union of the two populations.

Finally, Alexander had a constant need for additional soldiers to support his campaigns, and he obtained these men from the conquered peoples. He accepted both Persian soldiers and commanders into his companies. Preparing for the future, he also chose about 30,000 Asian boys whom he slated to learn the Greek language and the Macedonian fighting style. These boys would become the next generation of soldiers to fight for the king in a combined army.

Alexander's cultural blending disturbed those upper-crust Greeks and Macedonians who saw themselves as conquerors rather than as equals among the subject peoples. | Resentments | Indeed, while in Persia, Alexander adopted Persian robes and courtly ceremonies, including having his subjects prostrate themselves on the ground in his presence. Without a doubt, this ritual helped Persians accept their new king—but it also

| Intercultural marriages |

offended the proud Macedonians. Alexander's inclusion of Asians in the military elite only intensified Macedonian resentment. At one point, an outcry arose among Alexander's soldiers when the king apparently sought to replace some of them with Asians. Alexander squelched these objections decisively, executing 13 leaders and suggesting that the rest of them go home so that he could lead the Asian troops to victory. The Macedonians backed down, pleading for their king's forgiveness. Alexander resolved the incident with a lavish banquet of reconciliation, at which Asians and Macedonians drank together and Alexander prayed for harmony (sometimes mistranslated as "brotherhood") between them.

Alexander died too soon for historians to be certain of his exact plans for ruling his vast, multiethnic empire. For all we know, he might well have intended that Greeks and Macedonians would remain a ruling elite. The cities and colonies guaranteed a continued Greek presence, as did the invaders' weddings to local women. The conqueror's inclusive army might have been simply a practical means of ensuring a large enough force to fulfill his ambitions. Whatever his intentions, Alexander created a fertile combination by joining the cultures of the ancient Middle East and classical Greece.

Alexander's legacy included more than his political conquests—which in some regions hardly outlasted the young king himself. The memory of his accomplishments has endured in an embellished way far beyond even his most impressive victories. For example, Plutarch's interpretation | Alexander's memory | of Alexander's desire for a blending of peoples made this notion a foundational characteristic of Western culture, regardless of whether the king truly held this ideal. Moreover, a highly imaginative version of Alexander's accomplishments, titled *The Alexander Romance,* was translated into twenty-four languages and found its way from Iran to China to Malaysia. The idea of a great empire ruled by one king may have exerted an influence as far as the Han dynasty in China. It certainly shaped Mediterranean thinking, where would-be conquerors reverently visited Alexander's tomb in the spectacular Egyptian city of Alexandria that he founded.

THE SUCCESSOR KINGDOMS, 323–ca. 100 B.C.E.

Admirers across the world may have romanticized Alexander's supposed dream of a unified kingdom. In reality, however, brutal politics sullied the picture soon after the Great King's death. Legends preserve the probably false tale that as Alexander lay dying, he told his comrades that the kingdom should go "to the strongest." Even if Alexander never said this, the story reflects the reality of the violent fighting that broke out among the Macedonian generals shortly after the king died. Alexander's wife, Roxane, was pregnant when he succumbed, and presumably the empire should have gone to his infant son, Alexander IV. But within thirteen years of Alexander's death, both Roxane and her young son had been murdered. Moreover, the Macedonian generals had carved up the great empire into new, smaller kingdoms that became the successors to Alexander's conquests. **Map 3.2** shows the successor kingdoms.

Egypt Under the Ptolemies

Upon Alexander's death, one of his cavalry "companions," Ptolemy, moved toward Egypt with his own loyal troops to take control of that wealthy region. Ptolemy diverted the king's corpse, which was being returned to Macedonia for burial, and took it to Alexandria, where he erected an imposing tomb for Alexander. It seems that Ptolemy believed the presence of the conqueror's remains would help legitimize his own rule. Fending off attempts by Alexander's other generals to snatch the rich land of the Nile, Ptolemy and his successors ruled as the god-kings of Egypt for the next three hundred years.

The **Ptolemies** inherited a land with a long tradition of obedience to authority. Accordingly, the new kings wisely struck a bargain with the Egyptian priests, promising to fulfill the traditional duty of the pharaohs to care for the temples (and the priests) in exchange for protection of their legitimacy. Through most of their | Continuity of life | history, the Ptolemies lived in luxury in Alexandria, conducting official business in Greek while Egyptian peasants continued to obey the age-old dictates of the Nile, the priests, and the tax collectors. Life away from the court under the new order changed very little, which made it easier for the new dynasty to rule. The parallel practicing of both Egyptian and Greek ways continued throughout most of the Ptolemaic rule. In fact, the majority of these Greek kings rarely carried out traditional ritual functions, and some were probably not even formally crowned. For their part, the priests honored the Ptolemies while still governing in the traditional way.

However, in one significant way the Hellenistic rulers departed from their Egyptian predecessors—their queens took a more prominent role. Many of the Ptolemaic rulers engaged in brother-sister marriages as the ancient Egyptians had done, but many women were able to exert | Hellenistic queens | considerable power. Hellenistic queens derived much of their authority from controlling substantial wealth and spending it on public works (and on hiring large armies). The height of the

MAP 3.2

The Successor States After the Death of Alexander, ca. 240 B.C.E.

This map shows the breakup of Alexander's empire into three states and illustrates the relative sizes of the successor kingdoms.

Explore the Map

1. Based on your analysis of previous maps, as well as the information in the text, what were the historical and geographic reasons for the differing sizes of the successor kingdoms?

2. How might the movement of the Egyptian capital from Thebes to Alexandria have affected Egypt?

Hellenistic queens of Egypt came with the last one—Cleopatra VII—who challenged the growing power of Rome (discussed in Chapter 4).

Under the Ptolemies, the port city of Alexandria became the premier city of the Hellenistic world. It was a dynamic cosmopolitan city that by the end of the first century B.C.E. boasted almost one million inhabitants. Alexandria was a bustling port city where the main enterprise was the pursuit of wealth. The harbors were busy and the markets thronging, and international banks grew up to serve the people. To make sure ships could enter the port safely, Hellenistic scientists built a huge lighthouse on an island (Pharos) outside the harbor. The structure was 440 feet high, and the light from the lantern at the top was intensified by a system of reflectors. Ships

| Alexandria |

approaching the harbor were guided by the beam of the lantern. This lighthouse came to be regarded as one of the seven wonders of the ancient world.

For all its commercial value, Alexandria under the Ptolemies also became an intellectual and cultural center. The rulers established a world-famous museum (the word *museum* means "temple to the muses," the Greek goddesses who served as inspiration to creativity). At the museum, scholars from around the Mediterranean and Asia gathered to study texts and discuss ideas. The Greek rulers founded a great library as part of this museum and ambitiously designed it to stand as the West's first complete collection of published works. Well established by 280 B.C.E., the library boasted more than 700,000 volumes just one century later, making it the largest collection the ancient world had seen.

BIOGRAPHY

Arsinoë II
(315–ca. 270 B.C.E.)

Brilliant

and Ruthless

Queen of

Egypt

The Hellenistic dynasties created by the successor states to Alexander's empire (see **Map 3.2**) set new precedents for the ancient world by bringing strong women to power. These queens of all three dynasties (Seleucid, Antigonid, and Ptolemaic) derived their power from two main things: their descent from the original founders of the dynasties and their great wealth.

Many of these women strongly influenced the great events of the day. The story of Arsinoë II, queen of Egypt, reveals the violent world of Hellenistic politics and shows the fierce will for power that both men and women leaders often needed to rule effectively.

Arsinoë was the daughter of the first Ptolemy, Alexander's successor who took over Egypt. Like most Hellenistic princesses, she was well educated and raised to rule. She was married at age 15 to the king of Thrace, Lysimachus, an old companion-in-arms of Ptolemy. Lysimachus renounced his first wife in favor of the young, and very beautiful, Arsinoë. By the time Arsinoë was 30, she had borne three sons and had begun to plan for their (and her) future. To position her sons to inherit the throne, she accused Lysimachus's son by his first wife of treason and perhaps had him poisoned.

Yet despite Arsinoë's plans, her family became ensnared in one of the seemingly endless Hellenistic wars of power. First, Seleucus marched from Asia to Thrace to conquer Lysimachus. Amid the combat, Arsinoë's husband (now almost 80 years old) died. Then as Arsinoë fled with her children to Greece, her half-brother Ceraunus seized control of her old realm. Ceraunus well understood the benefits of legitimacy that Arsinoë's bloodline could provide, and the advantages of her great wealth. He offered to marry her and make her children his heirs. She agreed, but he betrayed her, killing her two youngest children in order to secure the kingdom for his own progeny. She and her eldest son managed to escape to Egypt to seek the protection of her brother, Ptolemy II.

Safe in Egypt, Arsinoë moved to rebuild her power. Not content to be simply sister to the king, she had Ptolemy's wife exiled and married him herself to assure herself the title of queen. From then on, she and her brother were known as "sibling-lovers" (*philadelphus*). If we are to believe the poets of the period, the couple genuinely loved each other. One poet wrote, "No more splendid wife than she ever clasped in bridal chamber her bridegroom, loving him from her heart, her brother and her lord." Satisfied with her newly secured position as the head of Egypt's ruling family, Arsinoë ignored her husband's many mistresses, although purportedly she quickly killed any political rivals who tried to reduce her authority.

The sibling marriage not only gave Arsinoë the power she craved but also helped consolidate the power of the dynasty by bringing the Ptolemies closer to traditional Egyptian practices; sometimes Egyptian pharaohs had married their sisters. However, the Greek Macedonians decried the practice as incest and forbade it. In marrying each other, Arsinoë and Ptolemy reclaimed an older form of legitimacy that had shaped the Egyptian ruling families. Artistic portrayals of Queen Arsinoë depict this movement toward traditional Egyptian practices. **Figure 3.2a** shows her in the traditional Macedonian fashion, crowned only by the slim band that

Eventually, however, the Ptolemies encountered both internal and external pressure to change. Under the reign of Ptolemy V (r. ca. 205–ca. 183 B.C.E.), a boy not yet in his teens, priests began demanding that the young king be more involved in religious rituals. The boy-king's problems only worsened when sub-Saharan Nubians (see Global Connections, Chapter 1), detecting his weakness, clamored for their own pharaoh. In addition, the armies of Alexander's successor in Asia were threatening Egypt's borders. Pressured on all sides, Ptolemy offered concessions to the powerful priests in return for their support in rallying the Egyptians to his cause. The young ruler reduced taxes on the peasants and increased payments to the priests. In return for his cooperation, the priests brought Ptolemy to Memphis, the traditional capital of the pharaohs, where they placed the great double crown of Egypt—the sign of royalty—on his head. Finally, they ordered that Ptolemy V be worshiped in every Egyptian shrine. To make good on this policy, they demanded that scribes write all the accomplishments of Ptolemy V "on a slab of hard stone, in the writing of the words of god, the writing of documents and the letters of the Northerners, and set it up in all the temples. . . ."

Figure 3.3 shows the **Rosetta Stone,** the tablet that resulted from this decree, which was unearthed in 1799. Demonstrating the presence of both Greeks and Egyptians in the kingdom of the Ptolemies, the stone records Ptolemy's deeds in three written versions: the sacred hieroglyphics at the top, Egyptian cursive administrative script at the center, and Greek ("the letters of the Northerners") at the bottom.

Rosetta Stone

FIGURE 3.2a Arsinoë

marked their rulers. **Figure 3.2b,** on the other hand, shows Arsinoë wearing the traditional headdress of the Egyptian rulers. The Macedonian queen had become an Egyptian one. During the next centuries, the Ptolemies in Egypt followed the precedent set by Arsinoë and Ptolemy. They preserved much of their Macedonian ways while adopting enough Egyptian traditions to let them rule the ancient country effectively. Historians have argued over how much political influence Arsinoë wielded. However, we should perhaps believe the ancient historian Memnon, when he wrote, "Arsinoë was one to get her own way."

FIGURE 3.2b Arsinoë

In addition, in a decree after her death, Ptolemy wrote that he followed the "policy of his ancestors and of his sister in his zeal for the freedom of the Greeks." Arsinoë's zeal for freedom stemmed more from her hostility to the Seleucid rulers (who had driven her from her lands in Thrace) than from any abstract ideals of independence. The queen wanted to be sure her Egyptian dynasty would be free from intrusion from the successors of Alexander coming from the north, so she even traveled to the front to survey the defenses. Furthermore, she and Ptolemy knew that their safety in Egypt would hinge on sea power,

so they expanded the Egyptian fleet significantly.

Even while securing the independence of Egypt, the Ptolemies did not forget the Greek love of learning that marked all the successor kingdoms. As their greatest accomplishment, they constructed an immense library in Alexandria, which served as the center of learning in the Mediterranean world for almost the next thousand years.

Egyptian priests followed Ptolemy's lead in worshiping Arsinoë as a goddess, and following her death in about 270 B.C.E., Ptolemy issued edicts and built shrines to stimulate her cult. Poets described Arsinoë as a special patron of sailors, claiming, "She will give fair voyages and will smooth the sea even in midwinter in answer to prayer." The veneration of Queen Arsinoë by Egyptians and Greeks alike ensured that the cultural blending that emerged during her lifetime continued long after her death.

Connecting People & Society

1. How did the reign of Arsinoë II contribute to the blending of Greek and Egyptian culture that marked the Ptolemaic dynasty?

2. How do the portrayals of the queen in art reflect the transformation of the Macedonian kingship?

In the hieroglyphic section the king's name is enclosed in circles, which supposedly protected his name and, because the names of pharaohs had always been so encircled, also signaled to all who saw it that Ptolemy was indeed the rightful god-king. Equally significant, the Rosetta Stone provided the key that finally let nineteenth-century scholars decipher hieroglyphic writing. Without the stone, the meaning embedded in the great carvings of the ancient Egyptians might still remain a mystery.

The Seleucids Rule Asia

In the violent political jockeying that broke out after the death of Alexander, one of Ptolemy's lieutenants, Seleucus, entered Babylon in 311 B.C.E. and captured the imperial treasure there. With this money,

Seleucus laid claim to the old heartland of the Persian Empire. Yet the extensive eastern lands that Alexander had conquered eluded his grasp. As early as 310 B.C.E. Seleucus gave northwest India back to its native rulers in return for five hundred war elephants, and by the third century B.C.E., eastern Asia Minor had fallen away. Nevertheless, Seleucus founded a long-standing kingdom that continued the Hellenizing process begun by Alexander.

Like Alexander, the **Seleucids** founded cities and populated them with imported Greek and Macedonian bureaucrats and colonists. Seleucia, about fifty miles north of Babylon, was established as the new capital of the kingdom, and Dura Europus, near the midpoint of the Euphrates River, was another important center. Their locations reveal that the Seleucid

Commercial cities

FIGURE 3.3 Rosetta Stone, 197 B.C.E. Greek-speaking Macedonian rulers had to communicate with Egyptians. Fortunately, the Macedonians wrote an edict in Greek and translated it into two Egyptian scripts on this famous stone. This translation provided the key to scholars' ability to read Egyptian hieroglyphs.

were exempt from paying taxes and even received free food until their first crops could be harvested. These colonists did not expect to work the land themselves; instead, resident dependent laborers farmed the land for their foreign conquerors. Again, as in Egypt, the resident peasantry served their Greek-speaking masters. Not surprisingly, the Seleucid kings gained a loyal following among the elite with these allocations of land.

Although Greek sovereignty faded quickly in the easternmost edges of the Seleucid lands, evidence remains of the impact of the Greek presence there. To illustrate, consider the great king of northern India Aśoka (r. ca. 268–ca. 233 B.C.E.). Aśoka is perhaps most remembered for spreading the ideals of Buddhism through inscriptions on stones. Like the Rosetta Stone, these Rock Edicts testify to the Hellenic presence in India, because Aśoka's sayings were preserved both in the Indian language of Prakrit and in Greek. In wise phrases such as "Let them neither praise themselves nor disparage their neighbors, for that is vain," the ideas of Buddhism met the language of Hellenism in the farthest lands of Alexander.

Antigonids in Greece

The Seleucid kings concentrated on ruling the western portions of their Asian provinces, ever watchful for opportunities to gain advantage over the Ptolemies or the Macedonian leaders who now ruled in Macedonia and Greece. These kings, known as the **Antigonids,** were descended from Antigonus the One-Eyed (382–ca. 301 B.C.E.), a general who had joined in the struggle for succession after Alexander's death. Antigonus failed to score a decisive military victory, however, and died on the battlefield at the venerable age of 80, still trying to win control of the entire Macedonian Empire. Nevertheless, his descendants eventually took power in Macedonia and Greece and introduced the Antigonid dynasty.

In the short run, Alexander's conquests profoundly affected Macedonian society and economy. At first, wealth | Life in Macedonia poured from the east into the young king's homeland. Indeed, near the end of his life, Alexander sent home one shipment of booty that proved so large that 110 warships were needed to escort the merchant vessels on their return journey. Numismatic evidence also confirms the volume of wealth that initially flowed into Macedonia, for its mint churned out about 13 million silver coins immediately after Alexander's reign. Much of this coinage came into wide circulation, for officials used it to pay troops and provide stipends for veterans' widows and orphans. Yet the money did not profoundly alter Macedonian society. By the reign of Antigonus's

kings recognized the crucial role of eastern trade in the prosperity of their kingdom. These cities controlled the trade routes through the Tigris-Euphrates valley and the caravan trails that crossed the desert from Damascus and, along with Antioch, became vital political and economic centers within the former Persian lands (see **Map 3.2**).

While the Ptolemies could depend on an established Egyptian priesthood to facilitate their control of their kingdom, the Seleucids had | Seleucid colonists | no such ready-made institution. Instead, they relied in part on Macedonian and Greek colonists to secure their hold on their Asian lands. After Alexander's death, the Seleucids settled at least 20,000 Macedonian colonists in Syria and Asia Minor. This number was supplemented by others from Macedonia who came looking for riches and privileges.

The Macedonian settlers viewed themselves as world conquerors and expected to maintain their high-status positions in the new lands. The Seleucid kings, who saw the colonists as the backbone of their armies, granted them considerable farmlands. Some charters from this time show that certain colonists great-grandson, Demetrius II (r. 239–229 B.C.E.), life in Macedonia had changed little from even as far back as Philip II's time. The army still consisted mainly of Macedonian nobles, who fought as companions to their king. Invaders from the north still threatened; indeed, in the 280s B.C.E. the Gauls, a tribe on the Macedonians' northern border, launched an attack that cost Macedonia dearly. To make matters worse, the Greeks to the south, who had never really accepted Macedonian rule, kept revolting.

The Greek city-states experienced more change than Macedonia did, for the traditional democracy of Athens and the other poleis had evaporated. The poleis relaxed their notions of citizenship, so many immigrants and freed slaves became citizens, but at the same time people had less attachment to their cities. Many jobs—from soldier to athlete—became the province of specialists, not citizens, and thus international professionals replaced the native competitors who brought glory and wealth to their cities. Furthermore, the new economy of the Hellenistic world widened the gulf between rich and poor, and the disparity undermined participatory government: Rich Greeks took over governance and frequently forgot that they had any responsibility to the poor.

Changes in Greece

Despite these tensions, outright revolution never materialized. The relentless warfare plaguing the poleis simply proved too distracting. In addition, Greeks from all walks of life continued emigrating to the other Hellenistic kingdoms in search of a better life, and this exodus helped ease population pressures at home. Bureaucrats and scientists headed for the Greek colonies to take advantage of the tempting opportunities there—for example, a talented mathematician, Apollonius, first worked in Alexandria, Egypt, and then was lured to the Seleucid kingdom in the east. The poleis, which in the old days had claimed people's loyalty, had given way to cosmopolitan cities. Now individuals sought to enhance their own fortunes in a wider world.

EAST MEETS WEST IN THE SUCCESSOR KINGDOMS

The vast breadth of the Hellenistic kingdoms stimulated the West's economy to new heights. Trade rhythms quickened, and merchants raked in unprecedented wealth. Under Alexander and his successors in the various kingdoms, Greek became the universal language of business. Now traders could exchange goods across large distances without confronting confusing language barriers. The Greeks also advanced credit, a business practice that let merchants ply their trade without having to transport unwieldy quantities of hard currency.

FIGURE 3.4 Hellenistic Coins Standardized currency facilitated trade among all the Hellenistic kingdoms and serves as fine historical evidence. Coin (a) is an eight-drachma coin of Ptolemy II of Egypt (r. ca. 284–ca. 247 B.C.E.). Coin (b) is a silver coin of King Orophernes (2nd century B.C.E.) from Cappadocia in the Seleucid kingdom.

Money in the New Cosmopolitan Economies

The Hellenistic kings standardized currency as well, another boon for trade. There were two weights of coins in the Hellenistic world: One was based on Alexander's standard, in which one drachma contained 4.3 grams of silver. The Ptolemies in Egypt abided by a different standard, using only 3.5 grams of silver in the drachma. Despite the dual standards, the consistency of both helped merchants buy and sell with ease throughout the extensive region. **Figure 3.4** shows two coins from this era. The gold coin from Egypt in **Figure 3.4a** is worth eight drachmas. It shows Ptolemy II with his wife Arsinoë II (featured in the Biography) on the front and Ptolemy's parents, Ptolemy I and Berenice, on the reverse. By showing two generations of royalty, the coin is proclaiming a dynastic succession that was traditionally important in Egypt. The silver coin in **Figure 3.4b** is a "tetradrachma," from Cappadocia in Asia Minor (modern Turkey). It shows King Orophernes, with the Greek goddess Athena on the reverse. These coins show that the Hellenistic kingdoms had much in common. Both coins show the monarchs in the style of Macedonian rulers, wearing the simple diadem that since Philip II's time had marked Macedonian kingship, and both are based on the drachma. They also graphically represent both the wealth that the Macedonian conquests generated and

Coinage and trade

the spread of Greek cultural influence throughout the region as trade intensified.

Goods moved briskly through the Hellenistic kingdoms, reshaping old patterns of trade and consumption. Athens initially benefited from the widespread demand for Greek goods like pottery and weapons, but a century after the death of Alexander, Alexandria had replaced Athens as the commercial capital of the eastern Mediterranean. The small islands of Rhodes and Delos also rose to prominence because of their advantageous locations along the routes that connected the north and southeast areas of the Mediterranean with Greece and Italy.

Heightened trade led to new approaches to agriculture as people rushed to develop and sell novel delicacies. As one example, Greek farmers began planting their precious olive trees and grapevines in the eastern kingdoms, permanently altering the ecosystems in those regions. In turn, eastern spices transformed cooking on the Greek mainland and in Egypt. Agricultural crossbreeding also became common, though it failed in some cases—even seeds imported from Rhodes to cross with Egypt's bitter cabbage could not sweeten that pungent vegetable of the Nile valley.

While commerce made countless merchants rich, the individual kingdoms also benefited—mainly by taking control of economic activity. **Command economies** In Egypt, where pharaohs traditionally controlled much trade and industry—a system called a command economy—the Ptolemies increased their controls to funnel the riches of the Nile valley into the royal treasury. They converted the most successful industries into royal monopolies, controlling such essentials as sesame oil, salt, perfumes, and incense. Their most successful venture, however, was the beer industry, which had been a royal monopoly since the Old Kingdom. The Ptolemies insisted that the millions of gallons of beer consumed each year in Egypt be manufactured in the royal breweries, though many women doubtless continued to brew the beverage for household consumption as they had always done.

Kings also levied taxes on imports and exports, such as grain, papyrus, cosmetics, timber, metals, and horses. These policies required a complex administrative system, which in turn led to the proliferation of Greek-speaking bureaucrats. Equally important, the kings used their new riches not only to live lavishly, but also to fund the expensive wars that ravaged the Hellenistic world.

Armies of the Hellenistic World

One of the most famous statues of the Hellenistic world, shown in **Figure 3.5**, is the Nike of Samothrace—called Winged Victory because Nike was the Greek goddess of victory—and it is a perfect

FIGURE 3.5 Statue of Nike (Winged Victory), ca. 190 B.C.E. This 8-foot-tall marble sculpture shows the goddess Nike descending through the wind to celebrate a victory at sea. The blowing draperies mark the Hellenistic style of flowing movement.

symbol of the war-dominated Hellenistic age. Originally part of a sculptural group that included a war galley, Nike strides confidently into the wind, certain of victory. However, the battles of the Hellenistic world seemed to bring endless suffering more often than clear victory.

The Macedonian kings thought of themselves as conquerors and derived their legitimacy in large part from their military successes. Like Alexander, whom they strove to emulate, these monarchs fully expected to participate in the hardships of battle and the dangers of combat. Consequently, they regularly made war on one another in hopes of gaining land or power. The ideal of conquest thus persisted after Alexander's death. However, the scale of warfare had broadened.

This broadening occurred partly because of the larger territories in dispute. Some boundaries now far surpassed the dimensions of the earlier Greek poleis. To cover these daunting distances, monarchs accumulated vast armies. Philip had conquered Greece with a force of about 30,000 men, **Mercenary armies** and Alexander had increased the numbers significantly as he moved east. Alexander's force in India may have exceeded 100,000—exceptional for ancient armies. The Hellenistic kings, however, regularly fielded armies of between 60,000 and 80,000 troops. These large armies consisted no longer primarily of citizen-soldiers but of mercenaries—who were loyal only to their paymaster and who switched sides with impunity. Tellingly, Hellenistic theater often featured mercenary soldiers who returned home with lots of money to spend and a newly cynical outlook.

The Macedonian armies were also influenced by their contact with the far eastern provinces. For example, in these distant lands they encountered war elephants for the first time. Just as horses had offered

War elephants

mounted warriors advantages of mobility and reach over foot soldiers, soldiers mounted on elephants had an even greater military advantage. Furthermore, elephants participated in the fray, trampling men and using their trunks as weapons. As mentioned previously, the earliest Seleucids had exchanged territory in India for the prized elephants, and these formidable animals eventually became part of the Hellenistic armory. The Seleucids tried to breed elephants in Syria but had to keep trading with India for more elephants when their efforts failed. To retain their advantage, the Seleucid kings cut off the Ptolemies' trade in Asian elephants, forcing the Egyptians to rely on the smaller, less effective African breed. The Greek historian Polybius (ca. 200–ca. 118 B.C.E.) described a confrontation between the two classes of pachyderms: The African elephants, "unable to stand the smell and trumpeting of the Indian elephants and terrified, I suppose, also by their great size and strength, . . . at once turn tail and take to flight." As impressive as the Asian elephants were, foot soldiers learned to dodge the beasts and stab or hamstring them. However, the massive animals remained a valuable tool for moving heavy siege engines to walled cities and attacking fortified positions.

Large, wealthy, and well-equipped armies now routinely toppled defensive walls, and kings followed Alexander's ruthless model of wiping out any city that showed even a hint of defiance. Mercenaries, too, cared little for civilians, and historical sources describe soldiers drunkenly looting private homes after a conquest. The countryside also suffered from the warfare, and peasants repeatedly petitioned kings to ease their burdens. Peasants faced increased taxes levied to fund expensive wars and then frequently confronted violence from marauding mercenaries. To an unprecedented level, civilians became casualties in wars waged between kings.

The incessant warfare also changed the nature of slavery in the Greek world. As we have seen, during the classical Greek period—as throughout the ancient world—slavery was taken for granted. Every household had one or two domestic slaves, and most manufacturing and other labor was done by slaves.

Slavery

Alexander's immediate successors generally avoided mass enslavement of prisoners, but traditionally it was customary to enslave losers in battle. Therefore, by the late third century B.C.E., prisoners began to be enslaved in huge numbers. This changed the scale of the institution of slavery and, ultimately, the treatment of the slaves themselves. By 167 B.C.E., the island of Delos in the Aegean Sea housed a huge slave market. Claiming that 10,000 slaves could arrive and be sold in a day on Delos, the Greek historian Strabo quoted a contemporary saying about the slave markets that suggested how quickly the slave-traders sold their human cargo: "Merchant, put in, unload—all's sold." Although these large numbers are surely an exaggeration, they testify to the huge increase in numbers of slaves that began to be moved around the eastern Mediterranean. Wealthy households now could have hundreds of slaves, and others worked in gangs in agriculture and mining. This new scale of slavery further dehumanized those who had been taken, and slaves joined civilians as a population suffering under the new kingdoms.

A True Cultural Blending?

Whether or not Alexander had envisioned a complete uniting of east and west, in reality a full blending of peoples never occurred in the lands he conquered. The Hellenistic kingdoms in Egypt and Asia consisted of local native populations ruled by a Greek/Macedonian elite who made up less than 10 percent of the population. However, this elite was not limited to people of direct Macedonian descent; it also included those who acquired Greek language and culture through formal or informal education. Alexander's conquests opened opportunities for people from many ethnic backgrounds to join the elite—a development that inevitably transfigured Greek culture itself.

The intermingling of East and West intensified with the movement of travelers, which the common use of the Greek language and the size of the kingdoms facilitated. Travelers included merchants and mercenaries and diplomats seeking political and economic advantages

Travelers

or opportunities to spy. Perhaps most instrumental in blending cultures were the artists and artisans who journeyed widely in search of patrons and prizes.

In this new, cosmopolitan world, even women traveled with a freedom unheard of in the classical Greek poleis. Female musicians, writers, and artists embarked on quests for honors and literary awards. One inscription on a commemorative stone recalls

"Aristodama, daughter of Amyntas of Smyrna, an epic poetess, who came to the city and gave several readings of her own poems." The citizens were so pleased with this poet's work that they granted her citizenship. During such readings, authors shared experiences from one part of the world with the people of another, enhancing the diversity that marked this vibrant time.

Such diversity showed up vividly in the art of the period. For example, classical Greek artists had sometimes depicted black Africans in their works. In the Hellenistic age such portrayals grew more frequent. **Figure 3.6** exemplifies the cultural blending that occurred in the visual arts of this period. This bronze figure was cast in the Greek style, yet

Diverse art

it shows a youth from sub-Saharan Africa, possibly Nubia, which partook in continued close interaction with Egypt (discussed in Global Connections in Chapter 1). The subject's pose suggests that he may have once held a lyre, a traditional Greek (not African) musical instrument. The young man might well have been a slave, given that the Hellenistic kingdoms traded heavily in slaves of all ethnic backgrounds. Or he might have been one of the many traveling performers who earned a living by entertaining newly wealthy, cosmopolitan audiences.

All travelers left some evidence of their visits in the farthest reaches of the Hellenistic world. In the third century B.C.E., for example, the Greek philosopher Clearchus discovered a Greek-style city, complete with a gymnasium at the center, on the northern frontier of modern Afghanistan. In the gymnasium, Clearchus erected a column inscribed with 140 moral maxims taken from a similar pillar near the shrine of Apollo at Delphi. Like the Rock Edicts of Aśoka, the pillar of Clearchus preserves in stone the mingling of ideas at the fringes of the Hellenistic world.

Struggles and Successes: Life in the Cosmopolitan Cities

The new cities founded by Alexander and his successors were in many ways artificial structures—they did not grow up in response to local manufacturing or commercial needs. Instead, they were simply created by rulers as showcases of their wealth and power. Expensive to maintain, these cities burdened local peasants with extra taxes and produced little wealth of their own. However, they played a crucial role as cultural and administrative centers, and they became a distinctive feature of Hellenistic life. Modeled on the Greek city-states, these cities still differed markedly from the poleis in several important ways, including the opportunities for women.

The travelers and the diversity of the cities helped break down the tight family life and female seclusion

FIGURE 3.6 African Musician, second century B.C.E. The Hellenistic kingdoms were characterized by a movement of peoples and a resulting cultural blending, exemplified by this African musician playing a Greek musical instrument.

that had marked traditional Greek cities. Women were more free to move about in public. Furthermore, many texts indicate that Hellenistic women had more independence of

Women

action than their Greek counterparts. For example, a marriage contract explicitly insists that a couple will make joint decisions: "We shall live together in whatever place seems best to Leptines and Heraclides, deciding together." These new opportunities for independence made possible the situation at the opening of this chapter, when the young working woman ran off with her lover.

The Hellenistic cities also differed from their Greek counterparts in that they owed allegiance to larger political entities, the king-

Cities and kings

doms. Now Greek monarchies had

thinking about

DOCUMENTS

DOCUMENT 3.2

Cities Celebrate Professional Women

Throughout the Hellenistic age, there is evidence of women whose public service brought them to the attention of their communities. The following three inscriptions commemorate women who served as a physician, a public official, and a musician. Notice that the inscription for the public official indicates that she was the first woman to serve, so this reflects a change from previous practice.

1. Physician and Midwife: Phanostrate of Athens, fourth century [B.C.E.] Funeral inscription

Phanostrate . . . , the wife of Melitos, midwife and doctor, lies here. In life she caused no one pain, in death she is regretted by all.

2. Public Servant: Phile of Priene, first century [B.C.E.] Public inscription

Phile daughter of Apollonius and wife of Thessalus, the son of Polydectes, having held the office of stephanephoros, the first woman [to do so], constructed at her own expense the reservoir for water and the city aqueduct.

3. Harpist: Polygnota of Thebes, Delphi, 86 [B.C.E.] Public inscription

Since Polygnota, daughter of Sokrates, a harpist from Thebes, was staying at Delphi at the time the Pythian games were to be held, but because of the present war, the games were not held, on that same day she performed without charge and contributed her services for the day; and having been asked by the magistrates and the citizens, she played for three days and earned great distinction in a manner worthy of the god and of the Theban people and of our city, and we rewarded her also with five hundred drachmas; with good fortune, the city shall praise Polygnota, daughter of Sokrates, a Theban for her reverent attitude toward the god and her piety and her conduct with regard to her manner of life and art; and there shall be given by our city to her and to her descendants the status of a proxenos, priority in consulting the oracle, priority of trial, inviolability, exemption from taxes, a front seat at the contests which the city holds, and the right to own land and a house. . . .

SOURCES:

1. *Inscriptiones Graecae* 2.3(2), 6873, in *The Ancient World: Readings in Social and Cultural History*, ed. D. Brendan Nagle (Englewood Cliffs, NJ: Prentice Hall, 1995), p. 174.

2. *Die Inschriften von Priene*, 208, in *Women in the Classical World*, ed. Elaine Fantham et al. (New York: Oxford University Press, 1994), p. 156.

3. *Sylloge Inscriptionum Graecarum* (3) 738, in ed. D. Brendan Nagle, p. 174.

Analyze the Document

1. What are the contributions of each woman, and how do their communities recognize their contributions (money, acclaim, and so on)?

2. What evidence do you see for the continued importance of families in the Hellenistic world?

3. What aspects of Hellenistic cities allow women to become prominent?

---

replaced Greek city-states as the influential political form in the developing history of the West. The relationship between the Hellenistic kings and the new cities derived from both Macedonian and Greek traditions. For example, during and after Alexander's reign, monarchs advocated democracy within the cities they founded. Cities were governed by magistrates and councils, and popular assemblies handled internal affairs. In return, the kings demanded tribute and special taxes during times of war. However, these taxes were not onerous, and a king might even exempt a city from taxation. In response, many cities introduced a civic religious cult honoring their kings. As one example, to show this dual allegiance to both their king and city, citizens of the city of Cos had to swear the following oath: "I will abide by the established democracy . . . and the ancestral laws of Cos, . . . and I will also abide by the friendship and alliance with King Ptolemy."

These cities flourished under the patronage of their kings, but they also struggled with all the problems endemic in any urban area. To feed the townspeople, city officials often

Urban problems

had to import supplies from distant sources. Following Hellenistic ideas of a command economy, these urban leaders set grain prices and sometimes subsidized food to keep the costs manageable. They also regulated millers and bakers to prevent them from making large profits from cheap grain. Finally, the cities suffered the unavoidable problems of what to do about sewerage and water drainage; the largest urban centers had drainpipes under the streets for these purposes. Gangs of slaves owned by the city maintained the drainage system and cleared the streets.

City leaders gave little attention to public safety. They hired a few night watchmen to guard some public spaces, but for the most part, they considered safety a personal matter. Consequently, people mingling in the crowded markets or venturing out at night were often victims of robberies, or worse. Danger lurked everywhere, but especially in the many fires that broke out from residents' use of open flames to cook and heat their wooden homes. Despite the perils of fire, crime, and lack of sanitation, however, cities still offered the best hope of success for enterprising people.

The greatest of the new cities—Alexandria, Antioch, Seleucia—drew people from around the world. No longer connected to the original Greek city-states, such newcomers felt little obligation to participate in democratic politics or to profess loyalty to a clan or polis. Greeks, Phoenicians, Jews, Babylonians, Arabs, and others gathered in the cosmopolitan centers to make their fortunes. As the most ambitious among them took Greek names, the old divisions between Greek and "barbarian" blurred. Traditional family ties dissolved, too, as we saw in the story that opened this chapter.

City dwellers improved their lot in several ways, some of them advancing through successful military activities. The Greek Scopas, for example, unable to find work in his home city, "turned his hopes toward Alexandria," where he got a job in the army. Within three years, Scopas had risen to command the armies of Ptolemy V. Women, too, had opportunities to participate in the public sphere. Document 3.2 offers examples of women who were remembered for their contributions to their cities.

New opportunities

Though cities opened up new opportunities, they also spawned miseries. Many poor people were forced to continue working well into their old age; indeed, the elderly market woman shown at the beginning of the chapter would have been a common sight in the Hellenistic period. The father in the chapter's opening story looked to his king to spare him an impoverished old age. His pleas probably went unheard, however; cities and their royal patrons tended to ignore the mounting problems of poverty. Slums cropped up, becoming just as characteristic of Hellenistic cities as the palaces of the wealthy and the libraries of the wise.

In some cities, destitute people designed institutions to help themselves. Artisans' guilds, for example, offered a sense of social connection to people bewildered by the large, anonymous cosmopolitan cities. Some people organized burial clubs, in which members contributed money to ensure themselves a decent interment at the end of lives that had little material security. Historical evidence suggests that some rich city dwellers worried about the possibility of social revolution. As one illustration of this fear, the citizens of a city in Crete were required to include the following statement in their oath of citizenship: "I will not initiate a redistribution of land or of houses or a cancellation of debts."

Patronage, Planning, and Passion: Hellenistic Art

The monarchs who were becoming fabulously wealthy did not spend much money on the urban poor. What did they do with the mounds of coins that filled their coffers? In part, they spent fortunes as patrons of the arts, commissioning magnificent pieces that continue to be treasured today. However, not all critics have admired the products of the Hellenistic artists. For example, early in the first century C.E., the prolific Roman commentator Pliny the Elder (23–79 C.E.) energetically discussed Greek art. A passionate admirer of classical Athenian art, Pliny claimed that after the accomplishments of Lysippus (ca. 380–ca. 318 B.C.E.), "art stopped." His dismissal of the Hellenistic world's artistic contributions has since been shared by many observers who admire the idealized poses of classical Greek works. But art did not stop with Lysippus; it merely changed as its center migrated from Athens to the great cosmopolitan centers of the East.

Classical Greek artists had been supported by public funding by democratic poleis. By contrast, Hellenistic artists received their funding from wealthy kings seeking to build and decorate their new cities. Royal patronage began with monarchs who wanted their newly established cities to reflect the highest ideals of Greek aesthetics. At the same time, this policy served the political agenda of promoting Greek culture. These rulers hired architects to design cities conducive to traditional Greek life, with its outdoor markets and meeting places, and employed artists to decorate the public spaces. Pergamum (see **Map 3.2**) posed a special challenge to architects: Its center was perched on a high hill, so city planners had to take the steep slopes into account in designing the city. In the end, they arranged the royal palaces at the top of the hill—visibly proclaiming the king's ascendancy—and the markets at the bottom. The layout of this magnificent city is typical of many Hellenistic urban centers.

Royal patrons

Citizens in Pergamum shopped in the colonnaded building shown at the lower left corner of **Figure 3.7.** Higher up the hill was an altar to Zeus and higher still, a temple to Athena that served as the entrance to the library. The heights were dominated by the royal palaces and barracks. (The temple shown at the center of the hilltop was built later by Roman conquerors.) On the left side of the model, there are theater seats built into the hillside, where some 10,000 spectators could gather to watch the latest dramatic productions. The city preserved the gracious outdoor life of the classical Greek cities, yet was dominated by the majesty and power of the new kings.

After cities were designed, kings commissioned sculptors to decorate the great public buildings, especially temples. Throughout the Hellenistic period, sculptors also found a market in the newly wealthy, who hired these artists to create works of beauty to decorate their homes. Hellenistic sculpture built on classical

Sculpture

models in the skill with which artists depicted the human form and in the themes that harked back to the age of Greek heroes and the Trojan War. Still, Hellenistic artists departed from the classical style in significant ways. Classical Greek sculptors sought to portray the ideal—that is, they depicted scenes and subjects that were above the tumult and passion of this world. By contrast, Hellenistic artists faced passion and emotion head-on. Their works exhibit a striking expressiveness, violence, and sense of movement, along with contorted poses that demonstrate these artists' talents for capturing human emotion in marble.

Hellenistic artists also portrayed themes that the classical artists in Athens would have considered undignified or even demeaning. These themes included realistic portrayals of everyday life. For example, classical artists, in their search for ideal beauty instead of imperfect reality, would have ignored subjects such as the market woman shown at the beginning of the chapter. The boxer in **Figure 3.8** also exemplifies the contrast to the Olympic heroism that we saw in Chapter 2. Here the artist shows his knowledge of Greek idealism in the perfectly crafted hair and musculature of the bronze figure. Yet this boxer is tired, not heroic. He rests his taped hands on his knees and his shoulders sag in exhaustion, or perhaps defeat. The marks of his contest show clearly on his face—his cheek bleeds, his nose is broken, and his ear is deformed from too many blows. Many art critics, like Pliny, who mourned the "death of art," have condemned Hellenistic artists for not striving to portray perfection. Nonetheless, they had

remarkable courage in showing the flawed reality of cosmopolitan life.

Resistance to Hellenism: Judaism, 323–76 B.C.E.

Much of Hellenistic art and life in the cosmopolitan cities reflected a deep and, in many ways, successful blending of classical Greek culture with that of the ancient Middle East and Egypt. Yet Alexander's desire to make "all mankind a single people" did not appeal to everyone in the Hellenistic world. Throughout their history, Jews had worked to preserve their distinctive identity, and this desire came directly into conflict with spreading Hellenism (ancient Greek culture). Although Judea remained an independent political unit under Alexander and the Ptolemies, the successor kingdoms offered opportunities for Jews from Palestine to trade and settle throughout the Hellenistic world. In the new multiethnic areas, urban Jews struggled to clarify and sustain their sense of identity. The most pious among them lived together in Jewish quarters where they could observe the old laws and maintain a sense of separate community. Alexandria and Antioch had substantial Jewish quarters, and most large cities had a strong Jewish presence.

Some Jews compromised with Hellenism, learning Greek and taking advantage of the opportunities available to those | Hellenized Jews | who at least had the appearance of Hellenism. As they learned to speak and write in Greek and studied the classical texts, some of their

FIGURE 3.7 Restored Model of Pergamum Hellenistic rulers built great new cities such as Pergamum in what today is the country of Turkey. The city spread over a high hill, from the royal palace at the top to markets at the bottom. A new style of life developed in the royal cities.

FIGURE 3.8 Seated Boxer, second century B.C.E. This bronze sculpture reveals much about the Hellenistic world. Hellenistic peoples still praised the Greek sports contests, but they recognized and documented emotions other than the joy of victory. This boxer, for example, appears to be dejected, tired, and bruised.

them that God would exact vengeance for their impiety. In an ironic twist, his text was translated into Greek by his grandson.

These uncertainties within the Jewish community came to a head when the Seleucid kings wrested Palestine from the Ptolemies in 200 B.C.E. The pace of Hellenization quickened after this pivotal event. Both Jewish and pagan historical sources claim that the Seleucid king Antiochus IV (r. 175–163 B.C.E.) intended to change Jewish observance in order to "combine the peoples"—that is, to Hellenize the Jews. According to an early Jewish text, even the high priest of Jerusalem supported the king and "exercised his influence in order to bring over his fellow-countrymen to the Greek ways of life." Antiochus established Greek schools in Jerusalem and went so far as to enter Jewish contestants in the Greek-style athletic games celebrated at Tyre. In 168 B.C.E., he ordered an altar to Zeus to be erected in the Temple of Jerusalem and sacrifices to be offered to the Greek god. The Roman historian Josephus (75 C.E.) later described the sacrilege: "He sacrificed swine upon the altars and bespattered the temple with their grease, thus perverting the rites of the Jews and the piety of their fathers."

Antiochus's policies proved too much for pious Jews, and in ca. 166 B.C.E., Judas Maccabeus (Judas the Hammer) led an armed revolt against the Seleucids. (See Document 3.3.) The account of the **Maccabean Revolt** is preserved in a text titled *The First Book of the Maccabees*, probably written in 140 B.C.E. by a Jew in Judea. The author articulated the goal of Antiochus clearly: "Then the king wrote to his whole kingdom that all should be one people, and that each should give up his customs." This decree of Antiochus is reminiscent of Plutarch's praise of Alexander quoted at the beginning of this chapter, and it confirms the differing, intensely felt opinions that people often have about cultural blending.

Maccabean Revolt

In the end, the Maccabeans prevailed. In 164 B.C.E. the Jewish priests rededicated the Temple, and the Jews celebrated the restoration of their separate identity. The historian of *First Maccabees* wrote that "Judas and his brothers and all the assembly of Israel determined that every year at that season the days of the dedication of the altar should be observed with gladness and joy for eight days." This declaration instituted the feast of Hanukkah, which Jews continue to celebrate today.

The Maccabean revolutionaries established a new theocratic state of Judea, which the Seleucids were too busy with war on their eastern borders to challenge. The reinvigorated Jewish state continued its conquests of neighboring states, including Greek cities in Galilee, and by 76 B.C.E. the Jews had established a kingdom almost as extensive as

Independent Judea

traditional beliefs changed, especially where they sought to reconcile Judaism with Hellenism. Sometime in the third century B.C.E., the Hebrew Scriptures were translated into Greek, in the influential document known as the **Septuagint.** (The name derives from the Latin word for "seventy," recalling the legendary group of 72 translators who were credited with the accomplishment.) In great cities like Alexandria, Jews gathered in synagogues to pray in a traditional fashion, but in many of these centers of worship, the Scriptures were read in Greek.

In Palestine, too, Jews and Gentiles, or non-Jews, met and mingled. Palestine had many Greek settlements, and even in Jerusalem Jews faced the question of what it meant for them to compromise with Hellenism. Jesus Ben Sirach, a Jewish scribe and teacher in Jerusalem, wrote a text called *Ecclesiasticus* (ca. 180 B.C.E.) in which he scolded believers who had turned away from the traditional Jewish Law of Moses and warned

DOCUMENT 3.3

Judas Maccabeus Liberates Jerusalem

In the first century C.E., the Jewish historian Josephus wrote a history of the Jews in which he described the revolt of Judas Maccabeus against the Hellenistic king Antiochus in ca. 166 B.C.E. As part of his desire to bring together his diverse peoples, Antiochus erected an altar to Zeus in the Temple at Jerusalem.

[Judas Maccabeus] overthrew the idol altar and cried out, "If," said he, "anyone be zealous for the laws of his country and for the worship of God, let him follow me"; and when he had said this he made haste into the desert with his sons, and left all his substance in the village. Many others did the same also, and fled with their children and wives into the desert and dwelt in caves; but when the King's generals heard this, they took all the forces they then had in the citadel at Jerusalem, and pursued the Jews into the desert; and when they had overtaken them, they in the first place endeavored to persuade them to repent, and to choose what was most for their advantage and not put them to the necessity of using them according to the law of war; but when they would not comply with their persuasions, but continued to be of a different mind, they fought against them on the Sabbath day, and they burned them as they were in the caves, without resistance, and without so much as stopping up the entrances of the caves. And they avoided to defend themselves on that day because they were not willing to break in upon the honor they owed the Sabbath, even in such distresses; for our law requires that we rest upon that day.

There were about a thousand, with their wives and children, who were smothered and died in these caves; but many of those that escaped joined themselves to Mattathias and appointed him to be their ruler, who taught them to fight even on the Sabbath day, and told them that unless they would do so they would become their own enemies by observing the law [so rigorously] while their adversaries would still assault them on this day, and they would not then defend themselves; and that nothing could then hinder but they must all perish without fighting. This speech persuaded them, and this rule continues among us to this day, that if there be a necessity we may fight on Sabbath days.

SOURCE: Josephus, "The Jewish Wars," in *The Great Events by Famous Historians*, vol. II, ed. Rossiter Johnson (The National Alumni, 1905), p. 247.

Analyze the Document

1. What religious motivations undergirded this war?

2. How did the Maccabees compromise their own religious beliefs to fight the war?

3. How did this conflict resemble modern controversies regarding fighting during Ramadan or Christmas?

that of Solomon (r. 970–931 B.C.E.) (see Chapter 1). Though they had revolted to preserve their cultural and religious purity, the new rulers proved intolerant of their Gentile subjects, forcing many to convert and insisting that non-Jewish infant boys be circumcised. These practices worsened the instability already plaguing the region.

THE SEARCH FOR TRUTH: HELLENISTIC THOUGHT, RELIGION, AND SCIENCE

Hellenistic rulers from Alexander on consciously spread Greek ideas and learning. To do this, they vigorously supported education, which they saw as key to the preservation of Greek ideals and the training ground for new Hellenized civil servants. Within these educated circles occurred most of the intellectual and cultural blending that created the brilliance of Hellenistic art as well as the struggles of cultural identity. However, these communities of the educated also proved a fertile ground for intellectual inquiry in which great minds eagerly sought truth about the world, religion, and the meaning of life.

A Life of Learning

Great speculations, however, began first in the schoolrooms. Families who wanted their boys to succeed invested heavily in education. At the age of 7, boys attended privately funded schools and practiced Greek and writing. The parchment samples of their

INTELLECTUAL LIFE

ca. 400–ca. 325 B.C.E.	Diogenes advocates Cynicism
ca. 342–ca. 292 B.C.E.	Life of playwright Menander
ca. 335–ca. 280 B.C.E.	Life of physician Herophilus
ca. 312 B.C.E.	Zeno founds Stoicism
ca. 310–ca. 230 B.C.E.	Life of Aristarchus, who posited heliocentric universe
ca. 306 B.C.E.	Epicurus founds school of philosophy
ca. 300 B.C.E.	Euclid publishes *Elements* on mathematics
ca. 220 B.C.E.	Archimedes advances engineering

KEY DATES

assignments reveal a strong anti-"barbarian" prejudice in which the culture of all non-Greeks was dismissed. Thus, even early schooling aimed to inculcate Greek values among non-Greek peoples. This indoctrination was reinforced by an emphasis on Homer's works as the primary literary texts.

At 14, boys expanded their education to include literary exercises, geography, and advanced studies of Homer. Successful students then continued their studies in the gymnasium, the heart of Hellenistic education and culture. Most cities boasted splendid gymnasia as their central educational institutions. Often the most beautiful building in the city, the gymnasium sported a running track, an area for discus and javelin throwing, a wrestling pit, and baths, lecture halls, and libraries. Here Greek-speaking boys of all ethnic backgrounds gathered, exercised naked, and finished an education that allowed them to enter the Greek ruling class.

Hellenistic kings cultivated education just as they served as patrons of the arts. They competed fiercely to hire sought-after tutors for their families and schools and to purchase texts for their libraries. The best texts were copied by hand on Egyptian papyrus or carefully prepared animal hide called parchment. (The word *parchment* derives from *Pergamena charta*, or "Pergamum paper," which refers to where the best-quality parchment was made.) Texts were prepared in scrolls rather than bound in books and were designed to be unrolled and read aloud.

This advocacy of education yielded diverse results. Many scholars produced nothing more than rather shallow literary criticism; others created literature that captured the superficial values of much of Hellenistic life; and some created highly sophisticated philosophy and science. The range of these works, however, contributed important threads to the tapestry of Western civilization.

Theater and Literature

The tragedies and comedies of classical Greek theater had illuminated profound public and heroic themes ranging from fate and responsibility to politics and ethics. Theater proved extremely popular in the Hellenistic cities as well. Though some cosmopolitan playwrights wrote tragedies, few of these works have survived. We do have many comedies from this era, which contrast so starkly with the classic Greek examples of this genre that this body of work is called New Comedy. Hellenistic plays were almost devoid of political satire and focused instead on the plights of individuals.

The best-known playwright of New Comedy is Menander (ca. 342–ca. 292 B.C.E.), whose works often centered on young men who fell in love with women who were unattainable for some reason. Most of these plots ended happily with the couples overcoming all obstacles. In general, New Comedy characters were preoccupied with making money or indulging themselves in other ways. **New comedies** This focus on individual concerns reflected the realities of cosmopolitan life—ruled by powerful and distant kings, individuals had limited personal power. Menander and the other playwrights of the age shed light on this impotence by focusing on the personal rather than on larger questions of good and evil.

A new genre of escapist literature—the Hellenistic novel—also emerged in this environment. The themes in these novels echo those of the plays: Very young men and women fall in love (usually at first sight), but circumstances separate them. They must endure hardships **Hellenistic novels** and surmount obstacles before they can be reunited. Surprisingly, most of these novels portray young women as resourceful and outspoken individuals. For example, a remarkable heroine in the novel *Ninos* dresses in gender-ambiguous clothing and leads a band of Assyrians to capture a fortified city. Although wounded, she makes a brave escape while elephants trample her soldiers.

Both the New Comedy and the Hellenistic novel sought to provide an escape from the realities of cosmopolitan life. Yet they also reflected new ideals in this society that often looked to the personal rather than to the polis for meaning. For example, unlike the writings of classical Greece, Hellenistic texts expressed an ideal of affection within marriage. The philosopher Antipater of Tarsus wrote, "The man who has had no experience of a married woman and children has not tasted true and noble happiness." The literature of the day also revealed an increased freedom of Hellenistic women to choose their partners. While families still arranged most marriages, some women (and men) began to follow their hearts in choosing a spouse. Woman also gained more freedom in divorce laws. Like men, they could seek divorce if their husbands committed adultery. One marriage contract from as early as 311 B.C.E. included clauses forbidding the husband to "insult" his wife with another woman. Taken together, all these themes expressed a new emphasis on love within the family.

Cynics, Epicureans, and Stoics: Cosmopolitan Philosophy

Like their literary counterparts, Hellenistic philosophers also narrowed the focus of their inquiry. Most of them no longer tackled the lofty questions of truth and justice that had preoccupied Socrates and Plato. Instead, they considered how an individual could achieve happiness in an age in which vast, impersonal kingdoms produced the kind of pain and weariness embodied by the market woman pictured at the beginning of the chapter.

The sensibilities of the Hellenistic age had been first foreshadowed by Diogenes (ca. 400–ca. 325 B.C.E.), an early proponent of the philosophic school called **Cynicism.** Diogenes was disgusted with the hypocrisy and materialism emerging around him in the transformed life of Athens as traditional polis life deteriorated. Diogenes and his followers believed that the only way for people to live happily in a fundamentally evil world was to involve themselves as little as possible in that world. The Cynics therefore claimed that the more people rejected the goods and connections of this world—property, marriage, religion, luxury—the more they would achieve spiritual happiness.

To demonstrate his rejection of all material things, Diogenes reputedly lived in a large tub. The carving in **Figure 3.9** shows him in the tub, oblivious to the lavish villa behind him. 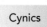 He is talking to Alexander the Great, enacting a likely apocryphal story in which Alexander offers the famous philosopher anything in the world. Diogenes simply asks Alexander to "stand out of my light and let me see the sun." The dog perched on top of the tub symbolizes Cynicism. (The word *cynic* derives from the Greek word *kunos*, which means "of a dog," or "doglike," because Cynics supposedly lived as simply and as filthily as dogs.)

Although Plato had dismissed Diogenes as "Socrates gone mad," Cynicism became popular during the Hellenistic period as people searched for meaning in their personal lives, rather than justice for their polis. Some men and women chose to live an ascetic life of the mind instead of involving themselves in the day-to-day activities of the Hellenistic cities. However, most found it difficult to reject material goods completely.

Other Hellenistic philosophies offered more practical solutions to the question of where to find personal happiness in an impersonal world. Epicurus (ca. 342–ca. 270 B.C.E.), for example, founded a school of philosophy that built on Democritus's (460–370 B.C.E.) theory of a universe made of atoms (described in Chapter 2). Envisioning a purposeless world of randomly colliding atoms, Epicurus proclaimed that happiness came from seeking pleasure while being free from pain in both body and mind. From a practical standpoint, this search for happiness involved pursuing pleasures that did not bring pain. Activities such as overeating or overdrinking, which ended in pain, should thus be avoided. In Epicurus's view, the ideal life was one of moderation, which consisted of being surrounded by friends and free of the burdens of the public sphere. His circle of followers included women and slaves. The Roman **Epicurean** Lucretius Carus (ca. 99–ca. 55 B.C.E.) articulated Epicurus's ideal: "This is the greatest joy of all: to stand aloof in a quiet citadel, stoutly fortified by the teaching of the wise, and to gaze down from that elevation on others wandering aimlessly in a vain search for the way of life." Of course, this "greatest joy" required money with which to purchase the pain-free pleasures that Epicurus advocated. His was not a philosophy that everyone could afford.

While Epicurus honed his philosophy in his private garden, the public marketplace of Athens gave rise to a third great Hellenistic philosophy: **Stoicism.** Named after *stoa*, the covered walkways surrounding the marketplace, the school of Stoicism was founded by Zeno (ca. 335–ca. 261 B.C.E.). Zeno exemplified the cosmopolitan citizen of the Hellenistic world, for he was born in Cyprus of non-Greek ancestry and spent most of his life in Athens.

At age 22, Zeno was a follower of Crates the Cynic, but later he abandoned his early connection to Cynicism, arguing that people could possess material goods as long as they were not emotionally attached to them. Indeed, the Stoic philosophers advocated indifference to external things. While this attitude paralleled Epicurus's desire to avoid pain, Zeno and

Cynics

Epicurus

Stoics

FIGURE 3.9 Diogenes and Alexander Diogenes argued that people should live a simple life, much like the dog shown sitting on the barrel in which the great philosopher lived. The artist included in this scene Alexander the Great, who reputedly admired the simple lifestyle that was so rare in the Hellenistic kingdoms.

The Search for Truth: Hellenistic Thought, Religion, and Science 99

the Stoics did not frame their philosophy in terms of the materialism of an atomic universe. Instead, they argued for the existence of a Universal Reason or God that governed the universe. As they explained, seeds of the Universal Reason lay within each individual, so everyone was linked in a universal brotherhood. In quasi-religious terms, this belief validated Alexander's supposed goal of unifying diverse peoples.

The Stoics' belief in a Universal Reason led them to explain the apparent turbulence of the world differently than the Epicureans. Stoics did not believe in random events but instead posited a rational world with laws and structures—an idea that would have a long history in the West. While individuals could not control this universe, they could control their own responses to the apparent vagaries of the world. Followers were implored to pursue virtue in a way that kept them in harmony with rational nature, not fighting it. The ideal Stoic renounced passions (including anger) even while enduring the pain and suffering that inevitably accompany life. Through self-control, Stoics might achieve the tranquillity that Epicureans and Cynics desired.

Cynicism, Epicureanism, and Stoicism had many things in common. Arising in settings where individuals felt unable to influence their world, they all emphasized control of the self and personal tranquility. Whereas the classical Greeks had found meaning through participation in the public life of their poleis, Hellenistic philosophers claimed that individuals could find contentment through some form of withdrawal from the turbulent life of the impersonal cosmopolitan cities. Moreover, all three philosophies appealed primarily to people with some measure of wealth. The indifferent, pain-free life of both the Epicureans and the Stoics required money, and the self-denial of the Cynics seldom appealed to really destitute people.

New Religions of Hope

For most ordinary people, the philosophies of the Hellenistic age had little relevance. These people looked instead to new religious ideas for a sense of meaning and hope. During this period, the gods and goddesses of the poleis gave way to deities that had international appeal and that were accessible to ordinary individuals—two features that marked a dramatic departure from previous religions of the West. Furthermore, the new religions offered hope in an afterlife that provided an escape from the alienation of the Hellenistic world. The international component paved the way for a blending of religious ideas—syncretism—and individuals felt a deeply passionate spiritual connection to their deities. The most popular new cults were known as **mystery religions**

because initiates swore not to reveal the insights they received during the highest ceremonies. The historical roots of these cults stretched back to early Greece, Egypt, and Syria, but they acquired a new relevance throughout the Hellenistic era.

Mystery cults included worship of fertility goddesses like Demeter and Cybele, and a revitalized cult of Dionysus. However, the most popular was that of the Egyptian goddess Isis, who achieved a remarkable universality. Inscription stones offering her prayers claim that Isis ruled the world and credited her with inventing writing and cultivation of grain, ruling the heavenly bodies, and even transcending fate itself—the overarching destiny that even the old Homeric gods could not escape. Isis reputedly declared: "I am she who is called Lawgiver. . . . I conquer Fate. Fate heeds me." In other inscriptions, worshipers claimed that Isis was the same goddess that other peoples called by different names: "In your person alone you are all the other goddesses named by the peoples."

Figure 3.10, a marble relief from Athens, demonstrates religious syncretism in action. The piece was carved in the classical technique showing an apparently traditional Greek family worshiping at an altar. At the right of the altar, standing before the veil of mystery, is the Egyptian goddess Isis, depicted in traditional Greek style. The god seated at the right resembles Zeus, but he is Isis's brother/husband Osiris, the traditional Egyptian consort of the goddess-queen. This figure shows the syncretic nature of the new Hellenistic religions, in which patron deities of particular cities acquired international appeal. In their worship of these mysteries, the people of the Hellenistic kingdoms may have almost achieved Alexander's rumored ideal of universalism.

Men and women who wanted to experience the mysteries of these new religions believed that they had been summoned by a dream or other supernatural call. They took part in a purification ritual and an elaborate public celebration, including a procession filled with music and, sometimes, ecstatic dance in which people acted as if possessed by the goddess or god. Finally, the procession left the public spaces and entered the sacred space of the deity, where the initiate experienced a profound connection with the god or goddess. Many mysteries involved sacred meals through which people became godlike by eating the flesh of the deity. Such believers emerged from this experience expecting to participate in an afterlife. Here lay the heart of the new religious impulses: the hope for another, better world after death. The mystery religions would continue to draw converts for centuries, and perhaps paved the way for Christianity—the most successful mystery religion of all.

Mystery religion

Hellenistic Science

The philosophic and religious longings of the Hellenistic world bred long-standing consequences for the future. People living in later large, impersonal cities turned to the philosophies of indifference and religions of hope. Equally impressive were the improvements on classical Greek science and technology that emerged in the Hellenistic learning centers. This flourish of intellectual activity was fostered in part by the generous royal patronage that made Alexandria and Pergamum scholastic centers, and in part by the creative blending of ideas from old centers of learning.

One scholar who benefited from the new Hellenistic world of learning was Herophilus (ca. 335–ca. 280 B.C.E.), who traveled to Alexandria from the Seleucid lands near the Black Sea to study medicine. The first physician to break the strong Greek taboo against cutting open a corpse, Herophilus performed dissections that led him to spectacular discoveries about human anatomy. (His curiosity even reputedly led him to perform vivisections on convicted criminals to learn about the motion of living organs.) His careful studies yielded pathbreaking knowledge: He was the first to recognize the brain as the seat of intelligence and to describe accurately the female anatomy, including the ovaries and fallopian tubes. However, all physicians were not as willing as Herophilus to treat the human body as an object of scientific study. Even in intellectually advanced Alexandria, dissection became unpopular, and subsequent physicians focused on techniques of clinical treatment rather than on anatomy. However, they made major strides in pharmacology, carefully studying the influence of drugs and toxins on the body.

In spite of these noteworthy advances, the most important achievements of the Hellenistic scientists occurred in the field of mathematics. Euclid (335–270 B.C.E.), who studied in Alexandria, is considered one of the most accomplished mathematicians of all time. In his most famous work, *Elements* (ca. 300 B.C.E.), Euclid presented a geometry based on increasingly complex axioms and postulates. When Euclid's patron, King Ptolemy, asked the mathematician whether there was an easier way to learn geometry than by struggling through these proofs, Euclid replied that there was no "royal road" (or shortcut) to understanding geometry. Euclid's work became the standard

Medical advances

Mathematics and astronomy

FIGURE 3.10 Isis and Osiris, later second century B.C.E. This sculpture is a votive relief, a carving that would have been placed in a temple and dedicated to fulfill a vow to a deity. Commissioned in Athens, it shows a family worshiping the Egyptian deities Isis and Osiris, who both look remarkably Greek in this rendering. The work illustrates the blending of religions that occurred in the Hellenistic world.

text on the subject, and, even today, students find his intricate proofs both challenging and vexing.

Euclid's mathematical work laid the foundation for Hellenistic astronomy. Eratosthenes of Cyrene (ca. 275–ca. 195 B.C.E.), for example, used Euclid's theorems to calculate the circumference of the earth with remarkable accuracy—he erred only by about 200 miles. Aristarchus of Samos (ca. 310–ca. 230 B.C.E.) posited a heliocentric, or sun-centered, universe (against prevailing Greek tradition) and attempted to use Euclidean geometry to calculate the size and distance of the moon and sun. Although Aristarchus's contemporaries rejected his work, he and other astronomers introduced a striking change into the study of the heavens: They eliminated superstition and instead approached their work with mathematics.

Many Greek thinkers combined theoretical science with practical applications. One of the most influential in this regard was Hipparchus of Nicaea (160–125 B.C.E.). A brilliant mathematician, Hipparchus invented trigonometry—the mathematics of measuring angles—and applied these insights to measuring the heavens and the earth. His accomplishments demonstrated once again the benefits of cultural blending, for he introduced into Greece the Babylonian mathematical convention of measuring the circle in terms of 360 degrees (see Global Connections, Chapter 1), the method by which we

thinking about
SCIENCE & TECHNOLOGY

Finding One's Way at Sea: The Invention of Latitude and Longitude

Long before the invention of global positioning system (GPS) devices, ancient mariners faced a nearly impossible task: finding their way when out of sight of land. To avoid disaster, sailors needed to be able to determine where they were in a vast ocean without any landmarks to guide them. But someone would first have to map and measure the earth before sailors would have the essential tools for calculating their location.

Hipparchus of Nicaea developed trigonometry, the mathematics of measuring angles, in the second century B.C.E. He used trigonometry to create an imaginary grid of latitude and longitude lines on the globe of the world (see **Figure 3.11**). Latitude (horizontal) lines measure the angle from the equator, and longitude (vertical) lines measure the angle from the prime meridian. All places on the earth have an address of sorts that we can express by their position on this grid, and because mathematics measures a circle in "degrees," we use this designation for the globe's address. Sicily, for example, is about 37 degrees north latitude and 14 degrees east longitude. This "address" is the same on Hipparchus's chart and in the GPS instruments we use today. Thus, with

trigonometry's invention, early sailors got the tools to compute their position on the global grid.

Yet mapping the earth and having the means to calculate one's position was just a first step. Mariners still had to determine their location on the global grid *while sailing on a vast, featureless*

FIGURE 3.11 Global Map Divided by Latitude and Longitude Lines

ocean. Calculating latitude was relatively easy, for that required only measuring the angle between the horizontal and a fixed location in the sky—either Polaris or the sun. Longitude was far more difficult to measure, because as the earth rotates during a 24-hour day, the

positions of Polaris and the sun move across the sky. One therefore has to know the exact time of day to calculate longitude. (For example, at the equator, a one-minute error in time causes about a 17-mile error in computing one's east-west position.)

Precise measurements of longitude while at sea would have to wait until the eighteenth century, when sophisticated clocks were invented that could compensate for the rough movements, caused by wind and waves, that had thrown off the accuracy of older clocks. Only then, with an accurate measure of the time of day, could a mariner calculate an exact reading of his longitude, just as we can do with our GPS devices.

Follow the development of navigation through the book. See, for example, the astrolabe in Figure 6.14 and the exploration of the world in Chapter 12.

Connecting Science & Society

1. How did Hipparchus's invention of trigonometry aid ancient sailors? What is the connection between measuring angles and finding one's way at sea?

2. What does the invention of latitude and longitude suggest about the relationships among science, people's practical needs, and inventions? What inventions (of new products or new processes) in your own lifetime show these relationships in action?

---

continue to measure the globe. Among Hipparchus's other practical applications were measuring the length of the lunar month within an error of one second, a stunning achievement, and being the first to use the ideas of latitude and longitude consistently to measure the earth. The map in Thinking About Science and Technology illustrates this significant application of trigonometry to empirical observation.

Another beneficiary of Greek mathematics was Archimedes (ca. 287–ca. 212 B.C.E.), often considered the greatest inventor of antiquity. Like so many cosmopolitan scholars, Archimedes, who was born in Syracuse, traveled

Archimedes

to Alexandria to study. He later returned to Syracuse, where he worked on both abstract and practical problems. He built further on Euclid's geometry, applying the theorems to cones and spheres. In the process, he became the first to determine the value of pi—essential in calculating the area of a circle. He also applied geometry to the study of levers, proving that no weight was too heavy to move. He reportedly coined the optimistic declaration "Give me a place to stand, a long enough lever, and I will move the earth."

Archimedes did more than advance theoretical mathematics: He also had a creative, practical streak. For example, he invented the compound pulley, a valuable device for moving heavy weights. His real challenge, however, came at the end of his life. As we will see in Chapter 4, Syracuse, the city of Archimedes' birth, was besieged by Rome, a rising power in the Mediterranean. Throughout the siege, Syracuse used both offensive and defensive weapons that Archimedes had invented. Yet the great man's inventions could not save the Sicilian city. The Romans ultimately prevailed, and in 212 B.C.E. Archimedes was struck down by a Roman soldier as he was drawing a figure in the sand.

Archimedes serves as an apt symbol for the Hellenistic world that produced him. He was educated with the best of Greek learning and combined it with the rich diversity of Asia and the Mediterranean lands—a blending that gave Western civilization dramatic impetus. The Hellenistic scientist died at the hands of a new people—the Romans—who embraced the practical applications of men like Archimedes and who next took up the torch of Western culture.

LOOKING BACK & MOVING FORWARD

Summary

The Macedonian kings Philip and Alexander permanently transformed the life of the polis that had marked the glory of Greece. Their conquests of Greece, and then Egypt and the Asian portion of the Persian Empire, created a unique blend of these ancient civilizations. By establishing a ruling elite of Greeks and Macedonians in cities from the Mediterranean to India, Alexander and his successors spread key elements of Greek civilization. Yet they also reshaped the culture of the polis. Political and cultural centers moved from the Greek city-states to bustling cosmopolitan areas, where people from all over the Hellenistic world mingled. Some benefited greatly from the new opportunities for personal enrichment that cosmopolitan life offered; many more sank to unprecedented levels of poverty. Some peoples embraced the cultural blending; others rejected it.

Though the armies of the Hellenistic kings competed endlessly for land and power, kings still had the resources to support culture and learning. Scientists, artisans, and scholars of this complex age made impressive advances. However, a new force was gathering momentum in the West, one that would profoundly impact the fate of Hellenistic civilizations.

KEY TERMS

Ptolemies, *p. 84*

Rosetta Stone, *p. 86*

Seleucids, *p. 87*

Antigonids, *p. 88*

Septuagint, *p. 96*

Maccabean Revolt, *p. 96*

Cynicism, *p. 99*

Epicurean, *p. 99*

Stoicism, *p. 99*

mystery religions, *p. 100*

REVIEW, ANALYZE, & CONNECT TO TODAY

REVIEW THE PREVIOUS CHAPTERS

In Chapter 1—"The Roots of Western Civilization"—we explored the beginnings of city life in Mesopotamia. Chapter 2—"The Contest for Excellence"—looked at the life, culture, and political fortunes of the classical Greek city-states.

1. Contrast the culture of classical Athens with artistic and philosophic ideas of the Hellenistic world, and consider what contributed to the transformation in ideas.

2. Review the urban experiences of Mesopotamia and Greece, and compare and contrast them with those of people in the cosmopolitan cities of the Hellenistic world. What do you think are the most significant differences, and what elements of urban life remained constant?

3. Chapter 1 summarized the early history of the Jews. Consider how their past contributed to the Maccabean Revolt under the Seleucids.

ANALYZE THIS CHAPTER

Chapter 3—"The Poleis Become Cosmopolitan"—describes the conquest of Greece by Macedonia and traces the spread of Greek culture as far east as India, as vibrant new monarchies combined Greek culture with the diversity of many other peoples to create the Hellenistic world.

1. What contributed to the conquest of the Greek city-states by Macedonia? Consider both the weaknesses of the poleis and the strengths of Macedonia.

2. What elements of Hellenic culture were most transformed, and in what ways were the cultures of the Persian Empire changed by contact with Greek culture?

3. Describe the changes in economics and warfare that were introduced in the Hellenistic world.

4. How did the opportunities for women change under the Hellenistic monarchies?

CONNECT TO TODAY

Think about some of the major issues the Hellenistic kingdoms faced—for example, cultural diversity, urban problems, and people's struggles to find meaning.

1. Does the United States, as a society, share some of these problems today? If so, how have the American people responded?

2. Do religious struggles such as those experienced by the Jews in Hellenistic times have parallels in the contemporary world? If so, how have countries responded?

BEYOND THE CLASSROOM

THE CONQUEST OF THE POLEIS

Borza, Eugene N. *In the Shadow of Olympus: The Emergence of Macedon.* Princeton, NJ: Princeton University Press, 1992. A chronological survey seeking to trace the emergence of Macedonia as a major force in the political affairs of the fourth-century B.C.E. Balkans.

Cartledge, Paul. *Alexander the Great.* Woodstock, NY: Overlook Hardcover, 2004. A riveting narrative of the life of Alexander that argues he was more concerned with his own glory than with a spread of Hellenism.

Harding, Philip. *From the End of the Peloponnesian Wars to the Battle of Ipsus.* New York: Cambridge University Press, 1985. A sophisticated analysis of the late Greek world before its conversion into the Hellenistic world by Alexander's conquest.

Worthington, Ian. *Philip II of Macedonia.* New Haven, CT: Yale University Press, 2008. Detailed biographical account, nicely illustrated with maps, offering a compelling argument that Philip is to be credited with the military innovations that Alexander put so effectively to use.

THE SUCCESSOR KINGDOMS, 323–ca.100 B.C.E.

Chaniotis, Angelos. *War in the Hellenistic World: A Social and Cultural History.* Hoboken, NJ: Wiley-Blackwell, 2005. Excellent discussion of military history and the ways almost-constant warfare shaped the Hellenistic world.

Grant, M. *From Alexander to Cleopatra: The Hellenistic World.* New York: Scribner, 1982. A general survey of the Hellenistic world.

Green, Peter. *From Alexander to Actium.* Berkeley: University of California Press, 1990. A complex analysis of the Hellenistic world's politics, literature, art, philosophy, and science.

EAST MEETS WEST IN THE SUCCESSOR KINGDOMS

Bartlett, John. *Jews in the Hellenistic and Roman Cities.* London: Routledge, 2002. A collection of essays offering a wide-ranging analysis of Jews in the classical world.

Billows, Richard A. *Kings and Colonists: Aspects of Macedonian Imperialism.* New York: E.J. Brill, 1995. An in-depth study of the problems of Macedonian imperial rule.

Cohen, Getzel M. *The Hellenistic Settlements in Europe, the Islands and Asia Minor.* Berkeley: University of California Press, 1995. A good general history of Hellenistic settlement—its founders, early history, and organization.

Dmitriev, Sviatoslav. *City Government in Hellenistic and Roman Asia Minor.* Oxford: Oxford University Press, 2005. An examination of city governments in the Hellenistic world and of the social and administrative transformation of Greek society.

Laks, Andre, and Malcolm Schofield. *Justice and Generosity: Studies in Hellenistic Social and Political Philosophy.* New York: Cambridge University Press, 1995. A comprehensive guide to the social and political philosophies in a period of increasing interest to classicists, philosophers, and cultural and intellectual historians.

Stewart, Andrew. *Faces of Power: Alexander's Image and Hellenistic Politics.* Berkeley: University of California Press, 1993. A remarkable look at art as a legitimate source of historical evidence.

THE SEARCH FOR TRUTH: HELLENISTIC THOUGHT, RELIGION, AND SCIENCE

Clauss, James. *Companion to Hellenistic Literature.* Malden, MA: Blackwell, 2009. Essays exploring the social and intellectual context of literature from the Hellenistic period.

Hicks, R.D., trans. *Diogenes Laertius: Lives of the Eminent Philosophers.* Cambridge: Loeb Classical Library, 1922. An excellent primary source on the giants of speculative thought in Greece.

Martin, Luther H. *Hellenistic Religions: An Introduction.* New York: Oxford University Press, 1987. A well-written survey of Hellenistic religions, their characteristic forms and expressions, differences and relationships, and their place in the Hellenistic system of thought.

Pollitt, J.J. *Art in the Hellenistic Age.* New York: Cambridge University Press, 1986. An accessible and well-illustrated look at Hellenistic art as an expression of cultural experience and aspirations of the Hellenistic age.

Sharples, R.W. *Stoics, Epicureans and Sceptics.* New York: Routledge, 1996. A readable account of the principal doctrines of these Hellenistic philosophies.

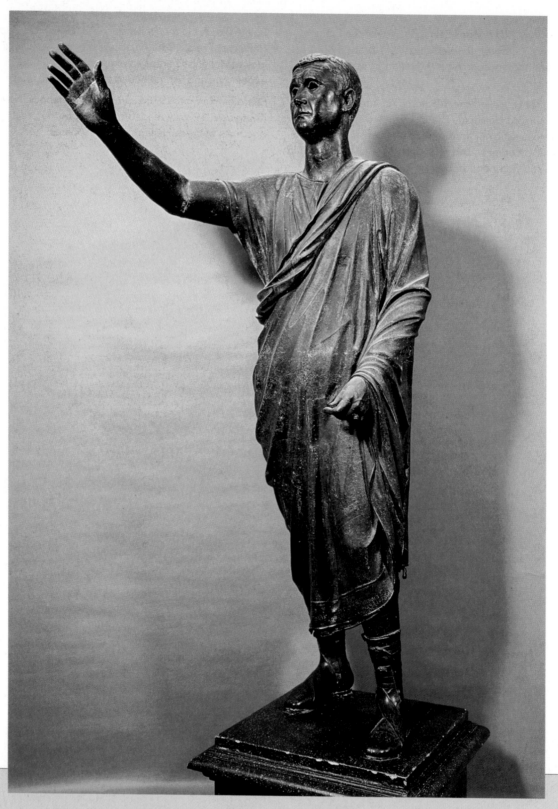

ORATOR ADDRESSING THE ROMAN PEOPLE

Romans lived public lives in which men were encouraged to serve their city in public office.
This calling required rhetorical skills to gain the support of Roman crowds, who gathered in the
Forum to listen to speeches and shout for their favorite speakers. Since the crowds were so large,
orators had to rely on broad gestures to sway masses outside the range of the human voice.
Rome grew great served by men such as Aulus Metellus, the orator depicted here in a life-size
bronze statue from the first century B.C.E.

Pride in Family and City

Rome from Its Origins Through the Republic, 753–44 B.C.E.

4

"No country has ever been greater or purer than ours or richer in good citizens and noble deeds; . . . nowhere have thrift and plain living been for so long held in such esteem." The Roman historian Livy (59 B.C.E.–17 C.E.) wrote a long history of Rome, in which he wanted to show how the heroic citizens of a small city-state became the masters of the world. He attributed their success to their upright character. At the same time Greek civilization was flourishing, a people had settled in the center of Italy, on the hills surrounding what would become the city of Rome. They were a serious, hardworking people who placed loyalty to family and city above all else. In time, this small group conquered the Italian peninsula, forging a coalition of peoples that enjoyed the benefits of peace and prosperity while relentlessly expanding through military conquest.

After overthrowing the monarchy, Rome developed a republican form of government, in which rich and poor citizens alike participated in a highly public legislative process. Within the city, men worked, relaxed, and talked in public spaces while noble women directed the household. Both nonnoble men and women worked in many areas of the city and contributed to an increasingly prosperous urban life.

Roman experience conquering and ruling the tribes of Italy prepared Roman armies to face foes farther afield. As Rome became a great power in the Mediterranean, it came into conflict with Carthage in North Africa. The two powers fought three wars—the Punic Wars—which destroyed Carthage. Rome was then drawn into wars in the eastern Mediterranean, in Greece, and into Asia Minor. These wars transformed Roman identity as Rome became a world power, in which an orator speaking in the Forum could hardly address the problems of the far-flung lands, and the republican form of government was no longer effective. Conquests funneled untold wealth and numerous slaves into Rome, and contact with Hellenistic civilization brought new culture, ideas, and values—causing Livy to lament the decline of "plain living" that he believed had made the Romans great.

At the end of this period, the stresses would prove too great, and the Roman Republic would end in civil war and murder. Yet despite its troubled demise, the Republic left a lasting legacy. Throughout the Mediterranean world, everyone knew of the proud city and its old families who had established laws, technology, and a way of life that exerted a continuing influence.

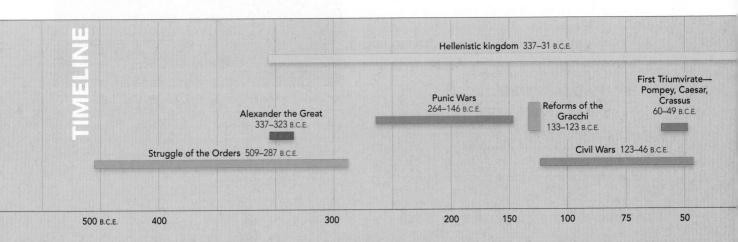

TIMELINE

Hellenistic kingdom 337–31 B.C.E.

First Triumvirate—
Pompey, Caesar,
Crassus
60–49 B.C.E.

Punic Wars
264–146 B.C.E.

Alexander the Great
337–323 B.C.E.

Reforms of the
Gracchi
133–123 B.C.E.

Struggle of the Orders 509–287 B.C.E.

Civil Wars 123–46 B.C.E.

500 B.C.E.   400   300   200   150   100   75   50

THE RISE OF ROME,
753–265 B.C.E.

On a warm spring day in 458 B.C.E., a Roman farmer was plowing the land adjacent to his small, round hut when the Senate recognized an imminent threat from a nearby tribe. In the face of such emergencies, the Roman Senate could offer one man supreme power for the duration of the crisis, giving him the title "dictator." The Senate offered the dictatorship to the farmer, Cincinnatus. He accepted the task and successfully led his armies to defeat the invaders. His grateful fellow villagers asked him to continue his leadership after the crisis, but he refused, preferring to return to his plow. Throughout the next centuries, this story of the strong, unassuming farmer Cincinnatus was told and retold by conservative Romans who looked back to the "ways of the fathers," *mos maiorum*, for models of virtue. (The American city Cincinnati was so named to honor George Washington—another savior farmer-general.) Romans preserved stories like this to remember their heroes and transmit their values to their families. Though they exist on the border between history and legend, these stories offer a glimpse of the origins of the greatness that would become Rome.

A Great City Is Founded

The historian Livy did not mind mixing history with myth, for he said: "There is no reason to object when antiquity draws no hard line between the human and the supernatural; it adds dignity to the past." Romans regularly remembered their history in terms of legends. Perhaps the most beloved of these stories told Romans how their city was founded. Like the story of Cincinnatus, the tale of the birth of Rome is filled with drama, conflict, heroes, and values. The tale begins with Aeneas, a Trojan hero who escaped from the destruction of his city after the Trojan War (described in Chapter 2). A royal female descendant of Aeneas decided to dedicate her life to serving the gods. She became pregnant by the god Mars and bore twin boys, Romulus and Remus. The princess's uncle did not believe in the miraculous conception, nor did he want her sons to threaten his rule, so he threw the infant boys in the Tiber River. Soon a shepherd found them being suckled by a wolf and raised them as his own sons. Many years later, after the boys had grown up, Romulus killed his brother during a quarrel and became the first king of the newly founded city of Rome. The traditional date of the founding of the city is 753 B.C.E., and archaeological evidence confirms the existence of a settlement there by this time.

Figure 4.1 shows a well-known statue from the fifth century B.C.E. that depicts the two brothers, Romulus and Remus, being suckled by the wolf that saved them. The age of the original statue—which was only of the nursing wolf—reveals how much the Romans treasured this myth of their city's founding. The twins were added about 2,000 years later, during the Renaissance, showing the continued attraction of the myth. Images like this helped Romans remember and carry on their valued traditions from generation to generation. Reflecting this sense of destiny and heroic action, Livy concluded that "with reason did gods and men choose this site for our city—all its advantages make it of all places in the world the best for a city destined to grow great."

FIGURE 4.1 Wolf of Rome, fifth century B.C.E. The Romans often looked back to their founding myth, in which a wolf nursed the brothers Romulus and Remus. This Roman statue celebrates that myth, though the nursing infants were a Renaissance addition. In ancient Rome, a live wolf was kept on the Capitoline Hill to remind Romans always to venerate their ancestors' history and ways.

Rome was located on hills overlooking a fertile, low-lying plain and the Tiber River, which afforded access to the Mediterranean Sea and to the inland regions. The geography of the surrounding Italian peninsula offered a number of advantages that would ultimately favor the growth of the young city. In contrast to Greece, whose mountainous terrain discouraged political unification, the large plains along Italy's western and eastern shores fostered trade, communication, and agriculture. The Apennine mountain range that marches down through the peninsula also creates abundant rainfall on the western plain. Therefore, Rome's fields were better situated for large-scale agriculture than had been possible for the Greek city-states. In addition, calm, accessible harbors along the western coast opened avenues for trade throughout the Mediterranean, which was further enhanced by Italy's central location in that important sea.

The initial settlers of Rome, like many of the other tribes in the region, were Indo-Europeans, those ubiquitous migrants from near the Black Sea whom we first saw in Chapter 1. They farmed, living in round huts and plowing their land. Cato the Elder (234–149 B.C.E.), a Roman political leader known for expressing traditional Roman values, summarized the Romans' pride in this way of life: "From farmers come the bravest men and sturdiest soldiers." Yet Rome also grew stronger through absorbing some of the culture and ways of its particularly talented neighbors. Greek colonies were well established in southern Italy and Sicily; Phoenician colonies prospered along the coast of North Africa. Most influential, however, were the Romans' immediate neighbors to the north, the Etruscans.

The Etruscan Influence

The Etruscans had appeared in Italy by 800 B.C.E., and for millennia historians argued about the origin of these peoples who did not speak an Indo-European language. Did they come from northern Europe, Italy, or North Africa? Modern DNA testing has confirmed the ancient historian Herodotus's claim that they arrived from Lydia in Asia Minor. The DNA evidence demonstrates that not only did the people come from modern Turkey, but they also brought their own cattle, setting that breed apart from the indigenous Italian cattle. The Etruscans settled the land and prospered. They traded all over the Mediterranean, importing luxury items and enjoying a good life.

Scholars have not yet deciphered all the Etruscan writings, so our best source of information about their daily life is their surviving artwork. **Figure 4.2** shows an Etruscan sarcophagus, or stone coffin, adorned by

FIGURE 4.2 Etruscan Sarcophagus, ca. 520 B.C.E. This sarcophagus (stone burial casket) was designed to hold cremated remains. The decoration celebrates the couple's life. They are shown reclining at dinner, an activity in which the wife and husband shared equal status.

a carving of a married couple. The couple recline together as they would have at dinner, and their poses suggest much affection between them. Indeed, women's active participation in this society surprised many of the Etruscans' contemporaries. The famous Greek philosopher Aristotle (384–322 B.C.E.), writing centuries later, described with some shock how even respectable Etruscan women joined in banquets with men.

Etruscan kings ruled Rome for a time, and the Romans learned a good deal from their civilization; indeed, much that we define as Roman was in fact Etruscan. For example, the Romans adopted Etruscan engineering and used their newfound skills to drain their lowland marsh, which formed the center of the growing city of Rome, and to build the great sewers that drained water from the city. They also adopted Etruscan architectural features—among them, the arch and vault construction—and modeled their temples on those of the Etruscans. Inside the temples, Romans learned to rely on divination—interpreting the will of the gods in the entrails of sacrificial animals—from Etruscan priests. Romans also adopted the toga, the white woolen robe worn by citizens, as well as the *fasces*, a bundle of rods surrounding an ax that was the powerful emblem of Roman authority.

Finally, the Romans acquired the Etruscan alphabet and began using it to write in their own Latin language. Note the statue of the orator shown at the beginning of this chapter. This perfect model of Roman life has his Roman name written in Etruscan letters on the bottom of his Etruscan-style toga. The Italian region of Tuscany is named after this early people who exerted an enduring influence on the growing culture of Rome.

The Roman Monarchy, ca. 753–509 B.C.E.

Like other ancient civilizations, the early Romans were ruled by kings, but to work out the details of the monarchy, historians have to struggle with combinations of history and legend. Romulus (ca. 753–ca. 715 B.C.E.) was the first king, and more unverifiable legends claim he was followed by four more monarchs. By the seventh century B.C.E., it seems, Rome was ruled by an Etruscan dynasty that governed for almost a century, from about 616 to about 509 B.C.E.

By the end of the sixth century B.C.E., the Roman aristocracy had come to chafe against the Etruscan kings' authority. Roman tradition holds that rebellion against the Etruscans erupted in response to the violation of Lucretia, a virtuous Roman matron. According to Livy, Sextus, son of the Etruscan king Tarquin the Proud, raped Lucretia at knifepoint. Her husband, Collatinus, told her not to blame herself, but

Overthrow of Etruscans

after extracting her husband's promise to exact vengeance, she committed suicide. She was remembered as a chaste, heroic woman who chose death over dishonor. After her death, Romans rallied around the leadership of an Etruscan nobleman—Brutus—who joined Collatinus in a revolt that toppled the monarchy. The story of Lucretia illuminates the values of bravery and chastity held by early Roman men and women, but it also became a symbol of Romans' revulsion against kings, which would be a continuing theme throughout their history.

The legend accurately concluded that the Etruscan monarchy was overthrown, but the historical reality was more complex. All Romans did not support the overthrow of the monarchy—many in the lower classes relied on the monarchy to control the power of the noble families (the **patricians**), and some patricians who were related to kings also supported the monarchy. With these competing social forces, simply overthrowing a monarchy would not resolve social issues. However, just as the Greek poleis had overthrown their own kings and replaced them with oligarchies of nobles during their early history, the situation was repeated in Rome. The erection of a stable governmental form would require time and struggle.

Governing an Emerging Republic, 509–287 B.C.E.

With the overthrow of the Etruscan monarchy, the Romans established a republic, a Latin word that meant "public matter" (often rendered "public realm" or "commonwealth" in English), which they distinguished from the "private realm" of the Etruscan kings. For Romans, this meant that power rested with the people assembled together and that magistrates served the state. This influential vision of government was in striking contrast to that of the Hellenistic kings, who generally viewed their kingdoms as their own property, their spoils of war, their private realm.

In practice, the Republic consisted of three parts—consuls, the Senate, and the assemblies. Executive authority rested with two male **consuls** who were elected annually by an Assembly of Centuries organized by army groupings of 100 men, or "centuries." The consuls were advised by a body of elder statesmen, the **Senate.** Finally, adult male citizens met in **assemblies,** outdoor public gatherings in which the participants voted—by group, not as individuals—on issues that had previously been presented to them by leading statesmen. Beyond this governmental structure, the Roman people were separated by two general social distinctions into groups called patricians and plebeians. The patricians, old families who composed about 6 percent of the population, were recognized as socially and legally superior to everyone else. The **plebeians,** who made up the majority of the population, were the Republic's working people; their numbers, however, did not include slaves. Although the republican system seemed to offer a balance of power, in reality authority rested with the patricians, who sat in the Senate, and with the wealthy men who dominated the Assembly of Centuries.

Perhaps not surprisingly given that so few dominated the many, some individual patricians found ways to enrich themselves and their families. Many abused their power and oppressed the commoners in their charge, even enslaving many because of debts they incurred. By the fifth century B.C.E., social relations between patrician and plebeian had deteriorated enough that a social revolution occurred, which historians have called the **Struggle of the Orders.** Two main issues fueled this controversy: First, the poor wanted guarantees against the abuses of the powerful, and second, the wealthy plebeians wanted a role in government. This struggle was not a civil war, but instead a series of political reforms forced on the aristocracy from about 509 to 287 B.C.E.

Struggle of the Orders

Plebeians began their revolution by establishing themselves as a political alternative to the patricians. They withdrew from the city, held their own assemblies, established their own temple to counter the patrician cults, and even elected their own leaders, called **tribunes,** who were to represent plebeian interests. Tribunes could veto unfavorable laws and represent plebeians in law courts, for example. Patricians also had a practical reason to listen to the voice of the people through their tribunes, because they needed the plebeians to fight in the infantry. Just as Greek citizens forced concessions from aristocrats who needed armies, Roman citizen-soldiers threatened to refuse military service unless some of their demands were met. This was an effective threat; slowly, plebeians gained in political skill and, through the pressure of their tribunes, extracted meaningful concessions.

Plebeians won a number of important rights: First they gained a written law code that could be consistently enforced. Between 451 and 449 B.C.E., the laws were written down and displayed in a form called the **Twelve Tables.** Subsequent Romans looked back proudly to this accomplishment, which established a Roman commitment to law that became one of Rome's most enduring contributions to Western culture. To mark the importance of the establishment of written law, Roman children continued to memorize the Twelve Tables for up to four centuries later. Plebeians also won the right to hold sacred and political offices. Although, in practice, offices more readily went to the wealthy, upward mobility was possible. Perhaps the greatest concession the plebeians eventually won was the right to marry patricians. This removed birth as the most serious impediment to the rise of talented and wealthy plebeians.

The plebeian struggle for representation culminated in 287 B.C.E., when the Tribal Assembly became the principal legislative body. **Figure 4.3** shows this new republican structure. This group was named because the assembly was organized in "tribes" or regions, urban and rural, where plebeians lived. Laws passed by the Tribal Assembly did not need Senate approval, but bound everyone—rich or poor. The resulting society in Rome contained three main social classes: patricians, wealthy plebeians—later called **equestrians** (or knights) because they could afford to be in the cavalry—and the poorer plebeians. Money and connections dominated Roman politics as patricians and equestrians fought to increase their power. In spite of these problems, Polybius believed the people retained important powers, as Document 4.1 describes.

Governing the Republic

As **Figure 4.3** shows, the Roman constitution was complex, but logical. All citizens participated in the two Assemblies that elected the magistrates who served the state. Roman men with money and influence could move through the *cursus honorum*, the career path of a successful public official. A man would be elected to each office for one year, and then (through the late Republic) automatically become a member of the Senate—that venerable institution which by now had no actual constitutional power but a great deal of influence. The Roman system probably worked in part because most of the political life took place within a more informal system.

Informal Governance: Patrons and Clients

From the earliest years of the Republic, Romans relied on semiformal ties to smooth social and even political intercourse. Powerful members of society, called patrons, surrounded themselves with less powerful people—clients—in a relationship based on informal yet profoundly important ties. Patrons provided clients with what they called "kindnesses," such as food, occasional financial support, and help in legal disputes. Clients consisted of people from all walks of life: aristocratic youths who looked to powerful patrons for help in their careers (or hoped to be remembered in a rich patron's will), businessmen who wanted to use a patron's political influence to profit in their enterprises, poets who needed money, or freed slaves who remained attached to their former owners. Because Rome remained overwhelmingly an agricultural society, the largest group of clients was small farmers, who depended on their patrons to help them survive in a land that was becoming dominated by powerful aristocratic landowners. Clients owed their patrons duties, such as financial and political support.

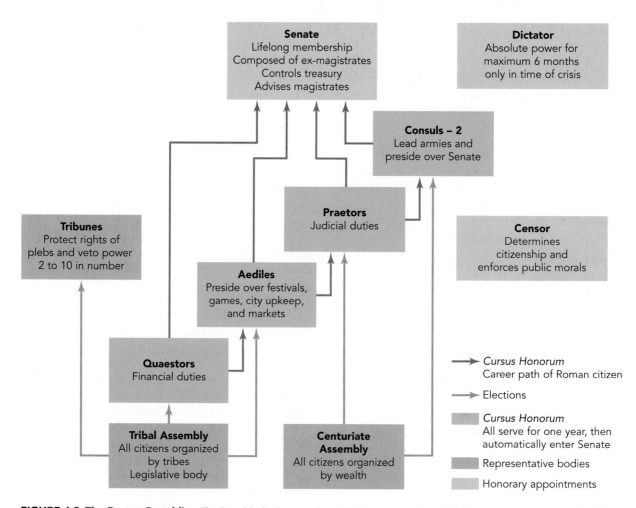

FIGURE 4.3 The Roman Republic The Republic had a complex political structure that still influences governments today. This chart illustrates both the representative bodies and the positions the Roman assemblies elected. It also shows the *cursus honorum*, that is, the expected political path of a Roman man as he rose in public office.

Many clients gathered at their patrons' doors every morning as the cock crowed—failure to appear would jeopardize one's tie of clientage. This mixed crowd numbering in the tens to hundreds received ritual gifts, ensuring that the poorest would eat and the richest were remembered, and everyone was invited into the patron's home to greet him. The patron was supposed to exert a moral authority over his clients, helping them to be good citizens. As the Roman poet Horace (65–8 B.C.E.) wrote, "A wealthy patron governs you as a good mother might do and requires of you more wisdom and virtue than he possesses himself."

| Clients' role |

In the public world of Mediterranean society, clients provided patrons visible proof of their authority. After the morning greeting, clients accompanied their patron to the center of the city, where the day's business took place. A patrician surrounded by hundreds of clients was a man to be reckoned with. Political life of the Republic was conducted in the **Forum,** a large gathering area surrounded by temples and other public buildings. The Forum included the Senate chamber, the people's assembly, and a speaker's platform—called

the Rostra—where politicians addressed the Roman people. **Map 4.1** shows the City of Rome with its important public spaces, including the Rostra and the Senate chamber. Clients would cheer their patron, shout down his opponents, and offer their votes to his agenda. An aristocrat who abandoned this public life that gave him stature and dignity was described sadly: "He will have no more entourage, no escort for his sedan chair, no visitors in his antechamber."

The Struggle of the Orders created a republic in which rich and poor both had a voice. In fact, it was a system dominated by wealth and an aristocracy that used its influence in the Senate and the Forum to preserve traditional privileges. However, the wealthy never forgot they needed the support of the Roman clients who gathered at their doors in the morning, shouted their support in the Forum, and manned Rome's armies.

Dominating the Italian Peninsula

As the Republic gathered strength, territorial wars between Rome and its neighbors broke out almost

DOCUMENT 4.1

The Power of Public Opinion

The Greek historian Polybius (ca. 200–ca. 118 B.C.E.) was a great admirer of the Roman constitution, which he described in his Histories. *He thought the republican constitution would ensure a stable government. After he described the roles of the Senate and all the officers of the state, he turned to the more informal power of the people of Rome.*

After this one would naturally be inclined to ask what part is left for the people in the constitution, when the Senate has these various functions, especially the control of the receipts and expenditure of the exchequer; and when the Consuls, again, have absolute power over the details of military preparation, and an absolute authority in the field? There is, however, a part left for the people, and it is a most important one. For the people is the sole fountain of honour and of punishment; and it is by these two things and these alone that dynasties and constitutions and, in a word, human society are held together: for where the distinction between them is not sharply drawn both in theory and practice, there no undertaking can be properly administered,—as indeed we might expect when good and bad are held in exactly the same honour. The people then are the only court to decide matters of life and death; and even in cases where the penalty is money, if the sum to be assessed is sufficiently serious, and especially when the accused have held the higher magistracies. . . .

Again, it is the people who bestow offices on the deserving, which are the most honourable rewards of virtue. It has also the absolute power of passing or repealing laws; and most important of all, it is the people who deliberate on the question of peace or war. And when provisional terms are made for alliance, suspension of hostilities, or treaties, it is the people who ratify them or the reverse. These considerations again would lead one to say that the chief power in the state was the people's, and that the constitution was a democracy.

SOURCE: Polybius, *The Histories of Polybius* (London: Macmillan, 1889), in eds. Brian Tierney and Joan W. Scott, *Western Societies: A Documentary History*, vol. I, 2nd ed. (New York: McGraw-Hill, 2000), pp. 102–103 (page citations are to second edition).

Analyze the Document

1. What powers does Polybius describe as belonging to the Senate and consuls?

2. What powers does he attribute to the people? Do you think he's right that these powers are substantial?

---

annually. What led Rome into these repeated struggles? Romans themselves claimed that they responded only to acts of aggression, so their expansion was self-defensive. The reality, however, was more complicated. Rome felt a continual land hunger and was ever eager to acquire land to establish colonies of its plebeians. Roman leaders also had a hunger for glory and plunder that would let them acquire and reward clients—victorious generals were well placed to dominate Rome's political life. Thus, farmers often had to drop their plows, as Cincinnatus did, to fight.

By the beginning of the fourth century B.C.E., Rome was increasingly involved in wars in the Italian peninsula. From an early period, Romans identified themselves with fellow Latin tribes as they fought together against surrounding hillside tribes. By the early Republic, this alliance was known as the Latin League. Under Rome's leadership, the Latin League successfully defended its borders during the fifth and fourth centuries B.C.E. However, Rome's allies became increasingly resentful of Rome's leadership and revolted in 340 B.C.E. Two years later, Rome decisively defeated the rebellious allies and dissolved the League. Here, however, Rome showed its genius for administration. Instead of crushing the rebellious states, Rome extended varying degrees of citizenship

Italian wars

to the Latins. Some received the rights of full Roman citizenship, while others became partial citizens who could earn full citizenship by moving to Rome. This benign policy allowed Rome with its allies to confront and conquer other peoples of the peninsula.

As **Map 4.2** shows, Rome acquired territories to the south and north. This was not a time of endless victories, however. In 390 B.C.E., the Gauls of northern Italy (a Celtic tribe) sacked much of the city before being bribed to leave with a large tribute payment, but it would be another eight hundred years before a foreign army once more set foot in the city. However, their invasion had weakened the Etruscan cities of the north, so by 295 B.C.E., Roman armies controlled the north of the peninsula. By the middle of the third century B.C.E., Rome dominated most of the Italian peninsula.

The Romans' successful expansion in part stemmed from their renowned courage and tenacity in battle. Most of their success, however, came from their generosity in victory. Although in **Map 4.2** it looks

Foreign policy

as if Rome had "united" Italy, in fact, the peninsula remained a patchwork of diverse states allied to Rome by separate treaties. These treaties were varied, but all were generous to conquered peoples. Romans allowed all the tribes to retain full autonomy in their own

MAP 4.1

Rome During the Republic

This map shows the city of Rome during the late Republic. The inset pinpoints the locations of the important features of the Forum.

Explore the Map

1. Which elements in the Forum and at the center of the city show how political life and religious institutions dominated life in Rome?

2. What were the political implications of the fact that the famous slum district, the Subura, was located so near the Forum and the Palatine Hill, where the wealthiest Romans lived?

territories and to elect their own officials, keep their own laws, and collect their own taxes. These peoples were required to supply troops for Rome's armies and to avoid pursuing independent foreign policy. Many

of the conquered peoples did have to give up some territory for Rome to use as colonies to feed their land hunger, but the colonies served to help Rome watch over and control its ever-widening borders of influence. As a result of Rome's leadership, the conquered territories at times enjoyed more peace and freedom than they ever had. Rome's sensible policy toward the territories bought the loyalty of many states and created a relatively cohesive unit that would fuel further imperial expansion.

FAMILY LIFE AND CITY LIFE

The great Roman orator Cicero (106–43 B.C.E.) wrote that the Romans were like other peoples except in their religious fervor: "In reverence for the gods, we are far superior." Perhaps more than other ancient civilizations, the Romans saw the world as infused with spirits; in their view, almost every space was governed by some divinity. Rome itself was guarded by three deities that protected the state—Jupiter, Juno, and Minerva—but there were gods for even smaller spaces. There were goddesses for the countryside, for the hills, and for the valleys. There were three gods to guard entrances—one for the door, another for the hinges, and a third for the lintel, the door's upper supporting beam. The remaining spaces within the home were equally inhabited by spirits that demanded worship and sacrifice.

A Pious, Practical People

Formal worship of the many gods and goddesses took place at the temples, where priests presided over sacrifices and divination officials looked for favorable omens in the entrails of sacrificial animals. The Vestal Virgins, six priestesses who presided over the temple of Vesta, goddess of the hearth, kept the sacred fire of the state hearth burning. (See the major Temple of Jupiter and the House of the Vestal Virgins in **Map 4.1.**)

According to the Roman people, their success hinged on proper worship, which meant offering sacrifices. Sacrifices could be as small as a drop of wine or a honeycake, or as large as an ox, but the Romans believed their destiny was deeply tied to their proper observation of religious rituals. When Rome was sacked by the Gauls in 390 B.C.E., Livy reported, one Roman general supposedly said, "All things went well when we obeyed the gods, but badly when we disobeyed them."

In addition to piety, Romans valued moral seriousness. These hardworking men and women prized duty to family, clients, patrons, and the Republic itself. They rejected the individualism of the Greeks and would have found the idea of Achilles sulking in his tent while his compatriots died incomprehensible.

Legend:
- Territory of Roman Citizens
- Roman Territorial Conquests
- Carthaginian Territories
- Greek Territories

MAP 4.2

Italy, 265 B.C.E.

This map shows the tribes of the Italian peninsula who were conquered by the Romans, the dates of the conquests, and the nearby Carthaginian territories.

Explore the Map

1. How would the location of the Tiber River yield advantages for Rome's developing trade?

2. How would Rome's expansion in the western Mediterranean begin to intrude on Carthaginian holdings?

3. Why would Messana's location (where Rome and Carthage would first clash) be strategically important?

These serious men and women, who stressed collective responsibility and obedience to both secular and religious authority, would one day rule the entire Mediterranean world.

Loyalty to the Family

Roman religion, duty, and loyalty began in the family. A father, in theory, had complete authority over everyone in his household, including his wife, children, slaves, and even ex-slaves. The father served as guardian of the family's well-being and shared with his wife the responsibility for venerating the household gods. In addition to recognizing all the spirits who guarded the home, families worshiped their ancestors, whom they considered the original source of their prosperity. The best families displayed busts of their important ancestors in niches in the home. **Figure 4.4** shows a Roman man holding the busts of his forefathers, revealing the piety and ancestor worship so vital to Romans at that time.

Marriages in early Rome were arranged, to make politically advantageous alliances between families and ensure the continuation of the family through children. A woman could be given Marriage patterns in marriage in two ways. Her family of origin might transfer her to her husband's control, in which case she became part of his family and participated in the worship of his ancestors. Or she might remain under her father's "hand," never becoming a full part of her husband's family. In this case, the woman's family of origin kept more political and financial control of her resources. **Figure 4.5** shows a modest, serious Roman couple with their child. They do not touch, and they stand together looking into the distance. The couple in this gravestone contrasts strikingly with the affectionate Etruscan couple shown in **Figure 4.2** and suggests that Romans considered marriage a serious duty.

Despite the authority of husbands, women still played an important role in the family. They instilled the values of Rome in their children and raised them to be responsible and obedient citizens. Historical evidence such as letters indicate that mothers exerted as much stern authority as fathers and therefore wielded some political power through their sons.

The Challenges of Childhood

Birth in a Roman home always involved great risk to the newborn. When a child was born, the midwife inspected it, even before the umbilical cord was cut, to judge whether it was physically perfect. If it was not, she would likely cut the cord too closely, thus killing the child. A healthy newborn was placed at the father's feet. If he accepted the infant, picking

FIGURE 4.4 Roman Patrician, first century C.E. The conservative Romans took great pride in their ancestors, whose lives, they believed, gave legitimacy to their descendants. Romans venerated busts of their ancestors, as this statue of a Roman holding two busts of his forebears shows.

up a boy or acknowledging a girl, then the child was raised. If he did not, the baby would be "exposed"—placed outside to die or to be taken in and raised as a slave. Roman law required the father to raise one daughter, but he could choose to raise all his daughters, as many families did. However, it is impossible to know how many children were exposed and how many died as a result. In one chilling letter, a soldier matter-of-factly instructs his pregnant wife to keep the child if it is a boy and to expose it if it is a girl. We can only conclude that the practice of exposure was not considered extraordinary.

When the child was accepted, however, he or she received endless attention. Influential physicians like Soranus and Galen (second century C.E.) detailed explicit instructions on how to raise an infant, and all the child-rearing advice focused on molding the baby to be shapely, disciplined, and obedient. Newborns were tightly bound in strips

Child-rearing practices of cloth for two months to ensure that their limbs would grow straight. Once a day they were unwrapped to be bathed in a tepid bath. Parents would then stretch, massage, and shape the screaming babies before tightly wrapping them again. Noble children were usually breast-fed by a wet nurse (a slave woman who had recently had a child), and many physicians recommended that children begin to drink sweet wine at 6 months. Infant mortality was high despite the recommendations of physicians and the attentions of loving parents—fewer than half of the newborns raised reached puberty.

At the age of 6 or 7, children were put in the care of tutors, and their formal education began. Patrician children of both genders were expected to receive an education so as to transmit Roman culture to the next generations. Girls also learned to spin and weave wool, activities that consumed much of their time in their adult years.

By age 12, boys had graduated to higher schooling, learning literature, arithmetic, geometry, music, astronomy, and logic. This general education prepared boys for public life—the honorable and expected course for a wealthy boy. If a boy was talented, at age 16 he began an advanced study of rhetoric. This skill would help him later to speak persuasively to the crowds that had so much influence on the political life of the Republic.

Life in the City

By the late Republic (ca. 50 B.C.E.), the population of Rome had reached an astounding 1,000,000. The richest lived on the hills (shown on **Map 4.1**), aloof from the bustle of the crowds and the smells of the lower city. They surrounded themselves with elegance and beauty and often decorated their houses with wall paintings called frescoes.

The painting in **Figure 4.6** adorned the inner wall of a house of a wealthy Roman and shows an urban scene where attractive houses range up the hills. This view not only gives us a sense of what the ideal city looked like but also reveals the degree to which Romans praised the urban life that formed the heart of Roman culture. The decorated door at the front of the painting demonstrates how separate the noble Roman's private space was from the public space of the colonnaded temple at the top of the illustration. At this front door, clients gathered in the hopes of

FIGURE 4.5 Family Gravestone, first century B.C.E.   This memorial stone of Lucius Vibius and his wife and child captures the qualities of the ideal republican Roman family: serious and modest, with no visible emotion.

being welcomed in. Even in this urban life, Romans did not forget their affection for the land—notice the potted plants near the door. The houses of the wealthy featured elaborate, well-tended pleasure gardens and fountains. Even landless renters kept potted plants on the terraces and balconies of their apartment buildings.

Below the hills, most city dwellers lived in small houses or crowded, multistoried tenements. The region of the city called Subura was the most notorious, and as **Map 4.1** shows, it was near the Forum and at the foot of the most prestigious house on the Palatine Hill. People brought water from the public fountains and heated their homes with open flames or burning charcoal. Waste ran down sewers and washed out of the city, but never with the efficiency that modern hygiene requires. Townspeople dumped garbage just outside city walls near the cemetery for the poor, where shallowly buried corpses rotted and carrion crows circled endlessly. Wealthy urban men and women carried little bouquets of fragrant flowers that they held to their noses to protect themselves from the smells of the city.

In addition to being the political center of Rome, the Forum was the economic and social center. Two rows of shops lined the large square, and merchants shouted, hawking their wares as slaves shopped for the household needs. In the afternoon, work ceased and the men headed for the baths. (Women, too, probably had public Life in the Forum bathing time set aside for them as well, but the historical evidence for the Republic does not explicitly discuss it.) The baths served much as a

FIGURE 4.6 Urban Scene Fresco, ca. 45 B.C.E. When Mount Vesuvius erupted in 79 C.E., it buried a beautiful villa at Boscoreale, near Pompeii. Excavations have uncovered magnificent frescoes such as this urban scene that was painted on a wall to give the illusion of looking out a window at the urban spaces the Romans designed and built so well.

modern health club. People exercised or played ball, swam, took steam baths, had massages, got their body hair plucked, and socialized. Then, in the late afternoon and evening, it was time for leisure. The crowds in the Forum strolled, chatted, and gossiped. Romans always included a political dimension in this informal talk, for here politicians gained nicknames like "knock-knees" or more obscene appellations. In the course of passing on rumors and jokes, Romans helped set future political fortunes.

In the afternoon and at home, men abandoned their togas (a huge length of unbleached wool, carefully wrapped around the wearer) and wore their undergarments: usually a tunic that came down to the thighs. Men who wore sleeves or long tunics were considered effeminate. Women, on the other hand, covered themselves with long, sleeved tunics that they wore under their dresses.

As in cities today, life in the urban heart of Rome was a mixture of ease and hardship, and of excitement, fellowship, and danger. Yet this complex, vibrant center marked the ideal of the Republic: a place where citizens met and mingled in a public setting, and where political and economic dramas unfolded. Unfortunately for the Romans, this appealing way of life could not last. As Rome expanded, its spectacular military successes brought changes that undermined the Roman civic ideal.

EXPANSION AND TRANSFORMATION,
265–133 B.C.E.

The Romans who enjoyed and contributed so much to the good life of the city represented only a part of the population. Rome's success derived primarily from its army. Over time, the army began to define the very structure of what was becoming an empire. As we saw in the example of Cincinnatus, the army of the Republic was made up of citizen-soldiers who set aside their work to fight for a season. When Rome's leaders believed they were threatened by foreign invaders, the consuls raised a red flag in the Forum. Then free householders throughout the territory—that is, tax-paying men between the ages of 17 and 46—had to report to the capitol within thirty days. From this large group, the consuls and military tribunes chose their army.

Weapons and discipline

The Romans' Victorious Army

By the early Republic, the army was organized in legions of about 4,000 men—about 40 companies of 100 men each, although the actual numbers that constituted a legion or a company varied over time. These were mostly foot soldiers fighting bare-legged in their tunics. All soldiers took an oath binding themselves to the army until death or the end of the war. The remarkable strength of this citizen army lay in its unequaled discipline. For example, commanders practiced decimation, in which one soldier in ten was killed if a unit disobeyed an order or failed badly. Traditionally, warfare in the Mediterranean was governed by informal rules that allowed surrender before either side suffered extensive losses. The Roman soldier, however, hated to return home defeated. The shame of it would prevent him from resuming his life in the city where everyone met face-to-face in the Forum.

The Roman army was an obedient, iron-willed fighting machine under the strict command of its leaders. Roman soldiers ate only wheat bread and drank only water while at war. In hot weather, they added some vinegar. Sometimes during campaigns in which the wheat ran out, the soldiers had to eat meat, but they feared the meat would "soften" them and erode their invincibility. They sneered at their opponents who slept heavily on wine and food, and this attitude probably gave them confidence in the heat of battles. The iron discipline extended to camp life, because soldiers could not rest until they had fortified their camp to make them impregnable to surprise attack. **Figure 4.7a** shows soldiers building such a camp after a long day's march.

The victorious republican soldier returned after a season of fighting with only a few gold coins in his

FIGURE 4.7(a)

Trajan's Column

This relief carving (a) is a detail of one of the winding panels from Trajan's Column, which was dedicated in 113 C.E. to celebrate the emperor Trajan's victories in war. The full column is shown on the right (b). Even though this column is from later than the republican period, it remains one of the important historical sources for Roman military life. The scene highlighted here depicts soldiers, dressed in battle armor (except

FIGURE 4.7(b)

their helmets), building a camp—a common daily activity for soldiers while they were on campaign.

Connecting Art & Society

1. What specific tasks are the soldiers performing?

2. Why do you think the artists included these tasks on a column celebrating a military victory?

3. How did these activities contribute to the might of the Roman army?

---

hand and the pride of victory in his heart. Through a relentless series of such victories, by 265 B.C.E. Rome had unified virtually the whole Italian peninsula (see **Map 4.2**). However, the Republic's growing wealth and power clashed with new foes outside the peninsula. These contests would transform the army, the Republic, and the Romans.

Wars of the Mediterranean

As we saw in **Map 4.2,** after Rome consolidated its hold on the Italian peninsula, it confronted Carthage, the other great power in the western Mediterranean. Carthage was founded around the same time as the city of Rome (ca. 800 B.C.E.) by a group of colonists from Phoenicia. The colony profited from its trade, prospered, and became a diverse and cosmopolitan

city as great as those of the Hellenistic kingdoms. At the height of its power, the population of Phoenician Carthage probably approached 400,000, of whom no more than 100,000 were of fairly pure Phoenician heritage. In the busy shops, merchants spoke Greek and many other languages of the Mediterranean as they sold wares drawn from the farthest reaches of the Hellenistic kingdoms.

The skillful Phoenician sailors even ventured outside the Mediterranean basin, trading along the western coast of Africa. The Greek historian Herodotus (ca. 484–ca. 424 B.C.E.) described how Carthaginian merchants traded with African tribes, relying on mutual trust instead of language skills. The merchants unloaded their cargo on the African shore, summoned local tribesmen by smoke signals, and then returned to their ships. The Africans approached and laid out what they thought would be a fair amount for the goods and then withdrew without taking the goods until the Carthaginians indicated their agreement on the price. As Herodotus wrote, "They say that thus neither party is ill-used; for the Carthaginians do not take the gold until they have the worth of their merchandise, nor do the natives touch the merchandise until the Carthaginians have taken the gold." By the third century B.C.E., the wealthy, enterprising Carthaginians had gained control of many territories in the western Mediterranean (see **Map 4.2**) and confronted the growing power of the Roman Republic.

Rome's expansion and growing alliances began to encroach upon the Carthaginians, who had controlled the western Mediterranean for so long, and it was only a matter of time before tensions came to a head. Rome's clash with Carthage began over who would control the Sicilian city of Messana, an area that the Romans saw as strategically vital to the security of southern Italy because it was on the straits between the island and the mainland (see **Map 4.2**). Carthage, for its part, resented the idea of Rome as a presence in Sicily. In 264 B.C.E., both sides sent troops in an effort to conquer the disputed island. This confrontation began the first of three hostile encounters between Rome and Carthage, called the Punic Wars. *Punic* meant "Phoenician," by which the Romans recalled the origins of the Carthaginians.

First Punic War

But to broaden their military efforts beyond Italy, the Romans needed ships. The city managed to raise some money and build a fleet, yet it had trouble finding admirals who had any solid seafaring experience. The Romans nevertheless demonstrated their famous tenacity and designed a new warship that would change the nature of naval battles. Before the Romans, the basic tactic at sea was ramming one ship into another, thus sinking the second. Sometimes sailors would board the opposing ship to engage the enemy, but not very often. The Romans changed this. They developed a new vessel that featured a special platform that allowed many infantrymen on board. When they approached an opposing ship, Roman soldiers could then board the enemy vessel and fight hand to hand, a style that was their specialty. In the Punic Wars, Carthaginian naval commanders did what usually brought them success—they rammed the Roman ships. Before the Carthaginian vessel could pull away, however, a platform descended and Roman troops swept across, taking the lightly manned Carthaginian ship. The Romans would then simply scuttle their own destroyed ship and seize the Carthaginian one. **Figure 4.8** shows one of these impressive warships with infantrymen poised to fight.

New Roman navy

FIGURE 4.8 Roman Warship The Roman infantry was unbeatable, but when Romans challenged Carthage, they had to learn to fight at sea. Instead of ramming an opponent's ship, Romans lowered a gangplank so that their infantry, shown here, could board the enemy ship and fight by hand.

In 241 B.C.E., Rome finally won a decisive sea battle against Carthage, and the First Punic War ended with a Roman victory. The Republic received control of Sicily and a large financial indemnity from the Carthaginians. But the larger question of who would control the western Mediterranean remained unresolved. A second contest seems to have been inevitable.

The Second Punic War (218–201 B.C.E.) began in Spain, where Rome and Carthage had signed a treaty dividing the spheres of influence at the Ebro River (see **Map 4.3**). However, the treaty left one issue unresolved: Who would control the city of Saguntum, which lay south of the Ebro? Under the terms of the treaty it was in Carthaginian territory, but Rome had an alliance with Saguntum that predated the treaty. The Carthaginian general, Hannibal Barca, attacked Saguntum and in the process began the Second Punic War. This war was different from the first one, for when war was declared, the Romans had control of the sea, so Carthaginians knew victory would come only if they brought war to Rome itself.

Second Punic War

The Carthaginians may have lacked a fleet, but in their general Hannibal they possessed one of the greatest military strategists in history. The confident general surprised the Romans by taking the war to Italy, moving his large Hellenistic-style army overland from Spain into the peninsula. Now Roman legions had to confront the military power of armies that included war elephants. Crossing the Alps with 30,000 to 40,000 men, 6,000 horses, and about 35 elephants was a difficult feat; many men and elephants fell and died in the dangerous passes. However, Hannibal emerged in northern Italy with enough of an army (complete with a dozen or so elephants) to shock the local population and win many victories.

Hannibal expected Rome's subject peoples to rise up in his support, and while some did, the inner

MAP 4.3

Expansion of the Roman Republic, 264–44 B.C.E.

This map shows the expansion of the Republic as it fought victorious wars against Carthage and the Macedonian and Seleucid kingdoms in the East. Notice the scale for distances.

Explore the Map

1. How hard would it have been for the Carthaginian general Hannibal to transport his army and elephants across the distances from Spain to Italy? Why?

2. Given Rome's expansion, how likely was it that the Hellenistic kingdoms of the Seleucids and Ptolemies would come into conflict with Rome?

3. How would Romans become influenced by Hellenistic culture in these conquests?

---

core of central Italy stayed loyal. The strong alliance system that Rome had built gave it a huge advantage. Nevertheless, the astonishing general handed Rome its worst defeat ever at the Battle of Cannae in 216 B.C.E., in which approximately 30,000 Romans died (see **Map 4.3**). Document 4.2 describes this significant battle and shows Hannibal's battle plan. Romans were shocked and frightened—for years Roman mothers would scare naughty children with the threat "Hannibal will get you"—and yet the Romans would not surrender. They adopted a defensive attitude of delay and refusal to fight while the Carthaginian forces marched up and down Italy for almost seventeen years—wreaking havoc along the way.

Finally, Rome produced a general who could match Hannibal's skill. Publius Cornelius Scipio (236–183 B.C.E.) had studied Carthaginian battlefield tactics and had the skill to improve on them. Scipio took Carthage's Spanish lands and then sailed to North Africa, bringing the war to Carthage. Hannibal had to leave Italy to defend his homeland, and he had to face the Romans virtually unaided. The

thinking about

DOCUMENTS

DOCUMENT 4.2

Hannibal Triumphs at the Battle of Cannae

The Battle of Cannae, 216 B.C.E.

Rome
→ Advance ■ Infantry
→ Retreat   ■ Cavalry

Carthage
→ Advance ■ Infantry
→ Retreat   ■ Cavalry

Cannae

Cannae

The Carthaginians, led by Hannibal, were able to inflict the single greatest defeat of the Romans in the history of their empire. By feigning retreat and convincing the Romans that they were abandoning Cannae, the Carthaginian army was able to surround the Romans and defeat them without mercy. This defeat caused great alarm to the citizens of Rome, as it left them nearly defenseless.

FIGURE 4.9 The Battle of Cannae, 216 B.C.E.

The Roman historian Florus (ca. 70–ca. 140 C.E.) wrote History of the Romans, *in which he recounted the long-remembered Battle of Cannae (216 B.C.E.), a turning point during the Second Punic War between Rome and Carthage. Military thinkers today still study Hannibal's winning battle strategy, but Florus notes Hannibal's mistake. Study* **Figure 4.9** *to understand Hannibal's winning strategy.*

The fourth and almost mortal wound of the Roman Empire was at Cannæ, an obscure village of Apulia; which, however, became famous by the greatness of the defeat, its celebrity being acquired by the slaughter of forty thousand men. Here the general, the ground, the face of heaven, the day, indeed, all nature conspired together for the destruction of the unfortunate army. For Hannibal, the most artful of generals, not content with sending pretended deserters among the Romans, who fell upon their rear as they were fighting, but having also noted the nature of the ground in those open plains, where the heat of the sun is extremely violent, the dust very great, and the wind blows constantly, and as it were statedly, from the east, drew up his army in such a position that, while the Romans were exposed to all these inconveniences, he himself, having heaven, as it were, on his side, fought with wind, dust, and sun in his favor. Two vast armies, in consequence, were slaughtered till the enemy were satiated, and till Hannibal said to his soldiers, "Put up your swords." Of the two commanders, one escaped, the other was slain; which of them showed the greater spirit is doubtful. Paulus was ashamed to survive; Varro did not despair. Of the greatness of the slaughter the following proofs may be noticed: that the Aufidus was for some time red with blood; that a bridge was made of dead bodies, by order of Hannibal, over the torrent of Vergellus, and that two *modii* of rings were sent to Carthage, and the equestrian dignity estimated by measure.

It was afterward not doubted but that Rome might have seen its last day, and that Hannibal, within five days, might have feasted in the Capitol, if—as they say that Adherbal, the Carthaginian, the son of Bomilcar, observed—"he had known as well how to use his victory as how to gain it." But at that crisis, as is generally said, either the fate of the city that was to be empress of the world, or his own want of judgment, and the influence of deities unfavorable to Carthage, carried him in a different direction. When he might have taken advantage of his victory, he chose rather to seek enjoyment from it, and, leaving Rome, to march into Campania and to Tarentum, where both he and his army soon lost their vigor, so that it was justly remarked that "Capua proved a Cannæ to Hannibal"; since the sunshine of Campania and the warm springs of Baiæ subdued—who could have believed it?—him who had been unconquered by the Alps and unshaken in the field.

SOURCE: Florus, *History of the Romans*, in *The Great Events by Famous Historians*, vol. II, ed. Rossiter Johnson (The National Alumni, 1905), pp. 186–187.

Analyze the Document

1. What are the tactics of ancient battles, and in what ways is Hannibal particularly skilled?

2. How much devastation is caused by the Battle of Cannae? Why does this destruction make the battle so traumatic to Romans?

3. Why does Hannibal not follow up with a decisive victory?

Roman control of the sea prevented the Carthaginian ally Philip V of Macedonia (of the Hellenistic Macedonian kingdom discussed in Chapter 3) from helping, and Carthaginian support in North Africa was weak. Scipio decisively defeated Hannibal at the Battle of Zama in 202 B.C.E. (see **Map 4.3**) and won the surname "Africanus" to commemorate his great victory that saved Rome. Carthage again sued for peace—giving up Spain and promising not to wage war without Rome's permission. But peace would prove temporary.

Carthage was placed in a difficult position, for Numidia, one of Rome's allies in North Africa, was encroaching on its territory. Yet Carthage could not wage war against Numidia without Rome's permission, and Rome withheld it. The Senate was led by Cato the Elder (234–149 B.C.E.), who was

Third Punic War

virulently anti-Carthaginian. Plutarch recorded his famous rousing speech in 150 B.C.E. as he tried to spur his countrymen to resume the fighting against Carthage. He reminded the Senate that Carthage was "only three days' sail from Rome," and he ended all his speeches with the phrase "Carthage must be destroyed." Cato spoke for many Romans who wanted to take on their old enemy again. The inflammatory language worked, and the Third Punic War began. After a long siege of the citadel at the top of the hill overlooking the town, Rome crushed the city of Carthage in 146 B.C.E. The Carthaginian general surrendered, and his wife, accusing him of cowardice, committed suicide by leaping with her two children into the flames of the burning city. The Roman general—another Scipio called Aemilianus—reputedly shed tears at the sight of the ruin of the great city. The once-shining city of Carthage would lie in ruins for a century until Rome itself recolonized it.

The wars against Carthage drew the Romans into battling in the eastern Mediterranean, leading to three wars against Macedonia between 215 and ca. 168 B.C.E. Romans felt drawn into the first war because the Macedonian king, Philip V (221–179 B.C.E.), had allied with Hannibal after the Roman defeat at Cannae. Following this indecisive war, Rome was again drawn into eastern affairs as some of the Greek poleis solicited Rome's help against a coalition between the

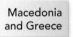

Macedonia and Greece

Macedonian and Seleucid kings. This time Rome won decisively and Macedonia agreed to stay out of Greek affairs. The third war arose when Macedonia again tried to reassert control over Greece. As a result of this war, Rome ruthlessly divided up Macedonia and eliminated any opposition.

At first, Rome left the Greeks "free," but there quickly arose a difference of opinion about the meaning of this term. The Greeks believed freedom meant to do as they liked; Romans believed it meant to act as obedient Roman clients. The Roman Senate finally ran out of patience and decided to annex the Greek mainland. To set an example to the recalcitrant Greeks, a Roman commander burned the city of Corinth, enslaved its inhabitants, and brought rich plunder back to Rome. The expansion eastward had begun, and it continued with the establishment of the province of Asia in 137 B.C.E., when the last king of Pergamum died, willing his land to Rome. Money, art, and slaves now flowed from the east to Rome, and the Republic had to decide how to govern its new far-flung conquests (see **Map 4.3**).

Historians still disagree about Rome's motives for continuing the warfare. Rome often marched to protect its allies—waging what they called "just wars." At the same time, some Romans were becoming rich in these enterprises, and Roman generals saw war as the road to upward mobility. Now the path to success for

an ambitious Roman lay not in impressing his fellow citizens in the Forum, but in leading victorious armies.

Rome did not always annex territories outright. Sometimes it operated through client states, leaving local rulers in place. Sometimes victorious Romans established the conquered territories as provinces—one in Africa, one in Asia, and later across the Alps in Gaul (southern France) in an area that is still called Provence. Within the provinces, people lived as they had in the past, but Rome's leaders expected these states to conform to their wishes (which at times caused friction). Governors were appointed by the Roman Senate to preserve peace and administer justice to Roman citizens. Other duties were given to private individuals, who could make fortunes performing administrative duties. For example, tax collectors received a contract to collect a certain amount of taxes, and they could legally keep some profits they squeezed from local populations. The governors were supposed to make sure tax collectors did not abuse their privilege, but, not surprisingly, many of them took full advantage of this system and extracted huge amounts of money from helpless residents. The conquests in Italy had yielded most profits from land. In the provinces, on the other hand, people made money from land, slaves, and graft. In the process, the Roman Republic itself was transformed in various ways by its military success abroad.

Administering provinces

An Influx of Slaves

In the ancient world, successful military campaigning earned a victor not just new territory and riches but also slaves. As Rome expanded, it accumulated more and more bondsmen and -women. After the Second Punic War, more than 200,000 men and women were captured as prisoners of war and brought to Italy as slaves. Numbers like these changed the nature of Roman society. Now, instead of each small householder having one to three slaves (as we saw was the pattern in

---

EXPANSION OF ROME

340 B.C.E.	Revolt of Latin allies
264–241 B.C.E.	First Punic War
263 B.C.E.	Rome rules Italian peninsula
218–203 B.C.E.	Hannibal fights in Italy
218–201 B.C.E.	Second Punic War
215–ca. 168 B.C.E.	Wars of Macedonia
149–146 B.C.E.	Third Punic War
148–146 B.C.E.	Macedonia and Greece become provinces

KEY DATES

ancient Greece), rich households might have hundreds of domestic slaves. By the end of the Republic, there were between two and three million slaves in Italy, an astounding 35 to 40 percent of the population.

Thousands of slaves labored in agriculture or mining, working in large anonymous gangs. However, in the cities, slaves and citizens often worked in the same occupations, and all could earn money through their labor. The most undesirable jobs—garbage collection, mining, acting, and prostitution—were generally reserved for slaves, although freed men and women, while technically citizens, were willing to do the most lucrative of these jobs. Often slaves dominated some of the higher-status jobs. After Rome's conquest of Greece (ca. 148 B.C.E.), most of the tutors and teachers to Roman children were Greek slaves. The Biography on page 125 describes the successful career of a playwright who had been a slave. Most physicians were either Greek or trained in Greece, and it was not unusual for physicians to be succeeded by their Greek slaves, whom they had trained and then freed to take their place.

Perhaps not surprisingly, Romans often feared their slaves. The Stoic philosopher Seneca (4 B.C.E.–65 C.E.) wrote that "the least of your slaves holds over you the power of life or death." As the numbers of slaves increased, Romans had more and more reason to worry, and they passed laws to try to protect themselves. For example, the punishment for murdering one's master was severe—all the slaves in the household were to be executed. The Roman historian Tacitus (ca. 56–ca. 120 C.E.) recorded an incident when an ex-consul was murdered by a slave. A senator arguing that the state should enforce the harsh law and kill the whole household said: "Whom will a large number of slaves keep safe, when four hundred could not protect Pedanius Secundus? . . . In every wholesale punishment there is some injustice to individuals, which is compensated by the advantage to the state." Not only did individual instances of slave treachery crop up, but large-scale slave rebellions broke out as well.

Three great slave uprisings disrupted Italy and Sicily between 135 and 71 B.C.E. The most famous was led by the gladiator Spartacus between 73 and 71 B.C.E. Spartacus escaped his master with 70 of his fellow gladiators. Many others joined them as the army of almost 70,000 slaves ravaged portions of Italy. They succeeded in defeating many of the soldiers sent after them. Some sources suggest that Spartacus even tried to take his army to Sicily to rally the slaves there but could not gather enough ships to cross the sea. Spartacus was finally killed and the rebellion crushed. Six thousand of Spartacus's followers were crucified—the brutal form of execution reserved for slaves. This revolt was suppressed, but Rome did not forget the potential for violence that simmered within the many men and women they had enslaved in their imperial expansion.

Economic Disparity and Social Unrest

Just as the expansion of Rome altered the nature of slavery, it transformed many other aspects of life in the Republic. These changes were noted sadly by many conservative Romans who watched their traditional way of life fade. One Roman (Silius Italicus) lamented the aftermath of Rome's victory in the Punic Wars: "[I]f it was fated that the Roman character should change when Carthage fell, would that Carthage was still standing." But such qualms were too late; the Republic was transmuting into something else entirely, even as some Romans mourned it.

One of the most noticeable changes came in the form of increasing disparity between rich and poor. Many of the upper classes had grown very rich indeed. Governors of provinces had the opportunity to make fortunes undreamed of in the Republic's earlier years. Other enterprising Romans made fortunes in shipbuilding contracts, banking, slave trading, and many other high-profit occupations. Rome had become a Hellenistic state like the successor states of Alexander the Great (see Chapter 3), with a growing distance between the rich and the poor.

While some Romans amassed great fortunes, others suffered a worsening of their economic situations. The example of Cincinnatus, who fought for only one season and then returned to his plow, was impossible to repeat when foes were far away and wars long. During the Punic Wars, military time was extended. As a result, more than 50 percent of adult males spent over seven years in the army, and some spent as long as twenty years. Throughout most of the Republic, the army was not formally paid, and this caused both some hardship and a particularly strong relationship between soldiers and their generals. By right, generals controlled all booty taken in war, and they distributed some of it to their troops. Thus generals acted as patrons to their client soldiers, who increasingly owed loyalty to their general rather than to Rome itself. Meanwhile, as soldiers stayed longer in the army, their family fields remained unplowed. Numerous farmers went bankrupt, and soldiers returned to their homes to find them sold and their wives and children turned out of the family farm.

Newly rich men and women eagerly purchased these neglected lands, and small landholders were replaced by large plantations worked by gangs of new slaves. Fields that had cultivated wheat were slowly transformed to produce olives and wine grapes, much more lucrative crops. Other great landowners in Italy grew rich on ranches that raised animals for meat, milk, or wool. Now Romans had to import their wheat from abroad, particularly North Africa.

Slave occupations

Slave revolts

BIOGRAPHY

Publius Terentius Afer (Terence) (ca. 190–159 B.C.E.)

During the peaceful interlude between the First and Second Punic Wars, a slave trader in Carthage purchased a young man named Terence. We have no idea how Terence came into the hands of a slave dealer; we do know he was not a prisoner of war. However, many North Africans were enslaved by the Carthaginians; Terence may have come from one such slave family. His surname, Afer, meaning "the African," suggests that he was not originally from Carthage. He was described as being "of medium stature, graceful in person, and of dark complexion," and some scholars have suggested that he was from a black sub-Saharan family. The ambiguity of Terence's background points to the cosmopolitan, highly diverse nature of the city of Carthage. It was one of the jewels of the Mediterranean—a bustling city where people mingled from all over and shared in a dynamic cultural life. Terence's early experience in the cosmopolitan city no doubt prepared him to contribute to Rome's growing interest in Hellenistic literature.

The young slave was brought to Rome and sold to a senator, M. Terentius Lucanus, who must have recognized the youth's promise. The senator had him educated as a freeman and then granted him his freedom. This is but one example of many talented slaves who were freed by their owners during the optimistic years of the Republic. Terence then pursued a literary career.

The intellectual gifts that had won Terence his freedom earned him the acceptance of an aristocratic circle of young men who were interested in literature. These educated youths were actively involved in fostering Greek literature, and such literary circles had much influence in Hellenizing Roman society.

At first, Terence was outside the guild of poets and the working playwrights. He made his artistic breakthrough when he got a chance to submit one of his plays for production to the aging but well-established poet Caecilius. Terence found out where the poet was dining and approached him as he reclined on his couch eating with friends. Because Terence was a stranger and plainly dressed, Caecilius invited him only to sit on a stool and recite from his work. After a few verses, however, the old poet was so impressed with Terence's talent that he invited him to join him on the couch and share the festive dinner. The budding playwright's career was launched.

Terence wrote six plays based on traditional Greek models, even specifying that they be performed in Greek dress. These plays show Terence's talent and understanding of both human nature and the social realities in Rome. Yet he received mixed reactions from the Romans. During his short lifetime, Terence was much criticized by other playwrights, and like so much else in Rome, these critiques were conducted publicly. Terence addressed his critics (and attacked other playwrights) in the prologues to the plays. These public debates tell us much about the openly competitive nature of the artistic world during the Republic.

Terence was accused first of plagiarism, meaning that someone else claimed to have been the first to translate Greek plays into Latin. In a prologue, Terence flatly denies "any knowledge of the play's previous Latinization." Terence was also charged with being "untraditional"—a serious insult to Romans. According to his accusers, he did not remain true to the Greek originals. Terence admitted that he combined plots and created interesting works of art rather than translations. As he put it, precise translations often turned "the best Greek plays . . . into Latin flops." These criticisms reveal a people struggling to discover a new art form and to determine the rules with which to judge it.

Terence challenged his audiences to judge his works on their own merits. Not surprisingly, many of his contemporaries appreciated his talent, for he did more than reproduce classic plays—he gave them his own stamp. For example, instead of simply relying on slapstick humor (as Plautus did), Terence developed a clever use of language to provide humor. He also used suspense as a dynamic device that would have a long history in the theater. His fame long outlasted him. Long after Terence's death, Cicero and Caesar, both known for their eloquence, praised his work as a model of elegant language. Audiences ever since have found his plays brilliant.

A Talented Slave

Unfortunately, Terence died while still in his prime. In 159 B.C.E., the 31-year-old undertook a journey to Greece, possibly to study theater or to escape the jealous rumors of his rivals. He died on the way, from either illness or shipwreck. He left a revered body of work that people still enjoy and appreciate today. Perhaps equally important, Terence exemplified the kind of upward mobility available to educated slaves during an age when Rome fell in love with Greek intellectual life.

Connecting People & Society

1. How does Terence's life demonstrate the Hellenizing of the Republic after the North African conquests?

2. What does this life reveal about the nature of Roman slavery?

3. What problems does Terence face, and what do they reveal about Roman culture?

Spurred by economic hardship, the displaced citizens flocked to the city. The population swelled with a new class of people—propertyless

New poverty

day laborers who were unconnected to the structures of patronage and land that had defined the early Republic. These mobs created more and more problems for the nobility because they always represented a potentially revolutionary force in the Forum. Aristocrats tried to keep them happy and harmless by subsidizing food, but this short-term solution could not solve the deeper problem of lost jobs taken by newly captured slaves and land seized by the newly rich. The situation had become volatile indeed.

THE HELLENIZING OF THE REPUBLIC

As if these social tensions were not disruptive enough, new intellectual influences further modified Rome's traditional value system. As the Republican armies conquered some of the great centers of Hellenistic culture from Greece to North Africa, Romans became deeply attracted to many of the Hellenistic ways. As the Roman poet Horace (65–8 B.C.E.) observed: "Captive Greece took her Captor Captive." With the capture of slaves from Greece, Greek art, literature, and learning came to Rome, and many in the Roman aristocracy became bilingual, adding Greek to their native Latin. Rome became a Hellenized city, with extremes of wealth and poverty and a growing emphasis on individualism over obedience to the family.

Cato the Elder (234–149 B.C.E.)—the anti-Carthaginian orator—was one Roman who feared the changes that came with the increasing wealth and love of things Greek, and when he held the office of censor (see **Figure 4.3**), he tried to stem the tide of Hellenization. The office of censor had come to be an influential one. During the early Republic, censors had made lists of citizens and their property qualifications, but in time the censors became so powerful that they revised the lists of senators, deleting

Resisting change

those whose behavior they deemed objectionable. To preserve the old values, Cato tried taxing luxury goods and charging fines to those who neglected their farms, but his efforts were in vain. Romans had added an appreciation of Greek beauty to their own practical skills, and they adopted a new love of luxury and power that seemed to erode the moral strength of old Rome. To men like Cato, the Republic was becoming unrecognizable.

Roman Engineering: Fusing Utility and Beauty

Most of the great building projects that so characterize Rome arose in the building boom during the early years of the empire, as we will see in the next chapter. However, the techniques that led to those projects were developed during the Republic and were refined by the influx of Greek ideas and artists during the wars of expansion in the third and second centuries B.C.E. During these years Rome developed a new aesthetic sense that combined its traditional love of utility with the Hellenistic ideals of beauty.

As we have seen, the Romans had learned much about engineering from the Etruscans, especially techniques for draining swamps and building conduits to move water.

Engineering

The early Romans had a strong practical side themselves and greatly admired feats of science and engineering. The Roman orator Cicero revealed this admiration when he traveled to Syracuse in 75 B.C.E. to visit the grave of Archimedes, the esteemed engineer we met in Chapter 3. When Cicero discovered that Archimedes' countrymen had forgotten him, he found the old engineer's grave and restored it.

Rome's military success stemmed in part from the engineering achievements that supported the legions. For example, armies had to forge many rivers, and the Roman engineers invented ingenious devices to help them. General Julius Caesar (100–44 B.C.E.), in his account of one military campaign, described how he had to sink heavy timbers into the fast-moving Rhine River to build a bridge. The task was completed in ten days, and the army crossed. Engineers could build pontoon bridges even faster by floating flat-bottomed boats down the river and anchoring them at the intended crossing.

Perhaps Rome's greatest military engineering lay in the area of siege engines. Caesar described how the Romans patiently built a tall, fortified mound and tower next to a city they were besieging. As some soldiers fought from the top of the tower, they protected others who were beneath sturdy beams below. These hidden soldiers were then able to dismantle the bottom of the wall, causing it to collapse so the army could enter and take the city. Some Roman siege engines were so impressive that even Chinese sources documented them.

Engineering skills also brought many benefits to civilian life. The arch is a key example. The Greeks used post and lintel construction, which limited the variety of structures they could build. By using arches, Romans enhanced the size, range, and flexibility of their constructions. The use of the arch can most readily be seen in the aqueducts—perhaps the greatest examples of Roman civil engineering. Aqueducts brought water from rivers or springs into cities.

Romans had a huge thirst for water. The first aqueduct, the Aqua Appia, was built as early as 312 B.C.E., and it brought water through underground pipes from about 8 miles

Aqueducts

outside Rome. Later aqueducts used both subterranean pipes and overhead pipes mounted on arches, which allowed the engineers to adjust the height of the aqueduct to regulate the rate of the water flowing through the channel at the top. The more than 46-mile-long Claudian aqueduct, finished in 52 C.E., cost a fortune, what would be millions of dollars today. By the end of the first century C.E., nine aqueducts directed an astonishing 22,237,000 gallons of water into the city each day. (**Map 4.1** shows the locations of Rome's aqueducts.)

Rome exported these marvels of engineering to cities throughout the Mediterranean world, and some of the best-preserved aqueducts are outside Rome itself. **Figure 4.10** shows the most spectacular surviving aqueduct, the Pont du Gard outside Nîmes in southern France, which spans the River Gard and its valley. The water flows through an enclosed channel on the top, and a roadway runs over the lowest row of arches. Structures like these were marvels of Roman engineering, featuring solid design, practical application, visual appeal, and durability.

FIGURE 4.10 Pont du Gard Aqueduct, late first century B.C.E. Roman engineers built monumental aqueducts to carry water over great distances into their cities. This aqueduct in southern France brought water from springs 30 miles away to serve the city of Nîmes. The careful engineering maintains a constant decline, allowing the water to flow freely and gently.

Concrete: A New Building Material

In the late third century B.C.E., Roman architects discovered a new building material that opened even more architectural possibilities than the perfection of the arch. Masons found that mixing volcanic brickearth with lime and water resulted in a strong, waterproof building material—concrete. With this new substance, architects could design large, heavy buildings in a variety of shapes.

Combining concrete construction with the knowledge of the arch allowed for even more flexibility than before. After they had mastered the arch, Romans built with barrel vaults, a row of arches spanning a large space. As early as 193 B.C.E., builders constructed a gigantic warehouse in Rome using this technique. Concrete and barrel vaults also made possible the design of large bathhouses, for the concrete was strong enough to withstand the heat of steam rooms. Finally, the new technology permitted the design of the oval amphitheaters that so characterized Rome.

Of course, people as religious as the Romans applied their architectural skills to their temples as well. Although most structures in Rome were made of brick or concrete covered with stucco, the growing Hellenization began to influence architectural tastes. Marble columns would soon grace the traditional buildings. In this new architecture, we can see the degree of the Greek slaves' influence on the Romans and Rome's own growing appreciation of Hellenistic art.

The fullest development of this temple construction took place early in the empire. The outstanding example of Roman religious architecture is the **Pantheon,** a temple dedicated to all the gods, shown in **Figure 4.11.** It was built in 125 C.E. on the site of a previous temple that had been constructed during the late Republic. The structure is a perfect combination of Roman and Hellenistic styles and thus embodies the transformation of republican Rome imposed by Hellenistic influences. The front of the temple has a classical rectangular porch with Corinthian columns (see **Figure 2.9,** on page 62) and a pediment, the triangular structure on top of the columns. From the front, the Pantheon resembles the Greek temples we saw in Chapter 2. Inside the temple, however, any resemblance to Hellenistic architecture disappears.

The interior of the Pantheon consists of a massive round space (visible in **Figure 4.11**) covered by a high dome, revealing the Romans' engineering skills. A heavy concrete base supports the weight of the whole, while the upper walls are constructed of a lighter mix of concrete. The center of the dome has an opening

Pantheon

FIGURE 4.11 The Pantheon, 125 C.E. The Romans' use of concrete permitted the construction of stunning, enduring structures such as the Pantheon, a temple devoted to all the gods. The dome's circular hole, called the *oculus* (eye), reminded visitors of the eye of Jupiter that watched them continuously.

that lets in natural light—and rain, though drainpipes beneath the ground (which still function today) took care of flooding problems.

Latin Comedy and the Great Prose Writers, 240–44 B.C.E.

In the third century B.C.E., Roman literature emerged. Written in Latin, it reflected the elements we have discussed throughout this chapter: Roman values, society, and the influence of Hellenistic culture. The earliest surviving examples of Roman literature are comic plays. Latin comedy flowered with the works of Plautus (205–185 B.C.E.) and Terence (190–159 B.C.E.), who wrote plays based on Hellenistic models but modified them for their Italian audience. Plautus and Terence wrote in verse, but unlike their Greek predecessors, they added a good deal of music, with flutes and cymbals accompanying the productions.

Like the Hellenistic plays, most comedies involved the triumph of love over obstacles. In Plautus's works particularly, the humor centered on jokes and elaborate puns within the stories and the plays were marked by slapstick, bawdy humor. For example, in one play Plautus described a confrontation in which a man threatened to beat a slave. The man said: "Whoever comes here eats my fists." The slave responded: "I do not eat at night, and I have dined; Pray give your supper to those who starve." The audience would have laughed at the play on words associating a punch with food, as well as the suggestion that the nobles were not really charitable to the starving. The plays included all types of Roman characters, from smart, scheming slaves to boastful soldiers and clever prostitutes, to many clients and patrons. Thus, Romans who watched these plays recognized and laughed at all the types of people that populated their world.

The Latin prose literature of the Republic emphasized the serious side of Roman character. The best of the prose writers were men who combined literary talent with public service—for example, Cicero and Julius Caesar.

Latin literature was shaped—indeed defined—by the writings of Cicero, whose career coincided with the decline of the Republic. His skillful oratory and strong opinions about Roman values placed him in the center of public life, but his long-standing influence derived from his prose, not his political involvement. His writings cover an extraordinary range of **Cicero** topics, from poetry to formal orations to deeply personal letters. From his more than nine hundred letters, we get a revealing picture of the personality of this influential man. He was deeply concerned about public affairs and political morality, writing, "our leaders ought to protect civil peace with honor and defend it even at the risk of life itself." At the same time, his letters reveal him to be vindictive, mercurial of mood, and utterly self-centered. Although scholars are ambivalent about the character of this complex man, there is no doubt about his influence. Cicero's writings defined the best use of Latin language, and his works were used as textbooks of how to construct elegant prose.

Julius Caesar's literary legacy also grew out of his active political life. As Caesar rose to power, he used literature to enhance his reputation in Rome. His accounts of his daz- **Caesar's writings** zling military campaigns in Gaul (across the Alps in modern France), vividly told in his *Commentaries*, intensified his popularity and have fascinated generations ever since. His Latin is clear and accessible, and his narrative vivid and exciting.

By the middle of the second century B.C.E., the Roman Republic had reached a crucial threshold. Vibrant, wealthy, and victorious in war, the Republic had established political and social structures that steadily fueled its success. But in crafting their society, the Romans had unwittingly planted the seeds of their own undoing. Their much-loved precepts, established in a simpler age, would prove unsustainable in a future where Rome boldly sought to extend its reach farther than ever before.

THE TWILIGHT OF THE REPUBLIC, 133–44 B.C.E.

In the mid-second century B.C.E., Rome suffered a sudden economic downturn. The wars of expansion had brought vast riches into Rome, and this wealth drove prices up. When the wars ended, the influx of slaves and wealth subsided. Furthermore, an unfortunate grain shortage made grain prices skyrocket. This shortage worsened in 135 B.C.E. with the revolt of the slaves in Sicily. Half of Rome's grain supply came from Sicily, so the interruption of grain flow threatened to starve the masses of people who had fled to Rome when their own small farms had been taken over. To stave off disaster, two tribunes of the plebeians, Tiberius and Gaius Gracchus, proposed reforms. (The brothers were known as the Gracchi, which is the plural form of their name in Latin.)

The Reforms of the Gracchi, 133–123 B.C.E.

The Gracchi brothers came from a noble family, yet they devoted their lives to helping the Roman poor. They credited their mother, Cornelia, with giving them the education and motivation they needed to use their privilege for the good of the Roman people. The Gracchi seemed to many Romans to represent the best of republican men—devoted to a public life. Of course, many modern historians have observed that helping the poor would increase their own clients and prestige. Regardless of the motivations of the brothers, they set themselves apart from many aristocrats who no longer obeyed the rigorous demands of public service, preferring private pleasures instead. There were too few nobles willing to sacrifice their own interests for those of Rome when Tiberius became tribune of the plebeians in 133 B.C.E.

In Tiberius's view, Rome's problems came from the decline of the small farmer, which in turn prompted migrations into the city and a shift to large-scale and cash-crop agriculture. Tiberius compassionately expressed the plight of the displaced soldier-farmers: "They are styled masters of the world, and have not a clod of earth they can call their own." Tiberius recognized an additional problem with the growing landlessness—Rome did not have a pool of soldiers, for men had to meet a property qualification to enter the army. Thus,

Tiberius's reforms

the newly poor could neither farm nor serve in the army—Rome had moved a long way from the days of the farmer-soldier Cincinnatus.

Tiberius proposed an agrarian law that would redistribute public land to landless Romans. The idea may have made a difference, but it alarmed greedy landlords. The law passed, but the Senate appropriated only a tiny sum to help Tiberius administer the law. Many senators were particularly worried when Tiberius announced he was running for reelection. Although in the distant past, tribunes had run for a second term, that had not been done for a long time, and Tiberius's opponents argued that it was illegal. In the ensuing turmoil, a riot occurred at an assembly meeting, and some senators with their followers beat Tiberius and 300 of his followers to death. With one stroke, a new element emerged in Roman political life: political murder.

Tiberius's land law continued to operate for a time, but not very effectively. In 123 B.C.E. Tiberius's brother Gaius became tribune in an effort to continue his brother's work, and he wisely appealed to a broad sector of the

Gaius's reforms

Roman people. He built granaries, roads, and bridges to improve the distribution of grain into the city, and these projects created jobs for many Romans. Gaius also tried to fix the price of grain to keep it affordable, and he appealed to the equestrian order by giving them more influence in the wealthy provinces. Gaius opened the new Asian provinces to equestrian tax collectors and placed equestrians in the courts that tried provincial governors accused of abusing their powers. Many senators believed these reforms were politically motivated to destroy the Senate (which had destroyed Tiberius), and it was true that cheap grain might weaken the patron-client relationship that represented the backbone of senatorial power. The Senate moved to undo his reforms as soon as Gaius was out of office, and he and some 250 supporters were murdered in 122 B.C.E.—their deaths were arranged by one of the consuls supporting the Senate.

The Gracchi's sacrifices did not solve the Republic's problems. Their careers focused Rome's attention on its worries, but the brothers had also established a new style of republican government. From their time on, a struggle unfolded in Rome between men like the Gracchi, who enjoyed popular support (*populares*), and *optimates,* who intended to save the Republic by keeping power in the Senate. The old image of a nobility surrounded by and caring for its clients became supplanted by a much more confrontational model. The Gracchi were only the first to die in this struggle, and perhaps the greatest legacy of the Gracchi was the subsequent violence that descended upon the political arena. Roman public life would not be the same again.

Populares vs. Optimates: The Eruption of Civil Wars, 123–46 B.C.E.

Even as Rome experienced violence in its political life, life in the provinces, too, seemed threatened. In North Africa, Rome's old ally Numidia caused trouble, and the Gauls threatened Italy from the north. Just as the military emerged as a primary instrument of political power, the generals, especially, had new opportunities to play a role in internal politics. The political struggle between the *populares* and the *optimates* catalyzed by the Gracchi was continued by popular generals.

The first general to come to power based on the support of the army was Gaius Marius (ca. 157–86 B.C.E.). An equestrian tribune, Marius took up the cause of the *populares*. To address the problem of the African wars and the shortage of soldiers noted by Tiberius, Marius initiated a way of enlisting new soldiers that would redefine the Roman military. He created a professional army, eliminating the previous requirement that soldiers own property. In addition, he formally put the soldiers on the payroll, making official the previous informal patron-client relationship between generals and their troops. Marius also promised them land after their term of service. In this way, he cultivated an army with many rootless and desperate men who were loyal only to him. Although Marius could not foresee the results, his policies established a dangerous pattern that continued through the rest of Roman history. With his new army at his back, the victorious general decisively defeated first the Numidians in Africa and then the Celts to the north. In his battles against Africans and Celts, Marius was accompanied by a brilliant young second-in-command, Lucius Cornelius Sulla (ca. 138–78 B.C.E.). In these wars that brought Marius so much power, Sulla felt that his brave exploits deserved some of the credit that Marius took, and he seethed with resentment.

New crises paved the way for the *optimates* to restore their own power under the aristocrat Sulla, who had learned warfare and resentment from Marius. The first threat to Rome's safety came from within Italy itself—the Italian allies who had first been conquered wanted a greater share in the prosperity that Rome's conquests were bringing. The violent fighting that took place between 90 and 88 B.C.E. finally forced Rome to give full citizenship to the Italian allies. This revolt by the Italian allies is called the "Social War" (from the Latin word *socii*, which means "allies"). The violence that devastated much of the countryside further weakened the Republic. As one of the consuls for 88 B.C.E., Sulla commanded six legions in the final stages of the Italian wars, and his successes earned him a governorship in Asia, where he was given the command to lead the armies against a second threat to Rome—Mithridates (120–63 B.C.E.), a king in Asia Minor who was threatening Rome's borders. However, fearing Sulla's growing strength, the assembly called Marius out of retirement and tried to give him control of Sulla's army. Perhaps Sulla's most dramatic moment came when he marched his army directly into Rome to confront Marius. The hostilities between the two generals made a permanent mark on the city, changing the peaceful Forum into a war zone. After defeating Mithridates, Sulla returned to Rome in 83 B.C.E. to take up the cause of the *optimates*.

Sulla assumed the long-dormant office of dictator (see **Figure 4.3**) but violated tradition by making the term unlimited. He also repealed laws that favored equestrians, and he killed off his political opponents. He buttressed the power of the Senate by passing laws to guarantee it, instead of allowing the tradition of Senate leadership to suffice. The venerable Roman constitutional system was becoming changed, and power politics began to fill the vacuum.

With the wars of Marius and Sulla, a new question confronted Roman politicians: how to protect the citizens from people seeking power and personal gain. Clearly, the old system of checks and balances no longer worked. The next group of popular leaders bypassed most of the formal structures and made a private alliance to share power. Modern historians have called this agreement the First **Triumvirate,** or the rule by three men. A contemporary called it a "three-headed monster."

The First Triumvirate (60–49 B.C.E.) was made up of three men who appealed to various sectors of Roman society. Pompey, beloved of the *optimates*, was a brilliant general who had won striking battles in the east against Sulla's old enemy, Mithridates, and Mediterranean pirates. Julius Caesar was probably an even more talented general and brilliant orator, who won wars in Gaul and Britain and had the support of the

RISE AND FALL OF THE REPUBLIC

509 B.C.E.	Defeat of Etruscan monarchy
509–287 B.C.E.	Struggle of the Orders
451 B.C.E.	Twelve Tables published
133–123 B.C.E.	Reforms of the Gracchi
90–88 B.C.E.	Social Wars—Rome vs. Italian allies
60–49 B.C.E.	First Triumvirate
49–ca. 46 B.C.E.	Civil war—Caesar vs. Pompey
44 B.C.E.	Julius Caesar murdered

KEY DATES

populares. The third man was Crassus, a fabulously rich leader of the business community who had also led armies (including defeating the rebel slave Spartacus). In keeping with tradition in Roman society, the political alliance was sealed by marriage between Pompey and Caesar's daughter, Julia. Instead of bringing peace, however, the triumvirate simply became an arena in which the three powerful figures jockeyed for control.

Events soon came to a head. Crassus perished leading armies to confront a new threat in Rome's eastern frontier. Julia died in childbirth, along with her infant. With her death, little remained to hold Caesar and Pompey together. *Optimates* in the Senate co-opted Pompey in their desire to weaken the popular Caesar, and they declared Pompey sole consul in Rome. Pompey accepted this command from the Senate, breaking his agreement with Caesar, ensuring retribution from the popular general. Caesar defied the Senate, which had forbidden him to bring his army into Italy, and in 49 B.C.E. marched across the Rubicon River into Italy. There was no retreating from this defiant act—a new civil war had erupted.

Julius Caesar, 100–44 B.C.E.

Julius Caesar came from one of the oldest noble families of Rome. As with the Gracchi, his family associated itself with the *populares.* In the civil wars to come, Caesar enjoyed a high degree of support from the plebeians, but before he could take power, he needed the backing of an army. This he achieved in his wars of conquest in Gaul. Both his military successes and his captivating literary accounts of them won him broad popularity. According to the ancient writers, this accomplished general was tall with a fair complexion and piercing black eyes. The bust of Caesar shown in **Figure 4.12** reveals his memorable strength of character. Clearly a brilliant man in all fields, he enthralls historians today much as he fascinated his contemporaries.

The civil war between Caesar and Pompey that began in 49 B.C.E. was not limited to Italy; battles broke out throughout the Roman world. Caesar's and Pompey's armies clashed in Greece, North Africa, and Spain. After losing a decisive

Civil war battle in Greece in 48 B.C.E., Pompey fled to Egypt, where he was assassinated. When Caesar followed Pompey to Egypt, he became involved with Queen Cleopatra VII (r. 51–30 B.C.E.) (also discussed in Chapter 5), who was engaged in a dynastic struggle with her brother. Caesar supported her claims with his army, spent the winter with her, and fathered her child; then he left in the spring to continue the wars that consolidated his victory over Pompey's supporters. In 46 B.C.E., Caesar returned to Rome.

FIGURE 4.12 Julius Caesar One of the most controversial figures from the late Republic was Julius Caesar. As was customary with old patrician families, his family commissioned this bust after his death so that they and others would remember his deeds.

Cleopatra joined Caesar in Rome as he took up a task harder than winning the civil war: governing the Republic. The new leader faced two major challenges. First, he had to untangle the economic problems that had plagued the Republic since before the Gracchi attempted reform. Second, Rome needed a form of government that would restore stability to the factions that had burdened the city with so much violence.

Caesar applied his genius for organization to these practical tasks. He reformed the grain dole and established an ambitious program of public works to create jobs for the unemployed. To help displaced peasants, he launched a program of colonization all around the Mediterranean. Caesar's policies extended widely. With the help of an Egyptian astronomer who had accompanied Cleopatra to Rome, Caesar even reformed the calendar. The new "Julian calendar" introduced the solar year of 365 days and added an extra day every four years (the prototype of the "leap year"). With modifications made in 1582, the Julian calendar has remained in use throughout the West.

DOCUMENT 4.3

Conspirators Assassinate Julius Caesar

The ancient biographer Plutarch (46–120 C.E.) carefully chronicled the lives and deaths of ancient heroes, and his account of the assassination of Julius Caesar remains an important one. As Julius Caesar, the dictator for life, walked to the Senate building, he was surrounded by conspirators who stabbed him to death. After the murder, chaos reigned.

When Cæsar entered the house, the senate rose to do him honor. Some of Brutus' accomplices came up behind his chair, and others before it, pretending to intercede, along with Metillius Cimber, for the recall of his brother from exile. They continued their instances till he came to his seat. When he was seated he gave them a positive denial; and as they continued their importunities with an air of compulsion, he grew angry. Cimber, then, with both hands, pulled his gown off his neck, which was the signal for the attack. Casca gave him the first blow. It was a stroke upon the neck with his sword, but the wound was not dangerous; for in the beginning of so tremendous an enterprise he was probably in some disorder. Cæsar therefore turned upon him and laid hold of his sword. At the same time they both cried out, the one in Latin, "Villain! Casca! what dost thou mean?" and the other in Greek, to his brother, "Brother, help!"

After such a beginning, those who knew nothing of the conspiracy were seized with consternation and horror, insomuch that they durst neither fly nor assist, nor even utter a word. All the conspirators now drew their swords, and surrounded him in such a manner that, whatever way he turned, he saw nothing but steel gleaming in his face, and met nothing but wounds. Like some savage beast attacked by the hunters, he found every hand lifted against him, for they all agreed to have a share in the sacrifice and a taste of his blood. Therefore Brutus himself gave him a stroke in the groin. Some say he opposed the rest, and continued struggling and crying out till he perceived the sword of Brutus; then he drew his robe over his face and yielded to his fate. . . .

Cæsar thus despatched, Brutus advanced to speak to the senate and to assign his reasons for what he had done, but they could not bear to hear him; they fled out of the house and filled the people with inexpressible horror and dismay. Some shut up their houses; others left their shops and counters. All were in motion; one was running to see the spectacle; another running back. Antony and Lepidus, Cæsar's principal friends, withdrew, and hid themselves in other people's houses. Meantime Brutus and his confederates, yet warm from the slaughter, marched in a body with their bloody swords in their hands, from the senate house to the Capitol, not like men that fled, but with an air of gayety and confidence, calling the people to liberty, and stopping to talk with every man of consequence whom they met. There were some who even joined them and mingled with their train, desirous of appearing to have had a share in the action and hoping for one in the glory. . . .

Next day Brutus and the rest of the conspirators came down from the Capitol and addressed the people, who attended to their discourse without expressing either dislike or approbation of what was done. But by their silence it appeared that they pitied Cæsar, at the same time that they revered Brutus. The senate passed a general amnesty; and, to reconcile all parties, they decreed Cæsar divine honors and confirmed all the acts of his dictatorship; while on Brutus and his friends they bestowed governments and such honors as were suitable; so that it was generally imagined the Commonwealth was firmly established again, and all brought into the best order.

But when, upon the opening of Cæsar's will, it was found that he had left every Roman citizen a considerable legacy, and they beheld the body, as it was carried through the Forum, all mangled with wounds, the multitude could no longer be kept within bounds. They stopped the procession, and, tearing up the benches, with the doors and tables, heaped them into a pile, and burned the corpse there. Then snatching flaming brands from the pile, some ran to burn the houses of the assassins, while others ranged the city to find the conspirators themselves and tear them in pieces; but they had taken such care to secure themselves that they could not meet with one of them. . . .

SOURCE: Plutarch, "Lives," in *The Great Events by Famous Historians*, vol. II, ed. Rossiter Johnson (The National Alumni, 1905), pp. 328–329.

Analyze the Document

1. How did the chaos and confusion after Caesar's death contribute to Rome's instability?

2. What caused the Romans first to support Brutus and then to reject him?

Despite his organizational skill, Caesar could not solve the problem of how to govern the Republic. In 48 B.C.E., he accepted the title of dictator, the venerable title Romans reserved for those who stepped in during a crisis. Unlike Cincinnatus (the Roman with whom we began this chapter), Cae-

Political titles sar did not renounce the title when the emergency was over, but ultimately proclaimed himself dictator for life, a shocking departure from the traditional six-month tenure. He reportedly refused the title of king to avoid offending the republicans, yet he took on many of the trappings of a monarch. He wore royal regalia and established a priesthood to offer sacrifice to his "genius"—what the Romans called each person's spirit. In 44 B.C.E., Caesar had his image placed on coins—perhaps the first time a living Roman was so honored. (Some historians believe Pompey may have beat Caesar to that distinction.) Some people began to question whether the Republic of Rome was changing too radically.

The Roman Republic Ends

The peace and order that Caesar brought to Rome pleased many, particularly the *populares* whose support had lifted Caesar to power. However, many

Conspiracy Romans, even among his supporters, were outraged by the honors Caesar took for himself. He had shrunken the role of the *optimates*, and peace seemed to come at the price of the traditional Republic and at the expense of the old power structure. Some conspirators were simply self-serving, hoping to increase their own power. Sixty senators with various motives entered into a conspiracy to murder their leader. Even Brutus, a friend and protégé of Caesar, joined in the plot. He would be like the Brutus of early Rome who had avenged Lucretia and freed Rome from the Etruscan kings. This Brutus would save Rome from a new king—Caesar.

Caesar was planning a military campaign for March 18, 44 B.C.E., so the assassins had to move quickly. On March 15, the date the Romans called the "ides," or middle of the month,

Caesar's murder they surrounded the unwary dictator as he approached the Senate meeting place. Suddenly they drew knives from the

FIGURE 4.13 Commemorative Coin Coins were struck to memorialize famous people and important events. Caesar's assassins produced this coin, marked with the Ides of March, the date of Caesar's murder, as well as the dagger that killed him.

folds of their togas and plunged them into his body. He died at the foot of the statue of Pompey, his old enemy. Most of the killers seem to have genuinely believed they had done what was best for Rome. They saw themselves as "liberators" who had freed Rome from a dictator and who would restore the Republic. In 43 B.C.E., they issued the coin shown in **Figure 4.13.** The coin depicts the assassins' daggers and reads "Ides of March." On the other side of the coin is a portrait of Brutus.

This attempt to celebrate a great victory on the coin was mere propaganda. The conspirators had no real plan beyond the murder. They apparently had made no provision for control of the army, nor for ensuring peace in the city. In the end, their claim to "save the Republic" rang hollow. Document 4.3 reveals the chaos that followed the assassination. After Caesar's death, one of his friends supposedly lamented, "If Caesar for all his genius, could not find a way out, who is going to find one now?" The republican form of government so carefully forged during the Struggle of the Orders crumbled under the stress of civil wars and murder.

LOOKING BACK & MOVING FORWARD

Summary   The Republic of Rome, with its emphasis on family and city, rose to great power from 509 B.C.E. to the death of Caesar in 44 B.C.E. By that year, Rome controlled much of the Mediterranean world, and a system of wealthy slave owners and a large standing army had replaced the citizen farmer-soldier who had laid the foundation for the Republic's success. Whereas the early Romans had emphasized the ties between citizens, now violent power struggles tore at the social fabric. A people who had preserved stories of serious Roman heroes began to treasure Greek models of beauty and individualism.

Julius Caesar became a central figure in Rome's transformation from republic to empire. Since Caesar's death, historians have argued about his qualities. Was he a great man who detected the inability of the republican form of government—designed to govern a city-state—to adapt to the changed circumstances of empire and social unrest? Or was he a power-hungry politician who craved control and blocked his fellow citizens from having any political involvement in the Republic? The truth no doubt falls somewhere between these extremes. One thing is certain: Despite the assassins' confident claims, Caesar's murder did not solve anything. More violence would ensue until a leader arose who could establish a new form of government that would endure even longer than the Republic.

KEY TERMS

patricians, *p. 110*

consuls, *p. 110*

Senate, *p. 110*

assemblies, *p. 110*

plebeians, *p. 110*

Struggle of the Orders, *p. 111*

tribunes, *p. 111*

Twelve Tables, *p. 111*

equestrians, *p. 111*

Forum, *p. 112*

Pantheon, *p. 127*

populares, *p. 129*

optimates, *p. 129*

Triumvirate, *p. 130*

REVIEW, ANALYZE, & CONNECT TO TODAY

REVIEW THE PREVIOUS CHAPTERS

Chapter 1—"The Roots of Western Civilization"—discussed the rise of the first empires of the West, the Assyrian and the Persian. In Chapter 3—"The Poleis Become Cosmopolitan"—we saw the rise of large Hellenistic monarchies throughout the old empires of the ancient world. Rome inherited much from these empires.

1. Review the Persians' and the Assyrians' treatment of conquered peoples and consider which most closely resembled the Romans' approach. To what degree did the Romans' treatment of their subjects contribute to their success as an imperial power?

2. Compare and contrast Roman and Greek governments.

3. In what ways do you think Rome came to resemble the great Hellenistic cities, and what problems did they share?

ANALYZE THIS CHAPTER

This chapter—"Pride in Family and City"—traces the rise of the small city of Rome to a Hellenistic power whose territory extended throughout the Mediterranean world. In the course of this expansion, the old values of Rome were transformed and new constructs were slowly and violently implemented.

1. Review these changes in early Roman life and values as the armies successfully expanded Roman influence. How did Romans struggle with their changing identity as Rome moved from city to empire?

2. Review the political structure of the Roman Republic. What were its strengths and weaknesses? How did the patron-client system contribute to the strengths and weaknesses of the political system?

3. What were the strengths of the Roman army? Consider how and why Rome expanded its territories so extensively.

4. What were Rome's contributions to the fields of art and technology?

CONNECT TO TODAY

The government of the United States looks back to the Roman Republic as its model of representative democracy.

1. Compare the power of the people in ancient Rome with that of Americans today. In which system do you think the people have exerted the most authority? Support your answer.

2. Romans found it impossible to maintain their republican form of government during their expansion. What similar stresses can you identify in world democracies today? Consider, for example, the flow of immigrants into European countries that has changed the face of traditionally homogeneous European populations, or the feeling among some U.S. citizens that the United States has grown so large, they have little say about what their legislators do in Washington, D.C. In what other ways might people feel disconnected from their government?

BEYOND THE CLASSROOM

THE RISE OF ROME, 753–265 B.C.E.

Bell, Sinclair, and Helen Nagy, eds. *New Perspectives on Etruria and Early Rome.* Madison: University of Wisconsin Press, 2009. Collection of essays exploring the latest archaeological discoveries yielding insights into early Italy; enhanced with maps and illustrations.

Garland, Lynda, and Matthew Dillon. *Ancient Rome: From the Early Republic to the Assassination of Julius Caesar.* London: Routledge, 2005. An accessible yet comprehensive summary that includes translations of documents and spotlights social and political developments during the Republic.

Meyer, J.C. *Pre-Republican Rome.* Odense, Denmark: Odense University Press, 1983. A highly illustrated archaeological look at pre-republican Rome.

Mitchell, Richard E. *Patricians and Plebeians: The Origin of the Roman State.* New York: Cornell University Press, 1990. A description of the separate patrician and plebeian systems.

FAMILY LIFE AND CITY LIFE

Aldrete, Gregory S. *Gestures and Acclamations in Ancient Rome.* Baltimore: Johns Hopkins University Press, 1999. An accessible, nicely illustrated, and fascinating discussion on the verbal and nonverbal communications between Roman crowds and their leaders.

Bradley, Keith R. *Discovering the Roman Family: Studies in Roman Social History.* New York: Oxford University Press, 1991. Essays that study the composition of the Roman family and household-central features of the Roman state.

De Albentiis, Emidio. *Secrets of Pompeii: Everyday Life in Ancient Rome.* Los Angeles: Getty Publications, 2009. A survey of how ancient Romans interacted in their public squares and marketplaces, decorated their homes, and spent their leisure time, as well as how they worshiped.

Gardner, J.F. *Women in Roman Law and Society.* Bloomington: Indiana University Press, 1986. An interesting look at the ways in which the practice of law affected women in various aspects of their lives.

Orlin, Eric M. *Temples, Religion and Politics in the Roman Republic.* New York: E.J. Brill U.S.A., 1996. An exploration into the relationship between the individual and the community.

Robinson, O.F. *Ancient Rome: City Planning and Administration.* New York: Routledge, 1994. A remarkable study of the level of organization, laws, and local governmental arrangements made to allow a large population to live together in the ancient world.

EXPANSION AND TRANSFORMATION, 265–133 B.C.E.

Bagnall, Nigel. *The Punic Wars.* London: Hutchinson, 1990. A detailed, chronological study of the different campaigns, studying them strategically, operationally, and tactically.

Goldsworthy, Adrian. *The Complete Roman Army.* New York: Thames & Hudson, 2003. A wonderfully comprehensive study of the development of the army from its days as a citizen's militia to the highly professional army that was the wonder of the Mediterranean world.

Mayor, Adrienne. *Greek Fire, Poison Arrows, and Scorpion Bombs: Biological and Chemical Warfare in the Ancient World.* Woodstock, NY: Overlook TP, 2008. A fascinating look at ancient weapons of mass destruction.

Ostenberg, Ida. *Staging the World: Spoils, Captives, and Representations in the Roman Triumphal Procession.* Oxford: Oxford University Press, 2009. Study of how Rome presented and perceived the defeated on parade, discussing what was displayed, how it was paraded, and observers' responses.

THE HELLENIZING OF THE REPUBLIC

Ogilvie, R.M. *Roman Literature and Society.* Harmondsworth, England: Penguin, 1980. A brief introduction to and fresh opinion of major Latin writers.

Rawson, Elizabeth. *Intellectual Life in the Late Roman Republic.* Baltimore: Johns Hopkins University Press, 1985. A summary intending to capture the full range of intellectual activity in the Republic.

THE TWILIGHT OF THE REPUBLIC, 133–44 B.C.E.

Lacey, W.K. *Cicero and the Fall of the Republic.* New York: Barnes and Noble, 1978. An in-depth study of all aspects of the man—speaker, author, philosopher—that shows how elements of Cicero's character developed over time in reaction to the social conditions of his age.

Langguth, A.J. *A Noise of War: Caesar, Octavian and the Struggle for Rome.* New York: Simon & Schuster, 1994. A chronologically organized focus on the personalities of these influential men.

Meier, Christian. *Caesar.* New York: Basic Books, 1997. A fine study that places Caesar, a remarkable individual, within his cultural context and encourages us to consider the relationship between the man and his times.

Shotter, David. *The Fall of the Roman Republic.* New York: Routledge, 1994. A brief survey of the elements surrounding the fall of the Roman Republic—a good introductory survey.

THE GEM OF AUGUSTUS (GEMMA AUGUSTEA), SARDONYX CAMEO, ca. 14 C.E.

This beautiful cameo was carved to praise a new order in Rome. At the top, Augustus is holding
the staff of emperor while he is crowned as a god by other deities. At the left, his heir, Tiberius,
descends from a chariot that he has ridden in triumph to celebrate his military victory in Germany.
In the lower level, the army raises a trophy of victory while watched by defeated Germans. This
piece shows how Rome had been transformed: No longer a republic, Rome was now led by a
living god whose family expected to succeed him, and the greatness of the empire depended on
soldiers and far-flung conquests.

" **. . .** [T]he newborn babe shall end that age of iron, [and] bid a golden dawn upon the broad world. . . ." With these words, the Roman poet Virgil foretold the birth of a child who would save the world from the civil wars plaguing the late Roman Republic. For many Romans, that child arrived in the person of Caesar Augustus, a talented leader whose political and economic policies introduced almost two hundred years of internal peace. But this *Pax Romana* was no cure-all. The Romans still faced the challenges of unifying a multiethnic empire while ensuring a succession of capable emperors. They also struggled to preserve their concept of private morality, and they grappled with the complexity of people's political involvement under an imperial system. In the third century C.E., economic and political hardship nearly wiped out the empire, as soldiers created military emperors who battled each other, often leaving Rome's borders at risk. In the fourth century, the reforms of two great rulers—Diocletian and Constantine—temporarily held Rome's extensive dominions together.

Meanwhile, another child born in the time of Caesar Augustus inspired a new creed that seemed to offer salvation. Followers of Jesus grew steadily in numbers through the first centuries C.E. At first, the empire ignored them and occasionally persecuted them, but it later adopted Christianity as its own. This fusion of Roman and Christian ideas created a new Christian empire that many ancient Romans believed fulfilled the promise of the child Virgil praised. Both empires—Roman and Christian—contributed a great deal to the continuing development of the West.

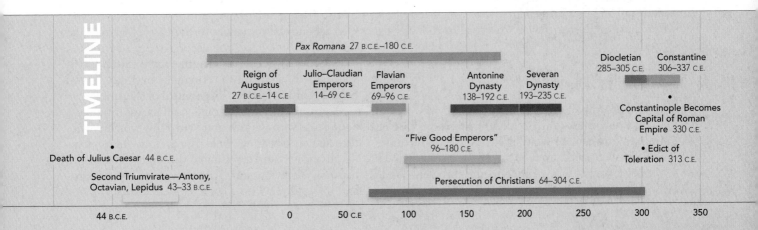

TIMELINE

Pax Romana 27 B.C.E.–180 C.E.

Diocletian 285–305 C.E.   Constantine 306–337 C.E.

Reign of Augustus 27 B.C.E.–14 C.E.   Julio–Claudian Emperors 14–69 C.E.   Flavian Emperors 69–96 C.E.   Antonine Dynasty 138–192 C.E.   Severan Dynasty 193–235 C.E.

Constantinople Becomes Capital of Roman Empire 330 C.E.

"Five Good Emperors" 96–180 C.E.

• Death of Julius Caesar 44 B.C.E.

• Edict of Toleration 313 C.E.

Second Triumvirate—Antony, Octavian, Lepidus 43–33 B.C.E.

Persecution of Christians 64–304 C.E.

44 B.C.E.   0   50 C.E.   100   150   200   250   300   350

FIGURE 5.1 Cleopatra VII, ca. 30 B.C.E. This bust portrays the famous Egyptian queen who bore Julius Caesar a child and seduced Mark Antony. Although Cleopatra was a Hellenistic ruler, the sculptor portrayed her face in the Roman manner.

THE *PAX ROMANA,*
27 B.C.E.–180 C.E.

On the eve of their wedding, a young Roman couple, Vespillo and Turia, paused during the celebration to reflect on a sad memory. Turia's parents had perished in the civil war that had elevated Julius Caesar to power, but the troubled times were not over for the young couple. During new civil wars, Turia had to sell her jewelry to help her husband escape the political strife in the city and even had to beg for a pardon for Vespillo. Finally, the wars were over, and the couple "enjoyed quiet and happy days" through forty-one years of marriage, although sadly they produced no children. They were representative of many Romans who struggled through the violence after Julius Caesar's death finally to enjoy a long **Pax Romana,** or Roman Peace, that was introduced by his successor.

Augustus Takes Power

In 43 B.C.E., three powerful men emerged who established a new triumvirate to rule the Republic. Unlike the first, the Senate legitimized this Second Triumvirate, which ruled from 43 to 33 B.C.E. and seemed to offer a way to bring peace to the turbulent land.

Marc Antony, who managed Caesar's vast fortune, was a strong general who seemed to challenge senatorial power. To balance his power, the Senate turned to Julius Caesar's grandnephew and adopted son, Octavian—a remarkably talented 19-year-old who played on popular sympathy for the murdered dictator by calling himself Caesar. The young Octavian offered respect to the Senate as he jockeyed for position against Marc Antony. The two brought into their partnership one of Julius Caesar's loyal governors and generals, Lepidus. At first, the three men controlled various parts of the empire: Octavian based his power in Italy and the provinces to the west; Lepidus held North Africa; and Marc Antony governed Egypt, Greece, and the provinces to the east. However, like the First Triumvirate, the second soon deteriorated into a power struggle among the three rulers. Octavian forced Lepidus into retirement in 36 B.C.E., and he and Antony vied for sole control of the empire.

As was traditional in Rome, politics was intimately bound up with family and with the women who, through childbearing, held the key to future family alliances. Not surprisingly, the political struggles between Octavian and Antony were to some degree played out in the bedroom. Having lost Julius Caesar, Cleopatra sought to continue her ruling dynasty through a new alliance with a new ruler of Rome. **Figure 5.1** is a portrait bust of Queen Cleopatra showing her regal bearing and her fairly ordinary looks. She seduced Antony with the wit and charm that had so impressed the ancient biographers and bore him twins. Antony, however, was not yet committed to an alliance with Egypt's ruling house. Octavian's popularity in Rome was too high for Antony to risk offending the Roman people. Rumors already circulated in Rome's Forum that Antony wanted to move the Roman capital to Alexandria, so Antony had to negotiate a marriage that would be more acceptable to the public.

Antony and Octavian finally negotiated a peace that was to be secured by Antony's marriage to Octavian's sister, the young, beautiful Octavia. Octavia soon became pregnant, so the two families had the opportunity to seal their agreement permanently. But | Civil war | Antony left Octavia and traveled to Egypt. It is uncertain whether he decided that a strong political ally like Cleopatra afforded better security against Octavian than marriage to his rival's sister, or whether he was driven by the Egyptian queen's allure. In either case, the alliance bound through marriage dissolved. Octavian and Antony resumed their battle over who would rule all of Rome.

The war between the two leaders finally came to a head in 31 B.C.E., when Antony and Cleopatra, surrounded by Octavian's forces, risked all on a sea battle near the city of Actium, off the western coast of Greece. During this famous battle, Cleopatra and Antony proved less determined than Octavian, for Cleopatra's squadron left for Egypt in the course of the battle, and Antony followed her. They abandoned their navy and about twenty legions of their troops. Octavian's navy destroyed the Egyptian fleet, and his land forces quickly occupied Egypt.

Antony committed suicide, and Octavian personally inspected his corpse to be sure his rival was dead. Cleopatra refused to be taken prisoner and, according to legend, ordered her servant to bring her a poisonous snake. She committed suicide by its bite. Although robbed of an imprisoned Egyptian queen, Octavian stood as sole ruler of Rome. With Cleopatra's death in 31 B.C.E., the last Macedonian kingdom fell, ending the Hellenistic age that had begun with the empire of Alexander the Great. Now the new empire of Rome dominated the Mediterranean world.

A New Form of Governing

Unlike his uncle, Julius Caesar, Octavian successfully established a form of government that let him rule without offending the traditions of conservative Romans. This delicate balance between his leadership style and the old ways earned him widespread popularity. On January 1, 27 B.C.E., the young general appeared before the Senate and claimed that he had | The principate | brought peace and was thus returning the rule of the state to the Senate and the people of Rome. Octavian acted in the spirit of Cincinnatus (see Chapter 4), the general who gave up rule to return to his plow, and the tradition-loving Romans appreciated his gesture. The Senate showed its gratitude by giving him the title Augustus, a name that implied majesty and holiness. It is by this informal title that his people addressed him and historians remember him. Augustus, however, modestly referred to himself as the *princeps*—that is, the "first citizen." The government he established was in turn called the **principate,** after the first citizen upon whom everyone depended.

The principate transformed the republican form of government, and historians roughly date the beginning of the Roman Empire from 27 B.C.E.—the date of Augustus's famous renunciation and acceptance of power. Under this new imperial form, the traditional representatives of government—the Senate and the | Governmental structure | Roman people—continued to exist and appoint the traditional magistrates to carry out their public business. The Senate continued to make disbursements from the traditional treasury and, in fact, slowly increased its power as it began to take over elections from the popular assemblies. The Senate also maintained control over some of the provinces—the older ones that did not require so many soldiers to guard the borders. In these ways, Augustus avoided offending the senators as Julius Caesar had done.

However, the vast extent of the empire and the increased complication of public affairs required a special magistrate—the princeps—to coordinate the administration of the empire and, more importantly, to control the army. By 70 C.E., the princeps was more often called emperor, a title with which troops had customarily hailed their generals. Building further on military precedent, Augustus established an imperial legion in Rome as his personal bodyguard. Known as the **praetorian guard,** this new body was named after the headquarters of the legion, or the *praetorium*. Roman generals had always had their own elite bodyguard, but because of its close association with the emperor, the praetorian guard, led by the praetorian prefect, became a powerful force on its own. The guard was unquestionably loyal to Augustus and worked to avert civil war such as the strife that had torn apart the Republic, but after his death a new political force had been created in Rome.

With these efforts, Augustus created a new structure on the remnants of the traditional Republic. Document 5.1 relates in Augustus's own words how

DOCUMENT 5.1

Augustus Tallies His Accomplishments

Shortly before he died in 14 C.E., Augustus left a number of state papers with the Vestal Virgins, including an account of his accomplishments that he wanted inscribed on bronze pillars to be installed in front of his mausoleum. Excerpts of this document give us a glimpse into this early period of the principate, which set the stage for subsequent imperial success.

3. I waged many wars throughout the whole world by land and by sea, both civil and foreign, and when victorious I spared all citizens who sought pardon. Foreign peoples who could safely be pardoned I preferred to spare rather than to extirpate. About 500,000 Roman citizens were under military oath to me. Of these, when their terms of service were ended, I settled in colonies or sent back to their own municipalities a little more than 300,000, and to all of these I allotted lands or granted money as rewards for military service. I captured 600 ships, exclusive of those which were of smaller class than triremes.

4. Twice I celebrated ovations, three times curule triumphs, and I was acclaimed *imperator* twenty-nine times. When the senate decreed additional triumphs to me, I declined them on four occasions. . . .

5. The dictatorship offered to me in the consulship of Marcus Marcellus and Lucius Arruntius by the people and by the senate, both in my absence and in my presence, I refused to accept. In the midst of a critical scarcity of grain I did not decline the supervision of the grain supply, which I so administered that within a few days I freed the whole people from imminent panic and danger by my expenditures and efforts. The consulship, too, which was offered to me at that time as an annual office for life, I refused to accept.

6. In the consulship of Marcus Vinicius and Quintus Lucretius, and again in that of Publius Lentulus and Gnaeus Lentulus, and a third time in that of Paullus Fabius Maximus and Quintus Tubero, though the Roman senate and people unitedly agreed that I should be elected sole guardian of the laws and morals with supreme authority, I refused to accept any office offered me which was contrary to the traditions of our ancestors. The measures which the senate desired at that time to be taken by me I carried out by virtue of the tribunician power. In this power I five times voluntarily requested and was given a colleague by the senate. . . .

15. To the Roman plebs I paid 300 sesterces apiece in accordance with the will of my father; and in my fifth consulship I gave each 400 sesterces in my own name out of the spoils of war; and a second time in my tenth consulship I paid out of my own patrimony a largess of 400 sesterces to every individual. . . . These largesses of mine reached never less than 250,000 persons.

17. Four times I came to the assistance of the treasury with my own money, transferring to those in charge of the treasury 150,000,000 sesterces. And in the consulship of Marcus Lepidus and Lucius Arruntius I transferred out of my own patrimony 170,000,000 sesterces to the soldiers' bonus fund, which was established on my advice for the purpose of providing bonuses for soldiers who had completed twenty or more years of service. . . .

22. I gave a gladiatorial show three times in my own name, and five times in the names of my sons or grandsons; at these shows about 10,000 fought. Twice I presented to the people in my own name an exhibition of athletes invited from all parts of the world, and a third time in the name of my grandson. I presented games in my own name four times, and in addition twenty-three times in the place of other magistrates. . . . Twenty-six times I provided for the people, in my own name or in the names of my sons or grandsons, hunting spectacles of African wild beasts in the circus or in the Forum or in the amphitheaters; in these exhibitions about 3,500 animals were killed. . . .

34. In my sixth and seventh consulships, after I had put an end to the civil wars, having attained supreme power by universal consent, I transferred the state from my own power to the control of the Roman senate and people. For this service of mine I received the title of Augustus by decree of the senate, and the doorposts of my house were publicly decked with laurels, the civic crown was affixed over my doorway, and a golden shield was set up in the Julian senate house, which, as the inscription on this shield testifies, the Roman senate and people gave me in recognition of my valor, clemency, justice, and devotion. After that time I excelled all in authority, but I possessed no more power than the others who were my colleagues in each magistracy.

35. When I held my thirteenth consulship, the senate, the equestrian order, and the entire Roman people gave me the title of "father of the country" and decreed that this title should be inscribed in the vestibule of my house, in the Julian senate house, and in the Augustan Forum on the pedestal of the chariot which was set up in my honor by decree of the senate. At the time I write this document I was in my seventy-sixth year.

SOURCE: Naphtali Lewis and Meyer Reinhold, *Roman Civilization: Sourcebook II: The Empire* (New York: Harper Torchbooks, 1966), pp. 10, 11, 14, 16, 19.

Analyze the Document

1. Why was Augustus so popular with the Roman people?

2. Which offices did he accept and which did he refuse? How did this help him avoid Julius Caesar's fate?

3. Notice the blurring of private and public funds. How do you think that blending contributed to Rome's stability and Augustus's office?

he balanced traditional offices with new demands. The document shows how he used his enormous personal wealth to balance the national treasury, to rebuild Rome, and to fund gladiator shows and other popular spectacles. In 2 B.C.E., the Senate awarded Augustus the title Father of the Fatherland. In a culture that depended on the father to guard his family's prosperity and honor, perhaps no other title could convey greater respect.

Of course, all these titles and honors, though significant, had little to do with the day-to-day practical problems of managing a large empire. Like any good father, Augustus ran the empire as one would run a household. He kept authority for himself, but the everyday business was handled by freedmen and slaves in his household. Although Rome itself remained governed largely by the traditional forms, Augustus made dramatic changes in governing the provinces.

Administering an empire

Augustus kept about half of the provinces—including wealthy Egypt—under his direct control, sending out representatives to govern there in his name. He began to create a foreign service drawn from the equestrian class (wealthy, upwardly mobile nonnobles), whose advancement depended upon their performance. This reform eliminated some of the worst provincial abuses that had gone on during the late Republic—for example, Augustus began eliminating private tax collectors. To keep the peace on the borders, Augustus stationed troops permanently in the provinces; the empire began to maintain fixed borders with military camps along the frontiers. Document 5.1 includes Augustus's own assessment of his accomplishments.

For all these reforms, even by ancient standards, the empire was astonishingly undermanaged—a few thousand individuals controlled some 50 million people. The genius of the system lay in a combination of limited goals on top—maintain peace, collect taxes, and prevent power from accumulating—with actual power exerted at the local level. Through its relative simplicity, the principate established by Augustus continued to function efficiently even during years of remarkably decadent rulers. The Roman people recognized Augustus's accomplishments by according him a level of respect almost suiting a god, and this veneration would dramatically shape the future of the principate.

Figure 5.2 reveals the Romans' love of this strong, wise leader. This famous statue—named for the villa of Augustus's wife, Livia, where the sculpture stood—captures the people's hopes for Augustus. In the statue, Augustus holds his right arm up in the fashion of a traditional republican orator. Compare this sculpture with the image at the beginning of Chapter 4, on page 106.

FIGURE 5.2 Augustus of Prima Porta, ca. 20 B.C.E. This idealized portrait of Augustus shows the first Roman emperor as a divine guardian of Rome.

The sculptor's interpretation of Augustus shows that the Republic had been transformed. Instead of a toga, Augustus wears the armor of a soldier, and in his left hand he holds the staff of an emperor, traditionally the commander of the army and now the leader of the state. He is also shown as more than a mortal hero. His bare feet indicate that he is a hero, perhaps even semidivine. The cupid astride the dolphin refers to the claim that Augustus's family was descended from the goddess Venus, mother of Cupid. The symbols on Augustus's breastplate—a victorious general and a generous Mother Earth—promise divine aid and prosperity. Although Augustus refused to let himself be portrayed explicitly as a god, these associations left no doubt about his near-divine status. Augustus allowed altars in his name to be erected in the provinces, but he refused to allow Romans to worship their "first citizen." His formal deification would come after his death.

This image of Augustus as a divine being was reinforced in the great literature produced under his patronage. Virgil's famous epic, the *Aeneid* (ca. 29–19 B.C.E.), is a mythological tale of the wandering of the Trojan hero Aeneas, who founded the city of Rome. However, in spite of the book's echoes of Homer, Aeneas was a kind of hero different from Achilles, and in this portrayal, Virgil was able to show that the virtues of the past could work in the new age of the principate. Aeneas refuses to yield to his weaknesses or his passions and is rewarded with a vision of the future in which his descendants will extend Rome's rule "to the ends of the earth." In his epic, Virgil promises:

Virgil's Aeneid

> . . . *yours will be the rulership of nations. Remember Roman, these will be your arts: to teach the ways of peace to those you conquer, to spare defeated peoples, tame the proud.*

The *Aeneid* did for Rome what Homer had done for classical Greece: It defined the Roman Empire and its values for subsequent generations, and in the process it contributed to the deification of Augustus. It was also a fine example of Augustus's talent for propaganda.

What Virgil did for Roman literature, Livy (59 B.C.E.–17 C.E.) did for the empire's recorded history. In his long, detailed work, *The History of Rome* (ca. 26 B.C.E.–15 C.E.), Livy recounted the development of his city from the earliest times to the principate, and he included many speeches that brought the past to life. Like Virgil, Livy emphasized Roman religion and morality, looking nostalgically back to republican values. And again like Virgil, the historian recognized that the future lay with the new imperial form of government. His history strongly influenced subsequent ancient historians and has remained a central source of information today.

Livy's Historia

The system established by Augustus was not perfect, but Augustus lived for so long that the principate became tradition. The Roman historian Tacitus (56–120 C.E.) wrote that by Augustus's death in 14 C.E., no one left alive could remember any other way to govern. For the next two centuries his successors ruled with the benefits of the imperial system that Augustus had established. But they also inherited major problems he left unresolved—Who should succeed the "first citizen"? How should one best govern such a large empire, and how would rulers handle such power?

Challenges to the Principate, 69–193 C.E.

Augustus's long tenure as emperor postponed the problem of imperial succession, but this weakness in the principate showed up soon after his death. The next four emperors all ascended the throne based on their ties to Augustus's family, and this succession showed how flimsy the concept of "first citizen" really was. An imperial dynasty had been established, and it did not matter that the rulers lacked the moral stature of Augustus or traditional republican virtues. During the Republic, leaders regularly confronted the Roman people in the Forum and yielded to the pressure of scorn or applause. However, the new rulers of the empire experienced no such corrective public scrutiny, and the successors of Augustus immediately proved that power corrupted. The historian Suetonius (69–130 C.E.) recorded the popular scandalous rumors that circulated about the decline of Augustus's successor, his stepson Tiberius (r. 14–37), shown celebrating his victory over the Germans in the chapter-opening art on page 136: "No longer feeling himself under public scrutiny, he rapidly succumbed to all the vicious passions which he had for a long time tried, not very successfully, to disguise." Tiberius "made himself a private sporting house where sexual extravagances were practiced for his secret pleasure," and in his isolation, Suetonius claimed, his paranoia grew. He even executed people for insulting his stepfather's memory if they carried a coin bearing Augustus's image into a lavatory or brothel. The Roman people believed that such excesses continued throughout the dynasty of Augustus's heirs.

Augustus's successors

One of the heirs in this dynasty was Caligula (r. 37–41), an irrational—if not insane—ruler who wanted to be worshiped as a god. The praetorian guard took matters into its own hands and assassinated Caligula. The guard then found Claudius, a retiring, neglected relative of Augustus, hiding in the palace and promptly declared him emperor. Claudius (r. 41–54) was regarded by many Romans as an imbecile subject to the whims of his wives, but the power of the connection to the family of Augustus prevailed to solidify his rule. The cameo in **Figure 5.3** is a beautiful piece of propaganda as well as art. It shows Claudius and his wife, Agrippina the Younger, in the foreground superimposed on Germanicus—Caligula's father—and his wife, Agrippina the Elder (the Younger's mother). The superimposition on the cameo emphasizes the family connections that gave Claudius the right to rule as "first citizen," and the horns of plenty on the front allude to the prosperity this dynasty promised to bring to the Romans. However, in contrast to the calm portrayal on the cameo, the dynasty only brought more family feuds.

FIGURE 5.3 Claudius and Agrippina the Younger This cameo gem depicts the emperor Claudius with his wife, Agrippina. In the background are his ancestors Germanicus and Agrippina the Elder. The design includes horns of plenty, symbolizing the prosperity the emperors were to bring to Rome.

Suetonius's history of those years tells of a series of murders within the family as members vied for the power of the princeps. Nero (r. 54–68) marked the most excessive of the murderers, for he killed many of his family members, mostly using his favorite means, poison. He even killed his mother, although it was not easy. He poisoned her three times, but she had taken a preventive antidote. Nero then tried to arrange for the ceiling of her room to collapse on her and for her boat to sink. When all these techniques failed, he simply sent an assassin to kill her and make it appear that she had committed suicide.

Nero was so despised that even his personal guard deserted him, and to avoid being captured and publicly executed, Nero commanded his slave to slit his throat, saying, "How ugly and vulgar my life has become!" It is not surprising that there were no more members of Augustus's family left to claim the succession, and the armies and the praetorian guard fought a bloody civil war to see which family would succeed to the imperial throne. Fortunately for Rome, Vespasian took power in 69 C.E. and restored some order to the empire, but even so fine an emperor could not ensure that his son would be equally competent. Each subsequent dynasty would eventually end through the weakness or corruption of one of the rulers, and the flaws in the succession policy were repeatedly highlighted. The assassination of Vespasian's murderous son Domitian (r. 81–96) introduced a new period, that of the "Five Good Emperors" (96–180). These rulers increasingly centralized their power at the expense of the Senate, but they ruled with a long-remembered

A new dynasty

integrity. From Nerva (r. 96–98) to Marcus Aurelius (r. 161–180), these emperors established a tone of modest simplicity and adherence to republican values.

Marcus Aurelius represented the highest expression of a ruler whose political life was shaped by moral philosophy. He was highly educated in law, poetry, and philosophy, but the latter was his greatest love. When he was only 11, he adopted the coarse dress and sparse life of Stoic philosophers (discussed in Chapter 3), and when he became emperor, he continued to act based on the self-containment embodied in Stoic principles. His ideas have been preserved in a collection of his contemplative notes, called his *Meditations* (171–ca. 180). Within these notes he wrote a caution that should have been followed by all who rose to great power: When one is seduced by fame and flattery, one should remember how flatterers are frequently wrong on other occasions, so one should remain humble. Unfortunately, too many emperors did not share Marcus's wise self-containment.

Through these years, the City of Rome was transformed from a center of republican power to a glorification of imperial power. As **Map 5.1** shows, the entertainment centers—baths, games—offered by the emperors began to dominate the city, and temples to divine emperors sprang up.

Throughout the reigns of emperors good and bad, the borders had to be guarded. Armies fought in the east and as far away as Britain. Centuries of Roman military presence along the frontiers had brought Roman-style cities and agriculture—indeed, Roman civilization—to the edges of the empire. This long-term presence of Rome in lands far from Italy served to add Roman culture to the growing Western civilization in the north of Europe as well as the Mediterranean.

Provincial defense

However, holding such extensive lands caused many of these soldier-emperors to be away from Rome for extended periods. Hadrian (r. 117–138) spent twelve of his twenty-one ruling years traveling around the provinces, establishing fortifications and checking on provincial administration. However, it was one thing to establish definite borders and quite another to hold them. The Stoic emperor Marcus Aurelius spent the better part of thirteen years in fierce campaigns to keep the border tribes out of the empire and he died while on campaign. His death brought an end to the era of the "good emperors," caused once again by a decadent son.

The long rule by good emperors may have been more the result of biological accident than anything else: Four of the emperors had no sons, so each of them adopted as his successor a man he thought best able to rule. However, Marcus Aurelius fathered a son, Commodus (r. 180–192), who unfortunately brought the age of the Five Good Emperors and the *Pax Romana* to an ignoble end through his cruel reign. Commodus

MAP 5.1

City of Rome During the Empire

This map shows the city of Rome during the empire and identifies the new buildings constructed by the emperors. Compare this map with **Map 4.1,** of Rome during the Republic. Notice how monuments of imperial power and establishments for entertainment dominated the city during the empire.

Explore the Map

1. What new buildings dominated the city? What were their functions? What do these buildings reveal about the cultural focus of the Roman people under the empire?

2. Where were the new fora (plural of *forum*) built by the emperors? Where was the imperial palace? In what ways do these features demonstrate how the emperors displaced old republican centers of power?

seems to have been a simpleminded man who loved the games. He even shocked Rome by fighting in the arena as a gladiator. With Commodus's murder (he was strangled by his wrestling partner), peace ended in Rome in a fresh outbreak of civil war.

A Vibrant, Far-Flung Empire

One must credit the genius of Augustus's political system and the steadfastness of the Roman administrators for the empire's ability to flourish even during

China's Han Dynasty and the Silk Road

In 206 B.C.E, while the Roman Republic was expanding, a strong Chinese military commander, Liu Bang, brought order to warring factions in China. Liu established the Han dynasty (named after his native land), which would endure for more than four hundred years. The Han emperors developed a centralized authority supported by a large bureaucracy, and they built an extensive network of roads and canals to facilitate communication throughout the realm. The emperors also knew the value of educated royal servants. Thus, in 124 B.C.E, Emperor Han Wudi established an imperial university. This university incorporated Confucianism as the basis for its curriculum, so the Confucian tradition took root in China. Like the Romans in the West, the Han emperors developed an influential body of law, written first on bamboo and silk. Their legal system became the most comprehensive and best organized in the world.

The centralized, ordered rule of the Hans facilitated trade. It also led to the development of the "Silk Road," which linked China and the West in significant ways. Luxury items moved from China and India to Mesopotamia and the Mediterranean basin. Incoming goods arrived through a complex series of trades. Roman sailors used the prevailing monsoon winds to sail their ships from Red Sea ports to the mouth of the Indus River in India at Barygaza. There, they traded their goods— mostly gold and silver— for Indian spices and silks. The Indian merchants took their share of the merchandise and proceeded to trade with the Han merchants.

Chinese traders shipped spices— ginger, cinnamon, cloves, and others— that Westerners craved both as flavorings and as medicines. However, the most prized commodity was Chinese silk, which gave its name to the trade route. By the first century C.E., Romans were willing to pay premium prices for the prized fiber. The Chinese knew how to feed silkworms on mulberry leaves and harvest the cocoons before the moths chewed through the precious silk strands. The silk traveled west in bales— as either woven cloth or raw yarn— and went to processing centers, most of them in Syria. There workers ungummed the rolls and unwound the fiber before weaving the fabric that sold for top prices throughout the Roman Empire. For hundreds of years, the trade flourished, bringing West and East into close contact. This contact sparked the exchange of ideas as well as goods. Unfortunately, it also spread diseases that dramatically reduced populations in China as well as in the Roman Empire.

Despite the thriving trade, the later Han emperors proved unable to maintain the centralization and prosperity that had marked the early centuries of their reign. In the face of social and economic tensions, as well as epidemic diseases, disloyal generals grabbed more and more power. By 200 C.E., the Han dynasty had collapsed and the empire lay in pieces. The trade along the Silk Road suffered too, but stories of the prosperous East continued to capture the imaginations of Westerners.

Making Connections

1. What did the Han emperors do to facilitate long-distance trade with the West?

2. What trade items flowed along the Silk Road?

3. What impact did this trade have on the Roman Empire?

MAP 5.2 The Silk Road, ca. 200 C.E.

MAP 5.3

The Roman Empire,
44 B.C.E.–284 C.E.

This map shows the greatest extent of the Roman Empire. Notice how much of this territory was acquired during the Republic, before Augustus's rule. The key also shows the major trade goods from the various parts of the empire.

Explore the Map

1. How long did it take for a rapid message to go from Rome to the farthest reaches of the empire? (The most rapid travel time was about 90 miles a day; average travel was 20 miles a day.) What difficulties did such vast distances create?

2. Which territories brought the most essential or expensive trade goods?

3. Which territories might the empire have first abandoned when under pressure? Why?

years of imperial decadence. In our age of rapid communication and many levels of administrators and financial managers, it is difficult to imagine how hard it must have been to govern, with a small bureaucracy, an area as large as the Roman Empire. **Map 5.3** shows the extent of the empire through 284 C.E. Although this map looks impressive, it still requires some imagination to understand the meaning

of these distances in the third century. For example, in good sailing weather, it took three weeks to sail from one end of the Mediterranean Sea to the other, and travel overland was even harder. Hauling goods by wagon train with escorts armed against bandits took so much time and manpower that it was cheaper to send a load of grain all the way across the Mediterranean than to send it 75 miles overland. Information moved almost as slowly as goods. What could hold the empire together against the centrifugal force of these distances?

The empire found a partial answer in Romanization. From the time of the Republic, Romans had established colonies for military veterans in the provinces, and such colonial expansion continued under the empire. Furthermore, to boost the strength of his army, Augustus recruited auxiliary troops from the noncitizen population all over the empire. After serving twenty-four years, these veterans were awarded with citizenship and land in the colonies. These auxiliary troops also served to spread Roman culture. Colonies became the cities that grew up in Britain, North Africa, Germany, and the East, bringing Roman culture to the most distant corners of the empire. The cities boasted all the amenities that Romans had come to expect: theaters, baths, a colosseum, roads, and townhouses. These urban communities had so much in common that they seemed to erase the huge distances that separated them.

Colonies

In these scattered, Romanized centers, local officials ruled. Town councils, for example, collected taxes and maintained public works, such as water systems and food markets. To collect taxes, officials maintained census figures on both the human population and agricultural produce and reported all to their superiors in Rome. This combination of local rule, Romanization, and some accountability to the central authority helped hold the fabric of the huge empire together.

Provincial administration

The provinces depended not only on the administrative skills of local officials but also on their philanthropy. In the best tradition of ancient Rome, men and women used their private resources for the public good. Inscriptions recalling private contributions survive in towns and cities all over the empire and reveal how essential such charity was to the maintenance of the Roman Peace. One woman in central Italy bequeathed one million coins in her will for the town to use to provide monthly child-assistance payments for all children until boys reached 16 years of age and girls 14. In another instance, the governor of the Asian city of Troy observed that the city was "ill-supplied with baths and that the inhabitants drew muddy water from their wells." The governor persuaded Emperor Hadrian to contribute three million coins to build an aqueduct, but when costs rose to seven million the governor paid for the difference from his own pocket. Philanthropists ensured that Roman life prospered all over the empire by contributing funds for baths, libraries, poor relief, and even public banquets.

The empire also remained unified through the marvels of Roman engineering. Fifty thousand miles of roads supplemented the great rivers as primary means of transportation. As is true today, the upkeep of roads posed a constant challenge and expense, and the empire used public and private means to fund them. The government collected tolls on goods in transit to fund road maintenance, but the toll payments seldom generated enough income. When in need, the empire turned to traditional philanthropy to make up the difference, asking local individuals and businesses to sponsor the upkeep of a particular portion of the road and erecting stones acknowledging their contribution. Such stones remain today in silent testimony to the philanthropy and organization that helped tie together the vast imperial lands.

Roman authorities also established a transportation system that provided travelers with horses and carriages and that monitored the movement of heavy goods. Regulations established maximum loads but were frequently ignored by inspectors, who often took bribes. With these elaborate networks of roads, lightly burdened travelers could cover an astonishing 90 miles a day—an extraordinary feat in ancient times.

Roads and transportation

During the early centuries of the empire, goods moved over great distances not only along the road network, for there was also a great deal of shipping. For the first time in the ancient world, the Roman navy kept the Mediterranean Sea relatively free of pirates, so shipping flourished. The sea had become a virtual Roman lake, and the Romans confidently called it Mare Nostrum (our sea) to show the degree to which the Mediterranean world was united under Rome.

The peace and unity of the empire allowed merchants to increase trade with the farthest reaches of Asia. The fabulous Silk Road brought spices and silks from as far away as China and only whetted the appetite of wealthy Romans for exotic goods from the East. Global Connections on page 145 discusses the Chinese empire that also profited from trade between the West and East.

Finally, the movement of people and armies also held the empire together. The Roman Empire boasted a remarkably multiethnic and multicultural population. Many educated provincials, for example, spoke at least three languages: Greek, Latin, and a local dialect. The imperial lands included a bewildering array of climates and geological features as well. **Figure 5.4** shows the 80-mile-long wall of Hadrian, the northern outpost of the empire in Britain built in the early second century. Here, Roman forts dotted the wall at 1-mile intervals. Roman soldiers peered into the damp fog, on alert against the fierce northern

Imperial diversity

FIGURE 5.4 Hadrian's Wall This photo shows the remains of the wall that marked the northern boundary of the Roman Empire on the British Isles. Ancient writers described the mist that hung on the wall through which soldiers watched for invaders from the wild north.

tribes who threatened to swarm across the imperial boundary. By contrast, **Figure 5.5** shows the forum of the ruins of Dougga, a Roman city in North Africa. You can see in the background the desert that marked the southern border of the empire. Beyond the great groves of olive trees that, together with abundant fields of grain, produced much of the agricultural wealth of North Africa, Roman legions stood watch against the Bedouin tribesmen who came galloping out of the desert to menace the edge of the empire.

With this remarkable diversity came the constant movement of people. Merchants traveled with their goods, and just as in the Hellenistic world, enterprising people moved about to seek their fortunes. Furthermore, to defend the empire's 6,000 miles of border, Roman authorities moved approximately 300,000 soldiers to wherever they were needed. The armies usually did not patrol their own regions. A garrison of black sub-Saharan Africans, for example, was stationed in the foggy north along Hadrian's Wall, and Germans from the north patrolled the desert. At the height of the *Pax Romana*, this flexible system seemed to ensure peace within Rome's borders.

As we will see, in time the centrifugal forces began to work against the ability of such a far-flung empire

to hold together. The expense and difficulties of long-distance trade caused more and more provinces to produce their goods locally. Outside the empire itself, more tribes wanted to enter and share Rome's prosperity, and the borders would become all too permeable. But for the first two hundred years of the empire, it seemed as if the promise of a glorious new age had been fulfilled.

LIFE DURING THE PEACE OF ROME

Just as Augustus wanted to return politics to the traditional morality of the Roman Republic, he also tried to revive the old morality in the private lives of Rome's citizens. However, the new wealth that poured into the pockets of well-placed Romans made the old morality seem quaint and antiquated.

A New Decadence

Although the growing separation between rich and poor that began under the Republic continued through the empire, those getting more wealthy began to flaunt their riches. Silks and embroidery replaced the rough wool of republican virtue, and satirists wrote

FIGURE 5.5 Roman Ruins The southern boundary of Rome was marked by a desert. These Roman ruins in the city of Dougga in modern Tunisia show how Roman culture extended to the dry southern lands.

scathingly of women sporting makeup, high heels, elaborate hairstyles, and lots of jewelry. Men, too, indulged in similar excesses to ensure their appearance reflected their wealth and status. Augustus and subsequent moralists would fight a losing battle against such decadent displays.

The new wealth from trade and peace extended beyond Rome itself to people living in other growing urban areas. **Figure 5.6** is a painting from the wall of a baker's shop in the city of Pompeii (about 150 miles south of Rome, near Naples). Pompeii was a prosperous city that was buried in 79 C.E. under the ash of a violently erupting volcano, Mount Vesuvius. The rain of ash froze the city and its people in time, allowing modern excavators to see individuals engaged in many activities of daily life. The image in **Figure 5.6** offers insights into the Italian peninsula's urban life, in which both men and women participated and grew wealthy in commerce.

The Problem with Population

During the Republic, marriage and family ties were central values of the Roman people, and Augustus used his power to support those values. The princeps promoted legislation that assessed penalties on people who remained unmarried and instituted strong laws against adultery. These laws, though intended to strengthen the family, fell far short of their mark. Morality is singularly hard to legislate, and the Roman historian Tacitus observed that many people simply

ignored the laws. Augustus himself experienced this phenomenon firsthand: Unable to control his own daughter's behavior (which he perceived as inappropriate), he ended up exiling her.

At heart, however, the laws were probably as much about children as about morality. The future of Rome, like the succession of the emperor, depended on offspring to carry on the family and other cultural traditions. Yet, throughout the empire, Romans had a particularly hard Birthrates time reproducing. Augustus even promoted a law that exempted women from male guardianship if they bore three children (four children for a freed slave). These numbers are a far cry from those in earlier times; Cornelia, mother of the Gracchi, earned praise for bearing 12 children! Fecundity in the empire certainly had plummeted to alarmingly low levels.

This phenomenon had cultural as well as physical causes. Wealthy Roman men and women often wanted few children, so as to preserve their inheritance intact. Yet, Augustus's law specifically tried to influence women. This law is particularly interesting in its assumptions: It recognized women's desire for freedom, and it assumed that women controlled their own fecundity. The former assumption may have been accurate, but the latter was only partially so. Sometimes women used birth-control methods based on herbs, spermicidal drugs, or douches. The texts also refer to abortion, although drugs strong enough to abort a fetus often endangered the life of the mother.

thinking about
ART

FIGURE 5.6

Wall Painting from a Baker's Shop in Pompeii, ca. 70 C.E.

This painting is from a baker's shop in the city of Pompeii, which was destroyed by the volcano Vesuvius in 70 C.E. Pompeii's preservation of small elements of Roman daily life makes it an important source of information about the past. The painting shows a prosperous, middle-class couple; the woman holds writing implements—a stylus and wax tablet—and the man holds a scroll (equivalent to an ancient book) with a label that identifies its contents. Notice how realistically the couple is portrayed.

Connecting Art & Society

1. Why might the couple have chosen to have themselves portrayed so realistically? What does the image indicate about what the couple valued?

2. What does this image suggest about the importance of literacy to a prosperous urban economy?

3. What does the image suggest about the woman's role in business, and in urban economy more generally?

The causes of Roman infertility lay in a full complex of medical misunderstandings combined with cultural practices.

Sexual and Medical Misunderstandings

Despite the scandalized commentary lamenting the sexual excess of "loose" women and decadent emperors, Romans in fact were very circumspect about sex. Medical wisdom warned men against the fatiguing effects of sexual activity, which they thought deprived the body of vital spirit. Roman physicians believed semen was made of brain fluid, and urged men to conserve it carefully.

By contrast, physicians did not believe that sexual intercourse weakened females. Indeed, medical advice for women focused on helping them to bear as many children as possible. Yet, medical misinformation actually contributed to Rome's falling birthrate. Physicians concluded, incorrectly, that women were most fertile soon after their menstrual periods, so they recommended reserving intercourse for that time. Furthermore, some doctors thought that women had to have intercourse before puberty in order to mature correctly. Medical misunderstanding about women's bodies and children's health care contributed to a low birthrate. These factors combined with other cultural issues—the desire to restrict children to keep from reducing inheritances, for example—help explain why Rome had so much trouble maintaining its population.

Despite the confusion regarding human reproduction, Roman medicine proved highly influential for the next 1,500 years. In particular, the physician Galen (131–201) popularized views that have prevailed even into modern times. Galen used some modern scientific techniques—for example, he performed vivisections on pigs to see the process of digestion—but his conclusions were strongly rooted in the classical world. He embraced the notion of moderation that was so central to ancient thought (recall Aristotle's "golden mean," discussed in Chapter 2) and therefore saw disease as the result of an imbalance, or excess. Galen believed that good health resulted from a balance among the four "humors,"

Galen

or bodily fluids—blood, bile, urine, and phlegm. He argued that each of these humors had its own properties—warm, cold, dry, and moist—and when a person was out of balance—that is, when one humor dominated—the cure was to restore an appropriate equilibrium. For example, if a person was feverish and flushed, he or she was considered to have an excess of blood. An application of blood-sucking leeches or the initiation of bleeding would reduce the blood and restore the balance. These ideas may not have improved people's health, but they formed the subsequent basis for medical treatment.

The Games

Families may have formed the basis of Roman society, but as we saw in Chapter 4, during the Republic, men forged critical ties in the world of civic affairs centered in the Roman Forum. Under the empire this focus changed; real power moved from the Forum to the emperor's household. Yet the Roman people still needed a public place to gather and express their collective will. Over time, they began satisfying this need at the great games and spectacles held in the amphitheaters across the empire. During the late Republic, wealthy men who craved the admiration of the people, and politicians who sought the loyalty of the crowd, spent fortunes producing chariot races in the Circus Maximus and hunts and gladiator games. After the time of Augustus, the emperors had a virtual monopoly on providing entertainment in Rome, although in the provinces others could produce spectacles. These games always had a religious significance to the Roman people, ritualizing Roman power and authority.

Figure 5.7 shows the Roman Colosseum, built by Emperor Vespasian (r. 69–79) as a gift to his subjects. **Map 5.1** shows its location within the city. This structure was the largest of its kind in the Roman world and held about 50,000 people. The photograph on the right (see **Figure 5.7**) shows what remains of the interior, including subterranean passages that held animals and prisoners. The photograph on the left shows the exterior, which dominated the skyline of Rome. Men and women flocked to the arena in the mornings to watch men hunt exotic animals that had been transported to Rome from the farthest reaches of the empire. Augustus proudly claimed to have provided a total of 3,500 animals in these hunts; other emperors were equally lavish in their displays.

From Forum to arena

The crowds then witnessed the public executions of criminals who were either set aflame or put in the path of deadly wild animals. Through such rituals, Rome displayed its power over its enemies. **Figure 5.8** shows a criminal being attacked by a leopard in the arena. This horrifying scene suggests that it was not easy to make animals attack humans; the victims had to be immobilized and the animals goaded into aggression. The very existence of the mosaic, however, which was displayed in a private home, reveals the Romans' pride in the empire's dominance over its perceived enemies. As we will see, these enemies would eventually include Christians.

Afternoons at the Colosseum were reserved for the main event, the gladiator contests. Gladiators were condemned criminals who were trained in the gladiator school near the Colosseum (see **Map 5.1**). They then received the right to live a while longer by fighting against each other in the arena. In time, the gladiatorial ranks were increased by slaves who were specifically bought and trained for this purpose. Gladiators armed with weapons were paired to fight until one was killed, and the winner won the right to live until his next fight. At first, gladiator contests were part of funeral rites, and the death blood of the losers was seen as an offering to the recently departed. Later, however, emperors sponsored contests featuring hundreds of gladiators. At the end of a gladiator contest,

Gladiators

FIGURE 5.7 The Colosseum   This magnificent building was inaugurated in 80 C.E. The concrete foundations were 25 feet deep to support the structure of concrete and marble. More than 50,000 spectators entered through numbered gates to their seats.

FIGURE 5.8 Condemned to the Beasts, ca. second century C.E. During the mid-afternoon at the games in the amphitheaters, criminals sentenced to death were attacked by beasts. This mosaic from a private home was designed to celebrate Rome's victory over its enemies.

the man who had been overpowered was supposed to bare his throat unflinchingly to the killing blade of the victor. Not all defeated gladiators were killed; those who had fought with extreme bravery and showed a willingness to die could be freed by the emperor's clemency.

It is easy to judge these activities as wanton displays of brutality. Yet, from the Roman perspective, these rituals actually exemplified and perpetuated Roman virtue. In the arenas, private honor and public good intersected: The private generosity that funded the games served the community's need for ritual, and the emperor's sponsorship strengthened the community's loyalty to its leaders. Finally, individuals learned to face death bravely by watching people die; as the historian Livy (59 B.C.E.–17 C.E.) wrote: "There was no better schooling against pain and death." Nevertheless, all these demonstrations of Roman largesse, prowess, and courage could not stave off the threats to the empire that came at the end of the *Pax Romana*.

CRISIS AND TRANSFORMATION,
192–ca. 400 C.E.

The violence that accompanied the assassination of Marcus Aurelius's decadent son Commodus in 192 transformed Augustus's principate. The armies had grown strong under the military policy of the Five Good Emperors, so armies even beyond the praetorian guard became the king makers. Septimius Severus (r. 193–211) was a new kind of emperor—a North African general who came to power because of his army's support. A military man to the core, he also embodied

the multicultural elements of the empire. He spoke Latin with a North African accent and seemed to feel more at home among provincials than among the old, wealthy families of Rome.

The Military Monarchy

Septimius transformed the political base for Roman rule. Under the principate as established by Augustus, the empire was ruled by a partnership between the emperor and the Senate; Septimius and his successors ruled with the support of the army, creating a military dictatorship. | Severan dynasty

Septimius enlarged the army until it contained several legions more than the army of Augustus. He also raised soldiers' pay, ensuring their loyalty. Septimius militarized the civil government as well, by making extensive use of generals in positions of power. With these changes, the route to high office lay through the emperor's army instead of the *cursus honorum* (described in **Figure 4.3**). Rome had changed indeed.

Septimius established a dynasty (the Severan) that uneasily held power until 235. His son Caracalla (r. 211–217) was ruthless and was murdered while on campaign. Strong women in the Severan family—Julia Maesa, Caracalla's aunt, and her two daughters—managed to ensure that two more incompetent boys took the throne, but both Elagabalus (r. 218–222) and Alexander (r. 222–235) were murdered.

In the fifty years that followed Alexander's death, Rome was beset with chaos. During this period, legions in various parts of the empire put forth their own claimants to the throne. This era of conflict—from 235 to 285—was dominated by what has come to be called "barrack-room emperors," men who had little allegiance to the ancient values of the city of Rome. From 235 to 285, the number of claimants to the throne exploded. In one nine-year period, the emperor Gallienus fought off as many as 18 challengers. A unit whose general became emperor increased its own status, so armies fought for the throne.

While armies were busy trying to create emperors, Rome's borders were threatened on all fronts. In the north, Germanic tribes (discussed more fully in Chapter 6) began to penetrate across the Rhine and Danube defenses. Soldiers and resources had to be moved north to try to stem the tide. Meanwhile in the east, Rome seemed so weakened that Zenobia, a powerful queen of Palmyra (a city in Syria), declared | Border wars

independence from Rome and led armies against the legions. Emperor Aurelian (r. 270–275) crushed Palmyra after two wars and brought Queen Zenobia in chains to Rome. The resourceful queen ended up living out her life in an extravagant villa near Tivoli in

Italy, but her city was destroyed. Rome was not as successful in other eastern campaigns, as the Persian Empire encroached on Rome's eastern provinces. A Persian rock inscription celebrates a Persian victory and indicates the stress on the empire during these dark days: "We attacked the Roman Empire and annihilated . . . a Roman force of 60,000."

This whole military era demonstrates the centrifugal force that had marked Rome's growth from the beginning. Emperors were created in barracks far from Rome, and territories on the edges of the empire were slipping from centralized control. As if these internal and external pressures were not enough, a severe economic downturn loomed.

Ravaged by Recession, Inflation, and Plague

At the height of the empire, certain families accumulated astonishing wealth. Even though they gave some of it back to the public in the form of monuments or games, they still lived lavishly. Not only did they buy jewels and fine silks, but they gave banquets featuring exotic (and expensive) 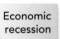 imported foods. One menu from a Roman cookbook recommends rare dishes from the far reaches of the empire: sow's udders stuffed with salted sea urchins, Jericho dates, boiled ostrich, roast parrot, boiled flamingo, and African sweet cakes.

This kind of luxury spending seriously damaged an already weakening economy for two reasons: It drained hard currency from the West and transferred it to the Far East, which supplied many of the luxuries; and it kept money from circulating, thus limiting the avenues for the growth of a prosperous middle class. As the poor in Rome received more and more food subsidies, the city had to spend more money on imported grain, further reducing the treasury. With the increase in imports from the East, the western centers of the empire began to suffer a shortage of hard currency, as money flowed to the great eastern centers that supplied most of the imports. As we will see, this shifting of wealth to the East had profound ramifications for the governing of the empire.

There was a further inherent weakness in the imperial economy: When territorial expansion stopped, there was little to bring new wealth into the empire. Instead, a growing bureaucracy, increased military expenses, and costly military rivalries served to drain money. The economy stagnated while expenses increased.

Emperors throughout the centuries tried to address the problem of a shortage of hard currency by debasing the coinage, which meant that plenty of money still circulated, but it was not worth as much as it had been before. Gold coins virtually disappeared from circulation, and by the mid-third century the silver content of coins had dropped to a negligible 1 percent. Not surprisingly, inflation struck. The price of grain climbed so much | Inflation | that a measure that cost two coins in 200 C.E. cost 330 coins just a century later. Inflation always hits the poor hardest, and many people turned to banditry out of desperation. The resulting fear and unrest further rocked life in the empire.

To worsen matters, plague from China spread through the empire along with the luxury goods that came along the Silk Road. (See Global Connections, page 145.) Just as in China, the disease caused intense suffering and depleted the already low Roman population. Labor became as scarce as hard currency. The Roman government turned to the tribes outside its borders to replenish its armies. Mercenaries crossed the borders to fight for Rome, and the legions of Rome increasingly came to resemble the "barbarians" from the outside. Structures like Hadrian's Wall no longer clearly separated the "civilized" from the "uncivilized."

All the problems of the late second and third centuries demonstrated that the Roman Peace was over. The borders between Roman and non-Roman had dissolved, and hungry, restless residents agitated within the empire. Medical knowledge was helpless in the face of pandemics like the mid-third-century plague, and Roman families could no longer populate the empire. The empire seemed to teeter on the brink of collapse.

The Reforms of Diocletian, 285–305 C.E.

Considering the many disasters facing the empire in the mid-third century, it is a wonder that the empire did not fall then. In fact, it was the dramatic measures of Diocletian, an autocratic new emperor, that helped Rome avert ultimate disaster—at least for the time being. Diocletian (r. 285–305) was a general who rose from the ranks to wear the imperial purple. Not content to be called emperor, he assumed the title "lord" and demanded that his subjects worship him as a living god. (See Document 5.2.) The change in title marked the formal end of the principate founded by Augustus—from then on, emperors were no longer "first citizens." Diocletian had a shrewd, practical side and used his considerable administrative talents to address the problems plaguing the empire. The new Roman lord was up to the task and stopped the decline.

Turning to the problems of communication, administration, and succession, Diocletian organized the government into | Tetrarchy | a **tetrarchy,** or rule by four men. Diocletian ruled in the wealthier eastern region of the empire, while assigning his partner, Maximian, to

thinking about

DOCUMENTS

DOCUMENT 5.2

Diocletian Becomes "Lord"

The Roman historian Aurelius Victor in the middle of the fourth century wrote a brief work titled Lives of the Emperors *in which he described the transformation of Diocletian from a "first citizen" like Augustus to a more aloof, godlike figure.*

By decision of the generals and [military] tribunes, Valerius Diocletian, commander of the palace guards, was chosen emperor because of his wisdom. A mighty man he was, and the following were characteristics of

his: he was the first to wear a cloak embroidered in gold and to covet shoes of silk and purple decorated with a great number of gems. Though this went beyond what befitted a citizen and was characteristic of an arrogant and lavish spirit, it was nevertheless of small consequence in comparison with the rest. Indeed, he was the first after Caligula and Domitian to allow himself to be publicly called "lord," and to be named "god," and to be rendered homage as such. . . . But Diocletian's faults were counterbal-

anced by good qualities; for even if he took the title of "lord," he did act [toward the Romans] as a father.

SOURCE: Aurelius Victor, *Lives of the Emperors*, in *Roman Civilization: Sourcebook II: The Empire*, eds. Naphtali Lewis and Meyer Reinhold (New York: Harper Torchbooks, 1966), p. 456.

Analyze the Document

1. How did Diocletian present himself to the Roman public?

2. What innovations does Aurelius Victor describe? Did this historian approve of Diocletian's actions?

3. Contrast this view of leadership with that of Augustus shown in Document 5.1. Why do you think the Romans were prepared to accept such a kinglike demeanor in Diocletian?

---

rule in the West. To address the issue of succession, each of these "augusti" adopted a "caesar" who would succeed him. In the Roman tradition dating back to Octavian, each caesar married his augustus's daughter, sealing the alliance through family bonds. **Figure 5.9** depicts the ideals behind the tetrarchy. The four emperors—all military men—rest their hands on their swords. They also embrace one another. The overall arrangement of their figures conveys the concept of a unified rule by four men. **Map 5.4** shows the territorial division of the tetrarchy.

Diocletian then turned his administrative talents to problems other than succession. He recognized that the military that had created so many emperors from the time of Septimius Severus onward was a threat to political stability. He brought the army under control in part by reversing Septimius's policy of uniting civil and military offices. He separated the two so that provincial governors could not command armies, thus making it harder for generals to aspire to the purple. To address the problem of incursions along the imperial frontiers, Diocletian rearranged the armies. Instead of placing his greatest martial strength along the borders, he stationed mobile legions deep inside the empire. That way, they could move quickly to meet a threat rather than just react as outsiders encroached. The Germanic tribes on the northern borders were particularly eager to enter the empire, looking for wealth. Diocletian recruited many of these Germans to serve in this new army, further diluting its traditional Roman character even as he made it more effective.

Military reforms

FIGURE 5.9 Tetrarchs, ca. 305 C.E. Diocletian's division of the Roman Empire's administration among four men might have seemed to some to fragment it. This statue from Venice shows the four tetrarchs embracing and thus strongly linked as one, assuring the viewer that the empire still stood united.

MAP 5.4

Diocletian's Division of the Empire, 304 C.E.

This map shows Diocletian's administrative reform of the empire and its division into four parts that would be governed by a tetrarchy (four men). Notice the primary division into east and west, with each unit ruled by an augustus.

Explore the Map

1. What geographic advantage led Diocletian to take the eastern portion of the empire?

2. Ravenna and Byzantium became the two new capitals of the empire, replacing Rome. What advantages did each city's location offer for trade and defense?

Finally, Diocletian turned to the severe economic problems troubling the empire. In the same way Augustus had tried to improve morality by decree, Diocletian issued economic edicts. He addressed the rampant inflation by freezing prices and wages, but these policies simply led merchants to withdraw goods from the open market to participate in informal black market exchanges. The emperor also raised taxes to pay for an expanding army, but he reformed the tax

| Economic reforms |

system so that it was partially based on payment in goods instead of in the inflated, scarce coins. This kind of authoritarian approach could not solve the empire's most deep-seated economic troubles, but it kept the economy from collapsing altogether.

The last problem that Diocletian addressed was the simple shortage of people to perform the tasks needed to keep the empire running. Again, he sought solutions in decrees. He identified "essential" occupations—ranging from soldier to farmer, baker, and tax collector—and froze people in these jobs. Furthermore, he made these occupations hereditary. His decrees had a serious unintended consequence: They weakened the willingness of well-off locals to contribute to the public works and the games that had so defined imperial life. Instead, great estates became more self-contained, pulling away from the central authority and maintaining their own mercenary armies. People increasingly complained about the tax collectors and the central government that seemed to ask more and more of its citizens while providing less and less.

The Capital Moves East

Diocletian's attempts to stabilize the succession barely outlasted him. He and his co-augustus stepped down in 305 as planned, leaving the empire to be ruled by their two caesars, but Diocletian's hopes for a smooth transition proved overly optimistic. There were years of intrigue and civil war as several rulers fought for the throne. Finally, one of the caesars was succeeded by an ambitious son, Constantine (r. 306–337), who defeated his rivals to assume sole control of the empire. The new emperor finally disbanded the powerful praetorian guards, who had backed his rival. Beyond that, he kept Diocletian's economic and military reforms but put his own unique stamp on the empire.

In 330, Constantine made a momentous decision for the future of the empire: He built a new urban center on the site of the old Greek city of Byzantium. Later the city would be called Constantinople, after its founder, and become a second capital to the empire, eclipsing Rome itself in power and grandeur. Rome was no longer a practical site for the capital of the empire because it was too far from the center of the military actions on the borders, and the conservative old Roman nobility made it very difficult for emperors to implement vigorous new ideas. Constantine could not have chosen a better site for a new capital city, which he called his "new Rome." It was easily defended and located along the rich eastern trade routes. Since Diocletian, when emperors ruled autocratically based in cities away from Rome, the great Roman Senate that had governed in concert with Augustus had shrunk to no more than a city council. The Roman Empire seemed to have little to do with Rome anymore and bore scant resemblance to the principate created by Augustus.

As the capital moved east, the western provinces came under increasing pressure from the Germanic tribes outside the empire. Great estates in the provinces—called *latifundia*—became more self-sufficient, needing nothing from the central authority. After the death of Constantine in 337, emperors reacted to Germanic invaders by inviting some

Constantinople

tribes into the empire to settle and become allies. The borders had already proved permeable, and with the continued population decline within the empire, there seemed to be enough space for everyone. This influx, however, carried the seeds of the empire's eventual disintegration. The Visigoths (more fully described in Chapter 6) were one of the tribes the Romans invited across the border to settle. However, the Romans treated them abysmally, giving them land they could not farm, raping their women, and forcing them to sell their children into slavery in return for food. The warlike tribe went on a rampage.

In 378, Romans under Emperor Valens (r. 364–378) confronted Gothic troops, and the resulting battle marked a change in military tactics. The Goths were heavily outnumbered by the heavy Roman infantry that had always seemed invincible. The Romans pushed the Goths back to their circled wagons, and defeat seemed imminent. Just then, Gothic cavalry dashed from the hills, smashing the Roman line. The infantry was no match for mobile cavalry, and the Roman army was destroyed. Emperor Valens was killed on the field. This battle dispelled the aura of invincibility that had surrounded the Roman legions for centuries and demonstrated the military importance of cavalry. It seemed that military might now lay in the hands of the "barbarians" rapidly pouring through the borders.

Even Rome itself was no longer the center of the empire, for by the fourth century, the emperors in the West had made Milan their capital. Then, in 402, Emperor Honorius fled from the invading Visigoths to create a new capital in Ravenna, behind defensible marshes. Ravenna was safe, but Rome was not, and in 410, the Visigoths plundered the "eternal city," Rome itself. Masses of panicked Romans (like Melania in the Biography on page 170) fled to Africa and the East.

It seemed that an era had passed and that the empire had finally fallen—but the end had not come quite yet. The Visigoths left Italy and settled in Spain as allies of the empire, just as many other tribes had done in other provinces. An emperor remained in the west, ruling from Italy, and a co-ruler continued to govern in the east, from Constantinople. But by 410 the western region had disintegrated so much that there seemed to be no point in referring to a Roman Empire in the West at all.

Twilight of the empire

For the last few centuries, historians have spent a great deal of thought (and paper) exploring what has come to be known as the "fall" of the Roman Empire that began in the turmoil of the third century. Historians point to dwindling population, economic problems, reliance on slave labor, civil warfare, and moral decay as the causes of the decline. All of these factors contributed to the transformation of the old Roman world, but perhaps more important than

Rome's "fall"

anything else was the great influx of peoples from the north who invaded the empire. These invasions (which we will explore in more detail in Chapter 6) caused the breakup of the huge empire that had dominated the Mediterranean world since the time of Augustus. The territorial empire was ending, but throughout these years of power and turmoil a religion arose that would give a new source of unity to the Mediterranean world.

THE LONGING FOR RELIGIOUS FULFILLMENT

As we saw in Chapter 4, the Romans were a deeply religious people who carefully linked their deities to cherished spaces. As the empire controlled more and more land, its subjects seemed increasingly distanced from their traditional gods. In part, worship of the emperor served as a unifying religious cult. By the middle of the third century, some twenty festival days honored deified emperors or their families each year. However, for all the reverence given to the emperors, a spiritual dissatisfaction still gnawed at the Roman people. Many Romans seemed to long for a closer relationship to a truly transcendent divinity, and Romans expressed this longing through a rise in various philosophic and religious movements.

We can see this attempt to bring the gods a little closer to earth in the increasing numbers of spells and charms that Roman men and women purchased. People tried everything from healing and love charms to curses placed on chariot racers. Prophets, magicians, and charlatans also proliferated. One late-second-century writer described a man who made a fortune by pretending to prophesy through a giant serpent that he wrapped around himself. However, all the religious movements of the Roman world were not as superficial as magical curses and false prophets.

Stoicism and Platonism

The Hellenistic philosophies (Chapter 3) all continued to offer religious satisfaction to some educated Romans. The great Roman Stoic Seneca (ca. 4 B.C.E.–65 C.E.) wrote that by focusing on their own ethical behavior, people could locate the divinity that dwells within each person. As mentioned earlier, the Stoic emperor Marcus Aurelius used this philosophy to bring meaning to the challenges of his life. Like the reflective emperor, many people found in Stoicism ethical principles to help guide their lives, and Stoicism exerted an important influence on both Christianity and Western ideas in general.

The most influential philosophical system, however, came with a new form of Platonism, **Neoplatonism,** that emerged during the late empire. In the third century, these Neoplatonists created a complex system that offered an explanation for the link between the divine and the human.

Like Stoics, Neoplatonists believed that each person contained a spark | Neoplatonism | of divinity that longed to join the divinity that had created it. Through study, contemplation, and proper living, people could cultivate that bit of divinity within themselves and thereby reduce the distance between the human and the divine.

These philosophies, though intriguing, had limited appeal. Just as they had in the earlier Hellenistic kingdoms, they attracted people with leisure, education, and a respectable income. Most people instead tried to satisfy their spiritual desires through one or more of the mystery cults that gained popularity in the second century.

Mystery Cults

The mystery cults that had become popular during the Hellenistic world (Chapter 3) had an even stronger appeal in the difficult times of the late empire. These cults had always offered hope to individuals seeking meaning in their lives and ecstatic celebrations that seemed to transport individuals outside themselves into the world of the gods. Some cults claimed to offer a universality lacking in many of the Roman deities, and many offered hopes of a better afterlife to people disenchanted with their current existence.

The ancient Greek cult of Dionysus is one example of a cult that promised all these things. In this popular worship, men and women celebrated the mysteries of the god of | Cult of Dionysus | wine and rebirth by drinking, engaging in sex acts, and ritually eating the raw flesh of beasts. **Figure 5.10** shows a painting discovered in Pompeii that probably depicts the worship of Dionysus. The young woman on the left is being whipped, probably to bring about an ecstatic state. The woman on the right dances in naked ecstasy with a cymbal while the woman before her prepares to hand her the staff marking her entrance into the mysteries. Such ceremonies appealed to people's need to feel personally connected with the divine.

The cult of Isis, the Egyptian goddess of fertility, enjoyed remarkable popularity throughout the empire. Septimius Severus and his wife portrayed themselves as Isis | Cult of Isis | and her consort, Serapis. As we saw in Chapter 1, the ancient Egyptians called Isis's husband Osiris, but in the Hellenistic period, when many of the Egyptian deities were assimilated into the Greek pantheon, Osiris began to be called Serapis. As the noted Greek biographer Plutarch (ca. 46–ca. 120 C.E.) explained, "Serapis received this name at the time when he changed his nature. For this reason

FIGURE 5.10 Mystery Religions, first century C.E. This fresco is from the Villa of the Mysteries near Pompeii, a site that was preserved by its burial in volcanic ash from the eruption of Mount Vesuvius. The image shows women participating in a sacred ritual, probably for the god Bacchus.

Serapis is a god of all peoples in common." In his new form as Serapis, the old god Osiris left his traditional home of the Nile and brought protection to wide areas of the empire. Thus, Serapis was an appropriate incarnation for Septimius, a North African emperor who wanted to combine imperial worship with that of a popular mystery religion to try to overcome Rome's lack of a single, unifying religion.

While some cults, like that of Serapis, strove for universal appeal, the worship of other deities was not intended to be for everyone. Instead, initiates prided themselves on participating in an exclusive and difficult worship. For example, some men and women celebrated the mystery of the Great Mother, the female goddess who brought fertility and comfort. In frenzied rituals, celebrants flogged themselves until their blood flowed, and some men castrated themselves as an ultimate sacrifice to the goddess. In another example, imperial soldiers felt particularly drawn to the mysteries of Mithraism, whose followers were exclusively men, and the religion's emphasis on

self-discipline and courage made it very popular with the armies of Rome. These soldiers gathered in special buildings, ritualistically ate bread and water, and awaited salvation.

These different mysteries practiced throughout the Roman world reflected the multicultural nature of the empire. People were willing to partake in mysteries of any origin, whether Egyptian, Syrian, or Persian. All these practices emphasized the irrational at the expense of the rational, in contrast to the Stoic or Platonist approaches. But in the ancient world, people did not feel compelled to choose only one path to spiritual fulfillment. The famous second-century author Apuleius, for example, was a magician, a Platonist, and an initiate into the mysteries of Isis.

The Four Faces of Judaism

Although Palestine had struggled for religious purity while under the Hellenistic kings, the Jews under Roman rule were not exempt from the religious angst

MAP 5.5

Israel at the Time of Jesus

This map shows the kingdom of Herod under the rule of Rome. It also illustrates how this kingdom reunited Judah and Israel and at the same time how much smaller it was than the old empire of King David.

Explore the Map

1. Where do the trade route lines go? What diverse influences did Judaism experience from the countless travelers who passed through the small kingdom?

2. Where were the major sites of Jesus' ministry? How close together were they? (Consult the scale.) How might these distances have contributed to the ministry?

that swept the empire. At the time of Julius Caesar, the kingdom of Judah had been ruled by descendants of Judas Maccabes (see Chapter 3), but the kingdom was swept into the turmoil of Rome's civil wars following the death of Julius Caesar. Finally, Herod, a member of a prominent family in Hebron, south of Jerusalem, rose to power and, with the support of Octavian, was made king of Judea and subject to Rome by the Senate of Rome. **Map 5.5** shows the kingdom of Herod and illustrates its central location in the trade of the Middle East. Herod was unpopular with the Jews, and during this kingdom, controversies grew. The struggles of four main Jewish groups shaped the religious and political future of this region and beyond.

The **Sadducees** largely comprised members of priestly families. They emphasized Jewish worship at the Temple in Jerusalem, which they saw as the cult center of the Israelites. (In Chapter 3 we saw that the Temple had been rebuilt in the sixth century B.C.E.,

| Sadducees and Pharisees |

and this structure—which had been further rebuilt in 19 B.C.E.—is known as the Second Temple.) The Sadducees were religious conservatives who rejected any "new" ideas that they did not find in the Torah—the first five books of the Bible.

These innovations included the ideas of angels and resurrection of the dead, both of which began to win more adherents. The Sadducees were also willing to compromise with the Hellenized world and the Roman rulers as long as the Temple cult remained secure. However, the Sadducees would not continue as a viable force after Titus destroyed the Temple in 70 C.E.

The **Pharisees,** on the other hand, emphasized Jewish purity laws. They refused all compromise with the Hellenized world and adhered strictly to dietary rules and rituals to reinforce their separateness from all non-Jews. However, the Pharisees did accept new ideas such as the resurrection of the just and the existence of angels. For Pharisees, Judaism centered not on public worship in the Temple but on the private observances of Jews all over the Roman world. The Pharisees also supported sayings and interpretations of Jewish scholars, such as the influential Hillel the Elder (ca. 30 B.C.E.–ca. 10 C.E.), that later became part of the Jewish tradition. It was the work of the Pharisees that would ultimately lead to the expanded writings that updated the practice of the Torah.

Although the Pharisees believed strongly in separating themselves from the surrounding non-Jewish world, they avoided political revolution. Another group in Palestine, the **Zealots,** took a different approach. This group looked back to the successful revolt of the Maccabees against Seleucid rule and urged political revolt against Roman rule as a way to restore Israel to an independent state. Not surprisingly, clashes between the Zealots and Roman troops broke out throughout the early first century C.E.

Despite their differences, all these groups were struggling in some way with the same question that had plagued Jews since the first Hellenistic conquest: how to maintain a separate identity within the Roman world. A fourth group, the **Essenes,** tried to avoid the problem altogether by withdrawing from the social world. The Essenes moved to separate communities and attempted to live pure lives, seemingly alienating themselves from the Temple cult. The Essenes have drawn much scholarly attention because they probably authored one of the most exciting archaeological finds in biblical history, the Dead Sea Scrolls.

In 1947, a shepherd boy discovered a deep cave containing ancient pottery jars holding hundreds of scrolls of texts dating from as early as 250 B.C.E. The scrolls include such valuable works as the oldest version of portions of the Hebrew Bible and other documents revealing the historical context of the biblical texts. Most of the works are severely damaged and have been reconstructed from hundreds of tiny fragments, which leaves lots of room for differing interpretations. Although many of the texts have been studied since the 1950s, there is still no scholarly consensus surrounding these precious scrolls.

Most scholars believe these texts were produced by the Essenes in their mountain retreat in Qumran (see **Map 5.5**)—a desert community fifteen miles from Jerusalem, near the Dead Sea—and hidden in the cave during the turbulent times when Rome was exerting its dominance in the region. All the writings were completed before 68 C.E., when the Romans destroyed the settlement at Qumran. Some scholars believe the writings came from a large library of various Hebrew documents, and thus they may reveal the origins of the many strains of Judaism, perhaps even the early Jesus movement. It is certain that continued analysis of these texts will shed a good deal of light on these early centuries that were so fertile to spiritual impulses.

In this time of spiritual longing, many Jews believed that a savior—a Messiah—would come to liberate them. Some believed that he would be a political figure who would liberate the Jews from foreign domination, and people like the Zealots were poised to fight for this political leader. Others, however, expected a spiritual savior—a Chosen One who would bring a kingdom of righteousness to earth. The Essenes may have withdrawn to the desert community to wait for the spiritual Messiah—their "Teacher of Righteousness." It was into this volatile religious time that Jesus of Nazareth was born.

The Jesus Movement

During the reign of Augustus (r. 27 B.C.E.–14 C.E.), at the beginning of the empire, a child named Jesus was born in about 4 B.C.E., possibly in Bethlehem (about 10 miles southeast of Jerusalem, shown on **Map 5.5**). This event dramatically influenced the empire by the fourth century. Thus, we must return to the time of Augustus to trace the fortunes of a small religious sect in Judea that would ultimately conquer Rome itself.

The information we have on Jesus' life and teachings is drawn largely from the Gospels of the New Testament of the Bible, which were written sometime after his death, probably by people who never knew him. (Estimates on the time of the composition of the Gospels range from thirty to ninety years after Jesus' death.) The Gospels offer little information about the first thirty years of Jesus' life. They do tell us that he was the son of a woman named Mary and a carpenter named Joseph and that he excelled in his religious studies, for he confounded the priests of the Temple with his knowledge of matters of faith.

According to the limited historical information available, Jesus drew from the rich religious environment in the Jewish lands. Like the Pharisees, he appealed to the poor, and many of his sayings resembled those of Hillel the Elder. His teachings also had some qualities in common with those of the Essenes, who had written of a coming Teacher of Righteousness. Unlike the Zealots, Jesus spoke of a heavenly kingdom rather than a violent revolution and attracted a large following of those who longed for a better life. Jesus began his ministry after being baptized by John the Baptist, and the Gospels tell the story of his activities after this defining event in some detail. For many, Jesus was the awaited Messiah who would save and transform the world. Many called him Christ—the Lord's Anointed, the Messiah.

While Jesus' ideas resembled those of some of his contemporaries, the totality of his message was strikingly new and changed the course of Western civilization. For about three years, Jesus preached in Judea and Galilee, drawing huge crowds to listen to his message of peace, love, and care for the poor and suffering. He was accompanied by a small group of devoted followers—the apostles—who carried on his message after his death. Many people also believed that he performed miracles and cures. His growing popularity alarmed both Jewish leaders and Roman authorities, who constantly watched for uprisings in Judea. In about 29 C.E., the Roman governor, Pontius Pilate, sentenced Jesus to crucifixion, the cruel death reserved for many of Rome's enemies. The Romans nailed a sign on Jesus' cross identifying him as the "king of the Jews," perhaps mistranslating the powerful notion of Messiah as king, and certainly underestimating the nature and appeal of Jesus and his message.

Jesus' brief, three-year ministry had come to an end. However, three days later, Jesus' followers believed they saw him risen from the dead and subsequently taken into heaven. They believed this proof of Jesus' divinity promised a resurrection for his followers, and the apostles wanted to spread this good news to other Jews.

A small group of Jesus' followers led by the apostles Peter and James formed a Jewish sect that modern historians call the Jesus movement to identify the period when followers of Jesus continued to identify themselves as Jews. The apostles appealed to other Jews by preaching and praying at the Temple and at small gatherings of the Jewish faithful. The earliest history of this Jesus movement is recorded in Acts in what Christians call the New Testament of the Bible. Like others throughout the Roman world, these Jews believed that prophecy and miracles marked the presence of the divine. Thus, the apostles, the followers who had known Jesus personally, began traveling to bring his message to others. They spoke in prophetic tongues and appeared to work miracles. They also began preaching in Jewish communities around the Mediterranean world.

| Apostles |

The early Jesus movement could have taken various different directions. Would Jesus' followers withdraw from society like the Essenes and John the Baptist had done? The apostle James moved to Jerusalem and centered his leadership of the church there, thus choosing not to lead a sect in the wilderness. A more thorny issue was the question of accepting Gentiles—non-Jews—into the new religion. James took a position of conservative Judaism, insisting that Christianity required its adherents to follow the circumcision and strict dietary laws that had marked the Jewish people. The apostle Peter seems to have been more willing to preach to Gentiles, particularly "God-fearing" Greeks who were interested in the ethical monotheism of the Jews. Peter believed they would not have to be circumcised or keep all the Jewish festivals, but they would have to follow the dietary restrictions.

However, the man who would be remembered as the Apostle to the Gentiles had not known Jesus before his crucifixion. Saul of Tarsus (ca. 5–64 C.E.), whom we remember by the name of Paul, was a Hellenized Jew and a Roman citizen who had at first harassed Christians. After he experienced a vision of the risen Jesus, he converted and took up the mission of bringing the Christian message beyond the particularity of the Jewish communities to the wider world of the Roman Empire and beyond. He moved beyond Peter by eliminating all dietary restrictions on Christians, and he traveled widely through the eastern portion of the empire establishing new Christian communities. **Map 5.6** shows where Paul journeyed and how the Christian message slowly spread throughout the Roman world. Paul's influence on the young church was immense, and his letters became part of the Christian Scriptures.

| Paul of Tarsus |

Religious tensions between Jews and Roman authorities in Palestine culminated shortly after the deaths of Peter and Paul. Rome finally decided to take strong action against those in Judea, including Zealots, who were rebelling against Roman rule. In the course of the suppression, the Essene community at Qumran was destroyed (but not before they had buried their precious scrolls, which we call the Dead Sea Scrolls), and then the armies proceeded against Jerusalem. In 70 C.E., the son of Emperor Vespasian, Titus (who later became emperor in his own right), led Roman legions into Jerusalem, burned the city, and destroyed the Second Temple. All that seems to have remained of Herod's great

| Destruction of the Temple |

*All dates are C.E.

THE ROMAN EMPIRE

14	Augustus dies
ca. 29	Jesus is crucified
64	Nero persecutes Christians
70	Titus destroys Jerusalem
193	Septimius Severus establishes military monarchy
ca. 285	Diocletian establishes tetrarchy
313	Constantine issues decree of toleration of Christians
ca. 385	Theodosius makes Christianity official religion
410	Visigoths sack Rome
ca. 420	Augustine writes *City of God*

KEY DATES

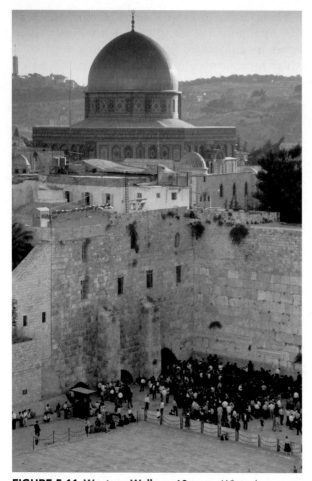

FIGURE 5.11 Western Wall, ca. 19 B.C.E. When the Romans destroyed the Jewish Temple in Jerusalem, all that was left standing was the western wall. This architectural remnant was called the Wailing Wall for centuries as Jews visited the site and lamented the loss of the Temple. Now people often refer to it simply as the Wall.

temple was the western wall. **Figure 5.11** shows this location, which has become an important symbol of Jewish faith and a location for prayer. For many years it was called the Wailing Wall, so designated to mark it as a mourning space for the destruction of the Temple. In the twenty-first century, it is more often called the Western Wall, and in Hebrew, it is simply called the Wall. (See Document 5.3.)

Titus returned to Rome in a triumphal procession and built a great arch celebrating his accomplishment. **Figure 5.12** shows a marble relief from that arch, in which Titus's troops return victorious from Jerusalem clutching spoils from the Temple. This figure shows soldiers carrying an important symbol of Judaism, the great menorah—a candelabra that held seven candles—which had been sacked from the holy place. The Temple was never rebuilt. Many Jews were scattered from Judea all over the Mediterranean after this devastation, and with them traveled numerous followers of the Jesus movement.

The destruction of the Temple inadvertently resolved the tensions within Judaism. The Sadducees, Essenes, and Zealots were all destroyed, and the Pharisees made peace with the Romans and recentered Judaism on synagogue worship. An emphasis on prayer and the law replaced sacrifices at the Temple. After 70 C.E., the Hebrew canon of scriptures came to be closed and the Hebrew Bible—what the Christians would call the Old Testament—was completed. Followers of the great teacher Hillel reached a compromise with the authority of Rome that let Jews maintain an identity within the empire, and future rabbis would study scripture and interpret the ways Jews should act while living among Gentiles.

> **Dispersion of Jews**

The conquest of Jerusalem also settled any question about whether Christianity was to be centered in Jerusalem. Early Christianity, like Diaspora Judaism, was to be a religion that was not bound to one city, and it began to claim universality. The Jesus movement within Judaism was transformed and was now more accurately called the early Christian church.

Early Christian Communities

The spread of Christianity was slow. Small groups of converts in the major cities of the empire gathered in one another's houses because there were no designated churches for the new movement. When members of the small communities met together at least once a week, people took turns reading scripture, praying, and offering other forms of worship. As Paul wrote: "When you come together, each one has a hymn, a lesson, a revelation, a tongue, or an interpretation" (1 Cor. 14:26). "Tongue" and "interpretation" refer to speaking prophetically, which people in the communities believed proved the presence of God in their midst. The culmination of the service was the Eucharist—the commemoration of Jesus' last supper—in which the faithful shared cups of wine and pieces of bread. Members then offered prayers of thanksgiving for Christ's sacrifice and death, which the faithful believed offered them salvation and eternal life.

The relatively small numbers of Christians grew consistently throughout the first few centuries after the death of Jesus. Some estimates suggest that the total number of Christians at the beginning of the third century C.E. was about 200,000, or less than 0.5 percent of the total population. Although this is a small percentage, the actual number is significant—Christians were slowly becoming more visible. The church father Tertullian (ca. 160–ca. 217) wrote that there were thousands of Christians in Carthage in about 200, and he was probably accurate—a few thousand Christians in a population of about 500,000. This small but growing number would periodically come into conflict with the power of Rome.

FIGURE 5.12 Marble Relief Depicting the Sack of Jerusalem, ca. 81 C.E. The Romans erected a triumphal arch to commemorate Emperor Titus's victory in Jerusalem. The scenes depict the treasures—which the Romans described as a "river of gold and silver"—that flowed from their conquest. They were most impressed, however, by the huge golden menorah from the Temple, shown prominently in this detail from the arch.

FROM CHRISTIAN PERSECUTION TO THE CITY OF GOD,

64–410 C.E.

Conservative Romans looked askance at any innovations, particularly religious novelties. It was one thing for Christians to worship someone who had died within living memory as a divinity, but it was quite another for them to reject the traditional Roman assortment of gods. Furthermore, early Christians seemed to violate the traditional Roman social order by including the poor, slaves, and women as equals in their congregations.

Christians, who gathered unobtrusively in communities, differed significantly from Pagan Romans in their views of what happened after the faithful died. They expected their bodies to be resurrected after death. This new attitude toward the dead transformed traditional Roman attitudes and practices toward corpses. Roman graves were considered polluting and were dug outside the walls of the city. We have seen (Chapter 4) that the bodies of the poor received little respect as they were buried shallowly by garbage. Christians wanted to keep their dead close to the community, and the **catacombs** dug under the city in about the second century to bury the Christian dead are one of the visible reminders of this dramatic change. **Figure 5.13** shows the burial spaces in a

catacomb. Here, rich and poor alike were interred to await resurrection together.

Looking for Christian Scapegoats

To quell accusations that he was responsible for a devastating fire in Rome, Emperor Nero looked for scapegoats and implemented the first large-scale persecution of Christians in Rome in 64 C.E. He executed hundreds of Roman Christians, possibly including the apostles Peter and Paul, and set a precedent that would be repeated periodically over the next two centuries. During the contentious years, provincial officials played a leading role in the persecutions. Some of these authorities chose to harass Christians; others ignored the new religion. Whatever their policy, however, the texts make it clear that when Christian men and women were brought to the arena, many died so bravely that some Roman spectators promptly converted.

During the third century when the empire confronted many internal and external problems, its policy toward Christians grew harsher. Under Emperor Decius (r. 249–251) and then again under Emperor Diocletian (r. 285–305), all imperial residents were to sacrifice to the emperor and receive a document recording their compliance. Diocletian, the autocratic emperor who legislated wages, prices, and military matters, thought he could decree religious beliefs as

DOCUMENT 5.3

Titus Destroys Jerusalem

In the first century C.E., the Jewish historian Josephus wrote a history of the Jews in which he described the violent destruction of Jerusalem in 70 C.E. by Titus. Josephus was an eyewitness who first fought against the Romans, then fled to the Roman camp and flourished in Rome after the war. In this excerpt, Josephus describes first the internal dissensions among the Jews (whom he calls the "seditious") and then relates the destruction that burnt the Second Temple.

The legions had orders to encamp at the distance of six furlongs from Jerusalem, at the mount called the Mount of Olives, which lies over against the city on the east side, and is parted from it by a deep valley, interposed between them, which is named Cedron.

Now, when hitherto the several parties in the city had been dashing one against another perpetually, this foreign war, now suddenly come upon them after a violent manner, put the first stop to their contentions one against another; and as the seditious now saw with astonishment the Romans pitching three several camps, they began to think of an awkward sort of concord, and said one to another: "What do we here, and what do we mean, when we suffer three fortified walls to be built to coop us in, that we shall not be able to breathe freely? While the enemy is securely building a kind of city in opposition to us, and while we sit still within our own walls and become spectators only of what they are doing, with our hands idle, and our armor laid by, as if they were about somewhat that was for our good and advantage. We are, it seems (so did they cry out), only courageous against ourselves [in mutual argument], while the Romans are likely to gain the city without bloodshed by our sedition." Thus did they encourage one another when they were gotten together and took their armor immediately and ran out upon the Tenth legion and fell upon the Romans with great eagerness, and with a prodigious shout, as they were fortifying their camp. . . . [After a long and bloody siege, the Romans finally entered the city.]

Now the number of those that were carried captive during this whole war was collected to be ninety-seven thousand; as was the number of those that perished during the whole siege eleven hundred thousand, the greater part of whom was indeed of the same nation [with the citizens of Jerusalem], but not belonging to the city itself. . . .

Now this vast multitude is indeed collected out of remote places, but the entire nation was now shut up by fate as in prison, and the Roman army encompassed the city when it was crowded with inhabitants. Accordingly the multitude of those that therein perished exceeded all the destructions that either men or God ever brought upon the world; for, to speak only of what was publicly known, the Romans slew some of them, some they carried captives, and others they made a search for underground, and when they found where they were they broke up the ground and slew all they met with. There were also found slain there above two thousand persons, partly by their own hands and partly by one another, but chiefly destroyed by the famine. . . . And now the Romans set fire to the extreme parts of the city, and burned them down, and entirely demolished its walls.

SOURCE: Josephus, *The Jewish Wars*, in *The Great Events by Famous Historians*, vol. III, ed. Rossiter Johnson (The National Alumni, 1905), pp. 151, 205–206.

Analyze the Document

1. How do the Jews' internal problems impede their defense of Jerusalem?

2. Why does Titus so thoroughly destroy the city?

3. How do you think the dissension among the Jews might have affected them after their dispersion?

---

well. But this wide-scale demand for conformity only provoked many more Christians to die for their beliefs. **Map 5.6** reflects the extent of Christian strength after the persecutions of Diocletian had ended.

Constantine: The Tolerant Emperor

In the long tradition of Roman emperors, Constantine looked for supernatural help in his wars with his rivals. According to the Greek historian Eusebius (ca. 260–ca. 340), as Constantine prepared for a crucial battle he saw in the sky a vision of a cross with Greek writing reading, "In this sign, conquer." That night he had a prophetic dream explaining that soldiers would triumph only if they fought under Christian symbols. He obeyed the dream and won a decisive victory. To the Romans, dreams and omens carried crucial religious messages, and Constantine's nighttime message convinced him of the power of the Christian God. In 313, he issued a decree of toleration (the Edict of Milan) for all the religions of the empire, including Christianity, and the martyrdoms ended.

Constantine did more than simply tolerate Christians. He actively supported the church. He returned property to Christians who had been persecuted, gave tax advantages to Christian priests, and let Christian advisors play a role in his court's inner circle. Constantine's support of Christians probably derived in part from his military victory under

> Constantine supports church

FIGURE 5.13 Christian Catacombs, ca. second century C.E. Unlike pagan Romans, who buried their dead outside the city, Christians longed to keep their "holy dead" close to the worship sites of the living. These catacombs were underground burial spaces for early Christians in Rome.

and state that moved Christianity in a new direction: It would continue to flourish and grow in the shadow of the imperial throne. It seems that the emperor finally committed to the new religion on his deathbed; he was baptized a Christian. His delay, however, has provoked much historical speculation. Had Constantine judged it politically unwise to become a Christian as he ruled, or had he not yet made up his mind? We do not know for sure, but we do know that subsequent emperors expanded his policies, moving from toleration toward a commitment to sole Christian worship.

The Empire Adopts Christianity

Theodosius I (r. 379–395) put the final cap on the movement toward Christianity by forbidding the public worship of the old Roman cults. With this mandate, Christianity became the official religion of the Roman Empire. Of course, everyone did not immediately convert to Christianity; Judaism remained strong, and those who clung to traditional Roman religious beliefs came to be called pagans. This word came from *pagani,* a derogatory term for backward peasants, and its etymology shows how Christianity spread first from urban centers.

This merging of a political and Christian empire irrevocably changed both Rome and Christianity. After the fourth century, Christian communities looked very different from those of two centuries earlier. Instead of gathering secretly in one | Christianity changes | another's homes, Christians met publicly in churches that boasted the trappings of astounding wealth. Indeed, where once people converted to Christianity in spite of the danger of persecution, the influential church father Augustine (354–430) complained, some people now converted only to impress the rich and powerful.

Figures 5.14 and **5.15** illustrate this shift in the status of Christianity. In **Figure 5.14,** a second-century statue of Christ depicts him as the Good Shepherd. He appears as an unpretentious peasant, wearing the typical shepherd costume of the day. The Good Shepherd was the most popular portrayal of Christ in the early, simple centuries of Christianity. **Figure 5.15** shows a very different Good Shepherd. In this fifth-century mosaic, Christ wears the royal purple cloth of emperors. Now the Lord, he watches over his flock rather than working to convert nonbelievers. The gold in the mosaic demonstrates the new wealth of

the sign of the cross. The women in his family exerted a strong influence on him as well. His half-sister Constantia and his mother, Helena, were both Christians. Whatever religious motives Constantine had for his support of Christianity, the emperor remained a shrewd politician. In fact, his support of the new religion included a practical political basis. For one thing, there were so many Christians in the empire that it would have been unwise to continue to marginalize them. Furthermore, Constantine's withdrawal of support for traditional pagan shrines permitted him to confiscate their gold to help standardize his currency.

Under Constantine's patronage, the Christian movement grew rich and powerful, and the emperor built beautiful churches in support of the religion. As part of the emperor's respect for Christianity, he decided to restore the Holy Places at Jerusalem and Palestine to Christian worship. Helena toured the region to identify the sacred spaces, but this was quite a feat, for since the destruction of the Temple, Jerusalem had become a Roman city that had lost all identification with its Jewish past. Nevertheless, Helena located what she believed were key sites in the life of Jesus, building great churches where he was born and where he died. With the backing of Constantine and his family, Jerusalem was revived as a holy place, and Christians began to make pilgrimages there. These journeys began a tradition of Christian claim on that land that would continue throughout the Middle Ages.

Constantine's support of Christianity throughout his life established a relationship between church

MAP 5.6

The Spread of Christianity to 311 C.E.

This map shows the areas of Christian strength by the fourth century and traces Paul's journey as he conducted his missionary work.

Explore the Map

1. Where were the areas of greatest Christian concentration? What might this clustering reveal about how influential Greek and Eastern thought was for the future development of the church?

2. Why did many of the Christian locations coincide with regions of commerce?

3. Why did Christianity spread mostly within the borders of the Roman Empire?

the church, as the image of Christ is transformed from that of a simple man to Lord of the universe.

As the empire embraced Christianity, the organization of the church began to duplicate the civil order of Rome. The emperor Diocletian had clustered provinces into larger units, called dioceses, for ease of administration. The church retained these divisions and placed bishops in charge of the major communities. Bishops were in charge of all aspects of church life, from finances to spiritual guidance, and as early as the third century in most regions they were paid by a church depending increasingly on

| Christian organization |

their administrative skills. For example, by 245 C.E. the province of North Africa had 90 bishops, and each was served by a well-developed hierarchy of priests and deacons. The ecclesiastical structure of the dioceses was divided into parishes, presided over by priests who reported to the bishops.

With Constantine's support, the church had become powerful. In the political world, power meant the ability to impose a uniformity of practice and even belief. Emperor Constantine tried to guide the church toward this kind of unity, and the church fathers began looking to authority figures to help them resolve differences. Prophecy—so important to the

FIGURE 5.14 Christ as the Good Shepherd, second century C.E. The earliest centuries of Christianity were marked by slow missionary work to gather new converts. The predominant image for this time and initiative was that of Christ the Good Shepherd gathering his flock.

In the eastern part of the empire, the relationship between bishops and emperor took a different turn. Beginning with Constantine, emperors in the East had involved themselves directly in religious disputes. Since the early third century, for example, Christians had quarreled over the nature of Christ. "Had he always existed," they asked themselves, "or did God bring him forth at a particular time?" In about 320, Arius, bishop of Alexandria, raised a furor when he argued that Jesus had been created by God. Arius's teachings polarized believers all over the empire, and Constantine did not want such a dispute raging in his lands. Therefore, he called a meeting that was the first "ecumenical" council—purportedly with representatives of the whole inhabited world. In 325, Constantine vigorously presided over the bishops he had summoned to the Council of Nicaea to resolve Arius's dispute over the nature of Christ. With the formulation of the Nicene Creed, which stated that Christ had always existed, Constantine and his bishops hoped to put that controversy to rest. However, as we shall see in Chapter 6, Arius's beliefs had already spread, and the church would have to face the problem of **Arianism** again. The council also set the precedent that orthodox Christians could exert their authority over those who believed otherwise.

Religious disagreements

Similarly in North Africa, Christians split over what to do about bishops and others who had "lapsed" during the years of persecution. This controversy was called the Donatist heresy, named after one of the protesting bishops. Church leaders believed it was essential to protect the notion that sacraments—like baptism and the Eucharist—were valid regardless of the behavior of the presiding priest, so they declared that bishops who had proven weak when threatened by torture could continue to hold their offices. The Donatists disagreed, saying that lapsed priests could *not* conduct the sacraments. Yet, passions had run so high over this issue that Donatists separated and tried to start a new church. The dispute catalyzed much violence in North Africa for centuries until the barbarian invasions created enough turmoil to move this issue to the background.

These and many other religious quarrels that spilled into secular politics raised the question of the relationship between church and state. In the early church, the relationship had been simple—Christianity focused on the next world while enduring an antagonistic earthly relationship with an unsympathetic state. Now, with church and state combined, the situation had become exceedingly complex. Many Christians felt ill at ease with all the resulting uncertainty. In his influential work *City of God* (413–427), Augustine tried to address these very complexities. Writing after the Visigoths had sacked Rome and terrified Romans had fled the city in waves, he explained that Christians

City of God

early church—became suspect, replaced by obedience to authority. As leaders began to look to a hierarchical organization for guidance in religious matters, it was perhaps inevitable that questions would arise over who should lead—religious or secular leaders. Ambrose (r. 374–397), the bishop of Milan in Italy, was one of the earliest bishops to challenge the power of the emperors and set a precedent for later bishops. In 390, Ambrose reprimanded Emperor Theodosius for massacring some rebellious citizens: The bishop excommunicated the emperor, forbidding him to participate in church services until he repented. Theodosius acceded to the bishop's demands, and later bishops of Rome (who came to be called popes) looked to this example of the church leading the state.

FIGURE 5.15 Christ as the Good Shepherd, ca. 450 C.E. After the Roman Empire became Christian, artists began to portray Christ with more imperial majesty. Here, Christ the Good Shepherd is shown clothed in gold and royal purple and presiding over his flock rather than working with his hands.

should not look at the current disasters with despair, nor see in them divine punishment. Instead, the church father drew from his strong background in Neoplatonism to explain worldly pain much as Plato had (described in Chapter 2), but with a Christian understanding. Augustine claimed that the world—and worldly cities—were made up of individuals who were constantly in struggle between their spiritual and earthly selves. Those people in whom the spiritual dominated belonged to a City of God, and those in whom the earthly dominated belonged to an earthly city. The perfect community of the faithful—the City of God—could exist only outside this world and would dominate at the end of time. In the meantime, all communities were mixed with members of both cities. Therefore, people ought to obey the political order and focus on the worthiness of their own souls rather than the purity of the reigning political institutions. They need not worry even when the city of Rome was sacked.

For Augustine and other religious thinkers, church and state were not incompatible. In fact, these men believed that the state should play an active role in ensuring the health of the church. In the early centuries of Christianity, **heresy** (expressing opinions that differed from official church doctrine) could

be considered treason punishable by civil sanctions. Augustine, for example, suggested confiscating the property of the Donatists to persuade them to conform. However, in the late fourth century, a Christian heretic (Priscillian) was sentenced to death. As the ultimate power of the empire was brought to issues of conscience in these ways, church members learned that the path to salvation lay in obedience. Inevitably, there were Christians who objected to this direction, but the majority saw in this Christian order a fulfillment of God's plan—a victory for the earthly church.

The New Roman

Like political institutions and the church itself, everyday Roman life was also transformed with the burgeoning strength of Christianity. As church fathers in many regions of the empire wrote on matters of religion, they also addressed the larger question of how the new Christian Roman was to behave. In some areas of life it was easy simply to prohibit certain behaviors. For example, the church fathers wrote that Christians should not attend gladiator shows or arena games. Over time, the great amphitheaters fell out of use. Instead, Christian Romans satisfied their appetite for spectacle with chariot races, which remained hugely popular for centuries. In other areas, religious leaders and the populace reached a compromise—Christians could read the beloved traditional literature, such as Virgil or Homer (even though it praised pagan gods and suspect morality), but they were to try to extract a Christian message from it. (This is a major reason why such literature has survived.)

Christians also reshaped the social fabric of Roman life. For example, they did not believe in exposing unwanted children. Indeed, through the early centuries, they actively rescued foundling infants and raised them as Christian. Furthermore, they placed enormous priority on caring for the poor and needy. By the middle of the third century, church records show, in Rome alone the bishop provided charity for more than 1,500 widows and others in need.

Views on sexuality also shifted with the influence of the church fathers. As we have seen, although the Romans showed a certain cautiousness in their sexual lives, they also passionately believed that people had a duty to marry and procreate. Some Christian leaders, on the contrary, strongly advocated celibacy as the ideal life. Numerous Roman men complied with this recommendation, and many women used Christian celibacy as a way to free themselves from the expectations that they would marry and bear children. The influential church father Jerome (ca. 348–420) surrounded himself with chaste women who studied and traveled with him and founded monasteries. The Biography featuring Melania the Younger tells of one such fourth-century woman who was famous and admired during her lifetime and who spent her vast wealth establishing enduring religious institutions.

The most influential writer on sexuality was Augustine. In his widely read work *The Confessions*, he described his inability to give up his mistress and his "habit" of lust. As he explained, only with God's help was he able to summon the resolve to renounce these vices. This experience convinced Augustine that human beings were born with original sin and that this sin was passed to subsequent generations through semen during sexual intercourse. Because of original sin, Augustine concluded, people had to keep constant vigil against the force of lust—even marital intercourse was somewhat suspect. Through this kind of thinking, religious leaders involved themselves in people's private lives, and this watchfulness continued for centuries through a growing body of church law. Hardly any aspect of Roman life was left untouched by the Christianization of the empire.

Christian sexuality *(margin note)*

THE HOLY LIFE

For early Christians, the path to God came through community; congregations of the faithful gathered together to help each other withstand the pressure of a hostile society. By the fourth century, some Christians were choosing another path to spiritual perfection. Men and women by the thousands left society to live alone in the deserts of Egypt and Syria, and their experiences profoundly influenced Christian life and thought.

Some Christians fled into the desert to escape the persecutions and chaos of the mid-third century. Others left during the fourth and fifth centuries because they objected to the union of church and state that developed after Constantine's rule. Still others fled the tax collectors. Whatever the reasons, the popularity of this movement reached enormous proportions. Historians estimate that by 325, as many as 5,000 men and women lived as hermits along the banks of the Nile, each in his or her own small cell. The fame of these holy people spread. Jerome advocated an ascetic life even for urban people and persuaded numerous wealthy Roman women to join him. Romans were scandalized when one of Jerome's young charges starved herself to death in her zeal for asceticism, but such was the passion for what many perceived was a holy life.

Flight to the desert *(margin note)*

Many of these holy men and women survived extraordinary feats of self-denial—enduring lack of food, sleep, and other basic necessities. Some people insisted on living for decades on platforms perched high on poles. Women in particular sealed themselves into tombs that had only a tiny opening through which they could receive a small loaf of bread, and they eked out their lives in cramped, filthy solitude. These people's contemporaries found their behaviors so unusual that they concluded that to endure such hardships, the holy men and women must be recipients of God's power.

Of course, the extreme deprivation of heroic abstinence was not for everyone. Some people wanted simply to withdraw from the distractions of the world so as to worship God without enduring the rigors of the desert hermits. Communal monasticism developed as a parallel movement to the hermit life and offered an appealing alternative to life in the thick of Roman society. Discipline was strict in these pious oases, but participants had contact with other people, and conditions were not as harsh as those in the desert. In time, communal monasteries were brought into the overall structure of the church. Monks and nuns took vows of obedience to the monastery head (the abbot or abbess), and the monastic leader answered to the local bishop.

Monastic communities *(margin note)*

The Influence of Holy People

The earliest holy people had been the Christian martyrs. Faithful observers witnessing their brave deaths concluded that God had invested their

BIOGRAPHY

Melania the Younger
(385–ca. 439)

FIGURE 5.16 Melania the Younger Icon.

A Model

of Holiness

Melania was born in 385, the daughter of a rich Roman patrician. By the time of her birth, Christianity was the official religion of the empire, and as a young girl she experienced the conflict of values that confronted so many Christian Roman families. Starting in her youth, Melania longed to follow a life of ascetic chastity like that of earlier holy women. As a daughter of Rome, however, she was expected to marry and bear children. As was the custom in a society in which women married young, when Melania was 14 years old her family arranged for her to marry Pinian.

The young bride begged her new husband to live chastely with her so they could better worship God. Pinian wanted first to ensure the worldly succession of his family, so he told Melania she must bear two children before he would consider her request. A daughter was born to the young couple. Melania became pregnant again, but during this pregnancy she practiced many austerities in her search for a holy life. For example, she repeatedly prayed on her knees all night against the advice of her physician and the pleas of her mother. Furthermore, as a symbol of her commitment, she began to wear rough wool under the smooth silk clothing of the upper class. It is ironic that this return to republican simplicity was seen as rebellion by her family.

Melania's father tried to exert his paternal authority and make her care for herself and her unborn child in the traditional ways, but Christian beliefs introduced competing loyalties into family life. The young woman disobeyed her father, and her son was born prematurely. The infant boy died shortly after being baptized. Melania and Pinian's daughter died soon after that. Like so many Roman families, this young couple was unable to produce heirs. They saw the will of God in their children's deaths, however, and at age 20, Melania persuaded Pinian to join her in a vow of chastity.

As her first demonstration of religious commitment, she sought to liquidate her property. Her biographer's description of the problems involved in this task suggest the scale of wealth that many imperial Roman families had accumulated. For example, Melania owned thousands of slaves that she could not free without contributing adversely to Rome's unemployment problem. Furthermore, her house was so expensive even the emperor could not afford to buy it. However, the turmoil of the times helped resolve the difficulties of disposing of her property. The Visigoths who sacked Rome burned Melania's home, and she was able to sell the ruined property easily. As she and Pinian fled to Africa in the wake of the invasion, Melania used her money to ransom captives and buy islands for fellow ascetics to use as holy retreats.

After liquidating most of her wealth, Melania escalated her personal renunciations. She began to fast regularly, eating only some moldy bread twice a week. Beyond that, she spent her days reading and writing. She knew both Latin and Greek and studied the scriptures and the writings of church leaders. As her reputation for holiness grew, people began to come to her to listen to her teach.

Melania and Pinian then traveled from North Africa to Jerusalem to tour the holy places that Constantine had identified. From there, they visited the holy men and women living in the deserts of Egypt. Finally, Melania decided to found monasteries in Jerusalem, where she and Pinian could embark on a communal life dedicated to spirituality. Joined by 90 virgins and some reformed prostitutes, Melania spent the rest of her life studying, teaching, and traveling to holy sites. Shortly after her death, the faithful began to venerate her burial place, where miracles reputedly took place.

Melania's life exemplifies the Roman world transformed. She began as a well-off young girl, wearing silk and expecting to carry on the traditions of an upper-class Roman. After the disastrous barbarian invasions, she settled in the Holy Land, wearing rough wool and embodying the new values of the Christian world.

Connecting People & Society

1. How does Melania's life reveal the conflict of values between pagan and Christian Rome?

2. How did the Visigoths' invasions affect Melania and her family?

3. Where did Melania settle, and what did she do? How might she have served as a model for others?

bodies with the power to withstand torture. People believed that martyrs' remains contained sacred power and saved and venerated their bones, or **relics.** One woman in North Africa was reprimanded by her bishop for bringing a sacred bone to church and kissing it repeatedly. This kind of veneration strengthened the notion of resurrection of the flesh, in which the tortured flesh itself would receive its reward. Christianity thus became a religion that accepted the body. Believers wanted the holy dead to be buried near them, and by the fourth century, most altars included relics. In a very short time, the faithful and the enterprising began to engage in a brisk trade in relics that would be lucrative and influential throughout the Middle Ages. Historians have uncovered letters in which people solicit relics to help increase the power of their churches, and some of the correspondence is quite poignant. Bishop Braulio in seventh-century Spain responded to one such request, writing that he had many valuable relics, but all the labels had been lost. He could no longer identify the bones, but asked if the correspondent wanted them anyway.

Relics were preserved, treasured, and displayed in reliquaries—containers, often covered in precious metals and jewels, that displayed the precious bones that lay within. These reliquaries spread | Saints' cults | all over Europe and became a visible feature of the growing religion. Exquisite jeweled containers were supposed to express both the power of the relic and the incorruptibility of heaven, where people believed the saint dwelled.

The desert fathers and mothers eventually supplanted the martyrs. They, too, seemed to embody holiness physically, and their *Sayings* reinforced the idea that people could not find spirituality without somehow sanctifying the flesh itself. Ironically, these holy people had traveled to the desert to find God and instead discovered their own humanity. They learned about the hunger that could drive one mad and about sexual urges that could relentlessly haunt their dreams. They even discussed nocturnal emissions and reflected on how to overcome boredom. The thinking of these spiritual people gave Christianity a profoundly human touch.

Like the martyrs, many of these holy people became venerated upon their deaths. The cult of saints became a strong part of Christian faith. Just as people believed that martyrs could intercede for them with God, so they felt convinced that prayer to a holy man or woman might also help | Ascetic influence | them attain their desires. Holy men and women who had learned so much about their humanity by transcending it seemed accessible even to the most ordinary of people. Saints gained reputations for doing everything from raising the dead and healing the sick to extending a too-short wooden beam so an overworked carpenter would not have to cut another. The conversion of the northern European countryside was inspired largely by living and dead holy people who had brought God's power down to the community.

The ascetic practices of the monasteries also shaped the lives of everyday Christians. Even for people who did not adhere to the strict rules of the monasteries, the luxuries of the Roman world seemed shameful when compared with the purity of the monasteries. Over time, people concluded that the ideal Christian life should be simple, and some Christians looked with disdain at those who surrounded themselves with comfort and pleasure. This tendency of monastic rigor to influence Christian life continued throughout the Middle Ages.

Monasteries always served both as havens during stormy political times and as outlets for those who sought a highly spiritual life. For centuries, these communities rejuvenated the Christian world and helped the church meet people's changing spiritual needs. Men and women in search of personal spiritual perfection would ultimately become powerful social forces for the medieval world.

LOOKING BACK & MOVING FORWARD

Summary The conservative Romans who mourned the death of Julius Caesar and celebrated the victory of his young nephew Octavian (Augustus) would hardly have recognized the world of Augustine or of the late-fourth-century emperor Theodosius. The great territorial empire governed four hundred years earlier by Augustus and his successors in the name of the Senate and the people of Rome was still impressive. However, it was now a Christian empire ruled from Constantinople by an emperor who governed in the name of God and was advised by bishops.

KEY TERMS

Pax Romana, p. 138

principate, p. 139

praetorian guard, p. 139

tetrarchy, p. 153

Neoplatonism, p. 157

Sadducees, p. 159

Pharisees, p. 159

The huge borders of the "civilized" world were still guarded by Roman legions, but by the fourth century these borders had become porous. The guarding legions more often than not wore the trousers of the Germanic peoples and rode horses instead of marching in the disciplined ranks of the tunic-clad Romans.

Sadly for Rome, the centrifugal forces pulling this radically transformed empire apart would prevail. As we will see in Chapter 6, the Roman Empire eventually split into three parts: Byzantium in the east, the Muslim world in the south, and the Germanic kingdoms in the west. However, the glory and accomplishments of Rome would remain in the West's memory and periodically inspire people to try reviving its greatness.

REVIEW, ANALYZE, & CONNECT TO TODAY

REVIEW THE PREVIOUS CHAPTER

Chapter 4—"Pride in Family and City"—described the rise and fall of the Roman Republic and the way expansion changed Roman life and values.

1. Review the "twilight of the Republic" that led to the civil wars and the murder of Julius Caesar. How did Augustus avoid the fate of Julius Caesar? What reforms did Augustus make to help the new empire endure?

2. Review the strengths and virtues that made the early Roman Republic so successful. Which of those were lost through the fourth-century reforms of Diocletian and Constantine? To what degree did these reforms contribute both to the decline of the empire and to its preservation?

ANALYZE THIS CHAPTER

Chapter 5—"Territorial and Christian Empires"—continues the story of the Roman Empire as it dominated the Mediterranean region for hundreds of years. The empire survived many crises and in turn was dramatically transformed by Christianity.

1. Consider the economic advantages of the great territorial empire of the Romans. Who benefited most from the Mediterranean trade? Who benefited least? What central weakness did the economy have during the empire?

2. What was the Silk Road? What goods traveled along it, and why was it so important to both the Roman and Han empires?

3. Describe the social, cultural, and medical ideas that contributed to Rome's declining population.

4. Review the situation in Judea and the various ideas within Judaism during the time of Jesus. How did the political and cultural environment in Judea affect the growth of Christianity?

5. Review the relationship between the early Christians and the Roman authorities. How did Christianity move from a persecuted sect to the religion of the Roman Empire?

6. The adoption of Christianity by the Roman Empire created profound transformations in both the early Christian church and the empire itself. Review these changes and consider which might have the longest-standing impact on the future of Western culture.

CONNECT TO TODAY

Think about the impact of the imperial Romans in establishing a multicultural empire, long-distance trade, and a revolution in religious life.

1. What similar issues is U.S. society struggling with today? In what ways might the study of the Roman Empire help citizens of the twenty-first century sort out and address public issues? In other words, what can we learn from the past?

2. What places in the world today are wrestling with changes in religion and with questions about the church-state relationship such as those that marked the late Roman Empire? How might people of opposing religious views avoid the violent religious struggles experienced by imperial Romans?

BEYOND THE CLASSROOM

THE *PAX ROMANA,* 27 B.C.E.–180 C.E.

Eck, Werner, et al. *The Age of Augustus,* 2nd ed. Cambridge, MA: Blackwell, 2007. A concise biography using varied sources to explain this revolution in the structure of Rome.

LeBohec, Yann. *The Imperial Roman Army.* New York: Hippocrene Books, 1994. A good description of the all-important Roman military.

LIFE DURING THE PEACE OF ROME

August, Roland. *Cruelty and Civilization: The Roman Games.* New York: Routledge, 1994. An exciting history of gladiators, chariot racing, and other games that offers an explanation of their appeal and function within society.

Dupont, Florence. *Daily Life in Ancient Rome.* Oxford: Blackwell, 1993. An informative interpretation of ancient Rome that describes and analyzes the everyday experiences of the Romans.

Jackson, Ralph. *Doctors and Diseases in the Roman Empire.* Norman: University of Oklahoma Press, 1988. A broad and concise account of classical medicine as it culminated in the Roman Empire.

Weidmann, Thomas. *Adults and Children in the Roman Empire.* New Haven, CT: Yale University Press, 1989. An interpretative analysis that traces changes in adult attitudes toward childhood.

CRISIS AND TRANSFORMATION, 192–ca. 400 C.E.

Gamsey, Peter D. *Famine and Food Supply in the Graeco-Roman World: Response to Risk and Crisis.* New York: Cambridge University Press, 1988. A study of the concerns and responses of both urban and rural dwellers to food crises, actual or anticipated.

Jones, A.H.M. *The Later Roman Empire, 284–602,* 2 vols. London: Blackwell, 1964. The most comprehensive classic study on the subject by a master historian.

Williams, S. *Diocletian and the Roman Recovery.* New York: Routledge, 1996. A vivid work that brings the emperor and his times to life and clearly explains Diocletian's military and civil reforms.

THE LONGING FOR RELIGIOUS FULFILLMENT

Riches, John. *The World of Jesus: First-Century Judaism in Crisis.* New York: Cambridge University Press, 1990. An examination of the ways in which Jewish figures and groups of the first century—including Jesus—reacted to the basic social, economic, and political realities of the time.

Turcan, Robert. *The Cults of the Roman Empire.* Cambridge, MA: Blackwell, 1996. A sound study of the cults during the Roman period.

FROM CHRISTIAN PERSECUTION TO THE CITY OF GOD, 64–410 C.E.

Brown, Peter. *Power and Persuasion in Late Antiquity: Toward a Christian Empire.* Madison: University of Wisconsin Press, 1992. Reopens the question of how the empire's transformation from paganism to Christianity affected its civic culture.

Carroll, James. *Constantine's Sword: The Church and the Jews.* Boston: Houghton Mifflin, 2002. An award-winning book that explores the relationship between Constantine's conversion, the adoption of the cross as a Christian symbol, and growing anti-Semitism. Provocative and fascinating reading.

Ehrman, Bart D. *Lost Christianities: The Battles for Scripture and the Faiths We Never Knew.* New York: Oxford University Press, 2003. A well-researched and clearly written look at the various early forms of Christianity that shows how they came to be suppressed or forgotten.

Frend, W.H.C. *The Rise of Christianity.* Philadelphia: Fortress Press, 1984. A comprehensive summary of the growth of Christianity, which includes the major figures and controversies of the movement.

Pagels, Elaine. *Beyond Belief: The Secret Gospel of Thomas.* New York: Vintage, 2004. An award-winning scholar of Gnosticism shows the diversity of the beliefs circulating in the early Christian communities.

Salisbury, J.E. *The Blood of Martyrs: Unintended Consequences of Ancient Violence.* New York: Routledge, 2004. A book that explores the ancient Christian martyrdoms that transformed many modern Western ideas, including images of the body, sacrifice, anti-Semitism, motherhood, suicide, and others.

Salisbury, J.E. *Perpetua's Passion: The Death and Memory of a Young Roman Woman.* New York: Routledge, 1997. A description of the cultural, social, and religious environment of early-third-century Carthage told through the story of a young martyr.

Stark, Rodney. *The Rise of Christianity: A Sociologist Reconsiders History.* Princeton, NJ: Princeton University Press, 1996. A controversial but influential analysis of how Christianity spread.

THE HOLY LIFE

Brown, Peter R.L. *The Body and Society: Men, Women, and Sexual Renunciation in Early Christianity.* New York: Columbia University Press, 1988. A classic study of the ascetic movements and their impact by the major scholar of late antiquity.

Bynum, Caroline Walker. *The Resurrection of the Body in Western Christianity, 200–1336.* New York: Columbia University Press, 1995. A fascinating look at the impact of martyrs and saints on ideas of the body and the afterlife.

GLOBAL CONNECTIONS

Wood, Frances. *The Silk Road: Two Thousand Years in the Heart of Asia.* Berkeley: University of California Press, 2004. A comprehensive and beautifully illustrated account that demonstrates the tremendous impact of the Silk Road in spite of relatively light traffic.

Looking Ahead to the Middle Ages, 400–1400

The breakup of the Roman Empire did not come easily. Warrior bands and official armies alike inflicted destruction and suffering on many throughout the old Roman Empire. From this violence arose what historians have come to call the Middle Ages (or medieval period), which extended from about 400 to about 1400. During that millennium, bloodshed intensified as three distinct cultural identities emerged in the Mediterranean basin and vied with one another for land, power, and affirmation of their faith. In the seventh century, the Prophet Muhammad and his followers established a new religion—Islam—that extended from the old Persian Empire in the east through North Africa and into Spain in the west. Byzantium—the eastern, Greek-speaking portion of the old Roman Empire—also developed its own language, religion, and politics, each of which distinguished it from the other two areas.

Meanwhile, the region in the northwestern portion of the old Roman Empire divided into disparate kingdoms that also boasted a unique culture. People living in these western realms called their region Christendom. Sometimes, but not always, they included the Christian Byzantine Empire in this designation. Byzantines, for their part, preferred to distance themselves from these "barbaric" westerners. Later historians (and geographers) would call the western region of Christendom Europe and Western civilization. However, just as in the ancient world, the West during the Middle Ages developed its distinctive character through interaction with the rest of the world.

But before the tenth century, Europeans' contact with other peoples diminished, as the disruptive violence caused them to withdraw from the great trade nexus that had marked antiquity. While the peoples of Islam and Byzantium maintained their cross-cultural contacts, western Christendom's inhabitants looked inward.

In the meantime, other parts of the world prospered. In the late sixth century, an ambitious ruler in northern China—Yang Jian—reunited China under centralized control after the centuries of fragmentation that followed the Han dynasty's collapse. The resulting succeeding dynasties—the Sui, Tang, and Song—organized Chinese society so efficiently that China became a leader in agricultural and industrial production.

These changes in China had a dramatic effect on the West after the eleventh century. Chinese inventions and innovations (from wheelbarrows to gunpowder) found their way west and transformed life in Christendom. In some cases, we can identify the agents of this transmission; for example, monks smuggled Chinese silkworms to Byzantium in order to implement a new cloth industry. In other cases, we cannot, though new ideas and inventions likely spread slowly from neighbor to neighbor across the Eurasian continent. Chinese technologies moved throughout east Asia as well, altering people's way of life in Korea, Vietnam, and Japan.

Even though India remained politically disunited during the early Middle Ages, the huge subcontinent molded cultures in south and southeast Asia. Over time, Islam attracted a popular following in India. Indeed, the new faith joined Hinduism and Buddhism as one of the major religions of the region. The connections between India and Islam remained strong through trade in the Indian Ocean, as Muslim merchants set up operations in all the major coastal cities in India. These mercantile centers remained fruitful sources of cultural exchange between Indians and Muslims in other lands, including Africa. Silk and porcelain from China; spices from southeast Asia; and pepper, precious gems, cotton, and many other goods from India swept through the Indian Ocean basin. All these goods—as well as exciting new ideas—eventually found their way

to Europe, transforming Christendom through commercial activity and the social interaction that often comes with it. Perhaps one of the most influential exports from India was "Arabic numerals," which probably originated in India and acquired the "Arabic" appellation later. These numbers, which we use today, replaced Roman numerals and facilitated advanced mathematical calculations.

Between about 1000 and 1450, many other peoples also established vast empires and huge trading networks. For example, Mongols, nomadic peoples from central Asia, created a great empire based in China that facilitated trade across Asia. Powerful states and empires emerged in Africa as well. In the kingdom of Kongo, for example, rulers built a strong central government. During these same centuries, the arrival of Islam in Africa transformed cultures there. Muslims from North Africa capitalized on the profitable trade across the Sahara Desert and down the African coasts. As they traded, they attracted Africans to their faith. By the tenth century, the kings of Ghana had converted to Islam, and other peoples followed. Over the next two centuries, tremendous wealth accumulated along coastal east Africa. Evidence indicates that a rich tradition of Muslim scholarship also arose in these cities.

Far across the oceans, peoples living in the Americas and Oceania were changing as well. In Central and South America, the Maya, Toltecs, Aztecs, and Incas all built impressive societies, with large populations, social hierarchies, and magnificent architectural structures. Through eastern North America, large populations of healthy communities built large earthen mounds in many places. One near the Mississippi River was a four-level mound bigger than the Great Pyramid at Giza. Pueblo and Navajo peoples practiced irrigation and skillfully constructed complex adobe and stone buildings that still

Medieval Empires and Two World Travelers

impress visitors. Modern scientists have reconsidered the view that the Americas were sparsely settled outside the regions of the empires of Meso-america; indeed, Amerindians settled throughout North and South America in large numbers. Perhaps even 40,000,000 people might have lived here before the diseases of Eurasia decimated the populations.

By 1000, a brisk trade had emerged among the islands in the south Pacific, testifying to the skill of navigators who could traverse the large spans of the Pacific. By 1100, even the more distant Hawai'ins and Tahitians had forged commercial ties.

What of the West in the face of such dynamic global developments? By 1000, Europeans were once again venturing out and interacting with others around the world. Scandinavian Vikings traveled overland, establishing settlements in eastern Europe and buying and selling goods all the way to China. They also journeyed west into Iceland, Greenland, and North America, where they both traded and fought with indigenous peoples.

By the twelfth century, interactions between Christendom and Islam exerted a particularly powerful impact on both cultures. Crusading Christian armies confronted Muslims on the battlefields of the eastern Mediterranean and North Africa. However, more fruitful exchanges took place in Sicily and Spain, where Muslims and Christians lived side by side in relative harmony. In these places, Christian scholars studied Muslim learning, and Christian artisans and farmers adopted and benefited from Muslim innovations, like improved irrigation techniques. Merchants in the Italian city-states also profited from extensive trade with Muslims all over the Mediterranean.

As the thirteenth century dawned, Europeans began making contact with peoples even farther from their borders. Merchants and others on the move began to roam across the Eurasian continent. Marco Polo, a Venetian merchant, worked at the Chinese court. Ibn Battuta, a Muslim judge, traveled from Mali (in Africa) to Spain, and across eastern Europe to China. These are only the most prominent examples of people who forged global connections during the Middle Ages. In spite of staggering distances and slow travel, the world seemed to be shrinking. It would appear to compress even further in the fifteenth century as Europeans ventured across the oceans.

Thinking Globally

As the center of Western civilization shifts north, how might this affect life in the West?

1. Refer to the map above. What do you notice about trade throughout the Eurasian landmass?

2. What might have been the advantages and disadvantages of travel by land or sea?

3. Notice the location of the large empires. How might these political units have facilitated trade and other interactions?

175

THE DOME OF THE ROCK, JERUSALEM, ca. 691

This Muslim pilgrimage site is located on the holiest place in Jerusalem. Jews revere the site as the place where they believe Abraham was told to sacrifice his son, Isaac. Muslims believe that the prophet Muhammad ascended to heaven from this spot. Christians respect it as the location of the Temple where Jesus walked. This building symbolizes the dramatic cultural transformations that unfolded as the Roman Empire dissolved, and it stands on one of the most contested pieces of land in history.

A World Divided

Western Kingdoms, Byzantium, and the Islamic World, ca. 376–1000

"The harsh nature of war! The malevolent fate of all things! How proud kingdoms fall, suddenly in ruins! Blissful house-tops that held up for long ages now lie torched, consumed beneath a huge devastation." These lines, written by Radegund, a nun living in sixth-century Gaul, poignantly express the turbulent world in which she lived. The Roman Empire was no longer a political unit that people could rely on for peace within its borders. The once mighty empire had fragmented into three culturally distinct parts separated by religion, language, and loyalties.

In the west, Germanic invaders established new kingdoms and converted to Christianity. Popes in Rome slowly became a force to be acknowledged in the West. In the East, the political form of the Roman Empire continued at least nominally for another thousand years. However, centered in the great city founded by Constantine, and separated from Rome, Byzantium began developing its own distinct character. The language of government changed to Greek, and people began to mingle more with the Slavic tribes to the north than with the Latins in the West. Finally, the desert of Arabia produced a prophet, Muhammad, who profoundly influenced the religious beliefs of millions. Followers of the new religion of Islam swept out of the desert and conquered the eastern and southern shores of the Mediterranean, as well as most of Spain. These three civilizations—the heirs of Rome—existed in uneasy, sometimes violent, proximity. Their differences and conflicts would remake the map of the Mediterranean basin and shatter the Roman unity that had graced the land for so long.

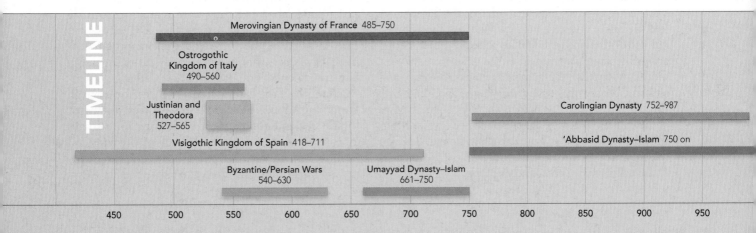

TIMELINE

Merovingian Dynasty of France 485–750

Ostrogothic Kingdom of Italy 490–560

Justinian and Theodora 527–565

Carolingian Dynasty 752–987

'Abbasid Dynasty–Islam 750 on

Visigothic Kingdom of Spain 418–711

Byzantine/Persian Wars 540–630

Umayyad Dynasty–Islam 661–750

450   500   550   600   650   700   750   800   850   900   950

THE MAKING OF THE WESTERN KINGDOMS,
ca. 376–750

Sidonius Apollinaris (ca. 431–ca. 480) was a Roman nobleman living in Gaul. He received a classical Roman education and wrote letters to his friends that brimmed with stories of the gracious life of a provincial Roman. In his missives, he described a lifestyle blessed by culture, ease, and luxury. Yet, Sidonius also witnessed much turmoil in his lifetime. In one letter he wrote, "Our town lives in terror of a sea of tribes which find in it an obstacle to their expansion and surge in arms all round it." He defended the walls of his town against the invading Visigoths and was imprisoned by the attackers. Later his captors released him, and he lived out the rest of his days tranquilly, serving as bishop in a town now governed by Visigoths. His Roman world had been reshaped, but not obliterated. To understand the changes that Sidonius experienced, we must first meet the Germans, who played such a major role in the remaking of the Roman Empire.

Life in a German Clan and Family

Who were these "Germani" that the Romans called "barbarians"? In about 500 B.C.E., when the earliest Romans were settling on the seven hills of their city and beginning their republic, groups of Indo-European Scandinavian people began to migrate south into the Baltic states and Germany and east into Ukraine. As they fanned out across the land, their tribes took on a bewildering array of separate names: East Goths (Ostrogoths), West Goths (Visigoths), Burgundians, Franks, Saxons, and so forth. These tribes traded with Rome and sometimes threatened its northern borders throughout the history of the empire. Whereas Chapter 5 focused on life within the empire, here we will move back in time to describe the culture of the early Germans and follow the fortunes of the tribes as they entered the empire.

Because the Germanic tribes had originally come from a small region in Scandinavia, they shared many cultural similarities. Their settlements were based on clans—families joined in kinship groups. A whole tribe made up of many clans might number no more than 100,000 people, including only about 20,000 warriors. Historians studying their early history are hampered by the fact that they did not write and thus left no written records. Instead, we must piece together their history from archaeology, Roman descriptions of the tribes, and texts based on imperfect memories written centuries later.

The earliest descriptions by Romans are not objective. Some Roman accounts depict the Germans as "barbarians" (outsiders) whose language sounded like babbling and whose personal hygiene was objectionable. One Roman wrote, "Happy [is] the nose that cannot smell a barbarian." However, the earliest and most famous text, Tacitus's *Germania*, written at the end of the | Roman sources | first century, praises the Germans in order to criticize Roman society by contrast. Therefore, Tacitus portrays the Germans as strong and brave people who cared for their families and raised sturdy children. He writes: "With them good customs are of more avail than good laws elsewhere." However, readers must be cautious not to accept his descriptions uncritically—he was no objective reporter, and he was interested in urging Romans to adopt more virtuous customs. Nevertheless, by carefully using these imperfect sources in conjunction with archaeological finds, we can piece together a picture of the lives of the early Germanic peoples.

Tacitus praised the Germans' devotion to marriage—"This they consider their strongest bond"—and the children it produced. Although Tacitus somewhat romanticized the marriage bonds, without a doubt they forged the essential ties that bound society together. Within marriages, men and women had clearly defined and equally essential roles. Men cared for the cattle (a clan's greatest measure of wealth) and | Marriage patterns | took primary responsibility for crop tending, iron working, and war making. Women owned property and received a share of their husbands' wealth upon marriage. Women also performed agricultural labor, but they were mainly responsible for pottery and textile production and household care. In addition, they brewed the all-important alcoholic beverages—honey-sweetened ale and mead, a fermented concoction of honey and water—that provided much of the caloric intake needed for survival. Preserving knowledge of herb lore, women also cared for the sick and injured members of the clan. Perhaps in part because of their knowledge of brewing and healing, women were reputed to have a gift for prophecy, so men often consulted their wise female elders regarding important forthcoming enterprises.

Women were considered "peace-weavers," for through their arranged marriages they were supposed to bring peace between two families. However, family feuds often transcended family ties. Because the purpose of marriage was to join families, men were not limited to one wife. On the contrary, the more wives a man had, the larger his kin network became. The meager sources suggest that many pre-Christian Germans were polygynous; men had as many wives and concubines as they could support. Under these polygynous marriages, husbands and wives did not necessarily live in the same household, so women had a good deal of independence and maintained close ties with their birth families. Although Tacitus claimed adultery was rare, anthropological studies indicate that polygyny may encourage infidelity among women, and there is no reason to doubt that adultery occurred among these tribes. Adultery, however, deeply threatened the strong kinship ties that marriage forged and was severely punished.

Figure 6.1 shows the corpse of a 14-year-old girl who was executed in the first century C.E. by drowning, probably for committing adultery. Such bodies— well preserved by the northern European bogs—offer a wealth of information about the lives of these early Germanic peoples. This young girl's head was shaved, and she was blindfolded before her death. Her right hand is frozen in an obscene gesture—perhaps her last act of defiance toward her executioners. This find offers eloquent, though silent, testimony to the importance of the marriage ties holding Germanic communities together, and the gruesome penalty for violation.

Germanic Clothing and Food

Germanic peoples differed from the more southerly Romans in more ways than family traditions. Their clothing styles and diets also set them dramatically apart. Germanic men wore trousers, a long-sleeved jacket, and a flowing wool or fur cape secured by a large brooch or pin (or even a thorn if the wearer was impoverished). With their elaborate, luxurious detail, some of these brooches signified wealth and prestige. **Figure 6.2** shows six examples of Germanic jewelry from the sixth century C.E. There are clasps (also called fibulae) to secure the capes and clothing and a

FIGURE 6.1 Germanic Girl's Corpse, first century C.E. In the peat bogs of the north, corpses were mummified. The well-preserved bodies provide detailed information about ancient life. When this girl was killed, her right hand was frozen in an obscene gesture toward her executioners.

silver belt buckle. The valuable gold pieces are inlaid with precious stones; the fibula at upper right is less valuable because it is partially made of silver. As the pieces show, most of the design work of the ancient tribes utilized patterns rather than representations, a preference believed to demonstrate the Germans' awareness of the complex patterns symbolizing how fate wove together people's destinies.

Germanic women wore ankle-length dresses of linen or woven wool, which they colored with vegetable dyes. Like the men, they wore capes for warmth. They also dressed their hair with elaborate combs and hairpins and wore patterned jewelry as marks of wealth and prestige.

The Germans' diets were not as elaborate as their fashion accessories. The German peoples raised cattle but seldom ate the meat—the animals were too valuable for the milk and labor they provided. Instead, most of the clans were primarily agricultural. They apparently invented a large, wheeled plow that only a team of six to eight oxen had the strength to pull. Unlike the small plows of the south that merely scratched the surface of the sandier land there, this plow could turn over the heavy clay soils of the north. Furthermore, it encouraged cooperation—for to use a plow of this size, members of the community had to work together. But even this technology did not yield enough grain for a healthy diet, for the northern growing season was short. In addition, the disruptions of wars—even raids—upset agriculture and led to frequent hunger.

Agriculture and diet

FIGURE 6.2 Germanic Jewelry, ca. sixth century C.E.
Gold jewelry was a mark of pride among the ancient Germanic tribes. These finely wrought pieces display the creative skills of the artisans.

Due to malnutrition, the average Germanic woman stood just under five feet; the average man, five feet six inches.

Heroic Society

Like the ancient Greeks, the Germanic tribes of the north cherished the heroic ideals. Warfare played a central role in this society. The Roman historian Tacitus remarked on the German preference for war over work when he wrote: "They think it tame and stupid to acquire by their sweat what they can purchase by their blood." Although Tacitus understated the agricultural productivity of the tribes, these warriors did prefer raiding and plundering. Through such adventures, they acquired both wealth and fame. In the evening gatherings after a day of war making, a poet might praise a particularly heroic deed, and the warrior's name would be permanently preserved in the "word-hoard" or poetry of his people.

Just as Homer had recorded the dramatic deeds of Achilles and Odysseus, anonymous Germanic poets composed works remembering the heroes of the north. The Anglo-Saxon poem *Beowulf* is a written version of one such heroic account. *Beowulf* not only tells of the accomplishments of the monster-killing hero but also gives us a glimpse into traditional Germanic society: The warriors gather in the hall to boast, drink, and prepare for their military feats; the women serve in the hall but also speak their minds; and the king takes responsibility for guarding his people and doling out gifts to ensure their loyalty.

A stunning hoard of Anglo-Saxon gold and silver objects dating from about 675 was excavated in 2009 in Staffordshire, England. This collection offers a recent confirmation of the accuracy of the accounts of the heroic society in *Beowulf*. The huge size of the collection—the gold alone weighs 11 pounds—suggests that Anglo-Saxon England was extremely wealthy. Most of the artifacts are war gear such as sword fittings, pommels, and helmets, and they may represent a victory hoard of the kind *Beowulf* refers to in documenting how warriors stripped the weapons of the defeated. The gold was probably buried to hide it from competing tribes and subsequently lost for over a millennium. Future archaeological finds will continue to fill in the gaps in the history of these elusive tribes who fought for gold and glory.

Each clan within the larger tribe was led by its own chieftain, who served as priest, main judge, and war leader. However, this was no absolute ruler, for the warrior elite (comitatus) was continually consulted in the decisions made for the whole clan. At times, small groups of warrior bands (usually less than 35 strong) set out to raid neighboring villages and bring back booty | Warrior bands and tales of bravery. Sometimes the whole tribe decided to move, bringing along all the related clans and escorting their women and children. According to Tacitus, women traveling with these fighting tribes stayed behind the battle lines, probably within a protective circle of ox carts. If their men seemed to be losing, the women goaded the warriors to victory by baring their breasts behind the battle lines to remind them of their responsibility to protect their dependents.

Infiltrating the Roman Empire, 376–476

While there was periodic, fierce fighting on the borders of the empire between the German tribes and the Romans, there was also a growing relationship based on mutual advantage. After the third century, Rome relied more and more on mercenaries to guard the empire's borders (described in Chapter 5). By the late fourth century, then, many tribes had a great deal of contact with the empire. Numerous young Germanic warriors no longer farmed but instead used Roman pay to support their families. Nearby tribes had learned to value Roman coins as much as cattle and jewelry (their traditional forms of wealth), and Rome had come to depend on the Germans' impressive skill in war.

This mutually satisfying relationship changed in the late fourth century when a Mongolian tribe

MAP 6.1

Germanic Invasions, Fifth Century

This map shows the routes of the various Germanic tribes as they invaded the Roman Empire and gives the dates of their invasions.

Explore the Map

1. Which tribes entered the empire, and where did they settle?

2. What regions might continue to be areas of contention following the invasions?

3. Notice the strategic location of Constantinople, whose walls protected it from invasion. Why would this city be able to control the important trade with the East?

---

originating in northern China came sweeping out of the steppes of Asia. These Huns (known as Hsiung-hu in their homeland) struck terror in the hearts of the Germanic tribes in their path. **Map 6.1** shows the route of the Huns as they galloped out of the east beginning in about 375. The Huns were a fierce people (even by Germanic standards) who charged across the continent

The Huns

on small ponies that seemingly needed no rest. Contemporary descriptions of the Huns reveal the dread and disgust generated by this wild and remarkably successful people. For example, the Roman historian Ammianus Marcellinus (ca. 354) wrote: They "are so prodigiously ugly and bent that they might be two-legged animals. Their shape, however disagreeable, is human." See Document 6.1 for an excerpt

DOCUMENT 6.1

The Huns Menace Rome

The mid-fourth-century historian Ammianus Marcellinus wrote a history of the later Roman Empire, including the invasions of the Germanic tribes. In this excerpt, Ammianus describes the fearful Huns, a nomadic people from central Asia who drove many of the Germanic tribes to flee into the empire. The historian pointedly describes the Huns as strikingly different from the "civilized" Romans.

At the very moment of their birth the cheeks of their infant children are deeply marked by an iron, in order that the usual vigor of their hair, instead of growing at the proper season, may be withered by the wrinkled scars; and accordingly they grow up without beards, and consequently without any beauty, like eunuchs, though they all have closely knit and strong limbs and plump necks; they are of great size, and bow-legged, so that you might fancy them two-legged beasts, or the stout figures which are hewn out in a rude manner with an axe on the posts at the end of bridges.

They are certainly in the shape of men, however uncouth, but so hardy that they neither require fire nor well-flavored food, but live on the roots of such herbs as they get in the fields, or on the half-raw flesh of any animal, which they merely warm rapidly by placing it between their own thighs and the back of their horses.

They wear linen clothes, or else garments made of the skins of field-mice; nor do they wear a different dress out of doors from that which they wear at home; but after a tunic is once put round their necks, however much it becomes worn, it is never taken off or changed till, from long decay, it becomes actually so ragged as to fall to pieces.

SOURCE: Ammianus Marcellinus, "History," in *The Great Events by Famous Historians*, vol. III, ed. Rossiter Johnson (The National Alumni, 1905), pp. 353–354.

Analyze the Document

1. Which characteristics of the Huns might the Romans have found most frightening?

2. How might this description have shaped Roman policy toward the Huns?

---

of this influential source. Some Germanic tribes fled across the boundaries of the empire in search of safer territory. One such tribe, the Visigoths, crossed into the empire looking for land and ended up sacking Rome itself in 410 (discussed in Chapter 5). As the map reveals, the Visigoths were only one of many Germanic peoples who crossed into the empire in the early fifth century.

As we saw in Chapter 5, by the late third century, the Romans faced severe economic problems that kept them from successfully defending their borders against these new encroachments. They could not even afford to pay for the minimum defense, for the empire spent about thirty gold pieces a year for each soldier. An army of only 30,000 would have cost the entire annual budget of the western empire, so the Romans had to develop a new, less expensive way to defend its borders. To address this need, the Romans offered some encroaching tribes a treaty that made them **federates,** or allies, of Rome. Through this treaty, the warrior tribes received permission to live within the borders of the empire, and in exchange, they agreed to fight the enemies of Rome. The Visigoths became federates for enough grain to feed their warriors and families; in return they agreed to fight their traditional enemies, the Germanic Vandals. The Visigoths were later called north to protect the Italian borders. As more tribes were awarded federate status, the western empire began to be transformed by the blending of peoples.

Federate treaties

The federate treaties allowed the Germanic tribes to live within the empire and govern themselves by their own laws and customs, using their own leaders. This model of separate, coexisting cultures almost immediately proved to be utopian. In most of the territories, such as Spain or North Africa, the Germans were very much in the minority, so their culture was transformed by contact with neighboring Romans. For example, tribal leaders began to be called and treated as kings, although competing German noblemen consistently resorted to assassination to maintain their traditional voice in tribal affairs.

In many cases, two religions also existed side by side. Some pagan tribes (Anglo-Saxons, for example) restored paganism to parts of the nominally Christian empire. Other tribes (Visigoths and Ostrogoths) were Christian but had been converted by a missionary named Ulfila (ca. 310–ca. 381), whose Christian ideas had been shaped before Arius's teachings had been condemned at the Council of Nicaea in 325 (see Chapter 5). Ulfila's parents had been captured by Goths, and he grew up speaking the early Germanic language, so he was the natural candidate to convert the Germans. By the fifth-century settlements, the Arian tribes associated their religious beliefs with their ethnic identity, and this impeded their relationship with the orthodox Catholics living in the disintegrating empire.

Arian Christianity

A fifth-century North African Catholic (Victor of Vita) chronicled the invasion of the Vandals, and he particularly lamented the religious strife that erupted. He wrote that the Vandals "gave vent to their wicked ferocity . . . against the churches, . . . cemeteries and monasteries, so that they burned houses of prayer with fires greater than those used against cities." Although Victor probably exaggerated the villainy of the Vandals, his description pointed to the disintegration of the empire. When the emperor could not protect his Catholic subjects from his Arian ones, the religious differences further splintered an already weakened central authority.

In addition to having disputes with the federate tribes, the empire lost some provinces altogether. In about 407, Rome recalled legions from Britain to help defend Italy against invaders. This left the Celtic Britons, who were Christian and lived in the Roman manner, alone to defend themselves against invaders from Scotland and from the Scandinavian countries. As **Map 6.1** shows, tribes of Angles, Saxons, and Jutes entered and settled the eastern portions of Britain, pushing most of the Celtic Britons to Wales and Ireland, the western edges of the British Isles. In the midst of these invasions, one British war chief won a great victory at the Battle of Badon (about the late fifth century) over the Anglo-Saxons. This victory stemmed the tide of the invasions, but only for a while. The deeds of this war chief, Arthur of Britain, were nevertheless remembered in the western Celtic lands and formed the basis for the famous Arthurian romances composed in the twelfth century (see Chapter 8). Britain was lost to Rome and became a mosaic of small Germanic kingdoms.

> Loss of provinces

North Africa also fell away from the empire. At first the Vandals were settled as federates in the northern lands of Africa, but they soon broke off their allegiance to Rome and created a separate kingdom with their capital in Carthage. By the middle of the fifth century, Rome had lost the rich tax shipments of grain and oil that had come in a steady stream from North Africa. Struggling with this and other territorial losses, the empire in the West was slowly disintegrating.

Did Rome "Fall"?

By the fifth century, the provincial armies in the West were dominated by Germans, so it is not surprising that many rose to military power in Rome itself. When the Visigoths invaded Italy, the Roman defense was led by a Vandal general, which shows how ineffective the Roman emperors in the West had become. During the invasion, the Visigoths' leader even captured Emperor Honorius's (r. 395–423) sister, Galla Placidia, and took her with him as he sacked Rome itself.

Finally, in 476, the military leader Odovacar deposed the last western emperor (who, ironically, was named Romulus Augustulus after Romulus, the founder of the city of Rome, and Augustulus, "little Augustus," after Augustus, the first Roman emperor). Odovacar disdained the practice of dual emperorship that the Romans had established and shipped the imperial regalia off to the east. He then appointed himself regent in Italy.

The western empire did not fall with a cataclysmic crash. People like Sidonius in Gaul probably did not even use words such as "fall" to describe the times. After all, the eastern regions still had an emperor to whom people could give their allegiance if they wished, and in fact, many in the east celebrated the fact that there was once again one emperor who ruled the Mediterranean world. However, Sidonius and his contemporaries knew that the Roman Empire overall had undergone a major shift. Historians frequently use the term "late antique" to describe this period during which there was so much continuity with the Roman world. But this world was changed.

> Transformation, not "fall"

The empire's declining population played a key part in this transformation. The shrinking populace left plenty of room for the Germanic tribes to settle without severely dislocating residents. Even after the Germanic settlements, as much as 20 percent of the arable land was abandoned in some areas of the empire. As we saw in Chapter 5, economic and social problems had also eaten away at the empire for centuries. Finally, plagues and warfare had decimated the already fragile population. The empire, therefore, did not fall; instead, it was transformed as new people moved into the territory that the Romans failed to populate.

The urban life that had so characterized Roman culture was the first thing to go. The violence of the times crippled the towns, and the Germanic preference for rural living shifted attention to the countryside. The urban tax base shriveled as powerful Romans began to refuse to pay taxes to Rome. The Germans, for their part, were not often vigilant in collecting them. The roads and bridges that connected the empire fell into disrepair, and people's focus narrowed to the local level.

There were always Romans like Sidonius who continued their correspondence with Romans elsewhere, but they became fewer and fewer. Even Roman clothing changed; the toga that had symbolized the civilized life of the city was abandoned in favor of trousers more suited to country life. (Churchmen continued to wear more traditional Roman robes. Indeed, to this day, Catholic vestments resemble the clothing of the ancient Roman upper class.)

Of course, change happens in both directions when different peoples intermingle. The Germans were as much influenced by the Romans as the Romans were by Germanic culture. Slowly, the Germanic pagans

FIGURE 6.3 Illustration from the Gospel of Matthew, ca. 660 This manuscript illustration of Matthew, Jesus' disciple, was probably created in Ireland. It reveals the Germanic love of intricate patterning, as well as discomfort with portraying the human form.

cloak resembles the gold work on the jewelry in **Figure 6.2.** The Germans and the Romans, through their mutual influence, were creating a whole new culture—that of the medieval west—and this illustration reveals the blending of the two ways of life. After invading, the Germanic tribes settled down and created new political entities—kingdoms instead of tribal units. These new entities formed the basis for the medieval kingdoms that defined the West in the centuries to come.

Rise and Fall of a Frankish Dynasty, ca. 485–750

In the sixth century, the Germanic Franks established a powerful kingdom in the old Roman province of Gaul (see **Map 6.1**). The Franks were ruled by the Merovingian family (named after a legendary ancestor, Merovech). The most famous Merovingian was Clovis (r. 485–511), a brutal man who murdered many of his own relatives to consolidate his rule. Clovis's descendants were no less brutal, and the accounts of subsequent reigns tell of feuds and assassinations involving Merovingian princesses as well as princes.

Clovis is significant not only because he unified large portions of the Frankish kingdom but also because he converted to Roman Christianity. According to Gregory, Clovis's wife, Clotilda, was a Christian and was influential in persuading the king to convert. In the tradition of Constantine before him, Clovis reputedly vowed to convert if he won a significant battle. He won and fulfilled his vow | **Christian Merovingians**

around the year 500 (although the date is controversial). Unlike the Visigoths and other Germans, Clovis converted to orthodox, not Arian, Christianity, and this began a long relationship between the popes and the Frankish kings. As was traditional with the German tribes, the conversion of the king meant the conversion of his people, which paved the way for the slow transformation of Germanic culture through the influence of the Roman church.

Figure 6.4 shows the baptism of Clovis—the defining moment during which the Frankish people (on the right) joined with the church hierarchy (on the left). In the center, an uncharacteristically innocent-looking Clovis is blessed by the dove of the Holy Spirit hovering above him. This illustration captures the king's central role in uniting the various groups in his society. The dove symbolized the Franks' belief that God had guided Clovis in his consolidation and conversion. This conversion also brought papal support to the Frankish kingdom. Like the manuscript illustration in **Figure 6.3,** this image testifies to the blending of Roman, Christian, and Germanic cultures that would characterize the early Middle Ages.

and Arians converted to orthodox Christianity and began to intermarry with resident Romans. In southern Europe, Germans began to speak the local Latin-derived dialects instead of their native Gothic. This is why the southern European languages (French, Spanish, Portuguese, Italian, Romanian) are called Romance languages—they are based on the language of the Romans. The Germans also became literate and began to produce written texts. | **Germans transformed**

Figure 6.3 shows a page depicting the beginning of the Gospel of Matthew, from a manuscript made probably in Ireland in about the seventh century. Whereas the theme of the image is Christian, the aesthetics resemble those of the Germanic tribes, which were shared by the Celtic inhabitants of Ireland. The beautiful patterning in the border and in the man's

In the Merovingian territory, Christianity made significant strides through the efforts of a number of royal women who founded monasteries and supported education. Radegund, whose poetry opened this chapter, is one example. This Merovingian queen, one of the several wives of King Clothar (d. 562), left her husband to found a convent. With her royal family ties, her financial independence, and the force of her personality, she overcame the anger of both her husband and the local bishop and established a house for women who wanted to dedicate themselves to God. She and her ladies spent their days praying, reading, copying manuscripts, and helping the sick and poor in the neighborhood. The king may have declared his people Christian, but leaders like Radegund did much more to win individual hearts to the new religion.

Although Clovis had been highly skilled in forging a Christian kingdom from the ashes of the Roman Empire in Gaul, the subsequent Merovingians were not as competent. By the seventh century, the authority of these kings had deteriorated—frequently, children inherited the throne and in turn died young, leaving the throne to another child. Real power began to be exerted by the "mayors of the palace," an office controlled by another noble family, the Carolingians. This enterprising family included a number of skilled leaders, and as we will see, the Carolingian Charles Martel won a great victory in 732 to save the land. His son, Pepin the Short (r. 747–768), forwarded the fortunes of the family. Pepin wanted more than just to rule; in fact, he craved the royal title as well. Just as Clovis had enhanced his authority through Christian ritual, Pepin looked to the spiritual leader of Christendom for help. The shrewd Carolingian wrote to Pope Zachary (r. 741–752), asking him who should hold the title of king: he who actually exercised the power or he who had the name of king but no actual authority. The pope favored Pepin, and the mayor of the palace then gathered all the Frankish bishops and nobles, who promptly proclaimed him their king. The last of the ineffectual Merovingian kings was forced to cut his long hair (a symbol of his power) and lived out his days in a monastery. Armed with the support of the church, the vigorous new dynasty was now in a position to bring centralized order to western Europe. We will follow the fortunes of the Carolingians in Chapter 7.

Fall of Merovingians

Accomplishments and Destruction in Italy, ca. 490–750

As the Franks established their kingdom in the sixth century, another Germanic kingdom took shape on the

FIGURE 6.4 King Clovis The violent Merovingian king Clovis is shown here as a model of piety at the moment of his baptism, which drew together church and state in the lands of the Franks.

Italian peninsula. The story began when Theodoric (r. 493–526), an Ostrogothic leader, ousted Odovacar (who had deposed the last Roman emperor) and declared himself ruler of Italy. Theodoric had received a Roman education and proved a talented and balanced ruler—at first. The Ostrogoths were Arian Christians, so Theodoric had difficulty uniting Goths and Romans in Italy. Nevertheless, he seems to have exhibited a surprising religious toleration in an age that had little.

Theodoric fostered learning at his court and supported a number of scholars who had a profound influence on Western culture. Boethius, for example—a high official in Theodoric's court—was a man of great education. He translated works of Aristotle from Greek to Latin, and these translations became the basis for the study of logic for centuries. He also had an inventive streak and built a water clock for his patron. But Theodoric's court was plagued with intrigue, and Boethius was unjustly accused of treason and jailed. He wrote his most influential work, *The Consolation of Philosophy*, while in prison. In *The Consolation*, Boethius thought about the injustices of life and found comfort in philosophy. This profound and sensitive work remains much studied today. However, it did not save Boethius, for Theodoric had him executed.

Fostering learning

Dionysius Exiguus, a Greek-speaking monk, was another respected scholar in Theodoric's Italy. A skilled mathematician, the monk calculated the date of Easter (which changes each year) and was apparently the first to suggest that calendars be dated from his estimation of when the Incarnation of Christ occurred (originally the B.C./A.D. system, which has turned into B.C.E./C.E.). Although modern scholarship shows that his dates were slightly wrong—Christ was probably born about 4 B.C.E.—Dionysius's dating system remains the basis of our Western dates. His student Cassiodorus (490–585) succeeded Boethius in the king's court, and his name is remembered much more than Dionysius's.

Thoroughly trained in Roman writings like the *Aeneid* and Livy's *History* (both discussed in Chapter 5), Cassiodorus seems to have recognized the power of historical writing to create and preserve a people's identity. Consequently, he wrote a historical chronicle, the *Origin of the Goths*, that was designed to show that the Goths had as impressive and ancient a history as the Romans. By showing that the history of the Goths resembled the epic scope of the Roman past, Cassiodorus helped

Historical writing

assimilate the histories of both peoples. Although the original of this seminal work is lost, excerpts survive in the quotations of later historical writings. Through this work and its subsequent emulators, the history of the Germans was incorporated into the history of the Roman Empire—the Germanic tribes were slowly but surely merging with the peoples of the old empire they had inhabited.

Theodoric was succeeded by his daughter, Amalasuintha, who ruled at first as regent for her young son and then as queen after the boy's death. She was well educated and well suited to rule, but

Fall of Ostrogoths

the unruly Germans were unused to being governed by a woman. Amalasuintha corresponded with the Byzantine emperor Justinian to gain support for her rule, writing: "We hope that the peaceful relations that you maintain toward us . . . may be extended." However, all her diplomatic skills could not save her from internal intrigue. In 535, she was murdered—according to Gregory of Tours, locked in an overheated steam bath where she was scalded to death.

Justinian used her death as an excuse to begin his reconquest of Italy as part of his ambitious plan to retake the western portions of the empire. The emperor's forces crushed the Ostrogothic kingdom. The scholar Boethius's widow seems to have received some satisfaction after the reconquest, for the emperor gave her permission to destroy statues of Theodoric as revenge for her husband's death. But few others celebrated the conquest that brought down the religiously tolerant and impressive rule of the Ostrogoths.

Justinian had overextended his resources, and the reconquest of Italy did not last long. A Germanic tribe that had fought as allies of the Byzantine army learned about the riches of Italy during the campaign against the Ostrogoths. In 568, these Lombards (longbeards) moved south and took over most of the peninsula (see **Map 6.1,** on page 181). Italy would now be ruled by a tribe much less Romanized than the Ostrogoths, and the slow struggle to achieve a synthesis between Germans and Romans began again. The fierce Lombards ruled the northern part of the peninsula until they confronted the growing power of the

Lombards

Franks in the north. Pepin conquered the Lombards in the mid-eighth century, and northern Italy came under the rule of the Frankish Carolingians.

Pepin did not forget his debt to the papacy that had supported his coronation, and when the Byzantines demanded that he return the Italian conquests to them, Pepin angrily refused. He said he had fought his war for St. Peter, and it was to Peter (that is, the papacy) that he would hand over his conquests. From this time onward, the pope ruled in central Italy as an independent monarch, and the "Donation of Pepin" marked the beginning of the Papal States, which endured until the nineteenth century.

The Visigoths in Spain, 418–711

The history of the Visigoths in Spain resembles that of the other growing kingdoms. Like the Ostrogoths, Visigoths were Arian Christians when they became federates of Rome, and the two cultures, Roman and Goth, lived separate though parallel lives in Spain. However, in the 580s the Visigothic kings converted to Roman Christianity and paved the way for a close church and state rule. Like the Ostrogoths, Visigothic kings fostered learning in their land. The most famous Visigothic writer was Isidore of Seville (ca. 560–636), who compiled collections of Roman works that preserved classical knowledge for subsequent generations.

Two flaws marred Visigothic civilization, however. The first was a delight in political assassination, which even the violent Franks called the "Visigothic curse." Church and state repeatedly condemned people who "turned their hand against the king," but the assassinations continued, weaken-

Visigothic weaknesses

ing the kingdom. The second problem was Visigothic persecution of Jews. Kings passed strict laws against the many Jews living in Spain, undermining their communities and dampening their loyalty.

The Visigothic kingdom was ultimately destroyed by invasions of Muslims from North Africa. As we will see later, followers of the new religion of Islam swept across North Africa, crossed the narrow straits known as the Pillars of Hercules (now the Straits of Gibraltar), and in 711 conquered most of the Iberian Peninsula.

Figure 6.5 shows Iberian Christians taken into slavery by the victorious Muslims. The conquerors include the mounted leaders in the background towering over their bound captives and the African foot soldiers in the foreground guarding the new slaves. The mules, cattle, and long-haired sheep on the right represent the great wealth of the Visigothic kingdom that now came into the hands of the Muslims. The only remaining Christian territory on the peninsula lay in the northwest hills. From there the Iberians would spend the next seven hundred years reconquering their land. The invasion, the interaction between Christians and Muslims, and the long era of reconquest left the Visigothic kingdom in ruins and shaped the subsequent history and culture of Spain.

The Growing Power of the Popes

As central authority fell away in western Europe, some people—especially in the cities—looked to their local bishops to handle things previously left to secular authorities. Bishops sometimes organized aqueduct repair or food relief, and perhaps not surprisingly, the bishop of the most prestigious city—Rome—began slowly to come to the fore. In these tumultuous centuries, the bishops of Rome began to claim earthly as well as spiritual authority and, in doing so, established precedents that would reach well into the future.

All Christian bishops were believed to be the successors of the original apostles and as such held the authority to guide the faithful. However, as early as the fourth century, the bishops of Rome began to assert their supremacy over all the other bishops. Many bishops during the early church period were called popes, based on the Latin word for "father," but the bishops of Rome slowly began to claim exclusive use of that title to set themselves apart from other bishops. On what did the popes base their claims of leadership? In part, the early-fourth-century popes claimed primacy because Rome had been the capital of the empire. However, as the imperial city faded in importance, the popes began pointing to biblical writings to justify their leadership of the church. They based their claim mainly on a passage from the Book of Matthew (Matt. 16:18–19) in which Christ said: "And I tell you, you are Peter, and on this rock I will build my church. . . . I will give you the keys of the kingdom of heaven. . . ." The early popes had claimed that Peter was the first bishop of Rome, so each subsequent pope claimed to be the spiritual descendant of Peter—thus also controlling heaven's keys.

Figure 6.6, an illustration from an early-eleventh-century manuscript, portrays Christ giving Peter the keys to heaven. A crowd of people stand behind Peter, suggesting their dependency on him. The claim that the supremacy of the pope is based on Christ's words to Peter is called the **Petrine doctrine** of papal

Petrine doctrine

FIGURE 6.5 Enslaved Christians As Muslims conquered the Iberian Peninsula, they amassed wealth in the form of sheep and mules, but they also took many Christian slaves, such as those shown bound at the front of the image.

supremacy. Not surprisingly, some people—especially the emperors in the east and some other bishops—disagreed with this interpretation of the Bible.

Since the fourth century, some popes had involved themselves in politics. As we saw in Chapter 5, Bishop Ambrose had forced Emperor Theodosius to bend to his will, and in the following century, Pope Leo I (r. 440–461) successfully negotiated with invading Huns and Vandals to spare Rome. At the end of the fifth century, Pope Gelasius (r. 492–496) tried to resolve this issue of who had power by describing authority on earth as two swords: one wielded by kings and the other by the church. In Gelasius's view, the church's sword was the greater because it was spiritual—popes were responsible for the souls of kings. In a metaphorical sense, then, Gelasius converted St. Peter's keys to heaven into an earthly blade.

However, these early popes could exert only sporadic authority, and they had little real power. It was Pope Gregory the Great (r. 590–604) who dramatically forwarded the case for papal supremacy, as much through his actions as with his words. A talented, energetic administrator, he defined the role of the pope in broad terms. For example, he took over the day-to-day administration of Rome, reorganizing estates and managing them in such a way as to generate extra revenue to feed the poor. When the Lombards invaded the peninsula, Gregory directed the defense of the city and negotiated the truce. Acting the part of a territorial ruler, he even exerted his authority outside Italy, writing letters to settle disputes

Gregory the Great

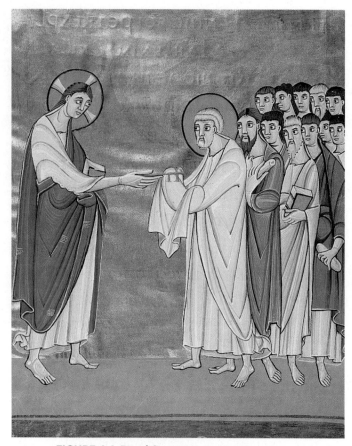

FIGURE 6.6 Papal Supremacy, ca. 1007 To argue for the supremacy of the popes over other bishops, some Christians looked to the biblical account of Christ giving the keys of heaven to his apostle Peter, an event that is shown in this colorful manuscript illustration.

and offering financial assistance to distant churches. Gregory's influence extended far beyond sixth-century Italy: In the ninth century, when the Anglo-Saxon king Alfred (see Chapter 7) selected seminal works to translate from Latin to Anglo-Saxon, Gregory's writings were prominently featured. With Gregory's precedent, popes of the eighth century and beyond were prepared to claim influence throughout western Christendom, although it would take until the thirteenth century for them to fully wield such authority over a Christian world.

Monasteries: Peaceful Havens

As the Germanic tribes were spreading into the western empire, many men and women sought refuge from the chaotic times in monasteries, where they could concentrate on their spiritual growth. As we saw in Chapter 5, communal monasticism began to appeal to many Christians throughout the empire. In the west, the most influential founder of communal monasticism was the Italian Benedict of Nursia (ca. 480–543). His twin sister, Scholastica, shared his calling and

Benedict of Nursia

founded monasteries for women. Like many other churchmen, Benedict disapproved of people who lived independently like the holy ascetics we met in Chapter 5. He feared that without guidance, such individuals might go astray, and he complained of wandering holy men, saying: "Whatever they think of or choose to do, that they call holy; what they do not like, that they regard as illicit." Instead, Benedict wrote a book of instruction—a *rule*—to guide monks and nuns in their communal lives.

Benedict eschewed the extreme fasts and bodily mortifications that had marked the eastern holy men and women, writing: "We hope to ordain nothing that is harsh or heavy to bear." Benedict's *Rule* required that people spend a balanced day divided into work and prayer, with moderate and regular meals. The requirement to work encouraged monks and nuns to study and copy the precious manuscripts that preserved classical learning. Benedict himself called his monastery a "schoolhouse for the Lord," which was an apt description for an institution that served a central role in education throughout the Middle Ages.

Although Benedict did not require heroic asceticism, the monk insisted that individuals ignore their own desires—whether for extra food, different work, or even extra hardships—and live in strict obedience to the head monk or nun. These monastic leaders, called abbots or abbesses, eventually became powerful figures in medieval life, extending their influence far outside monastery walls. By requiring a vow of obedience from monks and nuns, Benedict created an effective mechanism for bringing otherwise independent religious people into the Christian hierarchy.

Monasteries formed an effective avenue through which Christianity spread to the pagan outposts. In the early fifth century, a Romano-British Christian named Patrick (ca. 390–461) was kidnapped by Irish raiders and enslaved in Ireland. He later escaped to Britain, where he became a bishop. However, he decided his calling was to return to Ireland to convert the pagan Irish. He established monasteries in Ireland, and the Irish consider him the founder of Irish Christianity. The strong monastic tradition in Ireland created monks who made great strides in preserving learning and stimulating ideals of asceticism in the West. Furthermore, some Irish monks became missionaries to the pagan Anglo-Saxons in Britain. In fact, scholars give the Irish monks a great deal of credit for preserving the classical wisdom and transmitting it on to subsequent civilizations of the West.

Irish Christianity

Pope Gregory the Great—a monk himself—was also interested in converting the Anglo-Saxons and bringing them into the orbit of Roman Christianity. The pope sent monks to Britain in 597 to convert the natives—a task they slowly, but successfully, achieved. However, the monks sent from Rome came in contact with those sent from Ireland, and it became clear that the two strands of Christianity had developed differing opinions on certain points (the most important was the date of Easter). In 664, the Anglo-Saxon king called a council in Whitby to resolve the discrepancy. After ascertaining that all the monks agreed on the primacy of the apostle Peter, the king decreed that Peter's heir in Rome should prevail. Thus, the practices of Roman—instead of Irish—Christianity prevailed throughout Europe.

Conversion of Britain

Beyond their missionary roles, monasteries served as quiet havens from a tempestuous world. In these retreats, men and women worked, prayed, and studied—keeping ancient texts alive for a time when learning could again emerge from behind monastery walls.

THE BYZANTINE EMPIRE,
ca. 400–1000

As early as the beginning of the fourth century, Roman emperors had recognized the unique strategic and economic advantages of the eastern portion of the empire. During the turbulent fifth and sixth centuries, the eastern Roman Empire with its capital in Constantinople held firm as the western provinces fell away to the Germanic tribes. However, the eastern empire did not remain unchanged; instead, Constantine planted seeds that would later flower into a dramatically different empire. By the eighth century, the eastern Roman Empire had changed so much that historians call it the Byzantine Empire, or Byzantium, to distinguish it from the Latin Roman Empire that it succeeded. As with the emergence of the western Germanic kingdoms, the rise of the Byzantine Empire represented not a sudden break from the past but simply another aspect of the Roman Empire's transformation.

When the Visigoths sacked Rome in 410, the eastern emperor, Theodosius II, began to build a great wall to protect Constantinople from a similar fate. This structure stood firm even during the violent fifth and sixth centuries—inhabitants of Constantinople watched from the safety of the top of the wall as smoke rose from villages set aflame by the Germanic tribes and the Huns surging westward. The wall continued to protect the new capital for almost a thousand years.

The wave of invasions separated the eastern and western portions of the old Roman Empire. While the western portion adopted some aspects of Germanic culture, the easterners consciously rejected such changes. For example, at the end of the fourth century, residents of Constantinople were forbidden to wear Germanic clothing, such as pants and anything made from furs. Between 400 and 1000 C.E., the Byzantine

A separate empire

Empire distanced itself more and more from the concerns of the west and turned its focus north and east instead. One eastern emperor stood out as an exception to this tendency and turned his attention again to the west.

Justinian and Theodora, r. 527–565

Justinian was born in 483 to peasant parents living in a province near Macedonia. A promising youth, he was adopted by an uncle in the royal court. His uncle became emperor, which paved the way for Justinian to take the crown at his uncle's death in 527. The most influential person in Justinian's court was his wife, Theodora. She, too, had come from a humble background. She had been an actress, and according to the Byzantine historian Procopius (d. 562) (whose *Secret History* is biased against Justinian, so it may not be fully accurate), Theodora won the emperor's heart with her skill as an erotic dancer.

Early in Justinian's reign, Theodora established her role in the emperor's court when a violent riot (remembered as the Nika riot for the rioters' rallying cry "Nika" which means "victory") broke out in Constantinople between two rival political factions who supported different chariot racing teams. In an uncommon alliance, they joined forces to try to oust Justinian. When the rest of his advisors urged Justinian to flee the city, Theodora insisted that Justinian confront the rioters, saying, "For one who has been an emperor it is intolerable to be a fugitive." Justinian's forces brutally squelched the riot—probably 30,000 were killed—and this victory broke any political opposition.

Nika riot

During the Nika riot, much of Constantinople was burned, so Justinian and Theodora embarked on an ambitious reconstruction plan. The most impressive outcome of this effort was the design and construction of a massive church, the Hagia Sophia (Holy Wisdom). **Figures 6.7** and **6.8** show the great church that still dominates the city and awes visitors. The central dome, with its diameter of 101 feet, is the largest such structure in the world. Two half-domes double the interior length of the church to 200 feet. After the Muslims captured the city in 1453, the church became a mosque, and the spheres with the Arabic calligraphy date from the Muslim years. Today the magnificent structure is a museum, but it still showcases the impressive Byzantine engineering along with the blend of cultures that marks this region.

Rebuilding the city

Besides the Hagia Sophia, Justinian left another enduring contribution: the codification of Roman law. From the earliest codification—the Twelve Tables (Chapter 4)—Roman law continued growing and changing. Emperors and senators had passed decrees,

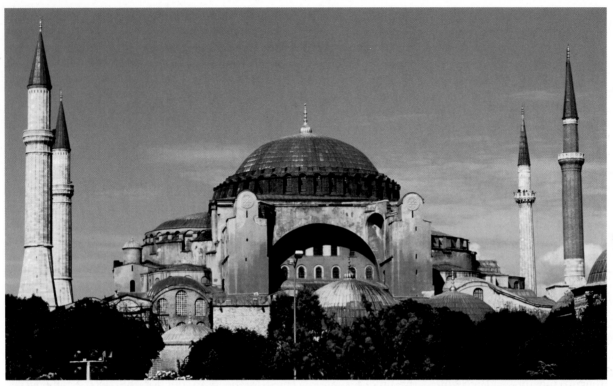

FIGURE 6.7 Hagia Sophia, 537 The Byzantine emperor Justinian commissioned this huge church in Constantinople. The structure's expansive domes and flowing lines long remained the wonder of the world. Builders added the four minarets in 1453 when they converted Hagia Sophia into a mosque.

FIGURE 6.8 Hagia Sophia, Interior, 537 Hagia Sophia's awe-inspiring interior prompted Justinian to declare that he was a greater temple builder than the biblical king Solomon. Others argued that the church's splendor demonstrated that Constantinople was superior to Rome. Buildings were key symbols in ancient power struggles.

judges had made precedent-setting decisions, and jurists had written complicated legal interpretations.

By Justinian's time, the collections were full of obscurities and internal contradictions, and the emperor wanted them organized and clarified. The enterprise was immense, as Justinian himself noted: "We turned our attention to the great mass of venerable jurisprudence and, as if crossing the open sea, we completed a nearly hopeless task." The results of this formidable project were published in fifty books called the *Corpus Iuris Civilis* (the *Body of Civil Law*) (ca. 533). In this form, Roman law survived and was revived in western Europe in about the thirteenth century. From there it has influenced Western legal codes through today.

Finally, as we have seen, after the murder of the Ostrogothic queen Amalasuintha, Justinian tried to reconquer the western territories that had fallen to Germanic tribes. In part, he wanted **Reconquering the west** to recapture lost tax revenues, but probably the ambitious emperor also hoped to resurrect the Roman Empire to its past glory. However, he succeeded only in taking North Africa from the Vandals and Italy from the Ostrogoths.

Under the newly established control of Justinian, a great church was built in the imperial capital of Ravenna, in the north of Italy. **Figures 6.9a and b,** in Thinking About Art, are sixth-century mosaics of Justinian and Theodora that adorned this Church of San Vitale, and they reveal much about how people perceived the royal couple. The mosaics were a worthy celebration of the victorious conquest of Italy, but the accomplishment proved more ephemeral than the magnificent mosaics.

Map 6.2 shows the extent of Justinian's reconquest. As impressive as it looked, it was destructive and costly. While the North Africans welcomed the rule of the orthodox emperor over the Arian Vandals, the Italians, who were governed by the tolerant Ostrogoths, were less thrilled. The new regime brought more violence and taxation. Worse, Justinian had to rely on German mercenaries to win these battles. As noted on page 186, this strategy paved the way for the Lombards to conquer Italy in 568. Although Justinian temporarily accomplished some of his goals, the reconquest led only to failure in the long run. He could not maintain a firm grip on the western provinces, and the constant battling drained the eastern empire of needed resources. Justinian's dream of reuniting and reconnecting with the empire's old homeland in Rome would vanish forever.

Constantinople: The Vibrant City

Constantinople not only was the administrative and cultural center of the east but also served as the economic hub. The great city's wealth stemmed in part from commerce: Trade routes to the Far East all passed through Constantinople, so spices, silks, rare woods, and perfumes poured into the Byzantine capital. These luxury items brought a fine profit to the men and women who resold them. Streets thronged with shopkeepers displaying their wares: goldsmiths, silversmiths, furniture makers, textile merchants, and so on. Shoppers bargained at the booths, and the sounds of commerce rang through the streets.

The Byzantine Empire also grew rich producing luxury items. Artisans in Constantinople and the other major cities of the east crafted expensive fabrics, fine jewelry, glassware, and ivory works. The empire **Lucrative industries** imported silkworms from China in the sixth century, which opened a new, lucrative industry. The royal court held a monopoly on silk production, and the finest silk was made in the emperor's palace itself. The court also controlled the profitable industry of purple dye, which was produced from mounds of shellfish left to rot on the shores of the eastern Mediterranean. As we saw in Chapter 1, everyone, from east to west, who wanted to demonstrate their nobility or royalty had to have purple dye. The long purple robes worn by Justinian and Theodora in **Figures 6.9a and b** testify to more riches than the couple's gold and jewels.

While great wealth was available in the bustling city, it came to only a few. The Byzantines had abandoned the ancient Roman tradition of offering free food to the urban poor, but officials offered food to those who worked in imperial bakeries or on aqueduct repair. The palace also established a number of charitable institutions for the needy, including poorhouses, hospitals, and the first orphanages recorded in Western tradition.

Prosperity brought temptation, and emperors and other highly placed officials began to favor eunuchs (castrated men) as a way to control corruption. Easterners from the time of the ancient Persian Empire believed that eunuchs were less prone to corruption than other men. Because eunuchs had no children, they were expected to have little motivation to acquire wealth to pass along to subsequent generations. As eunuchs gained favor in high places, some poor families even had a son castrated to prepare him for a prosperous career. In addition to the emperor's closest aides, highly placed bureaucrats, some army and navy commanders, and some high church officials were eunuchs. Doctors who were eunuchs were allowed to treat women, though some women's hospitals insisted on letting only female doctors attend to their patients.

A society and economy that so prominently featured eunuchs would have been unthinkable in the

FIGURE 6.9(A)

Mosaics in San Vitale, Ravenna, Italy, 548

In 540, Emperor Justinian's troops conquered Ostrogothic Italy, restoring the peninsula and its capital, Ravenna, to Byzantine control. As part of the celebration of this victory, the mosaics shown here were added to the Church of San Vitale in time for its consecration in 548. The images depict Emperor Justinian with his attendants (a) and his wife, Theodora, similarly accompanied (b). These works of art were brilliant propaganda pieces, intended to show the faithful a new order—one

FIGURE 6.9(B)

in which church and state were combined, with the imperial family at the head.

Connecting Art & Society

1. What elements in the images show the wealth and power of the royal family?

2. What might the halos around their heads indicate?

3. Why are Justinian and Theodora shown bringing gifts to the church? He carries a golden plate for communion wafers, and she brings a golden cup for the wine.

Roman Empire of Augustus. Yet, the Byzantines did retain some Roman characteristics. For example, the Roman tradition of public political involvement continued in Constantinople, as Justinian and Theodora discovered during the riots. In this vibrant city, people argued about the great religious questions, political issues, and the ever-intriguing chariot races. In Rome, men and women had gathered in the Forum or the Colosseum to express their collective opinion; in Constantinople they flocked to see the chariot races. The great race track—the hippodrome—could seat 40,000 people, and the emperor frequently addressed his people there. The two chariot teams, the Blues and the Greens, signified much more than simply a love of sports. People aligned themselves with the teams as we do with political parties—by wealth, religion, social class, and political inclination.

Chariot races

Military Might and Diplomatic Dealings

Constantinople's walls kept the empire safe from the Germanic tribes heading west, but external enemies still posed a threat. The Byzantines clashed regularly with the powerful Persians and kept a vigilant eye on the tribes to the north. As we will see, the Muslim people to the south also represented a constant danger. To withstand these challenges, the Byzantines carefully considered both military and diplomatic science.

While the emperors kept the administration of Constantinople in civilian hands, they entrusted the care of the provinces to military men. Rulers divided up their empire into about twenty-five provinces, called **themes,** governed by military commanders. (See **Map 6.3,** on page 194, for the theme divisions.) Assemblies composed of "heads of households" empowered to make judicial and financial decisions

MAP 6.2

Justinian's Conquests, 554

This map shows the size of the Roman Empire in 527 C.E. after the western provinces had fallen away, and it illustrates the extent of Justinian's reconquest.

Explore the Map

1. What was the extent of Justinian's conquest? How expensive do you think it was to control all that territory? Why?

2. What factors might contribute to the loss of these lands again? Compare this map with **Map 6.3** to see how fragile this reconquest proved to be.

administered the villages within each theme. Governors designated most village families as "military households," which meant they owed one fully equipped man to the empire's army. In this way, the provinces were guarded by armies made up of local residents who had a strong stake in the protection of their homes.

| Provincial organization |

The Byzantine army was disciplined, well paid, and thoroughly armed. Its backbone, the heavy cavalry, provided the army with extraordinary flexibility. Protected by mail armor and outfitted with lances and swords as well as bows and arrows, these fighters could shoot from a distance as archers or do battle at close range while heavily armed. The cavalry in turn was supported by an efficient infantry. Though only about 120,000 men at its height, this standing army was supplemented by a large number of camp followers.

| The army |

Slaves and engineers accompanied the infantry everywhere. Unlike the Roman legions, who constructed their own camps every night, the Byzantines depended on camp slaves to carry out such tasks. The army also developed a finely tuned medical corps, complete with ambulance carts that moved the wounded to safety.

In addition to its land army, the empire continued the Roman tradition of maintaining a strong navy. In the seventh century, Byzantine scientists invented "Greek fire," a deadly new weapon that gave the navy

MAP 6.3

The Byzantine Empire, Eighth Century

This map shows the extent and the organization of the Byzantine Empire in the eighth century and identifies the peoples who surrounded the empire. The map also indicates the internal structure of the empire—its division into themes.

Explore the Map

1. Why might the theme organization have been an effective way to manage the decentralized provinces?

2. Locate the many peoples of the Balkan region—Bulgars, Serbs, Croats, Slavs, and others. Do you think it was difficult for the Byzantines to withstand pressure from all those peoples? Explain.

3. What might be the long-term implications of the diversity of the peoples inhabiting the Balkans?

---

a crucial competitive edge. **Figure 6.10** shows a manuscript illustration of the use of Greek fire in a naval battle. The substance was made of combustible oil that was pumped through tubes or placed in containers to be launched from a catapult. The liquid then burst into flames on contact with the target. This weapon proved particularly effective at sea; because the oil floated, it kept burning on the water. Not surprisingly, the Byzantines closely guarded the secrets of Greek fire.

The Byzantines' military success stemmed from more than strategic and technical innovations. Unlike their western counterparts, the easterners continued

and improved the ancient Romans' highly developed diplomatic techniques to protect their empire. Many Byzantine emperors considered diplomacy as important as war, and therefore worthy of just as much Diplomacy investment. As a matter of policy, these rulers used spies, lies, and money to weaken their enemies, and sometimes even turned their enemies against each other. Indeed, today the term *Byzantine diplomacy* still connotes expedient and tricky negotiations. However, such complex diplomacy needed money to succeed. As long as the empire was wealthy enough to keep funding bribes, spies, and counterintelligence efforts,

FIGURE 6.10 Greek Fire The Greeks invented a combustible liquid that they pumped through tubes onto enemy ships. The liquid ignited the wooden hulls on contact and also floated on the water, killing sailors who attempted to escape. One enemy observed that the Greeks possessed lightning from the heavens to burn their enemies.

it stood firm. Later in the Middle Ages, the empire's diplomatic powers faded after an economic downturn. Nevertheless, the world learned much from the Byzantines about using diplomacy instead of war as a way to resolve conflict.

Breaking Away from the West

Emperors in the east saw themselves as heirs to the Roman Empire and frequently used images to demonstrate this continuity. However, it soon became apparent that the east was moving ever farther from the west.

Justinian was the last eastern emperor to use Latin as the official language. After the seventh century, the language of the Byzantine bureaucracy changed to Greek. This made sense given that the native language of most educated people in the east was Greek rather than Latin, but it accelerated the east's drift away from the west. The split became even more pronounced after people living in the Germanic kingdoms gradually forgot how to speak and read Greek. Men and women living in the two sections of the old Roman Empire could no longer converse except through interpreters.

During the late Roman Empire, Christianity had linked the faithful of many regions and backgrounds together in one worship. Greek was the language of scripture and worship in earliest Christianity, and as Christianity spread, people worshiped in their local languages. Usually that meant Latin in the west, and Greek, Syriac, Coptic, Armenian, and other languages in the east.

As people in the western portion of the old empire forgot how to speak Greek, the western church began to use Latin exclusively in worship services, while in the east church services continued to be conducted in local languages. Over time, these language differences drove the churches apart.

The question of who should lead the church posed another problem. As we have seen, the power vacuum caused by the invasions allowed the popes to emerge as independent political leaders. In the east, however, the self-styled sacred emperors were **Caesaropapist**; that is, they led both church and state. Note, for example, how the images of Justinian and Theodora in **Figures 6.9a** and **b** include religious symbols in addition to emblems of their secular offices. Emperors led the church, appointed the patriarchs (the eastern equivalents of the highest-ranking archbishops), led church councils, and involved themselves in theological controversies.

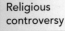

Just as Constantine had called the Council of Nicaea in 325 to discuss the origin of Christ (see Chapter 5), the Byzantine emperor Marcian called the Council of Chalcedon in 451 to resolve questions about the human and divine natures of Christ. The council decided that Jesus was both fully human and fully divine. This position seemed eminently logical to the pope in the west. Yet some men and women in portions of the east were shocked by this conclusion. In their view, this statement seemed to reduce the power of God by acknowledging that Jesus remained human. The anger catalyzed by this resolution further separated portions of the eastern empire from the west.

The Byzantine Empire, ca. 400–1000   195

In the eighth century, another religious controversy convulsed the east and brought the growing differences between the Latin and Greek churches to the forefront. From the fifth through the sixth centuries, the worship of the faithful in the eastern church had focused on icons—images of Jesus, Mary, and the saints. People viewed these depictions as more than simple portrayals; they believed that the images contained spirituality that had become material and thus could bring divine help. Byzantine monasteries in particular had amassed huge wealth by painting and selling icons. In the west, men and women also venerated images of saints, but not to the same degree.

Iconoclasm

The Byzantine emperor Leo III (r. 717–741) ordered all icons destroyed, and in an autocratic style, he intended for his decree to apply to all of Christendom, east and west. In part this dictate represented a belief common in the Asiatic provinces, that veneration of icons amounted to worshiping idols. Leo's policy also had a political side. The eastern emperors wanted to challenge the growing power of the monasteries that were producing most of the icons. This **iconoclasm** (icon breaking) controversy raged for a century in the east, during which time many mosaics in Constantinople and Asia Minor were destroyed, leaving Ravenna as the most important repository of the old mosaics. Finally, less controversial emperors withdrew their support from the iconoclasts (icon destroyers). In the meantime, however, the western popes did not acknowledge the emperor's authority, and Pope Gregory II (r. 715–731) defied Leo's edict. The tensions resulting from this struggle strained relations between the eastern and western churches even further.

Over the centuries, two branches of Christianity grew more and more apart until they became two separate churches—the Catholic west and the Orthodox east. The Orthodox church rejected the concept of papal supremacy that was growing in the west and preserved the idea that the church should be led by five bishops (called patriarchs) who presided in the five major cities: Rome, Constantinople, Jerusalem, Alexandria, and Antioch. Each of the five patriarchs—called the Pentarchs—exerted jurisdiction in his own area and met with the other patriarchs in council to regulate matters of dogma and church discipline. Over time, they rejected decisions made outside these councils by the popes alone. Questions of language, theology, hierarchy, and the wording of the creeds finally severed ties between east and west.

Orthodox church

In 1054, the two churches broke apart. The pope and the patriarch of Constantinople excommunicated each other, and the unified Christian church became two. (The mutual excommunications were finally withdrawn, but not until 1965.) Both the Roman Catholic and Greek Orthodox churches would grow and find adherents all over the world into the twenty-first century.

Converting the Slavs, 560–ca. 1000

Starting in the sixth century, the several Slavic groups settling along the Danube River, which had once formed the northeastern boundary of the Roman Empire, represented yet another challenge to Byzantine unity. These pagan tribes included Serbs, Croats, and Avars. In 679, the Bulgars, a Turko-Mongolian people, came out of the steppes of Russia and built a powerful kingdom just north of the Danube. **Map 6.3** shows generally where these peoples settled. In the ninth century, Scandinavian traders (and raiders) established a kingdom in Kiev (modern Ukraine) made up of Slavic people ruled by Scandinavian princes. (This principality, called Kievan Rus, became the origin of the name "Russia.") All these peoples alternately raided and traded with the eastern empire and personally experienced the famed Byzantine diplomacy. Some tribes were bribed into peace, some kings were offered Byzantine brides, and occasionally tribes were tricked into fighting each other.

The Byzantines sought a way to bring these peoples within the eastern empire's influence by converting them to Christianity. In 863, the Byzantine emperor Michael III (r. 842–867) sent two missionaries, Cyril and Methodius, to the Slavs. The missionaries realized that conversion depended in part on literacy. The Slavs, who had no written language, could not read the church services. Therefore, Cyril and Methodius developed a Slavonic written language based on the Greek alphabet.

Cyril and Methodius

Their mission was successful. Serbs and Russians embraced Greek Christianity, and the alphabet that Cyril and Methodius developed to transmit the religion became known as the **Cyrillic alphabet** (named after St. Cyril). It is still used in Russia and in portions of the Balkan peninsula today. The Bulgar leader also converted to Othodox Christianity in the 890s and adopted the Cyrillic alphabet.

The state of Kievan Rus was brought to Christianity by a bargain struck between the reputedly ruthless prince of Kiev, Vladimir (r. 978–1015), and the Byzantine emperor Basil II (r. 976–1025). Basil wanted to secure Vladimir's military assistance and bring the growing eastern Slavic state into Byzantium's sphere of influence. Vladimir agreed to convert to Greek Orthodox Christianity and help Basil if the emperor would give his own sister, Anna— a princess "born to the purple"—as Vladimir's bride. The Kievan prince already had several wives, but

Conversion of Russia

Basil had little choice. Anna went north and Vladimir established churches along the Byzantine model. Vladimir's "conversion" in 989 marks the traditional date for the beginning of Christianity in Russia.

Like its Byzantine counterparts, the Catholic church also sent missionaries who successfully converted tribes in portions of the east. The Poles, Bohemians, Hungarians, and Croats adopted Catholic Christianity and the Latin alphabet that came with it. These divisions in religion, loyalty, and alphabet divided eastern Europe, and, indeed, cultural divisions established during this period have continued to color the politics of the region into the twenty-first century.

By the tenth century, the Byzantine Empire had entered a sort of golden age. It had occupied and assimilated the strong Bulgarian kingdom, and the eastern emperor exerted his authority from the Adriatic to the Black Sea. The empire was prosperous and secure. The Byzantine culture and the western kingdoms would interact for centuries, during which time the West gained a great deal from Byzantium. The western legal system owed much to Justinian's codification, western scholars would gain from the Greek texts preserved in the east, and western kingdoms owed their survival to Byzantium's serving as a buffer state against incursions from the east. The eastern empire and the Orthodox church left an enduring cultural influence in eastern Europe that continues to affect political life today. In the seventh century, the Mediterranean world grew even more complex: A third great power was rising in the south and this new civilization would come to challenge both the west and Byzantium.

| Golden age |

ISLAM,
600–1000

In the early seventh century, the Arabian peninsula was part of neither the Byzantine nor the Persian Empire. The region contained both oases with settled populations and great reaches of desert. In the desert, nomadic Bedouin tribes roamed, living on milk, meat, and cheese from camels and goats; dates; and some grain from the oases. These tribes emphasized family and clan loyalty and fought, raided, and feuded with one another to protect their honor and their possessions. The Arabs were pagan, worshiping natural objects such as stones, springs, and a large ancient meteor that had fallen into the Arabian desert long before human memory.

The success of Bedouin life stemmed in large part from the use of domesticated camels. These magnificent desert animals could carry heavy loads for many miles without water and proved a speedy form of transportation in the raids of desert warfare. The Bedouins sold camels to the Arabs of the oases, who in turn used them for the long-distance trade that brought prosperity to the small cities of the oases.

During the wars between Byzantium and Persia (540–ca. 630), the land route to the Far East through Mesopotamia became dangerous. For safety's sake, some traders from Constantinople and Egypt decided to travel through Mecca in Arabia to reach a water route through the Red Sea. Others crossed the Arabian peninsula to leave by sea from the Persian Gulf. This trade brought even more wealth to the thriving oasis cities, the most important of which was Mecca. Mecca housed an important pagan shrine, the Ka'bah, containing the ancient meteorite, which drew Bedouins and other Arabs to gather in peace for trade. But trading had another consequence beyond stimulating commerce: It brought Arabs in contact with Christians and Jews, and, as a result, new ideas filtered into the Arabian peninsula.

The Prophet

The new ideas generated by Arab, Christian, and Jewish interaction came to be embodied in the person of a man named Muhammad. Muhammad (570–632) was an orphan who grew up in Mecca in the care of his uncle. He became a merchant and made an excellent marriage to a wealthy widow and businesswoman, Khadijah. The couple had seven children and lived a prosperous life. As a merchant, Muhammad earned a reputation for being a good and honest man. His nickname was "al-Amin"—"the trustworthy."

In his fortieth year, Muhammad began to have visions. First an angel appeared to him while he was sleeping and said: "Recite! Thy Lord . . . taught by the pen, taught that which they knew not unto men." When Muhammad

| The Qur'an |

GROWTH OF ISLAM

570	Muhammad born in Mecca
622	Hijra
628	Yemen converted to Islam
632	Muhammad dies in Medina
661	Murder of 'Ali
661–750	Umayyad dynasty rules from Damascus
ca. 691	Dome of the Rock built in Jerusalem
711	Muslims conquer Spain
732	Charles Martel wins Battle of Tours
750	'Abbasid dynasty begins
786–809	Harun al-Rashid rules

KEY DATES

awoke from this vision, he saw a huge man with his feet astride the horizon. This man claimed to be the angel Gabriel and told Muhammad to be the apostle to his people. According to Islamic tradition, Muhammad received an additional 114 revelations over the next twenty years. These revelations were recorded as the word of Allah (God) given in the Arabic language. Accounts of the revelations were collected after Muhammad's death and became the book of inspired scripture of the new religion. This scripture is called the Qur'an (sometimes written in English as "Koran").

Muhammad believed the God who spoke through him was the same God worshiped by Jews and Christians. Muhammad said that five major prophets had come before him: Adam, Noah, Abraham, Moses, and Jesus. Muhammad said each had brought truth, but Christians and Jews had departed from the prophets' messages—the Jews had ignored Jesus, and Christians had embellished the simple message of the Gospels by adding theological complexities. Therefore, Allah had decided to speak through Muhammad, who is known simply as the Prophet. The religion he founded is called Islam, and its followers are known as Muslims.

The Religion

The nature of Islam is as clear and stark as the Arabian desert itself. *Islam* means "surrender to God," and this idea lies at the heart of the religion, for a follower of the religion is called a Muslim—"one who submits." Christians had to study for years before converting and had to understand the subtlety of various creeds. For a man or woman to convert to Islam, he or she merely needed to testify, "There is no God but Allah and Muhammad is his prophet." Whenever children were born in Muslim lands, midwives and parents whispered this creed into their ears so that they would grow immediately into faith. After this simple creed, Muslims were to follow the Five Pillars of Faith.

The first pillar of faith is the profession of faith itself. Believers adhere to a strict monotheism. (For example, Muslims believe that the Christian belief in the Trinity of the Father, Son, and Holy Spirit signaled a departure from the command to have only one God.) Further, Muslims believe that the Qur'an represents the word of God. The power of the spoken and written word had come to light in Muhammad's first vision, which emphasized the importance of God's words brought through the Prophet. Many of the faithful memorize and recite the entire Qur'an (which is about as long as the Christian New Testament).

Figure 6.11 shows a page from the Qur'an. The beautiful calligraphy of the Arabic letters and the gold leaf make precious manuscripts like this one as much

FIGURE 6.11 The Qur'an Because images are forbidden to Muslims, writing became the most honored art in the Islamic world. Muslims considered beautiful calligraphy to be part of the revealed word of God, as shown in this manuscript page from the Qur'an.

works of art as religious objects. Muslims believe that the Qur'an must not be translated from the original language, so all the manuscripts are copied in Arabic. This figure shows how strikingly different the Arabic alphabet is from the Greek and Latin scripts that dominated in the West. This visual signal points to the language barrier that would separate Muslim from Christian lands.

The first pillar concerned private behavior, indicating the faith within, but the next four reinforced the first through public actions of all believers. The second pillar of faith is prayer, an activity that the faithful perform five times a day. In addition, every Friday, Muslims gather to pray together at the local mosque, called there by a human voice beckoning from the mosque towers, or minarets. (Christians are called by bells, and Jews by horns. Muslims believe the angel Gabriel told Muhammad to use the human voice to call his followers to prayer.)

Unlike Christian churches, mosques display no images of God. Muslims take the biblical prohibition against the idolatry of graven images literally. It may be that the Byzantine iconoclast movement was influenced by the example of the strict interpretation of the Muslims. Instead of images of God, mosques are decorated with beautiful geometric patterns. These designs are intended to help the faithful in their prayers by focusing their attention on the divine pattern of the universe. An example of mosaic patterning

Faith

Public rituals

appears on the photograph of the Dome of the Rock shown at the opening of this chapter.

The third pillar of faith is almsgiving. Muslims are to donate a portion of what they earn to the needy, and this giving purifies the rest of their earnings. The fourth pillar of faith is fasting. All Muslims fast during the month of Ramadan, a time based on the lunar calendar that comes at a different point every year, which commemorates the month Allah revealed the Qur'an to Muhammad. During this month, the faithful ingest no food or drink and do not engage in sexual relations during the day, but eat and celebrate every night after sundown. This month is much loved by Muslims because it lets them attend to spiritual matters and family in a concentrated way.

The last pillar of faith is pilgrimage. All Muslims try to make a journey to Muhammad's holy city of Mecca once in their lifetime. This trip—called the **Haj**—is made during a designated pilgrimage month, so the city throngs with Muslims from all over the world during this special time. Muslims today continue to follow all the pillars of faith, including the Haj.

The Spread of Islam

When Muhammad began to speak of his visions, his wife Khadijah became his first convert. However, aside from her and some close friends, few people living in the market city of Mecca paid any attention to his message. This city had grown prosperous in part because of pilgrims coming to worship at the pagan shrine of the Ka'bah, so the city leaders had little interest in the words of a new prophet.

In 622, Muhammad and his small group of followers fled Mecca to another city 250 miles to the north. This city was later named Medina, *Hijra* which simply means "the city." Muslims consider this flight, called the **Hijra** (or *Hegira*), the turning point in the acceptance of the new religion. Just as Christians mark the birth of Christ as a turning point by dating the calendar from that year, Muslims remember the Hijra by using the year 622 as the year 1 in their calendar. The dating system uses A.H. (*anno Hijrah*) instead of C.E. (common era).

From his new base in Medina, Muhammad spread his ideas to the desert Bedouins. Tribe by tribe, the Arabians converted and began to focus their warfare on "unbelievers" instead of on each other, eventually coalescing into a unified group. In 628, Muhammad returned victorious to Mecca, where the large numbers of his followers persuaded the urban dwellers that his message was true. He kept the great shrine at the Ka'bah, convinced that the large meteor within it was sacred to Allah. Pilgrims still journey to this holy place and it is the focal point of the prayer of Muslims worldwide.

Map 6.4 shows the extent of Islam at the death of the Prophet in 632. At first, Muhammad's closest followers proclaimed themselves **caliphs** ("deputies" or "successors") of the Prophet. The map shows how rapidly the first four caliphs spread the new religion. These successes continued, and only a century after Muhammad's death, Islam held sway in an area stretching from India to Spain. After this remarkable spread, many people who were not Arabs became Muslims, and although all learned to speak Arabic so they could read the Qur'an, sometimes tensions emerged between Arab and non-Arab believers. Nevertheless, the spectacular growth of this new creed obliterated the Persian Empire, shrank the Byzantine Empire, and conquered the Vandal and Visigothic kingdoms.

In the summer of 732, the forces of Islam drove through the passes of the Pyrenees into the Merovingian kingdom of the Franks. The army was made up of a large body of light cavalry and was a formidable force. Muslim generals [Battle of Tours] were confident of their ability to conquer the less-organized Franks. They easily swept through the southern lands, destroying the opposition and taking great plunder. As the Arab chronicler relates, "All the nations of the Franks trembled at that terrible army." The retreating forces approached the Merovingian household for help, and the great general Charles Martel (Charles the Hammer) led a force to a large grassy plain near Tours (see **Map 6.4**). The Arab chronicler recognized the momentous nature of this meeting: "The two great hosts of the two languages and the two creeds were set in array against each other." The battle was fierce and tens of thousands died, but Charles won a decisive victory. The remaining Muslim force retreated across the Pyrenees, and the storm of Islamic conquests in the west was halted.

In spite of Charles's victory, the Islamic conquests were impressive. Why did Islam spread so quickly? There are a number of reasons. In part, its success came from the military strength of the recently unified Bedouin and oasis Arabs. Forming a new "tribe" based on religion, these [Reasons for success] formerly separate groups now made an effective fighting unit. Islamic armies also benefited from believing that God supported their military expansion, for the Qur'an urged warriors to fight vigorously in the cause of monotheism: "Fight in the path of God with those who fight with you . . . kill them; such is the reward of the infidels. . . . Fight them till there be no dissent, and the worship be only to God." As Muslim armies swept to victory in what they believed was a holy war, or *jihad,* they may have forced pagans to convert or be killed.

The concept of jihad is a complicated one because the word has several meanings that have allowed for different interpretations and emphases over time.

MAP 6.4

The Expansion of Islam to 750

This map shows the expansion of Islam from the Arabian peninsula to the southern and eastern Mediterranean, with the dates of the expansion. It includes the cities of Mecca, Damascus, and Baghdad—each of which, in turn, would become the capital of the Muslim world.

Explore the Map

1. Which sections of the Byzantine Empire were lost to the Muslims?

2. Which regions might be most influenced by the changes in the capitals? Why?

3. Where were the Islamic rulers most likely to focus their efforts while based in each of the capital cities?

From the beginning, Muslims identified two kinds of jihad: The "greater jihad" is the ongoing struggle within each individual to strive *Jihad* against base desires. This inner struggle is more meritorious than warfare, and many scholars emphasize this greater jihad when discussing the concept. The "lesser jihad" is a military struggle conducted against infidels.

In the early Islamic expansion, the jihad against polytheism established Islamic territories, which were called the House of Islam. In theory, non-Muslim states were called a House of War that existed until they were subjugated or converted. Under early Muslim laws, jihad was to be a constant state of war against the infidels, but as we will see, this idea would change over time.

The expansion of Islam also drew strength from the relatively benign attitude of the Muslim conquerors.

Christians and Jews, whom Muslims called "people of the Book" because they all shared the same scriptural tradition and worshiped the same God that Muslims venerated, had only to pay taxes to the Muslim rulers. In one of the earliest political documents of Islam, Muhammad wrote a "constitution" for Medina in 622 outlining the policies of the new religion. In this document, he laid out the principle of toleration and mutual aid: "The Jews must bear their expenses and the Muslims their expenses. Each must help the other against anyone who attacks the people of this document." However, such toleration did not mean equality; it came with conditions, as shown in Document 6.2.

Many Christians, especially in Syria, Egypt, and North Africa, had rejected the policies of the Byzantine emperors and tolerated Islam. Within Byzantium, men and women whose beliefs had been declared

DOCUMENT 6.2

Christians Accept Caliph Umar's Terms

The caliph Umar I (r. 634–644) made an agreement with Christians in Syria, offering religious toleration. The following letter from the Christians outlines the agreed-upon terms and indicates what kinds of things Christians were forbidden.

We shall not build, in our cities or in their neighborhood, new monasteries, churches, convents, or monks' cells, nor shall we repair, by day or night, such of them as fall in ruins or are situated in the quarters of the Muslims. We shall not give shelter in our churches or in our dwellings to any spy, nor hide him from the Muslims. We shall teach the Qur'an to our children. We shall not manifest our religion publicly nor convert anyone to it. We shall not prevent any of our kin from entering Islam if they wish it. We shall show respect toward the Muslims, and we shall rise from our seats when they wish to sit. We shall not seek to resemble the Muslims by imitating any of their garments, the headgear, the turban, footwear, or the parting of the hair. We shall not mount our saddles, nor shall we gird swords nor bear any kind of arms nor carry them on our persons. We shall not engrave Arabic inscriptions on our seals. We shall not sell fermented drinks. We shall not display our crosses or our books in the roads or markets of the Muslims. We shall only use clappers in our churches very softly. We shall not raise our voices in our church services or in the presence of Muslims, nor shall we raise our voices when following our dead (in funeral processions). . . . We shall not bury our dead near the Muslims. . . . We shall not build houses overtopping the houses of the Muslims. We accept these conditions for ourselves and for the people in our community, and in return we receive safe-conduct. . . .

SOURCE: *Islam: From the Prophet Muhammad to the Capture of Constantinople*, vol. 2: *Religion and Society*, ed. Bernard Lewis (New York: Oxford University Press, 1987).

Analyze the Document

1. How were these prohibitions more lenient than what Christian heretics faced under Christian emperors? (Compare with Chapter 5.)

2. Why do you think Muslims chose these prohibitions?

3. What prohibitions do you think might have eventually encouraged many Christians to convert to Islam?

---

heretical had been forbidden to continue in their beliefs. Under the Muslims, who cared little about the subtleties of Christian theology, they could believe as they liked as long as they submitted to the conquerors. Jews, too, were free to practice their religion without the pressure they had experienced before, particularly under the Visigoths. In time, many Christians converted to Islam. The rise of Islam had created a whole new culture in the Mediterranean world.

Creating an Islamic Unity

The Muslim armies not only conquered large expanses of land but also quickly transformed the society and culture of these territories. Anyone traveling in the Mediterranean world today can see immediately that life in Algeria is strikingly different from life in Italy. This was not so during Roman times.

What was it about Muslim rule that made Islamic culture take root so powerfully in these formerly Christian regions? Language played a large role. Because the Qur'an was not to be translated, believers of Islam had to learn Arabic. Therefore, Arabic became the language of business, government, and literature in Islamic strongholds. Prayer and pilgrimage also served to solidify the Muslim world. As the faithful all looked to Mecca five times a day during prayer and made

Unifying elements

pilgrimages to the holy places, men and women broadened their attention and loyalties beyond their local kingdoms. Over time, they began to think of themselves as part of a larger group.

Law was another important unifying force. The Islamic governments were ruled by Muslim law based on the Qur'an and the Sunna, which is a collection of cultural traditions based on the life of the Prophet. These laws, administered by Muslim judges, governed most aspects of Islamic life. Uniform enforcement of the laws contributed to a growing cultural homogeneity.

Finally, the great Muslim trade network that extended from India to the Mediterranean powerfully united the Islamic world. The freedom that Muslim rulers allowed merchants and artisans fueled economic development. Arabic coins, dinars, began to replace Byzantine or Persian coins as the main trade medium, and the Muslims developed advanced banking techniques to facilitate trade. For example, they initiated the use of bank checks, which would not be employed in the West for another eight hundred years.

The Gracious Life

With large-scale trade came dramatic changes in Muslim society. The conquerors adopted the best of both the Persian and Hellenistic worlds and created a way of

Yemen: Monotheism Spreads to Southern Arabia

Trade is the greatest stimulant to human interaction. Throughout history, men and women have willingly journeyed vast distances to sell or acquire luxury items like jewelry, fine clothing, and spices, as well as to trade everyday, useful objects like pots, knives, and basic ingredients for meals. But as merchants and entrepreneurs talked business and conducted deals along the major trade routes, they transported ideas in addition to merchandise. The ancient trade between the Mediterranean world and the southernmost tip of Arabia brought together peoples separated by immense deserts and exposed them to one another's religious ideas and controversies. As notions of religion spread, the lives of peoples from these two markedly different worlds began to be inextricably connected. Of course, the shifting sands of southern Arabia's deserts and the monsoon winds that whipped across the Red Sea posed daunting obstacles to people seeking to travel from southern Arabia, or Yemen, to the Mediterranean. Yet, these enterprising individuals found ways to interact with their counterparts in the eastern Mediterranean.

Some scholars suggest that after Africa, Yemen was the area of earliest human migration out of the African continent. Bold Africans crossed the Arabian Sea at the narrow straits separating the Red Sea from the Gulf of Aden, and the human expansion out of Africa had begun. The fertile plateaus of Yemen's highlands and the abundant seacoasts allowed early villages to flourish. As far back as 1,000 B.C.E., several wealthy kingdoms cropped up in this promising new land. Historians of technology are particularly impressed by the ruins of the ancient Marib Dam that settlers built in about 500 B.C.E. This astonishing structure allowed the ancient residents of the City of Saba (the Sabeans) to irrigate about 25,000 acres of land—and secure their food supply for the next thousand years.

But Yemen's real wealth came from trade. The region grows rare, brushlike trees that produce strong-smelling resins from which ancient peoples produced frankincense and myrrh. These resins—used in perfumes, medicines, and religious ceremonies—were prized throughout the ancient Mediterranean world. By 1,000 B.C.E., domestication of the camel enabled merchants to trade extensively across the Arabian desert. As one result, demand for frankincense and myrrh spread widely in the northern parts of Arabia and throughout the Mediterranean basin. One ancient writer described a caravan of three thousand camels that would have extended over 25 miles as it arrived at Mediterranean ports laden with the precious incenses. Certainly the best-known caravan of cherished goods from Saba was brought by the queen of Sheba (Saba) to the court of the Jewish king Solomon (see Document 1.2). This trade mission is described in both the Bible (1 Kings 10:1–13) and the Qur'an (27:16–44). For centuries, people throughout the ancient world continued to value frankincense and myrrh: The Roman scholar Pliny the Elder noted that Emperor Nero burned an entire year's harvest of frankincense to mark his mother's funeral. Indeed, southern Arabia prospered so much during this earliest era that the Romans called it Arabia Felix, which translates to "Happy Arabia."

life that was comfortable and pleasant, at least for the wealthy. Muslim households built on traditions drawn from the Bedouin tribes combined with practices from the Persian Empire. Previously, men had been allowed to have an unlimited number of wives, as in the Persian harems. However, the Qur'an limited a man to four wives, and this only if he could demonstrate that he had enough money to provide each wife with her own quarters and her own slaves. If husbands and wives did not get along, they could appeal to a judge who acted as an arbiter. If arbitration failed to resolve a conflict, either the man or the woman could obtain a divorce. Women's status under Islam improved in other ways as well: They were no longer treated strictly as property as they had been in pagan Arabic tribal society, and under Islamic law, Muslim women could inherit and keep their property even after marriage.

Within the household, women were separated from the company of men, and this seclusion continued when they went outdoors. Muslim women continued an age-old Middle Eastern practice of wearing heavy veils to cover themselves, and this practice continues in many Muslim countries today. Within

Women

But even Happy Arabia was swept into the religious turmoil that raged through the Mediterranean world in the centuries after the birth of Christ. During the fourth and fifth centuries C.E., missionaries traveling the caravan routes began converting the southern Arabian tribes to monotheism. Their efforts spawned tensions. For example, in the early sixth century C.E., the Sabean king ordered all Christians in his realm to convert to Judaism. When twenty thousand of them refused, he ordered them executed. The Christian king of Ethiopia retaliated by seizing Yemen in 525 C.E. However, the Christian reign he initiated lasted just fifty years, crumbling when the Persians conquered the Yemeni kingdoms in 575. In 628, the Persian governor of Yemen embraced Islam, and the new religion spread quickly through the tribes of southern Arabia. As early as 630 (before the death of the Prophet), the first mosques rose in Yemen's cities. Still, the conversion of the Yemenis to Islam could not heal the religious divisions that had long plagued the region.

When the Muslim faithful split into factions (Sunni and Shi'ite) over the question of who should rule after the death of Muhammad, the faithful in Yemen also eventually took sides in the dispute. In the early eighth century, Shi'ites argued that the succession went to the grandsons of Husayn. Most of the Shi'ites recognized Husayn's elder son, Muhammad al-Baqir, as the fifth Imam. But some dissidents recognized the younger son, Zayd, as the legitimate successor. Both Zayd and his son were killed in subsequent battles and so could not fulfill their supposed destiny. However, many Shi'ites contended that while the next Imam must be a descendant of Husayn or his brother, Husan, he need not be the eldest of the siblings. This became one of several points of difference among the Shi'ite communities. Holding firm to their positions, a number of Zaydi sects emerged and formed a separate branch of the Shi'ite movement. In the late eighth century, some Zaydis fled to the mountainous region of Yemen. There, in 901, they established a Zaydi state. This long-standing branch of Shi'ism remains a significant minority in Yemen today.

As the centuries have unfolded, Yemen has continued to take part in the political and religious struggles marking interactions between the Western and Islamic worlds—from its conquest by the Ottoman Empire in the sixteenth century, to its engagement in Cold War politics during the mid-twentieth century. Religious tensions within Yemen have continued to affect interactions with the West: In 2000, extremists almost sank the U.S. battleship *Cole*, which was docked in one of its harbors, and in 2009, training camps in Yemen sent a 23-year-old Nigerian man to try to ignite an explosive on a U.S. airliner on Christmas Day. Fortunately the attack failed. In ancient times the trade in precious resins brought this land into close contact with the Mediterranean world, and its fortunes have remained intertwined with those of the West ever since.

Making Connections

1. What trade items brought Yemen into continuous contact with the Mediterranean world?

2. What religious ideas and controversies spread to Yemen?

3. How did the Shi'ite Muslims in Yemen split in disagreement?

---

the households, women presided over the many slaves generated from the conquests and subsequent trade and created a lifestyle that was the envy of many in the Mediterranean world.

Persians taught the Arabian Muslims to play chess and backgammon; from Syria, Muslims learned to wear wide trousers instead of the traditional Arab robes. They also began to eat at tables instead of sitting cross-legged on the floor. These seemingly small matters, when taken together, reflected a prosperous, relatively homogeneous society.

Daily life

Figure 6.12 reveals several unique aspects of Islamic society. In this illustration, two wealthy Muslim men are served wine by a Christian slave probably captured in Spain. (Islamic society depended heavily on slavery, just as the Persian and Roman cultures had.) This picture also captures Muslim attitudes toward alcohol. The Qur'an forbids drinking of wine, but many Muslims routinely violated this prohibition. Indeed, some beautiful Arabic poetry even extols the pleasures of good wine. As this illustration indicates, Muslim culture was developing into something very different from life in western Europe and Byzantium.

FIGURE 6.12 Spanish Muslims Muslim life included the enjoyment of many things, including a good game of chess. The game was probably developed in India and spread rapidly through Muslim lands into the West, where it was much beloved in the courts of Europe.

Forces of Disunity

For all its cultural commonalities, the Muslim world was not without strife. Two related problems led to conflict within the Muslim territories. One problem centered on ethnicity—specifically, relations between Arabs and other Muslim peoples. The other involved a pressing political question: Who would rule after the death of the Prophet?

Some Muslims believed that the caliphs should be spiritual leaders who based their authority on the Prophet's family. In the mid-seventh Shi'ite Muslims century, amid much controversy over the succession, the Prophet's son-in-law and cousin, 'Ali, became the caliph. 'Ali promoted the idea of equality for all believers, rather than privileged status for Arabs who had initially spread the Prophet's message. Although he hoped to serve less as a governor and tax collector than as a spiritual leader, 'Ali had to devote much of his reign to fighting political rivals.

In 661, as 'Ali was entering a mosque to pray, an assassin supporting another political faction plunged a dagger into the caliph, but 'Ali's notion of the caliphate remained alive. Men and women who followed his ideal were called **Shi'ites.** They continue to believe that the Islamic world should be ruled by **imams,** men descended from 'Ali who act as true spiritual heads of the community. The Shi'ite faithful proclaimed 'Ali's two sons, Hasan and Husayn, the second and third Imams. Husayn is particularly revered by Shi'ites today because followers of the caliph killed him and his infant son. Although Shi'ites look upon the usurpation of 'Ali's rights to rule as the beginning of their movement, Husayn's death—which they saw as a martyrdom—served as the emotional rallying point

for the Shi'ites. To this day, the death of Husayn is the most fervently celebrated event in the Shi'ite calendar. From these early centuries on, Shi'ites have believed that imams are endowed with the Divine Light Wisdom, which enables them to interpret complicated passages in the Qur'an. Shi'ites today are a significant minority in the Muslim world and continue to disagree with the Sunnis, who advocate a political, rather than purely spiritual, caliphate. The Global Connections on pages 202–203 shows how this struggle influenced events in southern Arabia (modern Yemen).

After the murder of 'Ali, the caliphate was taken over by the Umayyad family, who established a dynasty that lasted almost a century. The Umayyads located their capital in Damascus and created a govern- Umayyad caliphate ment that favored Arabs. This dynasty represented the traditional military and economic leaders of the Arabs. Nevertheless, dissent stirred even within the Umayyad caliphate. The Dome of the Rock (shown at the beginning of this chapter) was built by an Umayyad caliph in 691 who wanted to de-emphasize Mecca. He encouraged the faithful to visit the rock in Jerusalem from where Muslims believed Muhammad had ascended to heaven. He was successful; the Dome of the Rock today is a much-loved shrine. Unfortunately, it stands on land that Jews and Christians also venerate, and the site continues to generate controversy.

In 750, the 'Abbasids overthrew the Umayyad caliphate. They intended to restore more spiritual authority to the caliphate and to broaden authority from the Arabs to other believers, but most important, they moved the capital from Damascus to Baghdad. This newly built city, located on the banks of the Tigris River, was perfectly suited to take advantage of the rich trade from the Far East. Its land was rich, and the caliph was particularly impressed with its cool nights and freedom from mosquitoes. The founder claimed, "It will surely be the most flourishing city in the world," and 'Abbasid caliphate he was not wrong. The great city, fortified by three concentric round walls, was the administrative center of Islam and by the tenth century had a population of about 1.5 million people. This extraordinary city helped the Muslim world focus toward the old Persian provinces, with their rich trade routes to the east. Seen from this magnificent cosmopolitan city, rivaled only by Constantinople, western Europe seemed very primitive indeed. (See Global Connections in Chapter 7, on page 224.) However, the move to the east did not help the

Christians:
- Belonging to the Roman Catholic Church
- Belonging to the Greek Orthodox Church

Muslims:
- Under the Caliph of Baghdad ('Abbasid)
- Under the Caliph of Cairo (Fatimite)
- Under the Caliph of the Almoravids
- Under the Caliph of the Hammadites

(Stripes indicate blended religious groups)

MAP 6.5

Islam, ca. 1000

This map shows how the world of Islam was divided under the leadership of various rulers.

Explore the Map

1. What caliphate controlled the capital of Baghdad?

2. What caliphate focused on the East and the wealthy trade from India and China?

3. Given the distances involved, how difficult was it for the caliphate of Baghdad to exert authority over the Almoravids?

4. How might these divisions have weakened Islamic unity?

'Abbasids eliminate political dissension. The Umayyads continued to hold power in Spain, and the Shi'ites refused to support the 'Abbasids.

Beyond the disunity percolating within the ruling dynasties, there was the ever-present tendency toward local control. Caliphs in Baghdad growing rich on eastern trade had little authority over commanders as far away as Spain, and by the tenth century (fourth century of the Islamic calendar), military commanders, called **emirs,** were taking power in their local areas. Although they theoretically followed the rule of the caliphs, they frequently acted with a good deal of autonomy. As **Map 6.5** shows, the huge Muslim world, which formed a strong cultural unity, suffered

BIOGRAPHY

Avicenna (Ibn Sina)
(980–1037)

A Muslim

Scientist

Avicenna was born in 980, the son of a wealthy governor of an outlying province in modern-day Afghanistan. His father was Turkish and his mother Iranian. Because education played an important role in Muslim families, Avicenna and his younger brother Mahmud had tutors from a young age. Avicenna showed great intellectual curiosity and talent, and by the age of 10, he had memorized the entire Qur'an. Within his home, he also explored philosophy, theology, and mathematics. For a while, the avid scholar studied with an Indian surveyor, from whom he learned Indian mathematics.

A turning point came in Avicenna's life when his father hired a well-known philosopher to live with the family and tutor him. Avicenna learned so quickly that the tutor was stunned. The young man found medicine and natural science so easy that by the age of 16 he was practicing medicine and teaching other physicians. However, it was logic and geometry that captured the young man's imagination. After much struggle, Avicenna mastered Aristotle's logic and was so grateful for this new knowledge that he gave extra alms to the poor as a way to thank Allah. The young man so voraciously consumed all the works of the great thinkers that by the age of 18, he claimed he had mastered all knowledge. He accomplished this prodigious feat of learning without renouncing the pastimes that engaged other young men: He was well known for satisfying his passions for wine and women as well as for knowledge.

The young scholar became a court physician to a sultan when he was only 18, and he began his prolific writing career during these years. He wrote on subjects ranging from ethics to the law to the Qur'an. However, this happy time in his life came to a tragic end at age 22, when Avicenna's father died. Forced to earn a more substantial living, he entered government service, moving among the courts of various emirs. While he was still in his early twenties, Avicenna began to teach Abu 'Ubaid al-Juzjani, who stayed with him throughout much of the remainder of his life and who wrote Avicenna's biography. Al-Juzjani moved with the philosopher as he went from court to court, negotiating the complex Islamic political scene. He had resisted his father's attraction to Shi'ism and was imprisoned only once, for corresponding with an emir who was seen as a rival to the man he served.

---

from the centrifugal forces that separated all the ancient empires.

The many divisions within the House of Islam that had emerged by the tenth century led to a transformation of the idea of jihad. During the early expansion years, there had been a clear, twofold division of the world—the House of War and the House of Islam. Now, complex realities of political alignments caused some Muslims to argue for an intermediate area—a House of Peace—in which non-Muslim states could be exempt from attack. This legal device permitted travel and trade between Muslim and non-Muslim regions, and through the tenth century there was often a relationship of mutual tolerance established between the Muslim world and regions outside its borders.

Heirs to Hellenistic Learning

Despite all the political tensions, the Muslim world still managed to make astonishing gains in the arts and sciences, and in fact remained the intellectual center of the Mediterranean world for centuries. By the eighth century, the caliphs had collected Persian, Greek, and Syriac scientific and philosophical works and had them translated into Arabic. In the ninth century, the 'Abbasids ruling in Baghdad maintained this support of science. They built the House of Wisdom in Baghdad, which included a library, a translation center, and a school. This careful cultivation of learning and the blending of so many traditions led to remarkable accomplishments. Muslim scientists and physicians were by far the best in the Western world.

Muslim doctors did not slavishly follow the great classical physicians Hippocrates and Galen, even though the works of these men circulated widely. Instead, they combined this ancient wisdom with practical and empirical observation. Islamic rulers required doctors to be licensed, so the practice of medicine was well regulated. Some Islamic physicians wrote extensively and exerted a profound influence on Western medicine. Razi (865–925) (called Rhazes in the West) authored more than one hundred books on medicine. He was the first to diagnose smallpox and prescribe an effective treatment for it. Ibn Sina (980–1037) (known as Avicenna in the West) wrote *Canon of*

Medicine

FIGURE 6.13 Avicenna

Occupied with public affairs during the day, Avicenna at night continued his studies and writings. He composed treatises on arithmetic, music, and language and invented a unique form of rhythmic poetry that was emulated by subsequent poets. However, his most significant contributions came in the fields of medicine and philosophy.

When the Western universities recovered the works of Aristotle in the twelfth century, the texts included Avicenna's commentaries. In this way, the Muslim scholar's interpretations of Aristotle's ideas influenced the West's intellectual revival. Furthermore, Avicenna's *Canon of Medicine* served as the main medical text for more than six centuries and was copied throughout the Mediterranean world. In the West, the *Canon* was probably second only to the Christian Bible in the number of times it was reproduced. Some scholars suggest that his techniques of experimentation and observation gave birth to the modern scientific method.

In 1037 Avicenna fell ill. In hopes of stealing his money, one of his slaves tried to kill him by contaminating his food with opium. The scholar survived this attempt by treating himself. However, his illness killed him shortly thereafter. Nevertheless, Avicenna represented the best of the Muslim world that valued education and applied science. His theories on the sources of infectious diseases, his explanation of sight, his invention of longitude, and his use of the astrolabe have all caused modern scientists to praise his genius. The scholar accomplished all this while negotiating the hazards of a world dependent on uncertain politics and disloyal slaves. To this day, the outstanding body of work that he left behind continues to earn wide admiration and respect.

Connecting People & Society

1. How does Avicenna's life reveal the high respect for learning in the Muslim world?

2. How did the divisions within Islam affect Avicenna?

3. Why have some credited Avicenna with beginning the modern scientific method?

Medicine, an encyclopedia of medicine that laid the foundation for experimental science.

Muslim surgeons performed remarkably complex operations. They practiced vascular and cancer surgery and developed a sophisticated technique for operating on cataracts of the eyes that involved using a tube to drain the fluid from the cataract. This technique was employed even in modern times, until physicians developed procedures for removing the cataracts completely. A wide range of anesthetics, from opium mixed in wine to more sophisticated drugs, made surgery tolerable for Muslim patients. Hospitals, too, sprang up throughout the Muslim world and included outpatient treatment centers and dispensaries for the many medicines being developed. Thanks to the careful sharing of knowledge and the development of advanced procedures and study, Muslim physicians provided outstanding medical care between the seventh and twelfth centuries.

Scientists made dramatic progress in other areas as well. Mathematicians brought the use of "Arabic" numerals from India, and these replaced the Roman numerals that

Mathematics

FIGURE 6.14 Mariner's Astrolabe   Advances in Muslim mathematics allowed for the invention of the astrolabe, a device for measuring the angles of heavenly bodies. This new tool allowed navigators to calculate latitude more precisely in finding their way at sea.

had been used throughout the former empire. The major advantage of Arabic numerals was that they included the zero, which makes complex calculations

DOCUMENT 6.3

Shahrazád Mollifies a Murderous King

In the West, the best-known Muslim literary work is The Arabian Nights, *also called* The Thousand and One Nights, *which is set in the ninth-century court of Harun al-Rashid. This collection of tales circulated for centuries and was probably recorded in its present form in the fifteenth century. The story tells of a jealous king who marries a virgin each night and kills her in the morning so that his wives can never be unfaithful. The lovely Shahrazád escapes this fate by weaving a compelling story for the king every evening for a thousand and one nights. This excerpt explains what happened to Shahrazád after her years of storytelling.*

SHAHRAZÁD, during this period, had borne the King three male children; and when she had ended these tales, she rose upon her feet, and kissed the ground before the King, and said to him, O King of the time, and incomparable one of the age and period, verily I am thy slave, and during a thousand and one nights I have related to thee the history of the preceding generations, and the admonitions of the people of former times:

then have I any claim upon thy majesty so that I may request of thee to grant me a wish? And the King answered her, Request: thou shalt receive, O Shahrazád. So thereupon she called out to the nurses and the eunuchs, and said to them, Bring ye my children. According they brought them to her quickly; and they were three male children: one of them walked, and one crawled, and one was at the breast.

And when they brought them, she took them and placed them before the King, and, having kissed the ground, said, O King of the age, these are thy children, and I request of thee that thou exempt me from slaughter, as a favour to these infants; for if thou slay me, these infants will become without a mother, and will not find among women one who will rear them well. And thereupon the King wept, and pressed his children to his bosom, and said, O Shahrazád, by Allah, I pardoned thee before the coming of these children, because I saw thee to be chaste, pure, ingenuous, pious. May God bless thee, and thy father and thy mother, and thy root and thy branch! I call God to witness against me that I have exempted thee from every thing

that might injure thee.—So she kissed his hands and his feet, and rejoiced with exceeding joy; and she said to him, May God prolong thy life, and increase thy dignity and majesty! . . .

So they decorated the city in a magnificent manner, the like of which had not been seen before, and the drums were beaten and the pipes were sounded, and all the performers of sports exhibited their arts, and the King rewarded them munificently with gifts and presents. He bestowed alms also upon the poor and needy, and extended his generosity to all his subjects, and all the people of his dominions. And he and the people of his empire continued in prosperity and joy and delight and happiness until they were visited by the terminator of delights and the separator of companions.

SOURCE: Edward William Lane, trans., *The Arabian Nights' Entertainments—or The Thousand and One Nights* (New York: Tudor Publishing, 1927), pp. 962–963.

Analyze the Document

1. How might works of literature not only entertain but also reveal the values of the society that produce them?

2. What does this text say about early Muslim views of women?

3. What light does the story shed on the household of the caliph?

---

manageable. By the tenth century, Muslim mathematicians had perfected the use of decimals and fractions and had invented algebra. The word *algebra* comes from Arabic and means "the art of bringing together unknowns to match a known quantity." Today students all over the world continue to learn this art.

The mathematics of algebra allowed Muslim astronomers to calculate more precisely the angles of the sun and stars at different times of the year. Through algebraic computation, they made progress on the difficult challenge of finding their way at sea using the latitude portion of the grid of the world. (See Thinking About Science & Technology in Chapter 3.) With their new knowledge, they invented the mariner's **astrolabe,** shown in **Figure 6.14,** a heavy brass ring marked with degrees for measuring the angles of celestial bodies. The spread of this instrument to

Christian Europe in the twelfth century would transform navigation.

The accomplishments of Muslim society ranged far beyond science. The Qur'an is written in beautiful Arabic rhymed prose, and its study contributed to a lively appreciation for literature. Muslim writers throughout the Middle Ages would pen magnificent poetry that cele-brated beauty, love, and the sensual | Literature |

life. Perhaps the most famous literary work was *The Arabian Nights*. This widely admired collection of stories was set in Baghdad in the court of the most famous 'Abbasid caliph, Harun al-Rashid (r. 786–809), and has delighted readers in the East and West for centuries. Read Document 6.3 for an excerpt of this engaging work that reveals social attitudes of the early Muslim world.

Even the religious architecture developed by the Muslims put a unique imprint on the appearance of the southern Mediterranean cities. Whereas Christians emphasized religious images based on the human form, Muslims developed exquisite patterning designs. Domes and minarets gracing impressive mosques gave the skylines of eastern and southern cities their own distinct character.

Islam and the West

Before the seventh century, the story of the West unfolded rather organically from the Fertile Crescent around the Mediterranean basin and into northern Europe. Throughout these millennia, Western culture developed with contact from as far away as east Asia, until during the Roman Empire people identified themselves as participating in one empire—albeit a diverse, multicultural one. After Muhammad's visions and the spread of Islam, that experience changed. The Mediterranean world was split into two separate cultures. Historians have argued over the degree to which trade and travel were interrupted by the division, but none questions the cultural divide. From the seventh century on, Islam and the West would take two different paths, always interacting at some level, but always conscious of the difference between them.

LOOKING BACK & MOVING FORWARD

Summary   After the sixth century, the Mediterranean world of the old Roman Empire underwent a dramatic transformation. The Roman Empire in the west dissolved in the face of the rising Germanic kingdoms. The empire persisted in the east, but in a drastically changed form known as the Byzantine Empire. In the south, armies of the new religion of Islam conquered vast territories to create a new society and culture. Islam arose in part as a reaction to the Byzantine Empire and Christianity. Although they worshiped the same God as Christians and Jews, Muslims worshiped in a different way. Consequently, they developed a new way of life that led to a vigorous synthesis of the cultures of the many lands they conquered.

The emergence of this third culture in the lands of the old Roman Empire brought warfare, suffering, and religious tensions, but also a rejuvenated intellectual life. The West and Byzantium did not adopt Islamic religion, but they learned much from Muslim philosophers, scientists, and poets. From this time forward, the interactions among these three great cultures—western European, Byzantine, and Muslim—would profoundly shape the history of the West.

KEY TERMS

federates, *p. 182*
Petrine doctrine, *p. 187*
theme, *p. 192*
Caesaropapist, *p. 195*
iconoclasm, *p. 196*
Cyrillic alphabet, *p. 196*
Haj, *p. 199*
Hijra, *p. 199*
caliphs, *p. 199*
jihad, *p. 199*
Shi'ites, *p. 204*
imams, *p. 204*
emirs, *p. 205*
astrolabe, *p. 208*

REVIEW, ANALYZE, & CONNECT TO TODAY

REVIEW THE PREVIOUS CHAPTER

Chapter 5—"Territorial and Christian Empires"—followed the difficulties of the late Roman Empire and studied Diocletian's reforms, in which he tried to reorganize and preserve the empire, and Constantine's movement of the capital to the east.

1. What elements of Diocletian's reforms did the Byzantine emperors continue? Why did many of these reforms endure more in the east than in the west?

2. Review the reasons Constantine moved his capital. In what ways did his decision prove to be sound in the face of the events of the fifth and sixth centuries?

ANALYZE THIS CHAPTER

Chapter 6—"A World Divided"—shows how three distinct cultures emerged in the old territory of the Roman Empire.

1. Review the various characteristics of the societies of the Byzantine Empire, the Muslim lands, and the

western kingdoms. What are the strengths and weaknesses of each?

2. Compare and contrast the beliefs of Christianity, Judaism, and Islam.

3. What accounted for the rapid expansion of Islam?

4. As the Slavs converted to Christianity, they established cultural patterns that would affect Europe for millennia. Review the Slavic settlements and their conversion to Christianity.

5. Review the main elements of Muslim culture, including the forces of unity and disunity that helped shape the lands of Islam.

CONNECT TO TODAY

Think about the divisions of various cultures and religions that were described in this chapter.

1. How do the divisions within Islam, as traced in this chapter, continue to affect the world today?

2. How do you think the misunderstandings in this region might reflect the fragmentation that separated the Byzantine Empire from the West? Consider, for example, the split in the Christian churches and the use of differing alphabets by Greek and Latin speakers, as described in this chapter.

BEYOND THE CLASSROOM

THE MAKING OF THE WESTERN KINGDOMS, ca. 376–750

Brown, Peter. *The Rise of Western Christendom: Triumph and Diversity, A.D. 200–1000*. Boston: Blackwell, 1997. A highly readable narrative with a breadth of coverage presented by a master historian. Includes the Persian Empire and the differing development of the eastern and western church.

Glob, P.V. *The Bog People: Iron Age Man Preserved*. Translated by R. Bruce-Mitford. Ithaca, NY: Cornell University Press, 1969. A fascinating archaeological study of Iron Age people and their culture, based on the excavations of corpses from the bogs.

Heather, Peter. *The Fall of the Roman Empire*. New York: Oxford University Press, 2006. A convincing and elegant argument that Rome did not just fall but was dismantled by the German tribes, who had learned much in their centuries of living in Rome's shadow.

Noble, T.F.X. *The Republic of St. Peter: The Birth of the Papal State, 680–825*. Philadelphia: University of Pennsylvania Press, 1984. A clear study of the growth of the papacy in these early, little-studied centuries.

Russell, James C. *The Germanization of Early Medieval Christianity: A Sociohistorical Approach to Religious Transformation*. New York: Oxford University Press, 1994. An inquiry into Christianization efforts among the German peoples that considers the influence of the Germans on Christianity.

Wells, Peter S. *Barbarians to Angels: The Dark Ages Reconsidered*. New York: W.W. Norton, 2008. An examination of European culture after Rome's collapse, providing archaeological evidence to demonstrate the existence of a vigorous economic life during the early Middle Ages.

THE BYZANTINE EMPIRE, ca. 400–1000

Conte, Francis. *The Slavs*. New York: Columbia University Press, 1995. Summarizes the ancient Slavic world—its characteristics, internal and external contacts, and the influences that shaped its development.

Gregory, Timothy E. *A History of Byzantium*, 2nd rev. ed. Hoboken, NJ: Wiley-Blackwell, 2009. An extensively revised edition of a classic study that covers the empire from Constantine through the fall of Constantinople.

Hussey, Joan M. *The Orthodox Church in the Byzantine Empire*. New York: Oxford University Press, 1990. Explores the development of the church in the Byzantine Empire from the reshaping of the policies in the post-Justinian period of the seventh century to the fall of Byzantium in the fifteenth century.

Rodley, Lyn. *Byzantine Art and Architecture*. New York: Cambridge University Press, 1996. A well-illustrated introduction to the material culture of the Byzantine Empire.

ISLAM, 600–1000

Ansary, Tamim. *Destiny Disrupted: A History of the World Through Islamic Eyes*. New York: PublicAffairs, 2009. A lively survey of the history of Islam, showing how the relationship between Islam and the West has been mutually transforming.

Bidwell, Robin. *The Two Yemens*. Boulder, CO: Westview Press, 1983. An engaging history of Yemen from ancient to present times.

Esposito, John L. *The Oxford History of Islam*. New York: Oxford University Press, 2002. A collection of essays on various topics, from philosophy to history to art, that together offer a fine introduction to Islamic history.

Hillenbrand, Carole. *The Crusades: Islamic Perspectives.* New York: Routledge, 2000. A comprehensive, beautifully illustrated discussion of the Islamic sources, showing the changing idea of jihad, warfare, and life during the crusading period.

Momen, Moojan. *An Introduction to Shi'i Islam.* Oxford: George Ronald, 1985. A clear explanation of this branch of Islam written by a practicing Shi'ite.

Roberts, Robert. *The Social Laws of the Qur'an.* Atlantic Highlands, NJ: Humanities Press, 1990. A fine analysis of the laws in the Qur'an and how they impact society.

Stowasser, Barbara. *Women in the Qur'an: Traditions and Commentaries.* New York: Oxford University Press, 1994. A scripture-based examination of differing women's status in family and society.

FOUR EVANGELISTS, early ninth century

In the eighth century, after the waning of violence in the West, kings slowly began to restore order. In doing so, they looked to the learning of the past. This illustration of Matthew, Mark, Luke, and John comes from a Gospel book made in the palace chapel school at Emperor Charlemagne's court. The gracious folds of the tunics and the sparse but elegant landscape display classic artistry. At the top of the image, the artist shows the dawn breaking, promising a new order in the West that will be built on the literacy and the precious texts of the past.

The Struggle to Bring Order

The Early Middle Ages, ca. 750–1000

"Since I had not wherewith to feed and clothe myself, I wish to commend myself to you and to put myself under your protection. I have done so, . . . and as long as I live I shall never have the right to withdraw from your power and protection." With these words, drawn from a legal document, eighth-century noblemen placed themselves in a mutually binding contract with their superior. After the disruptions of the fifth, sixth, and seventh centuries, western Europeans struggled to restore order to their society, and they did it by trying to join all members of society in ties of law and loyalty. From the eighth to the tenth century, rulers worked to organize their kingdoms, and in doing so, they created a new culture that combined elements of the old Germanic tribes, the Roman Empire they inherited, and the Christian beliefs they embraced.

As kings worked to establish frameworks for their fragile new kingdoms, they discovered that written law codes and highly organized social structures gave their lands a relative peace that brought a growing prosperity. As law codes regulated people's behavior, nobles and peasants alike defined their relationships in terms of personal and contractual ties that stabilized day-to-day life for everyone. Kings also encouraged intellectual and cultural growth, which had stalled during the previous volatile centuries. Western civilization seemed poised to flourish again in a new form.

Anglo-Saxon England developed traditions of local government and law that planted the early seeds of constitutional government. However, the most successful combination of Germanic and Roman culture took place on the Continent, where Frankish rulers slowly consolidated an empire. With the peace brought by these new strong kings, the church, too, began to reassert its authority and its role in maintaining the Christian order. Although a new series of invasions in the tenth century undermined all these efforts, we can still find in them the roots of ideas and institutions that would shape the lives of men and women in the West for centuries.

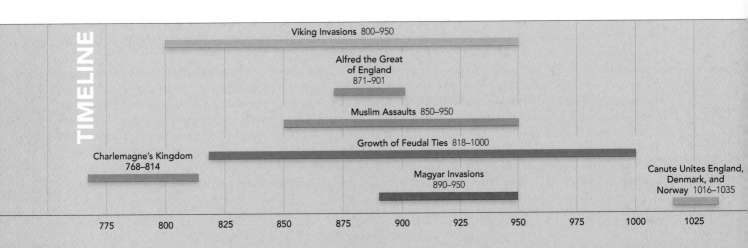

TIMELINE

Viking Invasions 800–950

Alfred the Great
of England
871–901

Muslim Assaults 850–950

Growth of Feudal Ties 818–1000

Charlemagne's Kingdom
768–814

Magyar Invasions
890–950

Canute Unites England,
Denmark, and
Norway 1016–1035

775   800   825   850   875   900   925   950   975   1000   1025

PREVIEW

BRINGING ORDER WITH LAWS AND LEADERSHIP

Early in the eighth century, in the northern England town of York, a small child was sent to the newly founded school at the church. As the young boy grew, he became an accomplished scholar who corresponded with Latin-speaking scholars all over western Europe. In time, his Anglo-Saxon name, probably Alhwini, changed to the Latin form of Alcuin, and it is by this name that he is remembered today. In 766, when Alcuin was about 30 years old, he became headmaster of the church school, and he never lost his commitment to education. The illustration that opens this chapter portrays scholars similar to Alcuin, writing with quill pens on parchment books.

As we will see, Alcuin's career did not end in York—he went on to travel and profoundly influence the most celebrated courts of the time, even encouraging the emperor Charlemagne to pass laws establishing schools for all freeborn children. In preserving and teaching Latin literature and working to strengthen the Christian church, Alcuin was instrumental in furthering the synthesis of Germanic, Roman, and Christian culture that shaped the early Middle Ages. Alcuin's career and dedication to learning were made possible in large part because the violence that had characterized the centuries after the fall of the Roman Empire was slowly being brought under control by talented kings.

The Rule of Law

Long before their penetration into the Roman Empire (see Chapter 6), the Germanic tribes had valued the force of law. Laws were not written down, however, nor legislated by king or council. Instead, laws constituted the customs of the past enforced by individuals and families. Traditionally, kings could arbitrate between conflicting parties, but people believed the law transcended any individual ruler, and law was administered by assemblies of the people. The German assemblies had developed some unusual means to help determine the truth in disputed cases. For example, they might consider the character (or value to the community) of the accused, and in a practice called **compurgation,** 12 honorable men testified to the character of the accused (without any necessary knowledge of the facts of the incidents under discussion). Or the assembly might appeal to the supernatural, in a process called **ordeal** (the word originally meant "judgment"). In an ordeal, the accused might pick up a red-hot iron or immerse his hand in boiling water. If the hand was not severely burned, the accused was judged innocent. Later in the Middle Ages, ordeals by battle would also be used to determine guilt, and in late witchcraft trials, women were thrown into the water to see if they sank. Floating—an indication that the water rejected the woman—was seen as a sign of guilt.

In the late fifth century, the kings from the western Germanic kingdoms—who inherited the Roman traditions of the lands they held—began to codify their people's laws, and they were helped by their Roman subjects trained in classical law. The ancient laws of the Germanic peoples began to be written down in Latin and began to incorporate some of the principles of Roman law. The laws of the land became yet another example of the slow blending of cultures that shaped the medieval world. The codes of the Franks, Lombards, Visigoths, and Anglo-Saxons offer historians important insights into these early kingdoms. The prologues of these codes continued to insist that the kings were not making laws, but simply recording the people's will—the old Germanic tradition of law was preserved.

In villages (which might have as few as a dozen families), the most respected people in the community assembled periodically to administer their local affairs. In many ways, these day-to-day decisions, made by people gathering together at a crossroads in the village, were more important to these people's lives than the larger policies set by kings. These villagers were participating in an ancient custom of

> Legal codes

self-governance at the most local level. Document 7.1 gives examples of rural legislation in the Visigothic code.

Like the villagers, the nobles of the Germanic tribes also had traditions for resolving disputes; they depended upon private vengeance for justice. According to the recorded laws, the principal preoccupation was to find ways to stop the bitter feuds that broke out between extended families who cherished their ability to protect their people and their honor above all else. The written law codes became a first step toward regularizing and perhaps controlling the violence to bring order to the growing kingdoms.

Feuding was slowly regulated by placing limits on the occasions where vengeance was allowed. For example, a family was not permitted to seek revenge if one of their number was killed while committing a crime. Nor could a family strike back before an offender from another family was proven guilty. However, the most important mechanism for regulating violence was persuading family groups to accept compensation (in money or goods) instead of vengeance. If a member of one's kin was killed or injured, for example, the guilty party had to restore the victim's monetary worth to his or her family. This amount of money was called **wergeld,** or "man gold"—in other words, the worth of a man. A free peasant was worth about 200 shillings; a nobleman, six times that. The Germanic laws used the techniques of ordeal and compurgation to determine who should pay wergeld.

The written Germanic law codes reveal rulers' hopes that wergeld would compensate peacefully for the various injustices that inevitably cropped up as people—especially heavily armed men who spent a lot of time drinking—lived together. Wergeld covered quarrels—offenders had to pay 30 shillings for cutting off an ear, 60 shillings for removing a nose, and 8 shillings for knocking out a front tooth—as well as damaged reputations. For slandering an earl, the penalty was 60 shillings; for cutting his hair to insult him, 10 shillings; for damaging his beard—his symbol of masculinity—20 shillings.

This intricate system of fines included outrages committed against all members of the tribe, from women and children to livestock. Wergeld was assessed for the rape of young women or nuns, for adultery committed with a married woman, and even for crimes as specific as watching a woman who was modestly hiding behind a bush to urinate. The early laws of the Franks penalized anyone who hit a pregnant woman, and the penalty was increased if the woman died, thus killing the unborn child. The laws recognized that part of a woman's value included her potential for bearing children; if someone killed a postmenopausal woman, he had to pay one-third of the fine for killing a woman during her childbearing years.

These law codes that so precisely reveal the details of life in the early Germanic kingdoms may appear strange to us because they put a price on everything from an insult to a toe injury. However, they represented an important step in the emerging synthesis between Germanic and Roman societies, as kings began to record the customs of the people. These records were intended to bring peace and order to the kingdoms, but in this they were only partially successful: The early medieval kings never succeeded in weaning their subjects completely from their need for vengeance. In spite of the efforts of kings, the eighth and ninth centuries remained an era of rampant lawlessness, largely because these laws were too difficult to enforce. However, important seeds were planted in the legal traditions that we have come to identify with Western civilization.

The eighth-century monarchs slowly insinuated themselves and their royal officers between feuding families, and written law codes became an instrument by which royal power could be slowly increased. Wergeld, compurgation, and trial by ordeal became major legal pillars of the early Middle Ages, adding to the judicial tradition left by the Romans. The Germanic custom of trial by assemblies became an important base for the growth of representative institutions that would emerge in the Middle Ages. The concept of the rule of law—in which law superseded individual inclination and played a central role in keeping order—proved highly resilient and helped consolidate these early monarchies.

ANGLO-SAXON ENGLAND: FORWARDING LEARNING AND LAW

As the eighth century opened, Anglo-Saxon England consisted of several kingdoms (shown on **Map 7.1**). The most powerful were Northumbria, Mercia, and Wessex. At this time, these kingdoms were separate and struggling to integrate their new Christianity and the new learning they inherited from the Roman texts that Christian leaders brought to the island.

The Anglo-Saxons had been converted to Christianity in the seventh century, and after the Synod of Whitby in 664 (discussed in Chapter 6), the English church began to be organized along the Roman model—with a clearer hierarchy of bishops and priests—instead of as a monastic, missionary organization. In 669, Pope Vitalian sent Theodore of Tarsus to be the archbishop of Canterbury, and this erudite man from the eastern Roman Empire significantly forwarded learning in Britain. He established a school at Canterbury and brought other scholars with him who founded Benedictine monasteries in the north of England—at Wearmouth-Jarrow—that also became centers of

DOCUMENTS

DOCUMENT 7.1

The Visigoths Lay Down the Laws

In about the seventh century, Visigoths began to write down their customary laws, which are excellent sources of information about ancient village life. The laws use the principle of wergeld, monetary compensation, to resolve conflicts between neighbors.

I. Where a Horse, or Any Other Animal, Which Has Been Tied Up, Is Removed, or Injured, in Any Way, Without the Consent of the Owner.

If any person should free a horse, or any other animal belonging to another, from its halter, or from its hobbles, without the knowledge of the owner, he shall pay him a *solidus*. If said horse, or other animal, should die, in consequence, said person shall give its owner another of equal value. If he should use said animal to travel, or to work with elsewhere, without the knowledge of the owner, he shall be compelled to give him another of equal value; provided the owner should find him on that day, or on the following one. If said animal should not be found by the third day, the person who took it shall be deemed guilty of theft.

III. Where the Mane or Tail of a Horse, or of Any Other Animal, Is Cut Off by Anyone.

Anyone who disfigures the mane of a horse belonging to another, or cuts off its tail, must at once give to the owner of the same another animal of equal value. Should any other animal be mutilated in this manner, the third part of a *solidus* must be paid for every one so mutilated.

IV. Where Anyone Castrates an Animal Belonging to Another.

Whoever castrates any quadruped used for racing purposes, without the knowledge or consent of the owner; or castrates any animal which ought not to be castrated; shall be compelled to pay double the value of said animal to the owner of the same, who has been damaged on account of his malice.

V. Where Anyone Produces an Abortion upon a Beast of Burden Belonging to Another.

Whoever produces an abortion upon a mare, shall give to the owner of the same a foal, one year old, by way of compensation.

XIX. Where a Dog That Has Been Irritated, Whether the Provocation Was Wanton or Not, Is Proved to Have Injured or Killed Anyone.

Where a dog bites another person not his owner, and said person is known to have been crippled or killed, in consequence thereof, no responsibility shall attach to the owner of the dog, unless it shall be proved that he caused said dog to make the attack. If, however, he should encourage his dog to seize a thief, or any other criminal, and the latter should be bitten while in flight, and should be crippled, or die from the effects of the bite, the owner of said dog shall incur no liability therefor. But if he should cause said dog to injure an innocent person, he must render satisfaction according to law, in the same manner as if he himself had inflicted the wound.

SOURCE: S.P. Scott, trans., *The Visigothic Code (Forum Judicum)* (Boston: The Boston Book Co., 1910), pp. 284, 285, 286, 291.

Analyze the Document

1. What kinds of animals did the villagers have?

2. What kinds of problems arose among neighbors?

3. How were these problems resolved?

---

learning. By the end of the seventh century, England was poised to be a center of intellectual activity.

The illustration in **Figure 7.1** was produced at Jarrow and shows the intellectual skill that had grown in this island outpost of Christianity. *Beowulf*, the most famous Old English poem that has immortalized the heroic values of the Germanic tribes (described in Chapter 6), was probably written down during this period of monastic scholarship. Although the English monastic schools created valuable manuscripts, their proudest creation was probably the greatest scholar since the decline of the Roman world: the Venerable Bede (ca. 672–735).

The Venerable Bede: Recording Science and History

In the early eighth century, Bede studied in Jarrow, and the young scholar mastered all the texts available to him. His writings interpreted the ancient works and made them accessible to his contemporaries. As a product of the monasteries, he wrote in Latin—the language of the church and of the educated—and his writings became essential to generations of subsequent Latin scholars. Bede was primarily a teacher who wrote a number of works intended as educational tracts. In these works he drew from previous scholars, thus preserving and expanding upon knowledge from previous centuries. For example, in an influential text—*The Nature of Things*—Bede incorporated much from the Roman encyclopedist Pliny the Elder (23–79) and the Visigothic scholar Isidore of Seville (ca. 560–636), but he added his own interpretations. For example, *The Nature of Things* attempted to explain the orbits of the earth, heavens, stars, and planets. In this widely copied and read work, Bede described the earth as a globe and discussed its geography, and this tract was counted among the most important scientific texts of the early Middle Ages.

Bede's most famous work, however, is the *Ecclesiastical History of the English People*, in which he tells the

Bede's *History*

history of early Anglo-Saxon England to ca. 731. This enterprise was pathbreaking in that he took as his canvas an entire nation—not just a local region, as was customary. This was all the more remarkable from a man who probably never went farther than 7 miles from the place where he was born. But his vision helped shape the English into a cohesive entity. Bede drew from sources that are now lost, so his work is invaluable to our understanding of this early period of the Middle Ages. Further, Bede was careful to distinguish between knowledge and rumor, so he established principles of historical writing that had been virtually forgotten since the Roman historians. Perhaps the most influential aspect of Bede's history was that he adopted Dionysius Exiguus's B.C./A.D. (now B.C.E./C.E.) dating system (described in Chapter 6). Not many people had read Dionysius's tract, but Bede's was read and translated for centuries, and our adoption of Dionysius's historical dating system can be largely attributed to Bede.

Centuries of readers were not captivated by these technical details. Instead, they were drawn to his powerful prose that brought to life the centuries in which the Germanic tribes seemed very foreign to Roman Christian missionaries. He wrote of how the first missionaries ordered to go to England in 596 by Pope Gregory recoiled at the prospect: "For they were appalled at the idea of going to a barbarous, fierce, and pagan nation, of whose very language they were ignorant." Readers followed these timid missionaries as they slowly converted the Anglo-Saxon kings and established monasteries that by the late seventh century could spawn a scholar of Bede's stature. The missionaries had done their work so well that when royal courts were ready, learning could leave the monasteries and enter secular life.

Governing the Kingdom

Like the other Germanic kings, the Anglo-Saxon kings developed detailed law codes that combined wergeld with some principles of Roman jurisprudence. Indeed, the small island developed an enduring legal tradition that has become known as **common law,** which differs from the **statutory law** that is based on mandates passed by a legislative body. The common-law tradition preserves a vestige of the Germanic tradition in which the customs of the people are law.

The Christian kings claimed to rule by the grace of God, but they did so with the approval and advice of the powerful men in their court. A

Witan

king could succeed to the throne only with the approval of the witan,

thinking about **GEOGRAPHY**

MAP 7.1

Anglo-Saxon Kingdoms, ca. 700

This map shows the seven Anglo-Saxon kingdoms that had emerged by the eighth century. It also locates the major intellectual centers—Canterbury and the monasteries at Wearmouth-Jarrow.

Explore the Map

1. Which of the three largest kingdoms was most vulnerable to invasion from Scandinavians from the north?

2. Which kingdoms were most likely to unite? Why?

3. What advantage was there to the location of the major intellectual centers at the northern and southern ends of the kingdoms?

or circle of wise men of the realm. (The full assembly was called the Witenagemot.) In addition, the king periodically called the Witenagemot to meet with him and discuss matters important to the governing of the realm. Like the laws themselves, the assembly had arisen through custom and tradition rather than from any constitutional authority. Moreover, its power ebbed and flowed in accordance with the king's power. For example, if a monarch were weak

FIGURE 7.1

Saint Matthew, from a Gospel Book, ca. 700

Medieval patrons from western European courts and monasteries commissioned colorfully decorated Gospel books. This illustration of Saint Matthew was part of a Gospel book made in Anglo-Saxon England in about 700. The work exemplifies how art could reveal the new synthesis of Germanic, Roman, and Christian elements that was forged in this era.

Connecting Art & Society

1. Compare the decorative design on the bench and in Matthew's robe's border with the Germanic gold filigree work in **Figure 6.2,** on page 180. What similarities do you find?

2. What elements of the image resemble Greco-Roman works of art?

3. How effective is this work in showing the synthesis of Germanic, Roman, and Christian culture that marked the Middle Ages?

time, however, all kings governed with the assistance of this body of powerful men.

In an age of slow communication, kings depended on other officials as well to govern their realms. Monarchs divided their kingdoms into shires (roughly the size of modern counties) and appointed royal representatives to govern in their name. These aristocratic earls had many responsibilities, including mustering the local men into armies if the king needed them and leading warriors into battle. Earls also served as the principal judges, presiding over shire courts and executing royal commands.

Some earls amassed so much power that they governed several shires. This tendency might have weakened royal authority and essentially created new kingdoms had not the Anglo-Saxon monarchs moved to name additional royal officials. For example, kings appointed shire reeves (who later were called sheriffs) to help the earls fulfill their duties, but the sheriffs answered only to the kings, not to the earls. In this way, rulers kept a firm grip on power, even down to the shire level.

Yet, in this preindustrial world, in which people had no mail system or telephone network to connect them, kings had to do more than just appoint earls and sheriffs to keep order. For instance, collecting taxes and resolving legal disputes were matters for face-to-face contact. These emerging kingdoms struggled to provide the means for such contact and the ways by which to control it. The Anglo-Saxons accomplished this feat not only by assigning royal representatives to govern at the shire level, but also by recognizing that some tasks were best handled at the local village level. Village laws enforced by community elders formed the basic level of administrative order, and parish priests and local tax collectors joined sheriffs and earls in structuring a network that could govern the new kingdoms.

Alfred the Great: King and Scholar

The administrative organization and the patronage of the arts flourished in England under the reign of King Alfred the Great (r. 871–901) of Wessex. Alfred is the only English king who has been called "the Great," in memory of his military victories and his support of learning and culture in his realm.

Alfred's contemporary biographer, Asser, offered an engaging picture of the young prince and emphasized his early love of learning: "As he passed through his childhood and boyhood he appeared fairer in form than all his brothers, and more pleasing in his looks, his words and his ways. . . . From his cradle, Alfred had been drawn to wisdom." Despite his intelligence, Alfred did not learn to read until he was 12 years old. In adulthood, he would make up for lost time.

(or young), the witan exerted a great deal of influence. A strong monarch, on the other hand, might call his lords together merely to confirm his decision. Over

MAP 7.2

England in 886

This map shows the division of England between Alfred the Great and Guthrum the Dane in the treaty of 886. Compare this map with **Map 7.1**.

Explore the Map

1. How many of the old Anglo-Saxon kingdoms were united by Alfred? Which were taken by the Danes?

2. What advantage might Alfred's southern kingdoms have had because of their proximity to the Continent?

He studied Latin, collected books, and invited scholars to his court. His interests extended to the arts, for he encouraged singers to fill his court with sacred music and traditional folk songs.

By the time Alfred became king, the political divisions shown in **Map 7.1** had been shaken by a wave of outside invaders—the Danes from across the North Sea. As early as the late eighth century, raiders from the Scandinavian countries had begun raiding northern England. The great monastery of Jarrow had been looted and destroyed, and the intellectual flowering in the north that had produced Bede came to an end. A Danish raid with some 350 ships plundered London, and it looked as if the Anglo-Saxon kingdoms would all fall to the Northmen.

However, King Alfred had reorganized the military to confront the invaders, and he built the first English navy to patrol the coast against the **Danelaw** raiders. After some English victories, the Danes and the English signed a treaty in 886. Under its terms, Alfred and the Danish king Guthrum agreed to divide England between them. **Map 7.2** shows the division the two leaders agreed upon. The northern lands later became known as the Danelaw to recognize that they were governed by laws different from those in the southern parts of the land. As part of this settlement, Guthrum agreed to convert to Christianity (which would

ultimately make it easier for the peoples to share the land). The treaty also paved the way for Alfred to forge a unified kingdom in the south and to focus on the laws and learning that were his passions.

Alfred worked to bring southern England into the intellectual world of wider Europe through literature. From his own educational experience, Alfred knew that Latin texts were not accessible to many inquiring minds. In a letter to one of his bishops, Alfred expressed the opinion (highly unusual in his time) that intellectual ideas should be available to everyone. He wrote, "It seems better to me for us also to translate some of the books which are most needful for all men to know into the language which we can all understand." The wise king followed his own advice and translated, or helped to translate, some of the great books of literature into

Alfred's translations

Old English so his own people could read them. Among other works, he translated Boethius's *The Consolation of Philosophy* (discussed in Chapter 6). Although Alfred valued the classical texts, he never lost his central interest in his own people, so his literary patronage extended to recording the history of their deeds. He translated Bede's *Ecclesiastical History of the English People* and initiated the writing of the *Anglo-Saxon Chronicle*, a history of England that continued Bede's effort to narrate the story of the English.

The rule of Alfred the Great marked the high point of the accomplishments of Anglo-Saxon England. Much of the southern portion of the island was ruled by this skilled king who brought the benefits of law and learning to his land. However, a century before Alfred's reign, across the English Channel, comparable developments had taken place on the Continent, where an even more powerful king had unified the lands of western Europe and established an empire that shone even more brightly than that of Alfred.

CHARLEMAGNE AND THE CAROLINGIANS: A NEW EUROPEAN EMPIRE

The Carolingian king Charles (later known as Charles the Great, or Charlemagne) earned that accolade by the force of his personality and the breadth of his talents. About six feet tall and physically powerful, Charlemagne boasted a full head of red hair and a prominent belly. Charlemagne the man has generated a lively debate among historians. His contemporary biographer, Einhard, left us with tantalizing bits of information about this man, who dominated the late eighth and early ninth centuries in western Europe, and who restored the centralized order that had disappeared with the fall of Rome. Charlemagne represented the high point in the process of the combining of classical, Germanic, and Christian cultural elements that we saw beginning in Chapter 6. **Figure 7.2** shows a ninth-century bronze statue that reputedly portrays this powerful ruler. In a conscious link with the classical past, the statue depicts him in the pose of the Roman emperor Marcus Aurelius—riding with no stirrups, as the Romans did, even though by Charlemagne's time the Germans did use stirrups. However, the rider also wears a Germanic cloak, a style that Einhard insists Charlemagne refused to abandon. In addition, he carries an orb representing his empire and wears a crown adorned with the symbol of office bestowed on him by the pope. In all these ways, this statue symbolizes the synthesis of cultures that restored a new kind of order to western Europe.

FIGURE 7.2 Charlemagne This bronze statue of the emperor portrays him in the pose of ancient Roman emperors, crowned and holding the orb of empire. The artist's intent was to communicate boldly that a new emperor reigned in the West.

Charlemagne's Kingdom

This impressive warrior undertook fifty-three campaigns throughout his reign—and won most of them. A pious man as well, Charlemagne established himself as a leader and reformer of the church. Finally, he had a deeply curious intellect. He knew the importance of education, recognized the worth of scholars like Alcuin, and energetically sponsored learning by establishing schools and hiring scholars. The political, ecclesiastical, and intellectual order that Charlemagne brought to the Continent has been called the Carolingian Renaissance, to emphasize the rebirth of learning that he initiated. As was the case in England, publicly fostered intellectual life depended upon a relatively ordered society, and in the early Middle Ages, this stability was purchased by military victories.

The map of Charlemagne's realm (**Map 7.3**) shows the vast span of territory—from northern Spain to the North Sea, from the English Channel well into Germany, and across the Alps into northern Italy—that this accomplished leader brought under his control. If we contrast this area with the smaller Anglo-Saxon kingdoms shown on

Administering the realm

MAP 7.3

The Empire of Charlemagne, ca. 800

This map shows the impressive kingdom of Charlemagne, with the dates of his conquests. Compare the size of this empire with that of the kingdom of Alfred shown in **Map 7.2**.

Explore the Map

1. What were the advantages and disadvantages of administering the two realms of such different sizes?

2. What aspect of Saxony's location might have given Charlemagne particular difficulties in administering that region?

3. What strategic advantage did the tributary peoples on Charlemagne's eastern border offer to the emperor?

Maps **7.1** and **7.2,** we can imagine the challenges Charlemagne faced in administering this territory.

Like his English counterparts, Charlemagne put noblemen in charge of the various provinces he controlled and tried to use laws to bring order to his lands. However, his approach differed from that of the Anglo-Saxons in that, instead of having fixed sheriffs at his command, Charlemagne sent traveling agents (called *missi dominici*) throughout his territory to examine conditions in his name and to redress certain abuses. These royal representatives traveled in pairs—a bishop and a nobleman, representing both the secular and religious arms of Charlemagne's realm. An edict issued by Charlemagne in 802 describes the high expectations he had for his officials, who were sent "throughout his whole kingdom, and through them he would have all the various classes of persons . . . live in accordance with the correct law . . . and let no one, through his cleverness or craft, dare to oppose or thwart the written law, as many are wont to do." The king knew that his rule depended upon his subjects obeying his laws.

Charlemagne enhanced his authority further by requiring his nobles to attend two assemblies a year. As the men gathered in the outdoor meeting fields, they listened to the emperor's latest decrees and

offered some opinions—but then went home and obeyed their ruler. In this way, Charlemagne moved from the original Germanic legal practice of the king simply recording the customs of the people; the Frankish king actually issued legal commands, and these carefully recorded capitularies serve as rich historical sources of his times.

In all these ways, Charlemagne departed from the Anglo-Saxon model and, in a strikingly new departure from traditional Germanic practice, sought to maintain a personal, centralized control over his unwieldy kingdom without appointing local administrators. Of course, personal rule hinges on the ruler's physical presence. Charlemagne met this requirement by traveling frequently throughout his lands, enjoying the hospitality of his noblemen. It is to Charlemagne's credit that this system worked as well as it did during his lifetime. As we will see, his administrative structure would not survive the loss of his personal attention.

Linking Politics and Religion

Charlemagne's political order had close links to his religious policies. He followed his father's lead in ensuring that his success as emperor was firmly tied to the fortunes of the church. This religious policy manifested itself in his treatment of the Saxons, a fierce people living on the northern borders of the empire. The Saxons had raided Frankish territory for generations. Charlemagne marched north in 772 and again in 775 and won decisive victories against the ferocious Saxons, but each time he left, they rose in revolt again. The emperor surmised that only by forcibly Christianizing the Saxons could he make them permanent members of his kingdom. In 785, after a particularly punitive campaign in which Charlemagne crushed the Saxon armies, the emperor forced the Saxon leader to convert to Christianity. Then Charlemagne established priests and monks in the conquered lands and punished relapses into paganism or other religious disobedience as treason. After some thirty years of religious coercion (which the scholar Alcuin opposed), Charlemagne's program worked—Christian Saxony no longer rebelled, again demonstrating how the church could serve his political ends.

As Charlemagne grew more powerful in the West, perhaps inevitably the question came up about his relationship with the Byzantine emperor in the East, and the two powers jockeyed for position. Charlemagne began to enter into many diplomatic contacts with the Byzantine court—he and Empress Irene of Byzantium engaged in ultimately unsuccessful negotiations to arrange a marriage between Charlemagne's daughter and Irene's son, the future emperor Constantine VI. However, in 797 Irene blinded and deposed her son Constantine, an act that made her the sole ruler. Charlemagne reputedly then proposed marrying Irene, thereby becoming the emperor himself, but these negotiations bore no fruit either. Instead, many wondered if Irene, a woman, could rule as emperor. If not, perhaps there was no emperor at all, and a new one should be named.

The turmoil in Byzantium contributed to one of the pivotal incidents in Charlemagne's reign, which showed his penchant for joining church and state. The event took place on Christmas Day in the year 800. The Carolingian king was in Rome; he had journeyed there at the request of Pope Leo III (r. 795–816), who had been attacked and brutally beaten while he conducted a procession through the streets of Rome. Charlemagne's armies restored the pope to power and calmed the violence in the city. While Charlemagne was in Rome, he must have visited Pope Leo's newly redecorated palace and seen the mosaics that the pope had commissioned, which had been completed in about 798, before the local rebellion.

One of those mosaics, shown in **Figure 7.3**, depicts the relationship between Pope Leo (on the left) and "King Charles" (on the right). Both kneel at the feet of Saint Peter, who was considered the founder and

Charlemagne's coronation

FIGURE 7.3 Pope and Emperor Charlemagne's crown did not resolve the question of who was superior: pope or emperor. This image tries to strike a balance, showing the two as equals as they kneel before Saint Peter.

guardian of the church of Rome. Peter hands Leo a priest's garment that marks his papal power and hands Charlemagne a spear with a banner of battle. The inscription on the bottom reads, "Blessed Peter, you give life to Pope Leo and you give victory to King Charles." Although the inscription was heavily restored in the eighteenth century, historians believe the original message was substantially the same. The mosaic offers a rough preview of the rebellion that threatened Leo's life, and of Charlemagne's subsequent military victory, but more than that it shows a certain relationship between the two men—they are separate, of equal stature, and both guided by religious principles.

When Charlemagne went to church in Rome on Christmas Day in 800, the relationship between pope and king was dramatically transformed. As the king of the Franks rose from prayer, the pope produced a crown and set it on Charlemagne's head. The watching crowds jubilantly proclaimed Charlemagne emperor. This event was of immense importance, for once again, a Roman emperor ruled in the West (independent of Byzantium), and he reigned by the might of his armies and with the blessing of God. The coronation reaffirmed the central alliance between the papacy and the Frankish kings, just as had been depicted on Leo's mosaic. A new prominence of the northern kingdom had begun. In his political activities and his personal life, the Frankish emperor personified the artful integration of God and politics.

Negotiating with Byzantium and Islam

As Charlemagne forged a new empire out of the fragmented kingdoms in the West, he naturally attracted the notice of the neighboring Byzantine and Islamic leaders. Not surprisingly, his taking the title of emperor irked the Byzantine court, but Irene ran out of time to object strenuously. She was overthrown in 802 by Nicephorus, a Byzantine aristocrat, who continued the diplomatic negotiations over the status of the Frankish ruler's title. Finally, in 813, both parties agreed that Charlemagne could be emperor of the Franks and the Byzantine emperor would be emperor of the Romans. This decision solved the immediate dispute, but the political split between east and west continued to widen. Einhard, friend and biographer of Charlemagne, summarized the uneasy relations between east and west by repeating a proverb he said was used in the east: "It is better that a Frank be your friend than your neighbor."

Charlemagne had more promising relations with the Islamic caliph in Baghdad, Harun al-Rashid (r. 786–809). Einhard said, "Charlemagne was on such friendly terms that Harun valued his goodwill more than the approval of all the other kings in the entire world." There were many diplomatic exchanges between the two courts, as it was in both their interests to forge a friendly bond against their mutual enemy, the Byzantine Empire. The Frankish sources say Harun even gave Charlemagne jurisdiction over the Christian holy places in Palestine, certainly a gracious, though empty, diplomatic gesture—Harun reportedly said, the holy land is "so far away that [Charlemagne] cannot defend it from the barbarians. . . . [Therefore] I myself will rule over it as his representative." Nevertheless, the two rulers exchanged many more tangible gifts to seal their friendship—among them an elephant that Harun gave Charlemagne in 802. The elephant lived eight more years and traveled with Charlemagne as he patrolled his kingdom, causing quite a stir among his subjects who had never seen such a beast. The Global Connections describes this relationship from the Muslim point of view.

Charlemagne's negotiations and the relative peace that came within his lands (in spite of almost incessant warfare on the borders) served to stimulate trade, which had declined during the previous tumultuous centuries. Through the ninth century, Venice, in Italy, had assumed a leading role in the southern Mediterranean trade. Venetian merchants sent grain, wine, and timber to Constantinople in exchange for silk cloth and other luxury goods. Other Italian cities also joined in the growing trade, and the Mediterranean trade that had been one of the hallmarks of the West continued to link the region and its varied peoples. More trade brought increased prosperity into Charlemagne's lands, and the great emperor used a portion of it to forward intellectual endeavors.

An Intellectual Rebirth

As memorable as Charlemagne's political and diplomatic victories were, his most enduring impact came in the area of intellectual achievement. Although Charlemagne himself had never learned to write, he had always shown a wide-ranging intellectual curiosity that as a powerful ruler he was able to indulge. Like the Anglo-Saxon cultural revival, the Carolingian rebirth built upon learning that had been preserved in monasteries. Furthermore, the cultural revivals in England and on the Continent were directly linked in the person of the scholar Alcuin.

In the late eighth century, Alcuin, the head of the library at York and a product of the same training that had encouraged the genius of Bede, sailed across the English Channel to visit the pope in Rome. On his way home, he met the young Frankish king, Charlemagne, who was so impressed by the English scholar that he asked Alcuin to visit his court and help him reform the education there. The 50-year-old Alcuin readily agreed to come, and he guided the revival of learning on the Continent under Charlemagne's patronage.

Charlemagne's motivation for fostering learning stemmed primarily from his concern for the religious health of his kingdom. (Charlemagne's letter in Document 7.2 tells of his motives in his own words.) The emperor had observed that even many of the **Establishing schools** priests serving in his parishes could not read well enough to recite the proper form of the liturgy. Nor were they sufficiently educated to guide their parishioners to what the emperor considered the correct understanding of a Christian life. To address these matters, Charlemagne issued an edict ordering that "In the villages and townships the priests shall open schools," and that the clergy must accept all interested children without charging them fees—although he did allow teachers to accept "the small gifts offered by the parents." From this pool of literate children, Charlemagne expected to produce a clergy educated, as one of his edicts said, "in the psalms, musical notation, chant, the computation of years and season, and in grammar."

Providing schools was not enough; Charlemagne noted that this education depended upon the proper

The 'Abbasid Caliphate and Charlemagne

Chroniclers during Charlemagne's reign proudly wrote about diplomatic contacts between the Carolingian king and the Muslim caliph Harun al-Rashid that took place between 797 and 802. This diplomacy was stimulated by the exchange of kind words and gifts, including the famous elephant, named Abulabbas, that the caliph presented to Charlemagne. Chroniclers of the 'Abbasid caliphate, on the other hand, never mentioned these interactions. To the sophisticated Muslims, Charlemagne must have ranked among the minor rulers who exchanged goods with Harun al-Rashid, whose name means "the well guided."

When the 'Abbasids conquered the previous caliphate, the Umayyads, they moved their capital from Damascus (in modern-day Syria) to a new city, Baghdad (in modern-day Iraq). (See **Map 6.5.**) Thus the heart of Islam moved east, away from the Mediterranean basin. The capital blossomed into a cosmopolitan city. One Muslim poet did not exaggerate when he described the magnificent city: "Baghdad, in the heart of Islam, is the city of well-being; in it are elegance and courtesy. Its winds are balmy and its science penetrating. In it are to be found the best of

everything and all that is beautiful." Harun al-Rashid (r. 786–809) guided the 'Abbasid caliphate at the height of its success. Another Muslim poet praised the leader, writing, "Did you not see how the sun came out of hiding on Harun's accession and flooded the world with light?" Indeed, the revered caliph fostered prosperity, science, and poetry throughout his lands.

By the late ninth century, the Persian Gulf had become the main trade route to the Indian Ocean and the East. Muslim traders grew immensely wealthy. Their ships sailed to Ceylon and other southeast Asian ports and brought jewels, spices, and even elephants back to Baghdad. So many spices became available through the trade that Islamic cookbooks recommended using liberal quantities of pepper, nutmeg, cinnamon, musk, ginger, and cloves for the sophisticated palates of Baghdad. According to the famous fictional account *The Thousand and One Nights* (see Document 6.3, on page 208), even Harun was a skilled cook. Considering the delicacies that graced Eastern tables and households, it is perhaps not surprising that Charlemagne's gifts of hunting dogs caused little stir among Muslim chroniclers.

Why did Harun al-Rashid bother to engage in diplomatic relations with Charlemagne at all? The answer probably lay in the Byzantine Empire, which bordered the 'Abbasid lands. As a teenager leading his father's armies, Harun had won some glorious victories over the Byzantine forces, and as ruler, he planned to continue his encroachments on the weakening Byzantine territory. Charlemagne, too, had provoked tensions among the Byzantines, particularly after he took the title of emperor. (The Byzantine emperor felt that he alone could claim that title.) Despite deep differences in religion and culture, Harun al-Rashid discovered that he had something in common with the Carolingian emperor: a shared enemy. Politics can create unlikely allies.

Making Connections

1. Whose court was more prosperous and sophisticated—Charlemagne's or Harun al-Rashid's? Explain.

2. Why did Harun al-Rashid engage in diplomatic relations with Charlemagne?

3. Why didn't the Muslim chroniclers mention the interactions between the two men?

---

books, ordering "all books used shall be carefully corrected." To accomplish this, the emperor gathered scholars from all over Europe to assemble a canon of corrected readings. When he invited Alcuin to his court, he was not disappointed, for Alcuin drew scholars from throughout the continent to visit the emperor and to share their wisdom. The scholars took up residence in the emperor's court and were very well paid for their labors—Alcuin, for example, ended his life an extremely wealthy man.

These scholars revived a curriculum (originally proposed by fifth-century scholars) that would dominate medieval universities and profoundly influence modern liberal-arts education. To create this course of study, they divided knowledge into seven liberal arts. The most basic of these were the **trivium,** in which students learned grammar, rhetoric, and logic. With these tools, students could read texts, explain them, and understand the way to think about them. Next came the more advanced curriculum, the **quadrivium:** arithmetic, music, geometry, and astronomy. Whereas to us these four subjects may not seem obviously related, to medieval thinkers they all shared one characteristic: They involved the patterns by which God organized the world. Because scholars of the Middle Ages saw this organization as consistent, they believed they could study music, for example, to understand mathematics or the movement of the heavens.

DOCUMENT 7.2

Charlemagne Promotes Educational Reforms

Charlemagne (here identified as Karl the Great) wrote many letters, which are preserved in large collections. In this letter written ca. 790, he describes how he valued education.

Karl, by the aid of God king of the Franks and Lombards and patricius of the Romans, to the clergy of his realm. . . . Now since we are very desirous that the condition of our churches should constantly improve, we are endeavoring by diligent study to restore the knowledge of letters which has been almost lost through the negligence of our ancestors, and by our example we are encouraging those who are able to do so to engage in the study of the liberal arts. In this undertaking we have already, with the aid of God, corrected all the books of the Old and New Testament, whose texts had been corrupted through the ignorance of copyists. Moreover, inspired by the example of our father,

Pippin, of blessed memory, who introduced the Roman chants into the churches of his realm, we are now trying to supply the churches with good reading lessons. Finally, since we have found that many of the lessons to be read in the nightly service have been badly compiled and that the texts of these readings are full of mistakes, and the names of their authors omitted, and since we could not bear to listen to such gross errors in the sacred lessons, we have diligently studied how the character of these readings might be improved. Accordingly we have commanded Paul the Deacon, our beloved subject, to undertake this work; that is, to go through the writings of the fathers carefully, and to make selections of the most helpful things from them and put them together into a book, as one gathers occasional flowers from a broad meadow to make a bouquet. And he, wishing to obey us, has read through

the treatises and sermons of the various catholic fathers and has picked out the best things. These selections he has copied clearly without mistakes and has arranged in two volumes, providing readings suitable for every feast day throughout the whole year. We have tested the texts of all these readings by our own knowledge, and now authorize these volumes and commend them to all of you to be read in the churches of Christ.

SOURCE: *Bibliotheca rerum Germanicarum*, IV, p. 372, in Oliver J. Thatcher and Edgar H. McNeal, *A Source Book for Mediaeval History* (New York: Charles Scribner's Sons, 1905), pp. 56–57.

Analyze the Document

1. What major problems does Charlemagne identify in this letter?

2. What steps did he take to correct the problems?

3. What role did Paul the Deacon play in the reform efforts?

4. How effective do you think these reforms would have been in achieving his goals?

The scholars also contributed much to text reform. Before the invention of the printing press, scribes copied books laboriously by hand onto animal skins (called parchment or vellum) with quill pens and ink. (The illustration on page 212 portrays such scribal activity.) Copyists sometimes needed a full day to copy just six to ten manuscript pages. Moreover, there was a shortage of these scribes. Today, we learn to read and write at the same time. During the Middle Ages, however, these two skills were considered separate. Although many people could read, not so many could write.

Correcting texts

The problems associated with handwriting only compounded these difficulties. Handwriting was not standardized, and copyists ran words together and employed contractions in an effort to use as little of the precious parchment as possible. Copyists not fluent in Latin (as few were) also made many mistakes. By the eighth century, these errors had been multiplying for several hundred years. The sample manuscript presented in **Figure 7.4a** shows how difficult this script was to read—words are connected and each small mark above the words means that one or more letters were deleted.

The scholars who gathered at Charlemagne's court school attacked these problems in two ways. First, they compared many versions of the same text to prepare a correct rendition. Second, they developed a standardized handwriting so that future copyists could accurately preserve the corrected text. **Figure 7.4b** shows a sample of Carolingian handwriting. Notice that the letters are well formed and the words more clearly spaced than in the Anglo-Saxon sample. This reformed handwriting style reduced errors, thus saving much wisdom for future generations. Moreover, the Carolingian handwriting style formed the basis for our own lowercase letters and the printing-press letters invented 600 years later. The scholars carefully working on texts played a crucial role in preserving the intellectual contributions of the classical world.

STRUGGLE FOR ORDER IN THE CHURCH

Established long before the Roman Empire disintegrated, the church had adopted the Roman administrative system in which bishops presided in dioceses (see Chapter 5). At the local level, priests in parishes cared for their flocks in manorial villages. Parish priests were accountable to their bishops, who in turn were accountable to archbishops, ruling in the largest urban center of the region. Archbishops called their subordinates together periodically to discuss church issues. During these meetings, bishops also learned about new church rules or ideas, which they then took back to their dioceses and communicated to their priests. This whole structure was designed to weave the Christian world and its administrators into a tight fabric of personal ties.

However, this structure sounds better on paper than it worked in practice during these tumultuous early medieval centuries. Communication among churchmen was always disrupted during warfare, and there was no certainty that competent priests and bishops would be appointed when a church office became vacant. Nor did the theoretical structure mean that the church operated independently of local warlords. Even during the years of relative peace under strong Carolingian kings such as Charlemagne, the church was dominated by monarchs, who felt responsible for bringing order to their churches. Nevertheless, during the eighth and ninth centuries, the church planted seeds of order that would fully flower in the High Middle Ages (see Chapter 8).

Monasteries Contribute to an Ordered World

Bringing structure to the ecclesiastical order was not limited to priests, bishops, popes, and kings. As we saw in Chapter 6, Benedict of Nursia (ca. 480–543) had established a monastic rule that brought men and women into obedience to their monastic leader, who in turn obeyed the local bishop. This kind of monastic structure had proved immensely popular. By the late seventh century, monasteries had sprung up throughout the northern regions of Europe, including Anglo-Saxon England. Monasteries for men and women provided one of the few avenues for social mobility for promising individuals, and for women, the monastic life offered the possibility of a voice in church affairs.

Monasteries performed an essential service in copying and preserving texts and learning. Bede and Alcuin were only two of numerous men and women who excelled in scholarship in an age that valued warfare more. The manuscript painting in **Figure 7.5** emphasizes the importance of this monastic learning. The illustration, taken from a Bible copied in a monastery, depicts the abbess (identified as Hitda in the image) offering a manuscript to the woman who commissioned its creation (identified as Saint Walburga).

(a)

(b)

FIGURE 7.4 Early Medieval Handwriting (a) Merovingian minuscule. (b) Carolingian minuscule. These two samples illustrate how important Charlemagne's handwriting reforms were to make texts legible. In the earlier one from the Merovingian era, each mark above a work indicates a contraction, making it difficult to translate. The Carolingian is more clear and easier to copy without mistakes.

FIGURE 7.5 Literate Nuns Women played a vital role in the preservation of learning in the monasteries as they copied precious manuscripts. Women's valuable contribution is shown in this illustration of Abbess Hitda presenting a manuscript to Saint Walburga.

Walburga was an eighth-century Anglo-Saxon nun who traveled to Germany to establish a monastery to carry out missionary work among the Germans, and this image emphasizes the importance of both monastic missions and the careful transmission of texts from one house to another.

Monasteries also became involved in the growing political issues of the day. As we have seen, nobles and kings exerted control over priests and bishops in their lands, and they believed they could exert the same authority over monasteries. To many spiritual reformers this seemed to subordinate spiritual values to secular politics, and in the early tenth century, reformers took a step to correct this imbalance.

Cluniac reform

In 910, a group of monks persuaded a duke in southern France to found a new monastery at Cluny. The Cluniac founding charter refined the Benedictine rule by insisting that the monastery was exempt from local control—owing only prayers for the donor and, as Duke William wrote in the founding charter, "subject neither to our yoke, nor to that of our relatives, nor to the sway of royal might, nor to that of any earthly power." To do this, Cluny was established to be directly subordinate to the pope, and all subsequent Cluniac foundations were to be accountable to the abbot at Cluny and, through him, the pope. This tenth-century movement established a strong, reinvigorated monasticism that helped increase papal authority (as we will see in Chapter 8). However, all these developments establishing order and hierarchy in the church would be shaken—and almost destroyed—by a new cycle of violence that engulfed western Europe.

ORDER INTERRUPTED: VIKINGS AND OTHER INVADERS

Although Charlemagne valued much of classical culture, such as education and even the title of emperor, his imperial rule was different from that of an early Roman emperor. His sense of empire remained highly personal. Like the innumerable German kings before him, he saw his kingdom as consisting of subjects loyal to him and to his family, not to an abstract political entity. He viewed his realm as his to divide up among his sons, not as an entity separate from himself and his family. This perception put him firmly in the Germanic tradition. However, in the end it undermined the order that he had built, as the emperor's descendants vied for control of the lands he bequeathed them.

Competing for the Realm: Charlemagne's Descendants

Charlemagne's only son, Louis the Pious (r. 814–840), inherited the empire, but during the course of his reign problems began to appear. Document 7.3 shows a contemporary witness's perception of the growing difficulties. However, the final disintegration of Charlemagne's empire took place after Louis' death, when his kingdom was divided among his surviving three sons: Charles the Bald (r. 843–877), Lothair I (r. 840–855), and Louis the German (r. 843–876). The three **Treaty of Verdun** brothers succumbed to the Germanic tendency toward civil war, each seeking to increase his power at the expense of the others. Their violent clashes struck at the foundation of what Charlemagne had constructed, and they brought untold hardship to the subjects of the once-unified kingdom (see Biography on page 233). **Map 7.4** shows the division of the lands established in the Treaty of Verdun in 843, which effectively destroyed Charlemagne's creation of a united western Europe.

The Treaty of Verdun anticipated some important nationalistic developments in western Europe,

DOCUMENT 7.3

A Comet Predicts Disaster

The collection of letters of the Carolingian dynasty includes correspondence to Charlemagne's son Louis the Pious. This letter, written in 837 to Louis, mentions the devastating raids that eroded his land's security and describes a comet that the author interpreted as a forewarning.

It is believed by almost all the ancient authorities that the appearance of new and unknown heavenly bodies portends to wretched mortals direful and disastrous events, rather than pleasant and propitious ones. The sacred scriptures alone tell of the propitious appearance of a new star; that is, that star which the wise men of the Chaldæans are said to have seen when, conjecturing from its most brilliant light the recent birth of the eternal king, they brought with veneration gifts worthy [of] the acceptance of so great a lord. But the appearance of this star which has lately arisen is reported by all who have seen it to be terrible and malignant. And indeed I believe it presages evils which we have deserved, and foretells a coming destruction of which we are worthy. For what difference does it make whether this coming danger is foretold to the human race by man or angel or star? The important thing is to understand that this appearance of a new body in the heavens is not without significance, but that it is meant to forewarn mortals that they may avert the future evil by repentance and prayers. Thus by the preaching of the prophet Jonah the destruction of the city, which had been threatened by him, was deferred because the inhabitants turned from their iniquities and evil lives. . . . So we trust that merciful God will turn this threatened evil from us also, if we like them repent with our whole hearts. Would that the destruction which the fleet of the Northmen is said to have inflicted upon this realm recently might be regarded as the sufficient occasion for the appearance of this comet, but I fear that it is rather some new distress still to come that is foretold by this terrible omen.

SOURCE: *Bibliotheca rerum Germanicarum*, IV, p. 459, in Oliver J. Thatcher and Edgar H. McNeal, *A Source Book for Mediaeval History* (New York: Charles Scribner's Sons, 1905), pp. 59–60.

Analyze the Document

1. What evidence does the author use to demonstrate that the comet reveals terrestrial events? What does the author conclude about the relationship between the comet and the Northmen's raids?

2. What do you learn about medieval attitudes from this letter?

---

because for the first time, linguistic differences that would divide the lands seemed to be solidifying. When Charles the Bald and Louis the German took oaths (called the Strasbourg Oaths) to support each other in this division, the oaths were recorded in two languages so that the subjects of each would understand them—Charles pledged in a Romance (Latin-derived) language, and Louis spoke in an early Germanic tongue. This showed how the two sections of Charlemagne's empire were already separating culturally and linguistically.

Map 7.4 further suggests how vulnerable the central lands were, because by 870, Charles the Bald and Louis the German had divided up the middle kingdom between them. These central lands—the modern regions of Alsace and Lorraine—remained in dispute off and on into the twentieth century.

Battered by the disruptions of war, the already local economy became even more isolated. The longdistance trade that had begun to enrich the Italian cities as well as the Carolingian kings virtually evaporated, and money went out of circulation. If it had even a brief respite from this dynastic turmoil, the Carolingian Empire might have recovered from mismanagement by Charlemagne's grandsons—but this was not to be. Instead, the weakened empire would succumb to new invaders from the north, south, and east.

Map 7.5 shows the impact of these invasions on Europe. Part of the pressure came from the south, as Muslim maritime raiders sailed across the Mediterranean Sea and penetrated most of the southern coasts of Europe. Sicily fell to the forces of Islam, as did the islands in the western Mediterranean. In spite of Charlemagne's foresight in establishing protective tributary peoples on his eastern flank, eastern Europe reeled from a serious blow with the invasion of the Magyars (now known as Hungarians, a name derived from one group of Magyars). Magyar warlords led their people in raids across Germany, France, and Italy before they settled down and established the kingdom of Hungary. The influx of Muslims and Magyars left an indelible imprint on Europe. However, the invaders who wreaked the most violence, and ultimately settled the most widely, came from the north—bands of Scandinavian warriors known as Vikings.

New invaders

"The Wrath of the Northmen": Scandinavian Life and Values

Back when Charlemagne had forcefully converted the Saxons to Christianity, the people living farther north, in what we know as Denmark, Norway,

Sweden, and Finland, remained pagan. For the most part, these Scandinavians lived on farms rather than in communal villages; they grew crops and kept cows and sheep. The short growing seasons of the north made agriculture especially challenging, and the people supplemented their produce by fishing in the cold, stormy waters of the North Sea. Over time they became skilled seamen and even engaged in long-distance commerce. They traded furs, amber, and honey for finely wrought jewelry, glass, cloth, and weapons. These rugged seamen from the north drew a fine line between trading and pirating and crossed it often. Still, their activities prompted the spread of goods from all over Europe to Scandinavian farms.

Who were these northern peoples? The Scandinavians were Germanic, so their way of life resembled that of the Germanic tribes who had earlier invaded the Roman Empire. The Scandinavians cherished heroic values and sought fame in notable deeds and through the works of poets who recorded those deeds. In their literature—both the poetry and the old Norse prose narratives called **sagas** that preserve their history—we can detect a people who valued words and wit as much as strength and courage. They worshiped gods similar in function to those of the ancient Greeks and Romans, but with different names—Wodin, Thor, and Freya are three deities whose names have been preserved in the English days of the week: Wodin's Day (Wednesday), Thor's Day (Thursday), and Freya's Day (Friday).

The powerful and violent Scandinavians shared another trait with the early Germanic people: a passion for revenge. Although these northerners tried to control their feuding through a system of compensation involving wergeld, they had much less success stemming their tendency toward violence than even the Anglo-Saxons had. A saying from Viking literature succinctly expresses how violent Scandinavian life could be: "A man should never move an inch from his weapons when out in the fields for he never knows when he will need his spear." The sagas, too, recount many a bloody feud. Indeed, it may have been this very violence that prompted numerous Vikings to leave Scandinavia in search of new, more peaceful lands overseas. Some may have left to avoid feuds, and the sagas suggest that others emigrated to escape the growing power of kings who tried to impose peace on many violent men who did not want to submit to authority.

All Northmen did not emigrate to avoid or seek violence. Many were drawn by the wealth that had accumulated in Europe during the prosperous years of the Carolingians and Anglo-Saxons. All these movements during the ninth and tenth centuries— ┤ Viking ships ├ raids, trading, and settlements—left a deep impact on European life.

MAP 7.4

Partition of the Carolingian Empire, 843—Treaty of Verdun

This map shows the division of Charlemagne's lands under his grandsons.

Explore the Map

1. Which of the three lands was most vulnerable to external attack? Why?

2. Which brother's lands were most susceptible to encroachment from the other kings? Explain.

3. Which of the lands was most desirable? Why?

Map 7.5 shows the Northmen's movements to the western and eastern edges of Europe. Their success in these campaigns stemmed largely from their innovative ships and their skill in navigating them. The Viking ships, one of which is shown in **Figure 7.6,** were marvels of engineering. They were highly valued possessions, guarded with honor and praised in

MAP 7.5

Invasions of Europe, Ninth and Tenth Centuries

The arrows on this map show the invasion routes of the major peoples who threatened Europe during the ninth and tenth centuries, along with the dates of their invasions.

Explore the Map

1. Which of the kingdoms shown on **Map 7.4** might have been most destabilized by the invasions?

2. Which rivers did the Vikings use for their invasions? How important was it for the Vikings to have ships that could easily navigate shallow rivers?

3. Based on the invasions (and subsequent settlements), where would you expect Muslim culture to influence the West?

Scandinavian poetry. Often built of oak and designed to flex with the rough waters of the North Atlantic, the vessels each carried between 50 and 100 men who manned oars on either side. A large sail, usually decorated in bright colors, completed the propulsion system.

Figure 7.6 also shows another unique feature of these ships: a shallow keel, the long timber that extended the length of the ship and supported the frame. This feature allowed the Vikings to pilot their ships up rivers during raids. It also let them beach the crafts easily and launch them back out to sea before their surprised victims could mount an effective counterattack. The ships and the ferocity and bravery of the men who sailed them earned the Scandinavians a widespread, fearsome reputation. A ninth-century chronicler wrote how Northmen "inflicted much harm," and he sharply captures the suffering: "The steel of the heathen glistened; excessive heat; a famine followed," as too many were dead to bring in a good crop. Many a European repeated the oft-quoted Anglo-Saxon prayer for God to "save us from the wrath of the Northmen."

Viking Travels and Conquests

As **Map 7.5** suggests, the unmatched navigational skills of the Vikings gave them access to many parts of Europe. Some Northmen traveled east down the Dnieper River to the Black Sea and the rich city of Constantinople, at times settling along this rich trade route. The oldest Russian chronicle contains the story of an invitation to the Northmen to come and rule, for there was no order in their land. As we saw in Chapter 6, the Scandinavians established a strong state centered in Kiev. Other Vikings traveled to Constantinople and served as soldiers of fortune in the Byzantine emperor's service. Throughout the tenth century, the emperor's personal guard—the Varangians—was composed entirely of Scandinavians. The most famous of these—Harald Sigurdson of Norway (r. 1046–1066)—grew so wealthy while serving in Constantinople that when he returned to Norway he became a great king. Archaeologists have discovered early-eleventh-century Byzantine coins in Norway that may have come from the hoard that Harald shipped home.

Harald's hoard of coins was not unique. Archaeologists have found some 1,700 treasure hoards, each containing on average about three hundred coins. These (primarily silver) coins were mostly eastern—Byzantine or Islamic. Great piles of treasure like these continue to draw our imagination, but the fact that so many were simply buried tells us that the Scandinavian eastern trade in the eighth and ninth centuries did not contribute much to the overall European economy. Most gold was not circulated; it was either hidden during the violence that dominated the age or used as jewelry to show status. For example, the coins shown in **Figure 7.7** on page 234 were joined to hooks so that the coins could be worn as jewelry instead of circulated as currency. This hoard of solid gold also indicates the volume of wealth that was plundered by the Vikings in their raids. However, great wealth like this may have contributed to the status of kings like Harald, but it did not improve the plight of hardworking Scandinavian farmers. Trade needs peace to benefit more people, and peace would have to wait.

Still other Scandinavians sailed west across the North Atlantic, seeking other lands and wealth. Although some Europeans may have imagined the world as flat, people who sailed westward out of sight of land and who watched ships return from the eastern horizon knew better. Like many ancients, Scandinavian sailors perceived the world as round. With these views, Scandinavians sailed confidently into the open seas in their sturdy, versatile ships. They established permanent settlements in Iceland and a settlement in Greenland that lasted for centuries. In the late tenth century, an expedition led by the Norwegian Leif Erikson (970–1035) traveled all the way to North America, which Erikson dubbed Vinland. Although the Vikings did not establish a permanent settlement there, their arrival on this distant coast counts as one of history's most extraordinary feats of sailing, and the difficult passage earned the captain the name "Leif the Lucky."

As the Vikings explored Greenland and North America, they naturally encountered peoples who already lived there. Because they considered these natives inferior, they called them by the contemptuous term *Skraelings*, which defies exact translation. They used this term to refer to Eskimos in northern Greenland and tribes they encountered in North America. The Scandinavians who settled in southern

Western explorations

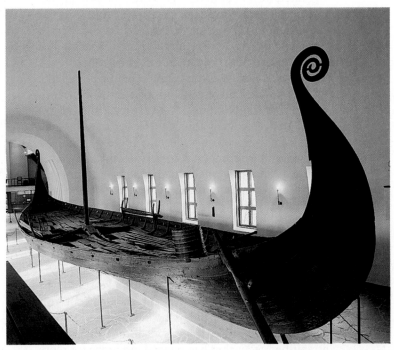

FIGURE 7.6 Oseberg Viking Ship, ca. 800 This splendid, sleek Viking ship was buried as part of a funeral ceremony. Two women were interred with the ship, along with their precious goods. They must have been highborn to have been buried in such lavish style.

Greenland mostly ignored their neighbors to the north. In North America, the encounter proved more dramatic. At first, these tribes and the Scandinavians engaged in some trading. Amerindians especially valued the Vikings' red cloth and milk. They also coveted the Scandinavians' weapons, but the newcomers refused to give them up.

Relations between the two peoples soon soured. Several confrontations occurred in which parties on both sides were killed. The sagas described one incident in which Amerindians in skin-covered boats and armed with arrows and catapults attacked. In another case, only the courage of a pregnant Scandinavian woman saved the day for the Vikings. According to the story, the woman picked up a sword and slapped it on her bare breast as the natives charged her. Unnerved by this odd sight, the attackers fled, and the woman won praise for her bravery. After this confrontation, the Vikings concluded that, although the North American land was bountiful, they could not live there safely because of the ferocity of its inhabitants. They abandoned North America and returned to Greenland, Iceland, and other areas where they could settle more easily.

Within western Europe, Vikings (or their descendants) made permanent conquests in northern France (Normandy), Sicily, and England. As previously mentioned, one group of Vikings, the Danes, had conquered most of northeast England by the middle of the ninth century, until they were stopped by Alfred the Great in 886. However, the British Isles remained a tempting target for the Northmen. In the summer of 1016, a great fleet led by King Swein of Denmark and his son Canute sailed for England. The Anglo-Saxon king Edmund Ironside (r. 1016) was beaten, and Canute became king of a united England. He was an able ruler and was one of many who demonstrated that the Northmen were effective administrators as well as skilled warriors. In 1066, the Norwegian king Harald Sigurdson—the enterprising Varangian who brought a fortune back from Constantinople—set himself a final goal of conquering all of England. He died in the attempt, and the sources say that the only English land he claimed was the "seven feet of soil" required to bury this tall warrior.

European settlements

An Age of Invasions: Assessing the Legacy

The invasions from the north, south, and east brought sporadic violence to western Europe for about two hundred years. With this kind of pressure, Viking, Magyar, and Muslim conquests all disrupted the newly established order that had reigned in Europe for more than a century. In Charlemagne's Frankish Empire, the onslaughts from many foreign fronts accelerated the disintegration initiated by the emperor's feuding

descendants, and the central authority envisioned by Charlemagne could not hold.

Learning also suffered as people devoted more and more attention and resources to war. Charlemagne's great palace school in Aachen, which had drawn scholars from all over Europe, ceased functioning. Again, learning took place primarily behind monastery walls. However, this time monks and nuns had the benefit of texts that had been corrected during Charlemagne's rule. In time, these carefully preserved sources of knowledge would once more play a role in centers of learning, but not until peace returned to western Europe.

Finally, order in the church crumbled under the tenth-century turmoil. In Ireland and on the western coasts of Britain, the magnificent Celtic monasteries were almost completely destroyed by Vikings looking for plunder. The invaders damaged monasteries in France as well. This violence took a massive personal toll on men and women seeking God. As just one example, texts tell of houses of women who feared that the Vikings would rape them and thus violate their vows of virginity. To avert this disaster, the women cut off their noses and lips as the Vikings approached their gates and greeted the invaders with mutilated faces.

The church structure of parishes and bishops under the control of the pope also deteriorated. Bishops and priests placed themselves under the protection of local lords instead of looking to Rome for help. Sometimes lords simply took over church lands, as a Frankish law declared: "because of threats of war and the invasions of some of the border tribes, we shall . . . take possession of a part of the land belonging to the church . . . for the support of our army." The church itself became fragmented in the service of

THE EARLY MIDDLE AGES

ca. 731	Bede, *Ecclesiastical History of the English People*
786–809	Harun al-Rashid caliph in Baghdad
800	Charlemagne crowned emperor in Rome
814	Death of Charlemagne
814–840	Louis the Pious rules
843	Treaty of Verdun divides Carolingian Empire
871–901	Alfred the Great rules England
910	Monastery at Cluny founded
ca. 1000	Leif Erikson travels to North America
1016–1035	Canute rules Denmark and England
1060	Norwegians convert to Christianity

BIOGRAPHY

Dhuoda, Bernard, & William

(ca. 840)

The political turmoil that marked the breakup of the empire assembled by Charlemagne destroyed the family of an educated, pious, remarkable woman named Dhuoda. This young woman was married at the palace of Emperor Louis the Pious in 824 to Bernard of Septimania, a relative of the emperor who served as a knight in Louis' court. Although marriage to such a high-born man seemed a good match, it was not to be a happy companionship. At first, Dhuoda joined her husband in his travels, but then Bernard sent her away to live in a small town in the south of France. The sources do not explain his reasoning—it could have been anything from personal to political. Nevertheless, he visited her periodically. In the meantime, Dhuoda spent her days quietly, immersed in books and prayer. She also followed the fortunes of her husband avidly, writing, "I rejoice in his campaigns." Dhuoda and Bernard had two sons: William, born in 826, and Bernard Jr., born in 841.

In spite of Louis the Pious's advocacy of marriage and his opposition to concubinage, his kinsman Bernard was one of many nobles who took it as their right to have many lovers. Bernard was not a loyal husband to Dhuoda during his absences, and he was particularly indiscreet in his choice of a companion. Accused of committing adultery with Louis' wife and of other treasonous conspiracy against his king, he lost the position of governor of Septimania. His relatives, too,

paid dearly for his transgressions. Bernard's sister, a nun, was accused of sorcery, sealed in a wine cask, and thrown into the river to drown. His brother was blinded and imprisoned after being accused of participating in Bernard's treason. In the Middle Ages, families were considered linked together in innocence and guilt, and even the life of a nun could be jeopardized by the misbehavior of her brother.

Bernard's fall from grace foretold his inability to negotiate the civil wars that erupted among Charlemagne's grandsons after Louis' death in 840. Just as Bernard's sister had paid the highest price for his infidelity, so Dhuoda and her sons would suffer because of Bernard's actions. In 841, Bernard returned to Dhuoda to attend the birth of their second son, Bernard Jr. He then took both boys from her and left. To curry favor with his new overlord, Charles the Bald, Bernard gave his 14-year-old son, William, to Charles as a hostage.

Dhuoda missed her boys acutely, especially William. In 841 she began writing a book of instructions for him, which she completed in 843. The book not only reveals her love for William but also reflects the central values of the ninth century. Dhuoda's writings urged her son to have faith in God and in the feudal ties that bound men together. She warned him, "Never let the idea of disloyalty against your lord be born or thrive in your heart." She also encouraged him to read, to give it the "same attention and zeal that others give to . . . a game of backgammon."

Yet all of Dhuoda's care and advice could not save this family caught in the crossfire of feudal conflict. Bernard shifted his allegiance from his own lord, Charles, to Pepin and was captured as he tried to leave for Pepin's army. Charles accused Bernard of treason and had him publicly beheaded. Fulfilling Germanic ideas of vengeance, young William tried to avenge his father's death, but Charles executed the 24-year-old youth. Like so many noble Carolingian families, Bernard, William, and Dhuoda were damaged by the jockeying for power wrought by the fall of Charlemagne's empire. In medieval families, political developments profoundly influenced personal matters. Even by devoting oneself to God, as Bernard's sister did, or studying and writing in solitude, as Dhuoda did, women could not escape political storms when their lives were joined to men who allied themselves with the wrong lord. Dhuoda's tender care and eloquent missives tell us of both the hopes and the tragedies of a typical Carolingian family. It is only through her love and thoroughness in writing to William that we have such a poignant glimpse of medieval life.

A Carolingian Family Tragedy

Connecting People & Society

1. How was Dhuoda's life affected by the turmoil of the breakdown of Charlemagne's central authority?

2. How important were marriage and family ties to medieval people, for both good and ill?

3. What does this life suggest about women's literacy?

---

war. In the end, the notion of a Christian Europe with both a pope and an emperor at its head disappeared into the wreckage of lives and property as the invasions dragged on.

In the eleventh century, the violence at last spent itself. The traditional Scandinavian farming and trading life was easier to conduct in peace than in war.

And as the invaders settled in newly conquered territories, they absorbed some of the structures already in place there. The Scandinavians also eventually converted to Christianity and thus became fully integrated into Christian Europe. Harald Sigurdson's brother, Olaf (r. 1016–1030), for example, converted the

Vikings convert

FIGURE 7.7 Viking Jewelry For a long time the Vikings, like the Germanic tribes, treasured precious metals like gold and silver and wore them as signs of status. This hoard reveals that even when the Vikings acquired gold and silver coins, they fitted them with clasps and wore, rather than spending, them.

together in personal relationships. In a modified version of the ties that bound the Germanic tribes, these structures were personal, tying each person to a superior. In the modern West, we often judge a society in terms of the freedom of its citizens, but in the Middle Ages, social order was defined by connections rather than degree of freedom. All men and women—from the peasantry all the way up to the king—were connected to someone above or below them in a contractual system of mutual obligations. The obligations did not fall equally on everyone, but each person had explicitly defined commitments to someone else. Everyone in society expected to live within a hierarchy that ordered nature, the church, and society. This social order was not a product of rational planning but instead developed slowly over centuries—and the chaos of the tenth century escalated the development.

Peasants and Lords: Mutual Obligations on the Medieval Manor

Manors developed from the agricultural estates of the old Roman Empire (described in Chapter 5) and the new divisions of the land made by early medieval kings. In various forms, manors existed throughout the Mediterranean world, including the Byzantine and Islamic empires. In western Europe during the Carolingian Empire, manors developed a characteristic pattern of **serfs** and lords that marked the medieval West for almost the next millennium. Virtually all manors consisted of the lord's home and outbuildings (barn, mill, etc.) and at least one village in which the peasants resided and worked.

Figure 7.8 shows the layout of a typical manor. Notice that unlike in today's farm communities, where farmers live on their cropland and travel into the village, medieval peasants lived close together in the village and traveled out to their fields. The fields were organized in strips, with each peasant family using some and the lord owning a large number himself. The church, too, owned some strips for the priest's support. However, the pasture, woodlands, and water were as important as the cultivated land, because they supported the village's animals.

The survival of the peasants depended not only on the crops they grew on their plowed strips but also on their wise use of the other spaces identified in **Figure 7.8.** Serfs grazed their oxen and working horses, as well as their sheep and goats, on the common pastureland. They relied on the large draft animals to help with the hard labor of plowing, especially in the heavy, clay soils of northern Europe. The animals also provided essential leather and wool for clothing and other uses. In our age of cotton and synthetic fabrics, it is easy to forget how important animals were for medieval clothing. Farm animals supplemented a grain diet

Norwegians by force of arms and his own charisma in the early eleventh century. Leif Erikson "the Lucky" introduced Christianity to Iceland and Greenland around the same time. Canute, who ruled England, Denmark, and Norway, converted to Christianity and brought priests from England to complete the conversion of the Northmen.

The Vikings may have settled down, but the centralization that had unraveled through the centuries of chaos would not be restored easily. However, throughout this time people had created another kind of order—one that was not imposed by royal officials, like Charlemagne's *missi dominici,* traveling through the land. Instead, people bound themselves to each other in solemn contracts like the one quoted at the beginning of this chapter. These local ties formed a new order from which the medieval world would build again.

MANORS AND FEUDAL TIES: ORDER EMERGING FROM CHAOS

As early as the eighth century, Carolingian nobles began to develop mutual contracts that bound people as well, with milk and cheese (especially from goats) and some meat. Peasants ate very little meat because their animals were too valuable to be disposed of in this way. However, sometimes the lord gave the peasants his unwanted portions of meat (tails, hooves, or entrails) to make soup.

The forests of the manor also played a key role in village life. Although the trees and the game animals belonged to the lord, peasants were allowed to gather fallen branches as firewood. Pigs could browse in the forest as long as the lord got a share of the pork. Finally, in times of hunger, villagers gathered acorns in the oak forests and ground them into flour to make bread.

Medieval European peasants were at the bottom of the social order in that they had obligations to people above them, but no one below them owed them any commitments. Most medieval peasants were personally free (that is, they were not slaves), but they were bound to the land. When a lord received a land grant from the king, he also gained the service of the peasants who worked the land. Peasants who were semifree in this way—that is, personally free yet not free to move from their village—were called serfs.

Beyond their obligation to remain on the land, serfs owed their lords many other things—roughly divided into goods and labor. For example, they had to give the lord a percentage of their crops or whatever livestock they raised—perhaps a tenth of their grain, a piglet, a number of eggs from their hens, or some of the cheese made from the milk of their goats. They also owed him their labor. On some manors, serfs had to work as many as three days a week on the lord's demesne lands, those set aside for his own consumption and use. Serfs had to plant his crops, build roads, erect walls or buildings, dig ditches, and do anything else the lord ordered. Serfs did not owe military service—fighting was the privilege of the nobility.

Peasant women worked as hard as the men. They did all the domestic chores, toiled in the fields, tended vegetable gardens, and fed the animals. In addition, they performed the time-consuming task of producing cloth. Women sheared the sheep, cleaned and prepared the wool, spun it into thread, and wove it into cloth. As serfs, women also shared the labor obligations of their husbands. They, too, owed the lord a portion of what they produced (from cloth to garden vegetables) and owed the lord and lady of the manor a certain amount of their labor for domestic chores, spinning, and weaving. Peasant children

| Serfs' obligations |

FIGURE 7.8 Medieval Manor This drawing of a hypothetical medieval manor shows how peasants lived in villages and worked strips of cultivated land. Notice all the important features of the manor, including pastures, mill, church, and woodlands.

bore obligations as well. Children as young as 6 were responsible for the care of their younger siblings, and older children worked in the fields alongside their parents.

In exchange for peasant services, lords provided things that required a large investment of capital: mills, barns, ovens, large draft animals, and the like. However, the lords primarily offered justice and protection to their serfs. In times of war, for example, the presence of a well-armed warrior and his followers could make the difference between a village's survival and its destruction. When an attacking army neared the vicinity, peasants with their flocks rushed inside the armed fortress of the lord to stay until the battle ended. However, they often had to watch as their crops and villages were raided and burned, and when the war ended they were left to begin again.

All serfs did not enter voluntarily into this contract in which they exchanged their labor for safety (especially since safety was never absolutely ensured). Sometimes armed lords who needed their lands cultivated forced peasants into servitude on their estates. Late in the Middle Ages, as we will see in Chapter 9, many serfs decided the benefits of protection were not worth the price. However, the newly restored order that established the medieval structure was built on the labor of peasants bound to work the land, which was divided up into manors—agricultural estates under the control of a lord.

Noble Warriors: Feudal Obligations Among the Elite

The medieval manors were structured and organized to provide food for everyone. However, in the medieval mind these manors served an additional function: They were the economic and agricultural base which supported the fighting forces that allowed rulers like Charlemagne and Alfred to conduct their campaigns. Armies were expensive. It took about ten peasant families to support one mounted soldier, so an efficient manorial organization was essential to produce an army. However, the Carolingians developed a way to organize the fighting men as well. Like the serfs, noble warriors were also bound to their lord in a system of mutual obligation. The legal formula that opened this chapter bound a noble fighting man. This system was a fluid one—each contract could be different, and some men might be bound to more than one lord. Nevertheless, a general system

slowly developed that was based on the exchange of land for military service. In its most general sense, this system—which historians in the sixteenth century called feudalism—formed the political structure of the elites in medieval society. Many historians today prefer to avoid the term *feudalism* because it seems to suggest a clearly organized structure instead of the loose system that varied from place to place. Regardless of modern disagreements, it is clear that medieval people saw themselves linked in a chain of mutual obligation; only the forms of those obligations were varied.

As we saw in Chapter 6, men in the Germanic tribes saw themselves as linked in loyalty to their chief. This was a personal tie that bound fighting men together. Charlemagne's grandfather, Charles Martel (r. 714–741) (who defeated the Muslims at the Battle of Tours, as we described in Chapter 6), seems to have at times joined these personal ties to the land that people occupied. Charles had seen the virtues of having an army made up of heavily armed men on horseback to replace the more lightly armed citizen foot soldiers that made up the Anglo-Saxon armies, for example. But armed, mounted knights were expensive. Instead of trying to raise money to support an army of this kind, Charles drew from what he had in abundance: land. He granted huge tracts of land, including the serfs who lived on them, to his followers in exchange for their military service. This process laid the foundation for a complex system that later brought order to the fighting men of the land.

The feudal system that grew out of Charles Martel's innovation bound men together in a series of mutual obligations, but what set it apart from other bonds of loyalty Lords and vassals was the linking of loyal service with land. When a nobleman bound himself in service to a lord, he swore a solemn oath of fealty (that is, to be faithful to his vows and his lord) by placing his hands between those of his lord. The nobleman now became the lord's **vassal**— bound to him for life. In return, the vassal would receive his **fief**—usually land, but it might be something else that would generate enough income to support the vassal. The illustration in **Figure 7.9** cleverly portrays

FIGURE 7.9 Vassal Receiving Fief This intricate drawing captures the complexities of the relationship between vassals and lords. The vassal points to the grain as a symbol of the land he receives in exchange for his loyalty, which he demonstrates by placing his hands between his lord's palms.

the solemn bonds. The standing vassal, shown with four arms, simultaneously places his hands between those of his lord and points to the stalks of wheat that stand for his fief.

The lord (who could be a king or any other man with land to bestow) gave away enough land to support the lifestyle of his noble vassals. These nobles' main function was warfare; they did not work the land as serfs did. Later, vassals took on other titles, like baron or duke, that showed their position relative to other greater or lesser vassals, but the word *vassal* remained a general term that applied to all noblemen bound in contract and loyalty to a lord. Theoretically, a vassal only held his fief as long as he was able to fight for his lord, but in fact, by the ninth century, vassals expected to be able to pass their fiefs on to their sons. A son was expected to place his hands between those of his lord and renew his father's vows before he took full possession of the fief, but as fiefs became hereditary possessions, the lord's control over his fiefs was reduced.

Each party owed something to the other. Lords owed their vassals "maintenance" (usually land) and military protection. In recalling the old Germanic legal principle of compurgation, the lord was also to act as his vassals' advocate in public court. Vassals owed lords "aid and counsel." The primary aid took the form of military service. Just as serfs owed their own lords labor, nobles owed their superiors specified periods of fighting time; these varied, but an average length of service might be forty days a year. Vassals also owed monetary aid. When a lord incurred certain expenses, such as for his daughter's wedding or his son's knighting, the vassals paid extra taxes to fund the event. In addition, vassals owed their lord counsel, or advice at the lord's command. This obligation, along with the witenagemot, paved the way for the parliamentary system that developed later in the Middle Ages (see Chapter 8). Both parties owed the other fealty—that is, good faith to do the other no harm—and this was granted by a solemn kiss that sealed the pact.

Because this was a system of mutual obligation, if either party breached the contract, the arrangement could be rendered null. For instance, if a vassal failed to fight or give counsel, the lord could declare his land forfeit and give it to someone else. Of course, enforcement became complicated when armies of men were involved, but the system did establish the idea of the primacy of contract law that bound people together in a more ordered society. However, because the feudal system varied from place to place and across time, historians disagree on exactly how formal or influential these contractual bonds were. Nevertheless, in the most general sense, feudal ties joined older kinship bonds in linking medieval warriors and their families together.

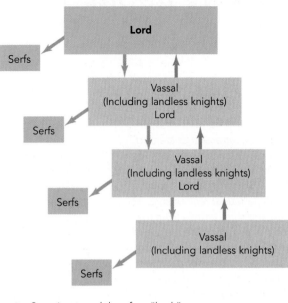

Superior to and therefore "lord."
Subordinate to and therefore "vassal."
The same man can be both lord and vassal.

FIGURE 7.10 Feudal Organization Medieval society was tied together by mutual obligations. This chart shows how vassals could be both lord and vassal, while serfs owed allegiance to only one master.

In this system, a nobleman could be both a vassal to someone over him and a lord to someone under him. A powerful vassal who had received large tracts of land from his overlord might offer portions of it to other nobles who, in turn, would become his vassals. The lowest vassal in this structure was still a lord to the serfs who worked the land (who were lords to no one). Medieval people did not find ambiguity in these flexible terms, because the words *lord* and *vassal* were not absolute—they expressed a legal condition that defined one person's relationship with another. The chart in **Figure 7.10** outlines the complexities of this relationship of superior and subordinate.

Feudal complexities

These feudal bonds were remarkably flexible because they were adapted to each place, time, and individual. Furthermore, the feudal ties kept society from disintegrating altogether in the face of the invasions and decentralization of the ninth century. In spite of these benefits, feudal ties also had features that further decentralized society, and even contributed to increased violence. In most cases, the vow of fealty was not necessarily exclusive, and in time the notion of personal loyalty became secondary to the idea of acquiring more property. Many vassals would serve different lords in exchange for different fiefs. Several sources showing the obligations and growing ambiguities of the feudal ties are excerpted in Document 7.4.

DOCUMENTS

Feudal Relationships Grow Complex

The following documents describe some legal contracts that created feudal ties. The first presents a legal form that arose in the mid-eighth century and that shows the establishment of the feudal relationship. The second and third entries from the early fourteenth century describe the later stages of the relationship: The second explains the mutual obligations established in the ritual of homage, and the third reveals that the vassal in this case held lands from four different lords, showing the increasing complexity of the feudal relationship.

1. To my great lord, (name), I, (name). Since, as was well known, I had not wherewith to feed and clothe myself, I came to you and told you my wish, to commend myself to you and to put myself under your protection. I have now done so, on the condition that you shall supply me with food and clothing as far as I shall merit by my services, and that as long as I live I shall perform such services for you as are becoming to a freeman, and shall never have the right to withdraw from your power and protection, but shall remain under them all the days of my life. It is agreed that if either of us shall try to break this compact he shall pay—solidi, and the compact shall still hold.

2. The tenant [vassal] should place his clasped hands between the hands of the lord; by this is signified, on the part of the lord, protection, defense, and guarantee; on the part of the vassal, reverence and subjection.

3. I, John of Toul, make known that I am the liege man of the lady Beatrice, countess of Troyes, and of her son, Theobald, count of Champagne, against every creature, living or dead, saving my allegiance to lord Enjorand of Coucy, lord John of Arcis, and the count of Grandpré. If it should happen that the count of Grandpré should be at war with the countess and count of Champagne on his own quarrel, I will aid the count of Grandpré in my own person, and will send to the count and the countess of Champagne the knights whose service I owe to them for the fief which I hold of them. But if the count of Grandpré shall make war on the countess and the count of Champagne on behalf of his friends and not in his own quarrel, I will aid in my own person the countess and count of Champagne, and will send one knight to the count of Grandpré for the service which I owe him for the fief which I hold of him, but I will not go myself into the territory of the count of Grandpré to make war on him.

SOURCE: *Formulae Turonenses*, no. 43; *De legibus et consuetudinibus Angliae*, 35; *Tabularium Campaniae*, in Oliver J. Thatcher and Edgar H. McNeal, *A Source Book for Mediaeval History* (New York: Charles Scribner's Sons, 1905), pp. 343–344, 364–365.

Analyze the Document

1. What were the mutually binding obligations that joined the parties to the relationship?

2. What responsibilities did each party have?

3. How did the vassal in the third document resolve potentially competing conflicts of interest?

The chart in **Figure 7.11** shows the complexities of vassals who served several masters. Of course, one can readily see the potential for divided loyalties built into this structure. What if both lords of one vassal were at war? Sometimes—very practically—a vassal followed the lord who gave him the largest fief. At other times, the vassal's first vow was the one that bound. Other vassals probably just tried to back the lord most likely to win the engagement. Beginning in the eleventh century in France and spreading from there over the next centuries, kings tried to establish the concept of **liege lord**—that is, the lord who could claim unreserved loyalty. Kings were able to enforce this with mixed success—the kings in England were successful, but in Germany they were less so. These systems of divided loyalty strained attempts to exert central authority in western Europe, so while feudal ties reduced the chaos, they still preserved some measure of violence. No doubt most people did not reflect upon these abstract considerations as they lived their lives. Feudal ties became simply one more reality of life in the Middle Ages.

Merriment, Marriage, and Medicine: A Noble's Life

The daily life of the nobility revealed the sense of community engendered by the feudal system. The feudal lords with their wives and children lived together with crowds of their own vassals and their servants. All ate together at long tables in the common hall of the manor house. The nobles amused themselves with music, dance, and games like backgammon, chess, and dice. Archaeologists have even found loaded dice in an Anglo-Saxon excavation, so cheating at such games is not a modern invention. In times of peace, both noblemen and noblewomen indulged their passion for hunting with hawks, horses, and hounds. Hunting was intended to keep their skills sharp for their real purpose: warfare.

Just as in the Germanic tribes, noble families in the feudal system were bound to each other by the important ties of marriage. Yet, the institution of marriage changed during the Carolingian years. In the tradition of the Germanic tribes, Charlemagne had taken a number of wives—

Marriage ties renouncing the marriage ties with one in order to marry another—and he even kept a number of concubines at the same time. However, under his religious son Louis the Pious, churchmen began to regulate the marriage bond, emphasizing monogamy and urging married men to give up their concubines. Although the church intruded more and more into the marriage relationship, it never persuaded all noblemen to make this sacrifice. Nonetheless, the church's interventions enhanced the status of the legal wife and made it essential that she, and only she, produce an heir. As a new bride came to the wedding with great ceremony, and as she emerged from the nuptial bedroom in the morning, crowds cheered the consummation of a marriage that everyone hoped would produce offspring. As highly placed wives, noblewomen exerted a significant degree of autonomy. Many texts suggest that such women were responsible for managing the royal treasury. Furthermore, when their husbands were away on military campaigns, noblewomen managed all the affairs of the manors—including defending the castles from hostile invaders when necessary.

Noble girls married young, many of them between the ages of 12 and 14, if not younger. A girl who was betrothed early might be raised in the household of her fiancé's family until she was deemed old enough for the marriage to be consummated. As they awaited their wedding day, girls learned household management, cloth making, and often reading and writing. Women could also inherit and hold land, but they still owed the feudal obligations that structured this society. If an unmarried girl's father died, she was placed under the wardship of the lord her father had served, because her future husband would become that lord's vassal. Widows, too, became wards until their lord arranged another marriage for them, but lords at times relinquished their rights of wardship in exchange for money, so wealthy widows might well control their own lives. Orphans were under the lord's control until they grew old enough to take their place in the lord's army or marry someone who could do so.

Germanic women had traditionally been responsible for medical care, and this continued through the early medieval period. Medicines consisted primarily

Medicine of herbs, as suggested by the manuscripts from this era that preserve

Superior to and therefore "lord."
Subordinate to and therefore "vassal."
Theoretically superior to all.

The same man can be both lord and vassal.

FIGURE 7.11 Feudal Complexities The chart in **Figure 7.10** illustrates the ideal feudal relationship. In reality, however, as this figure shows, vassals often had several masters and multiple vassals of their own. All were to owe allegiance to the liege lord. But the system's complexities, in the form of competing alliances, tended to promote violence and instability.

what are probably long-treasured medical recipes. Nasturtium, for example, was recommended for indigestion, wormwood for sleep disorders, and frankincense and oil for sore hands and fingers.

Even food was considered medicinal if prepared properly; therefore, women were also in charge of designing a healthful diet. Just as our notion of a balanced diet changes with the latest research, early medieval ideas about nutritious eating relied on contemporary understanding of health. For example, people during this period continued to hold the classical idea that health depended on a balance between the body's "humors": wet, dry, cold, and hot. A proper diet must be "tempered"—that is, feature a balance of foods in each category of humor. For example, beans were considered "cold," so they were supplemented by "hot" spices to balance them. Likewise, illness was treated by correcting an imbalance of the humors. For example, if a person was considered too hot, the patient was given predominantly "cold" foods to bring his or her humors back into balance. This system also applied to the preparation of food. Charlemagne's biographer tells about the emperor's growing "dislike" of his physician after Charlemagne was forced to forgo his beloved roast meat in favor of boiled fare. Food and medicine were considered interchangeable in this era, and knowledgeable men and women alike prescribed medicinal diets.

LOOKING BACK & MOVING FORWARD

Summary At the beginning of the eighth century, the Germanic tribes that had precipitated the collapse of the Roman Empire in the West established kingdoms and converted to Christianity. Monasteries revealed the intellectual treasures from the classical world that they had painstakingly preserved in their libraries. Kings began to forge an effective synthesis between Germanic, Roman, and Christian cultures and create vigorous new societies governed by the rule of law. The culmination of these developments was Charlemagne's assumption of the imperial crown; it seemed as if a unified empire would exist again in western Europe.

However, the ninth- and tenth-century invasions by Scandinavians, Muslims, and Magyars broke down this progress, introducing another dark period of violence and retreat to local authority. Yet, the settlement of the Northmen and their conversion to Christianity paved the way for a new restoration of European order. This time, rulers did not have to reinvent the political and economic structures of Europe; they simply had to restore them. They built on a decentralized order that had flourished in the dark days after the fall of the Carolingian Empire. This included a manorial system that secured effective agricultural production and a feudal system that supplied a political organization uniting people in law and loyalty. In the late eleventh century, it remained for kings, emperors, and popes to take charge and bring about the high point of medieval culture in western Europe.

KEY TERMS

compurgation, *p. 214*
ordeal, *p. 214*
wergeld, *p. 215*
common law, *p. 217*
statutory law, *p. 217*
trivium, *p. 224*
quadrivium, *p. 224*
sagas, *p. 229*
serfs, *p. 234*
vassal, *p. 236*
fief, *p. 236*
liege lord, *p. 238*

REVIEW, ANALYZE, & CONNECT TO TODAY

REVIEW THE PREVIOUS CHAPTER

Chapter 6—"A World Divided"—described the breakup of the Roman Empire into western kingdoms, the Byzantine Empire, and the Muslim world. It also described the three cultures as the old Mediterranean world split.

1. Review Germanic culture and values. Which elements did Charlemagne, Alfred the Great, and the Vikings retain?

2. Compare the illustration on page 212 with that in Figure 6.3. Both portray Saint Matthew, but in very different ways. Explain how the differences reflect Germanic and Roman culture.

ANALYZE THIS CHAPTER

Chapter 7—"The Struggle to Bring Order"—traces the slow establishment of order in Europe as kings instituted laws for their kingdoms and as Charlemagne forged a new empire in western Europe. It also describes new destruction as migrating tribes again wreaked havoc on the continent.

1. How did Alfred the Great and Charlemagne structure the administration of their respective kingdoms? How did the large size of Charlemagne's empire pose particular challenges for the ruler?

2. Review Charlemagne's diplomatic negotiations with the Byzantine Empire and the 'Abbasid caliphate. Why did each ruler act the way he/she did?

3. What was the basis for papal claims of supremacy over the church? What helped the church exert an order over its organization, and what forces prevented it from doing so?

4. Review the intellectual accomplishments of the Anglo-Saxon and Carolingian kingdoms.

5. Review the invasions of the ninth and tenth centuries. Who invaded? Where did they go, and what impact did they have on European society?

CONNECT TO TODAY

Think about the ways in which wars disrupt societies and the ways in which societies are once again reordered following warfare.

1. What similarities are there between the turmoil described in this chapter and the disruptions of war experienced by present-day countries such as Iraq, Afghanistan, and the Balkan nations? What differences are there?

2. What lessons can we learn from the past as we compare and contrast attempts to reorder societies today with the parallel efforts of the early Middle Ages?

BEYOND THE CLASSROOM

BRINGING ORDER WITH LAWS AND LEADERSHIP

McCormick, Michael. *Origins of the European Economy: Communications and Commerce*, A.D. *300–900*. Cambridge: Cambridge University Press, 2002. A comprehensive book on international trade that examines the patterns of Mediterranean commerce. Well written and engrossing—a brilliant piece of scholarship.

Meyers, Henry A., and H. Wolfram. *Medieval Kingship*. Chicago: University of Chicago Press, 1982. A solid study of the institution of kingship as it changed over time in western Europe.

Rio, Alice. *Legal Practice and the Written Word in the Early Middle Ages: Frankish Formulae, ca. 500–1000*. Cambridge: Cambridge University Press, 2009. A creative and fascinating study that uses legal formularies (model legal documents) to explore daily life in early medieval Europe.

ANGLO-SAXON ENGLAND: FORWARDING LEARNING AND LAW

Alexander, Jonathan J.G. *Medieval Illuminators and Their Methods of Work*. New Haven, CT: Yale University Press, 1993. A clear description of the techniques of manuscript illuminations with beautiful illustrations.

Bassett, Steven. *The Anglo-Saxon Kingdoms*. New York: St. Martin's Press, 1989. A clear and fascinating study of the origins of the Anglo-Saxon kingdoms and kingship.

Mayr-Harting, Henry. *The Coming of Christianity to Anglo-Saxon England*. University Park: Pennsylvania State University Press, 1991. A work that attempts to show how Christianity itself was changed in Anglo-Saxon society.

Smyth, Alfred P. *King Alfred the Great*. Oxford: Oxford University Press, 1995. A controversial look at the life and times of Alfred the Great that argues against the historical value of Asser's life of the king.

CHARLEMAGNE AND THE CAROLINGIANS: A NEW EUROPEAN EMPIRE

Barbero, Alessandro. *Charlemagne: Father of a Continent*. Berkeley: University of California Press, 2004. Engaging study that demonstrates Charlemagne's pivotal role in shaping medieval Europe and re-creates the details of the Carolingian world.

Bullough, David. *Carolingian Renewal: Sources and Heritage*. New York: St. Martin's Press, 1992. A clear and interesting study of the spirit of the age with a solid analysis of the sources.

Butzer, Paul L. *Science in Western and Eastern Civilization in Carolingian Times*. Boston: Birkhäuser Verlag, 1993. Skillfully juxtaposes the heritage of classical science in western Europe with the Byzantine and Arab traditions of astronomy and mathematics.

Dhuoda. *Handbook for William: A Carolingian Woman's Counsel for Her Son*. Translated by Carol Neel. Lincoln: University of Nebraska Press, 1991. A good translation with commentary on the letter by Dhuoda featured in the Biography.

GLOBAL CONNECTIONS

Clot, André. *Harun al-Rashid*. Translated by John Howe. New York: New Amsterdam, 1989. An easy-to-read biography based on the Muslim sources that ranges more widely than just the caliph's life to discuss the political, economic, social, and cultural times of the caliphate centered in Baghdad.

STRUGGLE FOR ORDER IN THE CHURCH

Knowles, David. *Christian Monasticism*. New York: McGraw-Hill, 1969. A short and clear look at monastic life and its literature—a classic.

Lawrence, Christopher Nugent. *The Age of the Cloister: The Story of Monastic Life in the Middle Ages*. Mahwah, NJ: HiddenSpring, 2003. Comprehensive study of monastic ways, including details of daily life and an examination of the monastic world's impact on Western culture.

ORDER INTERRUPTED: VIKINGS AND OTHER INVADERS

Clark, Helen. *Towns in the Viking Age*. New York: St. Martin's Press, 1994. An insightful archaeological investigation of early medieval towns in northern Europe.

Hall, Richard. *The World of the Vikings*. London: Thames & Hudson, 2007. A thorough and up-to-date overview of knowledge about the Vikings, with many illustrations.

MANORS AND FEUDAL TIES: ORDER EMERGING FROM CHAOS

Bloch, Marc. *Feudal Society*. Translated by L.A. Manyon. Chicago: University of Chicago Press, 1961. A classic study of the growth and nature of feudalism in its broad social context, but see Reynolds for a revised view.

Collins, Roger. *Early Medieval Europe, 300–1000*. New York: St. Martin's Press, 1991. A study of the people, politics, and religion of early medieval Europe.

Reynolds, Susan. *Fiefs and Vassals: The Medieval Evidence Reinterpreted*. Oxford: Oxford University Press, 1994. An important work that revises traditional approaches and considers whether the terms *fiefs* and *vassals* were used in the early Middle Ages as they are by modern scholars.

Strayer, J.R. *Feudalism*. Princeton, NJ: Princeton University Press, 1985. This work revises and refines the classic study of Bloch.

KING OSWALD WITH HIS BISHOP AIDEN, ca. 1200

This illustration shows the hierarchy of medieval society: The king and his bishop talk at the table while the poor laborers sit at the great men's feet, soliciting charity. A fortified castle frames the whole picture and represents the structure of the medieval order in which some fight (kings), others pray (bishops), and the rest work (laborers).

Order Restored

The High Middle Ages, 1000–1300

"From the beginning, mankind has been divided into three parts—men of prayer, farmers, and men of war. . . ." These words written by Bishop Gerard of Cambrai in the eleventh century capture the social order as the people of the High Middle Ages understood it. In this highly organized world, everyone was expected to keep his or her place, or "order." And these orders were arranged by their function—prayer, warfare, and labor on the land. This understanding of the world ignored the important role of commerce in the growing cities.

After the year 1000, medieval society began to expand in all respects. Agricultural advances spurred population growth; commerce quickened in thriving cities; fortified houses for the nobility sprang up across Europe. After the devastation of the tenth century, kings again tried to consolidate their rule, and nobles resisted their incursion. Intellectual life also flourished with the new prosperity of the age, and philosophers, poets, and artists created works that still inspire us today.

The church, too, grew stronger, and popes began to exert their authority over secular matters. Church leaders called for crusades against Islam, luring western Europeans far from their homelands. Finally, the church's growing role in secular life ignited criticism from some people, who felt that it had forgotten its true purpose. In the face of such criticism, religious leaders responded by both reforming some church policies and repressing those who complained. It was indeed a dynamic age.

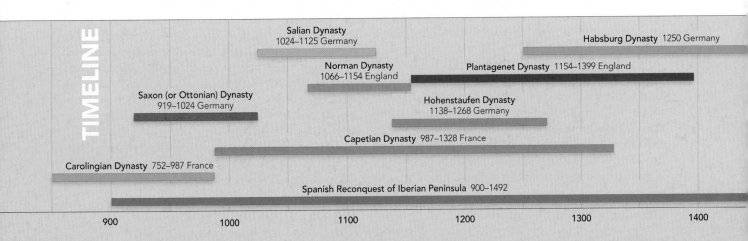

TIMELINE

Salian Dynasty 1024–1125 Germany

Habsburg Dynasty 1250 Germany

Norman Dynasty 1066–1154 England

Plantagenet Dynasty 1154–1399 England

Saxon (or Ottonian) Dynasty 919–1024 Germany

Hohenstaufen Dynasty 1138–1268 Germany

Capetian Dynasty 987–1328 France

Carolingian Dynasty 752–987 France

Spanish Reconquest of Iberian Peninsula 900–1492

900   1000   1100   1200   1300   1400

THOSE WHO WORK: AGRICULTURAL LABOR

In the late twelfth century, a noble knight, William Marshall, rested in the woods while on a journey accompanied only by his squire. He was awakened from his sleep by the sound of a woman's voice saying, "Ah, God, how weary I am." Opening his eyes, William saw a well-dressed couple riding along. William quickly mounted and rode to introduce himself and offer help, but the man was not pleased to see the knight. As the stranger drew his sword, his hood fell off and William saw by his tonsured hair that he was a monk—the handsomest one that he had ever seen. Filled with shame, the monk confessed he had run from his monastery with his lady love: "I have carried her off from her own country." William reprimanded the young woman and offered to escort her back to her brother so she would avoid the shame of the path she had chosen. She refused, and William did not persist. However, the knight did show continued concern, asking them how they would live. The monk showed a belt bulging with coins and said that they would lend money and live off the interest. The good knight William was horrified. "Upon usury? By God's sword, you shall not." He told his squire to take the money to save the couple from falling into the additional shame of moneylending. He sent the couple on their way (penniless) and took the money to the local inn, where William generously treated his friends to abundant food and drink with the purloined coins.

In this story of a noble knight—preserved in a long poem written by his son—we can see the Middle Ages coming into full flower. Knights acted with courtesy to help women who may have been in distress, and they were generous with money (that may not even have been their own). Wealth and love were to be had, and some people—even monks and women—began to explore new ways to live their lives. All this was stimulated by a technological and agricultural boom.

Harnessing the Power of Water and Wind

After 1000, Europeans used more mechanical power than any previous society had; and this power helped fuel the expansion of population, commerce, and political power in western Europe. Water mills provided the major source of mechanical power. In England in 1086, there were often as many as three mills for every mile of river. Water mills ground grain with extraordinary efficiency, and their technology spread rapidly across Europe. **Figure 8.1** shows two women bringing sacks of grain to a mill. The women must cross a bridge over the river that powers the great waterwheel. The nearby buildings reveal the prosperity of the mill owner—prosperity he has acquired by charging a fee for the use of the mill. In the picture, the man at the left stands ready to collect the women's fees.

How did the mills actually work? A cam, projecting from the axle of the waterwheel, converted rotary motion to vertical motion, which let mill workers accomplish tasks from forging iron to softening wool cloth to making beer and paper. By the twelfth century, creative builders had developed ways to bring mechanical power to regions without rivers to drive water mills.

In many parts of Europe, medieval peasants used windmills to generate power from wind. Although people had harnessed the wind much earlier in Asia and the Middle East, European engineers evidently invented these mills based on water mills. See **Figure 8.2** to analyze the independence of the invention. In addition, enterprising engineers managed to tap power from tides. As evidence, in 2009, archaeologists excavated a well-preserved tidal mill in Greenwich, near London, that had been built of huge oak trees cut down in 1194. The wheel diameter of this monumental engineering project is 16 feet. This huge mill drew water in as the tide rose and released it as it fell, powering the adjacent mill. This new find, which supplements excavations around the North Sea, demonstrates an early and wide use of tidal mills.

Harnessing all this power accomplished what technology in the ancient world had never achieved: It released human power for other uses.

New Agricultural Techniques

Peasants supplemented water power with effective use of animal muscle. In the early Middle Ages, as in the ancient world, people harnessed horses with the same kind of yoke they used on oxen. This device was highly inefficient on horses, however, because the yoke rested on their necks and impeded their breathing when they lowered their heads to pull. By the eleventh century, a new padded horse collar that had been developed in China appeared in western Europe. This harness rested on the animal's shoulders, making it possible for people to use horses for heavy plowing and pulling. Because horses can work 50 percent faster and two hours a day longer than oxen, the advantages were huge. Of course, now the peasant walking behind the team of horses also had to work longer and harder. Not surprisingly, the improvement was not as popular with workers as it was with their lords. Nevertheless, the amount of land under cultivation expanded dramatically with increased use of the horse.

FIGURE 8.1 Water Mill, 1470 The peoples of the Middle Ages saw the advantage of harnessing the power of running water. Over time, every community along a waterway had a mill. Women such as these brought their grain to be ground instead of grinding it by hand. Lords grew richer charging for the privilege.

The increased use of animal power required peasants to cultivate more land for fodder and hay. Traditionally—since Roman times—most peasants had used what is called a two-field system, in which half the land was left fallow (unplanted) while half was planted. The fertility of the fallow land was restored to yield more crops the following year. However, to accommodate the need to cultivate more land, manors slowly adopted a three-field system that further increased agricultural yields. In this system, plots of land were divided into thirds: One-third was planted in the spring and another in the fall, and the remaining third was left fallow. The three-field system also stimulated the growth of new crops that boosted production. Villagers began to plant legumes, such as peas and beans, which add nitrogen to the soil, thus fertilizing the subsequent grain crop. Legumes also provided an excellent source of protein, which vastly improved the villagers' diets.

Three-field cultivation

The Population Doubles

These agricultural improvements (and the declining violence after the ninth- and tenth-century invasions ended) led to unprecedented population growth. Although it is impossible to get exact figures, estimates of population growth indicate that from the eleventh through the thirteenth century, the population of Europe approximately doubled—from about 37 million to 74 million. Women in particular benefited from the addition of legumes to their diet because the iron in these foods helped replenish blood lost through menstruation and childbirth, and it enabled healthy women to have fewer miscarriages and nurse stronger babies. With such improvements, women began outnumbering men during these centuries, and even some medieval commentators noted this disparity, considering it a "problem."

Throughout this period, infant and child deaths remained high due to diseases and accidents, and the overall mortality rates were much higher than in modern times. But anyone surviving past the years normally devoted to warfare or childbearing could expect to live as long as people do today. Indeed, the Biography on pages 256–257 features a man who was vigorous well into his 80s. And in 1204, one 97-year-old representative of the pope participated in the Crusades. There were plenty of gray heads and seasoned minds in the villages, castles, and churches of the Middle Ages.

Life span

To accommodate the ballooning population, western Europeans expanded their settlements. Hardworking villagers on the northwest coast (later the Low Countries) built dikes to hold back the ocean itself to expand their agricultural lands. Sometimes groups of villagers left an overcrowded area and cultivated new land, a process called assarting. The resulting "assart" was great open fields that the peasants divided into strips as they established new villages and manors. Primarily they moved eastward. Probably as many as three thousand new villages were established in lands east of the Elbe River in modern-day northern Germany. As they migrated east, settlers spread western European culture into the lands of the

FIGURE 8.2(A) Vertical-Design Persian Windmill, ca. eleventh century

FIGURE 8.2(B) Horizontal-Design European Windmill on a Pivot, ca. thirteenth century

Catching the Wind: The Development of Windmills

The search today for alternative sources of energy has reawakened interest in wind power. It so happens that before the use of fossil fuels, people depended on the wind to power essential machines. The earliest windmills, developed in Persia and China, relied on a vertical rotating shaft; the wind turned a pole that was fitted directly into a stone or a pump to grind grain or to pump water (see **Figure 8.2a**). In contrast, in the West, engineers built windmills that employed a horizontal shaft with a propeller-like structure to catch the wind and turn the shaft (**Figure 8.2b**). In this method, gears were used to transfer the power from the horizontal shaft (to which the windmill's wind-catching panels, or "sails," were attached) to a vertical shaft. This gearing matched the familiar structure of the watermills that had earlier transformed power in Europe.

In one sense, the vertical-shafted windmill of Eastern design was easier to operate, because it could catch wind from any direction, whereas northern Europeans had to rotate their horizontal-model windmill so that the sails would catch the shifting winds. Notice in **Figure 8.2b** that the European windmill is on a pivot so that it may be turned to face the wind. In the case of windmills, Europeans favored a familiar design over an import that was simpler and might have been more efficient.

Connecting Science & Society

1. What factors, existing knowledge, and/or prior experiences might have entered into the decision of Westerners to develop a horizontal shaft for their windmills instead of adopting one of the vertical-shafted models that they had observed in their travels to the East?

2. Today engineers are attempting to design the best and most efficient windmills as alternative energy sources. What factors—social, economic, and/or other—do you think might influence the decision to use wind power as opposed to other power-generating technologies, such as steam and nuclear, in the present day?

3. How do you think the shift to and use of wind power influenced medieval society? How might an increased reliance on wind power influence the lives of people in the twenty-first century?

Slavs. **Map 8.1** shows some of the eastern settlements that were founded as western Europeans relentlessly sought new lands.

Why would peasants leave their established villages to go east and do the hard work needed to clear new agricultural lands? The texts show that people had

| New freedoms |

two motivations: the possibility of better lands and more freedom. The twelfth-century chronicler Helmod of Bosau described how Count Adolf II of Holstein (1128–1164) attracted settlers to his new lands: He insisted that "whoever might be in difficult straits because of a shortage of fields should come with their families to accept land which was excellent, spacious, fertile with fruits, abounding in fish and meat, and favorable to pastures." Still, the peasants drove a hard bargain—many surviving charters show that the new settlers gained many freedoms from the feudal obligations of serfdom. For example, the charter of the twelfth-century village of Lorris read: "No man shall pay a tax upon his food. Nor for measuring the grain which he obtains from his own labor or that of his animals. Nor shall he pay any tax on the wine which he obtains from his own vineyards." With such incentives, the spread to new lands blossomed, and western European culture flourished.

Few expansions offer unmixed blessings, and the population growth had dire environmental consequences. To build their new settlements, people clear-

| Environmental consequences |

cut huge swaths of forest, often using slash-and-burn techniques that left clouds of smoke and ash hanging in the air. The settlers also dumped human waste and the remains of slaughtered animals in the rivers. In the cities, coal burning poured clouds of dangerous pollutants into the air. Still, the population kept expanding, and more and more people appreciated being freed from the land to populate the burgeoning cities and towns.

THOSE OUTSIDE THE ORDER: TOWN LIFE

As we saw in the quotation that began this chapter, when medieval writers identified an ordered world of "those who work," they imagined agricultural laborers providing for the lords who ruled and the clergy who prayed. Yet, there were others who labored outside this well-defined hierarchy who did not fit medieval understandings based on a rural society. It was in these towns that people forged the real future of modern urban western European culture.

The few towns of the early Middle Ages were primarily administrative centers, serving as the residences of bishops or occasionally of a nobleman. These towns were walled for protection from

MAP 8.1

German Migration Eastward

This map focuses on the new eastern settlements from about 1000 to 1300. It shows a steady progress of migrants eastward over a long time period in search of promising agricultural lands.

Explore the Map

1. Where did the major cities grow?

2. What might be the impact of these cities on trade routes around the Baltic?

3. What do these settlements suggest about population growth in western Europe?

the surrounding violence of the feudal world. After 1000, more cities grew up and began to take on more commercial roles. In the process, they grew not only larger, but wealthier, and they developed new ways to govern their increasingly prosperous lives.

Communes and Guilds:
Life in a Medieval Town

People moved to towns that offered work in a thriving trade and a lively demand for goods. By present-day standards, most medieval towns were small. For example, of the 3,000 identified "towns" in late medieval Germany, 2,800 had populations of only about

1,000. Europe did have a few great cities, however. Cologne was home to some 40,000 people, and London's population approached that figure by the fourteenth century. The Italian cities of Florence and Venice boasted almost 100,000 residents each.

Men and women living in these small towns shared many ideas with the feudal society that surrounded them, like a belief in hierarchy and a sense of mutual ties. However, they expressed these ideas in ways that dramatically shaped urban life. To escape the many requirements imposed on village serfs, towns negotiated charters with the lords on whose lands the town stood. These charters granted townspeople freedom from labor obligations and freedom to travel at will. They also protected the growing town profits from unreasonable taxation and seizure, and some charters allowed the towns to run their own law courts. All these rights made towns islands of freedom in a tightly ordered world, and in return, the lords received money from the prosperous burgs. Towns also served as magnets drawing those who wished to escape from the ordered constraints of the feudal world. In most towns, if a serf could live for "a year and a day" without being caught, he had earned his freedom to stay in the town.

Sometimes townspeople could not peacefully obtain the liberties they desired, and they joined together in sworn associations called **communes** and staged violent revolutions to take communal liberties that they believed came with urban life. The communes elected their own officials, regulated taxation within the town, and generally conducted the business of running the urban centers. These communes were not democratic, for most people accepted it as natural that the rich citizens would govern the town. In Italy, the communes became so strong that the cities developed into independent city-states. In the French and English lands, by contrast, all the towns remained subject to the political authority of the king. In all cases, however, towns encouraged people to develop their skills, learn a trade, and make money.

Tradesmen within towns formed **guilds,** or organizations to protect their interests and control the trade and manufacturing within the towns. These guilds regulated the quality of such products as gold work, shoes, bread, and so forth; they managed their own membership and set prices. In part because urban women outnumbered men, they participated in the guilds, and families arranged marriages to cement bonds of loyalty and control of commerce. Widows in particular ran businesses and took their husbands' places in the trade organizations. Boys and girls served as apprentices in the shops until they learned their trade. Then they could work as "journeymen"—paid employees under the guidance of a master. Finally, journeymen would present a sample of their best work—whether a gold piece or a loaf of bread—to the guild masters to see if this "masterpiece" would qualify them to become full guild masters. In these ways, the guild could control both the quality of the products and the number of guild members involved in the trade.

For other groups, town life offered a more mixed set of opportunities and limits. Since the time of the Roman Empire, many medieval towns had a significant population of Jews. For centuries, Jews had played a vital role in town life as merchants, artisans, and members of many other professions. By the eleventh and twelfth centuries, however, Christian merchants and craftspeople began to view the Jewish community as competition. Slowly, they excluded Jews from guilds and, in some places, kept them from owning land. However, Jews still engaged in commerce and many Christians found them valuable—although separate—members of the town. For example, a late-eleventh-century charter was granted by a bishop (Rudgar) to Jews who were willing to settle in the German town of Speyer. He wrote that he thought "it would greatly add to its [Speyer's] honor if I should establish some Jews in it." He gave them a section of the city for their use (and walled it off to provide protection from less-enlightened Christians) and offered them special concessions for trading.

The bishop of Speyer also gave Jews the right to freely change coins, and, slowly, urban Jews such as those in Speyer began to enter into moneylending, which is essential to commercial enterprises. The Christian religion forbad its followers to collect interest on loans, for they believed that it was unseemly to make money from time, which belonged to God. While many Christians continued to engage in the lucrative practice of moneylending, slowly through the late Middle Ages, Jewish bankers increasingly began to take over the practice because Judaic practice contained no such strictures against lending money. The two urban groups thus depended on each other in an uneasy coexistence throughout most of the Middle Ages.

The Widening Web of Trade

The impetus for the growth of towns and wealth in the Middle Ages came not from manufacturing but from trade. Therefore, the most important towns were those that served as bustling centers for moving goods—throughout the Middle Ages most of the trade centered on luxury goods. Northern Italy, especially, became a significant nexus in southern Europe, and Venice, Pisa, and Genoa took the lead. As early as 998, Venetians had received charters from the Byzantine emperor that gave them complete freedom in Byzantine waters, and Pisa and Genoa had negotiated treaties with Muslim rulers that opened new markets. Thus, the way was paved for merchants to sail

Communes and guilds

Urban Jews

MAP 8.2

Trade Routes, Twelfth and Thirteenth Centuries

This map illustrates the major trading areas of the High Middle Ages, including the three principal zones of trade. It also shows the importance of sea and river routes and the Champagne fairs.

Explore the Map

1. Why were the Italian cities particularly well suited to take advantage of the southern trade?

2. What northern cities were well placed for sea and river trade?

3. In what respects were the Champagne fairs favorably located to bring together the northern and southern trade zones?

to the eastern Mediterranean and buy silks and spices passing through the great Muslim bazaars in Baghdad. They then brought the goods westward to Spain and southern France. Whereas the Mediterranean trade had been the commercial center during the Roman Empire, the medieval world opened a new trading hub in the north.

Cities in Flanders (particularly Bruges and Ghent) joined the Italian cities as commercial centers. They supplied fine wool cloth to all of northern Europe and acted as a supply center for Scandinavian products—particularly furs and hunting hawks—that were in demand all over Europe. The growth of the cloth industry, and the handsome profits to be made, led many northern men to replace at the looms the women who had dominated the industry. **Map 8.2** shows the three major trade zones, northern, southern, and the central overland route that distributed goods. However, through the eleventh century, there was no easy mechanism for joining the three zones.

Early in the twelfth century, the French count of Champagne saw an opportunity to make a large profit by hosting fairs in his lands at which merchants could sell goods from the three zones. He granted the right to various towns in his county to organize such gatherings. (**Map 8.2** shows the major towns of the Champagne fairs.) The counts of Champagne provided the space, set up booths, arranged for police to keep order, and invited moneylenders. Each day, the trade featured a different product, and the counts collected a sales tax from all the transactions made.

Champagne fairs

Figure 8.3 depicts one such medieval fair. At the booths, people gather to purchase animals, bolts of cloth, and fine artifacts. At the center of the illustration, the bishop of Paris opens the fair by bestowing God's blessing on the enterprise. The fairs featured products from all over Europe: leather from Spain, iron from Germany, copper and tin from Bohemia, and smoked fish and furs from Scandinavia. They also offered an outlet for local products such as cheeses and wines. The fairs also drew people from the medieval underbelly of society; thieves, con artists, actors, and prostitutes plied their trade among the bustling crowds.

In the late thirteenth century, many cities in northern Germany united to create the Hanseatic League, an association to capitalize on the prosperous northern trade. The cities formed a political as well as an economic power, and they were able to acquire a monopoly on the Baltic trade, replacing Flanders as the center of the northern trading zone. At its height, the Hanseatic League included seventy or eighty cities, led by Lubeck, Bremen, Cologne, and Hamburg. By the fourteenth century, they offered their own great fairs, which replaced the French fairs. By looking at **Maps 8.1** and **8.2,** we can see that the eastward settlements around the Baltic Sea helped spawn prosperous trade regions that brought centers of wealth ever northward from the Mediterranean Sea.

Hanseatic League

The Glory of God: Church Architecture

With the wealth that came pouring into the cities, townspeople built great churches to celebrate the glory of God and express their pride in their own towns. From about the tenth century until the twelfth, church architecture was dominated by the **Romanesque** style. Mostly monastic structures, these buildings were large and dark with long, central aisles made of barrel vaults and round arches. They seemed so solid and formidable, people often called them "fortresses of God."

Figure 8.4a shows the interior of the monastery church of La Madeleine at Vézeley in Burgundy. Built in the early twelfth century, this structure represents the highest achievement of Romanesque architecture. Because the barrel vault was high, it could not support the heavy stone roof by itself, so builders made the walls extra thick and the windows small. As a result, the church, and others like it, was dark inside.

In about 1140, Abbot Suger of the Church of St. Denis near Paris decided to change all this. He envisioned a majestic church built in a new style—a church that reached up toward the heavens and that was filled with light. Architects and builders set about making this vision a reality, and to do so, they adopted innovative techniques that came to be called the **Gothic** style. Instead of round arches, they used pointed ones, as shown in **Figure 8.4b**. Some scholars believe the use of the pointed arch originated in India and found its way through the trade networks to France. Regardless of its origin, the new arch style directed the weight of the roof down the building's massive columns instead of its walls. But such tall walls were vulnerable to cracking under the pressure of high winds. To guard against this danger, architects developed

Gothic architecture

FIGURE 8.3 Medieval Fair in France Merchants gathered at periodic fairs to sell their wares, and these fairs stimulated long-distance trade. Local people found goods and excitement at the fairs' temporary stalls.

FIGURE 8.4 Romanesque and Gothic Architecture Medieval church architecture reflected two main styles. (a) Romanesque design, with thick walls and round arches like those in La Madeleine at Vézeley (ca. 1104), shown here, was the earlier style. (b) Gothic style, featuring pointed arches and soaring heights as exemplified in Cologne Cathedral (begun in 1248), shown in this photograph, came later.

"flying buttresses," large braces that supported the outside of the building.

With these innovations, the walls no longer needed to be thick to provide the support for the church. Builders could therefore add large windows that let light fill the interior. Glassmakers gathered in nearby forests to burn the hardwood needed to blow glass, and they added metallic oxides to make rich primary colors. Artists fitted the colored glass into intricate lead webs to form magnificent pictures showing everything from biblical stories to scenes of medieval life. Abbot Suger himself contracted the stained-glass windows for his new church. Delighted with the result, he wrote, "The entire sanctuary is pervaded by a wonderful and continuous light." The thirteenth-century royal chapel in Paris shown in **Figure 8.5** contains some of the most remarkable examples of stained glass. The windows make up three-quarters of the wall surface.

Beginning in the mid-twelfth century, these immense Gothic cathedrals, with their pointed arches, stained-glass windows, and flying buttresses, began appearing in all the great cities of Europe. Designed to accommodate the entire population of a city (some can hold as many as 10,000 people standing during mass), they were also designed to attract admiring pilgrims. The cathedrals vied to acquire and feature relics of famous saints (see Chapter 5) that drew the faithful seeking solace and miracles. These pilgrims brought money to both the church and the city and helped stimulate movement throughout

> Stained glass

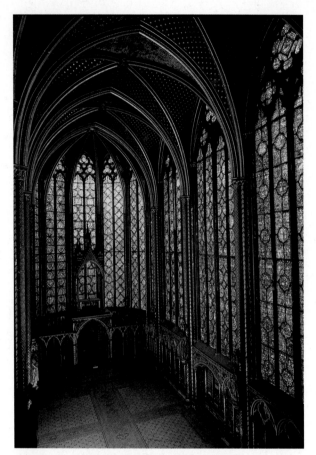

FIGURE 8.5 Stained-Glass Windows, ca. 1245 In the Gothic style, strong stone columns supported the weight of the cathedral's roof, thus freeing the walls from weight-bearing function. Skilled artisans installed stained-glass windows into those walls, such as these examples from the magnificent Sainte-Chapelle, Paris.

medieval Europe. The skylines of medieval Europe were reshaped by the towers of these striking new cathedrals.

The Rise of Universities

The cathedrals became more than just centers of worship and pilgrimage; they began serving as places of learning. Scholars and students gathered at cathedrals to study, and these cathedral schools became vibrant centers. It soon became clear that the informal organization of these schools was inadequate. Document 8.1 describes the drawbacks of some educators in the noble households. Townspeople frequently protested to the bishop against the students, who were often rowdy and sometimes violent. Students, on their part, resented the high prices that townspeople charged for rooms, food, and drink, and they needed protection against incompetent teachers. By the twelfth century, new structures were emerging to address some of these problems, establishing the beginnings of universities.

Just as townspeople founded guilds and used charters to protect their interests, students and scholars did the same. In some places (like Paris), masters grouped themselves into guilds, and in other cities (like Bologna), students organized themselves. These organizations were called universities—from the Latin word *universitas*, which means "guild." These universities received charters that confirmed the guild's autonomy and authority to license teachers.

Young men (some only 14 years old) from all social classes attended universities; wealthy younger sons of the nobility and promising young village boys could eventually hope for lucrative jobs in the church or courts. (Women were not permitted to attend universities.) Students completed the traditional course of study that had been established centuries before at Charlemagne's (r. 768–814) court. They studied the trivium—grammar, rhetoric, and logic—first and then the quadrivium—arithmetic, geometry, music, and astronomy. Upon completion, they would receive first a bachelor's degree and then a master's degree.

Advanced students interested in focusing on a specialized course of study could continue their studies and receive a doctorate degree. Students might study medicine in Salerno, where masters taught Arabic medicine and sometimes dissected human cadavers. Others might go to Bologna to study law based on Justinian's *Corpus* (discussed in Chapter 6) or study theology—the "queen of all the sciences"—in Paris. The many medieval universities of Europe are shown in **Map 8.3.** This map gives some idea of the potential for students to move from school to school as they sought different masters and different curricula. It also suggests how these institutes of learning served to link the intellectual life of such a broad geographic area.

The universities gave rise to a new kind of life for the young men who attended them. Many students eagerly devoured the ideas and knowledge that percolated at these centers of learning. The classroom pictured in **Figure 8.6** shows students with differing degrees of enthusiasm—those in the front listen attentively, while some in the back talk during the lecture and another in the foreground sleeps. The less serious students deeply enjoyed the freedom of university life, drinking in the local bars and brawling in the streets, raising the townspeople's ire. In Paris, a law was passed forbidding students to gamble with dice on the altar of the cathedral while mass was being said! All this freedom cost money; many letters in which students ask their parents to send more cash survive from this era. Yet, despite the occasional disruptions and distractions of life in the universities, students and teachers managed to engage in stimulating dialogues that led to exciting new ideas.

> Advanced degrees

Guibert of Nogent Describes His Education

In the early twelfth century, Guibert, the abbot of Nogent in France, wrote a remarkable autobiography that offers an intimate glimpse into twelfth-century life. His parents had promised him to the church at his birth and raised him to become a monk. In this account, he gives a rare description of child-rearing practices.

There was a little before that time, and in a measure there is still in my time, such a scarcity of grammarians that in the towns hardly anyone, and in the cities very few, could be found, and those who by good hap could be discovered, had but slight knowledge and could not be compared with the itinerant clerks of these days. And so the man in whose charge my mother decided to put me, had begun to learn grammar late in life and was the more unskilled in the art through having imbibed little of it when young. Yet of such sobriety was he, that what he wanted in letters, he made up for in honesty.

Placed under him I was taught with such purity and checked with such honesty in the excesses which are wont to spring up in my youth, that I was kept well-guarded from the common wolves and never allowed to leave his company, or to eat anywhere than at home, or to accept gifts from anyone without his leave; in everything I had to show self-control in word, look or act, so that he seemed to require of me the conduct of a monk rather than a clerk. For whereas others of my age wandered everywhere at will and were unchecked in the indulgence of such inclinations to their age, I, hedged in with constant restraints, would sit and look on in my clerical chasuble at the troops of players like a beast awaiting sacrifice.

Although, therefore, he crushed me by such severity, yet in other ways he made it quite plain that he loved me as well as he did himself. With such watchful care did he devote himself to me, with such foresight did he secure my welfare against the spite of others and teach me on what authority I should beware of the dissolute manners of some who paid court to me, and so long did he argue with my mother about the elaborate richness of my dress, that he was regarded as exercising the guardianship not of a master, but of a parent, and not over my body only, but my soul, too. As for me, considering the dull sensibility of my age and my littleness, great was the love I conceived for him in response, in spite of the many weals with which he marked my tender skin so that not through fear, as is common in those of my age, but through a sort of love deeply implanted in my heart, I obeyed him in utter forgetfulness of his severity.

SOURCE: Guibert de Nogent, *The Autobiography of Guibert, Abbot of Nogent-Sous-Coucy.* Translated by C.C. Swinton Bland (London: George Routledge & Sons, Ltd., and E.P. Dutton & Co., New York, 1926), p. 32.

Analyze the Document

1. Why did Guibert's mother have to settle for a mediocre tutor?

2. What methods of instruction did the tutor use?

3. What did Guibert think of his tutor?

4. How did medieval ideas of education differ from modern notions?

Scholasticism: The Height of Medieval Philosophy

The main goal of medieval philosophy was to reconcile faith with reason—that is, to understand with one's mind what one believed in one's heart. This philosophy was called **scholasticism.** The medieval thinkers applied a particular form of logic, called dialectic, which involves using logic to explore various sides of an issue, and these writings often take the form of questioning. The greatest thinkers drawn to the new universities in the twelfth century wrestled constantly with this problem and, in doing so, shaped both knowledge and faith.

The earliest medieval philosopher to explore the religious applications of dialectic was Anselm of Canterbury (1033–1109). Anselm's motto was "faith seeking understanding," and his most famous effort involved showing a logical connection between the belief that God is a perfect being and a proof (by the rules of logic) that God exists. He argued that because God was perfect he *must* exist, or else he would not be perfect (for Anselm, perfection demonstrated a real existence). Anselm wrote a number of works on logic, and his treatise *Why God Became Man* became the most important explanation of the central Christian mystery. Anselm established the exciting possibility that human reason could be brought to study the deep mysteries of Creation.

One of the most esteemed scholastic scholars was Peter Abelard (1079–1142), who taught in Paris. In his mid-thirties, Abelard was hired to tutor Heloise (ca. 1100–1163), the talented 17-year-old niece of a local church official. Teacher and student were soon lovers, and Heloise became pregnant. The couple married secretly because Heloise feared that a traditional marriage would hurt Abelard's reputation as a teacher, but her infuriated uncle had Abelard castrated. Leaving their child to be raised by relatives, both Heloise and

Anselm and Abelard

MAP 8.3

Medieval Universities

This map shows the numerous universities that were founded throughout the Middle Ages, as well as the years in which they were founded, where known.

Explore the Map

1. Which universities were founded earliest?

2. As time went on, how easy would it have been for students to move from school to school as they sought different programs of study? Explain.

3. Which region had the most universities? How might this clustering have affected the overall culture of that region?

Abelard entered monasteries, where they each continued brilliant careers of learning and influence.

Abelard established a method of applying critical reason to even sacred texts. His most famous work, *Yes and No* (*Sic et Non*), assembled a variety of authoritative sources, from the Bible to church fathers, that seemed to contradict one an other. From these, the scholar compiled 150 theological questions and the passages relevant to each question, which allowed scholars to consider the full range of the questions. Although his book has such provocative chapters as "Is God the Author of Evil, or No?" Abelard had no desire to undermine faith; on the contrary, he believed that this kind of inquiry would strengthen

FIGURE 8.6 Medieval Universities Universities were first founded in the Middle Ages. Scholars gathered at these new institutions to listen to lectures from famed masters. This image shows the students' diversity, as well as the youthfulness of many of them.

faith through the discovery of truth. This was an academic exercise in which students were expected to reconcile apparent contradictions.

Throughout the Middle Ages, there had always been people who believed that it was not possible or even desirable to reach God through reason. Abelard's adversary Bernard of Clairvaux (1090–1153) condemned many of Abelard's writings, primarily because he disapproved of the process of inquiry. Bernard wrote passionately: "I thought it unfitting that the grounds of the faith should be handed over to human reasonings for discussion." Although Bernard approved of rational inquiry in nonreligious areas, he firmly believed the way to God lay in faith and love—in other words, in emotion, not intellect. He wrote beautiful tracts on the mystic approach to God through feeling and faith, and many men and women chose to seek God through this mystic path rather than through logic.

Through the twelfth century, Islamic scholars also continued the great intellectual strides that had

been begun by scholars like Avicenna (980–1037) (in Biography, Chapter 6). Muslim scholars from centers as far apart as Baghdad in the east and Toledo in Spain studied the classical works of Aristotle and others with a sophistication lacking in the western kingdoms. The Muslim scholar Averroës (1126–1198) and the eminent Jewish scholar Maimonides (1135–1204) interpreted Aristotle's works and left extensive commentaries on the sophisticated ideas. These texts were discovered in Arabic libraries in Spain as Christians slowly reconquered Muslim territory, and the emergence of these commentaries along with the advanced logic of Aristotle generated much intellectual excitement in the university communities of western Europe.

Some of Aristotle's ideas as interpreted by these non-Christian commentators (such as his belief in the eternity of the world) seemed to contradict Christian faith. In spite of some controversy, many readers thrilled at the intellectual possibilities contained in such texts and felt confident that faith and reason could be reconciled. The Biography of Ramón Lull

BIOGRAPHY

Ramón Lull
(ca.1232–1316)

Troubadour,

Scholar, and

Missionary

to the

Muslims

Ramón Lull was born in about 1232 on Majorca, one of the Balearic islands off the east coast of Spain. As a young man, Ramón was deeply drawn to the love poetry of the troubadours. He composed songs and poems of love and the life of luxury. However, at about age 30, he had a transforming experience. One night, as he crafted a love song for his lady, he beheld a vision of Jesus hanging on the cross. After a few more such visions, Ramón decided to renounce his frivolous life and turn his efforts to religion. In his view, God had called him to convert the Muslims to Christianity.

Ramón began to train for his new vocation. To learn Arabic so he could preach to the Muslims, he bought a Muslim slave.

FIGURE 8.7 Ramón Lull, Balearic Islands, Mallorca

He studied with the slave for nine years and became fluent in Arabic. Toward the end of his studies, the slave tried to murder Ramón, perhaps to keep him from preaching Christianity to Muslims. The scholar survived the attack and had the slave arrested, but he felt torn about what to do with him. He did not want to order him killed, because that seemed unChristian. At the same time, he felt unsafe freeing him. As he wrestled with this problem, the slave committed suicide in prison. Ramón interpreted the suicide as God's way of releasing him from his dilemma. He concluded that the death of his Muslim slave confirmed the correctness of his own desire to convert the followers of Islam.

Ramón then set out to build the skills he saw as essential for carrying the Christian message to the Muslim world. He attended the university at Paris to study theology and honed his skill in the formal logic practiced by the scholastics. All this preparation revealed Ramón's passion for education. He founded a school in Majorca

---

(see above) tells of one remarkable man's expression of this passion for reason.

The scholastic enterprise reached its height in the thirteenth century with the works of Thomas Aquinas (1225–1274), an Italian churchman whom many regard as the greatest scholar of the Middle Ages.

Thomas Aquinas

Aquinas wrote many works, from commentaries on biblical books and Aristotelian texts to essays on philosophical problems and the *Summa Contra Gentiles*, a work probably intended for missionary use in converting heretics, Muslims, and Jews. However, his most important work was the *Summa Theologiae* (*Summary of Theology*), which was intended to offer a comprehensive summary of all knowledge available at the time.

Aquinas taught that faith and reason were compatible paths to a single truth, but that the mind by itself could grasp only the truth of the physical world. Faith (given by God's grace), however, could help reason grasp spiritual truths such as the Trinity. This central understanding—that faith and nature cannot contradict each other and that each can inform the other—has remained one

of Aquinas's most important contributions. The scholar wrote, "Our intellect is led by our senses to divine knowledge."

The most famous examples of his use of nature to yield divine truth were his "proofs" of God's existence, in which, like Anselm, he wanted to use logic available in the physical world to understand the mysteries of God. For instance, he showed that we can observe motion on earth and that all earthly motion is caused by some other motion. When we trace back all the motion that is caused, our logical mind leads us to the first mover that originated all other motion—the "unmoved mover"—who is God. Thus, our understanding of the physical world of motion, combined with faith, leads us to an understanding of one of the elements of God.

Aquinas's *Summa* remains one of the masterpieces of philosophy, but not all medieval thinkers found it satisfying. For some, it was too speculative and abstract. For all Aquinas's emphasis on using the natural world as a path to truth, he did not study the natural world very much. Instead, he read Aristotle's views on the natural world. Yet some of the great minds of the age turned directly to matters of the physical than four thousand oak trees in its construction. As the castle rose, its stone towers replaced the forests as the prominent feature of the landscape.

The Ideals of Chivalry

The contractual form of feudalism (see Chapter 7) persisted throughout the Middle Ages as a way to provide armies for lords and kings. However, the mutual contract did nothing to reduce the violence that continually plagued medieval society. Early in the eleventh century, churchmen meeting in councils tried to reduce the violence by advocating a Peace of God, which would impose rules of war—for example, exempting the poor and the clergy from the violence. In the middle of the eleventh century, churchmen tried to add a related concept, the Truce of God, which forbad fighting on Sundays and other holy days. Neither of these worthy movements fully quelled the violence.

By the twelfth century, the feudal tie had become interwoven with an elaborate code of values and symbolic rituals that served somewhat to tame the violent world of warriors. This code and culture of the ruling class was called **chivalry,** and its values became evident in church writings, romantic literature, and treatises. Ramón Lull, whose life was described in the Biography on pages 256–257, wrote *The Order of Chivalry,* one of the most famous of such treatises.

According to the texts, a knight should be strong and disciplined yet use his power to defend the church, the poor, and women in need. Knights were expected to possess the virtue of military prowess, but they also had to be loyal, generous, courteous, and "of noble bearing." In reality, knights probably violated these ethics as often as they adhered to them; the code of chivalry provided only a veneer of symbols and ceremonies that overlay the violence at the heart of "those who fight."

One activity required of chivalrous knights was participation in mock battles called jousts or tournaments. **Figure 8.9** shows a joust, which involved single encounters between two knights. (Tournaments were mock battles between teams of knights.) In this painted illustration, the knights display heraldic figures on their horses and shields that reveal their noble lineage and suggest the importance of noble blood to the ideals of chivalry. Women watch the contest and incite the men on to greater deeds of valor.

Jousts and tournaments

FIGURE 8.8 Caerphilly Castle, Wales Medieval warfare was largely defensive: Armor protected knights, and castle walls defended homes and borders. Wales was a frontier area, dotted with many castles built in the thirteenth century.

These were only mock battles, yet many combatants came away from them with debilitating—and sometimes fatal—injuries. The church repeatedly tried to ban tournaments, but the code of chivalry proved too powerful. Tournaments and jousts not only satisfied a profound social need but also provided a practical way for young men to win horses and armor—the victors in these contests took the equipment of the losers.

The very vehemence with which the aristocracy clung to demanding rituals of behavior points to a weakness in their rule. As the Middle Ages wore on, the public role of the nobility—defending and administering Europe—was weakening. Merchants had more wealth, so chivalry was in part a way to hold on to privileges that were eroding. Yet, the nobility convinced itself of its special place in the world through elaborate ceremonies, proper dress, staged battles, and a mania for genealogy. And in the evenings, members of the warrior class entertained one another with stories celebrating the chivalric ideals.

The Literature of Chivalry

During many of the evening gatherings, people listened to *chansons de geste,* or "songs of deeds," which celebrated the ideals of Christian knighthood in the eleventh and twelfth centuries. The most famous of these literary works are the French *Song of Roland* and the Spanish *Poem of the Cid.* Both poems extol the virtues of feudal heroes—Roland, a perfect vassal of Charlemagne; and Rodrigo Díaz de Vivar, known as El Cid (my lord), the perfect vassal of King Alfonso VI (r. 1065–1109) of Aragon. In both accounts, the knights embody the values of prowess and loyalty to a fault. Roland was too brave to call for help in the face

FIGURE 8.9 Joust Knights honed their skill in warfare by fighting in periodic mock battles such as the joust shown here. Elaborate heraldic markings conveyed the knights' noble lineage. The ladies who watched served as an admiring audience spurring on the combatants.

of overwhelming forces, and El Cid showed perfect fidelity to an unworthy lord. Both stories feature specific details of battle and bloody victories designed to delight an audience of warriors.

These poems also show another side of the chivalric ideal—men's strong emotional ties with one another. The loyalty and camaraderie formed on the battlefield pervaded many aspects of warriors' lives. Roland, for example, wept and swooned at the death of his friend Oliver. In these works, as in the many handbooks on chivalry, women played a peripheral role. They were expected only to incite men to greater deeds and existed mainly to be protected and to provide noble heirs. With the emergence of a new form of literature and a new social code, however, these attitudes shifted somewhat.

In Praise of Romantic Love

In the twelfth century, a new kind of poetry appeared in southern France that changed the social code between men and women—the poetry of the **troubadours,** or court poets. Historians are divided on why this new sensibility emerged at this time. Some postulate an influence of Arabic love poetry from Spain; others emphasize the patronage of wealthy noblewomen. Whatever its origin, the new poetry was highly influential in shaping people's ideas of love. In these works, the poets praised love between men and women as an ennobling idea worthy of being cultivated. Troubadour poetry is diverse, but from it we can distill some basic characteristics of this new romantic love. The ideal love was one in which a man grew more noble by loving and serving a highborn woman (not necessarily his wife and often somebody else's). As they complimented highborn ladies, poets wrote lines promising complete obedience: "And there's no task that's burdensome to me / If it should please my lady master." Knights who pledged this kind of service hoped to be rewarded ultimately with sexual favors: "Surely there'll some day be a time, / My lady beautiful and good / When you can pass me secretly / The sweet reward of a little kiss." This kind of love was meant to be difficult to attain, secret, and highly exciting.

In the twelfth century, Andrew the Chaplain wrote a book titled *The Art of Courtly Love* that paralleled earlier treatises on knightly chivalry. In this work, Andrew described how lovers must always turn pale in the presence of the beloved and stressed that secrecy and jealousy were essential for intensifying feelings of love. The ideal of courtly love was as much the exclusive property of the nobility as the ideals of chivalry had been. For example, Andrew wrote that if a nobleman fell in love with a mere peasant woman, "do not hesitate to take what you seek and to embrace her by force." Andrew and his noble patrons believed that only the nobility could love properly—that is, possess the leisure and money to engage in this elaborate game. Andrew warned of the consequence if peasants enjoyed romantic love: Their "farms may through lack of cultivation prove useless to us."

Historians have argued about whether the ideal of courtly love improved the actual treatment of women, given that men supposedly bettered themselves in order to win women's hearts. Certainly Andrew's advice about raping peasant women helps answer this question. The poetry written by women troubadours also reveals something about women's experience of this kind of love. Some of this poetry describes the tension between women and the men who claimed to love them but then left to embark on great deeds. The women's poetry shows a desire to have men remain present and attentive. As one poet wrote: "Handsome friend, as a lover true / I loved you, for you pleased me / but now I see I was a fool / for I've barely seen you since."

At least in the literature of courtly love, women occupied the center of the narrative. **Figure 8.10** shows a lady and her knight out hawking together. Unlike in **Figure 8.9,** the woman is in the forefront of the image. She holds the hawk and is courted by the

Courtly love

FIGURE 8.10 Noble Couple Hunting The nobility loved the hunt, which was one of their prerogatives. Here, a noble couple hunts with a trained hawk. Note how the artist incorporated elements demonstrating the couple's high status, including heraldic symbols at the top and the dapple-gray horse ridden by the woman.

attentive lover. The nobility of each is shown by the coats of arms above them. The artist also enhanced the woman's prestige by showing her on a dappled horse, the most expensive of the breed.

Troubadour poetry spread beyond France to other areas of Europe. Poets also wrote long romances describing the courtly love tradition. The earliest of these writers, Chrétien de Troyes, penned a number of romances set in the court of the imagined hero King Arthur. (The historical Arthur was the Celtic Roman general described in Chapter 6.) These works told of love, loyalty, and great deeds, and served to entertain a nobility that was as enthralled with courtly love as it was with chivalry. These stories and the ideal of romantic love profoundly influenced modern notions of the nature of love between men and women.

THE RISE OF CENTRALIZED MONARCHIES

While noblemen and noblewomen cultivated ideals of war and love, real warfare struck with relentless regularity. Kings were constantly trying to reestablish control over provinces that had drifted away during the turbulent tenth century. At the same time, nobles struggled to keep and even increase their own power. The repeated conflicts between monarch and aristocrat transformed the political map of Europe.

England: From Conquest to Parliament

In the early eleventh century, England had been ruled by the able Danish king Canute (r. 1016–1035) (see Chapter 7), but after his death his Scandinavian empire did not hold together. Before his death, Canute and the English nobility turned to a surviving member of the family of the Anglo-Saxon king Alfred. Thus, Edward the Confessor (r. 1042–1066) reestablished the Anglo-Saxon monarchy. However, a dynasty requires heirs to be stable, and Edward did not have any children. A new succession crisis would lead to the conquest of England.

In 1066, when Edward the Confessor died without an heir, the Anglo-Saxon witan crowned one of their own—Harold Godwinson—as king, and the Anglo-Saxon kingdom was poised to continue as it had before. However, two men believed they had better claims on the English crown. First, Harold Hardradi of Norway landed in the north of England. Harold Godwinson defeated him at the Battle of Stamford Bridge, but that was to be the last battle won by an Anglo-Saxon king. As Halley's comet streaked across the skies that year, seeming to predict disaster, the other claimant, Duke William of Normandy, prepared to sail. William was Edward the Confessor's cousin, and he also claimed that the Anglo-Saxon king had promised him the throne; he aimed to take what he believed was his right. William sailed a fleet across the English Channel and engineered the last successful large-scale invasion of England. The Anglo-Saxon king was killed at the Battle of Hastings and henceforth Duke William reigned as William the Conqueror (r. 1066–1087).

William brought a highly controlled feudal system to the island as he redistributed the Anglo-Saxon nobles' lands to his Norman followers. Although he allowed them to have subvassals, he required everyone to take an oath to him as liege lord (see Chapter 7), so the future Anglo-Norman kings could avoid some of the decentralization implicit in feudalism. William wanted to know exactly what lands he ruled, so he sent out royal officials to make a record of his holdings. The resulting text—the *Domesday Book*—is an invaluable historical record of the times. While William kept the local officials (like sheriffs) that had been so effective in Anglo-Saxon times, he replaced the Anglo-Saxon witan with his own assembly of vassals—the *curia regis*. In this assembly, or Great

Conquest of England

Council, vassals satisfied their feudal obligations to give the king advice and help him pass judgment. This advisory council would become one of the precedents for the growth of Parliament.

William's court spoke only ancient French, and the long coexistence of the two languages led to the incorporation of many French words into what became the modern English language. For example, the Anglo-Saxon words *pig* and *cow* turned into the French-derived *pork* and *beef* as they came to the table of the conquerors. Over the next centuries, however, the hybrid language that emerged was closer to Old English than to French.

The Norman conquest of England had implications for the French monarchy as well, for now the king of England held lands in France—Normandy—as vassal to the king of France. However, this English vassal was stronger than the French kings, and this ambiguous situation would lead to repeated tensions between the English and French royalty over these possessions in France (see Chapter 9).

Henry I (r. 1100–1135) was as able an administrator as William I. To make the *curia regis* more efficient, Henry created separate departments.

> **Henry I and II**

The financial department—known as the exchequer—with a chancellor at its head, became extremely important in making sure the crown remained fiscally solvent. Wealth remained the mainstay of power for the medieval monarchies; the other source was the law. Henry I used the law courts to maintain royal control over his vassals. However, a civil war over succession erupted after Henry's death, and during this time of troubles, the monarchy was weakened at the expense of strong nobles. It would take another strong monarch to restore the power of the kings. England found this monarch in Henry II (r. 1154–1189).

Henry II (who introduced the Angevin dynasty of English kings) left a permanent impact on the government and law of England. He continued Henry I's fiscal policies and expanded royal control of justice in the land. He sent traveling justices (called Justices in Eyre) empowered with royal authority around the countryside. They traveled regularly to the courts of the shire investigating and punishing crimes. Henry's legal reforms led to controversies with church courts (described later in this chapter), but they strengthened the power of the king.

Primarily through his marriage, Henry II greatly increased the English holdings in France. In 1152, Henry married Eleanor of Aquitaine, a great heiress (whose first marriage, to the king of France, had been annulled). She brought to the marriage her extensive family estates in France, and **Map 8.4** shows how much of France was under English control. This great English empire was increasingly threatening to the French kings, and it would have been even more so, but Henry and Eleanor's sons dissipated much of the royal wealth and power.

Henry's eldest son, Richard I (r. 1189–1199)—known as "the Lion-Hearted"—much preferred fighting to administering the land, and he spent all but ten months of his reign on campaign outside England. He died from a neglected wound received when he was besieging a castle, and the crown went to his younger brother, John.

The reign of John (r. 1199–1216) was marked by a series of humiliations. He fought costly wars in Normandy to try to defend his possessions against the French king's intrusions. To raise money, John departed from feudal custom in many regards; for example, he married heiresses to the highest bidders and even extorted money from his subjects.

Finally, in the spring of 1215, the barons, disgusted by John's high-handed behavior, staged a rebellion. They even took over London, forcing the king to retreat to a broad field south of the city. There, under

> **Magna Carta**

duress, John signed the **Magna Carta** (the Great Charter), which asserted that kings were not above the law. Beyond establishing this general principle, the charter was a feudal document that promised the king would not impinge on noblemen's traditional rights. However, the charter also included two principles that shaped the future of English (and North American) law: The king would impose no new taxes without the consent of the governed and would not violate the due process of law. This document is treasured as one of the precedents of constitutional law.

Another central institution that arose in the Middle Ages with special implications for England was **Parliament.** As part of their feudal obligations, nobles were to give advice to their lords, and kings all over Europe gathered their vassals and wealthy townspeople in councils—called parliaments—to discuss matters of the realm, which included everything from justice to collecting new taxes. In England in

> **Parliament**

KEY DATES

RISE OF PARLIAMENT IN ENGLAND

1066	William of Normandy conquers England
1066–ca. 1086	*Domesday Book* surveys English lands
1154–1189	Henry II strengthens royal laws
1170	Thomas Becket killed in Canterbury
1215	John signs Magna Carta; king not above law
1295	Edward I's Model Parliament

MAP 8.4

Medieval France, England, and Germany, Tenth through Fourteenth Centuries

This map shows England, with the major cities and battles of the eleventh century, and the patchwork of lands that made up France and Germany. It also traces the slow centralization of royal control in France.

Explore the Map

1. How did the French royal domain expand over the centuries? What do the fragmented acquisitions suggest about how the lands were acquired?

2. Where is Flanders? What geographic advantages made it a profitable outlet for English wool?

3. Why might it have been difficult to centralize the Holy Roman Empire?

Lands of the French and English Kings

- 987
- 987–1180
- 1180–1328
- English Holdings in France 1180
- English and its French Lands 1328
- Holy Roman Empire ca. 1200
- Battle Sites

the thirteenth century, this council took a significant turn and became an institution that was able to restrict the power of the king.

The English king Edward I (r. 1272–1307) desperately needed new taxes to finance his wars. Ordinarily English kings asked their nobles in parliament to give additional aid and then sent their agents to cities throughout the land asking for additional money from wealthy merchants. Edward simplified this process by calling for two knights from every county and two burgesses, or townsmen, from every city "to be elected without delay, and to . . . come to us at the aforesaid time and place."

This body with its expanded representation was called the Model Parliament, and it became precedent setting. As they gathered, the knights and the lower nobility sat with the burgesses and began to act together for their mutual benefit, while the clergy sat with the upper nobility. In time, the nobles would become the House of Lords, and the burgesses with the lower nobility, the House of Commons. At first, the House of Commons did little more than approve the rulings of the lords, but in time this institution came to rule England.

The Spanish Reconquer Their Lands

On the Iberian Peninsula, kings and nobles still fought over the issue of centralization, but a larger political problem—the reconquest of Muslim lands—overshadowed this concern. Land that in other countries might have been held by the nobility emerged as small individual kingdoms—Aragon, Leon-Castile, and Navarre (see **Map 8.5**). These kingdoms sometimes presented a united front to the Muslims and other times fought each other to increase their power. With the threat of the Muslims constantly lurking on their borders, they simply could not afford to focus on unifying the Iberian kingdoms. In the twelfth century, Portugal continued the forces of decentralization

MAP 8.5

Christian Expansion in Iberia

This map shows the location of the Christian kingdoms on the Iberian Peninsula, tracing their expansion southward into the Muslim territories, with dates.

Explore the Map

1. Why was Toledo so important strategically to the Iberians?

2. Where is Santiago de Compostela, an important pilgrimage site? How might its location have stimulated the reconquest?

3. Where is Majorca, the birthplace of Ramón Lull, who is profiled in this chapter's Biography? How does this location help to explain why Lull was drawn to North Africa?

Christian Territory, ca. 900
Reconquista, ca. 900–1150
Reconquista, ca. 1150–1250
Muslim Holdings, ca. 1250

when it emerged as a separate kingdom. Portugal had once been part of Leon, but King Alfonso VI (r. 1065–1109) gave it as an independent country to his illegitimate daughter and her crusader husband.

Map 8.5 shows the Iberians' slow reconquest of the peninsula from the Muslims. As the map indicates, each Iberian kingdom pursued its expansion southward at the expense of the Muslims. Kings then consolidated their hold on the new lands by establishing Christian settlers and building castles on the border lands. To encourage town settlements, which brought in profitable taxation, kings often gave privileges to Muslim and Jewish artisans and merchants. With this policy, the Iberian Peninsula became a hub for the fertile exchange of ideas among the three religious cultures.

| The reconquest

The miraculous tenth-century discovery of the bones of Saint James the Elder stepped up the crusading zeal of the Iberian Christians. A peasant discovered the relics after a vision of brilliant stars shining over a field revealed their location to him. A great shrine—Santiago de Compostela (St. James of the Starry Field)—was built to house the bones. This shrine became a renowned pilgrimage site, attracting the faithful from as far away as Scandinavia. Such pilgrims brought both money and arms, which supported

the Iberians' battle against the Muslims. Visitors to the shrine also brought artistic talent, and traveling builders designed and built great Gothic churches along the pilgrimage route. Christian warriors believed that Saint James appeared on a white horse at the front of Christian armies. Their faith seems to have spurred on their efforts.

The Iberian armies fighting in the culturally diverse land made a significant contribution to the intellectual life of western Europe, for in 1085, King Alfonso VI retook the important city of Toledo, which dominated the peninsula's central plateau. There, churchmen following Alfonso's army recovered the precious manuscripts of Aristotle and the Muslim and Jewish scholars (discussed earlier) that made such an impact on the universities of Europe. As **Map 8.5** shows, by the late thirteenth century, the Muslim lands had dwindled to the city of Granada in the south and the surrounding countryside.

France and Its Patient Kings

Late in the tenth century, the Carolingian family finally lost the royal title west of the Rhine. The descendants of Charlemagne had not exercised effective control of the great feudal princes for a hundred years, yet the title of king still brought some measure of prestige. In 987, Hugh Capet, the lord of the Île-de-France (the region surrounding Paris), was elected by the nobles to the French throne. The church legitimized his rule and a new dynasty was in place in France (see **Map 8.4,** on page 263). The rule of the Capetians involved a long history of slowly reasserting control over the great nobles of their lands. As **Map 8.4** also shows, the kings had to wrestle with the problem of the extensive English holdings in France.

The history of France from the tenth through the fourteenth century suggests the patience of the French kings. **Map 8.4** shows how they gained control over one province after another. These monarchs seldom resorted to war and conquest, but used the means provided under feudal contract law to bring regions back under their control. They also made prudent marriages with wealthy heiresses who brought their inheritances back into royal control. Perhaps most important, the Capetians were fortunate enough to produce sons to inherit their throne.

Philip II Augustus (r. 1180–1223) made great strides in centralizing his lands by directly addressing the English holdings. In wars against the English, Philip finally defeated King John and took over the English lands of Normandy, Maine, and Anjou (see **Map 8.4**). Through these conquests, Philip quadrupled the income of the French monarchy. This talented king recognized the need to develop new ways to maintain his control over the widely dispersed patchwork that was France. Instead of relying on the feudal hierarchy to govern locally, he appointed salaried officials—bailiffs—to collect taxes and represent his interests. These ambitious men, most well educated at the University of Paris, did much to strengthen royal power at the expense of the feudal nobility.

Capetian dynasty

The fortunes of the Capetians were dramatically forwarded by Louis IX (r. 1226–1270), whom many consider the greatest of the medieval kings. He was a pious man who went to church at least twice a day and cared for the poor and sick, and he achieved a distinction highly unusual for a king: he was proclaimed a saint by the church.

Louis IX

For all his piety, Louis did not neglect matters of the realm. Although he did not try to extend the royal domain, he nevertheless expected his nobles to be good vassals. He also took an interest in law and justice and wanted royal justice to be available to all his subjects. The king himself liked to sit in the open under a great oak to receive petitions. **Figure 8.11** shows Louis listening to the pleas of his humble

FIGURE 8.11 King Louis in Judgment   The French king Louis IX was known for the fairness of his personal judgments. In this two-part illustration, the guilty receive swift capital punishment by hanging (left), and Louis' subjects bring petitions to the king (right).

subjects—a monk and women. On the left, hanged criminals dangle from trees, demonstrating that the saintly king kept good order in his land. However, Louis did more than dispense personal justice; his advisors began to codify the laws of France, and he was the first king to legislate for all of France. Finally, Louis confirmed the Parlement of Paris—a court, not a representative assembly—as the highest court in France. (It held this position until 1789.) Saint Louis died while on crusade, and his successors continued to ride the Capetian momentum, slowly centralizing their authority.

King Philip IV "the Fair" (r. 1285–1314) believed that the greatest obstacle to his power was Edward I of England and his extensive French fief of Gascony (see **Map 8.4**). Philip engaged in intermittent wars against Edward from 1294 to 1302 and even tried to attack the important English wool industry by blocking importation of English wool into Flanders, but the Flemish towns revolted against him. All these wars were expensive and drove Philip to look for additional funds. The king tried to collect money from the church, which led to a protracted struggle with Pope Boniface VIII (described fully in Chapter 9).

Philip IV

In 1302, Philip needed the support of the realm in his struggles against the pope and to raise money, so he summoned representatives from church, nobility, and towns to the first meeting of the **Estates General.** As these men gathered to advise their king, they sat according to the medieval order—those who prayed, fought, and worked (including townsmen) deliberated separately. This triple arrangement, so different from the two houses of Parliament that grew up in England, helped diffuse each group's power, allowing kings to maintain tight control. This had dramatic consequences for the future of France.

By the end of the thirteenth century, the French monarchy was the best governed and wealthiest in Europe. It was a power to be reckoned with, but there were clouds on the horizon. The Flemish towns remained defiant, England continued to hold and contest lands in France, and the religious struggles had just begun. Philip's successors would face great difficulties.

The Myth of Universal Rule:
The Holy Roman Empire

Map 8.4 depicts a large, seemingly powerful neighbor—the Holy Roman Empire—looming to the east of France. But that empire was not as potent as its size might suggest. Early in the tenth century, the last direct descendant of Charlemagne died. The German dukes recognized the need for a leader and, in 919, elected one of their number (Henry of Saxony) to be king. His descendants held the German monarchy until 1024.

The most powerful of this line of kings was Otto I (r. 936–973), who restored the title of emperor. Otto in many ways resembled Charlemagne. He was a war-

Saxon dynasty

rior king who stopped the advance of the Magyars in 955 and won further conquests in northern Italy. Also like Charlemagne, Otto fostered a revival of learning in Germany in which literature and art flourished. (Otto had married a Byzantine princess, and she brought artists from Byzantium to enhance the German court.) Finally, the German king marched into Rome to receive the crown of the Roman emperor from Pope John XII, much as Charlemagne had done a century and a half earlier. For hundreds of years after this ceremony, an emperor would be proclaimed in German lands—later to be called the Holy Roman Empire. However, it is one thing to claim a far-flung empire and quite another to exert consistent control over it. Like other rulers in the west, Otto and his successors faced repeated challenges from the strength of the independent nobles within their lands. (**Map 8.4** shows many of the principalities within the empire.)

The Ottonian dynasty ended in 1024, and the German nobles selected Henry III (r. 1039–1056) from another branch of the Saxon

Salian dynasty

family. Henry began the Salian dynasty of Germany. He was an able king who looked for ways to exert more control in his lands, and he increasingly used bishops and abbots that he appointed as his administrators. When his son Henry IV (r. 1056–1106) tried to continue that

policy, he ignited a firestorm of debate called the investiture controversy (see page 267).

The Emperor Frederick I (r. 1152–1190), known as Barbarossa, or "red-beard," elected from the house of Hohenstaufen, came close to establishing a consolidated German empire. He planned to exert tight control over three contiguous regions that could form the core of royal lands. He had inherited Burgundy (see **Map 8.4**) and Swabia and invaded Italy to subdue Lombardy in the north. However, while this policy was theoretically sound, it proved ill

Hohenstaufen dynasty

conceived, and the German emperors were weakened by their continued involvement in Italian politics. Italy's city-states and a strong papacy refused to submit to German rule. The resulting, almost incessant, wars in Italy drained rather than strengthened the emperors' resources.

The rule of Emperor Frederick II Hohenstaufen (r. 1215–1250) effectively ended any chance of a unified German monarchy. Frederick was a brilliant ruler and patron of the arts, who had been raised in Sicily and had come to love the diverse Muslim and Christian cultures that coexisted in that sunny land. His policy was to confer upon the German princes and nobility virtual sovereignty within their own territories—he retained only the right to set the foreign policy of the empire. His goal was to take as much profit as possible from the German lands but focus his rule in Italy—particularly the Kingdom of the Two Sicilies in the south.

In southern Italy, he rigorously centralized his administration and imposed a monetary tax on all his subjects. He used Muslims as soldiers and was reputed to have a harem of Muslim women. He turned Sicily into a highly organized and culturally exciting monarchy, guided by his firm rule. Although many historians praise Frederick as the first modern ruler—highly organized and practically calculating—the pope and the northern Italian towns feared his expanding policies in Italy. Their fears were well founded, for Frederick led a campaign against the cities of northern Italy (the Lombard League) and scored some victories in 1237. The popes and the towns feared Frederick's encirclement. The pope excommunicated Frederick, and both sides conducted public relations campaigns to discredit the other. Frederick's attempts to unify Italy ended with his death in 1250.

The German princes wanted to preserve the freedoms they had acquired under Frederick II, so they elected a man they considered a weak prince—Rudolph of

Habsburg dynasty

Habsburg—as emperor. Eventually, the Habsburgs acquired the duchies of Austria, which became the chief foundation for the powerful Habsburg dynasty (see Chapter 11). Burdened by independent nobles and worn down by political trouble in Italy, medieval German emperors had little hope of holding their so-called empire together.

THOSE WHO PRAY: IMPERIAL POPES AND EXPANDING CHRISTENDOM

Like the monarchies that had seen their political power fragment during the tumultuous tenth century, the church, too, had decentralized. Local lords saw the churches on their manors as their own property and priests as their own vassals. Nobles sometimes treated bishoprics as rewards for loyal subjects rather than as religious positions. Critics of these practices began to voice demands for reform; and reformers sought an authentic leader who could preside over a universal Christendom.

A Call for Church Reform

One obvious candidate to reform the church was the Holy Roman Emperor. In 1046, when the German Henry III (r. 1039–1056) traveled to Rome to receive the imperial crown, he found the papacy dominated by Roman aristocrats and interfamilial disputes. When he arrived, three rival popes were vying for power. He deposed them all and established a pope (Clement II) loyal to Henry and a strengthened papal court. In the search for order in the Christian world, it seemed that the German emperors might preside over a unified Christendom.

But the eleventh-century popes also began to step forward as a force for reform. Pope Nicholas II (r. 1058–1061) began to free the papacy from military dependence on the German emperor by allying himself with the Normans in southern Italy. However, he also recognized that the church as a whole needed to be free from lay intervention. He was the first pope who expressly condemned the practice of lay investiture: Popes disapproved of a layperson (a secular ruler) giving a churchman the symbols of spiritual office (the ring and staff) because it appeared that the ruler was the source of spiritual authority. Nicholas was not able to stop that long-standing practice, but his voice would not be the last on this subject. However, he was able to move the selection of popes from lay interference, for he called a Roman council in 1059, which defined the principles by which popes were chosen by a college of cardinals, a practice that continues today. It seemed as if the popes might be able to preside over a unified Christendom.

Calls for church reform also came from another source: The ecclesiastical network of Cluniac monasteries that had been established in the early tenth century (see Chapter 7) began to raise its voice. From their foundation, Cluniacs had supported a strong papacy, and their influence increased even further when a cardinal highly sympathetic to the Cluniac order became Pope Gregory VII (r. 1073–1085). Gregory decided that popes, not kings or emperors, should guide Christendom. This outlook led him directly into conflict with the Holy Roman emperor Henry IV (r. 1056–1106).

The Investiture Controversy

The controversy between Gregory and Henry was triggered by the question of who should appoint or invest bishops in Germany, a matter that was as much political as religious. As we have seen, the emperors had used their right to choose bishops to appoint men to act as royal representatives throughout the lands of their independence-hungry nobles. The pope also understood the importance of having allies in distant lands, and he wanted his loyal men in the German churches. This controversy arose out of the dual allegiances bishops faced—to whom did they owe their principal loyalty, pope or king? Through the struggle, the two sides liberally wielded their weapons: Henry sent his armies marching into Italy; Gregory threatened to excommunicate the emperor (and indeed later did so), claiming that this action could free the ever-rebellious vassals from their feudal obligations. Gregory also had the support of a powerful patron, Matilda, Countess of Tuscany. This skilled tactician promptly challenged Henry's military strength, leading her own armies into battle against him.

Figure 8.12 shows a crucial incident in the investiture controversy. Henry IV kneels at Matilda's feet, while she is shown framed by her strong castle of Canossa. He begs her and Abbot Hugh of Cluny to intercede for him so that he may receive forgiveness from the pope, which Henry desperately needed to control his princes who saw this dispute as a way to gain more independence. This illustration also reveals the important roles both Matilda and the monks of Cluny played in the controversy, but the question of the independence of the church would not be easily solved. In a dramatic incident at Canossa, Henry waited three days in the snow dressed in the sackcloth of a penitent begging the pope's forgiveness. Gregory as a priest was obliged to forgive a sinner professing sorrow, so the two temporarily made peace.

Within three years, pope and king were again locked in combat. This time, however, when Henry invaded Italy, Gregory's Norman mercenaries caused so much damage in Rome that the outraged citizens forced the pope to abandon the city. He died in exile in 1085, bitterly convinced he had failed in forwarding papal authority. But Henry was unable to secure a decisive victory, either, and spent the remainder of his life trying to recover his authority in Germany. The issue of investiture was left for a later king and pope to resolve.

In 1122 the new emperor, Henry V, negotiated a compromise in the investiture controversy, the Concordat of Worms. Pope and emperor decided the pope could present new bishops with their symbols of office, indicating the priority of the church over its churchmen. However, the emperor could be present at and influence the elections of bishops. This compromise actually represented a victory for the popes, who now had an opening for exerting authority within the rising national monarchies all over Europe. But the papal victory would not come easily or unopposed.

Such tensions persisted between clergy and lay rulers who wanted to strengthen their own rule in their home territories. In England, the struggle took the form of a deadly clash between King Henry II (r. 1154–1189) and his archbishop and once best friend, Thomas Becket. Becket wanted to preserve the church's right to be exempt from the legal authority Henry was using to consolidate his power over his land. One day, a small group of knights seeking to please their king surprised Becket in his church at Canterbury and split his head with their swords. Becket died on the altar he had served so well. Their plan to eliminate the influence of the archbishop backfired, however: Becket quickly became a martyr in the battle for church autonomy. In the face of popular revulsion for the crime, Henry was forced to compromise with the pope to gain forgiveness for his archbishop's murder. Henry had to allow the papacy to be the court of appeal from English ecclesiastical courts, and this concession brought the English church more closely into the sphere of Rome.

FIGURE 8.12 Henry IV and Matilda of Tuscany, twelfth century This image captures the importance of the noblewoman Matilda of Tuscany in the investiture controversy, for it shows Holy Roman emperor Henry IV being forced to kneel before her and ask for her intercession. The stylized castle surrounding Matilda symbolizes her power.

The power of the popes grew; the example of Becket showed that their weapons of excommunication and spiritual leadership were impossible to fight with swords. As church power grew, the papacy developed structures that increasingly resembled the powerful medieval monarchies. Just as monarchs began to rely on bureaucracy, court systems, and money to consolidate their power, the pope created a papal curia—an administrative unit—to handle financial matters. He also created a branch to handle legal appeals with the growing body of canon law, which was the compilations of religious laws that slowly came to govern much of medieval life.

By the beginning of the thirteenth century, popes could with some accuracy claim that they presided over a universal Christendom, and one of the most powerful was Innocent III (r. 1198–1216). Innocent was able to exert leadership over princes of Europe: He reprimanded the kings of England, Aragon, Portugal, France, Poland, and Norway and insisted that they obey him. He vigorously fought heretics and wanted to clarify Christian belief. To accomplish the latter, he called the Fourth Lateran Council, which met in 1215. Among other things, this council identified exactly seven sacraments and reaffirmed their

THE MEDIEVAL CHURCH

1073–1085	Pope Gregory VII
1075–1122	Investiture controversy
1095	Urban II calls First Crusade
1198–1216	Pope Innocent III
1204	Fourth Crusade takes Constantinople
1209	Franciscan order established
1209–1213	Albigensian crusade
1212	Order of Poor Clares established
1215	Fourth Lateran Council; Dominican order established
1231	Inquisition founded
1291	Muslims retake Acre, ending Crusades

KEY DATES

essential role in reaching salvation. The council also pronounced on many other matters, from qualifications for the priesthood to monastic life and veneration of relics. With the clarity expressed by the council, the medieval church was firmly defined. In effect, the church had become an empire that superseded all other empires.

The Byzantine Empire Struggles

The Byzantine Empire had reached the height of its expansion and power in 1056, but in the late eleventh century troubles flared up. The Byzantine army, once built so firmly on the theme system (see **Map 6.3**), had deteriorated, and the emperors had begun to use mercenary soldiers, who were expensive to maintain. When the empire became vulnerable on several fronts in the late eleventh century, neither the army nor the treasury was prepared. The Normans threatened Byzantine provinces in southern Italy, and the Muslims menaced in the east.

Islam had gained strength from the movement of the Seljuk Turks, a fierce central Asian tribe whose members had converted to Islam and reinforced the Muslim armies threatening Byzantium. In the midst of succession problems, Byzantium elected a strong soldier—Ramonos Diogenes (r. 1068–1071)—as emperor. Diogenes led an army east in 1071 and challenged the Turks. However, he experienced a crushing defeat at the Battle of Manzikert, and this loss triggered another succession crisis in the capital. Meanwhile, the victorious Turks drove deeper into the empire, capturing all of Asia Minor and taking control of some of the Byzantines' richest lands.

In Byzantium's darkest days, a strong new emperor, Alexius Komnenus (r. 1081–1118), emerged and managed to halt the imperial disintegration. (See Document 8.2 for Princess Anna Komnene's description of the problems her father faced when he took power.) Alexius built a new army based on feudal ties, raised taxes, and desperately cast about for ways to check the Turkish advance. Remembering the skilled knights whom his forces had fought in Sicily, Alexius looked to the West for help. His appeal found fertile ground with a papacy looking for a cause.

Christians on the March: The Crusades, 1096–1291

From as early as the fourth century, Christians had begun to visit holy places, and with the prosperity of the eleventh century, these pilgrimages became even more popular. One of the favorite pilgrimage destinations (along with Santiago de Compostela, described earlier) was Palestine, where Jesus had lived. Sometimes bands of thousands traveled, and when they journeyed to the Holy Land, they passed through Byzantine lands to reach the Muslim territories that included the holy places. For centuries, these trips—albeit hazardous—were possible.

The Turks, who now controlled Jerusalem, did not consciously stop the pilgrim traffic, but they did impose taxes on travelers, and to many Christians it seemed that the Holy Land should not be controlled by these Turks. When Emperor Alexius sent an appeal to Pope Urban II (r. 1088–1099) pleading for help to supplement his forces, the pope was ready to respond. In 1095, Urban called for Christians to begin a holy war against the newly strengthened Muslims.

The text of Urban's speech was preserved by several (sometimes conflicting) chroniclers, yet all agree that it shows a clear perception of the needs of the West and the motives of crusaders. Urban reminds his audience that | Pope Urban's call western Europe is becoming too confining: "For this land which you inhabit, . . . is too narrow for your large population; nor does it abound in wealth; and it furnishes scarcely food enough for its cultivators." He further promised crusaders remission of sins if they undertook this journey. Urban's call was spectacularly successful, and members of the aristocracy began to plan the journey to the Holy Land.

Urban told departing soldiers to wear the sign of the cross on their breasts and encouraged them to earn the right to wear the symbol on their back when they returned, a symbol proving they had successfully fulfilled their vow to fight in this holy cause. The series of military engagements against the Muslims that continued for two hundred years are called the **Crusades,** named for the cross under which the Christians fought. People went on crusade for a number of reasons. Many were driven by sincere religious motivation, although their lofty purposes frequently deteriorated in the heat of battle. Some propertyless nobles hoped to find some land of their own, and other people sought wealth to bring home.

People responded to Urban's call with a fervor that surprised even the planners of the crusade. The first to respond included large numbers of peasants who followed two self-appointed leaders—Peter the Hermit and Walter the Penniless—to the east to free the Holy Land. Long before they reached the Holy Land, their zeal led to violence in the West. They terrorized local people, looting for food and supplies to take on their way. A contemporary chronicler also told how their religious fervor led to other violence: "Led by their zeal for Christianity, they persecuted the hated race of the Jews wherever they were found and strove either to destroy them completely or to compel them to become Christians." These early excesses would mark many of the subsequent crusades. When these peasants arrived in Constantinople, the emperor quickly shipped them over to Asia Minor, where they were massacred by the Turks.

DOCUMENT 8.2

Princess Anna Komnene Writes of Byzantium's Troubles

The Byzantine emperor Alexius's daughter Anna was a highly educated, skilled writer. In the twelfth century, she wrote The Alexiad, *a history of her father's reign. Anna was a valuable eyewitness to the First Crusade and to the growing animosity between western Europeans (whom she called Franks) and the Byzantines. In these excerpts, she offers a clear assessment of the weaknesses of the Byzantine Empire that led Alexius to seek help from the West.*

Book 3: IX   Alexius saw that the Empire was nearly at its last gasp, for in the East the Turks were grievously harassing the frontiers whilst in the West things were very bad. . . . Consequently the young and brave Emperor was desperate, and did not know which way to turn first, as each of his enemies seemed to be trying to begin war before the other, and thus he grew sorely vexed and disturbed. For the Roman Empire possessed only a very insufficient army (not more than the 300 soldiers from Coma cowardly and inexperienced in war, besides just a few very barbarian troops, accustomed to carry their swords on their right shoulder). And further there was no large reserve of money in the imperial treasury with which to hire allied troops from foreign countries. For the preceding Emperors had been very inefficient in all military and warlike matters and had thus driven the State of Rome into very dire straits. . . .

Book 3: X   Before he had enjoyed even a short rest, he heard a report of the approach of innumerable Frankish armies. Now he dreaded their arrival for he knew their irresistible manner of attack, their unstable and mobile character and all the peculiar natural and concomitant characteristics which the Frank retains throughout; and he also knew that they were always agape for money, and seemed to disregard their truces readily for any reason that cropped up. For he had always heard this reported of them, and found it very true. However, he did not lose heart, but prepared himself in every way so that, when the occasion called, he would be ready for battle. And indeed the actual facts were far greater and more terrible than rumor made them. For the whole of the West and all the barbarian tribes which dwell between the further side of the Adriatic and the pillars of Heracles, had all migrated in a body and were marching into Asia through the intervening Europe, and were making the journey with all their household. The reason of this upheaval was more or less the following. A certain Frank, Peter by name, nicknamed Cucupeter [Peter of the Cowl], had gone to worship at the Holy Sepulchre and after suffering many things at the hands of the Turks and Saracens who were ravaging Asia, he got back to his own country with difficulty. But he was angry at having failed in his object, and wanted to undertake the same journey again. However, he saw that he ought not to make the journey to the Holy Sepulchre alone again, lest worse things befall him, so he worked out a cunning plan. This was to preach in all the Latin countries that "the voice of God bids me announce to all the Counts in France that they should all leave their homes and set out to worship at the Holy Sepulchre, and to endeavor wholeheartedly with hand and mind to deliver Jerusalem from the hand of the Hagarenes [Muslims]." And he really succeeded. For after inspiring the souls of all with this quasi-divine command he contrived to assemble the Franks from all sides, one after the other, with arms, horses and all the other paraphernalia of war. And they were all so zealous and eager that every highroad was full of them. And those Frankish soldiers were accompanied by an unarmed host more numerous than the sand or the stars, carrying palms and crosses on their shoulders; women and children, too, came away from their countries. And the sight of them was like many rivers streaming from all sides, and they were advancing towards us through Dacia generally with all their hosts.

SOURCE: Anna Comnena (Komnene), *The Alexiad*, ed. and trans. Elizabeth A. Dawes (London: Routledge, Kegan, Paul, 1928).

Analyze the Document

1. What weaknesses in the Byzantine Empire does Anna Komnene describe?

2. Why, according to Anna, did the Franks come to crusade? Why do you think she does not attribute their arrival to Alexius's summons?

3. What characteristics does she attribute to the Franks?

4. How might a Western observer have described the same events?

The earliest crusaders were vividly described by the Byzantine emperor's daughter Anna Komnene in *The Alexiad*, a history of her father's reign. In addition to offering a first-person account of the crusaders, Anna sheds light on the mutual suspicion and ill will that divided Byzantines from westerners (whom she called Franks) and forecasts a future deterioration of the crusading ideal. In contrast to Komnene, western sources describe the crusaders as fulfilling a high purpose: "The Franks straightway began to sew the cross on the right shoulders of their garments, saying that they would all with one accord follow in the footsteps of Christ." These contrasting accounts underscored the widening split between East and West, which was fueled by a fundamental misunderstanding: The crusaders wanted land in exchange for their military

MAP 8.6

The Early Crusades, 1096–1192

This map shows the dates, routes, and major battles of the first three crusades.

Explore the Map

1. What were the advantages and disadvantages of the two routes to the Holy Land—by land and by sea?

2. How difficult would it have been to reinforce the crusader states and to hold that outpost given that it took the earliest crusaders about nine months to reach the Holy Land?

3. Which of the crusader states might have been the most vulnerable and first to fall? Why?

service (western-style feudalism), but Alexius just wanted to pay them and have them turn over the land to him. The Muslims wanted them all to stay away from their lands.

Anna Komnene's "soldiers of fortune" were highly skilled and successful warriors, and they relentlessly swept the Muslim forces out of the Holy Land. In 1099, when they took Jerusalem after a five-week siege, the carnage was brutal. The eyewitness Fulcher of Chartres tells of the bloodshed: "Within Solomon's Temple, about ten thousand were beheaded. If you had been there, your feet would have been stained up to the ankles with the blood of the slain." When the

violence died down, the crusaders took the Holy Land and established kingdoms there. **Map 8.6** shows the routes of the Crusades and the locations of the crusader states.

The crusader principalities served as outposts of western European culture in the East. They entertained pilgrims, fought skirmishes on their borders, and learned about life in the eastern Mediterranean. Generations of western Europeans living in proximity with Muslims were changed somewhat by the interactions. They learned to eat different foods, began to value bathing, and acquired a taste for urban life,

Crusader states

Those Who Pray: Imperial Popes and Expanding Christendom   271

unlike their rural cousins at home. Even a Muslim chronicler noticed the transformation: "Everyone who is a fresh emigrant from the Frankish lands is ruder in character than those who have become acclimatized and have held long association with Muslims."

However, the official relationship between crusader and Muslim was not friendly. On the Muslim side, the appearance of Christian soldiers reawakened the spirit of jihad that had receded from political policy. (See Chapter 6.) For example, a Syrian legal scholar in the twelfth century wrote a work called the *Book of Holy War,* in which he argued that it was the neglect of jihad that allowed the crusaders to conquer Jerusalem and surrounding areas. His solution was to call for a moral and military resurgence to respond to the crusading movement. But this work was not widely circulated; it established an ideal, but it took until later in the twelfth century for Muslims to rally against crusaders in the spirit of jihad.

The most important determinant of the relations between the two groups was probably geographic. **Map 8.6** shows the precarious location of the crusader states, surrounded by the Muslim world. These states would need constant support from the West to keep them from being retaken by the Muslims.

As early as the 1120s, the Muslims had begun to strike back, and Edessa fell in 1144. Christians in the west mounted further Crusades to support their fellows in the Holy Land, but the subsequent crusades were not as successful as the first, even though some illustrious western kings participated.

Map 8.6 shows the routes and dates of the two subsequent crusades. The Second Crusade was urged on

Subsequent crusades

by Bernard of Clairveaux (Peter Abelard's foe, described earlier), but the two leaders—King Louis VII of France and Emperor Conrad III of Germany—could not coordinate their efforts enough to make any difference.

Things became worse for the crusader states: The Muslims of Syria produced a vigorous leader named Saladin, who controlled Syria and Egypt. Using the newly invigorated spirit of jihad, Saladin conducted a coordinated force that retook Jerusalem in 1187. Saladin did not permit a massacre of civilians, and he even tolerated a continuation of Christian services, but the West was ablaze with calls for a new crusade. Three major monarchs responded: Emperor Frederick Barbarossa, Richard the Lion-Hearted of England, and Philip II of France. Everyone thought these pillars of chivalry could retake the Holy City, but they, too, had problems coordinating their efforts. After some stunning successes, Frederick Barbarossa drowned while swimming and his army went home. The French king also retreated after some losses, leaving Richard and Saladin to negotiate a settlement

whereby Christian pilgrims could have free access to Jerusalem. However, these concessions seemed humiliating to Christians in the West who unrealistically hoped for a decisive victory.

The Crusades spurred the emergence of new religious orders that followed a monastic rule and that served as a crucial part of the permanent garrison guarding the Holy Land. Their principal function was

Knights Templars

to serve God by fighting Muslims, and Muslims and Christians alike respected their military accomplishments. The Knights Templars, the most famous of these orders, protected pilgrims and served as bankers for those traveling to the Holy Land, but they grew so powerful that many began to resent their strength and organization. Saladin hated the Templars, saying, "Let us rid the earth of the air they breathe," but they remained a central force in the Holy Land. Again, the medieval social order blurred, as one group of those who prayed also began to specialize in warfare.

The noble ideal of crusading deteriorated over time as Christians began to focus less on the Holy Land itself and more on Christendom's perceived enemies. For example, crusading fervor led Christians in Europe to conduct more pogroms (massacres) against Jews in Europe.

Crusading armies also turned on Byzantine Christians as relations between them had continued to deteriorate. In 1182, the man who would become the Byzantine emperor Andronikos (r. 1183–1185), the last of the Komnenian dynasty, allowed a massacre of Latins in Constantinople. Westerners reacted to the slaughter with rage. Andronikos's death ended the strong Komnenian dynasty, and the Byzantine royalty once again was roiled by family feuding, negligence, and corruption. As you can see from **Map 8.7,** in 1204, crusaders were drawn into Byzantine politics and took advantage of the Byzantine disarray. The Fourth Crusade, short of money, first attacked the Christian city of Zara for the Venetians in exchange for their passage to the Holy Land. Then a pretender to the Byzantine throne offered crusaders money to place him in power, and crusaders attacked Byzantium itself. Successful in their mission, they sacked the great city, raping women (some of them nuns) and defiling altars. Despite the pope's condemnation, the westerners divided the empire among themselves and abandoned their plan to go to Jerusalem. They held Byzantium for fifty-seven years—until the Byzantines managed to retake it— but this interim badly weakened the empire, as well as the crusading ideal.

You can follow the continued fortunes of the subsequent crusades on **Map 8.7.** The Seventh and Eighth crusades, led by the saintly French king Louis IX (r. 1226–1270), went to North Africa, where the crusaders failed miserably. Louis died in Tunis.

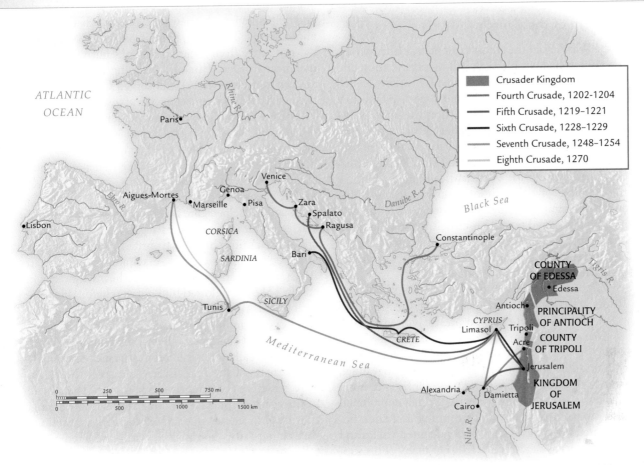

MAP 8.7

The Late Crusades, 1202–1270

This map shows the routes and destinations of the Fourth through the Eighth Crusades.

Explore the Map

1. Why were the county of Edessa and the city of Acre the first and last areas to fall back to the Muslims?

2. Why did several of these crusades never reach the Holy Land?

3. All of these crusades took the sea route to the east. What does this fact suggest about Venice's growth as a sea power?

Perhaps the height of misplaced religious zeal took place during the Children's Crusade (1212–1213), when some preachers argued that crusaders had lost God's help through their misdeeds, and only the innocent might save the Holy Land. The sources say thousands of innocent children died or were sold into slavery during this fiasco. (Some modern historians question whether this appalling incident really occurred.)

Finally, in 1291, the Muslims seized the last crusader outpost on the Asian mainland when the fortified city of Acre fell. This was a terrible military disaster for the West, and the last frightened Christians in the Holy Land paid ship masters fortunes for passage out of the doomed city. Knights Templars died courageously while guarding the evacuation of Christians from the burning city. Two centuries of Christian expansion into the eastern Mediterranean ended with few concrete results. Islam was as strong as ever; Byzantium had only weakened further. For centuries, however, the image of knights galloping across Europe to reclaim the Holy Land from the Muslims continued to captivate Christians throughout the West. The church lost prestige as crusaders lost the Holy Land, but

Crusaders expelled

even more devastating criticism emerged in western Christendom itself.

Criticism of the Church

In the West under the guidance of many skilled popes, the church had established a strong organization and wielded much authority. Yet some Christians, called heretics by the orthodox, disagreed with established doctrine and criticized the direction the church had taken. Some of these people believed that the church had erred in becoming rich as early as the reign of the Roman emperor Constantine (r. 306–337) (discussed in Chapter 5). These critics wanted to follow the example of the apostles described in the Bible and live a simple life by being poor, preaching, and reading the sacred text. This criticism also reflected a new reality in the West—there now existed a richer and increasingly urban world with the kind of visible inequities that seemed worth rejecting.

The best-known proponent of the simple life was Valdes of Lyons. (Later he became incorrectly called Peter Waldo, and he is often remembered by that name.) A rich merchant in his younger years, Valdes gave up all his material possessions in order to wander, beg, and preach. Many ordinary Christians were drawn to the holy simplicity of his life, but churchmen were threatened by his implicit criticism of churches decorated with gold. The pope condemned Valdes and his followers as heretics in 1181, but many of his supporters, called Waldensians, stayed loyal to their beliefs, and in fact, Waldensian churches exist today.

Several similar sects arose that advocated the apostolic life (called *vita apostolica*). Indeed, numerous men and women throughout the Middle Ages continued to consider wealth and Christianity incompatible. Taken together, such movements represented a growing discomfort with a church that seemed too powerful and too embroiled in the gritty details of the physical world to fulfill the spiritual needs of men and women. The thirteenth-century church met these criticisms with both accommodation and repression.

The Church Accommodates: Franciscans and Dominicans

New monastic movements had always been a source of reform for the church and an outlet for men and women who sought different ways of expressing their religious impulses. In the thirteenth century, popes approved two such movements, the Franciscans and the Dominicans, that promised to address the criticism that had arisen so strongly against the church. In previous monastic movements, men and women isolated themselves behind great walls to devote themselves to God. By contrast, the new religious impulses called for holy men and women to mingle among the people in the growing towns of Europe and help alleviate the new problems of urban poverty and suffering. Therefore, Franciscans and Dominicans did not retire from society as monks but were called **mendicant orders** (literally "begging orders," which alludes to their poverty) and served God by helping the needy within their villages and towns.

The Franciscan movement was founded by Francis of Assisi (1182–1226), the son of a wealthy Italian merchant. Like Valdes of Lyon, Francis had a conversion experience that inspired him to give up all his earthly goods to live in poverty. He survived by begging, and he helped care for the poor people of Assisi and other nearby towns. His gentle demeanor and charismatic preaching had broad appeal. Francis attracted a number of followers among the young in Assisi. One young woman, Clare, heard him speak, and in 1212 she followed him into a religious life. She established a mendicant order for women and presided over a group of women dedicated to the same ideals she had embraced. These Poor Ladies of Assisi, sometimes called Poor Clares, became the female counterparts of the Franciscans, but soon their lives were structured differently from that of their male counterparts: Instead of wandering and preaching, they lived in silence in enclosed convents. In spite of this change, this spiritual life still attracted many followers.

Although Franciscans in some ways resembled the Waldensians, who had been condemned as heretics, they differed in one significant respect: They believed in obedience to the pope. Because of this humility, Francis received papal dispensation to establish a new order of "friars," who would live in poverty and preach.

The Franciscans appealed to those who believed in a poor and humble church, but their work did not satisfy all the critics. Many people thought that the church had fallen into error because of ignorance. Another new mendicant order, the Dominicans, arose to address this problem. The Dominicans were led by the Spanish priest Dominic de Guzmán (1170–1221), an intellectual who believed that heresy could be fought through preaching. In 1215, Pope Honorius approved the Order of Preachers, or the Dominicans, who, like the Franciscans, took an oath of poverty and lived among the townspeople instead of in monasteries. However, they emphasized preaching rather than poverty and stressed study at universities to ensure that their preaching was strictly orthodox. The Dominicans thus appealed to people's minds, whereas the Franciscans spoke to their hearts.

Through permitting both of these orders, the church had responded to the spiritual needs of its followers by authorizing dedicated men and women to teach and practice among the people. Christians hungering for a more profound sense of spiritual connectedness welcomed the lessons they received from these pious teachers.

The Church Suppresses: The Albigensian Crusade and the Inquisition

The church did not always prove so accommodating in the face of criticism. In the late twelfth century, a heretical movement became very popular, particularly in southern France. This movement, called Catharism (from the Greek word for "pure"), was similar to Zoroastrianism (described in Chapter 1) in that it professed a system of two principles (or two deities)—light and darkness—fighting for supremacy. Adherents identified the god of darkness with the Old Testament deity who created the world and the god of light with the New Testament and spiritual salvation. They believed that people had to struggle to help the good principle trapped in everyone escape the evil world of the flesh. Because a center of this group was in Albi in southern France, they are also commonly known as Albigensians.

Albigensians were particularly threatening to the church because their ideas struck at the very heart of Christian belief, which considered the material world as good. Pope Innocent III first sent preachers to Albi to show people the error of their ways. However, in 1209, after some violence against papal representatives, the pope lost patience and called a crusade against the heretics. Northern French nobles, eager to break the power of the strong southern lords, participated avidly in the savage campaign. **Figure 8.13** shows Albigensians being expelled from one of the major heretical strongholds of Carcassone. This illustration contrasts the simplicity of the men and women heretics with the fierce crusaders, perhaps revealing some compassion for the heretics, because during the crusade's twenty years, thousands of people were massacred. In one especially tragic example, 7,000 men, women, and children of the town of Béziers took refuge from the crusaders in the local cathedral. When soldiers asked the papal representative how they could distinguish between heretics and the faithful, he reportedly replied, "Kill them all; God will know his own." All 7,000 of the townspeople—heretic and orthodox alike—died that day in the church's attempt to stamp out heresy.

Even after such brutal displays of power, church leaders still felt endangered by diversity of beliefs.

Albigensian Crusade

FIGURE 8.13 Albigensian Crusade The church turned the power of crusade against heretics in southern France, centered in Albi. This illustration documents the expulsion of the Albigensians from the town of Carcassone in 1209; their nudity symbolizes how they lost all their goods.

In the mid-thirteenth century, the church established a new court—the **inquisition**—designed to ferret out and eradicate threatening ideas. Unlike secular courts, which determined the guilt or innocence of actions, the inquisition aimed to detect wrong beliefs. The court recognized the difficulty in examining people's ideas and developed special means by which to determine what people were thinking. Often it relied on the Dominicans, with their training in understanding heresy, to serve as the inquisitor generals. These generals used questioning, starvation, and other forms of torture to force people to reveal their beliefs. Many unfortunate victims "confessed" to escape further torture or execution, and although they were released, many faced extreme "penances," such as renunciation of property or imprisonment. All self-confessed heretics faced severe social repercussions from their neighbors, who no longer wanted to associate with the "guilty." Those who were deemed guilty and unrepentant were turned over to the secular authority to be executed, usually by burning.

The inquisition

The inquisition swept through much of Europe, inflicting more damage in some communities than in others. Perhaps the only way to understand this phenomenon is to remember that people in the Middle Ages were deeply concerned about the state of their souls and their own salvation. They believed that exposure to incorrect religious ideas could jeopardize that salvation, and this was a risk they simply could not take. In their emphasis on community over the individual, they did not share modern beliefs that efforts to save one another from "wrong" ideas potentially put all ideas in peril.

By 1300, many in medieval Europe were convinced that order was established in the world. Bishop Gerard of Cambrai, whose quotation opened this chapter, elaborated on the three-part structure of this perfectly ordered society: Those who pray are able to enjoy this "holy leisure" because of the efforts of those who fight, who guarantee their security. Both of these groups are able to fill their functions because those who work see to the needs of their bodies. The world seemed perfectly appointed.

LOOKING BACK & MOVING FORWARD

Summary At the turn of the first millennium C.E., agricultural innovations sparked a dramatic surge in the European population. This growth fueled an expansion of western European civilization that represented the high point of the Middle Ages. During this time of expansion, western Europeans made great intellectual innovations—philosophical systems, engineering wonders, and creative literature. Kings slowly changed their feudal lands into national monarchies—sometimes by exerting their legal rights and sometimes by violent confrontations with their nobles. The church, too, increased its central power, ultimately claiming to rule over a Europe united in faith, although it had to resort to extreme measures to preserve this fiction.

Finally, the West was strong enough to expand its horizons and again confront the great cultures on its borders and beyond. With the violent Crusades in the eastern Mediterranean, Christians challenged the power of Islam and lost; with the reconquest of Spain, however, Christians prevailed over the Muslims. More significantly, Christians learned much about science, technology, and life from the Muslims. However, this ordered, prosperous age would confront dramatic challenges in the fourteenth century, when disasters would strike. Would medieval structures prove resilient enough to withstand the pressure?

KEY TERMS

communes, *p. 248*

guilds, *p. 248*

Romanesque, *p. 250*

Gothic, *p. 250*

scholasticism, *p. 253*

chivalry, *p. 259*

troubadous, *p. 260*

Magna Carta, *p. 262*

Parliament, *p. 262*

Estates General, *p. 265*

Crusades, *p. 269*

mendicant orders, *p. 274*

inquisition, *p. 275*

REVIEW, ANALYZE, & CONNECT TO TODAY

REVIEW THE PREVIOUS CHAPTER

Chapter 7—"The Struggle to Bring Order"—described manorialism and the feudal contract as the organizing structures of medieval life. It also described the invasions of the ninth and tenth centuries that undermined the developing order in the West.

1. Review the obligations of peasants and the nature of village life described in Chapter 7 and consider the strengths of these structures that allowed for the agricultural boom in the eleventh century.

2. Review the invasions by Vikings and others that caused a decentralization of power and the weakening of kings.

How did this decentralization influence the growth of England and France from the eleventh through the thirteenth century?

ANALYZE THIS CHAPTER

Chapter 8—"Order Restored"—traces the High Middle Ages and follows the fortunes of the social groups and political entities that made up the West.

1. Consider the growth of towns and the related developments of trade. How did towns govern themselves? How was the prevalence of Gothic cathedrals and pilgrimages related to the growing prosperity of towns?

2. One of the themes of this chapter is the struggle between popes and emperors or kings to decide who should lead a Christian Europe. Review these struggles and consider the advantages and disadvantages of each party's position.

3. Review the Crusades. Why did the crusaders go to the Holy Land, and what did they accomplish?

CONNECT TO TODAY

Think about the revolution in technology that fueled the West's growth in the Middle Ages.

1. Are there parallels in recent times with the medieval technological revolution? Explain.

2. What can we learn from the past about how to manage swift technological change?

Think about the long series of Crusades that the West initiated against Islam.

1. What world events today do you think reflect the long-standing Muslim–Western animosity fostered by the Crusades?

2. How do we use the word crusade today? How do you think that usage might contribute to mutual misunderstandings between Christians and Muslims?

BEYOND THE CLASSROOM

THOSE WHO WORK: AGRICULTURAL LABOR

Hanawalt, B. *The Ties That Bind: Peasant Families in Medieval England.* New York: Oxford University Press, 1986. An eminent historian provides a vivid and engaging picture of peasant life.

Schofield, Phillip R. *Peasant and Community in Medieval England, 1200–1500.* New York: Palgrave Macmillan, 2002. A study of peasant life, with an emphasis on interactions between the village and the outside world.

THOSE OUTSIDE THE ORDER: TOWN LIFE

Bennet, Judith M. *Ale, Beer, and Brewsters in England: Women's Work in a Changing World.* Oxford: Oxford University Press, 1999. An excellent discussion of the changing economic roles of women as the medieval economy grew.

Evans, G.R. *Philosophy and Theology in the Middle Ages.* New York: Routledge, 1993. A sound, comprehensive survey of intellectual thought, showing the ties between philosophy and theology.

Pounds, Norman. *The Medieval City,* 2nd ed. Westport, CT: Greenwood Press, 2005. An introduction to medieval towns emphasizing their historical development and functions.

Ridder-Symoens, Hilde de. *A History of the University in Europe: Universities in the Middle Ages.* New York: Cambridge University Press, 1991. Remains the only comprehensive history of medieval universities that includes their social and political context.

Wigelsworth, Jeffrey R. *Science and Technology in Medieval European Life.* Westport, CT: Greenwood Press, 2006. A discussion of the ideas and inventions that made a large impact on all facets of medieval daily life.

THOSE WHO FIGHT: NOBLES AND KNIGHTS

Bartlett, Robert. *The Hanged Man: A Story of Miracle, Memory, and Colonialism in the Middle Ages.* Princeton, NJ: Princeton University Press, 2004. A brief, brilliantly written account of the examination of a purported thirteenth-century miracle in which a hanged rebel was restored to life.

Gies, J., and F. Gies. *Life in a Medieval Castle.* New York: Harper & Row, 1974. A popular, illustrated work that offers a summary of noble life. Although not scholarly, it is nevertheless accurate and engaging.

Poly, Jean-Pierre, and Eric Bournazel. *The Feudal Transformation, 900–1200.* New York: Holmes & Meier, 1991. A scholarly and provocative detailed analysis of French sources to explore ideas of social hierarchy, war and peace, and medieval ideas.

Sanchez, Jose. *Medieval Knights: The Age of Chivalry.* Havertown, PA: Andrea Press, 2008. Beautifully illustrated and comprehensive account of medieval knights—their customs, military strategy, tactics, and social life.

THE RISE OF CENTRALIZED MONARCHIES

Fletcher, Richard. *Moorish Spain.* New York: H. Holt, 1992. A concise survey of the Iberian Peninsula from the Muslim invasion to the fall of Granada that shows the significant impact of the reconquest.

Furman, Horst. *Germany in the High Middle Ages, c. 1050–1200.* Translated by T. Reuter. New York: Cambridge University Press, 1986. A clear and engaging survey of a complex time.

Haines, Roy Martin. *King Edward II: Edward of Carnarfon, His Life, His Reign and Its Aftermath, 1284–1330.* Montreal:

McGill–Queen's University Press, 2006. A comprehensive narrative, backed by careful scholarship, that should remain the definitive work on this important period of English history.

Hallam, Elizabeth M. *Capetian France, 987–1328*. New York: Longman, 1980. A chronicle of the slow consolidation of these French kings as they expanded their power.

THOSE WHO PRAY: IMPERIAL POPES AND EXPANDING CHRISTENDOM

Ladurie, LeRoy. *Montaillou: The Promised Land of Error*. Translated by Barbara Brey. New York: Vintage Books, 1979. A classic study of the inquisition records of Albigensian villagers in southern France that reads like a novel with the insights of a master historian.

Lyons, Malcolm C. *Saladin: The Politics of Holy War*. New York: Cambridge University Press, 1985. A fine study of one of the most remarkable figures involved in the Crusades.

Maalouf, Amin. *The Crusades Through Arab Eyes*. New York: Schocken, 1989. An intriguing work using contemporary Arab sources to illuminate a perspective on crusading seldom discussed, with insights into today's controversies.

Madden, Thomas F. *The New Concise History of the Crusades*, 2nd ed. New York: Rowman & Littlefield, 2005. A thorough yet succinct history of the Crusades, with special attention on their impact on Islam and Byzantium.

Morris, Colin. *The Papal Monarchy: The Western Church from 1050–1250*. New York: Oxford University Press, 1991. Offers a balanced interpretation of the whole structure of the church in the formative central Middle Ages as the popes rose in power.

Peters, Edward. *Inquisition*. Berkeley: University of California Press, 1989. Traces the evolution of the concept of inquisition as represented in modern literature, art, and political theory.

Roach, Andrew. *The Devil's World: Heresy and Society 1100–1300 (The Medieval World)*. New York: Longman, 2005. A thorough examination of heresy that argues for a relationship between ideas and social and economic realities.

Sayers, Jane. *Innocent III: Leader of Europe, 1198–1216*. New York: Longman, 1994. Examines all aspects of this influential pontiff.

FOUR HORSEMEN OF THE APOCALYPSE, BEATO DE LIEBANA

MANUSCRIPT, ca. eighth century

In the fourteenth century, Europeans were struck with a series of disasters that seemed to foretell the end of the world, causing many to look to the images of the Four Horsemen of the Apocalypse, described in the Book of Revelation in the New Testament. The rider on the white horse with the bow brought conquest; the second, with a sword, brought war. The rider on the black horse with the scale brought famine and plague, and the final rider, on a pale horse, brought death, which followed close behind him. Survivors at the end of the fourteenth century lived through all these calamities that changed medieval society forever.

The West Struggles and Eastern Empires Flourish

The Late Middle Ages, ca. 1300–1500

"In the year of the Lord 1315, shall begin a great famine on earth. . . . Also the Church shall totter and the line of Saint Peter shall be execrated. Also the blood of many shall be poured out on the ground." A fourteenth-century priest, Jean de Venette, told of this prophecy that appeared in a dream, and it came all too true as the century brought a series of disasters that would break down the medieval order that had seemed so secure a century before.

At the beginning of the century, bad weather ruined harvests and introduced years of famine, which drove many people from their lands to search for food. This misery was compounded when a terrible plague swept in from east Asia and raged through western Europe, killing over a third of the population and bringing fear and despair to many survivors. Peasants in the countryside and urban workers responded by staging revolts that further seemed to attack the social order itself. In the High Middle Ages, people looked to the church and the pope to bring comfort and order, but in the fourteenth century the church too was split by controversy as disputed papal elections brought several popes to power at once. As these disasters swept over Europe, England and France engaged in a violent war—the Hundred Years' War—that brought destruction to civilians and mounted knights alike. In eastern Europe and beyond, new empires threatened western Europe from the outside.

At the end of a century and a half of devastation, the feudal, the manorial, and many of the intellectual structures of the medieval world had been undermined. Many people believed these disasters heralded the end of the world; instead, western Europe was transformed by the horrors that swept over it and moved in exciting new directions.

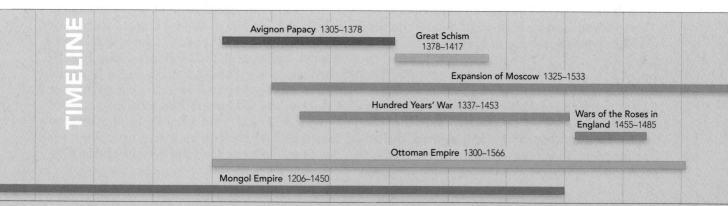

TIMELINE

Avignon Papacy 1305–1378

Great Schism 1378–1417

Expansion of Moscow 1325–1533

Hundred Years' War 1337–1453

Wars of the Roses in England 1455–1485

Ottoman Empire 1300–1566

Mongol Empire 1206–1450

1250 1275 1300 1325 1350 1375 1400 1425 1450 1475 1500

ECONOMIC AND SOCIAL MISERY

The town of Douai in medieval Flanders (now in France) was a prosperous place, where men and women produced woolen cloth in a booming cottage industry that made many merchants rich. Some people spun the wool, others wove it, and still others dyed the cloth. Then they turned it over to the merchants with whom they held their labor contracts. In prosperous times, there were good wages to be had, but early in the fourteenth century, hard times suddenly came. Years of bad harvests began in 1315, and the shops in Douai no longer had enough food to satisfy the town's needs. Tensions erupted in 1322, when rumors spread that the rich merchants were hoarding grain. Many of the cloth workers took to the streets, and in the legal records of the town, we learn that 18 workers—including two women—were arrested in the turmoil. The workers "in the full marketplace" had urged an assault on grain merchants to take the needed food from their warehouses. The two women were charged with being especially vocal, and in punishment they had their tongues cut off before being banished from the city for life. This was only one small incident in a century that brought suffering and despair to many in Europe.

Famine

The growth of European society stemmed mostly from agricultural innovations that had generated the boom of the eleventh century. By 1300, however, the burgeoning population began to put a strain on medieval technology. People were cultivating poorer lands, and crop yields were dwindling; on some marginal lands, farmers might harvest only three bushels for every one planted. After setting aside one bushel to plant the following year, the remainder was hardly enough to maintain a fixed population.

As the population grew, people tried to bring more and more lands into cultivation to make up for the scarcities, and this often resulted in plowing the common fields on which villagers grazed their animals. Unable to feed their livestock, people were forced to kill many of their animals—from one-quarter to one-third of their animals were slaughtered. This significant reduction of livestock also reduced the amount of manure for fertilizer, and yields fell again. By the beginning of the fourteenth century, farmers faced increasing difficulties accumulating a surplus of food—and then the weather worsened.

A series of years with too much rain began in 1310; lands were drenched. Chroniclers all over Europe wrote that the rains—with unusually deafening thunder and terrible lightning—were steady from April throughout the summer. **Bad weather** The winds and overcast skies made the whole growing season abnormally cool. The rains came when the seed had just been scattered—washing much of it away—and continued to fall through the summer, flooding the lower croplands. When farmers tried to harvest the meager crops, the rains came again. Rivers flooded, bridges were swept away, and the crops, with previously low yields, failed.

Famine began in 1315 and, in some parts of Europe, lasted until 1322. During these years, cold winters followed by cool and extraordinarily wet summers brought disastrous harvests. Aching hunger drove peasants from their lands in search of food, and according to some reports, starving farmers at times even resorted to cannibalism. Still, the disasters of this century were only beginning. Many who did not starve suffered from malnutrition and were susceptible to infection. Respiratory illnesses and intestinal ailments reached epidemic proportions in this century, but an even greater threat appeared.

The Black Death: A Pandemic Strikes

In the fourteenth century, a horrible pandemic swept in from the east and devastated Europe. The disease spread over vast areas, helped by increased trade from ships moving through the Mediterranean and by the expansion of the Mongol Empire. There is general agreement that the plague arrived in Europe in about 1348 on ships of Genoese merchants who traveled between Sicily and the Middle East, but the historical consensus about this pandemic ends here. What was this terrifying disease that people in the Middle Ages called the **Black Death?**

MAP 9.1

The Spread of the Black Death

This map tracks the progress of the plague as it spread gradually northward. It also shows how long it took the plague to travel north.

Explore the Map

1. How might weather and travel conditions have delayed the progress of the disease?

2. Compare this map with **Map 8.2.** What relationship do you think there was between trade routes and the plague's progress?

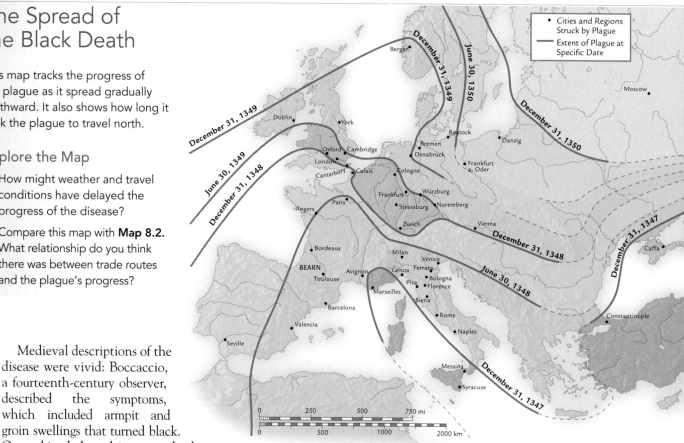

Medieval descriptions of the disease were vivid: Boccaccio, a fourteenth-century observer, described the symptoms, which included armpit and groin swellings that turned black. Once skin darkened in spots, death was virtually certain. This description causes most historians to identify the disease as bubonic plague, caused by a virulent bacillus (*Yersinia pesta*) that infected rodents in Manchuria, then spread to black rats. As we saw in Chapter 1, some of the most devastating diseases have been those that move from animals to humans, and this rodent disease was passed to humans from the bites of infected fleas. Bubonic plague can also reach a person's lungs, becoming pneumonic plague, which spreads rapidly through sneezing and coughing. Estimates are that between 30 and 70 percent of people who catch bubonic plague die, but almost 100 percent of those with pneumonic plague die.

The disease

In modern times, bubonic plague does not spread quickly, which causes some historians to question whether it was indeed the Black Death that brought such destruction. Some argue that this virulent form spread quickly to the lungs, becoming the deadly pneumonic form. Others suggest that several diseases—like smallpox—might have joined bubonic plague in sweeping through a population already weakened from famine. However, recent DNA studies confirm the presence of *Yersinia pestis* in plague cemeteries; so, although other diseases may have joined

forces with the plague in killing a weakened population, the Black Death did cause the devastation.

Whatever the exact disease, the pandemic raced through Europe. It spread quickly in the summer and declined in the winter months—the cold, wet summers helped the plague spread. **Map 9.1** shows the progress of the plague and the dates that the disease moved north from Italy to Scandinavia. The pandemic killed a shocking one-third to one-half of the population, but historians are uncertain of the exact numbers of the dead. Modern estimates agree that one-third of the population died, but they disagree on what that fraction means in actual numbers—estimates range from 20,000,000 to 35,000,000 dead. Disease hit the crowded cities hardest: Paris may have lost half its population and Florence as much as four-fifths. The eyewitness account in Document 9.1 describes the devastation in hard-hit Siena. These staggering numbers mean that everyone—especially in the cities where death rates were highest—saw neighbors, friends, and family members die.

The psychological impact of so great a plague was perhaps even more important than the actual loss of

DOCUMENT 9.1

Agnolo the Fat Survives the Plague

Agnolo di Tura del Grasso lived in Siena, Italy, when the plague struck in 1348. He wrote a chronicle of events from 1300 to 1351 that provides an eyewitness account of the horror. His description of the disease helped historians to identify it with bubonic plague.

The mortality began in Siena in May (1348). It was a cruel and horrible thing; and I do not know where to begin to tell of the cruelty and the pitiless ways. It seemed to almost everyone that one became stupefied by seeing the pain. And it is impossible for the human tongue to recount the awful thing. Indeed one who did not see such horribleness can be called blessed. And the victims died almost immediately. They would swell beneath their armpits and in their groins, and fall over dead while talking. Father abandoned child, wife husband, one brother another; for this illness seemed to strike through the breath and sight. And so they died. And none could be found to bury the dead for money or friendship. Members of a household brought their dead to a ditch as best they could, without priest, without divine offices. Nor did the death bell sound. And in many places in Siena great pits were dug and piled deep with the multitude of dead. And they died by the hundreds both day and night, and all were thrown in those ditches and covered over with earth.

And as soon as those ditches were filled more were dug.

And I, Agnolo di Tura, called the Fat, buried my five children with my own hands. And there were also those who were so sparsely covered with earth that the dogs dragged them forth and devoured many bodies throughout the city. There was no one who wept for any death, for all awaited death. And so many died that all believed that it was the end of the world. And no medicine or any other defense availed. . . . This situation continued until September, and it would take too long to write of it. And it is found that at this time there died in Siena 36,000 persons twenty years of age or less, and the aged and other people [died], to a total of 52,000 in all in Siena. And in the suburbs of Siena 28,000 persons died; so that in all it is found that in the city and suburbs of Siena 80,000 persons died. Thus at this time Siena and its suburbs had more than 30,000 men, and there remained in Siena (alone) less than 10,000 men. And those that survived were like persons distraught and almost without feeling. And many walls and other things were abandoned, and all the mines of silver and gold and copper that existed in Sienese territory were abandoned as is seen; for in the countryside . . . many more people died, many lands and villages were abandoned, and no one remained

there. I will not write of the cruelty that there was in the countryside, of the wolves and wild beasts that ate the poorly buried corpses, and of other cruelties that would be too painful to those who read of them. . . .

The city of Siena seemed almost uninhabited for almost no one was found in the city. And then, when the pestilence abated, all who survived gave themselves over to pleasures: monks, priests, nuns, and lay men and women all enjoyed themselves, and none worried about spending and gambling. And everyone thought himself rich because he had escaped and regained the world, and no one knew how to allow himself to do nothing. . . .

1349. After the great pestilence of the past year each person lived according to his own caprice, and everyone tended to seek pleasure in eating and drinking, hunting, catching birds and gaming. And all money had fallen into the hands of nouveaux riches.

SOURCE: Agnolo di Tura del Grasso, "Plague in Siena: An Italian Chronicle," *Cronica Maggiore* in *Black Death: A Turning Point in History?*, ed. William M. Bowsky (New York: Holt, Rinehart & Winston, 1971), pp. 13–14.

Analyze the Document

1. How did the devastation break down traditional social ties and rituals?

2. How did people react to all the deaths?

3. How did the survivors react?

4. How did the plague contribute to the breakdown of medieval society?

---

life. Law and tradition broke down, and many survivors saw no point in trying to preserve medieval customs. Boccaccio wrote: "In this sore affliction and misery of our city, the authority of the laws, both human and divine, was all dissolved and fell into decay," and he described how many sick died untended in the streets.

> Reaction

At the time, people did not realize that the disease was caused by bacteria and transmitted by fleas. Theories of the Black Death's etiology ranged from punishment by God to "bad air." Victims could expect only traditional treatments from physicians. In **Figure 9.1,** an ill king is attended by his doctors.

One holds his nose to indicate the belief that the disease left an offensive smell owing to the buildup of bad "humors." The physicians have applied leeches, used on previous patients, to the king to remove excessive blood—a lethal practice that is equivalent to sharing needles between patients who have a blood-borne disease.

As medicine failed to offer solace for this horrifying disease, many could only conclude that God's wrath brought the devastation. Responding to this notion, some people resorted to extreme measures to try to bring God's aid against the plague. One group—the

> Flagellants

FIGURE 9.1 Curing the Plague This illustration reflects popular attitudes about the Black Death. A physician holds his nose, expressing the general belief that one of the ways the plague spread was through bad air. Physicians have applied leeches to the king to draw his blood and reduce his fever.

FIGURE 9.2 Flagellants, fifteenth century Many people of the time believed that the plague was caused by the wrath of an angry God. Flagellants—individuals who beat themselves—tried to appease God by staging ritual parades of self-punishment.

flagellants—thought that by inflicting pain on themselves, they could ask God to relieve the suffering of others. **Figure 9.2** shows a group of flagellants banded together in a procession. In this image, the procession is led by men carrying a cross and a dragon as a mark of their brotherhood. Flagellants beat themselves three times a day with leather thongs tipped in lead. They marched from town to town "splashing the church walls with their blood," according to contemporary witnesses. This movement reflected the desperation of people searching for ways to appease a seemingly angry God.

In their fear, some people turned against their neighbors, and in many cities, Jews were accused of bringing the plague by poisoning wells. The persecutions fell particularly heavily on Jewish communities in Germany because periodically throughout the thirteenth century, the English and French kings had forced Jews out of their lands and many had moved eastward. Because there was a larger presence of Jews in Germany, their Christian neighbors used them as a focus of their fears. A contemporary chronicler (Jacob von Konigshofen) described a pogrom in Strasbourg that killed thousands of Jews accused of causing the plague: "On Saturday . . . they burnt the Jews on a wooden platform in their cemetery. There were about two thousand people of them. Many small children were taken out of the fire and baptized against the will of their fathers and mothers." In a practical aside, Jacob noted that the persecutors also had money on their minds, because they confiscated the property of

Attacking Jews

the Jews: "The money was indeed the thing that killed the Jews. If they had been poor and if the feudal lords had not been in debt to them, they would not have been burnt. . . ."

In spite of the foolishness of blaming people who were also dying from the plague, anti-Jewish persecutions spread. More than sixty major Jewish communities in Germany had been destroyed by 1351. Many Jews fled to eastern Europe—to Russia and Poland—where they received protection, and slowly many Jewish communities moved their homes even farther east. Popes would later condemn this irrational persecution.

The plague continued to ravage Europe in waves into the seventeenth and even early eighteenth centuries. These subsequent visitations of the disease also took a large toll on the population. It seems that the plague finally abated when the larger, meaner Norwegian brown rat (today's urban rat) displaced the European black rats. The brown rats had thicker fur, which resisted the flea bites of the black rat fleas, so the disease bacillus slowly lost its host pool. Even though the disease eventually disappeared, it left a legacy of fear and despair that haunted Europe for centuries.

Peasants and Townspeople Revolt

As an immediate result of the plague, the European countryside suffered a disabling shortage of labor. Desperate lords tried to increase their customary—and

FIGURE 9.3 Peasants' Revolt, 1381 The English preacher John Ball, shown on horseback, led peasants and knights in a revolt for better conditions for the peasantry. Although the uprising failed, rural conditions nevertheless improved.

already excessive—labor requirements in an effort to farm their lands. Free laborers, detecting an opportunity, began to demand higher wages, prompting some countries to pass laws freezing earnings. For example, a statute of laborers passed in England in 1351 said, "No one shall pay or promise to pay to anyone more wages . . . or salary than was accustomed." This policy enraged peasants across Europe. Determined to resist, they roamed the countryside, burning manor houses and slaughtering the occupants.

In some of these uprisings, popular preachers arose as leaders who combined social reform with religious hopes. Living in an age crippled by plague and famine, many believed that these "times of troubles" presaged a better world in which Christ would return. (See the Four Horsemen in the chapter opener on page 280.) The most famous of these preachers was John Ball of England, who rallied listeners by calling for the overthrow of the social order: "Oh good people, things . . . will not go well until everything is held in common and there are no more serfs or lords." His most famous couplet attacked the very hierarchical privilege that had marked the three orders of medieval society. He said simply: "When Adam delved and Eve span, where then were all the gentlemen?" When Adam and Eve lived in the Garden of Eden, both worked the soil and no one was a noble "gentleman."

John Ball

The illustration in **Figure 9.3** shows a confrontation between English peasants and the king's forces in 1381. John Ball rides the horse, and another popular preacher—Wat Tyler—stands in the foreground, holding a banner with the English coat of arms. This illustration shows two main things: First, the peasants had the support of well-armed and disciplined soldiers who had been trained to defend the English coast. Second, both sides hold the same royal banners, indicating that the peasants did not blame the king for their misery but remained loyal to the teenaged Richard II (r. 1377–1399). They blamed his advisors and the local nobility for their misery. Their loyalty made no difference in the outcome—the king joined in repressing the revolt.

French peasants, too, rose up against their lords, in a revolt called the **Jacquerie.** French chroniclers told in horror of peasants storming manor houses and brutally killing noblemen and their families. English peasants burned houses of aristocrats, lawyers, and government officials, at times burning the records that they believed contributed to their oppression. However, the peasants in all regions could not hold out for long against the aristocracy and its superior arms. Eventually, all the revolts were suppressed, with many peasants and their leaders massacred. Yet the violence, the labor shortages, and the prevailing belief that things were changing had begun to erode the old medieval manorial system. Over time, peasants who owed only rent gradually replaced serfs who had owed labor as well as rent. For these new peasants, their labor was now their own, giving them more freedom and opportunities to work for their own profit. Although the condition of many peasants improved, the trend was not uniform throughout Europe. The situation of peasants in western Europe improved more quickly than that of those in eastern Europe.

As the anecdote about the town of Douai that opened this chapter indicates, the unrest was not limited to the countryside. As population dropped, the declining demand for goods led to falling prices, and some industries suffered. Merchants and manufacturers responded by trying to limit competition and reduce the freedoms of the lower classes in the towns. Revolts broke out in many towns throughout Europe. In addition to Douai, violence erupted in Ghent, Rouen, and Florence. (This last was the famous Ciompi revolt in 1378—named for the wooden shoes worn by wool workers who rioted.) While some of these revolts led to short-term gains, most were crushed. Improvements for urban workers would eventually come with the labor shortages caused by the high death rates. But the rural and urban revolts of the fourteenth century set off social conflicts that periodically resurfaced throughout Western history.

Urban revolts

IMPERIAL PAPACY BESIEGED

Throughout these troubled times, many medieval men and women looked to the church, especially the papacy, to guide them. Yet the popes were grappling with their own problems, and these very troubles undermined people's confidence in the church. Early in the fourteenth century, the issue of the relative sovereignty of kings and popes resurfaced once more over the taxation of church lands and the clergy's claim to immunity from royal courts. This time, the French king proved stronger than the popes. In the course of this dispute, the French king, Philip IV (r. 1285–1314), ordered his troops to arrest Pope Boniface VIII (r. 1294–1303). Although the elderly pope was quickly freed by his supporters, he died soon afterward as a result of the rough treatment. Unlike Henry II of England after the death of Becket (described in Chapter 8), Philip IV was able to capitalize on the violence against the church. He brought pressure on the college of cardinals—which had elected popes since 1059—and they elected his favored French cardinal as pope.

FIGURE 9.4 Catherine of Siena, ca. 1447 This lavish painting by Paolo di Giovanni Fei documents the significant moment in the papal history when Saint Catherine of Siena persuaded Pope Gregory XI to leave his exile in Avignon and return to Rome.

Popes Move to Avignon

Philip expected this pope to support French interests, and to forward this aim, the king persuaded the pope to rule from Avignon, on the east bank of the Rhône River. Although the city was in the Holy Roman Empire, the French influence there was strong. The new pope, Clement V (r. 1304–1314), complied and set up his court in Avignon. The popes never again tried to exert authority of taxation and legal immunity over the French kings. However, the pope's absence from Rome raised serious issues. After all, the pope was the bishop of Rome and was obligated to be there to guide the faithful in his charge.

For seventy-two years after the election of Clement V, the popes ruled from Avignon—in the shadow of the French king. Many Christians objected to this **"Babylonian Captivity,"** as the Italian Petrarch (1304–1374) called it. Some people believed this shocking breach of tradition contributed to the subsequent plague, famine, and violence that accompanied the popes' residence in Avignon, and they urged the popes to resume ruling from Rome. The Avignon popes also expanded their administration, and they streamlined and made more efficient their collection of ecclesiastical taxes because they could not depend on the income from their lands in Rome. To many, it seemed that the church had become all too secular when the world was in desperate need of spiritual leadership.

An influential mystic, Catherine of Siena (1347–1380), felt called by God to intervene in this situation. Catherine had experienced a number of visions and was highly respected in her home city in the mountains south of Florence, in Italy. Catherine wrote a series of letters to Pope Gregory XI (r. 1370–1378) in which she urged him to return to Rome, and in 1376 she traveled to Avignon to urge him in person. The painting in **Figure 9.4** shows this emotion-charged meeting. Catherine kneels before the pope, pleading with him to once more take up his duties in Rome. He was persuaded, and in that year he tried to correct the decline in the papal prestige by returning to Rome. But the church's problems only increased.

Return to Rome

Things Get Worse: The Great Schism

Gregory XI died in Rome in 1378, and the situation was volatile. The citizens of Rome feared that the college of cardinals would choose another French pope who would return to Avignon. Indeed, the guard of the cardinals warned them that they "ran the risk of being torn in pieces" if they did not elect an Italian. The fearful cardinals elected an Italian,

MAP 9.2

The Great Schism, 1378–1417

This map shows how countries' loyalties were divided between the competing popes in Rome and Avignon.

Explore the Map

1. What regions supported which pope?

2. What political advantage might each country have achieved by its alliance?

3. Do the shifting alliances of the Holy Roman Empire demonstrate the lack of unity in that region? Explain.

Pope Urban VI (r. 1378–1389). Urban almost immediately indicated his plans to reduce the French influence in the college of cardinals, and, not surprisingly, the French cardinals—claiming that the election of Urban VI was invalid because they had been coerced by the Roman mob—left Rome. The dissenting cardinals elected a Frenchman—Pope Clement VII (r. 1378–1394)—who took up residence in the papal palace in Avignon. Now there were two popes, initiating what has been called the **Great Schism** of the church. (This is not to be confused with the schism of 1054, which divided the church into the Latin west and the Greek Orthodox east. See Chapter 6.)

Many people chose to follow one pope over the other based on political rather than religious motivations, and **Map 9.2** shows the respective alliances. Each pope denounced the other as the anti-Christ, and each tried to increase the revenues that now were split in half as Christians were divided in their loyalties. Many people began to criticize the church for its seeming concern for money over spiritual matters, and they advocated restoring a unified leadership to the divided Christendom. As the Black Death plundered Europe, the papacy lost its moral authority as the ruler of a united Christendom. Who could restore unity?

The Conciliar Movement

Church theorists had long speculated on who might rule the church if the pope should become incompetent. Some suggested the college of cardinals would be the logical body, but the college was split in two, so some theologians suggested that a general council of bishops might be able to restore the order and reform the abuses of the church. There was ample precedent for church councils to meet to resolve controversies, for as early as the fourth century, Emperor Constantine had called the bishops together at Nicaea (see Chapter 5). However, these new "conciliarists" wanted to convert the church to a kind of constitutional monarchy in which the power of the popes would be limited. This would be a dramatic step, but the times seemed to call for radical measures.

The first test of the **Conciliar movement** came at the Council of Pisa, convened in 1409 by cardinals of both Rome and Avignon. This council asserted its supremacy by deposing the two reigning popes and electing a new pope. Although this should have solved the problem, it only exacerbated it—the two previous popes would not step down, so now *three* popes reigned.

Finally, a second council was called. Some 400 churchmen assembled at the Council of Constance (1414–1418), which was the greatest international gathering in the Middle Ages. This august body deposed all three of the popes and elected a Roman cardinal—Martin V (r. 1417–1431). The Great Schism was finally over and the Western church was once more united under a single head. However, never again did the popes have the power that the medieval popes had, and church councils gathered periodically to address changes in the church.

New Critics of the Church

Not surprisingly, as men and women became disenchanted with the established church, they sought new ways to approach God so as to address the pressing challenges of the age. Criticisms of the church that had been expressed periodically throughout the Middle Ages appeared with more urgency in this age of crisis. The preacher John Ball was simply one of many who offered a different view of religion, and even the dreaded inquisition could not silence the new critics.

The Englishman and Oxford theologian John Wycliffe (ca. 1320–1384) offered a serious critique that struck at the heart of the organized church. Wycliffe argued that there was no scriptural basis for

papal claims of earthly power and that the Bible should be a Christian's sole authority. In the course of his writings, he attacked many of the practices of the medieval church (such as pilgrimages, the veneration of saints, and many of the rituals that had grown up over the centuries). Furthermore, Wycliffe argued that the church (and the popes in particular) should renounce earthly power, leaving it to kings. As he put it, "the pope [should] leave his worldly lordship to worldly lords." Wycliffe wanted a more simple church, led by a clergy that rejected all wealth. This would have been a major renunciation because the church was by far the greatest landlord in Europe. There was a great deal at stake.

John Wycliffe

Though Wycliffe's ideas were profoundly threatening to the established church, he had powerful protectors in the English court, who kept him unharmed until he died. Many of his followers (called **Lollards**) were condemned, but not until the early 1400s, when his ideas seemed to stimulate treasonous acts. One of the most famous proponents of some of Wycliffe's ideas was Jan Hus (ca. 1373–1415), a popular preacher and rector of the university in Prague. Hus and his followers demanded a reform of the church, and his ideas were joined to a desire for Bohemian freedom from German dominance. Hus was certain that his beliefs were correct and defended them before the influential Council of Constance. However, the Czech scholar was found guilty of heresy and was burned. An eyewitness to the execution wrote that Hus died bravely with the words of the Lord's Prayer on his lips. Many Czechs remembered Hus as a martyr both to conscience and to a growing desire for Czech independence. While the council could silence Hus, it could not silence the growing numbers of voices calling for a significant transformation of the medieval church. As we will see in Chapter 11, these calls for reform would eventually be heard.

Jan Hus

MORE DESTRUCTION: THE HUNDRED YEARS' WAR, 1337–1453

As if famine, plague, revolts, and religious controversy weren't enough, England and France entered into the **Hundred Years' War**—a century-long conflict that became the closing chapter in an age in which longstanding traditions and social contracts crumbled. The issue that triggered the conflict was the succession to the throne of France—the Capetians' good luck in producing male heirs finally ran out in 1328, when the last Capetian died. The nearest male relative was King Edward III of England, son of a Capetian king's (Philip IV) daughter (Isabel). The Parlement of Paris (the supreme court of France) claimed that a woman could not transmit a claim to the crown, so Philip VI of Valois, a first cousin of the previous ruler, became king. Edward at first did not dispute this decision, but he soon found cause to do so.

England vs. France

There were two other reasons for the two kings to clash: one was economic—urban revolts in Flanders gave Philip VI an excuse to interfere in the lucrative wool trade between England and Flanders. The Flemish asked Edward to assert his claim to the French crown so the rich trade could continue unimpeded. The second cause was feudal—the French king wanted to claim the status of liege lord over the lands in southern France held by Edward III. (See Chapter 8 to review how the English kings came to hold land in France as vassals to the king of France.) Edward, as a king himself, did not believe he should accept Philip as his liege lord. In response, Philip declared Edward's lands forfeit and Edward decided to exert his dynastic claim to be king of both England and France.

The long struggle began with some stunning English victories. The English first secured their communications across the channel with a naval victory at Sluys in 1340 (see **Map 9.3**); they

New weapons

then could turn to a land invasion of France. Although the French outnumbered the English, the English skillfully used new tactics and new weapons to supplement their mounted knights. In their wars against the Scots in the thirteenth century, the English learned of the effectiveness of the Welsh longbow and brought archers to fight against the French cavalry. The longbow was a simple yet highly effective device that had a greater range than the crossbow and could be fired with unprecedented speed. A longbowman could loose up to ten arrows a minute, compared with the crossbowman's two.

The English armies also took advantage of the pike—a weapon developed in Switzerland and used to good effect against the mounted armies of the Holy Roman Emperor. Foot soldiers wielded the long spears and braced them on the ground to fend off the charge of mounted knights. Some English foot soldiers brought pikes to France to support England's horsemen, who were outnumbered by the French cavalry.

While longbows and pikes challenged the ascendancy of mounted knights, their obsolescence was sealed with the spread of gunpowder from China. Iron shot appeared in England as early as 1346 and Italy in 1341, but the powder was unstable and did not explode immediately. Throughout the war, desperate soldiers used new (and frequently unreliable) guns to bring down knights, and equally desperate armorers tried to make plate armor stronger and curved so it could deflect bullets. However, the mounted knights simply grew too expensive and ineffective for the new warfare; the future lay with the infantry.

The English, led by Edward III, forged across the channel to confront the superior force of French mounted knights. Edward brought a strong infantry, loud guns, and lethal longbows, which eyewitness accounts of the Battle of Crécy in 1346 described as blackening the sky with English arrows. By the end

English victories

of the battle, the flower of French knighthood lay crushed, which struck a blow against feudalism itself when "those who fought" lost. In this victory, the English had secured Flanders and the important port of Calais. The strategy was repeated at Poitiers in 1356, and the exhausted French were forced to sue for peace (the Peace of Bretigny) in 1360. By the terms of this peace, King Edward renounced his claim to the French throne in exchange for Calais and enlarged holdings in Aquitaine.

The French were not willing to allow so much of their land to remain in English hands, so the war was reopened in 1369 under the French king Charles V (r. 1364–1380). He introduced a wise strategy of avoiding major military confrontation and, instead, wearing down the English forces on the Continent. During this phase of the war, soldiers on both sides devastated the countryside, plundering villages and ruining crops and vineyards. The illustration in **Figure 9.5** shows soldiers pillaging a house during the Hundred Years' War. They carry out chests and barrels, and some search for valuables hidden in pots and jars while others break open wine casks. This sort of civilian destruction contributed to the misery of the fourteenth century.

Edward III died in 1377, and Charles V in 1380. At this point, the English had almost been pushed out of France—they held only Calais and a small strip of land between Bordeaux and Bayonne. At first no formal peace was signed, but in 1396 a long truce ended this phase of the Hundred Years' War, and the monarchs turned their attention to internal affairs for a while.

Henry V (r. 1413–1422), who succeeded to the English throne in 1413, was an able soldier, eager to reopen the long-suspended war against France. His timing was good, because the powerful duke of Burgundy had used the turmoil to increase his own land at the expense of the French

Agincourt

kings (see **Map 9.3**). The Burgundians leapt into the fray on the side of the English, and with this new ally, Henry reasserted his claims to the French throne. In August 1415, he landed in Normandy with a substantial force of knights and about 6,000 archers, but his men were soon exhausted by casualties and dysentery. The bold king heard that the French army was marching against him, and he had to prepare for battle. Henry chose a troop formation in

MAP 9.3

The Hundred Years' War, 1337–1453

This map illustrates the Hundred Years' War between England and France. It shows that the major battle sites and areas of combat were in the north, even though the English claims in France lay in the south. The inset traces the Battle of Agincourt.

Explore the Map

1. What does the pattern of warfare (emphasizing the north) suggest about the significance of the various causes of the war?

2. What mistakes did the French make in the significant Battle of Agincourt?

3. Why do you think the location of Orléans (along the Loire River), where Joan of Arc made her decisive victory, proved to be strategically significant?

FIGURE 9.5 Pillaging Soldiers This illustration of rampaging soldiers during the Hundred Years' War shows them searching for valuables in a home and carrying them off. The war and its attendant plunder contributed to the woes of a society that was already beset by famine, plague, revolts, and religious controversy.

which the flanks were protected by gardens and orchards of two villages, and he arranged his men forming solid blocks flanked by the archers. (See inset in **Map 9.3**.) The French knights repeated the same tactics that had failed at Poitiers in 1356—a small body of dismounted men-at-arms took the center, followed by mounted knights and supported by crossbowmen, who were placed too far back to be useful. The English slaughtered the French knights in great numbers.

The French king was forced to sue for peace and declare his heir (called the **Dauphin**) illegitimate. England got direct control of northern France as far south as the Loire River and the promise that Henry's son would inherit the throne of France. For all practical purposes, France was defeated. The Dauphin could not accept these terms, but he seemed unable to rally any systematic resistance. In 1428, the English laid siege to Orléans, and its fall would have ensured English control of all the lands north of the Loire River. It seemed it would take a miracle to restore the French monarchy, and, many people believed they got one.

Joan of Arc

During these darkest days of France, a young peasant girl—Joan of Arc (1412–1431)—believed she saw visions in which angels urged her to lead the French troops to victory. She persuaded the Dauphin of the authenticity of her mission, and he gave her command of an army. Joan donned armor and almost miraculously stirred the determination of France's armies and lifted the siege at Orléans. Some accounts attribute her success to a skill in placing artillery, the new weapon of warfare. After this victory, she escorted the Dauphin to Reims—the city where French kings were

traditionally crowned—where he received the crown of France, thus renouncing the previous treaty. The French embraced the cause of their new king and the new national spirit seemed to revitalize the French armies. They rallied, and by 1453 only Calais was left in English hands.

However, Joan did not live to see the victory. She was captured in 1431 by the Burgundians, who turned her over to their English allies, who put her on trial for witchcraft and heresy. | Joan executed |
The Dauphin did not try to intervene, and his champion was put on trial. The record of her trial provides a fascinating glimpse into the experience of this extraordinary woman. She repeatedly restated her conviction that her voices were from God and that she was following a just cause. Ultimately, she refused to abandon her men's clothing and acknowledge that she had been wrong, so she was condemned to be burned at the stake. Document 9.2 reveals this deeply poignant episode in her trial. The French honored Joan of Arc as a savior of France, and in 1920 she was declared a saint of the Catholic Church.

Results of the War

The new weaponry that was used during the Hundred Years' War set European armies on a new course. Indeed, the weaponry and violence against civilians have caused many scholars to call this the first modern war. The feudal system that demanded knights' military service began to break down, and lords increasingly accepted money (called scutage) instead of military service. Now lords could hire professional armies—called **free companies** because they had no feudal ties and sold their services to the highest bidder—which were becoming more effective than traditional knights. (The knights continued to fight in their beloved tournaments long after they were less welcome on the battlefields.) Many kings had repeated difficulties paying their free companies, and soldiers ravaged the countryside in lieu of their pay. Under these pressures, the deterioration of the feudal system accelerated into what is sometimes called bastard feudalism, in which the old ties of loyalty were replaced with cash payments. Nobles, like kings, simply hired soldiers, dressed them in elaborate uniforms sporting the special colors of the noble families, and created their own private armies.

As a result of the Hundred Years' War, the English were expelled from French soil; the French king emerged more powerful than all his vassals, and the slow consolidation of royal rule was effectively complete. The monarchy had a permanent army, a strong tax base, and a great deal of prestige among people who were coming to see themselves as "French."

DOCUMENT 9.2

Joan of Arc Is Defiant

The record of Joan of Arc's trial offers a fascinating glimpse into both the inquisitorial proceedings of the late Middle Ages and the psychology of the accused. Earlier in her trial, Joan is found guilty and agrees to recant and renounce the voices that guided her in her battle against the English. This section begins with her recantation, which she later renounces.

Then, in the presence of all the aforenamed, in presence of an immense number of people and Clergy, she did make and utter her recantation and abjuration, following a formula written in French, which was read to her; . . .

". . . I, Jeanne, commonly called the Maid, a miserable sinner, after that I had recognized the snares of error in the which I was held, and [after] that, by the grace of God, I had returned to our Holy Mother Church, in order that it may be seen that, not pretending but with a good heart and good will, I have returned thereto; I confess that I have most grievously sinned, in pretending untruthfully to have had revelations and apparitions from God, from the Angels, and Saint Catherine and Saint Margaret; in seducing others; in believing foolishly and lightly; in making superstitious divinations; in blaspheming God and His Saints; in breaking the Divine Law, Holy Scripture, and the lawful Canons; in wearing a dissolute habit, misshapen and immodest and against the propriety of nature, and hair clipped 'en ronde' in the style of a man, against all the modesty of the feminine sex; . . ."

And the same day, **Thursday, May 24th, in the afternoon,** We [the judges] did repair to the place in the prison where Jeanne was to be found. . . . We told her to leave off her man's dress and to take a woman's garments, as the Church had ordered her. In all our observations Jeanne did reply that she would willingly take woman's garments, and that in all things she would obey the Church. Woman's garments having been offered to her, she at once dressed herself in them, after

having taken off the man's dress she was wearing; and her hair, which up to this time had been cut "en ronde" above her ears, she desired and permitted them to shave and take away.

Monday, May 28th, the day following Trinity Sunday.

We, the aforesaid Judges, repaired to the place of Jeanne's prison, to learn the state and disposition of her soul. . . .

And because Jeanne was dressed in the dress of a man—that is to say, a short mantle, a hood, a doublet and other effects used by men—although, by our orders, she had, several days before, consented to give up these garments, we asked her when and for what reason she had resumed this dress.

She answered us:

"I have but now resumed the dress of a man and put off the woman's dress."

"Why did you take it, and who made you take it?"

"I took it of my own free will, and with no constraint: I prefer a man's dress to a woman's dress."

"You promised and swore not to resume a man's dress."

"I never meant to swear that I would not resume it."

"Why have you resumed it?"

"Because it is more lawful and suitable for me to resume it and to wear man's dress, being with men, than to have a woman's dress. . . ."

And as We, the Judges, heard from several persons that she had returned to her old illusions on the subject of her pretended revelations. We put to her this question:

"Since last Thursday [the day of her abjuration] have you heard your Voices at all?"

"Yes, I have heard them."

"What did they say to you?"

"They said to me: . . . 'God had sent me word by St. Catherine and St. Margaret of the great pity it is, this treason to which I have consented, to abjure and recant in order to save my life! I have damned myself to save my life!' . . ."

"Do you believe that your Voices are Saint Catherine and Saint Margaret?"

"Yes, I believe it, and that they come from God."

"Tell us the truth on the subject of this crown which is mentioned in your Trial."

"In everything, I told you the truth about it in my Trial, as well as I know."

. . . After hearing this. We retired from her, to act and proceed later according to law and reason.

Wednesday, May 30th, towards 9 o'clock in the morning, . . .

We, the Bishop and Vicar aforesaid, having regard to all that has gone before, in which it is shown that this woman had never truly abandoned her errors, her obstinate temerity, nor her unheard-of crimes; . . . We have at last proceeded to the Final Sentence on these terms:

For the causes, declaring thee fallen again into your old errors, and under the sentence of excommunication which you have formerly incurred. WE DECREE THAT YOU ART A RELAPSED HERETIC, by our present sentence which, seated in tribunal, we utter and pronounce in this writing; we denounce thee as a rotten member, and that you may not vitiate others, as cast out from the unity of the Church, separate from her Body, abandoned to the secular power as, indeed, by these presents, we do cast thee off, separate and abandon thee:—praying this same secular power, so far as concerns death and the mutilation of the limbs, to moderate its judgment towards thee, and, if true signs of penitence should appear in thee, [to permit] that the Sacrament of Penance be administered to thee.

SOURCE: Saint Joan of Arc Center, Albuquerque, NM, "The Relapse, the final adjudication and the sentence of death," www.stjoan-center.com.

Analyze the Document

1. How did clothing—symbol of gender roles and obedience—play a significant part in the proceedings?

2. Why did Joan take back her confession?

3. What was the church's sentence?

4. What do you think of these events?

5. How might Joan have been treated today?

England had a longer struggle after its loss in the war. England's monarchy was seriously weakened as Parliament took more control of the purse strings after the wartime excesses. During the turmoil, the Lancaster and York families unleashed a civil war as they competed for the throne. Each family had a different color rose as its emblem, so this sporadic conflict was called the Wars of the Roses (1455–1485). The fighting perpetuated the worst aspects of feudal life as it degenerated into local skirmishes orchestrated by the nobility. The situation was made worse by mercenary soldiers unemployed after the end of the Hundred Years' War, who returned to England and sold their services to feuding families. Many old noble families were decimated in the course of this war.

Richard III (r. 1483–1485) took the throne from his 12-year-old nephew, Edward V, and had the young king and his brother imprisoned in the Tower of London, where they were murdered. This long-remembered act of cruelty stimulated a final resistance. Nobles rallied to the banner of Henry Tudor, a Lancastrian, and he finally vanquished Richard III at the Battle of Bosworth Field in 1485. He was crowned Henry VII (r. 1485–1509). To try to heal the breach between the noble factions, he married Elizabeth of York; at last the civil war was officially ended, but Henry needed all his skill to restore solid centralized control. He confiscated the lands of rebellious nobles and prohibited private armies. At the end of his reign, England was strengthened; and by the time of his granddaughter's rule, it was poised to expand beyond the seas (see Chapter 12).

RESPONSES TO THE DISRUPTION OF MEDIEVAL ORDER

As war and revolt have shown, one of the ways people responded to the fourteenth-century disasters was to consider new approaches to old problems. Wycliffe and Hus questioned church practices; Edward III of England thought of new battle strategies to confront French knights. These are only three of many famous and anonymous people who changed their world with creative new ideas. Philosophers, writers, and artists, too, produced works that dramatically changed the direction of Western thought.

William of Ockham Reconsiders Scholasticism

Within a century after Thomas Aquinas's synthesis (described in Chapter 8), a new breed of thinkers challenged the premises of scholasticism and questioned the ties between faith and reason. William of Ockham (ca. 1285–1349) was the most prominent of these thinkers. Scholasticism was based on the

idea that thinkers could extract general truths (or universals) from individual cases. Ockham was an English philosopher who argued that universals had no connection with reality, and this philosophy was called New Nominalism. (Ockham used **nominalism,** derived from the Latin word for "name," because he said that universals, or categories, were only convenient names for things.) New Nominalists believed that it was impossible to know God or prove his existence through reason—because God was all-powerful, he did not have to act logically.

So what should philosophers do? Ockham's studies spawned a decline in abstract logic, but a rise in interest in scientific observation that would bear much fruit in later generations. Ockham also discovered a fundamental principle that remained the basis of much scientific analysis. Called **Ockham's razor,** this principle says that between alternative explanations for the same phenomenon, the simpler is always to be preferred. People who have studied the material world ever since have looked to simple, elegant explanations to satisfy Ockham's razor. New Nominalism became popular in universities, and Ockhamite philosophy became known as the *via moderna* (modern way). Indeed, intellectuals were beginning to reject the old and look at the world in a new way.

New Literary Giants

In the fourteenth century, more authors began to write in the vernacular, their national languages, instead of Latin, which had been the language of great literature

A CENTURY OF DISASTERS FOR THE WEST

1305–1378	Babylonian Captivity of papacy
1315–1322	Famine
ca. 1320–1384	John Wycliffe
1337–1453	Hundred Years' War
1348	Arrival of Black Death in Europe
1358	Jacquerie revolt in France
ca. 1373–1415	Jan Hus
1378–1417	Great Schism
1378–1385	Urban revolts
1381	Peasant revolt in England
1414–1418	Council of Constance
1415	Battle of Agincourt
1431	Death of Joan of Arc
1455–1485	Wars of the Roses in England

KEY DATES

FIGURE 9.6 Domenico di Michelino, _Dante and His Poem, the Divine Comedy_ This illustration of the Italian poet Dante's famous _Divine Comedy_ was painted on the walls of Florence's cathedral. In addition to depicting Dante, it shows hell (on the left), a mountain of purgatory, and a celestial heaven.

throughout the Middle Ages. (Latin still remained the language of the church and of official government documents.) In the Middle Ages, romances and other poetry had been written in the vernacular (see Chapter 8), but in fourteenth-century Italy in particular, a new kind of literature emerged that explored people's place in the world. Italian poets from Tuscany made Italian a literary language and composed some of the greatest literature of all time.

The first of these writers was Dante Alighieri (1265–1321), who was born in Florence. In 1302, he became embroiled in the turbulent political situation of his city and was exiled. He always hoped to return to his beloved city but never succeeded, and he grew to be a bitter, disillusioned man wandering from city to city until he died in 1321. While in exile, he composed his masterpiece, now called the _Divine Comedy_. The work became so popular that a century after his death, Florence recognized his genius and commissioned the painting shown in **Figure 9.6** to honor the man they had exiled. He stands in the center holding

Dante

the book that brought such posthumous fame to the man and the city that spawned him.

The _Divine Comedy_ is a magnificent allegory of a soul's journey through despair to salvation. The lengthy work is divided into three sections—Hell, Purgatory, and Paradise—and the poet journeys through them all. He is first led through Hell by Virgil, the Roman poet whose works still formed the basis of a good education. Dante described the punishments of the damned in gruesome detail: In one location he saw "long lines of people in a river of excrement that seemed the overflow of the world's latrines," and in these pits Dante placed his contemporaries (as well as historical figures) who deserved punishment. The damned are shown in **Figure 9.6** on the lower left descending into Hell. Dante then leaves Hell and climbs the mountain of Purgatory (shown in the background of **Figure 9.6**), where sinners who would ultimately be saved were doing penance for their sins. Finally, Dante was led into Paradise by a mysterious woman—Beatrice—who was reputed to be the love of the poet's life.

thinking about

ART

FIGURE 9.7

Illumination from a Book of Hours, Fifteenth Century

This image is an illumination—an illustration within a hand-decorated, hand-colored manuscript—from a fifteenth-century Book of Hours. This work was commissioned by the wealthy Duke of Burgundy and used as a prayer book. The image is strictly hierarchic in structure: The castle is at the highest point, supported by hardworking peasants peacefully working a well-tended landscape and tending their flock. The whole scene unfolds under a well-ordered heaven.

Connecting Art & Society

1. Given the disasters of the fourteenth and fifteenth centuries, does the world that is depicted look realistic? Explain.

2. Why would this image have been particularly appealing to a noble patron?

3. What might this image indicate about one sort of human response to disasters and hardship?

Some scholars consider the *Divine Comedy* a perfect medieval work: It incorporates Aquinas's theology and Aristotle's science, and the whole work has the complexity of a Gothic cathedral or a *Summa Theologiae* (the philosophic summaries described in Chapter 8). Other scholars see in the work something new—a departure from the medieval world that shaped the poet. Dante, after all, was a layman who presumed to express theology of salvation. Furthermore, he articulated the growing criticism of the medieval church by placing many popes in Hell. Finally, his beloved guide through Hell and Purgatory was a classic poet—Virgil, who represented reason. His final tour through heaven was conducted by Beatrice, who was an allegory of faith. As we will see in Chapter 10, many thinkers who like Dante struggled with the despair of the age would find solace in pagan classics and faith in God's grace.

Another Florentine who had a profound impact on literature was Giovanni Boccaccio (1313–1375), who witnessed the devastating plague as it swept through his city. In his most famous work, *The Decameron*, Boccaccio offers a poignant eyewitness description of the plague, with insights into how various people responded to catastrophe, for he said some shut themselves off from everyone else, others prayed diligently in hopes of avoiding early death, and still others denied themselves nothing, "drinking and reveling incessantly from tavern to tavern." This description sets the stage for the heart of the book, in which ten young people escape to a villa outside Florence and decide to amuse themselves by telling stories. *The Decameron* is the collection of the stories they tell, and most are highly entertaining.

Boccaccio

The stories reflect a new, permissive attitude that arose in the wake of the plague, for the stories talk frankly of sex, lies, and ordinary people. The heroes are not knights or philosophers, but clever men and women who live by their wits, and their stories were intended more to amuse than to teach moral lessons. In his later years, Boccaccio became uneasy with his lighthearted works, and in a letter written in 1373 he urged someone to not let women read his stories, warning, "You know how much in them is less than decent and opposed to modesty." However, there was no return to a more modest, conservative age—the fourteenth century had disrupted much that was traditional, and many people welcomed a new way to look at life. In these dark times, many found a lighthearted tribute to pleasure particularly satisfying.

One typical way to react to disaster is to look back longingly to a "golden age"—in this case, to an imagined tightly ordered medieval world. **Figure 9.7** shows one such idealized world.

One of the world's most gifted poets—the Englishman Geoffrey Chaucer (ca. 1340–1400)—also looked longingly backward. Chaucer drew from tales like

Boccaccio's to offer a different view of the turbulent fourteenth century. His most famous work, *The Canterbury Tales*, was written in English and tells of a group of 29 pilgrims who journey from Southwark (outside London) to Canterbury to the shrine of Thomas Becket. Like Boccaccio's youths, Chaucer's pilgrims tell tales to pass the time on their journey, but unlike Boccaccio, Chaucer draws each pilgrim vividly, with a clear personality so each stands out as an individual. The stories are varied, from knightly romances to bawdy tales, and they still delight readers today.

 Chaucer

Chaucer's descriptions of the pilgrims offer a subtle, yet revealing, look at fourteenth-century society. He criticized corruption in the church by commenting on monks who would rather hunt than pray, or friars who were not interested in the poor: "He knew the taverns well in every town. / The barmaids and innkeepers pleased his mind / Better than beggars and lepers and their kind." However, Chaucer was also a medieval man who looked back to what he imagined was a golden age when knights were virtuous crusaders, priests cared nothing for money, and scholars loved only knowledge. If that golden age ever existed, it was gone by the fourteenth century—money was rapidly becoming the measure of success, and the future belonged to bright individuals with as much character as Chaucer's pilgrims.

A New View: Jan van Eyck

Just as Chaucer carefully and precisely created his pilgrims with words on a page, painters in Flanders began to re-create their world in paint with a precision that continues to astonish the viewer. One of the most famous of the Flemish artists is Jan van Eyck (ca. 1395–1441), who was among the first to use oil paint—a medium that allowed the artist to capture realistic details. In the painting of a husband and his bride shown in **Figure 9.8,** van Eyck portrays the scene with amazing realism, down to the witnesses to the marriage who are reflected in the mirror on the wall in the background. Both the new medium and the technical skill of the artist point to the new directions that European culture took in this period.

Like Chaucer and Dante, van Eyck was breaking new ground in the arts, but he also looked back to the Middle Ages and preserved much of their ideals. In the medieval world, people looked to intense and detailed symbolism to both reveal and explain their world, and van Eyck filled the painting shown in **Figure 9.8** with symbolism. The dog is a symbol of fidelity, and the carving on the bedpost is of Saint Margaret, the patron saint of childbirth. The

Realism and symbolism

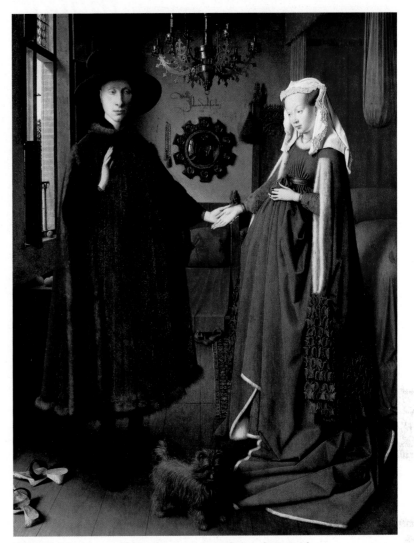

FIGURE 9.8 Jan van Eyck, *Giovanni Arnolfini and His Bride*, 1434 Painters who worked in Flanders in the fifteenth century were more innovative than their Italian contemporaries. Whereas the Italians favored tempera, a water-based paint, artists in Flanders preferred oil paint, which allowed them to depict highly lifelike details. Note the realistic qualities of this famous portrait, which is also brimming with symbolism.

single lighted candle indicates God's presence and blessing of the couple's wedding night. The combination of realism infused with symbolic meaning is characteristic of the late Middle Ages, and the Flemish painter captured this spirit perfectly.

The disasters of the long fourteenth century had caused many to question their traditional views and values. As the ordered world they had known was crumbling, however, room was being made for new ideas and new approaches. As we will see in the next chapter, the West would take a fresh and exciting path.

EMPIRES IN THE EAST

As the West struggled with disasters that fractured the medieval order, winds of change also blew from the Far East into Europe. New empires were forming

MAP 9.4

The Mongol Empire, ca. 1300

This map shows the greatest expanse of the Mongol Empire as it extended from the Pacific Ocean to the Black Sea. The scale indicates the vast distances of the empire.

Explore the Map

1. What problems did the Mongols face in governing an empire that encompassed so many cultures and religion?

2. How did the Mongolian conquests stimulate cross-cultural contacts between the West and non-West?

3. Locate Constantinople and Novgorod. Why were the Byzantine Empire and the Russian state threatened by the proximity of the Mongol Empire?

in the East that dominated the political landscapes of the regions for the next few centuries, and the West was brought into a new global relationship with lands as far away as east Asia.

Eastern Universalism: The Mongols

As early as the thirteenth century, while the West struggled between localism and centralization, dynamic conquerors swept out of Mongolia and established a new, unified empire extending from eastern Europe across Asia to the Pacific Ocean. In 1206, Genghis Khan (r. 1206–1227) united diverse nomadic groups and forged a formidable army that he led with consummate skill. He was an extraordinary figure who is

remembered for his appalling cruelty as well as for his wisdom and talent as a leader, for after the violence of his initial conquest, he established a peaceful, tolerant rule. He implemented the first Mongol written language and promulgated the first law code for his nomadic people. His grandson, Kublai Khan (r. 1260–1294), was an equally powerful ruler, whose wealthy empire, centered in China, offered a tantalizing lure to travelers from the West.

Map 9.4 shows the remarkable extent of the Mongol Empire in about 1300—from China and Korea in the east to Moscow and Ukraine in the west. The rulers of the Scandinavian/Slavic state centered in Kiev had already moved their capital to the far north in

Mongol Empire

DOCUMENT 9.3

A Franciscan Missionary Goes to China

John of Monte Corvino (1247–1328) was a Franciscan priest sent to convert the Mongols in China (called Cathay here). He wrote this letter in January 1305, asking for support from his fellow Franciscans in Italy, and the letter gives an idea of the difficulties of his assignment and of his successes.

I proceeded on my further journey and made my way to Cathay, the realm of the Emperor of the Tartars who is called the Great Khan. To him I presented the letter of our lord the Pope, and invited him to adopt the Catholic Faith of our Lord Jesus Christ, but he had grown too old in idolatry. However he bestows many kindnesses upon the Christians, and these two years past I am abiding with him. . . . In this mission I abode alone and without any associate for eleven years; but it is now going on for two years since I was joined by Friar Arnold, a German of the province of Cologne.

I have built a church in the city of Khanbaliq, in which the king has his chief residence. This I completed six years ago; and I have built a bell-tower to it, and put three bells in it. I have baptized there, as well as I can estimate, up to this time some 6000 persons; . . . And I am often still engaged in baptizing.

Also I have gradually bought one hundred and fifty boys, the children of pagan parents, and of ages varying from seven to eleven, who had never learned any religion. These boys I have baptized, and I have taught them Greek and Latin after our manner. Also I have written out Psalters for them, with thirty Hymnals and two Breviaries. By help of these, eleven of the boys already know our service, and form a choir and take their weekly turn of duty as they do in convents, whether I am there or not. Many of the boys are also employed in writing out Psalters and other things suitable. His Majesty the Emperor moreover delights much to hear them chanting. I have the bells rung at all the canonical hours, and with my congregation of babes and sucklings I perform divine service, and the chanting we do by ear because I have no service book with the notes.

Indeed if I had but two or three comrades to aid me 'tis possible that the Emperor Khan would have been baptized by this time! I ask then for such brethren to come, if any are willing to come, such I mean as will make it their great business to lead exemplary lives. . . .

I have myself grown old and grey, more with toil and trouble than with years; for I am not more than fifty-eight. I have got a competent knowledge of the language and character which is most generally used by the Tartars. And I have already translated into that language and character the New Testament and the Psalter, and have caused them to be written out in the fairest penmanship they have; and so by writing, reading, and preaching, I bear open and public testimony to the Law of Christ. . . .

As far as I ever saw or heard tell, I do not believe that any king or prince in the world can be compared to his majesty the Khan in respect of the extent of his dominions, the vastness of their population, or the amount of his wealth. Here I stop.

SOURCE: John Monte Corvino, "Letter of John Monte Corvino," in *Cathay and the Way Thither*, trans. and ed. Sir Henry Yule, 2nd ed. revised by Henri Cordier (London: Hakluyt Society, 1914), vol. III, second series, vol. 37, pp. 45–51, passim. Slightly abridged and reprinted in Leon Barnard and Theodore B. Hodges, *Readings in European History* (New York: Macmillan, 1958), pp. 107–108 (some spelling modernized). See also http:www.fordham.edu/halsal/source/corvino1.html.

Analyze the Document

1. Why do you think the pope was so eager to convert the Mongol khan?

2. How did the khan treat the Christians? Why did he treat them so?

3. What techniques did John use to convert the Chinese?

4. Do you think that the arrival of more Franciscans would have ensured the conversion of the khan?

5. Why do you think John argued this?

Novgorod, and this Russian state had to pay tribute to the Mongol Empire to its south. This empire encompassed an extraordinary diversity of peoples and religions—from Muslims to Christians to Buddhists—and it accommodated them seemingly without conflict. The popes were eager to convert the Mongols to Christianity and sent missionaries to China. Document 9.3 describes the trip of one such missionary.

This unified empire also created a huge trade area through which goods and ideas traveled easily. It is likely that Europeans learned the recipe for gunpowder from travelers through the Mongol Empire. (See Thinking About Science & Technology, Chapter 11.)

As we saw in Chapter 8, the Venetians in particular were well placed to take advantage of this trade. By the fourteenth century, the Venetians had established many trading posts where they could engage in a lucrative commerce. **Figure 9.9** on page 303 shows Venetian merchants trading cloth for oriental products—possibly spices—with traders who had landed in a Mediterranean port.

Certainly the most famous western Europeans who took advantage of the Venetian experience in trade were the Venetians Marco Polo (1254–1324) and his father and uncle, who traveled to the far reaches of

Marco Polo

FIGURE 9.9 Venetian Traders With the rise of the Mongol Empire came the facilitation of trade across the old Silk Road. Venetians such as Marco Polo and his family were well placed to take advantage of this lucrative business. Here, Venetian merchants trade cloth for spices.

the Mongol Empire. During several trading journeys, the Polos traveled all the way to the court of the great Kublai Khan in Khanbaliq. The journey took them three and a half years by horseback. The Polos stayed at the khan's court for seventeen years, and Marco apparently served as an emissary of the khan himself. When the Polos returned home to Venice, they brought back a wealth of spices, silks, and other luxurious curiosities. The extravagant items were so impressive that other merchants followed; by 1300 there was even a community of Italians living in China.

Perhaps Marco Polo's most important contribution was a book about his voyages, which has been translated into English as *The Travels of Marco Polo*. His writings told of things that people in the West found unbelievable. For example, the merchants found it extraordinary that the Chinese used paper money; as Marco wrote: "The coinage of this paper money is authenticated with as much form and ceremony as if it were actually of pure gold and silver." Even more astonishing, Marco described "a sort of black stone, which they dig out of the mountains. When lighted it burns like charcoal." The Chinese had been burning coal since about 100 B.C.E., but in the West such a feat seemed implausible. Few believed the exotic tales of the traveler, but the book did excite the imaginations of adventurers. It fueled the great age of exploration that followed—Christopher Columbus carried a well-marked copy of the book through his voyages.

The Ottoman Empire, 1300–1566

The political situation in eastern Europe changed permanently with the establishment of a new empire

at its borders. In the thirteenth century, a group of Asiatic nomads (later called Ottoman Turks) migrated westward from the expansive Asian steppes. Along the way, they converted to Islam and brought new vigor to Muslim expansion. The Turks were ruled by sultans, who were supposedly the successors of Muhammad and therefore empowered to interpret Muslim law. In this way, the sultans drew on seven hundred years of history to legitimize their authority.

As **Map 9.5** shows, the Ottoman Turks expanded slowly but steadily around the eastern Mediterranean. As they moved through the Balkans, the conquerors added to the diversity of the region's population. Even before the arrival of Muslim conquerors, the Balkans had been divided by culture and religion. Some countries, among them Hungary, were Catholic and used the Latin alphabet. Others, such as Serbia, were Greek Orthodox and used a Cyrillic alphabet. The Muslim invaders brought a new religion and a new alphabet into the already culturally diverse region, thus setting the stage for problems that would continue into the twentieth century. The Biography of Vlad III (1431–1476), king of Wallachia in what today is the country of Romania, sheds light on how the ongoing Muslim invasions destabilized the Balkans by causing a continually shifting balance of power.

The Ottoman expansion was powered by a formidable military at whose heart was an elite force called the janissaries. The janissaries were slaves who had been raised from boyhood and trained to fight for the sultan. As the Turks took over the Balkans, they forced the occupied peoples to pay a tribute of boys. These youths would be enslaved, converted to Islam, and trained to fight using the latest weapons, including artillery and guns.

By 1355, the Ottomans had effectively surrounded the Byzantine Empire, which had stood for so long as a powerful state and a buffer for the West. Finally, a powerful sultan, Mehmed II (r. 1451–1481), committed his government to a policy of conquest. The sultan turned to new technology to breach the walls surrounding Constantinople; he commissioned a gunner to craft an oversized cannon and smelted smaller weapons for the metal. The barrel, 26 feet long, could launch a stone ball weighing more than 1,000 pounds. Fifty yokes of oxen were needed to move the gun, and 700 men manned it. Constantinople's massive walls shook with the impact of the bombardment. The heavy stones that had provided an impregnable defense for so many centuries cracked. The city fell in 1453, and the last emperor, Constantine XI Palaeologus, died in the battle. Mehmed, now known as the "conqueror," made

Conquest of Constantinople

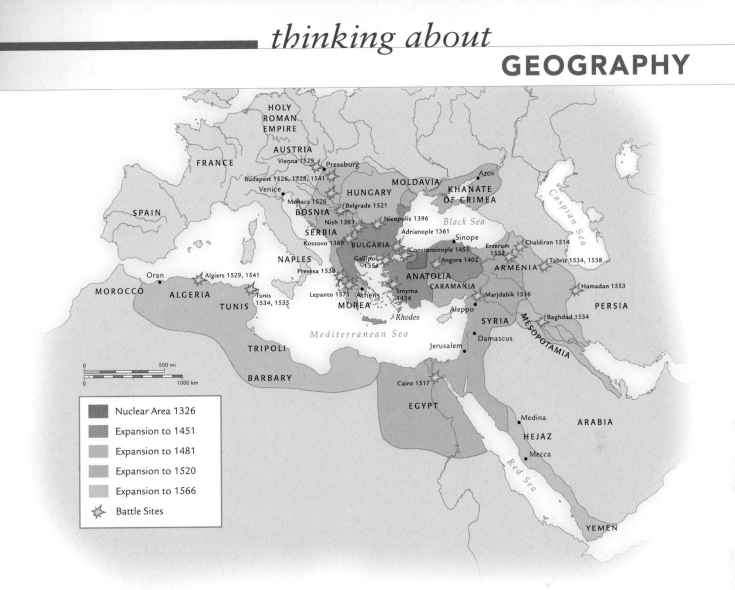

MAP 9.5

The Ottoman Empire, 1300–1566

This map shows the spread of the Ottoman Empire and identifies the major battles that marked its expansion.

Explore the Map

1. How did the nuclear area of the Turks in 1326 help them expand into the Byzantine Empire?

2. Notice how Constantinople had been surrounded long before its fall. Was there any chance that it could have avoided capture, even with external help? Explain.

3. How might western Europeans have felt threatened by the invigorated empire that extended well into the Balkans?

Constantinople his capital under the name of Istanbul, by which it is known today. (The name was not formally changed until 1930.) Mehmed extended his power around the Black Sea.

Almost a century later, the sultan Suleiman I the Magnificent (r. 1520–1566) brought the Ottoman Empire to the height of its power. As **Map 9.5** shows, the Ottoman Empire extended throughout the Middle East and into North Africa. In order to secure his

holdings in the eastern Mediterranean, Suleiman made the Ottomans into a major naval power. Suleiman's newly expanded navy had to confront the last Christian outpost in an otherwise Ottoman sea—the island of Rhodes (shown on **Map 9.5**), a highly fortified location held by the crusading order Knights of Saint John. The sultan lost many men in repeated assaults on the fortified island, but eventually his

Suleiman I

Nuclear Area 1325
Expansion to 1389
Expansion to 1462
Expansion to 1533
☆ Battle Site

MAP 9.6

The Rise of Moscow, 1325–1533

This map shows the expansion of the principality of Moscow as it grew from a small state in 1325 to a large empire in 1533. It also identifies the Mongol Khanate of the Golden Horde.

Explore the Map

1. In what ways was Russia well placed to take advantage of the Mongols' retreat from their westernmost province?

2. Compare this map with **Map 9.5.** Why would Russia have considered itself the logical heir to the Byzantine Empire as guardian of Christianity in the face of a growing Muslim threat?

artillery prevailed and the knights surrendered. They were allowed to leave the island with their weapons and they moved to the island of Malta in the central Mediterranean, where they continued to fight against Muslim expansion. However, Suleiman's victory consolidated his hold in the East, and Christian merchants seeking to capitalize on the rich trade with the East found themselves confronted by the sultan's ships and tax collectors. As we will see in Chapter 12, westerners became highly motivated to find new routes to the rich lands of east Asia.

With the sea secure, Suleiman turned his attention northward, and in 1529 he even threatened Vienna, in the heartland of Europe. From now on, the new monarchies of western Europe would have to conduct their diplomatic and military escapades with the Turks in mind, and, as we will see in the next chapters, the Turkish presence posed a significant threat to the West.

Russia: The Third Rome

At the beginning of the fourteenth century, Russia was divided into many principalities, each self-sufficient and independent. All of them, however, were subject to the Mongol khan of the Golden Horde, to whom they owed tribute and loyalty. The Mongols did not like the forested land of Russia, so they did not occupy it directly. Instead, they stayed in the steppes north of the Black Sea and simply collected tribute. One of the small principalities, the Duchy of Moscow, was able to take advantage of the Mongol overlords' absence to rise to a great empire. **Map 9.6** shows the small nuclear area of Moscow in 1325—three years before an enterprising prince, Ivan I (r. 1328–1341), came to power.

Ivan cultivated a relationship with the Mongol khan, offering loyalty and gifts. In return, Ivan received the right to collect the Mongol tribute within Russia. He grew so rich in the process (probably by withholding most of the money due the Mongols) that he earned the nickname Moneybags. This money fostered the growth of the Russian Empire in the fifteenth century, when the Mongols' fortunes declined. The khanate's hold on the territories of Russia and Ukraine loosened, and the Duchy of Moscow took the lead in overthrowing the last of Mongol rule.

Ivan I also wisely cultivated the Orthodox Church, gaining the support of that venerable institution. The Orthodox Church had flourished in Russia with the support of the Mongols, who gave the church immunity from taxation. Ivan I encouraged the Metropolitan Bishop of the Russian Church to make Moscow his permanent residence, so that city was well placed to lead the Orthodox Church when Constantinople fell in 1453.

Ivan III ("the Great") (r. 1462–1505) pushed back the final Mongol advance on Moscow in 1480 and established himself as the first ruler of the new Russian state. Ivan had married a niece of the last Byzantine emperor, so the Russian declared himself the heir to the Byzantine Empire—he proclaimed Moscow the Third Rome and took the title caesar, or tsar. The tsar strove to reestablish the greatness of the Byzantine Empire, and like the Byzantines, he closely allied with the Orthodox Church in his land. In 1589, the bishop of Moscow was proclaimed a patriarch—one of the five who presided over the eastern Orthodox Church. (See Chapter 6 for the origins of this church.) The Orthodox Church supported the tsar's claim that Moscow was the spiritual heir to Constantinople. Thus, religion and tradition supported the tsar's claim for absolute and universal authority.

Russia's empire stretched from Europe into the steppes of Asia, creating what would be a long-standing question in Russia: Where does its identity lie? Is it Western, Asian, or something else? Ivan III did not resolve this question by claiming the mantle of the Byzantine Emperor, and future Russian leaders would continue the discussion as they ruled the new conservative empire that had arisen in the East.

Ivan III

EASTERN EMPIRES FLOURISH

1206–1227	Mongol Genghis Khan
1260–1294	Mongol Kublai Khan
1328–1341	Russian tsar Ivan I
1451–1481	Ottoman Mehmed II
1453	Ottoman conquest of Constantinople
1462–1505	Russian tsar Ivan III the Great
1520–1566	Ottoman Suleiman I

KEY DATES

BIOGRAPHY

Vlad III Dracula (the Impaler), King of Wallachia

(1431–1476)

A Vicious, Controversial King

In the fifteenth century, eastern Europe was a region of complex and shifting loyalties. Then, as now, three religions—Greek Orthodox, Catholic, and Muslim—coexisted uneasily. The balance of power was changing as the armies of the powerful Ottoman Empire swept through the Balkans. The political situation took a shocking turn in 1453, when the Ottoman sultan Mehmed II conquered the ancient city of Constantinople, which had stood as a bulwark of orthodoxy against Islam. The fall of the Byzantine Empire and the rise of a strengthened Islam provoked Christian rulers to call for new crusading armies to protect Europe, but the political situation on the ground was never so simple, as Christians sometimes allied with Muslims to forward their own political aims. These tumultuous times brought to power one of the cruelest and most controversial kings of Europe, Vlad III, whose nickname, Dracula, would become linked in the nineteenth century with folklore accounts of a bloodthirsty vampire.

Vlad's father, Vlad II, was king of Wallachia, a region in what today is southern Romania. In the fifteenth century, Wallachia lay dangerously between two powerful neighbors—Hungary and the expanding Ottoman Empire. In 1410, during the height (and twilight) of chivalry, the king of Hungary founded a secret order of knights called the Order of the Dragon, whose members vowed to defend Christendom against the Turks. Vlad II was admitted to the order, and he proudly displayed its dragon emblem on his crest and his coins. *Dragon* in Romanian is *Drac*, so Vlad II was called Vlad Drac—Vlad the Dragon. His son, Vlad III, born in the neighboring region of Transylvania, was called Son of the Dragon, or Dracula, the name that would become so infamously linked with vampires.

Vlad Dracula did not hold his throne easily; throughout his life, he shifted alliances as unpredictably as the Balkan winds changed direction. In fact, he reigned three different times. He ruled first in 1448 with the support of the Turks, but he lasted only two months before a rival, supported by Hungary, drove him out. After the fall of Constantinople in 1453, Vlad made an alliance with Hungary, and he came to power again in 1456, promising to fight his former allies, the Turks. This time, he ruled until 1462, when invading Turks forced him to flee to Hungary, where he was imprisoned for years. Finally, he converted from orthodoxy to Catholicism, pleasing his Hungarian captors, who then supported his restoration to power in 1476. Throughout his turbulent reign, Vlad Dracula had to fear the threat posed by the local nobles—the *boyars*—who were themselves kingmakers and power brokers. He also had to deal with some powerful German merchants who seemed to be exploiting local Wallachians. How did Vlad respond to all these pressures in his brief rule? With terror and cruelty.

Indeed, Vlad Dracula developed a horrifying method of torturing and executing his enemies. He drove sharp stakes through the full length of their bodies and then erected the stakes in the ground, leaving the suffering victims to die slowly, some for hours and some for days. He often placed large rings of staked victims outside towns, where the decaying corpses served to terrify and appall his opponents. For his horrifying execution method, he won the infamous nickname Vlad the Impaler. Even the intrepid conqueror of Constantinople, Mehmed II, reputedly was sickened by the sight of 20,000 impaled Turkish prisoners outside the city of Tirgoviste, a spectacle that observers dubbed the Forest of the Impaled.

Vlad Dracula used his brutal execution technique against various enemies. Of course, he impaled military foes, from Turks to Hungarians. He also impaled Wallachians who violated his own ideas of justice: The *boyars*, for example, were frequent targets of his cruelty, and he kept them under control by his terror campaign. He also tortured thieves and merchants who cheated customers, in so doing earning the gratitude of peasants and others who longed for law and order. Vlad reputedly had strong ideas about the proper behavior of women, as he also impaled those whom he deemed unchaste or poor wives. Accounts indicating that Vlad Dracula impaled tens of thousands of people during his brief reign seem exaggerated—

indeed, the numbers are logistically improbable—but there is no doubt that he used this savage technique many, many times.

Evidently, Vlad did not practice torture simply as a political tool. Even Russian sources, which were generally favorable to him, describe how, when he was imprisoned, Vlad captured mice and birds, impaling their small bodies and watching them die in pain. Modern psychologists would surely identify him as a psychopath.

In 1476, when the Hungarians supported his return to power, Dracula invaded Wallachia with Transylvanian forces and took back his throne. However, the Transylvanians quickly went home, and Dracula was left with only a small army of supporters. When the Turks invaded to replace Vlad with a ruler of their choice, he was able to gather only about 4,000 troops, and he was killed near Bucharest in December 1476. There are conflicting reports of his death. Some suggest that he was slain by his own *boyars*; others maintain that he fell during a Turkish advance. We will probably never know the truth. The Turks took the king's head to Istanbul and displayed it on a stake to prove that Vlad the Impaler was dead. His body is reputedly buried at Snagov, an island monastery near Bucharest.

The historical sources describing Vlad Dracula vary in their assessment. German pamphleteers from the late fifteenth century describe him as a "monster" who tortured German merchants; **Figure 9.10,** from a German pamphlet, shows Dracula calmly eating while surrounded by a forest of the impaled. The Russians, whose czars were struggling to curb

FIGURE 9.10 Vlad III Dracula   German pamphlet, Nuremberg, 1499.

the power of their own *boyars,* called him a cruel but just prince who cared about his people. The Romanian folk tradition has embraced him as a national hero who defended his land from invading Turks and exploitative Germans. However, the characterization of Vlad that is most remembered, owing to the Irish writer Brad Stoker's novel *Dracula* (1897), is that of a vicious impaler. Most scholars of Stoker's work of fiction, which opens in Transylvania, believe that although the author drew from eastern European folktales on vampires, he based his character on the bloodthirsty Vlad Dracula the Impaler. These differing accounts show how historical records are shaped by the

political opinions of the writers and how, in a complex world of shifting alliances, a sadistic king can become a folk hero.

Connecting People & Society

1. How did the expansion of the Turks lead to instability in the Balkans?

2. How might such instability have contributed to the rise to power of a ruthless king?

3. Why might historians and other writers have come to different conclusions as they assessed Vlad Dracula's rule?

LOOKING BACK & MOVING FORWARD

Summary The fourteenth century brought with it a series of disasters in the West that broke down the medieval order that had prevailed before. Famine and plague killed millions, depopulating villages and towns. Revolts broke out in towns and across the countryside, not only bringing more violence but also raising the shocking specter of people attacking the very order of society. The manorial system in which serfs labored for their lords slowly broke down under the pressure, leaving a monetary system of rents and labor for hire. If one survived the disasters, life (at least in western Europe) might be better—higher wages and more opportunities awaited.

The papacy, too, fell prey to disasters. After new struggles with the kings of France, the popes lost prestige as they left Rome to live in Avignon and, subsequently, precipitated the Great Schism when disputed elections left two, then three, popes ruling at the same time. The medieval imperial papacy could not recover from such blows. Feudalism with its knights in shining armor also proved to be inadequate in the new age. During the devastating Hundred Years' War, infantry armed with bows and arrows, pikes, and later guns proved more effective than knights, and kings slowly began to prefer money to military service from their vassals.

In eastern Europe, new empires arose with strong, autocratic rulers, and with the strengthening of these empires East and West grew further apart. The tensions that emerged between the two profoundly influenced European life in the future. However, these eastern empires would soon face a western Europe with ideas and values dramatically different from those of the medieval West. What form would this new sensibility take?

KEY TERMS

Black Death, *p. 282*

Jacquerie, *p. 286*

Babylonian Captivity, *p. 287*

Great Schism, *p. 288*

Conciliar movement, *p. 289*

Lollards, *p. 289*

Hundred Years' War, *p. 289*

Dauphin, *p. 292*

free companies, *p. 292*

nominalism, *p. 294*

Ockham's razor, *p. 294*

REVIEW, ANALYZE, & CONNECT TO TODAY

REVIEW THE PREVIOUS CHAPTER

Chapter 8—"Order Restored"—described the three orders of the High Middle Ages and traced the fortunes of the social groups and the kings who ruled them. It also looked at the intellectual and religious accomplishments of that vigorous age.

1. Review the agricultural innovations that allowed for expansion during the High Middle Ages and consider why these no longer proved adequate in the fourteenth century.

2. Review the development of England and France in the High Middle Ages to see how they came to the violent confrontation of the Hundred Years' War in the fourteenth century.

ANALYZE THIS CHAPTER

Chapter 9—"The West Struggles and Eastern Empires Flourish"—traces the disasters of the fourteenth century that undermined the medieval structures, and it also shows the growth of empires in eastern Europe.

1. In the struggle between popes and kings over who should lead a Christian Europe, popes had dominated

in the thirteenth century. When the struggle reopened in the fourteenth century, the kings prevailed. Review the events that led to the Great Schism and its resolution.

2. How did the disasters of the fourteenth century undermine the feudal and manorial systems?

3. What were the eastern empires that came to power by the end of the fifteenth century, and what were their relative strengths?

CONNECT TO TODAY

Think about the chapter's discussion of the disruptions caused by natural disasters and disease. Also consider the growth of the Russian Empire and the spread of Islam into the Balkans.

1. What are some recent instances in which pandemics have disrupted (or have threatened to disrupt) societies? How have people responded to such threats?

2. The United States was involved in warfare in the Balkans during World War I and also later in the twentieth century. How might the events described in this chapter have contributed to the United States' involvement?

BEYOND THE CLASSROOM

ECONOMIC AND SOCIAL MISERY

Hilton, Rodney. *Bond Men Made Free*. New York: Methuen, 1973. A classic, highly sympathetic study of peasant unrest in the late Middle Ages.

Jordan, William Chester. *The Great Famine*. Princeton, NJ: Princeton University Press, 1996. A comprehensive study of this devastating event that looks at the causes, impact, and responses to the famine—certain to remain the classic work on the subject.

Kelly, John. *The Great Mortality: An Intimate History of the Black Death, the Most Devastating Plague of All Time*. New York: Harper Perennial, 2006. An extremely detailed and readable account of the plague that incorporates the latest findings.

IMPERIAL PAPACY BESIEGED

Blumenfeld-Kosinski, Renate. *Poets, Saints, and Visionaries of the Great Schism, 1378–1417*. Pittsburgh: Penn State University Press, 2006. A discussion of the calamity of the Great Schism in a wide sense, including an examination of artistic, visionary, and literary texts.

Swanson R.N. *Universities, Academics, and the Great Schism*. Cambridge Studies in Medieval Life and Thought, Third Series. Cambridge: Cambridge University Press, 2002. Analysis of the schism from the viewpoint of the academics who were prominent in the university rivalries, concluding with a look at their contribution to the Conciliar movement.

MORE DESTRUCTION: THE HUNDRED YEARS' WAR, 1337–1453

Allmand, Christopher. *The Hundred Years' War: England and France at War, ca. 1300–ca. 1450*. Cambridge: Cambridge University Press, 2008. A brief account that remains the best summary of this conflict.

Gillingham, John. *The Wars of the Roses: Peace and Conflict in Fifteenth-Century England*. Baton Rouge: Louisiana State University Press, 1981. A political and military history of this influential conflict.

Warner, Marina. *Joan of Arc: The Image of Female Heroism*. New York: Knopf, 1981. Examines Joan's life and legend.

RESPONSES TO THE DISRUPTION OF MEDIEVAL ORDER

Bergin, Thomas Goddard. *Boccaccio*. New York: Viking Press, 1981. A scholarly study of the life and thought of this influential writer.

Hicks, Michael. *Bastard Feudalism*. New York: Longman, 1995. A careful work that revisits the development of "bastard feudalism" in England, particularly in the fifteenth century, and shows that it is an acceleration of previous trends.

Huizinga, Johan. *The Waning of the Middle Ages*. New York: St. Martin's Press, 1967. A brilliant study of the mentality of the people in the late Middle Ages, including art, literature, and general outlook.

Lambert, Malcolm. *Medieval Heresy: Popular Movements from the Gregorian Reform to the Reformation*, 3rd ed. Oxford: Blackwell, 2002. A general explanation of the Hussite and Lollard movements placed within the larger context of other heresies.

Leff, Gordon. *William of Ockham*. Manchester, England: Manchester University Press, 1975. An authoritative study that makes the ideas of this difficult philosopher accessible.

EMPIRES IN THE EAST

Imber, Colin. *The Ottoman Empire, 1300–1650: The Structure of Power*. New York: Palgrave Macmillan, 2004. A detailed chronological survey that both introduces and summarizes the period.

Martin, Janet. *Medieval Russia, 980–1584*. New York: Cambridge University Press, 1995. A well-written, accessible account of the growth of Russia.

Morgan, David. *The Mongols*, 2nd ed. New York: Blackwell, 2007. A survey that stresses the impact of the Mongol Empire on eastern Europe.

PEDRO BERRUGUETE, *FEDERICO DA MONTEFELTRO AND HIS SON*
GUIDOBALDO, ca. 1476

This portrait shows the founder of the dynasty of Urbino—a soldier of fortune who was made
duke by the pope in 1474. The artist used oil paint and a new sense of realism to depict the duke
with everything that mattered to him: the armor of a soldier, the book of a scholar, the support
of the papacy, shown by the tiara in the upper left corner, and the presence of his son, an heir
to perpetuate his dynasty. Strong, well-rounded individuals such as this brought a dramatic new
spirit to the West.

A New Spirit in the West

The Renaissance, ca. 1300–1640

"This age is dominated by great men [who] labored much to aggrandize themselves and to acquire glory. And yet, would it not have been better if they had undertaken fewer enterprises and been more afraid of offending God and of persecuting their subjects and neighbors?" With these words, a contemporary biographer of Louis the Spider, king of France during the Renaissance, pinpointed both the strengths and weaknesses of this new age: Talented individuals accomplished much, yet often to the neglect of those in their care.

This rise of new talent first became evident in Italy during the disastrous fourteenth century, when some individuals responded to the troubled times with a clear-eyed realism that let them see opportunity amid the chaos. The transforming ideas of the era have been dubbed the Renaissance (meaning "rebirth"), and they promised a return to the spirit of ancient Greece and Rome that might restore the glory of the Roman Empire.

Political turbulence in the Italian city-states led visionary rulers to govern in new ways, developing innovative military strategies and novel diplomacy. This individual achievement in politics generated similar accomplishments in literature, architecture, and the visual arts as rulers became patrons supporting artists who mirrored their values. Just as these patrons stimulated artistic expression, intellectuals created a cultural movement that emphasized the study of Greek and Roman classics and praised realism and individual accomplishments. Perhaps the true greatness of the Renaissance lay in the application of these abstract ideas to real life. The innovative ideas that emerged in Italy subsequently spread throughout Europe as the ravages of the fourteenth century broke down old medieval structures and institutions.

Although these new ideas brought wealth and power to some, everyone did not benefit equally. Indeed, public policies in these centuries often worsened the lot of the poor and the powerless. Nevertheless, the Renaissance was an exciting, vibrant time that ushered Europe from the medieval world toward modern life.

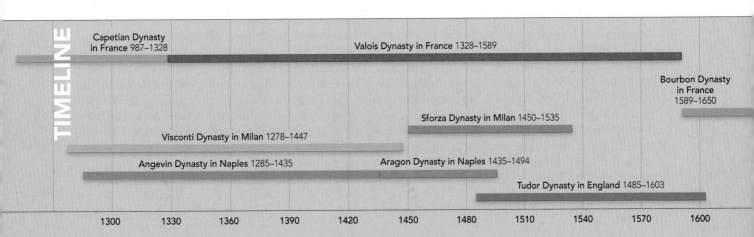

TIMELINE

Capetian Dynasty in France 987–1328

Valois Dynasty in France 1328–1589

Bourbon Dynasty in France 1589–1650

Sforza Dynasty in Milan 1450–1535

Visconti Dynasty in Milan 1278–1447

Angevin Dynasty in Naples 1285–1435

Aragon Dynasty in Naples 1435–1494

Tudor Dynasty in England 1485–1603

1300 1330 1360 1390 1420 1450 1480 1510 1540 1570 1600

A NEW SPIRIT EMERGES: INDIVIDUALISM, REALISM, AND ACTIVISM

In the late thirteenth century, Cimabue, an important painter from the Italian city-state of Florence, was walking in the countryside and saw a young shepherd boy drawing sheep on a rock. The painter recognized the boy's talent and took him on as an apprentice. The young shepherd, Giotto (ca. 1267–1337), flourished under his master's tutelage, and stories arose about the youth's talent for realistic painting—and his independent spirit. He was said to have once painted a fly on the nose of a face that Cimabue was painting, and the fly was so lifelike that the master tried to brush it off several times before he grasped his student's joke. Giotto grew up to vastly surpass his master and create paintings of such realism and emotional honesty that they helped change the direction of painting. As the new century dawned, there would be others like Giotto who creatively broke new ground.

The Renaissance: A Controversial Idea

For centuries historians have struggled with the very idea of whether this age beginning in the fourteenth century in Italy constituted a turning point—the **Renaissance.** People living in fourteenth-century Italy themselves identified this era as characterized by a return to the sources of knowledge and standards of beauty that had created the great civilizations of classical Greece and Rome. (Classical literature, as they defined it, covered a period from about 800 B.C.E. to about 400 C.E.) Francesco Petrarch (1304–1374), an Italian writer who studied the classics and wrote poetry, was an early proponent of Renaissance ideas. Petrarch lamented that he could find no one in his own time who could serve as a model of virtuous behavior—he mirrored the example of many in the fourteenth century who despaired of their time (see Chapter 9). However, through his studies, he came to revere figures from antiquity who seemed to understand proper values and follow them regardless of worldly distractions. Petrarch even wrote letters to ancient figures, and in one such letter to the Roman historian Livy, he wrote: "I only wish, that I had been born in your time or you in ours. . . . I have to thank you . . . because you have so often helped me forget the evils of today." Later Renaissance thinkers would follow Petrarch's example and see in ancient Greece and Rome the models to shape a new world.

Yet, they overstated their case—medieval scholars had never lost touch with the Latin texts, and no one gazing at the Gothic cathedrals and the magnificent illuminated manuscripts of the Middle Ages can doubt that medieval people had an exquisite sense of beauty. Indeed, most of the qualities that we identify with the Renaissance had existed in some form throughout the Middle Ages. For this reason, some modern scholars have suggested that the Renaissance should not be considered a separate historical era. Some see this era as part of a succession of "renaissances" that spurred the intellectual history of the West. Others argue that a different spirit clearly emerged during the period that we have come to call the Renaissance.

Medieval antecedents

In its simplest sense, the Renaissance was an age of accelerated change that began in Italy and that spread new ideas more rapidly than ever before. Many people, especially urban dwellers, questioned medieval values of hierarchy, community, and reliance on authority and replaced them with a focus on ambitious individualism and realism (both of which had to some extent existed in the Middle Ages but received new emphasis). Some no longer used the classic texts to reinforce the status quo, as had become common in the medieval universities; instead, they studied to transform themselves. Petrarch eagerly noted that the texts "sow into our hearts love of the best and eager desire for it." As they strove for excellence, the men and women of the Renaissance ushered in a new age.

Thus, many historians identify the Renaissance as a unique state of mind or set of ideas about everything from art to politics. Having first sprouted in Italy in the fourteenth century, these ideas slowly spread north as the prevailing medieval culture was rocked by the disasters of the fourteenth century. Just as historians disagree about the nature of the Renaissance, they also differ on exactly why these new ideas took root in Italy. What was it about the Italian situation in the early fourteenth century that made that land ripe for fresh ideas about individualism and realism and that fostered the rise of enterprising people?

Why Italy?

Because the people of the Renaissance themselves believed the heart of their rebirth was a recovery of the spirit of classical Greece and Rome, the ancient ruins provided a continuing stimulus for such reflections. As Petrarch mapped the ruins, he said the pastime was wonderfully pleasant "not so much because of what I actually saw, as from the recollection of our ancestors, who left such illustrious memorials of Roman virtue. . . ." For Petrarch and others, these ruins were an ever-present reminder of an age that they believed was dramatically different from their own—an age they sought to recapture.

The new appreciation of classical authors caused a resurgence of interest in the Greek classics that had been neglected in the West for so long. In 1396, the Florentines invited a Greek scholar from Byzantium to lecture at the University of Florence, but this first step received a huge impetus in the mid-fifteenth century when Constantinople fell to the Turks (see Chapter 9). Many eastern scholars fled to Italy, bringing their language skills and Greek manuscripts with them. Over the next decades, new translations of some of the greatest Greek works became fully integrated into Western culture. The study of Greek texts would make a dramatic impact on religious studies, as we will see in Chapter 11.

A fresh reading of the classics certainly stimulated in some literate Italians a desire to recover a spirit of classical greatness, but were readings alone enough to change a culture's sensibilities so dramatically? Some historians argue instead that the tumultuous politics of the Italian city-states particularly favored the growth of new ideas. Incessant warfare among the states opened the door for skilled, innovative leaders to come forward. These leaders in turn surrounded themselves with talented courtiers who willingly broke from tradition to forward their own careers as they pleased their princes. A new spirit found fertile ground in these ambitious, upwardly mobile men.

Others point to the Black Death, which entered Italy in 1348, as the catalyst that transformed the old order (see Chapter 9). The plague's drastic reduction of the population engendered huge economic changes. Prices plummeted, and trade in luxuries such as

Plague disruptions

silk, jewelry, spices, and glass quickened. Italy was ideally placed to profit from this commerce, for throughout the Middle Ages, the Italian city-states had dominated trade in the eastern Mediterranean. During the fourteenth century, individuals, families, and institutions accumulated a good deal of capital, and men and women used some of this money to support the arts. Some have vividly suggested that the Renaissance became one long shopping spree that supported the talented artists whose vision helped define this controversial era—the bridge that began to move Western history from the Middle Ages to modernity.

A Multifaceted Movement

At its core, the Renaissance emphasized and celebrated humans and their achievements. It thus revived an advocacy of individualism that the West had not seen since the time of the ancients. As the Italian writer Giovanni Pico della Mirandola (1463–1494) optimistically wrote in his *Oration on the Dignity of Man*, "Man is rightly . . . considered a great miracle and a truly marvelous creature," and in addition to this, Pico said that people could determine their own destiny. This optimistic faith in the human potential was an exciting new idea. Renaissance thinkers asserted a powerful belief in the human ability to choose right and wrong and to act on these choices.

Individualism

During the Renaissance, Europeans favored a biblical verse from Genesis that described humans as being created in God's "image and likeness." **Figure 10.1** shows one portion of the Italian artist Michelangelo's (1475–1564) revered painting on the ceiling of the Sistine Chapel. In this image, the realistic and beautifully proportioned figure of Adam mirrors the physical beauty of the Creator. Michelangelo also portrayed Adam as more than a piece of inert clay waiting for the divine spark to bring him life. Instead, Adam reaches up to God, meeting him halfway in the act of Creation. For Michelangelo and many other artists of the time, man was indeed created in God's image—not merely spiritually and morally, but also as a creator himself, shaping his own destiny. Here Michelangelo echoes Pico in expressing this idea that was the essence of Renaissance thought.

Renaissance men and women also prided themselves on their accurate view of the world. This form of realism appears vividly in the art of the period. Throughout the rest of this chapter, the various examples of artwork from these centuries show a realistic portrayal of the world.

Realism

Another prevailing theme in the Renaissance came with the emergence of activism. Petrarch himself succinctly expressed the energetic spirit of the age, writing, "It is better to will the good than to know the truth." In other words, being wise was not enough; one had to exert one's will actively in the world to make a difference. Leon Battista Alberti (1404–1472) expressed the same sentiment: "Men can do all things if they will." As we see, Michelangelo's

Activism

FIGURE 10.1 Michelangelo, *Creation of Adam*, 1508–1512 Michelangelo was commissioned to paint frescoes on the ceiling of the Sistine Chapel, the pope's personal chapel in the Vatican, Rome. This famous scene depicts God's work, with the shaping of Adam in His image.

Adam in **Figure 10.1** participates in his own creation by reaching up to receive the spark of life, and people were encouraged to imitate this active involvement.

A final characteristic of this new spirit was that it was secular—that is, it did not take place in the churches, monasteries, or universities that were dominated by religious thought. That is not to say Renaissance thinkers were antireligious, for they were not—Petrarch explained quite clearly: "Christ is my God; Cicero is the prince of the language I use." While most believed deeply in God and many worked in the church, their vocation was to apply the new spirit to this world, not the next.

> A secular spirit

Renaissance thinkers felt that the spirit of the classical worlds of Greece and Rome had been reborn before their very eyes. In part, they were right. This vital new age witnessed a renewed belief in human beings' capacity to perfect themselves, to assess the world realistically, and to act vigorously to make an impact on their society. The key to this transformation was education.

Humanism: The Path to Self-Improvement

The urban dwellers of the Italian cities knew that education was the key to success. Men entering business had to be trained at least in reading, writing, and mathematics. In Florence at the beginning of the fourteenth century, the number of students enrolled in private schools testifies to the value practical Florentines placed on education: Out of a total population of about 100,000, some 10,000 youths attended private schools to obtain a basic education.

Of those, about 1,000 went to special schools to learn advanced business mathematics. However, another 500 pursued a more general liberal education. From these latter emerged an educational movement that defined and perpetuated the Renaissance spirit and changed the course of Western thought.

Petrarch departed from the traditional medieval course of study and from his father's desire that he prepare for a career in law. Instead, he pursued a general study of classical literature. The cities of Italy spawned many young men like Petrarch, who wanted an education separated from the church-dominated universities that had monopolized learning for centuries. Such students sought to understand the causes of human actions through the writings of the ancients, and in turn improve themselves. After all, if they believed they were created in God's image, they had a responsibility to cultivate their capabilities. The humanities—literature, history, and philosophy—thus formed the core of the ideal Renaissance education, which aimed to shape students so that they could excel in anything. Proponents of this teaching method were called **humanists.**

> Humanist curriculum

Humanists stressed grammar (particularly Latin and Greek so that students could read the classics), poetry, history, and ethics. Following the ancient Roman model, humanists capped off their education with rhetoric, the art of persuasive speaking, which prepared men to serve in a public capacity. Although this course of study may not appear revolutionary, it proved to be.

The early humanists' passion for classical texts led them to search out manuscripts that might yield even greater wisdom from the ancients. As they read and compared manuscripts, they discovered that mistakes had crept into texts that had been painstakingly copied over and over in the medieval monasteries. So the early humanists carefully pored over the many copies of texts to compile accurate versions. These techniques established standards for historical and literary criticism that continue today. Our debt to these literary scholars is incalculable as we enjoy accurate editions of works written thousands of years ago.

The Renaissance emphasis on study inspired some writers to comment on educational theory. Christine of Pizan (1365–ca. 1430) was a professional writer who worked in the French court. She supported herself and

| Educational theory |

her children through her works of poetry and prose. Reflecting the interests of the times, she also wrote several pedagogical treatises: one instructing women on their roles in society (*The Book of Three Virtues*), a manual of good government for the French Dauphin (*The Book of Deeds of King Charles V*), and even a military handbook (*The Book of Feats of Arms and of Chivalry*).

In the same vein, many others authored books to help people learn to cultivate their talents. The best known of these is *The Book of the Courtier*, by the Italian author Baldassare Castiglione (1478–1529). In this popular work, the author summarizes the expected behavior of men of the court. For Castiglione, native endowments were only the beginning—a courtier had to cultivate military skills, a classical education, and an appreciation of art through music, drawing, and painting. Castiglione turned the Renaissance ideal of an active, well-developed individual into a social ideal of the aristocracy.

Other humanists proposed more formal educational settings. One educator (Guarino da Verona) established a model secondary school at Mantua, in Italy, called the Happy House, which taught humanities, religion, mathematics, and physical education. The school even included lessons on diet and dress; no facet of the whole human was neglected in the effort at improvement.

Urban families who prized education for their sons also expected their daughters to be educated, but not to the same degree. The eminent Italian humanist Leonardo Bruni (1374–1444) wrote an oft-quoted letter praising a humanist—but not a

| Women humanists |

full—education for women. For example, he argued that rhetoric in particular was inappropriate for women: "For why exhaust a woman with the concerns of . . . [rhetoric] when she will never be seen in the forum?" His comments reveal the crux of the matter: Women could be educated, but they were not to use their education in a public way, and since rhetoric was central to the humanists, educated Renaissance women were caught in a paradox.

As one example, Isotta Nogarola (1418–1466) earned much recognition from her family and some family friends for her learning. However, as soon as she tried to engage in a public dialogue (through letters), male humanists reprimanded her and deemed her immoral for her public display. She retired into the seclusion of her study, just as other women took refuge in convents to pursue their research.

Rulers, of course, were exempt from such prohibitions of public use of education, and royal women made good use of the latest Renaissance notions of study. Queens such as Elizabeth I of England (r. 1558–1603) and Isabella of Castile (r. 1474–1504) employed their education to rule effectively, support the arts, and encourage the new educational methods. The Biography of Isabella d'Este (on page 314) describes the life of one Italian woman who possessed so much political authority that she became a renowned patron of the arts and of education.

Humanists applied their skills in many areas of life. Some—called **civic humanists**—involved themselves in politics, treating the public arena as their artistic canvas. Others applied their skills at literary criticism to the Bible and other Christian texts. The most influential of these **Christian humanists** came from outside Italy. As we will see in Chapter 11, men such as the Spanish cardinal Ximénez de Cisneros (1436–1517) and the Dutchman Desiderius Erasmus (ca. 1466–1536) transformed the study of the Bible and paved the way for dramatic changes in religious sensibilities.

Humanist scholarship was crucial in shaping the new spirit of the Renaissance, but it was not sufficient in itself. Scholars and artists and talented young men would have made little impact without the generosity of patrons such as Isabella, who supported the new talent and assiduously purchased their productions. The spirit of the Renaissance thrived on the money that flowed abundantly (albeit unevenly, as we will see) in the Italian cities.

The Generosity of Patrons: Supporting New Ideas

The talented writers and artists of the Renaissance depended on generous patrons to support them. During the early Renaissance, cities themselves served as artistic patrons, stimulating the creation of art by offering prizes and subsidies for their talented citizens. Guilds, too, served as artistic patrons, commissioning great public monuments to enhance the spaces of their cities. The public art that graced the streets and squares enhanced the reputation of the city itself and in turn forwarded the new ideas of the gifted artists.

In time, warfare and internal strife caused cities to have less money to use in support of art, and patronage was taken over by wealthy individuals. In addition to Isabella d'Este, many other rulers, such as the Medici

BIOGRAPHY

Isabella d'Este
(1474–1539)

FIGURE 10.2 Isabella d'Este

Isabella d'Este was born the daughter of a duke in 1474 in the small Duchy of Ferrara, just south of Venice. She grew up in a court that both appreciated Renaissance education and art and succumbed to the violence that marked fifteenth-century Italy.

When Isabella was only 2, her father's nephew attacked the palace in an effort to seize power from the duke. Before Isabella was 8 years old, Venetian armies had invaded Ferrara to try to dominate the small duchy. Yet Isabella's father was a skillful diplomat and withstood these and many other challenges. In the process, his daughter began learning about Renaissance diplomacy.

Duchess of Mantua, Diplomat, and Patron of the Arts

The young girl was educated in the best humanist tradition. Her tutors taught her to read the great classics of the Roman world in the original Latin. She learned quickly and spoke Latin fluently at an early age. She also was an accomplished musician and excelled at singing and playing the lute.

When she was 6 years old, Isabella's parents began searching for a suitable future husband for her. They approached the family of the nearby Duke of Mantua to discuss a betrothal between Isabella and their eldest son, Francesco. When representatives of Francesco's family interviewed the young child, they wrote back to the prospective in-laws that they were astonished at her precocious intelligence. They sent Francesco's parents a portrait of the lovely black-eyed, blond child but assured them that "her marvelous knowledge and intelligence are far more worthy of admiration [than her beauty]." A betrothal was arranged that would unite the two houses trying to maintain independence from their powerful neighbors, Milan and Venice.

Isabella and Francesco were married in 1490, when she was 15. An elaborate ceremony joined the two families, and in her old age, Isabella proudly wrote of her memories of the gifts, decorations, and lavish banquet that marked this turning point of her life.

Under the skillful rule of Francesco and Isabella, Mantua rose to the foremost rank of the smaller Italian city-states. Isabella involved herself in the art of diplomacy throughout the couple's reign. She wrote more than two thousand letters—many of them to popes, kings, and other Italian rulers. In one letter to her husband, Isabella assured him that he could concentrate completely on military matters, for "I intend to govern the State . . . in such a manner that you will suffer no wrong, and all that is possible will be done for the good of your subjects." This talented woman was as good as her word, for when Francesco was captured in 1509 and imprisoned, Isabella ruled in his stead and valiantly saved the city from invasion.

Like other Italians influenced by Renaissance pseudoscience, Isabella avidly believed in astrology. She embarked on no important venture without consulting her astrologers. But she also took an interest in the real-world findings of the time. She received correspondence about Columbus's discovery of America and the "intelligent and gentle" natives he found there.

Yet the educated duchess is most remembered as a patron of the arts. She wrote explicit instructions for the works she commissioned: One painting prompted her to pen as many as forty letters. Recognizing excellence, she wanted to commission a work from Leonardo da Vinci, but the artist never found the time to oblige her. (See Document 10.1.)

With a love of literature nurtured since her youth, Isabella accumulated a library that became one of the best in Italy. She took advantage of the new printing industry to acquire the first editions of the great classics as well as the contemporary works of Petrarch and Dante. Her requests for these editions show her appreciation of beauty even in her search for literature: She asked for books printed on parchment (instead of paper) and bound in leather.

When Isabella was 64 years old, Francesco died. The aging duchess turned to her many children and grandchildren for comfort and companionship. She took particular delight in one grandchild who could recite Virgil at the age of only 5. Isabella died in 1539, a year after losing her husband. In the last months of her life, a great scholar of the age called her "the wisest and most fortunate of women"— an apt epitaph for someone who so personified the Renaissance spirit.

Connecting People & Society

1. What conclusions can you draw from this life about the importance of family ties in the Renaissance?

2. What opportunities did a wealthy woman have to participate in the intellectual life of the Renaissance?

3. What can you learn from this life about the importance of patronage to the arts?

DOCUMENT 10.1

Isabella d'Este Implores Leonardo da Vinci to Paint for Her

In 1504, Isabella d'Este of Mantua (see Biography in this chapter) wrote letters to Leonardo da Vinci soliciting a painting. Although she never received her painting, these letters show the tensions that often arose between purchasers' desires and artists' aesthetic inclinations and shed light on the all-important process of patronage.

Letter 1.   "To Master Leonardo Vinci, the painter. M. Leonardo,— Hearing that you are settled at Florence, we have begun to hope that our cherished desire to obtain a work by your hand may be at length realised. When you were in this city, and drew our portrait in carbon, you promised us that you would some day paint it in colours. But because this would be almost impossible, since you are unable to come here, we beg you to keep your promise by converting our portrait into another figure, which would be still more acceptable to us; that is to say, a youthful Christ of about twelve years, which would be the age He had attained when He disputed with the doctors in the temple, executed with all that sweetness and charm of atmosphere which is the peculiar excellence of your art. If you will consent to gratify this our great desire, remember that apart from the payment, which you shall fix yourself, we shall remain so deeply obliged to you that our sole desire will be to do what you wish, and from this time forth we are ready to do your service and pleasure, hoping to receive an answer in the affirmative." Mantua, May 14, 1504.

Letter 2.   On the 27th of May, Angelo del Tovaglia replied:—"I received the letter of Your Highness, together with the one for Leonardo da Vinci, to whom I presented it, and at the same time tried to persuade and induce him, with powerful reasons, to oblige Your Excellency by painting the little figure of Christ, according to your request. He has promised me without fail to paint it in such times and hours as he can snatch from the work on which he is engaged for this Signory. I will not fail to entreat Leonardo, and also Perugino, as to the other subject. Both make liberal promises, and seem to have the greatest wish to serve Your Highness. Nevertheless, I think it will be a race between them which is the slower! I hardly know which of the two is likely to win, but expect Leonardo will be the conqueror. All the same, I will do my utmost."

SOURCE: Julia Cartwright, *Isabella d'Este: Marchioness of Mantua, 1474–1539*, vol. 1 (New York: E. P. Dutton, 1903), pp. 324–327.

Analyze the Document

1. What painting does Isabella want? How do you think modern artists would react to getting such specific instructions? Why?

2. Letter #2 is from Leonardo's uncle. What does this fact indicate about the relationship among family ties, art, and patronage in the Renaissance?

---

in Florence and the Sforza in Milan, used their wealth to stimulate the creation of spectacular works of art. In return, patrons gained social and political status by surrounding themselves with objects of beauty or intellect.

Cosimo de Medici (1389–1464) offers a perfect model for the impact of patrons in the Renaissance. Cosimo supported intellectuals and artists and personally financed the acquisition of manuscripts. His fascination with the Greek philosopher Plato led him to make perhaps his greatest contribution to the intellectual life of the West: He founded the Platonic Academy, hiring the famous Neoplatonic scholar Marsilio Ficino (1433–1499) to guide the studies. Ficino translated the works of Plato and wrote works that demonstrated that Platonism and Christianity shared a belief that humans were permeated with divine love and that the goal of humanity was to rise upward toward the Divinity. These studies shaped the glorification of human accomplishments that were to be the hallmark of the Renaissance, and they were made possible by the powerful patronage of Cosimo and other leaders.

Not only rulers, but rising bourgeoisie could enhance their social status by owning works of art, and this activity served to spur the production of art. Document 10.1 describes Isabella d'Este trying to contract a painting.

The church also supported the arts. Religious fraternities commissioned many paintings, and popes financially backed numerous artists. Like cities and individuals, churches gained status through their patronage, but churches also recognized a religious purpose of art. Many people attributed miraculous power to visual portrayals of religious themes, and churchmen supported this belief. For example, the Florentines customarily brought an image of the Virgin Mary (called the *Madonna of Impruneta*) down from the hills to Florence in times of crisis, and in 1483, a procession of the Madonna was credited with stopping a destructive, monthlong rainfall.

Such ceremonies also served the civic purpose of bringing the faithful together in a public way. The painting in **Figure 10.3** shows a religious procession

> Religious patronage

FIGURE 10.3 Gentile Bellini, *Procession of Eucharist*, 1496 This painting shows the importance of religious festivals in the great St. Mark's Square of Venice, where pilgrims gathered to visit the relics of the famous saint.

in Venice, in which the sacred Eucharist was paraded through the square encased in a magnificently ornate carrier. The painting reinforces the way these religious festivities united the residents and indeed celebrated the beautiful public spaces of the city itself.

Thus, dynamic city life and a new emphasis on education stimulated new ideas, and generous patronage helped them grow. However, the new spirit spread rapidly by the late Renaissance owing to a revolutionary advance in technology.

The Invention of the Printing Press: Spreading New Ideas

Throughout the Middle Ages, precious texts had to be laboriously copied by hand, making books relatively scarce and expensive. As we saw in Chapter 1, one of the significant advantages to the growth of civilization is the ability for more people to read and have access to the written word. In Asia (China and Korea), inventors had developed a way to reproduce texts and pictures more quickly—wood-block printing. With this technique, images and some text were carved into wooden blocks and then could be mass-produced by printing. This technique had spread to the West by the late fourteenth century. By the early fifteenth century, Asian printers had replaced wooden type with bronze type, which was much more durable and offered a more consistent print. This method, too, rapidly spread to the West.

In the 1440s, these early printing techniques reached their culmination with the development of movable type and the adaptation of an oil press to print pages more rapidly. A German silversmith

named Johannes Gutenberg (ca. 1400–1470) is credited with bringing all these innovations together to produce the first printed Bible in 1455. Suddenly, literature became more available, thereby ultimately affecting all of Western civilization.

The development and proliferation of the printing press were a testimony to the growing confidence that there was a market for books. In addition to a demand for their product, print shops also needed something to print on. Paper technology gave them the necessary cheap medium to replace the expensive parchment used during the Middle Ages. The technique of papermaking came to Europe from China through the Muslim world. By the fourteenth century, Italian paper mills were using old rags to make inexpensive, yet high-quality, paper. Although some wealthy patrons, such as Isabella d'Este, often preferred the more traditional parchment, the future lay with the new paper.

Printing presses spread rapidly through Europe—by the 1480s many Italian cities had established their own presses, and by 1500 there were about a thousand presses all over the continent. Previously, valuable books, painstakingly copied by hand, belonged to the patron who paid for the copy. Now the literary world looked to a broader reading public for support, consequently igniting a rapid spread of ideas that carried the new spirit throughout Europe. Subsequent notions—from the excitement of international discoveries to intellectual challenges to religious ideology—also spread rapidly. The pace of change in Western civilization quickened as the European presses circulated ideas with unprecedented speed.

All the elements were in place for the transformation of thought that we have come to know as the

Italy in 1454

This map shows the political divisions of Italy in the fifteenth century. It also includes the locations of the major city-states of the north.

Explore the Map

1. Which of the city-states was most likely to be threatened by the expansion of the Papal States? Why?

2. Why was Venice so well placed to dominate trade in the eastern Mediterranean?

3. Which states were threatened by Venice's expansion into the peninsula?

4. What contributed to Naples's relative isolation from the politics of the northern states?

Renaissance. The study of classical texts had helped change people's views of themselves and their approach to the world. Money flowed in support of talented and enterprising individuals, and technology helped spread the ideas rapidly. Finally, men actively implemented these ideas in many fields, from art to business to politics.

THE POLITICS OF INDIVIDUAL EFFORT

The medieval power struggle between emperors and popes left an enormous power vacuum in northern Italy. This vacuum allowed small city-states, or cities that controlled the surrounding countryside, to become used to independence. As the fourteenth century opened, most of the northern cities were free communes (see Chapter 8) with republican forms of government, but as the fourteenth century progressed, changes occurred.

The Italian City-States

These city-states engaged in almost constant warfare over their borders and commercial interests, and within the cities, classes and political factions fought for control of the government. In such unstable times, most of the republican governments were under pressure, and strong men with dictatorial power took over. As we saw in Chapter 9, mercenary armies had become a significant feature of warfare, and they also became a force in Italian politics as city-states hired army captains (called *condottieri*) with their armies to come fight their wars. These mercenaries frequently ravaged the countryside, bringing more misery than protection to the population. Through the fourteenth and fifteenth centuries, city-states would see repeated internal and external strife as they wrestled with their neighbors and with internal governing. These turbulent times brought misery to many but opportunity to others. Sometimes strong, talented individuals rose to positions of authority without constitutional or hereditary legitimacy. The Duke of Urbino, portrayed in the chapter-opening illustration, was one such successful mercenary captain. These rulers introduced a new kind of politics and perhaps inadvertently stimulated the new spirit of the Renaissance.

Map 10.1 shows Italy in 1454. Notice that the northern areas consisted of a patchwork quilt of city-states. Among these, Venice, Milan, and Florence were the largest and most powerful. Popes controlled the large, central strip of the peninsula, and the Kingdom of Naples dominated the south. It was the competition among the northern states that fueled the politics of individual effort that so influenced Renaissance ideas such as individualism and activism.

The Italian city-states fell into two general categories: republics and principalities. Republics featured the institutions of the medieval city communes, in which an urban elite governed. For the most part, Venice and Florence preserved the republican form of government during most of the Renaissance. Principalities, on the other hand, were ruled by one dynasty. Milan and Naples were the most notable examples of this form of government.

Florence: Birthplace of the Renaissance

Florence at the beginning of the fourteenth century was a vibrant republic where Renaissance ideas seem to have been first fostered. Florence prided itself on its republican form of government, in which eligible men held office by random selection. But the city was an uneasy republic indeed, fragmented by local rivalries that always threatened to break out into violence within the urban spaces themselves. Only guild members could participate in the government, and an oligarchy of the leading families was frequently able to control it. Florence was badly hit by the plague—in 1348 alone, almost 40 percent of its population was killed, and its economy, too, was badly damaged as cloth production declined. Warfare with Milan in the early fifteenth century bankrupted many of the city's leading commercial families and created a massive public debt. In their troubles, the Florentines turned to the wealthiest banking family in Europe—the Medici. The republic got more than it bargained for.

In 1434, Cosimo de' Medici took control of the Florentine oligarchy and exiled his rivals. In the tradition of Caesar Augustus, whom he admired, Cosimo concentrated power in his household while ostensibly keeping a republican form of government.

The Medici

Under this shrewd family, Florence and the arts flourished. Cosimo's grandson, Lorenzo the Magnificent (r. 1469–1492), epitomized the ideal Renaissance ruler. A great statesman, he was also a patron of the arts, a poet, and an athlete.

Yet even Lorenzo could not bring peace to the contentious Florentine people. During his life he faced intrigue and assassination attempts and had to use all his diplomatic skills to preserve Florence from foreign foes. Late in his tenure, voices began to be raised against the Renaissance ideals that he so actively supported. Shortly after Lorenzo's death, the rule of the Medici could not withstand the growing pressures from outside and within the city.

In 1494, French armies invaded the countryside around Florence, and the city-state was again buffeted with financial and material woes. The French armies found an ally within the city in the person of a

Savonarola

fiery preacher who had objected to the rule of the Medici and to the passionate acquisition of money and art that had dominated the early Renaissance.

Girolamo Savonarola (1452–1498) was a courageous, yet uncompromising, man who had resented the rule of the Medici and accused the clergy of corruption from the papacy on down. He argued vigorously against the lust for money that motivated citizens in the high-tempo Florentine economy. Perhaps most of all, he despised humanism, which he believed poisoned everything from art to religion by placing humans in the spotlight. The passionate preacher clearly recognized the changing times, but he advocated a different response to these changes.

Helped by the disruptions caused by the French invasions, Savonarola was able to arrange for the Medici to be expelled from the city and for a republic to be reintroduced. But Savonarola also wanted to return people's sensibilities to those of what he perceived to be a more pious age. He preached against nude paintings and sculptures and in 1497 presided over a public "burning of the vanities"—a huge bonfire into which people tossed ornaments, pictures, cards, and other "frivolous" items. This event is described by an eyewitness in Document 10.2.

Eventually, the monk's zeal sparked opposition. The pope chafed at Savonarola's attacks and finally excommunicated him and forbad him to preach. Savonarola himself came to an ironic, fiery end: He was condemned and hung, and his body was burned in the public square of Florence—exactly where the "vanities" had been burned.

Like the other great figures of the age, Savonarola was a product of the Renaissance—he felt the same civic pride and shared the same love of education. But, instead of responding to these forces with a sense of humanism and realism, he looked for a spiritual reaction, a religious renewal that he believed should shape the future. In time, northern Europeans picked up Savonarola's call for religious renewal, but not yet. In Florence the Medici were restored in the sixteenth century, and the republic was formally dissolved in 1530.

At first glance, it may seem incongruous that the stormy political history of Florence spawned the creative ideas that we have come to identify with the Renaissance. However, the very environment that made people feel they had to be actively involved in their city and fight for their own interests stimulated the driving individualism that characterized this age. Politicians vied to prove themselves superior to

Friar Savonarola Ignites a "Bonfire of the Vanities"

Luca Landucci ran a small apothecary shop in Florence and kept a diary chronicling these turbulent times. This excerpt from 1497 describes the notorious incident in which the reforming friar Savonarola (whom Landucci calls Fra Girolamo) ordered his followers— young boys—to collect Florentine artworks and burn them in the square.

27th February (the Carnival). There was made on the *Piazza de' Signori* a pile of vain things, nude statues and playing-boards, heretic books, Morganti [poems], mirrors, and many other vain things, of great value, estimated at thousands of florins. Although some lukewarm people gave trouble, throwing dead cats and other dirt upon it, the boys nevertheless set it on fire and burnt everything, for there was plenty of small brushwood. And it is to be observed that the pile was not made by children; there was a rectangular woodwork measuring more than *12 braccia* [about 23 feet] each way, which had taken the carpenters several days to make, with many workmen, so that it was necessary for many armed men to keep guard the night before, as certain lukewarm persons, specially certain young men called *Compagnacci* wanted to destroy it. The *Frate* was held in such veneration by those who had faith in him, that this morning, although it was Carnival, Fra Girolamo said mass in *San Marco*, and gave the Sacrament with his hands to all his friars, and afterwards to several thousand men and women; and then he came on to a pulpit outside the door of the church with the Host, and showing it to the people, blessed them, with many prayers: *Fac salvum populum tuum Domine,* etc. There was a great crowd, who had come in the expectation of seeing signs; the lukewarm laughed and mocked, saying: "He is excommunicated, and he gives the Communion to others." And certainly it seemed a mistake to me, although I had faith in him; but I never wished to endanger myself by going to hear him, since he was excommunicated.

SOURCE: Luca Landucci, *A Florentine Diary from 1450 to 1516*, trans. Alice de Rosen Jervice (London: Dent, 1927), pp. 130–131.

Analyze the Document

1. What kinds of objects did the friar's followers collect?

2. Who supported the friar?

3. Was Landucci sympathetic to Savonarola?

4. Why was Florence a particularly appropriate place for this act?

---

their rivals, often by supporting artists whose products contributed to their own status. In the republican turmoil, the Renaissance was born.

Venice: The Serene Republic?

Venice preserved its republic with much less turmoil than Florence, although there, too, an oligarchy ruled. Venice's constitution called for only its aristocratic merchant families—numbering about 2,000— to serve in its Great Council. From among this number, they chose one man to serve as the council leader, or **doge,** for life, but most men were in their 70s before being elected to this office. This rule by the elders made political life in Venice remarkably stable—indeed, the city called itself the "Most Serene Republic." This title underplayed the ever-present factional strife that plagued the Italian cities, but Venetians were able to suppress the strife, and many believed their self-proclaimed myth of serenity.

This peace also stemmed from the prosperity generated by overseas trade, which Venice dominated owing to its advantageous location on the Adriatic Sea. **Map 10.2** shows how Venice's location perfectly situated it to take advantage of the lucrative

Overseas trade

trade in the eastern Mediterranean. From Venice's earliest history, it enjoyed a privileged position in the trade with Byzantium, and as we saw in Chapter 8, during the Fourth Crusade in 1204, the Venetians led in the conquest of Constantinople itself. Not only does the painting of St. Mark's Square in **Figure 10.3** show the wealth of Venice, but the domed church in the background reveals the continuing influence of Byzantium on the aesthetics of the city that was formed by interactions with the East. The end of the crusader kingdoms did not end the Venetian dominance of trade, and at the beginning of the Renaissance, wealth continued to pour into the Serene Republic. To consolidate its hold on the eastern Mediterranean, Venice built an empire of coastal cities and islands—as shown on **Map 10.2.**

Venice was built on a collection of islands in a lagoon, and the Grand Canal that continues to mark its main thoroughfare is a perfect representation of the city's maritime orientation. Of the city-state's total population of about 150,000 people, more than 30,000 were sailors. Venice's navy boasted forty-five galleys—large warships with sails and oars—and three hundred hefty sailing ships.

In the beginning of the fifteenth century, Venice began to engage in a policy of expanding into the

MAP 10.2

The Venetian Empire in the Fifteenth Century

This map shows the Venetian Empire, with the red lines indicating the main trade routes of Venice's prosperous commercial ventures.

Explore the Map

1. How would Venice's dominance of the Adriatic Sea and its control of Crete facilitate its ascendancy over the trade in the eastern Mediterranean?

2. Locate the Muslim cities of Tripoli, Tunis, Alexandria, and Beirut. How might Venetian trade with these centers have facilitated cross-cultural interactions?

Italian mainland—the city-state wanted to secure its food supply as well as its overland trade routes. **Map 10.2** shows the cities that became Venetian dependencies. Although this expansionist policy made sense to the Venetians, it understandably upset the neighboring states of Milan and Florence.

The Venetians perhaps should have looked more carefully at their maritime holdings, for Turkish expansion in the eastern Mediterranean (with the capture of Rhodes) seriously challenged Venetian supremacy in the seas. (See Chapter 11 for the subsequent confrontation.)

Through the Renaissance, however, this calm republic helped forward the progress of the new spirit. Its leaders wanted to grace their city with the magnificent new art, so their patronage brought talent to the fore, and their ships helped disseminate the new ideas along with the Italian trade goods.

Milan and Naples: Two Principalities

Milan's violent history mirrored that of Florence, but this city-state more quickly moved from a republican form of government to a hereditary principality.

During the thirteenth century, rival political factions in the city had constantly vied for power. In desperation, the commune invited a soldier from a family named Visconti to come in and keep the peace; he stayed on to rule as prince and established a dynasty that reigned in Milan from 1278 to 1447. The Visconti family recognized the volatility of Italian politics and focused on the military strength that had brought them to power in the first place. After fending off attempts to establish a republic, the Visconti established a principality that coveted the lands of the rest of northern Italy. Only the diplomatic and military talents of Florence, Venice, and its other neighbors kept this aggressive principality in check. Finally, in 1447, the Visconti dynasty ended when the prince died without an heir—the door was open for a new power struggle in Milan.

In 1450, another strong dynasty took power. The Sforza family kept the city-state's proud military tradition, yet also served as patrons of the arts to enhance their own political reputations. The Sforza continued to rule until the early sixteenth century, though always under the pressure of growing republican aspirations.

The Kingdom of Naples in the south was the only region of Italy that preserved a feudal form of government ruled by a hereditary monarchy. In the early fourteenth century, Naples was ruled by Angevin kings who were descendants of the king of France.

Naples | Under these kings, the ideas of the Renaissance came to the feudal and rural south. Giotto (the shepherd-painter whose story opened this chapter) and Boccaccio (see Chapter 9) spent time in Naples under the patronage of King Robert (r. 1309–1343), and even Petrarch called Robert "the only king of our times who has been a friend of learning and of virtue." However, after Robert's rule, Naples became a battleground with claimants from the Angevins and the Spanish Aragonese competing for the throne.

In 1435, the king of Aragon, Alfonso the Magnanimous (r. 1435–1458), was able to reunite the crowns of Naples and Sicily. He worked to centralize his administration but was unable fully to subdue his barons, and Naples remained a feudal kingdom. Alfonso was a passionate devotee of Italian culture and served as a patron of the Renaissance. However, the dynastic claims on this throne by other kings in Europe would disrupt Italian politics in years to come.

The Papal States

The Great Schism ended in 1417, when some 400 churchmen gathered at the Council of Constance and elected a Roman cardinal to be Pope Martin V. When he returned to Rome after the papal sojourn in Avignon (see Chapter 9), Martin found traditional papal lands under the control of neighboring states, and the city in sad disrepair. How was he to restore papal prestige? Should he focus on spiritual or secular leadership? These were the weighty questions that confronted the new pope, and his responses would shape the history of the church.

Martin's first decision was to take political control over central Italy. As one supporter of papal rule said, "Virtue without power would be ridiculous." **Map 10.1** shows the extensive Papal States, which spanned the peninsula. As rulers of central Italy, the popes had a particular advantage in that their rule was a **theocracy** that derived its legitimacy from God (and election by the college of cardinals), so issues of republicanism and tyranny did not apply. However, their religious role also brought complications. For example, as worldly rulers in the Italian tradition, they were expected to improve the fortunes of their families, so they frequently (and accurately) fell prey to the charge of nepotism as they created positions for their relatives. The popes also looked backward to their medieval struggles with the Holy Roman Emperors to control Italy (see Chapter 8), so many felt they had a right—indeed, an obligation—to expand papal lands on the peninsula. All these factors helped propel the popes into the frequently violent sphere of Italian politics. But they also leaped into the exciting, brilliant world of Renaissance creativity.

Martin V determined that the city of Rome itself should be a place of beauty and a beacon of papal power. Just as the Italian princes used art to enhance their prestige, popes began an ambitious—and expensive—building program that would underscore | Papal patronage | their authority. The culmination of this effort was the construction of the new St. Peter's Church in the

RENAISSANCE RULERS

1364–1380	Charles V the Wise, France
1434–1464	Cosimo de' Medici, Florence
1461–1483	Louis XI the Spider, France
1469–1492	Lorenzo the Magnificent de' Medici, Florence
1490–1539	Isabella d'Este, Mantua
1492–1503	Pope Alexander VI
1503–1513	Pope Julius II
1509–1547	Henry VIII of England
1515–1547	Francis I of France
1558–1603	Elizabeth I of England

KEY DATES

FIGURE 10.4 Melozzo da Forlí, *Sixtus IV Receives Platina, Keeper of the Vatican Library*, 1477 The popes were powerful patrons of the arts. This painting commemorates the founding of the Vatican library, which remains a major center of learning today.

Renaissance love of learning—as well as its penchant for nepotism and intrigue.

To increase (or even maintain) their secular power, the popes waded into the quagmire of Italian politics, and at the end of the Renaissance, a pope was elected from an influential family—the Borgia. **The Borgia family** Like many other Renaissance princes, the Borgia pope Alexander VI (r. 1492–1503) tried to reclaim his lands from his acquisitive neighbors. Alexander also proved worldly in his personal life; gossips gleefully circulated accounts of his sexual escapades. He still upheld the tradition of Renaissance family life, however, favoring his illegitimate children by placing them in advantageous positions. The pope's warrior son, Cesare Borgia (ca. 1475–1507), seemed a candidate for uniting Italy under Alexander's authority. For his daughter Lucrezia, Alexander arranged three marriages designed to advance the family's dynastic aims. Isabella d'Este (featured in the Biography on page 314) arranged one of these marriages to protect the Este family's interests. All these manipulations came to nothing, however: Alexander died suddenly, and the family's ambitions failed. The reputation of the papacy as a spiritual authority also declined.

One of the most memorable of the Renaissance popes, Julius II (r. 1503–1513) embodied the ambitious values of the times, but without the scandals that had plagued Alexander. Julius was as perfect a **Julius II** Renaissance ruler as Florence's Lorenzo de' Medici. A patron of the arts he made Rome a cultural hub on a par with the greatness of Florence. He was also an experienced warrior, personally leading his armies into battle as he carried on Alexander's expansionist policies. Julius II summoned Michelangelo to Rome and commissioned him to decorate the ceiling of the Sistine Chapel (see **Figure 10.1**). Michelangelo also worked on the new St. Peter's Church in Rome that was being built at the time. Although Julius and Michelangelo had a stormy relationship, the patron helped his artist produce some of the most beautiful work of the Renaissance.

later 1400s. Money flowed from all over Europe to build the new Rome, a development that angered many northern Christians. With these contributions, the popes transformed Rome into one of Europe's major cultural centers. **Figure 10.4** shows Pope Sixtus IV (r. 1471–1484) seated in as much grandeur and surrounded by as much wealth as any king. His courtiers talk among themselves while the pope receives the humanist Platina (kneeling in the center). This painting commemorated the founding of the Vatican library, to be run by Platina. Even today, the library remains a major learning center. The cardinal standing in the center of the painting later became Pope Julius II. The courtiers on the left are Sixtus's nephews, who later participated in a plot to murder one of the Medicis. This painting depicts the

The Renaissance popes achieved their ambitious agenda: They were powerful earthly rulers living in a magnificent city. As the papacy proved to be a stronger institution than the church councils, efforts were ended to give supreme authority to bishops meeting in councils. However, over time, the popes' territorial power would undermine papal claims of universality, as many people began to question why Italian princes should have authority over lands outside Italy. As we will see in Chapter 11, these same people would begin to criticize the popes for what some called worldly extravagance.

The Art of Diplomacy

The wars, shifting alliances, and courtly intrigue of Italian politics sparked a new interest (and expertise) in the art of diplomacy. Not since the early Byzantine state had courtiers devoted such attention to the details of successful diplomacy. States exchanged ambassadors to facilitate official communication and sent spies to maintain advantages.

The most noted writer on political skill and diplomacy was Niccolò Machiavelli (1469–1527), whose book *The Prince* still influences many modern-day political thinkers. Machiavelli recognized the danger confronting Florence in the fifteenth century as

| Machiavelli | French armies threatened the independence of the city-states, and he wrote to offer advice about how to |

survive—indeed prevail—in these turbulent times. His was an eminently practical guide that looked at politics with a cold-blooded realism that had not been seen before. For Machiavelli, the most important element for a successful ruler (the prince) was his strength of will. He insisted that while princes might appear to have such traditional virtues as charity and generosity, they could not rely on these traits to hold power. They must actually be ruthless, expedient, strong, and clever if they were to maintain their rule. As he said, "It is better for a ruler to be feared than loved."

Machiavelli's blunt description of political power articulated a striking departure from medieval political ideals. During the Middle Ages, the perfect ruler was Louis IX of France (r. 1226–1270) (described in Chapter 8), who proved so virtuous that he was made a saint. With the Renaissance, men like Cosimo de' Medici and Cesare Borgia—self-made rulers who methodically cultivated their talents and grasped power boldly—took power. Machiavelli's book captured the new statecraft and showed that realistic politics often meant a brutal disregard for ethics. Indeed, many Europeans living during the Renaissance showed a social indifference and personal immorality that we might find dismaying today.

INDIVIDUALISM AS SELF-INTEREST: LIFE DURING THE RENAISSANCE

In spite of efforts to hone their diplomatic skills to a fine art, many Italians still resorted to brute force to get what they wanted. In all the city-states, some individuals came to power by stimulating social strife among competing factions or even using violence to vanquish their rivals. Taking part in politics could also get one in deep trouble. Petrarch's father, for example, like many other men of his time, made the mistake of supporting a losing political struggle in Florence, and the victors punished him by amputating his hand. Individuals struggling to better themselves politically and economically often did so at the expense of their neighbors.

Aside from offering the occasional opportunity to improve one's social position, Renaissance cities still had a clearly defined social hierarchy. The Florentines referred to these divisions as the "little people" and the "fat people." The "little people" consisted of merchants, artisans, and workers and made up about 60 percent of the population. Slaves and servants assumed even lower status, beneath the "little people." The "fat people" included well-to-do merchants and professionals and made up about 30 percent of the population. The wealthiest elite—bankers and merchants owning more than one-quarter of the city's wealth—made up only 1 percent of the population.

Whenever there is a great disparity between rich and poor in a situation of some social mobility, crime tends to run high. This was true throughout Renaissance Europe. One Florentine merchant, Luca Landucci, who kept a detailed diary of the events of his age, regularly wrote | Rising crime | of crime and punishment as he heard his neighbors gossip about the shocking misdeeds of the day. In one diary entry, he repeats news of a young woman who killed a child for the pearl necklace the girl was wearing. In another, he tells of the townspeople watching as a man was beheaded for "coining false money." Luca's dreary lists of crimes seem endless.

Many people blamed wanderers for the alarming rise in crime. According to such observers, soldiers discharged from mercenary armies, the poor fleeing poverty in cities and countryside, and other displaced persons made the highways more dangerous than ever. Italy and other states tried to control crime, but their methods were usually ineffective as well as misplaced. As in other times of rapid social change, rulers increased the regulation of social behavior. For example, in England in 1547 a new law stipulated that vagabonds be branded and enslaved for two years. The law tells us a great deal about Renaissance society's intense fear of crime and strangers.

Growing Intolerance

Renaissance governments enacted harsh legislation on people they found threatening, from prostitutes to paupers. This same impulse contributed to an increasing intolerance of other religions and cultures, as evidenced by an intensifying prejudice against Jews. In Italy, Christians passed laws against sexual relations between Christians and Jews, and authorities in Rome reputedly burned 50 Jewish prostitutes to death for having intercourse with Christian men. Laws also restricted Jews to certain parts of cities and required them to wear identifiable clothing. In some instances the clothing included colors that had been set aside for prostitutes. This cruel association left Jewish women open to ridicule, criticism, and sometimes abuse from non-Jewish neighbors.

Persecution of Jews existed during the Middle Ages—thirteenth-century kings of England and France had expelled Jews from their lands, and communities of Jews had experienced periodic violence. (As we saw in Chapter 9, Jews were subjected to particular violence in the wake of the bubonic plague.) However, increasing prejudice in the fifteenth century led to large-scale expulsions of Jewish communities from many cities and countries. Vienna began expelling Jews in 1421, and many other German cities followed. **Figure 10.5** is taken from a fifteenth-century Hebrew manuscript, and it shows Jews driven from a German town. The group was allowed to take their animals and a wagon for the women, children, and elderly as they headed down the hills seeking a new home. Most German Jews moved eastward into Poland and Russia, and the center of Judaism shifted from western Europe to the East.

Ferdinand and Isabella forced all of Spain's Jews to leave in 1492, causing one of the largest movements of peoples in the era. Portugal did the same in 1497. Many Iberian Jews fled to the Muslim lands in North Africa, and some people today still trace their ancestry back to this exodus. As a result of this intolerance, western Europe lost the talents of the many Jews who had inhabited these lands for centuries.

Economic Boom Times

The new ideas of the Renaissance (both good and bad) developed against the backdrop of the fourteenth century crises but were fostered in the fifteenth century by a vigorous economic life. Individualism was stimulated by the economic potential, and excess money made the all-important patronage possible. Growing commerce and industries brought money into Italy, stimulating the local economy and allowing wealthy people to indulge their desire for beauty and comfort.

Venice shone as the greatest merchant city in the world, importing tons of cotton, silk, and spices every year and exporting woolen cloth and mounds of silver coins to pay for their imports. As the sixteenth century opened, 1.5 million pounds of spices came through Venice alone every year. Venetians did not simply rest on their commercial wealth; some enterprising citizens developed and manufactured new products—most prominently, forks and windowpane glass—that would in time sweep through the world.

By contrast, Milan and Florence were craft-industrial cities. Florence, with its 270 workshops, led the way in wool cloth making. Renaissance Italy also profited from another new industry: silk. As early as the twelfth century, travelers had smuggled silkworms into Italy from China so that Italians could begin to produce the precious fabric locally. But the industry really blossomed after the thirteenth century, when the Chinese silk loom appeared in Italy. Italians powered the looms with waterwheels and produced large amounts of silk cloth. In the fourteenth century, one city had a silk mill employing 480 spindles rapidly spinning the precious silk. By the fifteenth century, Florence boasted eighty-three workshops devoted to silk production. The wealth let Florence take part in the thriving economy generated by the cloth trade network that connected countries like Italy and the Netherlands all the way to the New World. In the wake of this prosperous trade, even a shopkeeper in Florence wrote excitedly about his first taste of sugar brought in from overseas.

But the most profitable industry was banking. Throughout the Middle Ages, the development of banking and commerce had been impeded by the Christian belief in the immorality of usury, or charging interest, but enterprising merchants found ways around the prohibition. Some people offered gifts in gratitude for a loan of money, thus effectively paying back more than they borrowed. However, the easiest way to collect interest was by changing money and making a profit on the exchange rate. By the thirteenth century, Christians all over Europe began to engage in the lucrative trade of money lending, but it was the Italian bankers of the Renaissance who really first perfected the art of using money to make money. In the process, many raked in fortunes—for example, the rich families in Florence purchased state-guaranteed government bonds that paid over 15 percent interest. It is not surprising that the "fat people" got even "fatter" as the Renaissance rolled on.

Slavery Revived

The booming economy of the Renaissance led to new institutional oppression—the revival of slavery in Europe. Why was slavery reintroduced precisely when even serfs were being freed from their bondage?

Some historians suggest that the labor shortage of the late fourteenth century caused by the bubonic plague drove people to look for fresh hands. However, this explanation is not satisfactory, because the new slaves were by and large not used in agriculture or industry. Instead, it seems that newly wealthy people trying to make their lives more comfortable looked to new sources for scarce domestic help.

Slavery had some complex facets. Renaissance families, for example, often considered slaves part of the household. One Florentine woman in 1469 wrote a letter to her husband asking him to acquire a slave girl to care for their young child or a "black boy" to become the child's playmate. Occasionally slaves bore children fathered by their owners, who sometimes raised them as legitimate heirs. **Figure 10.6** is a portrait of a slave named Katharina drawn by Albrecht Dürer (1471–1528), a popular engraver commissioned to render portraits of many famous people. Katharina was a slave of a Portuguese commercial agent living in Antwerp who became friends with Dürer in 1520. This portrait shows the high regard in which this owner held Katharina. She is well dressed, and the fact that she sat for a portrait shows that she was a valued member of the household.

FIGURE 10.5 Expulsion of Jews, ca. 1427 During the Renaissance, Jews were increasingly driven out of towns and countries. This image from a Hebrew manuscript depicts their expulsion from a German town.

The Venetians, positioned near the eastern Mediterranean, capitalized on this trade first, dealing mostly in Muslim and Greek Orthodox slaves obtained through warfare or simply taken captive. Between 1414 and 1423, Venetian traders sold about 10,000 slaves in their markets. Most of these slaves were young girls sold into service as domestic servants. The fall of Constantinople to the Turks in 1453 (see Chapter 9) led to a decline in slaves from Eastern lands, and Europeans began to look for new sources of captives. In the early fifteenth century, the Portuguese conquered the Canary Islands off the western coast of Africa, and what had been a trickle of African slaves into Europe swelled. In the following decades, Portuguese traders eager to compete with the wealthy Venetians brought some 140,000 sub-Saharan African slaves into Europe.

| Sources of slaves |

Many people questioned the reestablishment of slavery in Europe. The church disapproved of it, and numerous slaveowners considered it too expensive in the long run. Slavery gradually disappeared in Europe by the end of the Renaissance. However, the

precedent had been reestablished, and traders would later find a flourishing slave market in the New World (see Chapters 12 and 15).

Finding Comfort in Family

In the rugged world that emphasized individual achievement, the family assumed central importance as the one constant, dependable structure in Renaissance society. Men and women believed they could count on their kin when all else failed and highlighted these connections in art, literature, and the decisions they made in their daily lives. The emphasis on family loyalty was not limited to the upper classes. Artisan workshops, for example, were family affairs in which fathers trained sons and sons-in-law to carry on the family business.

Family ties also defined ethics in a world in which morality seemed relative. In a book about family written by Leon Battista Alberti (1404–1472), a Florentine architect, the author argued that whatever

| Marriage alliances |

FIGURE 10.6 Albrecht Dürer, *Portrait of Katharina*, 1520
This etching was commissioned by a Portuguese commercial agent living in Antwerp and is silent testimony to the enslavement of peoples in the early modern period.

different role than they did in real life. Frequently, following the medieval traditions of courtly love, women were given a prominent place as idealized beings who inspired men. Dante Alighieri (1265–1321) (discussed in Chapter 9), whose *Divine Comedy* stands at the cusp between the Middle Ages and the Renaissance, featured a young woman, Beatrice, as his guide into heaven. Petrarch devoted many sonnets to Laura, a young woman who served as his inspiration. Painters, too, portrayed numerous women, many of them nudes who represented idealized beauty and longing for perfection. Artists may have played with the notion of idealized women, but Renaissance men depended on real women to preside over the haven that was their family and their security for the future.

Children's Lives

Though idealized visions of women signaled the importance of the continuity that families provided, and Renaissance families wanted and loved their children, child-rearing practices undermined the hopes of many a proud parent. Privileged families of the Renaissance believed that it was unhealthy (and perhaps even unsavory) for women to breast-feed their infants. Therefore, they customarily sent their newborns to live with peasant women, who were paid to serve as wet nurses until the children were weaned. Some nurses took meticulous care of these infants; others were less attentive. Peasant mothers suffered from poor diets themselves and often had insufficient milk to nurse a fosterling along with her own infants. Foster babies faced other dangers in the villages as well: Criminal records tell horrifying stories of death in the countryside, such as that of a peasant man who murdered four children under the age of 8. Florentine city-dwellers hearing such tales sometimes worried about their children's safety in the countryside, but the force of custom sent infants away to depend on the kindness of strangers.

Wealthy urban parents reclaimed their children when they were weaned, at about 2 years old. These young strangers then had to fit into large households teeming with older children, stepchildren, and a host of other relatives. With busy parents and stepparents, children often formed their principal attachment with an older sibling or aunt or uncle. The artist Andrea Mantegna was commissioned to paint a cycle of frescoes for the Gonzaga family, who ruled the Duchy of Mantua, and **Figure 10.7** shows one portion of this magnificent work. Against the stunning background of the city, the painter shows a man with presumably three of his sons. The youngest, in the foreground, holds tightly to the eldest's hand, perhaps reflecting the situation in many crowded settings as older children cared for younger.

Childhood hardships

increased a man's power to help his family was good. Riches, however gained, fell into this category. Still, as Isabella d'Este proved, nothing beat a good marriage alliance for improving a family's standing.

Plans for such beneficial alliances began as early as the birth of a girl, when wealthy Florentine fathers would open an account with the public dowry fund, which paid as much as 21 percent interest. Family alliances depended on both parties bringing resources to the match. Wealthy families with sons wanted to be certain that their resources would not be diminished by marriage. Thus, parents of girls had to ensure that their daughters could bring enough money to an alliance to ensure a match with well-placed families. The dowry fund was implemented to guarantee that a girl had a sizable dowry when she reached marriageable age. Some Renaissance families could not afford dowries for all their daughters and encouraged some to enter convents (which required smaller dowries). Indeed, the number of convents in Florence increased from only five in 1350 to forty-seven in 1550.

Of course, all these efforts to secure important family alliances had an equal impact on men and women. In the literature and art of the period, too, both men and women appear, but here women play a strikingly

FIGURE 10.7 Andrea Mantegna, *The Cardinal Francesco Gonzaga Returning from Rome,* 1474 The painter was commissioned by the Marquis of Mantua to decorate a room with frescoes. The scenes show the marquis' family and are done with techniques of perspective that make the walls seem like windows on the world.

Child-rearing experts warned parents against pampering their offspring, and in general the parents obeyed. Ironically, in this culture of wealth and luxury, people raised their children with a degree of strictness that may seem extreme to us today. One writer (the Dominican Giovanni Dominici), for example, urged mothers to prepare children for hardship by making them sleep in the cold on a hard chest instead of a bed. To toughen them, parents fed children bitter-tasting objects such as peach-stones and sometimes gave them "harmless" nausea-inducing herbs so as to accustom them to illness. A humanist (Filarete) writing about an ideal school recommended that children be fed only tough meat so they would learn to eat slowly. This same writer recommended that children eat standing up until they were 20 years old. Many parents let their children sleep only six to eight hours a night to keep them from getting lazy.

Within these strict guidelines, boys and girls were treated quite differently. One humanist (Paola da Certaldo) advised feeding and clothing boys well. For girls, he recommended: "Dress the girl well but as for eating, it doesn't matter as long as it keeps her alive; don't let her get fat."

At about 7 years old, middle-class boys were sent to school to learn reading and mathematics and to ready themselves for the complex world of Renaissance economics. As the boys prepared for careers, fathers arranged marriages for their young daughters. Girls were married relatively young—between 17 and 20 years old (although sometimes younger)—to bridegrooms in their 30s who had established their careers. (See Isabella d'Este's biography.) Many brides, still children themselves when they began having babies, did not survive the experience of giving birth. One Florentine man recorded in his memoirs that, between 1390 and 1431, he had four wives who gave him a total of 24 children. The first three wives died in childbirth.

The harshness of childhood took its toll on many boys and girls; mortality among children reached astonishing rates. In fifteenth-century Florence, 45 percent of children died before the age of 20, most of them girls. The 1427 census in Florence showed a surprising gender ratio: 100 women to every 110 men. This statistic reversed the situation that had prevailed through the High Middle Ages, when women outnumbered men.

AN AGE OF TALENT AND BEAUTY: RENAISSANCE CULTURE AND SCIENCE

Renaissance life had its unsavory side—as rich men struggled to get richer, powerful men worked for more power, and small children sometimes suffered. But at the same time, Renaissance society produced some astonishingly talented people whose works have transformed not only our ideas about beauty but also the very appearance of the world we live in today. During the Renaissance—as in classical Athens—people expected art to be a public thing, to be available to and appreciated by people as they strolled through the cities. Public art nurtured civic pride.

Artists and Artisans

During the Renaissance, many upper-class boys pursued humanistic literary studies to prepare for the day they would play a public role in city life, but their families generally discouraged them from following careers in the visual arts. Filippo Brunelleschi (1377–1446), for example, greatly displeased his father when he declared his interest in sculpting and architecture; his family had fully expected Filippo to become a physician or a notary.

Michelangelo's father dismissed his son's interest in art as "shameful." Peasant boys, too, had little chance at a career in the arts, for without family connections, there was little chance of entry into the art world. If a country boy was a talented artist, he would probably not have the good fortune to be discovered like the shepherd Giotto whose story opened this chapter.

The majority of Renaissance artists came from artisan families. As boys worked as apprentices in artisan workshops, masters recognized and supported genius. Botticelli, the great Florentine painter, was apprenticed at age 13, as was Michelangelo. These examples were typical—a boy entering adulthood had to learn to take his place in the world, and that place often began in the artisan workshops. As a young man developed his skill, people began to recognize that he was no longer a simple craftsman, an artisan, making goods, but instead an artist, a creator of beauty.

Women ordinarily were excluded from taking this path. Yet, in spite of this lack of official acceptance, a number of female artists won renown during the Renaissance. Two, in particular, were highly respected by their contemporaries. Sofonisba Anguissola (ca. 1532–1625) achieved fame as an artist through her skill and the support of her wealthy, aristocratic father. More typical was the case of Lavinia Fontana (1552–1614), the daughter of an artist who trained in her father's workshop. Despite these successes, the public role of artists precluded many women from active careers in art. For example, Anguissola delayed marriage until she was in her late 40s so she could paint—a privilege that most Renaissance fathers did not grant.

Late in the Renaissance, artists overall gained new respect—wealthy patrons stopped viewing them as simply manual laborers and began to recognize them as artists. Michelangelo even earned the title Il Divino, the Divine One. Europeans during the Renaissance valued genius, and these artistic geniuses obliged by creating magnificent works.

Architecture: Echoing the Human Form

The most expensive investment a patron of the arts could make was in architecture, and artists competed for these lucrative contracts. In the process, they designed innovative churches and other buildings that contributed to the prestige of their cities. Where did architects learn these new ideas? Part of the answer comes from the training of architects. Artisans did not consider architecture a separate craft, so there was no direct apprenticeship for this profession that rigidly inculcated old design ideas. Indeed, the greatest architects had all trained for other fields: Brunelleschi, for example, was a goldsmith, and Alberti a university-trained humanist. The Renaissance passion for the glory of classical Greece and Rome led would-be architects to look carefully at the old ruins that had

stood for so long; their love of the individual caused them to put humans at the center of their enterprise. The resulting architecture, while looking back to classical models, was strikingly and beautifully new.

Instead of creating soaring Gothic cathedrals dominated by vertical heights, architects followed classical models of balance and simplicity and combined circular forms with linear supports to break up the monotony of vertical lines. Instead of creating structures that made humans seem small and insignificant before God, they built to glorify the human form and proportions. The fifteenth-century architectural drawings pictured in **Figure 10.8** show the ideal of buildings designed along human proportions. The drawing on the left shows a front view of a building with a man standing to indicate the proper proportions, while the one on the right shows a floor plan with the man lying down in the building.

The most influential architectural treatise, *On Building* by Alberti, dominated the field for centuries and expressed an architectural aesthetic that echoed that of the ancient Greeks. Alberti argued that buildings should mirror the human body in their supports and openings, and this sentiment is shown in **Figure 10.8.** Repeating the same principle, Michelangelo claimed that anyone who had not mastered anatomy and painting of the human form could not understand architecture. "The different parts of a building," he explained, "derive from human members." Thus, much of the architecture of the Renaissance was created in the image and likeness of the human form.

It is easy to miss the subtleties of human proportion within architecture as we look at the graceful buildings, but there is no overlooking one of the architects' debts to Rome—domes instead of Gothic spires now began to rise with more frequency over the skylines of Renaissance cities. **Figure 10.9** shows the cathedral of Florence, with its dome designed by Brunelleschi. The architect had admired the Pantheon dome in Rome (see Chapter 4), and he wanted to erect a massive dome to span the huge base of the new cathedral in Florence. However, Brunelleschi realized that the Roman dome was not suitable to the large space, so the architect creatively took the Gothic technique of using architectural ribs to create a magnificent new structure for the city. Brunelleschi designed the dome of the Florence cathedral with an inner and outer shell, both attached to the eight ribs of the octagonal structure. The drawing in **Figure 10.9** shows the structural design. Between the two shells the architect placed sixteen ribs to strengthen the dome. The two shells thus supported each other and shared the weight of the whole. Many Florentines predicted that the dome would collapse, yet Brunelleschi's handiwork continues to dominate the skyline of Florence.

Human architecture

Domes

FIGURE 10.8 Francesco di Giorgio Martini, *Trattato di Architettura,* 1480 As theoreticians of architecture considered the best proportions for designing pleasing buildings, they looked to the human form to determine the proper ratios. These drawings show these ratios superimposed on the front and floor plan of buildings.

The Renaissance study of architecture also extended beyond individual buildings to town planning in general. In the fifteenth century, planners began to dream of laying out towns in the simple and logical grid pattern that characterizes our modern cities. Indeed, older European cities still feature a medieval center with curved and random streets surrounded by tidy, post-Renaissance grids. In Latin America, by contrast, towns founded by fifteenth-century Europeans were created in a grid pattern centered on the town square. On the peripheries of such towns, however, streets wove randomly in the tradition of the villages that predated the Renaissance town centers. All these new ideas about buildings and street planning reshaped the cities of the West.

Town planning

Sculpture Comes into Its Own

Just as Brunelleschi's admiration of the ancients led him to re-create domed architecture, sculptors also drew from classical models. Italians, who had admired freestanding images from the ancient world, began to demand similar beauty for their cities. City communes and individuals commissioned life-size figures to stand free in the public spaces of cities.

Figure 10.10 shows Michelangelo's widely admired statue of David, the biblical figure who killed the giant Goliath. The statue stands more than 14 feet high and took the master three years to carve from a block of supposedly flawed marble. The work exhibits all the innovations of Renaissance sculpture: It is a huge, freestanding nude that depicts the classical ideal of repose, in which the subject rests his weight on one leg in a pose called **contra posto.** The figure exemplifies the confidence and the glorification of the human body that marked Renaissance pride.

Michelangelo's David

Michelangelo's statue shows another hallmark of Renaissance spirit—an exuberant praise of realism; the sculptor knew anatomy and realistically portrayed the human body. Renaissance sculptors had to look at life carefully in order to reproduce it with such accuracy, and the audience, too, was led to an appreciation of realism through admiring the great sculptures that graced the public areas.

The statue also carried a political message, a common characteristic of the civic humanism of the day.

FIGURE 10.10 Michelangelo, *David*, 1504 This spectacular sculpture, more than 14 feet high, was in its day the largest marble nude created since antiquity. It was commissioned by Florence to symbolize how the Florentine republic would stand—like David the "giant killer"—against neighboring political giants.

FIGURE 10.9 Florence Cathedral, 1420–1436 Brunelleschi's dome for the Cathedral of Florence was an architectural wonder. The drawing shows the ribbed structure that, despite Florentines' dire predictions that it would collapse, successfully held up the weight of the dome.

In 1494, when the French invasion of Florence caused a temporary fall of the Medici rule, the newly restored Republic of Florence commissioned Michelangelo to create a work with a patriotic theme—something that would celebrate the overthrow of the family that had dominated the city for so long. The sculptor chose David the "giant killer" to symbolize the republic's ousting of the goliath Medici. Michelangelo portrayed David before his fight with Goliath—the youth is confident and defiant, just as Florence saw itself confronting the rest of the world. In this masterpiece, art joined with politics in the best Renaissance tradition.

Painting from a New Perspective

The shepherd Giotto di Bondone (ca. 1267–1337), whose artistic talents were recognized by a Florentine master, was to revolutionize painting for Florence and the West. The young apprentice who fooled his master with a painting of a fly turned his talents to magnificent religious paintings, and he created realistic figures that showed a full range of human expression. For example, his images of the Virgin Mary were not done as remote queens of heaven, but instead painted as realistic young girls struggling to be caring mothers.

Figure 10.11 shows Giotto's fresco *Lamentation over Christ*, in which the faithful mourn the death of Christ. The painting looks back to medieval tradition with gold leaf on the halos and the theme of the painting. However, the painter points to the future with his three-dimensional figures and a new realistic portrayal of emotion. Giotto's talent was recognized during his lifetime, and his paintings were in great demand. Toward the end of his life, the city of Florence issued a proclamation that in part captures the painter's influence: "Many will profit from his knowledge and learning and the city's beauty will be enhanced." Painters following Giotto built on his techniques and further revolutionized this visual art.

Like architects and sculptors, Renaissance painters developed striking new techniques, including oil painting on canvas and the perfection of portraiture. However, perhaps their best-known innovation was **linear perspective,** which allowed painters to enhance the realism of paintings by creating the illusion of three-dimensional space on a two-dimensional surface.

Linear perspective

The Florentines—and Brunelleschi in particular—proudly claimed to have invented this technique of painting. Whether they did or not is probably irrelevant; regardless of who invented linear perspective, the Florentines perfected it.

Before beginning to paint, Brunelleschi organized the painting around a central point and then drew a grid to place objects precisely in relation to each other. His real innovation, however, came when he calculated the mathematical ratios by which objects seem to get smaller as they recede from view. In this way, he knew exactly how big to paint each object in his grid to achieve a realistic illusion of receding space. In commenting on Brunelleschi's creations, Alberti asserted that a painting should be pleasing to the eye but also should appeal to the mind with optical and mathematical accuracy. And here is the essence of these complex works: They used all the intellectual skill of the artists to create images profoundly appealing to the senses.

Perspective also grew from and appealed to the Renaissance emphasis on the individual, for it assumed that a painting would be viewed from one single spot in front of the work. As one art critic wrote, "Every painting that used perspective proposed to the spectator that he was the unique center of the world." In other words, the painter designed the painting with the eye of the beholder in mind. For the next four

FIGURE 10.11 Giotto, *Lamentation over Christ,* ca. 1305 Although Giotto painted many medieval themes, his contemporaries believed that he introduced a new style that brought "light to the darkness," as Boccaccio wrote.

hundred years, Renaissance ideas of perspective and space set the standard for Western painting.

The painter Raphael (1483–1520) was widely regarded as one of Italy's best painters of the High Renaissance (the late fifteenth and early sixteenth centuries). During his lifetime, he was much acclaimed as an artist who could portray transcendent themes with all the realism of fifteenth-century Italian life,

Raphael

and modern critics agree. His reputation gained him the coveted commission to paint a fresco for Pope Julius II's library, and **Figure 10.12** shows that fresco—*School of Athens*. Raphael created this fresco just as Michelangelo was painting the Sistine Chapel ceiling (see **Figure 10.1**).

Celestial Music of Human Emotions

Renaissance thinkers turned their attention to music in a quest to carry that art into the new age. Early humanists at first thought that music should imitate classical forms, but no one really knew what ancient Greek music sounded like. However, people did look to ancient mathematics to inform musical composition, for Pythagoras (ca. 569–475 B.C.E.) had postulated harmonious relationships among planets, and music intervals were supposed to echo the ratios of those relationships, creating what the ancients called a "music of the spheres." This search for heavenly music helped to standardize musical notation during the Renaissance and would continue into the seventeenth century.

FIGURE 10.12

Raphael, *School of Athens*, 1510–1511

Pope Julius II commissioned the painter Raphael to create a fresco for his library. The artist portrayed famous ancient philosophers, such as Euclid, Pythagoras, and Socrates, along with Plato and Aristotle in the center. Plato (looking remarkably like Leonardo da Vinci) is on the left, with his hand pointing in the air to remind viewers of the realm of ideas. He is speaking to Aristotle, whose hand presses downward, reminding viewers of his more earthly approach to knowledge. Raphael also included a self-portrait on the right (in the black hat) and a depiction of a brooding Michelangelo sitting in the center foreground, leaning his head on his hand.

Connecting Art & Society

1. Identify the following characteristics of the Renaissance in this image: individualism, appreciation of the classics, and perspective.

2. Why would the pope find the content of this fresco suitable subject matter for the papal library?

3. Why do you think Raphael included portraits of his artist contemporaries in the company of the philosophers?

On a practical level, composers drew from humanistic studies and put human feelings at the center of a piece so that the music itself would reflect the emotions of the lyrics. For example, if the lyric was sad, the pitch should descend and the tempo should slow down. Music also moved from the church to the courts in these centuries, and perhaps the best-known secular, emotional music was the **madrigals,** poetic songs usually about love. The attempt to link music, narrative, and emotion led to the invention of opera at the end of the sixteenth century.

Music became part of a well-rounded education. Castiglione, in his *Book of the Courtier*, wrote, "I am not pleased with the courtier if he be not also a musician." Music came into the households as well as the courts, and new instruments were developed to serve the home market. Noble households resonated with the sounds of instruments such as the viola da gamba (a bowed, stringed instrument), the whistle-like recorder, and the harpsichord (an instrument, like the piano, with strings that are plucked). The printing press helped to advance this popularization of music, as it allowed for the wide distribution of sheet music after the 1470s. Despite all the new instruments and the new technology of printing, however, the human voice, so expressive of human emotion, remained the central instrument of Renaissance music.

Science or Pseudoscience?

The Renaissance passion for direct observation and realistic assessment that led to such magnificent achievements in the visual, musical, and literary arts catalyzed a process that ultimately led to the scientific accomplishments of the seventeenth century. During the fourteenth and fifteenth centuries, however, much scientific inquiry was shaped by a desire to control as well as understand the world. This combination led to the pursuit of what we consider pseudoscientific studies.

As the Biography of Isabella d'Este indicated, astrology was extremely popular during these centuries. Even some popes hired their own astrologers. The bright appearance of Halley's comet in 1456 provoked a flurry of both dire and inspiring prophecies. For example, one humanist physician explained the outbreak of syphilis in Europe in terms of a conjunction of the planets Saturn, Jupiter, and Mars in the sign of Cancer. **Alchemy** was the early practice of chemistry, but the alchemists' interests were dramatically different from those of modern scientists. Their main goal was to find a "philosopher stone" that would turn base metals into gold. This science was perhaps even more popular than astrology.

Astrology and alchemy

Such pseudoscience aside, the Renaissance did succeed in combining visual arts with scientific observation. The study of linear perspective, for example, depended on an understanding of mathematics, and scholars spread the use of Arabic numerals to replace the Roman numerals that had previously dominated the West. The use of these numbers facilitated higher orders of calculations, like algebra, which was also learned from the Muslims. Musicians explored ratios and fractions to try to re-create celestial proportions. Realistic sculpture and painting required a study of anatomy, and this science also progressed. Amid these advancements, the Renaissance saw the birth of

Mathematics and anatomy

a man who came to represent the entire range and combination of talents that so defined this age.

Leonardo da Vinci: The "Renaissance Man"

Leonardo da Vinci (1452–1519) personifies the idea of the "Renaissance man"—the person who can supposedly do anything well. As a young man, he contributed to the architecture of Florence by helping to make the golden ball that topped Brunelleschi's dome (see **Figure 10.9**), but he excelled in much more than architecture and sculpture.

This multitalented Italian served in the courts of a number of patrons, from the Medici to the Sforza of Milan—even Isabella d'Este tried to woo him. At these courts, Leonardo painted magnificent portraits and beautiful religious works. **Figure 10.13** shows Leonardo's celebrated *Mona Lisa*, probably the most famous portrait from the Renaissance. Her famous hint of a smile and calm pose were strikingly original at the time and inspired many later portraits.

Painting

Although Leonardo's skill as a painter would have satisfied most men longing for greatness, he saw this medium only as a beginning, a means to a larger end. "Painting should increase the artist's knowledge of the physical world," he explained.

Leonardo left a collection of notebooks that showed his intense interest in the world. His drawings of plants revealed a skill and meticulousness that any botanist would envy, and his sketches of water in motion would have impressed the most accomplished of engineers. Leonardo's imagination seemed boundless—his sketches included tanks and other war machines, a submarine, textile machines, paddle boats, a "horseless carriage," and many other inventions that lay in the future.

Scientific notebooks

Leonardo also took an interest in the inner workings of the human body. Although some medieval physicians conducted dissections, the practice was not common. During the Renaissance, however, physicians and scholars began to approach the study of the human body empirically by regularly dissecting cadavers. At the time, both artists and physicians saw dissection as a way to improve their portrayal of the human form. Like many other artists, Leonardo dissected cadavers to understand anatomy and thereby make his paintings as realistic as possible (as well as to satisfy his insatiable curiosity). **Figure 10.14a** shows Leonardo's sketches and descriptions of human shoulders and arms, including the bones of the left foot and lower leg. The image demonstrates how he drew from cadaver studies as it shows the intricate connections of the ligaments in the joint as well as the various parts of the muscles as they encase the arm bones.

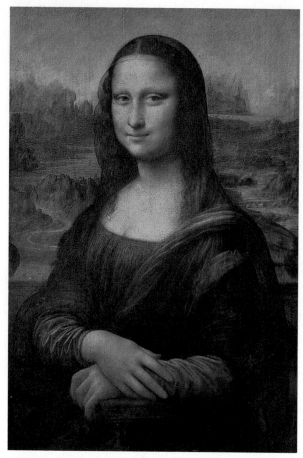

FIGURE 10.13 Leonardo da Vinci, *Mona Lisa*, ca. 1504
Leonardo's most famous painting displays his genius at portrait painting as well as landscape perspective (in the background). Notice that the form of the aqueduct by the subject's left shoulder is echoed in the drapery over that shoulder. This is only one way in which the artist connected the sitter to her environment.

Figure 10.14b, a depiction of a child in the womb, reveals the wide range of Leonardo's interests as well as his scientific curiosity. It is the oldest surviving illustration in the West of the actual position of an unborn child. To make this drawing, Leonardo secured a dispensation to dissect a deceased pregnant woman. In addition to capturing the correct positioning, the drawing explains the function of the placenta.

King Francis I of France (r. 1515–1547) once said of Leonardo, "No other man had been born who knew so much." Unfortunately for the future of science and engineering, Leonardo's voluminous notebooks were lost for centuries after his death. In retrospect, perhaps Leonardo's greatest achievement was that he showed how multitalented human beings could be. He proved the humanists' belief that an educated man could accomplish anything in all fields. Leonardo died at the court of Francis I, who had proudly served as his patron.

RENAISSANCE OF THE "NEW MONARCHIES" OF THE NORTH, 1453–1640

As we saw in Chapter 9, the medieval political structures of Europe began to fall apart under the pressures of the many disasters of the fourteenth century. The monarchies of the fifteenth century could no longer rely on feudal contracts and armies of mounted knights and began to search for new ways to rule their countries. To bypass their sometimes unreliable nobility, monarchs concentrated their royal authority by appointing bureaucrats who owed their status only to the will of the king or queen. As they looked for new sources of income to pay growing mercenary armies, kings and queens kept imposing new taxes and, in general, were receptive to new ideas to help them consolidate their power. Many hired Italians trained in the humanist tradition to work in their courts, and slowly and fitfully from the late thirteenth through the sixteenth century, the ideas of the Renaissance spread to northern European countries. As Renaissance notions traveled north and bore fruit in the courts of powerful rulers, the ideas were further transformed. This migration of ideas also accelerated the changes triggered by the disasters of the fourteenth century.

France: Under the Italian Influence

France offers a case study in how slowly and sporadically Renaissance ideas moved and how much this new spirit depended on the patronage of monarchs. The French king Charles V (r. 1364–1380), known as "the Wise," encouraged Renaissance learning among his subjects, gathering a circle of intellectuals around him. However, this early flowering of learning withered when his mentally unstable son, Charles VI (r. 1380–1422), took

FIGURE 10.14 Leonardo's Notebooks, ca. 1510 Leonardo, like many other artists at the time, studied dissections of cadavers to learn about humans and in doing so forwarded science as well as art. Figure 10.14a shows his drawings of a shoulder and arm. Figure 10.14b is the oldest drawing in the West of a child in the womb.

power. Integration of Renaissance ideals in this northern court would have to wait until the end of the Hundred Years' War in 1453 (discussed in Chapter 9).

France eventually triumphed in the Hundred Years' War, but a new threat from the neighboring state of Burgundy immediately arose. As we saw in Chapter 9, Burgundy had allied with England to weaken France, and England's defeat did not weaken Burgundy's land hunger. As **Map 10.3** shows, the rulers of Burgundy were trying to forge a state between France and the Holy Roman Empire, and their hundred-year expansion represented a real threat to France. Instead of leading armies in the old chivalric manner, however, the French king Louis XI (r. 1461–1483) skillfully brought a new kind of diplomacy to bear in confronting this next challenge. His contemporaries called him "Louis the Spider" because he spun a complex web of intrigue and diplomatic machinations worthy of Machiavelli—bribing his allies and murdering his enemies. Louis subsidized Swiss mercenaries, who eventually defeated the Burgundian ruler. France then seized the Duchy of Burgundy and added the sizable new territory to its lands. (As **Map 10.3** shows, the Low Countries remained in the hands of Mary, the Duke of Burgundy's

Louis the Spider

daughter, and they later formed part of the inheritance of her grandson, Charles V, whose fortunes we will follow in Chapter 11.) Louis left France strong and prosperous and well placed to play a powerful political role in the coming centuries. Document 10.3 offers a contemporary's view of this complex king.

As **Map 10.3** shows, the French kings succeeded in slowly taking the lands from the nobles who had retained their holdings since the Middle Ages. With its increasing strength, France next began expanding across the Alps into Italy to assert dynastic claims in Naples, because, as we saw previously, the French royal family was related to the rulers in Naples. However, the French came back with much more than wealth. Nobles leading mercenary armies in the Italian campaigns of 1494 came in search of land and left feeling dazzled by the cultural accomplishments of the Italian Renaissance. In a letter to his courtiers back home, the French king Charles VIII (r. 1483–1498) gushed about discovering the "best artists" in Italy. He returned home with some 20 Italian workmen whom he instructed to build "in the Italian style." The aesthetic ideals of Italy thus moved north with the retreating French armies, and the early Renaissance spirit in France was reawakened.

MAP 10.3

France in the Fifteenth and Sixteenth Centuries

This map shows the growth of the royal domain of the French kings from 1461 through 1559.

Explore the Map

1. Why did the Duchy of Burgundy pose a threat to the French kings?

2. Considering the location of Avignon, where the popes had lived so long, why did many in Europe accuse those popes of being pro-French?

DOCUMENT 10.3

A Courtier Describes a Suspicious King—Louis the Spider

Philippe de Commynes (ca. 1447–1511) served Louis XI and wrote an account of the king's reign shortly after Louis' death in 1483. Commynes had been raised at the court of Burgundy until he found it politically expedient to change sides and work for France. Thus, he was well placed to view the king with the eye of an outsider as well as a courtier.

The King had ordered several cruel prisons to be made; some were cages of iron, and some of wood, but all were covered with iron plates both within and without, with terrible locks, about eight feet wide and seven high. . . . I lay in one of them eight months together in the minority of our present King. . . . However, I have seen many eminent and deserving persons in these prisons, with these nets about their legs, who afterwards came forth with great joy and honor, and received great rewards from the King. . . .

It may be urged that other princes have been more given to suspicion than he, but it was not in our time; and, perhaps, their wisdom was not so eminent, nor were their subjects so good. They might too, probably, have been tyrants, and bloody-minded; but our king never did any person a mischief who had not offended him first, though I do not say all who offended him deserved death. I have not recorded these things merely to represent our master as a suspicious and mistrustful prince; but . . . that those princes who may be his successors, may learn by his example to be more tender and indulgent to their subjects, and less severe in their punishments than our master had been: although I will not censure him, or say I ever saw a better prince; for though he oppressed his subjects himself, he would never see them injured by anybody else. . . .

I knew him, and was entertained in his service in the flower of his age, and at the height of his prosperity, yet I never saw him free from labor and care. Of all diversions he loved hunting and hawking in their seasons; but his chief delight was in dogs. As for ladies, he never meddled with any in my time; for about the time of my coming to his court he lost a son, at whose death he was extremely afflicted, and he made a vow to God in my presence never to have intercourse with any other woman but the queen; and though this was no more than what he was bound to do by the canons of the church, yet it was much that his self-command should be so great, that he should be able to persevere in his resolution so firmly, considering that the queen (though an excellent princess in other respects) was not a person in whom a man could take any great delight. . . .

He was involved [in warfare that] . . . lasted till his death, and many brave men lost their lives in it, and his treasury was exhausted by it; so that he had but a little time during the whole year to spend in pleasure, and even then the fatigues he underwent were excessive. When his body was at rest his mind was at work, for he had affairs in several places at once, and would concern himself as much in those of his neighbors as in his own, putting officers of his own over all the great families, and endeavoring to divide their authority as much as possible. When he was at war he labored for a peace or a truce, and when he had obtained it, he was impatient for war again. He troubled himself with many trifles in his government, which he had better have let alone: but it was his temper, and he could not help it; besides, he had a prodigious memory, and he forgot nothing, but knew everybody, as well in other countries as in his own.

SOURCE: A.R. Scoble, trans. and annotator, *The Memories of Philip de Commines* (London: G. Bell & Sons, 1884), vol. II, pp. 75–81.

Analyze the Document

1. What qualities did Commynes value in the king and which did he criticize?

2. Would Machiavelli have considered Louis a good prince? Why or why not?

3. What qualities do you think made him a successful monarch?

Italian influence increased further with the substantial growth of the French court, which opened positions to Italian humanists and diplomats. France's kings employed more officials than any other state in Europe—one estimate places the number of bureaucrats at more than 4,000 during the reign of Francis I (r. 1515–1547). (Leonardo da Vinci was among those brought to France by this powerful and sophisticated patron.) Under Francis's rule, humanist literature flourished, and the new learning influenced university curricula from languages to mathematics to law. The king even ordered

Italians in France

Castiglione's *Book of the Courtier* to be translated into French and read to him nightly.

The French Renaissance did not merely copy the Italian movement. Indeed, many works by French artists and writers during this period show a unique blend of humorous skepticism and creative power. The imaginative humanist François Rabelais embodies this unmistakable French version of Renaissance ideals. His books *Pantagruel* and *Gargantua*—bawdy tales about giants with enormous appetites—are masterpieces of satire. Both stories continue to captivate modern readers. France had left its own mark on the Renaissance spirit.

English Humanism

When Henry VII (r. 1485–1509) became king in England after the Wars of the Roses (see Chapter 9), he succeeded in taming the rowdy and independent nobility and established a strong, centralized monarchy. Under the dynasty that he initiated, England again prospered. The English monarchs now turned their attention to the new spirit emanating from the south as they began to surround themselves with courtiers and art that served as the hallmarks of the courts of new monarchs. Delayed because of internal strife, the English Renaissance (1500–1640) gained momentum just as the Italian movement waned.

During the reign of Henry VII, English scholars intrigued by Renaissance thought traveled to Italy and studied under noted humanists. They frequented the newly established Vatican library and consulted with Platina, the papal librarian shown in **Figure 10.4,** and then returned home brimming with new ideas. By 1500, these scholars had so transformed the curriculum at Oxford that England could offer as fine a classical education as Italy. The forward-thinking English monarchs also brought back technological innovations. They embraced new artillery and set English engineers to work making gunpowder. Henry VII included a fireworks display at his wedding, in so doing importing this Italian skill into England and beginning a long tradition of English pyrotechnics. (See Thinking about Science & Technology in Chapter 11.)

Henry VIII (r. 1509–1547) proved an even more vigorous patron of Renaissance learning than his father. As we will see in Chapter 11, Henry met the French king Francis I and tried to outdo that Renaissance prince in splendor and patronage. The English king cultivated interest in astronomy, literature, and music—all the fields advocated by the humanists. Still, the talented monarch was outdone by his Lord Chancellor, Sir Thomas More (1478–1535).

More published a biography of the humanist Pico della Mirandola that revealed the author's debt to the Italian movement. The English scholar mastered classical learning and the humanist curriculum and applied his skills in public life in the best tradition of civic humanism. More's masterpiece, however, was *Utopia*, a work that commented on contemporary evils while offering a vision of a society free of poverty, crime, and corruption. More's work, with its visions of exploration and decidedly | Thomas More | political orientation, points to distinct characteristics of the English Renaissance. More's studies gave him strong views on religion, which, as we will see in Chapter 11, led to a fatal conflict with his king.

Many Englishwomen also wrote during this Renaissance. The first wife of Henry VIII, Catherine of Aragon (1485–1536), had grown up with a love of the new learning encouraged by her mother, Isabella of Castile. When Catherine came to England, she stimulated interest among courtiers and scholars in the proper education of women. Consequently, Englishwomen wrote more publicly | Renaissance queens | than their Italian counterparts. In fact, Italian travelers to England wrote disparagingly of the "brazen and violently assertive" Englishwomen. This tradition of education strongly influenced Queen Elizabeth I (r. 1558–1603), under whose rule England prospered and the Renaissance flowered.

Renaissance London: A Booming City

Sixteenth-century London—a vibrant city—scintillated during the English Renaissance, expanding physically and intellectually. Between 1560 and 1603, the population almost doubled, from 120,000 to more than 200,000, and travelers flocked there to see its wonders. **Figure 10.15** shows a 1616 painting of London by Claes von Visscher. In this cityscape, the great sailing ships that made London a bustling commercial hub waft by, along with small vessels that supplied the city's growing population. Rows of houses stand in front of St. Paul's cathedral, which dominates the skyline.

In the foreground of the painting is the south bank of the Thames, which had been a center of prostitution from the time of the Roman settlement of London. The south bank remained the unseemly quarter of the city, inhabited by criminals and prostitutes, and notorious for its | The south bank | violent forms of entertainment, such as bear baiting and dog fights. The south bank also housed private prisons, including the infamous "clink" that housed some of the fiercest criminals. Yet, the south bank was also home to the theaters where crowds gathered to watch the plays of the great Renaissance dramatists. The two tall, round structures in the foreground of **Figure 10.15** are examples of these theaters. The one on the right is inaccurately labeled "The Globe." Known as Shakespeare's theater, the building had burned down in 1613 because of sparks from fireworks set off as part of a play. This took place before Visscher painted his London scene. During the late sixteenth century, however, the Globe served as a backdrop for the work of the greatest writer England has ever produced, and crowds today gather to see plays performed in a newly rebuilt Gobe Theater on the south bank of the Thames.

England's Pride: William Shakespeare

The new social mobility of the Renaissance permitted William Shakespeare (1564–1616) to rise to prominence. William's father, a modest glove maker, a humanist education. At the age of 18, the young scholar married Anne Hathaway, about eight years his elder, who was pregnant with their first child. In 1592, William journeyed to London, where he worked as an actor and wrote comedies, histories, and tragedies.

This master of the English language articulated all the Renaissance ideals: Shakespeare's love of the classics showed in his use of Roman histories in his plays (*Julius Caesar*) and in his study of Roman playwrights that offered him models of theater. Furthermore, Hamlet's words "What a piece of work is man" expressed Renaissance optimism in human accomplishment; *Romeo and Juliet* re-created the story of "star-crossed lovers" (a reference to the Renaissance love of astrology) in the streets of Italy. *The Tempest* featured Renaissance magicians, and Shakespeare's histories described the fortunes of princes as surely as Machiavelli's analysis of history and politics had. His plays incorporated Renaissance music and modern warfare with cannons and fireworks. In Shakespeare's hands, the ideals of the Renaissance were given a new, enduring form—popular theater that reached the masses. However, some modern literary critics believe the great playwright accomplished much more than perfecting Renaissance ideas. Some claim that by expressing complex human emotions in magnificent language, Shakespeare created an understanding of humanity for the West. In this, perhaps, we can see the ideals of the Renaissance come full circle—the early humanists in Italy transformed themselves by the texts they read, and Shakespeare used the written word to shape our understanding of who we are. Western civilization was dramatically transformed.

FIGURE 10.15 Claes von Visscher, *Map of London* (detail), 1616 The south bank of the Thames is shown in the foreground of the image. In this seedy part of town, patrons came to see bear baiting and dog fights. But also here, in the circular theaters, Shakespeare and other playwrights created masterworks of English drama that have come down to us through the ages.

married a woman above his station, the daughter of a wealthy landowner. Shakespeare probably attended the local school in Stratford-upon-Avon and received

LOOKING BACK & MOVING FORWARD

Summary In the crucible of the fourteenth century—in which plague, famine, warfare, and religious instability swirled—new ideas percolated in the turbulent Italian city-states. Scholars and statesmen alike resuscitated a pride in human dignity, a confidence in human activism, and a fascination with classical ideals, and they expressed these ideas primarily in the secular arena. Writers, painters, and politicians looked with new realism at the world around them and strove to exert an impact on it. Although all these ideas had a precedent in the Middle Ages, their prevalence and novel applications created a new spirit that historians call the Renaissance.

KEY TERMS

This age of the Renaissance ushered in a period that had both great and shameful aspects. In booming economies, Italian city-states were able to support architects and artists who created masterpieces that have set Western standards of beauty for centuries. At the same time, many of these enterprising individualists turned a blind eye to social problems—increased crime, new slavery, and growing anti-Semitism.

The new ideas of the Renaissance flowed northward with humanist courtiers and talented artists and artisans. In the process, they helped transform the old feudal monarchies. At the same time, scholars in each country put their own stamp on the Renaissance spirit. For example, France gloried in court architecture and brilliant satire, and England most notably brought these ideas to the popular theater.

As we will see in Chapter 11, Spain and Germany, too, would mold the praise of individualism and literary criticism to their own interests. Like Savonarola in Florence, German humanists applied Renaissance ideas to spiritual matters. Their efforts would eventually bring about an upheaval in religion as great as the Renaissance revolution in art and ideas.

linear perspective, *p. 331*
madrigals, *p. 332*
alchemy, *p. 333*

REVIEW, ANALYZE, & CONNECT TO TODAY

REVIEW THE PREVIOUS CHAPTER

Chapter 9—"The West Struggles and Eastern Empires Flourish"—told of the disasters of the fourteenth century that contributed to the breakdown of medieval structures. It also told of the rise of empires in the East that would soon cast a long shadow on politics in the West.

1. Review the political order of northern Europe in the Middle Ages and contrast it with the political life of fourteenth-century Italy. How did the turbulent politics of Italy contribute to the growth of Renaissance thought?

2. Contrast medieval art, architecture, and literature with that of the Renaissance artists and humanists.

ANALYZE THIS CHAPTER

Chapter 10—"A New Spirit in the West"—considers the characteristics we have come to associate with the term *Renaissance*. It looks at the politics and social life of the Italian city-states that fostered these ideas and the magnificent accomplishments in the arts and science that accompanied them. It also follows the fortunes of the "new monarchies" of the north as Renaissance ideas spread.

1. Review the characteristics of the Renaissance and consider what contributed to the development.

2. One theme this chapter traces is the relationship between ideas—like individualism and realism—and actual events and accomplishments. Analyze some aspects of life and accomplishments of Renaissance Italy in light of these values, and consider how they were related.

3. How did Renaissance ideas spread northward, and how were they transformed in France and England?

CONNECT TO TODAY

Think about these key values of the Renaissance: individualism over community, realism over faith, and activism over passive obedience.

1. In what ways do contemporary U.S. society and culture also exhibit these values? In what ways are they expressed in public policy today?

2. Does the Western tradition of taking these values for granted prevent positive interactions with societies that do not share these values? Explain.

3. What examples can you cite from the world today wherein societies have censored religious criticism or suppressed individual liberties to strengthen the community? What do you think of such measures?

BEYOND THE CLASSROOM

A NEW SPIRIT EMERGES: INDIVIDUALISM, REALISM, AND ACTIVISM

Eisenstein, Elizabeth. *The Printing Revolution in Early Modern Europe.* New York: Cambridge University Press, 1983. Studies the shift from script to print and looks at the relationship between changes in communication and other developments.

Goldthwaite, Richard A. *Wealth and the Demand for Art in Italy, 1300–1600.* Baltimore: Johns Hopkins University Press, 1993. An original and important look at art in relation to the society and economy that produced it.

King, Margaret L., and Albert Rabil. *Her Immaculate Hand: Selected Works by and About the Women Humanists of Quattrocento Italy.* Asheville, NC: Pegasus Press, 1998. Presents writings of women humanists to illuminate an often-neglected side of the Renaissance.

Marek, G. *The Bed and the Throne: Isabelle d'Este.* New York: Harper & Row, 1976. A dazzling story of culture, art, and politics through the life of this talented ruler.

Naubert, Charles G. *Humanism and the Culture of Renaissance Europe,* 2nd ed. Cambridge: Cambridge University Press, 2006. A clear yet comprehensive description of the movement from its inception in Italy to its spread northward—definitely the place to begin.

THE POLITICS OF INDIVIDUAL EFFORT

Burckhardt, Jacob. *The Civilization of the Renaissance.* New York: Modern Library, 2002. A reissued edition of the nineteenth-century classic that began serious historical analysis of the Renaissance.

Femia, Joseph V. *Machiavelli Revisited.* Cardiff: University of Wales Press, 2002. Looks at the impact of Machiavelli's pivotal work, *The Prince,* while guiding the reader through the maze of contradictory interpretations.

Jones, P.J. *The Italian City-State: From Commune to Signoria.* Oxford: Clarendon Press, 1997. An impressive, scholarly study of the political history of the Italian city-states.

INDIVIDUALISM AS SELF-INTEREST: LIFE DURING THE RENAISSANCE

Brucker, Gene. *Florence: The Golden Age, 1138–1737.* Berkeley: University of California Press, 1998. A beautifully illustrated history by a prominent historian who brings the past vividly to life, including great families, common folk, wars, and artistic achievements.

Crum, Roger J., and John T. Paoletti, eds. *Renaissance Florence: A Social History.* Cambridge: Cambridge University Press, 2008. Comprehensive, accessible essays examining the social history of Florence and showing the ties between art and society.

Haas, Louis. *The Renaissance Man and His Children.* New York: St. Martin's Press, 1991. Sheds light on how Florentine parents (primarily fathers) viewed, reared, and cared for their children.

Katz, Dana E. *The Jew in the Art of the Italian Renaissance.* Philadelphia: University of Pennsylvania Press, 2008. A rigorous study of the portrayal of Jews in art, revealing animosity toward Jews even while some rulers upheld toleration legislation.

King, Margaret L. *Women of the Renaissance.* Chicago: University of Chicago Press, 1991. A short, accessible summary of women in the family, in the church, and participating in high culture.

McIntosh, Marjorie. *Controlling Misbehavior in England, 1370–1600.* Cambridge: Cambridge University Press, 2002. An in-depth study of the growing efforts of states to regulate behavior they deemed threatening to public order.

AN AGE OF TALENT AND BEAUTY: RENAISSANCE CULTURE AND SCIENCE

Baxandall, Michael. *Painting and Experience in Fifteenth-Century Italy: A Primer in the Social History of Pictorial Style.* Oxford: Oxford University Press, 1988. A brilliant work that shows the intersection between life in Florence and painters' expression of those experiences. A study of both painting and social history.

James, Frank A. *Renaissance and Revolution: Humanists, Scholars, Craftsmen and Natural Philosophers in Early Modern Europe.* New York: Cambridge University Press, 1994. A clear and engaging survey of the history of science and technology between 1400 and 1750.

RENAISSANCE OF THE "NEW MONARCHIES" OF THE NORTH: 1453–1640

Bloom, Harold. *Shakespeare: The Invention of the Human.* New York: Riverhead Books, 1998. A controversial but influential study of all Shakespeare's plays that argues that Shakespeare shaped the way we define ourselves.

Kendall, P.M. *Louis XI, the Universal Spider.* New York: W.W. Norton, 1971. A remarkable presentation of the French king Louis XI as one of the formidable personalities of Europe and one of the shapers of the modern world.

Martin, John J. *The Renaissance: Italy and Abroad.* New York: Routledge, 2002. A collection of essays that illustrates the current status of Renaissance studies, revealing its diversity and complexities.

Snyder, James, Larry Silver, and Henry Luttikhuizen. *Northern Renaissance Art,* 2nd ed. Upper Saddle River, NJ: Prentice Hall, 2004. Beautifully illustrated, comprehensive study of the artists and patrons who created the magnificent art of the northern Renaissance.

HANS HOLBEIN THE YOUNGER, *ERASMUS OF ROTTERDAM,* ca. 1523

As humanist ideas of scholarship and individualism spread north, they influenced a revolution in Christian thought, first led by the man portrayed here. Erasmus is shown resting his hands on a Greek book inscribed "The Labors of Herakles," a tribute to his Herculean task of revising biblical translations based on the study of ancient languages. He is placed in a room with hints of Renaissance design, reminding viewers of his debt to the Italian scholars. This quiet portrait reveals a pious man, seeking God alone. It does not reveal how this new approach to religion ripped at the social fabric as warfare and bloodshed tore through Europe.

"Alone Before God"

Religious Reform and Warfare, 1500–1648

"They used thumbscrews, which they cleverly made out of their pistols, to torture the peasants, as if they wanted to burn witches. . . . They put one of the captured peasants in the bake-oven and lighted a fire in it." This horrifying description of war in Germany (by a soldier, Jakob von Grimmelshausen) characterizes a period in European history when many innocents suffered horrible deaths. Rulers launched their armies at each other in an attempt to win new territory and enhance their power, and these armies fighting with new weapons unleashed untold misery.

At the same time, new ideas about how to worship God began to spread throughout Europe—religious reformers introduced an intellectual revolution that would not only alter how people viewed their relationship with God but also redefine their ideas about society, politics, and the very nature of human beings. However, as monarchs confronted the religious diversity boiling within their countries, they increased the violence: Civil wars over religion erupted and brought this period to a bloody close.

Out of this turmoil came a reform in religion that split the Christian body into many Christian churches. In the course of this reform, many men and women who were spared the bloodshed of warfare were killed for their beliefs. This religious reform also generated more subtle changes in society—ideas of love, marriage, education, and charity were transformed as some people rethought their relationship to God. The West was irrevocably changed.

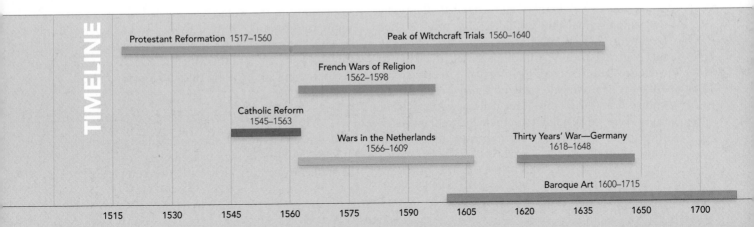

TIMELINE

Protestant Reformation 1517–1560

Peak of Witchcraft Trials 1560–1640

French Wars of Religion
1562–1598

Catholic Reform
1545–1563

Wars in the Netherlands
1566–1609

Thirty Years' War—Germany
1618–1648

Baroque Art 1600–1715

1515   1530   1545   1560   1575   1590   1605   1620   1635   1650   1700

THE CLASH OF DYNASTIES,
1515–1555

In 1520, two of the most powerful kings in Europe met in France to hold a tournament and discuss matters of state. Francis I (r. 1515–1547) of France had invited Henry VIII (r. 1509–1547) of England to his court to seek an alliance against his powerful enemy the Holy Roman Emperor Charles V (r. 1519–1556). Francis hoped to impress Henry with his extravagant wealth, but the ostentatious display generated only more rivalry. Each king approached the meeting with as much state as he could muster. The kings, their followers, and even their horses wore clothing made of silver and gold thread. Silk and gold decorated the walls of the French palace and even the tents on the palace grounds that offered shade from the noonday sun. The meeting was dubbed the Field of the Cloth of Gold. All this opulence underscored the character of the sixteenth century—there was money to spend and kings thought excess bought power. However, Francis had offended Henry by outspending him, and he did not get the alliance he sought. Instead, much to Francis's dismay, Henry met with Charles V, who approached the king in a frugal and reserved manner—and received his alliance. The struggle for land and power between Francis I and the Holy Roman Emperor would not take place on a golden tournament field; instead, these kings opened a violent century by warfare, while Henry waited to see who would be left standing. The Italian city-states—too small to compete

on fields of golden cloth—became the battleground in this bitter contest.

The kings of France and England ruled strong, unified states, but at the beginning of the sixteenth century, nation-states were not necessarily the ideal political form. Indeed, kings sought to extend their reach even further and acquire multinational empires like that held by the Holy Roman Emperor, Charles V. Ignoring considerations of common culture or the difficulties of holding large empires, each king believed simply that bigger was better.

Land-Hungry Monarchs

Charles V was the grandson of Ferdinand and Isabella of Spain (see page 360). Thanks to the prudent dynastic marriages of his ancestors, he had inherited a sprawling, multinational empire. **Map 11.1** shows the Habsburg lands of Charles V, which included the Netherlands, Spain, and lands in Austria, and highlights all the battles to indicate how warfare dominated Charles's reign. The map also shows the extensive empire of the Ottoman Turks, which threatened Charles in the East.

As we saw in Chapter 9, events in the eastern Mediterranean had complicated western European rivalry, for the empire of the Ottoman Turks had gained strength. After the Turks conquered Constantinople in 1453, they consolidated their rule and developed a sophisticated administration and a well-trained military. Under Suleiman I the Magnificent (r. 1520–1566), the Turks began to advance again, this time toward the very heart of Europe. **Map 9.5,** on page 302, shows the sixteenth-century advance of the Ottoman Empire and indicates why western Europeans felt threatened by the growing power of the Muslims.

Turkish expansion

In 1521, the Turks marched up the Danube valley and seized Belgrade and Hungary, creating a panic throughout central Europe. By 1529, they were outside the walls of Vienna, the core of the Austrian Habsburg lands. At the same time, Turkish ships proved so effective in the eastern Mediterranean that all the western rulers wondered how long they could hold on to their share of the lucrative sea trade in that area. For Charles V in particular, however, the Ottoman Empire had become a major, distracting presence in the east as he struggled to extend his empire in the west. All these monarchs had to grapple with new complexities in their seemingly endless struggles with one another, for the scale of warfare was increasing, and the old rules no longer applied.

The Changing Rules of Warfare

As we saw in Chapter 9, the mounted knights of the Middle Ages were being replaced by infantry, and by the sixteenth century, that trend was complete. The

MAP 11.1

Europe in 1526— Habsburg-Valois Wars

This map illustrates the political division of Europe in 1526 and highlights the Habsburg lands inherited by Charles V. It also shows the Ottoman Empire on Charles's borders.

Explore the Map

1. Why did the French king feel threatened by his powerful neighbor?

2. Why was Charles so concerned about the proximity of the Ottoman Empire?

3. Notice all the battles Charles fought. What might have been the impact of this warfare both on the people and on the emperor's ability to rule?

---

primary reason for this change was military technology. By 1500, Europeans had improved on the unreliable early guns of the Hundred Years' War. Now, guns with 50-inch-long barrels gave marksmen a good deal of power and accuracy, and soon the Spanish developed the musket, a 6-foot-long gun that could shoot lead bullets up to 200 yards. Armed with these weapons, soldiers could do a great deal more damage. As one observer noted: "Often and frequently . . . a virile brave hero is killed by some forsaken knave with a gun." Indeed, warfare was now dramatically changed, and kings had to pay the price in men and materials

for new armies. See Thinking About Science & Technology to see how the changes in gunpowder facilitated its widespread use.

The new weapons dictated different military strategies. Now, captains arrayed their troops in a series of long, narrow lines. The infantrymen carried muskets and were backed by tight formations of pike-wielding foot soldiers. In this new kind of warfare, sheer numbers often determined a king's success, so monarchs strove to bolster the size of their armies. At the beginning of the century, most armies had fewer than 50,000 men;

Growing armies

thinking about
SCIENCE & TECHNOLOGY

Destruction and Amusement: The Development and Uses of Gunpowder

By the tenth century, Chinese alchemists—recall that alchemy was the early practice of chemistry—were experimenting with mixing various substances for medicinal purposes. In the process, they invented an effective gunpowder. The formula was 75 percent saltpeter (potassium nitrate), which released chemically bound oxygen to support combustion; 15 percent charcoal to supply carbon to fuel the fire; and 10 percent sulfur to lower the temperature of ignition and speed up combustion.

Europeans adopted this recipe and began to use gunpowder on the battlefield in the fourteenth century. Then, in the fifteenth century, Western powder engineers developed a technique of binding the powder into small clumps called corned powder, which was easy to transport, to keep dry, and to load efficiently into guns and cannons. Importantly, the corned powder also was more stable; the corning technology prevented accidental dust explosions and detonation from static electricity and provided a more controlled burn rate. With the enhanced stability and transportability of the improved powder, large, mobile cannons could be brought into the battlefields, whereas previously they could only be mounted on ships and forts. From this moment on, battlefield violence increased dramatically, and foot soldiers faced devastating explosions as they charged. Gunpowder's impact would become starkly evident in the violence of the early modern wars and in the sea battles that would bring Europeans to power across the world.

People throughout history have found ways to adapt technological innovations for entertainment purposes, and this ingenuity was true for gunpowder. As early as the late fifteenth century in the West, gunpowder moved from wartime to peacetime uses as people set off gunpowder-powered fireworks to light up European night skies on special occasions. These displays were potentially hazardous, however; for example, the pyrotechnics that were lit during one of Shakespeare's productions ignited the fire that burned down the playwright's Globe Theatre in 1613. Even firemasters, individuals who made gunpowder, did not know exactly how gunpowder worked, and **Figure 11.1** shows the explosive results that often accompanied their experiments. This mystery stimulated scientific investigation for years to come, helping to move science from alchemy to chemistry as researchers finally identified the oxygen hidden in the saltpeter that fed the fires of what had long been believed to be a magic powder.

Remember the struggle for mastery of the chemistry of gunpowder so that when you learn about the Scientific Revolution in Chapter 14, you might consider again the relationship between practical utility and scientific theory.

Connecting Science & Society

1. Trace how the scientific experimentation behind the development and improvement of gunpowder led to the application of gunpowder technology for various purposes.

2. How did advances in the stability and transportability of gunpowder transform warfare?

3. Cite some instances in your lifetime where inventions of practical items or techniques have been later adapted for entertainment purposes.

INVENTIONS ILLUSTRES
La poudre

FIGURE 11.1 Experimenting with gunpowder.

Charles V's forces boasted a whopping 148,000 (although they were widely dispersed through Charles's extensive lands).

To enlarge their armies, rulers had to resort to creative new ways to fill their ranks. In part, kings relied on mercenaries, hiring soldiers of fortune who offered their services to the highest bidder, but these were never sufficient. Traditionally, kings claimed the right to draft an army from among the able-bodied men of the land. Originally, these draftees were required to fight only on their home soil, but in 1544 Henry VIII sent his conscripts overseas. No one objected, and a useful precedent was set that helped kings boost their foreign armies. Sometimes men did not wait to be drafted into the growing armies, but instead volunteered. These soldiers joined up for various reasons—some wanted to escape poverty or the hardships of village life; others sought adventure. Martin Guerre, described in the Biography, was one such villager; he volunteered for the wars probably to escape the responsibilities of family life.

Not surprisingly, armies made up of poorly paid mercenaries, conscripts, and volunteers brought new problems to the art of making war. Officers repeatedly complained of soldiers' lack of discipline, and they imposed drilling and strict penalties for disobedience. Military leaders developed other strategies as well to manage their expanding forces. The Spanish evolved a complex military administration, which included the first battlefield hospitals. The Dutch introduced standardized-caliber weapons to help solve the problem of supplying larger numbers of infantrymen. Feeding and outfitting armies were still no easy matter, however. Wives, children, prostitutes, and servants trailed behind the lines to take advantage of the regular pay that the armies offered their men. These followers also needed to eat, of course, and at times they plundered the countryside through which the army moved.

Modernized warfare carried a high price. Heavy artillery was especially costly for both offensive and defensive forces. Not only did armies have to spend valuable currency to equip their armies with cannons, but rulers had to rebuild cities into massive fortresses with forts and gun emplacements to guard against opposing artillery. The new warfare also required larger navies, and ships, too, were expensive. Between 1542 and 1550, England spent more than twice its royal revenue on military campaigns. Other European powers also bankrupted themselves on these incessant wars. For example, between 1520 and 1532, Charles V borrowed an astounding 5.4 million gold coins from rich merchants to pay his troops—still, he could not compensate them completely.

FIGURE 11.2 Pieter Brueghel the Elder, *The Cripples,* 1568
This painting shows the tragic reality of modern warfare. Many combatants lost their limbs to gunfire and were relegated to a life of poverty.

At his death, Francis I owed bankers one full year's income of all the crown lands.

Winners and Losers

Kings were seldom able to deliver a decisive victory in this seemingly endless warfare, and small victories were soon avenged. Therefore, very few combatants "won" these military contests or profited at all. However, some individuals were able to gain a huge profit. Bankers who lent money to kings recklessly supplying ever-larger armies struck it rich. Guns and ammunition manufacturers, especially in the Netherlands, also profited hugely.

Overall, however, losers vastly outnumbered winners in these wars. As armies ballooned, so did casualties. With the increasing use of bullets and gunpowder, the nature of combat injuries also changed. In the Middle Ages, battlefield surgeons had been skilled at treating sword injuries; in the sixteenth century, surgeons more often had to amputate limbs crushed by artillery shells (as happened to Martin Guerre; see the Biography). As one soldier wrote of the new guns: "Would to God that this unhappy weapon had never been invented." In **Figure 11.2,** a painting by the Dutch artist Pieter Brueghel the Elder (ca. 1525–1569), the wounded men's artificial limbs are depicted as particularly short. In this way, Brueghel emphasized the loss and disability that came with amputation. To survive, many legless or armless veterans resorted to begging in the towns and villages of Europe.

Casualties of war

BIOGRAPHY

Martin Guerre
(1524–1594)

Peasant,

Soldier, and

Reluctant

Family Man

In 1527, a peasant family moved from their village in the Basque country, on the border between France and Spain, to a village in southern France. The Guerre family prospered in their new home and by the time their young son, Martin, was fourteen, his parents had contracted a promising marriage for him with the daughter of a relatively well-to-do peasant family nearby.

Martin and his new bride, Bertrande, spent their wedding night in the Guerre household, where neighbor women gave them a heavily seasoned drink designed to stimulate their ardor and fertility. The potion failed. Martin remained impotent for eight years, while the village discussed whether he was under a spell and teased him mercilessly for not fulfilling his duty. Finally, an old woman told the young couple how to lift the spell through special prayers and cakes. The marriage was consummated, and Bertrande became pregnant immediately and bore a son. Martin, however, was not a happy young man. After quarreling with his father one day in 1548, the 24-year-old fled the village and was not heard from for years.

Martin traveled to Spain, where he served in the Spanish army in Flanders and France. During the fighting, he was shot in the leg; the limb then had to be amputated. Still, he sent no word to his village. In his absence, his parents died. Bertrande remained under the care of Martin's uncle Pierre as she raised their son and awaited the return of her husband.

Then, in 1556, a man strolled into the village and claimed to be Martin Guerre. He was actually an impostor, Arnaud du Tilh, who had left his own French village after a dissolute youth and joined the Spanish army fighting in Flanders. He had met Martin and learned about his life and marriage. Now, when Arnaud was ready to settle down into a new life, Martin's village seemed to offer that opportunity.

The village welcomed Arnaud as the lost Martin, and Bertrande took him in as her husband. If she had doubts about the newly passionate "Martin," she apparently set them aside. The couple harmoniously lived together for three years, during which Bertrande gave birth to two daughters.

Soon dissension arose in the village as Protestant ideas began to spread through the region. Bertrande's parents became Protestant, and Arnaud may have been drawn to Protestant ideas as well. As in so many villages throughout Europe, a split in religion caused tensions in previously unified villages, and these religious ideas may have exacerbated the suspicions that were growing in Bertrande's family. Arnaud and Martin's uncle increasingly began to quarrel over land and ideas, which caused Pierre to question Arnaud's very identity. Finally, Pierre had Arnaud arrested and charged him with impersonating his nephew. At Arnaud's trial, hundreds of villagers testified for both sides. Some were certain that Arnaud was the real Martin; others felt equally convinced that he was not. Most of them simply could not decide. The case went to appellate court, where the legal tide seemed about to turn in Arnaud's favor. However, one day during the appeal proceedings, the real Martin Guerre, outfitted with crutches and a peg leg, suddenly limped into the courtroom to reclaim his identity and his family.

The impostor was condemned to death, and Bertrande was judged an innocent victim of Arnaud's duplicity and returned to her husband. Over the coming years, Martin and Bertrande had two more sons. The historical records reveal nothing about Bertrande's response to Martin's return. In 1594, Martin died.

This extraordinary case was recorded by a contemporary witness, Jean de Coras, who was fascinated by the motivations of the various parties. Coras's account was widely circulated throughout France, although the author did not live long enough to enjoy the fame. The Protestant Coras was killed in the French wars of religion—a few months after the Saint Bartholomew's Day Massacre in 1572. Villagers related the tale of the impersonation of Martin Guerre for centuries.

Connecting People & Society

1. What does this biography tell you about how foreign wars disrupted families?

2. What does it reveal about changing religious ideas?

3. How does this life demonstrate the continuing belief in magic?

The wars of this period also contributed to inflation and ruined harvests, both of which tormented even noncombatants. Horrified contemporary witnesses repeatedly described the legions of poor, starving civilians who wandered the landscape in search of food and died along the way. One French writer told of "some thousands of poor people, . . . subdued like skeletons, the majority leaning on crutches and dragging themselves along as best they could to ask for a piece of bread." People weakened by hunger and traveling through the countryside also fell prey to all manner of diseases. In the sixteenth century, outbreaks of plague, typhoid fever, typhus, smallpox, and influenza took a terrible toll.

The Habsburg-Valois Wars, 1521–1544

All these costs of making war still did not deter kings from their drive for land and power, and the city-states of Italy—where both Francis I and Charles V had dynastic claims—became the battlefield. Thus began the Habsburg-Valois Wars, named after the ruling houses of Austria and France. These wars were fought sporadically for about twenty-five years.

The wars devastated the Italian city-states, demonstrating that only large states could successfully field large-enough armies for the new warfare. Charles also learned a hazard in using mercenary troops, for in 1527 the emperor was unable to pay them, and his enraged armies stormed Rome in search of booty to cover their pay.

Weary imperialists

Neither Charles nor Francis could win a decisive victory, so the two men finally negotiated a peace in 1544, and by its terms, Francis agreed to renounce his claim on Italy. Charles, too, wearied by all his problems, and in ill health, troubled by gout, decided to give up his imperial ambitions. He abdicated his various thrones between 1555 and 1556 and split his extensive holdings. He bestowed his Austrian and German lands on his brother Ferdinand I (r. 1558–1564) and the Low Countries, Spain, and Naples on his son Philip II (r. 1556–1598). Weary and disheartened, the ailing Charles V retired to a palace in Spain, where he died two years later. From this point on, these two branches of the Habsburg family went their separate ways.

During the wars, the kings had been willing to ally with unlikely partners. Sometimes Francis sought help from the Turks against Charles, and at times both Catholic kings courted critics of the church—"Lutherans"—to help against the other's Catholic forces. However, the treaty that ended the war attempted to present the Catholic kings as a united front against religious diversity that had flourished in their lands. Charles and Francis agreed to focus their energies on defeating "Muslims and Lutherans" who were threatening the Christian world. The Muslims had been a traditional enemy, but who were these Lutherans who appeared in the sixteenth century and who by 1544 seemed such a threat to the Christian kings?

A TIDE OF RELIGIOUS REFORM

The powerful medieval Christian church had called itself "Catholic," which meant "universal." In the hands of reformers, however, "Catholic" began to mean the traditional church, which even in the Middle Ages had come under criticism. Medieval critics had questioned some of the beliefs and practices of the church—its power, its wealth, and its insistence on obedience to the pope as necessary for spiritual salvation. The last point was central, because from the beginning, Christians had focused on salvation—everything from the best way to worship God to getting into heaven after death. As the sixteenth century opened, criticism began to intensify and many people wondered if their salvation was in good hands.

The Best Path to Salvation?

The church had promised Christians that the path to salvation lay in the hierarchy of the church and its sacramental system, which offered grace to the faithful through the seven **sacraments.** To further confirm this, the Fourth Lateran Council in 1215 (described in Chapter 8) had declared that there was no salvation outside the church. Churchmen also promised that the faithful would be supported by the community of Christians, including the Virgin Mary, all the saints, and the congregations on earth. No Catholic believer, the church claimed, would have to face God alone in the afterlife.

A new popular piety and personal mysticism, along with the spread of Renaissance ideas of individualism, began to raise questions about this path to salvation. Catholicism had emphasized the need for an ordained priest—a "father confessor"—to hear one's confession and offer absolution. This new sensibility of popular piety allowed individuals seeking God to seek Him directly through prayer, breaking the chain of mediators that had marked the Catholic church. Many men and women who called themselves the Brethren of the Common Life tried to create a devout personal relationship between themselves and Christ, to supplement the complex Catholic theology. This style of popular religion was called the **devotio moderna** (modern devotion), and it influenced many subsequent believers.

One pious follower of the *devotio moderna*, Thomas à Kempis (1380–1471), is reputed to be the author of the best articulation of their ideas, in *The Imitation of Christ* (1425). In this profoundly influential text, Thomas argued that personal piety and ethics were as important as religious dogma. In Thomas's view, individuals could work toward salvation by focusing on their own spiritual growth, and many agreed passionately with Thomas's assertion "Blessed is the soul which hears the Lord speak within it and receives consolation from his mouth." Many longed for this kind of personal contact with God that, as Thomas pointed out, would make society as a whole more spiritual. As devoted Christians began to experiment with new forms of a Christian life, intellectuals began to contemplate some of the more complicated aspects of Christian thought.

Desiderius Erasmus: "Prince of Humanists"

As humanism spread to northern Europe, scholars applied the techniques of humanist education to Christian thought. The greatest Christian humanist was Desiderius Erasmus (1466–1536), who became known as the "Prince of the Humanists." Erasmus (shown in the chapter-opening painting on page 342) knew firsthand that some elements of the church needed reform, because he was born in Holland as the illegitimate son of a supposedly celibate priest. He studied at a school that was the center of the Brethren of the Common Life and grew up imbued with the new devotion that called for people to approach God directly in their hearts. Erasmus became a priest and went to study in a traditional university in Paris, which he hated. He dropped out of school, complaining that the university offered "theology as stale as their eggs."

The young priest then went to England, where his intellect was awakened by the humanists in Henry VIII's London. Erasmus became great friends with Thomas More and began a course of study based on a humanist curriculum. His interests remained religious, however, and he turned the humanist emphasis on original texts to biblical studies. He learned Greek so he could immerse himself in the mental world of the New Testament, and like the Italian humanists, he insisted that language study had to be the starting point for any education: "Our first care must be to learn the three languages, Latin, Greek, and Hebrew, for it is plain that the mystery of all scripture is revealed in them." In this statement, we can see the literary work of the humanists applied to the highest Christian purpose.

Erasmus's greatest contribution to the intellectual life of the West was his critical edition of the New Testament. To approach this, Erasmus rejected the officially accepted version of the Bible—Jerome's (ca. 340–420) Latin translation, called the Vulgate—and returned to the Greek and Hebrew texts to create a new rendition. Erasmus even corrected portions of the Vulgate, and his edition became the basis for later translations of the Bible.

The humanist also criticized corruption in the church in many writings. For example, he wrote a satire, *Julius Excluded from Heaven* (1517), in which he showed the famous Renaissance warrior-pope Julius II (see Chapter 10) unable to enter heaven, even though popes had always claimed to hold its keys. His most famous satire, however, was *The Praise of Folly* (1511), in which he used his sharp wit to promote a greater spirituality in religion. In this book, his character, Folly, catalogs vices and in the process makes fun of the author himself, his friends, and the follies of everyday life. His attacks also

Religious satires

probed deeply into many of the religious practices of the day, and as readers laughed at his attacks on people who "worshiped" the Virgin Mary over her son and popes who did not live like Jesus, their ideas on worship itself began to change.

Perhaps even more than his disappointment at church corruption, it was his humanist love of education that led him to propose a radically different approach to Christian life. Erasmus argued that Christians should read the Bible directly, rather than relying on priests to interpret it for them: "I would that even the lowliest women read the Gospels and the Pauline Epistles. And I would that they were translated into all languages." A scholar to the core, Erasmus did not advocate separation from the church, but a contemporary of his recognized the long-term impact of the humanist's thought, saying that "Erasmus laid the egg Luther hatched." Revolution in religious thinking had been planted, and the letters in Document 11.1 reveal the anger that served as fertile ground.

Luther's Revolution

Martin Luther (1483–1546), the intelligent son of an upwardly mobile family in Germany, was an improbable revolutionary. His father, a successful mine owner, expected him to further the family fortune by becoming a lawyer, but young Luther's life took a dramatically different turn. During a fierce thunderstorm, Luther was struck to the ground by a bolt of lightning. Frightened, Luther cried out to Saint Anne (the Virgin Mary's mother): "Help me and I will become a monk." He survived the storm and fulfilled his vow (much to his father's initial disapproval). Luther threw himself into his new calling—becoming a monk, priest, and doctor of theology—but he remained plagued with a deep sense of sin and a deep fear of damnation. He even believed he actually saw the devil during the torments of his conscience.

For all Luther's study, prayer, and attempts to live a Christian life, he still did not believe he could ever be worthy of salvation. Even the church's promise of grace in the sacraments and "good works" of the church brought him no comfort. Finally, he found peace in the Bible, especially its statement that the "just shall live by his faith" (Rom. 1:17). Luther interpreted this statement as meaning that people were saved only through God's mercy, not through their own efforts to live as good Christians. Faith alone—not ritual—would save their souls. For Luther, Christ's sacrifice had been complete and for all time, so humans did not have to do anything else for their own salvation. This central point of Luther's belief is called "**justification by faith.**"

Inflamed by his newfound belief, Luther challenged church doctrine over the issue of **indulgences.** Through the Middle Ages, the Catholic Church had

DOCUMENT 11.1

Germans Rage Against Papal Exploitation

These two documents, written in 1480 and 1503, reveal that some in Germany raged against what they saw as exploitation of Germans by a distant pope. These documents show that Luther's critique launched in 1517 would find fertile soil.

1. Critique of Church Wealth, ca. 1480. Author anonymous.

It is as clear as day that by means of smooth and crafty words the clergy have deprived us of our rightful possessions. For they blinded the eyes of our forefathers, and persuaded them to buy the kingdom of heaven with their lands and possessions. If you priests give the poor and the chosen children of God their paternal inheritance, which before God you owe them, God will perhaps grant you such grace that you will know yourselves. But so long as you spend your money on your dear harlots and profligates, instead of upon the children of God, you may be sure that God will reward you according to your merits. For you have angered and overburdened all the people of the empire. The time is coming when your possessions will be seized and divided as if they were the possessions of an enemy. As you have oppressed the people, they will rise up against you so that you will not know where to find a place to stay.

2. Against Abuses in Indulgences, Myconius, 1512

Anno 1512. Tetzel gained by his preaching in Germany an immense sum of money which he sent to Rome. A very large sum was collected at the new mining works at St. Annaberg, where I heard him for two years. It is incredible what this ignorant and impudent monk used to say. . . . He declared that if they contributed readily and bought grace and indulgence, all the hills of St. Annaberg would become pure massive silver. Also, that, as soon as the coin clinked in the chest, the soul for whom the money was paid would go straight to heaven. . . . The indulgence was so highly prized that when the agent came to a city the bull was carried on a satin or gold cloth, and all the priests and monks, the town council, schoolmaster, scholars, men, women, girls and children went out in procession to meet it with banners, candles, and songs. All the bells were rung and organs played. He was conducted into the church, a red cross was erected in the center of the church, and the pope's banner displayed. . . .

SOURCE: Oliver J. Thatcher and Edgar H. McNeal, *A Source Book for Mediaeval History* (New York: Charles Scribner's Sons, 1905), pp. 336–340.

Analyze the Document

1. What are the main criticisms of the church expressed in these documents?

2. How will the angry rhetorical style of the documents contribute to the coming of the Reformation? Does the rhetoric make it increasingly difficult to compromise? Explain.

---

developed a complex understanding of how people are forgiven for their sins, including confession, penance, and absolution. As part of this process, churchmen claimed that people had to perform certain "works"—like prayers, fastings, pilgrimages, or similar activities—to receive forgiveness for their sins. If people died before completing full repentance for their transgressions, they could expect to suffer for them in **purgatory** before they could enter heaven, and late-medieval people had come to believe it would be virtually impossible for anyone to do full penance for their sins before death.

> **Attack on indulgences**

In the Middle Ages, the pope had begun to alleviate some people's fears by offering an "indulgence," a remission of the need to do penance for sins. The pope claimed to control a "treasury of merit"—an infinite supply of good works that had been done by the saints and the Virgin Mary from which he could draw to remit sins. These remissions came in the form of "indulgences," documents that popes gave people in return for certain pious acts. Dating from the fourteenth century, a pious act might be a contribution of money to the church.

In 1517, Pope Leo X had issued a special indulgence to finance the construction of a new St. Peter's Church in Rome that would replace an old, smaller one. Johann Tetzel, a well-known Dominican friar, appeared to sell these indulgences to rich and poor alike in Germany and sent the money to Leo. Tetzel was reputed to have used the crude words: "As soon as the coin in the coffer rings, the soul from purgatory springs." Luther, horrified by this apparent trafficking in God's grace, wrote a series of statements decrying the selling of these indulgences and protesting the flow of money from Germany to Rome.

Tradition says that Luther tacked his list of arguments—the Ninety-five Theses—to the door of the church in Wittenberg, but he may well have simply sent it to his bishop. It seems that Luther merely wanted to engage a scholarly debate on the subject, but too many people were profoundly interested in this topic. The inflammatory theses were soon translated

> **Ninety-five Theses**

into German and circulated even more widely than if they had been publicly posted on the church doors—they spread rapidly throughout Germany and beyond by way of the printing press. Their clearly drawn arguments and the passion that lay beneath them appealed to many intellectuals who criticized the church and to Germans who had begun to resent German money going to Italy. With Luther's strong words "It is foolish to think that papal indulgences . . . can absolve a man," the battle lines were drawn.

Luther's commitment to individual conscience over institutional obedience catalyzed major changes in his life that in turn shaped the emergence of the reformed church. It is somewhat ironic that within a generation, reformers would be enforcing institutional obedience with as much enthusiasm as the Catholics ever had. However, Luther himself pursued the logical consequences of his ideas. In Luther's new understanding, the monastic life made no religious sense; in the presence of God's grace, there was no need for heroic renunciations. Therefore, he left the monastery and married Katherina von Bora, a former nun, and wrote influential works on Christian marriage. He also composed moving hymns that transformed religious services. Furthermore, because he came to his understanding of religion through reading the Bible, he believed that it should be accessible to everyone, so he translated it into German. Indeed, this translation became his most influential legacy. Not only did it make the Bible available to an even wider group of readers; it also, through its popularity, helped shape the form of the developing German language.

Protestant Religious Ideas

Luther articulated a core of beliefs that subsequent religious groups would share, even as they departed from "Lutheranism." Christian churches (except the Roman Catholic and Eastern Orthodox) that share these beliefs today are called **Protestant.** The word derives from the protest of some German princes at the Diet (assembly) of Speier in 1529. Over the objection of the Lutheran princes, that body decided to protect the Catholic Church's right to offer services in Lutheran lands while denying the same privilege to Lutherans in Catholic lands. The name "Protestant" remained long after the issue had been resolved.

For Luther and subsequent Protestant reformers, at the heart of religious belief lay a faith in God's mercy that transcended the need for any good works. The Protestants thus conceived of a "priesthood of all believers," in which women and men were responsible for their own salvation. There was no need for an ordained priesthood to convey grace to believers by performing the sacraments.

Priesthood of all believers

Church leaders (whom Protestants called ministers, pastors, or preachers) could teach, preach, and guide Christian followers, but they could not help them achieve salvation. Each person stood alone before God throughout his or her life, and on judgment day prayers to saints and to the Virgin Mary were no more helpful than prayers offered by any other Christian. When people's spiritual quests combined with the Renaissance sense of individualism, it changed even the path to God.

With their emphasis on the individual's relationship to God, Protestants rejected many of the elements that had characterized the medieval church. No longer were the faithful to venerate saints or the Virgin Mary, so many claimed the relics of saints and martyrs that filled the churches of Europe were worthless. Protestant faithful would not become pilgrims traveling to the great cathedrals and saints' shrines in search of blessings or miracles. Indeed, the statues of the saints and other icons seemed to many Protestants to promote idolatry, and there was periodic Protestant **iconoclasm,** or destroying of the sacred images in the churches. (See **Figure 11.4.**)

Just as Protestants downplayed the importance of the priesthood and the intercession of saints, they restricted the significance and number of the sacraments. In the Middle Ages, Catholics had identified seven sacraments important for salvation (including marriage and the last rites at death). Most (but not all) Protestant reformers accepted only two sacraments—baptism and the Eucharist (the celebration of

Sacraments

Christ's Last Supper before his Crucifixion). Furthermore, they rejected **transubstantiation,** which said that the bread and wine offered up at mass were turned into the actual body and blood of Christ—a transformation that only an ordained priest could perform. Although Protestants may have rejected transubstantiation, they held various views on how Christ was present in the Eucharist, but because the bread and wine were not transformed, any believer could celebrate the Last Supper. As other Protestant groups branched off from Luther's initial thinking, they would emphasize some points of this theology over others. However, all of them shared the same basic principles: salvation by faith, not works; the Bible as the sole authority; and a "priesthood" made up of all believers.

These ideas spread rapidly in large part because they offered a simple and elegant answer to the question that had plagued so many: "How do I know I am saved?" Printing presses produced pamphlets and flyers offering these notions to the literate of towns and manors, and popular preachers told peasants in villages about Luther's challenge. Luther's seeds of revolution disseminated widely and found fertile soil.

The Reformed Church Takes Root in Germany

Luther's attack on tradition and hierarchy could not go unnoticed. In July 1519, at the Leipzig Debate, the Catholic theologian Johann Eck forced Luther to look at the logical consequences of his stand on indulgences and actually to deny the authority of popes and councils. After this turning point, Luther was more and more ready to make a full break with Rome. Finally, in 1521, Luther was called to appear before Charles V at the Diet of Worms to defend his views. Though confronted with over a thousand years of tradition, Luther nevertheless adhered to his understanding of scripture, and he reputedly made the famous reply: "To go against conscience is neither right nor safe. Here I stand, I cannot do otherwise." During the Middle Ages, many men and women who had similarly stood by their beliefs had been executed for their stance. The political situation in Germany in the sixteenth century saved Luther from this fate—and turned his personal stance into a religious revolution.

Under pressure from Charles V to recant, Luther sought and received the protection of his prince, the powerful Frederick the Wise of Saxony. **Figure 11.3** shows Frederick surrounded by Protestant reformers under his protection. Frederick, at the center of the image, has an imposing presence, with his gold chains and richly embroidered clothing. The reformers gather behind him, Martin Luther at the prince's right arm. This painting suggests the degree to which the Reformation drew strength from the support of powerful local leaders.

In addition to reasons of conscience, German princes had other motives for supporting Luther's ideas. The reformer's call to stop sending German money to Rome suited princes who felt the sharp sting of inflation. Princes could also benefit from confiscating wealthy Catholic properties (like churches and monasteries) in the name of religion. Luther's call for a break with Rome also appealed to a growing sense of German nationalism as distinct from the international Christendom represented by the Catholic Church. Some princes may have hoped that any weakening of the pope's authority would also diminish the power of the Holy Roman Emperor Charles V, whose authority derived in part from papal support. A weakened emperor meant more opportunities for the princes to bolster their own power.

Many poor, too, rallied to Luther's banner of religious reform, and this support took a particularly violent form in Germany. Spurred on by fiery preachers, peasants who suffered from hunger, inflation, and skyrocketing manorial dues made Luther's attack on religious abuses part of their revolutionary program. In 1524, German peasants circulated the Twelve

Peasants' war

FIGURE 11.3 Lucas Cranach the Younger, *Martin Luther and the Wittenberg Reformers,* **sixteenth century** The Reformation in Germany was not only a product of the skill and piety of Martin Luther, shown on the left. The movement and its leaders also drew strength from the protection and patronage of the powerful Prince Frederick the Wise of Saxony, center.

Articles, in which they demanded such things as a reduction of manorial dues and services and preservation of their rights to use meadows and woods. These wants dealt directly with the peasants' concerns, but they couched their demands in references to scripture—a direct consequence of Luther's call for people to conduct their lives in accordance with their biblical readings. The Twelve Articles claimed to "give a Christian reason for the disobedience or even the revolt of the entire peasantry" and further promised "[if any of] the articles here set forth should not be in agreement with the word of God . . . we will willingly recede from [it]." This widely circulated pamphlet linked Protestant theology directly with revolution, and Germany erupted.

In 1524, a violent peasant war broke out. As the peasants took up arms and stormed manor houses, they called for support from Luther's religious reformers. However, Luther was no John Ball (the religious leader who had led the peasant revolt in England in 1381). He advocated religious reform, not social revolution, for he believed the Bible called for people to obey secular rulers. Appalled by the violence in the countryside, Luther wrote a treatise called "Against the Robbing and Murdering Hordes of Peasants," in which he reprimanded peasants for defying legitimate government. He also urged those in power to "smite, slay and stab" rebellious peasants, but the nobility needed no urging from Luther to protect their privileges. The rebellion was brutally suppressed—more than 100,000 peasants were killed. The princes appreciated Luther's support of their repression and judged the movement perfectly consistent with their political needs. The Protestant Reformation thus found a warm welcome in the courts of many German princes.

By the time Charles V could turn his attention from the wars in Italy in the west and the Turkish threat in the east back to his German lands, the reformed church had taken firm root. At this point, Charles was in no position to uproot Lutheranism, which was supported by many of the great princes of the land. Furthermore, Charles's armies contained many Lutherans—as early as 1527, men among the rioting troops in Rome purportedly were calling for a silk rope to hang the pope. The emperor could not govern any longer without some accommodation.

Charles first tried to demand that his subjects come together under one religion. In 1530, he commanded all Lutherans to return to Catholicism or be arrested, but it was too late. Too many princes were willing to form a military alliance rather than obey. Then Charles tried compromise. In the 1540s, he encouraged talks between Lutherans and Catholics about the possibility of reconciliation, but these failed as well. By the 1550s, Lutheranism had captured about half the population of the empire.

In 1555, Charles's successor, Ferdinand, met with the German princes to negotiate a compromise to settle the religious turmoil. The resulting Peace of Augsburg established the Lutheran Church as a legitimate alternative to Catholicism in Germany. By this treaty, each | Peace of Augsburg | prince defined his principality as either Catholic or Lutheran. This compromise is known by the Latin phrase *cuius regio, eius religio*, which means "who rules determines the religion." Residents of any principality who did not agree with their prince's religious decision were free to move to a more congenial location. The Catholic emperor Ferdinand, the pope, and many churchmen did not like this concession to Lutheranism, which split the unity of the Christian church. However, they had no choice but to accept the compromise forced by the strong German princes.

The Augsburg treaty opened the door for the Reformation to fragment Christian Europe into a complex mix of different Christian sects. In addition, other monarchs and princes besides those in Germany saw the advantage in separating from Rome. Scandinavian kings, for instance, followed the example of German princes in supporting Lutheranism. These conversions left many problems unsolved—what about groups other than Lutherans? What about dissenting voices within either Catholic or Protestant principalities? What was the relationship between the state and religion? While these questions smoldered, the fire of religious reform continued to spread through Europe.

Bringing Reform to the States in Switzerland

While Luther's call for reform was the first to gain a large audience, his was not a solitary voice. Shortly after Luther's challenge, reformers in Switzerland successfully challenged old religious ideas. Switzerland consisted of a loose confederation of states (called cantons) in which many residents were ready for change, and the very independence of the cantons facilitated acceptance of new religious ideas. In addition, many of the young men from the Swiss cantons served as mercenaries in the seemingly insatiable armies of Europe, and service generated a growing disdain for the established order. Just as in Germany, dissatisfaction and growing national spirit combined with a desire for religious reform.

The first leader of the Reformation in Switzerland was Ulrich Zwingli (1484–1531), who lived in the northern canton of Zurich. Zwingli had been strongly influenced by | Zwingli | Erasmus's writings, and when he served as a chaplain with Swiss mercenaries, his longing for religious reform became joined with a desire to remove the Swiss confederation from the horrible wars.

In 1519 (a mere two years after Luther's challenge with his Ninety-five Theses), Zwingli became the priest of the main church in Zurich, and from there he began his own attack on traditional church practices. He believed Christians should practice only those things found in scripture, so his church in Zurich rejected such things as the veneration of saints, pilgrimages, purgatory, clerical celibacy, and most of the sacraments. In 1523, the city government in Zurich approved Zwingli's reforms, and Zurich became a Protestant city.

Zwingli and Luther shared many ideas, but would Protestants join together and form one church to oppose Catholicism? One German prince—Philip of Hesse—saw the advantages of consolidation and brought Luther and Zwingli together in 1529 at a meeting in Marburg to try to bring about an alliance. Although the two reformers agreed on virtually all points of doctrine, the meeting fell apart over their respective understanding of the nature of Christ's presence in the celebration of the Eucharist. Zwingli insisted the remembrance was symbolic, whereas Luther insisted that Christ's body was present as well as his spirit. As neither man could compromise with his conscience, there would be no united Protestant church or state. The new reformed churches would go their separate ways.

Just as in Germany, Protestantism came to the Swiss cantons with violence. In 1529, civil wars broke out between Protestant and Catholic cantons, and Zwingli himself died on the battlefield in 1531. The cantons reached a resolution similar to that of the later Peace of Augsburg in Germany—each canton would determine its own religion. However, the fires of reform stirred in more consciences and continued to spread, bringing both more hope and more violence.

Anabaptists: The Radical Reformers

The reforms of Luther and Zwingli appealed to many people but were implemented by princes or urban governments. However, many people saw power and religion as incompatible. New groups took a more radical turn in their efforts to reform the church and to keep it untainted by politics, and these reformers seemed threatening even to Protestants like Lutherans and Swiss reformers. Most members of these sects were referred to by their opponents as Anabaptists, meaning "rebaptizers" (although many of them preferred to be called simply Baptists), because they believed baptism should be reserved for adults, who could make a conscious choice to receive the grace of the sacrament. The radical sects drew heavily from peasants and artisans, especially those suffering from poverty and the relentless warfare of the period.

Confrontation between Anabaptists and the rest of society stemmed mainly from the Anabaptists' views on the relationship between church and state. Many radical reformers advocated a complete separation of these two institutions. They even argued that the "saved" (or the "elect") should not participate in government (including serving in the armies that were vigorously recruiting in the villages). One especially pacifist form of Anabaptism emerged in the Netherlands, developed by Menno Simons (1496–1561). Simons led his followers, the Mennonites, into Germany and Poland.

While most Anabaptist groups were pacifists, others became revolutionaries fighting for what they believed was a religious cause—the ushering in of a biblically promised age of peace and prosperity during which the "meek shall inherit the earth." Some saw the horrors of war and famine in the sixteenth century as the expected biblical disasters and chose to take up arms to help fight against those who had previously oppressed the poor. In Germany in 1534, a fiery preacher named Melchior established a sect (called the Melchiorites) that gained political control of their city of Münster. They burned all books but the Bible, abolished private property, and introduced polygamy as they settled down to await the expected second coming of Christ. Lutherans and Catholics alike believed this was a threat to society, so they captured the city and massacred the Melchiorites. Thereafter, the radicals were persecuted by Catholics and other Protestants alike.

Radical reformers

Calvinism and the Growing Middle Class

As we have seen, the Swiss cantons with their prosperous middle class had voiced religious longings and aspirations under the guidance of Zwingli. In the mid-sixteenth century, another voice also appealed to many of these well-to-do people in cities throughout Europe. Many people found intellectual and spiritual satisfaction in the teachings of the brilliant French scholar John Calvin (1509–1564). While preparing for a career in law, Calvin had studied many humanist writings, and in about 1533, Calvin read some of Martin Luther's works. He experienced a profound calling to Protestant theology, as he said: "God by a sudden conversion subdued and brought my mind to a teachable frame." The new reformer soon experienced pressure from royal authorities who in the reign of Francis I began a periodic suppression of reformers. Calvin had to flee France to avoid persecution and found a safe haven in the Swiss city of Geneva, where he published the first edition of his masterwork, *The Institutes of the Christian Religion* (1536).

What was the nature of Calvin's vision that appealed particularly to the hardworking and often prosperous middle classes? Calvin accepted the basic elements of Protestant belief that Luther had articulated, but he added his own emphasis. Whereas Luther had focused on salvation as the goal of human struggle, Calvin urged people to recognize the majesty, power, and justice of God. Perhaps Calvin's greatest contribution to Reformation thought was to redirect theological speculation from individual salvation to a larger question of humans' place in the universe.

When he turned to the question of salvation, Calvin again emphasized the power of God, shown in **predestination,** the belief that God preordained who would be saved or damned, even before a person was born. Calvin explained that if God were *only* just, everyone would be damned, for all people were sinful.

Church vs. state

Predestination

DOCUMENT 11.2

Marie Dentière Defends Reformation Women's Rights

In 1539, Marie Dentière (ca. 1495–1561) wrote a letter to Queen Marguerite of Navarre in which she defends the right of women to be active participants in the reformed churches. Selections from that letter appear below. Marie had been an abbess who left her monastery in the 1520s to come to Geneva and help bring about the Calvinist reform there. Within a few years, even the reformers in Geneva suppressed Dentière's work because it was written by a woman.

My very honored lady, since the true lovers of truth desire to know and understand how they ought to live in these very dangerous times, so too we women ought to know how to flee and to avoid all errors, heresies, and false doctrines, such as those of false Christians, Turks, infidels or others suspect in doctrine, as your writings have already very well demonstrated. . . .

I have not only wished, my lady, to write this letter for you but also to give courage to other women held in captivity, so that they will not fear exile from their countries, relatives, and friends, like I was, for the word of God. And principally I write for the poor little women, who desire to know and understand the truth; those who do not know which path, which way they ought to take, so that in the future they are not so tormented and afflicted within themselves, but rather they will rejoice, be consoled, and be moved to follow the truth, which is

the Gospel of Jesus Christ. And also [I write] to give courage to my little daughter, your god-daughter, to give the printers a small Hebrew grammar that she has written in French for the use and benefit of other little girls. . . . Because as you well know, the female sex is more shameful than the other, and not without reason. For until now, the scriptures have been hidden from them and no one dared say a word [about it], and it seemed that women should neither read nor hear anything of holy letters, which is the principal reason, my lady, that moved me to write to you, hoping in God that in the future women will no longer be so scorned as in the past. Because from day to day God changes the heart of his people for the better, which, I pray, will soon be so throughout the land. . . .

Not only would some slanderers and adversaries of the truth want to accuse us of too great audacity and boldness, but also some of the faithful say that women are too bold to write to one another about holy scripture. To them one can allowably respond that all those who have written and who have been named in holy scripture are not judged to be too bold, since several [women] are named and praised in holy scripture as much for their good morals, actions, behavior, and examples as for their faith and doctrine. . . .

Although there has been some imperfection in all women, nevertheless men have not been exempt from

it. Why is it so necessary to criticize women, seeing that a woman never sold or betrayed Jesus, but a man named Judas. Who are the ones, I ask you, who have invented and fabricated so many ceremonies, heresies, and false doctrines on earth, if not men? And the poor women have been seduced by them. Never was a woman found to be a false prophet, although they have been fooled by them. By this I do not wish to excuse the great malice of some women, which can surpass all measure, but there is no reason to make a general rule of it without any exception as some do daily. . . .

Therefore, if God has given grace to some good women, revealing something good and holy to them through his holy scriptures, will they dare not write, tell, or declare it to one another for the sake of the slanderers of the truth? Ah, it would be too impudent to wish to hinder them, and it would be too foolish to hide the talent that God has given us. He gives us grace to persevere until the end. Amen.

SOURCE: Marie Dentière, "A Very Useful Letter written and composed by a Christian woman from Tournai, sent to the Queen of Navarre, sister of the King of France, Against the Turks, Jews, Infidels, False Christians, Anabaptists, and Lutherans (Geneva, 1539)," trans. and ed. Elisabeth Wengler.

Analyze the Document

1. What does Marie say was the purpose of her writing? Notice she gives several reasons.

2. What arguments does she marshal in favor of women's studying and preaching?

3. Are her arguments consistent with the theology of the reformers?

4. Why do you think her writings were suppressed?

However, God tempered his justice with mercy, reaching down into the flames of damnation and plucking some souls out to share salvation. Calvin called these souls that were predestined to be saved the elect; the rest would experience eternal damnation. Many believers who, like Luther, felt that humans could do nothing to earn their salvation found comfort in the concept of predestination. Although predestination

was at the core of Calvin's beliefs, he never stressed it as much as his followers in subsequent generations did.

Many people seeking new paths to God were drawn to Geneva to join the exciting religious movement there. One such spiritual seeker was an ex-nun, Marie Dentière, who with her new husband was in the forefront of the reform movement in Geneva. Document 11.2, a letter from Marie to Queen

Marguerite of Navarre, reveals a tension that arose as part of the Reformers' theology: If all were responsible for their own salvation, did that mean women could preach and be leaders in the movement? Calvin, like Luther before him, rejected the idea that women should be leaders, but Marie expressed the ideas of many women—before and after her—that they, too, should be educated and preach the word of God.

As Calvinism took hold, Geneva became a vibrant center for Calvinist missionary work. Between 1555 and 1562, Calvin dispersed 100 preachers to the far-flung corners of Europe. Calvin had impressive organizational abilities, and he laid out directions for organizing congregations that explained how believers could establish underground groups to adopt Calvinism even where civil authorities were hostile. These techniques worked. The Netherlands were particularly receptive to Calvinist thought. In addition, many French cities soon amassed substantial Calvinist minorities, called **Huguenots.** German cities, too, began attracting Calvinist minorities—a problem because the Peace of Augsburg recognized only Lutheranism and Catholicism as acceptable religions. The Scot John Knox (1514–1572) was dazzled by Calvin in Geneva and returned to Scotland, where he established Calvinism as the predominant form of Protestantism. Like Knox, others from the British Isles were drawn to the exciting ideas of the reformers.

Spread of Calvinism

Protestant reliance on individual conscience made believers uncomfortable with much of the religious art that had dominated Christian worship in the West. In addition, many Protestants believed that religious art smacked of idol worship, drained precious resources better used on the poor, or simply distracted worshipers from focusing on the word of God. These concerns caused believers in many regions to attack religious art. Most of the Reformation leaders disapproved of such violence, but nevertheless, much religious art was destroyed in Protestant countries. This iconoclasm is reminiscent of the eighth-century conflict that had destroyed so much art in the eastern Orthodox lands. (See Chapter 6.) The engraving in Figure 11.4 shows people destroying religious art in the Netherlands. Statues are tumbled and precious windows broken while soldiers are unable (or unwilling) to stop the violence.

As a second-generation Protestant, Calvin moved the Reformation forward in important ways. In his

FIGURE 11.4 Destroying Images, 1566 Calvinists believed that the images that graced the churches were idolatry. This illustration from a work published in 1568 by Franz Hogenberg shows people in the Netherlands destroying these images in a riot.

writings and his life, he worked to establish a positive definition of Protestantism, that is, not simply as "not Catholic." In doing so, he articulated many of the theological principles that would define all Protestant churches. The passion for individualism and religious innovation kept Calvin (and anyone else) from uniting the various protest movements, but his intellect and strong faith made him an able advocate for Protestant thought.

Henry VIII and the English Church

In England in the 1520s, men with Protestant sympathies gathered to discuss some of Luther's writings that had been smuggled in. Perhaps even more exciting to the reformers was William Tyndale's English translation of the New Testament, which began to circulate in England in 1526. Protestant sympathies were growing on the island, but they would bear fruit from the actions of an unlikely ally—the king himself.

Henry VIII (r. 1509–1547), the proud king who appeared in state at the Field of the Cloth of Gold, was not initially a reformer. In fact, he had written an attack against Martin Luther in 1521 called the *Defense of the Seven Sacraments*, and Pope Leo X awarded him the title Defender of the Faith for his support. (Ironically, Protestant English monarchs still retain this title.) Although many English people wanted religious reform and some felt a strong antipathy toward the pope, it did not seem as if their king would lead them in a break with Rome. But Henry's desperate need for a male heir changed all this.

Remembering the devastating Wars of the Roses (Chapter 9) that had brought his Tudor dynasty to power, Henry believed he needed a male heir to secure the succession. His wife of eighteen years, Catherine of Aragon, had failed to produce one. Henry began to believe that God disapproved of this marriage, for he had married the widow of his brother (a practice normally forbidden) and had received special permission from the pope to do so. Henry also had fallen in love with a beautiful and bright young woman, Anne Boleyn. Anne did not want to become another of the king's mistresses, so she held off his amorous advances, insisting on a promise of marriage; first, Henry needed an annulment from the pope to end his first marriage.

Ordinarily, such royal annulments were easy to obtain because the popes had traditionally acquiesced to royal wishes. However, just as Charles V's absence from Germany in the Italian Habsburg-Valois Wars allowed Lutheranism to take hold, it also facilitated religious reform in England. Henry wanted his divorce in 1527, just as Charles V's troops were sacking Rome and virtually holding Pope Clement VII prisoner. The pope needed the goodwill of Charles to restore order and Henry's queen, Catherine, was Charles V's aunt. The pope dragged his feet in granting Henry his annulment.

In 1533, Anne Boleyn, persuaded that the king would marry her, became pregnant. Now Henry was running out of time for his annulment, for he wanted Anne's child to be born legitimate. Henry's two principal advisors—Thomas Cranmer, archbishop of Canterbury, and Thomas Cromwell—devised a way for Henry to get his annulment. Parliament passed an act making the archbishop of Canterbury the highest ecclesiastical official in England (cutting off the pope's authority). Then Thomas Cranmer ruled that Henry's marriage to Catherine was "null and void," so Henry was free to marry Anne. He did so, and three months later, much to the king's dismay, she gave birth to a girl, the future Queen Elizabeth. (Henry finally had a male heir by his third wife, after Anne was beheaded for adultery, but the king would eventually marry six women in his quest for heirs and personal happiness.)

Henry had gotten his annulment, but the force of religious reform he had unleashed continued its momentum. Parliament passed a number of measures designed to control the Catholic clergy and finally passed the Act of Supremacy (1534) that declared the king the supreme head of the Church of England. This break with the papacy established the Church of England as a separate church (which later was also called Protestant), but not everyone in England

welcomed this major reform. The most notable dissenter was the humanist Thomas More (1478–1535) (see Chapter 10), whose conscience would not allow him to obey a secular ruler in matters of faith, and he refused to swear an oath acknowledging the king's ecclesiastical supremacy. More was beheaded for his dissent, and this man of high integrity died blessing the king who had been his great friend, saying: "I die the king's good servant, but God's first."

Henry's position toward the reformers vacillated throughout his life. He did not support all the Protestant religious ideas—for example, he reaffirmed transubstantiation, which all the Protestants rejected. In fact, he considered himself a Catholic, although not a "Roman" Catholic. However, the powerful king readily implemented Reformation ideas that enriched his coffers and weakened the power of the Catholic Church. He shared the reformers' rejection of the monastic life and dissolved all the monasteries in England, confiscating their extensive lands and wealth. The king's treasury bulged from the confiscations, and many English religious reformers were satisfied with his new policies. However, the Church of England (also called the Anglican Church) really became Protestant under the reign of Henry's son.

Henry's third wife, Jane Seymour, finally bore him a son, Edward, in 1537. However, the boy was sickly when he took the throne upon Henry's death in 1547. Edward VI (r. 1547–1553) was a bright youth who was fond of Protestant theology, but he was young. Because of Edward's age, England was in fact ruled by a council of regents who wanted to solidify Protestantism in England.

The painting in **Figure 11.5** shows the young king at the center of the portrait, with his dying father on the left. The composition reveals the difficulties faced by the rule of a minor during these tumultuous times. The dying king, extending his right arm, transmits his blessing to rule, but the portrait includes many others with the father and son. On the right is the full Privy Council, which was to manage England during the boy king's minority. Seated next to Edward is his uncle, Edward Seymour, who served as the first Lord Protector of England. Seymour's successor, John Dudley, the Duke of Northumberland, is seated next to him. During Edward VI's brief six-year reign, both dukes would try to usurp power.

Beneath the young king in the painting, the pope and monks are crushed by the scriptures, while outside the window, iconoclastic Protestants destroy churches and images. Indeed, during the regency of the young king, Catholicism came under attack in England.

Archbishop Thomas Cranmer issued a Protestant manual of worship, *The Book of Common Prayer*, and Parliament issued the Act of Uniformity in 1549, making the prayer book's use mandatory for religious

FIGURE 11.5 Anonymous, King *Edward VI* (1537–53) *and the Pope*, 1568–1571 This work commemorates—and tries to ensure—the successful reestablishment of the Church of England by the young King Edward VI.

service throughout the kingdom. It seemed as if the Church of England was securely established, but the English would suffer more upheavals before religious peace reigned.

The 16-year-old Edward died without an heir, and the kingdom next went to his elder sister, Mary (r. 1553–1558), daughter of Catherine of Aragon, Henry's first wife. A staunch Catholic, Mary promptly set about undoing the Protestant reforms and returning England to the protective bosom of Rome. Although many prominent Protestants had fled to the Continent upon Mary's accession, the queen attempted to force remaining Protestants to renounce their beliefs. Bloody Mary ordered some 280 Protestants burned for "religious treason," including Archbishop Cranmer, who had originally granted Henry VIII his divorce. The English public was even more upset by her marriage to Charles V's son Philip II, the Catholic king of Spain. However, the marriage did not produce an heir who could continue her Catholic policies.

Upon Mary's death, the throne went to her half-sister, Anne Boleyn's daughter, Elizabeth I (r. 1558–1603), whose rule would earn her the affectionate nickname Good Queen Bess. Elizabeth (shown in **Figure 11.6**) proved a brilliant politician who

"Bloody Mary"

skillfully positioned herself at the center of a contentious court. As the portrait in **Figure 11.6** shows, she portrayed herself as a haughty, yet gracious queen who cared deeply for her subjects. She also remained unmarried (the ermine on her left arm in the painting is the symbol of virginity) and used that condition for her own diplomatic advantage by holding out the possibility of marrying into other European royal houses. Though arrogant and vain, Elizabeth was also a shrewd and frugal ruler who well deserved her people's grateful affection.

Elizabeth I

In matters of religion, Elizabeth did not worry about the fine points of theology. The young queen was appalled at the violence and destruction caused by the religious controversies, and she felt deeply responsible for maintaining peace in her realm while allowing people to follow their consciences. However, she was insistent on loyalty above all else, and she persecuted Catholics, who she felt had divided loyalties. She wanted to unify England around a Protestant core but also allow her loyal subjects latitude in religious practice and belief. For example, the prayer book that she instituted let people of differing convictions pray together in a national church. This moderate approach was effective: For a while, England basked in a time of peace that fostered an

FIGURE 11.6 Attributed to William Segan, *Portrait of Elizabeth I*, 1585 The shrewd Elizabeth brought a moderate approach to religious reform that allowed England to flourish. Her portraits both advertised her accomplishments and soothed her vanity.

intellectual flowering (see Chapter 10) and an era of international expansion (see Chapter 12).

Even as Elizabeth moved England toward moderation in religion, Scotland clung to the firm Calvinism preached by John Knox. In 1560, a Reformed Parliament gathered in Scotland and made a decisive break with Catholic France in favor of Protestant England. However, Scotland was to put its own mark on its church, which was established by the Scots Confession of 1560. Knox composed the church's liturgy, the *Book of Common Order*, which demonstrated how the Scottish church departed from the Anglican one. The Scots emphasized individual Christian conscience over ecclesiastical authority, and instead of placing bishops in authority, they established a Presbyterian form of organization that gave authority to pastors and elders of the congregations. The resulting Presbyterian congregations were more independent than the Episcopal congregations of the Anglican Church.

Scotland's church

By the end of the seventeenth century, the old medieval notion of a Europe united under the protection of a uniform Christianity had evaporated.

Map 11.2 shows the religious diversity that characterized Christian Europe at the end of the sixteenth century. Lutheran and Anglican churches were accepted by princes and rulers. Calvinists formed a solid minority in many areas. Many rulers struggled to grapple with even this degree of diversity. Yet Protestantism, by its very nature, had the potential to yield even more divisions. Once the door had opened for individuals to define their own way to God, there was no limit to the paths that people might create. However, the Catholic Church could not ignore these theological controversies and cries for reform, and in the sixteenth century, Catholicism searched its own conscience.

Europe divided

THE CATHOLIC REFORMATION

Even before Luther circulated his devastating criticism, many leaders in the Catholic Church were working to reform abuses and bring to Catholic worship new insights about textual criticism of Christian humanism. Girolamo Savonarola (1452–1498) in Florence, for example, had urged reform of the Renaissance papacy (see Chapter 10). His was not an isolated voice, though, for even popes in the early sixteenth century called councils and promulgated decrees aimed at reform. This movement of religious reform is called the Catholic Reformation by Catholics and the Counter-Reformation by Protestants, who saw these reforms as a response to the Protestant challenge. However, many of these religious reflections grew out of a continuing Catholic discussion that followed the Great Schism, the Conciliar movement, and the rule of the politically active Renaissance popes. Popes faced a tough challenge in implementing reforms at that time, because the Habsburg-Valois Wars occupied the attention of the Catholic kings Charles V and Francis I, who in normal times would have backed the papacy. These wars also carried a high financial price for the popes—during the sack of Rome in 1527, for example, imperial troops made off with mounds of gold coins from the papal treasury. To recover their losses, the popes stepped up the sort of fund-raising that had so incited Luther. Practical reform had to wait for peace.

The Stirring of Reform in Spain

In the fifteenth century, Spain emerged from its medieval decentralization and became a strong, unified kingdom. In 1469, Isabella (r. 1474–1504) and Ferdinand (r. 1479–1516) married, joining the kingdoms of Leon-Castile and Aragon (see **Map 8.5**). They immediately set about reducing the power of the nobility and establishing a centralized power. As part of their consolidation of royal authority, the two monarchs obtained permission from the pope to establish

MAP 11.2

Religions in Europe, ca. 1600

This map shows the distribution of the major centers of Catholics and Protestants in Europe at the end of the sixteenth century. Notice that there were strong Calvinist minorities in some countries.

Explore the Map

1. Where were Protestant minorities most likely to confront religious turmoil? Why?

2. Why might Catholics have felt threatened, even though Europe remained largely Catholic?

their own inquisition, directed against converted Jews and former Muslims who were suspected of secretly practicing their old faith. This newly established court brought great suffering to many of Spain's loyal citizens.

Ferdinand and Isabella became known as the "Catholic monarchs," emphasizing their faith and the degree to which they believed they carried the banner of an invigorated Catholicism. As part of their goal of a centralized and religiously homogenous Spain, they resumed the reconquest of the peninsula that had dominated the history of medieval Spain. The monarchs besieged Granada, the last Muslim stronghold in the south of Spain, and conquered it in 1492.

Ferdinand and Isabella

The religious zeal that grew out of the crusade against Granada continued after the fall of the city. In the same year, all Jews were expelled from Spain. Some 150,000 were given four months to leave. As we will see in Chapter 12, the same crusading zeal would extend across the Atlantic. By 1492, Spain was well placed to take the lead in fostering Catholicism against the forces of Protestantism.

As part of their dynastic aims, Ferdinand and Isabella had arranged marriages for their children to the leading families of Europe. Their daughter Joanna became the wife of the Habsburg archduke, and her son Charles V became heir to both Spain and the Habsburg lands. With such pious grandparents, it is not surprising that Charles V was so vigorous in his support of Catholicism.

The most influential religious figure in Spain during this time was Cardinal Ximénez de Cisneros 1436–1517). He was confessor to the queen, bishop of Toledo, Grand Inquisitor, and regent of Spain after Ferdinand's death. It was Ximénez who brought humanist ideas into Spain.

Ximénez was particularly impressed with Erasmus's emphasis on scholarly study of scripture and the works of the church fathers, and he wanted to strengthen this kind of education in Spain. In 1498, Ximénez received permission from the Borgia pope Alexander VI to found a new university at Alcalá de Henares that would feature humanist approaches to theological and ecclesiastical studies. The high quality of the scholarship at the school drew notice with the publication of the *Complutensian Polyglot Bible* (1520), an edition of the Bible written in three columns that compared the Hebrew, Greek, and Latin versions. This scholarship represented a high point in humanistic learning and new critical techniques in the study of the Bible.

Cardinal Ximénez

The Society of Jesus

Throughout its history, the Catholic Church had been reformed by monastic and mendicant orders that infused new life and ideas into the church. This pattern continued in the sixteenth century. Several new orders emerged, but the most influential was the Society of Jesus, whose members were called **Jesuits.**

The Society of Jesus was founded by Ignatius of Loyola (1491–1556), a soldier in the service of the Spanish monarch. In battle a cannonball shattered Loyola's legs, and he had a long and painful recovery—his legs had to be set and rebroken twice (without anesthesia) because they were healing crookedly. During his recuperation, Loyola read stories of Christian saints and decided to dedicate himself as a soldier of Christ. Loyola trained himself for a spiritual life with the same rigor that marked his military practice. In his quest, he was influenced by Thomas à Kempis's *Imitation of Christ* and wrote his own book that offered a Catholic version of the personal search for God. In the widely read work, *The Spiritual Exercises*, Loyola taught how spiritual discipline could satisfy people's desire to reach up to God while obeying the orders of the Catholic Church. Here was the perfect combination of Catholic orthodoxy and the longings expressed by Protestant reformers.

Jesuits established

In 1540, the pope established the Society of Jesus as a religious order, and the Jesuits, who vowed perfect obedience to the papacy, became the vanguard of reformed Catholicism. These men devoted themselves to education, sharing Cardinal Ximénez's belief that a Christian humanist education would combat the threat of Protestantism. Their schools became among the best in Europe, drawing even some Protestants who were willing to risk their children's conversion to Catholicism in exchange for the fine education. Document 11.3 contains a letter from Loyola that explains his recognition of the importance of education.

Jesuits also served as missionaries to bring Catholicism to the New World (see Chapter 12). However, in time the new shock troops of the papacy became controversial in their own right—the vigor with which they pursued their aims and the vehemence of their support of the papacy alienated some Catholics and Protestants alike. But there is no question that in the sixteenth century and beyond, the Jesuits would be a powerful force in the reformed Catholicism.

Figure 11.7, a painting by the Flemish artist Peter Paul Rubens (1577–1640), captures the spirit of reformed Catholicism. *The Miracles of St. Ignatius* was commissioned in 1620 to be placed in the Jesuits' first church in Antwerp in 1622 on the occasion of the canonization of Ignatius of Loyola. The painting shows the saint performing miracles: easing the pain of childbirth (on the right), reviving a suicide victim long enough for the dying man to take the last rites (in the foreground), and casting out demons (on the left). The image praises traditional Catholic doctrine, showing the efficacy of saints by representing them as

Ignatius Loyola Argues for Education as a Solution

In August 1554, Ignatius Loyola wrote a letter in which he reveals his desire to stop the growth of Protestantism. In this letter, he advocates education as the best way to stop Catholics from embracing the Protestant theology.

Seeing the progress which the heretics have made in a short time, spreading the poison of their evil teaching throughout so many countries and peoples . . . it would seem that our Society . . . should be solicitous to prepare the proper steps, such as are quickly applied and can be widely adopted, thus exerting itself to the utmost of its powers to preserve what is still sound and to restore what has fallen sick of the plague of heresy, especially in the northern nations.

The heretics have made their false theology popular and presented it in a way that is within the capacity of the common people. They preach it to the people and teach it in the schools, and scatter booklets which can be bought and understood by many, and make their influence felt by means of their writings when they cannot do so by their preaching. Their success is largely due to the negligence of those who should have shown some interest; and the bad example and the ignorance of Catholics, especially the clergy, have made such ravages in the vineyard of

the Lord. Hence it would seem that our Society should make use of the following means to put a stop and apply a remedy to the evils which have come upon the Church through these heretics.

In the first place, the sound theology which is taught in the universities and seeks its foundation in philosophy, and therefore requires a long time to acquire is adapted only to good and alert minds. . . . It would be good to make a summary of theology to deal with topics that are important but not controversial, and with great brevity. . . . In this way theologians could be produced in a short time who could take care of the preaching and teaching in many places. . . .

The principal conclusion of this theology, in the form of a short catechism [instructional manual] could be taught to children, as the Christian doctrine is now taught, and likewise to the common people who are not too infected or too capable of subtleties. This could also be done with the younger students in the lower classes, where they could learn it by heart. . . .

Another excellent means for helping the Church in this trial would be to multiply the colleges and schools of the Society in many lands, especially where a good attendance could be expected. . . .

The heretics write a large number of booklets and pamphlets, by means of which they aim at taking away all authority from the Catholics, and especially from the Society, and set up their false dogmas. It would seem expedient, therefore, that our Society here also write answers in pamphlet form, short and well written, so that they can be produced without delay and bought by many. In this way the harm that is being done by the pamphlets of the heretics can be remedied and sound teaching spread. These works should be modest, but lively. . . .

SOURCE: Ignatius Loyola, *Monumenta Ignatiana*, vol. 12 (Madrid, 1904), pp. 259–262, in Robert E. Van Voorst, *Readings in Christianity* (New York: Wadsworth Publishing, 1996), pp. 211–213.

Analyze the Document

1. What does Loyola argue are the main reasons for the spread of Protestant beliefs?

2. What solutions does he propose?

3. How effective do you think his suggestions will be?

4. What do you think will be other social effects of such an emphasis on education?

---

intermediaries between people and God. In the same way, Loyola is positioned in the vertical center of the painting. Rubens also affirms the importance of the sacrament of last rites (attacked by the Protestants) by depicting it as the occasion of a miracle. Finally, this work points out that, in less than a century, Loyola's accomplishments had earned him the status of sainthood and his Society of Jesus had become the army of the new Catholicism.

Rubens's painting is an example of a new style of painting (and the arts in general) called **baroque,** which also served to forward the ideas and spirit of reformed Catholicism. Baroque art was characterized by passion, drama, and awe and was designed to

Baroque art

involve the audience. Catholic patrons, in particular, spurred this art that spoke as eloquently of Catholic doctrine and passion as a Jesuit sermon. However, before either the new art style or the energetic order of Jesuits could be effective, the church had to agree on its doctrine in response to the Protestant critique.

The Council of Trent, 1545–1563

With the conclusion of the Habsburg-Valois Wars, the Catholic monarchs could focus on the divisive religious questions of the day. After the treaty of 1544 that ended the wars, church leaders from all over Europe

Reforming corruption

FIGURE 11.7 Peter Paul Rubens, *The Miracles of St. Ignatius*, 1620 Baroque artists portrayed the passions that accompanied the reformed Catholic faith. Here, Loyola, founder of the Society of Jesus, performs miracles as he stands as an intermediary between people and God.

church also affirmed the existence of purgatory and the power of prayer and even indulgences to free souls from their punishment.

These churchmen rejected Protestants by reaffirming their position that Christians needed both faith and good works to go to heaven. For Catholics, the sacraments by their very nature conveyed grace, so the council reaffirmed the existence of all seven rites. In further rejection of Protestant criticism, Catholics retained their idea of transubstantiation, by which priests presided over the transformation of the wine and host into the blood and body of Christ.

Like Rubens, the Spanish painter El Greco (the Greek) (1547–1614) was a baroque painter who reaffirmed Catholic theology. El Greco's painting *Burial of the Count of Orgaz* (**Figure 11.8**) is less about the burial of one man than about the theological stance of the Council of Trent. The dead count does not face his maker | El Greco |

alone. Instead, he is buried with the full ceremony of the church presided over by the bishop. El Greco also shows saints Augustine and Stephen miraculously appearing and helping with the burial. The count's way to heaven is paved by the prayers of the living who surround the scene and the Virgin Mary, who sits between the dead man and Jesus as an intermediary for the count's soul. The painting depicts heaven as filled with saints and the souls of other saved individuals, who also pray for the count and help him enter their community. By all these means, the picture visually reaffirms the theology established at the Council of Trent.

While debating and refining their beliefs, the churchmen used principles that had guided previous councils and looked to two authorities— scripture and tradition. Armed with these pillars of Christian thought, they prepared to answer Luther and the other Protestants, who recognized only their own consciences and the complete authority of the Holy Book. Catholics, the Trent council argued, could draw strength from the body of practices that the faithful had | Scripture and tradition | accumulated over the course of a millennium. With its doctrine thus established, the Catholic Church showed a new strength and confidence. Dissenters had gone to other sects, leaving a vigorous corps of dedicated believers to challenge the Protestants head-on.

Catholics on the Offense

Throughout this period, as we have seen with baroque art, many Catholics expressed their faith with more passion and mystical emotion than they had shown

gathered in northern Italy at Trent, and the council met intermittently from 1545 to 1563. Charles wanted the council to concentrate on reforming abuses, and it confronted this thorny issue honestly, establishing stern measures to clean up clerical corruption, ignorance, and apathy. They even banned the selling of indulgences and the office of indulgence-seller. But the real work of the council took place when it confronted the theological debate that had driven the Protestants from the church. As these leaders clarified their beliefs, it became obvious that there would be no compromise with Protestant Christianity.

The Council of Trent determined that Catholics did *not* stand alone before God. Rather, it claimed, the community of the faithful, both | Affirming doctrine | living and dead, could help a Catholic to salvation. Thus prayers to the saints and to the Virgin Mary *did* matter. The in centuries. Teresa of Avila, Spain (1515–1582), a sixteenth-century mystic who quickly became a saint, exemplified this newfound energy. The daughter of a converted Jew, Teresa entered a convent and experienced a series of visions. Not only a mystic, Teresa was an active reformer, establishing new convents for women as part of her dedication to a reinvigorated Catholicism. Her mystical writing, *Way of Perfection*, ensured her influence, for it inspired the pope to declare her a Doctor of the Church (which means that her writings were worthy of study). Soon she became the patron saint of Spain, replacing Saint James (Santiago), who had held that honor throughout the Middle Ages. The example of Teresa and other mystics offered the church a strong weapon to show skeptics the deep and passionate faith that came with Catholic worship. However, they also used stronger measures than the writings of gentle mystics.

Reinvigorated, and considering themselves at war with Protestants, the Catholics moved to repress opposition to their views. The Spanish Inquisition took a forceful role in this battle over religious diversity. (This court was separate from the papal inquisition that, as we saw in Chapter 8, had been introduced into Europe in the thirteenth century.) Inquisitors now added Lutherans and Calvinists to converted Jews and Muslims in their definition of suspect populations and launched a new round of public trials and executions. In 1542, the Inquisition was reestablished in Rome, as the popes also felt compelled to take extreme measures to protect Catholics themselves from incorrect ideas. In addition, the papacy began to publish an Index of Prohibited Books in 1557, which it updated and reissued regularly. (The index was finally abolished in 1966.)

While such measures aimed to control people's beliefs, the church looked to the Spanish king to champion the Catholic cause in the political and military arena. Philip II (r. 1556–1588), Charles V's heir to the kingdoms of Spain and the Netherlands, had an unparalleled zeal for both the Catholic religion and empire. Philip moved his capital from Toledo, a cramped medieval city, to the newly built city of Madrid, chosen because it was the geographic center of the Iberian Peninsula.

Philip faced two dire threats to the Catholic faith: the Turks in the eastern Mediterranean and the Protestants in the north. In 1571, he assembled a league that included a number of Italian city-states and set out to challenge the Turks' supremacy in the Mediterranean. The Venetians, who had a large fleet and were highly motivated by their trading

Spanish Inquisition

Philip II

FIGURE 11.8 El Greco, *Burial of the Count of Orgaz*,

ca. 1586 Reformed Catholicism disagreed with Protestant views in asserting that the dead can be helped by the prayers of the living and by the intercession of the dead themselves. The famous Spanish painter el Greco illustrated these beliefs in this scene of the burial of a count.

* = Catholic

PROTESTANT AND CATHOLIC REFORMERS

ca. 1320–1384	John Wycliffe
1415	Jan Hus executed
1511	Erasmus, *Praise of Folly*
*1515–1582	Teresa of Avila
1517	Martin Luther, Ninety-Five Theses
1519	Zwingli's reform in Switzerland
*1520	Ximénez, *Complutensian Polyglot Bible*, Spain
1521	Luther at Diet of Worms
1534	Henry VIII's Act of Supremacy in England
1536	Calvin, *Institutes of Christian Religion*
*1540	Loyola founds Society of Jesus
*1545–1563	Council of Trent

FIGURE 11.9 Anonymous, *The Battle of Lepanto*, 1571 This depiction of the famous Battle of Lepanto highlights the dramatic contrast between the old and the new warfare at sea. The Muslim ships' banks of oars are used to power the ramming of the enemy fleet, while the smoke of Spanish cannon fire from the high-hulled Spanish ships signals the naval combat of the future.

interests in the eastern Mediterranean, were particularly eager to join Philip's navy. Outfitted with 208 galleys—sleek warships rowed by slaves and armed with cannons—Philip's navy confronted the Turks' 230 warships at the Battle of Lepanto, off the coast of Greece. **Figure 11.9** depicts what the scene may have looked like. In this graphic image, cannons blaze and battering rams thrust forward as the galleys draw together.

When the smoke cleared after this spectacular battle, Philip's coalition had scored a decisive victory. The Turks lost two hundred warships, the Europeans only ten. Tens of thousands of men on both sides died in the fighting, and contemporary witnesses described the sea as running red with blood. Nevertheless, the success at Lepanto raised Catholics' spirits throughout the West. The navy had proved that Turkish power in the Mediterranean was not invincible after all. Indeed, some western Catholics began toying with the idea of invading the Ottoman Empire itself. But the Catholic monarchs had other adversaries in mind. Again, the kings of Europe went to war. This time, though, they marched against the Protestants in a series of battles that would drag on for a century and tear apart the soul of Europe.

EUROPE ERUPTS AGAIN: A CENTURY OF RELIGIOUS WARFARE, 1559–1648

The Reformation had done far more than just establish alternative Christian sects—it raised the possibility that individuals might follow their own consciences in matters of religion. In a society in which the church served as the central institution in people's lives, this radical new idea struck at the very foundation of European politics and social realities. From the time the Roman emperor Constantine supported the Catholic Church (see Chapter 5), people always assumed that there was an identity of belief between rulers and subjects. Political loyalty was considered a religious phenomenon; the Protestant Reformation questioned this assumption.

In fact, the wars of religion that scourged Europe from 1559 to 1648 involved much more than the proper way to worship God. They also centered on the question of what constituted a state—specifically, whether one state could encompass various religious expressions. Like the peasant wars in Germany in

1524, these new hostilities involved religion, but they had significant economic, political, and social dimensions as well.

French Wars of Religion, 1562–1598

By the 1550s, Calvinism had gained a good deal of strength in France among the peasants and in the towns of the south and southwest (including villages like that of Martin Guerre in the Biography). Although the French Calvinists (Huguenots) remained a minority—only about 7 percent of the population—they were well organized. Local congregations governed by ministers sent representatives to district assemblies that in turn coordinated their efforts with a national assembly and even mustered troops from local churches. This impressive minority even began to recruit members from the nobility—possibly 40 percent of French nobles had become Huguenots. Great noble families took the lead in forwarding their religious (and in turn political) interests—the Guises led the Catholics, and the Bourbons championed the Huguenots. By the mid-sixteenth century, French Protestantism was a force to be reckoned with and the French kings took notice.

Francis I (r. 1515–1547) and his heir, Henry II (r. 1547–1559), were both powerful kings who based their authority in part on a strong Catholic stance. However, this royal power was broken by a freak accident. King Henry was celebrating the wedding of his daughter by fighting in a joust (the war game still much beloved by the nobility), but during the last joust of the day, his opponent's lance shattered, gouging Henry's eye. Henry died of complications of this wound, leaving his widow, the Italian Catherine de' Medici, to rule as regent for her young sons from 1559 to 1589.

Catherine tried to preserve royal control, but her efforts were impeded by the struggle for power between the Guises and the Bourbons, both of whom had family ties to the monarchy and hoped to inherit the throne. Politics here intertwined with religion and the time was ripe for civil war.

Catholics vs. Huguenots Fighting broke out in 1562, when the Duke of Guise massacred a Huguenot congregation, and it continued for about thirty-six years (with brief respites). The Huguenot forces, though outnumbered, were too well organized to be defeated. The most infamous point of these wars was the Saint Bartholomew's Day Massacre, which took place on August 23, 1572, just when peace seemed imminent.

A religious compromise seemed to be on the horizon with a marriage between Catherine's daughter and the Bourbon leader of the Huguenots, Henry of Navarre. However, the mutual suspicions and desire for revenge had not subsided—the Guise family persuaded the young king Charles IX (r. 1560–1574) that the Huguenot gathering for the wedding was a plot against the crown. The king then ordered his guard to kill all the Protestant leadership. On the morning of St. Bartholomew's Day, the soldiers unleashed a massacre against Protestants.

Saint Bartholomew's Day Massacre

Although the young bridegroom escaped assassination, many others did not. Thousands were murdered, and the painting shown in **Figure 11.10** depicts a contemporary witness's memory of the slaughter. The massacre raged for six days, and as the image shows, it was particularly brutal. Women and infants were not spared, and the painting shows that even corpses were mutilated as religious fervor introduced a bloodbath. This violence did not end the wars, however. Civil war continued in France until King Henry III (r. 1574–1589) was assassinated, leaving no heir.

The next in line for the throne was Henry of Navarre—the Protestant bridegroom who survived the massacre. Recognizing that the overwhelmingly Catholic population would not accept a reformist king, he converted to Catholicism, reputedly **Peace in France** saying, "Paris is worth a mass." Sympathetic to both religions, the new king, Henry IV (r. 1589–1610), issued the Edict of Nantes (1598), which ended the religious wars and introduced religious toleration in France. However, a subsequent king (Louis XIV, discussed in Chapter 13) who believed that a nation was defined by loyalty to one religion would overturn Henry's policy. But for the time being at least, France gained a small respite from the violence of intolerance. The rest of Europe was not so lucky.

A "Council of Blood" in the Netherlands, 1566–1609

In addition to Spain, the Catholic king Philip II ruled over the Netherlands, which consisted of seventeen provinces. (Today these provinces are Netherlands, Belgium, and Luxembourg.) Trouble began when Philip began to exert more control over the provinces—he restructured the Catholic Church to weaken the local aristocracy, he insisted on billeting troops locally, and he levied new taxes, all of which offended the Dutch.

In response, riots broke out in 1566, and Dutch Protestants, though still a tiny minority, rebelled against their Spanish, Catholic overlords. In a spasm of violence, they destroyed Catholic Church property, smashing images of saints and desecrating the host. Philip was enraged. **Revolt breaks out** Vowing to silence the rebels, he sent the largest land army ever assembled into the Netherlands to crush the Protestants and bring the province

FIGURE 11.10 Françoise Dubois, *St. Bartholomew's Day Massacre*, ca. 1576 A massacre of French Protestants began on St. Bartholomew's Day (August 24, 1572) and lasted six days. Even this violence did not end the brutal struggle for religious supremacy.

back under his Catholic rule. In 1572, organized revolt broke out and war officially began.

Philip's crackdown ignited a savage forty-year contest in which the Spanish general, the "iron duke of Alba," presided over a slaughter of thousands of Protestants in what he called a "Council of Troubles," but what the Protestants called the "Council of Blood." Calvinist preachers retaliated by giving their congregations complete license to kill the invaders. To protect themselves, the towns of the Netherlands even opened their dikes to flood their country rather than give in to Philip's armies. The Dutch found an able leader in William of Orange, a nobleman known for his wise counsel, who took charge in 1580. William was assassinated four years later, and the murderer was publicly tortured to death as blood continued to flow in the Netherlands.

The defiance of the Dutch cost Philip more than the loss of soldiers and huge amounts of gold to finance the wars. It also diverted his attention northward, away from his victory over the Turks at Lepanto in 1571. Preoccupied by events in the Netherlands, he failed to ride the wave of widespread Christian antipathy toward the Turks and launch a decisive campaign against the enemy in the eastern Mediterranean.

Philip also tried to "save" England from the Protestantism that Henry VIII had introduced. Philip had married Henry's Catholic daughter, Mary (r. 1553–1558), and when she died without an heir, the Spanish king proposed matrimony to her sister, Elizabeth I. But the Protestant Elizabeth refused his attentions and even dared support the Netherlands against him. Philip struck back by hurling the full force of his navy against England, sending a huge fleet across the English Channel in 1588. What happened next stood in stark contrast to Philip's triumph at Lepanto. Instead of scoring an easy victory, the Spanish Armada was wiped out by the well-armed English ships and the sudden onslaught of violent storms in the North Sea (what the English would later call a "Protestant wind").

Armada against England

Philip never succeeded in subduing the Protestants in the Netherlands; the conflict dragged on until the deaths of both Philip and Elizabeth. In 1609, the two sides finally drew up an agreement that gave the northern provinces virtual independence. The final recognition of an independent Netherlands would have to wait until the Peace of Westphalia in 1648. After the final settlement, Protestants in the southern provinces moved north to escape continuing Spanish rule in the south, so the two provinces became divided along religious lines. The northern provinces became the Protestant Dutch Republic,

Netherlands split

and the southern (and French-speaking) Spanish Netherlands (which later became Belgium) remained Catholic. But this solution still could not quell the religious tensions tearing at Europe. Instead, the wars shifted east, where they culminated in the bloodiest engagement of them all.

The Thirty Years' War, 1618–1648

The Peace of Augsburg had only temporarily answered the question of religious diversity in the Holy Roman Empire. For fifty years after Augsburg, pressure mounted as more and more people followed their consciences and as diverse spiritual beliefs proliferated in the principalities. These tensions reached the boiling point in 1618, when a Catholic prince took over Bohemia (in the modern Czech Republic) and set out to vanquish the substantial Protestant minority in his state. Protestant Bohemian nobles responded by throwing the prince's representatives out of the castle window in Prague. The hapless officials landed unhurt in a pile of manure, but the Catholic explanation was that their fall had been broken by angels. The two sides seemed to have irreconcilable points of view.

But the Holy Roman Empire's political structure contained a unique feature that made religious tensions much harder to resolve than by merely pushing bureaucrats out of windows. The essential problem was that Protestant and Catholic electors (princes who elected the Holy Roman **War breaks out** Emperor) were roughly equal in number. If Bohemia went to a Protestant prince, the balance of power would shift away from the ruling Catholic Habsburgs. Fearing this possibility, the Holy Roman Emperor Ferdinand II (r. 1619–1637) went to war to reclaim Bohemia for Catholicism. His action provoked a civil war that began over the key issue of the authority of the emperor over the princes in Germany but that quickly turned international as Protestants and Catholics across the Holy Roman Empire faced each other in battle.

The first twelve years of the war were marked by the success of Emperor Ferdinand's forces, and it seemed as if the Catholic Habsburgs would be able to roll back the Protestant gains in the German lands. The powerful Catholic Maximilian of Bavaria put at Ferdinand's disposal an army that won a stunning victory over the Bohemians at the Battle of White Mountain in 1620 (shown on **Map 11.3**). The Bohemian rebels were killed or exiled, and it seemed as if the war was over. However, the Protestants continued their struggle, but with few gains.

In 1624, the emperor received considerable help when a soldier of fortune came to offer his services to the Catholic cause. Albrecht von Wallenstein, a minor Bohemian nobleman, recognized that the emperor needed a new army if he was to succeed, and Wallenstein offered to raise the force if he could billet it and raise its supplies wherever it happened to be stationed. Through these means, Wallenstein introduced a new way of funding wars. Previously, warriors had been paid **Wallenstein** largely by the losers—that is, through the victors' plunder and sacking of defeated peoples. Wallenstein's innovative requirements served as a kind of war tax levied on all princes and cities who supported the emperor. Now wars would be funded by potential winners as well as losers. This strategy not only funded a large army but also made Wallenstein one of the richest men in the empire. By 1627, Wallenstein's army had begun to conquer the northern region of the empire—the center of Protestant strength. Ferdinand grew so confident that he issued the Edict of Restitution in 1629, ordering all territories lost to Protestants since 1552 to be restored to Catholics.

By 1630, the tide and nature of the war had begun to change. With help from abroad, Protestants made gains, but the war began to shift from a religious struggle to a purely political quest—to weaken the power of the Habsburgs; for example, the Catholic French king was willing to **From religion to politics** join Protestants in support of this cause. Protestant forces found a worthy champion in the Swedish king Gustavus Adolphus (r. 1611–1632), who was appalled by Ferdinand's treatment of Protestants. At the same time, he feared a Habsburg threat to Swedish lands around the Baltic Sea (see **Map 11.3**).

Gustavus had a clear vision of modern warfare: It would be dominated by gunpowder. He drilled his men incessantly on lining up in squares so that the front line could fire and then move backward to reload while others replaced them. This system, which required ironclad discipline, allowed for sustained firing—an essential tactic for weapons that were still inaccurate. Gustavus also introduced the idea that cannons could be used on the battlefield against men, and in doing so he created the first effective field artillery.

Arraying his new army, Gustavus fought a decisive battle against Wallenstein at Lutzen in 1632. Amid the blinding smoke of gunpowder, Gustavus's armies beat Wallenstein's forces, but in the heat of battle, Gustavus himself was killed by gunshots. The king's death prevented the Swedish forces from following up on the victory. Meanwhile, Wallenstein's loss sealed his fate: The German princes eventually compelled Ferdinand to turn on his enterprising and wealthy general, and the emperor had Wallenstein assassinated a few months later.

MAP 11.3

The Thirty Years' War, 1618–1648

This map shows the major participants and the main battles of the Thirty Years' War, which took place on German territory.

Explore the Map

1. Based on geography, why did the king of Sweden become involved in this war?

2. Compare this map with **Map 11.2.** Which regions set aside their religious interests and fought primarily for political reasons?

3. Notice all the battles. How devastating was this war to the German people? Explain.

Gustavus's successes opened the final phase of the war (from 1632 to 1648), during which the emperor lost all his previous gains. The Protestant princes raised new armies, and by 1635, Ferdinand had to agree to suspend the Edict of Restitution and to grant amnesty to most of the Protestant princes. In return, the Protestants joined the imperial troops in driving the Swedes out of German lands. However, the Catholic French declared open war on Ferdinand in 1635, and for the next thirteen years, French and Swedish troops rampaged through the lands, causing destruction and devastation.

By the 1640s, the war had reached a stalemate. The kings and princes who had started the hostilities had all died, and their successors (as well as civilians) were exhausted. Both sides laid down their arms and took stock of their losses. This war

| Devastation | had raged with a violence that astonished even contemporary wit-

nesses used to sixteenth-century battle methods, for armies on both sides had swept through villages and towns and laid to waste everything in their paths. The war had exacted a staggering price: Germany's population had plummeted (although historians do not agree on the figures, some suggest a population loss as high as 30 percent). The economy, too, was damaged. Spain had gone bankrupt and would never recover its standing as a leader on the European stage. France and Sweden emerged somewhat victorious gaining some land at the expense of the exhausted German states.

Peace at Westphalia

The series of agreements that ended the Thirty Years' War are collectively known as the Peace of Westphalia, named for the region of Germany where the agreements were drafted. German princes now had the freedom to choose their own religion, but the religious desires of individuals within the states were still not accepted. However, for the first time, Calvinism was included among the tolerated faiths. The religious landmark of Europe was roughly established along north-south lines. The northwest—England, Holland, Scandinavia, and the northern German states—was Protestant, whereas the south remained Catholic.

The war had marked political overtones at the end, and the treaty accordingly addressed issues of power beyond religious choice. The peace set the political geography of Europe for the next century and estab-

| Political results | lished a precedent for diplomacy that would shape the way nations resolved political problems in the

coming centuries. **Map 11.4** outlines the aftermath of the Peace of Westphalia. The representatives at Westphalia conducted all these negotiations with an eye toward "balance of power," a relatively new principle that emerged in fifteenth-century Italy and was now applied to European politics. They believed that they could ensure peace by making all the European powers roughly as strong as their neighbors. This strategy would dominate European diplomacy for centuries.

LIFE AFTER THE REFORMATION

The early modern wars of religion were finally over. Christians with different beliefs would now have to learn to coexist. As the storms of religious rage subsided, Europeans began noticing the dramatic changes in other aspects of everyday life and thought that the Protestant Reformation had provoked.

New Definitions of Courtship and Marriage

When the Protestants excluded marriage as a sacrament, the institution changed in ways they could not have foreseen. After Martin Luther left the monastery and married Katherina, the couple formed a loving partnership and raised five children (along with caring for orphans). Luther explored this relationship in his writings and saw in marriage part of God's plan for humanity. Calvin, too, rejected the church fathers' "too superstitious admiration of celibacy" and extolled the benefits of conjugal partnerships. Although divorce was not easy in any of the Protestant groups, it was possible. With all these changes, the ideal of marriage shifted. Couples began to expect mutual love between man and wife, instead of simply duty that bound extended families together. The Catholic Church also was influenced by the new marital values, and in the late sixteenth century, church manuals began to use the word *love* to refer to conjugal relations.

POLITICS OF THE AGE OF REFORMATION

1521–1544	Habsburg-Valois Wars
1524–1525	German peasants revolt
1529	Turks besiege Vienna
1555	Peace of Augsburg, Germany
1562–1598	French wars of religion
1566–1609	Wars in the Netherlands
1571	Battle of Lepanto
1572	Saint Bartholomew's Day Massacre, France
1588	Spanish Armada attacks England
1618–1648	Thirty Years' War
1648	Peace of Westphalia

KEY DATES

Ottoman Empire	Swedish Dominions
Austrian Habsburgs	Brandenburg-Prussia
Spanish Monarchy	Boundary of the Holy Roman Empire

MAP 11.4

Europe, 1648

This map shows the political configuration of Europe after the Peace of Westphalia, which ended the Thirty Years' War.

Explore the Map

1. Which countries appear large and cohesive after the settlement of Westphalia?

2. Which countries control territories distant from their home center? Which of these remote areas might become centers of conflict in the future? Why?

People still did not marry just for love, however; instead, families continued to arrange suitable matches between young people. Arranged marriages were an essential and logical part of a view that valued family prosperity and continuity more than an individual's happiness. Individual's lives were seen as mere moments in the larger life of the family. Nevertheless, something new was going on in family relations. Although parents still negotiated a suitable match, prospective couples were allowed to consider their compatibility before marriage, and daughters had some

Courtship

say in vetoing disagreeable matches. Court-ship customs grew more complex, as men and women evaluated whether they would have a harmonious union. In **Figure 11.11,** a paint-ing titled *The Suitor's Visit*, a young man calls on a woman in one of many visits intended for the couple to get to know each other. Presum-ably, the suitor greets the young woman's mother, who will chaperone the courtship and approve the joining of the families that mar-riage still represented. The prospective bride is in the background playing her lute; young women in these years cultivated their skills at making music and clever conversation so as to beguile potential mates and convince them of their qualities as life partners.

Forging a Link Between Education and Work

The Christian humanists from Erasmus on urged everyone to learn to read. As we saw in Document 11.3, reformed Catholicism under the Jesuits also stressed education as central to a Christian life, and parochial schools and armies of nuns gave young children the rudiments of education. Protestants, too, urged study. As Luther and others emphasized Bible study as part of essential Christian behavior and translated the Bible into vernacular languages, the next logical step was to broaden literacy. Luther encouraged the cities and villages in Saxony to establish publicly funded schools, and many Protestants followed his call. A Bohemian reformer, Jan Amos Comenius (1592–1670), wrote: "All alike, boys and girls, both noble and ignoble, rich and poor, in all cities and towns, villages and hamlets, should be sent to school." This egalitarian notion would take centu-ries to implement, but it established a new educa-tional goal in the West.

The painter Jan Steen's depiction of an early-seventeenth-century classroom (shown in **Figure 11.12**) embodies the Protestant ideals of education. This is a village school where both boys and girls study. The strict schoolmaster slaps a boy's hand in reprimand for the poorly done assignment on the floor, while the boy cries. The girl on the boy's right smiles rather too gleefully at his distress. This scene must have played out repeatedly in the many small village schools that began to spring up as more chil-dren began to receive formal education.

Although education was intended primarily to help people study the Bible and learn to serve as their

Valuing literacy

FIGURE 11.11 Gerard Ter Borch, *The Suitor's Visit*, 1658 Many post-Reformation paintings captured the new courtship rituals—including conversations, letter writing, and musical performances—designed to ensure that married couples would be compatible.

own spiritual guides, it also had profound implications for the way people viewed work. In response to critics who complained about educating "rustics," the Bohemian educational reformer Comenius answered that universal education would help everyone avoid "that idleness which is so dangerous to flesh and blood." His words hinted at a new philosophy that stressed the value of work.

Valuing work

In the Middle Ages, "those who work" were rel-egated to the bottom of the social scale. The upper crust consisted of only those who could live off the income of their land and did not need to work to survive. The bourgeoisie—the middle class—that was becoming more and more prosperous since the Renaissance began to change that view and brought a new valuing of work into the consciousness of West-ern society. The Protestant reformers that appealed to many of the residents of these growing urban areas lent religious support to new ideas about work. In Luther's writings, even women were defined by the work they did. He described the ideal wife as fol-lows: "She likes working. . . . She girds her loins and stretches her arms, works with energy in the house."

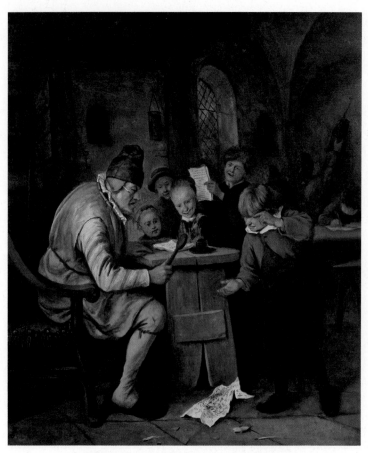

FIGURE 11.12 Jan Steen, *The School Master,* ca. 1655 The Reformation stimulated the spread of literacy. The intent was to help everyone to read the Bible. The modern world was born in small village schools—like the one immortalized in this painting—where children struggled under sometimes harsh teachers.

FIGURE 11.13 Jan Victors, *The Girls' Dining Hall on the Reformed Parish Orphanage,* ca. 1651 During the Reformation, the state began to take over the administration of charity from churches. This development gave rise to larger poorhouses, orphanages, and other such institutions.

Calvin, too, believed that men and women were called to work and that work itself was a virtuous activity. Centuries later, the German sociologist Max Weber, in *The Protestant Ethic and the Spirit of Capitalism* (1904), would argue that Calvinists' emphasis on work legitimized and therefore boosted the growth of capitalism in the West. Many Calvinists believed that hard work, efficiency, and frugality all indicated a person predestined to salvation. Not surprisingly, then, Protestants embraced what has come to be called the work ethic with fervor. Historians dispute the details of Weber's thesis, but his argument still offers us an insight into the way religious ideas shaped modern-day views of work in the West. In the Catholic Middle Ages, people had seen work as the curse of Adam laid on the damned; in the Protestant early modern period, work became God's gift to a saved humanity.

Anxiety and Spiritual Insecurity

The striking revolution in thought that the Protestant reformers introduced also prompted some spiritual anxiety and insecurity among Christians. In part, this unease stemmed from the hardship spawned by the relentless warfare of the period. The "community of the faithful" that Catholicism once represented had fragmented, and for Protestants encouraged to "stand alone before God," the new religious individualism often felt frightening.

The new mind-set began to raise questions about charitable institutions and their relationship with religious bodies. Where once the universal church had looked after the poor and widows and orphans, now separate congregations had to care for their own. The question of who was responsible for whom sometimes became quite murky, and a sense of individual responsibility for one's own plight slowly replaced a collective sense of charity. For example, civic authorities began to consider ways to help the needy, building workhouses for the poor and passing laws prohibiting begging. Such laws could never completely succeed, given the scale of need that we saw in the painting of the cripples in **Figure 11.2**. Yet, more and more societies tried designing institutional solutions to the problems of poverty.

Figure 11.13 depicts a girls' dining hall in a Protestant orphanage in Amsterdam. The painting emphasizes the institutional quality of charity

Charitable institutions

in the early seventeenth century. The orphans are dressed alike, for example, and the girls in the foreground serve watery soup for dinner while the matrons watch.

As communities redivided themselves along religious loyalties, many people's sense of personal anxiety increased. The Catholic Church had

Decline of "magic"

also provided community support and at least the hope of miraculous cures for the sick and troubled. Men and women could themselves pray to saints or the Virgin Mary for help, and priests could say prayers for members of their congregation in need. The Catholic Church even turned a blind eye to "white" magic (like that described in the village of Martin Guerre in the Biography), but Protestants rejected saints and any forms of "magic." As village rituals split apart, it became harder to define "community." As changing times and beliefs generated anxieties, some people began looking for scapegoats.

Searching for Scapegoats: The Hunt for Witches

Catholics and Protestants alike shared a long-standing, deeply held belief in charms and potions that could affect people. These might be as benign as healing magical cures and love potions, or as harmful as spells to bring bad weather, illness, or crop failure. Traditionally, Catholic priests offered prayers and countercharms to combat the power of people—often, but not always, called witches—who had the knowledge to cast spells. Protestant preachers argued regularly against "superstitious magical practices," but some remained attached to charms and spells, and in England witchcraft accusations usually remained tied to spell-casting.

In the sixteenth century, especially on the Continent, some people began to link a fear of witches to diabolism, or the idea that magical powers came because of a pact with the devil. Martin Luther himself claimed to have confronted the devil several times and constantly remained alert to the presence

Fear of the devil

of this evil being. Church authorities began to stress that witches were in league with the devil and performed mysterious ceremonies in his service. To stamp out the devil's assistants, many accused supposed witches, putting them on trial and executing them.

FIGURE 11.14 Salvator Rosa, *Witches at Their Incantations* (detail), late seventeenth century Religious insecurity stimulated more witch trials during the early modern period than there had been in the Middle Ages. This painting shows witches engaging in some of their reputed practices, such as performing magic and making pacts with the devil.

People in the sixteenth century were fascinated by the possibility of witchcraft. The best-known work on the subject was the *Malleus Maleficarum* (the "Hammer of Witches"), which had been written in the late fifteenth century (before the start of the Reformation) for inquisitors to try witches. However, by 1669 it had been reissued in fourty editions and had become extraordinarily popular, appealing to Protestants and Catholics alike. In France alone, 345 books about witchcraft were published between 1550 and 1650.

There is no real evidence that any of the convicted "witches" engaged in pacts with the devil. Instead, many people were forced to "confess" under torture. Others may have thought they were confessing to using simple charms only to discover that they were convicted of diabolism.

Figure 11.14, a painting from the seventeenth century, reveals the characteristics of witches as imagined by many Europeans of this period. Those accused of witchcraft were predominantly female (90 percent of those executed for witchcraft were women), many of whom were old. In this picture, the witches prepare magic potions drawn from body parts taken from the corpse hanging on the left and the heart impaled on the sword in the center. At the right, a witch carries an infant who will be killed and whose body will be used for magical purposes. In the center is a broomstick. People believed that witches rode these and used them to apply hallucinogenic potions to their vaginas.

Catholics and Protestants alike persecuted witches, and the trials in Europe peaked between 1560 and 1640. Although precise numbers elude us, more than 100,000 people were executed for witchcraft, and 200,000 may have endured trials. These trials are probably the most disturbing indicator of the rampant anxiety stirred by the intellectual and social changes of the sixteenth century.

Persecutions

By the eighteenth century, the witchcraft panic had ebbed and the trials gradually ceased, as men and women adjusted to the religious diversity that had split their countries and their communities. However, the ideals of the Protestant Reformation—individualism, a desire for marital harmony, an emphasis on hard work, and a staunch reliance on conscience—left a permanent mark on European society.

LOOKING BACK & MOVING FORWARD

Summary   Through the sixteenth century, the monarchs of the unified states of Europe—England, France, Spain, and the Holy Roman Empire—struggled to snatch power, wealth, and land from one another. The wars that resulted accomplished little except to bankrupt some of the kings, leave the European countryside in ruins, and inflict misery on the people. Meanwhile, religious revolutionaries stepped up their criticism of the thousand-year history of Christian tradition. These Protestants effected a reformation that spurred century-long religious warfare and that split Christendom as people followed their own paths to God. The religious quest had political ramifications as well—kings involved themselves in the Catholics' and Protestants' conflict in part to try to exert religious hegemony over their own lands and to gain land from their neighbors.

When the century of religious wars in Europe ended, it left a legacy of economic devastation, social and political change, and an intellectual revolution that transformed Western culture. More boys and girls in village schools began to read and write, men and women hoped to find love in marriage, and people began to take more pride in work over leisure. Nevertheless, the Protestant revolution failed to stop the competition for Christian souls. In the centuries to come, Europeans would take the battle between Protestants and Catholics across the seas, as they discovered lands that were new to them.

KEY TERMS

sacraments, *p. 349*

devotio moderna, *p. 349*

justification by faith, *p. 350*

indulgences, *p. 350*

purgatory, *p. 351*

Protestant, *p. 352*

iconoclasm, *p. 352*

transubstantiation, *p. 352*

predestination, *p. 355*

Huguenots, *p. 357*

Jesuits, *p. 362*

baroque, *p. 363*

REVIEW, ANALYZE, & CONNECT TO TODAY

REVIEW THE PREVIOUS CHAPTER

Chapter 10—"A New Spirit in the West"—described the characteristics that we have come to identify with the Renaissance. In addition, Chapter 10 discussed the complex political structure of Italy that engaged popes as well as princes in power politics.

1. Which Renaissance characteristics also describe the ideas of the Protestant reformers? Consider how the Renaissance influenced the Protestant Reformation.

2. Review the policies of Renaissance popes as they strove to become political powers in Italy. How did those policies contribute to the Reformation?

ANALYZE THIS CHAPTER

Chapter 11—"Alone Before God"—follows the expansion of warfare until it engulfed all of Europe in the sixteenth century. It also looks at the new religious ideas that split the Catholic Church and brought about a change in life in the West.

1. Review the various religious beliefs of the different Protestant sects and consider the relationship of these ideas to the different social and economic groups who were attracted to them.

2. How did the differing appeal help lead to the century of religious warfare? What were the results of this warfare?

3. Review the reform movements of the Catholic Church. How did the church respond to the critique of the Protestants?

4. How did the Reformation help contribute to changing social and cultural patterns that marked seventeenth-century Europe?

CONNECT TO TODAY

Think about this chapter's discussion of the ways in which changing religious ideas led to warfare and suffering. Also consider how the new technology of warfare increased the human cost.

1. Many individuals thought that the violence of the Thirty Years' War would prevent people from fighting about religion ever again. That expectation has not been realized. In what countries or regions of the world does religious warfare continue today? Why do you think such warfare has not ended in these locations?

2. Is the technology of modern warfare further increasing the human cost? Explain. How might technology *decrease* the human toll of war?

BEYOND THE CLASSROOM

THE CLASH OF DYNASTIES, 1515–1555

Bonney, Richard. *The European Dynastic States, 1494–1660.* Oxford: Oxford University Press, 1991. A rich survey that includes eastern as well as western Europe and provides an excellent overview (although it does exclude England).

Davis, Natalie Zemon. *The Return of Martin Guerre.* Cambridge, MA: Harvard University Press, 1983. The classic study of Martin Guerre (the subject of the Chapter 11 Biography).

Kelly, Jack. *Gunpowder: Alchemy, Bombards, & Pyrotechnics: The History of the Explosive That Changed the World.* New York: Basic Books, 2004. An engaging, detailed account of the development and use of gunpowder in artillery and fireworks, from its beginnings in China through the nineteenth century.

MacCulloch, Diarmaid. *The Reformation.* New York: Penguin, 2005. A comprehensive and brilliant intellectual history analysis of the Reformation that goes beyond traditional accounts of the period's main reformers.

Maltby, William. *The Reign of Charles V.* New York: Palgrave Macmillan, 2004. A concise, accessible summary of this significant ruler that shows his influence in Latin America as well as Europe.

Parker, Geoffrey. *European Soldiers, 1550–1650.* New York: Cambridge University Press, 1997. A short, beautifully illustrated look into the lives of European soldiers.

Reston, James. *Defenders of the Faith: Charles V, Suleyman the Magnificent, and the Battle for Europe, 1520–1536.* New York: Penguin Press HC, 2009. A vibrant re-creation of a pivotal period in the confrontation between the West and Islam, illuminating the ideas that underlay this struggle.

A TIDE OF RELIGIOUS REFORM

Bainton, Roland H. *Here I Stand: A Life of Martin Luther.* New York: Meridian, 1995. First published in 1950, remains the best and most sensitive study of the man and his impact.

Baylor, Michael G. *The Radical Reformation.* New York: Cambridge University Press, 1991. Collects letters and other documents to illustrate the rich diversity and the fragile unity that existed in the political thinking of some of the major radical reformers in Germany.

Belloc, Hilaire. *How the Reformation Happened.* Rockford, IL: TAN Books, 2009. A Catholic perspective on the causes of the Reformation, offering a concise thesis for these causes.

Haigh, Christopher. *English Reformations: Religion, Politics, and Society Under the Tudors.* Oxford: Clarendon Press, 1993. A scholarly work that draws on a wealth of primary materials from catechisms to churchwardens' accounts to offer a full picture of the English Reformation.

Scribner, R.W. *The German Reformation,* 2nd ed. New York: Palgrave Macmillan, 2003. A brief and accessible analysis of the appeal of the Reformation to common people.

THE CATHOLIC REFORMATION

Ahlgren, Gillian. *Teresa of Avila and the Politics of Sanctity.* Ithaca, NY: Cornell University Press, 1996. Considers Teresa's struggle in the context of a world that did not always look kindly on an outspoken woman.

Birley, Robert. *The Refashioning of Catholicism, 1450–1700: A Reassessment of the Counter Reformation.* Washington, DC: Catholic University Press, 1999. Offers a comprehensive, balanced, historical view of the Catholic Reformation by a prominent historian of Catholicism. Its strength is placing these ideas into the context of the times.

O'Malley, John. *Trent and All That: Renaming Catholicism in the Early Modern Era.* Cambridge, MA: Harvard University Press, 2002. The best overview of early modern Catholicism that explains the intellectual and historical developments in an engaging way.

EUROPE ERUPTS AGAIN: A CENTURY OF RELIGIOUS WARFARE, 1559–1648

Holt, Mack P. *The French Wars of Religion, 1562–1629,* 2nd ed. Cambridge: Cambridge University Press, 2005. A brief, clear description of the events of these wars as well as an analysis of the issues that formed the backdrop of the warfare, clarifying a complex time.

MacCaffrey, Wallace. *Elizabeth I: War and Politics, 1588–1603.* Princeton, NJ: Princeton University Press, 1992. Recounts the conduct of the war with Spain and describes the diplomacy of alliances of the period.

Wedgwood, C.V. *The Thirty Years War.* New York: NYRB Classics, 2005. A comprehensive, scholarly, definitive account of this pivotal war that engagingly draws from a full range of sources.

LIFE AFTER THE REFORMATION

Harrington, Joel. *Reordering Marriage and Society in Reformation Germany.* Cambridge: Cambridge University Press, 1994. A provocative and sound interpretation.

Russell, Jeffrey B. *A History of Witchcraft,* 2nd ed. London: Thames and Hudson, 2007. Fully revised classic study that places the sixteenth-century witchcraft craze in its historical context while drawing comparisons with modern sorcery.

Weber, Max. *The Protestant Ethic and the Spirit of Capitalism.* Los Angeles: Roxbury Publishing, 1998. Originally published in 1904, this study of how the Reformation helped create the modern world has generated much controversy but has also shaped much of the historical thinking about the Reformation.

PORTRAIT OF DON FRANCISCO DE AROBÉ, DETAIL FROM *THE MULATTO GENTLEMEN OF ESMERALDAS,* BY ANDRÉS SÁNCHEZ GALLQUE, 1599

Globalization changed the world beginning in the fifteenth century as Europeans and Africans encountered native peoples in the New World. This portrait is part of a larger portrait of three men in Ecuador in the service of the Spanish king Philip III. The subject here, Francisco, was of mixed African descent, a Christian, and the governor of a settlement in Ecuador. He represents the new blending of peoples and cultures, and this portrait, the oldest surviving signed and dated painting from colonial South America, reveals the kind of changes that came about as people moved across the seas.

Faith, Fortune, and Fame

12

European Expansion, 1450–1700

" To serve God and the King, to give light to those who are in darkness, and to grow rich, as all men desire to do." With these words, the Portuguese explorer Bartholomeu Dias (1450–1500) explained purposes that drove men to sail their ships across uncharted oceans during the sixteenth and seventeenth centuries. At the same time that Italian Renaissance ideas spread and the Reformation created new martyrs, daring Europeans ventured where they had never gone before. Kings and queens sponsored these explorers in the hopes that the new territories and riches they promised would give monarchs an advantage over their dynastic rivals.

The adventurers traveled by ship east to China, Japan, and other places in the Pacific, and west to strange new islands and continents. As they journeyed, they met peoples living in great empires in the East and in the mountains and jungles of South and Central America. They traded with many others from tribes and kingdoms in sub-Saharan Africa, the Caribbean, and North America. The interactions among the many cultures prompted the emergence of new markets and the discovery of unusual products that whetted Europeans' appetites for yet more novelties. Some men, like Don Francisco, shown in the chapter-opening portrait, were able to prosper in the new global environment, but not all were so successful. Sadly, the commingling also led to the transmission of deadly new diseases and other hardships. Europeans were irrevocably altered by these cultural contacts, and so were the cultures they encountered.

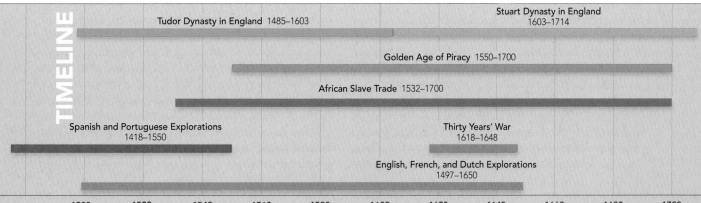

TIMELINE

Tudor Dynasty in England 1485–1603

Stuart Dynasty in England 1603–1714

Golden Age of Piracy 1550–1700

African Slave Trade 1532–1700

Spanish and Portuguese Explorations 1418–1550

Thirty Years' War 1618–1648

English, French, and Dutch Explorations 1497–1650

1500 1520 1540 1560 1580 1600 1620 1640 1660 1680 1700

PREVIEW

THE WORLD IMAGINED

In 1498, four Portuguese ships led by Vasco da Gama sailed south from Europe and rounded the southern tip of Africa to reach India in the east. Gaspar Correa accompanied this journey, keeping a careful chronicle that told of the exciting, frightening voyage. In order to sail south with prevailing northwesterly winds, the navigators could not hug the shore but instead had to direct the ships southwest, tacking into the wind and going far away from the sight of land into the unknown sea. For two months, Vasco da Gama tacked out to sea to make sure that when they turned to shore, the ships would "double the cape," skirting the African continent. Correa wrote of the hardships of this venture into the Atlantic: "The fury of the sea [made] the ships seem every moment to be going to pieces. The crews grew sick with fear and hardship, . . . and all clamored for putting back to Portugal. . . . At times they met with such cold rains that the men could not prepare their food. All cried out to God for mercy upon their souls." Vasco da Gama finally ordered the ships about and they sailed southeast again. They circled the southern tip of Africa and with much celebration they headed northeast toward India.

The ships were to face much more hardship. They pulled into great rivers in Africa looking for food and for people to tell them where they were. They ate unknown fruits—one so toxic it made their gums swell and their teeth loosen. The captain ordered his ill men to rinse their mouths with urine to ease their gums, and the cure worked. Somehow, through all the adversity the crews carried on and finally docked in India at a city where citizens flocked to the shore, amazed at the Western ships. Correa succinctly and accurately described the confrontation between East and West: "All were much amazed at seeing what they had never before seen." Vasco da Gama's crew was not unique in the fifteenth century; brave sailors sailed east and west from Europe, and the world was transformed as Europeans and indigenous peoples almost everywhere were amazed at their new confrontation.

The Lure of the East

Western Europeans had long coveted goods from the East, which they generally considered China and India. When they used the name "China," they also meant Japan and the other lands of eastern Asia. When they referred to "India," they included southeast Asia and the many islands dotting the Pacific, and although Vasco da Gama reached the mainland of India, he would have been content to land on any of the Pacific islands. More than just a geographic entity, though, the East, in many Europeans' minds, was the source of valuable luxury goods.

| Eastern trade |

Since the Middle Ages, Europe had lusted after the silks, fine carpets, pottery, and precious jewels produced in the East. Europeans were so impressed by these exotic goods that they praised the Chinese as the finest craftsmen in the world. Yet it was the spices from the Orient that riveted Westerners' attention. European diets were bland, and those who depended only on local seasonings—garlic, saffron, and the ever-present salt—found the food tiresome. Recipes of the time and records showing commercial demand reveal that people clamored for cloves, cinnamon, coriander, and pepper in particular—all available only in the East. Throughout the Middle Ages, these products came overland through the Byzantine Empire into western Europe.

But after 1400, intensifying warfare in eastern Europe and Asia made overland travel difficult. (See Chapter 9 for the increased threat posed by the Turks.) Europeans began looking for new trade routes through the eastern Mediterranean to satisfy their appetite for spice. They revived centuries-old memories of journeys to the East by reading accounts like that of the Venetian explorer Marco Polo (1254–1324), who wrote detailed descriptions of his visits to China (see Chapter 9). These works were incorrect in much of their geography, however; for example, Marco Polo believed that Japan was 1,500 miles east of China. Furthermore, most of these older accounts contained exaggerated descriptions of botanical and biological features of Eastern lands. Nevertheless, no tale of the exotic East seemed too far-fetched to fifteenth-century European imaginations.

Imagined Peoples

Since the time of the Roman scholar Pliny the Elder (23–79), people had heard of unusual races of people who inhabited parts of the world outside the Mediterranean. Pliny's works had been read, copied, and embellished over the centuries, and by the fifteenth century, explorers expected to find beings as bizarre as dog-headed humans, headless people, one-legged "sciopods," and—south of the equator—"antipods," whose feet reportedly faced backward.

Figure 12.1 shows an illustration from a fifteenth-century manuscript about the travels of Marco Polo. Although Marco Polo never claimed to have seen such creatures, later Europeans imagined that he did. On the left of the illustration is a blemmyae, a headless man whose face is located on his chest. In the center is a sciopod, a one-legged creature believed to use his large foot as a parasol against the sun. These two beings are greeted by a cyclops approaching from the right.

A more plausible person the explorers expected to meet was Prester John, supposedly a rich and powerful Christian king reigning in the heart of Africa. By the Renaissance, Europeans hoped to enlist this king as an ally against the Muslims. However, the search for both Prester John and the fascinating creatures in Marco Polo's tales was stymied by an inaccurate geographic sense of the world that, like the descriptions of the monstrous races, the explorers had inherited from the ancients.

Ptolemy's Map

During the fifteenth century, western Europeans acquired the *Geography* of Ptolemy (ca. 100–ca. 178). This guide had been translated from Greek, reproduced by the new printing presses, and widely distributed. Now Renaissance explorers had a picture of the world that they could use to venture into the Atlantic, or the "green sea of darkness," as the Arabic commentators called it.

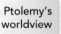
Ptolemy's worldview

Ptolemy portrayed the world as a globe, divided into the familiar 360 degrees of longitude. **Figure 12.2,** from a 1482 edition of the *Geography,* shows Ptolemy's map of the world. This ancient geographer believed that the world consisted of three continents—Asia, Africa, and Europe—and two oceans—the Indian Ocean and the Western Ocean. The map is surrounded by figures representing the many winds so crucial to a sailing society. In addition to mistaking the number of continents, Ptolemy made two major errors: He underestimated the extent of the oceans, suggesting that land covered three-fourths of the earth's surface, and

FIGURE 12.1 Monstrous Races, fifteenth century Influenced by writings of medieval travelers, explorers expected to see strange creatures such as those pictured here: the blemmyae on the left, a sciopod in the center, and a cyclops on the right.

he miscalculated the earth as being one-sixth smaller than its true size. With only Ptolemy's map to guide them, later explorers understandably expected the journey east to be shorter than it really was. During this age of discovery, however, the theories of Ptolemy dissolved in the face of experience.

THE WORLD DISCOVERED

The explorers expected to capitalize on Europe's desire for Eastern goods and bring back wealth for themselves and their sovereigns. Sixteenth-century rulers were desperate for money to field their expensive armies, and the conquest of Constantinople by the Turks in 1453 increased the price of the valuable spices as they imposed steep taxes on the goods. This costly trade siphoned precious metals away from an already coin-poor western Europe, and monarchs were willing to reward anyone who hunted for new wealth. Brave, enterprising men eager for fame and fortune took up the challenge.

Fame, Fortune, and Faith: The Drive to Explore

Though the lure of wealth motivated explorers and the sovereigns who funded them, some adventurers had other incentives for embarking on these risky travels. As Bartholomeu Dias implied in the quotation that introduced this chapter, religion also served as a major impulse for Europeans to seek new worlds. Christians during the fifteenth and sixteenth centuries felt besieged by the Islamic empire of the Ottoman Turks that loomed on Europe's eastern border (see Chapter 11). Some voyages aimed to find

FIGURE 12.2 Ptolemy's Map The ancient map shows the world as the explorers expected it to be: largely land, with little sea, and Europe at the center. The four winds in the corners reminded sailors of their source of power.

allies against the Turks. The Reformation within Europe also stimulated explorations and migrations, as Catholics sought converts to Catholicism overseas and Protestants looked for new lands where they could practice their faith. Faith joined with fame and fortune to drive Europeans across the seas.

New Technologies and Travel

Europeans had a passion for adventure, but they also needed strong navigational tools and skills if they were to survive these hazardous journeys. Fortunately for them, sailors in the Middle Ages had perfected instruments to help them sail out of sight of land. One

| Navigation instruments |

device, the **quadrant,** aligned with the fixed North Star at night to let navigators determine their latitude. However, this was not useful in the Southern Hemisphere, where the North Star was not visible. Sailors going south had to confront uncharted heavens as well as unmapped lands. During the day, sailors in both Northern and Southern hemispheres could check their calculations with the **astrolabe** (see **Figure 6.14**), which measured the height of the sun during the day or the altitude of a known star at night.

Finally, mapmakers had gained experience in charting the seas and lands and could graphically document their travels with some accuracy. Earlier skilled seafarers like the Vikings who first discovered North America lacked the cartography skills to allow them to reproduce their long sea voyages with as much certainty as did the sixteenth-century explorers. Navigators felt confident in their charts, and the newly discovered map of Ptolemy, though inaccurate, at least gave them a basic sense of direction.

Sailors lacked only the ships to carry them safely on long ventures. The galleys that had ruled the Mediterranean in the fourteenth century had large, square sails, but their locomotion came primarily from the many slaves who rowed the big ships. These ships were unsuitable for long distances and had little extra space left in their holds to store the provisions necessary for a lengthy sea voyage.

All this changed in the late fifteenth century, when the Portuguese built ships that marked the highest development of a long evolution of Mediterranean sailing ships. In the Middle Ages, shipbuilders had developed a new kind of sail rigging that allowed ships to maneuver near shore in uncertain winds. By

| Improved ships |

the sixteenth century, shipbuilders had improved the mobility of the sails and the rigging of the ropes so that the sails could be moved readily. **Figure 12.3** shows a sixteenth-century watercolor of Portuguese caravels—the small (70 to 80 feet long) ships that conquered the great seas. The large square sails allowed the ships to move in the direction of the wind, or downwind. The real secret to long-distance sailing, however, was the lateen, a triangular, mobile sail at the rear (furled in **Figure 12.3**). This device not only let the ship sail faster but also allowed it to sail at an angle to the wind and thus progress upwind—a crucial advantage for traveling into the prevailing westerly winds of the Atlantic. This ship, with its absence of oar banks, stands in striking contrast to the Mediterranean galleys shown in **Figure 11.9**. The ships had to be heavy to withstand the storms of the Atlantic, and this weight gave the West an unforeseen advantage: They could support heavy cannons, giving them a military advantage over the lighter ships of the East that sailed the calmer Indian ocean. On these innovative vessels, the Portuguese set out on voyages of discovery that changed the world.

The Portuguese Race for the East, 1418–1600

As the chronicler of Vasco da Gama's voyage described in the account at the beginning of this chapter, the Portuguese explorers had an immediate goal in mind: to venture south around Africa to the Indian Ocean and trade directly with natives in India for spices and other luxury items. This route would eliminate the troublesome role of the Ottoman Turks as key players in the eastern Mediterranean trade network. Beginning in 1418, Prince Henry the Navigator (1394–1460) of Portugal sponsored annual expeditions down the west coast of Africa. Bartholomeu Dias continued Henry's work with great success, rounding the southern tip of Africa in 1488. King John II of Portugal (r. 1481–1495), expecting this route to yield the riches of the East, named the tip the Cape of Good Hope. But Dias never reached India. His frightened crew had experienced the storms and hardships that Correa described, but Dias did not maintain the iron control that Vasco da Gama would, and his crew mutinied as he sailed north along the eastern coast of Africa. He was forced to return home.

In 1498, his countryman Vasco da Gama (ca. 1460–1524) set out with four ships to complete Dias's ill-fated voyage to India. He succeeded and returned to Portugal with ships laden with spices worth sixty times the cost of the journey. On his first trip to India, da Gama carried casks of honey, hats, and other trifles to trade for the precious spices. On his second voyage four years later, the explorer brought a new trading item that would transform commerce in the Indian

FIGURE 12.3 Portuguese Ships, sixteenth century Portuguese caravels, the subject of this informative watercolor, were sturdily designed ships that sailed the great seas. Powered by huge sails, the ships did not need banks of oars, so they could be stocked with water and food for long voyages.

basin: His casks were now filled with gunpowder. Soldiers in India had long known the recipe for gunpowder, but when they saw its use in da Gama's deadly cannons, a new arms race would begin that would fuel escalating violence in the age of exploration.

Portuguese explorers scored spectacular successes in opening up the trade to the East. As one pleasant surprise, they discovered that India was not simply one location—it included the Moluccas, "spice islands," from which wafted the delightful aroma of cloves as the Portuguese ships approached. As **Map 12.1** shows, the Portuguese established a string of trading outposts throughout the East. In these small settlements, Europeans lived peacefully near native settlements in a mutually profitable relationship. Portugal's successful entry into the Indian Ocean trade struck a dramatic blow to the economy of the Muslims, who had previously held a monopoly on that trade. At the same time, their neighbors, the Spanish, took a quite different approach. Spain's explorers sailed westward in hopes of reaching the

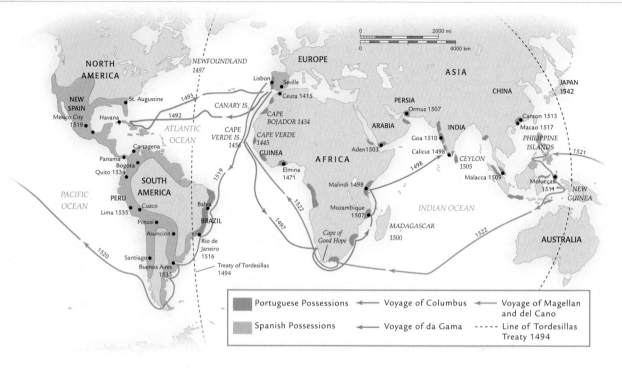

MAP 12.1

Exploration and Conquest, Fifteenth and Sixteenth Centuries

This map shows the routes and dates of the explorations of the fifteenth and sixteenth centuries, as well as the possessions claimed by the Spanish and Portuguese. It includes the Treaty of Tordesillas line, which divided the world between Portugal and Spain.

Explore the Map

1. What accounted for the differing settlement patterns in the Americas, Africa, and Asia?

2. How do you think the Treaty of Tordesillas influenced the differing settlement patterns of the Spanish and the Portuguese?

3. How were the small settlements around the coast of Africa useful for sailors and traders?

fabulous Orient, believing Ptolemy's claim that the land of plenty lay just over the horizon.

Spain's Westward Discoveries, 1492–1522

Christopher Columbus (1446–1506) perhaps best exemplifies Spain's travel ambitions. The son of an Italian (Genoese) weaver, Columbus traveled to Portugal in 1476 to learn about Portuguese shipbuilding and sailing. During his visit, he became captivated by the accounts of Marco Polo and the *Geography* of Ptolemy. Inflamed by images of glory and wealth, he asked the Portuguese king to sponsor him on a trip west to Asia. The king rejected him; like many others, he dismissed Columbus as a vague dreamer. Columbus then presented his idea to the Spanish monarchs

Ferdinand and Isabella. The queen, impressed with Columbus's proposal, made him an admiral in 1492 and financed his expedition.

Columbus embarked on his journey with three ships, the *Niña*, the *Pinta*, and the *Santa María*. In October, the small fleet landed on an island in the Caribbean Sea. According to the admiral's account, as he stepped ashore, Columbus "claimed all the lands for their Highnesses, by proclamation and with the royal standard displayed." According to Columbus, the many islanders who watched him did not object to his claims, so he accepted this as their tacit agreement—ignoring the language barrier that separated them. Subsequent explorers followed his lead, claiming ownership of already inhabited lands.

> Columbus's discoveries

FIGURE 12.4 Columbus's Discoveries   This contemporary woodcut shows the New World as Columbus wanted to portray it: populated by beautiful, naked peoples; lush with exotic plants; and all under the control of the Spanish king on the left.

Figure 12.4 is a contemporary woodcut that was intended to capture this incident, and it shows all the essential elements: The king of Spain, on the left, gives Columbus the authority for his voyage. The three ships are featured in the center, and Columbus is shown landing on an island to claim it for the king. The island is depicted as a place as fanciful as any in the literature of imaginative travel, with exotic trees and beautiful, naked natives. The reality of the landing proved much less idyllic.

Columbus made four voyages between 1492 and 1502, during which he established settlements on several more Caribbean islands and visited the northern coast of South America and Central America. On his third voyage, he brought women from Spain to ensure the permanence of the settlements. The explorer was not a good administrator, and when Spain sent a judge to look into a revolt in the new lands, Columbus was brought back to Spain in chains. Though he was later released and made a final fourth voyage to the New World, Columbus never received the riches and acclaim he sought. Throughout these years, the Italian adventurer apparently felt sure that he had found Asian islands. He even referred to the natives as Indians because he was certain he was in the general region of India. Columbus never realized that he had discovered a world unknown by virtually all Europeans. Instead, he clung to the image of the world he had imagined. His continued misconceptions encouraged other voyagers, who would soon prove him wrong.

As the Spanish and Portuguese both raced to claim lands on their way east, they inevitably came into conflict. The Catholic sovereigns of Spain and Portugal appealed to the pope to divide the world into two spheres of influence. In the 1494 Treaty of Tordesillas (shown on **Map 12.1**), the Spanish received exclusive rights to the lands west of Treaty of Tordesillas

a line drawn 370 leagues (about 1,200 miles) west of the Cape Verde Islands off the west coast of Africa, and the Portuguese received rights to the lands east of the line. This agreement (which was virtually ignored by the other European monarchs) was one of many attempts to apportion the world without regard for the opinions of indigenous residents.

Soon, subsequent travelers convinced Europeans that Columbus was wrong and that a great new landmass had been found. The most influential of these explorers was Amerigo Vespucci (1451–1512), an educated "Renaissance man" who worked for the Medici family of Florence (discussed in Chapter 10). In 1499, Vespucci set off on a voyage of discovery that took him westward from Spain and across the vast ocean to South America. During his voyage, he took careful navigational measurements and wrote colorful letters to his Medici patron, which were widely circulated. In the introduction to these works, Amerigo's publisher even suggested that Vespucci's name be given to the Mundus Novus (the New World) he had popularized with his maps and vivid tales of a continent across the ocean. The suggestion caught on, and the name "America" became attached to the western landmass that newly captured the European imagination. See Document 12.1 for an example of one of Vespucci's vivid descriptions.

After Vespucci's voyages, people set out purposefully to visit the new continent. For example, the Spanish adventurer Vasco Núñez de Balboa (1475–1517) trekked across the Isthmus of Panama, eventually reaching the Pacific Ocean on the   Circumnavigating the globe

other side. Besides adding to the evidence that a new continent existed, Balboa's discovery intensified the race to the riches of the East. New men with even bigger dreams of wealth joined the rush.

Ferdinand Magellan (ca. 1480–1521) was one of these men. A Portuguese explorer in the service of Spain, Magellan began the first expedition that succeeded in encircling the world. He sailed west from Spain in 1519 with three ships and discovered (and named) the Straits of Magellan at the southern tip of South America. The straits gave him access to the Pacific Ocean (which he also named). He and his crew braved the huge expanses of ocean and withstood mutinies. In 1521, Magellan was killed while interfering in a local war in the Philippines. His navigator, Sevastian Elcano (ca. 1476–1526), finished the

thinking about

DOCUMENTS

DOCUMENT 12.1

Amerigo Vespucci Describes the New World

In 1499, the naval astronomer Amerigo Vespucci wrote a letter to Lorenzo de' Medici of Florence (see Chapter 10) describing his travels. The letter serves as a valuable early source for European impressions of the new lands. It was particularly influential because of Vespucci's engaging style and sharp observations.

It appears to me, most excellent Lorenzo, that by this voyage most of those philosophers are controverted who say that the torrid zone cannot be inhabited on account of the great heat. I have found the case to be quite the contrary. I have found that the air is fresher and more temperate in that region than beyond it, and that the inhabitants are also more numerous here than they are in the other zones, for reasons which will be given below. Thus it is certain that practice is of more value than theory.

Thus far I have related the navigation I accomplished in the south and west. It now remains for me to inform you of the appearance of the country we discovered, the nature of the inhabitants, and their customs, the animals we saw, and of many other things worthy of remembrance which fell under my observation. After we turned our course to the north, the first land we found to be inhabited was an island at ten degrees distant from the equinoctial line. When we arrived at it we saw on the sea-shore a great many people, who stood

looking at us with astonishment. We anchored within about a mile of the land, fitted out the boats, and twenty-two men, well armed, made for land. The people, when they saw us landing, and perceived that we were different from themselves—because they have no beard and wear no clothing of any description, being also of a different color, they being brown and we white—began to be afraid of us, and all ran into the woods. With great exertion, by means of signs, we reassured them and negotiated with them. We found that they were of a race called cannibals, the greater part or all of whom live on human flesh.

Your excellency may rest assured of this fact. They do not eat one another, but, navigating with certain barks which they call "canoes," they bring their prey from the neighboring islands or countries inhabited by those who are enemies or of a different tribe from their own. They never eat any women, unless they consider them outcasts. These things we verified in many places where we found similar people. We often saw the bones and heads of those who had been eaten, and they who had made the repast admitted the fact, and said that their enemies always stood in much greater fear on that account.

Still they are a people of gentle disposition and beautiful stature. They go entirely naked, and the arms which they carry are bows and arrows and shields. They are a people of great activity and much courage. They are very excellent marksmen. . . .

Nearly half the trees of this island are dye-wood, as good as that of the East. We went from this island to another in the vicinity, at ten leagues' distance, and found a very large village, the houses of which were built over the sea, like Venice, with much ingenuity. While we were struck with admiration at this circumstance, we determined to go and see them; and as we went to their houses, they attempted to prevent our entering. They found out at last the manner in which the sword cuts, and thought it best to let us enter. We found their houses filled with the finest cotton, and the beams of their dwellings were made of dye-wood. We took a quantity of their cotton and some dye-wood and returned to the ships.

Your excellency must know that in all parts where we landed we found a great quantity of cotton, and the country filled with cotton-trees, so that all the vessels in the world might be loaded in these parts with cotton and dye-wood.

SOURCE: Amerigo Vespucci, "Letter to Lorenzo de' Medici," in *The Great Events by Famous Historians*, vol. VIII, ed. Rossiter Johnson (The National Alumni, 1905), pp. 351–356.

Analyze the Document

1. How did Vespucci's observations foster a scientific attitude?

2. How might this narrative have persuaded people that there would be profits to be made in the New World?

3. How might Vespucci's descriptions of the native peoples influence future interactions between them and the Europeans?

---

journey to Asia and through the Indian Ocean back to Spain. Elcano's voyage took three years and he returned home with only one ship. But that ship was packed with enough spices not only to pay for the cost of the expedition but also to make the crew very rich.

Magellan and Elcano's successful circumnavigation of the globe revealed not that the world was round (they knew that), but its true size. It also demonstrated the impracticality of sailing to the Orient

by way of the Pacific. The Spanish would have to search for new sources of wealth—this time in the New World.

The Northern Europeans Join the Race, 1497–1650

England, France, and the Netherlands came late to the race for the riches of the New World. Understandably, they were unwilling to accept the terms of the

Treaty of Tordesillas. Instead, they began their own explorations. They started by looking for a "northwest passage" to the East that would parallel the southern route around South America. In about 1497, the Genoese captain John Cabot (1450–1498) and his son Sebastian (1476–1557), who both had settled in England, received a letter from the English king Henry VII (r. 1485–1509) authorizing them to take possession for England of any new lands unclaimed by any Christian nation. So empowered, father and son sailed across the North Atlantic to Newfoundland and Maine. They found codfish so plentiful that their ships could not pass through the thick schools of fish. However, the voyage was immediately disappointing because they neither reached Asia nor returned laden with spices.

The French also hunted for a northwest passage to the East. In 1534, Jacques Cartier led three voyages that explored the St. Lawrence River in what is today Canada. He and his crew got as far **Settlements in Canada** as Montreal, but the great waterway led only inland, not out to the Pacific Northwest. An early settlement effort in the region of Quebec in 1541 failed, owing to the harsh winter and indigenes' hostility. In about 1600, Samuel de Champlain (ca. 1567–1635) made another try at establishing a settlement in North America. He founded Quebec, signing treaties with the natives to secure the settlement. Canadian settlements remained small in both size and number through the seventeenth century, but their existence ensured the continuous presence of European traders and missionaries in this northern land.

When the much-sought-after northwest passage proved elusive, northern Europeans shifted their journeys of discovery farther south and began to confront the Iberians directly. The Dutch established trading posts in the Spice Islands, and **Dutch colonies** Dutch warships proved their superiority and expelled the Portuguese from the islands that we now know as Indonesia. The Dutch also redesigned their ships to haul more cargo than the small Portuguese caravels that had first mastered the oceans. They then dominated the lucrative spice trade, founding colonies in strategic locations to protect their growing trade empire. As one example, they colonized the tip of South Africa to facilitate their Eastern trade and planted colonies in North America (most famously on Manhattan Island) and in the Caribbean.

The English, for their part, began to install settlements along the North American Atlantic seaboard in the seventeenth century: By **English colonies** 1700, about 250,000 colonists lived along the coast. Many of these people moved there to escape the religious persecution that swept Europe in the seventeenth century. For this reason, they traveled west with their entire families, with the intent to stay. Their presence irrevocably altered the face of North America. **Map 12.2** shows the status of the European colonization in about 1700, and it illustrates how the northern European countries had joined the Spanish and Portuguese in their race around the world.

CONFRONTATION OF CULTURES

When the Europeans arrived in the New World, it was already abundantly populated by peoples who had lived there in resilient societies for millennia. From as early as 35,000 B.C.E., small groups of people walked from Asia northward across a land bridge from Siberia to Alaska. Slowly, over tens of thousands of years, families, clans, and tribes moved southward and settled throughout North, Central, and South America. At first, all these tribes pursued a highly effective hunting-and-gathering existence, with devastating consequences for their future development. As the hunters came through North America, they confronted great herds of large mammals—horses, elephants, camels, and giant ground sloths. Within a few centuries of human arrival, all those large mammals were extinct, probably because of effective hunting. However, this meant that there were no more large animals in North America for domestication— this would represent a fatal disadvantage when the Amerindians confronted Europeans millennia later.

The Original Americans South of the Rio Grande

In about 5500 B.C.E., tribes in central Mexico first developed agriculture, which, as we saw in Chapter 1, allowed large settled populations to become established. These civilizations would become tempting, wealthy targets **Agriculture** for European explorers. Agriculture spread north and south from there, but very slowly. The differing latitudes and varied growing seasons of the large American continents caused agriculture to diffuse more slowly in the Americas than it had in Europe and Asia, where crops spread primarily within similar latitudes. In the Americas, for example, it took about 3,500 years for maize (what we usually call corn) and beans to spread 700 miles from Mexico to the southern farmlands of the modern United States, but spread they did.

With the early use of agriculture in Central America and the western mountains of South America, populations grew large and elaborate empires—the Maya, Aztec, Inca, and others—developed. These civilizations thrived mainly through the cultivation of maize. This highly nutritious, versatile crop originally grew wild in the New World but had been

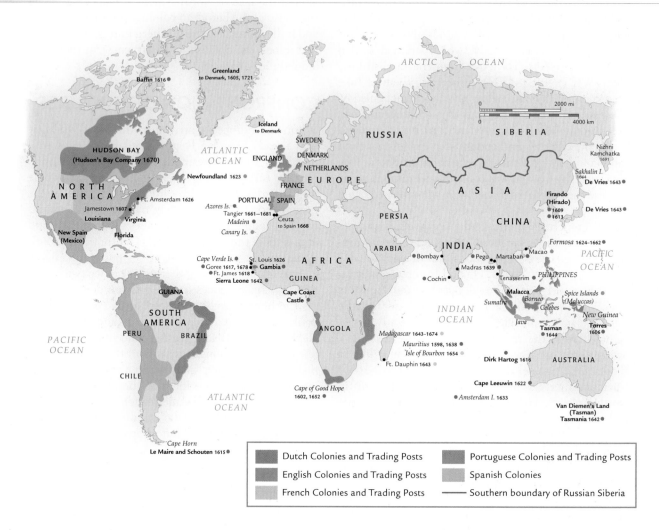

English Colonies and Trading Posts

French Colonies and Trading Posts

Portuguese Colonies and Trading Posts

Spanish Colonies

Southern boundary of Russian Siberia

MAP 12.2

European Expansion, ca. 1700

This map shows the world around 1700, when Europeans had expanded around the globe. Notice where the people from the various countries settled, and compare the different settlement patterns of the Americas, Africa, and Asia.

Explore the Map

1. What might account for the differences in settlement patterns?

2. Compare this map with **Map 12.1.** What are the major differences between the maps, and what caused these differences?

3. Why was North America so heavily settled compared to Africa?

cultivated for so long that it no longer grew without human help. Maize offered high yields with very little effort. Cultivators worked only about fifty days a year to produce an abundant crop that could be eaten even before it was ripe. In these maize-growing societies, men cut and burned brush to clear the land to plant the grain, and women ground the hard kernels into flour to make tortillas, or flat bread.

The Incas, a people living in the Andes Mountains of South America, also cultivated a crop indigenous to that region—potatoes. An excellent alternative to maize, which did not grow in the high country, this hardy vegetable grew easily in the adverse conditions and high altitudes of mountain ranges and provided a hearty food supply. Once planted, potatoes required little work to harvest and prepare. Incas living in the mountains dried potatoes for long-term storage.

The small amount of time required to cultivate and harvest maize and potatoes left many days free for other work, and the great Central and South American empires

Empire building

developed a religious and aristocratic culture that demanded human labor for immense building projects. The Maya, Aztecs, and Incas built magnificent cities and roads and imposing pyramids. These constructions seem even more remarkable when we realize that they were built with Stone Age technology and without use of the wheel and (in most places) without the help of powerful, domesticated animals. Among these civilizations, only the Incas had domesticated the llama and alpaca as beasts of burden; throughout the rest of North and South America, people raised only dogs and fowl.

Map 12.3 shows the locations of the large South American empires as they existed when the Europeans arrived in the fifteenth century. The illustration shows the narrow Isthmus of Panama, which formed an effective geographic barrier between the two major empires, and which also served to disadvantage the Amerindians in developing increasingly complex societies. For example, the Aztecs in Mexico invented a wheel, but because they lacked draft animals, the wheel remained a children's toy. The Incas had domesticated the llama but had no wheel to convert this animal into an effective beast of burden.

In Mexico, the Aztecs had located their capital at the great city of Tenochtitlán, built on a lake and accessible only by boat or causeway. (Tenochtitlán is the site of present-day Mexico

Aztec Empire

City.) The Aztecs called themselves Meshica, from which we get the word *Mexico*. The Aztecs had conquered all the surrounding local tribes and claimed tribute from the vanquished, including humans sacrificed to the demanding Aztec gods, who people believed claimed human blood to delay an inevitable destruction of Aztec society. Much of the visual information we have on the South American tribes comes from manuscripts written in the sixteenth century after the Spanish conquests. Authors included drawings within these books—many created by the Amerindians themselves. From these drawings, we can gain information about life before and after the Spanish invasions. **Figure 12.5** is one such drawing, which shows the ritual human sacrifice. In the sacrificial ceremony, victims were forced to the top of a pyramid and stretched over a stone. A priest then used a sharp stone knife to cut out the victim's heart and offer it—still beating—to the god. The voracious demand for

FIGURE 12.5 Aztec Human Sacrifice from the *Codex Magliabecchiano,* ca. 1570 Spanish conquerors took advantage of internal warfare among the tribes that generated human sacrifices such as that documented in this Aztec manuscript. The priest at the top removes the heart of the victims.

such tribute from the subject peoples catalyzed resentment among them—a force that the new conquerors from Europe would find useful in overpowering the Aztecs.

The Original Northern Americans

The spread of maize led to large, settled agricultural communities in North America. In the American Southwest, Pueblo and Navajo peoples adapted to their dry lands by irrigating crops of maize, beans, and squashes. They built permanent adobe buildings, and their populations grew. Farther north and east, Amerindians shaped their environments in different ways. They made extensive use of fire to burn underbrush in forests and, probably more significantly, to burn the great plains and prairies. In doing so, they created a huge pastureland for game, and their populations grew as well. **Map 12.3** shows the general patterns of the North American settlements.

The largest settled populations north of the Rio Grande spread along the Mississippi valley with the mound-building cultures. The largest surviving mound, at Cahokia near St. Louis, Illinois, is an astonishing structure, 100 feet high and 1,000 feet long. There were more than a hundred smaller mounds nearby. By 1250 C.E., the settlement surrounding these mounds probably reached between 15,000 and 38,000 inhabitants. These people grew prosperous from long-distance trade along the Missouri and Mississippi rivers, which brought seashells from Florida,

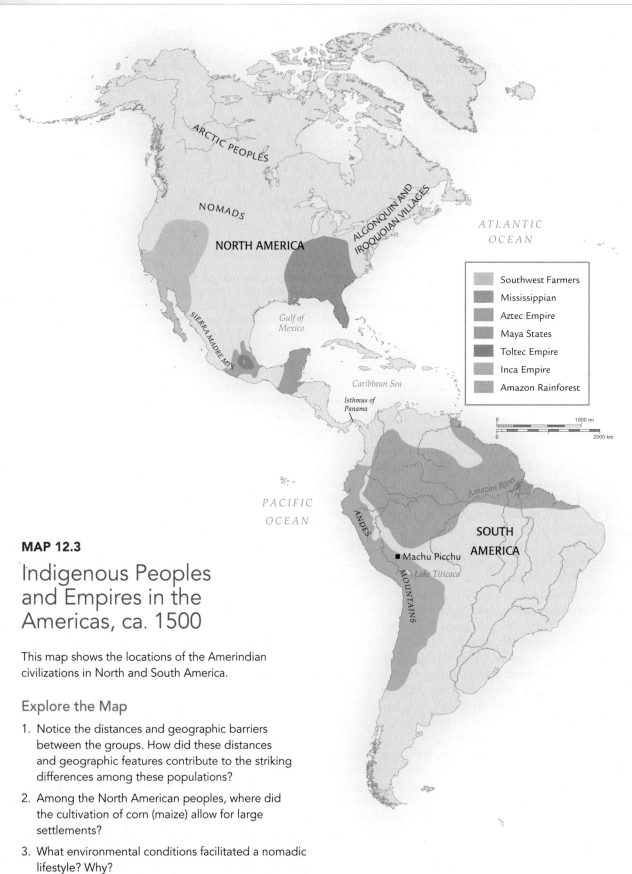

MAP 12.3

Indigenous Peoples and Empires in the Americas, ca. 1500

This map shows the locations of the Amerindian civilizations in North and South America.

Explore the Map

1. Notice the distances and geographic barriers between the groups. How did these distances and geographic features contribute to the striking differences among these populations?

2. Among the North American peoples, where did the cultivation of corn (maize) allow for large settlements?

3. What environmental conditions facilitated a nomadic lifestyle? Why?

copper from the Great Lakes, and other goods from all over the continent. The rise of Cahokia coincided with the spread of maize into the eastern part of the continent, a development that allowed the native populations to grow even more.

Fortunately, we have a visual record of the prosperity that eastern tribes of Amerindians enjoyed before their contact with Europeans, for an artist, John White, accompanied three voyages to the colony of Roanoke. White's detailed watercolors, copied by an engraver in the Netherlands and published in 1590, remain an excellent source of information about the lives and livelihoods of some North American tribes. The village White portrays in **Figure 12.6** is prosperous and orderly and has abundant food available. In the upper left of the etching, Amerindians hunt deer. In the hut at the upper right, a watchman makes "continual cries and noise" to frighten animals and birds from the fields, where maize and pumpkins (on the right) and tobacco (in the circular field on the left) grow. Villagers celebrate the abundance by dancing (lower right) and feasting (center).

There is much controversy over the size of these indigenous populations in North America, but certainly millions of people prospered in the American North. These flourishing cultures would be drastically affected by the arrival of Europeans.

Early Contacts

Christopher Columbus set the tone for the relationship between the original Americans and Europeans when he claimed land in the New World for the Spanish monarchs and when he treated the people as sources of revenue for the Spanish crown. With few exceptions, subsequent European explorers viewed the native peoples in the same way. Sometimes they traded with them; other times they used them as labor. Still other times, they killed or enslaved the men and women they found living in the new lands.

Explorers of the New World believed they had encountered a major problem: These lands lacked the spices and luxury goods of the East that had brought so much immediate wealth to merchants. These new explorers had to find other forms of riches to bring home. Sometimes they enslaved natives, but this was not particularly lucrative. Instead, they searched for silver and gold to take back to Europe. According to one contemporary observer, when an Amerindian asked a Spaniard what Europeans ate, the Spaniard responded, "Gold and silver." (We do not know whether this exchange actually took place, but the anecdote testifies to the insatiable European appetite for precious metals.) For the Europeans, all the early contacts involved questions of profit; for the Amerindians, such contacts brought suffering.

FIGURE 12.6 Amerindian Village from Theodore DeBry, _Grands et Petits Voyages_, 1590 This watercolor shows a well-ordered village in North America. Tribes grow tobacco, corn, and pumpkins.

Conquest of the Great Empires, 1520–1550

While in the Caribbean, the Spanish explorer Hernando Cortés (1485–1547) heard of a fabulously rich society to the west. Their curiosity aroused, he and 600 men sailed across the Gulf of Mexico in search of gold and glory. These Spanish soldiers of fortune were known as **conquistadors.** When Cortés landed on the Yucatán peninsula in southeast Mexico, the people he met there told him of a wealthy civilization in the interior (the Aztecs). As Cortés moved inland, he acquired a gift that proved more valuable to his quest than anything else—the slave woman Malinche.

According to later Spanish sources, Malinche was a princess whose father had died when she was young. The girl's mother gave her to local slave traders when the mother remarried, and the traders included the young woman in their gifts to Cortés. Malinche spoke four Amerindian languages, including the Nahuatl of the Aztecs, and she easily learned Spanish. She converted to Christianity and took the baptismal name

FIGURE 12.7 Cortés and Montezuma, from *Lecuzo de Tlaxcala*, sixteenth century, copied in eighteenth century Cortés is accompanied by his translator Malinche as he negotiates with the Aztec ruler Montezuma.

of Marina. Malinche was constantly at Cortés's side, interpreting and advising him on matters of policy and customs as he made his way west. The various peoples they encountered on their journey recognized her importance, calling Cortés "Malinche's Captain."

Eventually, Cortés's group marched 250 miles into the interior of Mexico and reached the Aztec capital of Tenochtitlán. There, Cortés and Malinche met with Montezuma II (1502–1520), the Aztec emperor. **Figure 12.7** depicts this meeting. This drawing was taken from a valuable cloth that was painted in the mid-sixteenth century by a Mexican tribe that helped Cortés conquer the Aztecs. (Unfortunately, the original cloth has disappeared, but a copy was made in Mexico in the eighteenth century.)

Confronting the Aztecs

By skilled use of images, the painter emphasized the role of Malinche in the conquest. In the illustration, Cortés and Malinche use the same gesture, showing that they speak with one voice. Montezuma sits in state, his nobles standing behind him. The Aztecs have gathered gifts for Cortés, drawn at the bottom of the page. The illustration foreshadows the coming European conquest: In the center of the picture, the Aztec royal headdress moves toward Cortés; in the upper-right corner, the hand of God reaches down to bless the proceedings.

Cortés knew that to transport the riches of the Aztecs back to Spain, he first had to vanquish this mighty civilization. With the help of Malinche, he garnered the support of nearly 100,000 people from neighboring tribes who were eager to throw off the Aztec yoke. Even with the advantage of gunpowder,

armor, horses, and fierce dogs, it took him nearly a year to subdue the empire, and contemporary witnesses captured the violence of the struggle. Bernal Díaz del Castillo described the capture of the last stronghold: "I have read of the destruction of Jerusalem, but I know not if that slaughter was more fearful than this—the earth, the lagoons, and the buttresses were full of corpses and the stench was more than any man could bear." In 1522, Cortés proclaimed the Aztec Empire "New Spain," and he prepared to rule. Although he had fathered a son with Malinche, he gave her as a bride to one of his soldiers and presented her with expensive estates to thank her for her help.

Aztecs conquered

The Inca Empire fell to another conquistador, Francisco Pizarro (ca. 1475–1541). In 1532, Pizarro landed on the west coast of South America and began to march to Cuzco, the Incan capital. (See Global Connections.) The Inca rulers had just endured a five-year civil war over a disputed succession, and the newly victorious ruler, Atahualpa, apparently underestimated the Spanish. Atahualpa came unguarded to meet with Pizarro, and he was promptly captured. He offered a roomful of gold as his ransom, which the Spanish accepted. After collecting the ransom, they killed their hostage. The Incas fought fiercely for a few years after the fall of their leader, but they were unable to overcome the Spanish technical advantages. A new order arose in South America.

Incas conquered

How did these small numbers of Europeans manage to conquer the impressive Amerindian empires? They gained a clear advantage from their steel weapons, horses, and high organization (including writing, which allowed them to communicate effectively). However, in the long run, their greatest weapon was biological—germs they brought from Europe. When previously isolated populations mingle, it is common for epidemics to break out, but the confrontation between Europeans and Amerindians was particularly devastating because the New World had no history of interaction with domesticated animals. The most devastating acute diseases that Eurasians faced came initially from their animals: measles, tuberculosis, flu, whooping cough, and, perhaps most deadly, smallpox. With thousands of years of exposure to these diseases, Europeans had developed immunities. Amerindians had not. In what turned out to be a biological tragedy that clinched the European conquest, disease and death followed the colonists everywhere they ventured. As one Huron woman said of the Jesuit missionaries, "They set themselves up in a village where everyone is feeling fine; no sooner are they there but everyone dies except for three or four people. They move to another place, and the same thing happens."

Germs

The Inca Empire Falls

Ten years after Hernando Cortés had sailed from Spain and conquered the Aztec Empire in Mexico in 1521, another conquistador, Francisco Pizarro, set off to seek his own fortune in the New World. He landed on the west coast of South America—which included the 2,500-mile border of the mountainous Inca Empire. (See **Map 12.3.**) The Inca ruler used a hierarchic bureaucracy to govern a population of about 11.5 million peasants.

Before Pizarro even landed in South America, the great Inca Empire had endured deep troubles. Powerful earthquakes accompanied by giant waves had pounded the coast. Lightning had struck the palace of Huayna Capac. Messengers had also told Huayna that strange beings with beards had landed on the coast. In the midst of these disasters, the ruler remembered a prophecy claiming that during the reign of the twelfth ruler, strange men would invade and destroy the empire. Huayna was the eleventh. On his deathbed, he purportedly advised his subjects to submit to the newcomers, who would surely arrive soon in fulfillment of the prophecy.

But the empire's ruling house had suffered other problems as well. Civil war between two half brothers over the succession erupted after the death of Huayna Capac. Atahualpa, Huayna's illegitimate son, challenged Huascar,

the legitimate heir. In 1533, Atahualpa captured Huascar, but resistance to Atahualpa's rule continued in the region of Cuzco. At this volatile moment, Pizarro arrived. Some of Huascar's supporters claimed that their god, Viracochas, had sent the armed men to place Huascar on the throne. This account of Inca beliefs on the eve of Pizarro's conquest was recorded in the early sixteenth century by the conquerors themselves. Historians have used it in part to explain how Pizarro—with a force of only 62 mounted men and 106 foot soldiers—could overwhelm between 100,000 and 400,000 armed Incas. Yet, it was neither their fatalism nor Pizarro's temporary alliance with Huascar that gave the Spanish the advantage; it was their technological superiority.

In the sixteenth century, warfare had honed both the weapons and the tactical skills of the Spanish. Their horses made a huge difference, adding power and reach to the mounted soldier. Pizarro wrote that the horsemen "did all the fighting, because the . . . Indians hold the footsoldiers in slight account." Furthermore, the Spanish fighters' steel swords, spears, and pikes so outmatched the Incas' most effective weapon, the sling, that the armored invaders could engage many Indians without much fear of injury themselves. Yet, even with these

advantages, the Spanish took seven years to fully conquer the extensive empire. Despite the Incas' lack of advanced weaponry, they quickly assessed the Spanish tactics and bravely exploited what weaknesses they could find.

Due to the cultural and technological chasm between the Spanish and the Incas, the conquest took on unprecedented brutality. One conquistador wrote, "I can bear witness that this is the most dreadful and cruel war in the world. For between Christians and Muslims there is some well-feeling. . . . But in this Indian war there is no such feeling on either side. They give each other the cruelest deaths they can imagine." After finally crushing the Incas, the Spanish had little inclination to treat their captives with any humanity. The early Spanish rule—with its forced labor programs—proved as brutal as the conquest itself.

Making Connections

1. How did technological differences between the Incas and the Spanish contribute to the brutality of the Spanish rule?

2. How did internal problems and Spanish military technology lead to the Incas' defeat?

North American Contacts

The fortunes of the northern Amerindians in the wake of Europeans' arrival are more difficult to recount because the first contacts between the Europeans and the northern tribes were indirect. Direct contacts in the north did not occur until twenty-five to one hundred years later than the South and Central American contacts. Thus we do not have as many eyewitness accounts for the early period in the north. Yet the effects of the Europeans' arrival were still powerfully felt there, because European

germs were able to spread to North America, where they brought diseases to the people and destroyed their societies on a large scale. Thus, when the first accounts of the northern contact were written, the authors described societies that had already been severely disrupted.

One example of the ravages of disease in the north following European contact came in the wake of the Spaniard Hernando de Soto's (ca. 1496/97–1542) landing in Florida in 1539. For four years, de Soto's small force wandered through Florida and Georgia and elsewhere in the South looking for gold. De Soto's band killed many Indians in the course of their travels, but the explorer eventually succumbed to fever and died. Many of de Soto's pigs remained to roam in the woods. As we have seen, domestic animals often served as sources of disease in early modern times, just as they do in the world today, as we are periodically confronted by animal-borne diseases such as swine flu and avian flu. De Soto's pigs similarly brought disease that spread widely through the human population. By the time the next Europeans traveled through the Mississippi valley a century later, the population had fallen steeply, by perhaps as much as 96 percent. Disease had emptied this rich land of its peoples.

Across the continent in southwestern North America, a shipwreck stranded another Spaniard, Álvar Núñez Cabeza de Vaca (ca. 1490–ca. 1560), with his three companions, who included an African slave. Cabeza de Vaca created a valuable account that told of a society already damaged by earlier contacts. For eight years, the travelers roved among the southern nomadic tribes until they encountered a Spanish colony in 1536. De Vaca wrote of hunger, hospitality, and warfare among the Amerindians, and his narratives shaped many Europeans' views of the native North Americans.

Some scholars believe that the rich environmental and animal resources the North American colonists found, from the fertile Great Plains to the innumerable buffalo herds, existed because the native peoples who had tended the land had died off, primarily from imported diseases. The North American world was transformed by the European arrival as surely as was the Southern Hemisphere.

Life and Death Under European Rule, 1550–1700

The goal of the newly established European colonial empires was to enrich the home countries. To meet this aim, the colonists exploited natural resources and Amerindian peoples to their fullest. The Spanish crown divided up the lands, placing viceroys in charge of each section. These royal representatives were responsible for delivering to the crown the profits taken from the new lands. The crown claimed one-fifth of all gold and silver mined in the New World, and the treasure ships departed the coasts of the Americas heavily laden.

To get the human labor he needed to search and mine for precious metals, Christopher Columbus proposed enslaving the native peoples. Queen Isabella rejected the plan, for she considered the New World peoples her subjects. Instead, the Spanish developed a new structure, called the **encomienda** system, to provide the conquerors with labor. Under this system, the

Enforced labor

crown would grant an encomienda, which gave conquistadors and their successors the right to the labor of a certain number of Amerindians. Theoretically, in exchange for labor, the Spanish owed the natives protection and an introduction to the Christian faith.

The encomiendas lasted only through the sixteenth century, but this system was replaced by other forms of labor servitude, like the *repartimiento*, which required adult males to devote a certain number of days of labor annually to Spanish economic enterprises, such as plantations (called **haciendas**) or mines. Sometimes these contracts stipulated a lifetime of labor (though the subject peoples remained personally free); other times, the Amerindians had to work for the Spanish for a fixed number of years. Life under these contracts proved extremely harsh— with hard labor and a shortage of food—and many laborers died while working for their new overseers.

For the Spanish, the arrangement yielded untold wealth, exemplified by the silver mine in Bolivia— the Potosí—shown in the painting in **Figure 12.8.** In the background of this picture, workers and packtrains climb steep peaks that lead to the veins of ore. The workers' homes are shown in the middle of the painting. In the foreground, other local Amerindians process the ore. First they watch a hydraulic wheel crush the raw ore; then they pound the ore with large hammers until it is reduced to powder. The waterwheel is fed by long canals that convey melting snow and rainwater from the mountain. The last step in the process was to mix the ore with mercury and convert it into a paste. This technique, brought from Europe in 1557, increased silver production tenfold. From 1580 to 1620, the great age of Spanish imperialism was financed by the silver extracted primarily from the Potosí mine.

Figure 12.8 also hints at the amount of work necessary to run sixteenth-century mines and the reason that the mine owners saw the enforced labor of the locals as essential. The Spanish crown gave the owners of the Potosí mine the conscripted labor of 13,300 Amerindians. These workers had to report to the mine on Monday morning and toil underground until Saturday evening. The mine owners did not provide meals; throughout the workweek, the men's wives had to bring them food. Many workers perished under the inhumane conditions.

Not everyone accepted this colonial brutality as a natural consequence of the need for silver. The most severe critic among these was the Dominican friar Bartolomé de Las Casas (1474–1566). In his book *The Tears of the Indians*, Las Casas wrote: "There is nothing more detestable or more cruel, than the tyranny which the Spaniards use toward the Indian." Historians have disagreed about the exact number of lives lost in the Spanish

Amerindian mortality

domination of Central and South America, but all the estimates are shocking. Diseases, overwork, and warfare took a terrible toll on indigenous people everywhere in the New World. When Columbus landed in 1492, for example, the population of the Caribbean Islands was about 6,000,000, and fifty years later, it numbered only a few thousand. The native population of Peru fell from about 1,250,000 in 1570 to just 500,000 in 1620. Mexico fared worse: About 24 million native individuals died between 1519 and 1605. Many fell victim to diseases, overwork, and the abuse that Las Casas had described. Some Europeans abhorred this destruction, but many saw it as merely a source of worry about where to get enough labor to work their mines and the plantations.

In another tragic turn of events, Las Casas proposed a solution that he thought might free the native workers from their burden of labor. He suggested that the king of Spain offer Spanish men and women a license to settle in the New World. In addition to land, each license would give permission for the holder to import a dozen African slaves to the Americas. In his old age, Las Casas recognized the problems with this policy. To his regret, the plan brought a shameful new injustice to the New World: the African slave trade.

The African Slave Trade

By the beginning of the seventeenth century, the new rulers in the Americas were facing alarming labor shortages. The original Americans had died in huge numbers just as colonists stepped up the need for labor in their profitable enterprises. As we saw earlier, mining required countless workers. The sprawling plantations built to exploit demand for new crops also desperately depended on large numbers of ill-paid workers.

Sugar is the overriding example. Although sugar-cane grew in Egypt and North Africa, it remained scarce and expensive. Europeans discovered that the cane flourished in the New World and began to cultivate it avidly in hopes of satisfying the intense European craving for its sweet flavor. Sugar also fueled a new vice—the alcoholic beverages (like rum) that it helped make. Throughout the Caribbean and in Brazil, colonists established grand sugar plantations and began using African slaves to work them. On the plantations, like the one in Barbados shown in **Figure 12.9,** workers tended the sugarcane and harvested it with large, sharp knives—a practice that often led to serious injuries. Then the cane had to be crushed to extract its juice. In this illustration, the cane is crushed in the background with grindstones.

Sugar plantations

FIGURE 12.8 Potosí Silver Mine, ca. 1584 This mine in Bolivia, worked by more than 13,000 conscripted Amerindians, supplied huge amounts of silver at great cost. The process used mercury, which polluted the waterways.

In the center, the crushed cane is cooked in vats to produce molasses, and then the product is distilled into rum (in the lower left). The whole process was guided by overseers like the one in the foreground holding his stick to beat any recalcitrant slaves.

Sugar and other plantations (for example, cotton in North America) were designed to produce enough of their specified crop to satisfy a world market. Plantation owners took a consuming interest in the success of these endeavors. Indeed, the German naturalist Maria Merian (see the Biography on page 405) wrote that she was ridiculed in the colony of Surinam, in South America, because she was interested in things other than sugar. This monoculture, or focus on a single crop, forced the plantations to trade with the rest of the world for all their remaining necessities, including labor.

As we saw in Chapter 10, slavery on a small scale began to be reintroduced into Europe during the Renaissance, and the sixteenth-century warfare escalating between Christians and Muslims stimulated even more enslavements in North Africa. For example, in 1627 Muslim pirates from the Mediterranean raided distant Iceland and enslaved nearly 400 descendants of the Vikings. Current studies suggest that between 1580 and 1680, some 850,000 Christian captives were enslaved in Muslim North Africa. Some of these captives who escaped or were ransomed engaged in their own slaving raids against Muslims as a form of revenge.

This growth of slavery between Christians and Muslims likely suggested to Europeans a solution for

FIGURE 12.9 Sugar Plantation, 1667 Sugar was the crop that brought the most wealth to plantation owners. Originally from Egypt, sugar was transplanted wherever it would grow, to satisfy soaring European tastes for sugar and rum. Slaves were brought to work the fields and the processing plants.

the labor shortages in the New World. In 1532, the first slave shipments departed from Africa to trans-

African slaves port slaves directly across the Atlantic to the plantations of the West Indies and Brazil. Before 1650, only about 7,000 slaves annually crossed the Atlantic, but the figure doubled to about 14,000 between 1650 and 1675. Before the 1680s, the Atlantic slave trade almost exclusively provided slaves for these sugar plantations. During the seventeenth century, blacks brought to North America came from the Caribbean, not directly from Africa—many had European surnames and knew a European language. A significant fraction of these early "servants for life" in North America became free, and some appear in the early records of the colonies (even in the South) as freeholders and voters. By the eighteenth century, the rise in plantations in North America caused slaves to be imported directly from Africa in large numbers (see Chapter 15).

The slave trade generated huge profits, not only for the Europeans, but also for African chiefs who sup-

Impact in Africa plied slaves to the traders. Because of long, but periodic, contact with Europe for millennia, Africans had substantial resistance to European diseases, so they survived in larger numbers than the Amerindians had. Slavery had always been part of African warfare, and as early as the seventh century, Muslims profited from slaves brought across the Sahara Desert. However, in the sixteenth century the huge profits created a new scale of trade—chiefs traded slaves to the Europeans in exchange for guns to gain advantage over their traditional rivals. Some tribes (such as the Congo in central Africa) were initially opposed to the trade but became heavily involved to stay competitive with their neighbors.

The political consequences of the trade in Africa varied. In the kingdom of the Congo, the Portuguese quest for slaves weakened the monarchy and led to local warfare and a decentralization of power. In the military kingdom of Dahomey on the west coast of Africa, kings made the slave trade a royal monopoly and profited enormously. When the trade ended, however, the resulting economic depression in Dahomey led to severe political disturbance. Although this discussion shows it is possible to treat the slave trade as one more manifestation of the growing world economy, one cannot ignore the fact that the trade of human beings rendered incalculable costs in human misery.

By 1700, traders were delivering about 30,000 slaves each year, and that number continued to escalate into the late eighteenth century. Packed tightly into the holds of ships and subjected to lack of food, water, and sanitary facilities, as many as 25 percent of these human beings died in transit. Anyone who survived the trip then faced new horrors: starvation and overwork and sometimes harsh physical discipline by their owners.

Some slaves ran away. In Brazil, in particular, many escapees fled into the forest and founded their own communities. The largest of the settlements was Palmares, which the Portuguese attacked in 1692 and destroyed three years later.

Slave rebellions Although it is impossible to get exact figures, it seems the community consisted of perhaps 10,000 fugitives who had formed a kingdom and designated a king and a council of elders. Other slaves devised more subtle forms of rebellion, including slow labor. In one interesting instance, an African woman in Surinam told the naturalist Maria Merian that the slaves practiced birth control to avoid bringing children into slavery. Although we know that Africans practiced some birth control in Africa, we cannot know for sure that it took a new purpose under slavery, but it may have.

Gathering Souls in the New Lands

Early explorers were partially motivated to travel by their desire to spread the Christian faith, and this desire only increased as Europeans found so many "heathens" around the world. Cultures all over the world became exposed to the Christian message. Many missionaries worked to alleviate the misery caused by the conquests, but others traveled from Europe with the zeal of crusaders and with the dogged insensitivity of the conquistadors. Some of them baptized natives in large groups, with no concern for their spiritual inclinations. Columbus and other early explorers, ignorant of native culture, wrote that the indigenous peoples had no religious sensibilities and thus should be easily converted. As a result, subsequent missionaries believed they were offering the benefits of religion to people who had none.

This attitude led to even further ill treatment of native peoples. In 1543, for example, the archbishop of New Spain (Mexico) tried 131 people for heresy, including 13 Aztecs, who he (rightly) believed practiced old forms of piety. In 1555, the Council of Mexico resolved not to ordain anyone of Indian, African, or mixed background—the priesthood was to be reserved for those of European descent. The suspicion extended even to churchmen sympathetic to native peoples. The Spanish crown had banned the writings of Bartolomé de Las Casas that decried Iberian treatment of Amerindians, and the Spanish Inquisition included them on its list of forbidden books.

A significant turning point in the conversion of the indigenous peoples of Mexico came in 1531, when a native convert named Juan Diego claimed to have seen the Virgin Mary. As **Virgin of Guadalupe** Diego explained it, Mary had commanded him to build a church in her honor, and when he needed proof of this command, the Virgin ordered him to gather roses within his cloak and take them to the bishop. Although it was not the season for the flower, Diego claimed to have found them and when he unfolded his cloak in the presence of the bishop, all claimed to see a miraculously formed image of the Virgin Mary left on the cloak. The Virgin of Guadalupe (named for the region near Mexico City where she reportedly appeared) became the patroness of Mexico, and Juan Diego's cloak with the Virgin's image remains in her shrine, where pilgrims gather to see it. **Figure 12.10** shows an eighteenth-century reproduction of the image on the cloak painted on wood. For many Mexicans, she lent credence to their belief that Christianity did not belong only to Europeans. Her shrine remains a major pilgrimage site today, and reproductions of the image have been widely circulated. Juan Diego, too, remained a venerated figure, and in 2002, he was declared a saint.

Some missionaries to the Americas proved acutely sensitive to the needs of the new converts and accommodated Christian practice to local religious ways. Las Casas was one such missionary; another was Marie de **Missionaries** l'Incarnation (1599–ca. 1669), a French nun who founded a convent in Quebec to teach native Canadian girls. Marie not only cared for the young women who came to her convent but also learned the Algonquin language and translated some religious writings into that language to make them accessible to the Algonquin-speaking peoples.

Missionaries generally paid more attention to the spiritual salvation of New World natives than to that of the African slaves brought to the Americas. A striking exception to this rule was the Portuguese missionary Pedro Claver (1580–1654), who has now been declared a Catholic saint. Claver settled in Colombia in 1610 and was horrified by the plight of the slaves who worked the plantations. From then on, whenever he signed his name, he added the vow "forever a servant to Africans." He lived up to that vow, converting many Africans to Christianity while caring for their physical needs. He even built and worked in a leper colony, caring for sick, neglected Africans.

Elsewhere across the world, European missionary work took on decidedly different forms than it did in the Americas. In Asia, the missionaries succeeded in their aims only after they acknowledged the validity and strengths of the local cultures. For example, some Jesuit priests in Japan adopted the status of Zen Buddhist priests and strictly observed Japanese etiquette. The Japanese were quite receptive to the missionaries, and by 1580, Jesuits claimed over 100,000 conversions in Japan. The goodwill ended in about 1600, when trade disputes unleashed a Japanese persecution of Christians that was so brutal it virtually stamped out Christianity on the

FIGURE 12.10 Virgin of Guadalupe In 1531, the Virgin Mary was said to have appeared to Juan Diego, a native convert in Mexico. This miracle was instrumental in bringing Christianity to the New World. This illustration of the Virgin of Guadalupe is by Pedro Antonio Fresquis, ca. 1790.

island. The Jesuit Roberto de Nobili in 1605 carried this policy of religious accommodation to its logical extreme in India by dressing in the robes of an Indian holy man, studying Sanskrit, and refusing all contact with fellow Europeans.

The Chinese proved more suspicious of the Westerners, at first denying them entry to their country. Nevertheless, a Jesuit—Matteo Ricci (1552–1610)—approached them with Western gifts (such as a mechanical clock) and gained admission to the court of the Ming emperor Wan-li (r. 1573–1620). While practicing his faith at the Chinese court, Ricci adopted much that was Chinese. He dressed as a Confucian scholar, for example, and preached the Christian message in terms consistent with Chinese ethics. By 1605, 17 missionaries were working in China. Not all the missionaries working in China were as tolerant as Ricci, and many condemned Confucianism as paganism.

As Christianity spread around the world, Christian practice changed as it accommodated the needs of new converts. Mexican Christians, for example, venerated the dark-skinned image of the Virgin of Guadalupe with a vigor unappreciated in Europe. Brazilian and Haitian converts worshiped in the Christian tradition, all the while acknowledging spiritual customs brought from Africa. Chinese Christians continued their practice of venerating ancestors, much to the chagrin of some European priests. In all these cases, the Catholic Church was itself transformed even as it transformed those around it. In time, Protestant worship, too, would be affected—the use of African rhythms in gospel music in modern North American churches offers one vivid example.

> Christianity transformed

THE WORLD MARKET AND COMMERCIAL REVOLUTION

Europeans had long traded over extensive distances; after all, it was the spices and silks of the Far East that had first lured them across the Atlantic. During the twelfth and thirteenth centuries, Europeans had enjoyed a growing commerce (see Chapter 8), creating northern and southern trade routes that brought goods through the Middle East from the farthest reaches of Asia. These centuries introduced a commercial revolution that greatly expanded the opportunities for many in the growing towns of the Middle Ages. However, the disasters of the fourteenth century (see Chapter 9) put the brakes on this growth, and this commercial contraction lasted almost until the middle of the sixteenth century. Now, the navigation of the seas and the exploration of new lands reopened and reshaped this pattern of production and commerce. By the end of the sixteenth century, Europeans were trading in a world market, on a scale larger than they had ever before experienced.

High Prices and Profits: Trading on the World Stage

In **Figure 12.11,** the Dutch artist Jan Vermeer (1632–1676) captures some of the themes of this new commercial age. Vermeer painted many everyday scenes praising the tranquillity and order of the prosperous Netherlands. However, these serene images also testify to the bustling world market that made middle-class townspeople so wealthy. Indeed, the lifestyle hinted at in this painting would have been unimaginable in the Middle Ages. Vermeer depicts a young woman gently grasping a water pitcher. The pitcher is made of silver, possibly from the Potosí mine in Bolivia (see **Figure 12.8**). The jewel box to the right of the pitcher lies open, revealing pearls, probably from the Orient. Both objects are set on a tablecloth of tapestry from India. The woman's clothing is made of oriental silk—an unusual luxury for everyday dress. Even the woman's movement to open a window suggests wealth, for expensive, leaded glass windows originally had been used only in churches. Vermeer completes this picture of prosperity with a leather map of the world hanging on the wall—a fitting symbol of the new global commerce.

What exactly stepped up the global demand for luxury goods? In part, the demand was fueled by population growth in the sixteenth and seventeenth centuries. During the sixteenth century, the number of Europeans expanded from about 80 million to 105 million as Europe recovered from the devastation of the Black Death. These increases continued. As the population steadily rose, goods became scarce. Demand intensified and drove prices up. In the sixteenth century, cereal prices escalated about fivefold, and the price of manufactured goods tripled. Contemporary witnesses repeatedly expressed shock at the inflation. As one sixteenth-century Spaniard lamented, "Today a pound of mutton costs as much as a whole sheep used to." People complained, but no one had concrete solutions to the problem.

> Inflation

At mid-century, some Europeans began blaming the influx of precious metals from the New World for their inflation woes. Their frustration was understandable. The Potosí mine alone yielded millions of Spanish coins a year, which poured unchecked into the European economy, moving rapidly from one country to the next. As just one example of the interconnected economy, the massive Spanish ships that transported silver across the Atlantic depended on French canvas for their sails. Silver coins from the New World paid for those sails. As one French author wrote, "They may have the ships, but we have their wings." Economists can trace Spanish silver from Europe to as far as China, where European merchants snapped up the silks and spices that initially inspired the explorations. Yet the flood of coins into Europe was only part of the picture. In truth, the price revolution stemmed from a combination of the new money, a surge in population growth, and unprecedented appetites for new goods.

The Rise of Commercial Capitalism

Inflation always hurts those with fixed incomes, but high prices also provide incentives for enterprising people to make a profit. The energetic sixteenth-

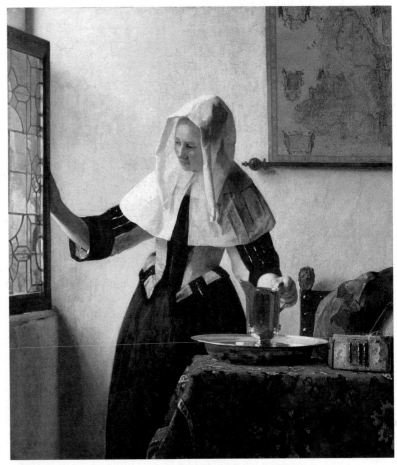

FIGURE 12.11 Jan Vermeer, *Young Woman with a Water Pitcher,* ca. 1664 The global trade brought wealth to new merchant classes. They could then afford beautiful art that celebrated their new acquisitions, such as glass windows, silver pitchers, woven tapestries, and even a world map for the wall.

century pursuit of trade stimulated new forms of production and economic concepts that together have been called the commercial revolution, but might more accurately be termed a commercial acceleration, during which trading practices developed in the Middle Ages spread and flourished. During this vital era, a set of business practices (and perceptions) arose that we know as capitalism. The word *capitalism* was actually not used until the nineteenth century. By the mid-seventeenth century, however, some individuals were called **capitalists,** a word indicating how they handled money. Capitalists were people who chose to invest their funds in business activities in order to make more money (capital). For these **entrepreneurs,** the most lucrative business opportunity was the growing world trade. Document 12.2 presents a seventeenth-century testimonial on the benefits of this long-distance trade.

Dutch entrepreneurs led the way in implementing capitalist ideas as they engaged in worldwide trade. For example, merchants in Amsterdam built huge warehouses to store goods so that they could control

Thomas Mun Praises Trade

Thomas Mun (1571–1641) was a director in the East India Company, and in 1630 he wrote "Discourse on England's Treasure by Foreign Trade," which was published in 1664. In this excerpt, Mun shows that he shared the mercantilist view that trade could enrich the kingdom.

Although a Kingdom may be enriched by gifts received, or by purchase taken from some other Nations, yet these are things uncertain and of small consideration when they happen. The ordinary means therefore to increase our wealth and treasure is by Foreign Trade, wherein we must ever observe this rule: to sell more to strangers yearly than we consume of theirs in value. For suppose that when this Kingdom is plentifully served with the Cloth, Lead, Tin, Iron, Fish and other native commodities, we do yearly export the overplus to foreign countries to the value of twenty-two hundred thousand pounds; by which means we are enabled beyond the Seas to buy and bring in foreign wares for our use and Consumptions, to the value of twenty hundred thousand pounds: By this order duly kept in our trading, we may rest assured that the kingdom shall be enriched yearly two hundred thousand pounds, which must be brought to us in so much Treasure; because that part of our stock which is not returned to us in wares must necessarily be brought home in treasure. . . .

Let Princes oppress, Lawyers extort, Usurers bite, Prodigals wast, and lastly let Merchants carry out what money they shall have occasion to use in traffique. Yet all these actions can work no other effects in the course of trade than is declared in this discourse. For so much Treasure only will be brought in or carried out of a Commonwealth, as the foreign Trade doth over or under balance in value. And this must come to pass by a Necessity beyond all resistance. So that all other courses (which tend not to this end) howsoever they may seem to force money into a Kingdom for a time, yet are they (in the end) not only fruitless but also hurtful; they are like to violent flouds which bear down their banks, and suddenly remain dry again for want of waters.

Behold then the true form and worth of foreign trade, which is *The great Revenue of the King. The honour of the Kingdom. The Noble profession of the Merchant. The School of our Arts. The supply of our wants. The employment of our poor. The improvement of our Lands. The Nursery of our Mariners. The walls of the Kingdoms. The means of our Treasure. The Sinnews of our wars. The terror of our Enemies.* For all which great and weighty reasons, do so many well-governed States highly countenance the profession, and carefully cherish the action, not only with Policy to increase it, but also with power to protect it from all foreign injuries; because they know it is a Principal in Reason of State to maintain and defend that which doth support them and their estates.

SOURCE: Thomas Mun, from *England's Treasure By Forraign Trade*, 1664, in *Modern History Sourcebook*, www.fordham.edu/halsall/mod/1664mun-engtrade.html.

Analyze the Document

1. What benefits does Mun say will accompany a vigorous foreign trade?

2. What does he consider a favorable balance of trade? How are these views consistent with mercantilist thought, and how do they differ from your understanding of modern economic life?

supplies and keep prices high. Through new strategies like this and through individual initiative (rather than through government policy), the Netherlands became the leading commercial center in Europe in the sixteenth century. Indeed, it was this very success that generated the wealth depicted in the households painted by Vermeer.

Capitalist ideas

Capitalist initiative gave rise to fluctuations in demand for goods. We can follow an early example of this economic cycle in the tulip industry. Tulips originally were imported into the Netherlands from Turkey, in the sixteenth century. A Dutch botanist discovered how to grow the many varied colors of this versatile flower. By 1634, buyers not only in the Netherlands but also all over Europe were so enthralled by the exotic and beautiful plants that one rare tulip bulb sold for 1,000 pounds of cheese, four oxen, eight pigs, twelve sheep, a bed, and a suit of clothes. Investors rushed to take advantage of the lucrative tulip market and the supply of the bulbs ballooned. Three years later, however, the increased supply drove down the price, ruining many who had gambled on the rare flower. Novice capitalists learned the hard way about the cruel whims of the market economy.

People with moderate means also yearned to participate in promising financial ventures. To accommodate them, businesses built upon medieval concepts of trading partnerships and developed an innovative entity called the **joint-stock company.** This new economic structure allowed ordinary investors to buy shares in commercial ventures that were run by boards of directors. With successes in such investments, modest capitalists might generate enough money to set out on their own and gamble on higher-risk opportunities. These joint-stock companies made

Joint-stock companies

it easier to raise enough capital for trading ventures around the world. Amsterdam was the site of the first stock exchange, and enterprising people in the colony of New York began trading shares at a tree at the end of Wall Street.

In the seventeenth century, English and Dutch merchants formed exceptionally efficient joint-stock companies that helped them dominate trade in Asia: the English East India Company, founded in 1600, and the Dutch United East India Company, known by its initials VOC (Vereenigde Oost-Indische Compagnie), founded in 1602. Although both companies enjoyed government support, they were privately owned by merchant investors. Their charters granted them remarkable powers—they could buy, sell, and even wage war in the companies' interests. These companies immediately generated huge profits, and both contributed to the early formation of a global network of trade.

Mercantilism: Controlling the Balance of Trade

With so much money at stake, western European governments attempted centralized regulation of their economies—**mercantilism**—to profit from the expanded global trade. Mercantilism was based on the assumption that the amount of worldwide wealth was fixed, so countries competed to get a larger piece of the pie. This was essentially economic nationalism, in which governments controlled their economies to increase their acquisition of hard currency. The simple principle "buy low, sell high" led these governments to discourage imports, particularly expensive ones, and encourage exports. In 1586, one Spanish bureaucrat asked King Philip II to forbid the import of candles, glass trinkets, jewelry, cutlery, and other such items, because these sorts of "useless" luxuries drained away precious Spanish gold. Such policies aimed to create a favorable balance of trade and fill bank vaults with gold.

Economic nationalism

Mercantilist governments passed laws to ensure a favorable trade balance. They imposed tariffs on imports and discouraged manufacturing in their colonies to force them to buy exports from the home country. Thus, hard currency would flow from the colonies to enrich royal treasuries in Europe. In fact, mercantilist policy encouraged the founding of new colonies to create new markets to purchase European exports. When other things failed, governments debased their coins to try to maintain a favorable balance.

Economic regulations

Some governments even tried to keep wages low so that citizens would have little discretionary income with which to buy expensive imports. All these efforts were meant to enrich the states, not the fortunes of wealthy citizens. Mercantilist policies placed the state before the individual. They achieved their goal, vastly enriching the powerful monarchies of western Europe. Sadly, they also financed the destructive wars that swept over Europe through the mid-seventeenth century (discussed in Chapter 11). Mercantilist economic policy would continue to shape government policy into the eighteenth century (as we will see in Chapter 15).

The Growth of Banking

Neither private capitalism nor mercantilism could have succeeded without innovations in banking practices. Medieval ideas that forbad charging interest and that kept royal treasuries locked in chests in royal bedrooms had become obsolete. In this new age, people needed easier access to a lot of money, and they refined banking techniques that had been developed in the late Middle Ages in the Italian cities of the Renaissance. Medieval bankers had developed bills of exchange and complex account books to facilitate commerce, but in the late fifteenth century, bankers added checks, bank drafts, and sophisticated double-entry bookkeeping to their skills, all of which made commercial ventures easier than ever.

Through the sixteenth century, private bankers handled most financial transactions. The Fuggers of Germany were the most successful at this profession, taking over a role that the Medicis in Florence had dominated in the fifteenth century. The Fugger family became so wealthy that they even lent money to Emperor Charles V. With the emergence of mercantilist ideas about economics serving the state, this kind of practice waned. Instead, government banks developed that controlled profits going to individuals. The Bank of Amsterdam was founded in 1609, followed by the Bank of Sweden in 1657, and the Bank of England in 1694. However, new banking policies could not ensure that even mercantilist governments would grow rich.

State banks

The Danger of Overspending: Spain Learns a Lesson

At first, Europeans believed that the wealth flowing into Europe from the New World was the primary payoff from their explorations. Entire countries became rich, and imperial powers grew in previously unheard-of ways. Spain immediately capitalized on the new wealth, its treasure ships offering unlimited prosperity and power to the monarchs. Yet, the vast influx of silver was deceiving, and the Spanish king spent it wastefully on the incessant wars that dominated the sixteenth and early seventeenth centuries.

Consequently, the Spanish crown had to declare bankruptcy several times in the course of the sixteenth and seventeenth centuries. Spain's financial troubles hurt merchants in Germany and Italy, but the real burden fell on the Spanish taxpayers, who were soon saddled with debt. Instead of relieving their debt burdens, the politics of empire only added to them. Domination of the New World passed to the governments of other countries (notably Holland and England) that proved more efficient in fiscal matters.

Ultimately, much of the gold and silver that motivated the expansionist countries did not even end up in Europe. A large percentage of this currency eventually flowed to the East for the purchase of luxury items. As Spain discovered, these precious metals were not enough to keep profligate governments in power.

Redefining Work Roles

The commercial revolution both enlarged the scale of business and redefined the way people viewed their work. While most people still worked the land, in the cities, which served as the nerve centers of the new economies, people experienced the most remarkable shifts in how they made | Women's work | their living. As the middle class rose to economic power on the dual waves of trade and hard work, the lives of urban women in particular diverged dramatically from earlier times. In the early Middle Ages, women had labored in the stores and workshops of Europe's cities. They dominated trades that they had controlled in the home—textile making and brewing, for example. Women had such a presence in these fields that feminine forms of certain words (ending in *ster*) derived from these jobs—for instance, *webster* (from *weaver*) and *brewster* (from *brewer*)—arose and even became common surnames. Women also owned taverns in such numbers that an instruction manual written for merchants in 1515 assumed that the innkeeper would be a woman and gave instructions on "how to ask the *hostess* how much one has spent."

Still, women's access to the workforce came primarily through their families. Daughters, like most sons, mastered trades in the family workshops, just as Maria Merian (in the Biography on page 405) learned printing from her stepfather. Wives worked with their husbands, and widows frequently ran businesses and took their husbands' place in the guilds. During the late Middle Ages, men slowly began to replace women in some of the most lucrative jobs, like cloth making, and just as in banking and commercial enterprises, this late-medieval trend accelerated in the early modern period.

Into the sixteenth century, as work generated more capital and power, it began losing its association with the family and became more linked to the public political arena. Many people (women and men alike) believed that public work and control of money were more appropriately managed by men than women. Late in the sixteenth century, cities accordingly began to issue ordinances restricting women's entry into guilds, which had taken on markedly political overtones. For example, a ruling in France in 1583 limited silk-making apprentices (who had previously been predominantly female) to only two males per master. In another example, a 1508 ordinance in the Netherlands referred to a "brotherhood and sisterhood" of a guild, but the reissued ordinance in 1552 mentioned only a "brotherhood of trimmers." By 1563, when the ordinances were again revised, even widows' rights had been omitted.

Similar examples emerged at local levels throughout Europe. As the commercial revolution spread and urban merchants grew powerful, the old divisions of those who worked and those who did not began to blur. Instead, the growing middle class began to divide the world between those who worked outside the home in the public, political arena and those who worked inside the home. Urban women, relegated increasingly to the domestic sphere, lost much of their visibility in the public arena.

Piracy: Banditry on a World Scale, 1550–1700

The expansion of trade into the Atlantic and Pacific brought with it another nettlesome problem: a rise in piracy. Piracy was as old as Mediterranean shipping, when seagoing robbers had preyed mercilessly on the ponderous merchant roundships that moved goods through the inland sea. As the pace of the world economy quickened, pirates moved to take advantage. From about 1550 to about 1700, a "pirate belt" developed that stretched from the West Indies to East Asia. The new entrepreneurial raiding coincided with the weakening of the great Turkish, Spanish, and Chinese empires that we saw in Chapter 11, because these navies could no longer effectively patrol their territorial waters.

Piracy as a way of life actually had a somewhat benign origin—monarchs had often issued licenses for people to steal from other countries in unofficial warfare. Before the seventeenth century, the word *pirate* rarely appeared. | Early privateers | Instead, seagoing raiders were called **privateers** or corsairs, terms meaning that they had the authorization of formal commissions from their rulers. Even as late as the eighteenth century, the

BIOGRAPHY

Maria Sibylla Merian

(1647–1717)

Maria Sibylla was born in Frankfurt, Germany, the daughter of a well-known engraver and publisher and his second wife, Johanna. Maria's father also had a keen interest in the explorations of the age. He published editions of *Grands et Petits Voyages,* which contained accounts of journeys to the New World (including the illustration shown in **Figure 12.6**). Although he died in 1650 when Maria was only 3 years old, she grew up to excel in the same fields that had so captivated her father. Maria's mother married a painter and art dealer, and the young girl cultivated her artistic interests and skills in her stepfather's workshop.

In her later years, Maria remembered acquiring an additional passion: "I have been concerned with the study of insects. This led me to collect all the caterpillars I could find in order to study their metamorphoses . . . and to work at my painter's art so that I could sketch them from life and represent them in lifelike colors."

FIGURE 12.12 Maria Sibylla Merian
Frontispiece to Merian, *Der Rupsen,* 1717.

Maria married Johann Andreas Graff, an artist and publisher, in 1665, and the couple had two daughters. Ten years later, she published her first book of copperplate engravings. This work consisted solely of illustrations of flowers and some insects. It contained no text but was used to provide patterns for artists and embroiderers, who preferred to work from an illustration rather than from life. This work established Merian's reputation as an artist and naturalist, and she was included in a contemporary book on German art.

A few years later, she published *Wonderful Transformation and Singular Flower-Food of Caterpillars.* This work contained her detailed observations and commentaries on the habits of caterpillars and was hailed as "amazing."

Yet Merian's scientific work was soon interrupted by dramatic changes in her personal life. In 1685, she was consumed with a fervor for religious renewal. With her elderly mother and two daughters, she joined a radical Protestant sect, the Labadists, in the Netherlands. The group established a community of the "elect," who held their property in common and lived in isolation from what they saw as a sinful world. When Merian's husband pleaded with her to return to him and bring home their daughters, she refused. He acquired a divorce and remarried.

After some years, the closed Labadist community must have felt too confining to the talented, curious Merian. She and her daughters left the group and settled in Amsterdam, the thriving port city that bustled with exotic goods and hummed with exciting tales of travel.

Recognized for her previous work, Merian was welcomed into the circle of naturalists in Amsterdam.

Despite the attractions of her new life, Merian continued to find fascination in insects. In 1699, she and her daughter Dorothea sailed from Amsterdam to Surinam, the Dutch colony on the northern shore of South America. The Labadists had established a community there, but it had failed due to the hardships of the tropics. Merian might well have heard about Surinam during her earlier stay with the Labadists and decided to go there to study tropical insects, butterflies, and plants.

The devoted naturalist lived in Surinam for two years. With the help of Amerindians and African slaves, she collected thousands of specimens and made hundreds of drawings of plant and insect species unknown in Europe. In 1701, she returned to Amsterdam, and several years later she published *Metamorphosis of the Insects of Surinam* in both Dutch and Latin. Her drawings were praised as "the most beautiful work ever painted in America" (see **Figure 12.15**). Merian lived the rest of her days in Amsterdam, consulted by other naturalists and continuing to seek out interesting new caterpillar specimens. Merian died in 1717, and in that year her daughter published a collection of her mother's work, including the image shown in **Figure 12.12.** Merian's books remained widely read by naturalists well into the next century.

Naturalist, Artist, and Traveler

Connecting People & Society

1. How did the Reformation and the age of exploration open up opportunities for Merian?

2. What evidence does this life offer about a growing scientific curiosity about the West?

3. What does this account tell us about the position of and opportunities for women?

United States Constitution gave Congress the right to issue letters of marque and reprisal, essentially to hire pirate ships. Privateers earned their profits from captured booty, and in the freewheeling raids that took place on the open seas, it was impossible to distinguish them from pirates acting on their own. The ships that were robbed probably did not draw any distinction between the two.

The difficulties of discerning pirate from privateer may be seen in the case of the famous early English privateers, particularly Francis Drake (ca. 1540–1596). By 1571, Drake had become a major force in the Caribbean, and this champion of the British was considered a ruthless pirate by the Spanish. Drake had numerous bases on land and gained the admiration and support of unconquered Amerindians and Spanish-hating escaped slaves. With the backing and affection of Queen Elizabeth I (r. 1558–1603), Drake and his fellow privateers relentlessly harassed the Spanish ships they found sailing in the Caribbean.

The fortunes of Drake's compatriot Walter Raleigh (ca. 1554–1618) showed how fragile royal support of these independent captains could be. Elizabeth backed Raleigh in his flamboyant enterprises, even knighting her champion. However, her successor, James I (r. 1603–1625) found the privateer less useful. As James began to have political difficulties with English Protestants, he sought an alliance with Spain (as we will see in Chapter 13). As a token of goodwill to Spain, James imprisoned Raleigh in the Tower of London and executed him in 1618.

Pirates included many Africans who had been captured as slaves, because after seizing wealthy slave-trading ships, pirates frequently gave the slaves the choice to continue on their way or join the pirate band. The eighteenth-century trial records of a pirate on the ship Pirate life *Whydah* indicate that about 30 to 50 of the men on his ship were African and 1 was an Amerindian. The freedom of the pirate life drew many who had few choices elsewhere.

With all its hazards—from fickle royal supporters to war on the high seas—the pirate life could bring amazing riches even for those without a royal patron. Pirate cities sprang up based solely on the illicit trade. For example, Algiers in North Africa became a prosperous Muslim pirate city, and Malta in the Mediterranean was its Christian counterpart. Other pirate cities dotted the Caribbean from the coast of the Yucatán to the islands of the West Indies. These cities served as havens for the violent, reckless sea raiders and their families. They also were places where talented outsiders could rise to positions of considerable power. For example, a poor North African shepherd boy rose through the pirate ranks to become "king" of Algiers in 1569. During the eighteenth century, several women even took command of pirate ships.

By the mid-eighteenth century, however, governments had begun expanding their navies and set out to suppress the buccaneers. The British admiralty discouraged privateering because it lured sailors away from serving in the navy. The age of informal warfare came to a close and accounts of the bandits' careers retreated to literary works that romanticized their lives. For example, literary pirates made their victims walk the plank; real pirates would not have wasted time on such rituals. If they wanted to kill their captives, they unceremoniously threw them overboard.

THE WORLD TRANSFORMED

The booming world market that stimulated the movement of goods and the enterprise of pirates also served to spread other aspects of European culture around the world. During the sixteenth century, more than 200,000 Spanish people, 10 percent of them women, migrated to Latin America. In the next century, comparable numbers of English, French, and Dutch settled in North America. These immigrants became a new ruling class that transfused much of European culture into the New World. They built cities featuring the grid pattern that marked Renaissance urban planning and placed their churches in the city centers.

KEY DATES

EXPLORING THE WORLD

1492	Columbus sails to North America
1494	Treaty of Tordesillas
1497	John Cabot lands in North America
1498	Vasco da Gama rounds Africa
1499	Amerigo Vespucci maps New World
1514	Portuguese reach China
1519–1521	Magellan's crew circumnavigates globe
1522	Cortés conquers Aztec Empire
1531	Virgin of Guadalupe appears
1532	African slave trade begins
1532	Pizarro conquers Incan Empire
1534	Jacques Cartier explores Canada
1577–1580	Francis Drake circumnavigates the world
1607	Jamestown colony founded
1620	English establish colony at Plymouth, Massachusetts

European Culture Spreads

The new immigrants brought their languages and religions, but also unique livestock, tools, plants, and other goods that transformed the lives of native peoples. When European horses escaped (or were stolen), for example, some indigenous peoples took them into their midst. The Plains Indians in the southwest of North America soon made horses central to their way of life. In time, guns, liquor, and many other goods also found their way into the many native cultures.

Plants from Europe, some of them intentionally cultivated, made their mark on the New World as well. For example, Europeans brought wheat to make the bread that had long served as their dietary staple. Along with their domesticated plants, they transported their traditional farming **Plants** methods. **Figure 12.13** shows Amerindians cultivating wheat on a Spanish plantation. The laborers use the same kinds of tools, including the overburdened donkey in the lower-left corner, that their European peasant counterparts had employed.

Europeans unwittingly altered the ecology of the New World in many other ways. As we have seen, they brought diseases that ravaged native populations. Less destructive but equally ubiquitous, plants transported to the New World spread with vigor. A sixteenth-century Inca observer (Garcilaso de la Vega) described how quickly the ecology of Peru had been transformed by invasive plants: "Some of them are becoming mischievous, such as the mustard, mint, and camomile, which have spread . . . [and] the first endives and spinach multiplied in such a way that a horse could not force its way through them." Inadvertent transportation of weed seeds also displaced native species. Dandelions are a particularly apt example of a European weed that spread accidentally as people, plants, and animals moved across the sea.

Europeans traveling and trading in Africa and Asia took New World plants to other regions of the world, transforming local consumption habits and economies. Africa, for example, received sweet potatoes and maize in the sixteenth century. In the Congo, the Portuguese introduced maize, although at first the tribes dismissed the vegetable as more suitable for pigs than human beings. In time, these plants became so central to the local culture that people no longer remembered that they were once strange imports. Because the societies of east Asia kept most Europeans at arm's length, they were less influenced by European culture than were the peoples of North and South America, and it would take several more centuries for European trade to exert its full impact in that region.

FIGURE 12.13 New Plants and Animals The spread of Europeans reshaped the New World's ecology. This image shows one such change as Amerindians plant wheat, a European crop, with metal tools, aided by an imported donkey.

Finally, the populations themselves mixed as immigrants settled among native societies. Because European men greatly outnumbered women from their home continent, many of them married native and slave women or **Population mixing** kept them as concubines. Generations of children born of mixed background, called *mestizos*, preserved aspects of both their parents' cultures. These generations ultimately made the Americas vastly different from Europe in spite of common languages, religions, and political structures.

Figure 12.14 reveals much about the cultural blending that marked the Americas.

European Culture Transformed

Europeans were as much transformed by contact with the New World as the original Americans were by their European conquerors. In one of the less savory examples of this exchange, the earliest explorers to the New World probably brought back a virulent form of syphilis. New archaeological excavations have revealed that some form of syphilis existed in Europe from classical times, but this new strain of the sexually transmitted disease ravaged Europe until the twentieth century, when the advent of penicillin offered a cure. The disease never took the kind of toll on Europeans that plagues such as smallpox and

FIGURE 12.14

Festival Scene Painted on a Screen, Mexico, ca. 1650

Many artists have a talent for portraying life at a particular time and documenting its distinguishing aspects. This painting by an unknown artist captures the blending of cultures that took place in the villages of Mexico in the seventeenth century. Notice the mestizos spinning on a pole in a traditional Amerindian celebration, and the hazy, dreamlike Spanish castles in the background.

Connecting Art & Society

1. What clothing do the participants wear? How is this evidence of cultural blending?

2. What other festival features can you identify, and how might such celebrations have served to join the community together?

3. What might the artist have intended by placing the castles of his homeland in this picture?

4. What conclusions can you draw about the blending of cultures in Mexico from this painting?

measles imposed on native populations. Nevertheless, its presence caused much misery and made some people more cautious about sexual activity.

New foods changed Europeans' diets and even the landscape. It is difficult to imagine Ireland without the hardy, nutritious potatoes that flourish today in that rocky land, but until the conquest of the Incas, the population of Ireland had to struggle to sustain **New foods** itself. The tomato—a New World fruit that people first rejected as poisonous—was eventually embraced as an aphrodisiac and became an often-used ingredient in European cuisine. Maize spread more slowly, for Europeans, like the Africans, did not initially view it as a food fit for humans. However, as early as 1500, it began thriving in Spain, from where it soon spread to Italy (near Venice) and eventually to the rest of Europe. Maize had immediate use as animal feed and peasant fare and allowed farming families to sell their more expensive wheat.

In addition to new staples, certain food stimulants from the Americas proved enormously popular in Europe. Chocolate, for example, came to Spain from Aztec Mexico in about 1520 in the form of loaves and tablets that were **New stimulants** boiled into a drink. A luxury at first, chocolate had become a common beverage by the eighteenth century. Tea, too, had been a rare treat in the Middle Ages, when some traders brought small amounts from China. Over time, more and more Europeans developed an unquenchable thirst for tea, making the East India Company rich in the process.

Coffee appeared in Europe for the first time in the early seventeenth century and replaced tea and chocolate as the most popular stimulant drink. Coffee seems to have first come from Africa and then spread to the Muslim lands—it was in Mecca by 1511, and Istanbul in 1517. By 1615, coffee had reached Venice, and merchants spread the product rapidly through Europe from there. Physicians praised the drink as medicinal for many ailments, from heart disease to "short breath, colds which attack the lungs, and worms." By the eighteenth century, coffee was so central to European society that even the social life of the West began to be centered at coffee shops.

But it was tobacco that made the biggest impression on European culture. Columbus saw Amerindians smoking it and brought the plant back home as an object of curiosity. Europeans cultivated tobacco at first for medicinal purposes—one sixteenth-century Parisian claimed **Tobacco** that it cured all ills—and the plant then spread rapidly all over the world. By the mid-seventeenth century, it had reached as far as China, where virtually the entire population took up the smoking habit. The difficulties of planting tobacco also stimulated settlement expansion. Because the crop rapidly depletes the soil, in an age without chemical fertilizers colonists seeking to profit from the lucrative crop constantly had to annex and cultivate new lands.

The New World's reshaping of European culture unfolded slowly. New products became available gradually, whetting appetites for yet more novelties. The commercial revolution stimulated the movement of goods all over the world, creating more and more demand, which fueled further explorations and commerce. Ironically, the demand for spices, and particularly pepper, that had originally served as the main force behind the voyages of exploration waned by the eighteenth century. Europeans had found other, more intriguing products to satisfy their restless desire for culinary novelties.

A New Worldview

When Europeans first set off across the seas, they had a false, though highly imaginative, view of what they would find. The world proved larger and far more diverse than they had ever imagined, and travelers began to study and write about the new reality. Amerigo Vespucci, the Italian mapmaker and chronicler we met earlier, wrote with awe in 1499 about New World flora: "The trees were so beautiful and so fragrant that we thought we were in a terrestrial paradise. Not one of those trees or its fruit was like those in our part of the globe." Such early descriptions were followed by systematic studies in the seventeenth century. For example, in 1648 a Dutch prince sponsored an expedition that published the *Natural History of Brazil*, followed by many other books by naturalists cataloging the wonders of the Americas.

Figure 12.15 shows an illustration from *Metamorphosis of the Insects of Surinam* by Maria Sibylla Merian (1647–1717) (see Biography). In this painstakingly rendered illustration, one can see both the detail that marked these kinds of studies and the artist's fascination with the exotic. Merian drew a guava tree (one of the fruits that Vespucci had found so strange) populated with spiders and ants. In the drawing, most of the spiders are eating ants. One of them, however, is shown attacking a nest of hummingbird eggs. Here Merian was illustrating a story told to her by the Surinam locals. (In fact, spider attacks on birds' nests are extremely rare.) This illustration, with its blend of careful attention to detail and elements of fantasy, typifies the European fascination with the newly discovered world.

The new maps created as explorers traveled the global coastlines and great rivers were almost as

Scientific observations

FIGURE 12.15 "Spiders and Ants on a Guava Tree," *Metamorphosis*, **plate 18, ca. 1705** Maria Sibylla Merian's careful study and drawings of New World plants and animals generated excitement and awakened scientific curiosity in Europe. She was just one of many such observers.

precise as the naturalists' drawings. These representations offered a much more realistic picture of the world than Ptolemy's map that guided Columbus. The map in **Figure 12.16** shows the globe flattened out. This projection method, which let sailors plot straight-line courses, was developed by the Flemish cartographer Gerhard Mercator (1512–1594), who first published it in 1569. Many modern European maps are still based on this technique.

Mercator maps

The **Mercator projection** was a huge step forward in mapmaking, but it still allowed for some measure of geographic illusion. By flattening out the map and placing Europe in the center, mapmakers could not help distorting their graphic representation of the world. Greenland, for example, appears much larger than it is, India becomes smaller, and Asia is divided, thus seeming to have less mass than it really does. Not surprisingly, the Mercator map encouraged the illusion that Europeans occupied the center of the world. This idea shaped Europeans' future mapmaking techniques and their attitudes and actions toward the rest of the globe.

FIGURE 12.16 Mercator Map, 1608   The explorers mapped the world and in doing so replaced Ptolemy's vision, shown in Figure 12.2. However, the popular Mercator map kept Europe in the center and skewed the perspective of the rest of the world.

LOOKING BACK *&* MOVING FORWARD

Summary   By the early sixteenth century, Western culture was no longer contained within Europe. Lured by faith, fame, and fortune, Europeans sailed all over the world. They also settled in the newfound lands, conquering and colonizing the Americas and establishing trading posts in the East. Merchants and entrepreneurs followed the explorers and established a world market that stimulated the growth of commercial capitalism, new banking techniques, and widespread popular interest in economic opportunity. Some governments began to set economic policy and tried to control the flow of money to and from their countries.

In this great movement of peoples and confrontation of cultures, Europeans generated enormous wealth—and equally unprecedented misery. Native populations were virtually eliminated by warfare, disease, and abuse, and hundreds of thousands of Africans were enslaved and taken by force from their homelands. The resultant blending of peoples, ideas, and goods profoundly affected the entire world and whetted European appetites for yet more exploration and conquest.

KEY TERMS

quadrant,   *p. 384*

astrolabe,   *p. 384*

conquistadors,   *p. 393*

encomienda,   *p. 396*

haciendas,   *p. 396*

capitalists,   *p. 401*

entrepreneurs,   *p. 401*

joint-stock company,   *p. 402*

mercantilism,   *p. 403*

privateers,   *p. 404*

Mercator projection,   *p. 409*

REVIEW, ANALYZE, & CONNECT TO TODAY

REVIEW THE PREVIOUS CHAPTERS

Chapter 10—"A New Spirit in the West"—analyzed the revolution in thought that we have come to call the Renaissance, and in Chapter 11—"Alone Before God"—we saw how the new ideas were put into practice in religion. Chapter 11 also told the story of the struggles of European states as they competed with one another to claim superiority.

1. Review the characteristics of Renaissance thought and consider how they contributed to the sixteenth-century interest in discovering previously unknown areas of the world.

2. Review the Chapter 11 discussion of sixteenth-century European warfare and religious reforms. How did these wars and reforms affect the global exploration that was occurring at the same time?

ANALYZE THIS CHAPTER

Chapter 12—"Faith, Fortune, and Fame"—describes and analyzes the European explorations and conquests that spread Western culture around the world and, in turn, transformed Europe.

1. Review the areas of Spanish and Portuguese exploration, and consider where these early efforts forced England, France, and the Netherlands to focus their attention. Which areas turned out to be most profitable in the long run? Why?

2. Consider the complex relationship between technology, commercial exchange, and the lure of exploration and conquest, and review how this relationship was expressed in this chapter.

3. What advantages did the Spanish have in their conquests in the New World? How did the Spanish perceptions of the natives shape their treatment of them?

CONNECT TO TODAY

Think about the ways in which the medieval world was changed through sudden globalization—the movement and spread of peoples, ideas, religions, and goods.

1. Have the high levels of global trade and immigration in contemporary times led to a similarly escalated global transformation? Explain.

2. Which of the transformations described in this chapter has had the largest influence on today's world? Why?

BEYOND THE CLASSROOM

THE WORLD IMAGINED

Friedman, John Block. *The Monstrous Races in Medieval Art and Thought.* Cambridge, MA: Harvard University Press, 1981. The best study on this subject—scholarly, fascinating, and well illustrated.

Russell, Jeffrey B. *Inventing the Flat Earth: Columbus and Modern Historians.* Westport, CT: Greenwood, 1991. Studies the origin of the myth that only Columbus believed the earth was round.

THE WORLD DISCOVERED

Greenhill, Basil. *The Evolution of the Sailing Ship, 1250–1589.* Annapolis, MD: Naval Institute Press, 1996. A clear explanation of the technology of sailing ships that does not get bogged down in unduly technical language.

Subrahmanyam, Sanjay. *The Portuguese Empire in Asia, 1500–1700: A Political and Economic History.* New York: Longman, 1993. A comprehensive look at the economic and diplomatic history of the whole Portuguese Asian empire.

CONFRONTATION OF CULTURES

Benjamin, Thomas. *The Atlantic World: Europeans, Africans, Indians, and Their Shared History, 1400–1900.* Cambridge: Cambridge University Press, 2009. Comprehensive, smart, and clearly written account of the human interactions that transformed the world.

Berlin, Ira. *Many Thousands Gone.* Cambridge, MA: Harvard University Press, 1998. A sensitive study of the changing nature of the history of African-American slavery in mainland North America.

Diamond, Jared. *Guns, Germs, and Steel.* New York: W.W. Norton, 1997. A Pulitzer Prize–winning analysis of the interactions of cultures around the world that is utterly riveting.

Fagan, Brian M. *Clash of Cultures.* New York: W.H. Freeman, 1984. Concentrates on the first period of European exploration and settlement beginning in 1488.

Fritze, Ronald H. *New Worlds: The Great Voyages of Discovery, 1400–1600.* Westport, CT: Praeger, 2003. A balanced history of European expansion showing the historical roots of the explorations and detailing the voyages of Henry the Navigator, Columbus, da Gama, and Cabot.

Karlen, Arno. *Men and Microbes: Diseases and Plagues in History and Modern Times.* New York: Touchstone, 1996. A detailed look at the history of diseases, demonstrating how infections are always part of the changing natural and social human environment. Particularly strong on modern times.

Standard, David E. *American Holocaust: Columbus and the Conquest of the New World.* New York: Oxford University Press, 1993. Describes in horrible detail the mass destruction of the New World societies in the wake of European contact.

GLOBAL CONNECTIONS

Rostworowski de Diez Canseco, Maria. *History of the Inca Realm.* Cambridge: Cambridge University Press, 1999. A thorough and readable account drawing from the latest scholarship.

Wachtgel, Nathan. *The Vision of the Vanquished: The Spanish Conquest of Peru Through Indian Eyes, 1530–1570.* New York: Barnes and Noble, 1971. A comprehensive, readable account sensitively drawn from the few sources giving the Indian point of view.

THE WORLD MARKET AND COMMERCIAL REVOLUTION

Braudel, Fernand. *Civilization and Capitalism, 15th to 18th Centuries,* 3 vols. Translated by S. Reynolds.

New York: Harper & Row, 1981. A celebrated author's detailed economic history that analyzes patterns in European and world economy—particularly rich in details.

Magnusson, Lars. *Mercantilism: The Shaping of an Economic Language.* New York: Routledge, 1994. A book that directly deals with how nations could increase their wealth specifically through international trade.

Omrod, David. *The Rise of Commercial Empires: England and the Netherlands in the Age of Mercantilism, 1650–1770.* Cambridge: Cambridge University Press, 2008. Scholarly contribution to the field of global economics that emphasizes the important connections that make up the webs of trade.

THE WORLD TRANSFORMED

Crosby, A.W. *Ecological Imperialism: The Biological Expansion of Europe, 900–1900,* 2nd ed. Cambridge: Cambridge University Press, 2009. Discusses the expansion of Europeans and the animals, weeds, and pathogens that accompanied them.

Davis, Natalie Zemon. *Women on the Margins: Three Seventeenth-Century Lives.* Cambridge, MA: Harvard University Press, 1997. Explores seventeenth-century culture through the lives of three women—a Catholic missionary, a Jewish storyteller, and the Protestant Merian (described in the chapter's Biography).

Fuentes, Carlos. *The Buried Mirror: Reflections on Spain and the New World.* Boston: Houghton Mifflin, 1992. A fascinating essay by one of Mexico's greatest writers on the blending of cultures of Spain and the New World.

CHARLES LEBRUN, *CHANCELLOR SEGUIER,* ca. 1670

Chancellor Pierre Seguier (1588–1672) was an ambitious courtier to the French king Louis XIV and a member of France's new nobility that earned position by service to the crown, the *noblesse de robe*. In this painting, Seguier's office is symbolized by the formal robes he wears, rather than by arms. Several well-dressed pages surround him, one holding an umbrella over his head as if he were a minor monarch. His face conveys a sense of pleased assurance with the position he has gained. Charles Lebrun (1619–1690), like several other leading artists of the day, served as painter to Louis XIV and for eighteen years created decorations for the king's Versailles palace.

The Struggle for Survival and Sovereignty

13

Europe's Social and Political Order, 1600–1715

"This poor country is a horrible sight," wrote the abbess of a French town in January 1649. "[I]t is stripped of everything. The soldiers take possession of the farms . . . there are no more horses . . . the peasants are reduced to sleeping in the woods . . . and if they only had enough bread to half satisfy their hunger, they would indeed count themselves happy." France had just emerged a victor from the Thirty Years' War (discussed in Chapter 11), only to find itself embroiled in a series of internal revolts. These revolts, like many others erupting throughout Europe, signaled new strains on European society from the bottom to the top of the traditional order.

For the vast majority—peasants who worked the fields—pressures came from powers outside their control. The landowning aristocracy required service and obedience; governmental officials demanded ever more taxes and military service; and the impersonal forces that most people attributed to luck, fate, or God brought bad weather, failed harvests, and plagues. Sometimes peasants fled their aristocratic masters or turned violently against isolated governmental officials. However, against the fates and well-armed soldiers, they were powerless.

For those at the top of society, the pressures came from central governments and monarchs. Kings, struggling with the increasingly heavy burdens of war and governance, chipped away at aristocratic independence year after year. They argued that "the royal power is absolute. . . . The prince [king] need render account of his acts to no one." Elites insisted that "our privileges and liberties are our right and due inheritance, no less than our very lands and goods." This contention between monarch and aristocrat sometimes broke out in violence, at other times led to compromises, and often severely strained the elite order.

These two struggles—the first faced by the vast majority on the bottom, the second by the dominant elites on top—colored the West's social and political life during the seventeenth and early eighteenth centuries. This chapter follows these intertwined conflicts in four areas—France, eastern Europe, England, and the Netherlands—where the story took different turns.

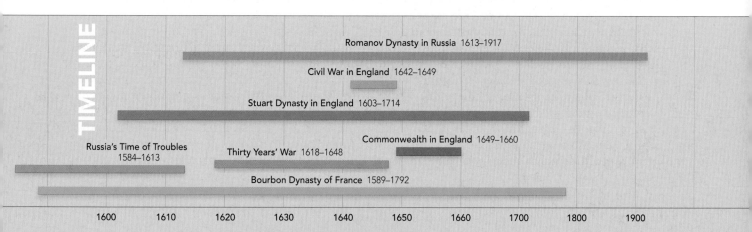

TIMELINE

Romanov Dynasty in Russia 1613–1917

Civil War in England 1642–1649

Stuart Dynasty in England 1603–1714

Commonwealth in England 1649–1660

Russia's Time of Troubles 1584–1613

Thirty Years' War 1618–1648

Bourbon Dynasty of France 1589–1792

1600   1610   1620   1630   1640   1650   1660   1700   1800   1900

STRESSES IN TRADITIONAL SOCIETY

"It is necessary that some command and others obey," explained a French judge and legal scholar in 1610. "Sovereign lords address their commands to the great; the great to the middling, the middling to the small, and the small to the people." This description captures the traditional social order that reigned in the West during the seventeenth century. Indeed, people took this order for granted. The structure was based on a hierarchy of ranks, and each rank, from nobility to peasantry, had its set status and occupations. Within each rank were subranks. For example, a hierarchy of titles and offices determined position among the nobility. Artisans divided themselves into masters, journeymen, and apprentices. Within the peasantry, landholders stood above laborers, and all looked down on serfs. Each rank distinguished itself through conventions, dress, duties, and etiquette. Finally, within all these ranks, position went hand in hand with family, itself ranked with men at the top, followed by women, and then children at the bottom.

Together the ranks made up the "body politic," with kings and nobles serving as the head and arms, and artisans and peasants as hands and feet. All worked together to perpetuate life as an organic whole. Everywhere, the church and religious sentiments sanctified this organic social hierarchy. Indeed, the social structure paralleled what Westerners saw as the larger, hierarchical order of the universe—the **Great Chain of Being.** In the Great Chain, everything—from God to the angels, humans, animals, and plants—existed in an ordered, permanent arrangement. During the seventeenth century, new forces tested the smooth running of this traditional society.

Mounting Demands on Rural Life

Facing new demands from many quarters, rural life declined. At the beginning of the century, life for most Europeans typically centered on small, self-sufficient villages that contained a few to a hundred families. A church or manor served as the center of communal activities. Strangers attracted intense scrutiny, and most authorities were local people whom everyone knew. When bad harvests, plagues, or war struck, the villagers received little help from the outside.

The majority of people lived in crowded one-room houses made of timber, thatch, and mud, with one or two narrow windows. At one end of the house stood a stone hearth used for light, cooking, and heat. Wood and peat, which fired the stove, were often in short supply, and the villagers struggled to stay warm during the winters. Grain, in the form of black bread and porridge, made up most meals, though in some areas meat, vegetables, fruits, and dairy products supplemented diets. A few treasured pots, pans, and utensils served all.

In **Figure 13.1,** Louis le Nain (1593–1648), a French artist known for his realistic paintings of peasant life, shows a farmyard scene in rural France. The faces of these people express a grimness; clearly they have known hard times and would endure difficulties again and again. Many seventeenth-century Europeans were poorer even than those in this painting. According to one observer in 1696, "They suffer from exposure: winter and summer, three-fourths of them are dressed in nothing but half-rotting tattered linen, and wear throughout the year wooden shoes and no other covering for the foot."

As in past centuries, the family functioned as both a social and an economic unit. Women and men married for practical as well as sentimental reasons. The land, wealth, skills, and position one held counted | The family | for much in a potential marriage partner. Husband, wife, and children lived together, and most marriages, whether happy or not, lasted until death. At various times, relatives, domestics, and laborers might live for a while in the household. Finally, although everyone worked together in the fields, men generally did the heaviest work, while women gardened, raised poultry, and supervised dairy producing.

Fathers, older children, and other relatives might also participate with mothers in raising and socializing young children. Nevertheless, children were not considered at the center of family life, and girls were less valued than boys. Indeed, parents often sent children away to other households to work as apprentices, domestics, or laborers if they could earn more there. Infant mortality ran high; of the five or more children to whom a woman was likely to give birth, only two or three lived beyond 5 years. Parents valued and cared for their children, but in a time of grinding poverty, it is not surprising that parents also viewed children as either assets or liabilities in the struggle for survival; great emotional entanglements with them were risky.

The stresses on these common people are strikingly revealed by the population decreases that occurred during the first half of the seventeenth century. The devastation from the seemingly endless wars took many lives, especially in German lands. The old enemies—poverty, disease, and famine—also roared through these decades. Unusually severe winters—advancing glaciers marked the 1600s as part of the "little ice age"—froze rivers and fields, and wet summers destroyed crops. Suffering, malnutrition, illness, and, too often, death followed. "The staple dish here consists of mice, which the inhabitants hunt, so desperate are they from hunger," reported provincial officials in northern France in 1651. "They devour roots which the animals cannot eat . . . not a day passes but at least 200 people die of famine in the two provinces."

| Population changes |

Bad times also meant postponed marriages, fewer births, and an increase in the number of deaths among infants and children. Europeans already married late compared to the rest of the world. On average, men waited until their late 20s to wed; women, until their mid-20s. Sometimes so many people died, wandered away in search of food, or fled to the cities that whole villages were abandoned. Conditions improved a bit during the second half of the century, though only enough for the European population to maintain itself and perhaps grow slightly. Life expectancy, which varied by social class and region, was probably less than 30 years (in part because of high infant mortality).

New demands from central governments cut into traditional patterns of rural life. With every new outbreak of war, governmental officials intruded more and more into villages in search of army conscripts. People resisted, and for good reason. Military service took men out of the fields, increasing the burden on the women, children, and elderly who had to shoulder the men's share of the labor. Soldiers embroiled in nearby battles plundered what they could from the villages they passed.

Officials also came with new tax assessments, even though peasants already owed much to those above them. Traditional taxes to the government, tithes to the church, and rents to large landowners used up more than half of the already scant wealth peasants produced. **Figure 13.2,** a mid-seventeenth-century print, caustically depicts some of the peasants' grievances. On the left, the well-dressed noble sits authoritatively on his padded chair to receive the peasant ("thin as the noble's terrier"), who is bringing money in his right hand, fruits and vegetables in his left hand, and a sack

FIGURE 13.1

Louis le Nain, *The Cart*, 1641

This painting by Louis le Nain provides a glimpse of everyday life in rural France during the mid-seventeenth century. Here, women and children of varying ages stand on a cart or tend a few animals. One woman sits with her baby on the ground; another has slung a large pot over her back, perhaps in preparation for gathering water. In the background stands a modest house.

Connecting Art & Society

1. What does this painting reveal about how these people spend their time?

2. What roles do women and children play in this rural economy?

3. Considering his portrayal of the figures and details in this painting, what impression of rural life do you think the artist wanted to convey to viewers?

of wheat at his feet. Above the noble are a spider and a fly caught in its web. As the caption on the lower left states, "The noble is the spider and the peasant the fly." The noble says, "You must pay or serve." The peasant can only reply, "To all masters, all honors."

Peasants avoided collectors and hid what assets they could. In countless incidents, peasants and city dwellers across Europe rose against increasing taxes and attacked the hated collectors. In the 1630s, for example, French peasants rose against tax increases

| Tax revolts |

FIGURE 13.2 The Noble and the Peasant, seventeenth century This print starkly laments the lot of the poor peasant. Here he brings money and the fruits of his hard labor to the rich noble, who sits arrogantly in a padded chair.

and forced temporary concessions from local officials, only to have those victories reversed by the state. Farther south, in 1647, women demanding more bread led riots that swept through the city of Palermo in Spanish-occupied Italy. Rebels in the city chanted, "Down with taxes!" As in France, government forces eventually reversed early victories and crushed the revolt.

Other intrusions further eroded the traditional isolation that characterized rural life. Officials and merchants ventured more and more often to the countryside to buy grain for cities, creating food shortages in rural villages. Moreover, as members of the local nobility departed for capital cities and the king's court, new officials appeared and began administering affairs and rendering judgments in courts. For good or ill, villagers found themselves increasingly drawn into the web of national affairs.

Pressures on the Upper Orders

Monarchs faced pressures of their own, especially the demands of war. In the competition for territory and status, kings won by fielding ever-larger armies and mustering the resources needed to support them. During the seventeenth century, armies doubled and redoubled in size, as did the central governments that supported them (see Chapter 11). The costs of making war and supporting government increased accordingly. Governments devoted half or more of their

income to the military, and monarchs desperate for money levied more and more taxes just to stay even. The ability to collect taxes could make or break a ruler. More than anything else, a king's unrelenting demands for more taxes sparked widespread resistance to his rule.

Competing centers of power added to the kings' problems. Independent town officials, church leaders, and provincial officials tried to hold on to their authority over local matters. Religious dissidents, for their part, guarded what independence they could. Finally, those who resented the royal tax collectors resisted the crown's reach. But the greatest threat to monarchical power came from aristocrats, who tried to retain as much of their social and economic dominance as possible. These nobles often challenged royal policies and decried royal "tyranny" as a violation of divine law. They guarded their traditional rights and local authority, and many of them refused to give up their tax exemptions. Should the crown falter, they stood ready to take back any powers they might have lost.

> Competing centers of power

Monarchs argued with, fought, and schemed against these forms of opposition. They justified their power as a divine right, because they represented God on earth, and surrounded themselves with compliant advisors and admirers. As Document 13.1 reveals, their favored supporters, such as France's court preacher and royal tutor Bishop Jacques-Bénigne Bossuet (1627–1704), backed them. Bossuet declared, "The whole state is included in him [the monarch], the will of all the people is enclosed within his own."

Yet the kings used more than words and "yes-men" in this power struggle. Bypassing representative institutions, they sent their royal law courts into the provinces as a way to extend their authority. Sometimes they appointed new local leaders to gain allies. Other times, they attracted aristocrats from the provinces to the royal court, thereby creating a power vacuum that they then filled with their own men. When great nobles resisted being turned into obedient officials, rulers often turned to the lesser nobility or members of the wealthy middle class—men such as Chancellor Seguier, whom we met in the opening of this chapter. Such royal servants received titles or land and were elevated to high office as compensation for their loyalty.

Women also became entwined in these struggles between monarchs and aristocrats. With the royal courts growing in size, many women became important friends and unofficial advisors to kings and influential aristocrats. They used their intelligence, wit, services, and advice to gain privileged positions in royal courts. There they won titles, offices, lands, money, and advantageous marriages for themselves and their families. Mothers encouraged their daughters

Bishop Bossuet Justifies Monarchical Absolutism

In their efforts to acquire as much power as possible, European monarchs and their supporters sought justifications for monarchical rights. One of the most explicit and influential justifications was written and preached by Jacques-Bénigne Bossuet (1627–1704), a French bishop and tutor to the son of Louis XIV. In the following excerpt from his Politics Drawn from the Very Words of Holy Scripture, *Bossuet argues for the divine right of kings.*

Article I

There are four characters or qualities essential to royal authority: First, royal authority is sacred; second, it is paternal; third, it is absolute; fourth, it is ruled by reason. . . .

Article II

Royal authority is sacred.

Proposition 1

God established kings as his ministers and rules peoples by them.

We have already seen that all power comes from God. "The prince," St. Paul adds, "is the minister of God to thee for good. But if thou do that which is evil, be afraid; for he beareth not the sword in vain; for he is the minister of God, a revenger to execute wrath upon him that doeth evil."

Thus princes act as ministers of God, and as his lieutenants on earth. It is by them that he exercises his rule. . . .

Proposition 2

The person of kings is sacred.

It thus appears that the person of kings is sacred and that to make an attempt on their lives is a sacrilege. . . .

The title of Christ is given to kings; and they are everywhere called christs, or the anointed of the lord. . . .

Proposition 3

The prince must provide for the needs of the people.

It is a royal right to provide for the needs of the people. He who undertakes it at the expense of the prince undertakes royalty: this is why it has been established. The obligation to care for the people is the foundation of all the rights that sovereigns have over their subjects. . . .

Article III

The royal authority is absolute.

. . . The prince is by his office the father of his people; he is placed by his grandeur above all petty interests; even more: all his grandeur and his natural interests are that the people shall be conserved, for

once the people fail him he is no longer prince. There is thus nothing better than to give all the power of the state to him who has the greatest interest in the conservation and greatness of the state itself. . . .

Proposition 4

Kings are not by this above the laws. . . .

Kings therefore are subject like any others to the equity of the laws both because they must be just and because they owe to the people the example of protecting justice; but they are not subject to the penalties of the laws; or, as theology puts it, they are subject to the laws, not in terms of its coactive power but in terms of its directive power.

SOURCE: J.B. Bossuet, *Politics Drawn from the Very Words of Holy Scripture* (1709), in *Western Societies, A Documentary History,* vol. II, eds. Brian Tierney and Joan Scott (New York: McGraw-Hill, 1984), pp. 11–13.

Analyze the Document

1. What, according to Bossuet, are the nature and properties of royal authority?

2. How does Bossuet justify the various qualities of royal authority?

3. How absolute is the power of kings?

---

not to let good marriage opportunities pass by. "It is true that [the proposed groom] is some fifteen years older than you," wrote one aristocratic mother in 1622. "[B]ut . . . you are going to marry a man . . . who has spent his life honorably at court and at the wars and has been granted considerable payments by the king." Royal mistresses also achieved important positions in the king's household. Françoise d'Aubigné (Marquise de Maintenon), mistress (and, secretly, wife) of France's King Louis XIV, influenced court appointments and founded a royal school for the daughters of impoverished nobles in 1686. Some mistresses even persuaded kings to acknowledge their children as "royal bastards" and grant them titles and privileges.

This system of elevated royal authority has been called **royal absolutism** because the kings of the day commanded more loyalty, control, and resources than their predecessors had, and because they justified | Royal absolutism |
their right to rule as an absolute. However, no monarch gained true absolute power. Most people understood that even the strongest ruler, divinely ordained, was vaguely subject to tradition and law. As one seventeenth-century French jurist explained, the king's power "seems to place him above the law, . . . [but] his rank obliges him to subordinate his personal interests to the general good of the state." Further, with so many local centers of power, with scores of nobles who persisted in their independent

ways, and with too much information to control, no king in this era could hope to dominate everything. Some monarchs even found themselves on losing ends of internal battles for power.

ROYAL ABSOLUTISM IN FRANCE

In western Europe, the efforts of French kings to maximize their power exemplified the development of royal absolutism. Building upon the work of predecessors who had enhanced the power of the monarchy, Louis XIV (r. 1643–1715) took personal control of the French monarchy in 1661. By then, France had supplanted Spain as the most powerful nation in Europe. Under Louis' long rule, royal absolutism reached its peak and inspired other monarchs to emulate his style.

Henry IV Secures the Monarchy

French absolutism had its immediate roots in the reign of Henry IV (r. 1589–1610). When Henry IV ascended the French throne in 1589, his country had endured several decades of wars between Protestants and Catholics, combined with conflicts between different political factions. Law and order had broken down, and powerful nobles had reasserted their authority. The finances of the central government lay in disarray, and French prestige abroad had sunk to a low level.

The talented, witty Henry, in his prime at 36, set out to change all this. He defused the religious turmoil by issuing the Edict of Nantes (see Chapter 11), which granted to Huguenots (French Protestants) religious toleration and control of some two hundred fortified cities and towns as a guarantee against future oppression. He appealed to the traditional nobility by developing an image as a cultured warrior-king who could be trusted to enforce the law. He catered to rich lawyers, merchants, and landowners by selling new governmental offices, which often came with ennoblement as well as prestige. This growing elite became known as the nobility of the robe because their robes of office, rather than the arms borne by the traditional nobility of the sword, represented their power (see p. 414). Many of these nobles gladly paid annual fees for the right to pass their offices on to heirs. For the peasantry, Henry suggested that prosperity should bring "a chicken in the pot of every peasant for Sunday dinner." Not surprisingly, Henry's authority and popularity soared.

With the help of his able, methodical administrator, the Duke of Sully (1560–1641), Henry also launched a comprehensive program of economic reconstruction. Agriculture and commerce benefited from the increased security of life and property brought by better law enforcement; from improved transportation facilitated by the repair of roads, bridges, and harbors; and from the freeing of trade, thanks to lower internal tariff barriers. The monarchy even subsidized and protected new industries that produced luxuries such as glass, porcelain, lace, silk, tapestries, fine leather, and textiles. Sully's efficient collection of taxes and administration of expenditures produced a rare budget surplus.

Henry also dreamed of making France secure from ambitious foreign states and of ensuring his country a supreme position in all of Europe. However, the powerful Spanish and Austrian Habsburgs on France's borders stood in his way. In 1610, he prepared to join his armies for a campaign against his rivals. Yet before he could set out, he was assassinated by a fanatic, and his plans died with him.

Richelieu Elevates Royal Authority

For several years after Henry's death, his Italian wife, Marie de Médicis (1573–1642), ruled as regent for their son, the young Louis XIII (r. 1610–1643). Marie kept opponents at arm's length but made little headway in strengthening the position of the monarchy. Then in 1624, one of her favorite advisors, Cardinal Richelieu (1585–1642), became chief minister and began exercising power from behind the throne. Having come from a minor noble family and possessing a keen intellect, the arrogant and calculating Richelieu handled the young king deftly and controlled others through a skillful blend of patronage and punishment. His twofold policy was to make royal power supreme in France and to maneuver France into a position of dominance in Europe. To Louis XIII, Richelieu promised "to ruin the Huguenot party, to abase the pride of the nobles, to bring back all your subjects to their duty, and to elevate your name among foreign nations to the point where it belongs."

With the royal army at his disposal, Richelieu boldly destroyed the castles of nobles who opposed the king; he disbanded their private armies and executed a number of the most recalcitrant among them. When Huguenot nobles in the southwest rebelled, Richelieu sent in the army and stripped the Huguenots of the special military and political privileges that Henry IV had granted them. Only their religious liberties remained intact. To dilute local centers of political power, the dynamic minister divided France into some thirty administrative districts, placing each under the control of a powerful *intendant,* who was an agent of the crown. He chose these *intendants* from the ranks of the middle class and recently ennobled people and shifted them around frequently, lest they become too sympathetic with their localities. Finally, Richelieu plunged France into the Thirty Years' War in Germany (see Chapter 11). His purpose was to weaken the Habsburgs, chief rivals of the French monarchs for European supremacy.

By the time of his death in 1642, Richelieu had firmly secured royal power in France and elevated France's position in Europe. Nevertheless, the imperious cardinal, having more than doubled taxes to promote his policies, had gained few friends. Far more French subjects rejoiced in his death than mourned his passing.

Mazarin Overcomes the Opposition

Richelieu was succeeded by his protégé, Cardinal Jules Mazarin (1602–1661). Louis XIII's death in 1643, a few months after that of his great minister, left the throne to Louis XIV, a child of 5. Mazarin, who began his career as a gambler and diplomat, played the same role in the early reign of Louis XIV and his regent, Anne of Austria (1601–1666), that Richelieu had played during the reign of Louis XIII.

Early on, Mazarin, Anne, and the child-king faced a series of wide-ranging, uncoordinated revolts that forced them to flee Paris. Known collectively as the **Fronde** (the name of a child's slingshot game, which implied that the participants were childish), these revolts stemmed primarily from French subjects' objections to high taxes and increasing royal power. Between 1648 and 1653, ambitious nobles, footloose soldiers returning from war, urban artisans, and even some peasants fought the monarchy and its supporters in what amounted to a civil war at times. Bad harvests added to the chaos and suffering: "People massacre each other daily with every sort of cruelty," wrote an observer in 1652. "The soldiers steal from one another when they have denuded everyone else . . . all the armies are equally undisciplined and vie with one

The Fronde

another in lawlessness." Nobles conspired and shifted alliances for their own gains, resulting in growing disillusionment with their cause. Gaining support from city dwellers and peasants longing for peace, and shrewdly buying off one noble after another, Mazarin quashed the revolts by 1653. The crown gradually reasserted itself as the basis for order in France.

The Fronde was paralleled by other revolts during the 1640s in Spain, the Italian states, and, much more seriously, England. In each case, the catalysts included new taxes, the demand for more men and supplies for the military, and monarchies' efforts to acquire more power. In the Spanish provinces of Catalonia and Portugal, as well as in the Italian states of Naples and Sicily, rebels murdered tax officials, peasants took up arms, and local nobles joined the fray. Localities demanded and sometimes got concessions, but many of these victories proved short-lived when the crown reasserted its authority. As we will see, matters grew much worse in England. Taken together, these mid-century rebellions served as a warning to monarchs not to push unpopular policies too far—and to the aristocracy not to underestimate the power of the crown.

The Sun King Rises

Upon Mazarin's death in 1661, the 23-year-old Louis XIV finally stepped forward to rule in his own right. "Up to this moment I have been pleased to entrust the government of my affairs to the late Cardinal," he announced. "It is now time that I govern them myself." With his regal bearing and stolid build, young Louis fit the part well. His lack of intellectual brilliance was offset by a sharp memory, a sense of responsibility, and a capacity for tedious work. "One reigns only by dint of hard work," he warned his own son. Haunted by childhood memories of fleeing in terror across the tiled rooftops of Paris during the Fronde revolts, he remained determined to prevent further challenges from rebellious aristocrats. By his mother, Mazarin, and a succession of tutors, Louis had been convinced that he was God's appointed deputy for France. Supporting him was the most famous exponent of royal absolutism, Bishop Bossuet, who argued that the monarchy "is sacred, it is paternal, it is absolute, and it is subject to reason . . . the royal throne is not that of a man but the throne of God Himself." As Document 13.2 indicates, Louis XIV learned these lessons well. In words commonly attributed to Louis, "*L'état, c'est moi*" (I am the state).

However, Louis could not possibly perform all the functions of government personally. The great bulk of the details were handled by a series of councils and bureaus and administered locally by the *intendants.* Distrusting the traditional nobility, Louis instead usually appointed members of modest noble backgrounds

DOCUMENT 13.2

Louis XIV Describes Monarchical Rights and Duties

For many, France's Louis XIV embodied the nearly all-powerful king—at least in his glorious appearance and style, if not always in his deeds. Louis XIV probably wielded more power than any other seventeenth-century European monarch. In the following excerpts from his writings, he describes his view of kingship to his son.

Homage is due to kings, and they do whatever they like. It certainly must be agreed that, however bad a prince may be, it is always a heinous crime for his subjects to rebel against him. He who gave men kings willed that they should be respected as His lieutenants, and reserved to Himself the right to question their conduct. It is His will that everyone who is born a subject should obey without qualification. This law, as clear as it is universal, was not made only for the sake of princes: it is also for the good of the people themselves. It is therefore the duty of kings to sustain by their own example the religion upon which they rely; and they must realize that, if their subjects see them plunged in vice or violence, they can hardly render to their person the respect due to their office, or recognize in them the living image of Him who is all-holy as well as almighty.

It is a fine thing, a noble and enjoyable thing, to be a king. But it is not without its pains, its fatigues, and its troubles. One must work hard to reign. In working for the state, a king is working for himself. The good of the one is the glory of the other. When the state is prosperous, famous, and powerful, the king who is the cause of it is glorious; and he ought in consequence to have a larger share than others do of all that is most agreeable in life.

SOURCE: J.M. Thompson, *Lectures on Foreign History, 1494–1789* (Oxford: Blackwell, 1956), pp. 172–174.

Analyze the Document

1. In what ways, according to Louis XIV, should a king take steps to maintain his authority?

2. How does Louis justify the obedience owed to kings?

3. In what ways do these views support an alliance between church and state?

---

to the important offices of his government. Well supervised by the industrious king, the administrative machinery hummed along.

To raise his stature, Louis XIV initiated massive public-works projects that glorified him, his government, and his reign. His greatest architectural project was a new palace. Hating the tumult of Paris, with its streets teeming with commoners, he selected Versailles, 11 miles southwest of the city, as the new seat of government. There, as many as 35,000 workmen toiled for more than forty years to turn marshes and sand into Europe's most splendid palace and grounds.

Figure 13.3 shows Versailles in 1668. Over the next forty-three years, successive teams of workers added rear gardens and more than doubled the size of the buildings. This painting, which shows the roads, paths, and gardens of Versailles geometrically laid out, gives a sense of the scale of the project. In the foreground to the right, the royal coach, with its train of followers, arrives at the front gates. The exterior of Versailles was designed in long, horizontal, classic lines. The interior boasted a lavish baroque style with richly colored marbles, mosaics, inlaid woods, gilt, silver, silk, velvet, and brocade. Ceiling-to-floor windows and mirrors and crystal chandeliers holding thousands of candles illuminated the salons and halls. In terms of sheer capacity, the palace could house 5,000 people and serve thousands more visitors each day. It faced hundreds of acres of groves, walks, canals, pools, terraces, fountains, statues, flower beds, and clipped shrubs—all laid out in formal geometric patterns symbolizing the triumph of engineering over nature. So dazzling was this hallmark of royal absolutism that other European monarchs soon attempted to copy it.

Louis used Versailles, images of himself, and symbols to enhance his authority among the nobility and everyone else. "The peoples over whom we reign, being unable to apprehend the basic reality of things, usually derive their opinions from what they can see with their eyes," he explained. **Figure 13.4,** a painting by an anonymous seventeenth-century artist, shows Louis—in the center astride a white horse—as he rides into the gardens at Versailles. His favored courtiers throng around him, hoping to be seen by him and others more than to see him. Servants mingle in the crowd as well. Above is the king's chosen symbol, the sun, with its light radiating out. As Louis put it, "The symbol that I have adopted and that you see all around you represents the duties of a Prince . . . endlessly promoting life, joy and growth." It is "the most dazzling and most beautiful image of the monarch."

The Sun King finally moved to Versailles in 1682. Once established there, he lured the men and women of the nobility away from their local centers

FIGURE 13.3 Pierre Patel the Elder, View of Versailles, 1668 A royal procession enters the grounds of Versailles in this aerial view. The new geometrically ordered palace and grounds became a monument to Louis XIV's reign and French royal absolutism.

of power where they might make trouble and turned them into domesticated court "butterflies." He subjected them to a complex system of etiquette and favoritism that made every aspect of Louis' daily life the center of their concern. Court became a theater where those already in favor, as well as aspiring favorites, had to scheme for gifts, patronage, and position. Winners might secure lucrative rewards, and losers might spend themselves broke trying to stay in the race.

Despite the grandeur of Versailles, this glittering monument to royal absolutism had its critics. In her novel *The Princess of Clèves* (1678), the Countess de Lafayette complained that at Versailles "everybody was busily trying to better their | Versailles' critics | position by pleasing, by helping, or by hindering somebody else." The court reportedly seethed with gossip, scandal, and intrigue. Critics such as Pierre Jurieu, a French Calvinist pastor who fled to Holland, lamented that the king "is the idol to which are sacrificed princes, great men and small, families, provinces, cities, finances and generally everything." Resentful nobles once proudly drawing high status from their lands

and lineage came to depend on the approval of and service to the king as the primary route to power. Many hard-toiling, heavily taxed French commoners also grumbled about living in the reflected glory of a pretentious monarch.

To enhance the glory of his court, Louis XIV subsidized and attracted to Versailles leading French artists and literary | Classical literature | figures. The elegance, the sense of order, and the formalism of royalty all found expression in much of the literature of this **classical style** in French culture. Pierre Corneille (1606–1684), for example, wrote elegant plays modeled on the ancient Greek tragedies. Human beings' conflicts with their own nature and with the workings of fate and the universe furnished the plots. Even more exquisite were the perfectly rhymed and metered couplets of Jean Racine's (1639–1699) dramas. Finally, in his profound comedies, Jean-Baptiste Molière (1622–1673) satirized pompous scholars, social climbers, false priests, and quack physicians. Louis and his court had little to fear from this literature. On the contrary, they appreciated its formal order and laughed along with other audiences at its satire, which was

FIGURE 13.4 Louis XIV at Versailles, seventeenth century
In this painting by an unknown artist, Louis sits on a white horse surrounded by his courtiers at his Versailles palace. Above him radiates his adopted symbol, the sun.

reflected their wealth and power. Yet during the second half of the seventeenth century, classicism, with its emphasis on control and restraint, began to gain favor. The appealing paintings of French artists Claude Lorraine (1600–1682) and Nicolas Poussin (1594–1665) helped classicism win official approval in France. Both men spent much time in Italy, studying the Renaissance masters and the Italian landscape. **Figure 13.5** embodies their style. In this painting, Lorraine has framed the foreground figures with trees under a radiant sky. The Italian landscape is geometrically balanced, the figures are in classic dress, and the scene exudes calm and discipline. Here is an idyllic vision, a scene designed to elevate the minds of viewers. Compared to the baroque, the classical style shows a logic that echoed the sense of order pervading the Versailles court of the Sun King.

Versailles, the arts, and all other aspects of government cost money. Louis assigned the talented Jean-Baptiste Colbert (1619–1683) to manage his finances. An engine of efficiency, Colbert toiled endlessly, supervising the details of the French economy while also promoting culture by founding the Royal Academy of Sciences in 1666 and subsidizing the arts. In keeping with his bourgeois origins, he chose service to the king as his means of advancement. His family shared in his success, becoming ministers, gaining high offices in the church, marrying well, and securing top positions in the military. | Colbert |

Promoting mercantilistic economic policies (see Chapter 12), Colbert protected industries with high tariffs while subsidizing exports and new industries. To encourage France's growing empire and the commerce it generated, he built a large navy. Finally, Colbert worked to ensure a worldwide reputation for the uniformly high quality of French products. He subjected manufacturing to the most minute regulation and supervision: So many threads of such and such quality and color must go into every inch of this textile and that lace. Although Colbert's restrictive mercantilistic controls in the long run stifled initiative and economic change, French products earned wide acclaim for their quality. By his death in 1683, Colbert had balanced the budget and promoted relative prosperity despite Louis XIV's lavish expenditures.

During the following decades, however, Louis embarked on policies that undermined much of what Colbert had accomplished. The king's demands for religious conformity and his military ambitions ranked among the most destructive of these policies. Huguenots (French Protestants) paid the highest price for his religious intolerance. In 1685, | Revocation of the Edict of Nantes |

aimed at humankind in general rather than at specific ruling regimes.

At court and elsewhere, many members of the elite also read historical romances. Perhaps the most popular of these was *Grand Cyrus* by Madeleine de Scudéry (1608–1701), a writer who rose from an impoverished background. The fact that this book was published under the name of the author's brother, Georges, hints at the difficulties women faced in expressing their cultural talents. Other forms of literature included letters and memoirs. The courtier Madame de Sévigné (1626–1696), for example, wrote almost two thousand letters to her daughter that reported what the king said and did as well as news of marriages, deaths, gossip, fads, and conspiracies that marked life at the court of Louis XIV. The Duke of Saint-Simon (1675–1755), who like many nobles felt slighted and grew to resent the king, chronicled life at Versailles in his forty-volume *Memoirs*.

While the literature of the seventeenth century amused monarchs, the visual arts of the period positively glorified them. Kings and aristocrats still favored the baroque style of painting and architecture (see Chapter 11). As they saw it, the baroque's swirling forms and massive, ornamental elegance perfectly | Visual arts |

Louis revoked the Edict of Nantes, which in 1598 had granted tolerance to the Protestant minority. Then he outlawed Protestantism and ordered Protestant churches demolished. The Duke of Saint-Simon lamented that the "ultimate results [of the reversal] were the depopulation of a fourth part of the kingdom and the ruin of our commerce . . . the country was given over to the authorized ravages of dragoons [armed troops], which caused the death of, literally, thousands of innocent people of all ages and both sexes." Although Huguenots were forbidden to emigrate, perhaps as many as 200,000 did, taking their wealth and skills with them to Protestant-friendly areas in Europe and America, "enriching them and causing their cities to flourish at the expense of France," according to Saint-Simon. Up to a million Huguenots who remained in France went underground.

Nor was Louis content to rule in peace as the leader of Europe's most powerful nation. During the last four decades of his 72-year reign, he fought four wars of aggression. The same old reasons prompted him to lead France into battle: more territory, more glory, and more wealth. He set his sights on the Spanish and Austrian Habsburg lands on France's eastern borders and on the Dutch, France's most powerful commercial rivals on the Continent. He put his war minister, the Marquis of Louvois (1639–1691), in charge of organizing France's huge military establishment on the model of a complex business, replete with supply depots and hospitals. While Louvois introduced strict discipline, uniforms, and promotions based on merit, Sébastien de Vauban (1633–1707) designed sturdy fortifications and brilliant siege operations. It was a common saying that whereas a city defended by Vauban was safe, one besieged by Vauban was doomed.

Louis initiated his foreign adventures in the War of Devolution (1667–1668), waged against Spain for French claims in the Spanish Netherlands and Franche-Comté (Burgundy). When victory seemed within reach, the United Provinces, England, and Sweden joined Spain to prevent France from upsetting the balance of power. The Treaty of Aix-la-Chapelle (1668) brought Louis only minor gains (see **Map 13.1**). In 1672, Louis turned against the Dutch, whom he blamed for organizing the alliance against him and who were France's chief trade competitors. The Dutch stopped the invading French only by opening the dikes and flooding the land. Dutch diplomacy brought Spain, Sweden, Brandenburg, and the Holy Roman Empire into an alliance against the French. Louis fought them to a standstill and gained some valuable territories in the Peace of Nijmegen (1679). In the following

| Wars of aggression |

FIGURE 13.5 Claude Lorraine, *The Marriage of Isaac and Rebekah (The Mill)*, 1640 This calm, balanced Italian landscape by a leading French artist exemplifies seventeenth-century classicism with its emphasis on control and restraint.

years, Louis made enemies of the Austrians by refusing to help in their war against the Turks, and he alienated Europe's Protestants by turning against the Huguenots. Fearful that he intended to upset the balance of power and dominate the Continent, much of Europe formed the Grand Alliance against him. The eight-year War of the League of Augsburg (1689–1697) gained France little territory at the cost of much bloodshed and misery. Louis' final struggle, the War of the Spanish Succession, was fought over French claims to the Spanish throne and the partition of Spanish holdings in the Netherlands and Italy. The war lasted eleven years (1702–1713), and the Grand Alliance defeated French and Spanish forces in a series of battles. Beaten, impoverished, and facing revolts fueled by despair and opposition to taxation, Louis XIV was forced to accept the Peace of Utrecht (1713), which ended Louis' ambitions to create a partnership of Bourbon monarchs in France and Spain—with France the senior partner. **Map 13.1** depicts France in 1661, when Louis XIV took control of the monarchy, and the territories he eventually acquired. In the end, he possessed little more than what he had started with some fifty years earlier, and he had even fewer holdings in North America.

Louis XIV died only two years after the Peace of Utrecht. He had long outlived his popularity. One widely circulated letter from an aristocratic critic, Archbishop Fénélon, complained that "for thirty years, your principal ministers have . . . overthrown all the ancient maxims of the state in order to increase your authority beyond all bounds. . . . For the sake of

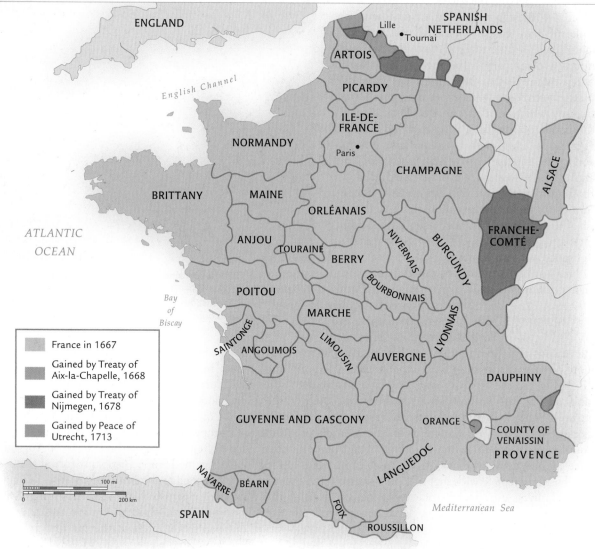

MAP 13.1

France Under Louis XIV, 1661–1715

This map shows France's provinces and the territorial gains the state made during the reign of Louis XIV. In four wars between 1667 and 1713, France fought against various rivals and coalitions of states to the south, north, and east.

Map legend:
- France in 1667
- Gained by Treaty of Aix-la-Chapelle, 1668
- Gained by Treaty of Nijmegen, 1678
- Gained by Peace of Utrecht, 1713

Explore the Map

1. Notice that most of Louis' gains came from Spanish lands and German states on France's eastern border. What might this pattern imply about vulnerable areas of Europe and changing power relationships at the time?

2. Consider how small France's gains were despite the almost endless, costly wars the state waged. What were the wars' likely consequences for France's finances and the popularity of its monarch?

getting and keeping vain conquests abroad, you have destroyed half the real strength of your own state." As the coffin carrying Louis XIV's body was drawn through the streets of Paris, some of his abused subjects cursed his name.

The Sun King had built the French state into the envy of Europe, and his glittering court at Versailles outshone all others. His success relied on knowing how to use the old system, modified by preceding state-builders such as Richelieu, to his advantage. He tamed rather than fought the nobility, who at the same time remained the crown's most important ally and potent competitor. Clearly, strong central governments enjoyed advantages, and none were stronger than France's under Louis XIV. For many monarchs, France under Louis XIV became the model of absolutism. However, his expenditures and wars created unprecedented misery for most commoners saddled with relentlessly rising taxes, more military service, and famines. Recognizing that the continued power of the state required some support of the people, Louis' successors would try to avoid his mistakes and ameliorate the worst threats to the lives of French people.

Assessing Louis XIV

THE STRUGGLE FOR SOVEREIGNTY IN EASTERN EUROPE

In eastern Europe, people struggled just as fiercely to survive and to define sovereignty as they did in the west. However, the two regions differed sharply, and those differences affected the outcomes of battles over these issues. States east of the Elbe River (see **Map 13.2**) were less commercially developed than those in western Europe. Instead of farms worked by legally free and mobile peasants, estate agriculture (large landed estates owned by lords and worked by their serfs) dominated those economies. By the sixteenth century, the nobles who owned these estates had reversed the medieval trends toward greater freedom for the peasantry and the growth of towns. Most people who worked the fields sank into serfdom, bound to the land and owing ever-increasing services to their lords. The middle classes in the towns also declined, failing to gain in numbers and wealth like their counterparts in western Europe. Finally, most central governments at the beginning of the seventeenth century proved weaker than those in western European states, as powerful nobles retained much independence. Despite all this, several monarchs decided to change things in their own favor.

Centralizing the State in Brandenburg-Prussia

In Brandenburg-Prussia, the "Great Elector" Frederick William (r. 1640–1688) inherited a scattered patchwork of poorly managed lands weakened by years of war and population decline. He faced a number of other problems as well. His army was tiny—too weak to keep foreign forces out of his lands or to discipline internal opponents. His nobles, or Junkers, had an independent streak and had found ways to avoid

most taxes. Finally, his cities remained uncooperative, asserting their long-established political and economic independence.

Frederick William set out to correct the situation. He believed that the key was to strengthen his standing army. Only then could he gain control of his lands and make Brandenburg-Prussia a desired ally in international affairs. During the 1640s, he more than tripled the size of his army. This new strength and effective diplomacy won him several new territories at the end of the Thirty Years' War (see **Map 13.2**). With energy and skill, he next centralized and administered the governments of his fragmented holdings—while continuing to boost the size of his army. He prevailed over the **Estates**—the representative assemblies of the realm—and acquired the crucial authority to collect taxes. He then used his newly powerful army to enforce tax payments and organize state resources. In a pivotal compromise with landed aristocrats, he allowed them complete control over their serfs in return for support and service in his bureaucracy and army. Through mercantilistic policies, he protected industries, improved communications, and promoted agriculture. Though Frederick William could not afford a lavish court like that of Louis XIV, his policies ratcheted up his power. "Hold fast to the eminence of your superior position . . . [and] rely on your own strength," he advised his son. At the Great Elector's death in 1688, Brandenburg-Prussia was well on the road to becoming a major player in European politics. He also left a legacy of military values and reliance on armed might that would influence much of Prussia's subsequent history.

In 1701, his son, Frederick I (r. 1688–1713), increased the dynasty's status by acquiring the title of King of Prussia in return for helping the Holy Roman Emperor in a war against France. He used state revenues to turn his Berlin court into a great social and cultural center. By his death in 1713, Brandenburg-Prussia had become a respected force in eastern Europe.

Austria Confronts the Ottomans and Expands Its Control

Austria's Leopold I (r. 1657–1705), facing extreme local, language, and ethnic differences within his diverse lands, could not hope to acquire the same power as that enjoyed by Louis XIV in France or even Frederick William in Prussia. Localities retained considerable autonomy, especially in matters of taxation. The practical Leopold focused on securing his own Habsburg lands, rather than cementing the minimal control he had over the Holy Roman Empire, and allied himself closely with the Catholic Church. He gained the allegiance of the nobles by making them his chief advisors and granting them rights to

MAP 13.2

Central and Eastern Europe, 1648

This map shows the border between the western and eastern agrarian zones, running from the mouth of the Elbe River south to Trieste on the Adriatic Sea.

Explore the Map

1. Which states lay to the east of this border?

2. What did this dividing line imply about social differences between eastern and western European states at the time?

3. What problems did these differences pose for eastern European states such as Austria and Brandenburg-Prussia, which controlled provinces to the west of this line?

exploit lands and the peasants on them. Some peasants revolted, but as elsewhere in Europe, they did not pose a serious challenge to authorities. With the help of Poland's king, Jan Sobieski (r. 1674–1696), Leopold also fought the Ottoman Turks, who controlled most of Hungary as part of their large and still-powerful empire.

During the fifteenth and first half of the sixteenth century, the Ottomans had enjoyed great power and relative prosperity. The sultans in Istanbul, wielding secular and religious authority, ran a strong autocratic state that could compete with any European power. Increasingly, they struggled to maintain authority in

The Ottomans

the face of competition from bandit armies, mutinous army officers, and squabbling elites, but seventeenth-century Ottoman rulers managed to maintain control. In 1683, Ottoman armies pushed into Austrian lands and laid siege to the capital, Vienna. Leopold and Sobieski's forces saved the city, however, and then brought most of Hungary under Austrian control (see **Map 13.3**). The loss shocked Ottoman elites, and for good reason. From that point on, the empire ceased to expand, and during the following decades, the Ottomans' sources of wealth dried up. Moreover, the military weaponry and tactics of Ottoman armies and navies lagged behind those of their European foes. Ottoman power and imperial leadership would deteriorate further as weakened rulers struggled against political corruption, provincial revolts, and military insubordination.

After his victory in Vienna, the Austrian king tried to install his own nobility in Hungarian lands and ally himself with powerful Hungarian nobles at the expense of the peasantry. He succeeded only partially, and the still-independent Hungarian nobles remained a thorn in the side of the Austrian monarchy. Facing west, Leopold helped build a coalition that stood against Louis XIV. By the Austrian king's death in 1705, the Habsburg state had become one of the most powerful in Europe.

Russia and Its Tsars Gain Prominence

Even farther east, the Russian monarchy slowly rose to prominence. Already in the sixteenth century, Ivan IV ("the Terrible") (r. 1533–1584) had added both to the authority of the Russian tsars (caesars, or emperors) and to the span of territories over which they ruled. He destroyed the remaining power of the Mongols in southeastern Russia and annexed most of their territory. Next, he began Russia's conquest of Siberia. Within his expanding state, Ivan ruled as a ruthless autocrat, creating his own service gentry to bypass powerful nobles and using torture and terror to silence all he saw as his opponents.

A difficult period known as the Time of Troubles (1584–1613) followed Ivan IV's death. Ivan's feeble-minded son Fyodor ruled ineffectively and left no successor upon his death in 1598. Great nobles vied for power among themselves and against weak tsars. To end the political chaos, a group of leading nobles in 1613 chose the 17-year-old Michael Romanov (r. 1613–1645) to rule as tsar. He began a dynasty that ruled Russia for over three hundred years.

The Romanovs

Despite the political stability Michael and his immediate successors brought, discontent among those below the tsar and the nobility mounted during the century as the authorities increasingly restricted the freedom of the masses. The notorious Law Code of 1649, for example, merged peasants and slaves into a class of serfs and gave the landowning nobility the power to treat them as property. In a spate of uprisings between the late 1640s and early 1670s, the lower classes rebelled against landowners and officials by killing them and looting or burning their estates. The discontent reached a climax in the late 1660s and early 1670s with the revolts of Cossacks (free warriors) in south Russia led by Stenka Razin. A shrewd, seasoned warrior, Razin claimed to "fight only the boyars and the wealthy lords. As for the poor and the plain folk, I shall treat them as brothers." His rebel army marched north, and many towns opened their gates to welcome Razin's forces, now swelling with the addition of discontented peasants and the urban poor. Russian soldiers finally caught, tortured, and executed Razin, and the uprisings tapered off.

By the final decades of the seventeenth century, the Romanov tsars had shored up the government's central administration and extended their authority throughout the country. Lured by visions of wealth from access to Siberian furs, Russians had driven eastward into Asia, establishing fortified settlements, bringing indigenous peoples under their control (in the process decimating them with raids and diseases such as smallpox), and planting their flag on the shores of the Pacific. Moreover, through increased trade and travel, Russia's commercial and cultural contacts with the West expanded, bringing new European goods and ideas into the country. The stage was set for a dynamic tsar to propel Russia more fully into European affairs.

Russian expansion

This new, energetic emperor came in the person of Peter I ("the Great") (r. 1689–1725). Standing nearly seven feet tall, Peter seemed born to rule. At the age of 17, he seized the reins of government from his elder sister. He soon concluded that the best way to bolster his own political and military power was to copy Western practices. To this end, he traveled to western Europe and learned as much as he could about Western politics, customs, and technology.

Peter the Great

Back home, Peter took decisive steps to solidify his authority. In 1698, he crushed a revolt of his bodyguards and silenced critics with a ruthlessness that cowed all potential troublemakers. "Every day was deemed fit and lawful for torturing," wrote an observer. He also made five years of education away from home and state service requirements for the nobility and allowed movement within the ranks only through merit. Peter applied the bureaucratic system of western European monarchs to both central and local government to secure his rule. He also brought Western technicians to Russia in large numbers and protected new industries with mercantilistic policies. Western social customs were introduced to the upper

Brandenburg-Prussia
Prussian Acquisitions in 1688
Russian Territory in 1693
Seized by Peter the Great from Sweden, 1694–1725
Austrian Habsburg Territory in 1657
Austrian Habsburg Territory in 1718
Ottoman Empire in 1699
Boundary of the Holy Roman Empire

MAP 13.3

Central and Eastern Europe, 1640–1725

This map shows the changing political landscape in central and eastern Europe during the seventeenth and early eighteenth centuries.

Explore the Map

1. Notice how Russia's expansion to the west increased its contacts with European commerce and affairs. How might these widening interactions alter the balance of power in Europe?

2. Consider the gains made by the Austrian Habsburgs against the Ottomans. What did the declining fortunes of the Ottoman Empire imply for the future of this part of the Western world?

3. Locate Poland-Lithuania. What problems did this country face, hemmed in as it was by three growing powers?

and middle classes of Russian society, such as bringing Russian women out of seclusion to appear in Western dresses at official dinners and social gatherings. In addition, Peter banned the long beards and flowing Oriental robes that Russian men traditionally wore. When the patriarch of the Russian Orthodox Church opposed the tsar's authority and some of his Westernizing policies, Peter took control of the church and confiscated much of its wealth. Henceforth, the Orthodox Church served as a powerful instrument of the Russian government.

All these reforms left the peasantry in even worse straits than before. Peasants made up 97 percent of Russia's population during Peter's reign, and they became tied down in a system of serfdom bordering on slavery. The taxes they were forced to pay ballooned by a whopping 500 percent, and their feudal obligations and military service increased. Nowhere was peasant life harsher than in Russia, and Peter's efforts to Westernize the nobility only widened the gap between the educated elites and the enserfed peasantry. "The peasants are perfect slaves, subject to the arbitrary power of their lords," wrote a British envoy to Peter's court. They are usually "transferred with goods and chattels; they can call nothing their own."

> Russia's military establishments

To keep Russia in step with the West and support his ambitions for territorial expansion, Peter devoted particular attention to his military establishment. He built a navy and patterned his expanded and modernized conscript army on the model of Prussia. Recruits were drafted for life and even branded with a cross on their left hand to deter desertion. Officials arbitrarily assigned serfs to work in mines and manufacturing establishments to supply the military with equipment and arms.

Peter meant to use his new military might. **Figure 13.6** depicts the clean-shaven tsar Peter the Great in heroic military pose. Clad in armor and carrying a sword, Peter asserts his authority over all potential rivals, who offer him their swords. Beneath the feet of his horse lies a defeated dragon. Above, an angel crowns Peter with divine authority. The tsar waged numerous military campaigns over his long reign, and he designed many of his great reforms to strengthen and modernize his armed forces. In the background of the painting, his troops surge to victory in a mighty battle.

Lacking warm-water access to the West, Peter tried to seize lands bordering the Black Sea that the Ottoman Turks held. Though they had weakened during the seventeenth century, the Ottoman Turks

FIGURE 13.6 Anonymous, *The Apotheosis of Tsar Peter I the Great* The painter portrayed the Russian tsar as a heroic, all-conquering military figure who is blessed with divine authority.

remained a formidable obstacle, and Peter's armies could not dislodge them. Frustrated, Peter turned northwest toward Sweden, which controlled lands bordering the Baltic Sea. Under King Gustavus Adolphus (r. 1611–1632), this Nordic country had become the dominant military power in northeastern Europe in the early seventeenth century (see Chapter 11). At the opening of the eighteenth century, Sweden held large areas east and south of the Baltic in addition to the homeland, and it ranked second only to Russia in size. Much of its success and the power of its monarchs came from the almost constant wars it fought during the seventeenth century. However, it lacked the population and resources to hold its far-flung territories for very long. Though Peter initially lost battle after battle to his brilliant Swedish adversary, Charles XII (r. 1697–1718), his persistence finally paid off. In the Battle of Poltava (1709), the Russians destroyed the Swedish army and managed to wound Charles.

> Conflict with Sweden

The Rise and Fall of the Mughal Empire in India

While monarchs in Europe struggled to consolidate their authority during the seventeenth century, powerful rulers rose in the Asian states. These emperors would become strong enough to rival the Western powers and control relations with European traders. The Asian leaders had a proud history. During the sixteenth century, the Mughals (Moguls), a fierce Islamic Turkish tribe, had swept into the Indian subcontinent and established a flourishing realm ruled by able emperors such as Babur (1483–1530) and Akbar (1542–1605).

In 1605, the 38-year-old Jahangir succeeded the great Mughal leader Akbar and assumed the title of "the world-subduing emperor." In his memoir, he described the lavish ceremonies accompanying his crowning. During the festivities, the high officials of the empire, "covered from head to foot in gold and jewels, and shoulder to shoulder, stood round in brilliant array, also waiting for the commands of their sovereign."

By that time, the Portuguese had already established a flourishing trading base on the west Indian coast. As the seventeenth century unfolded, the Mughals also allowed the English, French, and Dutch to establish trading bases in India, but without power to be of any concern. The Mughals themselves paid little attention to foreign trade but welcomed the revenues from the commerce into their treasuries.

Though Jahangir wielded power arbitrarily, he also felt compelled to follow certain traditions and laws. In his view, to bring "prompt punishment to the man who violates the laws of his country is an alternative with which no person entrusted with the reins of power is authorized to dispense." Jahangir also struggled to bring unruly sections of his empire more firmly under his control, at one time ordering a bloody campaign against rebellious Afghans. The Mughal emperor recorded how prisoners from one battle were paraded before him "yoked together, with the heads of the seventeen thousand slain in the battle suspended from their necks." Reflecting on the burdens of office, Jahangir lamented, "There is no pain or anxiety equal to that which attends the possession of sovereign power, for to the possessor there is not in this world a moment's rest." Nevertheless, the emperor gave his wife, Nur Jahan, a major role in running the government. He also managed to find time to support and enjoy sports, literature, and art as well as to smoke opium regularly. He completed his *Memoirs* before his death in 1627.

An eventual successor, Aurangzeb, became Mughal emperor in 1658 and held power for almost fifty years. One of his chroniclers, Bakhta'war Khan, claimed it was "a great object with this Emperor that all Muslims should follow the principles of the religion." The biographer also boasted that his emperor "has learned the Qur'an by heart."

But Aurangzeb's reign marked both the apex of Mughal power and the beginning of its end. By the time of his death in 1707, reckless spending, endless military campaigns, and persecution of Hindus and Sikhs had weakened the regime. Widespread rebellions broke out, which Aurangzeb's weaker successors failed to overcome. In the 1720s, one observer, Khafi Khan, reported that many townships "have been so far ruined and devastated that they have become forests infested by tigers and lions, and the villages are so utterly ruined and desolate that there is no sign of habitation on the routes."

As the Mughal empire disintegrated, rivals quickly took power. European traders also gained influence—especially the British and French, who were competing for the Indian trade in textiles, spices, and sugar. By the mid-eighteenth century, the land controlled by Aurangzeb's successors had dwindled to Delhi. Meanwhile, the British and French forged strategic political alliances with Indian states and jockeyed for a dominant position on the subcontinent.

Making Connections

1. What were the similarities between the European and Mughal monarchs, particularly Louis XIV of France and Aurangzeb of India?

2. What policies weakened their respective states?

Through the Treaty of Nystad in 1721, Russia received the Swedish Baltic provinces and some Polish territories (see **Map 13.3**). On the shores of the Baltic Sea, Peter triumphantly built a modern capital, St. Petersburg, that faced west. Reigning from this new court, he emulated the cultured, royal ways of the West to enhance his personal authority. At his death in 1725, Russia had taken its place as a major player on the European stage.

The Victory of the Nobility in Poland

Not all the eastern European states drifted toward monarchical absolutism. In Poland, the competition between the monarchy and the nobility took a different turn—with severe consequences for the nation. In the sixteenth and seventeenth centuries, Poland seemed poised to become a major power. Taking advantage of Russia's Time of Troubles (1584–1613), the Poles had captured Moscow for a few years until the Russians finally drove them out in 1613. In reality, however, the Polish nation, which included Lithuania in a dual kingdom, was far from strong. Sprawling over a large area between Russia and the German states, it had no natural, protective boundaries either to the east or to the west. Ethnic and religious divisions undermined the Polish rulers' hopes for unity, and the economy stumbled. In the late Middle Ages, a sizable overland commerce between the Black and Baltic seas had flowed across Poland. However, with the shifting of commercial routes and centers to the west in the sixteenth century, Poland's commerce withered. Worse, the Polish nobility, protective of its own power and fearful of an alliance between merchants and the king, deliberately penalized merchants by passing legislation to restrict trade. The great mass of the Polish people remained serfs, bound to the estates of the powerful nobility.

In the face of such forces, only a strong central government could have ensured stability for Poland. Yet this was precisely where Poland proved weakest. For many years, Poland's nobles had been gaining the upper hand, and they closely guarded their power to elect the king. When King Sigismund II died in 1572, ending the long-ruling Jagellon dynasty, the nobles saw to it that no strong king ascended the throne. They monopolized the legislative body (the Diet) and, to safeguard their rights, required a unanimous vote to pass any measure. This system guaranteed political anarchy in which, in the words of a mid-seventeenth-century observer, "there is no order in the state," and "everybody who is stronger thinks to have the right to oppress the weaker."

Over the course of the seventeenth century, revolts by Ukrainian Cossack warriors and wars with Russia, Sweden, and Brandenburg-Prussia resulted in the loss of Polish territories. Rivalries among the Polish nobles worsened the chaos. Moreover, Tatar slave raiders carried off many people. Incursions and internal wars destroyed towns, and the once-thriving Jewish populations were pushed from their homes and often slaughtered. Tens of thousands of Jews were murdered in the pogroms (organized persecutions) that swept through Poland between 1648 and 1658. Protestants also suffered at the hands of the Catholic majority. Not surprisingly, Poland's population declined sharply in these years. By the beginning of the eighteenth century, it lay vulnerable to surrounding powers that boasted stronger central governments.

THE TRIUMPH OF CONSTITUTIONALISM

As the tendency toward absolutism intensified in central Europe, another major struggle began to unfold in a small island nation far to the west. Kings desiring absolute power in England faced a situation significantly different from that in France. In France, the nobility had little history of common action between classes and lost their solitary struggle against absolutism. In England, however, there had been a tradition of joint parliamentary action by nobles and commoners who owned land, and this helped contribute to a different outcome in the struggle for sovereignty. Instead of government residing in the person of an absolute monarch, it rested in written law—constitutions, not kings, would come to rule.

The Nobility Loses Respect

For over one thousand years, the English had taken for granted the idea of separate social classes. Peasants and members of the middle classes showed the high nobility an unmistakable deference, turning out to greet them when they emerged, gazing downward and holding their hats respectfully in their hands. Even upwardly mobile landowners with some wealth (the gentry) knew that they ranked well below the peers (the old nobility). In England, there were only about four hundred noble families, and they jealously guarded their exclusive position. Commentators wrote that "nobility is a precious gift" and accepted this privilege as the natural order of things: "Men naturally favor nobility."

At the beginning of the seventeenth century, several disturbing incidents pointed to ominous cracks in the wall of privilege. One member of the gentry actually jostled and swore at an earl as the two passed in a narrow passageway, and some tenant farmers neglected to turn out, hats in hand, to welcome passing noblemen. Later, a Protestant sect, the Quakers, enacted a religious policy that forbad members to take off their hats to men in authority. Something had changed and nobles no longer seemed so essential or so noble.

What explained this apparent loss of respect for the English upper crust? We can find a partial answer in the shifting role of money. In the early modern world, the old wealth of the nobility had declined relative to the "new money" of merchants and other enterprising individuals. Furthermore, the medieval base of noble power, the military, had also declined. No longer were nobles in charge of defending the realm; mercenary armies made up of commoners now took care of these matters. England had a relatively large sector of independent craftsmen compared to other countries, and noblemen depended

New wealth

more on "free labor"—that is, on wage laborers who could enter into contracts for their labor. These differences led commoners increasingly to feel they could control their own lives rather than defer to their "betters." In addition, education had become the key to upward mobility. More and more, knowledge and service, rather than birth, seemed the measure of a man.

The members of the nobility did not relinquish their traditional place easily. Indeed, critics complained that noblemen were becoming more arrogant than ever in exerting their privileges. Sometimes, nobles even exceeded the bounds of propriety. In 1635, the Earl of Arundel lost his temper when the mayor of a city did not turn out to greet him in the traditional way. The earl sought out the mayor, grabbed his staff of office, and proceeded to beat him with it, shouting, "I will teach you to . . . attend Peers of the Realm!"

As early as the sixteenth century, laws throughout Europe had begun to supplement tradition in keeping the social classes separate, and the situation in England was no different. Governments issued **sumptuary laws** to regulate what kinds of clothing were appropriate for members of each social class. For example, an individual could not wear velvet unless he had an independent income of over 100 pounds a year, and laborers could not wear cloth costing more than 2 shillings a yard. These laws were supposed to preserve social distinction, but the newly rich recognized that the path to gaining social respect lay in part in *looking* noble. Thus, men and women insisted on purchasing luxurious clothing to rival that of the highest classes. In 1714, a Sicilian traveler observed: "Nothing makes noble persons despise the gilded costume so much as to see it on the bodies of the lowest men in the world." Now, it seemed, there was no visual marker of a person's noble status.

The nobles had more success in guarding their property rights than their fashion privileges. In 1671, Parliament passed game laws giving the nobility the exclusive prerogative to hunt on their own lands. The new mandates even allowed them to set lethal trapguns to kill poachers. Not surprisingly, these laws only exacerbated the common people's anger, as the poor continued to poach simply to survive in times of hunger. Still, many members of the nobility tried to hang on to their privilege while others pressed to undo them.

The portrait of James Stuart, a member of the royal family, shown in **Figure 13.7** captures the arrogance and complacency of the typical English nobleman of 1630, who was oblivious to the gathering social storm that would soon disrupt his idyllic world. James stands proudly dressed in the opulent clothing of the nobility that the sumptuary laws carefully tried to preserve.

Sumptuary laws

FIGURE 13.7 Anthony Van Dyck, *James Stuart, Duke of Richmond and Lennox,* ca. 1630 The English nobility worked to set themselves apart from lesser folk in their appearance and privileges. Here, James Stuart is shown in the lavish clothing that only the noble could wear, accompanied by the giant dog that accompanied him in the hunt, another privilege reserved for the nobility.

His stockings are made of the finest silk, and the lace at his throat is expensive and handcrafted. Adorning his jacket sleeve is a sun image embroidered in silver thread—an early forerunner of Louis XIV's trademark symbol. The painting portrays James with his huge hunting dog, again proclaiming his privileged position through his hunting rights. The dog gazes up adoringly at his master with the kind of deference that James had come to expect. Sadly for members of the nobility, they would receive fewer and fewer admiring glances from their fellow humans.

Protestantism Revitalized

A good deal of social criticism also came from Protestants, many of whom believed that the implementation of Reformation ideas in England had not gone far enough. Because many Protestants were involved in the increasingly lucrative commerce, their wealth helped make their concerns more visible. For many, the compromise of Elizabeth I (discussed in Chapter 11) that allowed worshipers of many beliefs to share one Church of England was unacceptable. These critics believed that the Church of England (the Anglican Church) should be "purified"—that is, trimmed of any practice that lacked biblical precedent or smacked of Catholicism. They especially objected to priestly garments and the elaborate rituals of the Anglican Church. Some wanted to eliminate bishops altogether, preferring rule by church elders instead. (This was the practice common in Scotland, where Protestant churches came to be called Presbyterian—"ruled by elders.")

In their zeal, many Protestants became increasingly anti-Catholic, and their political actions were shaped by this prejudice. Other Protestants even wanted to purify daily life, objecting to theater, cockfights, and other seemingly frivolous activities. Although individuals disagreed among themselves on exactly how they wanted the Church of England purified, they all concurred that change was essential. Many members of this loose group of critics, called **Puritans,** became influential members of Parliament.

Puritans in England reconsidered the political relationship between monarchs and their subjects, wondering about competing loyalties between law and conscience, for example. These questions formed the backdrop of a struggle for sovereignty that dominated the seventeenth century. As early as 1561, the Scottish reformer John Knox warned Queen Mary of Scotland that monarchs were responsible to their subjects: "If their princes exceed their bounds, Madam, no doubt they may be resisted, even by power." This was tantamount to a call to revolution. As Puritans gathered to discuss the purification of the church, they could not help but consider the possibility of political action.

James I Invokes the Divine Right of Kings

Because Queen Elizabeth I had died childless, the throne went to her cousin, the king of Scotland, who became King James I of England (r. 1603–1625). As soon as James heard of Elizabeth's death, he rushed to England brimming with great plans. He made promises to many who greeted him on his way south to London, rapidly knighted thousands of gentry, and even ordered an accused thief hanged without a trial—assuming incorrectly that as king he had the right to do so. Many of his subjects turned out to see their affable new monarch, but, unfortunately for him, he would not prove as popular, or as politically shrewd, as Good Queen Bess.

The honeymoon of the new monarch and his people faded rather quickly, for unlike his predecessor, he was unable to mollify the varying religious beliefs of his people. He was a Calvinist, yet he favored Anglicanism, and his most enduring heritage was the translation of the Bible he commissioned, the King James Bible, which remains widely admired as both religion and beautiful literature. However, the king managed to offend his subjects who hoped for his support for religious change. At the beginning of his reign, Calvinists approached the king, hoping to eliminate the Anglican episcopal system and bring it in line with the Presbyterian Scottish practice with which the king was familiar. They were sadly disappointed, for James threatened to "harry them out of the land" if they did not conform to Anglicanism.

James also offended his Catholic subjects, banning Jesuits and seminary priests. In 1605, a conspiracy of Catholics planned to blow up Parliament while it was in session. The plot failed and the conspirators were executed. Yet, the "gunpowder plot," as it came to be known, increased the anti-Catholic feelings in the country, which were exacerbated when James planned a political marriage between his son and a Catholic Spanish princess. Although the marriage negotiations fell through, the attempt alienated Calvinists and Anglicans alike.

Thus by 1610, there was much animosity between the king and many of his subjects. James thought the English ungrateful, and they found him arbitrary and arrogant. Unlike Elizabeth before him, James was disinclined to compromise his theoretical notions of divine right monarchy. Even before he ascended the throne, James had written two treatises in which he asserted the divine right of kings, and in 1610 he presented this position to a skeptical Parliament. As he put it, "Kings have power of . . . life and death; [they are] judges over all their subjects and in all causes, and yet accountable to none but God." This position was consistent with his hasty execution of the accused thief, but it offended many Puritans in the House of Commons, as well as many lords who viewed the king as subject to the law of the land.

During James's rule, the English colonies in North America grew. In part, the attention to the New World stemmed from James's financial difficulties: The first permanent English colony, named Jamestown after the monarch, was founded in Virginia in 1607. James hoped to generate new income from the Virginia colonies, which in 1619 had imported slaves from Africa to grow tobacco, an increasingly popular crop. Colonial settlement was also forwarded by James's high-handed attitude toward religious dissidents. When the king threatened to harry nonconformists out of the land, some took him literally and emigrated to North America to establish colonies.

They avoided Jamestown, which was sympathetic to the Church of England, and instead landed farther north, founding their first colony in Plymouth, Massachusetts, in 1620. The New World was not to be the solution to either James's religious or fiscal problems. He died leaving a shortage of money and an oversupply of ill will among both Parliament and Protestants.

Charles I Alienates Parliament

James's son, Charles I (r. 1625–1649), inherited both his father's rule and his policies. This sober monarch, continuing to invoke the divine right of kings, considered himself answerable only to God, not Parliament. His relationship with his subjects deteriorated rapidly. He approached Parliament in the same way his father had—calling it when he needed money and disbanding it when the members demanded concessions.

Showing a remarkable insensitivity to his Protestant subjects, Charles married a sister of the Catholic king Louis XIII of France. Soon after his wedding, Charles granted concessions to English Catholics, even allowing the queen and her entourage to practice Catholic rituals in the court itself. English Protestants were horrified at what they saw as outrageous behavior by the family of the titular head of the Church of England. Charles responded to critics by persecuting Puritans, whom he viewed as disloyal. More Puritans fled to North America, settling so many colonies in the northeast that the region came to be called New England. Meanwhile, the situation in old England grew more desperate.

| Concessions to Catholics |

As we saw in Chapter 11, warfare had become extremely expensive, and Charles's costly and fruitless wars with Spain and France had so strained his finances that he even tried to pawn the crown jewels. The king called Parliament several times in the 1620s, only to disband it repeatedly. Things came to a head in 1640, when the Scots, who also objected to the king's high-handed religious policies, invaded the north of England. To raise the army and funds he needed to fight the Scots, Charles called Parliament again. This time, Parliament forced him to agree that he could not disband it without the members' consent. The first crack in Charles's armor of divine right had appeared. The Long Parliament, as it came to be called, continued to meet from 1640 to 1653. Over time, it acquired a measure of power and established protections for the religious freedom of Anglicans and Puritans alike.

| Parliament gains power |

However, the temporary compromise between the king and Parliament came to an end when troubles in Ireland caused both to agree to send troops. However, their alliance ended there. The question of who would command the army remained. Parliament did not trust the king to suppress his religious sympathies to fight the Catholic Irish, and the king did not trust Parliament to share control of any army it raised. In the end, Parliament appointed officers to raise an army, and Charles withdrew from London to raise an army of his own. The Irish no longer seemed the immediate enemy for either side.

"God Made Men and the Devil Made Kings": Civil War, 1642–1649

As **Map 13.4** shows, the alignments in the English civil war show some divisions in English life. The rural areas were more likely to support the king, and the Puritan strongholds in the cities followed the forces of Parliament. In response to Charles's call for support, noblemen, cavalry officers, and Irish Catholics rallied to his banner. His royalist supporters were called Cavaliers, or horsemen, as a reference to medieval knights who fought for their kings. Back in London, Parliament recruited an army 13,000 strong, drawn from the commoners, merchants, a few noblemen, Scots, and Puritans. All these generalizations, however, are drawn in broad strokes, and frequently the choice to support one side or another derived from private decisions, based sometimes on religion and sometimes on long-standing personal grudges against neighbors.

The strength of the parliamentary forces, called **Roundheads** for their short haircuts, stemmed mainly from their skilled infantry, the support of major sections of the navy, and their religious conviction. Parliament's forces also benefited from the leadership of Oliver Cromwell, a Puritan who not only forwarded the cause of revolutionary change in Parliament but also took charge of the army and forged it into a formidable force called the New Model Army. The royalists had more experience in battles and more skilled generals. The lines were drawn—the royalist forces led by the king fought a civil war against the forces led by Cromwell.

By 1646, Parliament forces had won a series of victories, and Charles surrendered to the Scots, who later turned him over to Parliament in exchange for their back military pay. While the king was moved from prison to prison as royalists conspired to free him, leaders of Parliament confronted new challenges: a series of social upheavals as more and more people were drawn into the turbulent events of the 1640s.

| Charles captured |

Women from all social groups participated in unprecedented numbers in the English civil war. In their husbands' absence, a number of noblewomen defended their fortified castles against parliamentary

| Women in war |

forces, inspiring many accounts of great heroics considered surprising in the "weaker sex." Working women disguised as men also passed themselves off as Roundhead soldiers. In 1643, Charles issued a proclamation intending to prevent women from joining the army: "Let no woman presume to counterfeit her sex by wearing man's apparel under pain of the severest punishment which law shall inflict." However, the king was in no position to enforce this edict, and women continued to serve as soldiers. It is impossible to know exactly how many women fought for their cause, but the fact that Charles tried to legislate their exclusion suggests that at least he and his advisors thought the numbers significant.

Women were well suited as spies, because people expected them to be noncombatants. One such woman, Jane Whorwood, dedicated herself fiercely to the king's cause. The tall redhead repeatedly tried to free Charles during his imprisonment after 1646. She smuggled money to him and once brought in acid to weaken the metal bars so that he could break free. One of Charles's aides described Whorwood as "the most loyal person to King Charles I in his miseries."

Other previously uninvolved members of society also jumped into the fray. After 1646, radicals, both men and women, raised new | Levellers | demands for social justice. Their complaints stemmed mostly from the severe economic problems that had hamstrung England in the 1640s. A series of bad harvests caused food shortages and rising prices, and disabled soldiers returning home discovered they could no longer earn a living. Crime increased as people stole to feed their families, and the social order deteriorated. One contemporary observed: "Necessity dissolves all laws and government, and hunger will break through stone walls." From these difficult circumstances, groups of radical Protestants arose. Known as **Levellers,** they insisted that social justice become part of Parliament's agenda. A pamphlet sympathetic to their cause claimed that "God made men and the Devil made kings."

Levellers were as varied a group as the Puritans, encompassing people with a broad array of agendas. In general, however, they harked back to a tradition of English religious radicals like John Ball (see Chapter 9) and espoused as their goal to level social differences. To that end, they advocated some reforms of Parliament. For example, they believed Parliament should be chosen by the vote of all male heads of households, which would represent a dramatic broadening of the vote. Furthermore, they wanted members of Parliament to be paid, so that even those with no independent income could serve. Although these ideas may seem natural to us, they posed a major threat to those who believed that only property brought privilege.

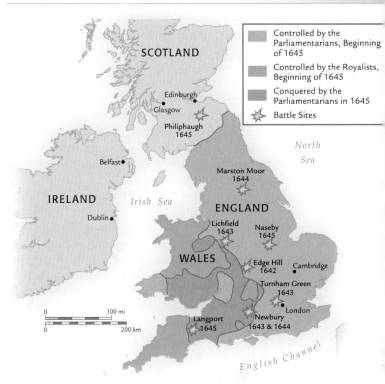

MAP 13.4

The English Civil War, 1642–1649

This map shows England during the civil war years, identifies the locations of the parliamentarian and royalist supporters, and pinpoints the major battles.

Explore the Map

1. Notice the scale of the map. How did the distances affect the progress of the war?

2. Why might the royalists have drawn from rural rather than urban centers?

3. Based only on the information on the map, does it seem possible for the royalists to have won without help from abroad? Explain.

The King Laid Low

In the midst of these controversies, the civil war broke out again in 1648 as Charles encouraged his supporters to rise up to free him. Cromwell's forces promptly crushed the uprisings, and some army leaders concluded that they would never come to peaceful terms with the king. With Cromwell's support, they demanded that Charles be tried for treason. The majority of Parliament members refused to take this extreme step, but in December 1648 invading soldiers purged Parliament of the cautious. The remaining members, scornfully called the Rump Parliament by opponents and historians, brought the king to trial.

The Rump Parliament tried Charles as a king, rather than deposing him first and then trying him as a private citizen. In other words, they wanted to find the *king,* not just the man, guilty. This bold act represented a direct clash between two theories of government—one claiming that the king stood above Parliament, the other declaring that he must answer to it. This unprecedented, highly public trial became the first in history to receive full press coverage. Newspapers had initially emerged in England in 1641, on the eve of the civil war; by 1649, six licensed newspapers recorded the testimony in the trial and provided differing opinions on the proceedings.

Charles was accused of claiming to rule by divine right: He who had been "trusted with a limited power to govern . . . had conceived a wicked design to . . . uphold in himself an unlimited and tyrannical power to rule according to his will. . . ." Though he genuinely believed in divine right, Charles refused to answer this or any other charge. Instead, he claimed that Parliament had no right to bring charges against him at all. He gained much popular support over the few days of the trial as he consistently reiterated his position, rising above a stutter that had plagued him all his life in order to express his views firmly and with dignity. He challenged Parliament to justify "by what power I am called hither." Both sides clearly understood the magnitude of the trial's central question: Who had sovereignty? Charles claimed that God had sovereignty and had delegated it to the king; the Puritans in Parliament claimed that they had sovereignty. There was no room for compromise, and neither side gave way. Charles was found guilty and sentenced to die.

On January 30, 1649, the condemned king was led to a scaffold erected in front of Whitehall Palace. His public execution inspired a rash of etchings and paintings. **Figure 13.8** depicts the crowds who gathered to watch, including women, whose interest in the execution seemed remarkable to contemporary commentators. Many in the crowd were sympathetic to their king. Jane Whorwood, for example, who had worked tirelessly to free Charles, ran forward to greet the king as he walked to the scaffold. **Figure 13.8** shows some of these sympathizers; note the old man in the foreground, leaning on his cane and crying, and the woman fainting in the center.

Charles bravely addressed the few people near him on the scaffold and repeated his views on sovereignty: "I must tell you that the liberty and freedom [of the people] consists in having a government. . . . It is not for having a share in government. Sir, that is nothing pertaining to them. A subject and a sovereign are clear different things." Charles then laid his head on the block, and the executioner severed it cleanly with one blow. The man on the side of the platform in **Figure 13.8** holds the king's head up to show the crowd. The monarchy had ended, and a new form of

Charles executed

FIGURE 13.8 Weesop, *Execution of Charles I,* **1649**   During the English civil war, King Charles I was put to death. This image documents the shocking event and shows how the audience was both attracted to and repelled by this act.

government arose to take its place: a republic in which sovereignty rested with representatives of those who owned property. England called its new republic the Commonwealth.

A Puritan Republic Is Born: The Commonwealth, 1649–1660

As the Rump Parliament began to rule the republic, chaos erupted throughout the realm. The new commonwealth faced warfare outside its borders and dissension within. Fortunately, Parliament had an able champion in Oliver Cromwell (1599–1658). While Parliament ruled, Cromwell with his army controlled the policies.

Rebellions broke out in Catholic Ireland and Protestant Scotland, and Cromwell led his army to those lands, putting down the revolts so brutally that the Irish still remember his invasion with anger. However, Cromwell was effective and brought Scotland and Ireland tightly under English rule. Yet Parliament had more to worry about than just these expensive wars.

Within England, Levellers continued to agitate for social reform, and many of their leaders were imprisoned. Then, in 1649, a gathering of women entered the House of Commons bringing a petition asking for "those rights and freedoms of the nation that you promised us." One member of Parliament taunted the women, saying their public stance was "strange," to which a petitioner responded, "It was strange that you cut off the king's head." These were odd times indeed, and many wondered whether Parliament's victory in the civil war had created more disorder than it had resolved.

| Domestic distress |

The 1649 cartoon in **Figure 13.9** expresses the fears of royalists and moderates alike during this difficult era and serves to illustrate the tumultuous times of the Commonwealth. In this complex image, ax-wielding men (representing the Roundheads) chop down the Royal Oak of Britain, England's longtime symbol of authority and tradition. The oak teeters, threatening to fall and take with it the Bible, the Magna Carta, and the traditional rule of law. Soldiers assist the woodsmen in destroying the tree and the order it represents. The pigs in the center symbolize the common people, being "fattened for the slaughter." Oliver Cromwell stands at the left, supervising the destruction. Below his feet is hell, although he is oblivious to how close he is to damnation. While this cartoon clearly vilifies Cromwell and all he embodied, it also reveals the disorder that had torn at England since the civil war began. Could the parliamentary forces under Oliver Cromwell resolve these fears and tensions?

FIGURE 13.9 *The Royal Oak of Britain,* **1649** Royalists and moderates feared that the civil war would destroy England and its traditions. This cartoon captures these fears as it shows revolutionaries chopping down the oak, symbol of Britain, and bringing down with it religion, the Magna Carta, and other texts hanging from the tree.

Parliament seemed incapable of uniting the various constituents that demanded action after Charles's death. In 1653, when the House of Commons considered a proposal to dismantle Cromwell's large army, the general lost patience. He disbanded Parliament altogether, named himself Lord Protector of the Commonwealth of England, Scotland, and Ireland, and established a military dictatorship—the republic remained only as an ideal. Cromwell faced the same problems that had confronted Parliament and the king—foreign wars and religious struggles. A pious Puritan, Cromwell set out to make England the model of a Protestant land, banning horse races, cockfights, and even theater. He ultimately proved as intolerant of Anglicans as they had been of Puritans, and he alienated most of the population with his intrusive policies. The brief experiment with a rule purely by Parliament had failed, and a military dictatorship could not be popular in a land with such a tradition of participatory government.

| Lord Protector |

Who Has the Power to Rule?

Charles's trial and execution, and the disorder that followed, did not resolve the issue of who had the ultimate power in England. In 1651, the English philosopher Thomas Hobbes (1588–1679) wrote a political treatise, *The Leviathan,* that offered an answer to this question in the form of a new theory of government.

| Thomas Hobbes |

Perhaps shaken by the chaos of the civil war, Hobbes harbored a pessimistic view of human nature. He claimed that everyone was driven by a quest for power and that given the chance, people would try to exercise their power at the expense of their neighbors—even if it meant taking their property and their lives. In this state of nature where there was no controlling authority, Hobbes described human life as "solitary, poor, nasty, brutish and short." However, he held out a ray of hope: Humans, he explained, recognized their inability to live peacefully, so they created a social contract by which they erected a ruler above them. By this contract, subjects willingly surrendered their sovereignty to a ruler who, in turn, agreed to rule over them absolutely.

With this explanation, Hobbes reconciled the Protestant views of sovereignty—in which the people held the right to rule—with absolute monarchy, where the ruler (the king or Lord Protector) possessed sole sovereignty. In the famous frontispiece of *The Leviathan*, shown in **Figure 13.10**, Hobbes visually portrayed the benefits of his system. The ruler is shown at the top wielding the sword and scepter of absolute power. Even more significant, he comprises all the people of the land—he is the body politic. The king derives his power from his subjects, without whom he would not exist. However, with this delegated power, he presides over an orderly and peaceful countryside and village. Church, state, the army, and Parliament are all neatly ordered along the sides of the page. This tidy, comforting vision stands in stark contrast to the chaos shown in **Figure 13.9** and reveals Hobbes's hope that absolute monarchy would guarantee peace in the land.

Hobbes omitted a key point in his thesis: Absolute rule is only as effective as the ruler. Although Cromwell preserved order (albeit while offending many), he failed to develop an institution that could maintain the Puritan republic. When he died in 1658, he named his son Richard his successor. However, the young man could not lead with the same energy and fervor that his father had shown. Under pressure from members of Parliament, Richard resigned, and the right to govern again returned to the people's representatives.

The Monarchy Restored, 1660–1688

Sobered by the chaos that had followed Charles's execution, Parliament decided to reinstate the monarchy. It invited Charles II (r. 1660–1685), son of the executed king, to resume the throne. Ships sailed from England to Holland to escort the king home from his place of exile. Among those in attendance when the king returned was Samuel Pepys (see Biography on pages 442–443), an English diarist who became noted

FIGURE 13.10 Thomas Hobbes, Frontispiece of His Work *The Leviathan*, 1651 Thomas Hobbes warned that only an absolute monarchy would save people from violence, a life he famously called "nasty, brutish, and short."

for the detailed accounts he kept of events from 1660 to 1669. According to Pepys, the people of England greeted their new king with much fanfare and excitement. Charles II came home to a restored monarchy that had all the luxury that his father had enjoyed—and all the problems that had plagued this troubled institution.

Samuel Pepys devoted several pages of his diary to Charles's coronation in 1661. "So glorious was the show with gold and silver," he wrote, "that we were not able to look at it, our eyes at last being so much overcome with it." Like most of his countrymen, Pepys drank ale with wild abandon during the celebration—the years of Puritan temperance seemed to melt away in a haze of drunkenness.

Yet, not everyone got caught up in the celebration. Former Cromwell supporters saw the Restoration in a very different light. John Bunyan (1628–1688), for example, who had John Bunyan fought with Cromwell, was imprisoned in 1660 for preaching against the Restoration. His original sentence of three months was extended to twelve years because he refused to stop preaching.

After his release in 1672, he continued to preach, and he wrote his masterpiece, *Pilgrim's Progress*, in 1678. Probably the most widely read book by an English author, *Pilgrim's Progress* tells of a hero named Christian and his search for salvation through an allegorical world. This tale of hope and confidence in the human power to prevail through times of tribulation was balanced by Bunyan's lesser-known work, *The Life and Death of Mr. Badman* (1680). In this allegory, Bunyan criticized the loose life of Restoration England by describing the journey of a man who goes straight to hell. Bunyan's works strongly suggested that the Restoration had definitely not solved the political struggles of England.

Charles II grappled with the same fiscal problems that had plagued James I and Charles I, but he had to face a Parliament that had proven its strength during the civil wars. The king was **Fiscal problems** bound by law to call Parliament at least every three years, and the members of Parliament had severely curtailed royal power over taxation. Like his predecessors, Charles needed money, and to buttress his revenues without the restrictions Parliament imposed, the new king tried to exert more control over the colonies in North America. He increased the customs duties permitted by the Navigation Acts (imposed in 1651) and fought a war with the Dutch in 1665. This conflict ended in a treaty that gave the English New York in exchange for Dutch control of Surinam in South America.

Charles's international dealings were hampered by disasters at home. In 1665, England **Plague and fire** experienced a plague of frightening intensity—70,000 people died in London alone. The following year, a devastating fire broke out in London, engulfing the city and destroying 13,000 dwellings and 87 churches, including the venerable St. Paul's Cathedral. After the fire had died out, Charles ordered the city rebuilt and hired the skilled architect Sir Christopher Wren to redesign the main buildings. Wren's masterpiece, the new St. Paul's Cathedral, still marks the London skyline.

In addition to these disasters, the issue of religion again came to the fore. Charles had Catholic sympathies, and to circumvent Parliament, he had several times turned to the Catholic king Louis XIV of France for help and money. The Protestant Parliament, wary of Charles's granting concessions to Catholics, passed the Test Act in 1673. The law required an oath of Protestant loyalties to prevent Catholics from holding public offices, but legislation could not affect the king's conscience, or alleviate Parliament's fears of Catholicism. In 1685, Charles died after converting to Roman Catholicism on his deathbed.

Charles's successor, his brother James II (r. 1685–1688), was not able to avoid direct confrontation with the Protestant Parliament. A Catholic, James demanded in vain that Parliament repeal the Test Act, and he proceeded to place Catholics in high office in violation of Parliament's law. Many English feared that James would adopt Louis XIV's policies against Protestants and even try to institute absolute rule. They may well have been right, but the members of Parliament were not going to wait and see. In 1688, when James's Catholic wife produced a Catholic heir to the throne of England, leading members of Parliament took action.

The Glorious Revolution

To preempt James, parliamentary leaders turned to the king's eldest daughter, Mary, a Protestant and the wife of William of Orange of the Netherlands. William staunchly opposed the policies of the Catholic **William and Mary** Louis XIV, so both his politics and his religion suited the English Protestants. William gathered a fleet and an army of 14,000 men and landed in England in November 1688. He marched slowly and peacefully toward London, while most of the English population rallied to his side. Recalling Charles I's fate, James decided to flee to France "for the security of my person." Louis XIV received his Catholic counterpart with kindness.

The Irish Catholics did not welcome the new Protestant king. Indeed, they thought of James II as a Catholic hero, and Irish leaders conspired with James to help him retake his throne while the French king helped fund this enterprise. Early in his reign, William led an army into Ireland and ruthlessly suppressed what he saw as Catholic treason. Abandoning both Ireland and his claim to the throne, James lived out his life in lavish exile in France, leaving the Irish to bear the brunt of William's wrath. The new king

ENGLISH CIVIL WAR

1625	Charles I becomes king
1629	Charles dissolves Parliament
1642	Outbreak of civil war
1649	Charles I executed
1649–1660	Commonwealth in England
1651	Hobbes, *The Leviathan*
1660	Restoration of monarchy with Charles II
1685	James II becomes king
1688	Glorious Revolution
1689	William and Mary become monarchs
1690	Locke, *Second Treatise of Government*

KEY DATES

BIOGRAPHY

Samuel Pepys
(1633–1703)

Enterprising

Clerk,

Member of

Parliament,

and Diarist

Samuel Pepys was born in London on February 23, 1633, the fifth of eleven children. Only he and two of his siblings survived childhood. Samuel's father was a relatively modest tailor and his mother was the sister of a butcher. Nevertheless, the family had relatives who included landed gentry, lawyers, and a physician. The Pepyses were Puritans, and although Samuel uncharitably recalled his mother as "quarrelsome and feebleminded" and his father as "always needing some kind of aid," the family did provide him with the educational opportunities he needed to succeed.

As a young boy, Pepys was sent to live with an uncle and attend the same grammar school where the young Oliver Cromwell had been educated. Samuel must have seemed a promising student, for when he was about 13 he returned to London to attend St. Paul's School, a stronghold of Puritanism and classical learning. He won scholarships to attend Cambridge University and received his bachelor's degree in 1654. After graduating, he found a job as secretary to a distant relative who had taken an important position in Cromwell's new Commonwealth.

A year later, Pepys married Elizabeth, the 15-year-old daughter of a French Protestant refugee. She brought no dowry to the marriage, though Samuel was probably drawn to her beauty—throughout his diary, he repeatedly made notes about attractive women. His domestic life proved stormy, but he wrote often about being pleased with his marriage during the more harmonious times in his household. Pepys complained that Elizabeth was untidy and that she mismanaged the household. For his part, Samuel was no model husband; he always kept his wife short of money and was relentlessly unfaithful to her. He recorded the details of his infidelities and of Elizabeth's pained reactions to them. Elizabeth died young and childless in 1669, and Samuel never remarried.

Through the late seventeenth century, Pepys was an active participant and a careful chronicler of the major events of the era. While still at Cambridge, he witnessed the execution of Charles I and supported the Commonwealth as a clerk. However, he must have harbored royalist sympathies, for his political career blossomed in 1660 with the Restoration. Pepys accompanied the fleet that escorted the new monarch back to England, and his contacts on that journey ensured him a position suited to his many talents.

Pepys began his diary in 1660 and for nine years detailed the events of his times, both great and small. In this extraordinary text, we have an eyewitness account of the devastating plague that scourged London in 1665, followed by the great fire the year after. Pepys juxtaposed historical events with the most intimate details of his daily life, from the food he ate

---

reduced Ireland to colonial status and offered new opportunity for English landlords to take possession of Irish Catholic lands. Irish anger toward the English festered and would grow, but William's victory was cheered in England.

William and Parliament turned to the immediate task of establishing the legitimacy of his kingship. Parliament decided that James's flight from England constituted an abdication of the throne. The sovereignty that, according to Hobbes, the people had surrendered to their king had been returned to Parliament, who now had the right to install a new monarch. Parliament determined to clarify its relationship with the king, and in 1689 it passed a Bill of Rights firmly stating that kings were subject to the laws of the land, thus creating a constitutional monarchy— the triumph of **constitutionalism.** Within the Bill of Rights, William agreed to "deliver this kingdom from

> England's Bill of Rights

popery [Catholicism] and arbitrary power" and to preserve freedom of speech, election, and the rule of law. The bill secured the position of Protestantism in England by ruling that "no person embracing Catholicism or married to a Catholic is eligible to succeed to the throne." Through this bloodless **Glorious Revolution,** Parliament had finally demonstrated that the power to rule rested with the people through their representatives, rather than absolutely with the king. After this, Parliament began to meet annually, which was a practical way to secure its authority.

Royalism Reconsidered: John Locke

Many English men and women were proud of their bloodless "revolution" that so peacefully changed their monarch, but others were uncertain about the legality of this step. The English philosopher John Locke (1623–1704) wrote an influential political

FIGURE 13.11 J. Hayls, *Samuel Pepys,* 1666

royal patronage under the reigns of Charles II and James II, but the Glorious Revolution of 1688 caused his fortunes to change. He lost the parliamentary election in 1689, and in the following year he was arrested on suspicion that he supported the deposed James II. Pepys had always been more interested in observing political events than in engaging passionately in them, and when he was released from prison he removed himself from political life. He spent the rest of his years reading, playing music, and exchanging letters with friends, including such eminent scholars as Isaac Newton. His last years were devoted to building a substantial library, which he bequeathed at his death to his alma mater, where it still remains intact and unaltered. He died peacefully in 1703.

Pepys wrote his diary in a shorthand that was used by clerks in the seventeenth century; Newton used the same shorthand for taking his notes. The four-volume, handwritten, leatherbound diary written in a forgotten code lay ignored on the library shelves until the nineteenth century. Then, an undergraduate of the college took on the gigantic task of transcribing the diary (omitting the erotic passages) and it became an instant success. Modern editions of the complete diary continue to engage readers with its direct picture of seventeenth-century England. It has ensured that Samuel Pepys will not be forgotten.

Connecting People & Society

1. How does Pepys's life reveal the impact of the Glorious Revolution and the growing power of Parliament on the individual?

2. What does this example show about the importance of educational opportunities in the seventeenth century?

to the arguments he had with his wife. He stopped keeping his diary in 1669 because his eyesight was failing him.

Pepys took an active role in political life by working in the naval office. In 1685, he was even elected to the House of Commons. He continued to receive the benefits of

---

tract—*The Second Treatise of Government* (1690)—to justify "to the world [and] the people of England" the Revolution of 1688 and proclaim the legitimacy of William. Locke did much more—he articulated a new relationship between king and subjects that provided a theoretical framework for constitutional forms of government. Like Hobbes, Locke believed that power originally rested with the people and that citizens themselves established a monarchy to keep order. However, whereas Hobbes had said that the people turned over their sovereignty completely to the monarch, Locke claimed that they retained it but created a contract of mutual obligations with their ruler. Locke argued that if the king broke the contract, the people had the right to depose him and install a new monarch, just as Parliament had done during the Glorious Revolution.

Locke's political theories were not intended to support full democracies—in his time, the "people" meant only those who owned property. He did not intend for individuals, such as the landless Levellers, to threaten property owners. Nor did he view women as sharing in the popular sovereignty of the privileged social order. Locke's highly influential rhetoric, in which he claimed natural rights of life, liberty, and property, actually applied to relatively few people in 1690. However, in time, his theory would broaden to form the basis for democracy as well as constitutional monarchy.

Parliament soon had the opportunity to exert its king-making authority once again. William and Mary died without an heir, so the crown went to James II's Protestant daughter, Anne. Queen Anne (r. 1701–1714) also died without an heir, whereby the Protestant Stuart dynasty evaporated. Parliament then passed the crown to George I (r. 1714–1727), a great-grandson of James I, who ruled the German principality of Hanover, introducing the Hanoverian dynasty

Hanover dynasty

MAP 13.5

The United Provinces and the Spanish Netherlands, 1609

This map shows the location of the Netherlands in Europe and its division into two separate states. Notice the scale of the map and consider how small the United Provinces were.

Explore the Map

1. How did the location of these states contribute to their wealth and importance in the seventeenth century?

2. How might the Catholic Spanish Netherlands have served as a buffer between Catholic France and Protestant United Provinces?

to England. This peaceful transition demonstrated once and for all that the struggle for sovereignty in England was over—Parliament ruled.

The Netherlands Maintain a Republic

The English nobles asserted their rights over the king by exercising their authority through a parliament that ruled over a highly centralized government. This struggle created a strong constitutional monarchy that preserved popular sovereignty while creating a state that would prove highly stable. Another way for people to preserve their sovereignty was to resist a strong central government in order to strengthen local institutions. In the seventeenth century, the Netherlands developed this political structure, which also gave power to the people instead of to absolute rulers. They instituted another form of constitutionalism that structured the government around consent of the propertied.

When the Low Countries split in 1609, the southern Catholic regions remained subject to the absolutist monarch, Philip III of Spain. **Map 13.5** shows the division of the Low Countries in 1609. The Spanish Netherlands of the south (now Belgium) formed a buffer between the United Provinces of the north and the divine right monarchy of France. In the United Provinces, which became largely Calvinist after the wars with Catholic Spain, a Protestant state developed that successfully resisted any attempts at royal absolutism.

The United Provinces—also known as the Dutch Republic—was the only major European power to maintain a republican form of government throughout the seventeenth century. Each province was governed locally by an assembly (called the State) made up of delegates from cities and rural areas. In reality, the States were dominated by an oligarchy of wealthy merchants. The union of the provinces was only a loose confederation, with each province sending deputies to the States General, a national assembly that implemented provincial assembly decisions.

Executive power at the local level was vested in governors (Stadholders) of each province. At the national level, executive power was given to the Council of State, made up of deputies drawn from the provinces.

This remarkable decentralization worked effectively for local issues but had some drawbacks for implementing foreign policy. During the 1650s, Holland—the largest province—began to take an informal lead in directing the state's foreign policy in the first two wars against England. After 1672, William III, a prince of the hereditary house of Orange, became the captain-general of the republic's military forces against France. The House of Orange had a permanent vote in the States General and served as a unifying point. However, William of Orange exercised more power once he became king of England in 1689 than he ever had in the Netherlands. Document 13.3 provides a description of the governmental structure of the Dutch Republic. The 1648 Treaty of Westphalia, which ended the Thirty Years' War (see Chapter 11), formally recognized the Republic of the United Provinces.

The United Provinces

An Ambassador Describes the Dutch Government

Sir William Temple (1628–1699) was an English diplomat who served as ambassador to the Netherlands in 1668 and again in 1674. He negotiated the marriage of William of Orange to Princess Mary of England. This political insider was an acute observer of the government of the United Provinces of the Netherlands as shown in this account.

In the first constitution of this government, after the revolt from Spain, all the power and rights of Prince William of Orange, as Governor of the Provinces, seem to have been carefully reserved. But those which remained inherent in the Sovereign, were devolved upon the assembly of the States-General, so as in them remained the power of making peace and war, and all foreign alliances, and of raising and coining of monies: in the Prince, the command of all land and sea forces, as Captain-general and Admiral, and thereby the disposition of all military commands, the power of pardoning the penalty of crimes, the chusing of magistrates upon the

nomination of the towns; for they presented three to the Prince, who elected one out of that number. Originally the States-General were convoked by the council of State, where the Prince had the greatest influence: nor, since that change, have the States used to resolve any important matter without his advice. Besides all this, as the States-General represented the sovereignty, so did the Prince of Orange the dignity, of this State, by public guards, and the attendance of all military officers; by the application of all foreign ministers, and all pretenders at home; by the splendor of his court and magnificence of his expence; supported not only by the pensions and rights of his several charges and commands, but by a mighty patrimonial revenue in lands and sovereign principalities and lordships, as well in France, Germany, and Burgundy, as in thy several parts of the Seventeen Provinces; so as Prince Henry was used to answer some that would have flattered him into the designs of a more arbitrary

power, that he had as much as any wise Prince would desire in that State; since he wanted none indeed, besides that of punishing men, and raising money; whereas he had rather the envy of the first should lie upon the forms of the government, and he knew the other could never be supported, without the consent of the people, to that degree which was necessary for the defense of so small a State against so mighty Princes as their neighbors.

SOURCE: *The Works of Sir William Temple,* vol. I (London, 1814), pp. 118–119 in *Modern History Sourcebook,* www.fordham.edu/ halsall/mod/17dutch.html.

Analyze the Document

1. Which powers remained in the hands of the prince and which in the assembly of the States General?

2. How does this division of rights compare with the governmental forms described in Document 13.1?

3. What might be the strengths and weaknesses of this form of government?

What were the special circumstances that led the Netherlands to develop and maintain this strong sense of local sovereignty when other areas of Europe were moving to centralized governments? In large part, such political independence was facilitated by prosperity. The seventeenth century has been called the golden age of the United Provinces, for this small region was a tremendous European and colonial power. Amsterdam became the commercial and financial center of Europe as ships brought huge quantities of herring from the North Sea, as well as sugar, tobacco, glass, and many other items from around the world, through the bustling port.

In addition to commerce, the Dutch prospered through skilled shipbuilding that was the wonder of Europe. Not only did they design remarkable ships that could sail with fewer crew members than more traditional ships; they also built them quickly and cheaply. They obtained timber, pitch, and rigging from the

Dutch prosperity

nearby Baltic regions, and they used the most modern technology for the assembly: mechanical saws, hoists for masts, and the manufacture of interchangeable parts. Contemporary witnesses were amazed to report that given two months' notice, Dutch shipbuilders could turn out a warship every week for the rest of the year. **Figure 13.12** shows an engraving of a Dutch shipyard that was the envy of the rest of Europe. It is no wonder that silver from the New World found its way into the coffers of Dutch builders.

The Dutch also grew rich from their activities as major slave traders in the New World. The population of Amsterdam grew from about 30,000 people in 1570 to 200,000 by 1660, and the growth was testimony to the wealth and opportunities people saw there. Its financial importance was secured in 1609 by the foundation of the Exchange Bank of Amsterdam, the greatest public bank in northern Europe. Europeans were astonished by the prosperity and enterprise of the Dutch.

FIGURE 13.12 Dutch Shipyard Even small states such as the Netherlands could become rich in the new global marketplace. Dutch shipbuilding was the wonder of Europe, and it was proudly depicted in many images, including this anonymous engraving.

FIGURE 13.13 Rembrandt van Rijn, *Syndics of the Cloth Guild,* ca. 1661 The painter Rembrandt had good reason to depict these wealthy merchants, for they had given him coal to heat his house when he had fallen on hard times.

court of Versailles. Furthermore, in the United Provinces, the Protestant faith cultivated an ideology of moderation—rather than the aristocratic excess that marked the nobility of other states. That is not to say that the seventeenth-century United Provinces espoused notions of egalitarian democracy—the nobility were as interested in trying to increase their power as those of other countries. They were just not able to exert much centralized control over the prosperous, Protestant residents that were the wonder of Europe.

Overall, the Dutch exhibited an unusual degree of religious toleration for their time. They even allowed Catholics and Jews to practice their religions, | **Religious toleration** | a policy that encouraged religious refugees to flock to the Netherlands from all over Europe. These refugees greatly enriched the cultural and economic life of the republic. Not only did the United Provinces attract intellectuals, such as René Descartes from France and John Locke from England, but the open-minded assemblies stimulated the spread of ideas through the press. The United Provinces became a leading center for book publishing and transmitted ideas, even revolutionary ones, all over Europe. In 1649, for example, an anonymous pamphlet published in the Netherlands attacked Cromwell's government for not supporting the ideas of the Levellers. The pamphlet called for an "equality of goods and lands" and condemned the government that "hangs a poor man if he do steal, when they have wrongfully taken from him all his maintenance."

The refugees streaming into the Netherlands included some destitute travelers and in some ways burdened the small country. The Dutch, however, generously assisted the needy, who never sank to the same depths of hardship that faced the poor in many other European cities. In his brief stay in the Netherlands, Samuel Pepys recorded in his diary the provisions the Dutch made for the poor. He observed a guesthouse, "where it was very pleasant to see what neat preparation there is for the poor." He further noted that there were special entertainment taxes to raise money for the needy.

The wealthy middle classes treated themselves well also. For example, they commissioned paintings that depicted their unique way of life. The Dutch artist Jan Vermeer (see Chapter 12) was one of several whose talents flourished in the free Dutch environment. Even more celebrated was the Dutch artist

The Dutch had other elements that contributed to their resistance of absolutism. The Dutch aristocracy was not as wealthy as that of England or France, for example. Their wealth lay more in commerce than in land, so the aristocracy had more in common with the merchants of their land than they did with the landed gentry in England or with the nobility at the

Rembrandt van Rijn (1606–1669), whose brilliant use of light and forceful expressiveness made him among the greatest of western European painters.

In the painting *Syndics of the Cloth Guild* (**Figure 13.13**), Rembrandt portrays the serious, successful merchants who had been chosen to manage the wealthy guild. The artist captures the proud intensity with which they work over a book on the table. In the uniformity in their clothing, they stand in striking contrast to the man in **Figure 13.7**, on page 434, who boasts luxurious designs and fabrics that set him apart from people precisely like these successful syndics. Rembrandt offered this painting to the cloth guild in thanks for their charity—the painter, who had fallen on hard times, needed coal to heat his house for the winter, and the cloth guild had provided it.

The preeminence of the Dutch began to wane by the beginning of the eighteenth century. The economies of England and France had gathered strength both in Europe and abroad and encroached on the commercial empire forged by the Dutch. Yet the two geographically small countries of England and the Netherlands had contributed much to the political development of the West. Both established the sovereignty of the people through constitutionalism—England through Parliament, and the Netherlands through local autonomy. For all their tremendous impact for the future, at the opening of the eighteenth century both nations seemed hardly whispers in a Europe dominated by strong monarchs proclaiming a divine right to rule.

LOOKING BACK & MOVING FORWARD

Summary   For upper-crust members of Western societies, the seventeenth century was a period of both comfort and struggle. The comfort came from these elites' continued dominance. From the beginning to the end of the century, they held most of the riches, status, and power. Those below them sometimes revolted, but the real threats came from competing colleagues and the monarch above. The efforts by monarchs to increase their power, to become "absolute" in both theory and practice, sparked intense struggles within states. In some places, such as France, Prussia, and Russia, strong monarchs offering order and stability won. In other places, such as Poland, England, and the Netherlands, powerful nobles—sometimes allied with commoners—overcame kings.

For the vast majority who toiled in the fields, the period offered struggle without much comfort. In western Europe, demands from expanding central governments for taxes and conscripts only aggravated the hardships wrought by unusually bad harvests and disease. In eastern Europe, landowning nobles added to these problems by burdening peasants under an increasingly heavy yoke of serfdom.

Thus the structure of this hierarchical society may have loosened enough for some people in western Europe to improve their lot. However, that structure only tightened in eastern Europe. For all of Europe, war, revolt, and even revolution shook societies without breaking the traditional hierarchies. Nevertheless, some traditions started to crumble. Important changes in science and thought were already afoot that would soon transform the intellectual foundations of Western society.

KEY TERMS

Great Chain of Being, *p. 416*

royal absolutism, *p. 419*

Fronde, *p. 421*

classical style, *p. 423*

Estates, *p. 427*

sumptuary laws, *p. 434*

Puritans, *p. 435*

Roundheads, *p. 436*

Levellers, *p. 437*

constitutionalism, *p. 442*

Glorious Revolution, *p. 442*

REVIEW, ANALYZE, & CONNECT TO TODAY

REVIEW THE PREVIOUS CHAPTERS

Chapter 11—"Alone Before God"—examines the Reformation, which shattered the unity of western Christendom, and the entwined religious and dynastic wars that followed. Chapter 12—"Faith, Fortune, and Fame"—told how several European powers expanded overseas during this same period and grew rich from the commerce developed in their colonies.

1. Analyze how the religious divisions and wars of the sixteenth and seventeenth centuries laid the groundwork for both the growth of absolutism in France and central Europe and the struggle against it in England and the Netherlands.

2. In what ways might the competition for overseas empires and the commerce that resulted have affected the power of central governments and their responsibilities? How might the Netherlands' political structure have contributed to its commercial expansion?

ANALYZE THIS CHAPTER

Chapter 13—"The Struggle for Survival and Sovereignty"—describes how kings and nobles battled for power, the resolutions of those struggles, and their impact on the millions of people outside the elites.

1. Analyze the ways monarchs tried to increase their power.

2. What groups opposed the increase in monarchical power, and what political theories were developed to support their positions?

3. In what ways might the term *absolutism* also apply to the Mughal emperors?

4. How do you explain why in some areas monarchs won the battle for sovereignty, whereas in others they lost?

5. Describe the struggles peasants throughout Europe faced during the seventeenth century. How did their conditions differ in western and eastern Europe?

CONNECT TO TODAY

Think about this chapter's account of the struggles for power between rulers and various groups, and consider the political theories that those in power developed to justify their positions.

1. Why might some people in today's world still find the idea of monarchy appealing?

2. Why would most people in the West today oppose monarchical rule? How might they justify their views?

3. What lessons from this chapter might today's political leaders do well to apply?

BEYOND THE CLASSROOM

STRESSES IN TRADITIONAL SOCIETY

Braudel, Fernand. *Civilization and Capitalism: The Structures of Everyday Life.* New York: Harper & Row, 1981. An excellent survey by an important historian that details the transformations in economic and social history.

Chartier, Roger, ed. *A History of Private Life, Vol. III: Passions of the Renaissance.* Cambridge, MA: Harvard University Press, 1989. Part of a fine series that describes the creation of the sphere of private life.

Gottlieb, Beatrice. *The Family in the Western World from the Black Death to the Industrial Age.* Oxford: Oxford University Press, 1994. A thorough survey of the transformations in family life.

Sturdy, D.J. *Fractured Europe: 1600–1721.* London: Wiley/ Blackwell, 2002. A comprehensive introduction, nicely organized around regions.

ROYAL ABSOLUTISM IN FRANCE

Bercé, Yves-Marie. *The Birth of Absolutism.* London: Macmillan, 1996. A solid examination of French absolutism from the reign of Louis XIV to 1789.

Phillips, Henry. *Church and Culture in Seventeenth-Century France.* Cambridge: Cambridge University Press, 2002. Excellent analysis of French culture and its connections with the Catholic Church.

Treasure, Geoffrey. *Louis XIV.* London: Longman, 2001. A well-written study of the king and his times.

THE STRUGGLE FOR SOVEREIGNTY IN EASTERN EUROPE

Goffman, Daniel. *The Ottoman Empire and Early Modern Europe.* Cambridge: Cambridge University Press, 2002. An informative survey of the topic.

Hughes, Lindsey. *Russia in the Age of Peter the Great.* New Haven, CT: Yale University Press, 1998. A recent study of this important figure.

Kirby, David G. *Northern Europe in the Early Modern Period: The Baltic World, 1492–1772.* London: Longman, 1990. A good survey of the region during this period.

Wilson, Peter H. *Absolutism in Central Europe.* London: Routledge, 2000. A good comparative study of absolutism in Prussia and Austria.

GLOBAL CONNECTIONS

Richards, John F. *The Mughal Empire.* Cambridge: Cambridge University Press, 1993. A solid, useful survey of Mughal history.

THE TRIUMPH OF CONSTITUTIONALISM

Braddick, Michael. *God's Fury, England's Fire: A New History of the English Civil Wars.* New York: Penguin Global, 2009. A splendid history of the civil wars that details events and people from the earliest rebellions through the execution of Charles. Gives careful attention to all parts of the United Kingdom.

Cust, Richard. *Charles I.* Harlow, UK: Pearson, 2007. Balanced exploration of this complex man whose reign spawned the civil war.

Fraser, Antonia. *The Weaker Vessel.* New York: Knopf, 1984. A detailed, illustrated, and comprehensive study of women in seventeenth-century England.

Gaunt, Peter. *Oliver Cromwell.* Cambridge, MA: Blackwell, 1995. A good study on the life and career of the Lord Protector.

Geyl, Pieter. *History of the Dutch-Speaking Peoples 1555–1648.* Phoenix, AZ: Phoenix Press, 2001. A fine historical summary that illuminates questions of national identity and the problems of a small country functioning in the shadows of great powers.

Hill, Christopher. *A Nation of Change and Novelty: Radical Politics, Religion, and Literature in Seventeenth-Century England.* London: Routledge, 1990. A history of the revolution by an eminent historian.

Miller, John. *Restoration and the England of Charles II,* 2nd ed. White Plains, NY: Longman, 1997. Clarifies the complex issues of the major political and religious themes surrounding the Restoration.

Purkiss, Diane. *The English Civil War: Papists, Gentlewomen, Soldiers, and Witchfinders in the Birth of Modern Britain.* New York: Basic Books, 2007. Vividly illuminates the details of everyday life and the personalities of the participants in the English civil war.

Sharpe, Kevin. *Culture and Politics in Early Stuart England.* Stanford, CA: Stanford University Press, 1994. A revisionist look at the culture and politics in England at this time.

van Deursen, A.Th. *Plain Lives in a Golden Age: Popular Culture, Religion, and Society in Seventeenth-Century Holland.* Translated by M. Ultree. New York: Cambridge University Press, 1991. A fascinating analysis of how laborers, peasants, and sailors made their living.

FRONTISPIECE TO MARCO VINCENZO CORONELLI'S ATLAS, 1691

In this frontispiece from an atlas, a globe and ship occupy center stage and represent the West's exploration of the world. Just above, the banner of a trumpeting angel reads, "Yet farther"— words that contrast sharply with the traditional medieval expression "No farther." Drawings of the numerous instruments that characterized the new age of exploration and science occupy the periphery of the image.

A New World of Reason and Reform

14

The Scientific Revolution and the Enlightenment, 1600–1800

In 1655, French scientist Blaise Pascal (1623–1662) retired from his studies and began recording his thoughts in writing. "Man is but a reed, the most feeble thing in nature; but he is a thinking reed," he wrote. "All our dignity consists, then, in thought . . . by thought I comprehend the world." Pascal's words hint at the changes emerging in scholars' thinking about ideas, the world, and the place of humans in it.

We can detect more clues about these changes in the artwork on page 450. The 1691 world atlas itself, published by the accomplished Venetian mapmaker and mathematician Marco Coronelli (1650–1718), echoes the overseas expansion of Europe, already two centuries old. It also reveals the underlying culture of the Renaissance, which stressed learning and exploration through reading and art. Coronelli chose this illustration to open his new atlas. With the images of a ship, the earth, and scientific instruments and the provocative phrasing "Yet farther," he declared the end of limits to the search for knowledge. The entire illustration suggests a people proudly using science to fuel their growing power—over other peoples as well as nature itself.

Buoyed by the accumulation of scientific discoveries, this optimism about the power of thought and the search for knowledge grew and spread throughout the West during the eighteenth century. Widening circles of intellectuals and the reading public learned about the new ways of thinking being applied to all fields, from politics and religion to economics and criminology. Despite resistance from church and state, this dawning of what became known as the Age of Reason would gather strength, filter down through the ranks of society, and form the intellectual foundation for life in the modern West. Certainly the West was not unique in reasoning about the world. In the centuries preceding Europe's Renaissance, the Chinese had made many scholarly and scientific advances. The Arabs not only had prized learning and science but also had provided Europeans with tools such as translations of Greek science and Arabic numerals that were essential for Europe's scientists. On the other hand, by the sixteenth century most European scientists had university educations, whereas non-Western civilizations lacked institutions comparable to the medieval universities in places such as Bologna, Paris, and Oxford. Moreover, during the seventeenth and eighteenth centuries, the Islamic, Chinese, Japanese, and other civilizations of the world declined to question their traditional ways. Only Westerners challenged the standard assumptions of their civilization. The power and attitudes that the West gained from this intellectual exploration helped redefine Western civilization and distinguish it from the non-Western world.

TIMELINE

- Copernicus 1543
- Kepler 1609
- Galileo 1630
- Descartes 1640
- Newton 1687
- Locke 1691
- Voltaire 1740
- Rousseau 1750

Enlightenment 1733–1789

Age of Ideologies

French Revolution and Napoleon 1789–1815

Scientific Revolution 1543–1687

1480   1550   1620   1690   1760   1830

PREVIEW

QUESTIONING TRUTH AND AUTHORITY
Learn why the old view of the physical universe changed.

DEVELOPING A MODERN SCIENTIFIC VIEW
Study the elements of the modern scientific view.

SUPPORTING AND SPREADING SCIENCE
Trace the spread of the Scientific Revolution.

LAYING THE FOUNDATIONS FOR THE ENLIGHTENMENT
Examine the roots of the Enlightenment.

THE ENLIGHTENMENT IN FULL STRIDE
Investigate how the Enlightenment developed.

QUESTIONING TRUTH AND AUTHORITY

On June 22, 1633, the well-known Italian scientist Galileo Galilei (1564–1642) knelt in a Roman convent before the cardinals who served as judges of the Inquisition. The cardinals informed Galileo that he was "vehemently suspected of heresy." They also showed him the customary instruments of torture, though they did not use them. Next, they ordered him to deny "the false opinion that the sun is the center of the universe and immovable, and that the earth is not the center of the same"—views that Galileo had supported in a book he published the previous year. Threatened with being tried and burned as a heretic, Galileo had to denounce his views as heresy. The court and papacy sentenced Galileo to house arrest in Florence for the rest of his life and forbad him to publish on the topic again. Nevertheless, Galileo would not change his mind. The sequence of events leading to Galileo's trial and conviction is a story of its own, but the conflict lay at the core of a major development of the age: the Scientific Revolution.

The Old View

Until the sixteenth century, most European scholars shared the standard medieval understanding of the physical nature of the earth and the universe. This understanding was based on a long legacy stretching back to the views of the fourth-century B.C.E. Greek philosopher Aristotle. His ideas had been modified in the second century C.E. by Ptolemy of Alexandria and then passed on through Byzantine and Arab scholars to medieval European thinkers. After the thirteenth century, Europeans translated Aristotle's works into Latin and merged his thinking with Christian ideas about the universe.

FIGURE 14.1 The Medieval View of the Universe, 1559
This woodcut shows the earth at the center of a stable, finite universe. A band with signs of the zodiac suggests the importance of astrology within this Christian understanding.

According to this Christian medieval understanding, illustrated in the woodcut in **Figure 14.1,** the earth rested at the center of an unchanging universe. Around it in ascending order rose the perfect spheres of air, fire, the sun, the planets, and the stars (the firmament), with God (the prime mover) just beyond. The signs of the zodiac are recorded on one band in the illustration, revealing the importance of astrology. Westerners accounted for the succession of day and night by explaining that this finite universe rotated in precise circles around the earth once every twenty-four hours. The heavenly abode of angels consisted of pure matter, and the earthly home of humans was made of changeable, corrupt matter. This universe was clear, finite, and satisfyingly focused on the earthly center of God's concern.

> The earth-centered universe

Common sense supported this worldview. A glance at the sky confirmed that the sun and stars indeed circled around the earth each day. Under foot, the earth felt motionless. To careful observers, the motion of planets, whose position often changed, was more perplexing. To explain this mystery, Ptolemy and others had modified their theories, concluding that planets moved in small, individual orbits as they traveled predictably around the earth. People had lived by the wisdom of the ancients and authoritative interpretations of the Bible for centuries. Accordingly, investigation of the physical universe generally consisted of making deductions from these long-accepted guides.

Undermining the Old View

During the fifteenth and sixteenth centuries, new problems began undermining this traditional view. Authorities of all kinds—including Aristotle—came into question during the Renaissance. Some of this questioning stemmed from the Renaissance search for classical writings, which led scholars to discover and read the works of Greek authorities who contradicted Aristotle. **Neoplatonism,** based on the ideas of Plato, stressed the belief that one should search beyond appearances for true knowledge; truth about both nature and God could be found in abstract reasoning and be best expressed by mathematics. Neoplatonic **Hermetic doctrine** provided especially powerful alternatives to Aristotelian thought.

According to Hermetic doctrine, based on writings mistakenly attributed to Hermes Trismegistus (supposedly an ancient Egyptian priest), all matter contained the divine spirit, which humans ought to seek to understand. Among many scholars, this doctrine stimulated intense interest in botany, chemistry, metallurgy, and other studies that promised to help people unlock the secrets of nature. The Hermetic approach also held that mathematical harmonies helped explain the divine spirit and represented a crucial pathway to understanding God's physical world. This approach encouraged scholars to use mathematics and to measure, map, and quantify nature. Moreover, Hermetic doctrine also held that the sun was the most important agency for transmission of the divine spirit and thus rightly occupied the center of the universe. Finally, these beliefs fostered the idea of the natural magician who could unleash the powers of nature through alchemy (the study of how to purify and transform metals, such as turning common minerals into gold), astrology (the study of how stars affect people), and magic. Scholars often saw no distinction between seeking to understand the harmony, oneness, and spiritual aspects of the natural world and what we would call scientific observation and experimentation. Although Hermetic doctrine often proved not useful, all these ideas encouraged investigators to question traditionally accepted knowledge.

Figure 14.2, an illustration from a book on alchemy by the German Heinrich Khunrath, shows these close connections between spiritual beliefs and

Hermetic doctrine

FIGURE 14.2 Heinrich Khunrath, *The Laboratory and the Chapel,* 1609 Amid the tools of his trade, an alchemist prays in a small chapel. This seventeenth-century illustration reveals the close connections between spiritual beliefs and alchemy.

the "science" or "Hermetic art" of alchemy. At the left, the author prays in a small chapel. Lettering on the drapery of the chapel states, "When we attend strictly to our work, God himself will help us." At the center, musical instruments and a pair of scales rest on a table, representing the links among music, harmony, and numbers so characteristic in alchemy. The inscription on the table reads, "Sacred music disperses sadness in evil spirits." On the floor lie containers and other apparatus used to mix materials, and at the upper right are flasks and other storage containers.

In addition to new ideas and beliefs, geographic exploration during the Renaissance also upset traditional assumptions. The discovery of the New World, for example, disproved Ptolemaic geography. Furthermore, overseas voyages stimulated demand for new instruments and precise measurements for navigation. This demand, in turn, encouraged research, especially in astronomy and mathematics.

Exploration

Finally, the recently invented printing press enabled even out-of-favor scholars to publish their findings, which spread new ideas and discoveries even further. Renaissance rulers supported all these efforts in hopes of gaining prestige as well as practical tools for war, construction, and mining. Church authorities did the same at times, especially backing

The printing press

research in astronomy in the hopes of improving the calendar to date Easter more accurately.

Like the Renaissance, the Reformation unleashed forces that provoked the questioning of long-held views. Most researchers had religious motives for their work, though those motives were not necessarily grounded in tradition. In particular, they yearned for insights into the perfection of God's universe. As we read in Chapter 11, the Reformation shattered confidence in religious authorities. By upsetting hallowed certainties, sixteenth- and seventeenth-century scholars hoped to establish new, even sounder certainties and thereby regain a sense of mastery over nature.

DEVELOPING A MODERN SCIENTIFIC VIEW

Even with these rumblings of change, no sudden breakthrough cleared away the centuries-old understanding of nature. Most scientific work still proceeded slowly, as did scholarly and public acceptance of its findings. Investigators had to demonstrate the effectiveness of their new methods again and again to convince even their colleagues. Indeed, few scholars suggested a wholesale rejection of traditional authorities; most simply chipped away at old notions. By the end of the seventeenth century, however, an entirely new scientific view of reality, initiated by just a handful of scholars, had replaced the traditional view. To understand this startling shift, we need to trace developments in astronomy, physics, and scientific methodology.

Astronomy and Physics: From Copernicus to Newton

During the sixteenth and seventeenth centuries, astronomy and physics attracted the most systematic attention from scholars. Researchers in these fields became particularly dissatisfied with the inability of Aristotelian theory to explain, simply and efficiently, careful observations and mathematical calculations of the stars. The Ptolemaic system for predicting planetary movements seemed overly complex and cumbersome to these scholars. Their findings would dramatically alter Westerners' perceptions of nature and of the earth's place in the universe. As the English poet John Donne complained in 1611, "New philosophy calls all in doubt."

Nicolaus Copernicus (1473–1543), a Polish clergyman with an interest in astronomy, astrology, mathematics, and church law, took the | Nicolaus Copernicus | first steps in this intellectual adventure. Like so many other northern European scholars, he crossed the Alps to study in an Italian university. There he became influenced by the rediscovery of Greek scholarship, Neoplatonism, and the Hermetic doctrine.

FIGURE 14.3 Andrea Cellarius, *The Copernican System*, 1661 This page from Cellarius's *Celestian Atlas* shows the "Copernican System of Planets," with the sun at the center of the universe and the planets circling around it.

Copernicus sought a simpler mathematical formulation to explain how the universe operated. His search convinced him that the earth was *not* at the center of the universe. Instead, he believed that the sun "sits upon a royal throne" in that location, "ruling his children, the planets which circle around him." Moreover, Copernicus concluded that the earth was not stationary: "What appears to be a motion of the sun is in truth a motion of the earth." According to Copernicus, the earth moved in perfect, "divine" circles around the sun, as did other bodies in the universe. Day passed into night because the earth turned on its axis. **Figure 14.3** shows this view of the universe. At the center is the sun, circled by the earth (showing night and day) and the other planets, (note Jupiter and its moons on the right). The signs of the zodiac are on the outer band, suggesting continuing beliefs in astrology. The figure on the lower right, holding a globe and a scientific instrument, is Copernicus. This change from an earth-centered (geocentric) to a sun-centered (heliocentric) universe would become known as the **Copernican revolution.**

Copernicus worked on his **heliocentric model** of the universe for almost twenty-five years. However, fearing ridicule and disapproval from the clergy, he waited until 1543—what became the year of his death—to publish it. Few people outside a limited circle of scholars knew of his views, and even fewer accepted them. Nevertheless, Catholic and Protestant authorities who were wedded to the earth-centered system soon recognized the threat to the Christian conception of the universe that these ideas represented. They denounced the Copernican system as illogical, unbiblical, and unsettling to the Christian faith. One Protestant associate of Martin Luther complained that "certain men . . . have concluded that the earth moves. . . . It is want of honesty and decency to assert such notions publicly. . . . It is part of a good mind to accept the truth as revealed by God and to acquiesce in it."

Still, Copernicus's thinking had some supporters. An Italian monk, Giordano Bruno (1548–1600), tested Catholic authorities by openly teaching and extending Copernican thought, arguing that "the universe is entirely infinite because it has neither edge, limit, nor surfaces." Bruno also professed a series of unusual religious notions. Outraged, the Catholic Inquisition burned Bruno at the stake. Nevertheless, Copernicus's views began to influence other scholars who were investigating the physical nature of the universe.

The Danish aristocrat Tycho Brahe (1546–1601) did not share Copernicus's belief in a heliocentric universe, nor did he grasp the sophisticated mathematics of the day. Still, he became the next most important astronomer of the sixteenth century. He persuaded the king of Denmark to build for him the most advanced astronomy laboratory in Europe. There he recorded thousands of unusually accurate, detailed observations about the planets and stars over a period of twenty years—all without a telescope. His discoveries of a new star in 1572 and a comet in 1577 undermined the Aristotelian belief in a sky of fixed, unalterable stars moving in crystalline spheres. Although Brahe mistakenly concluded that some planets revolved around the sun, which itself moved around the earth, other astronomers with better understandings of mathematics would use his observations to draw very different conclusions.

Tycho Brahe's assistant, Johannes Kepler (1571–1630), built on Brahe's observations to support the Copernican heliocentric theory. A German Lutheran from an aristocratic family, Kepler—like other Hermetic scholars—believed in an underlying mathematical harmony of mystical significance to the physical universe. He sought one harmony that would fit with Brahe's observations. Between 1609 and 1619, he announced his most important findings: the three laws of planetary motion. After determining the first law—which stated that the planets moved in ellipses around the sun—he excitedly wrote, "It was as if I had awakened from a sleep." The second law declared that the planets' velocity varied according to their distance from the sun. The third law concluded that the physical relationship between the moving planets could be expressed mathematically. Kepler thus showed "that the celestial machine . . . is the likeness of [a] clock," further undermining the Aristotelian view and extending the Copernican revolution.

Document 14.1 reveals that in 1597, Kepler responded to a letter from Galileo Galilei, the Italian astronomer, physicist, and mathematician discussed at the beginning of this chapter. Although Galileo expressed a reluctance to publicize his beliefs in Copernican ideas, Kepler encouraged him to take the risk. "Be of good cheer, Galileo, and appear in public. If I am not mistaken there are only a few among the distinguished mathematicians of Europe who would dissociate themselves from us. So great is the power of truth."

Galileo already believed that the world could be described in purely mathematical terms. "Philosophy," he wrote, "is written in this grand book, the universe, which stands continually open to our gaze. . . . It is written in the language of mathematics, and its characters are triangles, circles, and other geometric figures without which it is humanly impossible to understand a single word of it. . . ." Galileo also felt that harmonies could be discovered through experimentation and mathematics. By conducting controlled experiments such as rolling balls down inclines, he demonstrated how motion could be described mathematically. He rejected the old view that objects in their natural state were at rest and that all motion needed a purpose. Instead, he formulated the principle of inertia, showing that bodies, once set into motion, will tend to stay in motion. He thus overturned Aristotelian ideas and established rules for experimental physics.

Galileo, hearing about the recent invention of the telescope, then studied the skies through a telescope that he built in 1609 out of a long tube and magnifying lenses. He saw that the moon's surface, instead of being a perfect heavenly body, was rugged (like the earth's), with craters and mountains indicated by lines and shading. The telescope also revealed that Jupiter had moons and that the sun had spots. These observations confirmed the view that other heavenly bodies besides the earth were imperfect and further convinced him of the validity of Copernicus's hypothesis. For years, Galileo had feared the disapproval of the Catholic Church. Now, however, he was ready to publicly argue that "in discussions of physical problems we ought to begin not from the authority of scriptural passages, but from sense-experiences and necessary demonstrations." Galileo published his findings in 1610.

Six years later, the church attacked his proposition that "the earth is not the center of the world nor immovable, but moves as a whole, and also with a daily motion." This statement, the church said, was "foolish and absurd philosophically, and formally heretical." To back up its claim, the church cited the authority of both the Bible and itself. For the next several years, Galileo kept his thoughts to himself. In 1632, believing that the church might be more open, he decided again to present his views. To avoid challenging the church, he submitted his book to the official church censors and agreed to some changes they demanded.

thinking about
DOCUMENTS

Kepler and Galileo Exchange Letters About Science

Many leading European scholars of the Scientific Revolution feared publishing their views, which were often unpopular with religious authorities. Such scholars sometimes turned to each other for support, as the following late-sixteenth-century letters between Kepler and Galileo suggest. Here the two men discuss their beliefs in Copernican theory.

Galileo to Kepler: "Like you, I accepted the Copernican position several years ago. I have written up many reasons on the subject, but have not dared until now to bring them into the open. I would dare publish my thoughts if there were many like you; but, since there are not. I shall forbear."

Kepler's Reply: "I could only have wished that you, who have so profound an insight, would choose another way. You advise us to retreat before the general ignorance and not to expose ourselves to the violent attacks of the mob of scholars. But after a tremendous task has been begun in our time, first by Copernicus and then by many very learned mathematicians, and when the assertion that the Earth moves can no longer be considered something new, would it not be much better to pull the wagon to its goal by our joint efforts, now that we have got it under way, and gradually, with powerful voices, to shout down the common herd? Be of good cheer, Galileo, and come out publicly! If I judge correctly, there are only a few of the distinguished mathematicians of Europe who would part company with us, so great is the power of truth. If Italy seems a less favorable place for your publication, perhaps Germany will allow us this freedom."

SOURCE: Giorgio de Santillana, *The Crime of Galileo* (Chicago: University of Chicago Press, 1955), pp. 11, 14–15.

Analyze the Document

1. Why is Galileo reluctant to publish his views on the Copernican position?

2. How does Kepler respond to Galileo's concerns?

3. In what ways does Kepler's reply suggest that the Scientific Revolution was already a growing movement by the end of the sixteenth century?

Finally he published his *Dialogue on the Two Chief Systems of the World*—in Italian rather than the less-accessible Latin. This text advocated Copernicanism, portrayed opponents of the Copernican system (such as the Jesuits) as simpletons, and brought Galileo directly into public conflict with conservative forces in the Catholic Church. Because Galileo could show that his book had already been approved by church officials, prosecutors had to use questionable evidence against him. **Figure 14.4,** painted by an anonymous artist, shows Galileo, wearing a black suit and hat, sitting alone facing church officials. Behind him a man records the trial, while surrounding them are observers—some members of the clergy, others laypeople. In the lower left, two men discuss or argue the issues being decided within; above them some members of the audience look out toward the viewers and the greater world. As we saw at the beginning of the chapter, the Roman Inquisition ultimately forced Galileo to renounce his views.

News of Galileo's sensational trial spread throughout Europe, as did fear of publishing other radical views. Soon, however, his book was translated and published elsewhere in Europe, and his views began to win acceptance by other scientists. Even though Galileo admitted that the new science was beyond the grasp of "the shallow minds of the common people," he effectively communicated its ideas to his peers. By the time

FIGURE 14.4 Anonymous, *Trial of Galileo Before the Inquisition*   In 1632, Galileo came into conflict with conservative forces in the Catholic Church over his Copernican views. In this painting by an anonymous artist, Galileo sits facing the church officials who will judge him.

DOCUMENT 14.2

Isaac Newton: God in a Scientific Universe

Like Galileo and Descartes, Newton was well aware that his ideas had profound implications for theology. His views, he realized, might even be considered contrary to religious doctrine. Yet Newton was a deeply spiritual man and took pains to distinguish the appropriate realms of science and religion. In the following selection from Opticks (1704), his analysis of light, Newton emphasizes that his ideas and systems still allow room for God in the universe.

All these things being consider'd, it seems probable to me, that God in the Beginning form'd Matter in solid, massy, hard, impenetrable moveable Particles, of such Sizes and Figures, and with such other Properties, and in such Proportion to Space, as most conduced to the End for which he form'd them; and that these primitive Particles being Solids, are incomparably harder than any porous Bodies compounded of them; even so very hard, as never to wear or break in pieces; no ordinary Power being able to divide what God himself made one in the first Creation. . . .

It seems to me farther, that these Particles have not only a *Vis inertiae*, accompanied with such passive Laws of Motion as naturally result from that Force, but also that they are moved by certain active Principles, such as is that of Gravity, and that which cause Fermentation, and the Cohesion of Bodies. These Principles I consider, not as occult Qualities, supposed to result from the specifick Forms of Things, but as general Laws of Nature, by which the Things themselves are form'd; their Truth appearing to us by Phaenomena, though their Causes be not yet discover'd. . . .

Now by the help of these Principles, all material Things seem to have been composed of the hard and solid Particles above-mention'd, variously associated in the first Creation by the Counsel of an intelligent Agent. For it became him who created them to set them in order. And if he did not, it's unphilosophical to seek for any other Origin of the World, or to pretend that it might arise out of a Chaos by the mere Laws of Nature; though being once form'd, it may continue by those Laws for many Ages.

SOURCE: Sir Isaac Newton, *Opticks*, 4th ed. (London, 1730), pp. 400–402.

Analyze the Document

1. What is Newton's view of God's role in the universe?

2. What objections might scientists today have to these ideas?

3. What does Newton mean by "Principles" and "Laws"?

---

of his death in 1642, Europe's intellectual elite had begun to embrace the Copernican outlook.

In England, Isaac Newton (1642–1727) picked up the trail blazed by Copernicus, Brahe, Kepler, and Galileo. Late in life, Newton described his career modestly: "I do not know what I may appear to the world; but to myself I seem to have been only like a boy playing on the sea-shore, and diverting myself in now and then finding a smoother pebble or a prettier shell than ordinary, while the great ocean of truth lay all undiscovered before me." Newton may have held himself in humble regard, but his accomplishments were astonishing.

Isaac Newton

In 1661, Newton entered Cambridge University, where he studied the ideas of Copernicus and Galileo as well as the advantages of scientific investigation. He distinguished himself enough in mathematics to be chosen to stay on as a professor after his graduation. Like most other figures of the Scientific Revolution, Newton was profoundly religious and, as indicated by Document 14.2, hoped to harmonize his Christian beliefs with the principles of science. He also believed in alchemy and elements of Hermeticism.

Starting in his early 20s, Newton made some of the most important discoveries in the history of science. He developed calculus and investigated the nature of light; he also formulated and mathematically described three laws of motion: inertia, acceleration, and action/reaction. Yet he is best known for discovering the law of universal attraction, or gravitation. After working on the concept for years, he finally published it in 1687 in his great work *Principia* (*The Mathematical Principles of Natural Knowledge*). In the book, he stated the law with simplicity and precision: "Every particle of matter in the universe attracts every other particle with a force varying inversely as the square of the distance between them and directly proportional to the product of their masses." In his view, this law applied equally to all objects, from the most massive planet to a small apple falling from a tree.

Newton's *Principia*

Newton had managed to synthesize the new findings in astronomy and physics into a systematic explanation of physical laws that applied to the earth as well as the heavens. This Newtonian universe was infinite and had no center. Uniform and mathematically describable, it was held together by explainable forces and was atomic in nature. Essentially, everything in the universe consisted of only one thing: matter in motion.

The Revolution Spreads: Medicine, Anatomy, and Chemistry

Although astronomy and physics led the way in dramatic scientific findings, researchers in other fields made important discoveries as well. Many of these advances also had roots in the sixteenth century. For example, several scholars developed new ideas in the related fields of medicine, anatomy, and chemistry.

In medicine, a flamboyant Swiss alchemist-physician known as Paracelsus (1493–1541) strongly influenced the healing arts. A believer in Hermetic doctrine, Paracelsus openly opposed medical orthodoxy and taught that healers should look for truth not in libraries ("the more learned, the more perverted," he warned) but in the Book of Nature. "I have not been ashamed to learn from tramps, butchers, and barbers," he boasted. As a teacher and wandering practitioner, he treated patients, experimented with chemicals, recorded his observations, and developed new theories. Paracelsus concluded that all matter was composed of salt, sulfur, and mercury—not the traditional earth, water, fire, and air. Rejecting the standard view that an imbalance in the humors of the body caused disease, he instead looked to specific chemical imbalances to explain what caused each illness. He also encouraged research and experimentation to find natural remedies for bodily disorders, such as administering mercury or arsenic at astrologically correct moments. Though rejected by most established physicians, Paracelsus's ideas became particularly popular among common practitioners and would later influence the study of chemistry.

Paracelsus

Other researchers founded the modern science of anatomy. In the sixteenth century, Andreas Vesalius (1514–1564), a Fleming living in Italy, wrote the first comprehensive textbook on the structure of the human body based on careful observation. **Figure 14.5** shows the 28-year-old Vesalius displaying one of his studies on human anatomy from his 1543 treatise, *On the Fabric of the Human Body*. This figure is one of more than two hundred woodcut illustrations showing the composition of the body, stage by stage. Vesalius himself dissected cadavers, as suggested by the scalpel resting on the table. A notable aspect of this illustration is that Vesalius boldly looks the viewer in the eye, perhaps to challenge directly the old, authoritative assumptions about human anatomy. Nevertheless, his dissections of human bodies brought him into conflict with traditional physicians and scholars. Disgusted, he finally gave up his scientific studies and became the personal physician to Emperor Charles V.

Andreas Vesalius

Despite relentless criticism, other scholars continued anatomical research. A line from a poem written for the opening of the Amsterdam Anatomical Theatre

ANDREÆ VESALII.

FIGURE 14.5 Andreas Vesalius, from *On the Fabric of the Human Body*, 1543 Vesalius looks boldly out at the viewer while displaying one of his studies of human anatomy.

in the early seventeenth century reflects the sense that this research needed special justification: "Evil doers who while living have done damage are of benefit after their death." In other words, the body parts of criminals "afford a lesson to you, the Living." The most important of these researchers was William Harvey (1578–1657), an Englishman who, like Vesalius, studied at the University of Padua in Italy. Harvey dissected hundreds of animals, including dogs, pigs, lobsters, shrimp, and snakes. He discovered that the human heart worked like a pump, with valves that allowed blood to circulate through the body: "The movement of the blood occurs constantly in a circular manner and is the result of the beating of the heart." Yet, despite this mechanistic view, he also considered the heart the physical and spiritual center of life—in his words, "the sovereign of everything."

William Harvey

By the seventeenth century, anatomists and others benefited from several newly invented scientific instruments, such as the microscope. Anton van Leeuwenhoek (1632–1723), a Dutchman, became the chief pioneer in the use of this instrument.

In observations during the 1670s, he described seeing "little animals or animalcules" in water from a lake. "It was wonderful to see: and I judge that some of these little creatures were above a thousand times smaller than the smallest ones I have ever yet seen, upon the rind of cheese, in wheaten flour, mould and the like." Leeuwenhoek discovered what would later be identified as bacteria in his own saliva: "little eels or worms, lying all huddled up together and wriggling. . . . This was for me, among all the marvels that I have discovered in nature, the most marvellous of all."

Anton van Leeuwenhoek

Around this same time, Robert Boyle (1627–1691), an Irish nobleman particularly interested in medical chemistry, helped lay the foundations for modern chemistry. Drawing inspiration from Paracelsus, Boyle attacked many assumptions inherited from the ancients and began a systematic search for the basic elements of matter. Relying on the experimental method and using new instruments, he argued that all matter was composed of indestructible atoms that behaved in predictable ways. Boyle also discovered a law—which still bears his name—that governs the pressure of gases. His exacting procedures set a standard for the scientific practice of chemistry.

Robert Boyle

The Methodology of Science Emerges

The scientists who challenged traditional views in their fields also used new methods of discovery—of uncovering how things worked and of determining "truth." Indeed, this innovative methodology lay at the heart of the Scientific Revolution. Earlier techniques for ascertaining the truth—by referring to long-trusted authorities and making deductions from their propositions—became unacceptable to the new scientists. They instead emphasized systematic skepticism, experimentation, and reasoning based solely on observed facts and mathematical laws. The two most important philosophers of this methodology were Francis Bacon and René Descartes.

Francis Bacon (1561–1626), an English politician who was once lord chancellor of England under James I, took a passionate interest in the new science. He rejected reliance on ancient authorities and advocated the collection of data without preconceived notions. From such data, he explained, scientific conclusions could be reached through inductive reasoning—drawing general conclusions from particular concrete observations. "Deriv[ing] axioms from . . . particulars, rising by gradual and unbroken ascent, so that it arrives at the most general axioms of all. This is the true way," he proclaimed. In addition, Bacon argued that scientific knowledge would

Francis Bacon

be useful knowledge: "I am laboring to lay the foundation not of any sect or doctrine, but of human utility and power." He believed that science would benefit commerce and industry and improve the human condition by giving people unprecedented power over their environment.

Figure 14.6, the title page from Bacon's 1620 book, *New Instrument,* graphically depicts these views. The illustration shows a ship of discovery sailing out from the western end of the Mediterranean Sea into the unknown. Below is the quotation "Many shall venture forth and science shall be increased." Here is an optimistic assertion that knowledge is limitless and that science constitutes a voyage of discovery— a view that would be echoed again and again, as we saw in the picture at the beginning of this chapter. As **Figure 14.6** suggests, Bacon thus became a noted propagandist for the new science as well as a proponent of the **empirical method.**

FIGURE 14.6 The New Science   The title page of Francis Bacon's book *New Instrument* (1620) asserts optimistically that science is like a voyage of discovery with almost limitless potential.

Despite his brilliance, Bacon did not have a thorough understanding of mathematics and the role it could play in the new science. His contemporary René Descartes (1596–1650) would be the one to excel in this arena.

René Descartes

Born in France, Descartes received training in scholastic philosophy and mathematics at one of France's best Jesuit schools and took a degree in law. He entered military service and served during the Thirty Years' War. During his travels, he met a Dutch mathematician and became interested in the new science. An ecstatic experience in 1619 convinced him to commit to a life of the mind. He spent his most productive years as a mathematician, physicist, and metaphysical philosopher in Holland. In 1637, he published his philosophy and scientific methodology in the *Discourse on Method*—in French, not Latin. The book presented an eloquent defense of skepticism and of abstract **deductive reasoning**— deriving conclusions that logically flowed from a premise. "Inquiries should be directed, not to what others have thought, nor to what we ourselves conjecture, but to what we can clearly and perspicuously behold and with certainty deduce; for knowledge is not won in any other way."

Descartes questioned all forms of authority, no matter how venerable—be it Aristotle or even the Bible. He tried to remove systematically all assumptions about knowledge and advocated doubting the senses, which he claimed could be deceptive. Taken to its logical conclusion, his argument left him with one God-given experiential fact—that he was thinking. "I think, therefore I am" became his starting point. From there he followed a rigorous process of deductive reasoning to draw a variety of conclusions, including the existence of God and the physical world. He argued that there were two kinds of reality: mind, or subjective thinking and experiencing; and body, or objective physical matter. According to this philosophy, known as **Cartesian dualism,** the objective physical universe could be understood in terms of extension (matter occupying space) and motion (matter in motion). "Give me extension and motion," vowed Descartes, "and I will create the universe." He considered the body nothing more than "an earthen machine." In his opinion, only the mind was exempt from mechanical laws.

Descartes emphasized the power of the detached, reasoning individual mind to discover truths about nature. Unlike Bacon, he put his faith in mathematical reasoning, not in empirical investigation. By challenging all established authority, by accepting as truth only what could be known by reason, and by assuming a purely mechanical physical universe, Descartes established a philosophy and methodology that became the core of the new science.

SUPPORTING AND SPREADING SCIENCE

Only a small group of people actually participated in the **Scientific Revolution.** Of these, a handful of women managed to overcome barriers to take part as patrons for scientists or as scientists themselves. Men ignored or discounted their work, and scientific societies usually excluded them. The few women engaged in science, such as the naturalist Maria Sibylla Merian (see Biography, page 405) and the Germany astronomer Maria Winkelmann (1647–1717), had to rely on their own resources or work in collaboration with their husbands.

Few scientific scholars—whether male or female— got far without calling on a network of peers and soliciting the support of wealthy patrons. To spread their ideas, these scientists needed to publish their works, interact with like-minded colleagues, and gain the backing of prestigious elites. Fortunately for them, these elites were eager to comply.

Courts and Salons

Governments and wealthy aristocrats served as benefactors and employers of scientists. Kepler, for example, received help from the imperial court, serving in Bohemia as Rudolf II's official mathematician. Galileo became court mathematician to Cosimo de' Medici in Tuscany. Vesalius served as physician to Holy Roman Emperor Charles V, and Harvey as royal physician in England.

Queen Christina of Sweden, like several other monarchs, invited scholars and artists to her court. **Figure 14.7** shows her in 1649 with the French philosopher and mathematician René Descartes (on the

KEY DATES

right, pointing to papers). Books, papers, and instruments attest to the importance of the new science at this meeting. In this Protestant country, the religious figure on the far right seems to indicate that there is little conflict between science and religion. The artist portrays Christina, a deeply religious person (who would later become a Catholic), as an interested and gracious benefactor helping to bring to light scientific findings.

Rulers had their own motives—namely, practicality and prestige—for assisting scholars and scientists. Royals especially hoped that scholarship and scientific inquiry would yield discoveries that would enhance the strength and prosperity of the state. For example, they sought experts in building projects, armaments, mapmaking, navigation, and mining. They also tried to burnish their own reputations as powerful, educated people by patronizing scholarship, science, and the arts. In this way, support of science became a supposed hallmark of good government. Enticed by this assistance, learned people gathered at royal courts, which gradually filled rooms with new tools, machines, exotic plants and animals, and books.

Beyond the court, people formed private salons and local academies where those interested in science could meet. In the 1540s, the first academy for scientific study was established, in Naples. Women ran several important salons where scientists discussed their findings along with literature, art, and politics. Some scientists even found benefactors at these meetings.

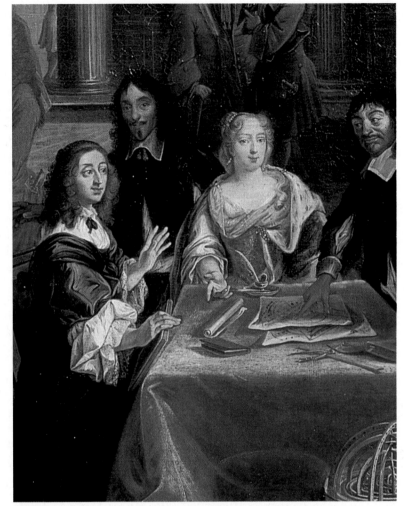

FIGURE 14.7 Queen Christina and Descartes The Swedish queen Christina displays her support of science in this depiction of a 1649 meeting with the French philosopher René Descartes.

The Rise of Royal Societies

During the second half of the seventeenth century, central governments stepped up their support of scientific experimentation, publications, and academies. In 1662, for example, Charles II chartered the Royal Society in England; four years later, Louis XIV's finance minister, Jean-Baptiste Colbert, founded the Académie des Sciences in France. These organizations, and others patterned after them, furnished laboratories, granted subsidies, brought scientists together to exchange ideas, published their findings, and honored scientific achievements. This governmental support of science added to the growing prestige of science and the scientific community.

Religion and the New Science

Religious organizations played a mixed role in the spread of the new science. Traditionally, the Catholic Church supported scholarship and learning in general, including, in natural science. Moreover, religious orders staffed most universities, and many key figures of the Scientific Revolution held university positions. Numerous leading scholars also felt a profound sense of spirituality. Copernicus, for example, who dedicated his work to the pope, was a cleric, as were many other natural scientists. Although we may be tempted to assume that the skepticism inherent in the scientific method would lead to atheism, the great scientists attacked neither faith nor established religion. Nor were they dispassionate investigators holding themselves apart from the spiritual nature of their age. They often believed in magic, ghosts, and witchcraft and typically considered alchemy, astrology, and numerology (predicting events from numbers) valuable components of natural science. Galileo, though he later decried his trial as the triumph of "ignorance, impiety, fraud and deceit," remained a believing Catholic. Even Robert Boyle, who like others came to think of the universe as a machine, attributed its origin to God: "God, indeed, gave motion to matter . . . and established those rules of motion, and that order amongst things . . . which we call the laws of nature." Newton agreed: "This most beautiful system of the sun, planets, and comets, could only proceed from the counsel and dominion of an intelligent and powerful Being. . . . He endures forever, and is everywhere present. . . ."

Nevertheless, the new science did challenge certain tenets of faith and the traditional Christian conception of God's place in the ordering of the world. Neither Protestant nor Catholic leaders welcomed Copernican ideas and the implications of the new science. The Catholic Church, itself ordered in a hierarchy that paralleled the old view of the universe, stayed particularly committed to established authorities. Moreover, the church's condemnation of Galileo in 1633 discouraged scientific investigations throughout much of Catholic Europe. Descartes was not alone in deciding not to publish ideas incorporating Copernican assumptions. As he explained in 1634, "It is not my temperament to set sail against the wind. . . . I want to be able to live in peace . . . out of sight." Although the French government would actively promote science, after the mid-seventeenth century most scientific work and publishing took place in Protestant areas—particularly in England and the Netherlands.

The New Worldview

By the end of the seventeenth century, the accumulation of convincing scientific findings and the support for those findings among the educated elites had broken the Aristotelian-medieval worldview and replaced it with the Copernican-Newtonian paradigm. According to the new view, the earth, along with the planets, moved around the sun in an infinite universe of other similar bodies. The natural order consisted of matter in motion, acting according to mathematically expressible laws. Scientific truths came from observing, measuring, experimenting, and making reasoned conclusions through the use of sophisticated mathematics. Religious truths still had their place, and the orderliness of nature reflected God's design (see Document 14.2, on page 457). However, science now claimed precedence in explaining the material world.

> The Copernican-Newtonian paradigm

In the sixteenth and early seventeenth centuries, great thinkers such as Copernicus and Galileo had been ridiculed and persecuted for their ideas. By the late seventeenth and early eighteenth centuries, Isaac Newton's fate revealed the acceptance of the new paradigm among educated elites. Famous and popular, Newton became a member of Parliament, served for many years as director of the Royal Mint, and was knighted by Queen Anne.

LAYING THE FOUNDATIONS FOR THE ENLIGHTENMENT

In the course of the eighteenth century, the ideas of the Scientific Revolution spread widely and were applied in stunning new ways. With this broadening, the eighteenth century witnessed the birth of a major cultural movement known as the **Enlightenment.** At the heart of this movement lay the firm conviction—especially among intellectuals—that human reason should determine understanding of the world and the rules of social life. "[H]ave the courage to use your own intelligence," and leave your "self-caused immaturity," exhorted the German philosopher Immanuel Kant (1724–1804). "All that is required for this enlightenment is freedom, and particularly . . . the freedom for man to make public use of his reason in all matters."

The Enlightenment hit its full stride in the middle decades of the eighteenth century, when it particularly influenced literate elites of Europe and North America. Yet, its roots stretched back to the end of the seventeenth century. At that time, the thinking that would characterize the Enlightenment emerged in the writings of people who popularized science, applied a skeptical attitude toward religious standards of truth, and criticized accepted traditions and authorities.

Science Popularized

Unevenly educated and facing challenging findings, members of scientific societies often struggled to understand one another's work. For the nonscientific public, the problem of communicating new, complex ideas was even worse. Late in the seventeenth century, several talented writers, nonscientists themselves but believing that science had established a new standard of truth, began explaining in clear language the meaning of science to the literate public. For example, the French writer Bernard de Fontenelle (1657–1757) enjoyed a long, brilliant career as a popularizer of science. In *Conversations on the Plurality of Worlds* (1686), he presented the Copernican view of the universe in a series of conversations between an aristocratic woman and her lover under starry skies. The English essayist and publisher Joseph Addison (1672–1719), in the March 12, 1711, issue of his newspaper, *The Spectator,* said that he hoped to bring "philosophy out of closets and libraries, schools and colleges, to dwell in clubs and assemblies, at teatables and in coffee-houses." He aimed his daily paper not only at men but at women "of a more elevated life and conversation, that move in an exalted sphere of knowledge and virtue, that join all the beauties of the mind to the ornaments of dress, and inspire a kind of awe and respect, as well as love, in their male beholders." Other writers also targeted women. In 1737, for example, *Newtonianism for Women* was published in Naples and was soon translated into English. Writings such as these helped make science fashionable in elite circles.

In the mid-eighteenth century, this popularization of science merged with another foundation of Enlightenment thinking: the belief that every educated man and woman should be familiar with the nature and methods of science. **Figure 14.8,** an illustration from a British book on the arts and sciences, depicts this connection between science and education. Here a teacher instructs three young men in the principles of astronomy by demonstrating the planetary movements on a new machine—the orrery. The stuffed animals hanging from the ceiling underscore the importance of natural history. Atop the bookcase and on the floor are seminal instruments of science—an air pump, a microscope, a telescope, and a globe. A human skeleton hangs in the closet.

Teaching science

Soon scientific ideas were being taught to children of the middle and upper classes. For example, the year 1761 saw the publication of *The Newtonian System of Philosophy, Adapted to the Capacities of Young Gentlemen and Ladies,* a book engagingly advertised as the "Philosophy of Tops and Balls." In it, a fictional boy named Tom Telescope gave lectures on science topics to children while also teaching the virtues of good manners and citizenship. The book proved immensely popular, going through many editions in Britain and in other countries.

Many of these books emphasized Newton—and for understandable reasons. Enlightenment thinkers saw this brilliant Englishman as the great synthesizer of the Scientific Revolution, an astute observer who rightly described the universe as ordered, mechanical, material, and set into motion by God. From Newton, they concluded that reason and nature were compatible: Nature functioned logically and discernibly; therefore, what was natural was also reasonable. Many writers of the day agreed with the spirit of a poem written for Newton by the English author Alexander Pope upon the scientist's death in 1727:

Glorifying Newton: reason and nature

> *Nature and Nature's Laws lay hid in Night.*
> *God said, "Let Newton be," and all was Light.*

In simple terms, Newton had become a European cultural hero, as **Figure 14.9** suggests. At the left center of this allegorical painting, a great urn "wherein is supposed to be deposited the Remains of the deceased Hero" is displayed. Above the urn shines a beam

FIGURE 14.8 Science, Education, and Enlightenment, 1759
Surrounded by scientific instruments and objects, a teacher instructs three students. This illustration reveals the growing sense during the Enlightenment that an educated person should be familiar with science.

of light, broken into the colors of the spectrum by a prism—a bow to Newton's famous prism experiments. At the right are pages filled with mathematical calculations; below them, a globe and measuring instruments. Various figures in classical dress admire these objects and perhaps discuss Newton's ideas. The entire painting glorifies not only Newton but all of science.

Enlightenment thinkers also admired the ideas of Newton's compatriot John Locke (1632–1704), who applied scientific thinking to human psychology. This English philosopher did not hold the mind exempt from the mechanical laws of the material universe. In his *Essay Concerning Human Understanding* (1690), Locke pictured the human brain at birth as a blank sheet of paper that sensory perception and reason filled as a person aged.

The psychology of John Locke

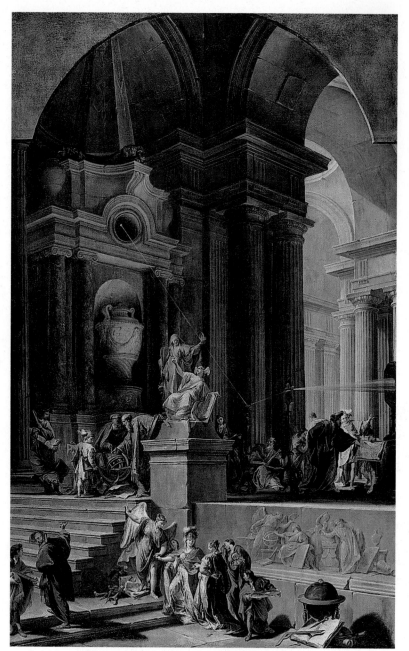

FIGURE 14.9 Giovanni Battista Pittori, *Allegorical Monument to Isaac Newton*, 1727–1730 This celebratory painting pays homage to Isaac Newton by glorifying the urn that stores his remains and highlighting his scientific discoveries.

ideas, like those of Newton and the Scientific Revolution, also set the stage for the skeptical questioning of received wisdom.

Skepticism and Religion

Locke's ideas, along with those of Newton and the Scientific Revolution, set the stage for the questioning of established wisdom that came to define the Enlightenment. Among several writers, skepticism—or doubts about religious dogmas—mounted. Pierre Bayle (1647–1706), a French Huguenot forced to flee to the Dutch Republic because of Louis XIV's religious persecutions, became the leading proponent of skepticism in the late seventeenth century. In his *News from the Republic of Letters* (1684), Bayle bitterly attacked the intolerance of the French monarchy and the Catholic Church. In most of Europe, where religious principles shared by ruler and ruled underlay all political systems, nonconformity was a major challenge. Therefore, the book earned him condemnation in Paris and Rome. Eventually, however, Bayle would have the last word. In 1697 he published the *Historical and Critical Dictionary*, which contained a list of religious views and beliefs that Bayle maintained did not stand up to criticism. Bayle cited human reason and common sense as his standard of criticism: "Any particular dogma, whatever it may be, whether it is advanced on the authority of the Scriptures, or whatever else may be its origins, is to be regarded as false if it clashes with the clear and definite conclusions of the natural understanding." Bayle also argued that "morals and religion, far from being inseparable, are completely independent of each other." For Bayle, a person's moral behavior had little to do with any particular religious doctrine or creed. With these stands, Bayle pushed much harder than Galileo in challenging the Catholic Church and other religious beliefs. He became recognized as an international authority on religious toleration and skeptical criticism of the Bible.

New information and arguments added weight to Bayle's criticism of biblical authority. For example, geological discoveries suggested that life on Earth had actually begun earlier than biblical accounts claimed. Investigators also began casting doubt on reports of miracles and prophecies. David Hume (1711–1776), a first-rate Scottish philosopher and historian, carried the skeptical argument even further. In *An Essay Concerning Human Understanding* (1748), he insisted that nothing—not even the existence of God or our own existence—could be known

Pierre Bayle

David Hume

"Our observation, employed either about external sensible objects or about the internal operations of our minds perceived and reflected on by ourselves, is that which supplies our understanding with all the materials of thinking." Locke's empirical psychology rejected the notion that human beings were born with innate ideas or that revelation was a reliable source of truth. What we become, he argued, depends solely on our experiences—on the information received through the senses. Schools and social institutions should therefore play a major role in molding the individual from childhood to adulthood. These for sure. Reality consisted only of human perceptions. To Hume, established religions were based on nothing but hope and fear. Reason demanded that people live with skeptical uncertainty rather than dogmatic faith.

Broadening Criticism of Authority and Tradition

Travel writing had a long history, and by the eighteenth century many Enlightenment thinkers had read explanations of China's lucid Confucian traditions as well as accounts of customs and beliefs in Islamic, Buddhist, and Hindu lands. Several writers—among them the Baron de Montesquieu (1689–1755), a wealthy judge in a provincial French court, and the French author Voltaire (1694–1778)—used comparisons of place and time to criticize authority and tradition during the early decades of the eighteenth century. Journeying abroad and writing about their experiences gave such people a new perspective on their home societies. Montesquieu and Voltaire, for their part, chastised European customs in general and French institutions in particular for being contrary to reason and good ethics.

Travel writings of Montesquieu and Voltaire

Both presented the traveler as an objective observer. In his best-selling book *Persian Letters* (1721), Montesquieu bitingly satirized the customs, morals, and practices of Europeans from the point of view of two Persian travelers. Through this comparative perspective, Montesquieu painted the French as lacking in both good morals and effective government. Voltaire, in his widely read *Letters Concerning the English Nation* (1733), similarly criticized French politics and Catholic intolerance. In the island nation, "one thinks freely and nobly without being held back by any servile fear." Like many people, Voltaire idealized England because it allowed greater individual freedom, religious differences, and political reform than most other countries, especially France. England was also enviably prosperous and was the home of Newton and Locke, so admired in France. Many French intellectuals wanted for their own country what the English already seemed to have.

Other writers took a new historical perspective to criticize tradition and trumpet rapid change. For them, the tools of science and reason enabled people to surpass their historical predecessors, even the admired Greeks and Romans of antiquity. History became a story of relentless human progress, and people living in the eighteenth century stood on the brink of unprecedented historical achievements. Some people, such as the American scientist and philosopher Benjamin Franklin (1706–1790), embraced the idea of progress with an almost religious

History and progress

fervor: "The rapid Progress of *true* Science now occasions my regretting sometimes that I was born so soon. It is impossible to imagine the Height to which may be carried . . . the Power of Man over Matter, . . . all diseases may by sure means be prevented, . . . and our lives lengthened at pleasure."

THE ENLIGHTENMENT IN FULL STRIDE

Building on the foundations of science, skepticism, and criticism, Western intellectuals systematically investigated the ethical, political, social, and economic implications of science after the 1730s. For them, nature—with its laws, order, simplicity, and rationality—served as a guide for human thought and society. "The source of man's unhappiness is his ignorance of Nature," claimed France's influential Baron d'Holbach (1723–1789). The Marquis de Condorcet argued, "The time will therefore come when the sun will shine only on free men who know no other master but their reason" (see Document 14.3). These optimistic intellectuals pushed for reform and change, using critical and empirical reasoning to back up their arguments. Specifically, they urged people to shrug off the shackles of tradition and custom and to participate in the accelerating progress of civilization. The spark of reason would soon dispel ignorance and enlighten all human understanding. Indeed, it was this image that lent the Enlightenment its name.

The *Philosophes*

Although Enlightenment ideas bubbled up throughout Europe and North America, France was the true heart of the movement. There Enlightenment thinkers came to be called *philosophes,* the French term for "philosophers." In a sense, the questions these thinkers grappled with were philosophical: How do we discover truth? How should we live our lives? Yet the *philosophes* were not traditional philosophers. Coming from both noble and middle-class origins, they were intellectuals—though often not formally trained by or associated with a university. They tended to extend, apply, or propagandize others' ideas rather than initiate new concepts themselves. They also wrote more plays, satires, histories, novels, encyclopedia entries, and short pamphlets than formal philosophical treatises. Finally, they considered themselves part of a common intellectual culture, an international "republic of letters" held together by literature, correspondence, and private gatherings. In the eyes of leading *philosophes* such as Jean Le Rond d'Alembert (1717–1783), this republic of letters should "establish the laws of philosophy and taste for the rest of the nation."

DOCUMENTS

Condorcet Lauds the Power of Reason

No one lauded the power of reason and the Enlightenment, or had more hope for the future—thanks to the Enlightenment—than the French mathematician and philosophe the Marquis de Condorcet (1743–1794). The following is an excerpt from his Sketch of the Progress of the Human Mind, *a book tracing human "progress" over time, which he completed in 1794.*

Our hopes for the future condition of the human race can be subsumed under three important heads: the abolition of inequality between nations, the progress of equality within each nation, and the true perfection of mankind. Will all nations one day attain that state of civilization which the most enlightened, the freest and the least burdened by prejudices, such as the French and the Anglo-Americans, have attained already? Will the vast gulf that separates these peoples from the slavery of nations under the rule of monarchs, from the barbarism of African tribes, from the ignorance of savages, little by little disappear? . . .

In answering these three questions we shall find in the experience of the past, in the observation of the progress that the sciences and civilization have already made, in the analysis of the progress of the human mind and of the development of its faculties, the strongest reasons for believing that nature has set no limit to the realization of our hopes.

If we glance at the state of the world today we see first of all that in Europe the principles of the French constitution are already those of all enlightened men. We see them too widely propagated, too seriously professed, for priests and despots to prevent their gradual penetration even into the hovels of their slaves; there they will soon awaken in these slaves the remnants of their common sense and inspire them with that smoldering indignation which not even constant humiliation and fear can smother in the soul of the oppressed. . . .

The time will therefore come when the sun will shine only on free men who know no other master but their reason; when tyrants and slaves, priests and their stupid or hypocritical instruments will exist only in works of history and on the stage; and when we shall think of them only to pity their victims and their dupes; to maintain ourselves in a state of vigilance by thinking on their excesses; and to learn how to recognize and so to destroy, by force of reason, the first seeds of tyranny and superstition, should they ever dare to reappear amongst us.

SOURCE: Jean Antoine Nicholas Caritat, Marquis de Condorcet, *Sketch for a Historical Picture on the Progress of the Human Mind*, trans. June Barraclough (London: Weidenfeld and Nicolson [Orion Books], 1955), pp. 236–237, 244.

Analyze the Document

1. What "hopes" does Condorcet have for the future of humanity?

2. According to Condorcet, what will open the door to such great progress?

3. In Condorcet's opinion, why are the French and the Anglo-Americans the most "enlightened" peoples?

The witty, versatile François Arouet, who took the pen name Voltaire (1694–1778), best represented the *philosophes*. The son of a Parisian lawyer, Voltaire received a fine classical education from the Jesuits and soon denounced their religious doctrine. He became the idol of French intellectuals while only in his 20s, and the enemy of many others. He soon ran afoul of state authorities, who imprisoned him in the Bastille for writing verses that criticized the crown. Released, he became embroiled in a dangerous conflict with a prominent nobleman and again landed in the Bastille. By promising to leave the country, he gained his freedom. In England, he encountered the ideas of Newton and Locke and came to admire English parliamentary government and the nation's religious tolerance. As we saw, he popularized Newton's and Locke's ideas and extolled the virtues of English society in his writings.

Slipping back into France, Voltaire hid for a time under the protection of Émilie du Châtelet (1706–1749), a wealthy woman who became his lover and

| Voltaire |

match. Châtelet had already shown brilliance as a child. By the age of 12, she could speak four languages and had already translated Greek and Latin texts. Her mother worried that she would not find a mate because she "flaunts her mind, and frightens away the suitors her other excesses have not driven off." In 1733, she insisted on joining a group of male intellectuals who met regularly at a Parisian coffeehouse, donning men's clothes after the management refused to admit her because of her gender. Voltaire lived openly with Châtelet and her husband. In the great hall of their country chateau, she hung rods, pipes, and balls from the ceiling for her experiments in physics. She made her reputation by publishing a three-volume work on the German mathematician and philosopher Leibnitz and translating Newton's *Principles of Mathematics*. A *philosophe*, accomplished scientist, and leading proponent of Newtonian thought in her own right, Châtelet helped Voltaire gain a better understanding of the sciences and their significance. When she died in childbirth in 1749, the despondent Voltaire accepted

| Émilie du Châtelet |

an invitation from King Frederick II of Prussia to join his court. However, they soon argued, and Voltaire returned to France.

Having made both a fortune in financial speculations and a rich network of friends and acquaintances, Voltaire was not without resources. He wrote poetry, drama, history, essays, letters, and scientific treatises—ninety volumes in all. The novel *Candide* (1759) became his best-known work. In this dark satire, Voltaire created the epitome of the "ivory-tower" intellectual, ridiculed the pretensions of the nobility and clergy, and skewered the naïveté of optimists who believed that "this is the best of all possible worlds and all things turn out for the best." He aimed his cynical wit especially at the Catholic Church and Christian institutions. His *Philosophical Dictionary* became the most famous, wide-ranging attack on supernatural religion and churches. Voltaire mounted several campaigns for religious toleration, coming to the defense of individuals attacked by prejudice. In his *Treatise on Tolerance* (1763), he attacked the mentality that led to the torture and murder of a Protestant merchant, Jean Calas, on the false charges of murdering his son for threatening to convert to Catholicism. "Christians ought to tolerate one another. I will go even further and say that we ought to look upon all men as our brothers. What! call a Turk, a Jew, a Siamese, my brother? Yes, of course, for are we not all children of the same father, and the creatures of the same God?" Voltaire was celebrated as a national hero and lionized internationally, and his popularity reveals the widespread acceptance of Enlightenment thought throughout the West by the late eighteenth century.

The *Encyclopedia*

No work better summarizes the philosophy of the Enlightenment than the *Encyclopedia*, a collaborative effort by many *philosophes* under the editorship of Denis Diderot (1713–1774) and Jean Le Rond d'Alembert. In the preface, the editors stated their aim: "to overturn the barriers that reason never erected" and "contribute to the certitude and progress of human knowledge." The *Encyclopedia* embodied the notion that reason alone could be used to discover, understand, or clarify almost anything. This massive work explored the complete spectrum of knowledge, offering articles on subjects ranging from music to machinery interpreted through the lens of the *philosophes*' criticism and empiricism. The authors wrote with supreme self-importance: "I can assure you," said d'Alembert in a 1752 letter, "that while writing this work I had posterity before my eyes at every line."

The first volume of the *Encyclopedia* was published in 1751. **Figure 14.10** shows one of its many

FIGURE 14.10 The *Encyclopedia*, 1751 This page from the *Encyclopedia* shows a chemical laboratory and a table with symbols for each chemical substance.

illustrations. In this image of a chemical laboratory, two chemists and their assistants work. Each piece of equipment is numbered in the illustration and labeled in the text. At the bottom of the picture is a "table of affinities," a system used to organize and symbolize each chemical substance. The illustration conveys a sense of both the practicality of chemistry and its ordered progress. Although the study of chemistry and the hundreds of other topics covered in the *Encyclopedia* at first glance may appear innocent enough, they were saturated with the philosophy of the Enlightenment. Church authorities and their governmental allies therefore saw the *Encyclopedia* as a direct threat to the status quo. They censored it, halted its publication, and harassed its editors. Thanks in great part to the persistence of Diderot, who fought the authorities and managed a difficult group of contributing authors, the project was finally completed in 1772.

Battling the Church

Diderot's struggle to publish the *Encyclopedia* was part of a wider conflict between the *philosophes* and the church. Both sides spent much time and effort attacking each other. In countries such as France and Italy, where clerics were strongly entrenched in government, officials censored the writings of the *philosophes* and threatened to imprison or exile them. Governmental censorship was usually more nominal than real. However, Diderot and others trying to publish "offensive" books constantly worried about these threats: "How many times did we awake uncertain if . . . we would be torn from our families, our friends, our fellow citizens. . . ." French authors often sent their works to Holland or Switzerland for publication, and private companies then made a business of smuggling the books back into France across Swiss or Dutch borders.

Sometimes the *philosophes'* "crime" was promoting toleration of religious minorities, whether Christian or otherwise. Montesquieu and Voltaire, in France, were among several who attacked discrimination against Jews, for example. These views were particularly controversial because religious tolerance—formal and informal—was not the rule. Most governments maintained a state religion, rooted in law and viewed as the custodian of received views, that discriminated against nonmembers. For example, Denmark barred Catholic priests from entering the country, and the Catholic Inquisition remained active in Spain.

Some *philosophes*, such as the Baron d'Holbach and David Hume, verged on atheism in their attacks on organized religion. "The Christian

Deism

religion not only was at first attended by miracles, but even now cannot be believed by any reasonable person without one," Hume claimed. However, few Enlightenment thinkers pushed matters that far. Most believed in some form of deism—that an impersonal, infinite Divine Being created the universe but did not interfere with the world of human affairs. The prominent author and political philosopher Thomas Paine (1737–1809) stated, "I believe in one God, and no more; and I hope for happiness beyond this life. . . . I do not believe in the creed professed by the Jewish church, by the Roman church, by the Greek church, by the Turkish church, by the Protestant church, nor by any church that I know of. My own mind is my own church." These ideas, like other ideas of the Enlightenment, gained momentum over the course of the eighteenth century. In the long run, the church probably lost more supporters among the upper and middle classes than it gained by so ardently attacking the *philosophes* and their ideas.

Reforming Society

The *philosophes* thought long and hard about reforming society. They wrote and argued

Political thought: Montesquieu and Rousseau

about the relationship between the individual and society and reevaluated the functioning of traditional social institutions. Applying their critical reasoning to fields from government to education, they generated influential ideas for reform.

The most important political thinkers of the Enlightenment—Montesquieu and the Swiss-born writer Jean-Jacques Rousseau (1712–1778)—built on John Locke's work. Locke had pleaded eloquently for the "natural rights"—life, liberty, and property—of

human beings. In his *Second Treatise on Civil Government* (1690), Locke had argued that to safeguard these rights, individuals agree to surrender a certain amount of their sovereignty to government. However, the powers of the government, whether it be monarchical or popular, were strictly limited. No government was allowed to violate the individual's right to life, liberty, and property. If it did, the people who set it up could and should overthrow it—something the English had done in their Glorious Revolution, according to Locke.

An admirer of Locke and the English system of government, the Baron de Montesquieu analyzed political systems from a relativistic perspective. In his widely acclaimed political masterpiece, *The Spirit of the Laws* (1748), Montesquieu argued that political institutions should conform to the climate, customs, beliefs, and economy of a particular country. For instance, limited monarchy is most appropriate for countries of moderate size, like France; and republics for small states, like Venice or ancient Athens. Each form of government had its virtues and vices.

Not only did Montesquieu approve of Locke's doctrine of limited sovereignty, but he specified how it could best be secured—by a separation of powers and a system of checks and balances. The alternative, he warned, was tyranny and an end to liberty: "There would be an end to everything, were the same man or the same body, whether of the nobles or of the people, to exercise those three powers, that of enacting laws, that of executing the public resolutions, and of trying the causes of individuals." This theory, equally applicable to monarchies and to democracies, became Montesquieu's greatest practical contribution to political thought. In North America, framers of the U.S. Constitution incorporated his ideas into their structuring of the United States government, creating separate executive, judicial, and legislative branches of government.

Rousseau offered a more radical political theory than Montesquieu's (see Biography). In his *Discourse on the Origin of Inequality* (1755), Rousseau argued that people in the "primitive" state of "noble savagery" were free, equal, and relatively happy. Only when some of them began marking off plots of ground, claiming them as their own and thereby founding civil society, did the troubles begin. Private property created inequality and the need for laws and governments to protect people from crime and wars. In *The Social Contract* (1762), Rousseau began by challenging his contemporaries: "Man is born free; and everywhere he is in chains." He then offered a solution to this conflict between individual freedom and social restrictions. In an ideal state, he argued, people entered into a compact with one another, agreeing to surrender their individual liberty, which was driven by self-interest, to the whole society. In return, the individual gained freedom by virtue of being part of the society's "general will," which was driven by the common good. "This means nothing less than that [the individual] will be forced to be free," explained Rousseau. Although Rousseau never made it clear just how the general will operated in practice, he believed that the people themselves—rather than a monarch or a parliamentary body—should make laws. His controversial ideas would powerfully influence the development of democratic theory over the next two centuries. For some, *The Social Contract* would support participatory democracy, whereas for others, Rousseau's emphasis on conforming to the general will would justify authoritarian political systems.

Although critical and combative, neither Rousseau, Montesquieu, nor the other *philosophes* were political or social revolutionaries. They did not champion the lower classes, whom they dismissed as ignorant, prone to violence, and, in Voltaire's words, "inaccessible to the progress of reason and over whom fanaticism maintains its atrocious hold." Diderot, of humble parents, admitted that he wrote "only for those with whom I should enjoy conversing . . . the philosophers; so far as I am concerned, there is no one else in the world." Most *philosophes* hoped for painless change from above rather than a revolutionary transfer of power to the still-unenlightened masses. Many shared Voltaire's belief that enlightened absolutism—rule by a well-educated, enlightened monarch—offered the best chance for the enactment of Enlightenment reforms such as religious toleration, rule subject to impartial laws, and freedom of speech (see Chapter 15).

If the functioning of the universe and politics could be described by understandable, rational laws, why should the same not hold true for economic activity? Several Enlightenment thinkers turned their thoughts to this question and attacked mercantilism, the system of regulated national economics that still operated throughout much of Europe. A group of French thinkers known as Physiocrats, led by François Quesnay, personal physician to Louis XV, began to teach that economics had its own set of natural laws. The Physiocrats believed that the most basic of these laws was that of supply and demand, and that these laws operated best under only minimal governmental regulation of private economic activity. This doctrine, which became known as *laissez-faire* (noninterference), favored free trade and enterprise. In France, the Physiocrats saw land and agriculture as the main source of national wealth. Other economists would build on their ideas and apply them to different settings.

In 1776, Adam Smith (1723–1790), a Scottish professor of philosophy who associated with the Physiocrats while traveling in France, published

Economic ideas: the Physiocrats and Adam Smith

Wealth of Nations. The book became the bible of laissez-faire economics. By nature, Smith argued, individuals who were allowed to pursue rationally their own economic self-interest would benefit society as well as themselves. Focusing on Britain's economy, Smith emphasized commerce, manufacturing, and labor rather than agriculture as the primary sources of national wealth. Anticipating the industrial age that would first emerge in Britain, he concluded that "the greatest improvement in the productive powers of labor . . . have been the effects of the division of labor." For Smith as well as the Physiocrats, laissez-faire economics held the key to national wealth—whether a nation was built on agriculture or industry.

What Smith and the Physiocrats did for economics, the Italian Cesare Beccaria (1738–1794) did for criminology and penology. Beccaria wrote *On Crimes and Punishments* (1764), an international best-seller, to protest "the cruelty of punishments and the irregularities of criminal procedures, . . . to demolish the accumulated errors of centuries." He argued that criminal laws and punishments, like all other aspects of life, should incorporate reason and natural law. Good laws, he explained, promoted "the greatest happiness divided among the greatest number." Criminal law should strive to deter crime and rehabilitate criminals rather than merely punish wrongdoers. In Beccaria's view, torture and capital punishment made no sense; indeed, only new penal institutions that mirrored natural law could transform convicted criminals.

Criminology, penology, and slavery

Other Enlightenment thinkers used similar arguments to denounce slavery. Abbé Guillaume Raynal (1713–1796), an outspoken and widely read critic of slavery, argued that this institution and many other practices of European and American colonists were irrational and inhumane. In the name of natural

THE ENLIGHTENMENT

1733	Voltaire, *Letters Concerning the English Nation*
1748	Montesquieu, *The Spirit of the Laws*
1751	The *Encyclopedia*
1759	Voltaire, *Candide*
1762	Rousseau, *The Social Contract*
1764	Beccaria, *On Crimes and Punishments*
1776	Smith, *Wealth of Nations*
1792	Wollstonecraft, *Vindication of the Rights of Women*

KEY DATES

BIOGRAPHY

Jean-Jacques Rousseau
(1712–1778)

Jean-Jacques Rousseau described himself as a "singular soul, strange, and to say it all, a man of paradoxes." A celebrity both admired and hated in his own time, he wrote more deeply on a wide range of subjects than any of his contemporaries.

"My birth was my first misfortune," Rousseau once stated wryly. His mother died shortly after he was born in 1712 in the Republic of Geneva. His father, a watchmaker, raised him to the age of 10 and then abandoned him to a series of homes where he served unhappily as an apprentice. One day in 1728, returning late from walking in the countryside, he found the gates of Geneva closed. Anticipating punishment from his master for his tardiness, he turned around and set off on the first of a series of wanderings that would mark the rest of his life.

Singular Soul, Controversial Thinker

He lived for much of the next ten years as the guest and lover of a baroness, Madame de Warens. In his own words, Rousseau became her "piece of work, student, friend. . . ." Rousseau addressed Madame de Warens as "Momma," and she referred to him as "my little one." This was the first of Rousseau's numerous relationships, many of them with older women. Yet he also lived as a recluse for long stretches of time during which he educated himself.

In 1742 the shy Rousseau arrived in Paris. He would often live there, though he harbored "a secret disgust for life in the capital," with its "dirty stinking little streets, ugly black houses, . . . poverty, [and] beggars." He first gained attention in Paris by writing about music and by joining the cultural circles. He also earned a modest income by serving as secretary to aristocratic patrons and by copying music. In 1745, Thérèse Levasseur, a young laundress, became his lifelong companion and ultimately his wife. The couple would have four children and abandon them all to a foundling hospital for adoption.

In 1749, Rousseau entered an essay contest that abruptly changed his life. He won the competition by arguing that progress in the arts and sciences corrupted rather than improved human conduct. Suddenly he was controversial and famous. "No longer [was I] that timid man, more ashamed than modest. . . . All Paris repeated [my] sharp and biting sarcasms. . . ." Buoyed by his newfound fame, he contributed several articles on music and political economy to the *Encyclopedia*, edited by his close friend Denis Diderot. He came to know and eventually quarrel with most of the leading figures of the Enlightenment.

Rousseau went on to publish several critical and widely circulated books, including *Discourse on the Origin of Inequality* (1755), *Julie, or*

---

rights, he called for a slave rebellion. An article in the authoritative *Encyclopedia* asserted similar views, declaring that all enslaved individuals "have the right to be declared free. . . ." These arguments, like the ideas of Beccaria and, in politics, of Montesquieu and Rousseau, would resound again and again through eighteenth-century Western society.

Becoming enlightened required education. Diderot claimed that the *Encyclopedia* was written so "that our children, by becoming more educated, may at the same time become more virtuous and happier. . . ." Many Enlightenment thinkers based their ideas on the psychological ideas of John Locke, which emphasized the power of education to mold the child into the adult. These thinkers often attacked organized religion in particular for controlling education.

Education

Rousseau became the outstanding critic of traditional education. In *Émile*, he argued that teachers should appeal to children's natural interests and goodness rather than impose discipline and punishment. "Hold childhood in reverence," he counseled. "Give nature time to work." He also pushed for less "artificial" schools, maintaining that nature and experience were better guides to independent thinking and practical knowledge—at least for males. "I hate books," he pointed out. "They only teach us to talk about things we know nothing about." By emphasizing practical education, learning by doing, and motivating rather than requiring the child to learn, Rousseau's *Émile* became one of the most influential works on modern education. His ideas on the education of females, however, were not so modern. Like most men of his time (enlightened or not), he believed that girls should be educated to fulfill their traditional domestic roles as wives and mothers.

In theory at least, the Enlightenment emphasis on individualism opened the door to the idea of equality between men and women. Several intellectuals explored this controversial issue. Early in the period, some challenging books on the "woman question" were published by female authors. In one of the best known of these, *A Serious Proposal to the Ladies* (1694), the English writer Mary Astell (1666–1731) argued that women should be educated

The "woman question"

The New Heloise (1761), *Émile* (1762), and *The Social Contract* (1762). These writings inspired not only learned responses but ardent mail from ordinary readers. One reader of *The New Heloise*, a novel focusing on the conflict between social demands and personal feelings, wrote, "Ever since I read your blessed book I have burned with love of virtue. . . . Feeling has taken over once again." Yet the books also inspired scorn. Peasants once stoned Rousseau's house, for example, after a pastor attacked him from the pulpit. Authorities issued more serious threats. In 1762, Parisian officials ordered *The Social Contract* burned and Rousseau arrested. He fled to Geneva, only to discover that officials there were also seeking his arrest. Again he escaped, moving from place to place and finding shelter with friends whom he quickly lost after bitter arguments. **Figure 14.11** shows him in the distinctive fur hat and collar he often wore during this period, when he was a guest of the English philosopher David Hume.

In the last fifteen years of his life, Rousseau felt persecuted and

FIGURE 14.11 Allan Ramsay, *Jean-Jacques Rousseau*, 1766

depressed. "I appear," he wrote, "as the enemy of the Nation." He published stunning, often exaggerated self-revelations in his *Confessions*, disclosing his affairs, lies, and quarrels.

A difficult man and a tortured soul, Rousseau was also a superb writer whose *New Heloise* became the most widely read novel of his age. He counts among the most important educational theorists in history and

became an accomplished composer and musical theorist. Author of one of the most striking autobiographical works ever written, he also proved an extremely influential philosopher and political theorist. "I am different," he wrote, "alone on earth. . . . Whether nature did well or ill to break the mould in which she formed me, this is something one can only judge after reading me." Sixteen years after Rousseau's death in 1778, France's revolutionary government moved his body to a place of honor near Voltaire's burial site in Paris.

Connecting People & Society

1. What were Rousseau's early life experiences, and how might they have colored the ideas in his writings?

2. What do authorities' and ordinary people's harsh reactions to Rousseau's socially critical works reveal about eighteenth-century society?

3. How did Rousseau's work and life reflect the ideas and efforts of other Enlightenment thinkers?

according to the ideas of the new science—reason and debate—rather than tradition. Later, she explained that men seem to know more than women because "boys have much time and pains, care and cost bestowed on their education, girls have little or none. The former are early initiated in the sciences" and "have all imaginable encouragement" while "the latter are restrained, frowned upon, and beaten." In other writings, she questioned the inequality of men's and women's roles: "If all Men are born Free, how is it that all Women are born Slaves?" Later in the eighteenth century, the British author Mary Wollstonecraft (1759–1797) published *Vindication of the Rights of Women* (1792), in which she analyzed the condition of women and argued forcefully for equal rights for all human beings. Like Astell, Wollstonecraft stressed the need to educate women: "If she be not prepared by education to become the companion of man, she will stop the progress of knowledge and virtue; for truth must be common to all, or it will be inefficacious with respect to its influence on general practice."

Few male writers went that far. Although some men supported better education for women, most held the traditional view that women were weaker than men and best suited for domestic rather than public affairs. According to Immanuel Kant, who spoke so optimistically and eloquently about education and enlightenment, "laborious learning or painful pondering, even if a woman should greatly succeed in it, destroy the merits that are proper to her sex." The editors of the *Encyclopedia* also ignored contributions from women, instead praising those who remained at home. Some of Rousseau's writings were particularly influential among women, primarily because they glorified child rearing, maternalism, and emotional life. Rousseau never suggested that women were independent beings equal to men. For him, "Woman is made to please and to be subjugated to man."

The Culture and Spread of the Enlightenment

The Enlightenment glittered especially in Paris, and salon meetings became the chief social setting for this intellectual culture. These meetings were hosted by wealthy Parisian patrons, usually women of the aristocracy or upper-middle class. In an environment lush with art, music, and wealth, the *philosophes*, powerful nobles, diplomats, statesmen, artists, and well-educated conversationalists gathered regularly to read, listen to, and debate the ideas of the Enlightenment. They also discussed—and sometimes influenced—economic policies, wars, and the king's choice of ministers. The German critic Friedrich Grimm (1723–1807), who published a private newsletter on Parisian life, described the salons of Julie de Lespinasse, who lived openly with the *philosophe* d'Alembert: "Her circle met daily from five o'clock until nine in the evening. There we were sure to find choice men of all orders in the State, the Church, the Court—military men, foreigners, and the most distinguished men of letters. Politics, religion, philosophy, anecdotes, news, nothing was excluded from the conversation." These salon meetings became self-conscious forums for arbitrating and molding public opinion through the open use of reason.

Salon meetings

As leaders, patrons, and intellectual contributors to these gatherings, women played a particularly important role in the Enlightenment. Independent, witty, powerful women governed the potentially unruly meetings and discussions by enforcing rules of polite conversation. One of the most famous of these patrons was Madame Marie-Thérèse Geoffrin (1699–1777), a rich middle-class widow who served as a model and mentor for other women leaders of salons. **Figure 14.12,** a painting by Anicet Charles Lemonnier, shows a salon meeting at her home in 1755. Madame Geoffrin, wearing a blue dress and looking at the viewer, sits at the left next to Bernard de Fontenelle, 98-year-old popularizer of science. Above is a bust of Voltaire, the Enlightenment hero living in exile at the time. Women with the right intellectual and social qualifications attended this and other salons, but the star invitees were usually men.

Smaller meetings in other French and foreign cities, from Berlin to Philadelphia, paralleled the Parisian salon meetings. Moreover, all these meetings went hand in hand with an extensive international correspondence carried out by participants. For some, letter writing, like good conversation in the salons, was an art. People also read and discussed Enlightenment ideas in local academies, Freemason lodges, societies, libraries, and coffeehouses. In addition, most municipalities had clubs where the social and intellectual elites could mingle.

Even bookstores, where people could purchase books or pay small fees to read recent works, became hotbeds of Enlightenment ideas. **Figure 14.13** shows

FIGURE 14.12 Anicet Charles Lemonnier, *An Evening at Madame Geoffrin's in 1755*, 1812 *Philosophes*, nobles, statesmen, and well-educated conversationalists often gathered in Enlightenment-age salons led by women such as Madame Geoffrin, shown here sitting on the right in a blue dress.

FIGURE 14.13

Léonard Defrance, *At the Shield of Minerva*, 1781

In this painting, French artist Léonard Defrance depicts a street scene in front of a bookstore in France. Notice the reference in the store's name to Minerva, the Roman goddess of poetry and wisdom. Also note the mix of people and the prominence of the clergyman (in white robes) among them.

Connecting Art & Society

1. What might the packages of books bound for, or being delivered from, Spain, Portugal, Rome, and Naples suggest about the spread of Enlightenment ideas throughout Europe?

2. In what ways does this painting imply that people of all classes were being touched by books—and perhaps by Enlightenment ideas?

3. Why do you think the artist included a member of the clergy in such a central place in this painting?

an eighteenth-century bookstore. In the doorway stand two women, reading books. Just outside are

Bookstores

packages of books being delivered from or to Spain, Portugal, Rome, and Naples. In the street, apparently drawn to the bookstore, are people of all classes, from a peasant with his scythe at the left to a cleric

in his white robes at the center. The name of the bookstore, "The Shield of Minerva," refers to the Roman goddess of wisdom. In a growing number of bookstores such as this, all sorts of works became increasingly available, from religious tracts and chivalric tales to new novels and Enlightenment literature.

These gatherings and interchanges spread the ideas of the Enlightenment throughout society and enhanced the social respectability of intellectuals. They also helped create a common intellectual culture that crossed class lines and political borders and that contributed to an informed body of public opinion. People who participated in these interchanges came to sense that they could freely express ideas as well as debate political and social issues. By the last quarter of the eighteenth century, Enlightenment ideas could be heard even in the camps of the *philosophes'* traditional opponents—the clergy, governmental officials, and monarchs. As we will see, these ideas pushed some monarchs to enact "enlightened" reforms and encouraged many other people to demand revolutionary change.

LOOKING BACK & MOVING FORWARD

Summary The great intellectual revolution of the seventeenth and eighteenth centuries was fueled by advances in science. Brimming with new scientific ideas and discoveries, Western civilization relinquished its medieval assumptions and embarked on an innovative journey unique among the cultures of the world. This change in direction became one of the main forces behind the power and dynamism that came to characterize the West. Through science, Westerners hoped to gain greater control over the material world and nature.

Enlightenment thinkers carried these daring aspirations further, self-consciously leading a mission of reform and freedom from the shackles of tradition. By striking the match of reason, they believed, people could at last dispel the darkness of the past and liberate themselves as never before. Thus enlightened, humanity as a whole could move from childhood to adulthood. As the *philosophe* Baron d'Holbach proclaimed, "The *enlightened man*, is man in his maturity, in his perfection; who is capable of pursuing his own happiness; because he has learned to examine, to think for himself, and not to take that for truth upon the authority of others."

Many participants in Enlightenment circles have since been criticized as self-concerned dilettantes reluctant to take on the risks of real reform. Most historians, however, see the *philosophes* as thoughtful, sincere, and sometimes brilliant thinkers. The *philosophes* clearly left a mark on Western culture. Their ideas, like those of the seventeenth-century scientists, threatened the traditional order, especially the church. As their primary legacy, they widened the gap between religiously influenced doctrines and accepted scholarly thought. Equally significant, they set the intellectual stage for a series of revolutions that would soon sweep America and Europe. Above all, their way of thinking—stressing reason, individualism, and progress—would form the intellectual foundation of modern Western society and further distinguish this civilization from its non-Western counterparts.

KEY TERMS

Neoplatonism, *p. 453*

Hermetic doctrine, *p. 453*

Copernican revolution, *p. 454*

heliocentric model, *p. 454*

empirical method, *p. 459*

deductive reasoning, *p. 460*

Cartesian dualism, *p. 460*

Scientific Revolution, *p. 460*

Enlightenment, *p. 462*

philosophes, *p. 465*

REVIEW, ANALYZE, & CONNECT TO TODAY

REVIEW THE PREVIOUS CHAPTERS

Chapter 12—"Faith, Fortune, and Fame"—told how several European powers expanded overseas during the fifteenth, sixteenth, and seventeenth centuries and grew rich from the commerce. Chapter 13—"The Struggle for Survival and Sovereignty"—focused on how kings and nobles battled for power, the resolutions of those struggles, and their impact on the millions of people outside the elite.

1. Analyze how the expansion of Europe might have stimulated scientific research.

2. In what ways did the effort of monarchs to increase their power and create stability relate to the promotion of science and the desire for greater intellectual certainty?

ANALYZE THIS CHAPTER

Chapter 14—"A New World of Reason and Reform"—examines the changing intellectual foundations of the West.

1. List and analyze the differences between the new scientific views of the world and traditional medieval views. How did standards for ascertaining the "truth" differ between these two perspectives?

2. Analyze the beliefs and motives of three central figures in the Scientific Revolution. What barriers did they have to overcome to present their views?

3. Do you think the Enlightenment merely popularized the Scientific Revolution, or did it accomplish something more?

4. In what ways did the Enlightenment threaten traditional views and authorities?

CONNECT TO TODAY

Think about the meaning of the Scientific Revolution and the values underlying the Enlightenment.

1. In what ways are our present-day assumptions about the physical universe and the workings of nature based on the ideas and discoveries of the Scientific Revolution?

2. What aspects of world politics today reflect Enlightenment values? What aspects of present-day global politics seem to be opposed to those values?

BEYOND THE CLASSROOM

QUESTIONING TRUTH AND AUTHORITY

Kuhn, Thomas S. *The Structure of Scientific Revolutions*, 2nd ed. Chicago: University of Chicago Press, 1970. A landmark analysis of the nature, causes, and consequences of transformations in scientific concepts.

Mandrou, Robert. *From Humanism to Science*. Atlantic Highlands, NJ: Humanities Press, 1979. A description of how the role of intellectuals changed between 1480 and 1700.

Teresi, Dick. *Lost Discoveries: The Ancient Roots of Modern Science—From the Babylonians to the Maya*. New York: Simon & Schuster, 2003. Focuses on discoveries from non-Western societies that predated Europe's Scientific Revolution.

DEVELOPING A MODERN SCIENTIFIC VIEW

Cohen, H.F. *The Scientific Revolution*. Chicago: University of Chicago Press, 1994. An analysis of when and where modern science began.

Dear, Peter. *Revolutionizing the Sciences: European Knowledge and Its Ambitions, 1500–1700*. Princeton, NJ: Princeton University Press, 2001. A survey of the main ideas of science and its new institutions.

Feingold, Mordechai. *The Newtonian Moment: Isaac Newton and the Making of Modern Culture*. New York: Oxford University Press, 2004. A well-illustrated book that focuses on Newton and how his ideas affected eighteenth-century culture.

Hall, Rupert A. *The Revolution in Science, 1500–1750*. London: Longman, 1983. A useful introduction to the developments in science during this period.

Schiebinger, Londa. *The Mind Has No Sex? Women in the Origins of Modern Science*. Cambridge, MA: Harvard University Press, 1990. An examination of the participation of women in science; stresses how science reflected male biases.

Shapin, Steven. *The Scientific Revolution*. Chicago: University of Chicago Press, 1996. A concise, new interpretation questioning whether there was a "scientific revolution."

Westfall, Richard. *The Construction of Modern Science: Mechanisms and Mechanics*. New York: Cambridge University Press, 1977. A good survey of scientific developments during the seventeenth century that emphasizes the importance of mathematics and mechanics.

SUPPORTING AND SPREADING SCIENCE

Jacob, Margaret C. *The Cultural Meaning of the Scientific Revolution*. New York: Knopf, 1988. Examines the evolution of science within its political, social, and cultural context.

Moran, Bruce T., ed. *Patronage and Institutions: Science, Technology and Medicine at the European Court, 1500–1750*. Rochester, NY: Boydell Press, 1991. Examines the role of royal courts in supporting and shaping science during this period.

LAYING THE FOUNDATIONS FOR THE ENLIGHTENMENT

Outram, Dorinda. *The Enlightenment*. Cambridge: Cambridge University Press, 2005. Presents the various interpretations of the Enlightenment.

Porter, Roy. *The Enlightenment*, 2nd ed. London: Palgrave, 2001. A solid, well-written survey of eighteenth-century intellectual life.

Sklar, Judith. *Montesquieu*. Oxford: Oxford University Press, 1987. A concise, well-written study of Montesquieu and his ideas.

THE ENLIGHTENMENT IN FULL STRIDE

Besterman, Theodore. *Voltaire*, 3rd ed. Chicago: University of Chicago Press, 1976. A useful biography of this major Enlightenment figure.

Darton, Robert. *The Business of Enlightenment: A Publishing History of the* Encyclopedia, *1775–1800*. Cambridge, MA: Belknap Press, 1979. A well-written social history and analysis of the publication of the *Encyclopedia*.

Gay, Peter. *The Enlightenment: An Interpretation*, 2 vols. New York: Knopf, 1966–1969. A classic study, exhaustive, but with a strong point of view.

Goodman, Dena. *The Republic of Letters: A Cultural History of the French Enlightenment*. Ithaca, NY: Cornell University Press, 1994. A study of the cultural and intellectual life of eighteenth-century France that concentrates on the role played by the salons.

Lougee, Carolyn. *Le Paradis des Femmes. Women, Salons, and Social Stratification in Seventeenth-Century France*. Princeton, NJ: Princeton University Press, 1976. Analyzes the foundations and importance of the French salons, emphasizing the role played by women in them.

Melton, J.V.H. *The Rise of the Public in Enlightenment Europe*. Cambridge: Cambridge University Press, 2001. Connects publishing and the reading public during the Enlightenment.

PHILIP VAN DIJK, *BRISTOL DOCKS AND QUAY*, ca. 1780
This painting shows the British port of Bristol, one of many European port cities that benefited from the lucrative overseas trade that grew during the eighteenth century. On the left, ships arrive and dock on the well-protected canal, where they are loaded and unloaded. On the quay are workers, merchants, and families—some of the many who directly benefited from the activity. Around them are well-kept shops, homes, and buildings that reflect the prosperity of this commercial center and the wealth drawn from Britain's colonial empire.

Competing for Power and Wealth

The Old Regime, 1715–1789

" A reasonable man is always happy if he has what is necessary for him according to his condition [social rank], that is to say, if he has the protection of the laws, and can live as his father lived before him," wrote a French observer in 1747. The political lesson behind these words was clear. "Essential . . . to the good of a nation is being governed in one constant and uniform manner." Most people living in the eighteenth century would have nodded their heads in agreement. Indeed, they actively upheld the social order—ranked, governed, and sanctioned as it was by tradition and Christian teachings.

Despite this affirmation of stability, change was afoot in these years. During the seventeenth century, kings and queens had struggled with nobles in their own countries for control and with other monarchs to increase their nations' sway. In their continuing competition for power and wealth, eighteenth-century kings and queens tried to strengthen their states while gaining status—often through war—in the international arena. Below them, ambitious aristocrats flexed their muscles, sometimes challenging their monarchs, sometimes forging alliances with them, and often reveling in the new wealth and culture that now lay within their reach. They, along with the growing number of commoners, began to see much promise in the new ways to produce food and organize manufacturing, all fueled by accelerating commerce—especially with overseas colonies, as reflected in the painting facing this page. Moreover, many elites—including some monarchs themselves—also recognized the strength of Enlightenment ideas and began to think of ways to institute "enlightened" reforms. At the base of Western society, the mass of peasants and workers toiled, as they always had. However, their numbers were increasing, and their ways of life were slowly adjusting to the pressures of change. This society and its politics would later be known as the Old Regime, but many living at the time detected the quickening pulse of a new era.

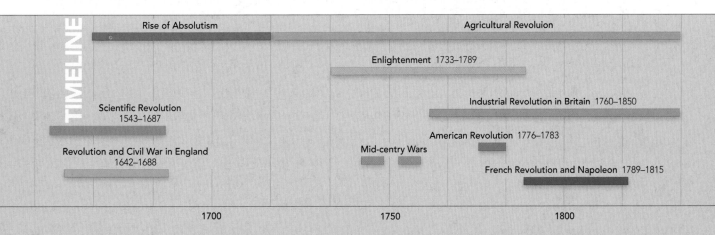

TIMELINE

Rise of Absolutism

Agricultural Revoluion

Enlightenment 1733–1789

Scientific Revolution
1543–1687

Industrial Revolution in Britain 1760–1850

American Revolution 1776–1783

Revolution and Civil War in England
1642–1688

Mid-century Wars

French Revolution and Napoleon 1789–1815

1700   1750   1800

PREVIEW

STATEBUILDING AND WAR

In August 1715, the old and sad Louis XIV fell ill. His legs swelled and turned black as gangrene set in. Remarkably, he had outlived both his son and grandson. On his deathbed, Louis warned his 5-year-old great-grandson, who would succeed him as Louis XV (r. 1715–1774), not to "imitate my love of building nor my liking of war." Neither Louis XV nor many other rulers of the time managed to follow this advice for long. War and building might cost lives and drain royal treasuries, but they made a spectacular show of power in a competitive world. The rulers of Europe clung to their statebuilding ways, straining to secure their central governments and ensure their own position at the top.

During the seventeenth century, this competitiveness had plunged Europe into a series of bloody conflicts—the very battles Louis XIV regretted on his deathbed (see Chapter 13). In western Europe, the violence stopped with the Peace of Utrecht in 1713–1714. Seven years later, the Treaty of Nystad (1721) ended the conflicts in eastern Europe (see **Map 15.1**). For a while, the two treaties held. Monarchs throughout Europe tried to adhere to the principle of a **balance of power** to prevent any one state or alliance from dominating the others. Nevertheless, anyone hoping for an extended period free of war would be sorely disappointed. Up-and-coming states such as

Prussia and Britain bristled with ambition and vied with their established competitors for power, prestige, and wealth. Their struggles spread beyond the borders of Europe to overseas colonies on continents from North America to Asia, in this sense turning European wars into global conflicts. As we will see, this competition subjected millions of people to a fresh round of hardship and irrevocably altered the fate and fortunes of nations throughout the West.

Rising Ambitions in Eastern Europe

Within Europe, the fiercest competition took place in eastern Europe. There, Russia and Brandenburg-Prussia were on the rise. Under Peter the Great, Russia had already defeated Sweden, grabbing much of the northeastern Baltic coast in the process. Russia next hoped to take advantage of the sprawling but weak Polish state farther west (see Chapter 13) and to benefit from the decline of the Ottoman Empire, which controlled the Black Sea to Russia's south. Brandenburg-Prussia also saw opportunities in Poland, which divided and bordered its lands. This militaristic state also coveted some of the holdings of the bloated Austro-Hungarian Empire to the south, which in turn intended to hold its own in the power struggle. Someone would have to pay the price for all these ambitions.

Peter the Great had done much to turn Russia toward the West and make it a great power. By the time of his death in 1725, he had modernized Russia's government and military, established Russia as the dominant power in northeastern Europe, and pressured the Russian nobility into the state bureaucracy and army officer corps. In the process, he made many enemies, from the peasants who paid dearly for Peter's accomplishments to all those who had a stake in the very social, cultural, and religious traditions that Peter attacked. His successors would have to face these enemies and shoulder the task of sustaining Russia's expansion to the south and west.

Six mediocre rulers followed Peter—including an infant, a boy of 12, and a mentally unstable tsar. Despite this shaky leadership, Russia held its ground. From 1725 to 1762, its population increased, and the landowning elite grew wealthier than ever. The nobility took back some of the authority it had lost to Peter, diminishing the service it owed to the state; in 1762, nobles freed themselves of all such obligations. Nevertheless, they still staffed the bureaucracy and military officer corps. Moreover, nobles cracked down even more on their serfs, reducing their status to that of mere property. The 1767 Decree on Serfs made the situation crystal clear: "Serfs and peasants . . . owe their landlords proper submission and absolute obedience in all matters."

> New leadership in expanding Russia

French Bourbon Lands
Spanish Bourbon Lands
Austrian Habsburg Lands
Prussian Lands
Great Britain
Boundary of the Holy Roman Empire

MAP 15.1

Europe, 1721

This map shows Europe after the Treaties of Utrecht (1714) and Nystad (1721).

Explore the Map

1. Although France and Spain were ruled by Bourbon monarchs, the two nations remained separate. How might a union between the two have altered the balance of power in Europe?

2. Locate the large states in eastern Europe. Which of these states, despite their size, were declining powers?

3. Identify the lands controlled by Austria. Why might this power's holdings have been vulnerable?

The decades of weak leadership ended when a dynamic new leader ascended the Russian throne. Catherine the Great (r. 1762–1796) grew up an obscure princess from one of the little German states. For political reasons, her family married her to young Peter III (r. 1762), the tyrannical and intellectually limited grandson of Peter the Great and heir to the Russian crown. He soon rejected her in all ways, and after he became tsar, he quickly lost most of his supporters as well. Catherine had no intention of languishing in obscurity. "I did not care about Peter," she later wrote, "but I did care about the crown." Less than a year after he took the throne, Catherine conspired with a group of aristocratic army officers, who assassinated him and declared Catherine tsarina of Russia.

Catherine the Great

The new empress used her striking intelligence, charm, and political talent to assert her own power and expand Russian territory and might. Well educated, she thought of herself as attuned to Enlightenment ideas. She often corresponded with French *philosophes* such as Denis Diderot, who spent some time at St. Petersburg as her guest. In 1766, she congratulated Voltaire for triumphing "against the enemies of mankind: superstition, fanaticism, ignorance, quibbling, evil judges, and the power that rests in their hands." Voltaire returned the favor with constant praise for Catherine. She relaxed the traditionally tight constraints on the press in Russia and she confiscated church lands—policies that seemed in line with Enlightenment thinking. Her educational reforms, by which she established new local schools, teachers' colleges, and schools for girls, also suggested a forward-thinking monarch. Most stunningly, Catherine convened a legislative commission, half of whose members were commoners (some even peasants), to reform Russia's legal code. She wrote the *Instruction* (1767) to that commission herself, relying on the works of key Enlightenment figures such as Montesquieu and Beccaria. Her *Instruction* called for equality before the law, the abolition of torture, and other liberal reforms.

These programs promised more than they delivered. The commission members squabbled among themselves, and in the end, the effort yielded only minor reforms before it was finally abandoned. Catherine's early talk of easing the burdens on the peasantry also came to little; in return for the support of noble landowners, she allowed them to subjugate the peasants even further. As Document 15.1 suggests, some observers criticized the treatment of Russia's serfs. For example, Alexander Radischev argued, "What good does it do the country that every year a few thousand more bushels of grain are grown, if those who produce it are valued on a par with the ox whose job it is to break the heavy furrow?" Catherine imprisoned him.

In 1768, Catherine provoked a war against the Ottoman Empire. The event seems to have signaled her turn away from enlightened reform and toward power politics. A massive insurrection by Russian serfs in 1773 under the leadership of a Don Cossack, Yemelyan Pugachev (1726–1775), further soured her on reform. Pugachev claimed to be Catherine's murdered husband, a "redeemer tsar," and promised his followers land and freedom. Thousands of serfs in southwestern Russia turned against their masters—slaughtering hundreds of landlords and officials—and demanded an end to their plight. Catherine's army managed to put down the rebellion, but only with great difficulty. When some disgruntled followers betrayed Pugachev, the army captured him and tortured him to death.

Catherine proved more successful in her ambitious foreign policy. She defeated the Turks in 1774, extending Russia to the Black Sea and the Balkan Peninsula. **Map 15.2** shows Russia's expansion to the south and west during the eighteenth century.

Catherine then turned on Poland. At the beginning of the eighteenth century, Poland was the third-largest country in Europe. Yet, as we saw in Chapter 13, it lacked natural boundaries and a strong central government. Weak and without allies, it became a power vacuum that proved all too tempting to its ambitious neighbors. In 1772, Russia, Prussia, and Austria—having plotted Poland's demise among themselves—annexed slices of Polish territory. This aggression at long last stirred the Polish government to action. The Diet passed sweeping reforms, improved the lot of commoners, and gave the central government power to act effectively. These changes came too late. Poland still could not match the combined armies of its enemies, and in 1795, the three aggressors divided the remainder of the hapless nation among themselves. **Map 15.2** shows the eventual dismemberment of Poland, which left Russia, Prussia, and Austria the dominant powers in eastern Europe. When Catherine died in 1796 after thirty-five years of rule, Russia had grown to an ominous size and had taken its place as a major power in world affairs.

The partition of Poland

Farther south, military defeats at the hands of the Russians marked the Ottoman Empire's continuing decline. Throughout the eighteenth century, the Ottoman economy suffered from falling population growth and a rising inability to compete commercially with Europeans. The English, French, and Venetians took over the trade from the East that used to pass through Ottoman hands. Sultans lost administrative authority to the Muslim clergy. Fearing cultural influences from western Europe, this conservative clergy hindered efforts to introduce European science and even printing presses into Ottoman lands for most of the eighteenth century. Unable to maintain their own armaments industry, moreover, the Ottomans had to rely on European suppliers to outfit the empire's army and navy. At the same time, the Ottomans faced uprisings in their Arabian provinces, where a religious reform movement, **Wahhabism,** challenged the sultans' authority. After mid-century, for good reason, many European elites began calling the Ottoman Empire the "sick man of Europe."

The decline of the Ottoman Empire

DOCUMENT 15.1

Landlords and Serfs in Russia

During the eighteenth century, Russian serfs probably fared worse than peasants elsewhere in Europe. Toward the end of the century, Alexander Radischev published a description of Russian serfs and their treatment by noble landowners. For this daring act, the author was imprisoned by Catherine II.

A certain man left the capital, acquired a small village of one or two hundred souls [i.e., serfs], and determined to make his living by agriculture. . . . To this end he thought it the surest method to make his peasants resemble tools that have neither will nor impulse; and to a certain extent he actually made them like the soldiers of the present time who are commanded in a mass, who move to battle in a mass, and who count for nothing when acting singly. To attain this end he took away from his peasants the small allotment of plough land and the hay meadows which noblemen usually give them

for their bare maintenance, as a recompense for all the forced labor which they demand from them. In a word, this nobleman forced all his peasants and their wives and children to work every day of the year for him. Lest they should starve, he doled out to them a definite quantity of bread. . . . If there was any real meat, it was only in Easter Week.

These serfs also receive clothing befitting their condition. . . . Naturally these serfs had no cows, horses, ewes, or rams. Their master did not withhold from these serfs the permission, but rather the means to have them. Whoever was a little better off and ate sparingly, kept a few chickens, which the master sometimes took for himself, paying for them as he pleased.

In a short time he added to his two hundred souls another two hundred as victims of his greed, and proceeding with them just as with the first, he increased his holdings year after year, thus multiplying the

number of those groaning in his fields. Now he counts them by the thousands and is praised as a famous agriculturalist.

"Barbarian! What good does it do the country that every year a few thousand more bushels of grain are grown, if those who produce it are valued on a par with the ox whose job it is to break the heavy furrow? Or do we think our citizens happy because our granaries are full and their stomachs empty?"

SOURCE: Alexander Radischev, *A Journey from St. Petersburg to Moscow* (1790).

Analyze the Document

1. In what ways does the landowner described in this excerpt treat his serfs?

2. How does the author criticize this treatment of serfs?

3. According to Radischev, is the main problem with this "certain man" or with the system of serfdom in Russia?

In east-central Europe, the small but rising Brandenburg-Prussia set its sights on the Austrian Empire, a large power struggling to maintain control over its far-flung lands. From 1713 to 1740, the vigorous Frederick William I ruled Prussia. The king was obsessed with unquestioned absolutism, centralized bureaucratic administration, and, above all, the military. His martial uniforms and preoccupation with Prussian soldiery earned him the label the Sergeant King.

Frederick William's mental image of the perfect military dominated his policies and Prussian society. While he employed his army for road and canal building as well as traditional military service, some 70 percent of the state's budget went to the armed forces, whose size he more than doubled during his reign. Rather than relying on mercenaries, the king required all men to register for military service in local units commanded by German noble officers. The localities, in turn, had to recruit and support these regiments, and soldiers were billeted among the civilian population.

> Forging a military state in Prussia

No other state in Europe could boast such a high proportion of men, from peasant to noble, in the military. Nor could any other state point to such a regimented society. In Prussia, the higher ranks of the military and state bureaucracy were reserved for the nobility; the middle classes were clearly prevented from rising to noble status; and the peasantry was a subordinate, overburdened people, often still serfs living in almost slavelike relationships to their land-owning masters.

Despite the martial tenor of life in Prussia, the king left a surprisingly progressive legacy. Frederick William I avoided wars, promoted a strong economy, welcomed Protestant and Jewish refugees, and filled the treasury. In 1740, he passed all that he had built, intact, on to his talented son Frederick II (r. 1740–1786), later known as Frederick the Great. The new king soon used this army—the fourth largest in Europe—and the money his father had accumulated to make a bold bid for Austrian lands.

In the same year that Frederick II ascended the throne in Prussia, Maria Theresa (r. 1740–1780) became empress of the Austrian Habsburg dominions.

Map legend:
- Boundary of Poland to 1772
- Boundary of the Three Powers at 1795
- Russian Gains 1721–1795
- Poland 1793–1795

MAP 15.2

The Expansion of Russia and the Partition of Poland, 1721–1795

This map shows eastern Europe during the eighteenth century, identifying the partition of Poland and the expansion of Russia and Prussia.

Explore the Map

1. In what ways did the partition of Poland benefit Russia, Prussia, and Austria?

2. How might Poland's decline change the balance of power?

3. Where might the rising powers of Russia and Prussia look for further expansion?

Austria was not a tightly controlled, militaristic state like Prussia. Rather, it had already lost most of the indirect control it once held over the central German states as head of the Holy Roman Empire. Austria's own lands contained a complex array of language groups and consisted of some semi-autonomous territories. Austria could barely control Hungary, and its nobility fully dominated its serfs, who paid most taxes directly to their lords rather than to the crown.

> **Austria tries to hold on**

As a result, Maria Theresa could afford only a relatively small army.

The empress's father had feared that these weaknesses might prove Austria's undoing when he died. Moreover, there was only weak precedent for a female ruler of Habsburg lands. Therefore, he spent the final twenty years of his life securing agreement among all the European powers (embodied in a document called the Pragmatic Sanction) that his daughter would succeed him without question. In spite of his diligence, when he died in 1740, competitors arose to challenge her authority. As for the principle of balance of power among states implying a desire for peace, Frederick II of Prussia dismissed the idea bluntly: "The fundamental rule of governments is the principle of extending their territories."

As soon as Maria Theresa took the crown, Frederick challenged her authority, a common occurrence when a succession was questionable in any way. Acting on his maxim that "the safety and greater good for the state demands that treaties should be broken under certain circumstances," the Prussian king marched his troops into Silesia (see **Map 15.3**), the richest of the Habsburg provinces. He also shrewdly forged alliances with other German states against Austria. His aggressive scheming plunged most of the major European states into a series of wars for the mastery of central Europe.

The mid-century land wars

The War of the Austrian Succession dragged on for eight years (1740–1748). Maria Theresa rallied Hungarian arms to her defense and repelled Prussia's allies—Bavarians, Saxons, French, and Spanish. The conflict eventually turned into a military stalemate, which led to a 1748 peace treaty that ended the hostilities. Maria Theresa had managed to preserve the Habsburg state as a major power, but she had been unable to dislodge Frederick from Silesia.

Neither she nor her advisors intended to tolerate this robbery of their fair province by the upstart Prussians—even if it meant starting negotiations for an alliance with their traditional rival, France. Frederick grew fearful of being isolated by his enemies and left vulnerable to invasions. In 1756, when he signed an alliance with Great Britain—Prussia's opponent only a few years earlier—Maria Theresa solidified a new alliance with France. Document 15.2 reveals how difficult the change of allies was for Maria Theresa. This astounding shift of alliances—the so-called Diplomatic Revolution—suddenly transformed former enemies into friends. Meanwhile, Maria Theresa shored up Austria's internal resources by honing her government's control over taxation, dimin-

The Diplomatic Revolution

ishing burdens on the peasantry, and reorganizing the bureaucracy. All this strengthened her position as a ruler who could command strong forces and who enjoyed backing from a powerful ally. **Figure 15.1,** a painting by Habsburg court artist Martin Meytens, shows the empress with her husband (seated on the left) and thirteen of her sixteen children. Her son Joseph, heir to the throne, stands in a favored place at the center of the star floor. As this painting suggests, even though she led Austria through wars, Maria Theresa often chose to present herself as a good mother to both her family and her nation.

Not one to wait for his enemies to strike first, Frederick reopened hostilities by overrunning Saxony in 1756, initiating the Seven Years' War (1756–1763). However, Frederick soon found himself at bay as France and Austria—now joined by Russia and Sweden, both of which hoped to gain lands at Prussia's expense—closed in on him from all directions. His only backing came from Britain, which saw an opportunity to weaken its longtime opponent, France. After holding off his enemies for six years, the exhausted Prussian king finally seemed near defeat.

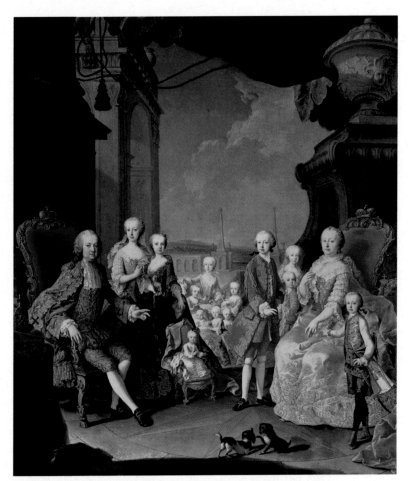

FIGURE 15.1 Martin Meytens, *Maria Theresa and Her Family,* 1750 The artist portrayed the empress with her husband and many children, suggesting that she was a good mother as well as a powerful ruler. To her right stands the heir to her throne, Joseph.

MAP 15.3

Prussia and the Austrian Empire, 1721–1772

This map shows two growing eighteenth-century powers, Prussia and Austria.

Explore the Map

1. Compare the holdings of these two states. Which do you think was stronger? Why?

2. What problems did both face in creating a strong, unified state?

3. To the west lay France, and to the east was Russia—both large and unified states. Where were Austria and Prussia most likely to compete with each other or to expand? Why?

"I believe all is lost," he confessed in private. Then in 1762 his luck revived. The Russian tsarina Elizabeth, one of his most reviled enemies, died. Her successor, the weak Peter III, happened to admire Frederick and suddenly pulled Russia out of the war. The remaining allies soon lost stomach for the fight. The peace in 1763 left matters much as they had been before the war began, but as we will see (pages 494–496), the fighting in Europe spread to India, the Caribbean, and North America.

Having narrowly escaped destruction, Frederick spent the remaining twenty-three years of his life reconstructing his war-ravaged territories. He encouraged agriculture, subsidized and protected industry, and invited immigrants into his well-governed territories. At no time, though, did he neglect his army or lose his sense of practicality. Indeed, in 1772 he joined Austria and Russia in the first partition of Poland. **Map 15.3** shows Prussia's expansion under Frederick, first at the expense of the Austrian Empire when he

DOCUMENT 15.2

Austria's Empress Explains the Diplomatic Revolution

During the eighteenth century, alliances among European states often shifted. They changed most dramatically in the 1756 Diplomatic Revolution preceding the Seven Years' War (1756–1763). In the following excerpt, Empress Maria Theresa of Austria explains why she turned toward her traditional adversary, France, to form a coalition against the newly allied Prussia and Great Britain.

"I have not abandoned the old system, but Great Britain has abandoned me and the system, by concluding the Prussian treaty, the first intelligence of which struck me like a fit of apoplexy. I and the king of Prussia are incompatible; and no consideration on earth will ever induce me to enter into any engagement to which he is a party. Why should you be surprised if, following your example in concluding a treaty with Prussia, I should now enter into an engagement with France?

"I am far from being French in my disposition, and do not deny that the court of Versailles has been my bitterest enemy, but I have little to fear from France, and I have no other recourse than to form such arrangements as will secure what remains to me. My principal aim is to secure my hereditary possessions. I have truly but two enemies whom I really dread, the king of Prussia and the Turks; and while I and Russia continue on the same good terms as now exist between us; we shall, I trust, be able to convince Europe, that we are in a condition to defend ourselves against those adversaries, however formidable."

SOURCE: Maria Theresa, William Coxe, *History of the House of Austria*, vol. 3 (London: Bohn, 1847), pp. 363–364.

Analyze the Document

1. Why does Maria Theresa forge an alliance with France?

2. What problems does she anticipate in allying Austria with France?

3. Why might Maria Theresa have identified the king of Prussia and the Turks as the "two enemies whom I really dread"?

---

took Silesia, and then at the expense of Poland as he used the territory to unify the main portions of his country. The map also shows Prussia's chief competitor, Austria, with its farther-flung territories. By the time of his death in 1786, Frederick had raised Prussia to the status of a great power and shared the leadership of central Europe with Austria.

Warfare in the Eighteenth Century

The nature of wars fought by these eighteenth-century nations had evolved and changed from earlier times. Now armies consisted primarily of professional forces whose size and elaborate organization mirrored the centralized, bureaucratic governments they served. Officers were paid as full-time servants of the state in both peace and war. However, the troops they commanded were not all so professional. Conscripts, volunteers, mercenaries, and even criminals made up their rank and file. In this sense, armies served as a depository for men without means and for those seen as threats to the social order. Officers tried to tame these motley groups by stressing harsh discipline and incessant drilling.

Weapons and tactics were also changing. Reliable muskets; bayonets that no longer hindered fire; mobile cannons; and skilled coordination of troops, artillery, and cavalry all made warfare potentially more destructive than ever. Still, generals typically avoided all-out battles, preferring to expend their resources judiciously.

"I do not favor pitched battles, especially at the beginning of a war," said Marshall Saxe, a leading French officer and writer on war tactics, in 1732. "I am convinced that a skillful general could make war all his life without being forced into one." Even Frederick the Great—not one to shy away from warfare—expressed this preference in his *Instructions for His Generals* (1747): "The greatest secret of war and the masterpiece of a skillful general is to starve his enemy." Instead of embarking on grand, decisive battles, then, eighteenth-century generals focused on building fortifications, initiating and maintaining sieges, securing supply lines, gaining superior positions, and piling up small advantages. Moreover, most military campaigns lasted only four or five months a year. Meanwhile, life outside the military—commerce, farming, culture, travel, and politics—went on as usual.

Yet, as Frederick the Great recognized, "war is [ultimately] decided only by battles and is not finished except by them." Outright fighting, when it finally occurred, took a heavy toll in human lives. Typically, soldiers arranged themselves in dense rows at least three men deep and fired their muskets, row by row, on command. Each side hurled artillery fire into the opposing troops and sent the cavalry charging in. Casualties mounted, but at the end of the day generals usually pulled their forces back from the battle with enough survivors to fight again.

Maritime battles cost fewer lives than land wars but could be crucial in the overall outcome of war.

FIGURE 15.2 An Eighteenth-Century French Warship This view of a French warship shows some of the weapons, men, animals, stores, and equipment carried by this powerful vessel of war.

The largest ships of war in the eighteenth century carried up to one hundred cannons. **Figure 15.2,** a cutaway view of a French warship, shows cannons poking out of the top three decks. Sailors are depicted at drill and at rest. At the upper right are officers' quarters, and the bottom decks house supplies, including livestock. Often firing at each other at point-blank range, many warships were destroyed or suffered grievous damage in these brutal clashes, and thousands of sailors perished.

A single battle, whether on land or sea, rarely led to a definitive outcome. More likely, the relentless draining away of money and men prompted diplomats to come to the bargaining table and end the war. This hemorrhaging of money and men was not missed by critics of the military, especially Enlightenment thinkers, who denigrated the old warrior culture as irrational and wasteful. Their criticisms, however, could neither prevent nor end wars in a society in which most people still regarded war as a normal—perhaps necessary—part of life.

Western Europe and the Great Colonial Rivalry

Like eastern Europe, western Europe experienced its own brand of statebuilding and rivalry for power. In this region as well as overseas, France and Britain uneasily shared dominance. Their seventeenth-century rivals, Spain and Holland, were declining. On the Continent, Spain—lacking the finances, manpower, and royal leadership that made it such a power in the late sixteenth and early seventeenth centuries—could no longer threaten France. Holland—damaged by three Anglo-Dutch wars and economic warfare with Britain during the seventeenth century—had

gradually lost much of its trade and international position. Overseas, however, Spain and Portugal had managed to hold on to most of their lands. In the Americas, they remained great colonial powers, controlling most of the territory stretching from Mexico to the South American continent. There, they dominated the Amerindians, disrupting their cultures and turning them into laborers on large plantations and in mines, which still produced massive loads of gold and silver for shipment to Europe. Holland also had retained its Pacific colonies, which supported a valuable coffee and spice trade. However, the Dutch had lost some of their empire in Asia and much of their sea power to the British. With Spain and Holland thus occupied, France and Britain became the primary colonial rivals (see **Map 15.4**).

Louis XIV had made France a model of absolutism. However, the French monarchy never again achieved the clout it had enjoyed under his guidance. To be sure, France remained a first-rank power with a large army, a centralized bureaucracy, and a growing economy. Yet, even during the last decades of his reign, Louis XIV's stature diminished. Thoughtful people criticized him for dragging France into what they saw as meaningless foreign conflicts. Louis' expensive wars and unreformed taxation policies also depleted the treasury. As Voltaire reported in 1751, "In the minds of the majority of his subjects, he lost during the last three years of his life all the prestige of the great and memorable things he had accomplished. . . ."

> The French monarchy in decline

After Louis' death in 1715, French nobles in governmental councils and France's *parlements*—the thirteen judicial courts that had to sign royal decrees before those documents could become

MAP 15.4

Overseas Colonies and Trade, 1740

This map shows Europe's colonies and overseas trade patterns during the mid-eighteenth century.

Explore the Map

1. Locate British and French holdings. Where were conflicts most likely to break out between these two powers? Why?

2. Describe the triangular trade across the Atlantic Ocean. What continents did this trade connect? Why was slavery so central to this system?

3. Which goods dominated trade? Which goods were Europeans most interested in selling and buying? Why?

law—angled for a restoration of the powers they had lost to the king. The *parlements* claimed to speak for the nation, though in fact they voiced only the interests of the elites. The nobles bargained with the crown, sometimes to the point of open defiance. They faced a stubborn opponent. The young Louis XV, who had ascended the throne at the age of 5, would rule for almost sixty years. Like Louis XIV, he asserted that "sovereign power resides in my person only . . . my courts [*parlements*] derive their existence and their authority from me alone . . . to me alone belongs legislative power without subordination and undivided."

Despite his longevity and support from some able ministers, Louis XV governed far less effectively than his predecessor had. Ignoring administrative matters, he allowed his royal bureaucracy to weaken. As resistance from the *parlements* ate away at the king's authority, France's fiscal pressures from old debts and continued military expenditures grew. The rising tensions centered on the issue of taxes. Specifically, the crown wanted to tap France's wealth by raising taxes, but the nobility sidestepped this move by using the *parlements* to protect their tax exemptions. Moreover, private tax farmers still controlled the collection of taxes, keeping one-third for themselves. Clearly, the monarchy was missing out on large sources of revenue. In 1716, the crown had tried to change this system. The effort led to the creation of a private bank, promoted by a brilliant Scottish financier, John Law, with the power to produce its own notes as legal tender and to monopolize overseas commerce. Within just a few years, however, overspeculation in his Mississippi Company had brought the bank to ruin the "Mississippi Bubble," leaving France saddled again with its inefficient old system.

Nothing drained money from the treasury more than wars. By avoiding major wars until 1740, the crown achieved relative financial stability. Thereafter the story changed, as France was drawn into a series of costly conflicts with Continental and colonial rivals. Struggling to fund these endeavors and lacking the appropriate financial institutions and taxable resources, France staggered under a relentlessly expanding debt.

In the 1770s, the king and his chancellor finally dissolved the *parlements* and tried to enact an ambitious program of reform. The move came too late. The inept Louis XV had never projected the image of a dynamic, reforming, enlightened monarch. On the contrary, he had a reputation for living lavishly within his opulent court. Underground pamphlets accused him of allowing his mistress and his sexual taste for girls to distract him from attending properly to courtly matters and the demanding business of managing the state. By the end of his reign, he had earned the dislike and even hatred of his subjects. Louis XV's death in 1774 was met with conspicuous silence, and his tardy reform program evaporated.

Hoping to gain popularity, Louis' successor, Louis XVI (r. 1774–1792), quickly restored the *parlements* and their powers. Again, these aristocratic bodies thwarted new plans for financial reform—even those offered by talented ministers. In France, unlike in most other European powers, the crown and the nobility failed to find a satisfactory way of working together. Again and again, reform efforts faltered, annoying those hoping for change. As frustrations

intensified, the crown became increasingly isolated from traditional sources of support within the country.

France needed all the strength it could muster to compete for colonies and stature with Great Britain, where a much different situation had evolved. In 1714, a year before Louis XIV's death, Queen Anne had died. The crown passed to George I (r. 1714–1727), the first of the German Hanoverian line. The British monarchy had already sustained damage from the civil war and revolution of the seventeenth century (see Chapter 13). Though the king remained the chief executive of the state, ordained by God and tradition, Parliament now had the upper hand. Divided into the House of Lords (for nobles only) and House of Commons (elected representatives of commoners), Parliament controlled critical functions such as taxation, lawmaking, and the process for bringing grievances to the monarchy. Clearly, king and Parliament had to find a way to work together rather than in opposition.

The answer came in the form of a new institution: the cabinet system. Under this structure, the king chose members of Parliament, usually from the House of Commons, to serve as his ministers. If he hoped to enact policies, he had to select ministers who could command plenty of votes. These men tended to be the leaders of the major groups, or parties, in the House of Commons. By the eighteenth century, two groups dominated the House. Whigs, favoring commercial interests and a strong Parliament, remained staunchly opposed to any return of the Catholic Stuarts to the crown. Whigs also championed popular rights more than the conservative Tories did. Tories usually favored large landowners and a strong monarchy and had stood less firmly against the Stuarts than the Whigs had.

Differences between the two groups came to a head in 1714. That year, the Tories considered supporting James, a Catholic Stuart raised in France, against George I. An unsuccessful rebellion in favor of James discredited the Tories in the eyes of the monarchy. In 1746, the English army put down another rebellion in Scotland that had attempted to support a Catholic Stuart. This latest fiasco further alienated the Tory leadership from the British crown.

For these reasons, George I and his son George II (r. 1727–1760) selected their ministers from the Whigs rather than the Tories. The two kings' lack of talent and public support made them all the more dependent on Whig leadership for governance. That leadership came in the person of Robert Walpole (1676–1745). Already recognized as a superb speaker and leading Whig in the House of Commons, Walpole became First Lord of the Treasury and the most important minister in George I's Privy Council in 1721. Much of Walpole's prominence derived from his successful handling of a financial crisis after an overseas

> Making the British system work

trading company collapsed in 1720 (the South Sea Bubble). After that coup, he brought in other Whigs who could control votes in Parliament. He flattered and "managed" the monarch to remain in favor. Through patronage—control over money, contracts, offices, and honors—and the manipulation of elections, he ensured the dominance of the Whigs and his own leadership for twenty years.

Many complained about this pattern of political corruption, which both Whigs and Tories used. One critic—the British artist William Hogarth (1697–1764)—produced many prints lambasting British political and social life. In **Figure 15.3,** one of a series of works on British elections, Hogarth shows a corrupt political campaign in progress. At the center, a voter emerges drunk from a riotous tavern. He has been bribed and is being instructed how to vote, which at the time was done publicly. At the left, the Tory candidate is purchasing cheap jewelry for a woman on the balcony. He makes his purchase from a Jewish merchant, despite his own anti-Jewish record in Parliament.

FIGURE 15.3 William Hogarth, *Canvassing for Votes—The Election,* 1754 This satirical scene of what went on during an election campaign shows an irresponsible candidate and his supporters bribing people for their votes.

Walpole's successors continued his strategy of patronage to ensure parliamentary support, and the Whigs held office for another twenty years. By the middle of the eighteenth century, a pattern had emerged. A group of ministers—themselves led by a prime minister, chosen from Parliament, who could command enough votes in the House of Commons to pass legislation—served the monarch and remained responsible to Parliament. Unlike in France, where most political debate took place outside the government, in Britain, debate occurred within Parliament between the party in power and the "loyal opposition." People thus perceived the nation as being governed by the rule of law rather than the whim of a monarch. This system often moved slowly, but it worked.

Although Britain's government may have been more representative than France's, it was far from democratic. Only some 200,000—most of them the wealthiest males—could vote. Rich landowners and powerful local elites staffed the government. Not surprisingly, Parliament listened most carefully to representatives of the 400 families whose massive estates included one-fourth of Britain's arable land. British officials did not seek to exempt themselves from taxation, as did most of their counterparts in France, but instead ruled along with the crown by controlling Parliament.

Prosperity formed the foundation of Britain's strong position in these years. The middle class in particular agreed with the popular British author and observer Daniel Defoe that "the greatness of the British nation is not owing to war and conquests . . . it is all owing to trade, to the increase of our commerce at home, and the extending it abroad." Goods poured into Britain from India and North America. The nation transformed itself into an agricultural exporter and a flourishing manufacturing center. By the middle of the eighteenth century, Great Britain had become Europe's leading economic power. It pursued its interest in European affairs through diplomacy, alliances, and the subsidizing of its allies' arms. Its naval dominance alone made it a formidable opponent. After 1740, Britain used both its economic strength and its military might in the great mid-century wars with France that stretched across three continents. To understand this story, we must shift our attention to the West's overseas colonies and the nature of trade among them.

More than anything else, France and Britain fought over colonies. For both countries, foreign trade quadrupled in the eighteenth century, and a large part of that increase derived from transactions with colonies. The two nations also made their greatest profits from trade across the Atlantic. However, their overseas presence differed crucially. The French had only 56,000 colonists living in North America in 1740—a fraction of the British colonial population. Yet French colonists carried out an extensive, highly profitable fur trade. Further, because of their small numbers and trade arrangements, they experienced limited conflict with Amerindians.

British colonists, clustered along the eastern seaboard, had a different experience. First, they grew rapidly—from 250,000 in 1700 to 1.7 million in 1760.

Colonies, trade, and war

As they occupied and exploited more and more land, they pushed the Amerindians out. Their expansion, combined with resistance from local tribes, led to savage battles. The fighting, in turn, convinced the colonists that removing or even exterminating the Amerindians was justified. As they became more firmly established, the British colonists bought manufactured goods from Britain in return for tobacco, rice, cotton, and indigo dye, much of which Britain re-exported to the European continent.

These North American colonists participated in the even more lucrative triangle of trade that connected Europe, Africa, and the Americas and that centered on the Caribbean (see

The triangle of trade

Map 15.4). The British and French, along with the Dutch and Spanish, held islands there that supported sugar, rum, coffee, and dyestuffs trade produced by slave labor. In particular, the demand for sugar and coffee seemed endless. European craving for these items grew so much that, for many, they became necessities rather than occasional luxuries.

At the heart of this thriving colonial commerce was the slave trade (see Chapter 12). Slavery was long common throughout Africa and in

The slave trade

other societies. For centuries, Islamic merchants had purchased slaves through well-established African networks and transported them by caravan across the Sahara Desert to the Mediterranean basin or by ship from east African ports across the Indian Ocean to Asia.

In the eighteenth century, the dramatic demand for slaves in the Americas shifted Africa's slave trade westward to the Atlantic coast. Ships from Europe carried manufactured goods (most notably, guns) and gin to western Africa and traded them for slaves—two-thirds of them males, because they best provided heavy labor. Usually captured by African middlemen, slaves languished in pens in towns or forts on the African coast. European trading ships then carried them across the Atlantic in a perilous two-month sea voyage known as the **Middle Passage.**

Figure 15.4, an 1846 watercolor, suggests what conditions were like belowdecks on a slave ship. Typically, slaves were packed like cargo into the holds of ships "where the light of day does not penetrate." As many as 700 slaves—naked, branded, and shackled—might be crammed into one ship. A French writer describing these voyages told of a "continuous state of alarm on the part of the white men, who fear a revolt, and . . . a cruel state of uncertainty on the part of the Negroes, who do not know the fate awaiting them." In Document 15.3, Olaudah Equiano, a captured African, describes how this Middle Passage experience soon made him "so sick and low" that he "wished for the last friend, death."

Traders took most of their slaves to the West Indies and Brazil; less than 10 percent went to North American destinations. After unloading their human cargo, the ships filled up with sugar, rum, and other goods—sometimes stopping farther north in the American colonies to take on additional products such as cotton, tobacco, timber, and furs. From there, the ships returned to Europe. Merchants then re-exported many of these products to other European nations.

Disease, abuse, and suicide took the lives of many slaves. In addition, African women often suffered the horror of rape by their captors. Those who survived the Middle Passage were then sold for profit and put to work on a plantation or in the mines or households of colonists. **Figure 15.5** depicts slaves harvesting sugarcane on a West Indies plantation. Men, women, and children share the difficult work. In the foreground, a manager on horseback gives orders to a slave, who looks up deferentially to his master. On the right, sugarcane is being loaded into a cart, to be carried to the mill in the distant background. Slaves suffered from poor diets, inadequate housing, broken families, and stiff corporal punishment. The uprooting, the trauma of transportation, and the harsh conditions in the colonies stripped much away from these people. Still, slaves often resisted their masters by working slowly, sabotaging equipment, running away, and revolting. Despite their lack of freedom, slaves built hybrid cultural traditions from African, American, and European sources.

Within the slave societies of Brazil, the West Indies, and North America, the notion of race was becoming tied to slavery, adding to earlier notions of racial prejudice. The unprecedented

FIGURE 15.4 A Transatlantic Slave Ship, 1846 This mid-nineteenth-century watercolor depicts a slave ship where the human cargo is packed tightly belowdecks.

DOCUMENT 15.3

Olaudah Equiano Describes the Middle Passage

The slave trade between Africa and the Americas involved the horrors of capture and the Middle Passage, a harrowing two-month voyage across the Atlantic. In the account below, Olaudah Equiano (1745–1797)—a west African who was captured by slave raiders when he was 10 years old—describes the ocean journey. He survived the voyage and twenty-one years of slavery before purchasing his freedom.

The first object which saluted my eyes when I arrived on the coast was the sea, and a slave ship which was then riding at anchor and waiting for its cargo. These filled me with astonishment, which was soon converted into terror when I was carried on board. I was immediately handled and tossed up to see if I were sound by some of the crew, and I was now persuaded that I had gotten into a world of bad spirits and that they were going to kill me. . . .

I was not long suffered to indulge my grief; I was soon put down under the decks, and there I received such a salutation in my nostrils as I had never experienced in my life; so that with the loathsomeness of the stench and crying together, I became so sick and low that I was not able to eat, nor had I the least desire to taste anything. I now

wished for the last friend, death, to relieve me; but soon, to my grief, two of the white men offered me eatables, and on my refusing to eat, one of them held me fast by the hands and laid me across I think the windlass and tied my feet while the other flogged me severely. I had never experienced anything of this kind before, and although not being used to the water I naturally feared that element the first time I saw it, yet nevertheless if I could have gotten over the nettings I would have jumped over the side, but I could not; and besides, the crew used to watch very closely over those of us who were not chained down to the decks, lest we should leap into the water, and I have seen some of these poor African prisoners most severely cut for attempting to do so, and hourly whipped for not eating. This indeed was often the case with myself. . . .

One day when we had a smooth sea and moderate wind, two of my wearied countrymen who were chained together (I was near them at the time), preferring death to such a life of misery, somehow made through the nettings and jumped into the sea; immediately another quite dejected fellow, who on account of his illness was suffered to be out of irons, also followed

their example; and I believe many more would very soon have done the same if they had not been prevented by the ship's crew, who were instantly alarmed. Those of us that were the most active were in a moment put down under the deck, and there was such a noise and confusion amongst the people of the ship as I never heard before, to stop her and get the boat to go after the slaves. However, two of the wretches were drowned, but they got the other and afterwards flogged him unmercifully for thus attempting to prefer death to slavery. In this manner we continued to undergo more hardships than I can now relate, hardships which are inseparable from this accursed trade.

SOURCE: Olaudah Equiano, *The Interesting Narrative of the Life of Olaudah Equiano, or Gustavus Vassa, the African, Written by Himself,* 2 vols. (London, 1789).

Analyze the Document

1. How are captured Africans treated on the slave ship?

2. In what ways do they try to resist?

3. Notice the date and place of publication. Why might a London firm have been interested in publishing this account by Equiano?

---

dependence on slavery and the associated development of racism would stain these societies in ways that persist to this day.

The consequences of the slave trade also rippled through sub-Saharan Africa. Traditional trade routes north to the Mediterranean and east to the Indian Ocean disintegrated as more lucrative commerce shifted west to the Atlantic coast of Africa. To supply more human cargo to the Europeans, west African kingdoms raided inland tribes. Bloody internal wars erupted—more deadly than ever thanks to the guns supplied by Europeans to the Africans.

Because many slaves perished in the Americas, and the plantations that depended on them kept expanding, the demand for fresh supplies of slaves

increased relentlessly. This rising need perpetuated the triangular commerce among Europe, Africa, and the Americas. European traders took 50,000 to 100,000 slaves across the Atlantic each year during most of the eighteenth century. By the time slave trafficking abated in the mid-nineteenth century, more than 11 million Africans had been ripped from their homes, transported across the Atlantic, and sold into slavery. Another 4 million died resisting seizure or while in transport.

Planters and merchants on both sides of the Atlantic profited from this trade, and European cities serving as slave-trade ports flourished, particularly in England. The coastal town of Liverpool, for example, grew from a small town to a major city in

FIGURE 15.5 A West Indies Sugar Plantation, 1823 This painting shows slaves cutting the sugarcane and loading it onto carts under the watchful eye of a manager, who is on horseback giving instructions.

the eighteenth century. In 1750, its slave merchants and fleet of almost two hundred ships carried almost half of Europe's slave trade. Thousands of men from Liverpool worked on both merchant and naval ships, and more than a dozen banks and several insurance companies served slave-trade merchants. The wealth spread outward from Liverpool, helping to finance Britain's burgeoning industry as well as its rising position on the world stage. "Our West-Indies and African Trades are the most nationally beneficial of any we carry on. . . . The Trade to Africa is the branch which renders our American Colonies and Plantations so advantageous to Great Britain," argued one British defender of the slave system in 1746. "The daily bread of the most considerable part of our British Manufacturers are owing primarily to the labor of Negroes." Although the statement may be an exaggeration, slavery generated much commerce and wealth in this eighteenth-century Atlantic economy, whether by direct or indirect means.

As Europeans' commercial activities, profits, and presence increased in the Americas, so did competition and friction, especially between the French and the British. In North America, British colonists along the eastern seaboard pushed inland, beyond the Appalachian Mountains into the Ohio Valley. The French strengthened their holdings by building forts along the Great Lakes and the large rivers of the St. Lawrence and Mississippi valleys. When the War of the Austrian Succession broke out in Europe in 1740, Britain and France soon locked horns on the Continent as well as overseas. Most of the fighting took place in the Americas, however.

Fighting on three continents

Wins and losses on each side balanced out, and by the time the conflict ended in 1748, each side had settled for what it had held in the beginning.

The peace would not last long. In 1755, war—sometimes known as the French and Indian War—erupted again, this time initiated by a British offensive against a French stronghold near Pittsburgh in North America. At the same time, the two powers were also competing in India, each trying to take advantage of the declining power of the Mughals (India's Muslim rulers—see Global Connections in Chapter 13). After 1715, the subcontinent had split apart into bickering, independent kingdoms. India became fertile ground for the British and French, working through their chartered trading companies and backed by their superior weapons of war, to make deals, gain influence, and line up allies among India's opposing princes and political factions. In 1759, British colonialist and soldier Robert Clive (1725–1774), representing Britain's East India Company, explained how a combination of force and bribery could gain the company and England "absolute possession of these rich kingdoms" in India that would provide "an income yearly of upwards of two million sterling." Moreover, he added, Britain would gain advantages over "the several European nations engaged in the commerce here," especially "against the French." This competition between the British and French for trade and imperial power developed into an undeclared war that, after 1756, coalesced with the hostilities breaking out across Europe (the Seven Years' War), the Caribbean, and North America.

In this widespread war, which involved Asians and Amerindians as well as Europeans, France invested most of its energy and resources in the European arena, whereas Britain focused on the battle overseas. Initially, the French, assisted by the Amerindian allies they had gained, held their own in North America. Then the British, with their superior navy and more extensive population, began capturing French strongholds one by one. The fall of Quebec in 1759 opened all of Canada to British forces. British naval power overwhelmed the French and their Spanish allies in the Caribbean as well. In India, the British also prevailed, crushing the French and subduing several resisting Indian states. During the succeeding decades, as **Map 15.5** reveals, the British increasingly took direct control over areas around their bases of power.

Figure 15.6 also attests to this British success. This late-eighteenth-century painting shows William Kirkpatric, a British officer, with his attendants—a group of Indian princes and merchants. Kirkpatric's prominence reflects his authority over those around him and his sword reveals the source of his power.

Western Africa, Brazil, and the Atlantic Slave Trade

Drawn by commercial opportunities, European vessels flocked to the west coast of Africa during the seventeenth and eighteenth centuries. The new trade, especially the lucrative and rapidly expanding commerce in slaves, turned west Africans' attention toward the Atlantic Ocean as well. European textiles, metal goods, and firearms poured into west Africa off the European ships. From Brazil and other lands in the Americas came new crops, such as manioc and maize, to supplement the yams, millet, and bananas that served as staples for sub-Saharan Africans. Prosperous port cities emerged, and west African states such as Dahomey and Asante gained power.

Other African societies weakened, and once-powerful kingdoms fell in the turmoil and wars provoked by slaving. In 1730, an officer of the Dutch West India Company involved in the slave trade concluded, "The great quantity of guns and powder which the Europeans have from time to time brought" to west Africa have caused "terrible wars among the kings, princes . . . of those lands, who made their prisoners of war slaves." Moreover, the profits from slaving made many Africans "forget all labor." Consequently, there was now "very little trade among the coast Negroes except in slaves." Other methods of obtaining slaves only worsened the turmoil and dislocations that were tearing African societies apart. According to Alexander Falconbridge, a British surgeon who served on slaving ships during the 1780s, "There is great reason to believe that most of the negroes shipped off from the coast of Africa are *kidnapped.*" As a result, "continual enmity is thus fostered among the negroes of Africa, and all social intercourse between them destroyed."

The slave trade shaped the Portuguese colony Brazil, as well. During the eighteenth century, Europeans shipped millions of slaves across the Atlantic; more than a third of them went to Brazil. Although most slaves worked on large plantations producing crops such as sugar and tobacco for export, many also served as domestics and manual laborers. The English navigator Captain William Dampier, stopping in Brazil, reported that everyone kept slaves in their houses except "people of the lowest degree of all." Tradesmen, he continued, "buy Negroes, and train them up to their several Employments," and "Many of the Portugueze, who are Batchelors, keep these black Women for Misses."

Another British traveler to Brazil, Henry Koster, reported that all slaves in Brazil "follow the religion of their master." Many were "baptized in lots before they left their own shores," whereas others were converted upon arrival in Brazil. "The system of baptizing the newly imported negroes," he reported, rendered the slaves "more tractable." Over time, these slaves learned to speak Portuguese, while "their own dialects are allowed to lie dormant until they are, by many of them, quite forgotten." Many slaves died from diseases such as yellow fever or from brutal working conditions and poor nutrition. However, Koster claimed that slaves adapted to "the habits of their masters." At the same time, their masters "imbibe[d] some of the customs of their slaves; and thus the superior and his dependent are brought nearer to each other."

The trans-Atlantic slaving connection between west Africa and Brazil continued into the nineteenth century. In 1888, Brazil—by then an independent nation—became the last state in the Americas to abolish slavery.

Making Connections

1. What were the consequences of the slave trade for the societies of western Africa and Brazil?

2. How did Brazilian masters deal with their slaves?

The British had to conquer native forces as well as the French to increase their holdings in the Indian subcontinent. The papers on the table represent the taxes collected by British authorities and suggest the imposition of British law over local states. In the background stands a magnificent estate, suggesting how colonial holdings and commerce created great wealth in the officer's homeland.

Maps **15.6** and **15.7** show the changing fortunes of France and Britain in North America between 1755 and 1763. The Treaty of Paris, which ended the fighting in 1763, gave Britain control of Canada and of France's holdings east of the Mississippi. Britain also received France's West Indian possessions, except for Guadeloupe and Martinique, and most of France's holdings in India. British control over most of India

MAP 15.5

India, 1756–1805

This map shows British acquisitions in India between 1756 and 1805.

Explore the Map

1. Notice where the British concentrated their holdings in the subcontinent. What connections might these holdings have had to trade and transportation?

2. Locate where the French and Portuguese maintained a presence. Why might that limited presence have been important to the French and Portuguese?

3. How might the British have maintained and extended their control over such large areas in India with a limited number of "settlers"?

dates from this period. France and several other nations still retained important overseas colonies, but Britain now reigned as the top colonial and commercial power. This "great war for empire" paved the way for the British to establish their worldwide empire in the nineteenth century.

THE TWILIGHT OF MONARCHIES? THE QUESTION OF ENLIGHTENED ABSOLUTISM

In both Britain and France, the eighteenth-century monarchies were in decline, but for different reasons. In Britain, the monarchs ruled in partnership with Parliament. However, the kings were undistinguished, and Parliament continued to gain the upper hand. In France, the successors to Louis XIV lacked the interest, talent, and support to make the monarchy dynamic or popular. The twin threats to the crown in these nations—the growing complexity of effective governance, and demands from elites to share power—arose elsewhere as well.

However, in several other nations, monarchs managed to maintain their authority—often by justifying their rule in innovative ways and instituting new policies. In the second half of the eighteenth century, some of these monarchs styled themselves as "enlightened," or attuned to Enlightenment beliefs and willing to initiate reforms for the good of the state and its people. Some historians have distinguished these rulers from their predecessors, calling them "enlightened absolutists" or simply "enlightened." Yet, how valid is this characterization? Several historians claim that these

FIGURE 15.6 The English School, *Dixton Harvesters*, ca. 1725 This late-eighteenth-century painting shows a British officer in India and his Indian attendants. It suggests the power and wealth gained by the British as they increased their presence on the Indian subcontinent.

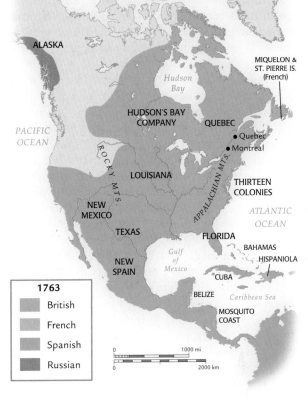

MAPS 15.6 and 15.7

North America, 1755 and 1763

These maps show North America before and after the Seven Years' War.

Explore the Maps

1. Notice France's large holdings in 1755. What advantages helped the British defeat France in this part of the world?

2. What new problems did Britain face as a result of its victory?

3. Identify what other competitors to the British remained in North America after 1763. How would you assess their relative strength?

monarchs primarily followed the long tradition of trying to buttress the central government's power and efficiency. Other historians argue that they genuinely initiated reforms in line with Enlightenment thinking.

The most sensational of the self-described enlightened monarchs was Frederick the Great (Frederick II) of Prussia. Even as a boy, Frederick loved music, poetry, and philosophy. After ascending to the throne, he still found time to perform in concerts as an accomplished flutist in his Palace of San Souci. There he also hobnobbed with towering cultural figures such as Voltaire, savored books in his library, and carried on a lively correspondence with leading French intellectuals. He knew and spoke the

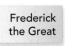

Frederick the Great

phrases of the Enlightenment. Like several other monarchs, he also wanted to display his awareness of culture and intellectual life to help justify his position as monarch. He described "the good monarch" as one who behaved "as if he were each moment liable to render an account of his administration to his fellow citizens." He claimed to act only in the common interest of the people, declaring himself to be "the first servant of the state" rather than a divinely appointed ruler.

At the end of the Seven Years' War (1756–1763), the second of his two wars of aggression, Frederick made some attempts at "enlightened" reforms. For example, he initiated codification of the laws, abolished torture, and ended most capital punishment.

Believing that "all religions, if one examines them, are founded on superstitious systems, more or less absurd," he proclaimed religious toleration. Nevertheless, he considered Jews "useless to the state" and taxed them heavily. He advocated public education but spent very little on it compared with what he spent on his army. In his economic policy, Frederick did share the Physiocrats' appreciation of the importance of agriculture and tried to introduce new methods of cultivation (see page 468). Yet he did nothing to free the serfs or lessen their burdens. Neither his wars nor his involvement in the partition of Poland revealed any hint of enlightened principles different from those of the monarchs who preceded him.

No one tried more sincerely to be enlightened than Joseph II of Austria (r. 1780–1790). "Since I have ascended the throne," he said | **Joseph II** | in 1781, "I have made *philosophy* the legislator of my empire." Viewing his rule as a moral and holy calling, Joseph issued thousands of decrees. Unfortunately, he lacked the practical sense of Frederick the Great. He did change laws that had previously limited freedom of the press and religion (including Judaism). He also restricted the death penalty, promoted education, and enacted and tried to enforce equality before the law.

Nevertheless, Joseph still ruled as an autocrat, antagonizing most of the powerful groups in his lands. Even peasants, unable to understand exactly what all the decrees meant, failed to support him. His well-meaning but ill-conceived efforts—to centralize the administration of the widely dispersed Habsburg territories, to replace the numerous languages of his subjects with German, to subordinate the strongly entrenched Roman Catholic Church, and to free the serfs in a society still based on feudalism—all backfired. Opposition and even open revolt swelled in his lands. In 1787, Joseph lamented, "[I] hope that when I am no more, posterity will examine, and judge more equitably . . . all that I have done for my people." His vision would not come to pass. Within a few years of his death in 1790, most of his reforms were abolished and the Habsburg lands reacquired their old, conservative ways.

Other monarchs, such as those of Sweden, Sardinia, Spain, and Portugal, attempted or enacted reforms that could be seen as enlightened. In Russia, Catherine the Great certainly prided herself on being enlightened (see page 482). She once described the true aim of monarchy as "not to deprive People of their natural Liberty; but to correct their Actions, in order to attain the supreme good." Ultimately, however, Catherine failed to put most of her reforms into practice. Instead, she resorted to the tried-and-true tactic of appeasing elites at a price paid by the peasantry.

Certainly these monarchs found it easier to manifest their "enlightenment" in style rather than substance.

Moreover, they rarely lost sight of traditional goals: to increase their own military and economic power. Few attempted to enact fundamental social, political, or economic reforms dictated by Enlightenment thought. Even those who tried, such as Joseph II in Austria, generally failed to overcome opposition to those reforms from tradition-minded people.

| **Style, substance, or survival?** |

Nevertheless, thoughtful observers of the eighteenth century—looking for tendencies and possibilities for reform rather than revolutionary change—believed that several rulers displayed the enlightened spirit of the times. Despite great obstacles to reform within the traditional order, some of these rulers made progress toward fulfilling the *philosophes'* agenda of promoting more religious tolerance, humane social institutions, and rational administration. In the eyes of contemporaries, they earned the label "enlightened".

Finally, from another perspective, **enlightened absolutism** also may have reflected a growing sense that, in the long run, monarchs could no longer *claim* to embody the state. The need for governmental efficiency had grown too much to be entrusted to a poorly qualified individual who happened to be a king or queen. Moreover, governments increasingly had to recognize the emergence of a public sphere within their lands where individuals and groups exchanged information, voiced ideas, and engaged in criticism. Public opinion became a potential tool that monarchs might use to their advantage—or a force they might ignore to their detriment. If the institution of monarchy were to survive, kings and queens had to justify their position in these new, ostensibly enlightened ways.

CHANGES IN COUNTRY AND CITY LIFE

Eighteenth-century European monarchs and officials faced not only the risky politics and wars of their times but also the changes unfolding in their very societies. Especially in western Europe, new economic and social forces began to upset old traditions (see Chapter 13). For some, these changes created a sense that life was improving and would continue to do so. For others, the changes only deepened their misery. The greatest shifts emerged in the countryside, where the vast majority of the population (some 80 percent) lived and depended on agriculture for their livelihood and very survival.

Historically, toiling in the fields within Europe's traditional subsistence economies produced little more than enough food to survive. During the late seventeenth and eighteenth centuries, new methods of agricultural production that had originated in

Holland spread to England and then to other areas of western Europe. These innovative methods allowed fewer people to work the fields and still produce far more food than they needed. The new techniques and the changes flowing from them became so important that they are known as the agricultural revolution.

The Agricultural Revolution

Most early-eighteenth-century farmers used methods that differed only marginally from those employed in previous centuries. They grew the same crops year after year, left one-third to one-half of the land fallow (unplanted) to allow the soil to replenish itself with nutrients for the next planting, and saved only enough fodder to feed small numbers of domestic animals during the winters. Individual families worked small strips of land, and large, uncultivated fields, brushlands, and forests (the commons) were reserved for general use by the community. Traditional community practices usually determined decisions about crops, animals, and land use. Overall, only a small minority of people made their living outside of agriculture, and an even smaller percentage had the good fortune to afford luxuries.

This traditional, agricultural economy had the potential to support a limited measure of population growth. In the eighteenth century, population increases stepped up the demand for food, and hence for hands to clear fields, drain swamps, terrace hillsides, carry water, and till the soil. Most of these efforts were simply an intensification of old methods for increasing agricultural yields, and the growing population consumed most of the extra food they produced. Something had to change if large numbers of Europeans hoped to increase their standard of living and provide enough food for people living in the cities as well as the countryside.

At the heart of the **agricultural revolution** lay two developments: first, the introduction of new crops and the use of new farming techniques that dramatically boosted agricultural yields; and second, the transformation of rural lands farmed for subsistence into large, controlled properties that produced crops for commerce. The primary agricultural advances came first in Holland and Britain, where farmers began experimenting with new crops such as clover, turnips, and legumes, as well as the potato from America. These crops replenished the soil rather than depleting it and therefore could be grown on lands that farmers periodically had to leave fallow. Farmers now used the new crops to feed livestock during the hard winters. More cattle meant more protein-rich dairy products; more horses and oxen eased the workload for humans and provided transportation; and more sheep produced more wool.

New crops and techniques

All this livestock, improving with new crossbreeding practices, yielded more meat, leather, and soap as well as manure with which to fertilize fields. Other new foods, such as nutrient-rich potatoes, also made the land more productive than ever before. Some landowners became renowned for their farming innovations. In England, for example, Charles "Turnip" Townshend (1674–1738) experimented with crop rotation and growing turnips. His compatriot Jethro Tull (1674–1741) advocated the use of a seed drill and manure, which made planting more efficient and productive.

Not all farmers adopted the new agricultural methods. For many, traditional ways were comfortably familiar. Even those who realized how much profit they might make by selling their surpluses in the cities and other distant markets needed money to fund the new farming methods. They also required control over larger tracts of land to introduce the new crops, apply the innovative methods, and specialize in certain products—whether sheep for wool, grain for flour, or cattle for meat and dairy.

By all means, fair and foul, these market-oriented landowners dispossessed individuals of their small plots and communities of their commons to enclose land with fences, hedges, and walls as their own.

Enclosures

Figure 15.7, a mid-eighteenth-century English painting, shows a large, rich estate in Gloucestershire, England. The fields are consolidated and enclosed. In the center, organized groups of men and women workers toil on the harvest while wagons haul away the produce, destined for commerce rather than local consumption. Other fields are carefully planned and managed for the marketplace. Gone are the small farms, subsistence crops, and open fields that used to dominate the English countryside. After 1750, Britain's Parliament furthered this trend by authorizing a wave of these **enclosures.** Over the decades, wealthy landowners created large, controlled tracts that yielded products for the market. They reserved only a small part of their land for their own needs or bought their food elsewhere. Through this process, thousands of small, independent landowners, sharecroppers, and tenant farmers lost their land—and the status and security that had come with it. Rural communities disintegrated, eroding the support and human interactions that had so characterized life in the country.

Manufacturing Spreads in the Countryside: Cottage Industry

The spreading agricultural revolution became one force pushing, forcing, or freeing people to work more in nonagricultural jobs. When families lost their self-sufficient farms, they had to find new sources of

FIGURE 15.7 Enclosed Fields in England, mid-eighteenth century Large, rich estates such as this one in Gloucestershire, England, consolidated and enclosed separate fields, transforming the countryside. This shift in agricultural practice enabled large landowners to raise crops more effectively for commerce.

income to supplement the meager day-labor wages their landowning employers paid them. Manufacturing seemed to offer a solution. Growing commerce, particularly overseas trade, had heightened demand for manufactured goods—and thus workers to produce them. Traditionally, well-paid urban artisans had done this sort of work. Now, with demand high and rural workers available by the thousands, merchants turned to the countryside to increase production and take advantage of the cheap labor. Moreover, by shifting more production itself to the countryside, merchants avoided urban guild regulations that historically had controlled wages and the quantity and quality of goods.

FIGURE 15.8 Cottage Industry, eighteenth century This illustration shows a rural family working together to produce textiles that will be collected for commerce.

All these changes stimulated the growth of **cottage industry,** also known as the putting-out system. This system, which had already existed in the sixteenth and seventeenth centuries but to a much smaller degree, worked in a specific way. An entrepreneur provided raw materials (usually for production of textiles such as wool or linen) and sometimes equipment (such as a handloom or a spinning wheel) to peasants. The entrepreneur might be anyone—from a city merchant to a rural landowner—who managed to amass enough money to make an initial investment in raw materials and perhaps equipment. Peasants, who sought employment during times of the year when there was less need for agricultural labor, worked in their homes (hence the term *cottage industry*) to turn these raw materials into finished products. Mainly, they spun wool into yarn and wove the yarn into cloth. Sometimes enterprising peasants contracted out raw material to other spinners to keep weavers busy, since weavers depended on spinners to provide a steady supply of yarn. Women and children often worked while men were off performing day labor for large landowners. The entrepreneur periodically returned, paid for the peasants' labor by the piece, and distributed the finished products to distant markets.

As **Figure 15.8** shows, whole families participated in cottage-industry work. Women and children usually washed, combed, and spun the raw material into thread, while men often wove the yarn on looms. In this print, members of a rural household in Ireland beat and comb flax into linen, which will later be spun and woven. The light streaming in from the open window, the smiling laborers, and the little girl playing with a dog all distract our attention from the realities of the work: the dark, cramped quarters of single-room cottages and the tedious nature of this labor.

Cottage industry spread rapidly during the eighteenth century, particularly in Great Britain and parts of France and Germany. In addition to textiles, all sorts of goods—from buttons and housewares to knives, nails, and clocks—were produced through this system. The quality of these products varied, and relations between merchants and laborers often broke down over accusations of theft and disputes over wages. Still, more and more people came to depend on the system. For many of these workers, cottage-industry labor changed from a part-time to a full-time occupation.

The primary appeal of the work was its availability. Cottage industry allowed many people to remain in rural areas in a time of shrinking demand for farm workers. It also helped large families keep up and enabled young people to get an earlier start on marriage. On the other hand, the pay rarely rose above starvation wages, and the labor was drudgery.

Wherever it spread, cottage industry extended the money economy and the web of the commercial marketplace. Along with the agricultural revolution, the growth of cottage industry helped set the stage for an even greater economic transformation that would eventually sweep from Britain throughout the West and into the non-Western world: the industrial revolution.

More People, Longer Lives

As these new economic and social forces began to alter traditional ways of life, Europe's population jumped from approximately 110 million in 1700 to 190 million in 1800. **Figure 15.9** reveals the population growth throughout most of Europe during the eighteenth century. Relatively large populations help explain the strength of three major powers—England (along with Ireland), France, and Russia (note that much of Russia's increased population came from territorial expansion). Earlier marriages, more and better food, and fewer plagues raised the birthrate and lowered the death rate. Agricultural and commercial prosperity, along with improvements in the transportation of food, reduced the number and severity of famines in many areas. In particular, the widespread cultivation of the potato during the second half of the eighteenth century made this cheap, nutritious food available to millions. A spate of good weather helped to improve harvests. In some areas, new urban sanitation practices—cleaning wells, draining swampy areas, and burying refuse—probably improved health as well.

Surprisingly, medical practices rarely contributed to better health. Certainly the medical field saw some

Population growth

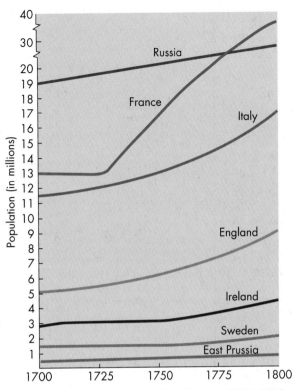

FIGURE 15.9 Population Growth in Europe, 1700–1800

advances. Inoculation against smallpox, for example, spread to Europe from the Middle East during the eighteenth century, although it was not used widely until the last decades of the century. Surgeons also made some improvements in the treatment of battlefield injuries. For instance, they learned to treat soldiers for shock before operating, and to clean wounds around the trauma.

Eighteenth-century medicine

Despite these signs of progress, eighteenth-century medicine was still dangerous. **Figure 15.10** provides a glimpse into a German hospital. In just one room, a bewildering array of medical procedures takes place. At the center, a surgeon saws off the leg of a patient. At the right lies a woman with a grotesquely swollen leg; just behind her, a woman prepares to give birth. At the far left, a priest administers last rites to a dying patient. In the background, women distribute food, men haul a body away, and sufferers lie crowded together in beds. French hospitals were no better. The French encyclopedist Denis Diderot described the Hôtel-Dieu in Paris, considered one of France's finest hospitals at the time: "Imagine a long series of communicating wards filled with sufferers of every kind of disease who are sometimes packed three, four, five or even six into a bed, the living alongside the dead and dying, the air polluted by this mass of unhealthy bodies, passing the pestilence of their afflictions from one to the other, and the spectacle of suffering and agony on every hand. That is the Hôtel-Dieu."

FIGURE 15.10 A German Hospital, 1746 This illustration from the mid-eighteenth century shows a hospital room and the kinds of activities—from amputations to food deliveries—that commonly took place there.

Deepening Misery for the Poor

The eighteenth-century population explosion exacted an ironic price. Stiffening competition for food drove prices up, while competition for jobs kept wages down. As a result, more and more people fell into poverty. A governmental commission in Austria reported to Empress Maria Theresa that "the peasants live in a condition of real slavery. . . . In their ruinous huts, the parents sleep on straw, the children naked on the wide shelves of earthenware stoves . . . all the charges of the Kingdom are born by the peasants, who are the sole taxpayers." Despite a widespread sense that people were better off than ever and that things would improve, in truth more people meant more misery.

In a desperate attempt to survive, poor people fled to the cities, hoping to find work in trade and manufacturing or as day laborers and domestics. Only some of them managed to find jobs; the rest were left to fend for themselves. A large percentage of urban dwellers missed out on the new wealth and opportunities of the cities. They eked out a living at little more than a subsistence level, and their lot worsened as more and more of them crowded in from the countryside.

Indeed, the surplus of workers; inflation; and disasters such as war, disease, and failed harvests hit the poor in cities and countryside alike. In France, economist Jacques Turgot (1727–1781) described the disastrous harvest of 1769: "The people could exist only by exhausting their resources, by selling at a miserable price their articles of furniture and even their clothes. Many of the inhabitants have been obliged to disperse themselves through other provinces to seek work or to beg, leaving their wives and children to the charity of the parishes. . . ." One Spanish official

described how "wives and children are without work, and all, piled together in cities or large towns, live at the expense of charity. . . ." Even for those who found steady employment, wages simply did not keep pace with escalating prices.

In bad times, food riots and tax revolts broke out in cities and rural areas across Europe. A rise in the price of grain often sparked attacks on merchants, granaries, and convoys of grain slated for armies. People turned on officials as well, blaming them for not keeping grain prices affordable or for allowing food to be shipped out to higher bidders elsewhere. Crime increased and more people slept along the sides of rural roads and city streets. Crowds of mothers pushed into foundling hospitals, desperate to leave children they could not care for. Some foundling hospitals established lotteries to determine which children they could afford to take in.

This deepening of poverty put a huge strain on traditional systems for aiding the poor, such as through the church or private charity. Some people were reduced to begging and to teaching their children this dubious art. Some authorities sympathized; others turned a blind eye. As one French official put it, "Beggary is the apprenticeship of crime; it begins by creating a love of idleness . . . in this state the beggar does not long resist the temptation to steal." A few countries devised legislation, such as the English Poor Laws, that required the impoverished to work on public projects or in workhouses. Officials used these sorts of laws more to control and discipline the poor than to help them. Often the same institution served as a workshop for the unfortunate, a hospital, and a prison. True, the poor had always suffered. Now, however, the population boom pushed their numbers to overwhelming new heights.

Prosperity and the Bourgeoisie

Like the agricultural revolution, urban growth made life worse for some and better for others. Those who gained most during this era were the middle and aristocratic classes, particularly those who seized opportunities in commerce and industry and in the expanding governmental bureaucracies. The urban middle class—in French, the *bourgeoisie*—expanded and found itself in a particularly odd situation. Wealthier than most, the bourgeoisie lived off their investments in trade, manufacturing, or land rather than working with their hands like their fellow commoners. They also found ways to avoid the restrictions of the guild system of production. While those laboring below them envied and resented their success, the bourgeoisie tried to distance themselves from "less respectable" commoners.

Middle-class people also had difficult relationships with those above them—the aristocracy. Successful members of the bourgeoisie resented the privileges enjoyed by the aristocracy, but—even more strongly—they wanted those privileges for themselves. They longed to join the aristocracy, and they were willing to spend money to do it. Money got them titles and offices, large estates, and judicious marriages—the trappings of success that they hoped would earn them acceptance into the ranks of the aristocracy. The aristocrats, for their part, viewed this method of social climbing—and the people who attempted it—with disdain. As they saw it, true nobility derived from birth, not wealth.

Nevertheless, the bourgeoisie persisted and thrived. These merchants, manufacturers, and professionals made money, expanded their businesses, invested in government bonds, and took chances on shaky financial schemes. They valued hard work and the accumulation of money. Moreover, they had the means to purchase a vast variety of luxuries, from coffee and chocolate to wallpaper, cotton clothing, and watch chains—goods produced outside the home, often even outside the country. For them, the market—rather than the household—supplied staples as well as conveniences and luxuries.

Over time, the richest among the bourgeoisie might manage to gain entrance into the aristocracy. Yet even if they could not get into the courts, estates, and homes of the aristocracy, the bourgeoisie developed a public culture of their own. They educated their children at universities and attended public theaters, music halls, and galleries. They filled tea rooms, coffeehouses, literary societies, and clubs and devoured newspapers, journals, and books written especially for them. Over time, they acquired their own sense of identity, as well as an impatience when further opportunities to rise in society were denied them.

THE CULTURE OF THE ELITE: COMBINING THE OLD AND THE NEW

The culture of the bourgeoisie and the aristocracy reflected the continuance of old trends along with the new developments that characterized the eighteenth century. For example, the courts of Europe still sponsored painters, composers, and musicians. In their private halls, aristocrats savored these artists' paintings, concerts, and operas. The prevailing spirit remained classical, inspired by the Greek and Roman appreciation for formal symmetry, proportion, and reason. On the other hand, artistic styles were changing. Several artists and authors put a new emphasis on emotion and nature in their works, an artistic trend sometimes referred to as the **cult of sensibility.** Audiences for these new cultural forms expanded, and the stream of literature being published for the growing numbers of literate Westerners swelled.

The Advent of the Modern Novel

Much of the reading public consisted of members of the middle class, and, not surprisingly, the modern novel reflected middle-class tastes. A compelling story, complex and varied characters, and realistic social situations formed the core of this new literary form. Novels also conveyed current ideas, manners, news, and information in witty and dramatic ways. In several popular novels, the English writer Daniel Defoe (1660–1731) wrote about individuals who planned ahead and used their entrepreneurial skills to meet challenges. The adventures of a character in a Defoe novel might take place at home in England or on exotic islands, as in *Robinson Crusoe* (1719). Similarly, Defoe's book *Moll Flanders* (1722) tells of a woman of lower-class origins who manages to navigate through all sorts of difficult situations, from prisons to a position in high society, in England and America.

Samuel Richardson (1689–1761) and Henry Fielding (1707–1754), also British, used the novel to analyze human personality, emotions, and psychology. In *Pamela, or Virtue Rewarded* (1740), Richardson recounts the story of a servant girl who tries to retain her virtue in the face of her wealthy employer's sexual advances. The book's characters and circumstances powerfully reflected contemporary realities, and the novel inspired a wave of similar works. Henry Fielding, for one, expanded on Richardson's effort, weaving a rich tapestry of English society in his novel *Tom Jones* (1749).

Many novels appealed particularly to women readers. British writer Fanny Burney (1752–1840) gained fame with the publication of her novel *Evelina or A Young Lady's Entrance into the World* (1778). The book portrays a provincial girl who makes a life for herself in London. Although the story ends with a marriage, it also reveals the social restrictions and dangers facing eighteenth-century women who tried to live an independent life. Burney would go on to publish several other popular novels.

During the second half of the century, novels and works of poetry by authors such as Jean-Jacques Rousseau in France and Johann Wolfgang von Goethe (1749–1832) in the German states emphasized emotion, relationships, and social problems. These authors presented the emotions as natural virtues, rejecting the artificiality of formal manners. Their style, which would become known as romanticism, grew in popularity during the last quarter of the century.

FIGURE 15.11 Antoine Watteau, *A Pilgrimage to Cythera*, 1717 Many of Watteau's popular paintings depicted aristocrats at play. In this scene, they wander through nature on a mythical island of love.

Pride and Sentiment in Art and Architecture

Unlike literature, the fine arts still typically reflected the tastes of the dominant aristocracy. Artists vied with one another for commissions to paint the portraits of royals and aristocrats, depicting their proud subjects adorned with plumes, buckles, silks, brocades, and laces. The scenes might include children and dogs and, in the background, lavish estate grounds. The distinctive clothing, haughty poses, and elaborate settings marked subjects as members of the landowning elite.

Many paintings showed intimate scenes of aristocratic private life—meetings, picnics, flirtations, and conversations among the upper classes. In Antoine Watteau's (1684–1721) popular paintings, for example, the context might be classical mythology, but the figures were eighteenth-century aristocrats. In *A Pilgrimage to Cythera* (a mythical island of love), shown in **Figure 15.11**, aristocrats wander leisurely through an idyllic garden of nature. Cupids at the left and Venus at the right bless the scene. The line between life, mythology, and the social roles played by the subjects blurs in this lush scene. The painting also has an underlying seriousness, as the lovers, reluctantly preparing to depart to the everyday world, enjoy a moment of life that will pass too quickly.

Whereas the aristocracy tended to populate Watteau's works, other artists painted well-received, sentimental scenes of ordinary people experiencing dramatic moments. **Figure 15.12**, a painting by the French artist Jean-Baptiste Greuze (1725–1805), shows one of these works. Here, the father at the left curses his departing son, who is determined to find his own way through life by joining the army. The young man's mother and other members of the family try in vain to reconcile the two men and to prevent the breakup of the family on such a painful note. In an accompanying painting, the grief-stricken son returns to find his father on his deathbed. William Hogarth's works (see **Figures 15.3** and **15.14**) also explored everyday experiences in the lives of ordinary people, but usually from a satirical or moralistic perspective.

Eighteenth-century architecture could not portray sentiments in the same detail as paintings, but buildings in the baroque style still expressed well the gaudy splendor of the eighteenth-century monarchs and their courts. At the same time, architects began deemphasizing size and instead relied on multiple curves and lacy, shell-like ornamentation to convey a sense of pleasing luxury. This style is usually referred to as **rococo**. Some new government buildings and urban residences followed a more neoclassical style, which stressed clarity of line and form modeled on Greek and Roman ideals.

Gardens complemented the buildings they accompanied, extending them and reflecting the mix of old and new tastes. As we saw in Louis XIV's Versailles palace (see Chapter 13), the French garden in particular emphasized rational, geometric forms marked off by hedges. Here, nature was shown completely tamed by human power and reason. By contrast, the eighteenth-century English garden looked freer and more natural. In fact, these gardens were not natural at all. Landscape architects designed them to imitate a vision of nature or to turn the grounds of an estate into an idealized version of nature. This managing of nature in English gardens was a compromise between old and new ideas about human beings' place in the natural world.

Reaching New Heights in Music

Of all the eighteenth-century arts, music left the most profound legacy. Much of it reflected the tastes of its royal, aristocratic, and ecclesiastical patrons. Composers and musicians, therefore, usually stuck to established forms, and music was typically heard as a pleasing background to conversations, balls, and other social occasions in the bastions of the aristocracy. Increasingly, however, music was played in public concert halls to a larger audience. Opera houses opened everywhere, and composers could now hope to make money from paying audiences as well as from court and aristocratic patronage. Several cities became well-known musical centers, but Vienna topped them all. This Austrian city became the musical heart of Europe, drawing hundreds of musicians who competed for favor there.

The first half of the eighteenth century saw the high point of baroque music, a style that had originated in the seventeenth century and that was still favored in royal courts and aristocratic homes.

The greatest practitioners of the baroque style were Johann Sebastian Bach (1685–1750) and George Frideric Handel (1685–1759). Bach was a member of a German family long distinguished by its musical talent. Noted in his own lifetime chiefly as an organist rather than a composer, he created a vast array of great music for organ, harpsichord, clavichord (forerunner of the piano), orchestra, and chorus. Sadly, much of Bach's work has been lost. Much of his music was religiously inspired, but he also wrote a large amount of secular music. Handel was born in central Germany in the same year and same region as Bach. He studied Italian opera in Germany and Italy and wrote forty-six operas himself. He also became court musician in Hanover. Later, he made his home in England, as did the elector, who became King George I of England. Handel wrote an enormous quantity of music—both instrumental and vocal—all of it marked by dignity, formal elegance, and harmony.

Baroque music

During the last decades of the century, the restrained baroque style gave way to the more melodic "classical" style, with its striking depth, structure, and emotion. Franz Joseph Haydn (1732–1809) and Wolfgang Amadeus Mozart (1756–1791) led the way. Their most stunning work was the symphony; by the end of their careers, they had created symphonies of rich harmonic complexity and emotional depth within the restrained classical form. During his long career in Vienna, Haydn wrote more than a hundred symphonies in addition to scores of compositions for other forms, particularly chamber music. Toward the end of his career, he became so popular that he left noble patrons and signed a lucrative contract with his music publisher.

The classical style

Haydn became a friend and a source of inspiration for the young Mozart (see Biography). **Figure 15.13** shows the 7-year-old Wolfgang playing the piano. Accompanying him are his father on the violin and his sister, who is singing. Here the performers are exquisitely dressed for their aristocratic audience. Ultimately, Mozart composed more than six hundred works and excelled in all forms, but he became most appreciated for his symphonies, piano concertos, and operas. His music was stunningly clear, melodic, elegant, and graceful. In his hands, the classical style reached its peak.

The Grand Tour

The music, art, and literature of the elites were part of a broader, cosmopolitan culture that spilled across national boundaries. This culture manifested itself in elaborate styles of dress, polished manners, and highly structured conversation. French was its international language. The growing popularity of travel and travel literature added to the sense of a common European cultural identity, at least among elites. Indeed, the

thinking about

ART

FIGURE 15.12

Jean-Baptiste Greuze, *The Father's Curse*, ca. 1778

In this eighteenth-century painting, French artist Jean-Baptiste Greuze depicts a dramatic family conflict between a father, issuing a curse, and his son, who is departing for the army. Hoping to hold the family together, the women and children plead with the father, on the left, and especially with the son, on the right. On the far right, a shadowy figure—perhaps an army recruiter who has influenced the son's decision—waits.

Connecting Art & Society

1. What does this depiction reveal about the roles of men, women, and children in this family?

2. Why might viewers of this scene be touched and fascinated?

3. Why might the father have been so disturbed by his son's departure?

4. How do the structure and lighting of the painting reflect the drama of its content?

wealthy often considered the **grand tour** a necessary part of education. Travelers on the tour stopped in main cities to indulge in coffeehouses, storefront window displays, public gardens, theaters, opera houses, and galleries. They might also visit art dealers or public auctions to purchase quality paintings. Family connections

BIOGRAPHY

Wolfgang Amadeus Mozart
(1756–1791)

Musicians quickly recognized the young Wolfgang Amadeus Mozart as a unique genius. His father, Leopold, a well-known Austrian composer and violinist, called him the "miracle which God let be born in Salzburg." Born in 1756, Wolfgang wrote his first compositions when he was just 5 years old. He embarked on the first of many tours throughout Europe as a 6-year-old child prodigy, playing the clavier with his elder sister, Nannerl, also a child prodigy, and his father (see **Figure 15.13**). They played at several royal courts for monarchs such as Louis XV of France, Maria Theresa of Austria, and George III of Britain. They also performed at the homes of leading nobles as well as in public theaters. Wolfgang's father, always eager to promote his young son, wrote that "our great and mighty Wolfgang seems to know everything at the age of seven that a man acquires at the age of forty."

Child Prodigy, Musical Genius

By the time he had reached 14, Mozart had composed several concertos, sonatas, and an opera. Announcements for his performances stressed his virtuosity. For example, for a concert in Italy, the 14-year-old would play "A Symphony of his own composition; a harpsichord concerto which will be handed to him, and which he will play on first sight; a sonata handed him in like manner, which he will provide with variations, and afterwards repeat in another key. . . ." The boy could play the organ and violin almost as well. After hearing Mozart in 1771, one well-known composer said, "This boy will cause us all to be forgotten."

FIGURE 15.13 The Mozarts

The prestigious Haydn, who strongly influenced Mozart's music, would later tell Mozart's father that "your son is the greatest composer known to me. . . ."

In 1781, Mozart settled in Vienna as a teacher and composer. Short, slim, with engaging blue eyes and a full head of fine hair, the young man enjoyed an active social life, including billiards and dancing. Yet music preoccupied him. He wrote, "You know that I am, so to speak, swallowed up in music, that I am busy with it all day—speculating, studying, considering." Keenly aware of his own talents, he at times arrogantly criticized other musicians' limitations. He felt certain that he could outshine any rival.

In 1782, despite the doubts of his father and sister, Mozart married Constanze Weber, a singer. Mozart wrote that "as soon as we were married, my wife and I both began to weep" for joy. Their marriage seems to have been happy. They would have six children, of whom only two survived. Neither parent managed the family finances well. Even though Mozart became brilliantly successful as a composer, a virtuoso pianist, and a teacher; received numerous commissions and fees; and attained appointment as royal chamber composer to Emperor Joseph II of Austria, he continually borrowed money to support his growing family.

Mozart could never quite satisfy his demanding and increasingly distant father. Hearing that Leopold had fallen seriously ill in 1787, Mozart wrote a letter of consolation that included his own views on death: "As death . . . is the true goal of our existence, I have formed during the last few years such close relations with this best and truest friend of mankind that his image is no longer terrifying to me but rather very soothing and consoling." Leopold died a month later. In July 1791, a stranger appeared at Mozart's door with a commission to write a requiem in secrecy. Mozart was still working on the project in December when he died in relative poverty. He was just 35. Although he probably had succumbed to an infection and fever, unsubstantiated rumors circulated for years that a competitor had poisoned him.

Connecting People & Society

1. How did Mozart's career reflect eighteenth-century society—still dominated by the aristocracy but with a growing middle class interested in the culture of the day?

2. In what ways did Mozart's family life influence his career as a musician?

3. What image of young Mozart do you think is projected in **Figure 15.13?**

offered them accommodations and introduced them to local society, Enlightenment salons, or potential candidates for marriage. The tour usually continued to historical ruins, which featured revered models of Greek and Roman antiquity that further strengthened the viewers' sense of a common cultural identity.

CULTURE FOR THE LOWER CLASSES

The lower classes were not without cultural outlets that fit their lives and provided a sense of common identity. For peasants, artisans, and the urban poor, culture typically came in the form of shared recreation, songs, tales, and the passing down of wisdom at gatherings and celebrations. Many of these activities also coincided with religious gatherings and celebrations.

Festivals and Popular Literature

Villagers worked together and celebrated together—at fairs, harvests, plowings, weddings, and religious holidays. Numerous festivals and public ceremonies had seasonal themes that were of particular importance and interest to people so dependent on agriculture. Other celebratory events related to the Christian calendar and centered on holidays, such as Christmas and Easter. Traditional weddings involved a community procession and festivities as well as a religious ceremony, and they featured music, dancing, feasts, games, and play. In the cities, artisans participated in their own organizations that combined recreational activities with mutual aid and religious celebrations.

Certain forms of literature also became popular among ordinary people. Literacy was growing, thanks to the printing press, the demands of business, and an increase in the number of primary schools. By the end of the eighteenth century, some 40 to 60 percent of the population in England and France could read (more men than women). With the rise in literacy, popular literature also expanded. Stirring religious tracts, almanacs, and tales of chivalric valor—typically, small, cheap booklets—circulated widely. More often, however, the "literature" of ordinary people was passed on orally. At night, people might gather to share folktales and songs that told of traditional wisdom, the hardships of everyday life, the hopes of common people, the dangers of life in the forests or of strangers who could be monsters or princes, and the ways to get along in life.

In the past, elites had fully participated in this popular culture, but during the eighteenth century they increasingly abandoned it to the lower classes. The "respectable" classes now often considered the leisure activities of ordinary people too disorderly and crude. Nevertheless, the middle and upper classes read some of the same popular literature enjoyed by the lower classes. Moreover, everyone—aristocrats and peasants alike—might be found at village festivals, fairs, and sporting events or enjoying jugglers, acrobats, magic lantern shows, and touring troupes of actors. Men of all classes watched and wagered on cockfights and dogfights. Other sports, such as soccer and cricket, gained popularity and drew large, animated crowds.

Gin and Beer

All the social classes also engaged in drinking—whether wine or brandy in the privacy of a wealthy home, or gin and beer in popular taverns. Especially in England, the ravages of drinking gin seemed to grow to alarming proportions. **Figure 15.14,** another moralistic work by William Hogarth, graphically depicts the evils of gin drinking in England. At the center a pox-ridden, impoverished, and drunken woman lets her baby fall over a wooden rail. Near her, a man slowly starves to death. In the background, workers haul bodies away, a man hangs himself in an upstairs tenement, children drink glasses of gin, and buildings collapse for want of repair. The scene is one of physical, social, and moral decay from excessive alcohol

GIN LANE.

FIGURE 15.14 William Hogarth, *Gin Lane,* 1750 In this disturbing scene, the British artist William Hogarth documented the physical, social, and moral decay that could result from excessive alcohol consumption.

consumption. Though this image is an exaggeration, the actual problems caused by drinking were so extensive that in 1751 the British government passed a heavy tax on cheap gin to curtail its consumption.

Religious Revivals

Popular culture also merged with deeply felt spiritual beliefs and religious activities. Despite the many secular trends of the period, Christianity still stood at the center of Western culture and life. Churches rather than the state ran the schools and hospitals. The poor, aged, and crippled relied on churches for social services. Church bells announced the time of day everywhere, and religious holidays marked the year.

Within this Western religious culture, popular piety persisted. Indeed, especially among Protestants, a sense grew among ordinary churchgoers that official

Pietism churches were becoming bureaucratized, complacent, and unresponsive to peoples' spiritual needs. In response, religious revivals spread from community to community and across national borders. In the German and Scandinavian states, **pietism**—which minimized dogma and formal ritual in favor of inner piety, holy living, and the private emotional experience of worshiping—gained strength. Revival movements in Britain and its North American colonies attracted thousands to huge gatherings.

The greatest of these revival movements was Methodism, founded in England by John Wesley (1703–1791). While studying for the Anglican ministry at Oxford, Wesley and a band of fellow students became disillusioned with the spiritual emptiness that had fallen upon the Anglican Church as well as its subservience to the government and the aristocracy. The group's lives became such examples of piety and moderate regularity that their fellow students branded them "Methodists" in derision. Methodism stressed humble faith, abstinence, and hard work. Barred from preaching in the Anglican churches, Wesley rode horseback from one end of England to the other until well into his 80s, preaching the "glad tidings" of salvation in thousands of sermons in streets, fields, and anywhere else he could find even a small audience. He claimed "to lower religion to the level of the lowest people's capacities."

Among Catholics, similar movements—such as Jansenism in France and Italy and Quietism in Spain—spread among elites and others. East European Jews had their own revivalist movement with the founding of the Hasidic sect in the 1740s. Hasidim (meaning "most pious") spread throughout Poland, rejecting formalism, stressing simplicity, and engaging in loud, joyful singing prayers. These religious movements revealed the power with which spiritual matters still influenced people in the West. Nevertheless,

like the broader cultural forms of the time, religious revivals left the overall social order intact.

FORESHADOWING UPHEAVAL: THE AMERICAN REVOLUTION

For most of the eighteenth century, neither wars, colonial rivalries, nor changes in country and city life upset the fundamental social and political stability of Western societies. In the last quarter of the eighteenth century, however, new forces erupted that would ultimately transform the West. The first of these disturbances occurred in Britain's thirteen North American colonies. This upheaval shifted the tide of events in North America and foreshadowed a far deeper and broader revolution that would strike at the heart of Europe itself.

Insults, Interests, and Principles: The Seeds of Revolt

By the mid-eighteenth century, more than two million people lived in the colonies. The seaboard cities in particular flourished, benefiting from a thriving commerce with Europe, Africa, and the West Indies. The colonists thought of themselves as British. Furthermore, the thirteen colonies in theory were part of Great Britain, governed in the same way and therefore subject to British trade regulations. In practice, however, the colonists often acted as they pleased, even if that meant quietly ignoring those regulations. They developed their own patterns of local government, manipulated British governors, and worked around British mercantilist policies.

Tensions between the island nation and these prospering colonies arose just after the Seven Years' War ended in 1763. Feeling that they had helped defend the American colonists against the hostile French and Indians, the British expected the colonists to help pay off the huge debt New commercial regulations and taxes incurred in the fighting. To tighten their control over the colonial empire for which Britain had just fought so long and hard, British officials enacted new commercial regulations and taxes. Perhaps the most irritating of these was the Stamp Act of 1765, which taxed printed documents such as newspapers, pamphlets, and wills.

The colonists reacted to the new policies with complaints, boycotts, protest meetings, outrage, and sometimes riots. Because colonists were not represented in Britain's Parliament, headlines in newspapers and pamphlets screamed, "No taxation without representation!" In their Stamp Act Congress of 1765, colonists announced that they were "entitled to all the inherent rights and liberties of his [the king's] natural born subjects within the kingdom of Great Britain." Local circumstances and the distance from Britain meant that "the only representatives of these colonies are persons chosen therein by themselves, and that no taxes ever have been, or can be constitutionally imposed on them, but by their respective legislatures." The British compromised, repealing most of the taxes, but many colonists were still not satisfied.

Both sides translated their disagreements into ideological terms. American newspapers, propagandists, and political groups, echoing Enlightenment ideas, argued that violation of their fundamental rights justified a fight for independence. Most people in Britain stood against rebellion and for parliamentary sovereignty as a matter of principle. They argued that they were making only reasonable and minimal demands on the colonies.

In the end, each side felt backed into a corner. The notion of full independence gained appeal among the colonists. American political leaders who were critical of British policies organized the First Continental Congress in 1774, hoping to persuade Parliament to abandon its efforts to directly control colonial affairs. In response, King George III increased British armed forces in America, convinced that "blows must decide whether they are to be subject to the Country or Independent."

A War for Independence

The first blows were exchanged in 1775 between British troops and American militiamen in New England. The Second Continental Congress appointed George Washington (1732–1799) its military commander, setting the course for armed rebellion and independence. On July 4, 1776, that Congress issued the Declaration of Independence, written primarily by Thomas Jefferson (1743–1826) and based on the ideas of John Locke and other Enlightenment thinkers. Citing "self-evident" truths; "inalienable" natural rights such as "Life, Liberty, and the pursuit of Happiness"; and "a long train of abuses" to reduce the people under "absolute Despotism," the Declaration passionately justified rebellion.

Odds favored the stronger British forces, and at first they had the upper hand. Indeed, many British leaders viewed the rebel troops with disdain, one official calling the rebels a "rude rabble without a plan." Nevertheless, despite much internal division, an American victory at Saratoga in 1777 persuaded the French to help the Americans with money, ships, and troops against France's longtime enemy. The Dutch and Spanish eventually declared war on Britain, increasing the stakes for the British. Now British possessions in the West Indies, the Mediterranean, and perhaps even India hung in the balance. In 1781, the victory of the French fleet off Virginia forced a large British army to surrender at Yorktown. This indignity convinced the British that the effort to keep the American colonies was not worth the costs. After two years of negotiations, the combatants drew up the Treaty of Paris in 1783. Britain agreed to recognize American independence and ceded to the United States the lands between the Mississippi River to the west, Canada to the north, and Spanish Florida to the south.

Creating the New Nation

In 1787, a new American constitution established a central government balanced by a separation of powers and strong states' rights. A Bill of Rights was soon enacted, protecting individual liberties and separating church and state. These principles, though lofty, did not apply to everyone. Although the Declaration of Independence had proclaimed that "all men are created equal" as a "self-evident" truth, one-fifth of the people remained slaves, and only property owners and men could vote. Nevertheless, the new nation had instituted—to an unprecedented degree—popular control, personal freedom, and formal toleration.

Some historians deem the American rebellion a war for independence, and others call it a revolution. At the time, people throughout the West—not just in America and Great Britain—viewed the events as dramatic and significant. A growing body of European readers avidly followed the action in newspaper accounts. Many of these readers saw the American Revolution as a victory for Enlightenment ideas. As revealed by **Figure 15.15,** a 1786 print, the French in particular celebrated the Revolution as a triumph in their own competition with their British rivals. In the center of the print, titled *Independence of the United States*, stands a monument topped by a rooster, symbolizing the French nation, and an image of French king Louis XVI. Below him are

> War for independence or revolution?

INDÉPENDANCE DES ÉTATS-UNIS.

FIGURE 15.15 *Independence of the United States* This eighteenth-century French print celebrates the "partnership" of the French and North American colonists against the British during the war for independence.

images of other heroes of the American Revolution, Franklin and Washington. To the right stands a noble savage, representing America and standing with a foot on the defeated British lion. To the left are ships, suggesting the aid France gave Americans in their fight against the British. Neither the anonymous artist, the king, nor the French people realized at the time that the debts incurred by France and the ideas promoted by the American Revolution would soon come back to haunt the French monarchy.

LOOKING BACK & MOVING FORWARD

Summary On the surface, life between 1715 and 1789 seemed to change only incrementally for most Westerners. The vast majority still lived in the countryside and worked the fields. Moreover, society and politics in the so-called Old Regime remained dominated by the aristocracy and, in most places, the monarchy. As in the seventeenth century, cultural forms still reflected elite tastes and the traditional values of commoners below them.

Below the surface, however, the West changed in crucial ways during this period. The political balance of power shifted as Russia and Prussia rose in the east while Britain gained prominence in the west. Success in the international arena often reflected how well central governments conducted their internal affairs. Some monarchs managed to dominate or work with the nobility, enact reforms, and even take on the trappings of "enlightened" rulers, whereas others—such as the French kings—failed in these ways. More important, mushrooming commerce, the agricultural revolution, and the spreading of cottage industry altered the ways by which millions of people earned a living, and these changes generated enormous new wealth. Finally, across the Atlantic in Britain's North American colonies, the American Revolution posed a challenge to the status quo that the French would soon take up in a much more fundamental way. These developments, combined with the spread of Enlightenment ideas, mark the eighteenth century as a period in which Westerners—knowingly or not—laid foundations for the great transformations to come.

KEY TERMS

balance of power, *p. 480*
Wahhabism, *p. 482*
parlements, *p. 488*
Middle Passage, *p. 492*
enlightened absolutism, *p. 498*
agricultural revolution, *p. 499*
enclosures, *p. 499*
cottage industry, *p. 500*
cult of sensibility, *p. 503*
rococo, *p. 504*
grand tour, *p. 505*
pietism, *p. 508*

REVIEW, ANALYZE, & CONNECT TO TODAY

REVIEW THE PREVIOUS CHAPTERS

Chapter 13—"The Struggle for Survival and Sovereignty"—told the story of kings and nobles battling for power, the results of those struggles, and their impact on millions of people throughout the West. Chapter 14—"A New World of Reason and Reform"—shifted focus to the changing intellectual foundations of the West.

1. In what ways was the eighteenth century a continuation of the struggle between monarchs and elites that had marked the seventeenth century?

2. Analyze how Enlightenment ideas—themselves stemming from the Scientific Revolution—affected Western society and especially politics during the eighteenth century.

ANALYZE THIS CHAPTER

Chapter 15—"Competing for Power and Wealth"—examines the battles of Western powers over land,

position, and commerce, as well as the economic and social changes affecting eighteenth-century life in the West.

1. Which nations do you think were the biggest winners and which the biggest losers in this period? How do you explain their varying fortunes?

2. How did eighteenth-century rulers try to shore up and justify their own powers and those of their central governments?

3. Analyze the impact of slavery on Africa, the Americas, and Europe.

4. Analyze the benefits and costs of the growing commerce, the agricultural revolution, and cottage industry.

5. Why might this period be considered one of both growing prosperity and deepening social misery?

6. Delineate the differences between elite and popular culture during this period. How do you explain those differences?

CONNECT TO TODAY

Think about the ways in which Western powers competed during the eighteenth century.

1. How are states in today's world competing politically and economically with one another, both in the West and in the world as a whole?

2. What connections are there in the world today between statebuilding and warfare—such as efforts to create a politically strong state, and policies that promote military buildup and willingness to go to war—that are similar to or different from those connections during the eighteenth century?

BEYOND THE CLASSROOM

STATEBUILDING AND WAR

Blanning, Tim. *The Pursuit of Glory: Europe: 1648–1815*. New York: Viking, 2007. A respected, topically organized survey.

Davis, Ralph. *The Rise of the Atlantic Economies*. Ithaca, NY: Cornell University Press, 1973. A survey of the early modern economic history of the countries on the western fringe of Europe and their colonies in North and South America.

de Madariaga, Isabel. *Catherine the Great: A Short History*. New Haven, CT: Yale University Press, 1990. A solid, useful study.

Jasanoff, Maya. *Edge of Empire: Lives, Culture, and Conquest in the East, 1750–1850*. New York: Knopf, 2005. A well-written reinterpretation of British imperialism and its consequences.

MacDonagh, G. *Frederick the Great*. New York: St. Martin's Press, 2001. A fine, comprehensive biography.

Manning, Patrick. *Slavery and African Life: Occidental, Oriental and African Slave Trades*. Cambridge: Cambridge University Press, 1990. A wide-ranging study that demonstrates how the external slave trade affected African societies.

Weigley, R.F. *The Age of Battles: The Quest for Decisive Warfare from Breitenfeld to Waterloo*. Bloomington: Indiana University Press, 1991. A study of the period between 1631 and 1815, when economic, social, and technological circumstances enabled governments to concentrate large forces in the field.

GLOBAL CONNECTIONS

Conniff, Michael, and Davis, Thomas. *Africans in the Americas: A History of the Black Diaspora*. New York: St. Martin's Press, 1998. Excellent coverage of the slave trade and the African diaspora.

THE TWILIGHT OF MONARCHIES? THE QUESTION OF ENLIGHTENED ABSOLUTISM

Gagliardo, John G. *Enlightened Despotism*. Arlington Heights, IL: AHM Publishing, 1967. A respected examination of the topic in its European context.

Scott, H.M., ed. *Enlightened Despotism*. Ann Arbor: University of Michigan Press, 1990. A book of essays by leading historians analyzing Europe's rulers and nobility.

CHANGES IN COUNTRY AND CITY LIFE

Blum, Jerome. *The End of the Old Order in Rural Europe*. Princeton, NJ: Princeton University Press, 1978. A comprehensive study of life in rural Europe from the early eighteenth to the mid-nineteenth century; especially good on the abolition of serfdom.

Clarkson, Leslie A. *Proto-Industrialization: The First Phase of Industrialization?* London: Macmillan, 1985. Stresses the importance of cottage industry for the beginning of industrialization.

Overton, Mark. *Agricultural Revolution in England*. Cambridge: Cambridge University Press, 1996. A survey of the transformation of England's agricultural economy between 1500 and 1850.

THE CULTURE OF THE ELITE: COMBINING THE OLD AND THE NEW

Black, Jeremy. *Eighteenth-Century Europe*. London: Macmillan, 1990. A thorough survey of the period.

Richetti, John. *The Cambridge Companion to the Eighteenth-Century Novel*. Cambridge: Cambridge University Press, 1996. Useful views on the origins of the novel and its cultural context.

CULTURE FOR THE LOWER CLASSES

Burke, Peter. *Popular Culture in Early Modern Europe*. New York: Harper & Row, 1978. A survey of popular culture from the Renaissance to the French Revolution.

Muchembled, Robert. *Popular Culture and Elite Culture in France, 1400–1750*. Baton Rouge: Louisiana State University Press, 1985. An examination of popular culture and the means higher authorities used to destroy it.

FORESHADOWING UPHEAVAL: THE AMERICAN REVOLUTION

Weintraub, Stanley. *Iron Tears: America's Battle for Freedom, Britain's Quagmire: 1775–1783*. New York: Free Press, 2005. A fresh look at the war from various perspectives.

Wood, Gordon. *The American Revolution: A History*. New York: Random House, 2002. A fine survey and important interpretation.

Moving into the Modern World

The world had changed dramatically since Europe began its "expansion" in the fifteenth century. By the mid-eighteenth century, the West had been sending out explorers, making new commercial contacts, establishing links, and racking up conquests in the non-Western world for almost three centuries. Had Europe's expansion changed the meaning of the West?

During the eighteenth century, the actual "boundaries" of the West did begin to shift. Russia brought under its direct control lands to the east in Siberia. By the second half of the century, Russians easily outnumbered those regions' indigenous inhabitants. It also pushed its borders south, particularly in the Caspian Sea region. Russia's growing empire blurred any line between the West and the non-Western world on the Eurasian landmass. Across the Atlantic, Europeans had colonized parts of the Americas so thoroughly that large sections of the Western Hemisphere were much more than mere outposts. Though thousands of miles away from Europe, they were becoming part of the West itself.

If not in control of other major regions of the world, people from the West were certainly in increasing contact with other cultures and civilizations across the globe. From the broadest perspective, Westerners shared important similarities with several of these civilizations. For example, all had economies based on agriculture and handicrafts; the factories, railroads, and steamships that would mark the industrial era in the West were yet to come. Moreover, several Asian civilizations had enough wealth and military might to put them in the same league as the European nations.

China, for instance, remained the dominant power in east Asia. By 1750, Qing emperors (1644–1911) had extended their control far into central Asia and the south. In those regions, they made Vietnam, Burma, and Nepal their vassal states. The long rule of the talented emperor Qianolong (Chi'en Lung) (1736–1795) marked the height of the Qing (Chi'ing) dynasty. Wealthy, sophisticated, well-organized, and powerful, Qing China controlled the degree of contact it had with the West and supported its own trading networks throughout east and southeast Asian lands. China and other east Asian societies benefited from the West's growing thirst for their unique products as well as from crops that originated in the Americas. Farther east, Tokugawa shoguns had unified the Japanese islands and secured their rule. Like the Chinese, they managed to keep Western people at arm's length while promoting their own conservative values, such as adherence to a carefully ranked society and Confucian principles.

By the dawn of the eighteenth century, three powerful Islamic empires governed by Turkish dynasties had come to dominate southern and southwestern Asia. The Mughals ruled most of the Indian subcontinent and commanded a formidable, cosmopolitan society. The Safavid dynasty reigned in Persia, prospering as a trade link between the East and West. The powerful Ottomans had expanded from their base in Anatolia into eastern Europe, southwestern Asia, and north Africa. As recently as 1683, they had mustered enough force to lay siege to Vienna, the capital of the Habsburgs' Austrian Empire. But the days of all three Islamic empires were already numbered. By 1750, the Safavid Empire had disappeared entirely, much of Mughal India was disintegrating and falling under British rule, and the Ottomans were losing control over various provinces.

Meanwhile, in the Western Hemisphere, the Spanish and Portuguese ruled most of Latin America. A varied mix of Europeans, Africans, and Amerindians populated those lands. In the Caribbean, Western administrators governed societies populated predominantly by African slaves. Farther north, firmly established British and French colonies were spreading west at the expense of indigenous peoples. The twin disasters of disease and violence had already reduced these natives to a fraction of their numbers from 250 years earlier.

In Africa, states and societies based on kinship groups continued to develop as they had for centuries. Societies in west Africa and on the east African coast maintained long-established trade with Muslims from the north and east. By the eighteenth century, Islam had spread through these African societies. But the growing slave trade to the west generated wealth in Atlantic port cities and power in west Africa's coastal kingdoms, while creating great turmoil and human loss throughout much of sub-Saharan Africa.

Most of Oceania remained scarcely touched by the West during this time. Only toward the end of the eighteenth century did Europeans begin settling in Australia and initiating substantial contact with that land's aboriginal peoples. During that same period, a number of Western explorers, merchants,

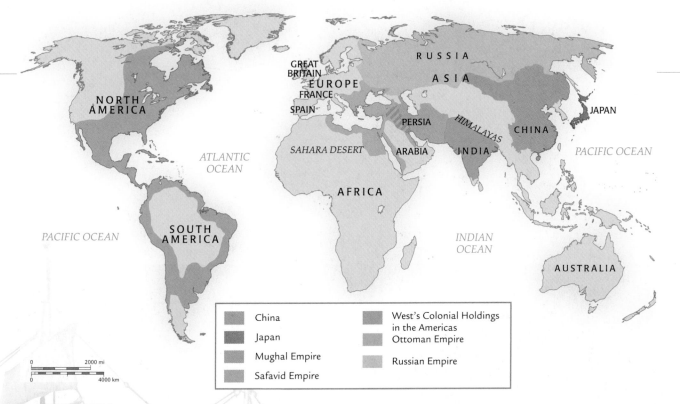

The World, ca. 1700

China

Japan

Mughal Empire

Safavid Empire

West's Colonial Holdings in the Americas

Ottoman Empire

Russian Empire

missionaries, and settlers arrived on islands throughout the Pacific.

In the mid-eighteenth century, European ships carried goods and people overseas in astounding numbers and with great regularity. Some sailed to Western ports; others, to lands beyond Europeans' control. Demand in the West for goods such as sugar, tea, coffee, and tobacco, along with demand in China for silver, fueled this long-distance commerce. As the same time, a burgeoning hunger for slave labor forced millions of enslaved Africans across the Atlantic into the Americas.

In some areas, Western nations were chipping away at holdings of competitors such as the Ottomans in southeastern Europe and western Asia and the Mughals in southern Asia. In other areas, such as North America beyond the Atlantic colonies and Oceania, Western societies were starting to overwhelm indigenous

peoples. But in vast regions of the world, eighteenth-century Europeans gained access only on coastlines. East Asian societies easily kept them at bay, remaining in control of their own affairs. Western newcomers had only recently made inroads into lands of the once-powerful Mughal and Safavid empires. The Ottomans, though declining economically and politically, nevertheless managed to retain control over most of their lands. And in Africa, much of the continent remained too difficult for the West to penetrate.

Western explorers still sailed and marched off in search of new opportunities. However, they were limited to the most remote regions—Oceania, the frozen stretches of the far north and south, jungle-choked lands in South America and sub-Saharan Africa. In many ways, the mid-eighteenth-century world was growing

more tightly interconnected. At the same time, that world was becoming a stage for widespread competition and conflict between states and civilizations.

Thinking Globally

1. In what ways had the meaning of the West changed by the eighteenth century?

2. How did the civilizations of the West compare to civilizations in the wider world?

3. In what regards might people of the times have looked at the Atlantic world (that is, areas with easy access to the Atlantic Ocean) as an interactive whole?

4. What geographic considerations might have helped to account for the West's lack of control over various areas of the globe outside the Atlantic world?

JEAN-PIERRE HOUEL, *THE STORMING OF THE BASTILLE*, ca. 1789

On July 14, 1789, a crowd of Parisians stormed the Bastille, a castle-prison that stood as a symbol of all that was oppressive under the Old Regime. For most people, this event marked the beginning of the French Revolution.

Overturning the Political and Social Order

16

The French Revolution and Napoleon, 1789–1815

France was beginning to stir. On October 17, 1787, Arthur Young, a British farmer and diarist traveling through France, described "a great ferment amongst all ranks of men, who are eager for some change, without knowing what to look to, or to hope for." People whom Young talked with in Paris concluded that "they are on the eve of some great revolution in the government."

Two years later, the French Revolution brought the French monarchy to its knees. During the following ten years, revolutionaries eliminated the monarchy, overturned the social system of France's Old Regime, and transformed France's institutions. Moreover, the Revolution, with its compelling banner of "Liberty, Equality, Fraternity," proved so potent that its impact spread far beyond the borders of France. It soon spawned wars that engulfed most of Europe for more than two decades. Riding the twin forces of revolutionary turmoil and war, one individual—Napoleon Bonaparte—would rise to a legendary pinnacle of power. He would rule over a new French empire and a nearly conquered continent. In the process, Napoleon spread the ideals of the French Revolution well beyond France. This tide of change, turmoil, and war mounted by the French Revolution and Napoleon would eventually subside, but for France—and for much of Western civilization—the course of history had shifted permanently.

TIMELINE

American Revolution 1776–1783

The French Revolution and Napoleon 1789–1815

Early Phases 1789–1793

The Terror 1793–1794

The Thermidorian Reaction 1794–1795

Restoration 1815–1830

Age of Ideologies

The Directory 1795–1799

Napoleon in Power 1799–1815

Enlightenment

Industrial Revolution in Britain

1787   1794   1801   1808   1815

"A GREAT FERMENT": TROUBLE BREWING IN FRANCE

Arthur Young recognized discontent percolating among the French population, but there was good reason for people everywhere to assume that any crises would pass without a fundamental change in the monarchy or social order. The French monarchy had remained intact for centuries. Both Louis XVI and his predecessor, Louis XV, ruled over the leading nation on the Continent—a country more populous, wealthy, and educated than ever. Although neither king could claim much popularity, Louis XVI could at least bask in the glory of supporting the American revolutionaries in their victory over the British, France's chief competitor.

Then what caused the "great ferment" in France described by our British traveler? Below the surface bubbled growing complaints within France's social orders. Members of the aristocracy and middle classes, many influenced by the ideas of the Enlightenment, wanted more rights and power from the monarchy. Peasants suffered hardships that could, as in the past, create disorder and uprisings. However, the immediate, visible problem came from a conflict over France's finances.

The Financial Crisis Weakens the Monarchy

When Louis XVI ascended the throne in 1774, he inherited a large—and constantly growing—national debt. Much of that debt had been incurred financing wars and maintaining the military (see Chapter 15). Yet this debt should not have broken a nation as rich as France. Great Britain and the Netherlands had higher per-capita debts than France, but these countries also boasted taxation systems and banks to support their debts. France lacked an adequate

The taxation system

banking system, and most of the national debt was short term and privately held. Moreover, France's taxation system offered little help. The French nobility, clergy, and much of the bourgeoisie controlled the bulk of France's wealth and had long been exempt from most taxes. Nearly all direct taxes fell on the struggling peasantry. There was no consistent set of rules or method for collecting taxes throughout the country, and private tax collectors diverted much revenue from the treasury into their own pockets. Unless something was done, royal bankruptcy loomed ahead.

To stave off financial ruin, Louis XVI appointed the Physiocrat Jacques Turgot (1727–1781), a friend of Voltaire, as his minister of finance in 1774. Turgot proposed to abolish guilds, eliminate restriction on the commerce in grain, institute a small new tax on landowners, and cut down on expenses at court. However, people who benefited from the old system soon engineered his dismissal, and his modest reform measures were rescinded. A succession of ministers tried all kinds of temporary solutions, but to no avail. Costs incurred to support the Americans in their war of independence against England made matters worse. Now interest payments on the debt ate up half of all government expenditures. Bankers began refusing to lend the government money.

Reform efforts

Desperate, Louis called an Assembly of Notables in 1787 and pleaded with these selected nobles, clergy, and officials to consent to new taxes and financial reforms. Still they refused, as did the judges (all members of the nobility) in the *parlement*, or law court, of Paris when Louis turned to them. Instead, leading nobles and officials demanded a meeting of an old representative institution, the Estates General. They fully expected to control these proceedings and thereby assert their own interests. With bankruptcy imminent and nowhere else to turn for help, the king gave in. No one knew it at the time, but Louis' decision set the stage for turning France's financial crisis into a political and social movement of epic proportions.

The Underlying Causes of the Revolution

Louis' financial woes were just the most visible part of France's problems. When these tensions combined with the conflicts tugging at the fabric of French society, a dangerous blend resulted. One of the most troubling conflicts stemmed from the relationship between the monarchy and the nobility. For centuries, the French nobility, less than 2 percent of the population, had been the foundation on which the monarchy established its rule. However, the nobility was also the monarchy's chief rival for power, and it had grown increasingly assertive during

Revolt of the nobility

the eighteenth century (see Chapter 15). Through institutions such as the *parlements* that they controlled, nobles resisted ministerial efforts to tax them. More and more, nobles claimed to be protecting their rights as well as France itself from "ministerial despotism." So, when the monarchy turned to this group for financial help, the nobles refused for two reasons. First, they wanted to protect their own financial interests. Second, they used the crisis to assert their independence. Indeed, they argued that they represented the nation. They established a price for their cooperation: a greater share of power. Understandably, France's kings refused to pay that price. Thus, when the Assembly of Notables turned a deaf ear to Louis' pleas in 1787 and instead demanded a meeting of the Estates General, the king faced a financial crisis that was linked to a virtual revolt of his own nobility.

Louis might have thought he could find allies within the middle class in his standoff with the nobility. After all, French and other European kings had occasionally turned to wealthy members of this class for support in the past. Nevertheless, as events would prove in the tumultuous months of 1789, the middle class had changed—it now nursed its own set of grievances. This growing social sector—having almost tripled during the century to some 9 percent of the population—had benefited greatly from France's general prosperity and population boom after 1715. Many talented, wealthy, and ambitious members of the middle class managed to gain the high offices, titles, and privileges enjoyed by the nobility. Others rubbed shoulders and shared ideas with the nobility in salons and did their best to copy the nobles' style of life. Moreover, most had found ways to avoid paying heavy taxes.

Middle-class demands

However, numerous members of the bourgeoisie—particularly younger administrators, lawyers, journalists, and intellectuals—had encountered frustrating barriers to the offices and prestige enjoyed by the nobility. They also had grown impatient with the monarchy's failure to enact reforms that would benefit them specifically. By 1789, many applauded broad attacks on the privileged orders and the status quo. An example of such an attack was Abbé Emmanuel-Joseph Sieyès' widely circulated pamphlet *What Is the Third Estate?* According to Sieyès, "If the privileged order should be abolished, the nation would be nothing less, but something more." The sorts of reforms that these middle-class critics had in mind were no more palatable to the monarchy than those of the nobility.

People from both the middle class and the nobility had begun expressing ideas and using highly charged political terms that profoundly threatened the monarchy. In the decades before 1789, salon meetings and new publications had spread key ideas of the

Enlightenment ideas and language

Enlightenment to an increasingly literate public, particularly the aristocratic and middle-class elite in Paris and other French cities (see Chapter 14). These ideas emphasized the validity of reason and natural rights and questioned long-established institutions. They also undermined notions of the divine rights of kings and traditional ways of life—all while intensifying expectations of rapid reforms. In addition, terms such as *nation, citizen,* and *general will* had increasingly cropped up in the political discourse and reflected a growing sense that politics should include more than the concerns of the monarch and a tiny elite. So, when nobles asserted their own interests against the king, they often used language and ideas that attacked monarchical absolutists as unjustified tyrants and that accused the king's minister of "despotism." Middle-class men and women shared these sentiments and later extended them to demands for legal equality.

Thus, given all the resentments brewing among the nobility and the middle class, Louis and his often unpopular ministers risked much after they exposed themselves to discussions of reform within the Estates General. Three other developments—all beyond the powers of the king, nobility, and middle class—added an underlying sense of disappointment, desperation, and disorder among the French people in these decades.

First, a gap opened between rosy expectations and frightening realities. Before 1770, France had enjoyed a long period of prosperity. This growing wealth engendered a sense of rising expectations—that economically, things would keep getting better and better. After 1770, a series of economic depressions struck, turning these high expectations into bitter disappointment and frustration. Worse, in 1788 the countryside suffered unusually bad harvests. In May and July of that year, hailstorms wiped out crops throughout France. Drought and then the most severe winter in decades followed. The price of bread soared, and with it came hunger, desperation, and even starvation. Droves of peasants crowded into the cities in search of jobs and help, but the agricultural depression had already spread there and had thrown thousands of artisans and laborers out of work. In the spring of 1789, peasants and urban poor looking for food turned to violence in France's cities and villages. Women led groups demanding grain and lower prices for flour. Desperate people attacked bakeries and stores of grain wherever they could find them. Arthur Young wrote, "the want of bread is terrible: accounts arrive every moment from the provinces of riots and disturbances, and calling in the military, to preserve the peace of the markets." The populace angrily blamed governmental figures and "parasitical agents" of the Old Regime for their plight.

Disappointed expectations

By 1789, many pamphlets and cartoons portraying the connection between suffering and France's privileged orders circulated throughout France. **Figure 16.1** is an apt example of these publications. This illustration shows the thin "common man," who represents the vast majority of the people, carrying three heavy figures from the privileged classes on his back. In front, wielding a whip and claiming feudal rights, is the king, representing oppressive royal power. Just above him is a clergyman in robes, brandishing papers representing the threat of an inquisition and clerical privileges. In back rides a judge with a list of the jealously guarded rights of the noble-controlled *parlements*. The illustration depicts the common man as a naked beast kept under control by reins, chains, and a blindfold. He crawls pitifully across barren fields, bleeding from the hands, knees, and loins, while his tormentors spur him on.

The second unsettling development came with the increasing demands for political participation and

Demands for political participation

governmental reform throughout the West in the years before 1789. These movements, arising in various countries, were led by ambitious elites. In Poland, agitation for independence from Russian influence surfaced between 1772 and 1792. Across the Atlantic, what started as a tax revolt in Britain's North American colonies turned into the American Revolution and war for independence that directly involved French aristocrats and common soldiers alike and led to government without a king (see Chapter 15). In the Dutch Republic, demands for reform in the 1780s erupted into open revolt in 1787. In the Austrian Netherlands (Belgium and Luxembourg), elites rose against the reforms initiated by Emperor Joseph II in 1787. Well-informed French elites, keeping abreast of these disturbances, began to surmise that they, too, might successfully challenge the political status quo.

The economic hardship and political uprisings across Europe were damaging enough. A third problem—the French people's disrespect for their own king—made matters worse. For much of the eighteenth century, France had been ruled by the unremarkable, unpopular, and long-lived King Louis XV. Unlike some of his European counterparts, neither he nor his successor, Louis XVI, managed to forge an effective alliance with the nobility or consistently assert their authority over it. Nor did they succeed in enacting reforms or even give the impression of being "enlightened" monarchs. Louis XVI had little particular taste or talent for rule, and his unpopular Austrian wife, Queen Marie Antoinette, increasingly drew fire for her supposed extravagance and indifference to those below her. According to a widely circulated story, she dismissed reports that the poor could not buy bread with the phrase "Let them eat cake!" Though the story was untrue, it reflected the growing anger against the king and queen.

Unpopular kings

Desperate to stave off the immediate threat of bankruptcy, the relatively weak Louis XVI looked for support. Instead of able allies, he found a jealous nobility, a disgruntled middle class, a bitter and frustrated peasantry, and an urban poor made desperate by hunger.

The Tennis Court Oath

In this ominous atmosphere, Louis XVI summoned the Estates General in 1788. This representative body, which had not met since 1614, was divided into France's three traditional orders, or estates: the first estate, the clergy, owned over 10 percent of France's best land; the second estate, the nobility, owned more than 20 percent of the land; and the third estate, the so-called commoners, included the bourgeoisie, the peasantry, and the urban populace. During the early months of 1789, elections of representatives to the Estates General were held. All men who had reached the age of 25 and who paid taxes could vote. In thousands of meetings to draw up lists of grievances to present to the king, people found

The Estates General

FIGURE 16.1 France's Privileged Orders, ca. 1789 This French cartoon shows an enslaved "common man" as a beast of burden carrying the merciless, privileged monarchy, clergy, and aristocracy on his back. Cartoons such as this example not only captured popular opinion but also served as propaganda that helped to fuel the revolution.

their political voices and connected their dissatisfactions with inflating expectations of reform. Hundreds of pamphlets appeared and public debate spread widely. Each of the three estates elected its own representatives. Because the third estate made up more than nine-tenths of the total population, Louis XVI agreed to grant it as many seats as the other two estates combined. However, by tradition, the three estates sat separately, and each group had one vote.

In April 1789, delegates began streaming into Versailles armed only with *cahiers*, or the lists of grievances from all classes of people, that had been called for by the king. Of the 600 representatives of the third estate, not one came from the peasantry. Except for a handful of liberal clergy and nobles elected to the third estate, these delegates—mostly ambitious lawyers, petty officials, administrators, and other professionals—were all members of the bourgeoisie. They fully expected to solve the financial crisis quickly and then move on to addressing the long lists of complaints that they had been accumulating for years. Most bourgeois representatives, like many liberal nobles, wanted to create a constitutional government with a national assembly that would meet regularly to pass taxes and laws.

After religious services and a solemn procession in Paris, the delegates met in Versailles on May 5. Immediately they debated the voting system. The two privileged estates demanded that, according to custom, the three estates meet separately and vote by order—that is, each estate cast one vote. This procedure would place power squarely in the hands of the nobility, which controlled most of the first estate as well as its own order. The third estate demanded that all the orders meet jointly and that delegates vote by head. This method would favor the third estate, for not only did this order boast as many members as the other two combined, but a number of liberal clergy and nobles in the first and second estates sympathized with the reforms called for by the third estate. All sides realized that the outcome of this voting issue would be decisive.

The delegates haggled for six weeks. Louis waffled from one side to the other. Finally, the third estate, backed by some clergy from the first estate, took action and declared itself the National Assembly of France on June 17 and invited the other two estates to join it in enacting legislation. Three days later, when the third-estate deputies arrived at their meeting hall, they found it locked. Adjourning to a nearby building that served as an indoor tennis court, they took the **Tennis Court Oath**, vowing not to disband until France had a constitution.

Figure 16.2 dramatizes and glorifies this act of defiance. The painting is based on a pen and ink drawing by Jacques-Louis David (1748–1825),

a talented contemporary painter and active supporter of the Revolution. In the center of the picture, the presiding officer, Jean-Sylvain Bailly (1736–1793) (soon to become mayor of Paris), raises his arm in a pledge and reads the oath aloud. Below him, from left to right, a white-robed Carthusian monk represents the second estate, a black-robed Catholic curate the first estate, and the brown-clad Protestant minister the third estate. These same three figures also stand for France's main religious groups: the secular clergy, the regular clergy, and Protestantism. All three figures join, symbolizing the transformation of the meeting into the newly formed National Assembly. Around these figures, representatives also take the oath. From above, light streams through billowing curtains as if blessing the heroic activities below, and members of the populace approvingly watch the scene.

On June 23, the king met with the three estates in a royal session. He offered many reforms but also commanded the estates to meet separately and vote by order. Then the king, his ministers, and members of the first two estates regally filed out. The third-estate representatives, however, defiantly remained seated. When the royal master of ceremonies returned to remind them of the king's orders, Count Mirabeau (1749–1791), a liberal nobleman elected by the third estate, jumped to his feet. "Go and tell those who sent you," he shouted, "that we are here by the will of the people and will not leave this place except at the point of the bayonet!" When the startled courtier dutifully repeated these words to his master, Louis XVI, with characteristic weakness, replied, "They mean to stay. Well, damn it, let them stay." A few days later, the king reversed himself and ordered the three estates to meet jointly and vote by head. The third estate had won the first round.

Storming the Bastille

The monarchy might have been able to reassert control had not the new National Assembly received unexpected support from two sources: the Parisian populace and the French peasantry. Both groups had been suffering from the unusually poor economic conditions initiated by bad harvests. Revolutionary events raised expectations in hard times, making these people in the city and countryside particularly volatile. The first important disturbances broke out in Paris, whose population of 600,000 made it one of the largest cities in Europe. In early July, rumors that the king was calling the professional troops of the frontier garrison to Versailles raced through the streets of Paris. Alarmed, residents concluded that the king meant to use force against them. Then Louis dismissed his popular finance minister, Jacques Necker (1732–1804). This move seemed to confirm the fears of the third estate, who saw Necker as an ally.

The National Assembly

"A Great Ferment": Trouble Brewing in France   519

FIGURE 16.2 School of Jacques-Louis David, *The Tennis Court Oath*, ca. 1792 On June 17, 1789, the third estate, dramatically declaring itself the National Assembly, took an oath to create a constitution for France.

At this critical juncture, the common people of Paris acted on their own. On July 14, riotous crowds of men and women searching for arms marched on the **Bastille,** a gloomy old fortress-prison in a working-class quarter. Few people were actually in the weakly guarded Bastille, but it symbolized the old order. Many died in the confused battle. With the help of mutinous troops, however, the crowd eventually took the Bastille, hacked its governor to death, and paraded around Paris with his head on a pike. "This glorious day must amaze our enemies, and finally usher in for us the triumph of justice and liberty," proclaimed a Paris newspaper.

The scene on page 514, one of many paintings and drawings made to celebrate this event, reveals the importance of this famous battle. The Bastille is portrayed as a massive castle that, against all odds, has come under attack by commoners and troops who have rallied to the side of the people. Only a few cannons seem necessary, for the people supposedly have heroic revolutionary spirit and numbers enough to surge forward and somehow storm across the bridge toward the Bastille entrance. The picture poignantly captures the symbolism of the act—the Bastille, representing the old feudal regime of the past, falls because of corruption within and the heroic power of an outraged people fighting under the revolutionary banner of "Liberty, Equality, and Fraternity." In fact,

this show of force by the artisans, shop owners, and laborers of Paris stayed the king's hand and sparked uprisings in other cities across France. Under pressure, royal authority began to crumble.

Uprisings in the countryside echoed events in Paris. That July and August, peasants throughout France revolted against their lords. Burning tax rolls, the peasantry attacked manors, reoccupied enclosed lands, and rejected the traditional rights of noble landowners—dues on land, flour mills, wine presses, and law courts, and the tithes (taxes) landlords charged their tenants. These revolts intensified with the spreading of unfounded rumors that bands of brigands, perhaps assembled by nobles, were on the loose in the countryside. Panicked by this "Great Fear," many nobles—including one of the king's brothers—fled France and became known as the *émigrés* (exiles).

> Peasant revolts

> The "Great Fear"

The End of the Old Order

Now the nobility as well as the monarchy was in retreat. The National Assembly—dominated by the middle-class deputies from the third estate but now including many deputies from the clergy and nobility—tried to pacify the aroused peasantry. On

DOCUMENT 16.1

New Laws End the Feudal System in France

During the summer of 1789, revolutionary activities swept France. On July 14, a mob stormed the Bastille, symbolizing a violent tearing down of the ancien régime. In the countryside, the peasantry rose against the nobility. Cracking under these pressures, nobles in the National Assembly moved on August 4 and 5 to abolish their own feudal rights and privileges. The following excerpts describe some of the laws passed to end the feudal system.

ARTICLE I. The National Assembly hereby completely abolishes the feudal system. It decrees that, among the existing rights and dues, . . . all those originating in or representing real or personal serfdom or personal servitude, shall be abolished without indemnification.

IV. All manorial courts are hereby suppressed without indemnification. . . .

V. Tithes of every description, as well as the dues which have been substituted for them . . . are abolished, on condition, however, that

some other method be devised to provide for the expenses of divine worship, the support of the officiating clergy, for the assistance of the poor, for repairs and rebuilding of churches and parsonages, and for the maintenance of all institutions, seminaries, schools, academies, asylums, and organizations to which the present funds are devoted.

VII. The sale of judicial and municipal offices shall be suppressed forthwith. Justice shall be dispensed *gratis*.

IX. Pecuniary privileges, personal or real, in the payment of taxes are abolished forever. Taxes shall be collected from all the citizens, and from all property, in the same manner and in the same form. . . .

X. . . . All the peculiar privileges, pecuniary or otherwise, of the provinces, principalities, districts, cantons, cities and communes, are once for all abolished and are absorbed into the law common to all Frenchmen.

XI. All citizens, without distinction of birth, are eligible to any office or

dignity, whether ecclesiastical, civil or military; and no profession shall imply any derogation.

SOURCE: James Harvey Robinson, ed., *Translations and Reprints from the Original Sources of European History*, vol. I, no. 5 (Philadelphia: University of Pennsylvania Press, 1898), pp. 2–5.

Analyze the Document

1. What conclusions about the grievances underlying the French Revolution might this document support?

2. What does this document reveal about the rapidly declining position of the aristocracy?

3. In what ways did these laws transform the *ancien régime*?

4. How did these laws change the relationship between commoners and nobility, as well as between citizens and the king?

August 4, during a night session of the National Assembly, one nobleman after another stood up and renounced his traditional rights and privileges in an effort to make the best of a bad situation. A leader of the Assembly hailed the "end of feudalism." As Document 16.1 shows, the National Assembly quickly decreed the end of serfdom, traditional dues owed to landlords, special taxation rights, and privileged access to official posts. The peasantry seemed pacified for the time being.

Success spurred the National Assembly to take further steps. The most important of these actions occurred on August 26, when the Assembly proclaimed the **Declaration of Rights of Man and Citizen.** Enlightenment ideas and phrases similar to those in the American Declaration of Independence filled this document. "Men are born and remain free and equal in rights," it stated. The natural rights included "liberty, property, security, and resistance to oppression." Sovereignty—supreme authority—rested with the nation as a whole,

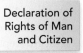
Declaration of Rights of Man and Citizen

not the monarchy. Enacted laws should express the "general will"—a term and idea made popular by Jean-Jacques Rousseau (see Chapter 14). The document proclaimed freedom of opinion "even in religion," freedom of the press, and freedom from arbitrary arrest. In 1791, this spirit would lead to the liberation of France's Jews from old legal disabilities.

Some of these rights, such as freedom of the press, applied to women as well as men, but only men gained the full measure of new social and political rights. In the months and years that followed, many women objected to this limitation. Organizing groups and writing petitions and pamphlets, these women demanded to be included. In 1791, Olympe de Gouges (1748–1793), a writer and strong supporter of the Revolution, wrote one of the best-known and more challenging pamphlets, the *Declaration of the Rights of Women*. She argued that women should have the same political and social rights as men: "The only limits on the exercise of the natural rights of woman are perpetual male tyranny; these limits are to be reformed by the laws of nature and reason." Some members of the government, such as the Marquis de Condorcet (1743–1794), voiced similar demands. However, their arguments fell on deaf ears.

Despite this rising tide of defiance, Louis refused to sign the August decrees. Instead, he once more assembled troops around Versailles and Paris. In answer to this new threat of force, on October 5 and 6, a huge crowd of Parisian women, already infuriated by high bread prices and food shortages, marched 11 miles through the rain to Versailles. The contemporary print shown in **Figure 16.3** depicts the marchers, armed with pikes, axes, swords, and cannon.

March to Versailles

FIGURE 16.3 The March to Versailles In this spirited scene from the times, determined Parisian women, carrying weapons and hauling a cannon, march to Versailles to confront the king with their demands and to force the royal family back to Paris.

With the exception of the well-dressed, reluctant figure at the left, their faces express a striking determination and authority. (Notice the woman riding in the cart with the cannon and the woman at the front to the far right).

At Versailles, the marchers surrounded the palace. With the help of members of the recently formed National Guard—units of armed civilians under Lafayette—they forced the king and his family to accompany them back to Paris, bringing him closer to the people and away from the protected isolation of Versailles and the king's aristocratic advisors. As the carriage bearing the royal family rolled toward the capital, where the royal family would be virtually imprisoned in the Tuileries Palace, the surrounding crowd of women and men shouted jubilantly, "We have the baker [the king], the baker's wife, and the little cook boy! Now we shall have bread!" Although this image of women taking political action into their own hands made them heroines of the Revolution in some eyes, others would nervously look back on the women's behavior as something inappropriate and even frightening. Most men were not ready to accept such a change in women's traditional roles.

A few days later, the National Assembly moved its sessions to Paris. The third estate, building on the anger and hunger of the peasantry and the urban poor, had triumphed. The old order had disintegrated.

THE CONSTITUTIONAL MONARCHY: ESTABLISHING A NEW ORDER

Flushed with success, the National Assembly now turned to the task of transforming French institutions. Guiding principles were represented by the revolutionary banner "Liberty, Equality, and Fraternity."

At that time, the idea of liberty meant freedom from arbitrary authority and freedom of speech, press, conscience, assembly, and profession. Equality meant equal treatment under the law and equality of economic opportunity—at least for men. Fraternity meant comradeship as citizens of the nation. During the next two years, the Assembly passed a series of sweeping reforms that altered almost all aspects of life in France.

Liberty, Equality, Fraternity

The central government, now based on national sovereignty, was transformed into what amounted to a constitutional monarchy. The National Assembly served as its legislature, and the king (still an important symbol of authority for many) remained its chief executive officer. Because only tax-paying males could vote and win election to office, the bourgeoisie firmly held the reins of power. For the time being, the governance of France was decentralized. To undermine old loyalties and the power of the provincial nobility, the National Assembly created eighty-three newly named departments, each almost equal in size and administered by locally elected assemblies and officials (**Maps 16.1** and **16.2**). Similarly, the National Assembly took France's judicial system out of the hands of the nobility and clergy. It created new civil and criminal courts, with elected judges. France's complex, unequal system of taxation was also swept away, replaced by uniform taxes on land and the profits of trade and industry.

Constitutional monarchy

The new government linked reform of the Catholic Church with the financial problems it faced. Repudiating France's debt was out of the question because part of it was owed to members of the bourgeoisie. To pay for its expenditures, the National Assembly issued what amounted to paper money called *assignats*. To back up the *assignats*, pay off the debt, and at the

MAPS 16.1 AND 16.2

Reorganizing France in 1789

These maps show France's historic provinces, each with its own political identity (Map 16.1, left), and the nation's revolutionary departments after 1789 (Map 16.2, right).

Explore the Maps

1. Why do you think France's Assembly reorganized the nation so that the old provinces were different sizes, while the newly created departments were almost equal in size?

2. Why do you think the Assembly eliminated the historic names of the provinces and renamed most of the new departments for geographic features (mountains, such as the Alps; rivers, such as the Seine)?

3. Would this sort of political and administrative reorganization inspire local resistance or undermine it? Why?

same time bring the church under governmental control, government officials confiscated and sold church property.

This seizure of property constituted a major step toward the nationalization of the church. Next the Assembly dissolved all convents and monasteries and prohibited the taking of religious vows. People would elect the clergy, including non–Roman Catholics, and the state would pay their salaries. These measures were incorporated in the **Civil Constitution of the Clergy,** to which all members of the clergy were required to take an oath of allegiance in order to perform their functions and

Civil Constitution of the Clergy

draw their salaries. This last step proved too much for many religious officials, for it threatened the very independence of the clergy. Pope Pius VI called the oath of allegiance "the poisoned fountainhead and source of all errors." Approximately half the clergy of France, including nearly all the bishops, refused to take the oath. This defection of the nonjuring clergy created a long-lasting division among France's Catholic population. Many, especially rural women, fought against this disturbance of their religious life, vowing to defend their faith "with the last drop" of blood. The Revolution would lose the support of many French citizens who felt loyal to the old church and their local priests.

The King Discredited

Louis XVI must have bitterly resented these changes, for they diluted his power and put Paris under the control of his former subjects.

Flight of the royal family

Nonetheless, he managed to make things even worse for himself. On June 20, 1791, the royal family, in disguise, escaped from Paris and headed by coach to France's northeastern frontier, where Louis hoped to find supporters and perhaps reverse the tide of events. Unfortunately for him and his family, a postmaster recognized them just before they could reach safety. Officials arrested the royal family in Varennes and returned them to Paris. To save face, the government concocted a thin story about the royal family being kidnapped, but in many eyes the king and queen had now become traitors.

In October 1791, the National Assembly gave way to the Legislative Assembly, with all new representatives elected under the new rules. In only two years, and with relatively little bloodshed, France had been made over. A written constitution ruled supreme over the diminished monarchy. The church lost its independence from the state. The nobility forfeited its special rights and privileges. Men gained individual rights and liberties and legal equality. Though excluded by the reformers, women would nevertheless continue to voice demands for political and social rights and play important roles as the Revolution evolved. France now boasted a more democratic electoral system than England or the United States. Events had already gone well beyond anything our British traveler, Arthur Young, might have imagined two years earlier.

Reactions Outside France

Outside France, writers and reformers in Europe and the United States hailed the French Revolution or the principles underlying it. In elegant salons, elites spiritedly discussed these dramatic events, and in newspapers and pamphlets, writers dissected and debated their meaning. Supporters established societies in Britain and in states along France's eastern borders. Some activists, such as the American writer Tom Paine, traveled to Paris to participate directly. In Britain, Charles Fox, a leader of the Whigs, called the Revolution "much the greatest event that ever happened, and much the best." Others argued against the French Revolution. The most famous attack was launched by Edmund Burke in his *Reflections on the Revolution in France* (1790). This British statesman argued that France moved too quickly in the name of abstract notions of natural rights and justice. As a result, revolutionaries replaced a despotic monarchy with anarchy. In his view, societies should evolve slowly, drawing reforms from the long historical experience of a national culture. Good government came from good habits. Reforms worked well when based on a nation's best traditions.

Most governments opposed the Revolution when they realized the threat it posed to their own security. If a revolution could rise in France, end aristocratic privileges, and undermine the monarchy, the same might happen elsewhere. Officials welcomed and listened to the aristocratic émigrés who fled France. They suppressed pro-revolutionary groups within their borders. Within a few years, most states joined coalitions to fight against the revolutionary armies.

TO THE RADICAL REPUBLIC AND BACK

The new government, launched with such optimism in October 1791, lasted less than a year. Up to that point, the bourgeoisie and the peasants had been the primary beneficiaries of the Revolution. The bourgeoisie had gained political control over the country and social mobility. The peasantry had won freedom from feudal obligations. To the many peasant landowners who owned their land before the Revolution were now added others who had seized the lands of émigré nobles or had purchased confiscated church lands (though many of these lands went to middle-class buyers).

However, other groups remained quite dissatisfied. The royal family and much of the aristocracy and high clergy yearned for the restoration of their traditional positions.

Sans-culottes

On the other hand, many Parisians urged a more radical approach to the Revolution. These shopkeepers, artisans, bakers, innkeepers, and workers had won little beyond theoretical rights and legal equality. Those who owned no property still could not vote, yet they had supplied much of the physical force and anger that had saved the third estate and made the reforms possible. Increasingly, these men and women formed organizations, held meetings, and intently discussed the numerous pamphlets, petitions, and newspapers printed daily in Paris. Some of these clubs became egalitarian meeting places for women and men; others, such as the Society of Revolutionary Republican Women, insisted that women should participate more fully in the Revolution. Many of the most politically active came to be known as the **sans-culottes** because they wore long pants instead of the fashionable knee breeches of the elites. A pamphlet described a *sans-culotte* as "a man who has no mansions, no lackeys to wait on him, and who lives quite simply. . . . He is useful, because he knows how to plough a field, handle a forge, a saw, or a file, how to cover a roof or how to make shoes and to shed his blood to the last drop to save the Republic." Typically the *sans-culottes* carried pikes and addressed people as "Citizen" or "Citizeness." Eventually they and their supporters gained control over the municipal government of Paris—the Commune.

Leadership for this urban populace fell into the hands of radical members of the bourgeoisie, who allied themselves with the *sans-culottes* and favored overthrow of the monarchy and extension of the Revolution. Well organized and ably led, these radicals came together in numerous clubs that formed to debate and plan political matters. The **Jacobin** Club, which had hundreds of affiliated clubs outside of Paris, became the most important of these political organizations. Its membership included more than 200 deputies, and over time, militant radicals gained strength within the organization.

The Jacobin Club

War and the Breakdown of Order

Events—particularly the rumors of war that had begun circulating throughout France—soon played into the hands of the Parisian radicals. The monarchs of Austria and Prussia, fearing the spread of revolutionary ideas to their own lands and urged on by French émigrés, began to make threatening moves and to issue meddlesome warnings to the French revolutionaries. In France, many groups welcomed the prospect of war, though for different reasons. The royal family and its supporters believed a French victory would enhance the prestige and power of the throne; even a French defeat could help by restoring the Old Regime and royal power. Radicals, who wanted to turn France into a republic, believed that war would expose the inefficiency and disloyalty of the king and topple the monarchy.

The war that broke out in April 1792 became the first of a series of conflicts that would span twenty-three years and ultimately embroil most of the Western world. At first, inflation, food shortages, and breakdowns of order hampered France's war effort. The French armies suffered from lack of experienced leadership; nearly all the high-ranking officers were members of the nobility and had either fled or been deposed. The Austrian and Prussian armies badly defeated the French and advanced toward Paris. Panic broke out in the city. "Everywhere you hear the cry that the king is betraying us, the generals are betraying us, that nobody is to be trusted . . . that Paris will be taken," exclaimed an observer. When the Prussian commander, the Duke of Brunswick, announced that he would deliver the royal family "from their captivity," French radicals rightly accused Louis XVI and Marie Antoinette of being in treasonable communication with the enemy. On August 10, local leaders in Paris organized a huge Parisian crowd of men

and women, who then attacked the king's palace. The royal family fled for their lives to the Legislative Assembly. The invading crowd wrecked the interior of the palace and slaughtered hundreds of the king's guards. The Legislative Assembly suspended and imprisoned the hapless Louis XVI. Under pressure from the people of Paris, it called elections—this time with almost all men enjoying the right to vote—for a National Convention to draw up a new, more radical constitution.

Meanwhile, one of the Jacobin leaders, Georges-Jacques Danton (1759–1794), used his great skills as an orator and organizer to gather recruits for the army and rush them to the front. As the recruits prepared to leave Paris to meet the invading Prussians, rumors—spurred by the propaganda of radical journalists like Jean-Paul Marat (1743–1793)—spread that reactionary clergy and nobles planned to murder their wives and children. Frightened and enraged people began murdering members of the nonjuring clergy (who would not swear allegiance to the new order) and nobles being held in the prisons of Paris. During the first three weeks of September 1792, more than a thousand fell victim to these massacres.

Panic and massacres

In the elections for the National Convention, held amid this hysteria, republicans—favoring elimination of the monarchy altogether and the creation of a French republic—won a sweeping victory. Document 16.2

National Convention

THE FRENCH REVOLUTION (1789–1799)

1787	Assembly of Notables
May 5, 1789	Meeting of the Estates General
June 20, 1789	Tennis Court Oath
July 14, 1789	Fall of the Bastille
August 4, 1789	Renunciation of noble privileges
August 26, 1789	Declaration of Rights of Man and Citizen
October 5–6, 1789	March to Versailles
June 20, 1791	Flight to Varennes
October 1791	Legislative Assembly
April 1792	War breaks out
September 1792	France declared a republic
January 1793	Louis XVI executed
1793–1794	The Terror
1795–1799	The Directory

KEY DATES

DOCUMENTS

The Jacobins' Revolutionary Politics

In the years following 1789, the Jacobin Club of Paris became the most influential political club in the city and, with many affiliated clubs outside of Paris, the most important in France. The Jacobins pushed politics in an increasingly more radical direction. The following document, which they circulated on September 12, 1792, reveals some of the club's evolving goals and tactics.

Since the 10th of August conspirators have expiated their offences; the public spirit has risen again; the sovereign, recovered possession of its rights, triumphs at length over the scoundrels leagued against its liberty and its welfare. Nevertheless, the people of Paris have felt the necessity of preserving an imposing attitude and of exercising a strict surveillance over the Minions and agents of the traitor, Louis the Last. Be apprehensive, brothers and friends, lest new intrigues shall follow the baffled intrigues. The head, the cause and the pretext of the machinations still lives! Despotism moves in the darkness; let us be ready to engage in a combat to the death with it, under whatever form it presents itself. . . .

Let us impress our minds then with the spirit of the orders of the electoral body of Paris; they alone can save us from all sorts of despotism and the dangers of convulsions too long a time prolonged, etc.

These orders are in substance:

The purgatorial examination of the National Convention, in order to reject from its midst the suspected members who may have escaped the sagacity of the primary assemblies;

The revocability of the deputies to the National Convention who have attacked or who attack by any motions the rights of the sovereign;

The sanction, or the popular revision of all the constitutional decrees of the National Convention;

The entire abolition of royalty and the penalty of death against those who may propose to reestablish it;

The form of a republican government.

These, friends and brothers, are the important matters which the electors, the Commune, and the Primary Assemblies of Paris, invite us to discuss earnestly in order to fortify and encompass the National Convention with your opinion upon these matters.

SOURCE: F.M. Anderson, ed., *The Constitution and Other Select Documents Illustrative of the History of France 1789–1901* (Minneapolis: H.W. Wilson Co., 1904), pp. 127–128.

Analyze the Document

1. What is the Jacobin Club's vision of the monarchy and its supporters?

2. What does the club stand for?

3. What tensions within France does this document expose?

---

reveals how the Jacobin Club of Paris, branding the king "Louis the Last," pushed for a republic and legislators who favored Jacobin views. Most of the conservative elements fearfully stayed away from the polls. This Convention ruled France for the next three years, taking the Revolution down a new, more radical road.

Radical Republicans Struggle for Power

The struggle for political dominance among the different Jacobin factions intensified after the election. The Girondins, so called because many of their leaders came from the vicinity of Bordeaux in the department of the Gironde, had once been the most powerful and radical faction of the Legislative Assembly. Because they had sat on the speaker's left, they had come to be known as "the Left." In the new National Convention, the Girondins found themselves on the Right as the more conservative faction. Now the Left consisted mostly of members of the Jacobin political club from Paris. These Jacobins came to be called "the Mountain" because they occupied the highest seats in the convention hall.

| Girondins and Jacobins |

On September 22, 1792, the National Convention declared France a republic. The government then disposed of the king, who had squandered most of his support since his flight to Varennes in 1791. The Convention tried Louis and found him guilty of treasonable communication with the enemy. An extended debate ensued over whether to execute the king, with most of the Girondins opposed and the Mountain in favor. On January 21, 1793, the Convention voted by a narrow margin to execute Louis.

| The Republic |

Figure 16.4 depicts the scene of Louis' execution. On the platform, Louis addressed the crowd for the last time: "I die innocent." An eyewitness described how the executioners "dragged him under the axe of the guillotine, which with one stroke severed his head from his body." The revolutionary government adopted the newly invented guillotine as its instrument of choice because it considered the device more efficient and therefore humane than other methods of execution, such as hanging and the ax. In the painting an executioner holds up the head of the king for the troops and crowd to view. An observer reported that a few seconds later, "cries of 'Vive la

| Execution of the king |

Républic' [long live the Republic] were heard . . . and in less than ten minutes this cry, a thousand times repeated, became the universal shout of the multitude, and every hat was in the air." The troops, with their backs to the crowd, are there to witness what is presented as a patriotic event. Although other executions would not have the same significance or draw the same crowds, this scene would be repeated thousands of times over the next two years. Beheadings not only served as affirmations of revolutionary justice but also provided entertainment—people often rented chairs and purchased food, drinks, and souvenirs, including miniature guillotines. Those who could not attend might purchase widely sold prints such as the one pictured.

FIGURE 16.4 Execution of Louis XVI, ca. 1794 In this depiction, an executioner holds up the head of Louis XIV, who has just been guillotined before a crowd of troops and other onlookers in central Paris.

Ten months later the queen, Marie Antoinette, followed Louis XVI to the guillotine. These executions sent a shudder of horror through the royal courts of Europe, as did the new French army recruits' surprising success against the Austrian and Prussian coalition. The hastily assembled revolutionary armies, swelling with numbers and enthusiasm, had checked the advancing Austrian and Prussian armies at Valmy in September 1792. France now went on the offensive. Alarmed, Britain, the Dutch Netherlands, Spain, Portugal, Sardinia, and Naples joined Austria and Prussia in a great coalition against France.

Internal and external enemies

This new external threat was compounded by internal threats to the revolutionary government. The peasants of the Vendée region in western France, stirred up by the nonjuring clergy and others, rebelled against the republican government. "We want our king, our priests and the Old Regime," cried the rebels. **Figure 16.5** shows a young aristocratic general leading the rebels in the midst of one of the close-quarter battles that often occurred in the Vendée revolt. Standing in tall boots and yellow pants, a white sash around his waist, and his wounded right arm in a sling, Rochejaquelein fires a gun at the enemy, so close in front of him that we see to the right the opposing bayonet just inches away. Behind Rochejaquelein stand his equally determined but more modestly dressed peasant guerrilla followers, one with a rifle, another with only a pitchfork to stress the popularity of this rebellion. Above flies the white flag of the rebel royalist cause that is echoed by the sacred heart pinned to the hero's chest. Rochejaquelein would survive this battle only to be killed in 1794. However, the uprising he helped lead spread until some sixty of the eighty-three departments suffered revolts. Lyons, France's second-largest

FIGURE 16.5 Pierre Narcisse Guérin, *Henri Duverger, earl of the Rochejaquelein* This painting portrays a heroic royalist leader during a bloody rebellion against the republican government in France's Vendée region.

BIOGRAPHY

Manon Roland
(1754–1793)

Manon Roland, describing herself as a "friend of humanity" and "lover of liberty," welcomed the French Revolution "with rapture." Born in 1754 into the family of a Parisian engraver, she learned to read by the age of 4. By her early 20s, she was fluent in two foreign languages, had mastered the Greek and Roman classics, and embraced the ideas of Rousseau. She also rejected her Catholic faith and formed a lasting hatred for the pretensions of the aristocracy—and of the royal family in particular. She married a lawyer twenty years her senior who gained a position as inspector of manufacturers in Lyons. At the outbreak of the Revolution in 1789, she was at the center of a group of idealistic intellectuals and admirers who met regularly in Lyons. She argued for a republic rather than a constitutional monarchy and demanded that the royal family be put on trial.

The turmoil of revolutionary events created opportunities for the couple. In 1791, the city government of Lyons sent Manon's husband to Paris as a negotiator. Manon accompanied him, thrilled to be at the political center of France. They attended meetings of the Jacobin Club, and Manon quickly gathered around her a social circle of men, including Robespierre, whom she would later describe as "ardent, jealous, avid for popularity." The Rolands also associated with Girondins.

Manon's husband often attended gatherings of this circle, and Manon let him do all the public speaking for both of them. Upholding the traditional, formal role of a proper wife, mother, and homemaker, she mostly listened. "I knew the role that suited my sex, and I never abandoned it," she noted.

Similarly, she did not argue for the rights of women or even invite other women to these gatherings, but she often resented men's attitudes toward women: It takes "a great deal of patience or vanity to hear with cool head, from men's own mouths, the value they attach to their superiority over us." Yet she was more politically and intellectually ambitious than her husband. Often, she was the force behind her husband's words and the author of writings that came out under his name. **Figure 16.6** shows this strong woman looking directly at the viewer, pen in hand.

In 1792, with the rise to power of the Girondins, Manon's husband was offered the high post of minister of the interior. She talked him into accepting it and, from behind the scenes, shared his new position of power and prominence. It was she who did most of the necessary writing—the instructions, circulars, and public announcements—and who accepted visitors eager to get an audience with the busy minister.

Events, however, moved too rapidly for Manon Roland as her life and the city, rose against the government in May. Toulon, the chief French naval base on the Mediterranean, invited in the British fleet to help in the fight against France's radical government. All-too-real enemies outside and within France's borders surged forward to fight against the Revolution.

The Terror

Faced with a seemingly inevitable demise of their cause and threatened by radical demands from the *sans-culottes*, the leaders of the Mountain decided to take drastic action. For support they turned to the Paris Commune, as the city government was called, which radicals and the *sans-culottes* controlled. The *sans-culottes* wanted to carry the Revolution even further, toward more direct democracy and governmental controls over the price of bread. Although the Mountain's leaders did not fully agree with the *sans-culottes*, they were willing to work with them to gain supremacy.

The National Convention, now dominated by the Mountain and surrounded by a threatening Parisian crowd of women and men urged on by *sans-culotte* leaders, voted the expulsion and arrest of their chief competitors, the Girondin leaders, on June 2, 1793. To pacify the *sans-culottes*, the National Convention also agreed to enact the Law of the Maximum to control the price of bread, flour, and other essentials. Finally, the Convention drafted a democratic constitution based on universal male suffrage that promised rights to education and even subsistence (a job or poor relief). However, the Convention soon suspended the constitution and formed the 12-member **Committee of Public Safety** to guide the country. The committee had two main tasks: to secure the Republic against its enemies—both internal and external—and to carry out a radical republican program. With the vast authority granted by the Convention, it enjoyed dictatorial powers. The committee came under the ideological leadership of the gifted and feared Maximilien Robespierre (1758–1794). A lawyer from the provinces when elected to the Estates General in 1789, he quickly rose to head the Jacobin Club in Paris. This stern, determined

Committee of Public Safety

FIGURE 16.6 Manon Roland

Revolution took more radical turns. She fell in love with Buzot, a young Girondin in her circle. She told her husband of her feelings, and although the two honored the form of their marriage out of a sense of propriety and discipline, they were miserable together. Manon made new political enemies, particularly Danton and the more radical Jacobins. The radical press called her a whore and her salon a hotbed of intrigue. Then the

Girondins began to lose power, and Manon's husband's career stumbled as well. He resigned from office two days after the execution of the king in early 1793. The Revolution had gone too far even for Manon Roland, who wrote that she was "ashamed of it. It has been dishonored by scoundrels." Over the next few months, both Rolands drew criticism from the press and their political enemies. Threatening groups of *sans-culottes* lurked in front of their apartment.

Too late, the Rolands tried to flee Paris. On May 31, 1793, Manon's husband, like many other Girondins, was arrested. He soon escaped, but then Manon suffered the same fate. After languishing in jail for months and writing her memoirs (modeled on Rousseau's *Memoirs*), she was tried on November 8, 1793, and found guilty of crimes against the Republic. That same day, she was escorted to the very guillotine where her longtime enemies Louis XVI and Marie Antoinette had perished. On the platform, she raised her eyes to David's statue representing liberty and lamented, "O Liberty, what crimes

are committed in thy name." Upon hearing of her death, her husband committed suicide. Just weeks later, her lover, Buzot, facing arrest himself, also committed suicide.

Revolutionary events that had drawn Manon to Paris and initially fulfilled her hopes quickly spun out of control. At the forefront of change in 1789, she found herself left behind and labeled an enemy of the Revolution just four years later. For Manon Roland and so many like her who rose with the Revolution, the wry statement of a moderate observer held true: "The Revolution . . . devours its children."

Connecting People & Society

1. What does Manon Roland's life reveal about the attitudes underlying the Revolution?

2. What does her biography reveal about the rapidly changing events that disrupted people's lives?

3. What does she mean by the words "O Liberty, what crimes committed in thy name"?

---

idealist was influenced by Rousseau and was bent on the creation of a virtuous republic. In pursuit of this dream, Robespierre and his fellow committee members struggled both to appease and to control the unpredictable, threatening *sans-culottes*.

To protect the Republic from its internal enemies and to satisfy demands from the *sans-culottes* for immediate action, the Committee of Public Safety instituted a Reign of Terror. "We must annihilate the enemies of the Republic at home and abroad, or else we shall perish," Robespierre warned. He justified the Terror by arguing that in this time of revolution, "the first maxim of our politics ought to be to lead the people by means of reason and the enemies of the people by terror." Accordingly, agents of the committee searched out and summarily tried anyone suspected of being counterrevolutionaries. Even those who had once supported the Revolution—such as the Girondins, whose views had fallen out of favor—were arrested and executed. Jean-Sylvain Bailly, shown leading the 1789 Tennis Court Oath in **Figure 16.2;** Manon Roland (see Biography); and Olympe de

Gouges, the woman who argued so strongly for revolutionary principles in the beginning, fell to the guillotine. Though many people became victims of arbitrary justice, officials used the Terror most often where real threats arose—regions in revolt and vulnerable areas near France's borders. During this violent phase of the Revolution, probably between 200,000 and 400,000 victims of the Terror went to prison. Some 25,000 to 50,000 died in jail or at the hands of executioners.

To secure the Republic against external enemies, the government ordered a **levée en masse,** or general call-up of all men, women, and children to serve the nation. As able-bodied young men were rapidly trained and rushed to the front, the army swelled to 850,000 men—a number that far exceeded the forces of France's opponents. Everyone else was supposed to contribute to the war effort by collecting or manufacturing supplies for the troops and by bolstering spirits. Women stitched clothing and served as nurses, children made bandages, and old men delivered stirring, patriotic speeches. This united activity for defense of

Reign of Terror

Levée en masse

the country produced an intense national patriotism. One soldier wrote home from the front to explain his feelings: "When *la patrie* calls us to her defense, we ought to fly there. . . . Our life, our wealth, and our talents do not belong to us. It is to the nation, *la patrie*, that all that belongs." With the officer corps now open to talent and the massive mobilization of men, materials, and spirit, the citizen armies turned back coalition forces by the end of 1793. By the summer of the following year, they had carried the war beyond France's borders.

The Republic of Virtue

While fighting this war, Robespierre and the Committee of Public Safety carried out their radical republican program. They attempted to reform institutions and infuse all aspects of French life with revolutionary politics. They intended to create a Republic of Virtue based on Rousseauian ideas of reason and natural law.

First, they targeted those institutions that, in their view, represented the worst of the Old Regime. Many officials saw the Catholic Church in this negative light and sold church buildings, turned them into warehouses, or rededicated them as "temples of reason." Angry radicals disfigured religious statues, even sending some wooden figures of saints to the guillotine and melting down church treasures. The most enthusiastic radicals searched out nonjuring clergy for prosecution and pressured even the clergy who had sworn to uphold the Revolution to leave their vocations. Some radical leaders hoped that the new festivals established to celebrate the Revolution would provide a sufficient substitute for Christian rituals. Other revolutionaries tried to create new beliefs, such as the Cult of Reason, to replace Christianity. Robespierre tried in vain to institute his own deistic Cult of the Supreme Being.

The National Convention also enacted legislation that took the rules governing family life and education away from the church and placed them in state hands. Marriage became a civil rather than a religiously ordained act. New rules for divorce allowed thousands of couples to end marriages they would have been bound to under church rules. Births were registered at city halls rather than local churches. Women could sue for equal inheritance for the first time. Education became a responsibility of the state. New legislation mandated free primary schooling for all girls and boys and state-run secondary schooling, though in fact the government had neither the funds nor enough trained teachers to support such a system.

Women—especially those living in the cities— welcomed the new marriage, divorce, inheritance, and education laws, for they increased women's rights.

Attacking the Catholic Church

Family life and education

However, the Jacobins had no desire to free women from their traditional role in the private sphere. Rather, they rejected women's participation in politics and outlawed female associations such as the Society of Revolutionary Republican Women. Jacobins declared that women's primary duties lay in nurturing children. They concluded that women had no proper role as active citizens and that women's political groups only disrupted the republican order. As one member of the government explained, "It is horrible, it is contrary to all laws of nature for a woman to want to make herself a man."

The new government went far beyond simply rooting out opponents of the Revolution and attacking institutions tied to the Old Regime. It also tried to create support for the Republic by infusing the objects and activities of everyday life with revolutionary symbols. The figure of Liberty replaced royal symbols on everything from coins and statues to plates and posters. Patriotic groups planted liberty trees throughout France. Women adopted the flowing robes and hairstyles of ancient Greece that reflected rejection of the traditional social order. People sported revolutionary ribbons on their hats. Songs such as the "Marseillaise," rallying the "children of the nation . . . against . . . the bloody standard of tyranny!" rang out among crowds and troops. Plays and paintings that supported the Revolution were encouraged. Officials promoted festivals that featured revolutionary symbols, mass loyalty oaths, and patriotic celebrations. Titles of all kinds were discarded and replaced with the terms "citizen" and "citizeness."

Revolutionary symbols

Pamphlets and posters spread throughout France, proclaiming what the Republic stood for. The 1792 poster shown in **Figure 16.7,** printed in 1794 (Year 2 of the French Republic), is a typical example. The poster announces principles at the core of the Republic: "Unity, indivisibility of the Republic. Liberty, equality, fraternity, or death." Above, the eye of God shines its blessings on these principles. Two female figures representing liberty and equality hold up laurel crowns of victory. On the two pillars are pikes, topped by red liberty caps and bound by fasces (rods) symbolizing the strong union of revolutionaries. Below is the new revolutionary calendar.

In the name of reason and revolutionary principles, the government revamped the calendar, making the months equal in length and naming them after the seasons. Weeks were made ten days long, with one day of rest. (This change eliminated Sunday, a day of traditional Christian importance.) September 22, 1792—the date of the declaration of the Republic— became the first day of Year I. The new metric system of weights and measures, based on units of 10, was introduced and eventually would spread beyond France's borders to countries throughout the world.

FIGURE 16.7 A Republican Poster, ca. 1794 Many pamphlets and posters such as this example, announcing principles such as liberty, equality, and fraternity and displaying symbols of the Republic, spread throughout France during the early years of the French Revolution.

The Revolution Spreads Outside of France

Since 1792, France had fended off various coalitions of European powers. After initial defeats, France's citizen armies had gone on the offensive. During the struggles that ensued, France incorporated lands on its northern and eastern borders, claiming that these additions conformed to France's "natural boundaries" of the Rhine and the Alps. By 1799, more victories on the battlefield enabled France to set up "sister" republics in Holland, Switzerland, and Italy. To these areas, the French brought their own Enlightenment-inspired revolutionary principles and legislation. However, the gains carried a tremendous price tag: Hundreds of thousands died in the fighting, and the constant warfare disrupted trade and created shortages of essential goods.

Sister republics

The Revolution also powerfully influenced opinion outside France. Initially, many groups in nearby countries supported the Revolution and its principles. However, part of that support rested on seeing France, a powerful rival, weakened. As people began to understand the seriousness of the attacks on monarchy and

Outside opinion

aristocracy and the threat to their own political independence, support waned. Still, many intellectuals and liberal political groups continued to uphold the ideals of the Revolution, at least until 1793, when the Revolution took a more radical turn.

The Revolution helped promote other developments farther away. In Poland, patriots tried to use inspiration from France to assert independence from Russia. Despite some initial successes, however, their efforts failed. In Ireland, the revolutionary doctrines of liberty, equality, and natural rights touched many, encouraging them to rise against their British lords and make Ireland a republic. Irish patriots even anticipated a French invasion to help their own rebellion, although the invasion never took place.

Uprisings

In the Caribbean, slaves in France's lucrative colony of St. Domingue (Haiti) took heart from revolutionary principles and revolted. As **Figure 16.8,** a French print, reveals, the 1791 slave uprising struck fear in the hearts of white settlers. Slaves, outnumbering white settlers, attack a plantation. Women and men fall under the knives, swords, and cannon of the slaves, while plantation buildings go up in flames. Reports from French settlers, such as the wealthy Madame de Rouvray, described how the slaves "slaughtered and torched much of the countryside hereabouts" and warned, "how can we stay in a country where slaves have raised their hands against their masters?"

After much maneuvering and the abolishing of slavery by the National Convention in February 1794, the rebel leader Toussaint L'Ouverture and his black generals gained control of St. Domingue. The determined group would go on to successfully oppose English, Spanish, and French armies, turning the island into the independent republic of Haiti in 1804.

Resistance to the Republic Rises

Despite the Reign of Terror and efforts to establish a Republic of Virtue, violent resistance to the Republic persisted and in some cases grew. Its leadership consisted primarily of local aristocrats and notables, officials who had fallen out of favor with the Jacobins, Girondin sympathizers, and members of the nonjuring clergy who had gone underground. They gathered additional support from remaining royalists, conservative peasants who had already gained most of what they wanted, opponents of military conscription, and the many citizens who remained loyal to Catholicism and their nonjuring priests. Of the many armed revolts that broke out across France, the most important occurred in the Vendée, a region in western France (see pages 527–528). In what amounted to a regional civil war that raged for most of 1793 and dragged on for years thereafter, both sides committed atrocities

FIGURE 16.8 Slave Rebellion in St. Domingue (Haiti) This French illustration depicts the 1791 slave rebellion in France's Caribbean colony as a bloody affair that cost white settlers their plantations and their lives.

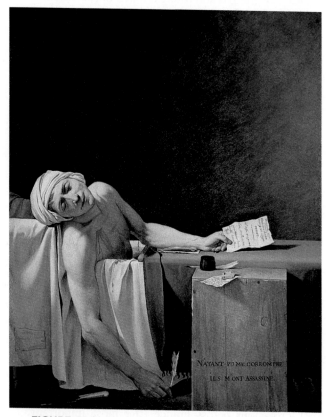

FIGURE 16.9 Jacques-Louis David, *The Death of Marat*, 1793 In this scene vividly capturing the French revolutionary conflict and resistance, radical journalist and deputy Jean-Paul Marat lies mortally wounded by an assassin while in a bath.

and thousands lost their lives before republican soldiers gained the upper hand.

Figure 16.9 reveals another form of resistance and the symbols of conflict during the radical phase of the Revolution. The painting, by the politically active artist Jacques-Louis David, depicts the death of Jean-Paul Marat, a journalist and leading radical deputy, in July 1793. Marat, ironically already suffering from a terminal skin condition, was working in his bathtub when Charlotte Corday, a supporter of the Girondins, assassinated him. Corday felt that it was her duty to kill Marat because of his persistent demands for more executions. This painting shows the mortally wounded Marat with pen and paper still in his hands and Corday's knife on the floor. David and others eulogized Marat as a martyr for the Revolution. On the side of his writing stand are the words "Not having been able to corrupt me, they assassinated me." Corday, widely denounced but convinced that she had "avenged many innocent victims," was soon guillotined.

Meanwhile, discontent with Robespierre and his policies increased. With the defeat of the invading coalition armies and the suppression of internal rebellion, most people no longer saw any need for the Terror—yet the Terror only intensified. When the influential Danton counseled moderation, Robespierre sent him and his most prominent followers to the guillotine. No one, not even the members of the National Convention, felt safe. Finally, on July 27, 1794 (9 Thermidor on the Revolutionary calendar, and thus referred to as the **Thermidorian reaction**), the Convention overthrew Robespierre. In an ironic ending, the Jacobin leader died by the guillotine: the same device to which he had sent so many others to their deaths.

> Thermidorian reaction

Reaction: The "White" Terror and the Directory

With the leader of the Terror now dead, the propertied bourgeoisie quickly gained control of the government. Eliminating the "Red" Terror of the Committee of Public Safety, they replaced it with the "White" Terror of reaction. They executed the former terrorists and imprisoned many supporters of Robespierre, including the painter, Jacques-Louis David. Armed bands of bourgeois hirelings roved around beating and killing Jacobins. Restrictive measures of Robespierre's regime were repealed, and many individuals, weary of the Republic's code of discipline and restraint, reveled in an outburst of licentious living. Middle- and upper-class women wore more revealing clothing; mistresses appeared more publicly, even in the political arena. On the other hand, women of the poor in the small towns and countryside often turned back to the Catholic Church. They hoped that a return to God would end the turmoil of the revolutionary years.

A new constitution in 1795 reflected conservative reaction. The right to vote for members of the legislative bodies was limited to the wealthier property owners. Executive functions were placed in the hands of five directors—the **Directory.**

Men of reasonable competence staffed the Directory (1795–1799), but they failed to restore tranquillity. War dragged on, governmental finances unraveled further, and brigands terrorized the countryside and the cities. The five directors tried to balance threats from the royalists on the Right and the Jacobins on the Left. They turned against the *sans-culottes* by removing price controls and had to be saved by governmental forces when the *sans-culottes* stormed the Convention in May 1795. Five months later, the government barely put down a royalist uprising, thanks to a quick-acting artillery officer named Napoleon Bonaparte. The directors finally resorted to purges to control the legislature and increasingly relied on the army for support. All in all, the situation was ripe for the arrival of a strongman who could bring both order at home and peace abroad.

NAPOLEON BONAPARTE

Within France, the Revolution provided unprecedented opportunities for ambitious soldiers of talent. Most prerevolutionary army officers had come from the nobility and had fled the country or lost their commands as the Revolution gathered momentum. This leadership drain, as well as the need to expand the army, created a huge demand for skilled officers. Napoleon Bonaparte, a talented artillery officer, stepped in to take full advantage of these opportunities.

Napoleon's Rise to Power

Born into a poor but well-known family on Corsica in 1769, just a few months after the Mediterranean island was transferred from the Republic of Genoa to France, Napoleon was hardworking, assertive, independent, and even arrogant as a youth. These qualities would stay with him for the rest of his life. The young Napoleon attended French military school (where he proved particularly strong in mathematics) and received his commission as second lieutenant when he was just 16. When the Revolution broke out in 1789, Napoleon was already familiar with Enlightenment ideas and resented the aristocratic pretensions of those around him. He quickly sided with the revolutionaries. In 1793, he attracted attention during the recapture of Toulon. Two years later, when he happened to be in Paris, the National Convention called on him to quell a threatening Parisian crowd.

Using artillery—his legendary "whiff of grape-shot"—Napoleon quickly dispersed the crowd and became the hero of the Convention. He fell in love with and married the politically well-connected Josephine de Beauharnais (1763–1814), a 32-year-old widow eager to provide security for her children.

Napoleon then used his growing prominence to secure command of the French army still fighting in northern Italy. Calling his forces "soldiers of liberty" and announcing to the people of Italy that "the French army comes to break your chains," he skillfully galvanized the lethargic French forces into defeating the Austrians and Sardinians. Along with loads of Italian art, Napoleon sent home glowing reports of his exploits. In 1797, he personally negotiated the favorable Treaty of Campo Formio with Austria, which recognized French expansion and the creation of the Cisalpine Republic in northern Italy (**Map 16.3**). Over the next two years, French armies moved south, helping to set up more French-controlled republics throughout the Italian peninsula. Napoleon's successes in Italy established his reputation as a brilliant military leader and able statesman.

Turning toward the British, Napoleon and the Directory concluded that an expedition to Egypt would deal a telling blow to British commerce with its colonies in Asia. Egypt could also serve as the foundation for a new French colony. Moreover, a conquest there might enhance Napoleon's image as a daring, heroic conqueror. Yet, despite some spectacular battlefield successes, the expedition failed; Admiral Nelson (1758–1805), who became one of Britain's most admired naval commanders, destroyed the French fleet at the Battle of the Nile on August 1, 1798. The French land campaign in Egypt and Syria persisted for a while, but it was doomed by a lack of supplies and reinforcements. Napoleon avoided personal disaster by slipping back to France with a few chosen followers, cleverly controlling the reports from Egypt and emphasizing the expedition's scientific explorations and exotic discoveries (he sent 165 scholars to Egypt in hopes that they might help him control the country) as well as its few victories.

Meanwhile, matters took a bad turn for France's government, the Directory. The expedition to Egypt prompted Great Britain, Austria, and Russia to join in a new coalition. These allies inflicted defeats on French armies and threatened to invade France itself. Eyeing this foreign threat, as well as bankruptcy, insubordinate army commanders, and disruptions in the countryside, rival factions within France vied for power. One conservative faction, led by a member of the Directory, Abbé Sieyès, concluded that a coup d'état would gain them needed control over the government.

Italian campaign

Expedition to Egypt

Coup d'état

MAP 16.3

France and Its Sister Republics

This map shows the expansion of France and the creation of its sister republics between 1792 and 1798.

Explore the Map

1. Notice the dates of annexation and of the creation of sister republics. Who do you think was most threatened by these developments? Why?

2. The arrow indicates Napoleon's invasion of Egypt in 1798. Why might Napoleon have moved against British interests in Egypt rather than against Great Britain itself?

This situation provided Napoleon with another opportunity to advance his career. Sieyès and others conspired with him to overthrow the Directory on November 9, 1799 (18 Brumaire). The conspirators expected that the 30-year-old military hero would make a popular figurehead representing authority, and they would actually govern the country. As events would prove, they were very mistaken.

Napoleon Consolidates Control

Napoleon quickly outmaneuvered his partners. He had a new "short and obscure" constitution drawn up and accepted by members of the old legislature. In a national **plebiscite** where people could vote to accept or reject the new constitution, the French overwhelmingly approved it (though the government falsified the results to give it a more lopsided victory). As one observer explained, people "believed quite sincerely that Bonaparte . . . would save us from the perils of anarchy." Napoleon named himself "first consul" and assumed the powers necessary to rule—all with the ready support of the Senate. The remaining two consuls, as well as voters and the handpicked legislative bodies they thought they were electing, had only minimal powers. Next, Napoleon placed each of France's eighty-three departments under the control of a powerful agent of the central government—the *prefect*. Thus, at both the local and the national levels, Napoleon ended meaningful democracy in France.

With the touch of a skilled authoritarian politician, Napoleon proceeded to gather support. He welcomed former Old Regime officials as well as moderate Jacobins into his service. By approving the end of serfdom and feudal privileges as well as all transfers of property that had occurred during the Revolution, he won favor with the peasantry. He gained the backing of the middle class by affirming the property rights and formal equality before the law that adult males had secured during the Revolution. He welcomed back to France all but the most reactionary émigrés, most of whom had come from France's old aristocracy. The educated elite admired Napoleon for patronizing science and inviting leading scientists to join him in his government. To deter opposition, he created a secret police force, suppressed independent political organizations, and censored newspapers and artistic works. Finally, for those who displayed the highest loyalty and the most spectacular achievements (particularly in the military), he created the prestigious Legion of Honor.

Keenly aware of the political and social importance of religion—once calling religion "excellent stuff for keeping the common people quiet"—Napoleon made peace with the pope and ended the ten-year struggle between the French revolutionary governments and the Roman Catholic church. Their Concordat (formal agreement) of 1801 declared the Catholic religion the religion of the majority of the French people but ensured freedom for Protestants. Later, Napoleon granted new rights to Jews, as well. Under his rule, the clergy was paid by the state and required to take an oath of allegiance to the state. Confiscated Catholic Church property was not returned.

First consul

The Concordat

Reforming France

Napoleon followed up this pattern of blending compromise and authoritarian control with a remaking of France's legal, financial, and educational systems. The Civil Code of 1804 (the **Napoleonic Code**), for example, generally affirmed the Enlightenment-inspired legal reforms that the early French revolutionaries had sought. Progressives throughout Europe and even overseas would embrace this law code. For men, the code guaranteed legal equality, careers open to talent, and paternal authority over women, children, and property. In particular, it catered to middle-class employers by forbidding strikes and trade unions. At the same time, the code rejected many of the rights and liberties gained in 1789 as well as the more radical measures enacted after 1792. For women, the code represented a clear defeat. Rather than granting them legal or political equality, it gave power over property and the family to men and left married women legally and economically dependent on their husbands. The code also severely restricted the right to divorce, particularly for women. These measures reflected Napoleon's belief that women belonged in the home and that their concerns should center on domestic life.

Napoleonic Code

To stabilize France financially, Napoleon established the Bank of France to handle governmental funds and issue money. To promote economic health, he involved the state in a huge program of public works, supported certain industries, and established price controls. To restructure educational institutions, he created a long-lasting system of secondary schools tied to the University of France and infused it with patriotic trappings. Napoleon also actively supported scientific research and rewarded surgeons, chemists, mathematicians, and other scientists with governmental posts and honors.

Finance and education

Creating the Empire

Napoleon's rise to power hinged on his ability to remove external military threats as well as internal disruptions. This he managed by crossing the Alps in

FIGURE 16.10 Jacques-Louis David, *Napoleon's Coronation* In this richly detailed canvas that took several years to complete, David, France's leading painter at the time, shows the newly crowned emperor Napoleon wearing a laurel wreath. Standing in front of Pope Pius VII, the new emperor prepares to place a crown on his kneeling wife, Josephine, to make her his empress.

THE AGE OF NAPOLEON

KEY DATES

1800 with a French army to crush the Austrian forces in northern Italy and knock Austria out of the coalition of powers opposing France. Next, he made peace with Russia and persuaded Great Britain to sign the Peace of Amiens in 1802.

In the first five years of his rule, Napoleon scored spectacular successes. Law and order reigned at home, and he secured peace abroad. Public morale was high. Napoleon's vision of a centralized, paternalistic state that would make France the model of a modern nation through reason, authority, and science seemed almost real.

However, two problems lurked beneath this promising exterior. First, Napoleon had an insatiable craving for public recognition and legitimacy. He satisfied this need at least partially with a bold move in 1804. That year, with the approval of the Senate and the French people in a lopsided plebiscite, Napoleon formally established France as an empire—and then crowned himself emperor.

Emperor Napoleon

As Jacques-Louis David's painting in **Figure 16.10** reveals, Napoleon controlled all aspects of the coronation. Although he invited Pope Pius VII (seated behind him) to preside over the ceremony, it is Napoleon—ever the self-made man—who takes matters into his own hands. As splendidly dressed spectators look on, Napoleon raises a crown, preparing to place it on the kneeling Josephine's head to make her his empress. He has already boldly crowned himself emperor with a laurel wreath that alludes back to Roman emperors and Charlemagne, crowned emperor by the pope in the year 800. Aware of the importance of details, Napoleon had shrewdly instructed his ardent supporter David to paint the reluctant pope raising his hand in blessing.

The new emperor then elevated members of his family to princely status and granted new titles and honors to his wealthy supporters who had proved themselves, usually as officers on the battlefield. Later, he divorced Empress Josephine, whose relationship with Napoleon became more formal than intimate, and who failed to produce a male heir. He married Princess Marie-Louise of Austria, giving him a stronger image as legitimate royalty.

In addition to his hunger for formal recognition, Napoleon had a second problem. He had risen to prominence and power through his military conquests. "I am an upstart soldier," he admitted. "My domination will not survive the day when I cease to be strong, and therefore feared." These martial ties would push Napoleon to seek still greater conquests on the battlefield. "Conquest has made me what I am; only conquest can maintain me." Yet even when battle after battle brought him victory, war also came at great cost and risk.

Need for conquests

War and Conquest

The interests of Great Britain and Napoleon clashed too often for their peace to last long. By the end of 1803, the two countries were again at war, and by 1805, the ambitious Napoleon had to battle a new coalition of European powers. That year, he marched to the English Channel with a huge army and seemed poised to invade England. Before him stretched 24 miles of water and British sea power. To overcome those barriers, Napoleon amassed a combined French and Spanish fleet and plotted his next move. Alert for any opportunity, he suddenly turned his army eastward, surrounded an exposed Austrian army, and on October 20, forced it to surrender. The next day, however, England's Admiral Nelson sighted the combined French and Spanish fleets off Cape Trafalgar on the southwest point of Spain and annihilated them. Although Nelson perished early in the battle, his navy's victory saved Great Britain from the menace of an invasion and limited Napoleon's conquests to the European continent.

Battle of Trafalgar

On land, Napoleon fared much better—in fact, he seemed invincible. His success stemmed in part from his independent units that could move quickly and then join in a mass attack. Equally important, he possessed an unusually talented officer corps and enjoyed the loyalty of a large number of nationalistic citizen-soldiers. The strategy of sending a mass of spirited soldiers in a column of attack aimed at dividing opposing forces served Napoleon well. Fighting alongside his troops, he cleverly used these military strengths to crush the combined forces of Austria and Russia at Austerlitz in December 1805. Prussia made the mistake of declaring war on France after it was too late to join the Austrians and Russians. As the French troops moved east through villages and cities, people reported how "the dreadful cry was heard in the streets, 'the French are coming!'" Napoleon virtually obliterated the Prussian forces. When the Russian troops began massing again, Napoleon moved eastward and decisively defeated them in the great Battle of Friedland (1807). Although the resulting Treaties of Tilsit (July 1807) were technically between equals, they actually left Russia only a junior partner to France. France commanded the greater resources, and Napoleon expected to have his way on the European continent.

Military strengths

Despite all these triumphs, Napoleon still could not find a way to get his troops across the Channel to attack England directly. He finally hit on an alternative plan—the **Continental System**—that he hoped would destroy his rival's commercial economy by preventing the importation of British

The Continental System

goods into continental Europe. To implement the plan, he ordered a continent-wide blockade against British ships, confiscated all British goods, and set French privateers upon British merchant ships. Britain responded with new regulations that amounted to its own blockade on shipping to continental ports. Now the naval war between France and Britain affected even neutral states, including the United States.

By 1810, Napoleon had redrawn the map of Europe (**Map 16.4**) and the political balance of power. He had dismembered Prussia and abolished the Holy Roman Empire. Now most German states were unified into the Confederation of the Rhine. Holland and the Italian peninsula had come under French control. Spain was a dependent state, and Austria, Russia, and a diminished Prussia had become reluctant allies of France. Only Great Britain and still-defiant parts of Spain and Portugal remained active opponents.

The new European order

In those areas annexed to France, Napoleon ruled directly and imposed all of France's laws and institutions. In dependent states, he installed French-controlled governments to rule with the help of local elites. He usually made members of his family monarchs in these areas—his brother Louis, king of Holland, his brother Jérôme, king of Westphalia, and his brother Joseph, king of Spain. As Document 16.3 suggests, some of France's "enlightened" institutions and policies were introduced. These usually included constitutional government, equality before the law, careers open to talent, the Napoleonic Code, civil rights to Jews and other religious minorities, and the creation of similar public works improvements—schools, roads, bridges—that Napoleon supported in France. Wherever Napoleon conquered, except Russia, he abolished serfdom. At the same time, the reforms included tax increases and conscription quotas to help finance and provide soldiers for Napoleon's armies.

The Impact Overseas

Naturally, Napoleon's policies exerted their greatest impact in Europe, but other areas—particularly in the Western Hemisphere and the British Empire—also felt the effects of his rule and expansion. In the Caribbean, Napoleon failed to put down the black population's struggle for independence and freedom in St. Domingue (Haiti) (see page 531). He also cut his losses in North America and sold Louisiana to the United States.

The Napoleonic Wars had dramatic consequences in the colonies of Spain and Portugal in the Americas. Discontent with colonial rule had been mounting

Revolt in Latin America

Map legend:
- French Empire
- Satellite Kingdoms
- Allies of Napoleon
- Hostile to Napoleon
- Confederation of the Rhine Boundary
- Major Battles

MAP 16.4

Europe, 1810

This map shows Europe at the height of Napoleon's empire.

Explore the Map

1. What was the extent of the area Napoleon controlled—directly and indirectly?

2. Where would you expect Napoleon's rule to have exerted the greatest impact?

3. What geographic problems did Napoleon face in trying to control his empire?

4. Locate the areas that remained hostile to Napoleon. How might geography help to explain why those areas retained their independence?

during the eighteenth century. In particular, the colonists resented the economic and political restrictions imposed by the mother country. As the native-born Creoles began to outnumber the Spanish and Portuguese-born settlers, the ties of loyalty to home countries weakened. The successful revolt of the English colonies to the north and the birth of the United States also impressed colonial liberals and intellectuals.

DOCUMENT 16.3

Napoleon Issues an Imperial Decree at Madrid

When Napoleon scored military successes outside of France, he demanded more from the conquered peoples than subservience to French rule. Typically, he applied some of the same reforms and institutions of the French Revolution to the conquered lands. This policy is shown in the following decree, issued from Napoleon's imperial camp at Madrid on December 4, 1808.

To date from the publication of the present decree, feudal rights are abolished in Spain.

All personal obligations, all exclusive fishing rights and other rights of similar nature on the coast or on rivers and streams, all feudal monopolies (*banalités*) of ovens, mills, and inns are suppressed. It shall be free to every one who shall conform to the laws to develop his industry without restraint.

The tribunal of the Inquisition is abolished, as inconsistent with the civil sovereignty and authority.

The property of the Inquisition shall be sequestered and fall to the Spanish state, to serve as security for the bonded debt.

Considering that the members of the various monastic orders have increased to an undue degree and that, although a certain number of them are useful in assisting the ministers of the altar in the administration of the sacraments, the existence of too great a number interferes with the prosperity of the state, we have decreed and do decree as follows:

The number of convents now in existence in Spain shall be reduced to a third of their present number. This reduction shall be accomplished by uniting the members of several convents of the same order into one.

All regular ecclesiastics who desire to renounce the monastic life and live as secular ecclesiastics are at liberty to leave their monasteries. . . .

In view of the fact that the institution which stands most in the way of the internal prosperity of Spain is that of the customs lines separating the provinces, we have decreed and do decree what follows:

To date from January 1 next, the barriers existing between the provinces shall be suppressed. The custom houses shall be removed to the frontiers and there established.

SOURCE: James Harvey Robinson, ed., *Readings in European History*, vol. II (Boston: Ginn, 1904), p. 512.

Analyze the Document

1. What benefits might Napoleon have been hoping for by issuing this decree?

2. In what regards are these measures consistent with the spirit of the French Revolution?

3. In what ways might this decree have inspired resistance within Spain?

Spanish colonists' attachment to Spain faltered further when Napoleon overthrew the Spanish king and placed his own brother, Joseph Bonaparte, on the throne. By 1810, many colonists were in open revolt.

Over the next ten years, Spain struggled to regain its colonies. In 1814, Argentina drove off a Spanish army and won its independence. Elsewhere, Simón Bolívar (1783–1830), known as The Liberator, led the fight for independence against Spanish forces. **Figure 16.11** shows him in heroic pose, probably to symbolize his military campaigns in Venezuela, Colombia, Ecuador, and Peru. The painting is modeled on a well-known work by David that portrays Napoleon leading his troops across the Alps. Bolívar points upward while a wind blows at his back—a traditional posture of victory.

As **Map 16.5** shows, by 1822 almost all of Spain's colonies, as well as Portugal's huge colony of Brazil, had gained their independence. Nevertheless, Bolívar's and others' hopes for unity within Spain's old colonies soon faded as various South American regions began dividing into separate states. Most of these new states would adopt the Napoleonic Code as their basis of civil law, and oppressive white minorities would rule them for many years.

FIGURE 16.11 Simón Bolívar Using a famous portrait of Napoleon as a model, an unknown artist portrayed The Liberator in a heroic military pose.

MAP 16.5

Latin America After Independence

This map shows that within a twelve-year period, Spain and Portugal lost most of their possessions in the Americas.

Explore the Map

1. In several areas there are differences between the date of independence from the colonial power and the date of separation from other states. What might these differences mean?

2. What territories were still held by European nations after 1830?

3. What might differentiate the territories that remained under European control from those that gained their independence?

Napoleon's dominance over the European continent inspired England to step up its overseas expansion and tighten control over its own colonies and areas of influence. Sea power enabled it to capture and take over French and Dutch colonies in Africa, Asia, and America. In addition, England began trading more briskly with South America. However, one of England's strategies—its counterblockade of Napoleonic Europe—had a major, unintended drawback. By enforcing the blockade, England ended up embroiled in the War of 1812 with the United States. That war, in turn, spread farther north when the United States attempted to invade Britain's loyal colonies in Canada.

> England's overseas expansion

In Egypt, Napoleon's invasion failed, but in its wake local elites rebelled against Ottoman overlords. In 1805, the Egyptian general Muhammad Ali was victorious, and he set himself up as effective ruler of Egypt for the next three decades. Using European models, he strengthened and modernized Egypt's army, which eventually became the most powerful force in the Islamic world.

In the decades that followed, states from Asia to the Americas that reformed their own governments and laws would look to the Napoleonic Code and adopt parts of it. In this way, some of the ideals of the Enlightenment and the French Revolution would be translated through the Napoleonic Code to many areas around the globe.

> Adopting the Napoleonic Code

Decline and Fall

Napoleon had an even more ambitious vision—to rule Europe as the head of a single imperial administration. Before he could make his vision real, new problems plagued him. Even at the height of his power, Napoleon and his empire suffered from dangerous weaknesses. Between 1808 and 1812, three crucial vulnerabilities—flawed policies, resistance to his rule, and overextension of his military reach—would intensify and erode Napoleon's power.

The Continental System that Napoleon devised to cripple England economically was not working well enough. With control of the sea, Great Britain applied an effective counterblockade against the

FIGURE 16.12

Francisco de Goya, *The Executions of the Third of May, 1808*

This 1814 painting by the great Spanish artist Francisco de Goya shows French soldiers executing Spanish citizens in retaliation for riots against French troops who had occupied Madrid. On the left, Spanish victims meet their end. On the right, French soldiers fire at terrifyingly close range. In the background, shrouded under a black sky, stands the monastery.

Connecting Art & Society

1. What message might Goya have been trying to convey to Spanish viewers by means of this painting?

2. What does this message suggest about the French occupation of Spain?

3. What associations might viewers of Goya's day have made to the central figure in white?

4. Why might Goya have decided to paint the sky over the monastery ink black?

Napoleon-dominated Continent. Port cities and industries relying on external commerce suffered. Smuggling further weakened the system. In some areas, such as Holland and Russia, the restrictions of the system | **Flawed policies**

became a constant source of irritation and resentment against the French. In the long run, the Continental System stiffened opposition to Napoleon on the Continent and failed to weaken England. Again and again, that island nation would finance Napoleon's enemies.

People across Europe had other reasons besides the Continental System to resist Napoleon's rule. In the wake of France's conquering armies, a new national spirit developed among many subject peoples. In Spain, for example, Napoleon had no sooner placed his brother Joseph on the Spanish throne than his unwilling subjects rose up against him. The painting in **Figure 16.12** by the influential Spanish artist Francisco de Goya depicts the popular resistance in Spain to the Napoleonic occupation and the reprisals that resulted. Here, in a night scene of May 3, 1808, a firing squad of anonymous French soldiers brutally executes citizens in retaliation for riots against French troops in Madrid. The magnitude of the French atrocity is emphasized by the central figure, who resembles a crucified Christ about to be shot. Monks and commoners, selected at random for execution, surround the man at the center, and the bodies of those already executed lie scattered on the bloody earth around him. Goya, who painted this scene six years after the actual event, intended the work as a statement against the evils of war.

Growing resistance

The Madrid rebellion and reprisals by Napoleon's soldiers inspired other Spanish uprisings and organized resistance against French troops in the years to come. Larger French armies, even when led by Napoleon himself, managed only limited success against the hit-and-run guerrilla tactics used by the Spanish. England took advantage of the situation by sending supplies and troops to Spain under the Duke of Wellington (1769–1852), the British commander who would plague Napoleon's forces to the end. Spain became a running abscess that drained Napoleon's military strength.

In Prussia, similar national sentiments encouraged the government—partly in secret—to modernize its army and civil institutions in preparation for liberation from France. In Austria, the government again declared war on Napoleon in a premature effort to free itself from subservience to the French emperor. In Holland, opposition to Napoleon's policies ran so strong that in 1810 he had to annex the country to France to bring it under control. All this resistance drained French forces and raised the specter of open revolt at the least opportunity.

Napoleon himself created that opportunity by overextending his imperial reach. Successes on the battlefield added to his growing dreams of creating an empire ruled from Paris that would encompass all of Europe. Russia, already chafing against the commercial restrictions of the Continental System and harboring its own ambitions for expansion in eastern Europe, stood as the main barrier to Napoleon's dreams. In 1812, these conflicting ambitions soured

Overextension

Invasion of Russia

the alliance between Russia and France. Against the advice of his closest associates, Napoleon decided to invade Russia. Amassing an immense army of more than 600,000, he plunged into the vastness of Russia. Half of his troops, however, were unenthusiastic conscripts from dependent states. The Russian army retreated into the interior of their huge country, following a scorched-earth policy and luring Napoleon ever farther from his base of supplies. "We believed that once in Russia, we need do nothing but forage—which, however, proved to be an illusion. . . . All the villages were already stripped before we could enter," wrote Jakob Walter, a German conscript in Napoleon's army. One of Napoleon's aides explained the deepening problem: "We were in the heart of inhabited Russia and yet we were like a vessel without a compass in the midst of a vast ocean, knowing nothing of what was happening around us." At Borodino, the Russians turned and made a stand. In one of the bloodiest battles of the nineteenth century—taking a toll of more than 80,000 casualties—the two armies fought until the Russians withdrew.

The French army may have won the battle, but it failed to destroy Russia's forces. In September, Napoleon's Grand Army, weakened by battlefield losses and even more so by hunger, fatigue, and disease, finally entered Moscow. Tsar Alexander I, however, refused to capitulate. The future looked even worse for the French when a fire destroyed much of Moscow, leaving the invaders without enough shelter or supplies to ride out the notorious Russian winter. "Here in the white country we'll all have to die of hunger," wrote Hohann Wärncke, a German soldier in Napoleon's army. Napoleon began his retreat, but too late. The winter caught his forces overburdened with loot. Tens of thousands of them froze, starved, or succumbed to disease. Russian Cossacks, riding out of the blizzards, cut down or captured thousands more. Many of Napoleon's men surrendered to Russian forces. Of the original 600,000 who marched into Russia, fewer than 100,000 struggled home.

Napoleon himself was able to dash back to France. Behind him, one nation after another, aided by British money, joined the Russians in a war of liberation. Back home, Napoleon raised new conscripts for his army and again rushed them eastward. At Leipzig in central Germany, in October 1813, allied armies at last decisively defeated Napoleon. The next year, the allies entered Paris and exiled Napoleon to the island of Elba, off the coast of Italy.

Defeat at Leipzig

Napoleon still had some fight left in him. While the allies squabbled over the peace settlement and discontent weakened France's new government under Louis XVIII, Napoleon escaped back to France. "Soldiers! In exile I heard your voice," he announced. "Now I have landed

Waterloo

[in France]." He quickly raised yet another army from the remains of his old, still loyal supporters. However, he was finally defeated in June 1815 by British and Prussian forces at Waterloo in Belgium. This time his captors imprisoned him on the bleak island of St. Helena in the South Atlantic. "Posterity will do me justice," he wrote while in exile. "The truth will be known; and the good I have done will be compared with the faults I have committed." Six years later, Napoleon died, probably of stomach cancer.

LOOKING BACK & MOVING FORWARD

Summary In 1815, a king from the old house of Bourbon again ruled France. Many aristocrats and royalists hoped to turn back the clock to the days before 1789, when they enjoyed unchallenged power and prestige. However, too much had changed. The Revolution had destroyed a French monarchy based on the divine right of kings. French aristocrats might still boast impressive titles, but the revolutionaries and Napoleon had secured legal equality for French men, if not women. Members of the middle class, though no longer enjoying the control they had exercised during the revolutionary years, would not relinquish the opportunities for position and prestige that they had gained. The peasantry, which had played such an important role during the early months of the Revolution, would never again be burdened by the traditional dues and services they once owed to lords. Finally, the Catholic Church had forever lost the lands and position it had possessed before the Revolution.

Napoleon's connection to the Revolution was contradictory. He subverted key elements of the Revolution by removing the substance from representative institutions and eliminating freedom of speech and press. On the other hand, he preserved other elements of the Revolution by affirming the end of feudalism, protecting the rights of property, and ensuring equality before the law for men; through his conquests, he spread the ideas and institutions of the Revolution beyond France's borders. When he maximized the political and military power of the state by rationalizing the government, he acted like an eighteenth-century enlightened despot.

Finally, the French Revolution and Napoleon created two potent, long-lasting images. First, people had learned that a popular revolution could topple the government and social order of even the most powerful country. This image would inspire revolutionaries and unnerve those representing the status quo for decades to come. Second, Westerners also saw in Napoleon a nationalistic, charismatic leader who could suddenly seize power and exert his will with ease. This compelling image would inspire other individuals who envisioned themselves as potential Napoleons. Perhaps even more important, it would seduce people who yearned for easy, decisive solutions to complex problems.

After 1815, the old forces of order tried desperately to reassert their control. Although they scored some temporary successes, the ideas and institutions of the Revolution, spread by the armies of the French Republic and Napoleon, had taken root permanently in France and beyond its borders. The French Revolution had become a watershed event, and those who ignored it did so at peril.

KEY TERMS

Tennis Court Oath, *p. 519*

Bastille, *p. 520*

Declaration of Rights of Man and Citizen, *p. 521*

Civil Constitution of the Clergy, *p. 523*

sans-culottes, *p. 524*

Jacobins, *p. 525*

Committee of Public Safety, *p. 528*

levée en masse, *p. 529*

Thermidorian reaction, *p. 532*

Directory, *p. 533*

plebiscite, *p. 535*

Napoleonic Code, *p. 535*

Continental System, *p. 537*

REVIEW, ANALYZE, & CONNECT TO TODAY

REVIEW THE PREVIOUS CHAPTERS

Chapter 14—"A New World of Reason and Reform"—revealed how Enlightenment ideas challenged traditional values and institutions in the West. Chapter 15—"Competing for Power and Wealth"—followed the battles of Western powers over land, position, and commerce as well as the economic and social changes affecting eighteenth-century life in the West.

1. In what ways were Enlightenment ideas reflected in the values and reforms of the French Revolution?

2. Do you think the French Revolution conformed to or contradicted the main political trends of the eighteenth century?

3. In what ways did Napoleon embody the eighteenth-century trend toward enlightened absolutism?

ANALYZE THIS CHAPTER

Chapter 16—"Overturning the Political and Social Order"—examines the great upheaval in France that shocked and transformed the West.

1. Analyze the roles of France's aristocracy, bourgeoisie, peasantry, and urban workers in causing the French Revolution.

2. What might Louis XVI have done to keep his throne?

3. Why do you think the Revolution turned more radical, resulting in the establishment of a republic and leading to the Reign of Terror?

4. How do you explain Napoleon's rise? Was his rise a logical consequence of revolutionary events?

5. Analyze Napoleon's accomplishments. Do you think they were worth the costs?

CONNECT TO TODAY

Think about the causes of the French Revolution, the events of 1789–1815, and the Revolution's consequences.

1. From the example of the French Revolution, what signs that a revolution is possible might we look for today?

2. How might the example of Napoleon and the circumstances that enabled his rise to power help to explain the appeal of other strong leaders in more recent revolutionary situations?

BEYOND THE CLASSROOM

"A GREAT FERMENT": TROUBLE BREWING IN FRANCE

Chartier, Roger. *The Cultural Origins of the French Revolution.* Translated by Lydia G. Cochrane. Durham, NC: Duke University Press, 1991. Examines the developments that contributed to the cultural destabilization of the Old Regime.

Doyle, William. *The Oxford History of the French Revolution.* Oxford: Oxford University Press, 2003. A thorough, highly respected survey.

Furet, François. *Interpreting the French Revolution.* Cambridge: Cambridge University Press, 1981. An important book that refutes the traditional theory of the French Revolution as a bourgeois revolution.

Landes, Joan. *Women and the Public Sphere in the Age of the French Revolution.* Ithaca, NY: Cornell University Press, 1988. Explores the historical evolution of the male-oriented public sphere and the consignment of women to the private realm of domesticity.

Lefebvre, Georges. *The Coming of the French Revolution.* Translated by R.R. Palmer. Princeton, NJ: Princeton University Press, 1947. A landmark analysis of the social structure of prerevolutionary France and the opening phase of the Revolution.

Schama, Simon. *Citizens: A Chronicle of the French Revolution.* New York: Random House, 1990. A popular, well-written narrative of events.

THE CONSTITUTIONAL MONARCHY: ESTABLISHING A NEW ORDER

Andress, David. *The French Revolution and the People.* New York: Continuum, 2004. A book that focuses on the impact of the Revolution on ordinary people.

Hunt, Lynn. *Politics, Culture and Class in the French Revolution.* Berkeley: University of California Press, 1984. Focuses on the political culture of language, dress, and festivals created by the revolutionaries.

Jones, P. *The Peasantry in the French Revolution.* New York: Cambridge University Press, 1988. Examines the role of the peasantry in the revolutionary events from 1789 to 1799.

TO THE RADICAL REPUBLIC AND BACK

Higonnet, Patrice. *Goodness Beyond Virtue: Jacobins During the French Revolution.* Cambridge, MA: Harvard University Press, 1998. A study of the Jacobins, their ideas, and the Terror.

Hufton, Olwen. *Women and the Limits of Citizenship in the French Revolution.* Toronto: University of Toronto Press, 1992. Analyzes attitudes toward women during the French Revolution that led to female exclusion from the rights of citizenship.

Kennedy, Emmet. *A Cultural History of the French Revolution.* New Haven, CT: Yale University Press, 1989. Examines the role of the arts, clubs, and intellectual institutions during the Revolution.

Lyons, Martyn. *France Under the Directory.* New York: Cambridge University Press, 1975. A brief yet wide-ranging survey of the Directory period.

Palmer, Robert R. *Twelve Who Ruled: The Committee of Public Safety During the Terror.* Princeton, NJ: Princeton University Press, 1970. A well-written account of the Terror and its leaders.

NAPOLEON BONAPARTE

Broers, Michael. *Europe Under Napoleon, 1799–1815.* London: Edward Arnold, 2002. Examines how Napoleon's rule affected people in conquered nations.

Connelly, Owen. *Blundering to Glory: Napoleon's Military Campaigns.* Wilmington, DE: Scholarly Resources, 1987. An assessment of Napoleon's military strategy and achievements.

Lyons, Martyn. *Napoleon Bonaparte and the Legacy of the French Revolution.* New York: St. Martin's Press, 1994. A solid reevaluation of Napoleon and his legacy.

Schom, Alan. *Napoleon Bonaparte: A Life.* New York: HarperCollins, 1998. An up-to-date, critical biography of Napoleon.

J. M. W. TURNER, *DUDLEY, WORCESTERSHIRE*, 1832

In his 1832 watercolor of Dudley, Worcestershire, a city of about 23,000 in 1831 in the heart of Britain's industrial Black Country, British painter J. M. W. Turner shows the transformation of old towns and traditional landscapes wrought by the industrial revolution. In the foreground on one of the canals that crisscrossed this region, barges laden with cargo—typically coal for fuel, iron ore for smelting, and lime for flux, all plentiful in the region and used in the production of iron—dock for unloading and wait to receive goods from factories along the banks. The vessel at the right carries hoops of sheet iron destined for one of Dudley's finishing shops. The numerous mills' chimneys and coal-fired hearths produce dense clouds of polluting smoke that dim the city and encrust it with soot. On the right, a white and orange glow bursts from iron furnaces. In the background, the church steeples and battlements of a ruined castle rise into the moonlit sky, indicating how the old town has had to adapt to the new realities of modern industry, where work never seems to stop. Charles Dickens (1812–1870), who visited the region during the 1830s, would describe it as "cheerless," a "mournful place" filled with "tall chimneys, crowding on each other and presenting that endless repetition of the same dull, ugly form," chimneys that "pour out their plague of smoke, obscured the light, and made foul the melancholy air."

Factories, Cities, and Families in the Industrial Age

17

The Industrial Revolution, 1780–1850

In 1828, a German visitor described Britain as a land where the "new creations springing into life every year bordered on the fabulous." These creations were the machines and factories of the **industrial revolution** that were replacing agriculture and handicrafts as the basis of the traditional economy. They turned industrial cities like Manchester into what the French writer Alexis de Tocqueville called "the greatest stream of human industry" that "flows out to fertilize the whole world."

However, this wave of industrial developments, which made Britain wealthy and envied, brought disturbing consequences in its wake: great swings of economic prosperity and depression and a new working class harnessed to the rhythm of machines. A British journal in 1826 spoke of a growing "accumulation of misery endured by thousands" in industrial areas. A few years later, the French consul in Edinburgh argued, "Who would want the prosperity of Liverpool and Manchester in France . . . beside these base miseries offered by manufacturing establishments?"

These "miseries" haunted not only the new factories and mines. Workers hoping for jobs crowded into unprepared cities. There, life for them, as well as for middle-class employers, professionals, and shopkeepers, was rapidly changing. In bad times, unemployment and business failures made urban life particularly harsh. In prosperous times, filth and disease still marked these cities. Here even the family, which for so long labored together as a cooperating unit of economic life, was shifting under the weight of new ideas and pressures. Western societies were entering the industrial age.

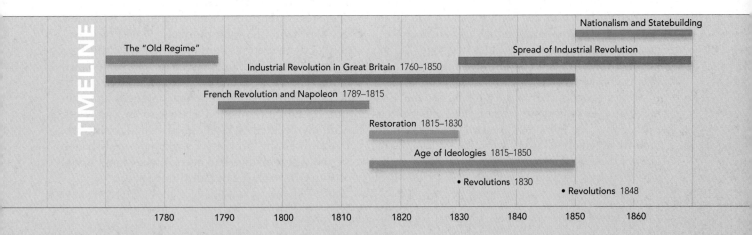

TIMELINE

Nationalism and Statebuilding

The "Old Regime"

Spread of Industrial Revolution

Industrial Revolution in Great Britain 1760–1850

French Revolution and Napoleon 1789–1815

Restoration 1815–1830

Age of Ideologies 1815–1850

• Revolutions 1830

• Revolutions 1848

1780   1790   1800   1810   1820   1830   1840   1850   1860

THE INDUSTRIAL REVOLUTION BEGINS

In this new era, Britain led the way. There a middle-class couple such as Richard and Elizabeth Cadbury (see Biography on pages 572–573) might expect to work hard and see the cloth and dry goods store they opened in 1794 support them and their several children. Thirty-five years later their sons, Benjamin and John, had become wealthy retailers and manufacturers.

Others did not consider the industrial age such a boon. One railroad worker told of a day when two thousand of his coworkers lost their jobs: "They were all starving, the heap of them, or next door to it." This worker had recently injured his leg at work and was laid up for one month, living "all that time on charity; on what the chaps would come and give me. When I could get about again, the work was all stopped, and I couldn't get none to do. . . . I went to a lodginghouse in the Borough, and I sold all my things—shovel and grafting-tool and all, to have a meal of food. When all my things was gone, I didn't know where to go. . . . Now I'm dead beat, though I'm only twenty-eight next August."

Stories about successful merchants like the Cadburys and less-fortunate laborers like this railroad worker give us a glimpse at the two faces of Britain's industrial revolution. Year by year, the work and home lives of these people and others changed only gradually. However, between the 1780s and 1850s—little more than a single lifetime—astonishing developments transformed economic and social life in Britain.

The scene pictured in **Figure 17.1** captures some of what that transformation meant to people. In the foreground of this 1851 painting is a romanticized vision of nature and the countryside, featuring trees, bushes, rock formations, hills, and a road winding around a lake. On the left, a couple, perhaps enjoying a picnic, relax with their dog—all apparently at one with nature. In the distance looms Manchester, which between 1780 and 1851 grew from a small country town to a large, industrialized city. Manchester's numerous factory chimneys belch clouds of smoke into the air. The sense of contrast is striking: In the city, people grind out the new wealth of this civilization, all while enduring crowds and filth away from the imagined delights of nature and the rural life they once knew.

In the mid-eighteenth century, most British people had lived in the countryside. Women and men who laboriously spun fibers into thread and yarn and then wove it into cloth with the aid of only simple tools and handlooms barely noticed the few new machines that could quickly spin American cotton into thread and weave it into cloth by the thousands of yards. At the edges of forests where wood was available for smelting iron, most ironmasters still forged metal using slow methods inherited from their ancestors. To transport their goods to markets, these people, like their predecessors from centuries back, relied on coaches drawn by horses over rutted dirt roads, and on wooden ships pushed by currents and winds across the seas. Steam engines, already present for several decades, were inefficient and rare outside of coal mines.

By 1850, things had changed dramatically. Over half of Britain's population, which had more than doubled during the period, now lived in cities. Cotton factories churned out hundreds of millions of yards of cloth that were sold throughout the world every year and were driving those who still made cloth the old way out of business. New mines, machines, and production techniques made vast quantities of iron cheap to produce, easy to work, and available everywhere. Railroads carried people and merchandise to their destinations quickly, inexpensively, and reliably. Recent generations of efficient coal-burning steam engines powered these factories, foundries, and railroads. Waves of inventions and innovations built on earlier breakthroughs cheapened production while improving quality. Entrepreneurs and business organizations applied these machines and production methods to other industries in Britain and elsewhere in the West. Although marked by periodic crises and downturns, a self-sustaining process of economic growth and technological change had been achieved and would continue through the decades after 1850.

FIGURE 17.1 William Wyld, *View of Manchester*, 1851 In this hazy vista, smokestacks in Manchester, England, stand in sharp contrast to the surrounding unspoiled rural landscape. By the time of this painting, the city had grown to become one of England's leading industrial centers.

What created this phenomenon—which French observers in the 1820s termed an industrial revolution—and why did it happen first in the West and particularly in Britain?

A Booming Commercial Economy in the West

Why the industrial revolution emerged first in the West rather than in other civilizations such as China or India is difficult to say. Before 1500, Europeans enjoyed no fundamental advantages in how they produced goods over their Asian counterparts; in some areas, such as iron and steel production, they even lagged behind. Many qualities, such as intellectual traditions and politics, differentiated Eastern civilizations from the West and may help explain the early appearance of the industrial revolution in the West. However, the rise of commerce during the sixteenth, seventeenth, and eighteenth centuries distinguished the West economically. Civilizations elsewhere usually participated in this growing commerce only reluctantly. China, for example, may have produced luxury goods dearly desired by Westerners, but, except for gold and silver, the Chinese wanted little in trade from the West (see Global Connections on page 550). Moreover, the occupation of merchant

The Western and non-Western worlds

had a low social status in China, further discouraging any potential bloom of commerce in that part of the world. In the West, however, the growth of commerce encouraged people to produce more agricultural and manufactured goods and sell them for a profit in the marketplace. Merchants and entrepreneurs became devoted to buying low and selling high, thereby amassing more and more wealth. The growth of commerce helped create the potential markets, producers, entrepreneurs, and capitalists that would fuel the industrial revolution in the West.

Britain's Unique Set of Advantages

Commerce also helps explain why Britain industrialized first. During the sixteenth and seventeenth centuries, commercial activity in England intensified along with English sea power and overseas holdings. In the eighteenth century, Britain became Europe's leading commercial and colonial power (see Chapter 15). Britain's economy efficiently turned out goods for export, and the island nation enjoyed considerable access to expanding markets—both internal, from its rapidly growing and relatively wealthy population, and external, from its colonies and established commercial connections.

Commercial vigor

Cross-Cultural Misunderstandings: China and Great Britain

As industrialization spread in England during the last decades of the eighteenth century, British merchants sought new markets across the globe for their manufactured goods. China constituted a huge potential market for trade. In 1776, the British economist Adam Smith concluded that China's home market was "perhaps in extent not much inferior to the market of all the different countries of Europe put together." Indeed, during the eighteenth century, China under the Qing (Ch'ing) dynasty enjoyed considerable peace, prosperity, and population growth. But the emperors had always limited European merchants' access to China. Moreover, the Qing, determined to minimize foreign influences on their society, imposed strict restrictions on Western commerce within China.

Eager to widen the opening to China, the East India Company persuaded the British government to send an experienced diplomat, Lord George Macartney, to China in 1792. There, Macartney presented a formal request from King George III for a lessening of trade restrictions. But Emperor Qianlong (Ch'ien Lung) (r. 1736–1796), a capable and humane ruler, rejected the request. In a letter to King George III, he stressed that China "possesses all things in prolific abundance and lacks no product within its own borders." Therefore, China had "no need to import manufactures

of outside barbarians [Europeans] in exchange for our own produce." Clearly, in the emperor's mind, it was the British who "yearned after the blessings of our civilization" and not the reverse. Indeed, Qianlong expressed sympathy for the British, condemned as they were to "the lonely remoteness of your island, cut off from the world by intervening wastes of sea." He went on to lament the persistent desire of Christian missionaries for greater access to China. The Chinese had no need for these missionaries, he argued. "Ever since the beginning of history, sage Emperors and wise rulers have bestowed on China a moral system [Confucianism] and inculcated a code, which from time immemorial has been religiously observed by the myriads of my subjects." The emperor ended his letter by denying all British requests for greater access to China. He also threatened to treat any future violations of his rules harshly: "Do not say that you were not warned in due time!"

Lord Macartney, in turn, criticized the Chinese. "Morality is a mere pretense in their practice, though a common topic of their discourse." As for science, the Chinese, he claimed, considered it a mere "intruder." However, Macartney admitted that China was "an old first-rate man of war, which a succession of vigilant officers has continued to keep afloat." And in the government as well as the family, he observed, authority was

"usually exercised with kindness and indulgence."

In 1816, the British tried again, sending Lord Amherst on a similar mission to China. This effort, too, met with failure. However, British observers had even more positive things to say about China than Lord Macartney had. One official under Lord Amherst noted that the "lower orders of Chinese seem to me more neat and clean than any Europeans of the same class." Many other Western observers who traveled in China during the first half of the nineteenth century agreed with Robert Fortune's conclusion: "In no country in the world is there less real misery and want than in China."

By this time, however, China's population growth was outstripping its economic growth. The government struggled to cope with its people's needs, but poverty worsened. Local banditry rose and rebellions broke out with alarming frequency. The weakening Qing empire was losing its ability to meet the growing challenges from the British and the West.

Making Connections

1. In what ways did British and Chinese views about China differ?

2. How did China try to defend itself?

3. How did Britain respond to China's isolation?

Commercial vigor, however, is not enough to answer the question of why Britain led the industrial revolution. Other areas of Europe enjoyed advantages that would be important for industrialization. For example, during the first half of the eighteenth century, Holland's agriculture and financial institutions were second to none. France was the wealthiest nation in the West. Britain, however, boasted a unique combination of advantages that, when added to its commercial leadership, laid a solid foundation for the birth of the industrial revolution.

Water transportation—far cheaper and quicker than overland shipping—played a crucial role in moving the coal, iron, cloth, and machines pumped out

MAP 17.1

Eighteenth-Century England

This map shows England's system of navigable waterways, as well as areas of coal and iron production in the eighteenth century.

Explore the Map

1. What were the advantages of England's natural resources for industrialization?

2. How did England add to those advantages during the second half of the eighteenth century?

3. Why were rivers and canals becoming so important during the eighteenth century?

Legend:
- Coal-producing Areas
- Major Areas of Metal Goods Production, ca. 1750
- Canals Built Between 1760 and 1800
- Navigable Rivers

| Transportation | by Britain's new factories and mines. Already crisscrossed with countless navigable rivers (see **Map 17.1**), Britain enhanced its natural internal transportation system even more by building an extensive network of canals after 1760.

Certain raw materials—especially coal, iron, and cotton—also had an essential part in the island's industrialization. Britain's American colonies harvested large quantities of cotton. Not only did | Raw materials | the British countryside contain plentiful deposits of coal, but they were often conveniently located near iron deposits where foundry workers used the two materials in the newer processes of smelting to make iron products.

An expanding population and a particularly large and mobile force of both skilled and unskilled workers gave Britain another advantage. | Labor | Already less tied to villages than others in many parts of the continent, this class of rural laborers grew as waves of enclosures in the eighteenth century made many small farmers landless (see Chapter 15). These men and women could fill the rising demand for cheap industrial labor in the cities.

Britain had the capital to invest in industry for several reasons. First, its growing agricultural and commercial prosperity made it one of the wealthiest countries—per capita—in Europe. Second, it gained an unusual ability | Capital | to amass and mobilize that wealth into capital for potential investment, thanks to the development of a national banking system. Third, unlike most of its continental competitors, Britain was long free of internal tariff barriers, had a uniform and stable monetary system, and—since the Glorious Revolution of 1688 (see Chapter 13)—had a government that sympathized with business interests. All this encouraged wealthy individuals and families to risk money on commerce and industry. Therefore, inventors, innovators, and those who saw an opportunity could more easily find the means to start an industrial enterprise in Britain than elsewhere in Europe.

Finally, and according to some analysts, most important, entrepreneurship—at the heart of industrialization—was more socially acceptable in England than elsewhere. "In

England commerce is not looked down upon as being derogatory, as it is in France and Germany," concluded an eighteenth-century Swiss observer. Members of England's aristocratic families—especially younger sons left without inherited lands—often sought careers in commerce and manufacturing. Social barriers between them and the business-minded middle class were lower than elsewhere. More than in most European nations, British merchants and **entrepreneurs** occupied a strong, respected place in society. On the other hand, in France, for example, most elites looked on commerce and industry as a means—often regrettable—to gain money to purchase office, estates, and aristocratic status; as soon as possible, French aristocrats usually left commerce or distanced themselves from their businesses.

> Entrepreneurship

In short, Britain had the most potential both to nurture and to take advantage of Europe's first industrial stirrings. Yet, what was it that finally transformed this potential into reality? Oddly, the crucial development came with advances in agriculture.

A Revolution in Agriculture

The agricultural revolution, with its new crops, methods of rotating crops, breeding of animals, and enclosures of open fields, spread in Britain during the late seventeenth and eighteenth centuries (see Chapter 15). Production increased, as did profits for the large landowners who shipped their crops to markets near and far. Declining food prices enabled more British families to purchase manufactured goods such as shoes, knives, and cloth. As the agricultural revolution picked up speed, fewer and fewer people produced more and more food. The new, large-scale farmers grew crops and livestock to feed the growing number of people working in factories, digging in the mines, and building their lives in the cities. Moreover, these well-to-do, enterprising landowners could use their profits to invest in the many business and commercial opportunities becoming available.

By 1850, the majority of Britain's population no longer raised food or lived in the countryside. Most lived and worked in cities and factory towns. Whether people were better off in these urban centers is a question we will turn to later. For now, the stage was set for Britain's industrial revolution.

NEW MARKETS, MACHINES, AND POWER

As wealth increased and people moved away from subsistence farming toward the burgeoning urban centers, the demand for manufactured goods reached unheard-of levels. Inventors and entrepreneurs rushed to fill this demand, dreaming up new machines and designing novel manufacturing methods. The machines, gaining complexity almost every year, seemed like mechanical wonders. The methods of production transformed the workplace. Coal and steam provided all the power necessary to make these machines and production methods work. Manufactured goods poured forth, available to all with the money to purchase them.

The Rising Demand for Goods

The old methods of production—slow, unreliable, and costly—could not satisfy the rising clamor for manufactured goods (see pages 498–500). In fact, the population growth in Britain and Europe alone created an ever-expanding pool of potential customers for low-cost clothing, nails, pottery, knives, and so forth. Eager overseas buyers, particularly in the colonies, offered raw materials in return for Britain's manufactured goods. At home, Britain's own successful farmers and merchants added to the demand.

Between the middle decades of the eighteenth century and 1850, inventors and entrepreneurs introduced new machines and methods that began to satisfy these hungry markets. Most inventors were practical men who embodied the widespread British interest in devices, gadgets, and machines of all kinds and had more talent as curious tinkerers than as scientific thinkers. Industrial entrepreneurs were also practical. Sometimes inventors themselves, they more often used the new devices and processes invented by others. Entrepreneurs purchased machines, employed workers, ran factories and mines, and found the necessary capital and markets.

> Inventors and entrepreneurs

Some entrepreneurs were landowning aristocrats; others rose from rags to riches. Many were Protestant dissenters, such as Calvinists and Quakers, who had been discriminated against by the dominant Anglican Church. Denied careers in government, they jumped at the opportunities presented by commerce and industry. Most, however, came from the middle classes. They took advantage of journals that promoted new techniques and ideas, divided and redivided the processes of production, and trained a work force unaccustomed to working with machines in factory conditions. Buying raw materials from both local and distant suppliers, they promoted their products to the public. Through their resourcefulness and sometimes outright greed, they pursued profits. Navigating a risky competitive environment, they often reinvested their profits in their shops and factories, buying new machines and boosting production. The story of how they took advantage of new markets in the early decades of the industrial revolution is a narrative of new developments in cotton, iron, and steam.

Cotton Leads the Way

Changes in cotton production came first and with dramatic results. Before 1750, most thread and yarn was spun by women and woven into cloth by men who worked in rural cottages or small urban shops. Using only simple spinning wheels and handlooms, these laborers produced thread, yarn, and cloth of uneven quality. How much they produced was limited by many things—the supply of fiber, farmwork that took them away from their spinning and weaving, the wages paid by the entrepreneurs who organized much of this work, and, above all, the tools and methods they used.

In 1733, John Kay (1704–1764) invented a device called the flying shuttle, which doubled the speed at

 Weaving and spinning

which cloth could be woven on a loom. The shuttle, in turn, intensified the demand for thread. In the 1760s, James Hargreaves (d. 1778) invented the spinning jenny, which revolutionized thread production. By 1812, one spinner could produce as much cotton thread as 200 spinners had in 1760. Other inventions, such as Richard Arkwright's (1732–1792) water frame and Edmund Cartwright's (1743–1823) power loom, allowed weavers to turn cotton into cloth in tremendous quantities. Two American developments added to the acceleration in textile production: Eli Whitney's (1765–1825) cotton gin (1793), which efficiently removed seeds from raw cotton; and the expanding slave plantation system in the South. Indeed, British manufacturers' growing demand for cotton became an important force perpetuating slavery in the cotton-growing areas of the United States.

By 1850, British cotton manufacturers had boosted cloth production from less than 40 million yards per year during the 1780s to more than 2,000 million yards per year. Cotton had become hugely popular and, alone, accounted for some 40 percent of British exports.

Iron: New Processes Transform Production

Machines for the new cotton industry were just one source of a growing demand for iron. Armies needed guns and cannons; civilians needed nails and pans. Until the eighteenth century, British iron makers were limited by the island nation's dwindling forests, for they knew how to smelt iron ore only with charcoal, which came from wood. Even during the days of plentiful charcoal, ironworkers had only their own and their animals' muscle power with which to work the iron into usable

forms. Most of this iron production came out of small family firms or homes of artisans.

In 1708, Abraham Darby discovered an efficient way to smelt iron with coal in a blast furnace. This innovation would make the iron industry a key driver of the industrial revolution. By the end of the century, other new processes enabled iron makers to double production again and again. As suggested by **Figure 17.2,** foundry workers began using steam engines to operate smelting furnaces, drive forge hammers to shape the iron, and roll the iron into sheets. The Coalbrookdale ironworks became one of England's **Smelting with coal** most important industrial centers, renowned for its production of pig iron and casting of cylinders for steam engines. In the center of Loutherbourg's painting, blistering flames and sulfurous clouds of smoke billow out from the coke hearth. To the right stand an engine house and a casting building. In the foreground, two dray horses haul a loaded cart along a road leading out from the ironworks. People standing along the road and to the left are dwarfed by the larger scene as well as the derelict industrial artifacts lying along the road. The painting suggests that the town—located in the rolling, wooded hills of central England—is being transformed into an industrial inferno. Ironworks such as these, with their tall, smoke-belching furnaces, were joining cotton factories as symbols of the industrial revolution.

The Steam Engine and the Factory System

Both the cotton and the iron industries created ever-higher demands for power. At the beginning of the

FIGURE 17.2 Philip James de Loutherbourg, *The Coalbrookdale Ironworks at Night,* 1801 Flames and smoke light up the night at Coalbrookdale, one of England's iron-producing centers.

eighteenth century, people had to rely on muscle, wind, and water to supply the energy to do their work. Early mills used water power, which meant that their owners had to build them near waterfalls. A drought in the summer or a cold snap in the winter could threaten to dry up or freeze this essential power source.

The steam engine, first used in the early eighteenth century to pump water out of deepening coal mines, provided a solution and would become the industrial revolution's most important technological advance. Portable and easily controlled, the earliest models were nevertheless not yet efficient enough for widespread application. Over the course of the eighteenth century, inventors such as Thomas Newcomen (1663–1729) and James Watt (1736–1819) improved the power and efficiency of these engines. Watt, a skilled craftsman backed by the daring entrepreneur Matthew Boulton (1728–1809), worked for years on the engine, making several design changes and eventually converting the reciprocal motion of the piston into a rotary motion. Now steam engines could be used not only to pump coal mines but also to drive the other new machines of the day, such as powering bellows for iron forges, mills for grains, and looms for textiles. The steam engine came to symbolize the new industrial age.

Reliable power from steam engines also made it possible for entrepreneurs to locate factories away from water power sites and build even larger cotton, iron, and other factories. In huge buildings, entrepreneurs hoped to guard their industrial secrets and mold a new labor force. Hundreds of workers, who produced goods in a repetitive series of steps and specialized tasks, tended rows of machines. The **factory system** had emerged. "The principle of the factory system . . . is to substitute mechanical science for hand skill, and the partition of a process into its essential constituents, for the division or graduation of labor," explained Andrew Ure, a professor of applied science, in 1835 (see Document 17.1). As we will see, factories generated unprecedented wealth for their owners and investors but brought new hardships for the people who toiled in them.

Figure 17.3 reveals the nature of the factory system. This realistic 1859 painting of a factory interior in France shows the mixture of raw materials (zinc ore), machines, and division of labor that epitomized factories in the industrial age. In the upper left and center, workers bring ore from the mines and dump it into machines for initial washing and processing. After the ore is split and sorted, workers shovel it into large ovens to be melted down. Men, women, and children work together in this hot, noisy building; the men have

FIGURE 17.3 François Bonhomme, *Workshop with Mechanical Sieves*, 1859   This interior view of a French zinc factory reveals the processing of raw materials, rows of machines, and division of labor that characterize the factory system.

DOCUMENT 17.1

Andrew Ure Defends Industrial Capitalism

From the beginning, industrialization had its critics and defenders. Andrew Ure, a British doctor, was one of the most effective public advocates of industrial capitalism. In the following excerpt from his 1835 book, The Philosophy of Manufacturers, *Ure focuses on the factory system and its consequences for workers.*

In my recent tour, continued during several months, through the manufacturing districts, I have seen tens of thousands of old, young, and middle-aged of both sexes, many of them too feeble to get their daily bread by any of the former modes of industry, earning abundant food, raiment, and domestic accommodation, without perspiring at a single pore, screened meanwhile from the summer's sun and the winter's frost, in apartments more airy and salubrious than those of the metropolis, in which our legislative and fashionable aristocracies assemble. In those spacious halls the benignant power of steam summons around him his myriads of willing menials, and assigns to each the regulated task, substituting for painful muscular effort on their part, the energies of his own gigantic arm, and demanding in return only attention and dexterity to correct such little aberrations as casually occur in his workmanship. The gentle docility of this moving force qualifies it for impelling the tiny bobbins of the lace-machine with a precision and speed inimitable by the most dexterous hands, directed by the sharpest eyes. Hence, under its auspices, and in obedience to Arkwright's polity, magnificent edifices, surpassing far in number, value, usefulness, and ingenuity of construction, the boasted monuments of Asiatic, Egyptian, and Roman despotism, have, within the short period of fifty years, risen up in this kingdom, to show to what extent, capital, industry, and science may augment the resources of a state, while they meliorate the condition of its citizens. Such is the factory system, replete with prodigies in mechanics and political economy.

The principle of the factory system then is, to substitute mechanical science for hand skill, and the partition of a process into its essential constituents, for the division or graduation of labour among artisans. On the handicraft plan, labour more or less skilled, was usually the most expensive element of production— *Materiam superaba opus;* but on the automatic plan, skilled labour gets progressively superseded, and will, eventually, be replaced by mere overlookers of machines.

By the infirmity of human nature it happens that the more skilful the workman, the more self willed and intractable he is apt to become, and, of course, the less fit a component of a mechanical system, in which, by occasional irregularities, he may do great damage to the whole. The grand object therefore of the modern manufacturer is through the union of capital and science, to reduce the task of his workpeople to the exercise of vigilance and dexterity,—faculties, when concentred to one process, speedily brought to perfection in the young. In the infancy of mechanical engineering, a machine-factory displayed the division of labour in manifold gradations—the file, the drill, the lathe, having each its different workmen in the order of skill: but the dexterous hands of the filer and driller are now superseded by the planing, the key-groove cutting, and the drilling machines; and those of the iron and brass turners by the self-acting slide-lathe.

SOURCE: Andrew Ure, *The Philosophy of Manufacturers* (Charles Knight, 1835).

Analyze the Document

1. What is the essence of the factory system?

2. How, according to Ure, does this system affect workers?

3. How might you argue that Ure's views are unfair?

---

the more authoritative and skilled jobs (a foreman sits in the rear to the left), while the women and children are assigned to sorting and splitting chunks of ore.

Coal: Fueling the Revolution

As the industrial revolution hit its stride, the demand for coal also intensified. Steam engines devoured coal as fuel. Iron makers required more and more coal to run their furnaces. Britain's doubling population needed coal to heat their homes.

People poured huge amounts of money and labor into digging mines, extracting the coal, and developing the roads, canals, and rails necessary to transport the mineral to waiting customers. Not only did coal fuel the industrial revolution; mining and manufacturing became so entwined that it was hard for people to think of one without the other.

Railroads: Carrying Industrialization Across the Land

The advent of the railroad age brought everything together. In the eighteenth century, horses had pulled carts along rails radiating out from mines, hauled barges along the growing network of canals, and pulled carriages along roads. Only wind in the sails of ships could move heavy cargoes and passengers across the seas.

During the 1820s, as steam engines began to power ships, the British inventor George Stephenson

FIGURE 17.4

William Powell Frith, *The Railway Station*, 1862

William Powell Frith's 1862 painting *The Railway Station* was viewed by thousands and helped make him one of England's most popular painters. It depicts the crowd in London's Paddington Station just before the departure of the Great Continental Express.

Connecting Art & Society

1. In what ways does this painting celebrate the connection between railroads and modern urban life?

2. What stands out about the various people in this depiction?

3. Why might viewers of the times have found this scene so interesting?

4. In what ways does the building enshrine the railroad and people in this scene?

(1781–1848) developed the practical modern railroad. In 1830 his new train, the Rocket, initiated the Liverpool-to-Manchester railway line. The Rocket's speed (16 miles per hour) and reliability excited the imaginations of everyone. People eagerly invested in railway companies, rode the new lines out of curiosity, and traveled by rail to vacation spots.

The railway carried heavy freight with unprecedented ease and speed. By 1850, trains were chugging over 2,000 miles of track in Britain, reaching astonishing speeds of up to 50 miles an hour. Steaming across bridges and through tunnels to the railway stations dotting the land, the new locomotives embodied the power and the promise that seemed to characterize the industrial age. Optimistic observers such as the British politician Edward Stanley argued that "of all the promoters of civilization, the Railway System of communication will be amongst the foremost in its effects, for it cannot fail to produce many and mighty changes in manufactures, in commerce, in trade, and in science."

Figure 17.4, by the popular British artist William Powell Frith, captures the drama and excitement of the railroad age. The Great Continental Express is about to depart from Paddington Station in London. At the center is a middle-class family. The mother kisses her son, who is holding a cricket bat and is being sent away to school with his brother. Farther right, a bearded foreigner whose dress suggests wealth haggles over the fare with a cab driver. A wedding party bids adieu to a bride and groom. Behind them, a boy sells newspapers to departing passengers, and a soldier in a red uniform kisses his plump baby good-bye. On the far right, two well-known London detectives arrest a criminal as he steps into the train. Behind them, workers load luggage onto carriage roofs. On the far left, working-class people hurry toward the third-class cars, and porters push luggage toward the train. Above the bustling platform and trains, the wrought-iron-ribbed ceiling and numerous hanging lamps mark the train station as one of London's appealing industrial wonders.

The railroad seemed to pull together all the trends that emerged during the industrial revolution. It ignited demand for an array of related products—coal-thirsty steam engines to power the trains, iron to build the rails and cars, cloth and leather to make furnishings, and bricks and glass to erect the new stations. Like the cotton factories, iron foundries, and coal mines, the railroad industry created new jobs while destroying old ones. In addition, it left its own permanent mark on the land and neighborhoods it affected. As Charles Dickens (1812–1870) described in *Dombey and Son* (1846), a new rail line meant that "houses were knocked down; streets broken through and stopped; deep pits and trenches dug in the ground; enormous heaps of earth and clay thrown up . . . everywhere carcasses of ragged tenements, and fragments of unfinished walls and arches, and piles of scaffolding, and wilderness of bricks, . . . mounds of ashes blocked up rights of way." All this "wholly changed the law and custom of the neighborhood," before the railroad "trailed smoothly away, upon its mighty course of civilization and improvement."

Finally, like the other new industries, the railroads could be a risky investment opportunity. Some owners

Effects of the railroad

and investors grew fabulously wealthy; others suffered devastating financial losses. Just as the cotton and iron industries continued to face competition from older methods such as the putting-out system (cottage industry), handicrafts, small family firms, and agriculture, the railroads had to fight to steal business from the roads and canal systems that were expanding across Britain at the same time. Those who had thrown their lot in with the railroads need not have worried too long about the wisdom of their investment, however. Like the cotton and iron factories, the railways were the wave of the future, and they rolled inexorably across the British landscape.

Britain's Triumph: The Crystal Palace Exhibition

In 1851, that shining future was put on display for all the world to admire. That year, London hosted the first international industrial fair at the glass and iron Crystal Palace. At this dazzling exhibit, millions of visitors came to gaze reverently at the British miracle.

Figure 17.5 shows the interior of the Crystal Palace—its arching glass roof like a cathedral, its steel framing a testament to modern engineering. Matthew

FIGURE 17.5 The Crystal Palace Exhibition Under a majestic glass and iron roof, visitors from around the world viewed commercial and industrial displays. This 1851 international fair marked Britain's new industrial might.

Wyatt, one of the directors of the exhibition, proudly described the construction of the palace as an industrial triumph: "But for the perfect system of discipline, which frequent practice in directing the labour of masses of workmen has now made general throughout England, it would have been impossible to have fashioned, in so short a time, so novel and so vast a structure . . . the gates of which may . . . be thrown open to the world at large, for many years to come." To Wyatt and many others in 1851, the Crystal Palace was at once an architectural masterpiece and a jewel of mass production that could not help but appeal to popular taste. In addition to admiring the building itself, visitors could view displays from various nations.

The awe-inspiring palace confirmed economic realities. Britain produced more than half the world's cotton cloth and iron, and, despite periodic downturns, the nation enjoyed sustained economic growth. Britain had become the world's first industrialized nation.

INDUSTRIALIZATION SPREADS TO THE CONTINENT

It was not until after 1830 that industrialization spread with much force outside Britain (see **Figure 17.6**). Before then, people from France, the German states, and elsewhere were interested in Britain's economic wonders. Some traveled to Britain to copy machines, and others enticed British technicians and capital to their own countries. A few modern industrial shops and machines sprang up on the Continent, but overall, agriculture and tradition still dominated economic life there.

After 1830, industrialization spread to certain regions, especially Belgium, northeastern France, the northern German states, and northwestern Italy (see **Figure 17.6**). These areas had plenty of urban laborers, deposits of iron and coal, and developed transportation facilities. Envious of British wealth, pressured by British competition, and recognizing the military potential of cheap iron and rail transportation,

Governmental aid

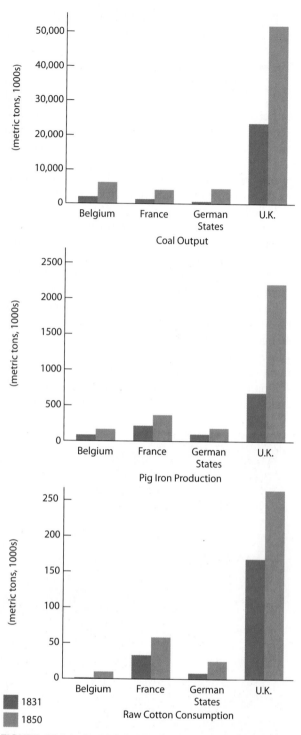

FIGURE 17.6 Industrial Production in Europe, 1831–1850

continental governments took a more active role in supporting industrialization than British rulers had. They enacted tariffs to protect their manufacturers from British goods, and they subsidized new industries. Railroads, partially financed by governments and foreign capital, led rather than followed the advent of other industries, widening markets and creating demand for coal and iron. These countries could not yet hope to catch up to Britain. At mid-century, a

MAP 17.2

The Industrial Revolution in Europe, 1850

This map illustrates the spread of industrialization in Europe by 1850.

Explore the Map

1. Locate the industrial areas. What connections are there among these areas, their resources—such as coalfields—and access to transportation by water or rail?

2. How does the extent of industrialization in England compare to that in the nations of continental Europe?

3. What does the location of railways suggest about the kinds of areas that early railways were intended to serve?

German official complained that Germany would never "be able to reach the level of production of coal and iron currently attained in England." But soon Germany and other nations would manage to industrialize more selectively and quickly, thanks to the groundwork that Britain had laid.

As **Map 17.2** indicates, by 1850 large industrial centers had arisen in Belgium, France, and those areas of northern Germany bounded by the 1834 Zollverein (a customs union that eliminated tariffs between independent German states). Other regions, particularly around Milan in northern Italy and in the northeastern United States, had also begun to industrialize.

Most of southern, central, and eastern Europe, however, remained virtually untouched by industrial development. Lacking well-placed resources, efficient transportation, mobile workforces, commercialized agriculture, and capital for investment, these regions retained their traditional and rural character. The vast majority of people in these areas remained in the countryside tied to subsistence farms or, especially in the east, large agricultural estates. Small villages rather than booming cities were the rule. Wealthy urban elites might purchase manufactured goods from industrial regions to the west, but their own countries could not produce them in the same way. Governments and perhaps a few ambitious and wealthy individuals sometimes imported the latest machines and built a few railroad lines, but these signs of industrialization primarily had symbolic or military value. Relying on old methods of production, merchants in these lands had trouble selling their manufactured goods in international markets. Nations, such as Spain and Russia, that once exported cloth saw their sales dry up in the face of British textiles.

Remaining traditional economies

There were a few exceptions in these traditional economies. For example, Austria's Bohemian lands developed a spinning industry, and a few factories sprang up around St. Petersburg and Moscow in Russia. Even so, British technicians and industrialists were often needed to support these limited efforts. On the whole, all these countries would have to wait before experiencing both the benefits and the burdens of the industrial revolution.

BALANCING THE BENEFITS AND BURDENS OF INDUSTRIALIZATION

How did industrialization affect everyday life for Europeans? To answer this complex question, we might first explore the impact of the new machines, factories, and railroads on people's work conditions, home lives, and social relationships. It is also important to ask who received the lion's share of the new wealth.

New wealth

Foreign observers marveled at Britain's wealth; indeed, to this day many of us associate machines, factories, and railroads with prosperity. Statistics seem to confirm this impression: Britain's national product increased more than threefold between 1780 and 1850. The population in Europe also surged during the same period and absorbed some of the new wealth. Probably thanks to better food supplies (especially cultivation of the potato), earlier marriages, and declining mortality rates, Europe's population ballooned from fewer than 175 million in 1780 to 266 million in 1850. During this same period, Britain's population more than doubled.

Population growth

These startling numbers suggest a sense of economic well-being on the part of Europeans, but they also frightened some contemporaries. In his influential *Essay on the Principle of Population* (1798), British economist Thomas Malthus (1766–1834) warned that population growth would inevitably outstrip food supplies. A few years later, another well-known economist, David Ricardo (1772–1823), argued that overpopulation would restrict wages to no more than subsistence levels.

Nevertheless, industrialization generated new wealth so rapidly that personal income rose faster than population growth in these years. Between 1800 and 1850, per-capita income skyrocketed by a whopping 75 percent in Britain. As other countries—such as Belgium, Germany, and France—industrialized, they too enjoyed similar gains. But who exactly was receiving these new riches?

The Middle Class

The middle classes (bourgeoisie), still a minority of the population even in Britain, prospered. The newest, most dynamic group within the middle classes was the industrial entrepreneurs—the factory and mine owners. They gained the most, some amassing enormous fortunes. Many bankers, smaller factory owners, professionals, merchants, and shopkeepers enjoyed more modest gains, as did those who earned interest and profits from investing their savings in industrial and commercial ventures. All investments, however, did not pay off. Some loans were not repaid. People took financial risks, and some lost their bets. Firms failed all the time, and periodic economic downturns spawned a string of losses and bankruptcies.

Still, over the long haul, the middle class as a whole benefited the most from industrialization. As their wealth and numbers grew, so did their prestige, political power, and cultural influence. The Scottish philosopher and scholar James Mill (1773–1836) claimed that the "heads that invent . . . the hands that execute, the enterprise that projects, and the capital by which these projects are carried into operation" all came from the middle class. Marked by their modest, sober clothing, the middle class gradually displaced the once-glittering aristocracy who were still tied by tradition to the land. This process unfolded slowly, and some aristocrats and landowners managed to adjust quite well to the change.

The Working Classes

The picture is far less clear for the working classes—those who labored in the factories, tended the machines, and toiled in the mines. For people who shifted from the agricultural life or jobs as artisans to work as factory laborers, industrialization may have hurt more than it helped, especially in its earlier decades. These people worked six days a week, twelve to sixteen hours a day, earning only subsistence-level wages. William Harter, a British silk manufacturer, justified the long hours to a parliamentary commission: Reducing the hours of labor "would instantly much reduce the value of my mill and machines . . . every machine is valuable in proportion to the quantity of work which it will turn off in a given time." In textile factories, whole families typically labored together. Women's earnings were between one-third and two-thirds of men's, and children's wages were a mere fraction of that. As a result, factory owners employed women and children whenever possible to save money, and they even contracted with orphanages to provide cheap child laborers.

Figure 17.7, an 1853 woodcut, shows the interior of a cotton factory. Here the supervisor of an English cotton factory whips a boy as a woman in tattered clothing looks on. Whipping was one way in which supervisors disciplined child workers to the rhythms of the machinery. In the scene's background, women and men tend the spinning machines while three other men talk, apparently unconcerned by the violence. Middle-class reformers such as Frances Trollope (1780–1863) used pictures like these to decry the harsh treatment of children in the cotton mills. One governmental investigation of child labor described how children "were rendered pale, weak and unhealthy" from "labouring for hours like little slaves." Employers, anxious to keep their machines running and wages low, replied that "it was absolutely necessary that the children should be employed within the mills from six o'clock in the morning till seven in the evening, summer and winter." Document 17.2 reveals some of the typical factory rules that employers insisted were necessary to keep their machines running smoothly and profitably.

| Factory labor |

After the 1820s, factory workers' wages started to climb. By the 1840s or 1850s, they were earning more than their agricultural counterparts. This change did not make them rich, however, for most of them had to spend some two-thirds of their income on food alone. In 1842, Flora Tristan reported that most workers in English factories "lack clothing, bed, furniture, fuel, wholesome food—even potatoes!" and that their bodies were "thin and frail, their limbs feeble, their complexions pale, their eyes dead."

Money was only one variable in the quality-of-life equation. Industrial workers faced job insecurity, physical dangers, and painful changes unique to their way of life. The worst insecurity centered on employment itself. Even in good times, some firms failed. During economic downturns and crises, such as the "Great Hunger" of the 1840s, wages plummeted below subsistence levels, and many workers lost their jobs.

| Insecurity |

FIGURE 17.7 Child Labor, 1853 New factories typically employed women and children. As this woodcut of a cotton factory interior suggests, supervisors sometimes used harsh methods of discipline.

For these industrial laborers there was no unemployment insurance to turn to, and no foraging, cottage industry, or gardening that people living in the countryside could resort to in hard times.

The work itself carried a high risk of severe physical injury. Factory owners made no provisions for safety. In cotton factories, children regularly climbed under and on top of the equipment to free jammed machines, collect cotton, and tie broken threads; many young workers suffered terrible injuries to their hands and even lost fingers. Long hours and exposure to chemicals, dust, smoke, and industrial residue all led to ill health. Indeed, industrial populations had a far shorter life expectancy and higher incidence of disease and deformity than rural populations. In the 1840s, the military turned down 90 percent of volunteers from some urban areas for health reasons—double the rate of rejection for rural volunteers.

| Risks of injury |

Besides job insecurity, injury, and ill health, the new industrial age brought lifestyle changes that are harder to evaluate. Industrial workers experienced

DOCUMENTS

Factory Owners Establish Discipline for Workers

Employers and overseers in the new factories needed workers who would labor in rhythm with the machines and according to the demands of industrial capitalism. To these ends, they instituted rules and disciplinary measures. The following document discusses such measures, which went into effect at a Berlin factory in 1844.

In every large works, and in the co-ordination of any large number of workmen, good order and harmony must be looked upon as the fundamentals of success and therefore the following rules shall be strictly observed.

1. The normal working day begins at all seasons at 6 A.M. precisely and ends, after the usual break of half an hour for breakfast, an hour for dinner and half an hour for tea at 7 P.M., and it shall be strictly observed. . . .

   Workers arriving 2 minutes late shall lose half an hour's wages; whoever is more than 2 minutes late may not start work until after the next break; or at least shall lose his wages until then.

4. Repeated irregular arrival at work shall lead to dismissal. This shall also apply to those who are found idling by an official or overseer, and refused to obey their order to resume work.

6. No worker may leave his place of work otherwise than for reasons connected with his work.

7. All conversation with fellow-workers is prohibited; if any worker requires information about his work, he must turn to the overseer or to the particular fellow-worker designated for the purpose. . . .

SOURCE: Sidney Pollard and Colin Holmes, *Documents of European Economic History*, vol. 1 (St. Martin's Press, 1968).

Analyze the Document

1. What problems do employers face, as suggested by these rules?

2. How might a labor union argue against some of these rules?

3. What do *you* think of these rules?

---

a new rhythm of labor that no longer bore any resemblance to the natural rhythms of daylight and seasonal changes. Now, workers toiled unrelentingly to keep pace with the machines and schedules of the factory owner. Employers and their stewards maintained workplace discipline with fines, curses, and whippings. Children who could not keep up were beaten at times (see **Figure 17.7**); some were even chained to their machines. There were no slack days, like the traditional Monday of preindustrial times. Wages took the form of cash, which workers had to save and apportion carefully over the week for food and housing despite the temptations of alcohol and other leisure activities. At the end of the long workday, laborers trudged home to poor housing clustered around noisy mills or mine entrances or to cheap, overcrowded rooms and cellars of industrial cities.

Lifestyle changes

The question remains: Did the overall quality of life improve for the working classes in the early decades of the industrial revolution? One way to judge is to ask what would have happened to these people without industrialization. Communal villages and agricultural labor had their advantages. In a widely popular poem, "The Deserted Village" (1770), Oliver Goldsmith lamented the loss of rural life:

Ill fares the land, to hastening ills a prey
Where wealth accumulated . . .
But a bold peasantry, their country's pride
When once destroyed, can never be supplied.

People growing up on farms and in small villages at least had traditions they could rely on. But this traditional life also had its own harsh side. Poverty was no stranger to the countryside, nor was child labor, cold, uncertainty, and squalor in windowless hovels. One contemporary, Frederick Eden, argued that the difficulties experienced by small farmers and villagers were only "temporary" and a small price to pay for "the greater good which may be expected from the improvement." However we evaluate all this, life in the city did give the working class something no one could have foreseen: a new sense of class consciousness, an awareness of their own unique burdens and hardships that emboldened them into action and alarmed the onlooking middle classes.

Developing Working-Class Consciousness

Because industrial workers lived in the same areas, labored in the same oppressive buildings, grappled with similar problems, socialized and commiserated together, and joined the same trade or civic organizations, they began to see themselves as a separate class. This sense of solidarity came partly from a tradition among artisans and craftsmen of membership in guilds. Although guilds were made illegal after 1791 and were opposed by middle-class people committed to gaining control over the workplace, other workers' organizations such as fraternal societies, trade organizations, and mutual aid societies

Workers' organizations

persisted. These groups laid the foundation for the emergence of trade unions, made legal (though severely restricted) in England in 1824 and elsewhere after 1850.

Figure 17.8, a nineteenth-century trade union membership certificate, reveals the pride and values in union labor during this industrial age. Like most unions of the period, the Associated Shipwright's Society—a British shipbuilders' union—was made up of skilled workers. Toward the top of this membership certificate is a blue shield; above it are two hands clasped in brotherhood, and below it are the words "WE ARE AS ONE." In the center is a construction site where ships are being built. Just above are pictures of ships, particularly the steamships that carried people and commerce throughout the world. On the bottom of the certificate are pictures of some of the typical benefits of union membership, including accident insurance, retirement income, and death payments. By mid-century, labor leaders had formed the beginnings of national unions, such as the Grand National Consolidated Trades Union in Britain in 1834, the National Trades Union in the United States in 1834, and the General Workers' Brotherhood in Germany in 1848.

FIGURE 17.8 A Trade Union Membership Certificate, nineteenth century This union certificate from Britain's Associated Shipwright's Society reveals the benefits and pride that labor union membership conferred during this industrial age.

Sometimes workers turned to violence against what they saw as threats from industrialization by destroying the new machines. After 1811, English hand weavers, losing their work to the new power looms, went on rampages, smashing the machines to pieces or campaigning to get rid of them. Glove makers destroyed the new stocking frames that threatened their jobs. These forms of protest came to be known as **Luddism** in honor of a legendary (and perhaps fictitious) leader, Ned Ludd. The British Parliament quickly named industrial sabotage a capital offense and heavily suppressed the violence. Nevertheless, sporadic episodes of violence continued to erupt for several years, not only in Britain but elsewhere as the industrial revolution spread. In the 1830s, silk workers in Lyons, France, rose up against attempts to lower their pay. In 1836, Spanish workers burned a textile factory in Barcelona. During the 1840s, several governments had to call out troops against strikers.

Most of these efforts brought few concrete results in the period before 1850. In addition to the power wielded by wealthier classes and governments, many internally divisive forces chipped away at the fledgling working-class solidarity. Labor leaders, for example, who usually came from the more skilled trades—the cabinetmakers, printers, tailors, masons, and blacksmiths—tended to look down on unskilled industrial workers. Most women were not invited to join worker organizations, though they forged some of their own trade associations. Other loyalties based on religion, region, trade, or even neighborhood undermined worker unity. Sometimes the only connection holding laborers together was a sense of shared problems, the belief that workers had a right to a just wage, and the impression that their employers were exploiters rather than economic partners.

Despite the forces dividing workers, their sense of themselves as a separate, unique class strengthened over time. Increasingly, members of the middle class began to see them as dangerous and even savage. As we will see in following chapters, with the sharpening of working-class consciousness, the power of the traditional artisan groups and the peasantry would decline—quickly in the decades after 1850, especially in highly industrialized places such as Britain, Belgium, and parts of Germany. The process would unfold more gradually in moderately industrialized places, such as France, and slowly in most of southern and eastern Europe.

For good or ill, industrialization was transforming everyday life across Europe. The economic and human balance shifted from the countryside to the city. Now the dramatic social transformations took place in the growing urban centers where, as one young worker described London in the 1820s, "a wilderness of human beings" lived.

LIFE IN THE GROWING CITIES

The unprecedented growth of cities from 1780 to 1850 stemmed from a combination of forces. Population was increasing in both urban

Urban growth

and rural areas. Enclosures of land by market-oriented landowners that dispossessed individuals of their small farms and communities of their commons further uprooted rural families. These pressures pushed people from the land. At the same time, the cities, with their promise of jobs and the lure of beer halls and theaters, attracted people in droves. Industrial towns sprang up where none had existed before. Towns ballooned into cities, and already large cities grew even more imposing. Some of the most spectacular urban growth happened in industrial cities, such as Manchester, which expanded from 25,000 in 1772 to 367,000 in 1850; and Birmingham, Leeds, and Saint-Étienne in France, which more than tripled in size. Other already substantial cities, such as London and Paris, became increasingly crowded and sprouted new suburbs.

Most cities flourished through industrial activity, such as mining and manufacturing. Other areas scarcely touched by industrialization, such as Naples, St. Petersburg, and Vienna, also grew dramatically through the expansion of governmental bureaucracies and traditional commerce.

The Promise and Pitfalls of Work in the Cities

Industry, however, had the strongest pull. It inevitably attracted new commerce and gave rise to a broad range of consumer and service needs. Women flocked to the textile factories, but even more women living in the cities worked as domestics. Many young women came for what jobs they could find, perhaps hoping to send home part of their pay and still save enough to start a new life. The building trades drew growing numbers of men, who sometimes left their wives and children in the countryside to survive on a patch of land and dwindling cottage-industry employment. Many men periodically returned to the countryside, particularly in winter, when construction slowed, or during planting and harvest times.

Living with Urban Growth

Industrialization and urbanization also altered the landscape that people traveled through to reach the cities. Forests shrank as people cut down more and more trees for construction of cities, mines, factories, and railroads. The same mines and railroads cut scars into the land, and the cities and factories ate up rural landscapes. Rivers once fit for fish or drinking became polluted with industrial and human wastes.

Approaching the cities, travelers saw smoke in the air from the dirty coal fires used to heat buildings and from the engines of industry. In the city, and particularly in the poor working-class areas, the air smelled foul, for there were no modern sewers, sorely inade-

Environmental changes

quate toilet facilities, and not enough clean water. Garbage and animal waste collected in the streets until heavy rains washed them away. In Manchester, only two-thirds of the houses had toilets, and many of those flushed into inadequate cesspools. Human and animal waste mixed in rivers that people used for drinking water. Charles Dickens's description of the fictionalized Coketown in his novel *Hard Times* (1854) would have struck a familiar chord for nineteenth-century travelers to Britain's industrial cities: "It was a town of machinery and tall chimneys, out of which interminable serpents of smoke trailed themselves for ever and ever. . . . It had a black canal in it, and a river that ran purple with ill-smelling dye, and vast piles of buildings full of windows where there was a rattling and a trembling all day long, and where the piston of the steam-engine worked monotonously up and down."

Overwhelmed by these surroundings, newcomers to the cities tended to settle in areas where they knew someone else. Whole neighborhoods grew up populated by people who had come from the same rural region. This tendency led to a sense of segregation and separate identities within the cities, as people familiar with one another clustered together.

Few neighborhoods were planned. Indeed, the expansion of most cities became increasingly uncontrolled. The rampant growth created far more problems for the working class than for anyone else.

Different neighborhoods

The middle classes, for example, most likely lived in lower-floor apartments in the more desirable sections of town and had the benefit of some running water. They also could afford to employ servants. It was in the working-class sections and poverty-stricken areas that the social ills and squalor of the age reached their worst levels. As the manufacturer and socialist Friedrich Engels (1820–1895) described, "The houses are packed from cellar to attic and they are as dirty inside as outside." In the Irish quarter of London, as many as 38 people crowded into small buildings down narrow alleys where the walls were crumbling, and "piles of refuse and ashes lie all over the place and the slops thrown out into the street collect in pools which emit a foul stench." In the bad quarters lived "the poorest of the poor. Here the worst-paid workers rub shoulders with thieves, rogues and prostitutes."

Document 17.3 describes conditions where poor workers lived. **Figure 17.9,** a mid-nineteenth-century woodcut by the French artist Gustave Doré (1832–1883), also portrays the squalor and crowding of a London slum. In the center, a young child carries a

DOCUMENT 17.3

A Middle-Class Reformer Describes Workers' Housing

During the first half of the nineteenth century, most urban workers gained little more than just enough to get by. Their dwellings reflected their precarious existence. The following is a description of housing in Nantes, France, during the 1830s.

If you want to know how he [the poorer worker] lives, go—for example—to the Rue des Fumiers which is almost entirely inhabited by this class of worker. Pass through one of the drain-like openings, below street-level, that lead to these filthy dwellings, but remember to stoop as you enter. One must have gone down into these alleys where the atmosphere is as damp and cold as a cellar; one must have known what it is like to feel one's foot slip on the polluted ground and to fear a stumble into the filth: to realise the painful impression that one receives on entering the homes of these unfortunate workers. Below street-level on each side of the passage there is a large gloomy cold room. Foul water oozes out of the walls. Air reaches the room through a sort of semi-circular window which is two feet high at its greatest elevation. Go in—if the fetid smell that assails you does not make you recoil. Take care, for the floor is uneven, unpaved and untiled—or if there are tiles, they are covered with so much dirt that they cannot be seen. And then you will see two or three rickety beds fitted to one side because the cords that bind them to the worm-eaten legs have themselves decayed. Look at the contents of the bed—a mattress; a tattered blanket of rags (seldom washed since there is only one); sheets sometimes; and a pillow sometimes. No wardrobes are needed in these homes. Often a weaver's loom and a spinning wheel complete the furniture. There is no fire in the winter. No sunlight penetrates [by day], while at night a tallow candle is lit. Here men work for fourteen hours [a day].

SOURCE: Sidney Pollard and Colin Holmes, *Documents of European Economic History*, vol. 1 (New York: St. Martin's Press, 1968), pp. 494–495.

Analyze the Document

1. What most bothers the author about workers' housing?

2. In what ways were housing conditions connected to public health problems?

3. How do you think a middle-class person might have responded to this account during the 1830s?

---

baby, perhaps because her mother is working. Around her in the alley, dejected men, women, and children stand listlessly. Dark tenements tower over them, and laundry sags from clotheslines. Though criticized for overdramatizing the plight of the poor, Doré effectively conveys the anguish of unemployment, poverty, and crowding marring this rich city. As this and works by novelists such as Charles Dickens, Elizabeth Gaskell, Frances Trollope, and Honoré de Balzac showed, the burgeoning cities were fostering a whole set of social concerns.

Worrying About Urban Society: Rising Crime

One of those social concerns centered on patterns of criminal behavior. People in the upper classes complained about crime and the social disorder it implied. Had cities become hotbeds of crime, as some middle-class observers claimed, or were these critics simply overly worried about their own safety and well-being?

Crime certainly plagued people in the West long before the industrial revolution. In rural areas, along highways, and in the preindustrial cities of Europe, crimes ranging from pickpocketing to murder occurred all too frequently. Professional thieves had reportedly run rampant in Germany, England, and France in past centuries.

In the early stages of industrialization, theft and robbery in particular did rise in the cities. Crowds provided prime opportunities for pickpockets. In urban taverns and dance halls, men sometimes fell into violent brawling, sometimes over women. In these establishments, alcohol flowed freely and almost certainly played a role in outbreaks of fighting. The widening gaps between rich and poor and the desperation of living in hard times also made tempers short. Finally, the anonymity of life in the city and the tempting array of luxury items to steal made crime harder to resist.

Whether justified by the realities of more crime or not, the specter of urban crime and fear of disorder prompted new efforts to improve law enforcement. In 1829, under the leadership of Robert Peel, Parliament passed a law establishing the first modern police force in London. Peel's new police, called "Bobbies" in his honor, emphasized regular patrols by uniformed officers as a way to deter crime and present a visual image of security. Both the middle and the working classes accepted the Bobbies, in part because the police were not allowed to be engaged for political purposes such as domestic espionage, and in part because people saw them as the first line of defense against all disorder. By the early 1830s, there were some 3,000 uniformed officers in the force.

Crime and law enforcement

**FIGURE 17.9 Gustave Doré, *A London Slum,*
mid-nineteenth century** Dark, crowded urban areas such as
the district shown in this woodcut were home to innumerable
poor workers and other impoverished individuals.

The frightening consequences of rapid urbanization were becoming all too apparent. Year by year,
the cities grew more densely packed and seemingly
more dangerous. In bad times, they teemed with
desperate people hoping to find jobs; in good times,

they drew even more people eager to take advantage
of the available work and other opportunities. Contemporaries associated the cities with overcrowding,
filth, crime, moral degeneracy, and an unruly working class. "They [the working class] live precisely
like brutes . . . they eat, drink, breed, work and die,"
complained a middle-class British observer in 1850.
"The richer and more intelligent classes are obliged
to guard them with police." Perhaps most disturbing,
however, were the disease and death that haunted
urban centers.

PUBLIC HEALTH AND MEDICINE IN THE INDUSTRIAL AGE

People had good reason to fear for their health and
safety in the growing cities, especially in the poorer
sections of town. On average, city dwellers fell ill
more often and died at a far earlier age than their
rural counterparts. Within the cities, the poor lived
half as long as the rich.

Industrialization itself was dangerous. The new
machines maimed factory workers, and cave-ins,
floods, and explosions killed miners. Various diseases
stemmed directly from mining and manufacturing.
Coal miners became ill and died from black-lung disease. Cotton workers developed brown-lung disease.
In textile factories, women suffered particularly high
mortality rates. Metalworkers, especially grinders,
developed lung diseases from inhaling shavings. Poi-
sonings from mercury, lead, and phosphorus used in
industrial processes also increased.

The Danger of Disease

The greatest danger came from infectious diseases.
They were the great causes of sickness and death
before the nineteenth century, and the rapid growth
of crowded cities that lacked sanitation facilities made
matters worse. People living in working-class quarters
and urban slums were most vulnerable. Tuberculosis
and diphtheria thrived in the most heavily populated areas and killed millions during the nineteenth
century.

Worse, plagues periodically swept through cities.
Cholera epidemics struck Europe several times, causing great panic as people in city after city awaited
the arrival of the illness (see **Map 17.3**). Suggested
remedies included taking several measures to restore
warmth to the body, giving laudanum (opium dissolved in alcohol), and seeking medical aid. In 1831
alone, cholera killed some 100,000 in France and
50,000 in England.

People disagreed about the causes of diseases.
Some observers blamed illnesses on physical weakness and immorality of individuals. In these

MAP 17.3

The Spread of a Cholera Epidemic

This map shows the spread of the cholera epidemic that originally broke out in eastern India in 1817.

Explore the Map

1. In what direction did the epidemic mainly spread over time?

2. What does this pattern reveal about growing connections between the Western and non-Western worlds?

Direction of the Spreading Cholera Epidemic

critics' view, disease was rooted in inferior genetic background, overindulgence, degenerate

Causes of disease

lifestyle, poor hygiene, and irresponsibility. Only self-help could solve the problem, they argued.

Other commentators and some doctors theorized that disease spread through contagion—that people caught diseases from one another. This theory had more to do with magic, belief in the devil, or a desire to keep the ill out of sight than any notion of modern germ theory. It seemed to explain sexually transmitted diseases like syphilis but could not answer the question of why some people contracted various diseases while others did not. In these commentators' minds, quarantine offered the best solution to fighting contagious diseases.

Most doctors eventually concluded that disease stemmed less from personal contact than from environmental forces. They believed in miasma, the centuries-old notion that people caught diseases by breathing fumes given off by human waste, rotting vegetables, decaying flesh, marshes, or stagnant ponds. They also blamed poor diets for weakening resistance to these sources of disease. In a widely respected 1840 study, the French physician Louis Villermé attributed the prevalence of disease in the working-class slums of Lille to the cellars and crowded rooms where "the air is never renewed," where "everywhere are piles of garbage, of ashes, of debris from vegetables picked up from the streets, of rotten straw," where "one is exhausted in these hovels by a stale, nauseating, . . . odor of filth, odor of garbage." This helped him and others explain why people living in barracks, workhouses, and the worst parts of cities more often fell ill and died.

Seeking Medical Care

None of these theories about disease aided individuals seeking medical care. Doctors may have been well-meaning, but in 1850, anyone visiting a doctor was more likely to be hurt than helped. Most people con-

Doctors

sulted physicians reluctantly and had little trust in the power of treatments or medicine. To our twentieth-century sensibilities, medicine in the early 1800s can indeed seem quite alarming. To alleviate a fever, for example, doctors often turned to traditional cures such as initiating bloodletting by opening a vein or applying leeches to the skin, or they recommended laxatives to purge the bad humors and fluids from the body. Physicians routinely prescribed pills that at best did nothing and more likely contained toxic substances such as mercury. Frequently, the addictive drug laudanum was suggested for the treatment of pain, sleeping problems, difficulties with children, and a variety of other complaints. Such treatments more often led to fluid depletion, poisoning, and addiction than any improvement of the patient's condition.

More benignly, doctors might recommend fresh-air cures or taking the waters at health spas. Many of the wealthy traveled to coastal resorts and centers in Caldas da Rainha in Portugal, Bath in England, and Baden-Baden in Germany for these health cures. They may have gained some temporary relief from conditions such as arthritis, but they more likely

FIGURE 17.10 Caroline Naudet, *Journey of a Dying Man to the Other World,* 1820 In this grim scene, doctors lead a dying man, a death-dealing surgeon, a sinister apothecary, and an undertaker. A harsh commentary on patients' fate under the care of early-nineteenth-century doctors, the work captures popular attitudes toward physicians.

enjoyed the lively social events and casinos that also attracted them to these spas.

Figure 17.10, an 1820 print by the French artist Caroline Naudet (1775–1839), reveals popular attitudes toward physicians. Titled *Journey of a Dying Man to the Other World,* the print depicts a wealthy doctor in black robes leading a procession that includes a dying man, a clergyman pointing up, a surgeon with a fluttering bat over his head, a sinister-looking apothecary carrying an enema device, and an undertaker. The solemn physician carries a banner that describes the traditional treatment for diseases: "To give a clyster [enema], after that to bleed, finally to purge."

Many sufferers looked for treatments opposed by ordinary doctors to cure their ailments. Homeopathy, which emphasized the use of herbal | **Alternative medicine** | drugs and natural remedies, gained in popularity during the period. Other options—from vegetable laxatives, claimed to be effective for all ills, to faith healers—saw wide use. These alternatives at least gave sufferers a sense of controlling their own health.

As for surgery, people turned to this option only as a last resort. Surgical methods became safer in the first half of the nineteenth century, but | **Surgery** | anesthesia and antiseptics still lay in the future. Those who managed to survive the pain of an operation faced a likelihood of dying from an infection afterward.

Promising Developments for Public Health

Despite all the dangers, the period had a few bright spots for the future of public health. Improvements in diet probably held the most promise. Many nutritious foods had become more available than ever, especially potatoes, which were an affordable, rich source of vitamin C and minerals; dairy products, which helped newborns survive infancy and childhood; and meat, which contained high-grade proteins. Inexpensive cotton underwear, thanks to the new cotton mills, kept people warmer and cleaner than before. The smallpox vaccine, developed during the eighteenth century and made into a safe form in 1796 by Edward Jenner in England, would virtually erase a disease that had once afflicted almost 80 percent of Europeans and killed millions. The discovery of anesthetics—nitrous oxide and, after 1846, ether and chloroform—began to make surgical trauma bearable.

Other developments showed some potential as well. Following the lead of a small group of influential French physicians, European doctors applied scientific methods to medicine and made great strides in pathology and physiology. Hospitals proliferated and increasingly became | **New developments in medicine** | places to observe the sick and gather information. New laboratories allowed doctors to conduct more experiments. Professional organizations and educational institutions for doctors and nurses formed, and governments, particularly in France, began taking some responsibility for medical education and licensing.

Many doctors no longer relied solely on a patient's description of the problem. Physical examinations became common—feeling the pulse, sounding the chest, taking the blood pressure, looking down the throat. Some doctors used the new stethoscope, which became a crucial tool for diagnosing bronchitis, pneumonia, and pulmonary tuberculosis (commonly called consumption). Among the upper classes, the family physician was even gaining some favor as a respected social contact and confidant.

In England, Edwin Chadwick (1800–1890) initiated a campaign to improve public health. In his 1842 report for a parliamentary commission, *The Sanitary Condition of the Laboring Population of Britain,* he emphasized that the accumulation of human and animal waste near people's dwellings was a crucial cause of disease. He proposed a system of underground tunnels that would allow constantly running water to carry waste out of the city.

Nevertheless, the gains from these promising new developments would not come until the second half of the nineteenth century. In Britain, one of every three people still died of contagious diseases in the decades surrounding 1850. Health, therefore, remained a great public and private concern. It was not the only concern that crossed the lines between public and private life, however. The day-to-day events in everybody's lives, whether in illness or health, unfolded within a crucial setting: the family. In this period of industrialization and urbanization, the family as an institution and the roles within it began to shift in the face of enormous economic and social pressures.

FAMILY IDEALS AND REALITIES

The ways that people come together into families and the roles they play in their families usually evolve slowly, if at all. During this period, however, the middle class redefined accepted notions of the family, and working-class families struggled under the new pressures beleaguering them. In subtle but important ways, family ideals and realities were changing.

Middle-Class Ideals: Affection, Children, and Privacy

With their numbers, wealth, and status in urban societies rising, the middle class not only developed its own ideas about what the proper family should be but also propagated those ideas as the norm for everyone else. The result was an evolution of, rather than a break from, old notions about the family. Compared with families of earlier times, the ideal middle-class family emphasized emotional bonds, attention to children, and privacy.

People were supposed to marry because of affection, love, and emotional compatibility. Social rank and wealth remained important, but 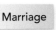 these values exerted less influence than they had in the past. Love could bridge social and economic gaps. Indeed, one of the great themes in the flood of new novels that appeared during the nineteenth century centered on this very conflict: the tension between love and money in marriage. In stories that ended happily, love won out—though most characters in these plots never were relegated to a life of poverty as a consequence of their choice.

The new middle-class family was smaller and more child centered than before. Europeans were choosing to limit the size of their families, and by mid-century this preference led to declining rates of population growth. Women gave birth to fewer children—two or three rather than the five or six of an earlier era—and more infants than ever survived the first, riskiest years of life. Unlike workers and peasants, middle-class parents did not have to view their children as economic assets—as hands to work the fields, help with the crafts, or labor in the factories. Wealthier urban parents could afford to raise perhaps just two or three children as fulfilling products of a good home. More than ever, children came to be seen as innocent, impressionable, vulnerable persons who should be separated from the corrupting influences of adult society. Mothers and fathers began investing more time, effort, and other resources in child rearing. Boys, especially, needed training and education designed to ensure their success as adults in the changing urban world. To arm them with these essentials, parents extended the time period of childhood and economic dependence. All this required planning and intensified emotional ties between parents and children. Parents increasingly centered their attention and family activities on children.

More than ever, mothers and fathers idealized their home as a private "haven in a heartless world," separate from and above the world of paid work. The home represented the reward for competing on the job—a protected, glorified place for a satisfying personal life. There husband and wife could enjoy the delights of material possessions and, hopefully, the rewarding intimacy of family life. As indicated by the growing number of popular books by authors such as Jane Austen (1775–1817), Mary Ann Evans (1819–1880) (writing under the pen name George Eliot), and Charlotte Brontë (1816–1855), home was a setting of many appealing, moralizing dramas where the virtues of prudence, love, sacrifice, self-reliance, and persistence could usually overcome all obstacles.

Separate Spheres: Changing Roles for Middle-Class Women and Men

With the rise of industrialization and urban life, the roles of middle-class husbands and wives grew more and more separate. In the seventeenth and eighteenth centuries, most middle-class families had worked together as one economic unit—sharing the responsibilities of running a shop or business and living near their place of work in back rooms, upstairs, or next door. During the nineteenth century, the tasks assigned to men and women, and the private world of home and the public place of paid work, became increasingly distinct. As the locus of work shifted from the home to the factory, store, or office, women lost their traditional employments that contributed to

FIGURE 17.11 Carolus Duran, *The Merrymakers*
Children became the center of domestic life for middle-class families of the industrial age.

the family economy. Paid employees working outside the home now occupied the role previously played by women who had run thriving family businesses. The new economic growth also allowed middle-class families to afford the homes, servants, and leisure previously reserved for the elite. Eventually, the ability of middle-class women to devote more time to their homes and families without having to do paid work, and to hire servants to lighten domestic burdens, became symbols of social success. The home became women's sphere, and within the home, child rearing began requiring far more maternal attention than ever. As the task of raising children and socializing them with the values and training needed for success expanded, so did the responsibilities of motherhood. Becoming "rational mothers," fully able to meet the new demands of child rearing, turned into a revered duty.

The man was supposed to be the respected economic provider who operated primarily in his sphere: The man's sphere the competitive world of work outside the home. He was expected to behave in an authoritative, competent, and controlled manner. These qualities reflected the legal and economic realities of the time. Under British common law and the Napoleonic Code on the Continent, for example, a man had legal authority over his wife and children. He also had control over his wife's personal property as well as over any money earned by her. Furthermore, only men could vote. Most positions in the middle-class world of work were reserved for men. Those jobs usually required specialized skills in planning and information managing—abilities that came primarily from formal schooling. Young men were more likely than women to receive a formal education in areas of study such as accounting or law. Through apprenticeships and clerkships in commerce, industry, or finance, men also found many opportunities to equip themselves for success in the growing industrial-urban economy.

Women faced a very different set of cultural expectations. A host of marriage manuals, medical tracts, advice books, and religious dictates reminded women that their place was within the domestic sphere. A The woman's domestic sphere woman should provide emotional support for her husband and cultivate a virtuous home environment to counteract the amoral, competitive marketplace. She should care for the children, make sure the house was clean and the meals served, supervise domestic servants (a requirement for any middle-class home), and manage other domestic tasks, from sewing to administering household accounts.

In the mid-nineteenth-century painting shown in **Figure 17.11,** Carolus Duran depicts two middle-class women at home. The center of the women's attention, and the painting, is a playful child sitting on her mother's lap and reaching for a pet bird or figurine. Across the table from the two well-dressed women, a maid or house servant leans toward the child with a folded paper figurine, perhaps in mock play with the bird. On the lower right are more petlike figurines. Indeed, middle-class families often considered pets as much a part of domestic life as the food and drink on the table.

In some ways, a middle-class woman's domestic sphere extended outside the home. She might manage the family's social life, for example, or lead in religious matters. If she had the time and means, she might also participate in philanthropic activities, social movements such as temperance or the abolition of slavery, and certain cultural events—but only as long as these activities added to her image as virtuous, dutiful, maternal, supportive, and sensitive. These activities put women in a position of power as representatives of the family in religious, social, and cultural matters and often gave them the last word on such matters within the family.

Involvement in politics was out of the question for most women. A few middle-class women joined movements to gain political and legal rights, but their efforts did not lead to real reforms during this period. Nor did paid work fit the domestic image. Although a woman might serve without wages as a clerk or secretary in her husband's store or office, paid work outside the home was considered inappropriate and generally not available to married women. Even for unmarried women, only occupations directly connected to the domestic role, such as governess, elementary school teacher, lady's companion, or seller of women's clothing, were deemed acceptable. There were exceptions, especially in cultural fields such as painting and writing, but most people raised a skeptical, disapproving eyebrow at women who had such careers.

At home, a wife was expected to be the counterpart to her controlled, strong husband. "In every thing . . . that women attempt, they should show their consciousness of dependence" on men, explained Elizabeth Poole Sandford in her widely read book, *Woman in Her Social and Domestic Character* (1842). Law hindered most married women from acquiring economic independence and generally placed them, as well as children, under the formal power and protection of men. Women were to be emotional and even frail, and therefore capable of only domestic tasks. The training of young women reinforced these qualities. Instead of a secondary schooling or professional education, women's formal training focused on religion, music, and perhaps languages. Any other skills a young woman might need, she picked up at home.

Educators and scientists generally agreed that women were ill suited for occupations outside the home and that they lacked the emotional control, mental acuity, and assertiveness of men. Doctors usually held the same views, and even believed that menstruation incapacitated women and that women had no interest in sex. Clothing, too, emphasized this vision of women's proper role. Middle-class husbands wore prudent and practical clothing for the world of work—trousers and jackets in modest black or gray. Their wives endured tight corsets and full decorative skirts more suited for display than action.

In short, the middle-class ideal was a small, private family bonded by love and authority. In such a family, the wife and husband willingly fulfilled the expected roles of their separate spheres. Families measured their success in achieving this ideal by the luxury items they bought, collected, and self-consciously displayed; by the accomplishments of their children; by how well their lives matched the uplifting dramas that the novels and paintings of the day depicted; and by their participation in appropriate social, religious, and philanthropic activities.

Middle-class success is well illustrated by the economic and social rise of wealthy commercial and industrial families such as the Cadburys (see Biography on pages 572–573). The 1824 drawing by E. Wall Cousins in **Figure 17.12** shows the still-modest Cadbury shops on Bull Street in Birmingham. To the right is Richard's original dry-goods (linens) store; to the left, his son John's tea and coffee shop. The plate-glass windows and the dress of people on the street indicate the store's intention to appeal to middle-class and wealthy clients. Above are the family's apartments, which include plants and pets. When the business expanded, the Cadburys moved away from this store to a suburban house, with separate nursery and schoolrooms for the children. The idea of separate rooms for children, and for eating, cooking, reading, and socializing, was new and reflected the growing wealth of the middle class and how the idea of differentiation—separate areas for

| Middle-class success |

different tasks and the division of labor—already spreading in the industrial world affected the domestic sphere as well.

Working-Class Realities

The middle class assumed that its vision of the proper family served as the standard for all. However, this vision did not fit the urban and industrial realities facing the far more numerous working classes.

Industrialization pulled many working-class women away from their homes and into factory jobs. Employers preferred to hire women because they worked for lower salaries and seemed more pliable than men. In the early decades, young children often accompanied their mothers, providing even cheaper labor and falling victim to the harsh, disciplined factory environment. During the 1830s and 1840s, public outcry against child labor (led by middle-class reformers, not the working class) prompted women to leave their younger children at home in the care of an older child or neglectful "babyfarmers," women who took in far too many children. Many mothers resorted to drugging their children with laudanum to keep them out of harm's way while the adults were at work.

| Women workers |

Middle-class critics demanded reforms that would limit women's ability to work away from home, although working-class women objected that they had no better alternatives. As one group of women factory workers from Manchester pointed out, "Hand loom has been almost totally superseded by power loom weaving, and no inconsiderable number of females, who must depend on their own exertions, . . . have been forced . . . into the manufactories, from their total inability to earn a livelihood at home." During recessions, women's plight worsened. Employers laid off the more highly paid men first, leaving women with the overwhelming burden of managing both a paid job and all the domestic tasks at home.

Working-class and peasant families were being pulled apart in other ways as well. Adolescent boys left home to seek work in the mines or cities. Daughters, too, sought jobs as factory laborers or as domestics in middle- or upper-class homes. In the cities, women were all the more vulnerable during economic downturns when low-paying jobs disappeared.

Prostitution

Hard times left unmarried and married women alike in particularly desperate straits. To survive, some women turned to prostitution, which grew along with Europe's mushrooming cities. In 1850, there were probably some 30,000 prostitutes in Paris and 50,000 in London. Unemployment and the dangers of solitude were probably the main forces driving women

BIOGRAPHY

The Cadburys

A Rising Middle-Class Family

By the late eighteenth century, the Cadburys were a well-established Quaker family of shopkeepers in western England. Young Richard Tapper Cadbury used his father's connections to find positions as an apprentice and journeyman to drapers (selling retail cloth and dry goods) in Gloucester and London. In 1794, his father helped him again, giving him money to start his own cloth and dry goods store on a main street in Birmingham, one of Britain's leading industrial cities.

In 1800, Richard, his wife, Elizabeth, and their growing family moved into an apartment above their shop on Bull Street. Middle-class families such as the Cadburys typically lived in the same building as their business until they could afford to buy a separate home. Elizabeth Cadbury, like most middle-class women of moderate means, worked in the family enterprise but had received no professional training. She picked up skills on the job, helping rather than leading, and taking over for her husband when he was away. As a married woman, Elizabeth had no independent legal identity and could not have owned a business on her own. Formally, their family business belonged to Richard, but like many businesses during the period, it also functioned as an informal partnership between the couple. In addition to working in the business, Elizabeth was also responsible for running the household, which included eight children and young apprentices.

Draper retailers such as the Cadbury family played a major role in the revolution of Britain's textile industries. Like producers, retailers benefited from the new sources of supply and expanding demand for cloth. The Cadbury shop expanded and brought in enough income for Richard and Elizabeth to rent a house and land for a garden on the outskirts of Birmingham in 1812. The younger children, their nurse, and their pets moved there. Elizabeth and her older daughters traveled back and forth, managing the two households.

Richard and Elizabeth's sons eventually apprenticed in retail businesses in different cities—Benjamin as a draper, John as a tea and coffee dealer. The daughters had no such training. Instead, they learned what they could from their mother as they helped in the shop, house, and garden.

John (1801–1889) opened a tea and coffee store next door to his parents' shop (see **Figure 17.12**). He and his first wife, who died in 1828, lived over the shop. When John accumulated enough money, he also opened a plant to manufacture the cocoa and chocolate for which the family name would become so famous. In 1834, John and his second wife, Candia, moved their home away from the city, with its filth and crowds, to a new, planned

---

to prostitution. Many prostitutes had come from outside the cities and had no family to help them. Others were out-of-work domestics, seamstresses in need of income during a slow season, daughters of unemployed workers, or women abandoned after being impregnated by masters or lovers. Low wages also led to prostitution; a woman earned as much money in one night prostituting herself as she could acquire in an entire week of work at the factory.

Many of these women worked as prostitutes for relatively short periods, and only part-time. While the work helped them financially, it also exposed them to venereal disease, which ran rampant during this period. Finally, in some people's minds, prostitution linked working-class women to images of urban crime and immorality. To middle-class moralists, prostitutes embodied unrestrained sexuality and therefore were the ultimate outcasts. However, despite its dangers, prostitution would persist as a sign of the difficulties that many working families faced in Europe's growing cities.

Stress and Survival in the Working Classes

The new tensions swirling through working-class family life had severe consequences for some. Peasant, artisan, and working-class families had worked together as economic units for longer than the middle class had, and industrialization and urbanization corroded this unity. The stresses proved so great that some families broke apart, leaving a growing number of women to work and manage households on their own.

However, the picture was not all bleak. As a rule, the family survived, providing a haven for workers and a home for children. Like peasants' and artisans' families, many working-class families clung to the old putting-out system or the newer piecework system, in which entrepreneurs distributed jobs, such as tailoring or decorating, to workers at their homes. Unions, better wages, and new social policies would ease the burdens on workers in the decades after 1850. In the end, most families adjusted and found ways to meet the many challenges of the industrial age.

middle-class suburb just outside of Birmingham. Candia generally stayed at home, busy with her domestic tasks and gardening, while John rode to town every day to take care of business and political affairs. Candia could not look after the family business as her mother-in-law, Elizabeth, had, for the demands of child rearing had grown and the training necessary for John's more complex business had increased. John's and Candia's spheres were much more distinct than the elder Cadburys' had been.

In 1861, John's sons, Richard and George, took over their father's failing business. They visited a chocolate factory in Holland that was using a new process to transform cocoa beans into cocoa and chocolate. In 1866, they successfully introduced that process into their own factory. This new technique helped them to break the near monopoly that French chocolate products had previously enjoyed in the British market. In the decades that followed, the brothers built Cadbury into a prosperous cocoa and chocolate manufacturing firm. Richard painted the designs for

FIGURE 17.12 E. Wall Cousins, *The Cadbury Shops*, 1824

fancy Cadbury chocolate boxes that idealized children and their innocence, using his own children as models.

In 1879, the brothers moved their firm from industrialized Birmingham to a rural site they called Bournville. There they introduced improved conditions for their workers and a private social security program, reforms well ahead of their time. George, holding firmly to the Quaker

views of his parents and grandparents, had long taught in a Birmingham "adult school" for workingmen. Concluding that poor housing lay at the root of many social evils, he began building high-quality working-class housing that featured gardens. By 1900, that community included 313 houses and served as a model for British "garden cities" and "garden suburbs."

In 1901, George and members of his family acquired the *London Daily News* and other newspapers, which they used to express their Liberal Party views. By this time, Cadbury, which had grown unevenly from the seeds planted by Richard and Elizabeth in 1794, had become a vast, worldwide company.

Connecting People & Society

1. Why did the Cadburys benefit so greatly from the industrial revolution?

2. In what ways did members of the family exhibit typical nineteenth-century middle-class values?

3. In what ways did the roles played by Elizabeth and Candia differ?

LOOKING BACK & MOVING FORWARD

Summary Industrialization meant unprecedented, sustained economic growth, and it soon became a measure of whether people considered a society "modern" or "traditional." Carrying in its wake fundamental changes in literally all aspects of life, industrialization altered the ways people worked, what they could buy, how they lived their lives, and where they stood on the social ladder. Its railroads, dams, bridges, factories, and mines transformed the land, the rivers, and the air. Nations that industrialized left others behind in the competition for wealth. That wealth was all too easily translated into power, leaving traditional agrarian societies in the West vulnerable to their industrialized neighbors.

The new riches pumped out by the machines of industry also propelled the West into an even stronger position to dominate over unindustrialized, non-Western societies throughout the world. Decade after decade, a widening gap of wealth and power opened up between the industrializing regions of the West and nonindustrializing regions of Asia, Africa, and Latin America.

KEY TERMS

industrial revolution, *p. 547*
entrepreneurs, *p. 552*
factory system, *p. 554*
Luddism, *p. 563*

At the same time, the cities grew. There, old ties to traditional communities and beliefs loosened; long-established religions even lost some of their influence. Despite a host of social problems, the cities had a vibrancy and an image of opportunity that continued to attract people. While some people lost when they migrated to the cities, others gained, whether by hard work, luck, or the advantages of birth. Perhaps life in the countryside, with its slower pace and simpler pleasures, simply could not compete with what the city promised.

Through these decades, most families found ways to adapt to new circumstances. Middle-class families responded to their improving positions by developing a compelling new set of ideals about how men and women should behave. Working-class families did their best to hold themselves together in the face of divisive forces; looking to the future, workers began seeing themselves as a new class of people who just might have the power to determine their own fate.

This growing awareness by both classes added to the fundamental changes being wrought by industrialism. Conflict—whether in an intellectual realm, at the work site, in the courts, or on the barricades—would often be the result. These conflicts, along with those stemming from the French Revolution, would profoundly shape social and political life in the West in the decades to come.

REVIEW, ANALYZE, & CONNECT TO TODAY

REVIEW THE PREVIOUS CHAPTER

Chapter 16—"Overturning the Political and Social Order"—examined the revolution that transformed France and whose consequences were felt throughout the West. The chapter also focused on the role Napoleon played during that period and the battles he waged throughout Europe until his final defeat in 1815.

1. Who do you think were the main beneficiaries of the French Revolution and the industrial revolution? Were they the same groups?

2. In what ways might the French Revolution and the industrial revolution be related?

ANALYZE THIS CHAPTER

Chapter 17—"Factories, Cities, and Families in the Industrial Age"—analyzes the industrial revolution and urbanization.

1. How do you explain why Britain industrialized before other European nations and non-Western societies such as China?

2. Compare the consequences of industrialization for the middle class and the working class.

3. In what ways did moving from the countryside to the city change people's lives during this period?

4. Analyze how the family and ideas about women's and men's roles altered within the middle class. In what ways were circumstances different for working-class families?

CONNECT TO TODAY

Think about the economic changes that industrialization brought, as well as the social consequences that followed in its wake.

1. Why might some people living in nonindustrialized countries today fear the prospect that their country might be industrialized—or have regrets when industrialization begins?

2. How might the changes involved in industrialization—such as the shift to factory production, technological advancement, and improved transportation—have influenced the globalization that we are experiencing today?

BEYOND THE CLASSROOM

THE INDUSTRIAL REVOLUTION BEGINS

Allen, Robert C. *The British Industrial Revolution in Global Perspective*. Cambridge: Cambridge University Press, 2009. An analysis of why the industrial revolution originated in Britain and not elsewhere.

Bayly, C.A. *The Birth of the Modern World, 1780–1914: Global Connections and Comparisons*. London: Blackwell, 2004. A highly regarded comparative approach to the period.

Landes, David. *The Wealth and Poverty of Nations*. New York: W.W. Norton, 1999. Connects cultures to economic development in a broad international context.

GLOBAL CONNECTIONS

Pomeranz, Kenneth. *The Great Divergence: China, Europe, and the Making of the Modern World Economy*. Princeton, NJ: Princeton University Press, 2000. A bold comparison of economic development in Europe and Asia.

NEW MARKETS, MACHINES, AND POWER

Deane, Phyllis. *The First Industrial Revolution*, 2nd ed. Cambridge: Cambridge University Press, 1979. A respected account of British industrialization and its consequences.

Landes, David S. *The Unbound Prometheus: Technological Change and Industrial Development in Western Europe from 1750 to the Present*. London: Cambridge University Press, 1969. A classic treatment of technological development in a broad social and economic context.

Mokyr, Joel. *The Lever of Riches: Technological Creativity and Economic Progress*. New York: Oxford University Press, 1992. An attempt to explain why technological creativity occurred in some places and not in others.

INDUSTRIALIZATION SPREADS TO THE CONTINENT

Pollard, Sidney. *Peaceful Conquest: The Industrialization of Europe, 1760–1970*. Oxford: Oxford University Press, 1981. Charts the process of industrialization as it spread from Britain to the European continent.

Stearns, Peter. *The Industrial Revolution in World History*. New York: Westview Press, 1998. A wide-ranging interpretation.

BALANCING THE BENEFITS AND BURDENS OF INDUSTRIALIZATION

Chinn, Carl. *Poverty Amidst Prosperity: The Urban Poor in England, 1834–1914*. Manchester: Manchester University Press, 1995. Focuses on the poverty created by the industrial revolution.

Gray, Robert. *The Factory Question and Industrial England, 1830–1860*. Cambridge: Cambridge University Press, 2002. An examination of the controversy over industrialization.

Thompson, E.P. *The Making of the English Working Class*. New York: Random House, 1966. A remarkable book of sympathy and insight that has been hugely controversial and influential.

LIFE IN THE GROWING CITIES

Lawton, Richard, and Robert Lee, eds. *Urban Population Development in Western Europe from the Late Eighteenth to the Early Twentieth Century*. Liverpool: Liverpool University Press, 1989. Examines urban growth throughout western Europe.

Traugott, Mark, ed. *The French Worker: Autobiographies from the Early Industrial Era*. Berkeley: University of California Press, 1993. Presents a working-class perspective on the effects of industrialization.

PUBLIC HEALTH AND MEDICINE IN THE INDUSTRIAL AGE

Porter, Roy. *A Medical History of Humanity*. New York: W.W. Norton, 1998. A wide-ranging and interesting survey that covers the period well.

FAMILY IDEALS AND REALITIES

Honeyman, Katrina. *Women, Gender and Industrialization in England, 1700–1850*. New York: St. Martin's Press, 2000. Analyzes connections between work and gender roles.

Maynes, Mary Jo. *Taking the Hard Road*. Chapel Hill: University of North Carolina Press, 1995. Examines German and French workers' lives during the industrial revolution.

Tilly, Louise, and Joan Scott. *Women, Work and Family*. New York: Holt, Rinehart and Winston, 1978. A classic study of the family as an economic unit, especially during the first half of the nineteenth century.

ANTON ZIEGLER, *THE BARRICADE IN MICHAELER SQUARE
ON THE NIGHT OF MAY 26TH,* 1848
This painting by the Austrian artist Anton Ziegler depicts the "glory days" of the 1848 revolutions. In the image, men and women of various classes in Vienna guard a revolutionary barricade made of paving stones, timbers, and carts. Behind the barricade, a community of people stands ready to help one another politely in the common effort (notice the man aiding a woman across a wooden footbridge). The atmosphere has an almost festive quality, and nothing in the picture hints at the violence and loss of life that came with this turbulent year.

Coping with Change

Ideology, Politics, and Revolution, 1815–1850

Prince Clemens von Metternich (1773–1859), Austria's conservative and powerful minister of foreign affairs, discussed ideas in candlelit salons as easily as he wielded power in somber cabinet meetings. Like other cosmopolitan aristocrats born into traditional eighteenth-century societies, he spoke French as well as the German of his birthplace. In 1820, five years after the fall of Napoleon, he wrote to his ally Tsar Alexander I (r. 1801–1825) of Russia. "Kings have to calculate the chances of their very existence in the immediate future," he complained. "Passions are let loose and league together to overthrow everything which society respects as the basis of its existence; religion, public morality, laws, customs, rights, and duties, all are attacked, confounded, overthrown, or called to question."

Metternich, Alexander I, and people everywhere were struggling to adjust to the political and social forces unleashed by the French Revolution and Napoleon's domination of Europe. The industrial revolution, wherever it set its roots, spawned another set of problems along with the wealth it created. Together, these waves of change were undermining traditional political, social, and economic orders.

Some, such as Metternich, fought to maintain the old order; others, displaying the "passions" Metternich complained about, fought for all-encompassing reforms. People on all sides turned to ideologies—sets of ideas, attitudes, and beliefs about how the world is and should be—to try to cope with the new realities of Western life in the nineteenth century. One of those realities was the possibility of revolution again raising its unpredictable head. The outcomes of these struggles of ideologies and politics would profoundly shape much of nineteenth-century history.

TIMELINE

Rise of Conservatism, Liberalism, Nationalism, Romanticism, and Socialism

• Revolutions

• Revolutions

Restoration

• Revolutions

French Revolution and Napoleon

Nationalism and Statebuilding

• Congress of Vienna

Industrial Revolution

1810   1815   1820   1825   1830   1835   1840   1845   1850   1855

THE CONGRESS OF VIENNA: A GATHERING OF VICTORS

In the autumn of 1814, the leaders of the powers who had finally vanquished Napoleon gathered to redraw territorial boundaries and fashion a lasting peace. The conference also attracted representatives of every state in Europe, hundreds of dispossessed princes, agents of every interest, and adventurers. Nearly everyone who thought he or she was somebody of importance in high circles attended. The representatives reveled in the glittering gatherings and entertainments. In addition to the public conferences, many private meetings took place—though just how private remains uncertain, for Austrian spies regularly opened letters and searched wastebaskets. Elsewhere, in newspapers from St. Petersburg, Rome, and Paris to London and even Boston, people closely followed the daily events in the beautiful Austrian capital. Something immensely important and exciting seemed to be unfolding there.

The four major victors over Napoleon—Great Britain, Prussia, Russia, and Austria—set peace terms with France around the time of Napoleon's overthrow in April, and these four dominated the congress. The able Lord Castlereagh (1769–1822) represented Great Britain and the experienced Baron Hardenberg (1750–1822) represented Prussia. Russia's tsar, the unsteady Alexander I, headed his own delegation. The elegant, arrogant Metternich led the Austrian delegation and became the most influential figure of the congress.

The victors

Jean-Baptiste Isabey's formal portrait of the principal figures at the Congress of Vienna (**Figure 18.1**) gives a sense of the seriousness of this event and the ideals that the victors represented. From left to right, Austria's polished Metternich stands before a chair, Great Britain's Castlereagh sits with crossed legs, and the elderly Talleyrand (1754–1838) of France rests with his right arm on the table. In a fine but business-like eighteenth-century salon, these powerful men are gathered around a table to participate in the reading and signing of crucial documents. Their clothing marks them as members of the aristocracy: Almost all the men sport gold trim and knee breeches with high stockings; some wear military coats and carry swords reflecting victory in the field over Napoleon. Most display medals symbolizing their achievements and position. Yet these clothes also hint at change: Most of the figures in the painting lack the more elegant clothing and wigs of the eighteenth century. Above the men, as if approving of what they are doing, hangs a symbol of the restoration of the old regime: a portrait of a king draped in regal robes.

As guiding principles in the negotiations, the conferees decided on legitimacy and stability. By *legitimacy* they meant that territories should once more be placed under the control of the old ruling houses of the traditional order. By *stability* they meant establishing and maintaining a balance of power within Europe, with particular focus on restraining France. The main powers agreed that the settlement should apply to all of Europe.

Legitimacy and stability

Yet the conferees proved lenient in their settlement toward France. Thanks to the victors' desire to turn France into an ally rather than a resentful enemy and to Talleyrand's diplomatic skills, France, the original force behind all the turmoil, escaped the proceedings with only light penalties. Having already restored the French throne to the Bourbons, the powers merely reduced France roughly to its 1789 boundaries. Because of Napoleon's 100-day return (see page 542), they also required France to pay an indemnity of 700 million francs, return stolen art treasures, and submit to occupation by allied forces until the indemnity was paid.

To confine France within its frontiers and discourage future French aggression, the powers established strong buffer states along France's borders. As **Map 18.1** shows, Prussia received a sizable block of territory along the Rhine; the Austrian Netherlands (Belgium) and the Dutch Netherlands were unified; Piedmont-Sardinia in northern Italy was enlarged; and the old monarchy was restored in Spain.

Territorial arrangements

Trading among themselves, the four main powers took new territories. Great Britain gained several strategic islands and colonies, all of which boosted its sea power and overseas dominance. Prussia added some areas in central Europe. Russia acquired control over a reduced, nominally independent Poland, thereby edging farther into the heart of central Europe. Russia also took Finland from Sweden, which in turn got Norway at the expense of Napoleon's ally Denmark.

FIGURE 18.1 Jean-Baptiste Isabey, *The Congress of Vienna,* **1815** Isabey's painting shows the main diplomats and governmental officials who negotiated the peace settlement after the Napoleonic Wars and suggests the principles that guided their decisions.

Austria gained Lombardy and Venetia in northern Italy as well as the permanent presidency over the weak German Confederation—the thirty-nine German states that remained after Napoleon's destruction of the Holy Roman Empire.

Although they displayed little concern for the wishes of the peoples being placed under the control of one power or the other, the conferees did produce a settlement that contributed to a century of freedom from Europewide war. Moreover, thanks to the persistent efforts of the British, the powers agreed in principle to abolish the slave trade. They also achieved—at least temporarily—their conservative goals of promoting legitimacy and stability that meant so much to them.

The Concert of Europe: Securing the Vienna Settlement

Metternich and his colleagues, pleased with their handiwork, set up the political machinery for perpetuating the Vienna settlement. Conveniently at hand was the Holy Alliance, conceived by Alexander I to establish and safeguard the principles of Christianity. Russia, Austria, and Prussia—the three bastions of conservatism—formed the nucleus of this alliance. Though Metternich and professional diplomats put little faith in it, the Holy Alliance did symbolize a commitment to preserving the Vienna settlement. Perhaps more important, it suggested a possible willingness to intervene in other countries in support of its conservative principles.

The Holy Alliance

The Quadruple Alliance, also known as the **Concert of Europe,** proved a much more earthly agency for perpetuating the Vienna settlement. Austria, Russia, Prussia, and Great Britain created this military alliance in November 1815 to guarantee the Vienna settlement. The powers agreed to hold periodic meetings to discuss common problems. In 1818, France completed its payment of indemnities and joined the Alliance.

The Concert of Europe

Soon this conservative partnership showed its strength. In 1821 it authorized an Austrian army to put down an insurrection in Naples against King

MAP 18.1

Europe, 1815

This map shows Europe after the Congress of Vienna in 1815.

Explore the Map

1. Compare this map with Map 16.4, on Napoleon's empire. What are the main changes that occurred in these years?

2. Locate the enlarged states—the Netherlands, Prussia, and Piedmont-Sardinia. Why did the Congress of Vienna strengthen these states?

3. Consider the effects of the settlement on the major European powers. Do you think the settlement severely punished France? Explain.

Ferdinand I. The Neapolitan liberal rebels, no match for the Austrian troops, were soon defeated and their leaders executed, imprisoned, or exiled. In 1822 the Alliance, despite Britain's withdrawal, authorized France to intervene against a liberal revolt in Spain. A French army streamed across the Pyrenees and easily crushed the rebellion. That same year, the conservative powers supported Alexander's proposal to send a Russian fleet to help put down the revolt of Spain's Latin American colonies (see Chapter 16).

The great strength of the Alliance, however, remained bound within the European continent. Across the Atlantic Ocean, President Monroe of the United States announced what would come to be called the Monroe Doctrine: The United States would regard any interference on the part of European powers in the affairs of the Western Hemisphere as an "unfriendly act." British support of the doctrine—stemming from Britain's own economic interests in Latin America—killed any further thought of Holy Alliance intervention in the Western Hemisphere, for Great Britain enjoyed unchallenged dominance of the seas.

IDEOLOGIES: HOW THE WORLD SHOULD BE

The principles underlying the settlement at Vienna and the international cooperation to enforce it reflected the deep conservatism of Metternich and many others during these years. Their conservatism was more than just a whim or political mood. Under the impact of the French Revolution and the industrial revolution, the centuries-old aristocratic order and agriculturally based society had started to crumble. Intellectuals in particular tried to grasp these changes by exploring ideologies, or sets of beliefs about the world and how it should be. These ideologies exerted immense power. People wrote, marched, fought, and died for them. Indeed, they fueled many of the struggles that would erupt in the years to come and ultimately would shape our very definition of the modern world.

Conservatism: Restoring the Traditional Order

The changes initiated during the French Revolution and supported by Enlightenment ideas threatened and even terrified conservatives. They wanted desperately to preserve the traditional way of life. **Conservatism** provided the ideas to refute Enlightenment and revolutionary principles and all those who stood behind them. At the heart of conservatism lay a belief in order and hierarchy. The social and political order, conservatives believed, should be based on a hierarchy of authoritative institutions whose legitimacy rested on God and tradition. As conservatives saw it, the revolutionary notion of equality was wrong. The elite were equipped to rule; the rest were not. The most formidable enemy was the bourgeoisie, "this intermediary class" ready to "abandon itself with a blind fury and animosity . . . to all the means which seem proper to assuage its thirst for power," according to Metternich. Conservatives also warned that the idea of individualism promoted by the Enlightenment and favored by the rising middle class would fragment society and lead to anarchy. In the mind of a conservative, all change was suspect. If change did come, it should take the form of slow evolution of social and political institutions.

In 1790, the influential Anglo-Irish writer and statesman Edmund Burke (1729–1797), horrified with the outbreak of the French Revolution, outlined some of the principles of conservatism (see page 524). He argued that the revolutionaries' radical reforms based on abstract reason and notions of equality unraveled hard-won victories against savagery: "[I]t is with infinite caution that any man ought to venture upon pulling down an edifice which has answered . . . for ages the common purposes of society." The monarchy and nobility should be preserved because they, like the church, were established links to an organic past and the best hopes for preserving the order necessary for societies to thrive.

> Burke

The French writers Joseph de Maistre (1753–1821) and Louis de Bonald (1754–1840) represented a later generation of conservative thinkers who proved more rigid and ultraroyalist than Burke. As Document 18.1 suggests, they attacked everything about the French Revolution and Enlightenment as contrary to religion, order, and civilization. De Maistre called the French Revolution an "insurrection against God." Both writers argued that authority rightly rests in the monarchy and the church, both of which derive that authority from God. "When monarchy and Christianity are both attacked, society returns to savagery," declared de Bonald. These conservatives felt that deep down, humans were more wicked than good, more irrational than rational. Only the time-tested traditions and institutions could hold the bad impulses of humans in check. All means, including fear and violence, should be used to roll back the changes from the French revolutionary and Napoleonic periods and return to societies dominated by monarchs, aristocrats, and clergy.

> De Maistre and de Bonald

Not surprisingly, people from these same three groups found conservatism most appealing. Conservatism also attracted many who believed in a Christian view of society, particularly members of the established churches rather than religious minorities. Some even

thinking about
DOCUMENTS

DOCUMENT 18.1

A Conservative Theorist Attacks Political Reform

Many conservatives resented the reforms sparked by the French Revolution. The extremely conservative theorist Joseph de Maistre was no exception. In the following excerpt from his Essay on the Generative Principle of Political Constitutions, *published in Russia in 1810 and then Paris in 1814, de Maistre attacks written constitutions and the reform of political institutions.*

Every thing brings us back to the general rule—*man cannot create a constitution; and no legitimate constitution can be written.* The collection of fundamental laws, which must essentially constitute a civil or religious society, never has been written, and never will be, *a priori.* It is only when society finds itself already constituted, without being able to say how, that it is possible to make known, or explain, in writing, certain special articles; but in almost every case these declarations or explanations are the effect of very great evils, and always cost the people more than they are worth.

. . . Not only does it not belong to man to create institutions, but it does not appear that his power, *unassisted,* extends even to change for the better institutions already established. . . . *Nothing* [says the philosopher, Origen] . . . *can be changed for the better among men, without God.* All men have a consciousness of this truth, without being in a state to explain it to themselves. Hence that instinctive aversion, in every good mind, to innovations. The word *reform,* in itself, and previous to all examinations, will be always suspected by wisdom, and the experience of every age justifies this sort of instinct.

. . . To apply these maxims to a particular case . . . the great question of parliamentary reform, which has agitated minds in England so powerfully, and for so long a time, I still find myself constrained to believe, that this idea is pernicious, and that if the English yield themselves too readily to it, they will have occasion to repent.

SOURCE: Scholars' Facsimiles & Reprints (New York: Delmar, 1977), reprinting of the edition of Joseph de Maistre, *Essay on the Generative Principle of Political Constitutions* (Boston: Little and Brown, 1847).

Analyze the Document

1. On what basis does de Maistre object to written constitutions?

2. Would any political reforms have merit, according to de Maistre?

3. Why might de Maistre be so concerned about "parliamentary reform"?

---

saw the revolutionary and Napoleonic periods as divine retribution for the presumption and evil that had long marred human beings. In the international field, conservatism was epitomized by Metternich's policies, the Holy Alliance, and the Concert of Europe. In domestic policies, this conservatism was characterized by the restoration of power to the traditional monarchs and aristocrats, the renewed influence of Christianity, and the suppression of liberal and nationalistic movements.

| Appeal of conservatism |

However, conservatives faced formidable opponents, even during the early years after the fall of Napoleon. The French Revolution had turned the ideas of liberalism into a powerful, persistent force. The clash between conservatism and liberalism had just begun and would endure into the twentieth century.

Liberalism: Individual Freedom and Political Reform

In contrast to conservatism, **liberalism** drew on the promises of the French Revolution and the Enlightenment. Conservatives sought to maintain traditional society; liberals fought to change it. Liberals wanted a society that promoted individual freedom, or liberty. However, many laws, customs, and conditions of the traditional order stood in their way. Liberals therefore opposed the dominance of politics and society by monarchs, aristocrats, and clergy, and governments' arbitrary interference with individual liberty. To the extent that these elements of the traditional order remained in place, liberals demanded reform and fought resisting conservatives.

From the Enlightenment and the theories of John Locke, liberals adopted ideas about natural laws, natural rights, toleration, and the application of reason to human affairs (see Chapter 14). From political thinkers such as Montesquieu, they took the idea that governmental powers should be separated and restricted by checks and balances. From the French and American revolutions, they drew on the principles of freedom, equality before the law, popular sovereignty, and the sanctity of property.

| Sources of liberalism |

Liberalism reflected the aspirations of the middle class, which was gaining wealth but lacked political and social power in the traditional order. Not surprisingly, then, liberals advocated government limited by written constitutions, the elimination of political and social privileges, and extension of voting rights to men of some property and education (most liberals stopped short of suggesting universal male suffrage or extension of the vote to women.) In addition, liberals desired representative institutions where none existed and an extension of the right to participate in representative institutions that remained the preserve of the aristocratic and wealthy elite. They demanded that governments guarantee the sanctity of property and individual rights, such as freedom of the press, speech, assembly, and religion.

Certain economic policies also had great importance to liberals and reflected the stake that the middle class had in commerce and industry. The Scottish economist Adam Smith (1723–1790) formulated the ideas that guided economic liberalism (see page 469). In *The Wealth of Nations* (1776), Smith argued that economics, like the physical world, had its own natural laws. The most basic economic law was of supply and demand, he explained. When left to operate alone, economic laws, like an "invisible hand," would keep the economy in balance and, in the long run, create the most wealth. According to Smith, self-interest—even greed—was the engine that motivated people to work hard and produce wealth: "It is not from the benevolence of the butcher, the brewer, or the baker that we expect our dinner, but from their regard to their own interest." Governments should therefore follow a policy of laissez-faire (hands-off), limiting their involvement in the economy to little more than maintaining law and order so that an unfettered marketplace could flourish.

Other liberal economic thinkers extended Smith's ideas. The British economist Thomas Malthus (1766–1834) cast gloom on hopes for progress among workers. He argued that population would always increase more than food supplies, resulting in poverty and death by "the whole train of common disease, and epidemics, wars, plague and famine." Malthus concluded that workers themselves were "the cause of their own poverty," because they lacked the moral discipline to avoid sexual activity. The politically influential Englishman David Ricardo (1772–1823) refined Malthus's arguments into the "iron law of wages," explaining that wages would always sink to subsistence levels or below because higher salaries just caused workers to multiply, thereby glutting the labor market and lowering wages. He emphasized that the economy was controlled by objective laws. The lessons for these "classical" liberals (to distinguish them from modern American liberals, who usually favor government programs to regulate certain economic and social affairs) were clear: no intervention in economic matters by government, no tariffs or unions that artificially raise prices or wages, and no restrictions on individual enterprise.

Over time, liberalism evolved and developed several variations. The English philosopher Jeremy Bentham (1748–1832) and his followers advocated a kind of liberalism that became particularly influential in Britain. Known as utilitarianism, it held that all activities and policies should be judged by the standard of usefulness. "Nature has placed mankind under the governance of two sovereign masters, *pain* and *pleasure*," explained Bentham. What was useful, the utilitarians decreed, was what created more pleasure than pain; the best laws and policies were therefore those that promoted "the greatest good for the greatest number" of people. Bentham's utilitarians fought for more governmental intervention in economic and social affairs than other liberals. For example, they supported reforms to protect women and children workers in factories and to improve urban sanitation. Democracy was implicit in utilitarianism, for the best way for the greatest number to maximize their own happiness was for each person to vote. Nevertheless, most liberals during this period actually opposed democracy. They feared the supposedly unruly "masses" and hoped to keep government in the hands of the propertied and well educated. They would not start to embrace democratic reforms until the middle of the nineteenth century. At that time, some of them, such as John Stuart Mill (1806–1873) (see Biography), would also begin arguing for major social programs to protect workers and even the right to vote for women.

As we saw earlier, liberalism appealed especially to the rising middle classes, who were prospering from commerce and industry and wanted political power along with their growing wealth and confidence. Liberals had faith that history was on their side, that liberalism, like progress, was inevitable and that the forces they opposed were of the past. That optimism gave them strength to fight against the conservative forces of tradition and rally to protect their gains.

Nationalism: A Common Identity and National Liberation

Like the liberals, nationalists harbored a spirit of optimism. They, too, were aroused by the French Revolution, for it promoted the idea that sovereignty rested not in a monarch or a church but in the people, and that they, banded together, constituted the nation. **Nationalism** promised to unify nations, liberate subject peoples from foreign rule, create a sense of fraternity among members of a national community, and lead that community to a common destiny. At its core was a feeling of cultural identity among distinct groups of people who shared a common language and traditions and who belonged in a nation-state of their own.

France became an early source of nationalist sentiments. There a sense of membership in the state

BIOGRAPHY

John Stuart Mill & Harriet Taylor
(1806–1873) (1807–1858)

Extraordinary

Victorians

John Stuart Mill and Harriet Taylor were one of the most famous and extraordinary couples of the nineteenth century. Born in 1806, John described his own childhood as "remarkable." His father, the well-known liberal philosopher James Mill (1773–1836), raised John according to the cut-and-dried principles of Jeremy Bentham's utilitarianism. John learned Greek at the age of 3, Latin when he was 7, logic at 12, and economics at 13.

On their daily walks, James encouraged little John to summarize assigned readings for him. He wanted to turn John's mind into a logical machine for radical thought and utilitarian reform.

In 1822, John and several other young men founded the liberal Utilitarian Society. John, like other liberals, had great faith in the power of knowledge and reason to right human errors: "Knowledge has triumphed. It has worked the downfall of much that is mischievous." For the young Mill, utilitarianism was virtually "a religion." In 1823, John took his first job with the East India Company, the vehicle of British rule in India. He would remain with that company for thirty-five years, reading dispatches from the company's agents in India and drafting replies.

In 1826 he suffered a "crisis." Recoiling from his sterile, intellectualized upbringing, John came to doubt the value of his education and ambition, concluding that neither of these qualities led to happiness. He turned to romanticism—a movement that featured the lush music and especially the writings of Wordsworth, Goethe, and other cultural icons of the day. In time, he came to believe that "poetry is higher than logic, and . . . the union of the two is philosophy."

During these same years, 19-year-old Harriet Hardy had married John Taylor, a wealthy partner in a wholesale drug firm. Taylor adored his intellectual wife, who was bolder and more brilliant than he. However, after giving birth to two children, Harriet began to lose interest in John. She increasingly found sex with him an unpleasant imposition and criticized marriage as a sexual contract that was unfair to women.

In 1830 Harriet Taylor and John Stuart Mill met. They became "intimate and confidential friends." Mill was a constant visitor to the Taylor household and a frequent companion to Harriet in London. Although their relationship created a scandal in London society, John Taylor, unwilling to see his wife unhappy, acquiesced in it.

In 1843, Mill published *A System of Logic*, the first of several major works that marked him as one of the leading thinkers of the nineteenth century. In 1851, Harriet published anonymously *The Enfranchisement of Women*, which argued for universal suffrage and more equal companionship between men and women. Mill would go on to publish *On Liberty* (1859), his most famous political work, in which he argued for freedom of thought and warned against the tyranny of the majority. In 1869, he published *The Subjection of Women*, which made him one of the leading feminists of the century. It is fundamentally wrong, he said, for society to "ordain that to be born a girl instead of a boy, any more than to be born black instead of white, or a commoner instead of a nobleman, shall decide the person's position through all life."

Mill was happy to describe most of his works as jointly produced by himself and Harriet. But Mill may have been too generous in his praise of her role.

The French Revolution

became especially important when the Revolution transformed the kingdom into a nation. Popular sovereignty, wider political participation, and the abolition of old provincial boundary lines gave the French a feeling of solidarity among themselves and with the national government. Universal conscription into the revolutionary armies added to feelings of fraternity in a righteous cause and helped make those armies strong. Powerful new symbols, such as the tricolor flag, stood for national unity and willingness to sacrifice for the sake of the nation.

Nationalism also moved people who did not yet share a state. In the German-speaking areas, for example, scholars and intellectuals developed a cultural basis for nationalism. Writers such as Johann Gottfried von Herder (1744–1803) fostered a sense of common national identity arising from German folk culture and oral traditions. Georg Wilhelm Friedrich Hegel (1770–1831) provided philosophical and historical bases for German nationalism and the importance of the national state. Romantics such as Ernst Moritz Arndt (1769–1860) urged Prussians, Austrians, Bavarians, and others with common roots to "be Germans, be one, will to be one by love and loyalty, and no devil will vanquish you." Groups and secret societies such as Young Germany—usually composed of students, intellectuals, and members of the middle class—promoted a sense of national identity and unity.

Cultural nationalism

In Italy, Poland, and elsewhere, nationalists formed similar organizations and intellectuals created interest in national languages and folk culture.

FIGURE 18.2 John Stuart Mill

Just how much she contributed has long been a matter of heated debate. In 1849, two discreet years after John Taylor's death, Mill and Harriet Taylor married. They were proud that their relationship was based on rationality, intellectual companionship, affection, and intimacy, but not sex. They imagined their marriage as a utopian union of equals. It lasted until 1858, when Harriet died.

In the years before his death in 1873, Mill was elected to the House of Commons, where he argued for liberal reforms such as the abolition of capital punishment, feminist reforms such as the extension of suffrage to women, and socialist reforms such as poor relief. **Figure 18.2** shows a caricature drawing of Mill that was published in the widely read journal *Punch* in 1867. Readers could easily recognize the famous liberal intellectual (depicted with an unusually large head). The illustration shows him leading women, who are demanding the right to vote, by pushing aside resisting men with his arm and his logical arguments. He concluded that "the social problem of the future" would center on "how to unite the greatest individual liberty of action with a common ownership in the raw material of the globe."

Thus Harriet and John embodied many nineteenth-century trends. Liberalism, romanticism, and socialism all played a role in their lives. In addition, what brought them together was the middle-class ideal—affection, companionship, the shared life at home. In other ways, however, they did not reflect the times at all. Their views on marriage and relations between men and women, for example, the long triangular relationship with John Taylor, and the intensity of their intellectual collaboration all alarmed many of their contemporaries. Only in the decades to come would these unusual views gain more favor.

Connecting People & Society

1. Why was Mill labeled a leading proponent of liberalism?

2. In what ways might the Mill family and the Cadbury family discussed in Chapter 17 (see Biography, pages 572–573) be compared?

3. In his life, writings, and politics, why is Mill considered a leading feminist of the nineteenth century?

Scholars resurrected and developed languages from previous eras and elevated myths to national histories. Schoolteachers taught these languages and histories to their students and thereby spread a sense of ethnic unity. Nationalists used this growing interest in language and history to proclaim their nation's special mission—for example, of the Czechs to become leaders of the Slavs, or the Italians to lead Europe again as it had during Roman times.

Nationalism promised a new sense of community as the old order with its traditional allegiances declined. 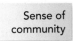 **Sense of community** It offered a sense of strength and unity that appealed to many peoples: to those threatened with foreign domination, such as the Spaniards and Italians under the French during the Napoleonic era; to those dissatisfied with the dominance of one ethnic group, such as Czechs, Magyars, or Serbs under the Germans within the Habsburg Empire; and to those feeling suppressed by what they considered foreign domination, such as the Greeks under the Ottomans, the Poles under the Russians, and the Italians under the Austrians.

From such sources, it was a short step to calls for national liberation and political unification. Nationalism soon acquired attributes of a religion and became a powerful political force. For example, the **National liberation and unification** Italian nationalist Giuseppe Mazzini (1805–1872), who founded the revolutionary Young Italy movement in 1831, called Italy "the purpose, the soul, the consolation of our thoughts, the country chosen of God and oppressed by men." Some nationalist leaders, such as Mazzini, began

Ideologies: How the World Should Be 585

demanding loyalty and solidarity from members of their organizations.

Before 1848, most nationalists supported liberal causes, for liberals also struggled for national rights. Both liberals and nationalists typically believed that sovereignty should rest with the people, united by common loyalties and language. They also had faith that change would bring political, social, and economic progress. Campaigns by liberals to promote agricultural improvement and industrial development often merged into German, Italian, and Hungarian calls for national unity.

Later, nationalists would ally themselves with conservatives, for both believed in the value of historical traditions and in an organic society over the rights of the individual. Nationalism would also become more entwined with notions of national superiority and special national missions that so often appealed to conservatives. All nationalists, however, insisted that each nation of people, unified into a self-governing state, should be the primary focus of political loyalty and that the political boundaries of the state should be the same as ethnic boundaries of the people. The widespread political and emotional appeal of nationalism made it an increasingly powerful ideology over the course of the century.

Romanticism: Freedom, Instinct, and Spontaneity

The origins of nationalism in literature and history also made it attractive to believers in **romanticism.** This ideology became the dominant spirit in literature and art during the first half of the nineteenth century. Its significance stretched beyond culture, however. Romanticism reflected a new recognition that human beings were complex, emotional, and only sometimes rational creatures. In a civilization that was growing ever more scientific, materialistic, industrial, and urban, romanticism became a counterweight for the human experience. It stood against eighteenth-century classicism and the Enlightenment and the ideals of reason and order that so characterized those eras. Instead, romanticism emphasized individual freedom and spontaneity.

The origins of romanticism can be traced back to Jean-Jacques Rousseau, the acclaimed writer and philosopher we met in Chapter 14. Though a central figure of the Enlightenment, Rousseau had stressed feeling, instinct, emotions, and love of nature. He described walking away from the city into the fields and woods, stretching himself out on the ground, digging his fingers and toes into the dirt, kissing the earth, and weeping for joy. In several of his most widely read writings, he seemed to idealize love, childhood, and "the noble savage."

| Rousseau |

Other strands of romanticism came from the German "Storm and Stress" (Sturm und Drang) literature of the late eighteenth century. German writers gave much weight to inner feelings fully experienced and expressed by sensitive individuals. Johann Wolfgang von Goethe provided a model of the emotional individual searching for love and self-understanding in his novel *The Sorrows of the Young Werther* (1774). Like Rousseau, Goethe had many interests. He delved into philosophy, science, and public affairs as well as literature. His masterpiece, the philosophical drama *Faust*, featured a medieval scholar who, dissatisfied with the fruits of knowledge, sells his soul to the devil in return for earthly pleasure and wisdom. In Goethe's medieval interests, his emotional spontaneity, and his love of nature and of individual personality, this renowned writer exemplified the heart of romanticism.

| "Storm and Stress" literature |

All these qualities explored by Rousseau and Goethe came to characterize the work of succeeding romantic writers and artists. Many romantics expressed a new interest in the Middle Ages. They revived the popularity of medieval tales, Gothic architecture, the Knights of the Round Table, and heroic figures, thereby turning the medieval era from the Dark Ages into the Age of Faith.

| Reviving the Middle Ages |

This fascination with the Middle Ages reflected romanticism's passionate concern with the drama of history. Written by scholars such as Thomas Babington Macaulay (1800–1859) in Great Britain, history was literary and exciting, featuring heroic individuals, great accomplishments, and national struggles. These same themes were explored by the Prussian philosopher Hegel. In Hegel's view, history was a great spiritual drama of heroic individuals that would lead to a new sense of national identity and freedom.

| History |

Romanticism also stressed the emotion of Christianity and the mystical presence of God in nature. According to romantic theologians, the important part of religion was the feeling of dependence on an infinite God rather than religious dogma or institutions. In his widely read book *The Genius of Christianity*, the French writer François Auguste-René de Chateaubriand (1768–1848) described in lush words how "every thing in a Gothic church reminds you of the labyrinths of a forest; every thing excites a feeling of religious awe, of mystery, and of the Divinity." In part, religious revivals during the late eighteenth and early nineteenth centuries, with their stress on piety and emotional outpourings, reflected these spiritual qualities of romanticism.

| Christianity |

The connections among the love of nature, the spiritual presence of God, and the power of emotions were most striking in the romantic literature, art, and music of the period. In the literary realm, the English poets William Wordsworth (1770–1850) and Samuel Taylor Coleridge (1772–1834) became closely associated with the beautiful lake country of northwest England—Wordsworth by birth and Coleridge by adoption. Together the two men traveled to Germany, where they fell under the influence of German romanticists. They collaborated on *Lyrical Ballads* (1798), which included Wordsworth's "Lines Composed a Few Miles Above Tintern Abbey" and Coleridge's "Rime of the Ancient Mariner." Both writers glorified nature and sensed a brooding, mystical presence of the divine. Wordsworth saw in nature a higher wisdom than what scholars might offer:

> One impulse from a vernal wood
> May teach you more of man,
> Of moral evil and of good
> Than all the sages can.

Wordsworth's and Coleridge's ardent appreciation of nature, their introspective concern for the individual, and their preoccupation with the spiritual rather than the material made them leaders among Britain's many romantic poets.

In France, Germaine de Staël (1766–1817) led the romantic movement in literature. Although she admired the passionate Rousseau, she attacked most Enlightenment thinkers for not being free enough. She turned to writing in order to grapple with her own emotional experiences with several lovers and to argue for living the passionate life. Often writing about female heroes and genius in works such as *Corinne*, de Staël also looked to history for a vision of another, better world. She and other romantics created an image of the ideal romantic heroine who followed her emotions rather than tradition or reason—a model that some tried to follow in life. Also in France, George Sand (Amandine Dupin Dudevant) (1804–1876) became an extraordinarily creative writer and an unconventional, even threatening woman. Abandoning her tyrannical husband for an independent life in Paris, Sand became an intellectual leader whose private life included several love affairs with well-known people. At her own convenience, she dressed as a man or a woman. Like several other women writers, she also took a male pseudonym to add legitimacy to her writings. Several of her novels explored romantic love and featured strong, intensely emotional heroines.

Leading romantic painters also stressed emotional images. **Figure 18.3,** an oil painting by the German artist Karl Friedrich Schinkel, shows an idealized image of a medieval town at twilight. In the center stands a magnificent Gothic cathedral, its spires stretching toward the heavens above. The parting clouds and setting sun seem to bless this church and town. Below, humble workers bring abundant supplies from the river. They are dwarfed by the cathedral, the central stairs leading up to the cathedral, the high-arching bridge that echoes the arches of the cathedral, their finely built town on the right, and nature above. The painting contains the key elements of romanticism: glorification of nature, religious mysticism, adoration of an idealized medieval era, and expression of emotion.

The romantic love of magnificent landscapes can be found in **Figure 18.4.** This 1817 painting emphasizes the theme of the poet both immersed in nature and conjuring up a majestic natural setting like a god. Here the robed poet with his harp stands on a cliff, his arm stretched out to the swirling heavens above. Below him, waters rage and a knight on a white horse (lower left) gallops off into the distance. In the background stands a medieval castle built into the mountains.

In music, a number of romantic composers followed in the footsteps of Ludwig van Beethoven (1770–1827). The music of this famed German composer overflowed the bounds of classic forms, becoming freer, more individualistic, and more emotional than anything that had come before. Beethoven composed his *Pastoral Symphony* as a musical link to nature. "How happy I am," he wrote in 1810, "to be able to stroll in the woods, among the trees, bushes, wild flowers and rocks. No one can love the country as much as I do." The lyrics to one of his choral works explain his feelings about music:

> When the magic of sound holds sway
> and works bring inspiration,
> glorious things must appear,
> darkness and turmoil become light.

One critic explained that romantic music should "paint to the eyes of the soul the splendors of nature, the delights of contemplation, the character of nations, the tumult of their passions, and the languor of their sufferings. . . ."

The painting by the Austrian artist Josef Danhauser shown in **Figure 18.5** brings together leading figures of romantic art and literature. At the center, the Hungarian virtuoso and composer Franz Liszt plays the piano for his friends. Standing, from left to right, are the French writer Victor Hugo, the Italian violinist Niccolò Paganini, and the composer Antonio Rossini. Sitting are the French writers Alexandre Dumas, George Sand (characteristically in men's clothing), and Daniel Stern (Marie d'Agoult, who had a long-term liaison with Liszt). Above the group are a portrait of Lord Byron and a bust of Beethoven, the deceased "saints" of romantic poetry and music.

FIGURE 18.3

Karl Friedrich Schinkel, *Medieval Town on a River*, 1815

In this 1815 painting, Karl Friedrich Schinkel depicts an imaginary medieval town. A stunning Gothic cathedral, blessed by the setting sun, dominates the people below as well as the scene itself. The town in the background appears well ordered, as do the town's citizens, working calmly and enjoying the fruits of this civilization.

Connecting Art & Society

1. What impression of medieval life do you think the artist intended to convey to viewers?

2. In what ways does this painting represent romanticism?

3. Why do you think Schinkel chose to make the cathedral so prominent?

4. How might the scene in this painting contrast with a realistic urban scene of the nineteenth century?

Through much of romanticism, strands from all the ideologies combined and recombined in a variety of ways. Nationalism, for example, played a prominent role in some romantics' lives. In the 1820s, England's romantic poet Lord Byron (1788–1824) fought for Greek national independence against the Turks (see **Figure 18.7**). Some of Frederic Chopin's (1810–1849) dramatic music

> **Connections to nationalism**

self-consciously evoked nationalistic sentiments for his native Poland, which was still under Russian rule. The Italian Giuseppe Verdi (1813–1901) and the German Richard Wagner (1813–1883), who developed the opera into a fully integrated art form of music, theater, ballet, and special effects, were among many other composers whose works brought together romantic and openly nationalistic themes.

Liberals, too, found comfort in various aspects of romanticism, which helps explain the movement's wide appeal. By breaking sharply with past forms, romanticism attracted liberal and revolutionary spirits. Indeed, many romantic writers and artists sided with liberal causes. Germaine de Staël, for example, in her own life as well as in her novels, histories, and political tracts, fostered romanticism and liberalism in France. Few liberal romantics, however, were more popular than the French writer Victor Hugo (1802–1885), who idealized the masses of underprivileged humanity and preached redemption and purification through suffering.

Connections to liberalism

At the same time, certain dimensions of romanticism appealed to conservatives as well—especially the return to the past, the emphasis on Christianity, and the stand against the rationalism of the Enlightenment. Sir Walter Scott (1771–1832), who in novel and verse glorified the Middle Ages and his native Scotland, was a conservative. So was the French writer François Auguste-René de Chateaubriand, who advocated a return to mystic Catholicism and dreamed of noble Indians in tropical America.

Connections to conservatism

Romanticism found expression in many cultural forms—in the new English gardens that imitated nature rather than confining it to geometric forms, in the image of the artist as a nonconforming genius, in the glorification of walks down wooded lanes, in the popularity of the Grimm fairy tales that evoked images of medieval life, and in the sentimentalization of love in life and literature. In its qualities, its popularity, and its persistence, romanticism proved to be more than a casual change of taste or a mood. It reflected the revolutionary social, political, and intellectual developments of the era.

Early Socialism: Ending Competition and Inequities

Romantics questioned the existing system from cultural and emotional perspectives. **Socialists** questioned it from social and economic perspectives. As socialists saw it, the common people—the workers—were missing out on the astounding power and wealth generated by the industrial revolution. Socialists called for a reordering of society so as to end the competition and class divisions that caused inequalities and suffering. Such calls made the socialists enemies of both the conservative and liberal camps.

During the early decades of the nineteenth century, a few intellectuals—some of whom came to be

FIGURE 18.4 John Martin, *The Bard*, 1817 This vision of a poet immersed in nature in a dramatic medieval landscape exemplifies the romantic impulse in art.

FIGURE 18.5 Josef Danhauser, *Liszt at the Piano*, 1840 This painting, rich with symbolism, brings together images and portraits of leading writers, musicians, and composers of the romantic era.

called Utopian Socialists—contended that society should be based on cooperation rather than competitive individualism and that property should be owned communally. One of the first of these early socialists was the French nobleman Henri de Saint-Simon

(1760–1825). During the French Revolution, Saint-Simon abandoned his noble title. Turning to land speculation, he made and lost a fortune. He and his followers believed that society should be reorganized on the basis of a "religion of humanity," that all people should work, and that the inheritance of private property should be abolished. In Saint-Simon's ideal world, women would be elevated from their inferior social positions. Superior artists, scientists, engineers, and businesspeople would be rewarded according to the formula "from each according to his capacity, to each according to his deserts." Saint-Simon's influential followers became convinced that the best scientists and managers could use their expertise to plan and run prosperous societies for the benefit of everyone.

Utopian Socialists

Saint-Simon

Charles Fourier (1772–1837) was also an early Utopian Socialist who, like Saint-Simon, gathered a following. A Frenchman who had been a traveling salesman, he advocated doing away with economic competition, which he saw as the very source of evil. In his utopian society, agriculture and industry would be carried on by voluntary cooperatives whose members would pool their resources and live in communal apartment houses (*phalansteries*). Housework and child care would be a shared responsibility of the community. Women, like men, would have the right to work and to control their own money. Fourier also considered traditional marriage too restrictive sexually. Work and pleasure would merge as people did as they pleased while still carrying out the tasks their society required to survive. People would be paid according to the labor, capital, and talent that each contributed.

Fourier

In fact, the communities that Fourier's followers established in the United States and Europe rarely lasted for long. Fourier's ideas, however, inspired many people looking for a more joyful, communal alternative to the competitive industrial societies spreading in the West.

Robert Owen (1771–1858) had different ideas. Born in Wales, Owen quickly made an industrial fortune in Manchester and bought large cotton mills in New Lanark, Scotland. Early in the nineteenth century, he set out to make New Lanark a model community. He raised wages, shortened work hours, improved working conditions, abolished child labor, provided educational and recreational facilities for employees, and established sickness and old-age insurance. Productivity in his mills soared, and profits rose. Owen spent years drawing up plans for model socialist communities, which he envisioned as being located in rural settings and as mostly self-sufficient.

Owen

The plans called for community members to raise children together and for women to share in governing. Like Fourier, Owen advocated loosening the bounds of marriage to create greater sexual freedom for women and men. Several such communities were established in America, most notably New Harmony, Indiana. However, all soon succumbed to internal disagreements and economic difficulties. The efforts cost Owen most of his fortune. He retained his fame, especially within the labor movement and among those establishing modest workers' cooperatives. However, he died in 1858 without having created a lasting alternative to the harsh industrial capitalism he deplored.

In the 1830s, several Frenchwomen began linking socialist demands with calls for the emancipation of women. The most famous of these women was Flora Tristan (1801–1844), who was influenced by Fourier's ideas. French law discriminated against women in many ways, including automatically awarding custody of children to fathers after a marital separation. When Tristan's abusive husband was awarded their children, she fought back. Eventually she turned this dispute into a campaign to end discrimination against women within marriage, in the law, and on the job. She traveled throughout Europe and Latin America, speaking passionately for unions and the creation of centers for the care and education of workers. In her *Worker's Union* (1843), she argued that equality between women and men could free the whole working class and transform civilization.

Tristan

These and other early socialists recognized both the significance of the industrial revolution and its possibilities. They attacked the unbridled pursuit of profits in an unregulated, industrial economy. Only a well-organized society, they explained, could eliminate the misery of industrial capitalism and promote happiness. Most also attacked middle-class restrictions on women, emphasized the importance of sensual pleasure, and questioned traditional Christianity. The wave of socialist thought that these leaders unleashed became profoundly influential by the middle decades of the nineteenth century. As it evolved, it took on a more revolutionary quality, and it bore the distinctive stamp of one of the most authoritative thinkers of the nineteenth century: Karl Marx.

"Scientific Socialism": Karl Marx and *The Communist Manifesto*

"A specter is haunting Europe—the specter of Communism," announced Karl Marx (1818–1883) in 1848. "Let the ruling classes tremble at a Communist revolution." Born into a German middle-class family, his father was a Jewish lawyer who had converted to Christianity. A brilliant student, Marx attained his doctorate in philosophy and history, but he was denied an academic position because of his radical views. After embarking on a career in journalism, he was exiled from Germany for his attacks on censorship and his economic views; later, France exiled him because of his revolutionary socialist ideas. He spent the last thirty-four years of his life in London researching, writing, and trying to build organizations to put his ideas into action. Marx collaborated with his friend Friedrich Engels (1820–1895), son of a wealthy German manufacturer, in writing the seminal work *The Communist Manifesto* (1848). This treatise, along with the later *Das Kapital*, contained the fundamentals of what Marx called "scientific socialism."

Marx argued that economic interest, more than anything else, drove human behavior. He also thought that the dominant characteristic of each historical epoch was its prevailing system of economic production—how people made a living. In his view, politics, religion, and culture were all shaped mainly by economic and social realities.

Economic interest

Marx also described how human societies in each historical era became divided into the "haves" and the "have-nots." The haves owned the means of economic production—in nineteenth-century Britain, for example, the industrial capitalists who owned the machines and factories. They also controlled the state and the ideas that dominated their societies. The have-nots were the exploited laborers—for example, Britain's industrial working class. Each side consisted of classes of people with opposing interests. As Marx wrote, "[T]he history of all hitherto existing society is the history of class struggle." At a certain point, economic and social change would bring these class struggles to a revolutionary crisis. The French Revolution, he explained, was an example of one of those conflicts coming to a violent head, as the bourgeoisie (the middle-class capitalists) overcame the aristocracy (the feudal landlords.)

Class struggle

Marx focused much of his analysis on his own industrial society of the nineteenth century. In this society, he explained, the bourgeoisie (capitalists) exploited workers by paying them only subsistence wages rather than compensating them for the true value created by their work. "These labourers, who must sell themselves piecemeal, are a commodity, like every other article of commerce," Marx lamented. At the same time, Marx saw capitalists as locked in a competitive struggle with one another. This contest forced them continually to introduce new, costly machines and build larger factories: "Constant revolutionizing of production, uninterrupted disturbance of all social conditions, ever-lasting

Industrial capitalism

uncertainty and agitation distinguish the bourgeois epoch from all earlier ones." Soon, Marx warned, greater and greater quantities of goods would be produced by a system running out of control. Eventually, the relentless competition and the periodic economic crises that plague industrial societies would thin the ranks of the bourgeoisie. At the same time, the working class would grow stronger as its numbers and consciousness increased. Inevitably, the workers—with "nothing to lose but their chains" and with "a world to win"—would revolt, seize the factories, destroy the capitalist system, abolish private property, and establish a classless socialist society.

Marx only hinted at the general nature of this new socialist society. His writings suggest that the elimination of capitalism would end the division of society into classes of haves (capitalists) and have-nots (workers). The state itself would eventually wither away, for its only purpose was to protect the interests of the haves against the have-nots. Freed from exploitation and the pressures of capitalist competition, all people would lead more varied, cooperative, creative lives—in this sense, free and truly human.

Socialist society

Marx's socialism gained immense appeal. Because he based much of his analysis on evidence and logic, it attracted intellectuals and students. Because his socialism reflected the social and emotional turmoil being produced by the industrial revolution, especially the suffering of the working poor, it spoke convincingly to workers and their leaders. During the second half of the nineteenth century, Marx's socialism would become a major force in the West.

Appeal of socialism

RESTORATION AND REPRESSION

Socialism as well as the other ideologies reflected the political and social realities of their era, particularly the efforts of people to understand and cope with changes that either threatened them or offered promise. In the three decades following 1815, however, socialism played only a limited part in the great struggles for policies and power. During these years, it was the forces representing conservatism, liberalism, and nationalism that instead took center stage.

The struggles for influence and power among believers of these ideologies took place in pamphlets and newspapers, in courts and parliaments, in universities and police barracks, and in streets and fields throughout Europe. In the first years after the defeat of Napoleon, conservatism held sway in international and diplomatic affairs. The Vienna agreements and the cooperative arrangements to repress the threat of revolution in Europe epitomized this ideology. Conservatism also prevailed in domestic politics across most of Europe.

The Return of the Bourbons in France

When the victorious armies of the coalition powers entered France and deposed Napoleon in the spring of 1814, they brought "in their baggage" the members of the Bourbon royal family who had fled the Revolution. In their wake trooped the émigré nobility. The brother of the guillotined Louis XVI was placed on the throne as Louis XVIII (r. 1814–1824). (The son of Louis XVI, who had died in prison without having ruled, was considered Louis XVII.)

Louis XVIII

The "restored" king ruled with an odd mixture of conservatism and moderation. He issued a charter that retained Napoleon's administrative and legal system as well as civil and religious liberties. He also placed lawmaking in the hands of a two-chamber legislature. However, only a small, wealthy elite could vote, and the king kept most of the power.

Nevertheless, Louis XVIII used his authority with moderation, thinking that a mild leadership style would help ensure his hold on the crown and tranquillity in France. Most of the returned émigrés, however, had little appreciation for his relaxed rule—they were more conservative and angry than he was and wanted action. Led by the king's younger brother, the comte d'Artois, these ultraroyalists controlled the legislature. Through the rest of Louis XVIII's reign, they agitated for a return of their privileges and indemnification for their lost lands.

After Louis XVIII's death in 1824, d'Artois was crowned King Charles X (r. 1824–1830); he followed more conservative policies that favored the old aristocracy and the Catholic Church. He offered money to indemnify those who had lost land in the Revolution and gave the church greater control over education. Those policies provoked growing opposition to his rule. When elections increased the size of the opposition, he dissolved the Chamber of Deputies. In the face of still-increasing opposition, he abolished freedom of the press and drastically restricted the right to vote.

Charles X

Reaction and Repression in the German States

The German states in 1815 consisted of thirty-seven little states and two large ones—Prussia and Austria. All belonged to the German Confederation, which lacked an army, a treasury, and even a flag. Austria and Prussia politically dominated the German lands. Both states were firmly conservative, if not reactionary.

In multilingual Austria, the Habsburg emperor and Metternich, the conservative diplomat we met at the beginning of the chapter, held sway. The Austrian leaders had good reason to fear liberalism and nationalism like the plague, for the empire included many ethnic groups—including Hungarians, Czechs, Serbs, and Italians—with their own languages and customs. In the wake of the French Revolution, they began to stir with national consciousness. Metternich used all means—police, spies, censorship, and travel restrictions—to ensure the status quo. The only possible threats to conservative control came from within some of the small states in the weak German Confederation, and Austria enjoyed permanent presidency over that organization.

Metternich

When students and professors formed organizations and staged festivals that supported liberal and nationalistic principles, conservative officials became alarmed. "We want a constitution for the people that fits in with the spirit of the times and with people's own level of enlightenment," explained one student. "[A]bove all, we want Germany to be considered *one* land and the people *one* people."

The murder of a conservative dramatist by a member of a student organization, Karl Sand, gave Metternich his opportunity to strike. After Sand's trial and public execution, Metternich called the princes of the leading German states to Carlsbad and had them draw up a set of harsh decrees outlawing the organizations. He also issued an ominous warning: "The duty of especial watchfulness in this matter should be impressed upon the special agents of the government." The Carlsbad Decrees established strict censorship and supervision of classrooms and libraries. Spies and police terrorized liberal students and professors. Although Sand became a political martyr in the eyes of many young nationalists, the crackdown worked: The small liberal and nationalistic movements evaporated.

Carlsbad Decrees

In Prussia, the conservative, militaristic Hohenzollern kings reigned. Behind them stood the equally conservative landed aristocracy, the Junkers. The Junkers served as officers in the Prussian army and filled the key posts in the civil service and administration. They had no sympathy for any reforms that seemed even faintly liberal or nationalistic, and they reversed many of the changes of the Napoleonic era. However, to better connect its separated territories, Prussia began making commercial treaties with its smaller German neighbors, providing for the free flow of trade among them. By 1834, nearly all the states of the German Confederation except Austria had joined the Prussian-sponsored **Zollverein** (customs union), which would prove of great importance in the march toward national unity.

Prussia

Restoration in Italy

Austria dominated Italy even more completely than Germany. Metternich described Italy as only a "geographical expression." Austria annexed the northern states of Lombardy and Venetia outright. Most other states were ruled by Austrian princes or under Austria's protection and guidance. Piedmont-Sardinia in the northwest was free from Austrian control, but its ruling House of Savoy was no less conservative than Metternich.

In 1815, the deposed aristocracy and clericals trooped back to the Italian states intent on regaining their old positions. They and their Austrian masters soon sent nearly all the Italian intelligentsia to prison or exile. When revolts in Naples, Sicily, and Piedmont flared up in 1820, the forces of order quickly used overwhelming force to put them down.

The Papal States in central Italy were no exception in this period of restoration. Pope Pius VII revived the Inquisition, reconstituted the *Index* of prohibited books, annulled Napoleonic laws of religious toleration, and even did away with French innovations such as street lighting. His successor, Pius VIII, followed equally conservative ideas. In 1829, he condemned almost everything even faintly liberal, including secular education and civil marriage.

Conservatism in Russia

Russia remained a vast agricultural nation with a feudal social structure and a tiny urban bourgeoisie. The Orthodox Christian Church, dominated by an upper clergy drawn from the aristocracy, served as an arm of the government. After fighting against the French, suffering a ravaging invasion in 1812, and playing a major role in Napoleon's defeat, Russia commanded considerable respect and power in Europe. Russia's tsar was the unstable Alexander I—at first a man open to reform, such as granting the Poles a constitution and proclaiming religious toleration, and later more of a reactionary mystic who resumed religious repression. He fell under the influence of Metternich in international affairs and his own aristocratic magnates at home. At his death in 1825, Russia remained a champion of autocracy and conservatism.

His successor, Nicholas I (r. 1825–1855), was an austere autocrat whose military career wedded him to the concepts of discipline and authority. When he assumed the throne in December 1825, a group of his young liberal military officers—hoping to write a constitution and free the serfs—revolted. Nicholas immediately crushed these "Decembrists" and bitterly turned against any hints of liberalism. He followed a policy of demanding submission of everyone to the autocracy and to the Orthodox Church. Although the Decembrists would later gain a reputation as liberal political martyrs, Russia's government now stood as a bastion of conservatism and would remain so for many decades.

Holding the Line in Great Britain

Although Great Britain had for years been a home of representative government, conservatives dominated its government in 1815. Property qualifications so severely restricted the suffrage that only about 5 percent of adult males could vote. The distribution of seats in Parliament was so distorted that a relatively small number of families dominated the House of Commons. Furthermore, the emerging industrial cities of the north were scarcely represented at all. The conservative landed aristocracy and the Tory Party, which had seen the country through the Napoleonic Wars, had a firm grip on power.

Things became even more restricted when an economic depression left thousands of returning veterans jobless. Luddite riots (see page 563) and the specter of revolutionary | Peterloo Massacre | activity prompted the government to take strong measures against the restless workers. The climax came in 1819 when troops charged on a crowd that had assembled in St. Peter's Fields, outside Manchester, to listen to reform speeches. A number were killed and hundreds injured in this Peterloo Massacre.

Figure 18.6, a print by George Cruikshank, shows the troops of the conservative British government breaking up this rally for liberal and radical political reform. On the platform, women and men

FIGURE 18.6 George Cruikshank, *The Peterloo Massacre,* 1819 Cruikshank's print shows Britain's conservative forces violently breaking up a rally for liberal and radical reform.

wave banners demanding universal suffrage, religious freedom, and liberty; a banner is topped with liberty caps, a radical symbol from the French Revolution. This depiction of the violence that erupted at St. Peter's Fields near Manchester seeks to evoke sympathy for the reformers. It portrays merciless troops on horseback striking down and trampling nonresisting women, men, and children. An army officer on horseback repeats orders from a higher authority: "Cut them down." A participant confirmed this depiction: "Women, white-vested maids, and tender youths, were indiscriminately sabred or trampled. . . . In ten minutes from the commencement of the havoc the field was an open and almost deserted space." Parliament would not back down. It soon passed the Six Acts of 1819, which further restricted public meetings and facilitated prosecution of radicals.

The government treated the Irish no less harshly. The Irish had long been ruled and exploited as a conquered people. In the 1801 Act of Union, Britain formally absorbed Ireland into the United Kingdom. In this predominantly Catholic land, the Protestant minority controlled most of the land and political power. The Catholic peasantry suffered from such acute poverty that the threat of famine was not uncommon. Irish nationalists organized to agitate for the right to send elected Catholic representatives to Parliament. In 1829, fearing a civil war in Ireland, the conservative British government reluctantly passed the Catholic Emancipation Act, which allowed Roman Catholics to become members of Parliament.

A WAVE OF REVOLUTION AND REFORM

Despite conservative efforts to maintain order and halt change during the years after 1815, liberal and nationalistic causes simmered just under the surface. The demands for greater political participation and recognition of national identity strengthened and spread. Moreover, Europeans could no longer ignore the changes stemming from early industrialization and urbanization. In some cases, revolts and revolutions broke out. In other cases, people clamored for and gained major reforms.

The Greek War for Independence

A hint of the problems to come occurred during the 1820s, when Greeks mounted a national liberation movement against their Ottoman Turk overlords. The Ottoman Empire still sprawled over vast territories, from the north African coast and southwest Asia to southeastern Europe, but it had been weakened by internal dissension and external threats. By 1815, revolts had enabled Serbia to gain virtual independence, and in Egypt, Mehemet Ali ruled with only nominal subordination to the Ottomans. The Greek revolt began in 1821, which resulted in the death of many defenseless Turks. After the Turks met Greek insurrections with force and atrocities, romantic and liberal idealists formed an international movement to support Greek independence. Britain's well-known romantic poet Lord Byron was one of several who traveled to Greece to contribute to the cause. He brought money and enlisted in a regiment but lost his life to malaria at Missolonghi.

Figure 18.7, by the romantic French artist Eugène Delacroix (1798–1863), captures Greece's struggle for independence. The year is 1826, during the months when the Turks laid siege to the Greek stronghold of Missolonghi and the garrison of 4,000 finally succumbed to 35,000 attackers and the Ottoman fleet. The remaining defenders blew up the city and

FIGURE 18.7 Eugène Delacroix, *Greece Expiring on the Ruins of Missolonghi,* 1827   In this canvas capturing Greece's struggle for independence, a woman symbolizing Greek liberty kneels in the ruins of a Greek city in a plea for help against Turkish overlords.

themselves rather than surrender to the Turks. Greece is represented as a beautiful, defenseless peasant woman and a classical symbol of liberty. Under a dark, foreboding sky, she kneels on what are both the ruins of Missolonghi's city walls and the stone remains of Greek culture in a desperate, mute appeal for aid. But it is already too late for the martyred freedom fighter (perhaps evoking the memory of the fallen Byron), whose arm is thrust forward toward the viewer. Behind the woman, a Turkish soldier strikes a victorious pose. The painting, like the Greek cause in Europe, blends the themes of romanticism, liberalism, and nationalism that so characterized the era.

In the end, intervention by Great Britain, France, and Russia finally secured Greek independence. Although Europeans thought of Greece sympathetically as Christian and as the birthplace of European civilization, these countries' motives had more to do with their own greedy hopes of gains at the expense of the Turks than with genuine support for the Greek revolutionaries. They achieved their objective, but this dramatic chapter in Greek history still revealed the strength of nationalistic movements and the power of liberal and romantic ideals to fuel these movements.

FIGURE 18.8 Horace Vernet, *The Duc d'Orléans Proceeds to the Hôtel de Ville, July 31, 1830*, 1833   In this high-energy scene portraying the July Revolution in France, Louis-Philippe, carrying the hopes of the revolutionaries, rides victoriously to Paris's city hall.

Liberal Triumphs in Western Europe

In 1830, a new series of revolutions tested and sometimes overwhelmed established governments. In France, a struggle arose for liberal reforms against the reactionary King Charles X. Since ascending the throne in 1824, Charles had tried to reverse the moderate policies of his predecessor, Louis XVIII, and return France to the days before the French Revolution. He aligned himself with the most extreme ultraroyalists and the Catholic Church, angering the wealthy bourgeoisie and even the peasantry with his reactionary policies. Support for his regime weakened and he lost control over the Chamber of Deputies, the most representative of France's two-chamber legislature. His efforts to dissolve the Chamber, censor the press, and narrow the electoral laws only stiffened liberal opposition. In July 1830, things came to a head. Liberals in Paris joined with workers outraged by rising food prices. Workers took to the streets of Paris and set up barriers against the king's unenthusiastic troops. Uprisings—fueled by hunger, suspicions of hoarding, and resentment against taxes—spread throughout France. After three days of haphazard fighting, the insurgents gained the upper hand. Charles X, the last Bourbon king of France, fled to Great Britain.

The July Revolution in France

Figure 18.8, a painting by Horace Vernet, reveals how the victors in France's revolution of 1830 interpreted the dramatic events of that year. In the center of the painting, the new constitutional monarch, Louis-Philippe, rides victoriously to the Hôtel de Ville (city hall), the seat of power in Paris. Before him a man carries the French revolutionary tricolor flag, replacing the old Bourbon flag of Charles X. Louis-Philippe's horse picks its way through the paving stones, which the people of Paris had used to construct barricades and hurl at the royal troops. In the foreground, rich and poor walk arm in arm with regular and irregular soldiers in victory; a wealthy man stops to drop alms into a basket for the poor or fallen. Women and men of all classes hail the new king and the revolutionary cause.

While many in France had hoped for a republic to replace the Bourbon monarchy, more conservative liberals took control and created a constitutional "bourgeois monarchy" under Charles X's cousin, Louis-Philippe (r. 1830–1848). Recognizing that a new, more liberal era had dawned in France, Louis-Philippe assumed the role of "citizen king," casting aside the clothes and ornaments of royalty and dressing in the style of his Parisian upper-middle-class supporters. He reduced property qualifications for voting, thereby doubling the electorate (though still only the property-owning elite could vote).

The year 1830 also brought revolutionary trouble in the Belgian provinces of the kingdom of the Netherlands. The union forced on

Revolution in Belgium

Belgium (predominantly Catholic) and the Netherlands (mainly Calvinist) at Vienna had never been a happy one. Although numerically a minority, the Dutch staffed most of the country's political institutions. As one Belgian nationalist put it in 1830, "By what right do two million Dutchmen command four million Belgians?" Desires for national liberation combined with tensions over high food prices to fuel a revolt in August 1830. When the halfhearted efforts of the Dutch government failed to suppress the revolt, Austria and Russia threatened to intervene. Britain and France resisted the intervention and secured Belgian independence. Belgium soon adopted a liberal constitution.

By that time, liberal reformers had also scored successes in Switzerland, making that

Switzerland and Spain

country the first to grant universal male suffrage. In 1834, a new constitution introduced at least the form of liberal institutions to Spain as well.

Testing Authority in Eastern and Southern Europe

As **Map 18.2** shows, revolutionaries also tested regimes in eastern and southern Europe. In November 1830, a Polish nationalistic move-

Poland

ment led by students and army cadets tried to end Russian rule. They managed to establish a provisional government in Warsaw, but conflict within different social groups and among reformers weakened that government. Russian troops soon defeated the revolutionaries. Nicholas sent thousands of Poles to Siberia in chains and began a harsh program of Russification to crush any hint of Polish independence.

In Italy, nationalists began gathering in secret societies called *Carbonari*. (The word means "charcoal burners," suggesting an image of

Italy

common people meeting around charcoal fires.) The Carbonari had long plotted for political freedom and national unification. In 1831, liberal and nationalist revolutions broke out in central Italy, but Austrian forces promptly suppressed them. The movement again went underground but was kept alive under the leadership of the romantic nationalist Giuseppe Mazzini.

Liberal Demands in Great Britain

In Britain, conservatives had to contend not only with demands for liberal reforms but also with pressures rising from early industrialization and urbanization.

Despite the Peterloo Massacre and the restrictive Six Acts, Britain had already shown signs of political flexibility in response to public opinion in the 1820s. By 1822, it had deserted the conservative Concert of Europe. The government repealed laws preventing laborers from organizing unions and removed civil restrictions against nonconforming Protestants and Catholics. Yet these measures, however encouraging to liberals, did not get at the fundamental issue that had raised reform demands for decades: broadening popular participation in the government.

Now the industrial middle class, gaining in wealth and number, added weight to radicals' demands to extend the right to vote and relocate political strength from the

Reform Bill of 1832

countryside to the underrepresented industrial cities. However, the conservative Tories, who controlled Parliament, remained unwilling or unable to effect electoral reform. In 1830, elections brought the more liberal Whigs to power. These Whigs believed that moderate reform rather than reactionary intransigence was the best way to preserve elite institutions from revolutionary change. Worried that the July Revolution in France might spread to Britain, and facing increasing public demonstrations for reform as well as violent acts of protest, the Whigs decided to bend rather than break. They introduced the Reform Bill of 1832, which answered some of the demands. Speaking in favor of the bill, the English historian and politician Thomas Babington Macaulay warned that "now, while the crash of the proudest throne of the Continent [France] is still resounding in our ears . . . now, while the heart of England is still sound," the Reform Bill must be passed. After considerable effort, the Whigs finally enacted the new law.

The Reform Bill did not grant the universal manhood suffrage called for by radicals, but it lowered property qualifications so that most upper-middle-class men (still a small minority) could vote. More important, the bill redistributed electoral districts, taking power away from the "rotten boroughs" (no-longer-important towns and rural areas) and giving it to the underrepresented cities where commercial and industrial elites dominated. The political struggle to pass the bill enabled the House of Commons to gain power over the House of Lords, which had opposed the law. The long era of dominance by the conservative landed aristocracy was ending. More liberal property owners, including the commercial and industrial bourgeoisie, rose to power. From that point on, Britain's leading political groups realigned themselves into the modern Conservative and Liberal parties.

Britain's government soon turned to other reforms. Britain had for several decades led in the antislavery movement, abolishing its own slave trade in 1807 and pushing the Congress of Vienna to declare against the trade in 1815. Europeans, however, often violated principled declarations against slavery and shipped hundreds of thousands more African slaves to the Americas—especially to the Carib-

Antislavery bean and Brazil. In 1833, Parliament bowed to humanitarian radicals and Protestant reformers and abolished slavery in Britain's colonies. Fifteen years later, France would follow suit by abolishing slavery in its colonies, and in 1888, Brazil joined the list, ending slavery in the Americas.

Britain's Parliament and reformers also tried to cope with growing pressures exerted by the industrial revolution. Several new laws

Economic and social reforms aimed to ease some of the disturbing harshness of industrial employment. Between 1833 and 1847, Parliament forbad the employment of women and children in underground mines, prohibited the employment of children under 9 in textile mills, and limited children 9 or older and women to ten hours a day in those factories. Other legislation also reflected the British economy's shift from agriculture to industry. In the name of free trade and lower bread prices, liberals mounted a major attack on the Corn Laws, which imposed tariffs on grain imports. An anti–Corn

Corn Laws Law movement spread throughout the country, accusing the aristocratic landowners who benefited from the Corn Laws of being enemies of the middle and working classes. Victory for the movement came in 1846 with the repeal of the Corn Laws. The repeal reduced the price of bread, but it also opened up the possibility that employers—knowing that workers could afford the cheaper bread—would slash wages.

These liberal principles and reforms, however, only added to the suffering of millions facing the horrible

Irish famine potato famine in Ireland. This mostly rural and impoverished population relied on the potato for food. In 1845, a new, unknown fungus attacked potato plants, ruining the crop. Famine spread as the crops failed year after year. Despite some charitable assistance, Britain's liberal government concluded that the state should not meddle in the economy. More than a million died in Ireland and another million fled overseas while Britain's liberals—often sympathetic and believing that the free market would alleviate the distress—held fast to their principles and did little.

Nor were liberal reforms enough for the hard-pressed urban workers. They were bitterly aware that

Chartism they had been bypassed by the Reform Bill of 1832: "The Reform Act has effected a transfer of power from one domineering faction to another, and left the people as helpless as before," explained one of their leaders. They also complained that Britain's

MAP 18.2

European Revolts, 1820–1831

This map shows the locations of revolts in Europe between 1820 and 1831.

Explore the Map

1. What was the geographic extent of these revolts?

2. What problems might the scope of the uprisings have posed for the efforts of the Concert of Europe to maintain the status quo through international cooperation?

3. Which of these revolts do you think had the most lasting consequences? Why?

unprecedented national prosperity had not benefited workers: "With all these elements of national prosperity, and with every disposition and capacity to take advantage of them, we find ourselves overwhelmed with public and private suffering." In 1838, working-class leaders took action and drew up The People's Charter. The document called for several democratic reforms, including universal male suffrage, election by secret ballot, and the removal of

A Wave of Revolution and Reform   597

property qualifications for office. "We perform the duties of freemen; we must have the privileges of freemen," announced the charter.

The so-called **Chartists** presented their demands twice to Parliament, which summarily rejected them. Nevertheless, the movement persisted within the working class for years. Women aided the cause by raising money and passing petitions for signatures. They also, unsuccessfully, demanded that the charter include provisions for female suffrage. Finally, in April 1848, the Chartists planned a huge demonstration in London to back up their petition. The frightened government and middle classes prepared to use force to control the gathering, as they had several times against strikes and workers' protests. However, when the reforms were refused once more, only a few mild protests arose, and the Chartist movement sputtered out. Nevertheless, Britain's political parties were becoming aware of the growing influence of the working classes and began considering ways to win their favor.

In Britain, then, reforms designed to meet demands for broader representation and manage the social consequences of industrialization and urbanization were under way by the 1840s. Under pressure, Britain's government bent enough to satisfy much of the middle class. The discontented working classes were not yet powerful enough to force their views on the resisting government. Liberalism, the strongest ideology challenging Britain's traditional order, remained a force for reform rather than revolution.

On the Continent, however, nations followed a different path. Throughout western Europe, liberal and nationalistic movements gained stunning successes in these same years. In eastern and southern Europe, these two ideologies also rose and served notice, but, with the exception of Greece, the conservative forces of order beat them down. In 1848, however, the complicated interplay among all these movements finally reached a volatile turning point.

THE DAM BURSTS,
1848

On New Year's Day, 1848, one could look back to 1830 and conclude that the forces that had opened the gates to a wave of revolutions and reforms had since been held under control. In February 1848, everything would change.

Trouble had already been brewing across Europe. In 1846 and 1847, poor harvests had driven up food prices and even brought famine. These disasters, along with financial crises, undermined markets for manufactured goods, created business failures, and left thousands of workers jobless. Governments tried to maintain order, but the growing resentments of liberals, nationalists, and now socialists, who blamed governments for failing to enact overdue reforms, made things even more difficult.

Antigovernment groups had also begun taking on a disturbing complexity and variety. Some protesters wanted only to widen political participation and institute accepted liberal reforms; others demanded full democracy. Several ethnic groups desired national autonomy; workers wanted jobs and rights. Together, the potential opposition to established governments not only loomed large but also cut across class and ideological lines. Intense, shared opposition to the status quo masked any differences these groups might have had. As the pressure of their frustration mounted, the economic crisis threatened to unlock the floodgates.

The "Glory Days"

The dam broke first in France. Louis-Philippe's constitutional monarchy had allied moderate conservatives and moderate liberals into a regime of wealthy property owners. | France |
Presenting itself as the bearer of national patriotism and political caution, the government managed to quiet both conservative and radical opponents during the 1830s. However, beneath the surface of this apparently stable regime, discontent grew. The king and his chief minister during the

KEY DATES

COPING WITH CHANGE

1814–1815	Congress of Vienna
1815	The Quadruple Alliance (Concert of Europe)
1819	Carlsbad Decrees
	Peterloo Massacre
1820	Revolts in Naples, Sicily, and Piedmont
1822	Revolt in Spain
1825	Decembrists revolt in Russia
1829	Greek independence
1830–1831	Revolutions in France, Belgium, Poland, and Italy
1832	British Reform Bill
1833	Britain abolishes slavery in its colonies
1834	Zollverein founded
1838	Chartist movement begins
1846	Repeal of Corn Laws in Britain
1846–1848	Irish famine
1848	*The Communist Manifesto*
	The revolutions of 1848

1840s—the moderately liberal historian François Guizot (1787–1874)—opposed any further extension of the suffrage. Workers, who had not shared in the relative prosperity of the period, clamored for the right to vote and the right to organize unions but got neither. The poor harvests and financial crises in 1846 and 1847 heightened frustration with the regime. In Paris, more than 40 percent of the workforce was without a job. One Parisian radical complained, "While half of the population of Paris dies of starvation, the other half eats for two."

The parliamentary opposition and bourgeois reformers began holding banquets to rally support for widening the right to vote. When a banquet to be held in Paris on February 22 in honor of George Washington's birthday (the United States served as a symbol of democracy in this period) promised to attract thousands of sympathetic workers, the government tried to prohibit the event. Opposition erupted in the Parisian streets. King Louis-Philippe tried to quiet people by dismissing his unpopular prime minister, François Guizot. Long in office, Guizot's response to those not rich enough to have the right to vote was "Get rich, then you can vote." The king's effort at appeasement failed. A shot fired during a brawl between a crowd and troops guarding government houses unnerved the troops, who fired a murderous volley into the mob and set off a full-scale insurrection. Barricades against governmental troops flew up all over Paris, and when the king's citizen militia, the National Guard, began taking the rebels' side, Louis-Philippe followed Guizot into exile.

Figure 18.9 depicts the triumph of the revolutionaries and the already simmering political battles to come. In the center, the well-dressed liberal and romantic poet Alphonse de Lamartine (1790–1869) stands with his arm raised in front of the Paris city hall. He persuades the crowd to keep the tricolor flag to represent the new republic rather than the more radical red flag, carried by a woman in plain dress riding a white horse on the left. On the right, troops and ordinary citizens march under the flag in unity. On the left, citizens bring objects of wealth gathered to support the new republic. At the bottom are the paving stones used in the battle and a fallen victim of the struggle.

Lamartine and a group of bourgeois liberals proclaimed the Second Republic and hastily set up a provisional government. The new ruling body was republican in sentiment, but, tellingly, it had only one prominent radical member: the socialist writer Louis Blanc (1811–1882). The provisional government immediately called for the election by universal male suffrage of an assembly to draw up a new constitution. Yet that government turned down demands for political and economic rights by the new woman's newspaper, *The Voice of Women*, and by women's political clubs. Under pressure from the Paris populace, the provisional government did admit workers to the National Guard, there by giving them access to arms.

Document 18.2 reveals that the government, in response to popular demand for the right to work, also set up national workshops. The workshops—an idea once proposed by Louis Blanc—however, were a parody of Blanc's socialist vision. Blanc lamented that they were deliberately planned so as to ensure failure. In this ill-designed undertaking,

National workshops

FIGURE 18.9 Henri-Félix Emmanuel Philippoteaux, Revolutionary Triumph in Paris This vibrant painting shows the poet and liberal leader Alphonse de Lamartine triumphantly saluting a Parisian crowd in 1848.

DOCUMENTS

France's Provisional Government Issues Decrees

Shortly after the 1848 revolution that ended the July Monarchy in France, the victors established a new provisional government. They issued the following decrees relating to workers on February 25, 1848—the day after creating the provisional government.

The provisional government of the French republic decrees that the Tuileries shall serve hereafter as a home for the veterans of labor.

The provisional government of the French republic pledges itself to guarantee the means of subsistence of the workingman by labor.

It pledges itself to guarantee labor to all citizens.

It recognizes that workingmen ought to enter into associations among themselves in order to enjoy the advantage of their labor. . . .

The provisional government of the French republic decrees that all articles pledged at the pawn shops since the first of February, consisting of linen, garments, or clothes, etc., upon which the loan does not exceed ten francs, shall be given back to those who pledged them.

The provisional government of the republic decrees the immediate establishment of national workshops. The minister of public works is charged with the execution of the present decree.

SOURCE: James Harvey Robinson, ed., *Readings in European History*, vol. II (Boston: Ginn, 1904), pp. 560–561.

Analyze the Document

1. What do these decrees suggest about the possible causes of the 1848 revolution?

2. What might have been the advantages and disadvantages of issuing these decrees?

3. How do you think French businessmen reacted to these decrees?

---

laborers were assigned to hastily arranged projects. When more laborers enrolled than could be used, the surplus workers were paid almost as much as the employed ones to remain idle. To make matters worse, tens of thousands of job-hungry laborers rushed to Paris to join the workshops. The resulting demoralization of labor and the cost to the taxpayers frightened peasant and bourgeois property owners alike. Elections held in April 1848 swept conservative republicans and monarchists back into office.

As **Map 18.3** reveals, the February explosion in Paris set central Europe aflame with revolt. One core of the revolutions settled in Vienna, | Austria | the seat of the Habsburg government. After news of the Paris events arrived in Vienna, Austrian students, middle-class reformers, and workers charged into the streets, clamoring for an end to Metternich's system. There, as elsewhere in the streets of Europe's cities, women joined men in the effort, building the barricades, taking care of the wounded, supplying the fighters with meals, and sometimes taking part in battles against armed forces. The painting on page 599 captures the flavor of this revolutionary activity. As the uprising gained momentum, Metternich fled for his life. The Habsburg emperor, Ferdinand I, hastily abolished the country's most repressive laws, ended serfdom, and promised constitutional reform.

In Hungary, the Magyars, under the leadership of the eloquent Louis Kossuth (1802–1894), rose and demanded national autonomy from Austria. The Czechs followed suit in Bohemia and called for a Pan-Slavic congress to meet at Prague. In Austria's Italian provinces of Lombardy and Venetia, the rebellious populace drove the Austrian forces into defensive fortresses and declared their independence. By June 1848, it appeared | Hungary | that the Habsburg Empire was splintering along ethnic lines and that its German core would commit to liberal reforms.

When the Hohenzollern ruler of Prussia, Frederick William IV (r. 1840–1861), heard of events in Austria, he granted some reforms and promised a liberal constitution. Nevertheless, as Document 18.3 suggests, the | Prussia | news from Paris and Vienna sent middle-class liberals and artisans demonstrating in the streets of Berlin, the capital of Prussia. Frederick William sent in the troops, but their brutality stiffened support for the revolutionary cause. A few days later, he withdrew his troops and promised more reforms and support for German national unity. Hohenzollern Prussia, like Habsburg Austria, appeared on the road to liberal government.

In several other German states, rulers quickly gave in to revolutionary demands. Then a self-appointed group of liberal leaders made a bold move: They called for a popularly | Frankfurt Assembly | elected assembly representing all German states to meet at Frankfurt to construct a liberal German nation. "[A]t last the great opportunity had arrived for giving to the German people the liberty which was their birthright and to the German fatherland its unity and greatness," explained a participant. Three crucial questions confronted the Frankfurt Assembly: (1) whether German-speaking portions of the multilingual Habsburg Empire and other states should be included in the projected German nation, (2) what should be done with non-German ethnic groups living within German states, and (3) who should head the new nation. After almost a year of debate, the assembly decided on a smaller Germany and offered the crown to the king of Prussia.

Meanwhile, in Italy several states established new constitutions. The movement for national unification **Italy** kept alive by the idealist Giuseppe Mazzini found additional strength. He backed up his ideas with action: "Insurrection—by means of guerrilla bands—is the true method of warfare for all nations desirous of emancipating themselves from a foreign yoke," he explained. Just one year after the first revolt broke out in France, popular demonstrations brought down the papal government and forced Pius IX to flee Rome. Mazzini soon gained a foothold as head of the newly formed Republic of Rome.

The Return to Order

For the revolutionaries of 1848, a new, victorious age seemed to have dawned. Within a few months, the old governments almost everywhere had been swept from power or seriously weakened. The upheavals were so widespread that at one point Tsar Nicholas I of Russia exclaimed to Britain's Queen Victoria, "What remains standing in Europe? Great Britain and Russia." Unfortunately for the revolutionaries, however, the forces of order showed resiliency and even new strength when events took more radical turns.

In France, divisions rose among those once unified against the monarchy. The more conservative peasantry and landowners in the coun-**June Days in France** tryside stepped back from the radical reforms demanded by Parisian artisans, shop owners, and intellectuals. The gap also widened between the middle class, which felt that reforms had gone far enough or even too far, and workers, who agitated for more social programs. These divisions reached a boiling point when the Constitutional Assembly, which had been elected in the late spring of 1848, abolished the national workshops. Officials told the workers to join the army or go look for work in the provinces. The desperate men and women of the Paris working class resorted to arms and barricades. For four days, war raged in the streets of Paris between the working class, armed with National Guard rifles, and the regular army. The French liberal writer and politician Alexis de Tocqueville (1805–1859), an observer of the events, described the "June Days" as "the revolt of one whole section of the population against another. Women took part in it as well as men . . . and when at last the time had come to surrender, the women were the last to yield."

thinking about
GEOGRAPHY

Sites of Revolts, 1848–1849

Boundary of German Confederation

MAP 18.3

European Revolts, 1848–1849

This map shows the locations of the 1848–1849 revolutions.

Explore the Map

1. What possible reasons might there have been for the eruption of so many revolutions over this wide geographic area?

2. Compare this map with **Map 18.2.** What do the two maps reveal about the breadth of revolutionary activity between 1820 and 1849 and the challenges faced by the conservative forces of order?

Figure 18.10 depicts the fate of the revolutionary workers of Paris during the June Days of 1848. Here the paving stones used so successfully for the barricades in February 1848 are scattered in the rout of the revolutionaries. The revolutionaries and the radical demands they represent—symbolized by the red, white, and blue of a fallen fighter's clothing—lie crushed by army troops, who this time have willingly fired on the people. The artist, Meissonier (1815–1891), witnessed these defenders "slain, shot down,

DOCUMENT 18.3

German Liberals and Nationalists Rally for Reform

The February 1848 revolution ending Louis-Philippe's regime and establishing a republic in France inspired many others throughout Europe who thirsted for reform. In Germany, liberals and nationalists rallied in hopes of uniting the German states and initiating liberal reforms. In the following selection, the journalist Carl Schurz (1829–1906) describes his participation in those events and the feelings he shared with others.

One morning, toward the end of February, 1848, I sat quietly in my attic-chamber, working hard at my tragedy of "Ulrich von Hutten" [a sixteenth-century German knight], when suddenly a friend rushed breathlessly into the room, exclaiming, "What, you sitting here! Do you not know what has happened?"

"No; what?"

"The French have driven away Louis Philippe and proclaimed the republic."

I threw down my pen—and that was the end of "Ulrich von Hutten." I never touched the manuscript again. We tore down the stairs, into the street, to the market-square, the accustomed meeting-place for all the student societies after their midday dinner. Although it was still forenoon, the market was already crowded with young men talking excitedly. There was

no shouting, no noise, only agitated conversation. What did we want there? This probably no one knew. But since the French had driven away Louis Philippe and proclaimed the republic, something of course must happen here, too. . . . We were dominated by a vague feeling as if a great outbreak of elemental forces had begun, as if an earthquake was impending of which we had felt the first shock, and we instinctively crowded together. . . .

The next morning there were the usual lectures to be attended. But how profitless! At last we closed with a sigh the notebook and went away, impelled by a feeling that now we had something more important to do—to devote ourselves to the affairs of the fatherland. And this we did by seeking as quickly as possible again the company of our friends, in order to discuss what had happened and what was to come. In these conversations, excited as they were, certain ideas and catchwords worked themselves to the surface, which expressed more or less the feelings of the people. Now had arrived in Germany the day for the establishment of "German Unity," and the founding of a great, powerful national German Empire. In the first line the convocation of a national parliament. Then the demands for civil rights and liberties, free speech, free press, the right of

free assembly, equality before the law, a freely elected representation of the people with legislative power, responsibility of ministers, self-government of the communes, the right of the people to carry arms, the formation of a civic guard with elective officers, and so on—in short, that which was called a "constitutional form of government on a broad democratic basis." Republican ideas were at first only sparingly expressed. But the word democracy was soon on all tongues, and many, too, thought it a matter of course that if the princes should try to withhold from the people the rights and liberties demanded, force would take the place of mere petition. Of course, the regeneration of the fatherland must, if possible, be accomplished by peaceable means. . . . Like many of my friends, I was dominated by the feeling that at last the great opportunity had arrived for giving to the German people the liberty which was their birthright and to the German fatherland its unity and greatness, and that it was now the first duty of every German to do and to sacrifice everything for this sacred object.

SOURCE: Carl Schurz, *The Reminiscences of Carl Schurz* (New York: The McClure Co., 1907), vol. 1, pp. 112–113.

Analyze the Document

1. Why did the fall of Louis-Philippe in France have such a strong effect on Schurz?

2. What reforms does Schurz long for?

3. What does Schurz mean by a "constitutional form of government on a broad democratic basis"?

thrown from the windows, covering the ground with their corpses, the earth not yet having drunk up all the blood." Meissonier intended his painting to serve as "a sober warning to the rebels of the future." When the last barricade had fallen during the bloody June Days, some 1,500, mostly workingmen, had perished. Several hundred were sent overseas to French colonial prisons. Louis Blanc fled to Great Britain. The events widened the cleavage between radical urban Paris and conservative rural France—a cleavage that would long complicate France's public life. As a final insult to the revolutionaries, the December presidential elections swept Louis-Napoleon Bonaparte

(1808–1873), nephew of Napoleon Bonaparte, to victory. Promising something for everyone and projecting an image of order and authority, Louis-Napoleon held office for three years and then destroyed the republic in 1851 by taking power for himself in a coup d'état.

In Austria, the revolutionaries' inexperience and the rivalries among various ethnic groups gave the Habsburgs the upper hand. Playing one group against another and using their still-formidable military force, the Austrian rulers beat down the liberal and national revolts one after the other. In Hungary, they had the help of the reactionary

Austria and Hungary

Nicholas I of Russia, whose army overwhelmed the Magyar rebels. In Italy, Austrian might (and in Rome, French arms) eventually prevailed.

In Prussia, Frederick William IV fell under the influence of his militaristic and reactionary Junker advisors.

Prussia

Heartened by the news from Vienna that the Habsburgs had regained their position, he spurned the German crown offered him by the Frankfurt Assembly, contemptuously calling it "a crown from the gutter." His rejection of the crown blasted the Frankfurt Assembly's hopes for a united, liberal Germany. He accused liberals in the Frankfurt Assembly of "fighting the battle of godlessness, perjury, and robbery, and kindling a war against monarchy," and his Prussian troops drove the point home by ousting the few remaining liberals determined to keep the assembly alive.

Figure 18.11 reveals much of what happened in Prussia and elsewhere. The painting by Adolph Menzel shows a funeral that the city of Berlin staged for the fallen on Sunday, March 22, 1848. More than 300 people had lost their lives in the fighting that raged during the early days of the revolution. Caskets are piled in a monumental pyramid. To the left of the church, the black, red, and gold flags of a (hopefully) united Germany flutter outside the optimistic townspeople's houses. To the left, university students, who played a vital role in the revolution, stand at attention. To the right, people energized by the revolution watch the procession, discuss recent events, and read announcements. Groups of the newly armed militia and mourners who supported the revolutionary cause move across the square. Victory once seemed to be in the revolutionaries' grasp. As the only sketched-in figures on the far left suggest, when the revolutionaries suffered reversals a few months later, Menzel lost the heart to finish the painting. His canvas stands as a testament to this "unfinished" revolution.

What Happened?

By 1850, the conservative forces of order had regained control. What happened? How could so many victories by liberals, nationalists, workers, and students be turned into defeats so quickly?

There are several explanations. First, the alliances among middle-class liberals, radicals, socialists, artisans, and workers was one of convenience (based on their shared opposition to the status quo) rather than genuine fellowship. After revolutionary forces gained power, the interests of the various groups proved too divergent for the alliances to endure. These divisions emerged most clearly in France, where the frightened middle class and conservative peasantry broke with the Parisian working classes. Lamartine, a poet and leading politician at the time, explained how the revolutionaries

Internal divisions

FIGURE 18.10 Jean-Louis-Ernest Meissonier, *Memory of Civil War (The Barricade)*, 1849 Revolutionary workers lie mortally wounded in the streets of Paris after the forces of order crushed the uprising in June 1848.

were divided into two groups: the republicans "were inspired by the hatred of royalty," while the socialists "were inspired . . . by the progress of humanity. The republic and equality was the aim of the one; social renovation and fraternity the aim of the other. They had nothing in common but impatience . . . and hope. . . ."

Second, liberal and nationalistic forces worked best together when out of power; in power, they often stood at cross-purposes. This lack of harmony between liberals and nationalists was particularly pronounced in central Europe, where the nationalist aspirations of German, Polish, Magyar, Croatian, Serbian, and other groups conflicted with efforts to form new governments with liberal institutions. For example, liberals in the Frankfurt Assembly who sought to unify Germany turned against other nationalities who rose up against German rule in Austria and Prussia.

Holding power: liberalism vs. nationalism

Third, the strength of conservatism should not be underestimated. With industrialization just beginning to emerge in central Europe, the middle and working classes—both discontented with the conservative status quo—were still weak. Revolutionary leaders were inexperienced as well. In Germany, for example,

FIGURE 18.11 Adolph Menzel, *The March Casualties Lying in State,* 1848 On March 22, 1848, Berliners gathered in a somber funeral procession to honor those who died in the early days of the revolution against the Prussian government.

the journalist Carl Schurz explained the failure of the Frankfurt parliament: "That parliament was laboring under an overabundance of learning and virtue and under a want of . . . political experience."

Conservatism

Finally, once the shock of initial defeat at the hands of revolutionaries had faded, the seasoned leaders of the forces of order marshaled their resources, drew on their own armies and those of allies, and overcame the divided revolutionary forces. After they reestablished control, conservative leaders tore up most of the reforms and imprisoned, executed, or exiled revolutionaries. In December 1848, Pope Pius IX summarized the views of angry conservatives: "We . . . declare null and of no effect, and altogether illegal, every act" of reform during 1848. In fact, a few liberal reforms, such as the abolition of serfdom in Austria and Hungary and the limited constitutions in Piedmont and Prussia, would survive, but the great changes and power that for a few months seemed within the grasp of revolutionaries were gone.

Force

LOOKING BACK & MOVING FORWARD

Summary   In 1815, the conservative forces of order tried to secure their own survival by repressing all those heartened by the principles and reforms of the French Revolution and the Enlightenment. Change became the enemy of conservatives, but the industrial revolution and the growing strength of ideologies such as liberalism, nationalism, and socialism strengthened demands for change.

In the early 1820s, a cycle of revolution and reform timidly emerged. In 1830, revolutionary forces posed a broader challenge, gaining some important victories in western Europe. The cycle returned in full force in 1848, as revolutions broke out through Europe and scored victory after victory. Those victories proved short-lived. By 1850, conservatives were back in power. This quick reversal of fortunes has led many historians to call the revolutions of 1848 "the turning point at which modern history failed to turn."

Yet the revolutions of 1848 left several important legacies. In a few cases, some liberal reforms were retained; in other cases, reforms in modified forms would be passed in succeeding years. Moreover, the overall failure of 1848 did not necessarily ensure a permanent victory for conservatism. As industrialization

KEY TERMS

Concert of Europe,   *p. 579*
conservatism,   *p. 581*
liberalism,   *p. 582*
nationalism,   *p. 583*
romanticism,   *p. 586*
Socialists,   *p. 589*
The Communist Manifesto,   *p. 591*
Zollverein,   *p. 592*
Chartists,   *p. 598*

and urbanization spread year by year, traditional life and the old order it represented kept crumbling. Perhaps most significant, participants and observers had witnessed the power of ideologies, as well as economic and social realities, to galvanize people into political action.

However, the reestablished governments had learned important lessons from 1848, too, and would try to secure their positions with new vigor. They repaired the dam that broke in February 1848. For the time being, at least, everything seemed under control.

REVIEW, ANALYZE, & CONNECT TO TODAY

REVIEW THE PREVIOUS CHAPTERS

Chapter 17—"Factories, Cities, and Families in the Industrial Age"—analyzed the industrial revolution and urbanization. Chapter 16—"Overturning the Political and Social Order"—examined the revolution whose consequences were felt throughout the West.

1. In what ways might the developments described in Chapter 18 be considered a reaction to the French Revolution and industrial revolution discussed in the previous two chapters?

2. What forces stemming from the French Revolution and industrial revolution did conservatives try to repress or contain? To what extent do you think conservatives succeeded?

ANALYZE THIS CHAPTER

Chapter 18—"Coping with Change"—analyzes the struggles between competing ideologies and political forces during the period between Napoleon's fall and the revolutions of 1848.

1. Analyze the ideas of conservatism and policies of the forces of order in the years between 1815 and 1830.

2. In what ways did the ideas and actions of liberals, nationalists, and socialists challenge conservatives between 1815 and 1850?

3. In what ways did romanticism become a new cultural movement and an important ideology?

4. Analyze the commonalities in the several revolutions and movements for reform that developed between 1820 and 1848.

CONNECT TO TODAY

Think about the ideologies and revolutions discussed in this chapter.

1. What struggles in recent times—within Western countries or elsewhere in the world—might be comparable to those that occurred between competing ideologies and political forces in the first half of the nineteenth century?

2. What lessons from the revolutions of 1848 might apply to today's world?

BEYOND THE CLASSROOM

THE CONGRESS OF VIENNA: A GATHERING OF VICTORS

Bridge, F.R. *The Great Powers and the European States System, 1815–1914*. London: Longman, 1980. A thorough diplomatic history of the period.

Chapman, Tim. *Congress of Vienna: Origins, Processes, and Results*. London: Taylor & Francis, 1998. A well-written study that covers the topic well.

IDEOLOGIES: HOW THE WORLD SHOULD BE

Arblaster, Anthony. *The Rise and Decline of Western Liberalism*. Oxford: B. Blackwell, 1984. An analysis of the evolution and key components of liberalism.

Beecher, Jonathan. *Charles Fourier: The Visionary and His World*. Berkeley: University of California Press, 1986. Traces the development of Fourier's ideas through his early years to his emergence as a political prophet and founder of one of the most significant early socialist movements.

Breckman, Warren. *European Romanticism*. London: Bedford/St. Martin's, 2007. A useful, brief history of romanticism, with documents.

Smith, Denis Mack. *Mazzini*. New Haven, CT: Yale University Press, 1999. A biography of this important figure by a well-known historian.

RESTORATION AND REPRESSION

Jardin, André, and André-Jean Tudesq. *Restoration and Reaction, 1815–1848*. Cambridge: Cambridge University Press, 1988. A solid survey of France during this period.

Sheehan, James J. *German History, 1770–1866*. New York: Oxford University Press, 1989. A comprehensive, exhaustive examination of the changes in German social, political, and economic history.

Sked, Alan. *The Decline and Fall of the Habsburg Empire, 1815–1918*. London: Longman, 1989. Studies the growing problems facing the Habsburg Empire during the nineteenth century.

A WAVE OF REVOLUTION AND REFORM

Church, Clive. *Europe in 1830: Revolution and Political Change*. London: Allen & Unwin, 1983. Examines the revolutions that swept across Europe in a comparative context.

Fortescue, William. *Revolution and Counter-Revolution in France, 1815–1852*. London: Blackwell, 2002. A useful survey of the topic and France during this period.

THE DAM BURSTS, 1848

Rapport, Michael. *1848: Year of Revolution*. New York: Basic Books, 2009. A well-written narrative.

Sperber, Jonathan. *The European Revolutions, 1848–1851*, 2nd ed. Cambridge: Cambridge University Press, 2005. A brief yet thorough account that covers the tumultuous events throughout Europe.

ADOLPH MENZEL, *THE DEPARTURE OF WILLIAM I FOR THE ARMY ON JULY 31, 1870*, 1871

This 1871 painting by German artist Adolph Menzel suggests that the inhabitants of Prussia's capital, Berlin, greeted a statebuilding war against France with an outburst of Prussian patriotism and broader German nationalism. Menzel depicts King William I's departure on July 31, 1870, from Berlin to his military headquarters in Mainz to help lead the war against France. On the left, in a white satin-lined coach, the king and his wife pass under cast-iron and glass street lamps along the fashionable tree-lined avenue Unter den Linden. The monarch salutes the crowd, while the tearful queen covers her face with a handkerchief. The crowds are celebrating not only the king but also their own success and anticipated victory. Flags billow in the breeze—both the Prussian and the black, white, and red German flags, signaling a moment of growing national unification. In the distance stands Berlin's new redbrick city hall, evidence of Prussia's growing political and economic power that supports the bold military effort.

Nationalism and Statebuilding

Unifying Nations, 1850–1870

On May 31, 1860, just three weeks after landing in Sicily, the Italian nationalist leader Giuseppe Garibaldi toured Palermo, Sicily's main city. He entered the city at the head of a band of one thousand volunteer soldiers to begin the liberation of southern Italy from the old, Austrian-supported Bourbon king. He called for "Italians" to "put an end, once and for all, to the miseries of so many centuries," and "prove to the world that it is no lie that Roman generations inhabited this land." An eyewitness described how "the popular idol, Garibaldi, in his red flannel shirt, with a loose colored handkerchief round his neck . . . was walking on foot among those cheering, laughing, crying, mad thousands." As he moved through the streets, "the people threw themselves forward to kiss his hands, or, at least, to touch the hem of his garment, as if it contained the panacea for all their past and perhaps coming suffering."

In the decades between 1850 and 1870, millions of others in the Italian states—and in regions ranging from the Americas in the west to the Ottoman Empire in the east—would rally, fight, and die in the name of national unity. In Europe, maps had to be redrawn as new nation-states emerged. In the United States, a wrenching battle was entered into in the name of preserving the Union. Political leaders would use nationalistic appeals to build stronger states as well as to tear apart multinational empires. Nationalism was evolving from the ideals of earlier decades to the realities of power politics.

TIMELINE

Drive for Italian Unification

Drive for German Unification

Second Empire in France

Crimean War 1854–1856

U.S. Civil War 1861–1865

New Imperialism

Age of Ideologies

Spread of Industrial Revolution

• Franco-Prussian War

| 1850 | 1855 | 1860 | 1865 | 1870 |

PREVIEW

BUILDING UNIFIED NATION-STATES

"Every German heart hoped for it," wrote the Baroness Spitzemberg in Berlin in 1871. "United into one Reich, the greatest, the most powerful, the most feared in Europe; great by reason of its physical power, greater still by reason of its education and the intelligence which permeates it!" So the baroness expressed her longing for national unification, a passion felt by many others in the West.

In the two decades after 1850, no political force was stronger than nationalism. It pushed people toward national unity in Italy and Germany and threatened to tear the Habsburg and Ottoman empires apart. In the United States, the principle of national unity helped spark a brutal civil war. In France and elsewhere, rulers enacted major reforms designed to bolster national unity and their authority as leaders of a nation of citizens. All these efforts were intended to build strong, unified nation-states led by central governments that could enjoy the support of their citizens.

> Nationalism

Unlike in 1848, however, the nationalist political figures were neither revolutionaries nor idealists. As one advocate of Italian unification observed, "To defeat cannons and soldiers, cannons and soldiers are needed." From positions of established power, this

> Political realism

new generation of leaders molded nationalism to fit harsh political realities. They focused their eyes on practical policies, not ideals. They gambled, compromised, manipulated, and fought to achieve their goals. Few struggled more persistently and cleverly than Count Camillo di Cavour (1810–1861).

THE DRIVE FOR ITALIAN UNIFICATION

Cavour was born into a well-to-do, noble family living in Piedmont-Sardinia, a small but relatively powerful independent state in northern Italy that also included the island of Sardinia. As a young man, he gambled, played the stock market, experimented with agricultural techniques, and succeeded in business—a pattern of taking calculated risks he would later try to follow in politics. By the 1840s, he had become committed to Italian unification. Shortly before the revolution of 1848, he founded the newspaper *Il Risorgimento* (*The Resurgence*), which passionately argued for a unified Italy. In 1850, Piedmont-Sardinia's King Victor Emmanuel II (r. 1849–1878) made Cavour his minister of commerce and agriculture and, two years later, prime minister.

> Cavour

Cavour's goals were clear. First, he wanted to modernize Piedmont economically and thereby win strength and respect for his homeland. Second, he sought to make Piedmont the central engine of the drive for national unification. Third, he advocated forming a new Italian state as a constitutional monarchy under Piedmont's king rather than a democratic republic or a confederation under the pope. To achieve all these ends, Cavour lowered tariffs, built railroads, and balanced Piedmont's budget. He supported the nationalistic Italian National Society and its Feminine Committee, which worked toward national unification with Piedmont at the helm. Finally, he employed diplomacy and Piedmont's relatively small army to gain international support for the struggle against the primary obstacle to unification—Austria.

> Cavour's leadership

When the Crimean War broke out between Russia and the Ottoman Empire in 1854, Cavour saw an opportunity. He brought Piedmont in on the side of Great Britain and France, countries that had joined the Ottoman Turks against Russia. Cavour hoped to gain the friendship and support of France and Britain and thereby elevate Piedmont-Sardinia's status among the European powers. "I believe that the principal condition for the improvement of Italy's fate," he explained to the Parliament of Piedmont in 1855, "is to lift up her reputation once more . . . to prove that Italy's sons can fight valiantly on battlefields where glory is to be won." Victory in the east, he claimed, "will help the future state of Italy more than all that has been done by those people who hoped to regenerate her by rhetorical speeches and writings."

His risky plan may have paid off. At the Paris Peace Conference in 1856, which ended the war, he pleaded Piedmont's case against Austria so skillfully that he captured the attention of the international community. Two years later, Cavour and France's Emperor Napoleon III met at a French resort to discuss ways to move against Austria, a competitor of France on the Continent and the chief barrier to Cavour's hopes for Italian unity. The two decided to provoke Austria into a war against Piedmont and thereby bring France into the fray. "Together we began to . . . search of those grounds for war which were so difficult to find," explained Cavour in a note to his king. Then "we discovered what we had been trying so hard to find," a way to manipulate Austria into a war that "would not alarm the other continental powers." After Austria declared war, France would help Piedmont drive the Austrians out of Lombardy and Venetia, and these two states would then be annexed to Piedmont-Sardinia. In return, Piedmont would cede the two small, French-speaking provinces of Savoy and Nice to France and allow a kingdom of Central Italy to be created for Napoleon III's cousin.

In 1859, after Cavour mobilized the Piedmontese army and refused an Austrian demand to reverse the act, the unsuspecting Austrians declared war on Piedmont. French armies, using new railroad lines, poured across the Alps to fight alongside the Piedmontese. In the bloody battles of Magenta and Solferino, the French and Piedmontese ousted the Austrians from Lombardy. But to the dismay of Cavour, Napoleon III suddenly made a separate peace at Villafranca with Austria that gave Piedmont Lombardy and left Venetia in Austrian hands. Cavour's side now had momentum, however. Nationalists in other Italian states, inspired by Piedmont's success, rose to the cause of national unity. By early 1860, most of northern and central Italy had joined Piedmont voluntarily.

At this pivotal point in the action, the rawboned nationalist Giuseppe Garibaldi (1807–1882) made a daring exploit. Garibaldi had long struggled to create a unified and republican Italy—organizing people, conducting campaigns of guerrilla warfare, and leading insurrections. Often in exile, he had become a well-known figure in Europe and the Americas. In May 1860, accompanied by a thousand civilian warriors dressed in red shirts, he sailed for Sicily in southern Italy, where many peasants had already launched a revolt. "It is the duty of every Italian to succor them [the Sicilians in revolt] with words, money, arms, and above all, in person," he announced (see Document 19.1). Garibaldi's goal was nothing less than the conquest of the Kingdom of Naples, the largest and most populous of the Italian states, and then Rome itself. Cavour officially condemned the seemingly foolhardy expedition but secretly assisted it.

As **Figure 19.1** suggests, Garibaldi's exploits read like an adventure novel. He heroically lands at the island of Sicily to fight for Italian unification. In the background, his band of volunteer soldiers (the "Red Shirts") pours from three ships and marches in rough formation. Carrying a sword and a flag representing Italian unity, Garibaldi is welcomed by admiring children, women, men, and a priest. In rapid succession, Garibaldi conquered Sicily, crossed the Strait of Messina, and triumphantly entered Naples (see **Map 19.1,** on page 614). The opposing troops had little heart for their own cause. Many, along with civilian women and men by the thousands, joined Garibaldi after his first victories. Made ever bolder by his conquests, the confident Garibaldi advanced north toward Rome.

Not wanting to lose control of the rapidly changing situation and fearing that an attack on Rome by Garibaldi might lead France and Austria to come to the aid of the pope, Cavour sent troops southward in September 1860, gained control over the Papal States, and then skirted the area around Rome. King Victor Emmanuel, marching at the head of his army, met Garibaldi's forces south of Rome. Garibaldi yielded to Victor Emmanuel and his Piedmontese troops. Two years later, Garibaldi, hoping to annex Rome as the capital of Italy, fomented an unsuccessful uprising. The gallant patriot soon retired to his farm on the rocky island of Caprera.

The Kingdom of Italy was formally declared in March 1861, with Victor Emmanuel II as monarch and the Piedmontese Constitution of 1848 as the national charter. The king, along with a parliamentary government elected by limited suffrage, would rule. The red, white, and green Piedmontese flag now flew over all of Italy, from the Alps to Sicily, except in Venetia and Rome (see **Map 19.1**). These two provinces (with the exception of the Vatican palace) joined the Italian state in 1866 and 1870, respectively.

Sadly, Cavour did not live to enjoy the fruits of his labors. Less than three months after the birth of his beloved Italian nation, he died. Paunchy, with ill-fitting glasses, he had never cut an impressive figure. Nor had he made a particularly powerful orator. "I cannot make a speech," he once said, "but I can make Italy."

War with Austria

Garibaldi

Kingdom of Italy

Garibaldi Appeals to Italians for Support

The campaign that resulted in the unification of Italy required not just idealism but also a realistic outlook and daring action. With his political manipulations, Cavour provided the realism. With his invasion of Sicily in 1860, Giuseppe Garibaldi provided the daring action. To support the invasion, Garibaldi issued his Proclamation for the Liberation of Sicily.

Italians!—The Sicilians are fighting against the enemies of Italy, and for Italy. It is the duty of every Italian to succour them with words, money, and arms, and, above all, in person.

The misfortunes of Italy arise from the indifference of one province to the fate of the others.

The redemption of Italy began from the moment that men of the same land ran to help their distressed brothers.

Left to themselves, the brave Sicilians will have to fight, not only the mercenaries of the Bourbon, but also those of Austria and the Priest of Rome.

Let the inhabitants of the free provinces lift their voices in behalf of their struggling brethren, and impel their brave youth to the conflict.

Let the Marches, Umbria, Sabina, Rome, the Neapolitan, rise to divide the forces of our enemies.

Where the cities suffice not for the insurrection, let them send bands of their bravest into the country.

The brave man finds an arm everywhere. Listen not to the voice of cowards, but arm, and let us fight for our brethren, who will fight for us tomorrow.

A band of those who fought with me the country's battles marches with me to the fight. Good and generous,

they will fight for their country to the last drop of their blood, nor ask for other reward than a clear conscience.

"Italy and Victor Emmanuel!" they cried, on passing the Ticino. "Italy and Victor Emmanuel!" shall re-echo in the blazing caves of Mongibello.

At this cry, thundering from the great rock of Italy to the Tarpeian, the rotten Throne of tyranny shall crumble, and, as one man, the brave descendants of Vespro shall rise.

To Arms! Let me put an end, once and for all, to the miseries of so many centuries. Prove to the world that it is no lie that Roman generations inhabited this land.

SOURCE: Public Documents, *The Annual Register*, 1860 (London, 1861), pp. 281–282.

Analyze the Document

1. How does Garibaldi appeal to Italians outside Sicily for support?

2. In what ways does this proclamation echo the appeal of nationalism?

3. Who does Garibaldi identify as his enemies? Why?

GERMANY "BY BLOOD AND IRON"

Like Italy, Germany as we understand it did not exist in 1850, except in the hearts of nationalists. Most of the many German states belonged [Prussian leadership] to the loose Germanic Confederation, but this organization, under the dominance of Austria, did not function as a unified nation. Would someone like Piedmont's Count Cavour rise to overcome the obstacles to German unification? By 1860, no one of this caliber had yet stepped forward.

The best hope for German unity rested with Prussia, which had achieved a position of strength thanks to its economic expansion and leadership over the Zollverein, a German customs union that fostered industrialization in Prussia and the Rhineland (see page 592). By 1853, every German state except Austria had joined the Zollverein. However, Prussia was torn by the political struggle between liberals in the legislature and the conservative aristocracy. The two sides fought over plans to strengthen Prussia's military. When Prussia's new king, William I, and his military advisors proposed to double the size of the

army, the liberals, who distrusted Prussian militarism and hoped to gain a stronger role for the legislature in the Prussian government, defeated the measure. Faced with a deadlock between these uncompromising forces and convinced that his royal authority was being threatened, William I called on Otto von Bismarck (1815–1898).

"I was born and raised as an aristocrat," Bismarck once explained. He would remain loyal to Prussia's landowning aristocracy his whole life. As a young man, Bismarck showed little promise of future greatness. While attending university, he spent more time [Bismarck] gambling than studying. A religious conversion in 1846 and marriage seemed to give him more of a sense of purpose. He entered politics in 1847 and came to believe that only an alliance of conservatism and nationalism could preserve the aristocracy and strengthen Prussia. His enemies were the liberals, who had failed in 1848, and Austria, Prussia's chief competitor and supposed senior partner within the German states.

Bismarck assumed the office of prime minister of Prussia in 1862. With the backing of the king, the aristocracy, and the army, he promptly defied the

FIGURE 19.1

Garibaldi Landing in Sicily

This painting illustrates Giuseppe Garibaldi and his band of soldiers landing in Sicily in May 1860. This event and the campaign that followed it played an important role in the unification of Italy. Notice the spirit and mood captured by the artist.

Connecting Art & Society

1. How has the artist depicted Garibaldi, who stands in the center of the picture, and the "Red Shirt" soldiers behind him?

2. In what ways does this depiction glorify Garibaldi's exploits and the unification movement?

3. How has the artist presented the people surrounding Garibaldi?

liberals in the legislature, violated the constitution, and ordered taxes collected for military reform. "Necessity alone is authoritative," he argued. He would pursue a policy of realism—**Realpolitik**—to achieve his goals. "Not by speeches and majority resolutions," Bismarck rumbled, "are the great questions of the time decided—that was the mistake of 1848 and 1849—but by blood and iron." As the prime minister argued, Germans looked to Prussia for leadership not because of its liberalism but because of its power.

Like Cavour in Italy, Bismarck sought out political opportunities, created them when they failed to materialize, and did not hesitate to take calculated risks, including war. In 1864, Denmark provided his first opportunity when it tried to incorporate Schleswig and Holstein, two small provinces lying between Prussia and Denmark. The provinces' legal status had been disputed for decades. Posing as a defender of German nationalism, Prussia promptly declared war on Denmark, pulling Austria—anxious to retain leadership of the German Confederation—in as Prussia's reluctant ally. In the complicated settlement—Schleswig and Holstein were to be ruled jointly by Prussia and Austria—Bismarck shrewdly planted the seeds for a future conflict with Austria.

> Wars for unification

Bismarck soon used this unworkable arrangement to stir up trouble with Austria. He obtained the

MAP 19.1

The Unification of Italy

This map shows the unification of Italy in the years after 1859.

Explore the Map

1. Locate Lombardy and Nice. Do you think Piedmont gave up too much for what it gained in its bargain for French support? Explain.

2. Find the route of Garibaldi's campaign. Why were Garibaldi's exploits so important—and threatening—to Piedmont's plans to unify Italy?

3. How important were the territories still outside the Italian state in 1860? Explain.

support of Italy by promising Austria's province of Venetia as a prize. He gained Russia's sympathy by supporting its intervention against rebellious subjects in Poland. He neutralized Napoleon III by personal persuasion and deception. Finally, as Document 19.2 suggests, he manipulated domestic politics to achieve his ends. In 1866, Bismarck took a

Austro-Prussian War

risk by using threats and maneuvers to provoke Austria into declaring war on Prussia. Austria was twice the size of Prussia, with double the population, and had long dominated central Europe. Nevertheless, Prussia's modern and mobile armies managed to overwhelm the surprised Austrian forces in just seven weeks. Austria suffered four times as many casualties as Prussia, in great part because of the fast-firing needle-guns used by Prussian troops and the army's use of railroads to move forces quickly to battlefields. Bismarck boldly expelled Austria from the German Confederation and even annexed several German states that had sided with Austria. Nevertheless, hoping for Austrian support in the future, Bismarck refused the desires of Prussia's king and army leaders to annex Austrian territories.

Prussia now controlled the newly created North German Confederation. Despite some democratic

forms, such as a legislative body (the Reichstag) elected by universal male suffrage, the government was fundamentally an **autocracy.** The legislature had no control over the chancellor— appointed by and responsible only to the king or his cabinet—and lit-

Franco-Prussian War

tle control over the budget or armed forces. However, some of the southern German states, with larger Catholic populations than Prussia had, still lay outside Bismarck's grasp (see **Map 19.2**). He wisely recognized that these remaining, reluctant states might join the fold if German nationalism could be rallied against a common, foreign threat. France, Bismarck decided, might just fit the bill.

Bismarck's opportunity to confront France came in 1870 when the Spanish crown was offered to a Hohenzollern prince—a relative of Prussia's William I. When Bismarck persuaded the reluctant prince to accept the Spanish offer, the French immediately

DOCUMENT 19.2

Bismarck Masters Politics in Prussia

Like Cavour in Italy, Otto von Bismarck became a master of both politics and war in his effort to unify Germany under Prussia. Just before Prussia's war with Austria in 1866, Bismarck, despite his conservatism, instituted a constitution that included universal male suffrage. In the following excerpt from his Memoirs, Bismarck describes his support for universal suffrage.

Looking to the necessity, in a fight against an overwhelming foreign Power, of being able, in extreme need, to use even revolutionary means, I had had no hesitation whatever in throwing into the frying-pan, by means of the circular dispatch of June 10, 1866, the most powerful ingredient known at that time to liberty-mongers, namely, universal suffrage, so as to frighten off foreign monarchies from trying to stick a finger into our national omelette. . . .

The acceptance of universal suffrage was a weapon in the war against Austria and other foreign countries, in the war for German Unity, as well as a threat to use the last weapons in a struggle against coalitions. In a war of this sort, when it becomes a matter of life and death, one does not look at the weapons that one seizes, nor the value of what one destroys in using them: one is guided at the moment by no other thought than the issue of the war, and the preservation of one's external independence; the settling of affairs and reparation of the damage has to take place after the peace. Moreover, I still hold that the principle of universal suffrage is a just one, not only in theory but also in practice, provided always that voting be not secret, for secrecy is a quality that is indeed incompatible with the best characteristics of German blood. . . .

The counterpoise to this lies in the influence of the educated classes, which would be greatly strengthened if voting were public, as for the Prussian Diet. It may be that the greater discretion of the more intelligent classes rests on the material basis of the preservation of their possessions. . . . Every great state-commonwealth that loses the prudent and restraining influence of the propertied class, whether that influence rests on material or moral grounds, will always end by being rushed along at a speed which must shatter the coach of state, as happened in the development of the French Revolution.

SOURCE: Otto von Bismarck, *The Memoirs,* trans. A.J. Butler (Howard Fertig, 1890).

Analyze the Document

1. What exactly does Bismarck mean by "universal suffrage"?

2. Why might he support this apparently democratic institution?

3. To what groups of people does he particularly appeal? Why?

---

took alarm at the prospect of being surrounded by Hohenzollerns. The French exerted heavy pressure on Prussia, and both the prince and King William yielded. However, the unsatisfied French ministers demanded more. After a meeting at Ems between the French ambassador and the Prussian king, the chancellor saw an opportunity to provoke the French into war. Cleverly editing the Ems telegraph dispatch so as to make it appear that the French ambassador and the Prussian king had insulted each other, he published it to the world. The French government was offended and walked into Bismarck's trap. Buoyed by public demands for action, France declared war.

The chancellor had taken his greatest risk, for France seemed to possess enough military might and economic resources to humble Prussia. As France's confident prime minister stated, "We go to war with a light heart." Again, however, the able Prussian troops quickly scored resounding successes. One French army was surrounded at the fortress city of Metz. The Prussians encircled another French army at Sedan, forcing it to surrender. Napoleon III himself was one of the captives. When this news reached Paris, the liberals overthrew the government of the Second Empire and declared the Third French Republic. Paris held out for a few more months, surrounded by the Germans, but finally surrendered in January 1871.

On January 18, 1871, Bismarck called the heads of all the German states to Versailles in France. Gathering in the Hall of Mirrors, the dignitaries proclaimed Prussia's King William I emperor of the new German Empire; he would rule until 1888. **Figure 19.2** celebrates that moment. In this well-known painting by Anton von Werner, who witnessed the event, Prussian officers hail William, who stands at the left. But the center of the painting belongs to Bismarck, dressed in white, the architect of this historical moment. He alone holds the document proclaiming the new empire that he, more than anyone else, had built. The dramatic scene is set in France's historic symbol of monarchical power, the Versailles palace. By choosing this location, Bismarck drove home the point that Prussia had achieved German unity by defeating France in war. He also wanted to make it crystal clear that Germany, now in possession of France's rich provinces of Alsace and Lorraine and owed a war indemnity of 5 billion francs in gold from the French, had replaced the humiliated France as Europe's leading continental power.

MAP 19.2

The Unification of Germany

This map shows the steps taken to achieve German unification in 1871.

Explore the Map

1. Notice the changes in 1866 and 1867. How do you explain this expansion of Prussian control?

2. How do you explain Prussia's ability to add more territory to the south and west in 1871?

3. Who might have been most threatened by a powerful Germany after 1871? Why?

The constitution that Bismarck had drafted for the North German Confederation became the constitution for the new German Empire. Its twenty-five states retained control over many domestic matters, but Prussia dominated the union. Known as the Second Reich (Germans honored the old Holy Roman Empire as the First Reich), the powerful nation included a large and rapidly growing population, a vibrant industrial economy, and a feared military. Bismarck, of course, remained chancellor and lived to rule over his creation for the next nineteen years. In Germany, as in Italy, a clever, realistic political leader had employed diplomacy and war to transform the unruly forces of nationalism into German unification.

FIGURE 19.2 Anton von Werner, *Proclamation of the German Empire*, 1885 After defeating France on the battlefield, Bismarck and other dignitaries salute Prussia's King William I, now the emperor of the new German Empire, in this scene celebrating German unification.

THE FIGHT FOR NATIONAL UNITY IN NORTH AMERICA

The struggle for unification flared up in other parts of the West besides Italy and Germany. Between 1800 and 1861, the United States' political institutions had evolved along democratic and nationalistic lines. Almost all white men had gained the right to vote. A modern, broad-based political party system had formed and wrestled political power from the elite circles of the old colonial well-to-do. The nation had expanded westward to the Pacific Ocean, conquering the Amerindians and displacing them to reservations. When Mexico stood in the way of expansion, it also lost its lands to the United States armed forces. Commercial interests led the United States across the Pacific to Japan. Finally, American culture began to free itself from strictly European influence. Citizens proudly thought of themselves and their institutions as having a distinct flavor within Western civilization.

However, as the nineteenth century progressed, the nation labored under growing regional differences. The North was an expanding, urban, industrial society based on free labor. **Figure 19.3,** a lithograph of the Stillman, Allen & Co. Novelty Iron Works of New York City, illustrates one of the many manufacturing facilities growing up in the North's cities in the middle decades of the nineteenth century. The South remained agricultural, dependent on plantation crops such as cotton, and based on slave labor. **Figure 19.4,** a painting by Charles Giroux, portrays this rural society with its large population of slaves. The North enjoyed a growing population and generally favored federal over state power. The South, worried that its influence over national policies was slipping away, emphasized states' rights over federal power. In the decades before 1861, these two regions, with their increasingly different societies and interests, clashed politically on several occasions.

It was the issue of slavery, though, that gave these clashes a dangerous emotional intensity and tied together the other problems dividing the North and the South. By the early 1800s, the northern states had eliminated slavery. However, the institution persisted in the South, where agriculture, and especially cotton plantations, reigned supreme. There, slaveholders viewed slaves as the very basis of their wealth, power, and status. Meanwhile, in the free-labor North, antislavery sentiment grew. "[T]his government cannot endure permanently half slave and half free," declared Abraham Lincoln (1809–1865) in 1858, just two years before the nation elected him president.

In 1861, all these regional differences, fueled by the question of whether to abolish slavery, ignited a bloody war between the North, led by Lincoln, and the South, under Jefferson Davis (1808–1889). The conflict raged for four years until the North finally defeated the Southern armies. Ultimately the war took more than 600,000 lives, making it the bloodiest conflict in the Western world since the end of the Napoleonic Wars. Lincoln had achieved his primary goal: to reestablish national unity and affirm the power of the national government. In the aftermath, slavery was abolished in the United States.

Farther north, a different struggle for national independence and unity had been unfolding in Canada. William Lyon Mackenzie (1795–1861), a nationalist politician, called for Canadians to "put down the villains [the British] who oppress and enslave our country" and gain "freedom from British tribute." Britain responded to a rebellion in 1837 by

FIGURE 19.3 A Northern Factory The smokestacks and busy harbor activity in this print illustrate the U.S. North's industrial might, which played a crucial role in the Civil War.

FIGURE 19.4 Charles Giroux, a Southern Plantation, ca. 1850s The economic strength and social structure of the U.S. South were represented by cotton plantations such as the one immortalized in this painting.

granting Canada some control over its own domestic affairs. Nevertheless, the Canadian territories were not yet joined into a single nation, and Canadians feared the growing power of the United States. Demands for union and complete nationhood increased. Finally, in 1867, the British North American Act united Canada into a single nation with its own constitution.

DIVIDED AUTHORITY IN THE AUSTRIAN AND OTTOMAN EMPIRES

Nationalism pulled Austria's multiethnic empire apart rather than bringing it together (see **Map 19.3**). Czechs, Serbs, Romanians, Magyars

Austria

(Hungarians), and other ethnic groups wanted to form their own, independent nations rather than rally behind Austria, which was predominantly German.

Austria's emperor, Francis Joseph (r. 1848–1916), was no reformer or politician in the mold of Bismarck, Cavour, or Lincoln. Under pressure from liberals and nationalists, he agreed in 1860 to a moderate decen-

tralization of the empire and the creation of a parliament. After Austria's defeat by Prussia in 1866, the dominant German minority in Austria compromised with the assertive Magyars rather than fight them over issues of nationality. Their agreement, the Compromise of 1867, set up the **Dual Monarchy** of Austria-Hungary. Each country had its

Austria-Hungary, 1867

own separate parliament, but the two were united under a common ruler, the head of the House of Habsburg. This arrangement was essentially an alliance between the Germans of Austria and the Magyars of Hungary against other competing ethnic groups. The empire therefore divided authority in an effort to control even more threatening movements for national independence. This arrangement did not please other national groups, especially the Czechs, who would persistently demand equality with the Hungarians.

Like the Austrians, Ottoman rulers also had to struggle with the divisive forces of nationalism. In 1850, at least nominally, the Ottoman Empire was still extensive. From its base in Anatolia, it maintained varying degrees of control

The Ottoman Empire

over much of southeastern Europe, as well as over provinces stretching from North Africa to the Persian Gulf. However, the empire was already in decline. Its North African provinces—Egypt, Libya, Tunisia, and Algeria—were virtually autonomous. Egyptian rulers in particular tried to modernize the army, bureaucracy, and economy using western European models; Mehemet Ali (r. 1805–1848) at one point had become strong enough to threaten Ottoman control in Syria and Anatolia. To the north, powerful, ambitious neighbors—especially the Russians, who attacked the Turks in 1853 and again in 1877—maneuvered to take advantage of the Ottomans' weaknesses: lack of economic development, declining finances, internal dissension, and difficulties instituting reforms. But the greatest threats to the empire's integrity came from its restless Balkan provinces in southeastern Europe. In this area, nationalism rose, producing the same sorts of movements for independence that had weakened the Austrian Empire.

By 1830, the Ottoman Empire had already lost Serbia and Greece to independence movements (see **Map 19.4**). Nationalism had fueled an unsuccessful revolt by the Romanians in 1848 as well. In 1856, the

Balkan nationalism

Romanians gained international support as part of the settlement of the Crimean War. Over the next twenty years, they pressed the Ottomans for their freedom, finally winning full independence in 1878.

Nationalist movements also cropped up among the Bulgars. Encouraged by Serbia and Russia, the Bulgars revolted in 1876. Each side in the conflict

MAP 19.3

Language Groups of Austria-Hungary

This map shows the concentrations of language groups in Austria-Hungary at the end of the nineteenth century.

Explore the Map

1. What does this map reveal about the difficulties facing the Austro-Hungarian Empire in an age of growing nationalism?

2. In what areas was the empire most vulnerable? Why?

3. Notice the surrounding states. What language groups might have found support from outside the empire's borders?

committed atrocities, but those committed by the Turks especially shocked Europeans. That year, Bosnia and Herzegovina also rose against the Turks. Serbia and Russia then joined forces against the Ottoman Empire. By 1878, international agreements, most notably the Treaty of Berlin, had secured the independence of Bulgaria and placed Bosnia and Herzegovina under Austro-Hungarian rule. Movements for national independence, with the aid of powers eager to take advantage of the empire's declining strength, had ended Turkish control throughout most of the Balkans. However, these developments also left a jumble of dissatisfied groups and nationalities—a few who had their own states, some who longed for political independence, and others who did not like being annexed by Austria-Hungary.

USING NATIONALISM IN FRANCE AND RUSSIA

The power of nationalism to motivate people to join revolutionary organizations, form new political allegiances, follow powerful politicians, and go to war in the name of national unity made itself clear in Italy and Germany. Under different conditions, nationalism weakened and dismembered long-established multinational states such as the Austrian and Ottoman empires.

Nationalism also pushed governments in well-established states to reach out to citizens for support. These governments tried to justify and sustain their authority by performing public services, and they bolstered their power by promoting the idea of national greatness. They paid more attention to everyday life

MAP 19.4

The Decline of the Ottoman Empire, 1683–1914

This map shows the loss of territory from the Ottoman Empire between 1683 and 1914.

Explore the Map

1. Who were the Ottomans' main European rivals in this region?

2. What areas in particular were lost during the nineteenth and early twentieth centuries?

3. Why did the growth of nationalism become such a threat to the empire?

Legend:
- Ottoman Empire Boundary in 1683
- Areas Lost 1683–1815
- Areas Lost 1815–1878
- Areas Lost 1878–1912
- Areas of Ottoman Empire Lost in Balkan Wars 1912–1913
- Ottoman Empire in 1914
- Anglo-French Interventions, 1853 and 1854

so as to maintain social peace and cultivate loyalty to the nation—and especially to its leaders. These efforts to channel nationalism into statebuilding are especially well illustrated by the paths that France and Russia took after 1850.

Napoleon III and the Second Empire

In France, Louis-Napoleon Bonaparte, nephew of Napoleon Bonaparte, promised reform while creating a regime based on authoritarian nationalism. Louis-Napoleon was originally elected president of France's Second Republic in 1848 (see page 602). He benefited from his illustrious name, his appeal to property owners longing for order, and his well-publicized promises to link democracy from below with reforming leadership from above. When the National Assembly refused to change the constitution so that he could run for a second term, he organized a coup d'état and seized power on December 2, 1851. Resistance was limited, although hundreds were killed and thousands were arrested and deported. He quickly granted universal male suffrage, and during the following year, he held two plebiscites in which more than 90 percent of the voters supported him, establishing the Second Empire and making him hereditary emperor—Napoleon III. "I believe," he

[Napoleon III]

confidently wrote, "that there are certain men who are born to serve as the means for the march of the human race. . . . I consider myself to be one of these."

Building on his uncle's legend, Napoleon III tried to convince citizens that he would lead the nation to new heights in domestic as well as foreign affairs. Napoleon III kept the elected legislature firmly under his thumb by minimizing its authority over his ministers and manipulating the electoral machinery. When it served his purposes, he encouraged industrialization and economic growth by promoting railroad construction, public works, and financial institutions—policies that appealed to the middle and working classes. His prefect of Paris, Georges Haussmann (1809–1891), rebuilt Paris into an envied model of a modern, wealthy, powerful capital (see Chapter 20). To project a progressive image, Napoleon also directed the building of hospitals, nurseries, and homes for the aged. To gain support from workers, he kept bread prices low, instituted a system of voluntary social insurance, encouraged cooperatives, and partially legalized labor unions.

The French emperor's foreign adventures gained him prestige at first but lost him everything in the end. He brought France into the Crimean War and played the glorious host to the peace conference that ended that conflict. In addition, he tried to increase French influence on the Italian peninsula by joining Piedmont in a war against Austria, but he underestimated the strength of Italian nationalism; that nation unified without becoming beholden to France. In 1862, his armies marched into Mexico City and set up a Habsburg prince, Maximilian, as puppet emperor for France. A few years later, problems at home and a threatening army from the United States forced Napoleon to withdraw his troops, leaving the doomed Maximilian to the mercy of Mexican forces. French artist Edouard Manet (1832–1883) depicts the scene on June 19, 1867 (**Figure 19.5**). In an arena with spectators looking over the brick wall, as if this were a ritual killing at the end of a bullfight, a Mexican firing squad aims and fires at point-blank range, executing Maximilian and two of his generals. However Maximilian did not die immediately; the soldier on the far right is casually reloading his rifle as if anticipating that the emperor would have to be given a final degrading coup de grâce. The soldiers are in uniforms similar to those of the French army to emphasize France's role in this affair. The Mexican fiasco added to the growing unpopularity of Napoleon III with the French people.

Meanwhile, declining prosperity further weakened Napoleon's position within France. Trying to allay the mounting discontent of liberals and workers, he made one concession after another. By 1870, the liberal parliament had begun gaining the upper hand. That year, the ailing and discouraged Napoleon III blundered into a war with Prussia. Defeated and captured, he and his government fell.

Fall of Napoleon III

FIGURE 19.5 Edouard Manet, *The Execution of Emperor Maximilian*, 1868 In this violent scene, Mexican troops execute Maximilian, the emperor set up by France in their failed Mexican adventure during the 1860s.

Alexander II and Russia

Napoleon III had stood for order, reform from above, and national grandeur. Until he faltered, the French gave up their liberal sentiments for those ends. In Russia, Tsar Alexander II made similar appeals in an effort to overcome that country's troubles.

By 1850, Russia had earned a reputation as the most conservative of European powers. Its government remained autocratic under the tsar, its feudalistic society still bound serfs to the land and their lords, and its large army enjoyed an aura of near invincibility. After the Crimean War, it became clear that things would have to change.

Russia's autocracy

In 1853, war broke out between Russia and the Ottoman Turks. Although the causes for this outbreak of hostilities were complex, Russia hoped to snatch territory from the weakening Ottoman Empire. In addition, Russia sought to gain shipping access to the world from the Black Sea through the Turkish Straits and gain influence in the Near East. Early the next year, after the Russian navy sank the Ottoman fleet in a single devastating battle, France, Britain, and Piedmont-Sardinia, driven by their own ambitions rather than principles, joined the Ottoman Turks and poured their military forces into the Black

Crimean War

NATIONALISM AND STATEBUILDING

1851	Louis-Napoleon becomes emperor of France
1854–1856	Crimean War
1860	Italian unification
1861	Russia frees the serfs
1861–1865	U.S. Civil War
1866	Austro-Prussian War
1867	Canadian independence and unification
	Creation of Austro-Hungarian Dual Monarchy
1868	Meiji Restoration in Japan
1870	Franco-Prussian War
1871	German unification

BIOGRAPHY

Florence Nightingale
(1820–1910)

In October 1854, a British journalist in Constantinople reported the successes enjoyed by the British army in the Crimean War. He also described in dramatic detail the horrendous condition of the army's medical facilities where the wounded and sick languished and died.

One of the many readers outraged by the report was Florence Nightingale. Just three years earlier, in a private note, she had written,

"Angel of the Crimea" and Medical Reformer

"What am I that their [other women's] life is not good enough for me? . . . why, oh my God, cannot I be satisfied with the life that satisfied so many people?" The war, which was causing so much suffering on and off the battlefield, suddenly created an opportunity for Nightingale to take control of her own life, gain fame as "the Lady with the Lamp," and be hailed as a national heroine.

Born in 1820 into an upper-class family, she received an unusual classical education—including several languages, philosophy, history, and science—from her father. Her mother tried to train her to conform to the domestic responsibilities of her class—the domestic rituals, long meals, and formal sociability Florence resisted. She complained that "daughters are now their mothers' slaves . . . they are considered their parents' property, they are to have no other pursuit, nor power, nor independent life, unless they marry." She rejected suitors, explaining, "I have a moral and active nature which requires satisfaction, and that would not find it in his [a husband's] life."

Instead, she pleaded with her family to allow her to train as a nurse. They responded with rage, for at the time nursing was considered a menial occupation reserved for the lowest classes. Her society offered few opportunities for "respectable" women to gain independence, and Florence described the suffering caused by these restrictions: "I see the numbers of my kind who have gone mad for want of something to do."

Her frustration and torment with family life became entwined with her anguished spiritual life. She first reported hearing God speak to her when she was 16. The depth of her despair is revealed by her petitions to God: "Forgive me, God & let me die—this day let me die." But she also looked to God for purpose: "God has something for me to do for him—or he would have let me die some time ago."

Her chance for a purposeful life came in 1854 when reports of the lack of proper medical care for sick and wounded British soldiers in the Crimean War appeared in the newspaper. Despite her family's opposition, Nightingale had managed to gain some training as a nurse in Germany, France, and Ireland. Now she was serving as superintendent of the Hospital for Invalid Gentlewomen in London. Using her family's wealth and political connections, she obtained from the British government a commission to lead a team of 38 nurses to Turkey.

On November 4, 1854, they arrived at the barrack hospital at Scutari—a suburb outside Constantinople near the Black Sea (see **Map 19.4**). In a November 14 letter, she described conditions at Scutari: "We have no room for corpses in the wards. . . . Not

---

Sea. They laid siege to Russia's naval base Sebastopol, on the Crimean peninsula.

The war dragged on until 1856, and both sides fought with gross incompetence. The flavor of this war, and in particular one suicidal charge by the British light cavalry, would be immortalized in a poem by Alfred, Lord Tennyson:

> *'Forward, the Light Brigade!'*
> *Was there a man dismay'd?*
> *Not tho' the soldier knew*
> *Some one had blunder'd:*
> *Their's not to make reply,*
> *Their's not to reason why,*
> *Their's but to do and die:*
> *Into the valley of Death*
> *Rode the six hundred*

Thanks to new telegraph lines and expanded press coverage, the public in the West could follow the conflict closely. People learned almost immediately, in graphic detail, about the horrific loss of life both on the Crimean battlefield and in the pitifully inadequate medical facilities (see Biography). More than 250,000 soldiers died, most of them from disease caused by poor sanitation, starvation, and lack of medical assistance. In the end, no one could claim much of a victory, but Russia, whose massive military no longer looked so formidable, was humbled.

Even before the Crimean disaster, peasant revolts and workers' protests had plagued Russia. In all of Europe, only Russia still allowed serfdom, which left millions tied to the land. Russia's serfs deeply resented the labor and dues they owed for the right to farm lands, and protests and insurrections broke out with

FIGURE 19.6 J. A. Benwell, *Florence Nightingale in the Military Hospital, 1856*

on *Nursing* (1859) became a primary text for nurses, and the nursing school she established in London (1860) became a model for similar institutions in Europe, Australia, and North America. Suffering from what she called "nervous fever," she spent much of the rest of her life in her own sickbed battling the sense of despair that had risen during her youth. Nevertheless, she used her prestige, political connections, and writings to campaign for reform of military health care, public sanitation, and social policy. In 1907, three years before her death, she was honored as the first woman to be awarded the British National Order of Merit. The Angel of the Crimea had revolutionized nursing and transformed military and public health care in the West.

Connecting People & Society

1. How does Nightingale's experience reveal the different ways in which war can alter people's lives?

2. How does her life illustrate the problems caused by the social limitations on women during this period (see Chapter 17)?

3. What impressions does **Figure 19.6** convey about the hospital and Florence Nightingale?

a sponge, nor a rag of linen, not anything have I left. . . . These poor fellows have not had a clean shirt nor been washed for two months before they came here. . . . I hope in a few days we shall establish a little cleanliness." She advocated fresh air, sunshine, hygiene, and diet. **Figure 19.6,** a lithograph of a ward at Scutari, shows Nightingale holding up her lamp and organizing care for the patients. Images such as this gave her the label "Lady with the Lamp."

Within six months and despite opposition, incompetence, and corruption within the British army, she transformed the medical facility, and the death rate fell from 40 percent to 2 percent. Her fame quickly spread. The *London Times* declared, "There is not one of England's proudest and purest daughters who at the moment stands on as high a pinnacle as Florence Nightingale."

The end of the war in 1856 did not end her efforts. Her best-selling *Notes*

alarming frequency. Between 1825 and 1855, more than five hundred serf rebellions occurred in Russia. Food shortages struck all too often, yet most aristocrats took little responsibility for the suffering of their serfs. Many within the privileged class feared rebellion.

The peasants' low standard of living is revealed in **Figure 19.7,** a photograph of peasants in a Russian village during the second half of the nineteenth century. The man on the left wears tattered clothes. He and all the others stand barefoot in the mud street and beside the simple houses. This image contrasts sharply with **Figure 19.8,** an 1861 photograph that shows a noble landowner standing on the front steps of his mansion and reading a decree to some of his assembled serfs. Well-dressed members of his family watch from the stairs and the second-floor balcony, while household servants stand by attentively.

Not surprisingly, serfs conscripted into Russia's armies showed a distinct lack of enthusiasm. Their sullenness finally helped make Russia's leaders see that their country was being left behind by the other powers. The country simply lacked the social support, armaments, and railroads (it took Russia months instead of weeks to move troops and supplies to the Crimean front) to win a modern war. Moreover, because serfs were bound to the land, Russia lacked a large mobile labor force to support industrialization and thereby keep up with nations to the west.

The new tsar, Alexander II (r. 1855–1881), was a complex, well-educated individual who recognized Russia's problems from the moment he took office. He was determined to introduce reforms to strengthen and modernize Russia and prop up his own rule. Like Napoleon III's policies, Alexander's **"Great Reforms"**

FIGURE 19.7 Peasants in a Russian Village The mud streets, rude housing, and worn clothing in evidence in this photo from the second half of the nineteenth century suggest the low living standard of Russia's peasants.

FIGURE 19.8 A Noble's Estate in Russia, 1861 In this mid-century photograph, a Russian landowner reads a decree to his assembled serfs.

came from above but proved much more far-reaching and dramatic. In 1861, Alexander freed Russia's 22 million serfs and, a few years later, 25 million state-owned peasants. "It is better to abolish serfdom from above than to wait until the serfs begin to liberate themselves from below," he told a group of his nobles. This bold move, occurring at almost the same time that millions of slaves were emancipated in the United States, put an end to a notorious form of human bondage and transferred land to the freed peasantry. In **Figure 19.8,** the noble landowner is reading the decree that abolished serfdom. Document 19.3 reveals one serf's reactions to this decree. However, emancipation did not make the peasants fully independent and self-sufficient. In general, they received the poorest land, owed payments for their land and freedom, and were tied by collective ownership to their village commune, the *mir,* whose elected officials assigned parcels of land and determined what could be planted.

> Alexander II's "Great Reforms"

Other reforms made the judicial system more independent, created local political assemblies (*zemstva*) with elected officials, encouraged primary and secondary education by opening thousands of new schools, and reduced military service. However, expectations for further reform rose too fast for Alexander and

came to haunt him. His efforts to relax control over Poland and grant amnesty to thousands of Poland's political prisoners seemed only to provoke a major Polish revolution in 1863, leading Alexander to repress the divisive nationalistic uprisings there and elsewhere within Russia's empire. To counter budding nationalism among minorities, he tried to force them to adopt the Russian language and culture. The universities he reopened became centers of intellectual discontent. Nor did his emancipation of the serfs end peasant rebellions.

Alexander intended to transform Russia into a modern authoritarian state that could command the allegiance of its citizens and wield power through a reformed, supported military. At best, he succeeded only partially. Certainly some of his reforms created important, long-lasting changes, but he did not turn his nation into a modern, national monarchy. Alexander himself, though called the "tsar liberator," was never popular. After an assassination attempt in 1866, he became more close-minded and increasingly turned Russia into a police state. Unrest still simmered among Russia's different nationalities. In addition, dissatisfaction among the peasantry and growing dissent among Russia's intellectuals, middle classes, and workers spelled trouble for the years ahead.

DOCUMENT 19.3

A Serf Reacts to the Russian Emancipation Proclamation

In 1861, Tsar Alexander II issued a dramatic proclamation emancipating Russia's serfs. Many people anticipated great changes stemming from this proclamation. The following excerpt depicts the reaction of Aleksandr Nikitenko, a former serf.

5 March. A great day. The emancipation manifesto! I received a copy around noon. I cannot express my joy at reading this precious act which scarcely has its equal in the thousand-year history of the Russian people. I read it aloud to my wife, my children and a friend of ours in my study, under Alexander II's portrait, as we gazed at it with deep reverence and gratitude. I tried to explain to my ten-year-old son as simply as possible the essence of the manifesto and bid him to keep inscribed in his heart forever the date of March 5 and the name of Alexander II, the Liberator.

I couldn't stay at home. I had to wander about the streets and mingle, so to say, with my regenerated fellow citizens. Announcements from the governor-general were posted at all crossways, and knots of people were gathered around them. One would read while the others listened. I encountered happy, but calm faces everywhere. Here and there people were reading the proclamation aloud, and, as I walked, I continually caught phrases like "decree on liberty," "freedom." One fellow who was reading the announcement and reached the place where it said that manor serfs were obligated to their masters for another two years, exclaimed indignantly, "The hell with this paper! Two years? I'll do nothing of the sort." The others remained silent. I ran into my friend, Galakhov. "Christ has risen!" I said to him. "He has indeed!" he answered, and we expressed our great joy to each other.

Then I went to see Rebinder. He ordered champagne and we drank a toast to Alexander II.

SOURCE: Aleksandr Nikitenko, *The Diary of a Russian Censor* (1893).

Analyze the Document

1. How did various people react to the tsar's proclamation, according to Nikitenko?

2. In what ways does their response reveal aspects of Russian culture?

3. How might members of Russia's aristocracy have reacted to this proclamation?

LOOKING BACK & MOVING FORWARD

Summary By the 1870s, the most successful political leaders had learned new lessons about the power of nationalistic sentiment. Nationalism was a mighty force more easily used than opposed. It could fuel successful movements for national unification, disintegrate multinational empires, enhance existing unity in already established nations, and strengthen central governments.

Shrewd political realists, rather than the idealists of earlier times, led successful nationalist struggles. These leaders relied on power politics, war, and diplomacy to achieve their aims. But such politicians, sometimes viewed as heroes who gamely shouldered the burden of unification, stood on ground that idealists and revolutionaries had broken in the years before 1850. Moreover, the hardest work was often carried out by nationalist groups, students, soldiers, intellectuals, journalists, and others who rose to the call of national unity. The costs for everyone were high. Many Italians, for example, lost their lives in the struggle for independence. Also tragic, those Italians who survived these turbulent years were left with a new nation that was far from rich and that still suffered from regional and political differences. Germany bought its unification with arms. From that point on, German nationalism remained linked with military prowess rather than liberal ideals. In the United States, Lincoln had preserved the Union—but only after a four-year nightmare that would mar American society for generations and cost Lincoln his life.

KEY TERMS

Realpolitik, *p. 613*
autocracy, *p. 614*
Dual Monarchy, *p. 618*
"Great Reforms," *p. 623*

Other leaders, such as Napoleon III and Tsar Alexander II, recognized that reforms initiated from above could foster needed national unity and win them greater power. Moreover, Napoleon saw that real power flowed upward from a nation of citizens who deeply identified with their state and government. Increasingly, however, the cry "for the good of the nation" served as the only rationale for such leaders' policies and whims. As the era unfolded, even war could be presented to an unwary public as an act of national will and politics.

REVIEW, ANALYZE, & CONNECT TO TODAY

REVIEW THE PREVIOUS CHAPTER

Chapter 18—"Coping with Change"—analyzed the struggles between competing ideologies and political forces during the period between Napoleon's fall and the revolutions of 1848.

1. In what ways do you think the politics of this era reflect the efforts of governments to adjust to the changes initiated by the French Revolution and the industrial revolution?

2. How did the ideological struggles initiated during the first half of the century continue during the following decades?

ANALYZE THIS CHAPTER

Chapter 19—"Nationalism and Statebuilding"—examines the efforts to build national unity and strength between 1850 and 1870.

1. Analyze the methods used by leaders such as Cavour and Bismarck to achieve national unity. How do they compare with efforts during the revolutions of 1848?

2. How did leaders such as Napoleon III in France and Alexander II in Russia try to link nationalism and statebuilding?

3. In what ways was nationalism divisive in the Austrian and Ottoman empires?

CONNECT TO TODAY

Think about the force of nationalism and problems related to it.

1. In what ways is nationalism still a potent force in today's world?

2. What do you think are nationalism's benefits in our times? What are its drawbacks?

BEYOND THE CLASSROOM

THE DRIVE FOR ITALIAN UNIFICATION

Clark, Martin. *The Italian Risorgimento*. New York: Pearson, 1998. A well-written, succinct summary.

Coppa, Frank J. *The Wars of Italian Independence*. New York: Longman, 1992. A thorough discussion of the subject.

Mack Smith, Denis. *Cavour*. London: Weidenfeld and Nicolson, 1985. An excellent biography of this important figure in Italian unification.

GERMANY "BY BLOOD AND IRON"

Blackbourn, David. *A History of Germany, 1780–1918*. London: Blackwell, 2002. An excellent political history and a fine analysis.

Carr, William. *The Wars of German Unification*. London: Longman, 1991. Analyzes the three wars that led to the unification of Germany.

Pflanze, Otto. *Bismarck and the Development of Germany. I: The Period of Unification, 1815–1871*. Princeton, NJ: Princeton University Press, 1990. An exhaustive biography and history of Germany during the period.

THE FIGHT FOR NATIONAL UNITY IN NORTH AMERICA

Bensel, Richard Franklin. *Yankee Leviathan: The Origins of Central State Authority in America, 1859–1877*. Cambridge: Cambridge University Press, 1990. A discussion of state formation and the extension of central state authority during the Civil War and Reconstruction.

McPherson, James. *Battle Cry of Freedom*. New York: Oxford University Press, 2003. A well-written one-volume history of the American Civil War.

DIVIDED AUTHORITY IN THE AUSTRIAN AND OTTOMAN EMPIRES

Shaw, Stanford J. *History of the Ottoman Empire and Modern Turkey. II: Reform, Revolution and Republic: The Rise of Modern Turkey, 1808–1875*. Cambridge: Cambridge University Press, 1983. An effective analysis of the causes for the Ottoman decline during the nineteenth century.

Sked, Alan. *The Decline and Fall of the Habsburg Empire, 1815–1918*. London: Longman, 2001. A particularly strong analysis of the Habsburg Empire during this period.

USING NATIONALISM IN FRANCE AND RUSSIA

Edgerton, Robert. *Death or Glory: The Legacy of the Crimean War*. New York: Perseus, 1999. Covers the war and its significance.

Kolchin, Peter. *Unfree Labor: American Slavery and Russian Serfdom*. Cambridge, MA: Harvard University Press, 1987. A comparative study of the two experiences.

Lincoln, W. Bruce. *The Great Reforms: Autocracy, Bureaucracy, and the Politics of Change in Imperial Russia*. DeKalb: Northern Illinois University Press, 1990. Puts the social reforms during the reign of Alexander II in a broad political, social, and intellectual context.

Price, Roger. *People and Politics in France, 1848–1870*. Cambridge: Cambridge University Press, 2004. Clearly surveys the politics of the Second Empire in France.

OPENING OF THE SUEZ CANAL, 1869

In 1869, after ten years of construction, the Suez Canal—linking the Mediterranean and Red seas—opened. This drawing of the opening ceremony shows a crowd of traditionally dressed local inhabitants on the banks watching the line of new European boats, powered by steam as well as sails. European dignitaries, separated from this crowd, also attended the ceremonies. The canal, built by the French and later acquired by the British, shortened the sea route from Europe to India and the Far East by thousands of miles, and the new, large, smoke-belching steamboats carried cargo more rapidly and reliably than ever, facilitating the West's imperial expansion.

Mass Politics and Imperial Domination

20

Democracy and the New Imperialism, 1870–1914

"We have conquered for ourselves a place in the sun," announced Germany's Kaiser William II (r. 1888–1919) in 1901. Addressing an audience from Hamburg's business community, he boasted that "it will now be my task to see to it that this place in the sun shall remain our undisputed possession, in order that the sun's rays may fall fruitfully upon our activity and trade in foreign parts, that our industry and agriculture may develop within the state." William was referring to Germany's territories, gained in the scramble for overseas conquests that had been going on over the previous two decades. His audience and many others in the industrialized Western world expected to gain wealth from this recent imperial expansion.

He also may have been reminding his listeners that the German nation had been unified in the 1860s through war and conquest (see Chapter 19). Indeed, underlying his words was an appeal to pride in the growing power of this new nation. Like other political leaders in the West, William had learned to use nationalism to gain support from listeners and readers.

Politicians such as William could no longer ignore public opinion, for democracy was on the rise. Between 1870 and 1914, demands for democracy, or political participation by common people, spread as more and more people struggled to gain access to politics. Now the new politics of nationalism combined with industrialism to multiply the power of the West and push it outward into Africa and Asia in a great imperial expansion. The West was rising to a new level of world dominance.

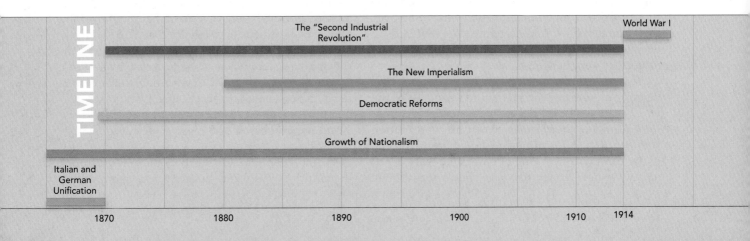

TIMELINE

The "Second Industrial Revolution"

World War I

The New Imperialism

Democratic Reforms

Growth of Nationalism

Italian and German Unification

1870   1880   1890   1900   1910   1914

DEMANDS FOR DEMOCRACY

In 1896, the Russian statesman Konstantin Pobedonostsev (1827–1907) published what would become a widely read attack on democracy. "What is this freedom by which so many minds are agitated, which inspires so many insensate actions, so many wild speeches . . . ?" His answer was democracy, "the right to participate in the government of the State." He complained that "the new Democracy now aspires to universal suffrage—a fatal error, and one of the more remarkable in the history of mankind."

However, between 1870 and 1914, it became increasingly clear to those who had long enjoyed political power in the West that, sooner or later, the beliefs of the masses would count in politics. Since the French Revolution in 1789, a widening pool of Europeans had tasted political power, a trend that ruling elites feared. Some politicians, such as Pobedonostsev, tried to turn their backs on democracy. Others tried to tame it, and still others flourished with it.

During the 1870s and 1880s, three developments became entwined with demands for democracy. First, many governments established national systems of free and compulsory public education at the primary-school level. With this | Public education | policy, they hoped to create more patriotic citizens. They also wanted to provide citizens with the skills and discipline needed by modernizing economies and military establishments. Moreover, they wanted their voting electorate to be educated. To liberals especially, access to the schoolhouse and democracy went hand in hand.

Second, educated, voting citizens could read newspapers, and popular journalism responded to the call. Before 1850, newspapers were | Popular journalism | few, small, expensive, and written for a limited readership. By the end of the century, a new kind of newspaper had popped up everywhere—one that was cheap, sensational,

and wildly popular. In the United States, publishers such as Joseph Pulitzer (1847–1911) and William Randolph Hearst (1863–1951) built influential newspapers featuring screaming headlines, flag-waving patriotism, an easy style, sensational news, and attention-getting columns. Other newspapers throughout Europe, especially in the capital cities, followed the same pattern. They catered to the newly educated public's hunger for news and, in turn, powerfully molded public opinion.

Third, politicians realized they had to appeal to the new voters. They devised innovative campaign strategies, such as crisscrossing the country by railroad and delivering | Political campaigns | stirring campaign speeches to cheering crowds in large halls and outdoor forums. They listened to newly formed interest groups—whether business organizations, reformers, or labor unions. These interest groups held rallies on their own, to gather support and gain influence through newspaper coverage of their meetings. Finally, politicians began creating all sorts of state institutions, from census bureaus to social security administrations, to satisfy the demands of their politically aroused societies and persuade new voters to support them. All these changes vastly reshaped parliamentary politics.

Such developments put pressure on politicians to adjust the way they conducted themselves, for democratic reform meant more than widening the right to vote and bringing new faces into government. To succeed in the new world of mass politics, politicians had to learn to monitor—and navigate—the shifting tides of public opinion. More and more, rising to and staying in political office meant pleasing interest groups, journalists, educated readers, and newly enfranchised voters.

Liberal Democracy in Western Europe

Would European societies ease toward a liberal democratic consensus? Many people hoped so, particularly in western Europe, where Great Britain and France had experimented with democratic reforms, but in different ways.

Great Britain started the second half of the nineteenth century in a strong, stable position. It had avoided the revolutionary turmoil that swept over the European continent between 1848 and 1850, largely because the British adapted just enough to contain the pressures for radical change (see Chapter 18). Liberalism—stressing little governmental involvement in economic and social affairs, low taxes, and free trade—seemed to work well in Britain, and the island nation boasted the most modern economy in the world.

For most of the 1850s and 1860s, liberals controlled the British government. But they were more willing to call on national pride, sympathize with movements for national liberation abroad, and parade British naval might than to accommodate those who demanded entry into the political system. It was the Conservative Party, under Benjamin Disraeli (1804–1881), that finally decided to bend and take the credit for democratic reform before the Liberals themselves could grab it. The Conservatives passed a new measure—the Reform Bill of 1867—which doubled the electorate and gave the vote to the lower-middle class for the first time. In addition, they gathered support from the working class by passing laws that limited working hours, established sanitary codes, created housing standards, and aided labor unions. In 1884, the Liberal Party, under William Gladstone (1809–1898), countered by pushing through another reform bill that gave two-thirds of adult males the vote. To sweeten the deal even further, the Liberals opened the army and civil service to talent and made primary education available to all.

Reform bills of 1867 and 1884

Having both jumped on the reform bandwagon, British Conservatives and Liberals now had to compete for power in new ways. For the first time, politicians such as Gladstone used the railways to campaign throughout the nation, speaking before crowds of thousands. A growing corps of journalists followed the campaigns, shaping public opinion by reporting speeches and scandals daily in cheap newspapers with mass circulation. New interest groups, mostly from the middle class, bent the ears of politicians who wanted their support in return.

Figure 20.1, a painting by Alfred Morgan, reveals some of these trends in British politics. The artist depicts the political leader William Gladstone (wearing a tall hat, sitting stiffly, and staring straight ahead) riding in an omnibus. This form of transportation, which carried more than two dozen passengers at a time, was relatively inexpensive and available to all classes of people. The man (holding a newspaper), women, and children who share the bus with Gladstone are dressed well but are not members of Britain's wealthy elite (who still rode in small carriages such as the one seen through the rear window). As this image indicates, Gladstone tried to appeal to the growing electorate by portraying himself as an upright, hardworking individual who allied himself with the people. Britain was moving toward democracy, but in ways that worried traditional politicians used to deciding things among their "own kind."

France's path toward democracy took more violent turns than Britain's. A birthplace of democracy, France nevertheless started the 1870s on a turbulent

FIGURE 20.1 Alfred Morgan, *An Omnibus Ride to Piccadilly Circus, Mr. Gladstone Travelling with Ordinary Passengers,* 1885   In the scene illustrating the politics of democracy, British political leader William Gladstone joins middle-class riders in a bus, thus presenting himself as a man allied with the people.

note. The Franco-Prussian War of 1870 spelled the end of Napoleon III's Second Empire and the emergence of the Third French Republic (see Chapter 19). The first elections, held in February 1871 after Napoleon III's fall and the surrender of Paris, resulted in a victory for the monarchists, who hoped to limit democracy and open the door for the restoration of a monarchy. Still the city of Paris refused to submit to the domination of conservative, rural France. It demanded home rule and set up its own city government, or commune.

France's Third Republic

The **Paris Commune** would gain a reputation as a democracy out of control or as an experiment in Marxist socialism. In reality, the Commune stood for decentralizing power in France, self-governance, support of working-class organizations, and greater equality for women. Its roots lay in the city's resistance to the Germans between September 1870 and January 1871. During those horrific months, Parisians had braved starvation and isolation in the face of the German siege. Most of the rich fled the city. The lower classes not only resented this exodus but also took over positions of power that the wealthy had abandoned. The February 1871 elections ended the German siege, but not the division between Paris and the rest of the nation. Parisians felt betrayed by France's new conservative government when it concluded the peace with Germany. When government troops tried to disarm them, they rebelled and fighting erupted. The government troops withdrew, and again Paris was put under siege, this time by

The Paris Commune

FIGURE 20.2 The Paris Commune, ca. 1871 This altered photo portrays executions during the Paris Commune period. It was used by government troops as propaganda against Communards.

French troops. Two months later, the government troops attacked, killing some 25,000 Parisians, arresting thousands more, and deporting more than 5,000 to distant penal colonies.

Both sides in the Paris conflict committed bitter reprisals. The "photograph" shown in **Figure 20.2** purports to show Communards—including women and nonuniformed men—executing 62 hostages. In fact, the "photograph" is a photomontage—a composite photograph—used by government troops to justify retaliation against Communards.

The fall of the Paris Commune ended the immediate threat to the integrity of France, but not the political and social uncertainties that still lurked below the surface. A period of restless political struggle followed. At first, monarchists almost regained power, but they failed to agree on which of three possible royal houses (the Bourbon, the Orleanist, or the Bonaparte) they should rally around. By the end of the 1870s, liberals, elected by universal male suffrage, controlled the French Republic. Conservatives, however, refused to give up. In the late 1880s, they joined nationalists, supporters of the military, and opponents of parliament to rally around a handsome man on horseback, General Georges Boulanger, who became so popular that he might have overthrown the Republic had he been bolder and more skillful or had the republican leaders been less courageous. As it turned out, when he was summoned to answer charges of treason against the Republic, he fled to Belgium and eventually committed suicide on the grave of his late mistress.

Meanwhile, several forces reoriented politics toward the wider voting public. First, public schooling spread throughout France. Republican teachers replaced Catholic teachers, bringing in a common secular curriculum and promoting patriotism and republican virtues. Second, military service became compulsory and

| Spread of democratic institutions |

helped turn young, rural men into French citizens with new political awareness. Third, a popular national press took root in Paris and attracted readers throughout the nation. These papers reported all the political scandals, especially the sensational and far-reaching **Dreyfus affair** (see page 637), and soon readers in the provinces began avidly following national politics. In France, as in Britain, democratic institutions were spreading throughout the nation and redefining the nature of politics.

For and Against Democracy in Central and Eastern Europe

In contrast to the western European governments, national leaders in central and eastern Europe were more autocratic. Monarchs and their ministers in these regions had the last word in political decision making. Like nations in western Europe, those in central and eastern Europe struggled with pressure to institute democratic reforms. In some cases, these nations took reluctant steps toward democracy; in others, they declined to change. In addition, the tensions between autocratic and democratic forces in central and eastern Europe became particularly entwined with aggressive nationalism. The cases of Germany, Austria, and Russia provide apt examples of the various ways in which this struggle manifested itself.

In Germany, the constitution stipulated universal suffrage, but real power rested with the king and his ministers. Bismarck, who dominated as Germany's chancellor between 1870 and 1890, supported universal male suffrage from the beginning only because "in a country with monarchical traditions and loyal sentiments" such as Germany, "universal suffrage would lead to . . . eliminating the influence of the liberal bourgeois classes." Bismarck believed that most workers and peasants would vote for his conservative policies.

| Germany under Bismarck |

Bismarck solidified the German states and people under Prussia. He also brought the law codes, currencies, and military forces of the lesser states into conformity with those of Prussia. He then turned to issues of ethnic divisions and cultural unity. Laws and schools pressured non-German language groups to give up their languages and traditions. In 1872, Bismarck struck out against Roman Catholics for being insufficiently nationalistic. Known as the *Kulturkampf* (the struggle for civilization), the roots of Bismarck's attack lay in Germany's Protestant-Catholic religious divisions and the newly vigorous papacy of Pius IX, who declared papal infallibility in 1870, opposed cooperation with Protestantism, and attacked the growth of state power. With support from

| Conflict with Catholic Church |

liberals, Bismarck passed laws asserting the state's right to restrict religious orders, require civil marriage, and bring all education (including schools run by the Catholic Church) under state control. When the Roman Catholic clergy resisted, authorities arrested hundreds of priests and six bishops. Many of these measures backfired, however: They made the Roman Catholic Center Party stronger. In 1878, Bismarck repealed the most severe of the anti-Catholic laws, but only because he wanted support for a more important struggle—the fight against the democratically minded and socially radical Socialists.

Conflict with Socialists

In a twelve-year crusade against the Socialists, who attacked the autocratic nature of Germany's government and were gaining popularity in elections, Bismarck outlawed the Social Democratic Party's publications, organizations, and meetings and set the German police force on them. When his repressive tactics did little to diminish Socialist votes, Bismarck tried to undercut the party's appeal to the working class by removing "the causes for socialism." Borrowing some of the Socialists' programs, between 1883 and 1889 he established a comprehensive system of social insurance that provided accident, sickness, and old-age benefits.

Ironically, in fighting against the Social Democrats, the conservative Bismarck made Germany a leader in enacting progressive social policies. Nevertheless, Bismarck's campaign against the Social Democratic Party would fail. The Socialists had built a solid following and continued to gain public support. In 1890, two years after the death of Kaiser William I, the new monarch, Kaiser William II, dismissed the aging chancellor. William II, eager to rule himself, "dropped the pilot" of the German ship of state and ended an era in German history.

In Austria, liberalism spread during the 1870s along with the rise of the bourgeoisie in that country. Liberals supported the constitutional monarchy, parliamentary government, and restricted suffrage. They also believed that it was possible to hold a multinational empire together. In the 1880s, nationalistic demands from different language groups began to overwhelm liberals and play into the hands of conservatives. Parliamentary sessions in Austria frequently degenerated into shouting matches, in which representatives from different language groups hurled inkstands at one another. This nationalistic discontent proved even more intense in Hungary than in Austria. Moreover, the partnership between Austria and Hungary threatened to disintegrate altogether (see page 618). The introduction of universal male suffrage in 1907 only made the empire more difficult to govern. More often than not, the emperor and his advisors bypassed parliament and ruled by decree.

Nationalistic discontent in Austria

In Russia, Alexander II's "Great Reforms" did little to open the doors to democracy beyond the local level (see pages 623–624). Indeed, they may have sparked more dissatisfaction than celebration. For serfs, liberals, and intellectuals, the reforms did not go far enough. A group of sons and daughters of the aristocracy and middle classes decided to take action. In a well-intentioned but ill-fated movement, they traveled to rural areas in an effort to uplift the lives of country dwellers. They received a rude welcome in several ways: Rural people resented what they saw as condescending attention from inexperienced urban intellectuals, and the tsar's police promptly repressed them.

Radical action in Russia

Some of the young idealists fled; others remained and turned to terrorism. One group, The People's Will, defined terrorism as "the destruction of the most harmful persons in the Government, the protection of the party from spies, and the punishment of official lawlessness and violence." Vera Zasulich became an early heroine in this movement when she attempted to assassinate the St. Petersburg chief of police in 1878. Her action initiated a series of violent eruptions and assassinations, in which terrorists killed numerous bureaucrats and police officials, and the government brutally suppressed the rebels. The cycle of terrorism and repression turned Alexander II to a more conservative course, and he halted all further reforms. In 1881, members of The People's Will retaliated by murdering Alexander II with a bomb.

The new tsar, Alexander III (r. 1881–1894), blamed his father's death on softness and set out to erase every trace of liberalism and democracy in Russia. His secret police arrested thousands of suspects, and the tsar himself initiated a sweeping program of Russianization. Authorities forced minority groups to use the Russian language and persecuted followers of non-Orthodox religions, especially Jews. Russia, much more so than Austria, would not yet bend to the democratic winds blowing from the west.

Reaction under Alexander III

INSIDERS AND OUTSIDERS: POLITICS OF THE EXTREMES

During the late nineteenth century, those democratic winds in the West spread beyond what had been the mainstream of politics. New groups and causes emerged to challenge the established center of liberal and conservative politics. These new groups gained strength and complicated the trend toward democracy. To the political left of liberals stood the unions, socialists, and anarchists. To the political right of conservatives were anti-Semites and ultranationalists. Still outside, without the vote, were women, who increasingly demanded a voice in national politics.

These groups and causes appealed to large numbers of people, particularly those who had previously been left out of politics. They became so prominent that established political leaders could not ignore them. With the political spectrum widening, it seemed less and less likely that Europe's nations would find some consensus or social peace.

The Spread of Unions

Until the 1880s, labor unions were limited chiefly to skilled workers, organized by crafts, who proved moderate in their aims and methods. In the 1880s, unionization spread rapidly to unskilled workers. These new union members adopted more radical methods and turned toward socialist programs. Seeking more than mutual aid, they demanded a say in working conditions and wages. They went on strike and flexed their political muscle through the vote. One worker described an 1890 strike of textile workers in Bradford, England, that dragged on for six months. "Twice and sometimes three times a week we had processions of the workpeople marching from near the millgates by several routes to the center of Bradford. The women strikers established a well-conducted soup kitchen, and the sympathy of the shopkeepers was very broad and the butchers gave their bones and greengrocers and grocers and bakers gave peas, lentils and loaves, and thus children were fed." As a man who employed thousands of dockers in Marseilles, France, explained, "The days of the employer's arbitrary power are past, unfortunately. . . . For long we

Strikes

could hope to subdue these trade unions that rose against our authority. . . . That too is finished, over."

Figure 20.3 captures some of the ideals of the new unions. This strike at Saint-Ouen, near Paris, France, is sympathetically portrayed by the artist, Paul Louis Delance. Workers, young and old, stream from smoke-belching factories carrying red flags, the symbol of their cause and of socialism. Their faces convey suffering and grim determination. The welfare of a woman and child—the core of the typical working-class family—represents the strikers' goal. The strikers are supported by humble people, heads bowed, upon whom a few rays of sunshine fall as if in blessing for the nobility of their cause.

As the end of the century approached, organized labor became a formidable force. Labor unions in Great Britain formed the National Trades Union Congress and became identified with the new Labour Party. In Germany, unions, especially among the unskilled workers, grew dramatically and coalesced into a national Marxist organization. In France, various unions banded together into the giant General Confederation of Labor, with a radical political program. In the United States, the abundance of cheap immigrant labor and the determined resistance by industrial capitalists hindered the emergence of unions. In 1886, however, Samuel Gompers founded the American Federation of Labor—the first successful national labor organization in America. By 1914, unions had become sufficiently large and organized to make them a major power, both in the workplace and at the polls.

Socialism Gains Strength

Like the labor unions, socialism also became a major force within the working class and in politics during the late nineteenth century. Most socialists looked to the ideas of Karl Marx for inspiration (see Chapter 18). Marx had argued that modern industrial society was splitting into two opposing classes: the capitalists, or owners of the means of production, and the workers. Capitalism, he explained, was bound to be replaced by a socialist system through revolution by the working class. Marx helped union organizers to form the International Working Men's Association (the First International) in 1864. The organization fell apart in the 1870s, but in 1889, socialists formed the Second International. These organizations helped socialists unify and spread their cause. A sense of shared struggle and beliefs inspired them to form unions, create political parties, and fight powerful employers and strong politicians.

The First International

Yet, the strength of socialism varied in each country. In Britain, established politicians

FIGURE 20.3 Paul Louis Delance, *Strike*, 1908 Under red flags symbolizing their cause, striking French union members stream out of distant factories.

excluded the working classes or socialist thinkers from politics until the 1880s. Then a group of well-known intellectuals formed the **Fabian Society,** which advocated the adoption of socialist policies through politics rather than revolution. Beatrice Webb (1858–1943), one of the founders of the Fabians, explained that she became a socialist because of "the physical misery and moral debasement following in the tracks of the rack-renting landlord and capitalist profit maker in the swarming populations of the great centres of nineteenth century commerce and industry." Webb could see no way out of "the recurrent periods of inflation and depression—meaning for the vast majority of the nation, alternate spells of overwork and unemployment."

The Fabians

During the 1890s, both unions and socialists in Britain developed enough political muscle to form the Labour Party and elect members to Parliament. By 1906, Labour had pressured the Liberals, led by David Lloyd George (1863–1945), to adopt new policies providing accident, sickness, old-age, and unemployment insurance for workers. As Labour members of Parliament argued, these old men and women were "the veterans of industry, people of almost endless toil, who have fought for and won the industrial and commercial supremacy of Great Britain. Is their lot and end to be the everlasting slur of pauperism?" To pay for the new policies, the Liberals shifted the "heaviest burden to the broadest backs." A steeply graduated income tax and high taxes on inheritances landed on the rich. When Conservatives in the House of Lords resisted, the Liberal and Labour parties passed a bill that stripped the House of Lords of most of its former power.

Britain's Labour Party

In France, socialism gained strength during the 1890s. During the following decade, socialist parties helped push France's republican government to enact a limited program of unemployment, old-age, accident, and sickness insurance for workers. By this time, the different wings of the French socialists had joined to form the United Socialist Party under the leadership of scholar-orator Jean Jaurès (see Biography). By 1914, the United Socialist Party numbered 1.5 million voters and had 110 seats in the Chamber of Deputies.

France and Jaurès

Socialism enjoyed its greatest success in Germany. In 1890, Germany's main socialist party, the Social Democrats, won the vote of 20 percent of the electorate. Officially the party adhered to the idea that revolution was historically inevitable. A party leader, August Bebel, expressed the optimism of this view: "Every night I go to sleep with the thought that the last hour of bourgeois society strikes soon." In practice, however, the party usually followed the ideas

German Social Democrats

of the "revisionist" socialist Eduard Bernstein (1850–1932). This German writer and politician urged socialists to cooperate with the capitalist classes to obtain immediate benefits for labor and advocated a gradual approach to socialism. By 1914, the Social Democrats polled some 4.5 million votes, making it the largest political party in Germany.

Even in conservative Austria, socialists gained strength in industrial areas for the same reasons they did elsewhere in the West. The plight of workers was their top priority. Anna Maier, who started a life of work in a tobacco factory when she was 13, captured this concern when she explained that "young girls were often abused or even beaten" on the job. One day Maier read a copy of the *Women Workers'* newspaper smuggled into the factory by one of the older women. Eventually, she managed to join the Social Democratic Party. After she had taken part in demonstrations, her factory manager took her "off a good job" and put her "in a poorer one," but as she later reported, "nothing stopped me." When the tobacco workers union formed in 1899, she joined them and became "a class-conscious fighter." Maier's story was repeated by many other workers throughout the West in the decades before 1914.

Anarchism: Freedom from All Authority

While sometimes associated with socialists, **anarchists** made more radical demands. Drawing on the ideas of leaders such as the Russian activist Mikhail Bakunin (1814–1876) and Russian theoretician Pyotr Kropotkin (1842–1921), they stressed the elimination of any form of authority that impinged on human freedom. "So long as there exist States, there will be no humanity," Bakunin argued. "The masses of the people will be de facto slaves even in the most democratic republics." Anarchists believed that human beings, once freed from the corrupting institutions that oppressed them, would naturally cooperate with one another. "Life will be open to all," an anarchist leader explained. "Everyone will take what he needs—this is the anarchist ideal."

Bakunin

Anarchism became particularly influential in Spain, Italy, and France, where it appealed to trade unionists, artisans, agricultural laborers, and shopkeepers suffering from unemployment and declining wages. Its supporters favored direct action through unions and cooperatives rather than parliamentary politics. After the turn of the century, many anarchists hoped the grand solution to their problems would come with a "general strike," as described by the popular French writer Georges Sorel (1847–1922). Such a strike, they believed, would force the capitalist system to grind to a sudden halt. A small wing of the anarchist movement went beyond hoping

BIOGRAPHY

Jean Jaurès
(1859–1914)

One observer described the French politician Jean Jaurès as such a spellbinding orator that "he could raise the masses and enchant the elite at the same time." **Figure 20.4** shows Jaurès standing beneath the red flag of socialism, addressing a crowd in 1913. Jaurès's speeches in France's Chamber of Deputies sometimes lasted for hours. He also wrote so prolifically that it would take ninety volumes, four hundred pages each, to amass all his writing. Some called him an obvious genius. He called himself "a cultured peasant." Certainly an intellectual, he wore the typical middle-class long, black overcoat. However, the coat was usually dirty, his pants always too short, and his pockets forever stuffed with books and papers. Between the 1880s and 1914, he became one of France's most respected politicians.

Orator and Socialist Politician

Born in 1859 to a rural, middle-class family of little wealth, Jean excelled at school, winning a series of prizes and scholarships. He became a teacher in 1881 and then a professor of philosophy at the University of Toulouse in southern France in 1883. In 1885 he was elected to the Chamber of Deputies as an unaffiliated republican. Just 25, he was France's youngest deputy. That year he met Louise Bois, the daughter of a merchant, and a year later the couple married. Attracted to Paris by the political activity there, the couple settled in an apartment and eventually had two children.

FIGURE 20.4 Jean Jaurès

Defeated in his 1889 bid for reelection to parliament, Jean became interested in socialism and made it the subject of his doctoral dissertation. He won fame for his support of striking miners at Carmaux in 1892. After this event, he was reelected to the Chamber of Deputies, this time as a socialist. He accepted the possibility of socialism by evolution rather than revolution: Class struggle might properly be replaced by democratic political struggle. To Jaurès and a growing number of other socialists, the forces of history suggested that socialism was inevitable. He rose in the Socialist Party, becoming a leader by 1900. In 1904, he helped found a newspaper, *L'Humanité*, which became France's chief socialist periodical. By 1908, he had solidified the party.

Jaurès became increasingly concerned with the problem of war. He argued that France wasted its resources on military preparations. "What will the future be like when the billions now thrown away in war preparations are spent on useful production to increase the well-being of the people?" he asked. He saw the West's recent imperial expansion into the non-Western world as a primary cause for wars. "The fever of imperialism has become a sickness. It is the affliction of a badly organized society which cannot utilize its energies and productive forces at home." More and more, Jaurès championed pacifism and Franco-German reconciliation, but his stand won him and his followers ridicule and accusations of treason, particularly by right-wing nationalists.

During the evening of July 31, 1914, Jaurès began composing an antiwar appeal. At 9:00 P.M., he and a group of other socialist journalists met and decided to dine at a crowded café on the rue Montmartre. At 9:40 a young man who was affiliated with a nationalist group burst in and fired two shots, killing Jaurès. The French socialist leader was murdered on the very eve of the war he warned against.

Connecting People & Society

1. In what ways does Jaurès's life reflect the promises of democracy?

2. How is it representative of the political problems faced by people in this era?

3. What does his life suggest about the nature and strength of socialism during this period?

for a general strike and turned to violence. Among its victims were President Sadi Carot of France in 1894, King Umberto I of Italy in 1900, and President William McKinley of the United States in 1901.

Anti-Semitism and Ultranationalism

Usually at the opposite end of the political spectrum from socialism and anarchism, **anti-Semitism** often appealed to conservative nationalists. Followers of Judaism had long suffered from anti-Semitism—hostility toward or hatred of Jews. Since the Middle Ages, Jews had been accused of murdering Christ, segregated into special quarters known as ghettos, and persecuted. However, between 1789 and the 1870s, the spreading ideals of the Enlightenment and the French Revolution had enabled Jews to gain new rights and a degree of legal equality, though rarely full acceptance. At least in western and central Europe, this progress led many Jews to believe that finally they could join their nation-states as full citizens.

During the last decades of the nineteenth century, however, nationalism took on militant and authoritarian tones. All too easily, this spreading strain of nationalism strengthened racist and anti-Semitic thought. Comte de Gobineau (1816–1882), a Frenchman, and Houston Stewart Chamberlain (1855–1927), an Englishman who became a German citizen, wrote widely read tracts arguing that race determined much of history. The two men helped formulate the Aryan myth, which held that Germans belonged to a special race and therefore possessed superior qualities: "[T]he Germanic races belong to the most highly gifted group, the group usually termed Aryan. . . . Physically and mentally the Aryans are pre-eminent among all people; for that reason they are by right . . . the lords of the world." Chamberlain's ideas veered off into anti-Semitism, as did the thinking of other well-known racist writers. Their pseudoscientific thought—which labeled Jews as a separate, inferior race—became increasingly popular, as indicated by this excerpt from a speech delivered by an anti-Semitic member of the German parliament: "A Jew who was born in Germany does not thereby become a German; he is still a Jew. Therefore it is imperative that we realize that Jewish racial characteristics differ so greatly from ours that a common life of Jews and Germans under the same laws is quite impossible."

During the same period, anti-Semitic politics gained force, especially among artisans, small shopkeepers, rural workers, and others who felt threatened by liberalism and capitalism and saw Jews as being linked to both. These people scornfully called Jews outsiders and capitalists and blamed them for their own economic ills and fears. Ultranationalist politicians used anti-Semitism to rally crowds, shift the blame for failed policies away from themselves, and win votes.

Right-wing newspapers such as *La Libre Parole* popularized scandals as well as anti-Semitic stories that coalesced most dramatically in the Dreyfus affair. People throughout France followed every development of "the affair" day after day and year after year. In 1894, a group of bigoted army officers falsely accused and convicted a Jewish captain, Alfred Dreyfus, of treason and sent him to solitary imprisonment on Devil's Island in South America. Three years later, evidence of Dreyfus's innocence appeared. Nevertheless, high-ranking officers refused to reopen the case. Newspaper articles, sensational trials, accusations, and huge public demonstrations divided the nation between the political Left and Right. Republicans, socialists, and intellectuals, inspired by the famous French writer Émile Zola, who attacked the judgment of the military and judiciary in the case, rallied for Dreyfus. Nationalist, conservative, monarchist, and anti-Semitic forces supported the army. In 1899, a second court-martial again convicted Dreyfus, despite evidence of another officer's guilt in the affair. The president of the Republic pardoned Dreyfus, but it took seven more years to get Dreyfus fully acquitted.

The Dreyfus affair marked not only the battle over anti-Semitism but the evolution of French politics. The victory for Dreyfus became a victory for republicanism and anticlericalism. Electoral victories made republicans strong enough to separate church and state in 1905 and initiate a program of social legislation. Socialists, who had joined republicans in the Dreyfus case, gained greater legitimacy and popularity. The political power of monarchists and the Catholic Church had been dealt a debilitating blow.

For Jews, persecution was worse in central and eastern Europe. These regions had the highest Jewish population and the most aggressive strain of nationalism. Nationalistic anti-Semitic organizations, such as the Pan-German Association and the Christian Social Workers' Party, emerged in Germany. Anti-Semitic journals warned of the dangers to "the native-born Christian population" as Jews gained access to the press, to state offices, and to professions such as teaching and law. One anti-Semitic deputy in Germany's parliament explained in an 1895 speech that "every Jew who at this moment had not done anything bad may nevertheless under the proper conditions do precisely that, because his racial qualities drive him to do it."

In Austria, the Christian Socialist Party and the German National Party took a decidedly anti-Semitic stand. By the 1890s, a new breed of politics based on symbols, charisma, nationalism, racism, anticapitalism, and anti-Semitism had arisen. The election of Karl Lueger in 1897 as mayor of Vienna symbolized this political trend; Lueger campaigned

FIGURE 20.5 Samuel Hirszenberg, *The Black Banner,* 1905 flee anti-Semitic attacks (pogroms) in Russia-dominated Poland. Horrified and grief-stricken Jewish people, bearing their dead,

on an anti-Semitic platform and triumphed even in this bastion of Austrian liberalism.

Some of the most violent anti-Semitic acts occurred in Russia. Tsars Alexander III and Nicholas II (r. 1894–1917) sanctioned the persecution of Jews and required them to live in designated areas. Officials labeled Jews as outsiders and excluded them from mainstream society. Whenever anyone wanted to assign blame for their problems, they could point to the Jews. This hostility culminated in a series of pogroms, or organized mass attacks on Jews, led by anti-Semitic groups and government officials. **Figure 20.5** shows a procession of Hasidic Jews in Russian-dominated Poland carrying a coffin, which contains one of the victims of an anti-Semitic pogrom. The faces of people in the procession reflect shock, horror, and desperation as well as mourning, and the sky echoes the ominous dangers still facing these people. The title of Hirszenberg's 1905 painting refers to "The

Black Hundreds," who were the armed gangs of the "Union of the Russian People"—a right-wing, anti-Semitic political movement founded in 1905—and to *The Russian Banner,* the newspaper of this organization, which also received "black money" from Russia's tsar. Between 1870 and 1914, these persecutions helped push more than 2 million eastern European Jews out of their homes and to the west, particularly to the United States (see **Map 20.1**).

Concerns about persecutions in eastern Europe as well as the weakening of Jewish identity through assimilation in western Europe gave rise to **Zionism,** a Jewish nationalist movement to create an independent state for Jews in Palestine—the ancient homeland | Zionism and Herzl
of the Jews. The Hungarian writer Theodor Herzl (1860–1904) became the leading figure in the Zionist movement. While in Paris covering the Dreyfus affair for an Austrian newspaper, he gained a greater sense of the strength of anti-Semitism and his own identity as a Jew. In 1896, he published an influential pamphlet, *The Jewish State: An Attempt at a Modern Solution of the Jewish Question,* urging formation of an international movement to make Palestine a Jewish homeland. He envisioned the homeland transformed into a socialist community of hardworking cooperatives. The following year he led the new World Zionist Organization to prominence. He gained a large following in eastern Europe, found financial support from several sources, and won cautious political support from British governmental officials. "It might be many years before the founding of the State is under way," Herzl warned. "In the meantime, Jews will be ridiculed, offended, abused, whipped, plundered, and slain in a thousand different localities." After Herzl's death in 1904, other leaders advanced his aims and secured more support—including the financial aid of donors such as the French banker Baron de Rothschild, and the cooperation of Arthur Balfour (1848–1930),

MAP 20.1

Jewish Migration, 1870–1914

This map shows areas and cities with large Jewish populations and traces typical migration routes to the west and south.

Explore the Map

1. In what cities and areas of eastern Europe were Jews most heavily concentrated?

2. What was the significance of the particularly harsh anti-Semitic policies in these areas?

3. Why might Jews have migrated primarily to the west and south?

The Pale: Area Where Russian Jews Were Allowed to Live

Other Areas of Large Jewish Population

• Cities with Large Jewish Population

← Typical Migration Routes

Britain's prime minister. By 1914, some 85,000 Jews had immigrated to Palestine, primarily from eastern Europe.

Still Outsiders: Women, Feminism, and the Right to Vote

By 1914, most of the political groups that had been outside the mainstream of politics had gained a political voice. In the majority of Western countries, universal male suffrage had become the rule by 1914. However, women still remained on the political sidelines, hampered by an ideology that left them unequal economically, trapped in their own "separate sphere" by laws that declared them legally inferior, and excluded by political institutions that deprived them of the vote. Few men in any of the political parties, movements, or unions offered their support for women's suffrage.

During the last decades of the nineteenth century, many women finally turned to political activism. Numerous women—whether as individuals or as activist group members—were already Political activism calling themselves "feminist." Groups of feminists organized several movements to promote women's issues, demand legal equality of the sexes, and advocate social and political change. In 1878, representatives of these groups from twelve nations came together in Paris at the International Congress of the Rights of Women and initiated a period of increased activism and international cooperation. Although feminists were still a minority

among women, their strength grew dramatically. In Britain and the United States, women with middle-class and aristocratic backgrounds fought especially hard for the right to vote. They argued that without the vote, women would continue to suffer from a range of inequalities. "The idea that the possession of political rights will destroy 'womanliness,' absurd as it may seem to us, is very deeply rooted in the minds of men," British writer Frances Power Cobbe (1822–1904) pointed out in 1884. Men, Cobbe explained, "really prize what women now are in the home and in society so highly that they cannot bear to risk losing it by any serious change in their condition." A few years later, Elizabeth Cady Stanton (1815–1902) expressed the views of many Americans in the women's suffrage movement: "If we are to consider [a woman] as a citizen, as a member of a great nation, she must have the same rights as all other members."

Another group of feminists tried to gain equality through social reform—focusing on the needs of the working class and often voicing socialist sympathies. Led by women such as Louise Michel (1830–1905) in France and Clara Zetkin (1857–1933) in Germany, they argued that only when workers as a whole gained freedom from economic and social oppression would women achieve justice. In 1885, Michel looked forward to a transforming revolution that would introduce a new era "when men and women will move through life together as good companions, and they will no more argue about which sex is superior than races will argue about which race is foremost in the world." Ten years later, Zetkin explained that proletarian women could attain "salvation only through the fight for the emancipation of labor."

The strongest women's suffrage movements arose in Great Britain. The movement was exemplified by organizations such as the National Union of Women's

Suffrage movements

Suffrage Societies, led by Millicent Fawcett (1847–1929), and the more radical Women's Social and Political Union, led by Emmeline Pankhurst (1858–1928) and her two daughters. The leaders of these movements had reached a crucial conclusion: Being polite was not going to win them the right to vote. They worked as other political groups did, forming organizations, presenting petitions, pressuring politicians, forging alliances, holding demonstrations, publishing newspapers, and marching for the franchise. They continued despite scorn from men, ridicule by newspapers, rejection by politicians, cold shoulders from labor unions and socialists, and force

by the police. **Figure 20.6** shows a policeman arresting Emmeline Pankhurst. "We have tried every way," explained Pankhurst. "We have presented larger petitions than were ever presented for any other reform, we have succeeded in holding greater public meetings than men have ever had for any reform . . . we have faced hostile mobs at street corners . . . we have been ridiculed, we have had contempt poured upon us . . . we know that we need the protection of the vote even more than men have needed it."

In 1908, a rally for female suffrage drew some 250,000 women to Hyde Park in London. After 1910, feminism in Britain took a more public and violent turn as women resorted to window smashing, arson, assaults, bombing of railway stations, and chaining themselves to the gates of Parliament. Police arrested them, judges imprisoned them, and, when they went on hunger strikes, authorities force-fed them.

Still the British government as well as most other Western authorities refused to give in to the feminists' demands. Finland granted women the right to vote in 1906—the first victory for the women's suffrage movement—but other victories would take years. Women would not gain the vote until after 1918 in Britain, Germany, and the United States; until the 1940s in France; and until the 1970s in Switzerland.

EMIGRATION: OVERSEAS AND ACROSS CONTINENTS

By 1914, most Western societies had taken great, often reluctant, steps toward democracy. A swirl of forces—the growing pressures of nationalism, the spread of industry and commerce, and the competition for military might—fueled those steps and molded the politics that resulted. Some of those same forces also pushed a new wave of Europeans and their governments across the globe.

After the mid-nineteenth century, a great migration of people from Europe gained momentum. Europeans streamed overseas and across continents, hoping to start new and better lives. As they fanned across the globe, they brought money and great quantities of manufactured goods to nonindustrialized areas. Their governments did the same: Imperial powers raced to carve up Africa and establish control in Asia. With their new presence, wealth, and power, Europeans dominated the world as never before.

Leaving Europe

Ever since the first sixteenth-century settlements, Europe had sent a sizable trickle of emigrants to the Americas. The trickle became a flowing stream in the mid-nineteenth century. Great numbers of British, Irish, and then German immigrants landed in the United States during the 1840s, 1850s, and 1860s.

FIGURE 20.6 The Women's Suffrage Movement in Great Britain, 1914 Police arrest suffrage leader Emmeline Pankhurst during a demonstration for the franchise.

FIGURE 20.7

Eugène Laermans, *The Emigrants*, 1896

This triptych (three-paneled painting) by Eugène Laermans shows stages in the process of emigration that many Europeans experienced. In the right-hand panel (*The Exordium*), a parish priest addresses the crowd of departing villagers for the last time. For the priest, the news seems bad; this departure of his flock may mark the decline and possibly death of his village. In the background lies the village under dark clouds. The central panel (*The Exodus*) shows a seemingly endless line of humble men, women, and children carrying their meager belongings and dragging their pets. They march along the road and, for the last time, look back at their homeland and village in the distance. In the left-hand panel (*The Exile*), they crowd into the port. The darkening clouds to the west warn of a difficult voyage across the Atlantic and their unknown fate in new lands.

Connecting Art & Society

1. What is the apparent mood of the emigrants in each panel?

2. According to what you see in this painting, why do you think these people might be emigrating?

3. In what ways might this painting be considered a realistic rather than an idealistic depiction of emigration across the Atlantic?

After 1870, the stream swelled to a rushing torrent, as peoples from southern and eastern Europe joined the flow. Between 1870 and 1914, some 30 million Europeans left their homelands and emigrated, mostly to the Americas and Australia.

What explains this immense movement? As suggested in **Figure 20.7** by Belgian artist Eugène Laermans (1864–1940), many of the vast numbers of peasants and workers who emigrated overseas left Europe reluctantly. They felt pushed by the difficulties of their lives on the land and in the villages more than pulled by the apparent opportunities in foreign lands. In several parts of Europe, such as Scandinavia, the British Isles, and southern Italy, the land could no longer support the expanding population. Moreover, the shift to commercial agriculture throughout Europe had left a flood of small farmers landless or unable to com-

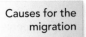
Causes for the migration

pete. Natural catastrophes also played a part. A deadly potato famine in Ireland in the late 1840s forced many Irish to flee their homeland to escape starvation. These hardships impelled people—even in relatively rich western European countries such as Laermans's Belgium—to head for more promising shores. Many emigrated to the Americas, especially between 1880 and 1892.

Many opportunities, both real and imagined, also beckoned from across the oceans. Visions of free or cheap land, already taken away from native peoples, attracted Europeans to the Americas, Australia, and New Zealand. People heard news of plentiful jobs in America's growing cities. Steamships and railroads made the trip faster and cheaper than ever, though not pleasant for the crowds who traveled in ships' bottom compartments with baggage and supplies.

Unfortunately for these hopeful travelers, reality often proved far less appealing than their dreams.

DOCUMENT 20.1

Kaiser William II Links Nationalism and Imperialism

For many people, the distance between the increasingly assertive nationalism of the late nineteenth century and the new imperialism of the period was short. The following speech at Hamburg in 1901, delivered by Kaiser William II of Germany, exemplifies this view.

In spite of the fact that we have no such fleet as we should have, we have conquered for ourselves a place in the sun. It will now be my task to see to it that this place in the sun shall remain our undisputed possession, in order that the sun's rays may fall fruitfully upon our activity and trade in foreign parts, that our industry and agriculture may develop within the state and our sailing sports upon the water, for our future lies upon the water. The more Germans go out upon the waters, whether it be in the races of regattas, whether

it be in journeys across the ocean, or in the service of the battleflag, so much the better will it be for us. For when the German has once learned to direct his glance upon what is distant and great, the pettiness which surrounds him in daily life on all sides will disappear. Whoever wishes to have this larger and freer outlook can find no better place than one of the Hanseatic cities.[1] What we have learned out of the previous history of our development amounts really to what I already pointed out when I sent my brother to the East Asiatic station (Dec. 15, 1897). We have merely drawn the logical conclusions from the work which was left us by Emperor William the Great, my memorable grandfather, and the great man whose monument we have recently unveiled. These consequences lie in the fact that we are now making our

efforts to do what, in the old time, the Hanseatic cities could not accomplish, because they lacked the vivifying and protecting power of the empire. May it be the function of my Hansa during many years of peace to protect and advance commerce and trade! . . .

As head of the empire I therefore rejoice over every citizen, whether from Hamburg, Bremen, or Lübeck, who goes forth with this large outlook and seeks new points where we can drive in the nail on which to hang our armour.

SOURCE: C. Gauss, *The German Kaiser as Shown in His Public Utterances* (New York: Charles Scribner's Sons, 1915), pp. 181–183.
[1] *The Hanseatic cities formed a league in the late Middle Ages to facilitate trade.*

Analyze the Document

1. How does William II connect nationalism and imperialism?

2. By what means does he hope to spread German influence throughout the world?

3. In what ways might this speech appeal to both liberals and conservatives?

New arrivals usually got only the most remote or poorest lands and the lowest-paying jobs. Lonely or adrift in their new world, they sent letters and money back home, maintaining ties to old communities for a while or asking others to join them. Millions gave up the search for a better life or found reason to turn back; about one-third of those emigrating overseas from Europe eventually returned home.

THE NEW IMPERIALISM: THE RACE FOR AFRICA AND ASIA

In the 1880s, this mass migration of individuals was paralleled by an expansion of Western power into non-Western parts of the world. European nations raced to gain control over Africa and Asia especially. They subdued local opposition and reshaped the existing societies to fit their own purposes. They brought Western culture and institutions to Africa and Asia whether those peoples wanted them or not. By 1914, imperial powers had seized most of Africa and much of Asia, taking direct or indirect control over almost half a billion people.

Imperialism was not new. Since the fifteenth century, Europeans had been extending their influence over the globe. Increasingly during the eighteenth and nineteenth centuries, Western nations developed and mobilized the ships, weapons, and finances that gave them advantages over other civilizations. Spurred on by competitive rivalries among themselves for power and wealth, European states used these advantages to impose their will again and again in Asia and Africa. But the burst of expansion between about 1880 and 1914 was so rapid and extensive that historians call it the **new imperialism.**

Money and Glory

There were many forces driving this wave of imperialism. For one thing, as Document 20.1 indicates, people thought they could make money from it. "It is in order to foster the growth of the trade of this country, and to find | Economic causes an outlet for our manufacturers and our surplus energy, that our far-seeing statesmen and our commercial men advocate colonial expansion," concluded a British colonial administrator. Industrial nations hungered for new markets, cheap raw materials, and juicy investment opportunities. Western manufacturers, merchants, financiers, shippers, investors, adventurers, and settlers thought they would find all these things in Africa and Asia, and European workers believed that the guaranteed markets would keep them employed. Political leaders, egged on by other pressures as well, usually agreed.

Yet the race for riches often proved more difficult than people expected. Many colonies cost European governments far more to acquire and maintain than riches received. The colonizing process got complicated politically as well. Imperial powers took some colonies not because they saw them as money-makers but because they wanted to protect the borders of other, more lucrative colonies. In many such buffer colonies, loans were never paid off, mines never yielded enough minerals to cover their expenses, and markets proved not worth the cost of building railroads to reach them. But in the beginning, people hoped for great profits or at least security for money-making ventures in distant lands. Competition and the optimistic taking on of risks were at the heart of capitalism, and this led many Westerners and their nations into Africa and Asia.

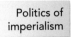
Politics of imperialism

A different, probably more powerful competition—the drive for international prestige—also drove governments, cheered on by millions of their citizens, to snap up colonies. The renewed burst of imperialism came at precisely the time when nationalism was on the rise in Europe. As Document 20.2 suggests, nationalistic sentiment easily translated into a new struggle for imperial conquest—for remote islands, barren deserts, and impenetrable jungles as well as for more lucrative prizes. Governments used such conquests to display their muscle, especially when such a display was lacking at home. France's expansion, for example, helped French citizens feel compensated for losses suffered in the Franco-Prussian War. Italian conquests overseas promised to make up for Italy's failure to acquire first-rate power status on the Continent. Gaining colonies became a measure of status, proof of a nation's political and economic prowess. To be left behind in the imperial race marked a nation as second class. "[A]ll great nations in the fullness of their strength have desired to set their mark upon barbarian lands, and those who fail to participate in this great rivalry will play a pitiable role in the time to come," the nationalist German historian Heinrich von Treitschke announced. People in the West avidly followed the race for colonies. Newspapers reporting on incidents and conquests in Asia and Africa framed these developments as adventures and patriotic causes. Thrilling stories about action overseas sold countless papers. In books and classrooms, people could see their national colors spreading across oceans and continents.

Nationalism and imperialism

This competition for economic gain and international prestige gained a life of its own, a momentum that became hard to curb. When one nation moved into a new area, others followed, for fear of being left with nothing. To protect established colonies, imperial powers seized adjoining territories. To ensure supply lines to distant colonies, nations grabbed up islands, ports, and bases. To form alliances and collect bargaining chips for when disputes arose, imperial powers made colonial claims.

Finally, people found ways to justify imperialism. Westerners saw themselves as bringing "blessings" of their civilization to "backward" peoples. The British writer Rudyard Kipling (1865–1936) expressed the belief of many Westerners when he wrote of the "white man's burden" to civilize the "lesser breeds" of the earth. Missionaries took to heart the injunction to "Go ye into all the world and preach the gospel to every creature."

Justification

Figure 20.8, a cover illustration from a French Catholic magazine, *The Pilgrim*, reveals Westerners' idealized views of imperialism. Here a member of the White Sisters, a Catholic order, teaches already converted Ugandan girls how to use a sewing machine. The image plainly contrasts the devoted, beautiful

Une Sœur Blanche, missionaire d'Afrique, apprend la machine à coudre et la couture aux petites chrétiennes noires de l'Ouganda. (Dessin de Guénac.)

FIGURE 20.8 A European Vision of Imperialism This pro-imperialism publication depicts a member of a Catholic order teaching Ugandan girls how to improve their lives.

DOCUMENT 20.2

Economics and Imperialism in Africa

With new conquests made in the scramble for Africa, many people expected commerce to accelerate and new markets for manufactured goods to emerge. This attitude shows up in Lord Lugard's account of his experiences in colonial service. A British soldier and administrator, Lugard helped bring large parts of Africa into the British Empire.

The Chambers of Commerce of the United Kingdom have unanimously urged the retention of East Africa on the grounds of commercial advantage. The Presidents of the London and Liverpool chambers attended a deputation to her Majesty's Minister for Foreign Affairs to urge "the absolute necessity, for the prosperity of this country, that new avenues for commerce such as that in East Equatorial Africa should be opened up, in view of the hostile tariffs with which British manufacturers are being everywhere confronted." Manchester followed with a similar declaration; Glasgow, Birmingham, Edinburgh, and other commercial centres gave it as their opinion that "there is practically no middle course for this country, between a reversal of the free-trade policy to which it is pledged, on the one hand, and a prudent but continuous territorial extension for the creation of new markets, on the other hand." . . .

This view has been strongly endorsed by some of our leading statesmen. Space forbids me to quote extracts from speeches by our greatest politicians, which I might else adduce as proof that they held the opinions of the Chambers of Commerce, which

I have quoted, to be sound and weighty. . . .

The "Scramble for Africa" by the nations of Europe—an incident without parallel in the history of the world—was due to the growing commercial rivalry, which brought home to civilised nations the vital necessity of securing the only remaining fields for industrial enterprise and expansion. It is well, then, to realise that it is for our *advantage*—and not alone at the dictates of duty—that we have undertaken responsibilities in East Africa. It is in order to foster the growth of the trade of this country, and to find an outlet for our manufactures and our surplus energy, that our far-seeing statesmen and our commercial men advocate colonial expansion. . . .

There are some who say we have no *right* in Africa at all, that "it belongs to the natives." I hold that our right is the necessity that is upon us to provide for our ever-growing population—either by opening new fields for emigration, or by providing work and employment which the development of over-sea extension entails—and to stimulate trade by finding new markets, since we know what misery trade depression brings at home.

While thus serving our own interests as a nation, we may, by selecting men of the right stamp for the control of new territories, bring at the same time many advantages to Africa. Nor do we deprive the natives of their birthright of freedom, to place them under a foreign yoke. It has ever been the key-note of British colonial method to rule through and by the natives, and it is this method, in contrast to the arbitrary

and uncompromising rule of Germany, France, Portugal, and Spain, which has been the secret of our success as a colonising nation, and has made us welcomed by tribes and peoples in Africa, who ever rose in revolt against the other nations named. In Africa, moreover, there is among the people a natural inclination to submit to a higher authority. That intense detestation of control which animates our Teutonic races does not exist among the tribes of Africa, and if there is any authority that we replace, it is the authority of the Slavers and Arabs, or the intolerable tyranny of the "dominant tribe." . . .

***

So far, therefore, as my personal experience goes, I have formed the following estimate: (1) No kind of men I have ever met with—including British soldiers, Afghans, Burmese, and many tribes of India—are more amenable to discipline, more ready to fall into the prescribed groove willingly and quickly, more easy to handle, or require so little compulsion as the African. (2) To obtain satisfactory results a great deal of system, division of labour, supervision, etc., is required. (3) On the whole, the African is very quick at learning, and those who prove themselves good at the superior class of work take a pride in the results, and are very amenable to a word of praise, blame, or sarcasm.

SOURCE: Captain F.D. Lugard, *The Rise of Our East African Empire*, vol. I (London: William Blackwood and Sons, 1893), pp. 379–382, 473.

Analyze the Document

1. How does Lugard connect nationalistic and economic motives for imperialism?

2. How does he respond to arguments against imperialism?

3. What are Lugard's perceptions of Africans?

European woman and the humble, well-behaved children. The implied promise is that the West will bring the benefits of its technology, faith, and civilization to a new generation of thankful Africans.

Some people put imperialism in a less rosy context. These observers described colonial competition and conquest as part of an unavoidable, Darwinian struggle

for survival of the fittest (see Document 20.3). In such a struggle, the white "race" would surely prevail, they believed. France's prime minister even claimed that "the superior races have rights over the inferior races," a view supported by many.

There were people who opposed imperialism. Intellectuals, reform clubs, and politicians such as

DOCUMENT 20.3

Progress and the Struggle of Race with Race

During the late nineteenth century, ideas about social Darwinism and eugenics—the study of hereditary "improvement" by selective breeding—spread in the West and were used to justify competition, war, and imperialism. Karl Pearson (1857–1936), trained as a mathematician, became an outspoken proponent of eugenics, claiming the best scientific thinking backed it. The following is an excerpt from his 1901 book, National Life from the Standpoint of Science.

History shows me one way, and one way only, in which a high state of civilization has been produced, namely, the struggle of race with race, and the survival of the physically and mentally fitter race. . . . The struggle means suffering, intense suffering, while it is in progress; but that struggle and that suffering have been the stages by which the white

man has reached his present stage of development, and they account for the fact that he no longer lives in caves and feeds on roots and nuts. This dependence of progress on the survival of the fitter race, terribly black as it may seem to some of you, gives the struggle for existence its redeeming features; it is the fiery crucible out of which comes the finer metal. You may hope for a time when the sword shall be returned into the plowshare, when American and German and English traders shall no longer compete in the markets of the world for their raw material and for their food supply, when the white man and the dark shall share the soil between them, and each till it as he lists. But, believe me, when that day comes mankind will no longer progress; there will be nothing to check the fertility of inferior stock; the relentless law of heredity will not be

controlled and guided by natural selection. Man will stagnate; and unless he ceases to multiply, the catastrophe will come again; famine and pestilence, as we see them in the East, physical selection instead of the struggle of race against race, will do the work more relentlessly, and, to judge from India and China, far less efficiently than of old.

SOURCE: Karl Pearson, *National Life from the Standpoint of Science* (London: A & C Black, 1901).

Analyze the Document

1. In what ways might Pearson's ideas justify imperialism?

2. How should competition and struggle take place, according to Pearson?

3. In what ways might Pearson's ideas be considered racist today?

Jean Jaurès called it an unjustifiably cruel and costly exploitation. However, such voices did not carry enough weight. Powerful economic interests and politicians had found imperial expansion irresistible, and most citizens were all too willing to support the adventure. Moreover, imperial conquest became so easy it seemed foolish not to take advantage of it.

Opposition to imperialism

The Tools of Conquest

Before 1850, it was either too difficult or not worth the effort for Westerners to penetrate into Africa's interior or extensively expand colonial holdings in Asia. After 1850, science and technology gave the industrialized nations the tools they needed to conquer and control nonindustrialized lands.

Steam-powered iron ships conveyed messages, materials, and people across oceans quickly and cheaply. Smaller steamboats took travelers up rivers. Railroads carried them across vast stretches of land. The Suez Canal cut thousands of miles off journeys to Asia, and the Panama Canal promised much the same (see the drawing on

Transportation facilities

page 628). In 1800, mail took as long as one year to get from London to India. In 1880, a telegram took just hours.

Innovations in weaponry also gave the West new clout. Europeans had long possessed more firepower than non-Western peoples. The new breech-loading rifles and machine guns multiplied that advantage. Local societies resisted, but with the destructive power of these new weapons, European soldiers numbering only a few hundred annihilated local forces in the thousands. Winston Churchill, Britain's future prime minister and an observer of the 1898 Battle of Omdurman in the Sudan, described the effects of the machine gun on natives: "It was not a battle but an execution. . . . The bodies were . . . spread evenly over acres and acres." In that particular battle, 11,000 Muslim tribesmen died, whereas only 28 British soldiers lost their lives. Many other battles, large and small, took place in the series of open and guerrilla wars over the years. Imperial powers usually prevailed, but conquest and control came with much bloodshed and brutality. As the British novelist Joseph Conrad wrote in his 1902 classic, *Heart of Darkness*, "The conquest of the earth, which mostly means the taking it away from those who have a different complexion

Force

or slightly flatter noses than ourselves, is not a pretty thing when you look into it much."

Disease, more than distance or resistance, had also kept Europeans out of most of Africa. But by 1830, the French had discovered the power of quinine to protect their soldiers from deadly malaria long enough to take Algeria in North Africa. After 1850, explorers, missionaries, traders, soldiers, and officials came into sub-Saharan Africa armed with the new medicine.

Medicine

Various Europeans used these tools of conquest at different times. Sometimes missionaries and explorers entered new lands first; at other times, traders or even military officers made decisions on their own to move in. Once there, they called on home governments to provide support, enforce contracts, and protect private interests. Newspapers reported "atrocities" committed against the unwelcome intruders and stirred up European cries for revenge and protection of national honor. Western governments that had requested the cooperation of local political leaders and had been refused turned to force. Indirect control could quickly turn into direct control as problems arose. Control expanded even more as neighboring areas attracted the interest of the intruders.

Patterns of conquest

The Scramble for Africa

Imperial control spread most dramatically in Africa. In the early nineteenth century, Africa was the seat of several vital civilizations. In the north were the long-established Islamic societies. In sub-Saharan Africa—particularly in the western and central Sudan, where the Sahara Desert gave way to grasslands and trade flourished—a rich array of societies and states had developed over the centuries. In most kingdoms of the Sudan and western Africa, Islam had become a major cultural influence. Trade and contact with Europeans affected Africa, but except for coastal and certain other limited areas, such as South Africa, most of Africa remained free from European control.

By the middle decades of the nineteenth century, however, the French had conquered and annexed Algeria in North Africa and had pushed their way up the Senegal River in the west. The British had taken the Cape Colony in South Africa from the Dutch during the Napoleonic Wars, and the Dutch settlers had moved northward into the interior (see **Map 20.2**). In the late 1870s, two developments initiated an international scramble to carve up Africa.

North Africa

The first occurred in Egypt. This North African state had long interested France and Britain as a market for European goods and investments and as a bridge to Asia. European bankers financed the construction of port facilities, railroads, and telegraph lines in Egypt,

granting high-interest loans to Egypt's government. In 1869 the Suez Canal, built by a French company, opened and became the vital link from the Mediterranean Sea through Egypt to the Red Sea and the Indian Ocean (see the drawing on page 628). The British desired control over the canal so as to secure their lucrative position in India. In 1875, Great Britain took advantage of the Egyptian government's financial distress and purchased the Egyptian ruler's, or khedive's, controlling portion of the canal stock. Four years later, France and Britain seized Egypt's treasury to secure their investments. When nationalist groups in Egypt revolted, British troops occupied Egypt. Formally, the khedive remained in office, but after 1882, Britain held most of the real power. By then, 3,000 ships a year passed through the Suez Canal.

The British reshaped Egypt's economy so that it produced cotton, silk, and wheat for export in return for manufactured goods. They also disrupted local work life by hiring Egyptian laborers for their own projects—whether as railroad builders or servants. Worse, they insulted unfavored groups—such as Muslims and Arabs—by paying them less than favored groups.

The French reluctantly acquiesced to British control in Egypt in return for Britain's support of French ambitions in northwestern Africa. In the following years, Britain expanded south to secure Egypt and east to maintain its position in India and China. For similar reasons, France expanded from its stake in Algeria to Tunisia, Morocco, and most of northwestern Africa.

At the same time, King Leopold II of Belgium (r. 1865–1909), set out to get "a slice of this magnificent African cake." Hungry for ivory, rubber, hardwoods, palm oil, and glory, he initiated a new competition for acquisitions in sub-Saharan Africa by devouring the Congo. He had claimed that his purpose was "to open to civilization" central Africa, "to pierce the darkness which envelopes whole populations." In fact, his troops killed and mutilated thousands of local peoples in the process of conquest. An American missionary described the brutality with which Leopold's officials forced people into the forest to collect rubber: "The soldiers drive the people into the bush. If they will not go they are shot down, and their left hands cut off and taken as trophies."

Worried about missing out on the land grab, the other European powers voiced their own claims. The French centered their efforts in western Africa, the Germans in eastern Africa, and the British up and down the center, "from Cairo to Capetown." The Berlin Conference of 1885 formalized this scramble for Africa, setting ground rules for territorial acquisition on that continent. According to the conference, colonizers were supposed to have enough physical

Sub-Saharan Africa

MAP 20.2

Imperialism in Africa, ca. 1885

Comparing **Map 20.2,** which shows European holdings in Africa in 1885, with **Map 20.3** on page 648, which shows European holdings in 1914, reveals the results of the Europeans' grab for African lands.

Explore the Maps

1. Which European nations became the main imperial powers in Africa?

2. Notice the dates of acquisition by the European powers. What do these dates reveal about the timing of the scramble for African lands?

3. Locate Britain's possessions. How do these holdings reflect Britain's concern to protect its routes to India?

---

presence to control and develop an area before they could claim it. They also agreed to treat Africans according to humane standards, although they often used that declaration to disguise the exploitation and abuse they continued to commit.

By 1914, most of the huge continent had been carved up by the various European powers (see **Map 20.3**). The main exception was Ethiopia. There, Emperor Menelik II (r. 1889–1913) cleverly played one European power off another. In the process, he

MAP 20.3

Imperialism in Africa, 1914

manipulated the Europeans into supplying his country with modern arms, which he then used to defeat the invading Italians in 1896.

For the Europeans, the costliest struggles occurred among themselves. The imperial powers averted most conflicts by diplomacy. In South Africa, however, even the most skilled diplomacy failed to keep the peace. British settlers began to move into the South African Cape Colony early in the nineteenth century. The Dutch Boers (Afrikaners), who had settled there in the seventeenth century and resented Brit-

ain's abolition of slavery, trekked northward far into the interior, slaughtering the resisting Zulus in their way. Eventually, the British recognized the independence of the two Boer states, Transvaal and the Orange Free State.

However, when rich gold mines were discovered in Transvaal in the 1880s, British immigrants flooded in. The British entrepreneur and empire builder Cecil Rhodes (1853–1902), backed by powerful interest groups concerned about the growing German presence

Boer War

MAP 20.4

The Middle East and Central Asia, 1850–1914

This map shows the Middle East and parts of Central Asia where Russia and Britain expanded their areas of control and influence during the second half of the nineteenth century.

Explore the Map

1. Where were Russia and Britain most likely to come into conflict? Why?

2. Where were the Ottomans and Persians put on the defensive?

3. Why might the Russians and British have been so concerned about Afghanistan that they nearly went to war over it in 1884–1887?

---

in southwestern Africa, decided to brush aside the two little Boer republics. But what the British thought would be an easy victory took three years (1899–1902) of military effort and involved severe casualties and enormous costs. Backed by 300,000 troops from India and the homeland, Britain finally won the brutal contest and in the end treated the defeated Boers leniently. The British took them into partnership in the Union of South Africa, and the Boer hero General Louis Botha (1862–1919) was elected the Union's first prime minister. Botha's government announced that it would "permit no equality between colored people and the white inhabitants," a policy that South Africa would hold on to for the next eighty years.

Europeans usually ruled directly over African societies so they could create the economic conditions they wanted. Colonial administrators trained cooperative tribes as their clerks, soldiers, and favored workers. These preferences often sparked bitter tribal jealousies and rivalries. Throughout Africa, Europeans made it clear by their words and actions that they considered themselves, their civilization, and their "race" superior to the Africans. Their dominance established, Europeans prided themselves on bringing Christianity and civilization to the "dark" continent. They had scant appreciation for the qualities of African societies and dismissed the Africans as inferior peoples useful only for manual labor. Often they treated them little better than slaves. They also established new political boundaries that ignored the long-standing

> Dominance, conflict, and consequences

social, cultural, and political realities of local peoples. Some officials even worked to "submerge" Africans from different societies "into a single colored working class," a policy that prevented Africans from maintaining kinship and community ties. Those Africans who resisted might be decimated in armed battle or dispossessed and forced onto reservations. Yet resentment and desperation led many Africans to rebel against their conquerors, despite the hopelessness of their situation. A warrior in South Africa explained the reasons for one of these rebellions: "Our King gone, we had submitted to the white people and they ill-treated us until we became desperate and tried to make an end of it all. We knew that we had very little chance because their weapons were so much superior to ours. But we meant to fight to the last, feeling that even if we could not beat them we might at least kill a few of them and so have some sort of revenge."

Establishing Control in Asia

In Asia, Western powers usually got what they wanted by ruling through local elites. In these large, well-organized societies, where the potential for effective resistance remained great, Westerners' tampering with the established power structure was risky.

India was as linguistically and regionally diverse as Europe. Nevertheless, by the nineteenth century, the British had brought together a variety of states, territories, and tribal groups to create an Indian state under British control. The Indian subcontinent became Britain's richest imperial prize. Nearly twenty times larger than Great Britain and more than seven times as populous, India bought and sold more goods than any other British colony. Britain directed much of its imperial policy toward preserving this lucrative colony. Part of the reason Britain annexed new colonies in Africa and widened its sphere of influence in the Middle East was to protect India from other European states. One of these was Russia, which was expanding its control in areas near India (**Map 20.4**). Competition for power and influence in these lands brought Russia and Britain to the brink of war in 1881 and again in 1884–1887.

Until 1858, the British East India Company, a private-stock company, governed much of India. However, the great Sepoy Mutiny of 1857, the first large-scale uprising of Indians against British rule, almost drove the British out of India. This prompted the British government to take direct control. Instead of meddling with the structure of Indian society, the British used India's elites to support their rule. They employed a half-million Indians to administer the huge country and built railroads, canals, ports, schools,

> The Middle East and India

and medical facilities. In one sense, India benefited in that population increased rapidly. On the other hand, living standards for most fell as population increases outstripped economic growth. The British paid low wages and labeled Indians as inferior—at best, in the words of the British historian and politician Thomas Macaulay, "a great people sunk in the lowest depth of slavery and superstition." Through use of tariffs, they forced India to collapse its own cotton industry and accept British imports of cotton cloth instead. They restructured India's economy to specialize in products the British wanted, such as jute, raw cotton, opium, tea, and wheat. As one Indian nationalist explained, "*Pax Britannica* [Britain's peace] has been established in this country in order that a foreign government may exploit the country."

Britain permanently altered this ancient civilization by creating a national unity, whether the Indians desired it or not. Moreover, British men and women in India imported their own cultural standards, lived separately from the "inferior" native societies, and expected the Indians they dealt with—from elites to servants—to adjust to British ways. For example, in her book *The Complete Indian Housekeeper and Cook* (1898), British author Flora Annie Steel boasted that "to show what absolute children Indian servants are," she has "for years adopted castor oil as an ultimatum," adding that this is "considered a great joke, and exposes the offender to much ridicule from his fellow-servants." **Figure 20.9,** a photo of Indian servants catering to a British gentleman, indicates the gulf between the British ruling class and the Indians they governed. It also reveals the appeal of foreign service to the British, who at home may have enjoyed only modest social positions.

The British showed no inclination to grant India self-government. As a result, nationalism—already a potent force in Europe—rose in Asia. Indian dissatisfaction with British rule mounted steadily. In 1885, the nationalist Indian elite formed the Indian National Congress, which would launch a long struggle for Indian independence.

France followed the same pattern as Britain in its southeast Asia colonies. By the 1860s, open resistance to the intruding French had become hopeless. As one of Vietnam's leading statesmen explained in 1867, "The French have come, with their powerful weapons of war . . . no one can resist them. They go where they want, the strongest ramparts fall before them." During the 1880s and early 1890s, France took what would become Vietnam, Cambodia, and Laos and grouped them into the Union of Indochina under French control. As in India, medicine, sanitation, canals, roads, and other projects financed by the French led to population growth in Indochina. French rule also spawned economic

> Southeast Asia

dependence and resentment against the European assumption of superiority. A southeast Asian elite arose that, as in India, would struggle to expel Western rule.

China, with its highly structured society, strong central government, and large armed forces, had long kept Western-

China

ers at arm's length. Although the Chinese admitted some European traders and Christian missionaries in the sixteenth and seventeenth centuries, they closed their doors rather tightly thereafter. At the beginning of the eighteenth century, China ranked among the world's most prosperous and powerful societies. The Chinese still considered their huge, populous country the center of civilization surrounded by lesser civilizations. As late as 1793, China's emperor could easily dismiss a proposed trade agreement with Britain: "Our Celestial Empire possesses all things in abundance. We have no need of barbarian products."

However, during the nineteenth century, population explosion, famine, rebellions, and poor leadership under the declining Qing (Ch'ing) dynasty weakened the ancient civilization. The country became a power vacuum that proved all too tempting to the Western powers. Armed with their guns and goods, Westerners streamed into China.

First, the British forced themselves on the Chinese. During the 1830s, Britain began trading Indian opium in China for tea, silver, silk,

Opium Wars

and other products. Soon opium became one of Britain's most important commodities (see Global Connections). Chinese officials tried to stop the economic drain, addiction, and criminal activities stemming from the opium trade by making the drug illegal. As the Chinese official in charge exclaimed to the British, "You do not wish opium to harm your own country, but you choose to bring that harm to other countries such as China. Why?" In response, Britain sent gunboats and troops armed with modern weapons. They easily defeated the Chinese in a series of clashes known as the Opium Wars. By the terms of the Treaty of Nanking (1842), which ended the conflict, the Chinese ceded Hong Kong to the British, opened several tariff-free ports to foreign trade, exempted foreigners from Chinese law, and paid Britain a large indemnity.

At mid-century, disaster struck. China suffered a devastating civil war—the Taiping Rebellion (1850–1864). Subsequent rebel-

Taiping Rebellion

lions extended the internal conflict another ten years. In the end, these wars took perhaps fifty million lives, and the famines that followed cost the lives of millions

FIGURE 20.9 The British in India This period photo showing Indian servants attending to a British man suggests both the gulf between these peoples and the appeal to the British of going overseas to imperial holdings.

more. All this strife weakened the Qing dynasty and revealed the government's inability to control a nation threatened by external enemies and internal upheaval.

In the years that followed, China fought a series of wars against foreigners. It lost them all, and each defeat chipped away at its sovereignty and racked up

IMPERIALISM AND THE NON-WESTERN WORLD

1839–1842	Opium Wars in China
1850–1864	Taiping Rebellion in China
1853	United States forces opening of Japan
1868	Meiji Restoration in Japan
1869	Suez Canal opens
1885	Berlin Conference
1896	Ethiopians defeat Italians
1898	Spanish-American War
1899–1900	Boxer Rebellion in China
1899–1902	Boer War
1904	Russo-Japanese War

KEY DATES

Opium and the West in China

Opium, a narcotic derived from the opium poppy, was known and used—especially for medical purposes—in China for centuries. However, not until the nineteenth century did its use become so widespread that millions of Chinese became addicted to the drug. The West was not free from opium, either, for Europeans and Americans increasingly resorted to opium-based products such as morphine and laudanum to calm their nerves, ease aches and pains, and control their noisy children. During the nineteenth century, most of China's opium supply was imported by British merchants from colonial holdings in India.

Chinese officials made only halfhearted attempts to restrict the opium trade until 1838, when Emperor Daoguang finally banned importation of the drug. In 1839, an imperial official, Lin Zexu, wrote a letter to Britain's Queen Victoria complaining about the destructive impact of opium on China. "Unscrupulous" merchants, Lin wrote, were "so obsessed with material gain that they have no concern whatever for the harm they can cause to others." These merchants had flooded China with so much opium "that this poison has spread far and wide in all the provinces." Lin asked the queen to stop the trade and "destroy and plow under all of these opium plants." When Lin began confiscating and destroying imported opium, the British responded with force. As one of China's discouraged commissioners reported, "The ships of the barbarians are sturdy and their cannons fierce." By 1842, British firepower had

overwhelmed the Chinese, and the Treaty of Nanjing legalized the opium trade and granted concessions to Britain and other Western powers.

The struggle against the British over opium was only the beginning of the wars and other upheavals China suffered during the nineteenth and twentieth centuries. Internal problems also increasingly plagued the vast country, weakening the government's ability to resist the West. In 1852, Zeng Guofan, a perceptive scholar and high official in Emperor Xianfeng's government, commented on the situation. Taxes, Zeng claimed, were overwhelming the people. Therefore, "people are complaining and angry, and often the resistance to tax payment bursts forth and mushrooms into full-fledged riot." More and more impoverished people were resorting to banditry to survive. Yet attempts to stop the lawlessness were useless because governmental soldiers "have always been in collusion with the bandits," Zeng maintained, and would soon release the bandits "in return for a handsome bribe." Moreover, people had lost faith in the justice system because so many "innocent men are condemned" and the people "[are unable] to have a wrong redressed." The next year, a series of disastrous uprisings struck China, the worst of which came with the Taiping Rebellion. Over the following ten years, the conflicts devastated large parts of the country. While the government eventually crushed the rebels, the country soon began losing lands and control to imperial powers.

Meanwhile, the destructive consequences of the opium trade

mounted. Isabella Bird Bishop, a British traveler in China during the 1890s, reported on the situation. In addition to noting the continuing importation of opium into China by the British, Bishop observed that "The area devoted to the [opium-producing] poppy in Sze Chuan [province] is enormous." Moreover, its culture was "encroaching on the rice and arable lands" so much that "there was no longer a margin left on which to feed the population in years of a poor harvest." Even though the Chinese regarded the opium habit as a disease, Bishop continued, in that province "opium houses are as common as gin shops in our London slums." In the large cities of that province, she noted, 80 percent of men and 40 percent of women were opium smokers. "It is obvious," she concluded, "that opium has come to stay."

To other observers throughout China and the West, it seemed equally clear that China was caught in the tightening grip of Western and Japanese imperialists as well as a powerful and addictive narcotic.

Making Connections

1. How did Chinese officials try to restrict the opium trade?

2. What do you think of the British response?

3. In what ways did British merchants' selling of opium help to undermine the authority of China's government?

---

yet more indemnities. The Western powers grabbed up spheres of influence and semi-independent treaty ports where all foreigners were exempt from Chinese jurisdiction. In addition, they built railroads to penetrate farther into China's heartland. As shown on Map 20.5, they also took lands on the huge country's periphery. By all these means, the French and British added to their possessions in south Asia, Russia gained territory in the north, and Japan snapped up Korea and Taiwan in the east.

MAP 20.5

Imperialism in Asia, 1840–1914

This map shows the expansion of imperialism in Asia by the Western powers and Japan.

Explore the Map

1. Which powers had gained the largest territorial interests in Asia by 1914?

2. Which lands in particular were controlled by Russia, Britain, and Japan?

3. Where do you think conflicts were likely to break out among Russia, Britain, and Japan? Why?

The United States joined in the frenzy, grabbing the Philippine Islands after a war with Spain in 1898 and a long struggle against Filipino nationalist forces that cost the lives of perhaps 200,000 Filipinos. President William McKinley explained that the United States had the duty "to educate the Filipinos and uplift and Christianize them." To protect its commercial interests in Asia, the United States called for an "Open Door" policy that would avoid further territorial annexations by the imperial powers. Rivalry among the great powers themselves, as much as Chinese resistance, saved China from complete loss of its independence.

Meanwhile, Chinese nationalism rose in response to foreign aggression. In 1899–1900, the Boxer

The Philippines

FIGURE 20.10 John Clymer, *The Boxer Rebellion,* 1900 This dramatic painting shows U.S. marines firing on the Boxers, who in 1899 staged a rebellion against foreign influence in China.

Rebellion, a serious uprising against Western influences, erupted. Furious at those who had betrayed Chinese religion and customs, the Boxers, a secret organization that believed in the spiritual power of the martial arts, killed thousands of Chinese Christians and a number of foreigners—all with the encouragement of China's dowager empress. **Figure 20.10,** a painting by American artist John Clymer, depicts a battle between the Boxers—in the center, with swords and spears—and U.S. marines—in the lower right, with modern machine guns, rifles with bayonets, and revolvers. The Boxers, represented as wild and bloodthirsty, seem to burst out of the heavily populated Chinese society, while the steadfast U.S. marines fire from the outside into that society. Combined forces from the imperial powers brutally suppressed this nationalist movement and forced China to pay large indemnities.

[Boxer Rebellion]

Even propped up by imperial powers, the corrupt Chinese central government could not last. In 1911, reformers led by Sun Yat-sen (1866–1925), a Western-educated doctor, launched a revolution aimed at freeing China from foreign exploitation and modernizing its society. Rebellions swept most of China and pushed the corrupt, inept, disintegrating dynasty to its final collapse. Sun proclaimed a republic, but power soon dispersed among imperial generals, who became warlords. China's struggles to cope with the encroaching world and its internal problems were far from over.

Japan, even more than China, had long refused direct contact with the West. At the beginning of the nineteenth century, the island nation remained in great part a feudal society ruled by the shogun—a strong military governor—and his military chieftains.

The Japanese emperor had only limited powers. Though long influenced by Chinese culture, Japan also had a sharply defined sense of identity: "[O]ur country is the source and fountainhead of all other countries, and in all matters it excels all the others," explained one Japanese writer.

[Japan]

In 1853, however, the Japanese witnessed an imposing sight: a squadron of well-armed, steam-powered American ships under Admiral Matthew Perry (1794–1858) sailing uninvited into Edo (Tokyo) Bay. Perry's instructions from the American government stressed the United States' desire to "establish commercial intercourse with a country whose large population and reputed wealth hold out great temptations to mercantile enterprise." If friendly negotiations should fail, the instructions continued, Perry should "change his tone" and threaten force. Perry took the charge to heart: "The World has assigned this duty to us," he asserted.

Japan's efforts to resist Perry's encroachment proved futile. Soon the well-armed Western ships intimidated the Tokugawa government into signing unequal treaties with the United States. Japan also inked agreements with Britain, Russia, France, and the Netherlands that opened the country to trade and foreign presences.

Fifteen years after Perry's arrival, the 250-year-old Tokugawa shogunate collapsed in a revolution led by powerful aristocrats who ushered into power the boy emperor Meiji (Enlightened Rule). Weakened by decades of population growth, declining agricultural productivity, popular revolts, and failed efforts at reform, the shogunate gave way. According to Count Ito, a leader of the **Meiji Restoration,** members of the new government "set themselves to the task of introducing Western civilization into Japan." These leaders quickly dismantled the country's traditional military and social order. Using French, German, British, and American ways, they created a new conscript army, introduced universal education, established a written constitution, and began industrializing the economy. In 1889, Ito declared success: "If we . . . compare the present state of affairs with that which existed some twenty years ago, we shall not exaggerate if we say that the country has undergone a complete metamorphosis."

[The Meiji Restoration]

Within a few decades, Japan had transformed itself on its own terms. Once a feudal society with a preindustrial economy, it was now a modern industrialized nation. **Figure 20.11,** a photograph of a Japanese silk-working factory, reveals how intensively—in form and substance—Japan adopted Western industrial methods: Men dressed in formal Western attire

FIGURE 20.11 Japanese Silk Factory, 1905 This photograph features a Western-clad man supervising women in a large Japanese silk factory.

supervise women who work on row after row of tightly spaced machines.

The industrialized nation soon began flexing its new muscle in Asia. Japan viewed China no longer as a source of culture to be respected but as a weakened land open to conquest and exploitation. In 1894, the Japanese invaded China, forcing it to pay a large indemnity and give up Korea and Taiwan. In 1904, after Russia angered Japan by increasing its presence in China's northern province of Manchuria, the Japanese attacked the tsar's troops. To the world's surprise, Japan defeated the inept Russian forces both on land and at sea and became the dominant power in Manchuria. Industrialized, militaristic, and imperialistic, Japan had taken its place alongside other world powers by 1914.

Russo-Japanese War

The Legacy of Imperialism

With its technology, its industrial capitalism, and above all its aggressive nationalism, the West had subjected most of Africa and Asia to its domination between 1870 and 1914. In Australia and New Zealand, European powers had already established large settler colonies. As in North America, contact and clashes with the incoming settlers proved disastrous for the indigenous populations. In the Pacific, the pattern of imperial conquest that the West had established in Africa and Asia held true. Western adventurers, missionaries, traders, gunboats, troops, and businesses came, took over, and destroyed the world that native peoples had long known. Worse, the Westerners carried diseases that decimated Pacific populations.

Certainly, life in non-Western lands had not been idyllic before the intrusion of the West. As one Ndebele warrior in South Africa put it, "Even in our own time there were troubles, there was much fighting and many innocent people were killed." Many from the West in these lands may have been well meaning, and they may have brought elements of Western civilization that were of some benefit to people in the non-Western world. In 1900 Lord Curzon, the celebrated British viceroy of India, wrote about the consequences of British rule over India: "I do not see how any Englishmen, contrasting India as it now is with what it was . . . can fail to see that we came and have stayed . . . in obedience to . . . the decree of Providence, ... for the lasting benefit of millions of the human race." In India, British rule probably prevented internal wars and promoted order. In Africa, Europeans did abolish slavery. Imperial powers built ports, railway lines, hospitals, schools, and sanitation facilities. Colonized peoples also learned about Western politics, economics, and education, eventually making use of them to assert their own liberation from imperial powers.

Yet, rather than striving to understand and appreciate non-Western societies, most people in the West viewed them from a condescending, arrogant, or downright racist perspective. The colonized peoples had to endure being treated as menials and subordinates by men and women whose only necessary qualification was being Western. The insults to local peoples' self-respect and their relentless humiliation fueled resistance to Western control.

Western powers not only forcibly drew non-Western lands into a world economy but also exploited the natural and human resources of the conquered lands and profoundly undermined the cultural, social, and religious traditions of the African and Asian peoples. In addition, they distorted non-Western economies to serve the demands of their own commerce. They imposed what one observer called "the European system of monotonous, uninterrupted labour," in which industries such as mining and railroad building subjected native laborers to inhumane and dangerous working conditions. Forced to migrate to find jobs in the alien economy, local workers left behind shattered families and communities. Political structures that had long functioned effectively in these lands broke down in just a few years.

By 1914, tens of thousands of colonial administrators, soldiers, and settlers relied directly on imperialism for their careers, status, and livelihood. They, along with Western tourists, enjoyed a sense of privilege and superiority over Africans and Asians. Many also enjoyed, though less often discussed, sexual contact with their colonized peoples. Indeed, most Westerners had come to view imperialism as normal and harmless. In their home countries, some people in the West visited the proliferating zoos with "exotic" animals, studied anthropology, viewed new works of art, and read literature that reflected interaction with non-Western lands. But few recognized how destructive it could be—not only to colonial peoples but also to themselves. In Asia, for example, Russia's expansion south brought it to the borders of British India and nearly ignited a war with that nation. Farther east, Russia pushed to the Sea of Japan and Manchuria; the action sparked hostilities with Japan. More than once, Britain, France, and Germany narrowly avoided war in Africa. Imperialism extended the already intense economic and political competition among the European states, heightening the potential for major conflict among these powers.

LOOKING BACK & MOVING FORWARD

Summary   In the years 1870–1914, more and more Westerners gained access to the political process. Nationalism opened these doors for them, as did the movement toward democracy. But the combination of nationalism and democracy had its dangers. In Britain, J. S. Mill warned that "the sentiment of nationality so far outweighs the love of liberty that the people are willing to abet their rulers in crushing the liberty and independence of any people not of their race or language." Many political leaders recognized nationalism and democracy as forces that they could use to their advantage. Others simply adjusted to them. Those who resisted did so at their own peril.

Europeans were also moving, not only to their own cities but out of Europe by the millions. Industrialization and the promise of wealth in new places combined with nationalism and mass politics to push the imperial West throughout the world as never before. As a result, Western power—economic, political, military, and imperial—expanded in an environment of intense international competition.

In the years just before 1914, the strain of this competition on Western societies grew obvious. Labor unrest, the movement for women's suffrage, politics of the extremes, civil violence, diplomatic crises, military threats, and a growing sense of uncertainty all pointed to trouble in the making. Yet this was a complex era. During this same period, the civilization that produced such uncertainty also created new engines of wealth, transformed its cities, and supported an explosion of creative thought and culture.

KEY TERMS

Paris Commune,   *p. 631*
Dreyfus affair,   *p. 632*
Kulturkampf,   *p. 632*
Fabian Society,   *p. 635*
anarchists,   *p. 635*
anti-Semitism,   *p. 637*
Zionism,   *p. 638*
new imperialism,   *p. 642*
Meiji Restoration,   *p. 654*

REVIEW, ANALYZE, & CONNECT TO TODAY

REVIEW THE PREVIOUS CHAPTER

Chapter 19—"Nationalism and Statebuilding"—analyzed the efforts to build national unity and strength between 1850 and 1870.

1. In what ways did nationalism remain a powerful force in the decades after 1870?

2. Analyze how nationalism evolved during these later decades, comparing it with the nationalism of 1850–1870 as well as the ideology of nationalism of the early nineteenth century.

ANALYZE THIS CHAPTER

Chapter 20—"Mass Politics and Imperial Domination"—examines the spreading demands for democracy and the West's imperial expansion between 1870 and 1914.

1. In what ways were large numbers of people incorporated into politics during this period?

2. Why were some areas and groups still left out of the political arena in 1914?

3. Analyze the various causes for the rise of imperialism during this period.

4. For both Western and non-Western peoples, what consequences flowed from imperialism?

CONNECT TO TODAY

Think about the development of democratic institutions throughout the West, and consider the many political and economic consequences of imperialism in the non-Western world discussed in this chapter.

1. What difficulties might nondemocratic societies encounter while trying to institute democracy in today's world?

2. What consequences of imperialism might still be influencing world affairs today?

BEYOND THE CLASSROOM

DEMANDS FOR DEMOCRACY

Mayeur, Jean-Marie, and Madeleine Réberioux. *The Third Republic—From Its Origins to the Great War, 1871–1914.* Cambridge: Cambridge University Press, 1987. A solid survey of France during this period, stressing the politics of the republican government.

Rapport, Michael. *Nineteenth-Century Europe.* London: Palgrave, 2005. A reliable, recent survey with much information and analysis.

Wehler, Hans-Ulrich. *The German Empire, 1871–1918.* Leamington Spa, England: Berg Publishers, 1985. An important and controversial work that argues for continuity between the Second and Third reichs.

INSIDERS AND OUTSIDERS: POLITICS OF THE EXTREMES

Hause, Steven C., and Anne R. Kenney. *Women's Suffrage and Social Politics in the French Third Republic.* Princeton, NJ: Princeton University Press, 1984. Examines all aspects of the women's suffrage movement in France from its origins to the years after the end of World War I.

Lindemann, Albert S. *A History of European Socialism.* New Haven, CT: Yale University Press, 1983. An overview of the European socialist tradition from the Enlightenment to the 1980s.

Offen, Karen. *European Feminisms, 1700–1950.* Stanford, CA: Stanford University Press, 2000. A survey of European feminism with good coverage of the late nineteenth and early twentieth centuries.

Pulzer, P. *The Rise of Political Anti-Semitism in Germany and Austria.* Cambridge, MA: Harvard University Press, 1988. Studies the role of anti-Semitism in the world of central European politics.

Schorske, Carl E. *Fin-de-Siècle Vienna: Politics and Culture.* New York: Knopf, 1980. A classic study of the creative intellectual climate of Vienna that emphasizes the connections between culture and politics.

EMIGRATION: OVERSEAS AND ACROSS CONTINENTS

Hoerder, Dirk, and Leslie Page Moch, eds. *European Migrants—Global and Local Perspectives.* Boston: Northeastern University Press, 1996. A collection of articles by several scholars on the migrations of Europeans across the land and overseas.

Wolf, Eric. *Europe and the People Without History.* Berkeley: University of California Press, 1983. An important cross-cultural perspective on the process and consequences of imperialism.

THE NEW IMPERIALISM: THE RACE FOR AFRICA AND ASIA

Doyle, Michael W. *Empires.* Ithaca, NY: Cornell University Press, 1986. A comparative examination of imperialism.

Headrick, Daniel R. *The Tentacles of Progress: Technology Transfer in the Age of Imperialism, 1850–1940.* New York: Oxford University Press, 1988. Argues that the poorer countries failed to develop under imperial rule despite the transfers of Western capital and technology.

Hochschild, Adam. *King Leopold's Ghost: A Study of Greed, Terror, and Heroism in Colonial Africa.* Boston: Houghton Mifflin, 1999. A chilling story of imperial brutality.

Wesseling, H.L. *Divide and Rule: The Partition of Africa, 1880–1914.* New York: Greenwood, 1996. A solid, well-written survey of this imperial conquest.

GLOBAL CONNECTIONS

Gelber, Harry. *Opium, Soldiers and Evangelicals.* London: Palgrave Macmillan, 2004. Revises standard views of the Opium Wars.

WILLIAM P. FRITH, *MANY HAPPY RETURNS OF THE DAY*, 1856

In this painting, a family gathers for a birthday. The rich clothing, carpeting, paintings on the
wall, heavy curtains, solid bricks showing through the window, and attentive servant on the left
all mark this as an urban middle-class home. In the center, haloed by a wreath, is the innocent
"angel" birthday girl. Here is the ideal of the happy home, the center of private life where men,
women, and children celebrate together. Yet the scene also reflects the contrasting gender
spheres: The women and children gather comfortably. But the father and grandfather—reading a
newspaper—sit close to the window and to the outside, public world of the modern city.

Modern Life and the Culture of Progress

Western Society, 1850–1914

I n 1864, an observer described Milan in northern Italy as vibrant "without being feverish like Paris or London." Though Milan had become one of the great cultural centers in the newly unified Italian state, workers still lived along narrow, winding streets in the heart of this city. Everyone knew each other and spoke the local Milanese dialect. Citizens "huddled around the cathedral, like a family warming itself at the hearth."

This quaint image would not last long. Over the next thirty years, wide avenues and expensive "great white houses, all straight," replaced Milan's narrow streets and old dwellings. Each year thousands of immigrants—mostly peasants and artisans—streamed into the city looking for jobs and all kinds of other opportunities. In just one decade, the city's population grew by almost a third. By the 1890s, the center of Milan teemed with people from the city's outlying quarters and suburbs who traveled there to work, shop, or amuse themselves. They spoke the common Italian language and shoved "on and off the trams . . . day and night." More people purchased goods in the huge new department store near the cathedral than prayed in that Gothic church. Nearby, in the newly built Gallery, musicians, singers, businesspeople, shoppers, and diners congregated in the shops and cafés under a magnificent glass roof. Milan—like Paris, London, and other great cities in the West—had become a center of industry, growth, and culture—a thriving embodiment of modern life.

In the decades after 1850, industrialization pulled masses of Westerners to new jobs in cities like Milan. Urban growth began to overwhelm the West's centuries-old land-based society. In cities, the continuing spread of liberal ideas and the optimism of wealthy urban leaders created a culture of progress. Dominated by science, which seemed to promise so much, and by competitive values that served the up-and-coming middle class so well, this urban culture altered the ways people thought about the world and their place in it. Those who recognized these engines of change saw their civilization being pushed to modernity. In 1850, however, few understood what modernity meant or even how difficult the ride there could be.

TIMELINE

Romanticism

Italian and German Unification

"Second Industrial Revolution"

Industrial Revolution

The New Imperialism

Spread of Democratic Reforms

Realism and Naturalism

World War I

Impressionism

Expressionism

1850   1860   1870   1880   1890   1900   1910   1914

PREVIEW

THE SECOND INDUSTRIAL REVOLUTION

"Steam and electricity have conquered time and space to a greater extent during the last sixty years than all the preceding six hundred years," gushed a special issue of *The Illustrated London News* in 1897. Yet in 1850, most people knew little about the industrial revolution. Outside Britain and a few limited areas in the West, more people still lived in the countryside than in the cities, and more worked at home or in home workshops than in factories. Most had never set foot in a railway car. Even in the cities, people probably made their living much as their parents had—as helpers in shops, domestics, artisans, merchants, and day laborers.

By 1914, this scenario had changed so drastically that even Britain had been left behind. Between 1850 and 1870, the coal mines, iron foundries, textile factories, steam engines, and railroads that had made Britain an industrial giant spread broadly into western and central Europe and North America. After 1870, new inventions, manufacturing processes, and methods for getting products to market and selling them rendered the earlier milestones of industrialization out-of-date. Science, technology, and industry marched hand in hand. Large-scale factories dwarfed the textile mills and iron foundries of the early industrial era, and huge department stores displayed endless goods to entice consumers. For the first time in history, people began to expect continuing economic growth. According to some historians, these developments created a "second industrial revolution."

Steel Leads the Way

Steel led the way in this new wave of industrialization. The Bessemer processes for removing impurities from molten iron speeded up and cheapened steel production, transforming it from an expensive luxury product into a strong, affordable improvement over iron. **Figure 21.1,** an 1880 photograph of the Krupp Steelworks, reveals the new technology and massive factories that produced steel and enabled countries such as Germany to become industrial leaders. On the left are the huge converters that turned iron into steel. Dwarfed in comparison, workers (in the foreground and around the converters) toil to keep the process going. By 1914, the annual production of steel had risen more than fiftyfold since 1850. **Figure 21.2** charts the growth of steel production between 1882 and 1912 and the countries that led in the creation of this crucial industrial material. Out of this steel, manufacturers made efficient tools and machines to fabricate metal, textile, leather, and wood products.

With advances in chemistry, textile manufacturers could now use inexpensive synthetic dyes to color their cloth, and paper manufacturers could process wood pulp more efficiently than ever. By 1914, Chemicals new chemical-based fabrics and processes had spawned a host of infant industries. Germany's chemical laboratories and their development of industrial uses for chemicals helped propel that nation ahead of Great Britain as an industrial leader.

FIGURE 21.1 The Krupp Steelworks, 1880 This photograph of a German steel factory shows the powerful new machines that helped make Germany an industrial leader.

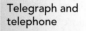

FIGURE 21.2 Steel Production (thousands of metric tons)

Electricity and petroleum became practical sources of power, thanks to the invention of the electrical dynamo, the steam turbine, and the internal combustion engine. By the end of the century, electric lamps glowed in city streets, large stores, and wealthy neighborhoods throughout Europe. Electricity powered factories and workshops and was the magic behind the refrigerators and vacuum cleaners starting to appear in middle-class homes.

> Electricity and petroleum

New Transportation and Communication Networks

Getting around, moving things, and communicating became dramatically easier as well. Before 1850, few people had seen more of the world than they could view on foot or by cart or horseback. By 1914, millions traveled enormous distances each year. Even in China, Turkey, and Brazil, trains chugged along, hauling people for astonishing stretches. This was the greatest era of railroad building in history, and with the railroads came hundreds of bridges and long tunnels. At the same time, huge steamships with steel hulls, turbine engines, and screw propellers replaced sailing ships. The opening of the Suez Canal (between the Mediterranean Sea and the Indian Ocean) in 1869 and the Panama Canal (between the Atlantic and Pacific oceans) in 1914 cut thousands of miles off long sea voyages and brought the Western and non-Western worlds into closer contact.

> Railroad building

However, the future lay with yet another revolutionary invention: the internal combustion engine. In 1887 the German inventor Gottlieb Daimler (1834–1900) attached his little combustion engine to a wagon—and the automobile was born. Two decades later in the United States, former bicycle mechanic Henry Ford (1863–1947) introduced the assembly line to the automobile industry. By 1914, cars, taxis, and trucks jammed city streets in Europe and America and created new demand for oil, rubber, and concrete.

> Internal combustion engine

Just as these new means of transportation linked millions of people physically, the telegraph and telephone connected them in a giant communication network. In 1844, Samuel Morse sent a message by wire 40 miles from Baltimore to Washington. In 1866, ships laid telegraph cable across the Atlantic, enabling news to travel from London to New York as quickly as it had moved from one side of London to the other. Ten years later, Alexander Graham Bell (1847–1922), an American born in Scotland, invented the telephone.

> Telegraph and telephone

The Birth of Big Business

These telephone companies, railroads, shipping lines, steel mills, chemical plants, and new factories became too large for all but a very few individuals to finance. Capitalists now raised money by organizing corporations and selling shares of stock—partial ownership—to investors. Governments helped out by passing laws that limited stockholders' risk to only the money they invested. Luck helped, too, for the discovery of gold in California and Australia in the 1850s and 1860s, and in Alaska and South Africa later in the century, increased the supply of money. This was big business, and it was controlled by large banks and wealthy executives. These executives functioned much as heads of state, conferring with boards of directors and lesser executives. Under them were layers of managers who specialized in areas such as sales, finance, and production and who hired, fired, and supervised employees.

In this new world of business, the big and strong often destroyed the small and weak. Corporations combined into gigantic, monopolistic trusts (called "cartels" in Germany) that commanded markets, prices, and wages. Rockefeller's Standard Oil trust in the United States and the I. G. Farben chemical cartel in Germany are examples of the spectacular business successes of the age. By 1914, big business controlled a large share of industrial production in the West. In Japan, too, which adapted quickly to Western industrialization, five giant corporations dominated three-quarters of that nation's industry.

> Monopolies

The Lure of Shopping

With all the new technology, manufacturers habitually churned out more products than they could sell.

So, merchants found new ways to create customer demand. Grandiose department stores, such as the

Bon Marché in Paris and Bocconi's in Milan, rose up in major cities across the West. The stores displayed a dazzling array of enticing goods—ready-made clothes, furniture, rugs, umbrellas, stationery, toilet paper—a cornucopia of foreign and domestic temptations. Prices were fixed and aimed at the middle classes, but even members of the working class might afford some items. Posters announced "sales" to draw more people to their stores' massive glass and iron emporiums. Glossy catalogues mailed to potential customers in other cities and the countryside encouraged people to order the practical goods and the luxuries of modern urban life for delivery by the new national postal services.

As **Figure 21.3** suggests, the stores become tourist attractions, places to spend leisure time, and leading promoters of consumption. This Parisian department store, with its dramatic central staircase, was designed like a theater for visitors as well as a building where a huge variety of goods could be purchased. Men, women, and children—themselves on display as much as the goods for sale—stroll through this monument to prosperity. By 1900, more than 15,000 people passed through the doors of the Bon Marché in Paris every day. Equally amazing, this shoppers' mecca was only one of twelve Parisian department stores that together employed almost 10,000 people. Department stores had come to represent the materialism of the cities.

Winners and Losers in the Race for Wealth

In this intense economic struggle, some people flourished, others fell behind, and many worried about their future. Cycles of prosperity and recession made economic life precarious. New economic powers such as Germany and the United States

rose to challenge and sometimes surpass mighty Great Britain, which failed to invest sufficiently in new processes and marketing techniques. Industrialization spread unevenly east to Russia—St. Petersburg alone would sprout more than nine hundred factories by 1914. Areas in southern and eastern Europe that held on to old ways of making a living fell further behind, although even in these poorer regions industrialization gained some footholds. Overseas, Australia and Canada began to industrialize, and Japan—with its new machines, factories, and railroads—became a major industrial power.

However, most of Latin America, Africa, and mainland Asia scarcely entered the industrial race before 1914. Although Latin American nations boasted some railway lines and substantial foreign trade, they lacked the machinery and manufacturing that marked industrial economies (see Global Connections). A similar pattern held in mainland Asia and most of Africa, which produced cash crops and raw materials to trade to the industrialized West for manufactured goods but were unable to develop industrial economies.

Did this second industrial revolution make life better overall for Westerners? As we saw with our discussion of the first industrial revolution in Chapter 17, this question is difficult to answer. Statistically, the

answer is yes. It certainly paid to be living in the industrializing nations of the West. In these thriving regions, most people benefited from the new wealth—even those living outside the cities. Food prices came down, and larger farms, chemical fertilizers, and threshing machines boosted harvests and lowered costs. Agricultural producers in North America, Argentina, and Australia sent inexpensive grains and meat in new, refrigerated ships. Prices for manufactured products also dropped as the new machines and processes made production more efficient. With declining prices came a rise in real wages for workers, which almost doubled in Britain between 1850 and 1914. Meat, dairy products, sugar, tea, and coffee were no longer luxuries. People snapped up previously out-of-reach manufactured goods. With care and luck, they even saved a bit of money for hard times.

FIGURE 21.3 A Paris Department Store New stores in large cities, such as the Bon Marché in Paris, offered shoppers a huge choice of products from around the world.

Economic Transformation in Latin America

In 1855, the Yankee speculator and entrepreneur Henry Meiggs arrived in Santiago, Chile, with ambitious plans to introduce railroads into that South American nation. By 1867, his company had built more than 200 miles of railroad lines, many of them across Chile's difficult coastal mountain range. A year later, Meiggs moved north to Peru, which had only 60 miles of track under operation. At a banquet attended by the social elite of Lima, Peru's capital, he promised that his railroads would lead to "a great social revolution." He described the locomotive as "that irresistible battering ram of modern civilization" whose "whistle will awaken the native race from . . . lethargy. . . ." By the time of Meiggs's death in 1877, this man whom Peruvians called the Messiah of the Railway had built more than 700 miles of track, most of them up into the steep Andes and along 2-mile-high plateaus. The entrepreneur had enlisted the help of capital and experts from Europe; machinery from the United States; and more than 20,000 workers from Peru, Chile, Bolivia, and China.

Chile's and Peru's experience with Meiggs and his railroads mirrors similar developments unfolding throughout Latin America between 1850 and 1914. People, money, and machinery flowed from western Europe across the Atlantic to the Americas, and international trade mushroomed. Latin America's subsistence economies blossomed into market economies that exported crops and raw materials to Europe—such as bananas, coffee, sugar, tobacco, nitrates, copper, rubber, cocoa, wheat, and beef. In exchange, Europeans sent industrial goods. This transformation required new railroads, steamships, utilities, communications, harbors, refrigeration facilities, and banks. However, Latin American countries lacked the capital to finance these investments. Spotting a hot opportunity, British, French, German, Belgian, and North American investors sent their money (sometimes in the hands of men such as Meiggs) to fill the voids.

Some larger Latin American countries flourished, thanks to all this trade and economic development. Argentina's economy, for example, expanded at about 5 percent per year between 1880 and 1914. And the population of major Latin American cities such as Montevideo, Uruguay; Buenos Aires, Argentina; São Paulo, Brazil; and Rio de Janeiro, Brazil, more than tripled during the generation that preceded World War I. Not surprisingly, the large landowners and elites in these cities benefited the most from the new economic activity. So did foreigners. British companies owned most of Argentina's meat-processing plants, railways, and telegraph lines as well as many of its banks and merchant houses. This pattern showed up elsewhere in Latin America as well. In Mexico, for example, Belgian, Yankee, and English investors put up much of the money for that nation's railroads. The French controlled the large Mexican department stores; the Germans, the hardware business. North Americans dominated the cement industry, and the Spanish and French ran the textile industry.

Not everyone applauded these developments. "No one can deny the benefits that the railroads, the gas plants, the street cars, and the telegraph and telephone lines have brought to us," admitted the Argentine socialist Juan Bautista Justo in 1896. But "our country is tributary to England. Every year millions of gold pesos leave here and go to the stockholders of English enterprises that are established in Argentina." Others voiced the same sentiments elsewhere. Francisco García Calderón, a Peruvian diplomat and writer, complained, "South America cannot dispense with the influence of the Anglo-Saxon North, with its exuberant wealth and its industries."

Despite such lamentations, there was no turning back. During the decade that followed World War I, Rudyard Kipling described São Paulo as "a metropolis" where "cars and trucks move everywhere, like electrons in the physics texts, across grids of streetcar lines." Outside the city, coffee plantations stretched "as far as the eye could reach, the evenly-spaced twelve-foot trees and their reddening berries covered the rolling hills." The wave of economic transformation that began in western Europe had swept through Latin America and was headed for the rest of the world.

Making Connections

1. What effects did the "second industrial revolution" have on Latin American nations?

2. What problems did this economic transformation create for Latin America?

Those hard times visited some more than others, and here the old pattern held true. The middle classes benefited more than the working classes, skilled workers more than unskilled, and owners of large farms more than agricultural laborers. Nor did the new wealth end misery for those at the bottom of the socioeconomic ladder. Many people remained mired in poverty. Among workers, few could expect to retire without sinking into dependence or impoverishment, let alone ease into the dream of a comfortable cottage with a small garden. The gaps between rich and poor were all too apparent. The upper 20 percent of the population generally received more of a nation's income than the remaining 80 percent. Every day the urban poor could see but not afford the fine apartments, carriages, and clothes of the wealthy.

| Hard times |

THE NEW URBAN LANDSCAPE

City life became the new norm for masses of people in the West. Many rural villages declined or died, slowly in some areas, quickly in others. People from outside the local community moved in, bought the land, and hired migrant laborers to work it. Residents flocked to the cities, and those who had established themselves there stayed. An observer in 1899 reflected the experience of millions: "[T]he most remarkable social phenomenon of the present century is the concentration of population in cities." Europe's population ballooned from 270 million in 1850 to 450 million in 1914, and well over half of western Europeans lived in cities. In Britain, only 8 percent of the workforce remained in the countryside. London, Europe's greatest urban center, grew from 2.5 million in 1850 to more than 4.5 million in 1914.

Rebuilding Cities

As these numbers multiplied everywhere, even the physical foundations of cities changed. Urban centers grew out, up, and belowground. Milan, the thriving Italian center described at the beginning of this chapter, was not the only city to rebuild. Governments, entrepreneurs, and speculators tore apart centuries-old housing and winding streets in Paris, Vienna, Brussels, Stockholm, Barcelona, Cologne, and Mexico City. In place of these older features, they constructed broad, tree-lined avenues, parks, fashionable apartment houses, department stores, fancy cafés, government buildings, museums, hospitals, opera houses, schools, and libraries. New neighborhoods, open spaces, transportation systems, and underground water and sewer systems transformed the face and substance of city life.

Paris led the way in this wave of reconstruction. In the French capital, Emperor Napoleon III and his technocratic administrator, Baron Haussmann, initiated the most ambitious plans for demolishing some of the oldest and poorest neighborhoods. According to Napoleon, Haussmann, and their advisors, these reconstruction efforts offered several important benefits. Doctors and reformers argued that filth from overcrowding caused the diseases that often swept through Paris. Wide streets and open spaces, they explained, would let in much-needed fresh air. But those wide streets also gave governments a political advantage: They deterred people from again throwing up revolutionary barricades to fight the forces of order, as they had in 1848, and afforded troops ready access to working-class areas. Finally, reconstruction projects generated untold wealth for investors, speculators, influence brokers, schemers, architects, engineers, and workers from all over France.

As in Milan, the new construction drove the poor out of the center of Paris to the east end or into working-class suburbs. Wealthier Parisians felt little sympathy. After all, they reasoned, the capital city represented the nation in the eyes of citizens and visitors alike. As Haussman explained, "The splendor of this city reflects on the whole country." The power, wealth, beauty, and modernity of Paris must not be marred by images of poverty and misfortune.

Sewers and Subways

Below Europe's city streets, less glamorous but no less important projects hummed along. In 1850, most houses in Europe's major cities did not have running water. Sewage in cities such as Berlin still ran in open gutters, creating an atmosphere of filth and tremendous stench. During the following decades, these standards began to change. First in London and then elsewhere, engineers and workers built water and sewer systems. Doctors, reformers, and planners led the drive to bring in freshwater in aqueducts or pipes from sources upstream and to create hundreds of miles of underground sewers to carry waste downstream. These measures made urban life healthier and more comfortable than before.

More than water and waste moved below the city, however. In 1863, London's underground railway opened. Over the next fifty years, Paris and New York built subways of their own. Along with carriages, trams, and railroads, the efficient, predictable subways enabled people to shop and work in places farther from home than ever. People moved their residences out of crowded urban centers to city fringes and suburbs—whether upscale neighborhoods for the middle class or less expensive areas for workers.

CITY PEOPLE

Who were these people filling the cities of the West? How did they make their way in life, so far away from the land and surrounded by industrial advances and new wealth? Part of the answer is revealed in **Figure 21.4,** a mid-century engraving of a typical Parisian apartment house. At this time, the city's various social classes still lived in close proximity but in different conditions. The drawing portrays the wealthy bourgeoisie living on the first (American second) floor in luxurious comfort; above them lives a bourgeois family of lesser means. The lower classes and aspiring artists—dancing and drinking instead of working, having too many children, and being unable to pay their bills—live on the bottom and upper floors in increasing poverty, thanks to their imprudence.

On Top of It All: The Urban Elite

At the top of the urban social order was a small, elite class of wealthy aristocrats and the richest of the bourgeoisie—the millionaire factory owners, merchants, and bankers. Amounting to less than 1 percent of the population, these people socialized together, turned to each other for help, and intermarried. Through strategic matchmaking, new wealth from the daughter or son of an American captain of industry or banker might enable an aristocratic family to maintain its position. More often, however, aristocrats kept their positions by making shrewd investments, serving governments, holding on to top spots in the military and diplomatic corps, and wisely managing their lands and businesses. They, along with members entering their ranks, had prestige but not the formal privileges that their eighteenth-century predecessors had enjoyed.

Those who had been born into aristocratic families clung to what was left of the old lifestyle. Those aspiring to the aristocratic life used their money to copy that lifestyle. These newly rich bought estate houses in the country and opulent townhouses along the best avenues and parks, attended fancy balls, took hunting trips to Africa, and supported large staffs of servants. They also kept up with the latest fashions and made grand gestures toward cultural and philanthropic activities. However, a few rules of the aristocratic game had changed. Obvious arrogance was frowned upon, as this elite made an effort to comply with middle-class morality. At the very least, they strove to appear responsible, domestic, and religious. Of course, their children got the best of everything. In every way, these elites were truly the upper crust, on top and intent on staying there.

FIGURE 21.4 The Urban Classes, mid-nineteenth century In a typical Parisian apartment house such as this, people from various social classes lived in different circumstances but in close proximity.

Pride and Success: The "Solid" Middle Class

Well below this upper crust, the "solid" bourgeoisie held the better jobs, lived in the finer apartments, dined at fashionable restaurants, and commanded at least one good servant. These were the families of small factory owners, merchants, managers, doctors, druggists, local bankers, lawyers, professors, and architects who earned and spent more money than most.

Worried about competitors from below, many middle-class men established "professional" associations designed to keep standards up and rivals down. Nor did they open their professions to women (see Document 21.1). Wives and daughters, they intoned, "best" not work for pay. Beliefs that women and men belonged in "separate spheres"—women at home, men in the public world of work—persisted. "Of all those acquirements, which more particularly belong to the feminine character," explained Isabella Mary

Women and work

DOCUMENT 21.1

John Stuart Mill Argues for Women's Rights

During the last decades of the nineteenth century, a number of observers commented on the position of women in Western societies and argued for women's rights. One of the most prominent and influential was John Stuart Mill, who published his essay "The Subjection of Women" in 1869. In the following excerpt from that work, Mill places the question of women's subordination within the context of human progress and morality.

The principle which regulates the existing social relations between the two sexes—the legal subordination of one sex to the other—is wrong in itself, and now one of the chief hindrances to human improvement; and that it ought to be replaced by a principle of perfect equality, admitting no power or privilege on the one side, nor disability on the other.

. . . The masters of all other slaves rely, for maintaining obedience, on fear; either fear of themselves, or religious fears. The masters of women wanted more than simple obedience, and they turned the whole force of education to effect their purpose. All women are brought up from the very earliest years in the belief that their ideal of character is the very opposite to that of men; not self-will, and government by self-control, but submission, and yielding to the control of others. All the moralities tell them that it is the duty of women, and all the current sentimentalities that it is their nature, to live for others; to make complete abnegation of themselves, and to have no life but in their affections. . . .

For what is the peculiar character of the modern world—the difference which chiefly distinguishes modern institutions, modern social ideas, modern life itself, from those of times long past? It is, that human beings are no longer born to their place in life, and chained down by an inexorable bond to the place they are born to, but are free to employ their faculties, and such favourable chances as offer, to achieve the lot which may appear to them most desirable.

If this general principle of social and economical sciences is . . . true, we ought to act as if we believed it, and not to ordain that to be born a girl instead of a boy, any more than to be born black instead of white, or a commoner instead of a nobleman, shall decide the person's position through all life. . . .

SOURCE: John Stuart Mill, "The Subjection of Women," *Three Essays* (Oxford: Oxford University Press, 1975).

Analyze the Document

1. In Mill's view, why is the legal subordination of one sex to the other sex wrong?

2. Other than laws, what means are used to subordinate women, according to Mill?

3. In what ways is the liberation of women related to "the peculiar character of the modern world"?

Mayson Beeton in her best-selling advice book for women, "there are none which take a higher rank . . . than such as enter into a knowledge of household duties; for on these are perpetually dependent the happiness, comfort, and well-being of a family."

Some women managed to swim against the current, however. They engaged in philanthropic activities—in support of the poor and uneducated, or against alcohol and prostitution. British philanthropist Angela Burdette-Coutts (1814–1906), for example, gave away a fortune to schools and housing for the poor. In France, many wealthy women followed the example of Empress Eugénie (consort of Napoleon III), who supported societies that provided assistance to new mothers. In the United States, educated middle-class women staffed hundreds of settlement houses in urban centers that helped immigrants adjust to the customs and language of their new country as well as middle-class values. Only a few women managed to carve out careers in business, teaching, writing, or painting. Exclusion from universities kept most ambitious upper-middle-class women from pursuing lucrative professions, though schools such as Queens College in Britain and the Female Medical College of Pennsylvania promised some professional opportunities to women.

If not arrogant, this bourgeoisie was proud. Who else better represented their civilization? As they saw it, success flowed from character, ability, and effort; in a world open to talent, rewards came from achievement. These people praised discipline, control, and respectability, while attacking public drunkenness, emotional outbursts, and—especially in **Victorian Britain**—open displays of sexual affection. In addition, they respected Christian morality and marital fidelity. Cleanliness went hand in hand with purity and modernity, as did running water for regular baths and several changes of clothes. Certainly, they argued, all good people should live up to these standards, at least in appearance.

Values

Hardworking and Hopeful: The Lower Middle Class

Those just below the solid bourgeoisie probably tried as hard as any group to succeed in modern society. These lower-middle-class people performed skilled services as tellers in banks, sorters in mailrooms, and salespeople in department stores. Reading, writing, and mathematical skills (and for more and more, the new typewriter) enabled thousands to become schoolteachers, postal workers, and clerks in places from government agencies and insurance firms to accounting offices and train stations. Some of these lower-paying "white-collar jobs" became open to educated women, particularly if they were unmarried.

Lower-middle-class people made their living in settings that sometimes resembled factories. **Figure 21.5** shows clerks working in the offices of Cadbury's, the chocolate firm described in Chapter 17. In this huge room, all the chairs, desks, and tasks seem the same. All the clerks are men, and even their clothes look almost identical. **Figure 21.6** shows a French telephone exchange, also set in a large room in which the chairs, fixtures, and activities are similar. Here the employees are all middle-class women, with the exception of male supervisors and a boy who delivers messages. As this image shows, even when jobs opened for middle-class women, they were often separate from men's work and of lower status.

With the heightening tempo of industrialization, these lower-middle-class occupations multiplied. People might move up the economic ladder, and better-off workers could hope to see their educated children rising into this class. In turn, a few children from lower-middle ranks might move into the also-expanding solid middle class. Although moving up remained more the exception than the rule, the possibilities were far greater than before 1850. By 1914, the middle classes overall had grown from between 3 and 10 percent of the population to more than 20 percent in much of the West.

Social mobility

FIGURE 21.5 Modern Office Work for Men Many lower-middle-class clerks worked in large offices featuring row after row of desks, as in this photo of Cadbury's chocolate firm in England.

FIGURE 21.6 French Telephone Exchange, late nineteenth century In this large telephone office, almost all the employees are middle-class women.

The "Other Half": The Working Classes

Unlike the elites and the middle classes, the working classes lived on crowded side streets, the poorer east side of cities such as London or Paris, or the edge of town where land and rents were cheaper. Though better off than before 1850, they still faced the threat of job loss, which could send them into poverty in an instant.

Even employed workers struggled to make ends meet. A new demand for certain skilled work helped some. Those who could read directions; could build or repair machines; or were printers, plumbers, or cabinetmakers earned respectable wages. They might also join unions and demand reforms. Other skilled workers lost out, for factory owners fit laborers to jobs that had become nothing more than mindless, repetitive tasks. Automaker Henry Ford expressed the views of

many industrial managers toward this kind of labor: "I could not possibly do the same thing day in and day out, but . . . to the majority of minds, repetition holds no terrors. . . . The average worker, I am sorry to say, . . . wants a job in which he does not have to think." Whether former artisans with obsolete skills or migrants from the countryside, these workers earned paltry wages and worked at an exhausting pace. They and their children tended to remain low-paid industrial laborers for the rest of their lives.

Despite legislation restricting women from certain jobs, many labored outside and inside the home. Jeanne Bouvier, a Frenchwoman born in 1865, worked as millions of other working-class women did. When she was 11 years old, she took her first job in a silk factory near Lyons. Three years later, she

FIGURE 21.7

Léon Frédéric, *The Stages of a Worker's Life*, 1895–1897

In 1897, Belgian artist Léon Frédéric completed these three panels depicting urban workers. In the left panel, he focused on men. In the right, he depicted the woman's world. Children and families occupy the central panel.

Connecting Art *&* Society

1. In what ways does the content of this work fit with its title, *The Stages of a Worker's Life*?

2. What are the differences among the roles played by men, women, and children in this painting?

3. What impression of working-class life do you think the painter intended to convey to viewers?

4. What is your own reaction to this painting?

moved to Paris, where she worked as a domestic and then in the hatmaking industry. Later, she worked a twelve-hour day as a seamstress and did piecework on her own.

In addition to their jobs in factories and small shops, many women took in work at home finishing clothes, polishing items for sale, wrapping chocolates, or decorating toys. Some of the new machines of industry even added to the demand for this older piecework. For example, Singer's sewing machine, invented in the 1850s, enabled entrepreneurs to hire women for low wages to work at home or in small "sweatshops." Such women proved especially appealing to these employers because they were easy to fire and posed little threat of forming a union or going on strike.

Still more women worked in traditional urban jobs. Domestic servants could count on meals and housing and perhaps even some savings from their salaries. On the other hand, they suffered from the whims of their employers and the threat of sexual abuse. Women in laundries labored at drudgery for low wages, although some of them enjoyed the sense of comradeship that came with the job at times.

The growth of cities may have increased the work available to these women, but the machinery of the industrial revolution did not yet ease job conditions for them.

Léon Frédéric (1856–1940), for a time Belgium's most famous painter, tried to encompass all stages of a worker's life in a large triptych (**Figure 21.7**). In the foreground of the central panel, children on the right play cards, while on the left they carry and nibble on bread. Their parents and young couples stand just behind them, and in the background are the aged members of the working class whose ultimate fate is marked by the distant but approaching funeral coach. The left panel depicts the man's work world, where men of all ages, from adolescence to old age, engage in manual labor or observe it. In the foreground they are digging, and in the middle ground they struggle with heavy beams. Behind them are the factories where they work. The right panel shows the women's world, all mothering and nurturing with babies in their arms and at their breasts. Behind them are market stalls where they shop. Here is a vision of workers' lives in a nutshell: hard manual labor for men, child rearing and food preparation for women, and at the end, old age and death for all.

What to Do About "Them"

Members of the middle classes looked upon their working-class counterparts with a mixture of fear and sympathy: fear that these were dangerous people who might rise in revolt, commit crimes, or create disorder, and sympathy for the harshness of working-class life. Most middle-class people agreed with the popular writer Samuel Smiles that the working classes suffered from their own faults rather than injustices in the social system: "no laws . . . can make the idle industrious, the thriftless provident, or the drunken sober. Such reforms can only be effected by means of individual action, economy, and self-denial."

However, other members of the middle class—especially younger, college-educated people who were also connected to religious causes—joined organizations to ease the plight of the urban poor. With high optimism and idealism, they established clinics, settlement houses, and maternal-wellness societies. Thousands of middle- and upper-class women visited the poor; ran schools; and inspected asylums, workhouses, and prisons. One Spanish charity worker wrote a guide for visitors to the poor: "In viewing their faults, vices, and crimes, we must ask ourselves this question: Would the poor be what they are, if we were what we ought to be?" Some of these workers spread birth-control information; others touted the benefits of religion. Women's groups in particular distributed prayer books to the poor or sold Bibles to raise money to aid the needy—a reflection of the still-close link between the churches and charitable work. Still others tried to help the poor through political activism, joining socialist organizations such as the Fabian Society in London, which decried the capitalist system as unjust and inefficient.

SPORTS AND LEISURE IN THE CITIES

Building Character Through Athletics

For turn-of-the-century Europeans who had the time and money, city life could be fun. New forms of recreation and sports not only offered entertaining diversions but also built character values important for industry and war. Soccer, rugby, and cricket, once games only for schoolchildren, became extremely popular, competitive team sports for adults. In 1901, more than 100,000 attended a championship game of soccer in Britain. The emphasis on teamwork, competition, and discipline in the sports world reflected the qualities of industrial work and military service so prized during the era. Other new sports, such as

bicycle and auto racing, stressed the speed and power of machines; by no coincidence, industrial firms sponsored some of these contests. Even the growth of scouting and, in Germany, the "wandering youth" clubs revealed the belief that good character required physical vigor and outdoor living. Accordingly, the modern Olympic games—stressing competition and nationalism—were established during this period, with the first games held in Athens in 1896.

Women's sports were less professional and less competitive than men's. Even scouting for girls was designed to instill homemaking values. But women did take to bicycles, despite warnings from the old guard that the loose clothing necessary for bicycling was unfeminine, that the activity would damage enthusiasts' ability to have children, and that women might inappropriately experience sexual pleasure from riding.

The New Tourist

Increasingly, people vacationed away from the cities. More and more, people left town. Those who had the means might imitate the eighteenth-century aristocratic habit of visiting the great cities, museums, and monuments of Europe. Others traveled to resorts on the Mediterranean coast, the Alps, or the shores of the Baltic Sea. By 1890, some 100,000 people visited the resort town of Vichy in central France to "take the waters" (cure their ills), relax, and socialize. Tourism became so popular that special books appeared, and professionally organized tours formed to guide people on their travels.

Workers usually lacked the time or money for such luxuries. Some managed short trips on trains that left cities every day for the coast, perhaps to Dieppe in France or Brighton in England, where piers and amusement parks beckoned. Most, however, stayed in the cities. There, some went to café concerts to see singers, comedians, jugglers, and acrobats. Others attended theaters featuring fast dancing or enjoyed boxing matches, vaudeville shows, and (after the turn of the century) movies.

PRIVATE LIFE: TOGETHER AND ALONE AT HOME

As the tempo of life in factories, stores, government offices, and streets increased, private life grew more precious. The individualism trumpeted by the liberal bourgeoisie accentuated the longing to withdraw from the public arena into the family, the home, and the self. The personal—one's body, sexuality, and internal life—became a subject of intense fascination. The home—the realm of the family protected by walls and locked doors—was the center of private life.

Family: The Promise of Happiness

People believed in the family. Like a religion, the family promised happiness in a difficult world, a meaning that would extend beyond death, and a sacred place free from intrusion by the outside world. As much as their means permitted, people celebrated the family through daily gatherings at meals and special occasions such as weddings, vacations, and birthdays (see the painting on page 658). For individuals, these occasions marked points in their own life cycles. At more private moments, the family home served as a place where individuals shared emotions, or perhaps confessed silently to themselves or in a diary in the solitude of a bedroom.

More than ever, people recorded moments of private life in letters, diaries, and photographs. Families exchanged thousands of letters over a lifetime that told of children, deaths, visits, and health. Such correspondence held **Recording private life** the family together when travel and migration to different cities threatened to pull it apart. Diaries of the day reveal much self-concern and introspection. One Frenchwoman explained, "When I am alone, I have plenty to do in following the movement of my ideas and impressions, in exploring myself, in examining my dispositions and my various ways of being, in drawing the best out of myself, in registering the ideas that come to me by chance or that are suggested to me by my reading." People took photographs to capture family occasions—from baptisms to Sunday meals and partings—especially after the invention of the small Kodak camera in the 1880s. They carefully enshrined these photographs in frames and collected them in well-organized albums.

A Home of One's Own

The dream of family life and privacy required having a home of one's own—a private kingdom apart from city and society. But home had another purpose as well: It announced the material success of the bourgeoisie and the pleasures of private life.

As revealed in the 1877 painting of a Paris interior shown in **Figure 21.8,** the typical bourgeois apartment resembled an antique shop, overdecorated in no particular style and bulging with possessions. Heavy drapes hang over the walls and windows, multiple carpets cover the floors, fabrics ornament the mantelpieces and furniture, and tassels dangle everywhere. In such a home, family members could gaze at the many prints and paintings, enjoy music played by an elder daughter on the piano, read a novel in the library, and stay informed by subscribing to journals. Small, private gardens or potted plants and painted landscapes completed the picture by offering a way to appreciate nature.

Servants shared middle-class homes but remained on the fringes of the family's private life. Relegated to their own small quarters in the attic or basement, servants had little freedom to move about the house at their **Servants** leisure or take part in their employers' lives. Indeed, with the era's emphasis on both individualism and privacy, employers increasingly saw servants as potential intruders into private life. The bedroom and bathroom became off-limits, and people complained about how hard it was to find "good," affordable servants. By the turn of the century, many middle-class families managed with just a single female domestic, or none at all.

For the typical middle-class man, home was a retreat from public life, to be savored at the end of the workday or on weekends. For the middle-class woman, it was much more. Society glorified her domestic role **Women's roles** more than ever. No longer would she be praised for doing "productive" work such as managing a husband's shop. Instead, she orchestrated every aspect of the family's home life, managing the meals, chores, visits, and guests. Her highest duty, however, was to bear and raise children. No longer was reproduction regarded as simply a natural function: It had become a complex, demanding activity. Most likely, a middle-class woman had fewer children than her

FIGURE 21.8 Mihaly Munkacsy, *Paris Interior*, 1877 Middle-class apartments in large cities typically bulged with possessions.

DOCUMENT 21.2

Beeton's Guide for Women

Mrs. Beeton's Book of Household Management became the most popular "guidebook" for the proper middle-class woman in Victorian England. It covered topics from account keeping and the importance of cleanliness to strategies for hiring domestics. In the following selection, Isabella Beeton describes the overall role of the "mistress of a house," proper dress, and the correct treatment of servants.

1. As with the Commander of an Army, or the leader of any enterprise, so is it with the mistress of a house. Her spirit will be seen through the whole establishment; and just in proportion as she performs her duties intelligently and thoroughly, so will her domestics follow in her path. Of all those acquirements, which more particularly belong to the feminine character, there are none which take a higher rank, in our estimation, than such as enter into a knowledge of household duties; for on these are perpetually dependent the happiness, comfort, and well-being of a family.

***

13. The Dress of the Mistress should always be adapted to her circumstances, and be varied with different occasions. Thus, at breakfast she should be attired in a very neat and simple manner, wearing no ornaments. If this dress should decidedly pertain only to the breakfast-hour, and be specially suited for such domestic occupations as usually follow that meal, then it would be well to exchange it before the time for receiving visitors, if the mistress be in the habit of doing so.

***

19. The Treatment of Servants is of the highest possible moment, as well to the mistress as to the domestics themselves. On the head of the house the latter will naturally fix their attention, and if they perceive that the mistress's conduct is regulated by high and correct principles, they will not fail to respect her. If, also, a benevolent desire is shown to promote their comfort, at the same time that a steady performance of their duty is exacted, then their respect will not be unmingled with affection, and they will be still more solicitous to continue to deserve her favour.

SOURCE: Isabella Beeton, *Mrs. Beeton's Book of Household Management* (London: Chancellor Press, 1982).

Analyze the Document

1. What does Beeton mean when she compares the mistress of a house to "the Commander of an Army"?

2. What qualities does Beeton stress?

3. What attitudes toward women does this selection reflect?

---

mother, but she was expected to lavish greater attention on them. Her children would probably remain at home through adolescence, though many families sent their offspring to boarding schools. To help women meet all these expectations, books, magazines, pamphlets, and advice columns offered tips on how to attract a man and marry well; manage a household; sharpen "home economics" skills; and cultivate an appropriate social life that included teas, afternoon visits, and dinner parties.

At the same time, disturbing crosscurrents started to undermine this picture of the home and women's role in it. As Document 21.2 indicates, prominent people circulated new ideas about the restrictions imposed on women. Many women demanded more independent lives, even choosing to live outside the confines of the middle-class home. The British reformer Florence Nightingale (1820–1910) complained of "the petty grinding tyranny of a good English family," refused to marry, and helped found the modern profession of nursing (see Biography in Chapter 19). A few occupations outside the home were gradually opened to middle-class women, and some women entered universities and professions. Growing numbers of "new women" lived in women's clubs or apartments, dressed more practically, and did more "daring" things such as traveling alone and entering the public space as activists.

Poor Housing

Workers could not afford to draw such sharp lines between public and private life. Their homes, typically only one or two rooms in deteriorating buildings, rarely fulfilled all their needs. Often they relocated from one residence to another, carrying what they could. In some cases, they moved so as to search for something slightly better; in others, they sought to avoid a landlord demanding back rent.

The loss of a job might well doom a family to homelessness. With little hope of saving enough to pay for decent housing, workers tended to spend their extra money on clothes to "cut a good figure" and thereby present a well-groomed image in their public lives. For them, the city streets held far more promise than the buildings in which they lived. While the bourgeoisie retreated into homes or private clubs, workers used the public buildings, streets, and spaces of the city for their social and even private lives.

Working-class women enjoyed neither the space, furnishings, nor servants that graced the typical middle-class home. They usually worked at a factory or did poorly paid piecework at home, where they could care for their children. If their children seemed more unruly and independent than those of the middle classes, moralists condemned these mothers for failing to create a proper home life. Such critics ignored the fact that working-class women lacked the money needed to cultivate the "ideal" family life. Worse, this disapproval helped employers justify paying these women less than men and treating them poorly.

Working-class women

Intimacy and Morality

Private life for working-class families was burdened by tensions involving basic survival. Middle-class families experienced tensions, too, but of a different sort. Founded on love, companionship, and intimacy, the middle-class family could become a pressure cooker of conflicting feelings and desires, of guilt and shame, of misunderstood communication and resentment. Family members often fought over money, but the confining expectations of intimacy could be worse. "Do not admit anyone else into our private life, into our thoughts," counseled a French man to his prospective wife in 1873. People understood such warnings. The home was a center of secrecy. More often than not, at the heart of that secrecy was sex.

For Britain's middle classes in particular, this era witnessed the height of Victorian sexual morality. Sex was supposed to be little discussed and limited to the marriage bed, enclosed in a separate "master" bedroom with locked doors. Sexual problems "shouldn't arise," but if they did, "enlightened" sufferers might turn to their doctor—the expert on sex, hygiene, and morality all rolled into one. Mixing moralisms with an image of scientific authority, most doctors confirmed the standard views of other commentators: Healthy and prudent sexuality could take place only within the marriage. Affairs risked scandal (especially for the woman) and illegitimacy. Sex with prostitutes was unhygienic and somehow dangerous to the race. Doctors vaguely connected prostitution, syphilis, tuberculosis, and alcoholism as physical and social "scourges," all resulting from "venereal excesses." Most often, they blamed women for being prostitutes, for forcing their husbands to visit prostitutes, or for having inappropriate sexual appetites.

Victorian morality

Masturbation also caught the attention of doctors, priests, and parents. Physicians warned men that masturbation would drain their strength. They condemned masturbation by females even more strongly. To prevent youths from "abusing themselves," they prescribed orthopedic devices, special bandages, and belts.

As for homosexuality, people viewed it in an even worse light. Doctors labeled it a sickness or psychological disorder. Newspapers added to the public condemnation of homosexuality by reporting "scandalous" affairs among public figures and "uncovering" homosexual subcultures. The trial and imprisonment for gross indecency of the famed British author Oscar Wilde (1854–1900) in 1895 promoted a new awareness of homosexuality while revealing how far officials and the public would go to denounce it.

Sexual Realities

Despite these idealized, restrictive notions about proper sexual conduct, reality was quite different. Somehow people, especially the middle classes, discussed sex enough to limit births. While many used the old methods—abstinence and withdrawal—new information and methods also became available. Men began using condoms, and women douched or used diaphragms and sponges soaked in disinfectants. Many resorted to abortion as a method of birth control, particularly in cases of illegitimacy.

Birth control

These methods seem to have worked. The birthrate declined in these years. In France, for example, it dropped from 33 per 1,000 in 1800 to 19 per 1,000 in 1910. Many people chose to limit births for economic reasons. As people moved from farms to the cities, they no longer needed so many children to help with the work. In the cities, the increasing costs of raising children deterred couples from having large families. Yet successful birth control among the middle classes caused concern, for many worried that the "best" of society were not reproducing themselves as quickly as the "poor" and "uncompetitive." Commentators argued that "good" families needed more children. Nationalists complained that competing states or "alien peoples" would overwhelm their nation or "race" if "the fittest" did not increase their fertility.

Certainly actual sexual behavior failed to live up to the standards of Victorian moralists. The "best" people had affairs, and illegitimacy remained high. Deadly sexually transmitted diseases rose and spread widely among all classes. In addition, prostitution thrived in many urban areas. Tens of thousands of prostitutes in the largest cities displayed themselves on streets and in city parks and in windows and doorways. Some worked in bars or elegant brothels for a more select clientele. Working-class women who lost jobs, domestic servants dismissed because of pregnancy, or young women on their own might turn to prostitution to survive. Men of all classes patronized prostitutes. Governments tried to control prostitution, requiring medical exams of prostitutes and limiting its practice to certain districts. Worse than these inconveniences were the risks of this life. Prostitutes were often subjected to violence, the most famous example of which was the serial killings committed by Jack the Ripper in London in the late 1880s.

By the end of the century, new attitudes, or perhaps the weight of reality, had broken down some of the more restrictive notions of Victorian sexual propriety. More people accepted and expected mutual sexual enjoyment within marriage, and people became educated about the physical facts of sexual contact. Books, pamphlets, and talks about sex enabled women and men to read about the subject and sometimes even discuss it openly. Doctors, psychologists, and intellectuals began to study sex and see that it played a major role in individuals' sense of identity.

New attitudes

Psychic Stress and Alcoholism

Growing concern with sex and private life in this period reflected a broader preoccupation with psychological well-being. Anxieties and emotional disorders seemed all too common. Women especially suffered from fits, paralysis, convulsions, numbness, headaches, oversensitivity to light, digestive disorders, and fatigue. Doctors listened, prescribed pills, and suggested expensive cures such as surgery and health-spa retreats. They sometimes blamed the complexities of city life or the noise and speed of modern life for these disturbing health problems. Other commentators suggested different causes. Within the confines of middle-class life, perhaps people worried too much about being judged by others. Or maybe the rapid changes of the era led to insecurity. Whatever the causes, the evidence of psychic stress was growing in diaries, in the rise of psychoanalysis, in the new descriptions of proliferating "mental illnesses," in the spread of psychiatric clinics, and in the mounting number of chronic patients in insane asylums.

Was widespread alcoholism a sign of psychic stress? **Figure 21.9,** an 1876 painting by Edgar Degas (1834–1917) of a woman drinking absinthe (a strong alcoholic beverage) in a Parisian café, seems to indicate a link between drinking and stress. Although a man sits nearby, the woman's face suggests that she is alone and gloomy. In this evocative image, lines separating social drinking, addiction, and psychic stress blur. Drinkers now seemed more depressed than jovial, and drunkenness appeared to be everywhere—in the streets, at work, in bars, and, increasingly, behind closed doors. New temperance movements attacked the "scourge" of alcohol, and with legitimate reason. In France, the average person consumed more than 60 gallons of wine a year, not including brandy, beer, and the more addictive absinthe shown in this painting. Even drugs such as opium, morphine, heroine, cocaine, and hashish gained footholds, especially among artists. Fear of drug-induced suicides led France to ban such drugs in 1908.

By no coincidence, the practice of **psychoanalysis** emerged during this period (see pages 683–684). Vari-

FIGURE 21.9 Edgar Degas, *Absinthe*, 1876–1877 This painting of a woman drinking a strong alcoholic beverage in a Paris café suggests links between drinking and stress.

ous other movements also focused on psychic stress. One of the best known and popular of these was Christian Science, founded in America by Mary Baker Eddy (1821–1910). Having suffered interminable ailments and nervous disorders as a youth, Eddy turned to a spiritual approach to healing in her adult years. As she explained in her best-selling book *Science and Health* (1875), "mind healing" could dispel sickness and pain. Whatever the causes and supposed cures, stress and emotional pain seemed too widespread to ignore, and many observers connected them to the pressures of modern life.

SCIENCE IN AN AGE OF OPTIMISM

Despite these concerns about the pressures of modern life, most observers embraced the new age enthusiastically. "I see no limit to the extent to which intelligence and will, guided by sound principles of investigation, and organized in common effort, may modify the conditions of existence, for a period longer than that now covered by history," announced British biologist T. H. Huxley (1825–1895) in 1893. "And much may be done to change the nature of man himself," he added.

The eighteenth-century optimism about science spread during the second half of the nineteenth century. Many people—especially members of the rising middle classes—felt certain that their generation would find solutions to the problems that had plagued human beings from the beginning. Scientists confirmed this optimism by making discoveries that answered fundamental questions and that could be translated into practical products, such as industrial goods and medicines. Intellectuals proffered new ways to explain the world and human beings' place in it. Writers and artists found answers to similar questions by looking hard at the lives of people in their changing world. These scientists, intellectuals, and artists thrived in big cities such as London, Paris, Berlin, Milan, and Vienna. In these cultural hubs, some taught in universities or conducted experiments in laboratories. Others might debate in learned societies, do research in libraries, or paint in studios. Still others chatted in cafés or simply wrote in back rooms. Their work generated provocative ideas and added to the sense that life could be understood more fully than ever before.

Science, Evolution, and Religion

The best news came from science. After 1850, word of scientific advances spread from elite circles to the broader public (see Thinking About Science & Technology). Stunning discoveries emerged and directly affected people's lives. However, certain conclusions that appealed to some provoked outrage in others.

No one became a greater hero, or villain, than Charles Darwin (1809–1882). Born into a distinguished British family, Darwin studied medicine and theology. Yet these disciplines failed to challenge him. Instead, the world of plants and animals became his consuming passion. His answer to a single question— how have all living species come to be as they are today?—caused an intense controversy that still continues in some circles.

| Darwin |

In 1831, Darwin, despite frail health, began a voyage around the world as a ship's naturalist on the *Beagle*. He observed and collected fossils and specimens in different environments. He made his most important finds in South America and the Galápagos Islands off the coast of that continent. Gradually he developed his theory of evolution, which, for him, answered his question. In *On the Origin of Species by Natural Selection* (1859), he described the slow evolution of present plant and animal species from earlier, simpler forms through a process of natural selection. Survival, he explained, came from struggle. In the competition for survival, those that possessed the most useful characteristics in a given environment— for example, the horse with the longer legs—survived to produce the most offspring. Through this process, they transmitted their successful qualities to future generations.

These ideas were not completely new. By the mid-nineteenth century, many intellectuals had accepted the concept of a slow and gradual development of the earth's crust and its inhabitants. Liberalism included ideas about the competitive struggle among human beings for food and survival, something that Thomas Malthus had written about at the beginning of the century (see Chapter 17). In addition, Enlightenment thinkers had already popularized the notion of "progress." Many in the mid-nineteenth century already embraced the sense that the present had evolved in progressive stages from a lower past. But no one had ever before supplied an all-encompassing explanation, supported by convincing evidence, for the origin of plants and animals.

What about human beings? Most people believed that humans remained a species apart from all others. At first Darwin avoided the delicate question. In his 1871 work, *The Descent of Man*, he finally took the bold step of arguing that humans evolved from more primitive species by the same process as plants and animals. "Man still bears in his bodily frame the indelible stamp of his lowly origin," he proclaimed. No longer could people "believe that man is the work of a separate act of creation." **Figure 21.11,** one of many satirical cartoons on this topic, ridicules Darwin's idea that humans descended from other species by showing Darwin holding up a mirror to his close relative—a monkey—and depicting Darwin with the body of a monkey.

Though many people already believed in evolution, Darwin's claims became front-page news. Few ideas have provoked such widespread controversy. To some people, his ideas made sense. Much of the scientific world, for example, quickly accepted Darwin's theory of evolution. Dominant social groups everywhere also derived comfort from it. The rising bourgeoisie, for instance, seized upon evolution as a way to explain and justify its own success. Scientists, including Darwin, also found confirmation for their views that women were inferior to men and destined to play a dependent domestic role in the male-dominated family.

| Controversy |

As Document 21.3 suggests, philosophers and scholars also expanded Darwin's thesis and applied it to all human behavior, a doctrine known as **Social Darwinism.** British philosopher Herbert Spencer (1820–1903) built a whole system of influential ideas around the concept of evolution; he and other Social Darwinists extended Darwin's theory far beyond its scientific foundations by making it the key to truth and progress. Spencer even saw the notion of survival of the fittest as justification for the harsh competitiveness of human society: "Under the natural order of things society is constantly excreting its unhealthy, imbecile, slow, vacillating, faithless members," he explained. Helping such people "encourages the multiplication of the reckless and incompetent . . . and discourages the multiplication of the competent and provident. . . ." Other Social Darwinists, such as British criminologist Francis Galton (1822–1911),

| Social Darwinists |

Universities and the Professionalization of Science

Were science and universities always as closely connected as they are today? Several European universities had been established during the Middle Ages, well before the Scientific Revolution. Some of the early giants of science, among them Copernicus and Kepler, worked primarily outside universities. During the seventeenth and eighteenth centuries, many individuals who investigated the natural world may have been associated with a university or learned society. But the professionalization of science—as an organized program of university study or as a career—lay in the future.

In the closing years of the eighteenth century, institutions such as the École Polytechnique in France and the Royal Institution in England started teaching science in a formal way. After the first decade of the nineteenth century, German universities began offering the study of natural science. **Figure 21.10** shows one such institution, the University of Halle-Wittenberg, in 1836. These schools advanced scientific knowledge in two main ways. First, they promoted scientific research; that is, instead of teaching only established knowledge, professors also conducted research and encouraged their students to do the same. Second, universities helped train future teachers, physicians, and other professionals, who in turn would spread scientific thinking and the fruits of science throughout society.

During the second half of the nineteenth century, the model of the German research university was adopted in the United States and elsewhere. At the same time, polytechnic schools were founded in several Western nations to train students in the application of science to technology and industry. With the advent of the polytechnics, universities could focus more on pure science— that is, science that is concerned not with practical applications but with the development and testing of new theories—and advanced research.

The connections among schools, universities, and science strengthened during the twentieth and twenty-first centuries, particularly with the development of "big science," which we will examine in Chapters 25 and 26.

Connecting Science & Society

1. In what ways did universities and polytechnic institutions help to develop a professional identity for scientists?

2. Generally speaking, why might government and industry support universities and the professionalization of science? How would government and industry benefit?

3. How have societies benefited from universities' training of teachers, scientists, and other professionals?

FIGURE 21.10 The University of Halle-Wittenberg, 1836

suggested that the human race could be improved through selective breeding, or eugenics.

Darwin's ideas threatened many people wedded to traditional Christian beliefs. He tried to reassure his alarmed readers: "I see no good reason why the views given in this volume should shock the religious feelings of anyone." Though many Christians accepted some of Darwin's ideas, his views offended numerous others. Specifically, the notion of a long and mechanistic evolution of all present species, including human beings, from simpler forms seemed to contradict the account of divine creation given in the Bible: "If the Darwinian theory is true," complained one theologian, "Genesis is a lie, the whole framework of the book of life falls to pieces,

Darwinism and religion

FIGURE 21.11 Darwin and a Monkey This satirical cartoon reveals the controversy over Darwin's theories after the publication of his books.

and the revelation of God to man, as we Christians know it, is a delusion and a snare." Evolution, Darwin's critics cried, left God out of the world and diminished the uniqueness of human beings in it.

Some of Darwin's opponents suppressed his books and the teaching of evolution in schools. The Catholic Church angrily rejected Darwin's theory along with many other ideas of the time. In 1864, Pope Pius IX (1846–1878) issued a *Syllabus of Errors* attacking the idea of evolution and secular education. He also railed against religious toleration, free speech, and much else: It is "an error to believe that the Roman Pontiff can and ought to reconcile himself to, and agree with, progress, liberalism, and modern civilization." In 1870, the First Vatican Council bolstered the pope's authority by declaring that, under certain circumstances, the pope's statements on issues of morality and faith should be considered divinely sanctioned truths.

Darwin's allies rushed to his defense. Thomas Huxley, a biologist, surgeon in the British navy, and president of a leading scientific society, popularized Darwin's work in dozens of vigorous and lucid books and pamphlets. Heaping withering scorn on opponents, Huxley called himself "Darwin's bull-dog." Alfred Russel Wallace (1823–1913), a British naturalist, claimed that Darwin "is the Newton of natural history" who "established a firm foundation for all future study of nature."

Over time, many of Darwin's critics moderated their hostility to Darwin's findings. Toward the end of the century the Catholic Church, under Pope Leo XIII (1878–1903), even began taking the position that natural science was not the province of the church, that evolution could be taught as a hypothesis, and that parts of the Bible should be taken figuratively.

Mysteries of the Material and Human World

Research multiplied in many fields besides natural science. Scientists focused especially on the nature of matter. Discovery after discovery in chemistry and physics led them to conclude that all matter was composed of atoms, that each atom was **Physics and chemistry** in turn made up of smaller particles that moved in circles like a miniature solar system, and that each chemical element of matter had a specific atomic weight. In 1870, the Russian chemist Dmitri Mendeleev (1834–1907) compiled a new chart showing the atomic weight of all the known elements and indicating by gaps the other elements that remained to be discovered. Chemists and physicists proved him right. Year after year, researchers discovered new elements that fit into the periodic table. In the 1870s, James Clerk Maxwell (1831–1879) analyzed the relationship between light, magnetism, and electricity. His ideas led to a greater sense of physical unity in the universe and practical developments such as the development of the electronics industry.

The successes of Darwin and of chemists, physicists, and others in the natural sciences encouraged scholars to apply the same scientific techniques and principles to psychology, or the study of human **Psychology** behavior. One of the first to bring this discipline into the laboratory was Wilhelm Wundt (1832–1920). In his laboratory at Leipzig, Wundt and his enthusiastic students tested human reactions and carried out carefully controlled and measured experiments on cats and dogs, assuming that the findings would also apply to human beings.

The Russian scientist Ivan Pavlov (1849–1936), pursuing Wundt's line of inquiry, discovered the conditioned reflex. Pavlov showed meat to a hungry dog

DOCUMENT 21.3

Walter Bagehot on Natural Selection and Human History

Social Darwinism and related doctrines spread, especially among liberals, during the second half of the nineteenth century. The Englishman Walter Bagehot (1826–1877) won notice for presenting views shared by his liberal, middle-class contemporaries. The following is a selection from his 1873 work, Physics and Politics.

. . . Three laws, or approximate laws, may, I think, be laid down. . . .

First. In every particular state of the world, those nations which are strongest tend to prevail over the others; and in certain marked peculiarities the strongest tend to be the best.

Secondly. Within every particular nation the type or types of character then and there most attractive tend to prevail; and the most attractive, though with exceptions, is what we call the best character.

Thirdly. Neither of these competitions is in most historic conditions intensified by extrinsic forces, but in some conditions, such as those now prevailing in the most

influential part of the world, both are so intensified.

These are the sort of doctrines with which, under the name of "natural selection" in physical science, we have become familiar; and as every great scientific conception tends to advance its boundaries and to be of use in solving problems not thought of when it was started, so here, what was put forward for mere animal history may, with a change of form but an identical essence, be applied to human history. . . .

The strongest nation has always been conquering the weaker; sometimes even subduing it, but always prevailing over it. Every intellectual gain, so to speak, that a nation possessed was in the earliest times made use of—was invested and taken out—in war; all else perished. Each nation tried constantly to be the stronger, and so made or copied the best weapons, by conscious and unconscious imitation each nation formed a type of character suitable to war and conquest.

Conquest improved mankind by the intermixture of strengths; the armed truce, which was then called peace, improved them by the competition of training and the consequent creation of new power. Since the long-headed men first drove the short-headed men out of the best land in Europe, all European history has been the history of the superposition of the more military races over the less military—of the efforts, sometimes successful, sometimes unsuccessful, of each race to get more military; and so the art of war has constantly improved. . . .

SOURCE: Walter Bagehot, *Physics and Politics* (New York, 1873), pp. 44–46.

Analyze the Document

1. How does Bagehot connect natural selection and human history?

2. In what ways might someone use Bagehot's argument to justify war or imperialism?

3. In what respects do Bagehot's views reflect nineteenth-century liberalism?

---

until the dog's mouth watered. Then Pavlov rang a bell while showing the meat. Eventually, the dog's mouth would water when only the bell was rung. The implication was that many of our human responses are purely mechanical reflexes prompted by stimuli of which we are often unaware.

The field of sociology also acquired status as a social science. Auguste Comte (1798–1857) named the new discipline. He argued that humankind was entering a stage of history in which truths would be discovered by the scientific gathering of factual data. Humans and society, he said, are as susceptible to scientific investigation as minerals, plants, and the lower animals are. He believed that his philosophy, which he called **positivism,** would reveal the laws of human relations and allow social scientists to engineer harmonious societies. Comte's followers, eager and numerous during the second half of the nineteenth century, placed great faith in statistics and amassed copious statistical data on numerous social problems.

Sociology

Like Comte, most of them believed that sure social knowledge would enable people to remake society for the better.

Historians such as the German Leopold von Ranke (1795–1886) strove to turn history into a social science. Ranke rejected history based on tradition or legend. He also attacked the notion that history could come in the form of a purposeful story about the progress of humanity, the working out of God's will, or other such themes. He argued that historical accounts should be based on an exhaustive accumulation and analysis of documentary evidence. Conclusions could be drawn only from facts, he insisted. In this way, Ranke believed, history would become coldly scientific and morally neutral. His attitude and methodology spread widely, particularly in Germany and the United States.

These scholars believed that individual and social behavior could best be studied by careful, objective observation, experimentation, and analysis.

History

Like scientists, they considered themselves professionals with specialties rather than amateurs. They also formed societies and published their findings in their own journals. Part of what drove them was their faith that these findings would point the way to improving the quality of human life, and they conveyed that faith to a wider public. In this sense, these scholars and scientists shared and promoted the optimism of the period.

Germs, Cures, and Health Care

No field of science promised more new understanding and dramatic applications than medicine. At mid-century, medicine entered a golden age. The most important discovery came not from a doctor but from a chemist. Louis Pasteur (1822–1895), the son of a French tanner, became interested in what happened to wine and beer during the fermentation process. In the 1860s, he discovered the airborne microorganisms responsible for fermentation and showed that bacteria caused milk to sour. He demonstrated that heating milk—"pasteurizing" it—destroyed the bacteria that caused diseases. His long years of work eventually enabled him to identify disease-producing organisms in humans and create vaccines to prevent diseases such as rabies. Here, finally, was the explanation for how people caught infectious diseases: germ theory.

> **Pasteur and germ theory**

Many doctors and scientists, still wedded to old ideas and practices, dismissed Pasteur's findings. The German scientist Robert Koch (1843–1910) confirmed the French chemist's conclusions, convincing doctors that bacteria indeed caused diseases. In the early 1880s, Koch discovered the bacteria responsible for two of the most deadly diseases of the time: tuberculosis and cholera. His students used the same research methods to find microbes that caused a list of other diseases from pneumonia and meningitis to syphilis.

Modern doctors of the late nineteenth century now understood that specific microorganisms (germs) caused specific infectious diseases. In addition to this realization, new tools increased physicians' stature as scientists and improved their ability to diagnose ailments. The thermometer, for example, allowed them to measure body temperature, and the stethoscope let them hear what was going on inside the body. The microscope permitted examination of tissue samples, the X-ray (1896) revealed the body's internal structures, and the electrocardiograph (1901) recorded the workings of the heart.

The most advanced doctors realized that although they may have known more about illnesses and the inner workings of the body, they still could do little to cure diseases. Aspirin (1899) reduced fever, inflammation, and minor pain; morphine controlled more serious pain; and barbiturates might induce sleep— but none of these constituted a medical cure. The first great exception was an antitoxin against diphtheria developed in Robert Koch's Berlin laboratory in 1891. For most diseases, however, cures lay in the future. The best that doctors could do was to stop prescribing poisonous pills and dangerous procedures such as bloodletting and purges.

> **Remedies**

Within medicine, the field of surgery saw especially remarkable progress. During the 1860s and 1870s, the British surgeon Joseph Lister (1827–1912) developed procedures that included the use of antiseptics during operations. These procedures dramatically lowered the risk of infection from the operation itself. Over the following decades, surgeons applied Lister's methods with great success. No longer did they operate in dirty, blood-splattered back rooms, wearing black coats or street clothes. Increasingly, they washed their hands, worked in relatively sterile environments, and wore white surgical gowns, face masks, and rubber gloves to lessen the risks of infection.

> **Surgery**

In **Figure 21.12,** an 1890 painting of an operating room in a Vienna hospital, a patient is being prepared for surgery. The doctors wear white coats rather than street clothes, and the patient is being anesthetized. However, old practices died slowly. Even though Joseph Lister had developed antiseptic procedures more than twenty years earlier, the surgeon and his assistants in the painting do not wear masks or gloves, and the surgical instruments have not been sterilized. Everyone in the scene is male; most medical schools still denied access to women. The picture also lacks religious symbols. All in all, it conveys a sense of solid confidence in modern science.

KEY DATES

WESTERN SOCIETY, 1850–1914

1853	Beginning of the rebuilding of Paris
1857	Flaubert, *Madame Bovary*
1859	Darwin, *On the Origin of Species*
1860s	Pasteur's germ theory
1864	*Syllabus of Errors*
1870	Periodic table developed
1876	Telephone invented
1896	Modern Olympic games
1905	Einstein's theory of relativity
1913	Stravinsky, *Rite of Spring*

FIGURE 21.12 Albert Seligmann, *Operation by German Surgeon Theodor Billroth*, 1890 This painting of a Viennese operating room reveals a growing confidence in modern science but the persistence of old patterns in medical practice, including the absence of surgical masks and gloves, the use of unsterilized instruments, and males' dominance of the profession.

Medical advances also made a huge difference in the field of nursing. In hospitals, emergencies, and war, nurses often had the most direct contact with sufferers and the wounded. During the Crimean War (1853–1856), Florence Nightingale transformed nursing into a modern profession (see Biography in Chapter 19). Her reforms stressed cleanliness, fresh air, and discipline and helped make nursing an attractive path to independence and service. A few years later, the philanthropist Dorothea Dix (1802–1887) led similar reform efforts in the United States during the Civil War, and in Switzerland a banker established the International Red Cross, creating new demand for professional nurses.

Nursing

By the turn of the century, much in medicine had gained the authority of science and was "professionalized." Better nursing gave the wounded a fighting chance at survival. Doctors who understood diseases and surgeons who performed operations safely now helped more than hurt their patients. Even so, many doctors insisted on practicing traditional medicine, and most remained too expensive for working-class families to afford except when they were in dire need. Many working-class women were forced to prescribe their own curative regime or find some inexpensive "cure."

CULTURE: ACCEPTING THE MODERN WORLD

Faith in science and technology reflected a growing sense that people could observe the facts of everyday life carefully, understand them, and use that understanding to control the world more successfully than ever before. Writers and artists also closely observed contemporary life in their books and paintings. During the second half of the nineteenth century, their focus included the methods of science and the realities of urban life. The romanticism of early-nineteenth-century culture—which had idealized love, religion, and the exotic—gave way to a gritty sense of realism (see Chapter 18). Realists felt free to look modern life full in the face and both praise its successes and criticize its failings.

Realism and Naturalism: The Details of Social Life

The age witnessed the rise of realistic and naturalistic literature, which explored the social dislocation brought about by the industrial revolution, commercial values, and city life. Eugène de Vogüé (1848–1910), a nineteenth-century French writer, explained that a realist "observes life as it is in its wholeness and complexity with the least possible prejudice on the part of the artist. It takes men under ordinary conditions, shows characters in the course of their everyday existence." Authors, often focusing on the unpleasant, sordid side of human nature and society, examined how environment and heredity together shaped people's lives. With scientific thoroughness, these writers examined people's public and private lives, their individual and social failings, and the hypocrisy of their religious and moral values.

Literature

The French novelist Gustave Flaubert (1821–1880), for example, deftly captured the full flavor of **realism.** His *Madame Bovary* (1857) related the illicit sex life of the wife of a small-town French physician in such full and unblushing detail that it scandalized a public not yet accustomed to such unrestrained revelations. *Madame Bovary* became a model for other novelists. Few writers, however, were as popular as Charles Dickens (1812–1870). As we saw in Chapter 17, Dickens's novels presented realistic descriptions of the middle and lower classes in Britain's urban, industrial society. For example, in *The Old Curiosity Shop*, he refused to shy away from the realities of nighttime in impoverished sections of cities, "when bands of unemployed labourers paraded in the roads . . . when carts came rumbling by, filled with rude coffins . . . or when orphans cried, and distracted women shrieked and followed in their wake, . . . when some called for bread, and some for drink to drown their cares. . . ."

Mary Ann Evans (1819–1880), writing under the pen name George Eliot, also wrote popular novels examining the realities of British social life. In *Middlemarch*, for instance, she linked psychological conflict to the determining social realities surrounding her characters. The Norwegian playwright Henrik Ibsen (1828–1906) presented another perspective on such realities. Ibsen ridiculed bourgeois society in his popular dramas. In *A Doll's House*, probably his best-known play, the heroine, Nora, rebels against her expected role in the "doll's house" that her stodgy, hypocritical, middle-class husband, Helmer, has created for her:

NORA: What do you consider my holiest duties?
HELMER: Need I tell you that? Your duties to your
    husband and children.
NORA: I have other duties equally sacred.
HELMER: Impossible! What do you mean!
NORA: My duties toward myself.
HELMER: Before all else you are a wife and a mother.
NORA: That I no longer believe. Before all else I
    believe I am a human being just as much as you are.

The French writer Émile Zola (1840–1902) explained that the naturalist novel, having evolved from the realistic novel, "substitutes for the study of the abstract man . . . the study of the natural man, governed by physical and chemical laws, and modified by the influences of his surroundings; it is in one word the literature of our scientific age. . . ." He wrote in almost clinical detail about the social problems spawned by industrialism. In one series of novels, he portrayed several generations of a working-class family battered by the forces of heredity and the environment. They struggle to survive, fighting poverty, strikes, alcoholism, and conflict among themselves.

Russia produced some especially talented writers who created stunning realistic literature. An example is Leo Tolstoy (1828–1910) and his masterpiece *War and Peace* (1865–1869). This sweeping novel about Russia during the Napoleonic Wars features scores of characters who battle impersonal social forces and the overwhelming details of everyday life. Even the strongest individuals in the story become ensnared in forces beyond their control. In other writings that reflected the social realities of his own times, Tolstoy attacked capitalism and materialism: "Money is a new form of slavery, and distinguishable from the old simply by the fact that it is impersonal. . . ."

Fyodor Dostoyevski (1821–1881), another legendary Russian author, focused more on psychological and moral realities in his novels. His characters—such as the anguished student Raskolnikov in *Crime and Punishment* (1866), who murders an old woman—struggle with moral conflicts in an age marked by spiritual bankruptcy. Like other realistic writers, Dostoyevski shone a spotlight on the harshness of modern life, particularly its power to overwhelm individuals.

Innovative painters turned to realistic depictions of life on their canvases. The French artist Gustave Courbet (1819–1877), who believed that an artist should "never permit Art sentiment to overthrow logic," led the attack on romantic art by painting sober scenes of urban life and rural labor. In *The Stone Breakers* (**Figure 21.13**), he portrays rural laborers as a passerby might see them. Courbet claimed he "saw these people every day on my walk." Here an old worker—with patches on his pants and holes in his socks—breaks up stones, probably for use in building a road. His young assistant, who is "suffering from scurvy" according to Courbet, carries the stones away in a basket. The two men's tattered clothing and averted faces make them seem anonymous and therefore representative of many other workers. While there is dignity in their work, Courbet does not glorify either the stone breakers or nature. The scene, like the men's lives, is harsh. The image suggests that the

FIGURE 21.13 Gustave Courbet, *The Stone Breakers*, 1849 A man and his young assistant break up stones for a road in this realistic painting of rural life.

young assistant is likely to end up the same as his old companion. Courbet and other realistic artists depicted everyday life on large canvases and thereby earned the wrath of those artists and critics who believed that only paintings of historical, mythological, religious, or exotic scenes should be considered great art.

Impressionism: Celebrating Modern Life

Like the realists and naturalists, impressionist painters embraced modern life—but in a different way. Specifically, they applied a new understanding of color, light, and optics to their work. Their paintings—with their informal quality and emphasis on angles—suggested randomness of reality. Such artists ventured outside their studios to paint scenes. They especially sought to convey the impression of a view that the eye actually sees at first glance—the impression created by light reflected off a surface at a single moment—rather than what the knowing brain interprets from visual cues, hence the name **impressionism** for this school of painting. The French artist Claude Monet (1840–1926) (see Biography) described the way he painted: "Try to forget what objects you have before you—a tree, a house, a field, or whatever. Merely think, here is a little square of blue, here an oblong of pink, here a streak of yellow, and paint it just as it looks to you . . . until it gives your own naive impression of the scene before you."

Monet's *The Docks of Argenteuil* (**Figure 21.14**) is an example of many paintings of the suburban countryside—the places to which the urban bourgeoisie might travel on Sundays or vacations. In this scene near his home just outside of Paris, middle-class women carrying parasols stroll down a wide, tree-lined path bordering the Seine or wander over to a dock on the right where boats might be rented. Sailboats on the river suggest pleasure; a bridge in the distance implies that the city is not far away. The bourgeoisie purchasers of Monet's paintings would recognize this sort of place, where civilization and countryside meet under a broad sky.

Impressionists also painted psychologically subtle portraits, bedroom and dance-hall interiors, urban parks, and city streets. *Boulevard des Italiens, Morning, Sunlight* (**Figure 21.15**) by Camille Pissarro shows one of the straight, wide, tree-lined fashionable boulevards constructed in Paris during the Second Empire under Napoleon III. Pissarro, often regarded as the father of the impressionist movement, needed only a few brushstrokes to suggest people, buses, carriages, storefronts, and building details—the impression that one might get glancing out an upper-floor window at an anonymous but vibrant urban scene below.

FIGURE 21.14 Claude Monet, *The Docks of Argenteuil,* **1872** This vivid impressionist painting shows an appealing suburban scene just outside Paris.

FROM OPTIMISM TO UNCERTAINTY

The impressionists' delight in the beauty and charm of modern life fit well with the continuing belief in reason, individual rights, and progress that marked the decades after 1850. Economic growth, improving conditions in the cities, and new conquests by science buoyed a broad sense of moderate optimism about the world. However, from the 1880s on, signs of a disturbing new undercurrent rose to the surface of Western culture. Some of the West's best intellectuals, writers, and artists injected themes of pessimism and painful introspection into their work. They emphasized how strongly irrational forces guided human behavior. Though still a minority, these thinkers and critics undermined rather than overwhelmed the prevailing certainty and optimism of the period. They added to the growing social and political tensions of the turn-of-the-century decades described in Chapter 20.

Everything Is Relative

In part, this disillusionment stemmed from the growing feeling of uncertainty creeping into elite scientific circles—the sense that the more people learned, the less solid and reliable the material world became. The work of Albert Einstein (1879–1955) exposed this uncertainty in physics. A German who later fled to America, Einstein assailed time-honored concepts about the stability of matter and the nature of the physical universe. In 1905, while still earning a living as a patent clerk in Switzerland, he proposed

BIOGRAPHY

Claude Monet
(1840–1926)

Impressionist

Painter

As a boy growing up in Le Havre on France's north coast, Oscar Claude Monet was rebellious and daring. "My youth was essentially that of a vagabond," he wrote. "Never would I bend to a rule."

That pattern of assertive rebellion would stay with him. In 1857, the 16-year-old Claude announced to his father, a prosperous merchant, that he was going to Paris to become a painter. His father refused to help him financially, but Claude left home anyway. In Paris, he rejected academic art training, instead working with other young artists such as Pissarro and Renoir, with whom he would remain connected for many years.

In 1864, he met the 18-year-old Camille Doncieux, and the two moved in together. That year, Claude had his first paintings accepted at the official Salon, where prominent artists entered their paintings to be judged and—if accepted—offered for sale. Success at the Salon meant the possibility of earning a living as an artist. Despite this triumph, financial problems plagued the young Monet. He often had to hide in Paris or flee to the suburbs to escape from creditors. He perpetually wrote letters begging his family, friends, and other artists for money.

In the following years, Monet enjoyed some successes but was disappointed whenever his paintings were turned down by the Salon. Depression often haunted him: "I am like a man going down the third time. . . . I see everything black. . . . Money is always lacking. Disappointments, insults, hopes, new disappointments." But in good times, he lived the bourgeois life and experienced private joys. In 1868, he wrote: "I am surrounded here by all that I love. I pass my time outdoors on the flint beach when the seas are heavy or when the boats go off to fish, or I even go into the country, which is so beautiful here. . . . I find in my tiny house a good fire and a good little family." Though he had a one-year-old son, Jean, with Camille, it took the prospect of money from an inheritance by Camille, guaranteed by a contract, before he finally married her in 1870.

In 1872, the Monets moved to Argenteuil, twenty minutes from Paris by train. Camille played the role of a middle-class housewife, rising early to serve breakfast to her husband and son, shopping, buying bread just before lunch, cleaning the house, preparing dinner, and reading the newspapers daily. Their son, Jean, dressed in long skirts, as was the style of the time and riding his tricycle with a stuffed horse mounted on its front end, appeared on several of Monet's canvases, as did Camille. Every day, Monet painted by the shore of the river, sometimes accompanied by other visiting impressionists.

By 1874, Monet had turned his back on the official Salon. That year, he and other artists formed a group and mounted their own exposition. Monet was at the head of the group, which included Renoir and Pissarro. Critics attacked the paintings at the exposition, particularly one by Monet titled *Impression: Sunrise*, for rejecting accepted standards of good art. Yet the group continued to paint and show together, earning a reputation for being rebellious artists and "bohemians" with inappropriate lifestyles.

In 1878, the ailing Camille gave birth to a second son. A year later she died. Soon Monet became involved with another woman, Alice Hoschede, already married to a successful merchant and the mother of several children. The couple soon moved in together.

Monet was happy living with Alice, and his paintings began to sell well. He stopped showing his paintings with the other impressionist painters and moved to Giverny, northwest of Paris. There he created a large garden and pond, which he would paint for the rest of his life.

Monet gained a public reputation for being both brilliant and unyielding. When the government tried to award him the Legion of Honor, he refused. By 1890, he was recognized as France's premier painter, far more popular than any of his colleagues. His paintings commanded high prices. Now sporting a long, white beard, he became a revered figure. Despite his failing eyesight, he painted almost up until his death in 1926.

Monet made the bourgeoisie both the subject and the assumed audience of his paintings. Many of his landscapes featured the suburban fields, gardens, walks, and riverbanks that the bourgeoisie loved to visit (see **Figure 21.14**). Even his landscapes of southern France or the north coast were presented from the point of view of a tourist. Monet always emphasized the "modern" in his work. There was no horror in his depictions of the city, only a celebration of its boulevards, railway stations, and parks.

Connecting People & Society

1. How do Monet's life, paintings, and popularity reflect European society during the second half of the nineteenth century?

2. Does this profile of Monet's life suggest that art was a business much like other businesses? Explain.

3. Why did Monet and other artists come to be viewed as "bohemians" with inappropriate lifestyles?

FIGURE 21.15 Camille Pissarro, *Boulevard des Italiens, Morning, Sunlight,* 1897 Impressionist painters such as Pissarro depicted city scenes such as this interpretation of a bustling boulevard in Paris.

what would become the seminal theory of relativity. According to this theory, time, space, and motion are relative to one another as well as to the observer—they are not the absolutes scientists had believed in for so long.

Building on the work of the German physicist Max Planck (1858–1947), who had shown that heated bodies emit energy in irregular packets (quanta) rather than a steady stream, Einstein also derived a groundbreaking formula, $E = mc^2$ (E = energy; m = mass; c = speed of light). This formula blurred the distinction between mass and energy and described the immense energy contained within each atom. The atomic energy in a lump of coal, for example, was revealed to be some three billion times as great as the energy obtained by burning the coal. This unsettling notion later contributed to the development of the atomic bomb. By showing that matter could be transformed into energy, Einstein again challenged Newtonian physics. More conservative scientists, wedded to time-honored Newtonian physics, dismissed his theories. Eventually, however, Einstein's views gained support, further undermining scientists' assumptions about the physical nature of the universe.

Sex, Conflict, and the Unconscious

Ideas about the human mind—the internal, mental universe—also took a disturbing turn in these years. Sigmund Freud (1856–1939), the Viennese neurologist, concluded that nervous disorders stemmed from psychological causes, not physiological sources as most doctors had believed. Basing his ideas on the words, experiences, and dreams of troubled patients, he founded psychoanalysis, which he described as "the scientific method by which the unconscious can be studied."

Freud argued that much of human behavior was irrational, unconscious, and instinctual. Conflict, he claimed, was a basic condition of life, particularly when it occurred between people's innate biological drives (such as sex or aggression) and their social selves. According to Freud, these conflicts developed

Freud and psychoanalysis

on a mostly unconscious level and in stages during childhood. At war within all people are what Freud called the id, the superego, and the ego. The id is the source of our basic desires, the most important and disturbing of these being sexual. The superego imposes socially acceptable standards of behavior on the individual. The ego tries to find ways to satisfy both the demands of the id and the restraints of the superego. Typically, the mind responds to this conflict by repressing the id's desires from consciousness. However, the unconscious psychic struggle continues, creating a mental life of great tension.

Freud added fuel to his already controversial ideas by emphasizing the importance of sexual conflicts originating in childhood. He argued that children inevitably come into conflict with their parents, competing with the same-sex parent for the love of the opposite-sex parent. At an unconscious level, he claimed, this competition for the parent of the opposite sex strongly shapes the development of an individual's personality.

Freud believed that much psychic pain and many emotional disorders stemmed from the suppressed and frustrated drives of early life—frustrations that then festered outside of people's awareness. He concluded that the correct therapy for such disorders was to make the sufferer conscious of the facts and circumstances of his or her original frustration. Hence, he encouraged patients to talk about their dreams, for by interpreting dreams the unconscious could be revealed.

Freud's controversial explanation of human behavior had several disturbing implications: Neither adults nor children are innocent beings after all; too few people lead happy lives; sex and aggression play powerful roles in children and adults alike; people cannot escape from internal conflict and frustration. Although he hoped that reason and understanding would ease humanity's psychological plight, Freud was far from an optimist. He eventually concluded that "the price of progress in civilization is paid in forfeiting happiness."

Fear of Social Disintegration

The French scholar Émile Durkheim (1858–1917), a founder of modern sociology, offered a different sort of warning about trends in modern society. Though a strong believer in science, Durkheim argued that industrial society—especially with its competitive individualism and lack of collective values—was weakening the ties that connected people with one another. As people became more concerned with their own freedom and advancement, he believed, the restraints and the spiritual beliefs that held traditional societies together would break down. This trend toward social disintegration, Durkheim warned, disoriented individuals, made them feel cut off from others, and left them without a sense of purpose. As a result, more and more people were experiencing despair, which in turn led to rising suicide rates. Like Freud, Durkheim believed that advancing civilization left psychic pain in its wake.

Disenchantment Sets In

Perhaps the deepest sense of disenchantment with the optimistic, bourgeois, urban society of the nineteenth century emerged in philosophy. Friedrich Nietzsche (1844–1890), a brilliant German philosopher, is one example. Reason could not solve human problems, Nietzsche concluded. Instead, he believed in "will," which in his view enabled people to survive and the strongest among them to achieve power. Great leaders, he argued, rose through strength, intelligence, and above all, "the will to power." Nietzsche further claimed that if a superior society were to emerge, it would have to come about through the efforts of gifted individuals who would rise to positions of leadership because of their superior strength, will, and intelligence. Anything that contributes to power is good, he explained—be it strength of will, boldness, cunning, or intelligence. Likewise, whatever leads to weakness is bad—be it gentleness, modesty, generosity, or compassion.

In Nietzsche's view, Christianity stood in the way of a better human society. "Christianity has taken the side of everything weak, base, ill-constituted; it has made an ideal out of opposition to the preservative instincts of strong life," he announced. "God is dead; we have killed him." For Nietzsche, the idea of the death of God was liberating: Now humans could cast off all conventions. Nietzsche also decried democracy for amounting to rule by the supposedly mediocre "masses . . . or the populace, or the herd, or whatever name you care to give them." He went on to attack many other accepted tenets of nineteenth-century civilization, such as liberalism, rationalism, and science. Although Nietzsche was not a nationalist or racist himself, others would later use his ideas to support militant nationalism and racism.

In France, the philosopher Henri Bergson (1859–1941) also questioned the limits of rational and scientific thinking. Gaining a large following by lecturing at the University of Paris, he argued that truth is best grasped through intuition and unconscious feelings rather than reason: "Science can teach us nothing of the truth; it can only serve as a rule of action." Society, Bergson said, needs the energy that only a spontaneous following of the "life force" can provide. His views, like those of Nietzsche and others, reflected a growing criticism of the dominant ideas of middle-class society in the West.

Art Turns Inward

Many talented artists also turned away from the mainstream of nineteenth-century civilization.

Expressionism Their work grew more pessimistic and critical of middle-class life. The slogan "Art for art's sake" reflected the trend of various artistic movements, such as **expressionism** and symbolism. They self-consciously attacked social and artistic taboos in ways that mystified much of the public. Their often introspective works proved understandable mainly to themselves and a small artistic elite. The Russian abstract expressionist painter Wassily Kandinsky (1866–1944) spoke for many of his fellow artists when he explained that his work was not intended to represent how things looked. "Look at the picture as a graphic representation of a mood and not as a representation of objects," he suggested.

Many artists focused on peripheral members of a society that seemed to be disintegrating, painting prostitutes, solitary drinkers, blind beggars, and circus performers. Moreover, threatening symbols of science, machinery, and speed began to crop up on canvases. Photography had already displaced traditional representation art. The French poet Guillaume Apollinaire (1880–1918) explained that modern painters "avoid any representation of natural scenes . . . since everything is sacrificed by the artist to truth." Now avantgarde painters created distorted, subjective, and abstract images.

We can see evidence of these trends in expressionist paintings such as those by the Belgian artist James Ensor (1860–1949). In *Christ's Triumphant Entry into Brussels* in 1888 (**Figure 21.16**), Ensor shows a parade and a mob of people whose faces are in coarse caricatures or masks that reflect pretense and false smiles. Behind their masks lurk isolation and anxiety. They march under banners that cynically proclaim "Long Live Socialism," "Political Spectacles Always Succeed," and "Long Live Jesus."

Like Ensor, the Norwegian artist Edvard Munch (1863–1944) expressed a deep current of horror in middle-class life, but in a deeper, more personal way. In *The Scream* (**Figure 21.17**), a wide-eyed figure standing on a bridge lets out a terrified shriek. The land, water, and sky—all distorted and painted in alarming colors—echo the cry of the figure. Munch described the feelings that inspired the scene: "I was

FIGURE 21.16 James Ensor, *Christ's Triumphant Entry into Brussels*, 1888 Expressionist artists such as the Belgian painter James Ensor often attacked the pretenses of everyday life in their paintings.

FIGURE 21.17 Edvard Munch, *The Scream*, 1893 Much late-nineteenth-century expressionist art focused on themes of horror and anguish in middle-class life.

tired and ill—I stood looking out across the fjord—the sun was setting—the clouds were colored red—like blood—I felt as though a scream went through nature. . . ." In this painting, themes of death, anxiety, loneliness, and fear coalesce. Munch once exclaimed, "How much of my art I owe to suffering!"

Many other artists painted similarly anguished scenes, emphasizing social anxieties, urban loneliness, violence, horror, and a turning inward toward the unconscious. Their paintings penetrated through surface-level appearances into a deeper, disturbing psychic reality.

In music, expressionism also challenged artistic conventions and public tastes. The Russian composer Igor Stravinsky (1882–1971) led this movement in his music for the ballet *The Rite of Spring*. The premiere of the ballet on May 29, 1913, in Paris has been called the most notorious event of the twentieth century. Upon hearing the music—with its offbeat rhythm and unrestrained, dissonant sounds—the audience rose in outrage. Fights broke out, and many listeners stormed from the theater after complaining loudly. Yet among certain elites, Stravinsky became the leading composer of the day.

Like science and philosophy, art and music were slipping away from the grasp of ordinary people. The new understandings of modern life that had seemed so promising a few decades earlier now appeared shadowed by doubt and even foreboding.

Music

LOOKING BACK & MOVING FORWARD

Summary   By 1914, industrialization, urban growth, and the culture of progress had pulled much of the West into new territory. Life in large parts of Europe and North America had undergone a huge transformation. Someone who had lived during the late eighteenth century would have found virtually everything about the turn-of-the-century West strange or even shocking. Most of us, however, would readily recognize early-twentieth-century Paris, Berlin, or New York as modern. Those cities—like our cities today—were part of a widespread urban society and culture dominated by the middle classes and marching to the quickening pace of economic transformation. The variety of public and private life within those cities has persisted to the present day.

People have called the years 1850–1914 the Age of Progress. The reasons are clear. Income for most people rose at least a little, and for some quite considerably, while the machines of industry pumped out endless new products that promised to ease the burdens of everyday life. Science promised even more and delivered findings that seemed to unlock the mysteries of both the physical and social worlds. Many of the cultural forms of the period gazed directly at the modern world and embraced it. In the 1920s, the French would look back to the two decades surrounding the turn of the century as La Belle Époque—the beautiful era.

Yet, as we have seen, darker forces of change simmered below the optimistic surface during these same years. Just how much progress was achieved in politics is not so clear. Events in the summer of 1914 would expose that sense of dangerous uncertainty as all too well founded. Whether progress was made in the West's relations with the rest of the world is also in doubt. From outside the West, some observers questioned the very value of Western civilization. "In order to estimate the value of a civilization," explained a high Chinese official educated in European universities, "the question we must finally ask is not what great cities . . . it has built . . . what clever and useful implements . . . it has made . . . what institutions, what arts and sciences it has invested: the question . . . is what type of humanity, what kind of men and women it has been able to produce." These complex questions, too, would be immediately recognizable to us today. Modern times had arrived.

KEY TERMS

Victorian,   *p. 666*

psychoanalysis,   *p. 673*

Social Darwinism,   *p. 674*

positivism,   *p. 677*

realism,   *p. 679*

impressionism,   *p. 681*

expressionism,   *p. 685*

REVIEW, ANALYZE, & CONNECT TO TODAY

REVIEW THE PREVIOUS CHAPTER

Chapter 20—"Mass Politics and Imperial Domination"—traced the spreading demands for democracy and the West's imperial expansion during the second half of the nineteenth century.

1. How did politics adjust to the new industrial and urban realities of this period?

2. In what ways did imperialism support and reflect both the nationalism and industrialism of this period?

ANALYZE THIS CHAPTER

Chapter 21—"Modern Life and the Culture of Progress"—traces the changes stemming from new industrial transformations and urban growth, as well as the culture of the West.

1. Considering the material in this chapter and Chapter 17 (which focused on the industrial revolution), why do you think industrialization so quickly doomed traditional society in the West?

2. Analyze the impact of spreading industrialization on the various social classes during this period.

3. How did people adjust to the opportunities and pressures of life in the West's modernizing cities?

4. Do you think the title "Modern Life and The Culture of Progress" is an apt description of Western culture during this period? Why or why not?

CONNECT TO TODAY

Think about the new industrial transformation, urban growth, and cultural development between 1850 and 1914.

1. In what ways is the period of rapid industrialization we examined in this chapter similar to contemporary times?

2. In what regards is this historical period different from the experience of recent times?

3. Why do you think that so much of the culture—especially ideas, art, and literature—of the period 1850–1914 remains influential and popular in today's world?

BEYOND THE CLASSROOM

THE SECOND INDUSTRIAL REVOLUTION

Hobsbawm, Eric J. *The Age of Capital, 1848–1875.* New York: New American Library, 1979. Includes detailed sections on industrialism as well as its social consequences.

Ville, Simon P. *Transport and the Development of the European Economy, 1750–1918.* Houndmills, UK: Macmillan, 1990. A comparative study of the major forms of transportation from 1750 to 1918 and their relationship to economic development.

Williams, Rosalind H. *Dream Worlds: Mass Consumption in Late Nineteenth-Century France.* Berkeley: University of California Press, 1982. An exploration of the mental evolution of consumer society in late-nineteenth- and early-twentieth-century France.

THE NEW URBAN LANDSCAPE

Olsen, Donald J. *The City as a Work of Art—London, Paris, Vienna.* New Haven, CT: Yale University Press, 1986. A well-illustrated examination of nineteenth-century urban growth and design.

Pinkney, David. *Napoleon III and the Rebuilding of Paris.* Princeton, NJ: Princeton University Press, 1972. A classic study of one of the most important urban renovations of the nineteenth century.

GLOBAL CONNECTIONS

Chasteen, John Charles. *Born in Blood and Fire: A Concise History of Latin America.* New York: Norton, 2001. A useful survey covering the period.

CITY PEOPLE

Joyce, P. *Visions of the People: Industrial England and the Question of Class, 1848–1914.* Cambridge: Cambridge University Press, 1991. An examination of working-class culture and language.

Pilbeam, Pamela. *The Middle Classes in Europe, 1789–1914.* Chicago: Lyceum Books, 1990. A thorough treatment of middle-class life in the major European nations.

PRIVATE LIFE: TOGETHER AND ALONE AT HOME

Gay, Peter. *The Bourgeois Experience: Victoria to Freud,* 2 vols. New York: Oxford University Press, 1984–1986. Exhaustively researched volumes dealing with the varied experiences of middle-class life in America and Europe.

Perrot, Michelle, ed. *A History of Private Life, IV: From the Fires of Revolution to the Great War.* Cambridge, MA: Harvard University Press, 1990. Richly detailed and well-illustrated essays on the nineteenth century and its division between public and private life.

Peterson, M. Jeanne. *Family, Love, and Work in the Lives of Victorian Gentlewomen.* Bloomington: Indiana University Press, 1989. A portrayal that defies the stereotype that Victorian gentlewomen led productive lives, were well educated, and were sexually knowledgeable.

SCIENCE IN AN AGE OF OPTIMISM

Bowler, Peter J. *Evolution—The History of an Idea*, rev. ed. Berkeley: University of California Press, 2003. An outstanding survey of the subject that argues that the Darwinian revolution never really occurred.

Bynum, W.F. *Science and the Practice of Medicine in the Nineteenth Century.* Cambridge: Cambridge University Press, 1994. Examines the impact of the sciences on medicine.

Kern, Stephen. *The Culture of Time and Space, 1880–1918.* Cambridge, MA: Harvard University Press, 1983. A lively discussion of the impact of the new technology.

CULTURE: ACCEPTING THE MODERN WORLD

Dale, Peter A. *In Pursuit of a Scientific Culture: Science, Art, and Society in the Victorian Age.* Madison: University of Wisconsin Press, 1989. Examines the connections between science, culture, and society during the second half of the nineteenth century.

Thomson, Belinda. *Impressionism: Origins, Practice, Reception.* London: Thames and Hudson, 2000. A well-written study of the history of impressionism.

FROM OPTIMISM TO UNCERTAINTY

Burrow, J.W. *The Crisis of Reason: European Thought, 1848–1914.* New Haven, CT: Yale University Press, 2000. An excellent survey of the subject.

Gay, Peter. *Freud—A Life for Our Time.* New York: Norton, 1988. A standard biography of Freud.

Hughes, H. Stuart. *Consciousness and Society: The Reorientation of European Social Thought, 1890–1930.* New York: Vintage Books, 1979. A classic examination of the intellectual revolt against scientific certainty.

OTTO DIX, *WAR*, 1929–1932

The German expressionist painter Otto Dix (1891–1969) fought in the trenches of World War I and was wounded several times. In this triptych he depicts the destructiveness of war. In the panel on the left, soldiers march toward the bleak battlefront. Their fate is depicted in the following panels: the gore and destruction of the front lines, trenches that serve as coffins for the numberless dead, and the endless haunting nightmares of those who somehow survive. This painting all too accurately captured the reality of the period as experienced by millions of people.

Descending into the Twentieth Century

22

World War and Revolution, 1914–1920

"**M**illions of men are going to be massacred in a War of the Worlds." As late as the first days of August 1914, only a few Westerners voiced such ominous warnings as these words by the French writer Marcel Proust. In 1917, the third year of the war that Proust had foretold, the young British poet and soldier Wilfred Owen became trapped in a hole on the still-raging battle lines with the shattered body of a fellow officer. As Owen put it, the officer "lay not only near by, but in various places around and about." Owen returned to England suffering from "shell shock," as nervous breakdowns were known. Yet, a year later, he chose to return to the front. In a letter to his mother, he explained why: "I came out in order to help these boys. . . ." He hoped "by watching their sufferings that I may speak of them as well as a pleader can."

Suffer the young soldiers did, and much of Western civilization agonized along with them. The Great War ended the era that had begun 125 years earlier with the French and industrial revolutions. It spawned a new round of revolution, destroyed several empires, and altered politics and society for the rest of the twentieth century. The consequences of this war even spread into the non-Western world, drawing in troops from Asia and Africa and changing how people around the globe viewed the West.

Why did entire nations send their people into this conflict? After all, the war was not inevitable, nor was it an accident. At the same time, some of the combatants reasoned that they had no choice in the matter. Indeed, the outbreak of the war seemed to pivot on something that happened one June day in 1914. By itself, that event would not have led nations to commit to such a costly endeavor. But people turned the event into a spark that ignited a deadly fire they could not put out.

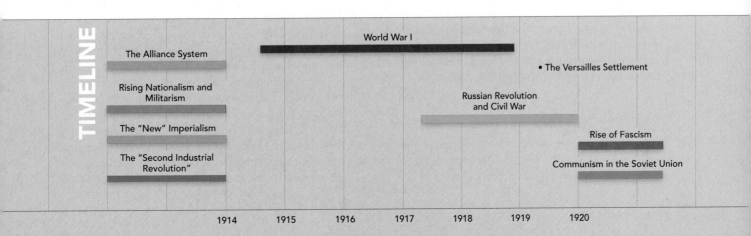

PREVIEW

ON THE PATH TO TOTAL WAR

On June 28, 1914, 19-year-old Gavrilo Princip, gun in hand, waited along a parade route in Sarajevo, the capital of the Austro-Hungarian province of Bosnia. Princip was a member of a Bosnian nationalist organization that had been trained by the Black Hand, a Serbian terrorist group. He was not alone. That day, Archduke Ferdinand, the heir to the Austro-Hungarian throne, was visiting Sarajevo. Princip, waiting with several conspirators, planned to kill the archduke to promote Slavic liberation from Austro-Hungarian control. As Ferdinand's open car passed by, Princip's co-conspirators lost their nerve and did not shoot. Then Ferdinand's driver took a wrong turn. Realizing his mistake, he stopped the car and, by chance, backed up to where Princip stood. Princip fired, killing Ferdinand and his wife.

In those years, several political leaders had been assassinated without great risk of war. Yet in just four weeks, this incident would lead Austria-Hungary, a second-rate power, to declare war on Serbia, a third-rate power in the southeast corner of Europe—the Balkans. Within one more week, most of Europe was engulfed by war. How could this incident in Sarajevo, far from the heart of Europe and not directly involving any of Europe's major powers, result in an all-out war that would end an era and transform Western society?

Rivalries and Alliances

Part of the answer lies in the national, economic, and imperial rivalry percolating in Europe at the time. Militant nationalism, intensifying since the mid-nineteenth century, encouraged countries to view one another as dangerous rivals in the struggle for power and prestige. Politicians used this nationalism to glaze over domestic problems and win public support. The growth of industrial capitalism created an environment of competitive economic struggle as nations tried to promote their industries and gain markets. The outburst of imperialism in the decades before 1914 pitted these rivals against one another in a race to acquire colonies and expand their arenas of influence around the world.

These rivalries fueled international affairs and pressured European states to form a system of alliances among themselves. The German statesman Otto von Bismarck initiated the alliances in the 1870s. Concerned about being | The alliance system | encircled by enemies, he allied Germany with Austria-Hungary and Russia to avoid any possibility of a two-front war—to the east against Russia and to the west against France. After forcing Bismarck's retirement, the new German kaiser—hoping to extend German influence over areas of concern to Russia—allowed the reinsurance treaty with Russia to lapse. This opened the door to major shifts in international relations. New alliances formed as European states tried to protect themselves and pursue their ambitions. Italy, looking for support against France in the competition for colonies, joined Germany and Austria-Hungary in 1882 to form the Triple Alliance. Russia, hoping to expand into southeastern Europe and gain access to the Mediterranean at the expense of the declining Ottoman Empire, came into conflict with Austro-Hungarian and German ambitions in the Balkans. By 1894, Russia had joined in a new alliance with France, which eagerly sought an ally in case of a clash with Germany. In 1904, Britain, threatened by the rise of Germany as a new naval, industrial, and imperial power, joined its old rival France in an alliance called the Entente Cordiale. In 1905 and again in 1911, German challenges to French sovereignty over Morocco in North Africa created international crises that drew France and Britain closer together.

By 1914, Europe had divided itself into two powerful alliance systems: the Triple Entente, comprising France, Russia, and Great Britain; and the Triple Alliance, made up of Germany, Austria-Hungary, and Italy. On the one hand, these alliances may have encouraged Europeans to believe that they could avert major wars. Between 1870 and 1914, a balance of power did generally prevail. Statesmen solved most conflicts diplomatically, and military scuffles remained brief and local. On the other hand, the alliance system gave smaller powers an opportunity to influence the decisions of larger powers; everyone feared that losing an ally—even a relatively weak supporter making decisions in its own interests—would upset the balance of power and make strong nations vulnerable.

Meanwhile, military might played a large part in politics in this world driven by competition and a struggle for international stature.

Military buildup Germany built a new navy; Britain kept ahead and in 1906 launched the *Dreadnought,* the first of a new class of battleships armed entirely with big guns; and most powers reinforced their armies. Between 1870 and 1914, France and Germany more than doubled the size of their standing armies by requiring citizens to serve for set periods of time. Politicians justified huge expenditures for the military buildup with nationalistic slogans and claims that military spending promoted industry, jobs, and trade. Military staffs made plans emphasizing quick offensive thrusts and drew up timetables for mobilizing their forces in case of war. Most people assumed that any war that broke out would be short, like the Franco-Prussian War of 1870 (see pages 614–615), and that their own nation would win it. This armaments race and military planning only heightened the suspicion and fear brewing between nations. It also made national leaders feel ever more dependent on their allies for support in case of war.

Crises in the Balkans

These rivalries and hardening alliances became enmeshed in a series of crises that exploded in the Balkans (see **Maps 22.1** and **22.2**). Why the Balkans? This was Europe's most unstable area—a land of strong nationalistic aspirations felt by several peoples who had been long dominated by the declining Austro-Hungarian and Ottoman empires. As the Ottoman Empire disintegrated during the late nineteenth and early twentieth centuries, various Balkan peoples, such as the Romanians, Bulgarians, and Serbs, had established independent nations. Peoples still under Ottoman or Austro-Hungarian rule agitated for their own independence or sought support from their linguistic kin—especially the Serbs—in these new Balkan states. The Ottoman Turks had long struggled to maintain what power they still retained in the area. Their efforts to modernize economically, reform the government, and maintain unity in the face of demands for a constitution failed to reverse the empire's decline. In 1908, a coup overthrew the sultan and brought the nationalistic Young Turks to power, but their efforts to make Turkish the official language in Balkan areas and to increase Turkish control made the region more volatile. The Austro-Hungarians feared dismemberment of their multinational empire by these nationalistic sentiments. They hoped to expand into the Balkans and thereby weaken any movements for independence among their own ethnic minorities. These hopes brought Austria-Hungary into conflict with Russia, which had long hungered for influence and expansion in the Balkans and wanted to secure a port into the Mediterranean. Russia had fought two limited wars in pursuit of these aims during the second half of the nineteenth century. It also envisioned itself as the honorable, fraternal protector of Slavic peoples in the Balkans.

The first Balkan crisis erupted in 1908, when Austria-Hungary suddenly annexed two provinces, Bosnia and Herzegovina, which were home to Serbs, Croats, and others. Serbia had wanted to annex these territories, peopled by its own linguistic kin. Serbia appealed to Russia, and Russia threatened Austria-Hungary, whereupon Germany joined its ally and forced Russia to back down. The second Balkan crisis occurred in 1912–1913. The various Balkan states defeated Turkey in a war and then fought among themselves over the spoils. Victorious Serbia longed for more territory. Austria-Hungary thwarted the small country's expansion to the Adriatic Sea and threatened to annihilate Serbia. Again Serbia appealed to Russia, and again German pressure forced Russia to back down.

The assassination of Archduke Ferdinand on June 28, 1914, precipitated the third Balkan crisis. The government of Austria-Hungary, certain of Serbian involvement in the assassination, decided to crush Serbia and establish its own dominance in the Balkans once and for all. But this plan would require the backing of Germany, for Russia might come to the support of its Serbian allies and defend its own interests in the Balkans. At a fateful conference in Berlin eight days after the Sarajevo shooting, the German government encouraged Austria-Hungary's scheme with a "blank check" of full support. Emboldened by Germany's backing and advice to act quickly, Austria-Hungary presented Serbia with an ultimatum that Serbia could not hope to meet. The Austrians may not have wanted a Europe-wide war, but they felt they needed a war with Serbia. Upon hearing of Austria's demands on Serbia, Russia's foreign minister told Austria's ambassador, "You are setting fire to Europe." On July 28, even after Serbia had yielded on all but one of the ultimatum's terms (which would have allowed Austria to investigate Serbian involvement in the assassination plot), Austria-Hungary declared war.

To back Serbia against Austria-Hungary, Russia ordered its clumsy military establishment to mobilize. However, Russian military planning, which assumed a war against Mobilization both Austria and Germany, did not allow for only partial mobilization against Austria. Russia's order of full mobilization on July 29 was almost the same as a declaration of war—especially to German military leaders.

MAPS 22.1 AND 22.2

The Balkans, 1878 and 1914

Map 22.1 shows the Balkans in 1878 and highlights fighting and territorial changes to 1913. **Map 22.2** shows the same region in 1914, after new warfare had resulted in further territorial changes.

Explore the Maps

1. What specifically do the red arrows in the two maps indicate about shifting alliances and battlefronts?

2. Who gained the most and who lost the most? Explain.

3. Why might this region have been such a complex political and military cauldron?

Germany's main war plan assumed a two-front war against Russia and France, requiring the German army to knock France out of the fighting before Russia could bring the weight of its slow-moving forces against Germany. Therefore, Germany mobilized and sent ultimatums to Russia, demanding demobilization, and to France, requiring a declaration of neutrality. When Russia failed to reply and France gave an unsatisfactory response, Germany declared war on Russia on August 1 and on France two days later. On August 4, when German troops violated Belgian neutrality on their way to attack France, Great Britain declared war on Germany.

Thus the great powers of Europe were sucked into a general war they did not want by the very alliances they had formed to protect themselves and feared to violate. The growing tensions in European societies—violent domestic politics, strikes, threats from the political Left and Right, and themes of uncertainty and disintegration expressed in the arts—all worsened matters.

One of the most ominous expressions of the growing tensions in the air came from German expressionist Ludwig Meidner (1884–1966). In his 1913 canvas *Apocalyptic Landscape* (**Figure 22.1**), the sky seems to explode as if under bombardment. Below, buildings shatter as the land quakes. People run in all directions over streets that echo the violence above. In the artist's words, this painting shows "big city life" where "life is lived at fever pitch" and reflects a time when "the great world storm was already baring its teeth and casting its harsh shadow over the whimpering land which was carrying my brush." These tensions made many Europeans, including many intellectuals and well-known observers, welcome war as a quick, all-encompassing relief. Facing these perils and tensions, Europe's stunningly inept political and military leaders made decisions based more on blind optimism and fear of humiliation than on reason and concern for their nation's well-being. That "great world storm" described by Meidner soon arrived. At the time, few Europeans guessed how long the brutality would last.

THE FRONT LINES

Off to Battle

Almost everywhere in Europe, people greeted the declarations of war with outbursts of nationalistic joy. As the Austrian writer Stefan Zweig (1881–1942), a volunteer himself, recalled, "There were parades in the street, flags, ribbons, and music burst forth everywhere, young recruits were marching triumphantly, their faces lighting up at the cheering." Young men volunteered in droves, "honestly afraid that they might miss this most wonderful and exciting experience of their lives; that is why they hurried and thronged to the colors, and that is why they shouted and sang in the trains that carried them to the slaughter." **Figure 22.2,** a photograph of German volunteers marching down a Berlin street during the first weeks of the war, reveals the enthusiasm, optimism, and naïveté of the young men. Well dressed and raising their hats, they announce their bravery and celebrate their good fortune at being able to fight for their nation.

Here, suddenly, was a way to end domestic divisions and renew one's sense of purpose in the world. Political opponents set their differences aside and came together to support the war effort. As Document 22.1 reveals, even socialists, long opposed to war and nationalistic calls, joined in the effort to promote national defense. In Germany, the socialists voted for war credits and agreed to suspend strikes until the end of the war. In France, socialists joined their old opponents to support a government of national defense, called the Sacred Union. Russia's leading socialist party proclaimed, "Our first duty is to preserve our nation's unity and integrity, and to defend her position as a world power." Most feminists also suspended their political demands and offered ardent support for the military cause. The troops, people assumed, would surely be home by Christmas. Indeed,

Celebrating war

FIGURE 22.1 Ludwig Meidner, *Apocalyptic Landscape,* **1913**
Disturbing social tensions during the years preceding World War I are captured in many works of the period, including this dark, chaotic urban scene.

the British government promised that life would go on as usual with no shortages and no new regulations. Each combatant expected to win.

Nations initially on the sidelines soon enlisted with one side or the other (see **Map 22.3**). Hoping to gain territory in a victorious fight, Turkey and Bulgaria joined Germany and Austria-Hungary to become the **Central Powers.** Italy, long a member of the Triple Alliance with Germany and Austria-Hungary, had declared its neutrality at the beginning of the war, claiming that Austria had violated the alliance by launching a war of aggression on Serbia. Italy shifted

DEVELOPMENTS LEADING TO WORLD WAR I

1882	Triple Alliance
1894	Franco-Russian Alliance
1904	Entente Cordiale
1905	First Moroccan crisis
1908	Revolt in Ottoman Empire
	First Balkan crisis
1911	Second Moroccan crisis
1912	Second Balkan crisis
1914	Assassination of Archduke Ferdinand

thinking about
DOCUMENTS

A Russian Socialist Supports the War Effort

At the beginning of World War I, there was tremendous popular enthusiasm and unity behind governments for the war effort. Even socialist parties—which had long argued that they would not support a nationalistic war entered into by a government dominated by capitalists—joined the effort. The following letter from V. Bourtzeff, a Russian socialist, appeared in the London Times *about six weeks after the outbreak of the war in 1914.*

To the editor of "The Times":

Sir—May I be allowed to say a few words in connection with the excellent letter by my compatriot, Professor Vinogradov, which appeared in your paper today (September 14)? Professor Vinogradov is absolutely right when he says that not only is it desirable that complete unity of feeling should exist in Russian political circles, but that this unity is already an accomplished fact.

The representatives of all political parties and of all nationalities in Russia are now at one with the Government, and this war with Germany and Austria, both guided by the Kaiser, has already become a national war for Russia.

Even we, the adherents of the parties of the Extreme Left, and hitherto ardent anti-militarists and pacifists, even we believe in the necessity of *this* war. *This* war is a war to protect justice and civilization. It will, we hope, be a decisive factor in our united *war against war*, and we hope that after it, it will at last be possible to consider seriously the question of disarmament and universal peace. There can be no doubt that victory, and decisive victory at that (personally I await this in the immediate future), will be on the side of the Allied nations—England, France, Belgium, Serbia, and Russia.

The German peril, the curse which has hung over the whole world for so many decades, will be crushed, and crushed so that it will never again become a danger to the peace of the world. The peoples of the world desire peace.

To Russia this war will bring regeneration. . . .

All the parties without any exceptions have supported the Government without even waiting for it to make any definite announcement about these crying needs. This is the measure of the belief of the people in the inevitableness of liberal reforms. The Government unfortunately still seems irresolute, and has up till now only done the minimum to justify the popular belief in it, but we are convinced that circumstances will develop in such a way that the Government will not be able to delay for long that which has become for Russia a *historical necessity*. And the sooner this happens the better.

SOURCE: Frank A. Golder, *Documents of Russian History, 1914–1917,* trans. E. Aronsberg (Prentice-Hall, 1927), pp. 38–39.

Analyze the Document

1. Why does Bourtzeff support the war effort?

2. How does Bourtzeff justify his opposition to the government's policies and his support for the government in the war?

3. What might this document suggest about the political advantages of going to war?

---

its loyalty to France and Britain after receiving better promises of victory spoils. This side, eventually joined by many other nations from the Americas and the non-Western world, became known as the **Allies.** The Allies had the advantage of sheer numbers, but the Central Powers were led by Germany's better-equipped, well-trained army and could more easily move troops and coordinate military strategies.

> The Central Powers versus the Allies

The Schlieffen Plan

Anticipating a confrontation with both Russia and France, the German high command resorted to a military strategy known as the **Schlieffen Plan.** This plan called for a holding action against the slow-moving Russians while the main German forces thrust through neutral Belgium to knock out France. Then the Germans could concentrate on destroying Russia. Great Britain, her allies hobbled, would sue for peace, the Germans expected.

Day after day, the Schlieffen Plan worked. Four weeks after the outbreak of hostilities, German forces arrived just outside Paris ahead of schedule. Some

FIGURE 22.2 German Volunteers, 1914 This photograph shows German men optimistically celebrating as they march off to war.

MAP 22.3

World War I

This map shows the two alliances and the major fronts in World War I.

Explore the Map

1. What does this map reveal about the surrounded position of the Central Powers and the importance of Turkey during the war?

2. Locate the major areas of fighting on the western and eastern fronts. What do these reveal about the different natures of the wars on these two fronts?

3. Which areas in Europe were most directly affected by the fighting?

MAP 22.4

The Western Front

This map shows the western front at various stages of World War I.

Explore the Map

1. How far did the Germans penetrate in their 1914 offensive?

2. How close did the Germans come to capturing the French capital?

3. Describe the location of the western front at the beginning of 1915—that line would change little over the next three years.

4. What countries were most directly affected by the fighting on the western front?

their best troops under generals Hindenburg (1847–1934) and Ludendorff (1865–1937) and sent them east to fight the Russians, who had invaded Germany with unexpected speed. Nearing Paris, the German First Army detoured from its planned route in order to concentrate its force on the French capital. This move opened a gap in the Germans' eastern flank and exposed its western flank. At this juncture, the desperate French armies seized the opportunity and turned on the Germans. Parisian taxicabs rushed army reserves to the front in the effort to save Paris. Units of Britain's army arrived to enter the fray at a crucial moment. In the bloody seven-day Battle of the Marne, the Allies at last halted the Germans, drove them back several miles, and shattered German hopes that the Schlieffen Plan would succeed. As **Map 22.4** indicates, both sides extended their lines more than 400 miles from the Swiss border to the North Sea and dug in for the winter. Germany was now stuck with what it had tried so hard to avoid—a war on two fronts.

Slaughter and Stalemate on the Western Front

The defensive lines proved superior to offensive thrusts. To the surprise of almost everyone, the armies on the western front fought a war of attrition from their networks of trenches protected by barbed wire, | Trench warfare | mines, and machine guns. The trenches became filled with mud, rats, human bodies, lice, waste, poison gas, and the stench of death. But they also served as homes and protection for troops under fire, as shown in **Figure 22.3**. Along with their rifles and grenades, soldiers carried wire cutters and gas masks. Between the trenches, mortar and massive artillery bombardments created a barren, pockmarked landscape of mud and death that few soldiers could cross and still hope to live. The British introduced tanks in 1916 but did not manage to use them effectively to cross trenches until the last year of the war (see Thinking About Science & Technology).

Despite the defensive advantages of **trench warfare,** military commanders remained wedded to notions of an offensive breakthrough. Again and again, they sent troops scrambling out of their trenches, over the top and into no-man's-land, where enemy machine-gun fire mowed them down by the thousands. Fritze Franke, a German soldier, described his experience of trench warfare in a November 1914 letter: "Every foot of ground contested, every hundred yards another trench; and everywhere bodies—rows of them! All the trees shot to pieces; the whole ground churned up a yard deep by the heaviest shells; dead animals; houses and churches ... utterly destroyed.... And every troop that advances in support must pass through a

surprises, however, lay in store for them. Stubborn Belgian resistance had held up the Germans long enough for the French to redeploy their forces to the north and for the British to send their small army across the Channel. Germans suffered unanticipated casualties and transportation problems. At a critical moment, the German command detached 100,000 of each time the human costs were staggering. "We lie under the network of arching shells and live in a suspense of uncertainty," wrote German war veteran Erich Maria Remarque (1898–1970) in his novel *All Quiet on the Western Front.* "Over us Chance hovers." The wartime life expectancy of a frontline officer such as Wilfred Owen was only two months. After a year and a half of this mutual slaughter, nothing had changed.

In 1916, the Germans tried for a draining victory by attacking the French fortress at Verdun (see **Map 22.3**). Their plan was, in the words of the German commander, to "bleed to death" the French by forcing them to sustain massive casualties defending this historic strongpoint. During the ensuing nine-month battle, the Germans sometimes fired as many as a million shells in one day. The French managed to hold off the Germans, but 700,000 men on both sides lost their lives in the effort. "You found the dead embedded in the walls of the trenches, heads, legs, and half-bodies, just as they had been shovelled out of the way by the picks and shovels of the working party," recalled one French soldier.

That same year the British attempted a breakthrough in the Battle of the Somme in northeastern France (see **Map 22.3**). They suffered 60,000 casualties, with more than 20,000 killed in just the first day. "As far as you could see there were all these bodies lying there—literally thousands of them. . . . It didn't seem possible," wrote a British soldier. By fall, Britain had endured 400,000 casualties; France, 200,000; and Germany, 500,000, in this one battle. It ended in a stalemate. "Here chivalry disappeared for always," wrote the German Ernst Jünger. In the Passchendaele offensive (see **Map 22.3**), the British again tried to break through the German "crust," losing some 400,000 soldiers in the effort. Like other great battles in the west, Passchendaele scarcely moved the front lines at all.

Neither the politicians nor the generals found the will to call a halt to the slaughter. Anything short of complete victory, they feared, would mean that all the deaths and casualties were in vain. The troops were not so stubborn. Sometimes they agreed to avoid battles. They even occasionally fraternized across the trenches, sang together, and allowed each other to eat meals in peace or collect the bodies of fellow soldiers in no-man's-land. They also were capable of making their outrage known to their superiors. After a new, disastrous offensive ordered by France's commander General Nivelle in April 1917, mutinies broke out in almost half the French divisions on the front. Thousands of soldiers were court-martialed and more than 500 sentenced to death, although most executions were never carried out. New commanders and troops tacitly agreed to stop these hopeless offensive onslaughts.

> Great battles of 1916

FIGURE 22.3 Trench Warfare   Rows of men in gas masks wait in trenches protected by barbed wire in this war of attrition on the western front.

mile of this chaos, through this gigantic burial ground and the reek of corpses." Fololiyani Longwe, an African serving in the British army on the western front, described how soldiers stood "buried in a hole with only your head and hands outside, holding a gun" for days with "no food, no water," and "only death smelling all over the place." Wilfred Owen, the British poet whom we met at the beginning of the chapter, related how the brutal reality of the war wiped out old images of its glory. Owen warned that anyone who saw the suffering

> . . . would not tell with such high zest
> To children ardent for some desperate glory,
> The old Lie: Dulce et decorum est
> Pro patria mori. ("It is sweet and proper
> to die for one's country.")

Military leaders failed to realize that machine guns, modern artillery, mass mobilization, and trenches had utterly changed the nature of warfare. Acting on old assumptions and oblivious to these new military realities, generals ordered offensives again and again. Each time the charges moved lines only yards, if at all, and

thinking about
SCIENCE & TECHNOLOGY

FIGURE 22.4 British Mark 1 Tank, 1916

The Invention of the Tank

Efforts to build movable protective devices for use as offensive weapons in warfare go back thousands of years. A modern form of these devices is the tank, a vehicle first developed during World War I. Trench warfare created a demand for an armored, self-propelled weapon that could bridge trenches, maneuver across the cratered battlefields of the western front, and enable the infantry to break through enemy lines to victory.

The British and French led efforts to develop this weapon. Manufacturers' early models were unreliable, and the tank's use on the battlefield was questionable—and sometimes led to outright failure. Too easily, the vehicles became mired and exposed in difficult terrain. Moreover, the heat and fumes that built up inside often made crews sick—and even lose consciousness. But the British and French inventors persisted, modifying the vehicle's design and tactical features. They eventually came up with a practical tank that used iron armor for defense, an internal combustion engine for power, caterpillar tracks for mobility, and cannons and machine guns for weapons.

The British first employed these practical tanks at the Battle of the Somme in 1916 but with only limited success. The photo in **Figure 22.4** shows the British Mark 1 tank spanning a trench at that battle. The tanks proved to be of greater effect during the last year of the war. However, because the slow-moving vehicles were vulnerable to artillery and antitank weapons, they required support from accompanying infantry and ground-attack aircraft.

As we will see in Chapter 24, the tank would become a much more potent and decisive weapon in World War II.

Connecting Science & Society

1. In what ways is the invention of a practical tank an example of the industrialization of warfare?

2. What role did inventors, producers, and the government, working together, play in the development of the tank?

3. How might an earlier development of a practical tank have altered the nature and course of World War I?

Figure 22.5 illustrates how all means, old and new, were used to fight this war. Here soldiers with plumed helmets sit astride horses while an airplane, used for bombing and intelligence, flies overhead. Armies would use poison gas, flamethrowers, and tanks for the first time. Even dogs—75,000 of them—were employed to search for wounded men on the battlefronts.

On the seas, both sides in the war hoped for decisive victories. The British navy set up a blockade of Germany, and the Germans responded with the submarine. Germany and Britain never met in a conclusive naval showdown, however. In the Battle of Jutland, the only major naval battle of the war, the British fleet prevented the German fleet from breaking the blockade—but suffered serious losses as a result. Most of the massive struggle took place on the ground. After three years of fighting, neither side could break through on the western front. By then, the French alone had sustained more than 3.5 million casualties. Yet the war dragged on.

Victory and Defeat on the Eastern and Southern Fronts

As **Map 22.3** indicates, the war proved far more mobile and offensive on the eastern front than in the west. In eastern Europe, the terrain did not favor trench warfare, and in any case the Russians lacked the resources to sustain such a defensive effort. Initially, Russia, with its huge but inadequately supplied army, pushed into German and Austro-Hungarian lands. At the end of August 1914, however, the reinforced German armies, bolstered by their superior technology and leadership, trapped the Russians at Tannenberg and administered a crushing defeat. The Russian commander, General Samsonov, committed suicide on the spot. Farther south, the Russians defeated an Austro-Hungarian army at Lemberg only to bring in a German army that delivered a series of hammer blows to the Russians. The Germans drove deep into Russia and inflicted immense casualties, making Generals Hindenburg and Ludendorff heroes. In the Balkans, German, Austrian, and Bulgarian forces had eliminated Serbia from the war by the end of 1915. That same year, a disastrous Anglo-French effort to help the hard-pressed Russians by landing at Gallipoli and breaking through Turkish defenses at the nearby Dardanelles was beaten back by the Turks with heavy losses to the Allies (see **Map 22.3**).

In 1916, Russia made one more great effort against the Austro-Hungarian forces in the south. Under General Aleksei Brusilov, Russian armies almost forced the Austro-Hungarians to withdraw from the war. The Austro-Hungarians resorted to recruiting men over the age of 50 into the army and, in the end, kept going only with German support. But the Russians could not sustain the effort. Lack of effective leadership, insufficient supplies, and desertions plagued Russia's armies. "Half of them have no rifles," Tsar Nicholas admitted, "the troops are losing masses and there is nobody to collect them on the battlefields." Germany's renewed push in 1917 resulted in massive Russian losses. These losses, along with internal strife that toppled the tsar, his government, and the succeeding provisional government (see pages 710–715), knocked Russia out of the war in December 1917. Nevertheless, for more than two years, the Russian effort had drawn German troops east, weakening the German forces in the west.

Russia's military collapse

Meanwhile, in northeastern Italy, Austrian and German troops won some costly battles, but the Italian forces limited the Central Powers' advances (see **Map 22.3**). Farther south and east, Allied forces attacked the Ottoman Empire. In 1915, after an Anglo-French fleet failed to open the Dardanelles strait so that Russia could receive supplies in her Black Sea ports, a 400,000-man force of British, French, Australian, New Zealand, and other troops

Southern fronts

FIGURE 22.5 Old and New Means of Warfare In World War I, all means, from the traditional cavalry horses to the new airplanes, were used on the battlefront, as this period photograph documents.

landed at Gallipoli. The invaders suffered terrible defeats at the hands of the Turkish defenders and were forced to evacuate. Even more crippling, malaria, cholera, dysentery, and other diseases spread among the troops fighting in the Middle East. Eventually, the British, most notably the charismatic officer and writer T. E. Lawrence (1888–1935), stirred up Arab resentment into a desert revolt against the Ottoman Turks in Palestine and Mesopotamia. Together, British and Arab forces gradually gained the upper hand against the Ottoman Turks.

The War Spreads Across the Globe

The war itself soon spread outside of Europe and the Mediterranean basin, in great part thanks to the West's colonies and imperial interests throughout the world. In the South Atlantic, British and German naval forces clashed off the Falkland Islands. In Africa, minor battles erupted around Germany's colonies. In East Asia, Japan joined the war on the Allied side and promptly seized German holdings in the Pacific and China. When Russia seemed on the verge of falling apart, Japan also sent soldiers into the tsar's far eastern provinces. Britain and France drew troops from Canada, Africa, Asia, and Australia to fight on several fronts. More than 1 million Indian soldiers served under the British, particularly in the Middle East campaigns, and hundreds of thousands of African soldiers from French colonies served in Europe. The Western nations also called on workers from these lands, including a 200,000-man labor battalion from China, to work in France and elsewhere in the war effort.

However, non-Western peoples often resisted the European powers' efforts to gain their support. Nomadic tribes fled Russia's central Asian provinces rather than serve in the tsar's army. In French West Africa, local tribes revolted when the French tried to mobilize labor brigades. Moreover, non-Westerners did not automatically favor the Allied cause. Most of those who followed the conflict in Asia viewed World War I as a European civil war. In addition, they were likely to favor Germany over France and Britain, two nations that had a tradition of Asian conquest. Indeed, for the most part, the first world war remained a European affair. Raging on year after year, the conflict shattered the lives of soldiers and civilians alike.

WAR ON THE HOME FRONT

No Western society could come through such a protracted war unscathed. As the toll on lives and supplies climbed, whole societies had **Total war** to mobilize to support the military effort. In this sense, World War I became the first **total war,** blurring the traditional distinctions between combatants and civilians and between battle lines and the home front. The first world war transformed whole economies, societies, and governments, as well as the lives of soldiers.

Mobilizing Resources

After the first few months of hostilities, armies began to run out of ammunition, supplies, and troops. The French alone were firing more than 100,000 artillery shells a day—far more than their armaments factories could supply. Entire economies were reorganized to churn out huge quantities of bullets, guns, and machines in just days and weeks rather than the usual months and years. The war effort required untold quantities of other materials as well—everything from food and uniforms to trucks and coffins. Overall, the war demanded unprecedented industrial capability and organizational agility to produce and move supplies for the armed forces.

To varying degrees, the governments of the major powers took control of their economies. Government agencies, rather than the free marketplace, determined production, consumption, wages, and prices. In Germany, the War Raw Materials Board located, rationed, and distributed raw materials. To meet the need for products that Germany

Governments take control

could no longer import, such as rubber, the board helped develop synthetic substitutes. In Britain, the Ministry of Munitions, led by David Lloyd George, supervised the armaments industry. The ministry's bureaucracy of 65,000 clerks controlled prices, supplies, and production of war materials.

This tightly controlled mobilization of resources also included people. Not only were men drafted into the armed services, but women and men on the home fronts were often required to work in accord with priorities determined by the government. Labor unions were brought into partnership with business and government. In addition, governments suspended laws limiting the length of the workday and controlling workplace conditions. People were thus forced to work longer hours under dangerous circumstances.

Demand for troops on the front lines and labor on the home front altered traditional social and national boundaries. Although the war did not eliminate class conflict, social distinctions blurred as people from all walks of society joined the war effort and worked or fought side by side. Conventional national distinctions were sometimes violated: For a while, the hard-pressed Germans forced thousands of Belgians to move and work in German factories. The war effort could even include children: Some German teachers organized their students to go through garbage and collect anything that might be useful. Perhaps most striking, officials challenged traditional gender roles by calling women into the labor force.

New Gender Roles

Gender roles changed radically under the pressures of all-out war. At first, many women were left on their own financially as their husbands marched off to battle. Later, when economies began straining with the war effort, women got new jobs previously reserved for men. **Figure 22.6** shows women working in a large British armaments plant, producing the huge quantity of shells needed on the battle lines. Such women participated in all aspects of the munitions industries. They became army clerks and streetcar conductors and drove taxis and ran farms. Some served as firefighters at home and as nurses at the front. Others gained entry into white-collar jobs in banks, commercial businesses, and urban offices. In Great Britain, the number of women working outside the home had increased twentyfold to some five million by 1918. In Russia, women made up over 40 percent of the labor force. Similar patterns held in other European countries.

These shifting labor patterns created new tensions over women's roles as men began fearing they would lose their jobs to women permanently. "Workmen have to be handled with the utmost tenderness and caution lest they should actually imagine . . . that women could do their work equally well," wrote a female British munitions factory worker in 1916. Women themselves often had conflicted feelings about their new role. Many gained a new sense of independence from earning a paycheck. Some displayed their newfound freedom by living alone, going out socially on their own, wearing shorter dresses, cutting (bobbing) their hair, and smoking cigarettes. Others felt torn by the dual demands of service and family. "What exhausts women in wartime is not the strenuous and unfamiliar tasks that fall upon them, nor even the hourly dread of death for husbands or lovers or brothers or sons," recalled British writer Vera Brittain (1896–1970), who served as a nurse in France. "It is the incessant conflict between personal and national claims which wears out their energy and breaks their spirit." By no coincidence, several nations would grant women the right to vote at the war's end.

Maintaining the Effort

As the war persisted, governments became more involved in manufacturing consent and less tolerant of dissent. Propaganda specialists tried to inspire support for the war and hatred for the enemy. The more the propaganda succeeded in its aims, the harder it became for governments to compromise or withdraw from the conflict. Officials deliberately manipulated information and censored private letters to shape public opinion about the war. In particular, they tried to create the impression that their own country was completely virtuous and that it was the other nations that were committing crimes against humanity. To combat war weariness, governments painted the enemy as evil incarnate and whipped up people's sense of outrage. There was no way, political leaders declared, that "good" people could ever make peace with such diabolical opponents.

Figure 22.7, a cover from a French magazine, is an example of such propaganda. The image depicts Germans as having committed atrocities during their march through Belgium and northern France. Here an innocent, horror-stricken, assaulted woman kneels on a blood-soaked crib and cradles the body of her

FIGURE 22.6 Women War Workers This interior view of a British armaments plant reveals how mass production, supported by women workers, created the huge quantity of materials needed for the war effort.

murdered child. The empty wine bottles and helmet scattered on the ground around her leave no doubt that immoral German soldiers have committed these acts. The illustrator also blames the Germans for setting the homes and church of this village on fire while passing through. The glaring headline exhorts people to "Let Us Never Forget."

Governments also tried to promote dissent among their opponents and turn neutral countries into allies. Germany supported the Irish in their 1916 Easter Rebellion in Dublin for Irish independence, which British forces brutally crushed. Germany also aided the Bolsheviks against Russia's government. The British promoted rebellion among the Arabs against the Turks and used propaganda to help bring the Americans in on their side.

Victories or defeats on the front lines reflected the abilities of civilian societies to mobilize effectively for the war effort—materially, politically, and psychologically. Those nations less able to develop and sustain this vast home-front effort—such as the Austro-Hungarian and Russian empires—faltered first. They lacked the solid industrial base and organizational strength of Germany, France, and Great Britain. Over time, however, even the strongest nations weakened under the strains of total war. Food shortages spawned malnutrition, disease, and high infant mortality, especially in Germany, which acutely felt the impact of Britain's naval blockade. Governments tried to pay for the war by printing more money, thereby creating an inflation of prices.

By 1917, hunger and war weariness were igniting strikes and domestic disorders throughout Europe. Beleaguered governments suspended civil liberties,

thinking about
ART

FIGURE 22.7

Let Us Never Forget

Numerous propaganda posters were produced on all sides of the war. This French poster depicts the fate of the Belgians when the Germans conquered the nation on the way to their main western adversary, France.

Connecting Art & Society

1. What kind of response do you think this scene was intended to stir in the viewer?

2. Why does the scene focus on a woman and her child rather than, for example, a battle scene?

3. In what ways has the artist used visual clues to prompt the viewer to read this picture as a dramatic series of events that have just occurred?

4. Why might propaganda posters such as this example be effective in influencing public sentiment?

ignored democratic procedures, and ruled by emergency police powers. In France, Georges Clemenceau (1841–1929) became a virtual dictator after November 1917. He sent troops against strikers and arrested those agitating for peace. "I wage war," he declared. | Rising dissent |
"I wage nothing but war!" In Austria, political unity unraveled as different nationalities clamored for independence. In Germany, some socialist and Catholic legislators came out for peace, and Generals Hindenburg and Ludendorff assumed control over the German war effort. By the end of 1917, Russia's whole war effort had collapsed. Clearly, World War I would be won or lost on the home front as well as on the battle lines.

TO THE BITTER END

Early in 1917, the German high command grew desperate to bring the draining war to a victorious conclusion. The generals decided to launch an unrestricted submarine campaign against enemy and neutral shipping alike. Germany's leaders knew this policy could bring the United States into the war. Up to that point, the United States had remained neutral but had become increasingly invested in the Allied cause through trade and loans. The sense that Germany and its partners were the aggressors, along with the 1915 sinking of the passenger liner *Lusitania* during a German submarine blockade of Britain, had also nudged American public opinion toward support of the Allies. Now Germany's high command gambled that they could defeat Britain and France before the Americans could send enough supplies and troops to Europe to make a difference. Indeed, Ludendorff and Hindenburg promised victory within only six months.

At about the same time, British intelligence turned over to the United States an alarming note that it claimed to have intercepted. In that document, called the Zimmermann note, Germany offered to grant U.S. | The U.S. enters the war |
territory to Mexico—the very territory lost by Mexico in the 1848 Mexican-American War—if Mexico agreed to attack the United States. When German submarines began sinking American cargo ships, U.S. entry into the conflict was ensured. On April 6, 1917, the United States declared war on Germany. President Woodrow Wilson promised to "make the world safe for democracy."

The Germans had good reason to think that they might prevail. At the beginning of 1918, the United States' contribution to the war was still relatively small. In addition, the Italians had suffered a disastrous blow at the Battle of Caporetto, almost putting them out of the war. Romania had been defeated, and Russia had withdrawn from the war. Now Germany could at last focus its efforts on a one-front war. In the

Atlantic, its U-boats (submarines) were sinking one-fourth of all ships taking supplies to Britain—350 ships went down in one month alone.

On the other hand, Germany's allies—the Austro-Hungarian and Ottoman empires—were teetering, and Germany was suffering from lack of materials and food, thanks to Britain's naval blockade. The British had also discovered a way to foil the U-boats by using heavily escorted convoys armed with depth charges. Now the race was between Germany and the United States. Germany transferred troops from the Russian front in an effort to overwhelm Great Britain and France before waves of American troops could arrive, while the United States struggled to raise, train, and transport sufficient forces to France to stem the German tide.

In March 1918, Field Marshall Ludendorff launched, on the western front, the first of a series of massive German blows designed to end the

| Final battles | war. The British and French were

driven back with heavy losses. Desperate, they finally agreed to a unified command under France's General Ferdinand Foch (1851–1929). By mid-June, after the fourth of the great drives, the Allied lines were so badly battered that when the climactic fifth drive began along the Marne River in mid-July, Ludendorff wired the kaiser: "If the attack succeeds, the war will be over and we will have won it." When Foch heard the opening German barrage, he wired his government: "If the present German attack succeeds, the war is over and we have lost it." The Allies stopped the Germans by a narrow margin. Foch, now receiving a swelling stream of fresh American soldiers—more than 250,000 soldiers a month—immediately ordered a counterattack. British tanks helped break through German lines. The balance shifted. Suddenly, the Germans were in retreat. German strength and morale waned rapidly. That spring and summer, Germans suffered more than 2 million casualties.

At the end of October, Germany's Bulgarian and Turkish allies surrendered. On November 3, Austria-Hungary, its ethnic minorities in revolt, also surrendered; a week later, the last Austro-Hungarian emperor abdicated. The next day, mutiny broke out in the German navy and spread to workers in German cities. Popular uprisings brought down the kaiser's government, and on November 9 he fled the country. On November 11, the new German Republic government accepted an armistice.

For many, however, even the last days of the war were too long. In Britain, Wilfred Owen's mother, like so many others, received news of her son's death (he was machine-gunned in a final attack) just as church bells began ringing for victory. Those last days would also leave a haunting legacy in Germany. German commanders manipulated reports from the front so

that most of Germany's population remained unaware of the extent of their country's military collapse. The new civilian government of republicans and socialists in Germany would later be blamed by many Germans for the surrender. This development would in turn set the stage for future charges that Germany had not really lost the war but had been stabbed in the back by the very political forces that would rule Germany during the 1920s.

ASSESSING THE LOSSES

The war had shattered much of Europe. Some 10 million soldiers and perhaps another 7–10 million civilians had perished from the war and its hardships. Russia lost almost 2 million soldiers, as did Germany. Serbia lost some 15–20 percent of its population. All across northern France and Belgium, war cemeteries spread, many with unmarked graves, others with elaborate monuments to the fallen such as those in **Figure 22.8**. Europe lost the cream of a generation of its future leaders. Colonial troops from Asia and Africa also suffered. **Figure 22.9,** showing a Senegalese soldier learning to use artificial limbs with the help of a Red Cross nurse, indicates the price many such veterans paid for their service.

For those left behind, the hardships persisted. Many survivors would have to spend the rest of their lives in veterans' hospitals. In many places, mutilated people, widows, and spinsters seemed the rule rather than the exception. Many survivors would remain obsessed with the experience of this war, like the British poet Siegfried Sassoon, who wrote, "The rank stench of those bodies haunts me still, And I remember things I'd best forget" (see Document 22.2). In addition to all the death and misery, the fighting brought incalculable financial and material losses. The war laid to waste a tenth of the richest region of France and devastated the most developed part of Russia. It also saddled European nations with heavy debts, especially to a new international creditor—the United States. Finally, it was difficult not to merge the losses from the war with the tens of millions of deaths caused by the 1918 flu pandemic. That flu, which spread rapidly around the globe, was not *caused* by World War I, but the close quarters of troops and the mass movements of people spurred by the war probably added to the suffering and the staggering death toll.

THE PEACE SETTLEMENT

No peace settlement could make up for the losses of World War I. Nevertheless, delegates who gathered at Versailles near Paris in January 1919 and the people they represented expected a resolution that could somehow justify those losses. Other burdens

BIOGRAPHY

Käthe Kollwitz
(1867–1945)

Artist and Witness to War

By the eve of World War I, Käthe Kollwitz's prints, drawings, and posters had made her one of Germany's leading artists. "[M]y art has purpose," she said. "I want to be effective in this time when people are so helpless and in need of aid."

Käthe Schmidt was born in East Prussia in 1867. As a child, she often suffered from periods of depression, and these episodes continued well into her adulthood. Early on she learned to express her feelings in art. In 1891, Käthe married Dr. Karl Kollwitz, whom she would praise years later as her "life's comrade." Karl shared Käthe's socialist sympathies. That year, the couple moved to Berlin, where Karl took a job as a physician for a workers' health insurance fund and where Käthe gave birth to Hans in 1892 and Peter in 1896. Reflecting on the role of love in her life, she would later describe silently falling in love with women as well as men and the influence of bisexuality on the themes in her art.

Käthe earned her first public success as an artist between 1895 and 1898 with the publication of a series of prints, *The Weavers*. These images recorded a doomed revolt of handloom weavers in the 1840s. Indeed, most of her works explored the plight of victims of social injustice, the cause of peace, and the sufferings of war and death. Not surprisingly, her art often offended the authorities, including the kaiser.

In early August 1914, just after World War I broke out, the Kollwitz family heard German soldiers singing as they marched in the streets (see pages 695–696). Käthe wept in horror. During those same days, her youngest son, Peter, only 18 years old, volunteered for the army. On August 27, 1914, she wrote, "Where do all the women who have watched so carefully over the lives of their beloved ones get the heroism to send them to face the cannon? I am afraid that this soaring of the spirit will be followed by the blackest despair and dejection." A month later, she wrote, "It seems so stupid that the boys must go to war . . . how can they possibly take part in such madness?" Three weeks later, on October 22, 1914, Peter was killed in the war.

This loss of her son haunted Käthe for the rest of her life. In letters and diaries, she expressed endless grief for her fallen boy. She expanded her sorrow to embrace grieving mothers in all countries. Reflecting on the causes of the war, she described how Peter and others she knew had "subordinated their lives to the idea of patriotism. The English, Russian and French young men have done the same. The consequence has been this terrible killing and the impoverishment of Europe."

After her son's death, Käthe began a long struggle to create monumental sculptures in memory of Peter and other sons killed in the war. It would take her ten years to start work on the final forms for these sculptures and another eight years before the figures were completed in stone. **Figure 22.8** is a photograph of the two sculptures. At the opening ceremony, held in the Belgian cemetery where Peter was buried, Käthe stood before her stone figure of the mother: "I looked at her, my own face, and wept and stroked her cheeks."

When the war ended, she worried that "the peace will probably be very bad." For her the war, fought by Europe's youth, had destroyed "all that is most beautiful in Europe." In 1919, she became the first woman elected to the Prussian Academy of Arts. In 1928, she was further honored by being

---

weighed on the delegates as well. The end of fighting did not stop wartime hatred and suffering. Starvation threatened central and eastern Europe. In addition, a growing fear of revolutionary communism haunted the delegates, who primarily represented the forces of order and wealth in their nations. Already in power in Russia, communists had a real chance of triumphing in Germany and in the newly independent states of eastern Europe.

Gathering at Versailles

Although all thirty-two of the victorious Allies participated in the peace conference, the leaders of France, Great Britain, the United States, and Italy made the major decisions. Representatives of colonized peoples, ethnic and religious groups, women's organizations, and various national groups went to Versailles hoping for a hearing but received none. The vanquished Germany and Austria-Hungary were excluded from the talks, as was Russia, which had dropped out of the war a year earlier.

Premier Georges Clemenceau, the aged Tiger of France, headed the French delegation. As host of the conference and leader of the nation that had done the most to defeat Germany, Clemenceau expected to dominate the decision making. The eloquent and fiery Prime Minister David Lloyd George led the British delegation. He also intended to dominate the conference. Premier Vittorio Orlando (1860–1952), head of the Italian delegation, wanted all the territory that the Allies had promised in the first place

FIGURE 22.8 Käthe Kollwitz, *The Mourning Father and Mother*

appointed head of a master class for graphic arts. In 1930, as the Nazis rose in strength, she wrote that "evil reaction is creeping into all areas." Käthe was forced to resign her prestigious position when Hitler came to power in 1933, and the Führer banned her work. In 1940 her grandson, Peter, the namesake of her son Peter killed in World War I, joined Germany's army as World War II erupted. He was killed on the Russian front in 1942. She continued her work almost until her death on April 22, 1945.

Like so many other people, Käthe Kollwitz had witnessed the great enthusiasm as soldiers first marched off to the Great War in August 1914. Also like countless millions of people, she had lost a loved one in that conflict. She, too, would live long enough to witness a terrible renewal of war. In her last letter, she wrote, "the war accompanies me to the end." She, along with far too many in the West, would never fully recover from the scars of World War I.

Connecting People & Society

1. How does Kollwitz's life reflect the impact of World War I on European society?

2. How does Kollwitz explain the causes and enthusiasm for the war?

3. What are your reactions to Kollwitz's sculptures?

---

to draw Italy into the war. The idealistic President Woodrow Wilson (1856–1924), expecting approval of his Fourteen Points as the basis for peace, led the American delegation. The United States had attained much prestige during the war and was the first non-European country in centuries to influence the fate of European nations.

A Victors' Peace

A fundamental and bitter clash immediately developed between Clemenceau, who wanted a "hard" peace that would render Germany harmless, and Wilson, who wanted a "just" peace free of vindictiveness. Wilson and his advisors feared that a harsh settlement would leave Germany resentful, eager for revenge, or ripe for takeover by extreme political forces. He also believed that secret diplomacy and the alliance system had caused the war in the first place, and urged "open covenants of peace, openly arrived at." In his Fourteen Points, Wilson also called for the self-determination of peoples, armaments reduction, and a "general association of nations" to guarantee the safety of "great and small states alike." Lloyd George often sided with Wilson but, like Clemenceau, wanted a victory worthy of the sacrifices made during the war.

It took six months of hard work and wrangling to draw up the peace terms. Although the Treaty of Versailles reflected many of Wilson's ideals, it was more of a victors' peace reflecting France's desire

| Wilson's Fourteen Points |

FIGURE 22.9 Casualty from the Colonies A nurse helps one of the many soldiers from Europe's colonies who became casualties of the war.

for security and an eagerness to punish Germany. In what came to be known as the **war guilt clause,** the agreement forced Germany and its allies to accept full responsibility for the war. Germany lost all its overseas colonies and concessions; several victorious nations gained control over these territories in Africa and the Pacific. France regained Alsace and Lorraine, lost in the Franco-Prussian War of 1870. In addition, the victors would occupy German territory on the west bank of the Rhine for the next fifteen years. The Polish-speaking areas of eastern Germany were ceded to the resurrected Polish state, and a "Polish corridor" was cut through German territory to give Poland an outlet at Danzig to the Baltic Sea. Germany's armed forces were limited to 100,000 soldiers and saddled with severe armament limitations. Finally, Germany was held liable for reparations that in 1921 were set at $33 billion.

Redrawing the Map of Europe

As **Map 22.5** reveals, the treaties dealt the harshest blow to Germany's allies because the territorial rearrangements were usually based on the principle of unifying national language groups. Austria-Hungary was cut down from a polyglot empire of 50 million—second in area only to Russia among the nations of Europe—to an Austria of 6.5 million German-speaking Austrians and a Hungary of 8 million Magyars. Many in Austria wanted their new country to merge with Germany, but the settlement specifically forbad this arrangement. The Czechs and Slovaks

were joined into the new state of Czechoslovakia, which included sizable German and other minorities. Serbs, Croats, Slovenes, Bosnians, and others populated the new state of Yugoslavia. The Ottoman Empire was dismembered, and parts of its Anatolian homeland were occupied by British, French, Italian, and Greek forces. Perhaps unavoidably, all these new national boundaries created many internal ethnic divisions and pockets of discontent that would breed future conflicts.

Woodrow Wilson had placed his chief hopes for peace in an association of countries—the **League of Nations**—that he expected would guarantee borders and peaceably settle the tensions and conflicts that were certain to arise in the future. The League was incorporated into the treaty with Germany but had no military forces at its command. Its only weapons were economic sanctions and moral condemnations. Though perhaps well intentioned, the League was doomed almost from the beginning. The exclusion of Germany and the Soviet Union from the association weakened its potential effectiveness. In addition, the self-righteous President Wilson—reluctant to compromise with political opponents back in the United States and physically weakening—failed to persuade the isolationist American Senate to ratify the peace accords and join the League. What little faith Great Britain and France had in Wilson's ideas quickly disappeared.

The League of Nations

Legacy of the Peace Treaty

The peace settlement negotiated in Paris satisfied no one and left a legacy of deep resentments. France's Clemenceau considered the terms too lenient. Moreover, both Great Britain and the United States refused French pleas to join France in a defensive alliance. Not surprisingly, the French felt betrayed and abandoned. The Germans, for their part, considered the terms outrageous. Many Germans refused to believe that their armies had lost the war. The Germans also resented not being allowed to participate in the talks. Their representatives were presented with a humiliating settlement that they signed only after the Allies threatened to invade. Italy's leader, Orlando, walked out of the conference to protest broken Allied promises of more territorial gains.

Nationalists in Turkey, led by their wartime hero of Gallipoli, Mustafa Kemal (1881–1938), refused to accept the Treaty of Sèvres, which had been negotiated by the Allies and the sultan's tottering regime in 1920. That treaty allowed foreign powers to occupy eastern and southern Anatolia.

DOCUMENT 22.2

In the Trenches and Beyond

Some of the most poignant accounts of experiences on the front lines come from poets who have served in the military. Unlike many poets, such as Rupert Brooke and Wilfred Owen, Siegfried Sassoon (1886–1967) survived World War I. But the experience would haunt him for the rest of his life. The following are excerpts from "The rank stench of those bodies haunts me still" and "Does it Matter?"

The rank stench of those bodies haunts me still

The rank stench of those bodies
    haunts me still,
And I remember things I'd best forget.
For now we've marched to a green,
    trenchless land
Twelve miles from battering guns:
    along the grass
Brown lines of tents are hives for
    snoring men;

Wide, radiant water sways the
    floating sky
Below dark, shivering trees. And
    living-clean

Comes back with thoughts of home
    and hours of sleep.

To-night I smell the battle; miles away
Gun-thunder leaps and thuds along
    the ridge;
The spouting shells dig pits in fields
    of death,
And wounded men, are moaning in
    the woods.
If any friend be there whom I have
    loved, speed
God (send) him safe to England with
    a gash.

               ***

Does it Matter?

Does it matter?—losing your
    legs? . . .
For people will always be kind,
And you need not show that you
    mind
When the others come in after
    hunting
To gobble their muffins and eggs.

Does it matter?—losing your
    sight? . . .
There's such splendid work for the
    blind;

And people will always be kind,
As you sit on the terrace
    remembering
And turning your face to the light.

Do they matter?—those dreams
    from the pit? . . .
You can drink and forget and be
    glad,
And people won't say that you're
    mad;
For they'll know you've fought for
    your country
And no one will worry a bit.

SOURCE: Siegfried Sassoon, "The rank stench of those bodies haunts me still" and "Does it Matter?" in *The Penguin Book of First World War Poetry*, 2nd ed., ed. Jon Silkin (London: Penguin Books, 1979), pp. 124–125, 131–132.

Analyze the Document

1. Which images most vividly convey the war experience?

2. How does Sassoon describe the lives of maimed soldiers who return to society?

3. What do you think Sassoon means by "Does it Matter?"

Mustafa Kemal's national army drove out the occupying troops, toppled the sultan's regime, and established the Republic of Turkey—an act affirmed by the Allies in the Treaty of Lausanne (1923).

In areas of North Africa and the Middle East, Arabs were outraged by decisions of the Allied powers. Arab nationalists had been promised independence by the British and French during the war. Now mandates from the League of Nations authorized the French to exercise administrative control over Lebanon and Syria, and the British over Mesopotamia and Palestine (see **Map 22.6**). According to the League of Nations, these peoples were "not yet able to stand by themselves" and their "tutelage . . . should be entrusted to the advanced nations." Making matters worse, Britain had promised Jewish nationalists a homeland in Palestine.

China refused to sign because the Treaty of Versailles gave the Japanese rights in the Chinese mainland, and Japan left offended because the conference refused to declare formally the equality of all races.

Russia, which had suffered huge losses, had not even been invited to the conference, and the U.S. government failed to ratify the treaty.

John Maynard Keynes (1883–1946), an influential British economist who attended the talks, perhaps best summed up the flaws in the Paris agreement in his book *The Economic Consequences of the Peace* (1919) (see Document 22.3). "[T]he treaty," Keynes warned, "includes no provisions for the economic rehabilitation of Europe—nothing to make the defeated Central Empires into good neighbors, nothing to stabilize the new States of Europe, nothing to reclaim Russia. . . ."

World War I had unleashed passions and destruction of such magnitudes that possibly no settlement could have sufficed. Nowhere in the West did those passions rage stronger than in Russia, defeated by Germany in 1917 and still reeling from internal upheavals. There, revolution and civil war were forging a new union that would alter world affairs for the rest of the twentieth century.

MAP 22.5

Europe, 1923

This map shows Europe after the settlement that ended World War I.

Explore the Map

1. Notice the territorial losses suffered by the German, Russian, Ottoman, and Austro-Hungarian empires. Do these losses support the argument that the Versailles settlement was a harsh one?

2. What areas might suffer from instability stemming from these new territorial arrangements?

3. What strategic problems faced the new eastern European states that hoped for support from France and Great Britain?

REVOLUTIONS IN RUSSIA

In 1914, the Russian tsar Nicholas II and his advisors hoped that a short, painless war in the Balkans would overcome domestic divisions within Russia, strengthen the tsar's regime, and improve Russia's international stature. Instead, the "short, painless" fight turned into a massive conflagration that only compounded Russia's internal discord and revealed how far Russia had fallen behind other powers to the west. In addition, the greatest fears of the tsar, his government, and the aristocracy whose interests he

MAP 22.6

The Middle East, 1923

This map shows the Middle East in the years just after World War I.

Explore the Map

1. Notice what has happened to lands once ruled by the Ottoman Empire. How might Arab nationalists have reacted to these changes?

2. Consider the location of this region and its natural resources. Why might politics in this area of the world be so important?

DOCUMENT 22.3

Keynes Warns of the Economic Consequences of the Peace

The various parties involved in the peace treaty talks after World War I came to agreements only after painful, protracted negotiations. Much of the debate centered on how to deal with Germany. In the following excerpt from his influential book The Economic Consequences of the Peace *(1919), economist John Maynard Keynes—an advisor to British prime minister Lloyd George at the Versailles Conference—assesses the different attitudes toward the peace terms.*

By fixing the Reparation payments well within Germany's capacity to pay, we make possible the renewal of hope and enterprise within her territory, we avoid the perpetual friction and opportunity of improper pressure arising out of Treaty clauses which are impossible of fulfilment, and we render unnecessary the intolerable powers of the Reparation Commission.

***

It would be objected, I suppose, by some critics that such an arrangement might go some way in effect towards realizing the former German dream of Mittel-Europa.

***

If we take the view that for at least a generation to come Germany cannot be trusted with even a modicum of prosperity, that while all our recent Allies are angels of light, all our recent enemies, Germans, Austrian, Hungarians, and the rest, are children of the devil, that year by year Germany must be kept impoverished and her children starved and crippled, and that she must be ringed round by enemies; then we shall reject all the proposals of this chapter, and particularly those which may assist Germany to regain a part of her former material prosperity and find a means of livelihood for the industrial population of her towns. But if this view of nations and of their relation to one another is adopted by the democracies of Western Europe, and is financed by the United States, heaven help us all.

***

I pass to a second financial proposal. The requirements of Europe are *immediate*. The prospect of being relieved of oppressive interest payments to England and America over the whole life of the next two generations (and of receiving from Germany some assistance year by

year to the costs of restoration) would free the future from excessive anxiety. But it would not meet the ills of the immediate present—the excess of Europe's imports over her exports, the adverse exchange, and the disorder of the currency. It will be very difficult for European production to get started again without a temporary measure of external assistance. I am therefore a supporter of an international loan in some shape or form, such as has been advocated in many quarters in France, Germany, and England, and also in the United States. In whatever way the ultimate responsibility for repayment is distributed, the burden of finding the immediate resources must inevitably fall in major part upon the United States.

SOURCE: John Maynard Keynes, *The Economic Consequences of the Peace* (Harcourt, Brace, and Howe, 1919).

Analyze the Document

1. What would be the consequences of high reparation payments from Germany, according to Keynes?

2. What role was the United States expected to play in the future?

3. Do you agree with Keynes that Germany should have been helped to "regain a part of her former material prosperity"? Why?

---

represented came true: World War I devastated Russia militarily and brought the centuries-old Romanov dynasty crashing down.

The First Warnings, 1905

Long-simmering discontent made Russia ripe for violent upheaval. This discontent had its roots in the Russian government's historical resistance to change. Throughout the nineteenth century, Russia's government had usually tried to ignore rather than adapt to the liberalizing movements that swept most of Europe. The tsar ruled autocratically, relying on the nobility, the church, the army, and the bureaucracy without allowing a hint of political participation to the vast majority of Russian society.

Industrialization, initiated in the 1880s and surging in the 1890s—encouraged by the aggressive policies of Sergei Witte (1849–1915), the finance minister, and an infusion of foreign capital into Russia—stimulated the growth of the middle and working classes in cities such as Moscow and St. Petersburg. These people chafed against Russia's traditional society and archaic government. Frustrated Russian intellectuals turned to revolutionary doctrines and even terrorism in an effort to promote rapid change. Others hoped for more moderate liberal reforms. Still the tsarist government, particularly under Nicholas II (1894–1917), refused to bend.

A turning point came with the embarrassing defeat of the tsar's army and navy by Japan in the 1904–1905 Russo-Japanese War. The various liberal and radical groups took advantage of the government's weakness and clamored for reform. The mounting pressures for change finally exploded early in 1905. On Sunday, January 22, thousands of workers gathered in front of the tsar's palace in St. Petersburg to protest economic hardships. "We have become beggars; we have been oppressed; we are burdened by toil beyond our powers; we are scoffed at; we are not recognized as human beings; we are treated as slaves who must suffer their bitter fate and who must keep silence," complained the petitioners. Marchers sang "God save the tsar," but the tsar's troops fired on them, killing and wounding hundreds of women, men, and children. The violent event, known as Bloody Sunday, was dramatically depicted by the Russian artist N. Vladimirov (**Figure 22.10**). On the right, a line of Tsar Nicholas II's troops shoot at the procession of workers. On the left, the unarmed workers, who sought to present peacefully a petition to the tsar at the Winter Palace in St. Petersburg, fall. Their blood darkens the snow as well as faith in the tsar as a protector of the people. In response, Father Georgi Gapon, a radical Orthodox priest, warned the tsar: "A sea of blood—unexampled—will be shed. Because of thee, because of thy whole family, Russia may perish."

Demands for reform increased, and in October, a general strike paralyzed the country for ten days. In the cities, workers organized themselves into councils, or **soviets.** Sailors mutinied on the battleship *Potemkin,* as did soldiers in the army. At the same time, peasants in the countryside revolted and attacked wealthy landowners. Several officials were assassinated. With much of its army pinned down thousands of miles away in the Russo-Japanese War, the tsar's government wavered. Surrounded by dissension and revolt, Nicholas II yielded at last and issued a manifesto that promised civil liberties, a popularly elected Duma (parliament), and legalization of unions. These concessions had little lasting meaning, however. The return of the Russian troops from the Far East and a fresh round of governmental repression had restored order by 1907. The tsar and his advisors reduced the Duma to a nondemocratically elected body.

The Fall of the Tsar

The few halfhearted reforms were not enough, and discontent persisted in the years after 1905. In the months before the outbreak of World War I, strikes proliferated in Russia's cities. This turmoil probably encouraged the tsar to bring Russia into the war, for he immediately banned strikes and suspended the Duma, whose members still agitated for liberal reforms. As we saw earlier, Russia soon suffered staggering losses at the hands of the German armies. Its leadership, transportation facilities, supplies, and armaments simply could

FIGURE 22.10 N. Vladimirov, Bloody Sunday, 1905 On January 22, 1905, Russian soldiers opened fire on thousands of workers protesting economic hardships in front of the tsar's palace in St. Petersburg.

not withstand the demands of total war. Moreover, many non-Russian subjects living within the empire became more interested in establishing their own independent states than supporting the war effort.

In August 1915, a desperate Nicholas made a fatal mistake: He left the capital to take personal command of the army. The severity and depth of this error are revealed by the reaction of Russia's war minister. Reporting on the dire military situation to the council, the minister concluded, "Considering the present situation at the front and in the rear of the armies, one can expect an irreparable catastrophe momentarily." However, he added, "a far more horrible event threatens Russia." His stunned colleagues on the Council of Ministers waited for the grim news. "This morning, His Majesty told me of his decision to personally assume the supreme command of the army." As a result of Nicholas's actions, the Russian people blamed the tsar for their country's military losses. Equally problematic, the inept, unpopular government in the capital now fell under the sway of Nicholas's wife, Alexandra. When the tsarina came under the influence of Grigori Efimovich Rasputin (ca. 1871–1916), a corrupt Siberian mystic who claimed to have the power to heal the tsar's hemophiliac son, things took a more bizarre turn. Even the tsar's aristocratic supporters, a group of whom finally murdered Rasputin late in 1916, demanded fundamental change.

In early March 1917, the dam broke. The strains of war drove hungry workingwomen to initiate strikes and demonstrations. With industrialization, Petrograd (St. Petersburg), Moscow, and other Russian cities had grown rapidly. Women, who made up more than half of the labor force in Petrograd,

> The March revolution

FIGURE 22.11 Demonstrations in Petrograd, 1917 Marches such as this one in March 1917 by Petrograd women led to the revolution that overthrew Russia's tsar and his government.

had to work long hours for low wages and then stand in long bread lines to buy food for their families. Rising prices and shrinking supplies, especially during the winters, translated into hunger and starvation. **Figure 22.11** is a photograph of one of these demonstrations. Here women march down a Petrograd street demanding an increase of rations to soldiers' families.

Women rightly blamed the government for Russia's continuing involvement in the war and for the food shortages. On March 8, in recognition of International Women's Day, they made their voices heard. That day, 10,000 women marched into Petrograd, shouting, "Down with war and high prices! Down with starvation! Bread for workers!" The protesters also demanded an end to the rule of Nicholas II. Thousands of sympathizers, both women and men, joined the demonstrations in the wintry days of March 1917. Yet police and troops were reluctant to fire on the crowds, especially because so many of them were women. Many troops actually joined the demonstrators. The French ambassador to Russia reported watching "a disorderly mob carrying a red flag" marching toward an oncoming regiment of troops. But instead of restoring order, "the army was fraternizing with the revolt." Too many people had lost their respect for the rigid, poorly led autocracy. As Russia's minister of foreign affairs put it, "The Emperor is blind!" Many of his colleagues agreed. On March 12, the Duma organized a provisional government, and three days later Nicholas II abdicated. Railroad workers took him and his family into custody.

The Provisional Government

Most members of the provisional government hoped that Russia would move toward constitutional parliamentary democracy. Led by moderate liberals Pavel Milyukov (1859–1943) and Prince Georgi Lvov (1861–1925), these politicians represented the upper classes. The provisional government enacted into law civil liberties, religious freedom, equality before the law, union rights, and other liberal reforms. They also promised more fundamental social reforms and a constitution.

However, in addition to its inexperience, its rival factions, and the intensifying pressures for change, the provisional government labored under three key burdens. First, it had to share power with the soviets—the political organizations of workers, soldiers, and radical intellectuals—particularly the strong Petrograd soviet. The soviets favored socialist self-rule and stood against the upper classes represented by the provisional government. Second, the government chose to continue Russia's draining involvement in World War I. The links between these first two burdens came to light with the Petrograd soviet's issuance of Order Number 1 on March 14. This significant mandate declared that military officers would be democratically elected by soldiers and that military decisions would be democratically made. Order Number 1 further unraveled authority and discipline within Russia's armed forces. Third, neither the provisional government nor the soviets could control the peasantry, which made up some 80 percent of the population. Peasants refused to wait for the land-redistribution legislation that the government had promised. They seized land and hoarded food for themselves, worsening hunger in the cities as prices rose and supplies became more scarce. The peasantry's defiance also attracted soldiers, who deserted the front to make land claims of their own.

The provisional government failed to satisfy many. The peasants wanted still more land, and workers demanded more bread. Russia could no longer support the unpopular war effort, yet the government could not find a way to withdraw gracefully from it. Again and again the provisional government tried to rally the Russian troops to victory. In desperation, it even created the Women's Battalion of Death in an effort to shame male soldiers into greater effort. More than 80 percent of these women became casualties. The desertions continued.

The soviets

In May, the liberal heads of the provisional government resigned and the moderate socialist Alexander Kerensky (1881–1970) became the leading figure in the government. Kerensky, however, faced new political divisions, for by this time many radical intellectuals had returned to Russia from the west, where they had fled from the tsar's repression, or rose from Russia's social ranks. They tried to push ideas and events in one direction or the other. Those who proved most influential came from a group of Marxist revolutionaries, the Social Democrats—in particular their minority faction, the Bolsheviks. This faction was led by Vladimir Ilich Ulyanov (1870–1924), known by his revolutionary name, Lenin.

Kerensky leads

The Rise of the Bolsheviks

Marxism had become influential among some Russian intellectuals, revolutionaries, and groups critical of Russia's tsarist autocracy toward the end of the nineteenth century. In 1898, Russian Marxists had formed the Social Democratic Party, whose principal leaders were Georgi Plekhanov (1857–1918) and his disciple Lenin. Repression by the tsar's government forced the Social Democrats into exile. At a London conference in 1903, the radical Bolshevik wing under Lenin split from the more moderate Mensheviks.

Until 1917, Lenin's **Bolsheviks** remained only a minor party within Russia. Its leaders were hunted down by the state police and shot, imprisoned, or exiled. For seventeen years, Lenin remained in exile in Switzerland, keeping his party alive from a distance and plotting the eventual overthrow of the tsar's government. During that time, he developed theoretical and tactical principles that the Bolsheviks would later use. Three of these principles set forth the most crucial guidelines and, for the most part, set Lenin's Bolsheviks apart from other Marxist organizations. First, the party should be an elite, highly trained, and constantly purged (cleaned of disloyal ideas and people) group of dedicated Marxist revolutionaries capable of instructing and leading the masses. This elite would not be seduced by short-term gains. Second, contrary to what Marx had argued, the socialist revolution need not include only the industrial working class. In Russia, it could be a dual revolution of workers and poor, land-hungry peasants—all part of an even broader socialist revolution that would sweep through other European countries. Third, the party should firmly oppose participation in the war, which Lenin considered a product of imperialist rivalries and a continuing civil war among capitalists.

In April 1917, the German government secretly transported Lenin from his place of exile in Switzerland to a Baltic port, from which he made his way

Lenin's principles

to Russia, in an effort to worsen the chaos in Russia and remove Russia from the war. The Germans had good reason to consider Lenin a threat to stability in Russia. John Reed, a sympathetic American journalist and observer, described Lenin as "a strange popular leader—a leader purely by virtue of intellect; colorless, humorless, uncompromising and detached; without picturesque idiosyncrasies—but with the power of explaining profound ideas in simple terms, of analyzing a concrete situation." Back in Russia, Lenin refused to cooperate with the provisional government. Instead, he unleashed a barrage of compelling slogans, such as "Peace to the Army," "Land to the Peasants," "Ownership of the Factories to the Workers," and "All Power to the Soviets." He argued that the time was ripe for a socialist revolution against capitalism. To achieve this revolution, he urged his followers to gain control over the soviets, particularly the powerful Petrograd soviet.

When Kerensky failed to extract Russia from the war, Bolshevik influence grew, especially among the Petrograd workers and soldiers. In July 1917, a massive popular demonstration against the provisional government erupted in that city. Most members of the Bolshevik Party supported the demonstration, though in the end the leadership did not. In these bloody July Days, the provisional government put down the demonstrators with force. The Kerensky government arrested many Bolsheviks and impelled others, including Lenin, to flee to Finland.

Russia's July Days

Yet Kerensky soon suffered a fresh round of failures in the war as well as the threat of an impending coup d'état by General Lavr Kornilov (1870–1918). To avert disaster, in September the desperate Kerensky released the Bolsheviks and relied on the soviets to defend the capital against Kornilov. Kornilov's plans failed when most of his soldiers refused to follow his orders to attack Petrograd.

By October, many leading figures from larger socialist parties had become discredited through their association with the provisional government. This turn of events helped the Bolsheviks, under the leadership of Lenin and the brilliant Leon Trotsky (1879–1940),

THE RUSSIAN REVOLUTION

1904–1905	Russo-Japanese War
1905	General strike and revolution
1917	March revolution
	November revolution
1918	Treaty of Brest-Litovsk
1918–1920	Civil war

KEY DATES

finally gain control over the Petrograd and Moscow soviets. Bolshevik women created a network to call for demonstrations, organize women in factories, and do paramilitary work. Lenin judged the time right for his next move.

On November 6, he and Trotsky launched a well-organized seizure of power. His Red Guards (workers' | The November revolution | militia units) took over crucial control centers and arranged for the transfer of power to the soviets and Lenin. Within just hours, the deed was complete. Kerensky, unable to reorganize his forces, fled. Although some of the fighting was violent, the success of the Bolshevik revolution stemmed mostly from the revolutionaries' organizational talents, a lack of effective resistance by the provisional government, and Trotsky's success in portraying the uprising as *defense* of the soviets rather than a Bolshevik *offensive*.

On November 7, the Bolshevik majority enthusiastically elected Lenin the head of the new government. The revolution won the endorsement of soviets throughout Russia. **Figure 22.12,** a painting by the Russian artist Vladimir Serov, shows Lenin, with Stalin standing behind him, proclaiming to the revolutionary forces the Bolsheviks' assumption of power in 1917. In this idealized re-creation of events, the artist has elevated Stalin to a prominent position just behind Lenin. The artist also portrays Lenin as a powerful orator towering above all others. The serious, impassioned crowd below, made up of women, sailors, soldiers, and workers, listens intently. The red flag of communism is held aloft in victory.

Communism and Civil War

The Bolsheviks, who now called themselves Communists, immediately moved to fulfill their promises and consolidate their power. In place of the old tsarist hierarchy, they set up a pyramid of people's soviets, or councils. These councils were elected by universal suffrage but were actually dominated by relatively few Communist Party members. When national elections failed to return a Communist majority to the Constituent Assembly, Lenin had armed sailors disperse that elected body. Capitalism was abolished outright. A barter system of exchange replaced money, the value of the ruble having been destroyed by inflation and devaluation. Committees of workers responsible to party commissars took over management of industry and commerce. The government nationalized the land and turned over its management to local peasant committees, who then distributed it to individual peasants to be worked by their own labor. All crop surpluses were to be given to the state. Finally, the state expropriated church lands and enacted laws to establish the legal equality of the sexes—the first Western government to do so.

To buy time and free the new regime for the enormous task of refashioning Russian society, Lenin immediately opened peace negotiations with Germany. The Germans, realizing Russia's helplessness, demanded the harshest of terms. Lenin attempted to stall them, but in March 1918, when the Germans threatened to attack Petrograd and Moscow, he signed the Treaty of Brest-Litovsk. Russia lost Finland, Estonia, Latvia, Lithuania, the Ukraine, Bessarabia, the Polish provinces, and some of the Trans-Caucasian territory. Lenin had paid a high price for peace. These lands contained one-third of Russia's European population, three-fourths of its iron, and nine-tenths of its coal. In addition, Germany compelled Russia to pay a heavy indemnity. Lenin gambled that a socialist revolution in Germany would reverse some of these losses and provide the support that the fledgling socialist system desperately needed to survive in Russia.

Nevertheless, these hard peace terms were not the worst of Lenin's woes. A bitter civil war broke out in Russia following the peace with Germany

FIGURE 22.12 Lenin Proclaiming Soviet Power This propagandistic painting by Vladimir Serov shows Lenin, backed by Stalin, announcing the Bolshevik victory in 1917.

MAP 22.7

Civil War in Russia, 1919

This map shows Russia during the civil war.

Explore the Map

1. What different forces threatened the area controlled by the Bolsheviks?

2. Why might the Bolsheviks have emerged from this period with a sense of isolation from the West?

3. What strategy might have helped the forces opposing the Bolsheviks?

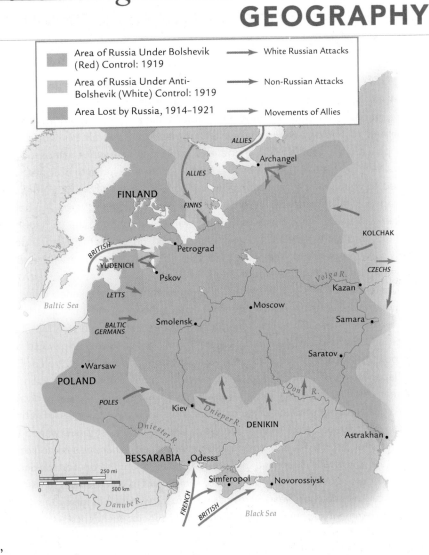

Legend:
- Area of Russia Under Bolshevik (Red) Control: 1919
- Area of Russia Under Anti-Bolshevik (White) Control: 1919
- Area Lost by Russia, 1914–1921
- White Russian Attacks
- Non-Russian Attacks
- Movements of Allies

(see **Map 22.7**). The Russian aristocracy, including most of the higher army officers, launched a series of uncoordinated attacks against the Bolshevik regime. These "White" forces were aided by various other groups disaffected by the revolution. They also had the support of French, British, Greek, Polish, Japanese, Czech, and U.S. troops that were in Russia for various reasons, but in great part to oppose the anticapitalist Bolshevik government. For decades afterward, the Communists would remember how the outside world had turned against them during this vulnerable time.

Creating an emergency policy of "war communism," the Bolshevik government mobilized Russia's economy and society for the civil-war effort. Urban workers and troops swept through the countryside and confiscated grain from the peasantry to feed the cities and the army. The Bolsheviks sharply suppressed any internal opposition. A secret police force—the Cheka—unleashed the Red Terror to hunt down "class enemies" and ensure internal conformity to the Bolshevik regime. To avoid the possibility of White forces freeing the imprisoned Nicholas II and his family, the Bolshevik government ordered them executed. However, the Red armies faced numerous obstacles in their all-out effort to defeat the Whites. When peasants realized

that the government intended to seize their surpluses, for example, they resisted or refused to raise more crops than they needed for themselves. Moreover, the government had to contend with violent ethnic hatreds that further divided the country. Only with the greatest difficulty did the Red armies, well organized by Trotsky, finally defeat the Whites. In doing so, the Bolsheviks regained the Ukraine.

By 1920, World War I and the Russian civil war had ended. In addition to the two million Russian soldiers who died in the world war, some four to six million had lost their lives in the civil conflict. The once-powerful nation lay defeated, impoverished, and exhausted. Starvation hung like a specter over millions. The fighting was over, but Russia and other Western nations now faced the challenge of rebuilding social stability in an environment of continuing political and economic turmoil.

LOOKING BACK & MOVING FORWARD

Summary   British historian Arnold Toynbee said that in the years before 1914, his generation expected that "life throughout the World would become more rational, more humane, and more democratic . . . that the progress of science and technology would make mankind richer . . . that all this would happen peacefully." World War I shattered that vision. The very technology and industrial prowess that had fueled the West's growth and sense of progress were turned to unimagined destruction. The war ended dreams of heroic battles and courageous military deeds: "Words such as glory, honor, courage, or hallow [became] obscene" in the face of how the war was fought and the carnage that resulted, wrote the American author and veteran Ernest Hemingway. Indeed, many survivors of World War I were haunted for the rest of their lives with a sense of belonging to a "lost generation."

Along with millions of human lives, the war destroyed or weakened European empires. The German, Austro-Hungarian, and Ottoman empires collapsed. Military losses and revolution ended the Russian empire, replacing it with the Soviet Union and Communist rulers who were transforming that society and would alter the political landscape throughout the world in the next decades. In the Far East, the Japanese gained lands and stature by expanding their empire at the expense of German colonies and China. In the Middle East, Africa, and Asia, the war and vague Allied declarations in support of national liberation stimulated struggles for national rights and independence. Even in the West, faith in imperialist ideals waned during and after the war. As one Indian diplomat explained, "there was no conviction left of the Europeans' superiority or sense of vision." From the outside looking in, Europe now seemed shrunken, vulnerable, and subject to unreasonable passions.

The calamities of those years were not limited to the war itself. In Turkey, the nationalistic government responded to Armenian demands for independence by deporting some 2 million Armenians from eastern Turkey. Probably one-third of these were massacred in what amounted to modern mass genocide; another third may have died during the forced march to Syria. In 1918, an influenza epidemic hit, killing some 50–100 million people worldwide. In central and eastern Europe, postwar starvation threatened millions despite relief efforts by the United States and the International Red Cross. The peace treaties "to make the world safe" and "to end all wars" left a legacy of disappointment and resentment. In the next two decades, these sentiments would draw Europe and the world once again into a maelstrom of violence.

KEY TERMS

Central Powers, *p. 695*

Allies, *p. 696*

Schlieffen Plan, *p. 696*

trench warfare, *p. 698*

total war, *p. 702*

war guilt clause, *p. 708*

League of Nations, *p. 708*

soviets, *p. 713*

Bolsheviks, *p. 715*

REVIEW, ANALYZE, & CONNECT TO TODAY

REVIEW THE PREVIOUS CHAPTERS

Chapter 20—"Mass Politics and Imperial Domination"—analyzed nationalism, the spreading demands for political inclusion, and imperialism during the second half of the nineteenth century. Chapter 21—"Modern Life and the Culture of Progress"—examined new industrial transformations and urban life during this same period.

1. In what ways did nationalism, industrialism, and imperialism create the forces underlying World War I?

2. After the experience of World War I, why might people have looked back on the decades preceding the war so longingly?

ANALYZE THIS CHAPTER

Chapter 22—"Descending into the Twentieth Century"—tells the story of World War I and the Russian Revolution.

1. How might it be argued that several nations should bear responsibility for plunging the West into World War I? Which countries, if any, do you think were most responsible?

2. Why was this war so devastating, physically and psychologically?

3. Analyze the role of the home fronts. How did problems at the home fronts relate to problems on the battlefronts?

4. It is perhaps easier to understand why there was a revolution in Russia that toppled the tsar than why the Bolsheviks came to power several months later in a second revolution. How do you explain this?

CONNECT TO TODAY

Think about the themes of war and revolution that are discussed in this chapter.

1. What insights from studying World War I might we use to analyze the potential causes of wars and to anticipate how a war, once started, unfolds?

2. Is one lesson from this chapter that any major war in modern times may result in a revolution that itself has unanticipated consequences? Explain.

BEYOND THE CLASSROOM

ON THE PATH TO TOTAL WAR

Ferguson, Niall. *The Pity of War: Explaining World War I.* New York: Basic Books, 1999. A thoughtful reassessment of the causes, course, and results of World War I.

Stevenson, David. *Cataclysm: The First World War as Political Tragedy.* New York: Basic Books, 2004. An excellent and comprehensive one-volume study of the war.

Strachan, Hew. *The First World War.* Oxford: Oxford University Press, 2003. A fine, very well written, up-to-date survey.

THE FRONT LINES

Ellis, John. *Eye-Deep in Hell: Trench Warfare in World War I.* New York: Pantheon Books, 1989. An examination of the daily experiences of the trench soldier.

Keegan, John. *The First World War.* New York: Knopf, 1999. A highly respected military historian examines the realities of warfare, stressing experiences on the western front.

WAR ON THE HOME FRONT

Brayborn, Gail, and Penny Summerfield. *Out of the Cage: Women's Experiences in Two World Wars.* London: Pandora Press, 1987. Analyzes women's experiences in the two world wars and finds that the wars were economically and socially liberating for women.

Coetzee, Frans, and Marilyn Shevin-Coetzee, eds. *Authority, Identity and the Social History of the Great War.* Providence, RI: Berghahn Books, 1995. A comparative study of the experience and significance of the war in people's lives, especially for those on the home fronts.

Williams, John. *The Homefronts: Britain, France and Germany, 1914–1918.* London: Constable, 1972. Studies the effect of the ongoing struggle on the British, French, and German populations.

TO THE BITTER END

Becker, Jean-Jacques. *The Great War and the French People.* New York: St. Martin's Press, 1986. An examination of the impact of the war on the French.

Schmitt, Bernadotte E., and Harold C. Vedeler. *The World in a Crucible, 1914–1918.* New York: Harper & Row, 1984. Analyzes World War I as a total war and traces its economic, social, cultural, and diplomatic consequences.

ASSESSING THE LOSSES

Fussell, Paul. *The Great War and Modern Memory.* Oxford: Oxford University Press, 1975. A fascinating study of the British experience on the western front from 1914 to 1918 and the literary means by which it has been remembered.

Winter, J.M. *The Experience of World War I.* New York: Oxford University Press, 1988. A well-written examination of how the war was experienced by the peoples of the belligerent nations.

THE PEACE SETTLEMENT

MacMillan, Margaret. *Six Months That Changed the World.* New York: Random House, 2002. A new, very comprehensive account of the talks and the settlement.

Sharp, Alan. *The Versailles Settlement: Peacemaking in Paris, 1919.* New York: St. Martin's Press, 1991. A balanced overview that stresses the difficulties facing participants at the conference.

REVOLUTIONS IN RUSSIA

Fitzpatrick, Sheila. *The Russian Revolution, 1917–1932,* 2nd ed. Oxford: Oxford University Press, 1994. A brief and insightful treatment of this complex subject.

Lincoln, W. Bruce. *Red Victory: A History of the Russian Civil War.* New York: Simon & Schuster, 1989. Examines the Bolshevik triumph over internal conflicts.

Pipes, Richard. *The Russian Revolution.* New York: Vintage Books, 1991. Argues that the Bolshevik revolution was an authoritarian coup d'état.

GEORGE GROSZ, *THE PILLARS OF SOCIETY*, 1926

In *The Pillars of Society*, German expressionist artist George Grosz (1893–1959) sarcastically and ominously depicted the leaders of Germany during the 1920s. The swastika on his tie, the sword in one hand and beer mug in the other, and the dreams of combat pouring out of his head identify the "old-guard" man in front as a Nazi. Behind him, in suits and ties, stand two other members of the dominant middle class. One, a dull journalist with a chamber pot on his head, holds a blood-stained palm leaf that suggests his hypocritical pacifism. The other, a parliamentarian with a head full of excrement, mindlessly clutches a German national flag. In the background, a corrupted military chaplain offers his blessings while murderous soldiers look on. The soldiers remind viewers of how violence and the catastrophic Great War provided a backdrop to German society in the 1920s.

Darkening Decades

Recovery, Dictators, and Depression, 1920–1939

"The Storm has died away," wrote French poet Paul Valéry in the years just after World War I, "and still we are restless, uneasy, as if the storm were about to break . . . we do not know what will be born, and we fear the future. . . ." Many in Europe shared Valéry's sense of "terrible uncertainty." The Great War was finally over, and people longed for the return of normal life. In 1919, almost any memory of the days before the war seemed rosy. Too much had changed, though; the pre–World War I era was gone forever.

In fact, the immediate postwar years would bring frustration and turmoil. In the victorious democracies, growing disillusion and political bickering rather than dynamic action seemed the rule. Moreover, some of these nations faced dramatically rising resistance to foreign rule in their overseas holdings as colonial people, led by nationalistic intellectuals who combined Western ideas with their own cultural traditions, agitated for independence. Millions of people living in communist Russia still struggled just to survive, let alone transform that troubled nation. Elsewhere in the West, union, socialist, and communist movements alarmed those who feared change. As suggested by the painting on the facing page, many Europeans, especially in Italy, Germany, and east-central Europe, turned to right-wing leaders who attacked parliamentary government and raised the compelling banner of militant nationalism. Ahead, still unseen by most, lay the very dangers that people thought were over when the Great War ended.

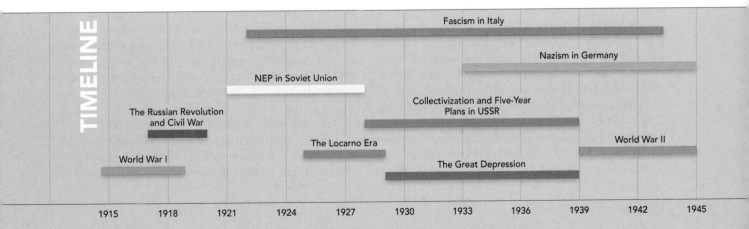

TIMELINE

World War I

The Russian Revolution and Civil War

NEP in Soviet Union

The Locarno Era

Fascism in Italy

Nazism in Germany

Collectivization and Five-Year Plans in USSR

The Great Depression

World War II

1915   1918   1921   1924   1927   1930   1933   1936   1939   1942   1945

PREVIEW

TRYING TO RECOVER FROM THE GREAT WAR, 1919–1929

In a haunting preview of troubles lurking over the era, Erich Maria Remarque, a German author and war veteran, described his life in Berlin during the early 1920s. "Prices have been soaring everywhere" and "poverty is greater than it was during the war." One afternoon he heard that demonstrations had been called for. In the streets, ominous rumors circulated that "troops have been concentrated at the barracks." Groups of strikers began marching through the streets. A disturbance broke out, people were yelling, and on corners speakers harangued small crowds. "Then suddenly everywhere is silence." A procession of maimed and wounded war veterans in the "faded uniforms of the front-line trenches" moved slowly toward him. Men with one arm carried white placards: "Where is the Fatherland's gratitude? The War Cripples are starving."

For Remarque and millions of others living in the post–World War I West, reality soon undermined the sense of liberation that the end of the war had brought. Families tried to care for their wounded sons, fathers, and brothers, and to endure the loss of those who had perished in battle. Many veterans came home angry. They had been promised moral purification during the war and compensation for their service after. Now they sensed that, in some ways, civilians did not fully appreciate their sacrifices. Too often, their old jobs

had disappeared. For some, their wives or lovers had deserted them or developed a new, disturbing sense of independence. Many veterans, returning to homelands whose economies lay in ruins, struggled just to get enough food.

Indeed, economic uncertainty had settled like a pall over most of Europe. In the decades after the war, nations struggled to retool their economies from wartime needs back to ordinary requirements and to reestablish international trade. Enormous sums in veterans' pay, war-widow benefits, and unemployment insurance burdened government treasuries. In vain, the victors had hoped that high reparation payments from Germany would be enough to help them rebuild their economies or at least cover debts from the war. So, governments borrowed when they could and printed money that had no basis in actual wealth. The resulting inflation hurt the middle classes in particular. They watched in panic as rising prices drained away their life savings. Between 1914 and 1928, France's currency alone lost four-fifths of its value. Still more unlucky were the thousands of western European investors, especially in France, who had invested in Russian bonds and saw them turn worthless when the Bolsheviks came to power.

Across Europe, recessions followed short periods of relative prosperity all too quickly. Unemployment persisted—in Britain, it remained above 10 percent in both good times and bad. Governments and employers pressured women to give up their wartime jobs or accept lower-paying positions so as to make way for men. Inflation and unemployment spun Germany's economy out of control. Among the Western powers, only the United States emerged from the war richer than ever. In Asia, Japan also emerged from the war stronger and richer—a new competitor looking to expand in East Asia and gain recognition as a great power. Europeans now looked to their governments for relief and leadership.

The Victors Just Hold On

Solutions to Europe's economic problems depended greatly on the politics of the postwar era. However, within the democracies, no one seemed to step forward with innovative ideas for change. Some people hoped that the addition of women to the voting roles in these countries (with the notable exception of France, Italy, and Sweden) would improve politics. In fact, however, women's suffrage seemed to change politics little, if at all. Most women voted as men did, and relatively few women gained political office.

International relations showed the same lack of innovation as domestic politics. Although the dominant military power on the Continent, France still

> Economic uncertainty

feared a resentful Germany and defensively held on to what it had salvaged in the Versailles treaty following the war. The nation fiercely resisted

Defensive France

any efforts by colonized people to move toward independence in its overseas holdings. Various conservative parties generally held power and domestic policies changed little from the prewar period. The conservatives concentrated on rebuilding France and trumpeting anti-German nationalism.

Great Britain might have worked with its ally France to find solutions to postwar problems, but each nation usually acted alone or in opposition to the other. Various political parties—Conservatives, Laborites, and Liberals—alternated in

Britain and its empire

power in Britain. Sometimes they formed coalitions with each other, but none came forth with fresh solutions to the economic and diplomatic problems plaguing the British. Instead, Britain pulled away from extensive involvement in European affairs and tried to solve the Irish problem and to hold on to its restless colonies in Asia and Africa.

In the decades before World War I, British governments had attempted in vain to enact home rule for Ireland to quell growing demands for Irish independence. Leaders such as Constance Markievicz (1868–1926), a founder of republican and women's organizations, called on the Irish to "fix your mind on the ideal of Ireland free, with her women enjoying the full rights of citizenship in their own nation," warning that "our national freedom cannot, and must not, be left to evolution." In 1914, Parliament had finally passed the Irish Home Rule Bill, but it postponed the bill's implementation until after the war. In 1916, impatient Irish nationalists in Dublin rose up against the British but were crushed (see page 703). Executed leaders quickly became national martyrs, and the extremist organization Sinn Fein (Ourselves Alone) gained leadership in the nationalist cause. Its military wing became the Irish Republican Army. When the Sinn Fein Party declared Irish independence in 1919, fighting broke out between the IRA and the British army. With the British cast in the role of oppressors, the bloodshed persisted for two years. In December 1921, a treaty created the Irish Free State, although the six predominantly Protestant counties of Ulster (Northern Ireland) remained tied to Great Britain. Even then, a civil war broke out between protreaty and antitreaty forces. This legacy of violence would haunt the British and Irish again and again.

The British also faced nationalist problems elsewhere in the world. In West Africa, nationalistic leaders pressured the British to establish representative institutions; the British agreed to new constitutions in Nigeria in 1923 and the Gold Coast in 1925. In North Africa, opposition to foreign rule forced the British to grant independence to Egypt in 1923. In the Middle East, Britain faced uprisings in Iraq and conflicts in Palestine, where Zionist immigrants bumped up against native Arabs. In Asia, nationalist parties developed into powerful political forces. Perhaps the strongest movement for national liberation emerged in India. Many Indians, hoping they would be rewarded with self-government, had fought for Britain in World War I, and the Indian economy had grown with India's support of Britain's war effort. Indian leaders, such as Mohandas Gandhi (1869–1948) and Jawaharlal Nehru (1889–1964), who had been Westernized by education and experience while employed by British rulers, led the drive for independence. Gandhi used the tactic of civil disobedience—publicly and nonviolently breaking the law—to promote widespread sympathy for his cause. Even Britain's leaders, reacting to these pressures, began talking about granting self-rule to India.

The United States, for its part, could have taken a leadership role in international affairs. However, it refused to ratify the Versailles treaty, join the League of Nations, or involve itself extensively in tensions overseas. Europe's troubles came to center more and

The U.S. turns inward

more on events in Germany, an unstable nation that would soon become enmeshed in a round of political and international turmoil.

Continuing Crises in Germany

Germany emerged from World War I defeated and angry. However, it had the potential to regain its strength quickly. More populous than France, Germany still had an intact industrial infrastructure. It also occupied an advantageous position in the postwar rearrangement of the European map. On its eastern borders lay weak nations newly created at the end of World War I. Farther east, Russia was isolated and preoccupied with shoring up its struggling new communist society.

Soon after the war, the Germans set up the **Weimar Republic** (named after the city where its constitution was drawn up) as a model liberal democracy. Moderate Social Democrats led the republic, but they had

The Weimar Republic

inherited the taint of defeat from the outcome of the war. Moreover, many officials in the bureaucracy, judiciary, and army were the same people who had occupied these positions before 1918. They were not particularly dedicated to the new republic. Nationalists and right-wing parties looked on the new parliamentary system with contempt.

Challengers within Germany arose almost as soon as the Social Democrats came to power. From the Left, Rosa Luxemburg (1870–1919) and Karl Liebknecht (1871–1919) led an uprising of radical

Marxists (Spartacists). The government responded with repression, using the Free Corps—right-wing paramilitary groups made up mostly of veterans—to murder the two leaders and put down the communist threat. Nevertheless, communists continued to stir discord for several more years. In 1920, the German government faced a new threat, this time from right-wing nationalists under Wolfgang Kapp (1858–1922). A general strike by workers in support of the government paralyzed the economy and ended Kapp's effort to take over Berlin.

Then economic and international crises added to Weimar's political woes. In January 1923, after the German government defaulted on the huge war reparations bill, French and Belgian troops responded

Wild inflation by occupying the Ruhr Valley, Germany's richest industrial area. The Germans struck back with passive resistance—opposing the occupiers in every way but with violence. Enraged, the French tried to create a secession movement from Germany in the Rhineland. Although the occupying forces failed to collect any reparations, the occupation paralyzed Germany's economy, and wild inflation swept the country. At the crest of the inflation wave, four trillion German marks were worth only one dollar. People literally took wheelbarrows full of money to go shopping. **Figure 23.1** reveals the extent of the inflation. Here children, apparently unaware of the economic turmoil throughout Germany, play with stacks of their nation's nearly worthless paper money. Within days, the inflation wiped out countless Germans' life savings. With a frightening hint of future events,

FIGURE 23.1 German Inflation, 1923 In November 1923, these German children play with stacks of paper money made nearly worthless by ruinous inflation.

Document 23.1 reveals some of the fears and political turmoil engendered by this uncertainty.

Conciliation and a Glimpse of Prosperity

Germany's international and economic picture looked bleak in 1923. But near the end of that year, a series of events unfolded that held out hope for international cooperation and a return to prosperity, not only for Germany but also for other nations in the West. In August, Gustav Stresemann (1878–1929) rose to leadership in the German government and offered to reconcile the country's differences with France. Having lost more money and international standing than it had gained from its occupation of the Ruhr, France reversed its policy and agreed to cooperate with Stresemann. An international commission headed by Charles Dawes (1865–1951) of the United States drew up a plan for the occupying forces' withdrawal from Germany. The commission also arranged for international loans to Germany and set up a system by which Germany would pay lower reparations in installments. In 1925, Germany signed the Treaty of Locarno with France, Great Britain, Italy, and Belgium—an agreement that guaranteed Germany's existing frontiers with France and Belgium. Optimistic headlines in the *New York Times* declared, "France and Germany Ban War Forever." In 1926, the League of Nations admitted Germany and elected Stresemann its president. With inter-national relations apparently normalized, France retreated, hoping that alliances with smaller eastern European states and the **Maginot Line**—a string of defensive fortresses on the French/German border it began building in the late 1920s—would contain the economically revived Germany.

The Dawes plan

Most of the remaining Western economies also perked up after 1924. In several countries, automobile manufacturing, aviation, synthetics, and electronics took off. Vacuum cleaners, washing machines, refrigerators, and electric irons—now often purchased on installment plans—became the norm in middle-class homes. New production techniques spread, especially among big-business employers who began using the principles and methods of "scientific management" promoted by the American efficiency engineer Frederick W. Taylor (1856–1915). After conducting time and motion studies, Taylor and other industrial psychologists recommended a sharper division of labor and detailed control over every aspect of work in order to boost worker productivity. Taylor especially emphasized the division between thinking by managers and physical labor by workers: "We do not want any initiative [from workers]," he wrote. "All we want of them is to obey the orders we give them, do what we say and

Uneasy prosperity

DOCUMENT 23.1

Postwar Strains in Germany

Postwar dislocations and economic difficulties put enormous strains on European nations, particularly Germany. One of these hardships took the form of explosive inflation that struck Germany in 1923. This 1923 speech by Adolf Hitler—a minor but ambitious political figure at the time—reveals some of the anger and political uncertainty spawned by the inflation.

"Germany is a people of children; a grown-up people would say: 'We don't care a fig for your paper-money. Give us something of value—gold! What have you after all to give us? Nothing? Thus have you defrauded us, you rogues and swindlers!' An awakened people with its last thirty marks—all that is left of the millions of its glory—would buy a rope and with it string up 10,000 of its defrauders!" Even the farmer will no longer sell his produce, "When you offer him your million scraps of paper with which he can cover the walls of his closet on his dung-heap, can you wonder that he says, 'Keep your millions and I will keep my corn and my butter.'" "The individual and the nation are delivered over to the international capital of the banks; despair seizes the whole people. We are on the eve of a second revolution. Some are setting their hopes on the star of the Soviet: that is the symbol of those who began the Revolution, to whom the Revolution has brought untold wealth, who have exploited it until to-day. It is the star of David, the sign of the Synagogue. The symbol of the race high over the world, a lordship which stretches from Vladivostok to the West—the lordship of Jewry. The golden star which for the Jew means the glittering gold."

"And when the people in its horror sees that one can starve though one may have milliards of marks, then it will perforce make up its mind and say: 'We will bow down no longer before an institution which is founded on the delusory majority principle, we want a dictatorship.' Already the Jew has a premonition of things to come: . . . he is saying to himself: If there must be a dictatorship, then it shall be a dictatorship of Cohen or Levi."

SOURCE: Adolf Hitler, *The Speeches of Adolf Hitler*, vol. I, trans. and ed. by Norman Baynes (Oxford: Oxford University Press, 1942), pp. 72–73.

Analyze the Document

1. What explanation does Hitler offer for the painful problems confronting Germans?

2. What solutions does he suggest for those problems?

3. Are there any inconsistencies between this statement from 1923 and Hitler's later actions? Explain.

---

do it quick." These techniques may have made production more efficient, but for laborers, work became more mindless, dull, and repetitive than ever.

Outside of manufacturing, many people found jobs in the fast-growing service and housing sectors. Women in particular took positions as salesclerks, social workers, nurses, telephone operators, manicurists, hairdressers, and processors of convenience foods such as pudding mixes and dried cereals. Housing projects with indoor plumbing, electricity, and central heating sprang up throughout Europe—many of them boasted common-use day-care centers, laundries, and gardens. With all these developments, the West seemed to be back on the path of material progress that characterized the decades before World War I.

At the same time, several industries declined, unable to keep up with the new products, enhanced technology, and stiffer competition. Britain, especially, clung to its old expertise in metals and textiles and failed to invest in the rising new technologies. Its coal industry sank dramatically, sparking massive strikes that in 1926 turned into a general strike by miners and other industrial workers. The economies of nations outside of Europe—particularly in the United States, Canada, Australia, and Japan—benefited at Britain's and Europe's expense.

The Roaring Twenties?

The popular culture of the 1920s reflected these complex political and economic changes of the postwar era. This uneasy, worrisome time has been called the Jazz Age and the Roaring Twenties. Both terms convey the exuberance of the period's popular culture. They also hint at the superficial nature of the gaiety. This glittering culture had an edgy, frenetic quality that suggested a people haunted by a profound insecurity.

In **Figure 23.2,** a depiction of a cabaret scene, the German expressionist painter Otto Dix captures these contradictions of life during the 1920s. Berlin in particular became famous for cabarets such as this. In the painting, a couple dances to the music of a jazz band made up of black and white musicians, probably from America. European interest in American jazz and culture reflected the new international stature of the United States. To the right poses a "flapper," a fashionably thin woman whose dress and hair are cut short. She and the woman behind her smoking a cigarette stand alone, apparently independent. The scene suggests sexual abandon, yet the expressions on most people's faces are stiff, even apathetic. The picture conveys more of a sense of frenzy, decadence,

FIGURE 23.2 Otto Dix, _Grosstadt (Big Town)_, 1927–1928 These scenes from just outside (left) and inside (right) a Berlin cabaret show the contradictions of postwar life as impoverished, crippled veterans on the street look in on revelers frolicking on the dance floor. The painting suggests artificial celebration and underlying misery more than joy.

and artificial celebration than relaxed happiness. The artist's deeper message is especially clear in the left panel of this painting. In this smaller section, a crippled veteran leans on a crutch outside the cabaret and begs for assistance as the revelers pass him by with scarcely a glance in his direction. The canvas echoes a description of Berlin in that era by a leading German journalist, Hans Sahl: "It was a time of great misery, with legless war veterans riding the sidewalks on rolling planks, in a nation that seemed to consist of nothing but beggars, whores, invalids, and fat-necked speculators."

While millions of people read the proliferating practical books, popular fiction, and newspapers, no new forces of popular culture shaped and reflected national attitudes more than the radio and movies. In France, the first radio broadcast station opened in 1920. It transmitted poor-quality sound to a limited audience, but by 1939, the number of radios in France had reached almost five million. The movie industry also flourished, particularly in Germany, Russia, France, and the United States. More than 100 million people saw a film each week.

> The radio and movies

Filmmaking itself became an art form, a visual record of social attitudes, and an account of people's ambitions and dreams. Films were thoughtfully and cleverly edited to promote drama and show scenes from different perspectives. Increasingly, creating movies involved specialized roles, such as producer, director, and editor. Marketed actors became envied celebrities, and millions followed the lives and careers of these movie stars. Many filmmakers projected their nations' self-images in stunning, creative ways—perhaps none more so than the legendary Russian Sergei Eisenstein (1898–1948). His epic films about the 1905 and 1917 revolutions in Russia represented the Soviet view of events in those "heroic" years.

Other films revealed deep-seated concerns about modern society. **Figure 23.3,** for example, shows an eerie, futuristic scene from the German director Fritz Lang's (1890–1976) film _Metropolis_ (1925). This image emphasizes the overwhelming power of urban architecture and technology and demonstrates cinema's potential to serve as an artistic medium. Here a solitary airplane flies through the stark canyons of buildings in a futuristic city. Humans are dwarfed out of sight in the impersonal world they have created. The image seems to complement visually lines from "The Waste Land" (1922), a work by one of the period's leading poets, T. S. Eliot (1888–1965):

> _Unreal City,_
> _Under the brown god of a winter dawn,_
> _A crowd flowed over London Bridge, so many . . ._
> _And each man fixed his eyes before his feet._

On another level, this scene also hints at other harbingers of modernity: the advent of skyscrapers, already rising in New York City, and the daring flights being made in small planes. Just two years after this film was made, the solo flight across the Atlantic of the American pilot Charles Lindbergh (1902–1974) won acclaim on both sides of the ocean. Americans and Europeans alike saw embodied in Lindbergh and New York the promise of something young, exciting, and dynamic that just might push the West forward into a bright future.

Indeed, throughout the West, cities such as Berlin, Paris, and New York became even more dazzling cultural centers than before. Office buildings and skyscrapers shot up, some of them displaying striking new trends in architecture. The most influential architect was the German Walter Gropius (1883–1969), who in 1919 founded the **Bauhaus** school of art in Germany. This school created new standards for modern architecture and for the design of ordinary objects, from chairs and lamps to dishes. In 1925, Gropius designed the building shown in **Figure 23.4.** Emphasizing clean, functional lines, this international style of architecture symbolized acceptance of the modern, industrial world. These buildings unabashedly displayed their efficient structure, prefabricated materials, and steel and glass features. Many architects would follow this new style over the next half-century in creating office buildings, workers' housing, and private homes.

| The Bauhaus school |

In addition to trends in entertainment and the arts, the phrase "Roaring Twenties" implied new attitudes toward sex. Especially in leading cities, clothing fashions, often popularized in movies, exhibited these changing attitudes. Women's clothing, featuring thinner fabrics, shorter skirts, and tight-fitting styling, became more revealing. Along with fashion, women's hairstyles grew progressively shorter as well. Women discarded confining corsets that had long been in fashion and even donned trousers for sporting activities. Bathing suits, too, became increasingly skimpy. The "flapper," whom we saw in **Figure 23.2,** was now the new symbol of the ideal, free, sexually liberated woman.

| New attitudes toward sex |

The new focus on body image and sexual appeal intensified concerns about hygiene. People began regularly using toothbrushes, deodorants, and cosmetics. In addition, they bathed more often than before and shaved more closely. Tanned, thin women and muscular men became the new standards of health and sexual attractiveness.

As sex became more openly discussed and encouraged, governments also searched for ways to revive declining birthrates and thereby replace the lives lost during the war. In France, for example, the government

FIGURE 23.3 Movies and Modern Life This scene from Fritz Lang's film *Metropolis* (1925) shows a plane flying through the canyons of a modern city. It suggests the power of the cinema to convey images and ideas about modern life.

made distributing birth-control information illegal and abortion punishable by death. The French proclaimed a new holiday, Mother's Day, an innovation that other Western countries soon copied. Many governments provided maternity benefits, and increasingly, births took place in hospitals under the control of specialized nurses and doctors. Separate rooms for testing, labor, delivery, and recovery made the process of giving birth almost factory-like. Doctors, nurses, and social workers told women the "best" way to care for their children, and child-rearing courses for girls became compulsory in some countries.

The Anxious Twenties

Of all the forms of culture that gained currency during these years, high culture most powerfully reflected the stressful undercurrents of the postwar period. Many writers, intellectuals, and artists emphasized the uncertainty of the era and explored the widespread feelings of insecurity that people harbored.

Several philosophers, reacting to the horrors of the Great War, attacked nineteenth-century optimism and rationalism. These thinkers expanded on the ideas set forth earlier by Friedrich Nietzsche in Germany and Henri Bergson in France (see page 684). The most widely read of the post–World War I philosophers was a German, Oswald Spengler (1880–1936). In his book *The Decline of the*

| Sense of decay and crisis |

FIGURE 23.4 The Bauhaus Building Designed in 1925, this building represented the new international style in architecture and symbolized acceptance of the modern industrial world.

West (1918), Spengler argued that all civilizations were like biological organisms, each with its own life cycle. Western civilization, he claimed, had passed its high point, and World War I signaled the beginning of its end. This sense of decay and crisis emerged in many other works, most notably in the Spanish writer José Ortega y Gasset's (1883–1955) *Revolt of the Masses* (1930). Gasset lamented the decline of liberal elites and the "accession of the masses to complete social power." The masses, he warned, were not equipped to lead, yet they now took control from qualified elites and demanded a dangerous conformity: "Anybody who is not like everybody, who does not think like everybody, runs the risk of being eliminated."

Sigmund Freud's ideas (see Chapter 21) about the irrational, unconscious, and instinctual aspects of human thought and behavior—which had first emerged just before World War I—gained more acceptance during the 1920s. The unconscious and irrational played particularly prominent roles in the most acclaimed literature of the postwar era. The Irish writer James Joyce (1882–1941), German author Franz Kafka (1883–1924), and French writer Marcel Proust (1871–1922) created disquieting, introspective works of literature that elevated personal psychological experience over reason. In *Ulysses* (1922), Joyce in particular mastered the stream of consciousness technique, which displayed to the reader the rambling thoughts, free associations, and erotic fantasies going on in the mind of a character. At first critics and the public dismissed the novel as "morbid," "nonsense," and "foul." Eventually, however, this book about a single day in the lives of a group of Dubliners, which also served as a commentary on the human condition, was hailed as one of the century's greatest works of literature. In her novel *Mrs. Dalloway* (1925), British author Virginia Woolf used similar techniques to describe one day in the inner life of a woman, including fragmented conversations, partial remembrances, and fantasies (see Biography).

Novels and memoirs of the Great War also proliferated during these years. As in *All Quiet on the Western Front* by the German author Erich Maria Remarque, these works emphasized themes of brutality and suffering, disillusionment with civilian life, and a sense that the war had spawned a generation of lost souls. At the same time, Remarque's and others' books revealed a longing for the sense of purpose and comradeship that so often arises during a war effort but subsides in times of peace.

Similar themes marked artistic styles of the day. The **Dada** movement stressed the absence of purpose in life. Surrealist painters explored dreams and the world of the subconscious. Other painters, such as Käthe Kollwitz (see the Chapter 22 Biography) and Otto Dix (**Figure 23.2**), created moving images of suffering, destruction, and social despair.

In the 1920s, then, Western democratic societies struggled mightily both to come to terms with the consequences of the war and to move on to better days. In the early postwar years, the difficulties seemed overwhelming. Even with the revival of healthier economies and easing of international tensions after 1923, underlying doubt and insecurity persisted and made themselves plain in the period's cultural expression.

TURNING AWAY FROM DEMOCRACY: DICTATORSHIPS AND FASCISM, 1919–1929

The sense of unease and the difficult realities clearly burdened politics in the Western democracies, but things were far worse on the political front elsewhere in Europe. Among the states of east-central and southern Europe, the strain of the postwar years became too much for the fragile democratic systems budding there.

Authoritarianism in East-Central Europe

In 1919, Admiral Miklos Horthy (1868–1957), the reactionary former commander of the Austro-Hungarian navy, led forces, aided by anticommunist Allies and ambitious Romanians, that overthrew the newly formed regime led by the communist Béla Kun (1885–1937) in Hungary. Horthy's rule, like other right-wing authoritarian regimes that followed in Poland (1926) and Yugoslavia (1929), amounted to a dictatorship backed by the nation's military and conservative forces—the bureaucracy, high church, and wealthy elites. Why did these east-central European

BIOGRAPHY

Virginia Woolf
(1882–1941)

In 1938, the British writer Virginia Woolf looked back on her life and described herself as "fundamentally an outsider." By then, however, literary critics and the public alike had accepted this sensitive author's extraordinary works and honored her widely.

Born in 1882, Virginia Stephens was raised and educated within the Victorian literary world by her scholarly, well-connected parents. "Think how I was brought up!" she said, describing her isolated childhood. "No school; mooning about alone among my father's books; never any chance to pick up all that goes on in schools—throwing balls; ragging; slang; vulgarities; scenes; jealousies!" In adolescence, the gifted Virginia suffered from depressions and endured the first of the nervous breakdowns that would haunt her for the rest of her life.

In 1912, she married Leonard Woolf, also a writer and intellectual. They remained close over the years, the patient Leonard taking care of Virginia when she fell ill. The two also founded the Hogarth Press, which would publish works by some of the most important writers of the twentieth century, including T. S. Eliot, Sigmund Freud, and E. M. Forster. Their house in Bloomsbury became a gathering place for an influential group of writers, artists, and intellectuals who came to be known as the Bloomsbury group. Woolf acquired a reputation as a bit of a social snob, admitting that she enjoyed rubbing shoulders with the aristocracy because "the aristocrat is freer, more natural, more eccentric than we are." Within this group of intellectuals and social elites, some of her closest friends and lovers were women.

Woolf began her career as a writer in 1905 and published her first novel in 1915. Over the next twenty-five years, her many novels and essays gained critical and public recognition.

Reflecting the growing interest in psychology and the life of the mind, she focused on England's intellectuals like herself, experimented with stream-of-consciousness narration in her novels, and emphasized the psychological and emotional underpinnings of her characters. After writing *Jacob's Room* (1922), she felt she had finally come into her own: "There's no doubt . . . that I have found out how to begin (at 40) to say something in my own voice." In some of her works, the action took place over just days. These included *Mrs. Dalloway* (1925), centering on a fashionable society woman, and *To the Lighthouse* (1927), her most autobiographical work of fiction. Other books, such as *Orlando* (1928) and *Between the Acts* (1941) covered large sweeps of English history. Woolf's characters embodied the traumas and challenges of the postwar years. For example, in *Mrs. Dalloway*, a shell-shocked war veteran, Septimus Smith, represents the millions of soldiers killed or maimed—in one way or another—in World War I.

Woolf's best-known nonfiction work, *A Room of One's Own* (1929), focuses

FIGURE 23.5 Virginia Woolf, 1925

on the role of women in literature, education, and twentieth-century society. "A woman must have money and a room of her own if she is to write fiction," she wrote. She went on to explore the hindrances faced by women writers and their need to depart from traditional literature "made by men out of their own needs for their own uses."

During the 1920s and 1930s, Woolf closely followed world events. Having lived through the Great War of 1914–1918 and anticipating the upcoming conflagration that would become World War II, she argued that men—with their power and need to demonstrate their masculinity—caused wars. As a pacifist and antifascist, she became disgusted with the rise of rulers such as Hitler and Mussolini: "His eyes glare," she wrote. "His body, which is braced in an unnatural position, is tightly cased in a uniform. Upon the breast of that uniform are sewn several medals and other mystic symbols. His hand is upon a sword. He is called in German and Italian Führer and Duce; in our language Tyrant or Dictator."

Woolf's fears came true with the outbreak of World War II in 1939. She survived the terrifying bombing raids and threat of German invasion during the Battle of Britain. But she never broke free from her bouts of mental illness. On March 28, 1941, she filled her pockets with stones and drowned herself near her home. "I feel certain that I am going mad again," she had written in her suicide note. "And I shan't recover this time."

Writer and Self-Conscious Observer

Connecting People & Society

1. Why do you think Virginia Woolf described herself as "fundamentally an outsider"?

2. Why do you think Woolf has won renown as a great writer and leading feminist?

3. What connections are there between Woolf's ideas and historical developments in the decades after World War I?

nations, most of which emerged from the dissolution of the Austro-Hungarian Empire during World War I with new democratic regimes, turn away from parliamentary democracy?

Part of the answer may be that the newly created nations in this area faced enormous economic problems. Although the old Austro-Hungarian Empire had suffered from ethnic and political divisions, it had functioned as an economic whole—its industrial areas trading with its agricultural regions. Now split up, the individual nations were mostly agricultural and too unproductive to create prosperity. Only Czechoslovakia, whose parliamentary system would survive the longest, boasted an advanced industrial economy.

Struggling with these problems, the new democratic regimes seemed divided and ineffective. Many conservative groups feared the kind of change represented by liberal democracy, socialism, and communism. Such changes promised to dilute conservatives' power, diminish their economic base, and undermine their beliefs in the traditional social order. This lack of experience with democracy and the strength of these conservative groups made these nations vulnerable to authoritarian men like Horthy, who promised order and advocated nationalism backed by armed force. One by one, the democratic governments fell to authoritarian takeovers. As in Horthy's regime, the new rulers sometimes used "White Terror" to silence opponents and often repressed Jews and other minority groups.

To the south, Turkey became a republic in 1923 under the leadership of the nationalist Mustafa Kemal and displayed some of the same authoritarian characteristics. Kemal soon became known as Atatürk (Father of the Turks). Theoretically, the nation was a constitutional democracy based on universal male suffrage, but in fact, Atatürk acted as an authoritarian ruler. He secularized Turkey completely, separating the state, legal system, courts, and schools from the Muslim religious establishment. In 1934, women gained the right to vote. Many of Atatürk's reforms, including the importation of the Roman alphabet and Western clothing, were based on European models. Yet, although Kemal was a modernizer, his regime became a one-party dictatorship that promoted Atatürk—a military man who was willing to use brutality to get his way—as the all-important nationalistic hero.

This rise of authoritarian governments during the 1920s spread to the West. The most dramatic and ominous move came in Italy. There, the charismatic Benito Mussolini (1883–1945) took power, bringing with him a new governance system and ideology: **fascism.**

The Rise of Fascism in Italy

At its core, fascism in practice meant dictatorship by a charismatic leader. However, it was more than that. It included a set of antidemocratic, anti-individualistic, and anticommunist ideas or attitudes. Fascist doctrine hailed the people while denouncing the principles of the French Revolution. Fascist leaders such as Alfredo Rocco (1875–1935) viewed the state as a living organism and rejected liberal democratic forms of government, complaining that the liberal state "is dissolving into a mass of small particles, parties, associations, groups and syndicates that are binding it in chains." The fascist call was to nationalism and military prowess. In Italy, people angry and dismayed by events following World War I heard this call and followed it.

| Fascist doctrine |

Italy had emerged from World War I a battered, disappointed victor. Its armies, on the verge of collapse, had nevertheless managed to hold on and ultimately contributed to the final Allied victory. However, the Treaty of Versailles denied Italy some of the territories on the Adriatic coast that the Allies had promised in return for Italy's contribution to the war effort. Many Italians felt that at Versailles, their nation lost its rightful status as a great power. All this left Italian nationalists bitter and convinced many more Italians that the war had not been worth the price Italy had paid.

| Turmoil in Italy |

Near chaos within this troubled nation multiplied these disappointments. Italy's already weak economy staggered under a huge national debt. Its inflated currency, together with a shortage of consumer goods, made prices skyrocket. Hundreds of thousands of veterans could find no jobs. In the summer of 1919, disorder spread. Farmworkers threatened property owners by joining unions called red leagues. Veterans and poor families began seizing idle lands. Banditry in the south grew out of control, and strikes plagued the cities. During the winter of 1920–1921, workers seized control of several hundred factories. Socialists and communists gained strength within industrial and rural unions.

Italy's newly elected government, plagued by political divisions, seemed powerless in the face of these pressures. Frightened landlords and factory owners, along with thousands of veterans and a middle class ravaged by inflation and insecurity, longed for vigorous leadership and a strong, dependable government. The vigorous leader who stepped forward was Benito Mussolini. The strong government was his fascist dictatorship.

Mussolini was born into a family of socialist artisans; he received enough education to become a teacher and then a radical journalist. At

| Mussolini takes power |

the outbreak of World War I, he used the socialist paper he edited to advocate antimilitarism and to demand that Italy remain neutral during the war. A year later, he changed his mind, now convinced that "only blood makes the wheels of history turn." He broke from his socialist allies, started a new newspaper, and joined the army. After the war, he organized mostly unemployed veterans into the National Fascist Party—the term *fascist* alluding to Roman prowess, unity, and justice. His Fascist Party soon attracted enough support to bring down Italy's parliamentary government.

Why did Mussolini's political movement hold such appeal? The answer to this question is complex. Fascism attracted veterans hoping for a sense of renewal

| The appeal of Fascism |

after the disappointments of the war and the immediate postwar years and appealed to young men who felt they had missed out on the war experience and therefore responded to the call of wounded national pride. "When I returned from the war—just like so many others—I hated politics and politicians, who . . . had betrayed the hopes of soldiers, reducing Italy to a shameful peace," explained Italo Balbo, a future associate of Mussolini. These men became the members and muscle of the new party. Factory owners, merchants, and landowners also embraced fascism when Mussolini vowed to save Italy from communism. These groups provided Mussolini with money when he organized squads of black-shirted Fascisti to terrorize radical workers and their liberal supporters. Finally, those who blamed the parliamentary government for Italy's postwar woes warmed to fascist promises to act decisively and create unity through nationalistic policies. Fascism seemed to offer a third way—a path above socialism and conventional parliamentary democracy—to security and success for Italy.

Figure 23.6 reveals some of the qualities that made Mussolini's Fascist movement attractive. Mussolini

FIGURE 23.6 Mussolini and His Black Shirts Mussolini and his Black Shirt followers raise their arms in a military salute, capturing the flavor of Italian fascism.

stands on a platform dressed in a white paramilitary uniform, his arm raised in the Fascist salute of exaggerated bravery. Below him stands his bodyguard of black-shirted party members in their paramilitary uniforms, holding knives up in the disciplined salute. All are posing for the crowd of onlookers to the left and photographers. The whole scene has been self-consciously set up to present an image of strong leadership and military prowess, and it suggests the appeal of ritual and participation in a mighty movement. Similar scenes would become common as fascist movements and authoritarian governments spread across Europe.

In 1922, building on this support, squads of black-shirted Fascists marched on Rome under Mussolini's vow that "either we are allowed to govern or we will seize power." The indecisive Italian king Victor Emmanuel III (r. 1900–1946) buckled under the pressure and appointed Mussolini prime minister. With great speed, the Fascist leader acquired extraordinary powers.

Between 1924 and 1926, Mussolini turned his office into a dictatorship. Under his rule, only the Fascist Party could engage in organized political activity. Il Duce (the leader)

| The Fascist system |

sent his secret police everywhere. "Everything within the State," he demanded, and "Nothing outside the State." Mussolini next struck a deal with the powerful Catholic Church and signed the Lateran Treaty of 1929. In return for money and the right to teach religion in the public schools, the papacy finally recognized the existence of the Italian state. The agreement ended the sixty years of division between the church and the state since unification.

To guide Italy's economy toward self-sufficiency and industrialization while carefully protecting private property and profits, the Fascists worked closely with business leaders. They organized the different industries and trades into confederations, or corporations. Each corporation included a syndicate of workers and one of employers, each in turn headed by a Fascist official. The Fascists also abolished all independent labor unions, strikes, and lockouts. Instead, compulsory arbitration under the party's direction now settled issues of wages and working conditions and disputes between labor and management. The complicated economic and political machinery that Mussolini put in motion for these purposes became known as the corporate state, or corporatism.

Although the state would gain a controlling hand in several major industries, Mussolini's corporate state mainly enlarged the bureaucracy and hamstrung workers' unions. A few well-publicized achievements, such as new railroads, highways, building projects, and educational reforms, hid more fundamental deficiencies. His ambitious agricultural policies generally failed to improve per capita output. People of property fared well, but workers, especially women, suffered declining income. Even though women flocked to hear him, Mussolini cut their wages by decree and banned them from several professions. Those who did not heed his call to take up their maternal duties were pushed toward low-paying jobs. Nevertheless, growing numbers of Italian women still managed to enter universities and find positions in the world of paid work.

By 1929, Mussolini stood unchallenged. Using films, radio addresses, biographies, newspapers, and schools, he amassed a huge following of supporters who repeated his reassuring phrase "Mussolini is always right." Some artists and intellectuals supported at least his image of dynamic leadership. Mussolini also won a reputation among groups throughout Europe, South America, and the United States as someone who could "make the trains run on time," gain peace with the Catholic Church, and stand up to communist threats.

In reality, Mussolini—like many twentieth-century politicians—was more of an actor able to manipulate appearances than an effective ruler who could solve domestic or international problems. Many people immune to his charm saw him as merely a strutting, boasting carnival performer. Mussolini's vision of historical destiny—to create a Second Roman Empire and turn the Mediterranean into an Italian lake—perhaps most revealed a disturbing lack of touch with reality. Even with Il Duce in control, Italy was no major power.

To the east, the situation was entirely different. Russia had been a major power and might well rise again. Now transformed into a communist state and reformed into the Soviet Union by the Bolsheviks, its radical left-wing policies represented an even more frightening threat to capitalist democracies than the extreme right-wing politics of Italian Fascism.

TRANSFORMING THE SOVIET UNION, 1920–1939

In 1920, Russia's bloody civil war had finally ended. The suffering, however, dragged on. Industrial production sank to only 13 percent of pre–World War I levels. A famine struck, taking four to seven million lives. Countless thousands of veterans and city dwellers roamed the countryside in search of food, shelter, and employment. "Green Armies" of peasants revolted against forced requisitions of their crops and restrictions against selling products at market prices. Workers struck against declining wages and lack of control over the factories. Sailors at the Kronstadt naval base mutinied, demanding political liberty. Many Communist Party and union members called for more democracy. How could Lenin's still vulnerable Communist government survive?

Lenin's Compromise: The NEP

Lenin retreated. In 1921 he launched the **New Economic Policy (NEP),** a "temporary" compromise with capitalism. This policy allowed peasants to manage their own land and sell their own crops. In addition, small-scale industries could operate under private ownership, and money and credit were restored. Although the state still supervised the economy, the NEP provided enough capitalist incentive to pull the Russian economy out of chaos.

Lenin's retreat did not extend to politics, however. Russia remained a "dictatorship of the proletariat," symbolized on Russia's flag by the red of socialism, the hammer of industrial workers, and the sickle of peasants. Lenin and the Communist Party elite maintained a tight grip on power and brutally suppressed any opposition. Local soviets submitted to the central government in Moscow, dominated by its 16-person Politburo and, above all, the secretariat of the Communist Party. The formal creation of the Union of Soviet Socialist Republics (USSR, or Soviet Union) in 1922 paid only lip service to desires for autonomy in "republics" such as the Ukraine, Armenia, and Georgia. Russia, home to four-fifths of the USSR's total population, dominated the Union.

Soviet society in the 1920s reflected its revolutionary origins as well as the temporary compromise with capitalism. The Communists had eliminated the old aristocracy, church, and traditional class distinctions. But party, military, and cultural elites enjoyed higher standards of living, better housing, and more educational opportunities than anyone else. Some peasants who took advantage of NEP opportunities also became relatively wealthy, as did their urban counterparts running small businesses.

Moreover, women enjoyed unprecedented legal equality. In addition to the right to vote, they received the right to equal pay, education, and professional opportunities. The government set up programs and agencies such as the Women's Bureau to promote equality, day care, housing, medical care, and information on birth control and divorce. Alexandra Kollontai (1872–1952), head of the Women's Bureau, urged collectivization of child rearing and a new family form: "The narrow and exclusive affection of the mother for her own children must expand until it embraces all the children of the great proletarian family. In place of the indissoluble marriage based on the servitude of woman, we shall see rise in the free union [of two people] . . . equal in their rights and in their obligations. . . ."

These new policies all showed promise, but in fact the burdens on Soviet women probably increased. Programs to help them lacked the resources to make a real difference. Greater access to jobs rarely translated into higher-level positions. Women were still expected to retain their traditional burdens at home, their "second shift."

Although the NEP was a retreat from strict Communist policies, Lenin's regime still envisioned itself as leading the world into modernity. The government turned churches and great mansions into museums and meeting halls. Cultural activities promoted proletarian pride, the benefits of technology, and the glories of the future. Avant-garde artists created utopian visions by connecting images of mass production and social justice.

The NEP may have encouraged the outside world to end its isolation of Russia. Between 1922 and 1924, all Western nations recognized the Soviet Union except the United States, which remained aloof until 1933. Indeed, to many socialists throughout the West, the Soviet Union stood as a source of hope and inspiration.

The Struggle to Succeed Lenin

Lenin would not live to witness the results of the NEP. After a series of paralytic strokes, he died in 1924. Three of his chief associates—Leon Trotsky (1879–1940), Nikolai Bukharin (1888–1938), and Joseph Stalin (1879–1953)—jockeyed to succeed him. Most observers assumed that the brilliant but arrogant Trotsky, who had led the Red Army during the civil war, would win. He argued that the Soviet Union must promote revolutions elsewhere in the West to survive and that the Soviet economy should

be tightly controlled and massively industrialized from above. By contrast, the popular Bukharin, who had been appointed by Lenin to lead the NEP, argued for socialism by slow, careful steps. The shrewd political manipulator Stalin claimed a middle-of-the-road position between these two but believed that Russia must survive alone—"socialism in one country." His opponents vastly underestimated him.

Stalin (a pseudonym meaning "man of steel") was born in Georgia the son of poverty-stricken ex-serfs. His mother managed to get him into an Orthodox seminary school, where he received a formal education. Expelled from the seminary because of his Marxist views, he joined revolutionary groups. Repeatedly arrested, he kept managing to escape. In 1917, he took advantage of the revolutionary turmoil and hastened to Petrograd from his exile in Siberia. A poor speaker and writer, he used daring and organizational talents to rise in the party. He played a prominent role in Russia's civil war and became executive secretary of the Communist Party. In this key position, he made himself master of the all-important party machinery and pursued his drive for power.

Joseph Stalin

Toward the end of his life, Lenin warned that "Stalin is too rude" to lead. Nevertheless, after Lenin's death, Stalin cleverly played on the Soviet people's love of Lenin by posing as his heir and leading a movement to deify him. He also brought into the party new people, who thereby owed him a debt. Playing his rivals against each other, he used his control over the Central Committee of the Communist Party to edge the overconfident Trotsky and his supporters on the Left out of powerful positions and, in 1927, expel them from the party. The next year, he turned against Bukharin and the Right. Party members who had doubts about Stalin accepted the need for party loyalty. By the end of 1928, Stalin had maneuvered himself into a position of dominance over the Communist Party and of dictatorship over the Soviet Union. Now he set out to transform the nation.

Stalin's Five-Year Plans

By 1928, Soviet industry had probably attained little more than 1913 levels of production. Stalin and his party leadership wanted much more. That year, he ended the NEP and launched the First **Five-Year Plan**. The fundamental goal of the plan could not have been more ambitious: "We do not want to be beaten. . . . Old Russia . . . was ceaselessly beaten for her backwardness. . . . We are fifty or a hundred years behind the advanced countries. We must make good this lag in ten years . . . or they crush us." The plan called for the rapid, massive industrialization of the nation. Goals included more than doubling industrial production, increasing the generation of electric

FIGURE 23.7 *The Five-Year Plan in Four Years,* 1930s This propaganda poster portrays Stalin as leading efforts to industrialize the Soviet Union rapidly. He faces the old "enemies" of the Communist Party.

power almost fivefold, and building 1,500 new factories within five years. To achieve the goals, the State Planning Commission, or Gosplan, would strictly regulate all aspects of production, including targeting crucial industries such as steel, regimenting the industrial labor force, and hiring foreign engineers to help build the new factories. The 1930s Soviet propaganda poster shown in **Figure 23.7,** "The Five-Year Plan in Four Years," portrays the idea that Stalin will lead Soviet industrial development against the threatening reactionary forces of capitalism and religion. As if preparing for another war, Stalin ordered the USSR's entire society to mobilize for industrialization.

To help accomplish the Five-Year Plan's goals (which included doubling agricultural production),

Collectivization

the state took agriculture out of the control of individual peasants by consolidating their lands into huge collective farms that used modern machines. Elected managers and party officials ran the farms. Individuals could own tools, keep small gardens for fruits and vegetables, and raise pigs and chickens for private use or sale. By determining prices and distribution of crops, the state expected to use agricultural "surpluses" to pay for industrialization—to buy the equipment to build factories, transportation facilities, and power plants. **Collectivization,** it was believed, would also push peasants to become industrial workers in the cities.

As Document 23.2 suggests, the process of collectivization proved ruinous. Hundreds of thousands of peasants, especially wealthier landowners derisively called kulaks, powerfully resisted the new policies. In protest, they even destroyed their own crops

and livestock—some 50 percent of horses and cattle between 1929 and 1933. Officials terrorized such resisters into submission. "The expropriation of the kulaks is an integral part of the formation . . . of the collective farms," announced Stalin. The kulaks should be "eliminated as a class." Hundreds of thousands of peasants were killed and far more were exiled to Siberia, never to return. This violent battle of wills was accompanied by plummeting agricultural production and government pressure to increase agricultural exports at all costs to finance industrialization. The results were disastrous: Between 1930 and 1933, famine struck, taking the lives of four to six million people. An observer reported that in Ukrainian villages, peasants resorted to eating "dogs, horses, rotten potatoes, the bark of trees, grass—anything they could find . . . and no matter what they did, they went on dying, dying, dying." The effort to collectivize agriculture and the deadly hunger tore apart rural families, communities, and established ways of life. Nevertheless, Stalin finally got his way: More than half the land was collectivized within the first year, and over 90 percent after ten years. As one Communist Party worker put it, "It took a famine to show them who is master here. It has cost millions of lives, but the collective farm system is here to stay."

To industrialize the Soviet Union, planners had to start almost from ground level and build up. They concentrated on producer goods such as engines and tractors rather than consumer goods such as shoes and clothes. Gradually, steel mills, dams,

Mobilizing for industrialization

power plants, foundries, mines, refineries, chemical factories, and railroads appeared all over the Soviet Union. Technocrats and officials faced pressure to produce targeted results. The government fostered a sense of emergency to inspire people, especially the young, to work hard. Presenting the effort as a great adventure, officials pointed out that those who most contributed to the industrialization drive could achieve a status similar to that of the heroes of the 1917 revolution. The government moved "shock brigades" of enthusiastic, efficient workers from factory to factory to stimulate production, while the press celebrated new "Heroes of Labor" who exceeded production targets. Officials encouraged women to work both on the collective farms and in factories; by 1940, women made up almost half the labor force.

All elements of Soviet society were mobilized to support the effort to make the USSR an industrial power. Schools, adult education classes, newspapers, union meetings, and youth associations became saturated with official doctrines of Soviet communism, efficiency, and class pride. "We must make every school child aware of . . . how the great people of

DOCUMENT 23.2

Stalin Collectivizes Agriculture

As part of his campaign to collectivize agriculture, Stalin used massive coercion against the Russian kulaks (relatively rich independent peasants). Widespread destruction and death resulted. In the following excerpt, Lev Kopelev recounts his own participation in this collectivization drive.

A team consisting of several young kolkhozniks [collective farmers] and members of the village soviet . . . would search the hut, barn, yard, and take away all the stores of seed, lead away the cow, the horse, the pigs.

In some cases they would be merciful and leave some potatoes, peas, corn for feeding the family. But the stricter ones would make a clean sweep. They would take not only the food and livestock, but also "all valuables and surpluses of clothing," including icons in their frames, samovars, painted carpets and even metal kitchen utensils which might

be silver. And any money they found stashed away. Special instructions ordered the removal of gold, silver and currency. . . .

We were raised as the fanatical [believers] of a new creed, the only true *religion* of scientific socialism. The party became our church militant, bequeathing to all mankind eternal salvation, eternal peace and the bliss of an earthly paradise. It victoriously surmounted all other churches, schisms and heresies. The works of Marx, Engels and Lenin were accepted as holy writ, and Stalin was the infallible high priest.

. . . Stalin was the most perspicacious, the most wise (at that time they hadn't yet started calling him "great" and "brilliant"). He said: "The struggle for grain is the struggle for socialism." And we believed him unconditionally. And later we believed that unconditional collectivization was unavoidable if we were to overcome the capriciousness and uncertainty of

the market and the backwardness of individual farming, to guarantee a steady supply of grain, milk and meat to the cities. And also if we were to reeducate millions of peasants, those petty landowners and hence potential bourgeoisie, potential kulaks, to transform them into laborers with a social conscience, to liberate them from "the idiocy of country life," from ignorance and prejudice, and to accustom them to culture, to all the boons of socialism. . . .

SOURCE: Lev Kopelev, *The Education of a True Believer* (New York: Harper & Row, 1980), p. 123.

Analyze the Document

1. Why was this aspect of collectivization so devastating?

2. How does Kopelev justify his participation in the drive?

3. What insights into Soviet life during the early 1930s does this document provide?

---

our epoch—Lenin, Stalin, and their companions in arms—organized the workers in the struggle for a new and happy life," explained a Soviet text on teaching methods. Officials, minor bureaucrats, and members of the secret police ranged everywhere and monitored progress. Within families—the "school for socialism"—mothers were urged to raise their children to fit into communist society. Earlier policies supporting women's choices were reversed. The state made abortion illegal and promoted traditional marriage and relationships. In this more repressive era, homosexuality became a crime.

The state also tightened controls over cultural productions, ending the experimentation of the 1920s. The Central Committee of the Communist Party told publishing houses that "books must be an instrument for the mobilization of the workers for the tasks of industrialization and collectivization." A government ministry took control over filmmaking to make sure movies promoted revolutionary enthusiasm and favorable views of the communist state. Socialist realism became the required orthodoxy in art. In this style, approved murals, art, and literature portrayed realistic images of people carrying out the dreams of a communist society. **Figure 23.8** is an example of this effort

to make art relevant and compelling to the working masses. In this idealized image, an older man (reminiscent of an aged Lenin) shows a boy the achievements of Stalin's programs. Above the two smiling figures is a well-known nineteenth-century painting of poverty-stricken peasants and workers hauling a ship up a river by ropes. By contrast, the new social reality can be seen outside the window, where steamships haul barges up a river and in the distance modern facilities attest to the creation of modern industry. The eager boy, in a comradely embrace, wears the uniform of a Stalinist youth organization and represents the glowing future.

THE SOVIET UNION

1918–1920	Civil war
1920–1921	Famine
1924	Death of Lenin
1928	Beginning of First Five-Year Plan
1930–1933	Famine
1934	Beginning of Great Purges

KEY DATES

FIGURE 23.8 Promises of Soviet Society, 1930s This poster shows an idealized scene of Soviet accomplishments and announces, "People's Dreams Have Come True!"

At the end of 1932, Stalin announced that all goals of the First Five-Year Plan had been accomplished several months ahead of time. He recited a list of accomplishments in iron, steel, tractors, automobiles, machine tools, chemicals, and aircraft production. "Our country has been converted from an agrarian into an industrial country," he proclaimed. These gains, however, came at a high price. For the hard-pressed workers, consumer goods beyond the necessities remained scarce. Clearly, some Soviet citizens—namely, party members—benefited more than others. One refugee cynically compared life before and after the Bolshevik Revolution: "In Tsarist times there were the rich and the poor; under Soviet power there were the party members and the nonparty members." Similar Second and Third Five-Year Plans would follow, this time with more emphasis on consumer goods and armaments. The terrifying Great Purges would also follow.

Blood and Terror: The Great Purges

In 1934, Leonid Nikolayev assassinated Sergei Kirov (1888–1934), a high Soviet official. Stalin used the murder as an excuse to eliminate potential rivals. The incident introduced a long period of party purges, marked by terror, house arrests, bizarre show-trials, torture, imprisonments, and executions—all approved by Stalin.

Historians still debate Stalin's motives for the **Great Purges.** Stalin and party officials blamed difficulties during the five-year plans on many—engineers, technocrats, army officers, older party members, regional nationalists, foreign conspirators, saboteurs—and purged the accused. Lower-level officials probably contributed to the waves of purges by trying to rise at the expense of higher-level officials. Stalin himself was extremely suspicious. He saw enemies everywhere. Certainly he worried about threats from within the party. He eradicated all potential opposition—real or imagined, and even on foreign soil. In 1940, Soviet agents assassinated Trotsky in Mexico.

By the time the Great Purges ended in 1939, authorities had killed some one million people. Another seven million died or languished in forced-labor camps; still more had been sent into exile. The terror spread throughout Soviet society, for everyone knew of someone accused and arrested. Almost all the original Bolshevik leaders and the Red Army's top officer corps were gone. New, younger figures beholden to Stalin now staffed the government, the Communist Party, and the military.

In the end, Stalin got most of what he wanted. By 1939, the Soviet Union had a fully planned economy, with the state determining production, prices, and distribution. Although officials announced successes whether they occurred or not, the USSR had in fact become the third-greatest industrial power in the world. More than 90 percent of peasants lived on collective, mechanized farms. Millions more had moved to the cities, where new housing, schools, libraries, and hospitals had sprung up. For the first time, most of the population could read. Within the Soviet Union, no one dared oppose Stalin, and now he had the armaments to face a new challenge already rising in the west. But the cost had been tremendous. Between 15 and 20 million people (some scholars argue that the figure might be much higher) had died from starvation, execution, or the harsh conditions in forced-labor camps, and far more had suffered as a result of Stalin's policies.

THE GREAT DEPRESSION,
1929–1939

The forces to the west creating that challenge to the USSR had begun to coalesce and gather momentum, and the Soviets were not the only ones threatened by them. As we saw earlier, authoritarianism and fascism—fierce opponents of communism—had already started to rise in the 1920s. In 1929, a new crisis struck the Western democracies: the **Great Depression.** Reeling from years of hard times and pulling much of the world with them, Western societies began edging toward a new darkness that would more than rival the horrors of World War I.

Crash!

In October 1929, the New York stock market crashed. In one month, stocks lost almost two-thirds of their value. The financial crisis quickly spread from the United States, the world's leading industrial nation and creditor, to Europe, where nations depended heavily on American loans and trade. The crash ended the relative prosperity since 1924 and provoked an unprecedented global depression. Within two years, thousands of banks and businesses throughout the West failed. Spending, production, employment, and income all dropped sharply. Plant closings, farm foreclosures, and joblessness haunted the Western nations. People's confidence in the economy died, and too often with it went their faith in themselves.

A complex series of events had led to the disaster. The postwar economic order was built on a fragile foundation of international credit, reparations payments, and foreign trade. Much of Europe remained dependent on the United States for credit. Germany in particular relied on American loans to support its reparation payments.

Causes of the economic collapse

In 1928, American investors began pulling their money out of Germany and demanding repayment of loans to invest in the unregulated, soaring U.S. stock market. Credit dried up in Germany and in east-central European nations tied to the German economy. The 1929 crash sent people running to banks to withdraw funds, further undermining credit. Soon the West's entire economic house of cards collapsed.

The collapse took much of the globe with it. Over the years, non-Western lands had become important suppliers of raw materials—such as rice, cotton, cocoa, rubber, oil, copper, and tin—for Western industry and urban populations. With their economies more and more dependent on international trade, these regions were now tied to the economic fate of the West. Ties to the West particularly marked industrialized Japan's economy. The lure of increasing trade with the United States during the 1920s had persuaded Japan to halt its imperial expansion in Asia. The Great Depression—which quickly slashed exports to the United States in half and left three million people unemployed—brought an end to Japan's prosperity and revived its imperial ambitions.

Effects in non-Western lands

Japan's leaders looked to make East Asian markets their own, by conquest if necessary.

In the Teeth of the Depression

By 1932, Europe's economies had shrunk to one-half their 1929 size. Unemployment in the West rose to a shocking 22 percent, leaving 30 million people out of work. Along with their jobs, people lost their savings, their farms, and their homes. In Germany, Heinrich Hauser described how "an almost unbroken chain of homeless men extends the whole length of the great Hamburg-Berlin highway." One British woman echoed the feelings of many: "These last few years since I've been out of the mills . . . I've got no spirit for anything." Masses of people sank into poverty, and malnutrition and diseases spread. Families suffered from new tensions as men lost their traditional role as breadwinners. "When he was out of work," lamented a woman from Liverpool, "we were always having rows over the children."

Scenes of despair could be found everywhere. **Figure 23.9,** a painting by Isaac Soyer, shows people in a New York employment agency. Their faces reveal little hope as they wait—reading a newspaper, looking away in distraction, or staring ahead in resignation. The dreary room offers no consolation, and the scene through the window suggests there is little to look forward to on the city streets.

In eastern and central Europe, hard-pressed farmers and unemployed workers looked for scapegoats. They blamed Jews, whom they saw as controlling the

FIGURE 23.9 Isaac Soyer, *Employment Agency*, 1937 Despair among unemployed workers such as these in the United States became common as the Great Depression wore on.

banks, bureaucracy, jobs, and policies responsible for the depression. People also pointed their fingers at socialists, communists, big business, and even modernity. Ethnic groups and major powers turned on one another, and throughout the West, popular protests by desperate, angry people spread.

Searching for Solutions

At first, governments met the depression the old way: by balancing the budget and increasing tariffs on imported goods. However, these policies just made matters worse by dampening spending and hindering trade. A moratorium on reparations and war debts in August 1931 came too late to do much good. Imperial powers such as Britain and France turned to their colonial holdings for secure trade and profits, only to meet rising demands for independence in India, Iraq, Vietnam, Algeria, and elsewhere. The British economist John Maynard Keynes (1883–1946) argued for new policies—more government expenditures financed by budget deficits to stimulate consumer spending and raise employment—but few listened to his still little-known ideas.

After 1932, new regimes in the United States, Britain, and Germany adopted policies to increase government spending and provide some relief. Similar policies had already enabled Scandinavian democracies to weather the depression with relative ease. However, even with these measures, most Western democracies recovered slowly and not fully until the late 1930s, thanks to spending for rearmament. **Figure 23.10** indicates that France and the United States in particular had difficulty raising industrial production to figures approaching pre-1929 levels. By then, these democracies faced new threats that made even the anxious 1920s look like "roaring"

good times. The most ominous menace came from Germany.

NAZISM IN GERMANY

In 1928, Germany's fascist party, the Nazis (National Socialists), won less than 3 percent of the vote in national elections. Five years later, the party and its leader, Adolf Hitler, gained power and ended German democracy—all through legal means. How did this happen?

The Young Adolf Hitler

The story of Nazism's rise begins with the life of Adolf Hitler (1889–1945). Hitler was born to a middle-aged Austrian customs official and his much younger wife. When his father died in 1905, Hitler quit school and traveled to Vienna, where he hoped to become an artist or architect. Denied admission to the art academy, he lived on his orphan's pension, selling postcards and hanging wallpaper. He compulsively followed daily routines and would do so for the rest of his life. He also picked up nationalistic, anti-Semitic, and racist ideas circulating in Vienna that he embraced with deadly seriousness.

When World War I broke out, Hitler "thanked heaven out of an overflowing heart." For this ardent German nationalist, here was a righteous crusade to end a life of drifting. He served as a courier in the German army and was decorated three times. War's end found him in a hospital recovering from a poison gas attack. He revered World War I as "the greatest of all experiences." As for Germany's defeat at the end of the conflict, he blamed Jews and Marxists, who he felt sure had "stabbed Germany in the back."

The Birth of Nazism in Germany's Postwar Years

Hitler spotted opportunities in Germany's turbulent postwar years. Several right-wing groups had formed that offered extreme solutions to Germany's problems and that threatened the newly formed parliamentary government of the Weimar Republic. In 1919, while working in Munich as an informer for the army, Hitler joined one of those groups—the German Workers' Party. A year later, he rose to leadership in the party and renamed it the National Socialist German Workers' Party, or the **Nazi Party** (despite the party's name, it was neither socialist in the traditional sense nor well supported by urban workers). Hitler also organized a paramilitary wing—the SA "stormtroopers"—to back the party. Copying Mussolini's techniques, the SA troopers wore brown shirts and carried pagan symbols (the swastika). They marched through the streets,

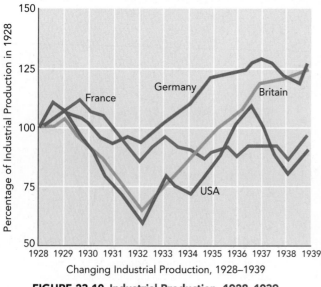

Changing Industrial Production, 1928–1939

FIGURE 23.10 Industrial Production, 1928–1939

sang patriotic songs, and beat up communists, socialists, and anyone else they considered their opponents.

Nothing yet marked this small group as destined for success. Nevertheless, in 1923 Hitler and the popular war hero Field Marshal Ludendorff made an ambitious grab for power. From a beer hall in Munich, the Nazis marched on the local government. Republican troops easily put down this "Beer Hall Putsch," and Hitler, after a highly publicized trial, spent nearly a year in jail. While in prison, he wrote *Mein Kampf* (*My Struggle*), a work that set forth the core of his Nazi doctrine.

Nazism, like other brands of fascism, assaulted the liberal, democratic tradition in the West. According to Nazi doctrine, the political order should be dominated by a single party headed by a dictatorial leader (Hitler) who appealed to the masses. In addition, the doctrine reflected the sense among many Germans of being haunted by defeat in World War I and "humiliated" by the settlement that followed, and it fostered the belief that Germany therefore should rearm and redress the "injustices" of the Versailles treaty. At the center of Hitler's beliefs lurked biological racism and anti-Semitism. He glorified the mythical German "Aryan race" as superior and destined to conquer all other peoples in the struggle for racial supremacy. He also condemned the Jews as corrupt, landless parasites who created Marxist communism, caused Germany's humiliating defeat in World War I, and propagated liberalism. Underlying this element of the Nazi doctrine was a sense that everything in politics and in life was a constant struggle between peoples. Perils and enemies—whether from Jews, Poles, Bolsheviks, or others—lurked everywhere, plotting Germany's destruction. These fears seemed to justify ambitions to conquer the Slavic people to the east, to gain living space (*Lebensraum*), and to follow policies to rid Germany of all opponents.

Nazi doctrine

The Growth of the Nazi Party

Hitler exited jail in 1924 determined to acquire power from within, legally. Between 1925 and 1929, the Nazi Party grew in numbers somewhat but still remained a small splinter group. Then in October 1929, Germany's foreign minister, Gustav Stresemann, whose effective leadership for five years held center parties of the Weimar Republic together, died. That same month, the New York stock market crashed. Soon the Great Depression had Germany in its grip. It spelled the end of American loans and ignited unemployment and panic. Internal divisions immobilized parliamentary government, and the political extremes on both the Left and Right rapidly gained strength.

In 1930, the aged president Paul Hindenburg, Germany's military commander during World War I and no friend to democracy, authorized rule by decree over Germany's unstable parliament. In elections held that year, the Nazis won a startling 18.3 percent of the vote—up from 2.6 percent in 1928. Hindenburg turned to conservative politicians to lead the republic, but they failed to govern effectively. The moderates, socialists, and communists, for their part, could not unify into a strong political force. In 1932, the Nazi Party became the largest political organization in Germany, winning an astonishing 37.3 percent of the vote. In elections for the office of president, Hitler gained 13.5 million votes against Hindenburg's 19 million.

The Appeal of Nazism

Nazism offered certainty to confused, frightened people; a sense of emotional belonging and unity in a time of crisis and anxiety; and action in a time of political immobility and conflict. Hitler and the doctrine of Nazism captured the imaginations of many Germans, especially young people and displaced veterans eager to achieve some measure of social stature in the new elite. Indeed, Hitler presented Nazism as "the organized will of the youth." For some, this included the appeal of being part of a street gang. He also appealed to the millions of Germans—the lower-middle class in particular—who had been traumatized by the Great Depression.

Much of Hitler's appeal stemmed from the alluring promises he made—promises that offered comfort and reassurance to a people in desperate need. He claimed that he would get rid of the despised war reparations, economic hardship, incompetent leadership, threats from the Left, and parliamentary government. In addition, he vowed to restore national unity and order in Germany and revive both the German people's shattered pride and their military might. Document 23.3 suggests how Hitler and the Nazi Party used nationalism and anti-Semitism to gain support.

To wealthy industrial leaders and landowners who feared the growing strength of unions, socialists, and communists, Hitler and his party held less of a personal attraction. Instead, Nazism represented the lesser of two distasteful options in the minds of these groups. Many such people who voted for the Nazis did so as a way to vote *against* the Weimar Republic, the terms of the Versailles treaty, and the communist path, rather than *for* the Nazi ideology. Indeed, most of these Germans probably would have preferred to elect more traditional conservatives, but none of the existing candidates passed muster.

Whatever the appeal, those drawn to Hitler and the Nazis either ignored the party's strident nationalism, racism, and anti-Semitic fervor or embraced those sentiments. After all, such calls had been heard throughout central and eastern Europe for decades.

DOCUMENT 23.3

Goebbels's Nazi Propaganda Pamphlet

Propaganda was strongly emphasized by the Nazis as a method of acquiring and maintaining power. Joseph Goebbels (1897–1945), an early leader in the Nazi Party, was made chief of propaganda in 1929, minister for propaganda and national enlightenment in 1933, and a member of Hitler's cabinet council in 1938. The following is an excerpt from a 1930 pamphlet, written by Goebbels, describing why the Nazis are nationalists and against Jews.

WHY ARE WE NATIONALISTS?

We are NATIONALISTS because we see in the NATION the only possibility for the protection and the furtherance of our existence.

The NATION is the organic bond of a people for the protection and defense of their lives. He is nationally minded who understands this IN WORD AND IN DEED.

Today, in GERMANY, NATIONALISM has degenerated into BOURGEOIS PATRIOTISM, and its power exhausts itself in tilting at windmills. It says GERMANY and means MONARCHY.

It proclaims FREEDOM and means BLACK-WHITE-RED.

WE ARE NATIONALISTS BECAUSE WE, AS GERMANS, LOVE GERMANY. And because we love Germany, we demand the protection of its national spirit and we battle against its destroyers.

***

WHY DO WE OPPOSE THE JEWS?

We are the ENEMIES OF THE JEWS, because we are fighters for the freedom of the German people. THE JEW IS THE CAUSE AND THE BENEFICIARY OF OUR MISERY. He has used the social difficulties of the broad masses of our people to deepen the unholy split between Right and Left among our people. He has made two halves of Germany. He is the real cause for our loss of the Great War.

The Jew has no interest in the solution of Germany's fateful problems. He CANNOT have any. FOR HE LIVES ON THE FACT THAT THERE HAS BEEN NO SOLUTION. If we would make the German people a unified community and give them freedom before the world, then the Jew can have no place among us. He has the best trumps in his hands when a people lives in inner and outer slavery. THE JEW IS RESPONSIBLE FOR OUR MISERY AND HE LIVES ON IT. . . .

WE ARE ENEMIES OF THE JEWS BECAUSE WE BELONG TO THE GERMAN PEOPLE. THE JEW IS OUR GREATEST MISFORTUNE.

It is not true that we eat a Jew every morning at breakfast.

It is true, however, the he SLOWLY BUT SURELY ROBS US OF EVERYTHING WE OWN.

THAT WILL STOP, AS SURELY AS WE ARE GERMANS.

SOURCE: From Louis L. Snyder, *The Weimar Republic.* Reprinted by permission of D. Van Nostrand Co. (New York, 1966), pp. 201–203. Copyright © 1966 by Litton Educational Publishing, Inc.

Analyze the Document

1. How does this document reflect the character of life in Germany during the 1920s?

2. To whom was this document designed to appeal? Give evidence for your answer.

3. In what ways might this excerpt be a convincing piece of propaganda?

However, many Germans failed to detect the especially virulent quality of the Nazis' version of these feelings. Even experienced politicians never saw the danger in the situation. In fact, some conservative leaders, such as Franz von Papen, supported Hitler under the assumption that they could control him. As they would discover, they were greatly mistaken.

Hitler Takes Power

In January 1933, President Hindenburg offered Hitler the chancellorship, and the Nazi leader accepted. Jubilant stormtroopers marched through Berlin's streets, holding their blazing torches high. In his new position, Hitler immediately called for another round of parliamentary elections. Now in official control of the state police and the agencies of information, the Nazis used propaganda and terror to confuse and frighten voters. As Hitler explained it, "Terror at the place of employment, in the factory, in the meeting hall, and on the occasion of mass demonstrations will always be successful."

Five days before the elections, Hitler discredited the communists by accusing them of burning the Reichstag building. He used the fire to justify the suspension of civil liberties and the arrest of many communists. On election day, the Nazis gained 44 percent of the vote; with their nationalist allies, they now had enough for a majority. The Reichstag quickly passed an enabling act granting Hitler the power to make laws on his own for four years. He soon outlawed all other political parties, and when Hindenburg died in 1934, Hitler became the sole leader of the German government. That same year, Hitler ordered Heinrich Himmler (1900–1945) and a handpicked private armed force, the elite **SS,** to "blood purge" his own paramilitary organization, the SA. Hitler saw the leader of the SA, Ernst Röhm (1887–1934) as a rival with plans to establish control over the army. That Night of the Long Knives eliminated potential opponents to Hitler within the party and the powerful SA as a rival to the reviving German army. Now the army swore allegiance to Hitler. The Nazi leader's dictatorship was complete.

Life in Nazi Germany

His power consolidated, Hitler proceeded to turn Germany into a police state. The government abolished freedom of speech, press, and assembly. An elaborate and all-powerful secret police, the Gestapo, uncovered and destroyed opposition. Nazi officials took over top positions in the government and pressured churches to conform to the new order. Professional organizations of doctors, teachers, lawyers, and engineers were transformed into Nazi associations. Officials even pushed people into joining Nazi leisure-time organizations.

The Nazis set out to bring family and private life under their control. As one step, the German Women's Bureau established guidelines for "proper" womanhood. Women, the bureau proclaimed, 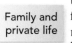 belonged at home, where they could fulfill their primary duties as homemakers, as subordinates to their husbands, and as producers of children. According to Guida Diehl, the leader of a pro-Nazi women's organization, "A woman's honor rests on the province specifically entrusted to her . . . love, marriage, family, motherhood. . . . The German man wants to know . . . that it is worthwhile to live and die for such German womanhood." Officials launched campaigns to honor and reward pregnant women, prevent birth control, and improve racial stock. The government provided subsidies for large, racially German families. Women who gave birth to more than four children received the bronze Honor Cross of the German Mother; more than six warranted a silver medal, and more than eight, the coveted gold. In 1937, the Nazi Art Council of the Reich demanded that painters cease depicting families with only two children. A new program in 1938 went so far as to encourage SS soldiers to breed children with "racially fit" women outside of marriage.

Nazi youth organizations such as the Hitler Youth and the League of German Girls expanded rapidly, absorbing the majority of teenage boys and girls by the late 1930s. Boys were molded into Nazi supporters with military values and sometimes encouraged to spy on their teachers and parents. "I don't want an intellectual education" for

FIGURE 23.11 Adolf Hitler at Buckeberg, 1934 Carefully organized mass rallies such as this one from the mid-1930s helped create a sense of belonging among the German people and increased Hitler's power.

boys, Hitler said. "They must learn in the face of the most difficult trials to conquer the fear of death for my sake." Girls were trained to become housewives and mothers, which the Nazis saw as the perfect complement to the loyal, fearless German soldier.

Hitler inspired and manipulated people with his stirring, inflammatory speeches, rallies, parades, and symbols. His organizers choreographed mass meetings such as the one at Buckeberg in 1934, shown in **Figure 23.11,** to whip up excitement and a sense of belonging among the populace. In this photograph, Hitler leads a procession of Nazi elites between two lines of honor guards and swastika banners. At such rallies, Hitler made a carefully staged, dramatic entrance and delivered a long, emotionally charged speech. "It is the belief in our people that has made us small men great, that has made us poor men rich, that has made brave and courageous men out of us wavering, spiritless, timid fold," he proclaimed at the Nuremberg rally in 1936. Listeners described feeling "eternally bound to this man." The ministry of propaganda, under Joseph Goebbels (1897–1945), reinforced the psychological power of the rallies by controlling information and spreading Nazi ideology through the press, radio, films, textbooks, pamphlets, and posters. For example, the ministry commissioned Leni Riefenstahl (1902–2003) to create the documentary film *Triumph of the Will* (1935), which portrayed the Nazis and their leaders as awe inspiring and gloriously on the march. Goebbels also painted an image of Hitler as the people's heroic leader, the one who could even be trusted to limit any

thinking about
ART

FIGURE 23.12

Felix Nussbaum, *Self-Portrait with Jewish Identity Card*, 1943

This painting depicts the German artist Felix Nussbaum within prison walls and holding up his Jewish identity card. Although this painting dates to 1943, the Nazis subjected Jews in Germany, such as Nussbaum, to increasingly harsh repression during most of the 1930s.

Connecting Art *&* Society

1. What do the yellow Star of David and the identity card indicate about the evolving Nazi policy toward Jews in Germany?

2. Why might the artist have portrayed himself looking out at the painting's viewers so directly?

3. What feelings might viewers of the times have experienced upon seeing this painting?

excesses by overzealous extremists within the Nazi Party itself.

In addition to promoting enthusiasm for their leader and ideology, the Nazis attacked "decadent" modern art and the popular culture of the Jazz Age. Only those whose works conformed to Nazi tastes—usually sentimental, pro-Nazi subject matter—could exhibit, publish, or perform. Officials promoted the burning of liberal books, sometimes even those of Germany's greatest literary figures of the eighteenth and nineteenth centuries, such as

Goethe and Schiller. The Nazi minister of culture told university professors, "From now on it will *not* be your job to determine whether something is true but whether it is in the spirit of the [Nazi] revolution." Although some intellectuals and artists supported these policies, many opposed them and left Germany.

Both to solidify their power and to carry out their racist ideas, the Nazis targeted many groups for repression. For example, they sent communists, socialists, resisting Catholics, Jehovah's Witnesses, and the Roma (Gypsies) to concentration camps. Mixed-race children, criminals, prostitutes, alcoholics—all considered genetically inferior or "community aliens"—became candidates for sterilization. Homosexuality warranted at least incarceration or castration. A frightening glimpse of the future for all these groups came in 1939 when the Nazis created euthanasia programs designed to eliminate the mentally ill, handicapped, aged, and incurably ill.

> Nazi repression and persecution

No group, however, was more systematically repressed than the Jews. According to Joseph Goebbels, Jews had "corrupted our race, fouled our morals, undermined our customs, and broken our power." He blamed them as "the cause and the beneficiary of our misery." In 1933, the government excluded Jews from higher education and public employment. By 1935, most Jewish professionals in Germany had lost their jobs. That year the **Nuremberg Laws** took citizenship away from Jews and forbad marriage or sexual relations between Jews and non-Jews. In 1938, an episode of unrestrained violence revealed the mounting intensity of the Nazis' anti-Semitism. Incited by Goebbels, who blamed Jews for the assassination of a German diplomat in Paris, Nazi stormtroopers vandalized Jewish residences, synagogues, and places of business, smashing windows and plundering shops during the night of November 9–10. The troops then attacked Jews themselves, killing dozens and imprisoning tens of thousands in concentration camps. After this attack—known as **Kristallnacht**, or Crystal Night, for its images of shattered glass—the Nazi government increasingly restricted Jews' movements, eliminated their jobs, and confiscated their assets. By 1939, over half of Germany's Jews had emigrated, even though they had to leave their possessions behind, pay hefty emigration fees, and face rejection in other countries. Soon, though, it became too late to escape Germany.

Figure 23.12 depicts the repression closing in on the Jews. The man in this painting—a self-portrait of the German artist Felix Nussbaum (1904–1944)—grimly regards the viewer. In one hand, he holds up his identity card, which in red letters states that he is Jewish. The yellow Star of David on his coat also identifies him as Jewish to the public. The walls of a prison yard tower above him. Beyond the walls, barbed wire, a truncated tree, and a blackening sky all hint at the dark future facing this man and others like him. Nussbaum completed this painting in 1943 while in hiding from the Nazis; less than a year later the Nazis arrested, imprisoned, and then killed him, along with his parents and brother.

What did ordinary Germans think of this repression and persecution? Historians still debate this question. Although many people seemed to share Hitler's attitudes, at least to a degree, most people outside the persecuted groups may not have understood Hitler's extreme, ultimate purpose. Certainly some knew and many should have known. A few Germans objected. However, open resistance was dangerous. For those who disagreed with Hitler, it was much easier and safer to retreat into private life and apathy. Moreover, they, and many other Germans, found reason to overlook Hitler's repressive measures and support him in his efforts to revive their prostrate nation.

Rebuilding and Rearming the New Germany

Governmental expenditures fueled economic recovery, but Hitler's main goal was rearmament. Superhighways, hospitals, sports stadiums, and apartment houses sprang up all over Germany; so did rearmament plants that created jobs for millions. To make Germany self-sufficient in case of another war, the Nazis supported the development of synthetics for the manufacture of such items as rubber and petroleum that Germany would otherwise have to import. The planned conquest to the east, Hitler hoped, would provide needed raw materials and eventually pay for Germany's governmental expenditures.

For the most part, the Nazis left business organizations and the capitalist economy alone. However, big business, forced to bow to the will of governmental policy, did lose some freedom. The real assault was on independent labor unions, which the government abolished and replaced with the Nazi Labor Front.

All these efforts worked. Germany regained the economic and military strength to make it a great power. By 1935, Hitler had taken Germany out of the League of Nations and the Geneva Disarmament Conference. Unwilling to back the letter of the Versailles treaty with force, the Allies offered only muted opposition to Hitler's renunciation of the Versailles disarmament provisions. The next year, Hitler initiated a secret Four-Year Plan to prepare Germany for war. By 1939, the Nazis had increased armaments expenditures thirtyfold. Hitler felt ready to flex his newly developed muscles. His aggressive ambitions, combined with disturbing events outside Germany, were pushing the world toward war.

LOOKING BACK & MOVING FORWARD

Summary   During the 1920s, the West struggled to recover from the terrible World War I years. But any optimism generated by the end of the war was quickly tempered by problems such as inflation and unemployment in much of Europe. In southern, central, and eastern Europe, political turmoil created even more uncertainty. In the Soviet Union, crippled by the war and a devastating civil war, the Bolshevik regime faced an overwhelming task of rebuilding and creating a new kind of society. Even among the victors in western Europe and North America, the search for some return to "normalcy" brought frustrations and, at best, temporary moments of vibrancy, stability, and renewal. Most of the strong moments ended with the stock market crash of 1929, which ushered in the Great Depression.

By the early 1930s, the West had divided into three camps: the capitalist democracies, the fascist and authoritarian nations of central and eastern Europe, and the communist Soviet Union. As hardships from the Depression deepened and persisted, the capitalist democracies weakened, the authoritarian nations became ominously belligerent, and the communist Soviet Union under Joseph Stalin pursued—at terrible cost—its ambitious policies of agricultural collectivization and industrial five-year plans. But no country seemed to grow stronger, and for many in a more frightening way, than Germany under Adolf Hitler and the Nazis. The decade would not end before a return to the horrors that so many had hoped were behind them when that terrible storm lifted in 1918.

KEY TERMS

Weimar Republic, *p. 723*

Maginot Line, *p. 724*

Bauhaus, *p. 727*

Dada, *p. 728*

fascism, *p. 730*

New Economic Policy (NEW), *p. 732*

Five-Year Plan, *p. 733*

collectivization, *p. 734*

Great Purges, *p. 736*

Great Depression, *p. 736*

Nazi Party, *p. 738*

Lebensraum, *p. 739*

SS, *p. 740*

Nuremberg Laws, *p. 742*

Kristallnacht, *p. 742*

REVIEW, ANALYZE, & CONNECT TO TODAY

REVIEW THE PREVIOUS CHAPTER

Chapter 22—"Descending into the Twentieth Century"—told the story of World War I and the Russian Revolution.

1. In what ways were the forces unleashed by World War I responsible for the rise of authoritarian governments in Europe?

2. How might one argue that during the 1920s and the 1930s, the West never recovered from World War I?

ANALYZE THIS CHAPTER

Chapter 23—"Darkening Decades"—traces the rise of fascism, the development of the Soviet Union, and the trials of nations struck by the Great Depression.

1. Do you think the 1920s was a period of real recovery and cultural flowering or more of a haunted, anxious decade? Why?

2. Analyze the main qualities of German Nazism. How do you explain its rise and the acquisition of power by Hitler?

3. Why do you think Stalin initiated the Five-Year Plans? What were the purposes of those plans?

4. In what ways was the Great Depression much more than an economic downturn?

CONNECT TO TODAY

Think about the rise of fascism and Nazism, the transformation of the Soviet Union, and the hardships of the Great Depression.

1. In today's world, what might be some of the consequences of another serious economic depression?

2. What circumstances in the present day might facilitate the rise of regimes like the dictatorships or fascist governments of the 1920s and 1930s?

BEYOND THE CLASSROOM

TRYING TO RECOVER FROM THE GREAT WAR, 1919–1929

Kitchen, Martin. *Europe Between the Wars: A Political History*. London: Longman, 1988. An economic and political history of the interwar period.

Mommsen, Hans. *The Rise and Fall of Weimar Democracy*. Chapel Hill: University of North Carolina Press, 1996. Argues that Weimar collapsed because of a skewed political culture inherited from imperial Germany.

TURNING AWAY FROM DEMOCRACY: DICTATORSHIPS AND FASCISM, 1919–1929

Paxton, Robert O. *The Anatomy of Fascism*. New York: Knopf, 2004. A fine, comparative analysis of fascism and fascist movements.

Payne, Stanley G. *A History of Fascism, 1914–1945*. Madison: University of Wisconsin Press, 1995. Excellent in its European and global perspective on fascist movements.

Wasserstein, Bernard. *Barbarism and Civilization: A History of Europe in Our Time*. Oxford: Oxford University Press, 2007. An excellent survey emphasizing dark developments during the period 1914—2007.

TRANSFORMING THE SOVIET UNION, 1920–1939

Applebaum, Anne. *Gulag: A History*. New York: Doubleday, 2003. Vividly analyzes the Soviet Union's forced-labor camps.

Lewin, Moshe. *The Making of the Soviet System: Essays in the Social History of Interwar Russia*. London: Methuen, 1985. A thoughtful analysis by a noted scholar.

Thurston, Robert W. *Life and Terror in Stalin's Russia, 1934–1941*. New Haven, CT: Yale University Press, 1996. An attempt to revise accepted interpretations of Stalin and the Great Terror as the product of an evil mastermind.

Tucker, Robert C. *Stalin in Power: The Revolution from Above, 1928–1941*. New York: Norton, 1990. The second volume of an exhaustive and acclaimed analysis of Stalin, stressing the policies of collectivization and industrialization.

THE GREAT DEPRESSION, 1929–1939

Eichengreen, Barry. *Golden Fetters: The Gold Standard and the Great Depression, 1919–1939*. New York: Oxford University Press, 1992. Argues that the gold standard was the obstacle to financial stability and economic prosperity in the interwar period.

Kindleberger, Charles. *The World in Depression, 1929–1939*, 2nd ed. Berkeley: University of California Press, 1986. A wide-ranging account that argues that problems in the system of international exchange played the most important role in causing the Great Depression.

NAZISM IN GERMANY

Evans, Richard J. *The Third Reich in Power, 1933–1939*. New York: Penguin, 2005. An excellent examination of life in Nazi Germany during the 1930s.

Fischer, Klaus P. *Nazi Germany: A New History*. New York: Continuum, 1995. A highly regarded examination of Nazi Germany.

Kershaw, Ian. *The Nazi Dictatorship*, 3rd ed. London: Edward Arnold, 1993. A thoughtful examination of the historiography of Nazism.

Koonz, Claudia. *Mothers in the Fatherland: Women, the Family, and Nazi Politics*. New York: St. Martin's Press, 1987. Studies Nazi ideology regarding women as well as women's responses to it.

HORST STREMPEL, *NIGHT OVER GERMANY*, 1945

This 1945 painting by German artist Horst Strempel (1904–1975) depicts the fate of Germany in World War II. More broadly, it conveys the human suffering brought on by that horrendous conflict. In the left panel, a man huddles in terror and stares out from a confined space. Behind him mysterious figures loom in the darkness. In the right panel, a family peers out of a similar space, despair etched in their faces. The figures in the central panel mutely express that same despair, while the background hints at the misery and destruction of war. Below these individuals huddle more people, seemingly trapped but perhaps hoping for rescue. Strempel's painting, like World War II itself, has roots in World War I and echoes the stunning depiction of that conflict by Otto Dix, shown on page 690.

Into the Fire Again: World War II, 1939–1945

I n September 1938, British prime minister Neville Chamberlain flew home from a conference with leaders of France, Germany, and Italy. At the airport north of London, he announced to cheering crowds that an agreement at that meeting, known as the Munich Conference, had achieved "peace for our time." British newspapers proclaimed him a hero.

Less than a year later, Chamberlain delivered another speech on the same topic. But this time, he made a painful admission to Britain's House of Commons. "This is a sad day for all of us, and to none is it sadder than to me," he confessed. "Everything that I have worked for, everything that I have hoped for . . . has crashed into ruins." The events that had devastated Chamberlain had just taken place in eastern Europe. On September 1, 1939, Germany had invaded Poland. Now Chamberlain was announcing Britain's declaration of war against Germany. He made his point clear: "I trust I may live to see the day when Hitlerism has been destroyed and a liberated Europe has been reestablished."

Chamberlain, who died in 1940, would not see that day. War raged in Europe and across the globe for more than five years. Some viewed this conflict as a chance to reverse the results of the Great War of 1914–1918. Others deemed it a dreaded return of that "war to end all wars." But for most, this new contest would prove unique in its horrors and far worse than World War I. Inhumanity—from indiscriminate bombing to programmed genocide—gained the upper hand in the West, Asia, and the Pacific between the late 1930s and 1945. In the end, the conflict would take the lives of tens of millions of people and leave lasting scars on many nations and individuals. The painting shown on the facing page not only echoes Otto Dix's image of World War I (see page 690) but also evokes the suffering of those who survived the violence and hardship inflicted by World War II.

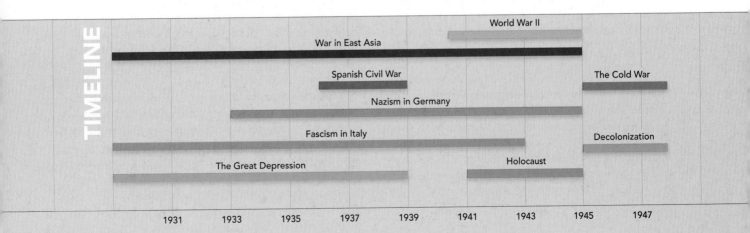

TIMELINE

World War II

War in East Asia

Spanish Civil War

The Cold War

Nazism in Germany

Fascism in Italy

Decolonization

The Great Depression

Holocaust

1931 1933 1935 1937 1939 1941 1943 1945 1947

PREVIEW

THE ROAD TO WAR,

1931–1939

"For us Germans the dictated Treaty of Versailles is not a law," announced Hitler to the German Reichstag on September 1, 1939. Throughout his speech—in which he sought to explain why German forces has just invaded Poland—Hitler jumped back and forth between the Great War of 1914–1918 and the present conflict, referring to himself as "the first soldier of the German Reich." He made clear his intent to reverse the results of World War I: "I have once again put on that uniform which was always so sacred and dear to me. I shall not lay it aside until after the victory—or I shall not live to see the end. . . ." What happened in the West and the world that led to that moment?

As we saw in Chapter 23, in the tense years of the 1920s and 1930s a new wave of authoritarian governments had washed across eastern and southern Europe; by 1938, only Czechoslovakia remained a parliamentary democracy. Many of these regimes included elements of fascism, but most were simple dictatorships by royal or military figures. Fascist movements, such as the Cross of Fire organization in France and the "Rex" Party in Belgium, also sprouted up in western Europe.

The democratic nations turned inward as they grappled with the depression and political divisions within their own borders. After 1934, communists in those nations sought to form alliances with socialists and moderates against the growing strength of fascism. The **Popular Front** in France is an example of such a partnership. The Front governed from 1936 to 1938. It was unable to pull the nation out of the depression, however, and ultimately fell from power. Its defeat left France more politically divided and discouraged than ever.

International Affairs Break Down

For France and the other democracies, international affairs soon slipped out of control. Rearmament spread, aggression became the order of the day, and neither the democratic powers nor the League of Nations responded forcefully to stop it.

In 1931, Japan initiated the new pattern. Many in Japan had long viewed China as their immediate rival—an enemy with the potential to stand in the way of their ambitions for economic and political dominance in east Asia. On the orders of young officers, the Japanese army invaded Manchuria in northern China and began a drive for conquest. Crowds in Japan cheered the news of the Manchurian campaign, and a heightened sense of nationalistic militarism gradually pervaded Japanese political life. The League of Nations condemned Japan but took no action. By 1937, China had managed to shake off the most onerous Western controls over the country but still bore the scars of decades of a sporadic, bloody civil war. China's dominant Nationalist Party, under Jiang Jieshi (Chiang Kai-shek) (1887–1975), had expended much of its strength opposing the growing Chinese Communist Party, led by Mao Zedong (1893–1976). In the early 1930s, Jiang had almost vanquished the Communists, but Mao and the core of his movement held on.

In 1937, Japanese troops invaded China proper. Less than six months later, the Japanese Imperial Army captured Nanking, capital city of China's Nationalist government. Over the following six weeks, Japanese army officers gave their troops free rein of the city. An American reporter in Nanking described the Japanese victory as "accompanied by the mass killing of the defenders, who were piled up among the sandbags, forming a mound six feet high." Victory did not end the slaughter: "Thousands of prisoners were executed by the Japanese . . . the killing of civilians was widespread . . . Nanking's streets were littered with dead." In what probably amounted to a deliberate policy, the Japanese carried out mass killings and executions of up to 300,000 Chinese soldiers and civilians and raped thousands of women.

Appalled, the rival Chinese Communists and Nationalists finally forged an alliance against the Japanese, and the Soviet Union provided military assistance to China against its powerful rival in the east. Nevertheless, city after city in China fell to Japanese bombs and invading armies. With its expanding industrial economy hungry for new markets, Japan

Japan on the march

was determined to create "a new order in East Asia," under its domination. To secure its position, it moved to form an alliance with two other aggressive, authoritarian states: Italy and Germany.

In 1935, Mussolini ordered his troops to invade Ethiopia in East Africa, hoping to win popularity at home despite the unemployment 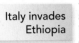 and failing social policies there. Ethiopia appealed to the League of Nations for protection. The League condemned Il Duce's actions, but the democratic powers did not follow up with enough action to stop him. Indeed, these responses to his aggression only pushed Mussolini toward Hitler, and in 1936 the two leaders agreed to a friendship alliance—the Rome-Berlin **Axis.** In 1939, that alliance solidified into the military Pact of Steel. To show unity with Hitler, Mussolini promptly adopted anti-Semitic racial laws for Italy. To further his own military ambitions, he invaded Albania.

Civil War in Spain

In 1936, civil war broke out in Spain. Five years earlier, Spain had become a democratic republic for the first time. But when the Popular Front, made up of radicals, socialists, and communists, won election in 1936, a group of generals led by the conservative Francisco Franco (1892–1975) launched an armed rebellion against the new government. Franco's nationalist rebels enjoyed the support of the fascist Falange Party, the army, the church, and most of the wealthy elites; nevertheless, they could not easily overturn the popular Loyalists—the supporters of the Popular Front government.

The Spanish civil war soon became an international battlefield. Hitler and Mussolini, spotting an opportunity to advance the cause of fascism, gain an ally, and test their new weapons, sent arms and troops to aid Franco. At one point in 1937, Germans manning new airplanes on behalf of Franco's nationalists attacked the small Spanish town of Guernica, raining death on the civilian population there. The slaughter became the subject matter of one of the most haunting paintings of the twentieth century, *Guernica* (1937), by the Spanish artist Pablo Picasso (1881–1973). This 25-foot-long mural in black and white (**Figure 24.1**) captures the worst features of this war—terror, brutality, disjointedness, lack of direction, and despair. On the left, a woman shrieks while holding a dead child. In the center, a warrior and horse lie shattered into fragments as the wounded sorrowfully look on. On the right, a woman plummets from a burning building. The image expresses both a wailing lament and a warning: modern war not only kills indiscriminately but targets civilians in order to terrorize all into submission.

The Loyalists appealed to the other Western democracies for aid, but no help came. These nations hoped to maintain good relations with Italy and Germany and thus committed to a policy of neutrality, even though the fascist powers only pretended to agree. Unofficial Loyalist support came from some 40,000 idealistic volunteers, such as the Garibaldi Brigade and the Lincoln Brigade, who traveled to Spain from abroad and fought as individuals in the Loyalist cause. Otherwise, only the Soviet Union (until 1938) and Mexico provided assistance. The Loyalists also suffered from internal divisions between competing communists, anarchists, and liberals. In 1939, after three years of slaughter and atrocities on both sides, Franco's rebels finally beat down the last of the Loyalist resistance (see **Map 24.1**). The authoritarian Franco ruled Spain until his death in 1975.

Trying to Cope with Germany

In March 1936, Hitler gambled by ordering his armed forces into the Rhineland, that part of Germany on the west bank of the Rhine River that the Treaty of Versailles had deemed a demilitarized zone (see **Map 24.2**). France fretted and fumed but, lacking Britain's support, did nothing. Hitler's bold gamble paid off. With a new confidence, he turned to the three countries that bordered Germany to the east: Austria, Czechoslovakia, and Poland.

In 1938, the Nazis incorporated Austria without opposition, annexing the 6.5 million Austrians to the German Reich (empire) (see **Map 24.2**). Hitler then claimed a portion of Czechoslovakia—the Sudetenland—that included 3.5 million German-speaking people. The Czechs, however, surprised him by rushing to their defenses. For months, Hitler churned out a barrage of propaganda that painted the German-speaking Czechs as a persecuted minority. He threatened and roused his people to readiness for war, finally vowing to march if the Sudetenland was not surrendered to him.

A difficult question now arose for the rest of Europe as it watched Hitler's actions: What should be done? For complex reasons, no one opposed Hitler with force. For one thing, World War I had made many Europeans reluctant to risk general war again. In addition, disagreement swirled over the justice of Hitler's demands. Some people agreed with Germany that the Versailles treaty was too harsh and sympathized with those who wanted to appease Germany's injured feelings. Many other people saw Hitler as sometimes reasonable and as a force that at least might be used to stop the spread of communism. British prime minister Neville Chamberlain (1869–1940), aware of Britain's lack of armed forces and public support to halt Hitler, tried for a compromise with the German ruler.

FIGURE 24.1

Pablo Picasso, *Guernica*, 1937

Pablo Picasso's painting reveals the horrors of the Spanish civil war by focusing on a 1937 bombing raid on the town of Guernica. Here, Picasso uses symbols and images of people who are broken and suffering, with most of the faces looking up to the sky where destruction has rained down upon them.

Connecting Art & Society

1. What impressions of war was Picasso seeking to convey to viewers?

2. How does this painting differ from a traditional battle scene?

3. In what ways might details of this painting serve as a warning?

On September 29, 1938, the leaders of Germany, Italy, France, and Britain met in Munich to resolve the Sudetenland question. In the end, the two democratic powers chose **appeasement**—giving in to Hitler's demands in hopes of satisfying him. Hitler grabbed the piece of Czechoslovakia that he wanted. British and French leaders, underestimating Hitler's territorial ambitions and determination to go to war, felt pleased with the agreement. Their nations still suffered from the Great Depression and could not endure another conflict, they told themselves. Moreover, many Europeans—particularly the British and French—considered a renewal of horrors akin to those of the Great War of 1914–1918 unacceptable. However, the Czechoslovak and Soviet governments expressed outrage; they hadn't been invited to attend the conference. The agreement would force the Czechs to capitulate. For Stalin, the deal confirmed the continuing unwillingness of the Western democracies to unite with the Soviet Union against the growing fascist threat.

> Appeasement at Munich

Back in Britain, Chamberlain announced that the **Munich Conference** agreement had "saved Czechoslovakia from destruction and Europe from Armageddon." Across Europe, crowds cheered, celebrating what they saw as the preservation of peace. But a few months later, Hitler showed his true colors: With no warning, he sent forces to overrun the remainder of the Czechoslovakian Republic (see **Map 24.2**).

When Hitler next threatened Poland, Great Britain got tough and promised to come to Poland's aid. They turned to the Soviets for help, but it was too late. Isolated or excluded for too long from international affairs and disillusioned by France's and Britain's weak response to German aggression, Stalin stunned the world by signing a nonaggression pact with Hitler on August 23, 1939. In return for the Soviet Union's neutrality while Germany carved up Poland, Hitler gave Stalin a free hand to reannex territories in eastern Europe—including eastern Poland—that Russia

> Nazi-Soviet nonaggression pact

MAP 24.1

The Spanish Civil War, 1936–1939

This map shows the evolution of the Spanish civil war between 1936 and 1939.

Explore the Map

1. What was the route of Franco's forces? Where did they begin and end up? Why?

2. Why was France's unwillingness to help the Loyalist forces so important a factor in the war's outcome?

had lost during World War I (see **Map 24.2**). By making this cynical pact with his greatest ideological enemy, Nazi Germany, Stalin may have gambled that the Soviet Union could stay on the sidelines, growing in strength, while the fascist and democratic capitalists destroyed one another.

At dawn on September 1, the Germans launched an all-out attack on Poland by land, sea, and air. Hitler remained convinced that France and Britain would not go to war over Poland. He was wrong. Two days later, Great Britain and France declared war on Germany. In a poem titled "SEPTEMBER 1, 1939," poet W. H. Auden (1907–1973) moaned that

The unmentionable odor of death
Offends the September night

World War II had begun.

AXIS VICTORIES,
1939–1942

Perhaps the war initiated in 1914 never quite ended, and the 1920s were just a pause in three decades of fighting and crises after 1914. Maybe if the depression had not struck, Hitler and the Nazis would not have come to power, the democracies would have continued to grow, and war could have been averted. Tragically, the war that did break out in September 1939 would blaze six long years and encompass the globe as never before.

Triumph of the German Blitzkrieg

The German **blitzkrieg**—a "lightning war" of highly coordinated air strikes and rapid deployment of tanks and motorized columns—overwhelmed Polish forces.

MAP 24.2

German Expansion, 1936–1939

This map shows German expansion between 1936 and September 1939, as well as the territory annexed by the Soviet Union thanks to the Nazi-Soviet nonaggression pact of August 1939.

Map legend:
- International Boundaries, 1936
- Germany in 1933
- Remilitarized in 1936
- Annexed in 1938
- Satellite States, March 1939
- Conquered by Germany in September 1939
- Annexed by Soviet Union in September 1939

Explore the Map

1. In what ways did these developments leave Poland vulnerable?

2. What distinguishes the steps in Germany's expansion?

3. What nations might have felt most threatened by further German aggression?

But that did not end matters within Poland: German occupiers and Germans already living within Poland soon began destroying the Polish people, actions that would form a pattern to be repeated and magnified in the years to come. The French and British mobilized their armies along the German border, and the British fleet blockaded Germany by sea—all to no avail.

For the next six months, in what became known as the "phony war," almost no military action took place.

France and Great Britain seemed paralyzed. Meanwhile, the Soviet Union took advantage of its agreement with Hitler and reannexed territories in Poland and eastern Europe—including Estonia, Latvia, and Lithuania—that Russia had lost in World War I. When Finland refused to yield strategic territories, the Soviets attacked. The Finns put up a determined resistance, and it took several months for the Soviet army finally to defeat these stubborn soldiers.

In April 1940, the Germans suddenly overran both Denmark and Norway. German planes fended off Britain's fleet, inflicting heavy losses. The next month, German armies assaulted Luxembourg, the Netherlands, Belgium, and France. Tiny Luxembourg offered no resistance, while the Dutch fought heroically but fell after six days. To support the beleaguered Belgians, the British army and a large part of the French army moved into Belgium. The French trusted that their fortresses—the Maginot Line—would hold along the German border. However, the line proved useless against the highly mobile German tanks. The Germans skirted the fortresses to the north through the Ardennes Forest. German general Erwin Rommel recalled the breakthrough: "The tanks now rolled in a long column through the line of fortifications. . . . Our artillery was dropping heavy harassing fire on villages and the road far ahead. . . . Engines roared, tank tracks clanked and clattered . . . civilians and French troops, their faces distorted with terror, lay huddled in the ditches." And then, he noted, "the flat countryside lay spread out around us under the cold light of the moon. We were through the Maginot Line."

The Battle of France

The German blitzkrieg drove quickly to the English Channel, cutting off Allied armies in Belgium and then trapping them at Dunkirk, a seaport in northern France. A flotilla of military and civilian ships, including fishing boats and pleasure craft, rescued 330,000 British and French troops off the beach at Dunkirk.

The Battle of France ended after only five weeks. Although almost equal in numbers to the Germans, the French seemed demoralized from the beginning of the war. According to one French journalist, they felt abandoned by the British, "who were ready to fight to the last French soldier." On June 16, 1940, the aged, right-wing Marshal Philippe Pétain became premier of France and quickly surrendered to Hitler. **Figure 24.2** shows triumphant German troops on the march through Paris that year. In the background stands France's Arch of Triumph, a reminder of past victories now vastly overshadowed by Germany's occupying forces. With the surrender, Germany took the northern half of France and the entire Atlantic coast. The new authoritarian French regime would govern the remaining unoccupied portion of France from the city of Vichy. French general Charles de Gaulle escaped to Great Britain and declared himself leader of the Free French government in exile.

FIGURE 24.2 France in Defeat, 1940 In this stark photograph, German troops parade down France's celebrated Champs-Élysées boulevard after the fall of Paris in 1940.

France's collapse left Great Britain to face Germany alone. The audacious and eloquent Winston Churchill (1874–1965), who had replaced Neville Chamberlain as prime minister, warned his people of the serious struggle to come: "This is no war of chieftains or of princes, of dynasties or national ambition; it is a war of peoples and of causes." The Germans, determined to gain control of the English Channel and prepare for an invasion of Britain, unleashed massive air attacks against Britain in July 1940. As the Battle of Britain erupted, Churchill rallied his country, offering his "blood, toil, tears, and sweat" and vowing "we shall never surrender."

The Battle of Britain

For almost two months that fall, the Germans bombed London every night. A British civilian described some of the ordeal: "Bombs fell by day as well as by night. We became accustomed to the sudden drone of an airplane in the middle of the morning, the screech of a bomb, the dull crash of its explosion and the smell of cordite that filled the air a moment later." **Figure 24.3** reveals some of the effort involved in the Battle of Britain. A group of three women and one man pull in a barrage balloon. Weighted cables dangling beneath the balloon hinder low-level flights by German bombers. In the background are buildings destroyed by bombings, but numerous smokestacks in the distance indicate that Britain's ability to fight survives. In cellars and subway stations, the British people holed up while their planes and antiaircraft guns,

FIGURE 24.3 Laura Knight, The Battle of Britain, 1943 Women and men pull in balloons used to hinder flights by German bombers during the Battle of Britain.

now aided by radar, fought off the Germans. Boosted by the high morale of the people, the increased output of aircraft factories, and Churchill's leadership, the island nation miraculously held. By November, the British had prevailed.

War in North Africa and the Balkans

Even though Italy was not yet ready to take on another major war, Mussolini did not want to miss out on the spoils of an easy victory. He, too, invaded France as it fell to the Germans. Then in September 1940, his armies in Africa moved east from Libya into Egypt. A few weeks later, they attacked Greece from Albania.

However, Mussolini's forces met disaster at every turn. Mobile British forces routed Italian armies in North Africa, and British planes crippled the Italian fleet in southern Italy. The Greeks also contributed to the rout, driving the Italians back into Albania.

In response, Germany's forces streamed into the Balkans and North Africa. Hitler had several goals in mind for this move. He coveted the Balkans for their rich supplies of raw materials, especially the Romanian oil fields. He also hoped to save the Italian forces in North Africa and take the Suez Canal, Britain's lifeline to its empire. Hungary and Romania yielded to Hitler's threats and joined the Axis alliance in November 1940; Bulgaria did the same in March 1941. Yugoslavia and Greece refused, and they were overrun by German forces within a few weeks.

Germany's Afrika Korps drove the British back into Egypt. Pro-German movements broke out in Iraq, Iran, and French Syria. At this point, however, Hitler hurled his main forces against the Soviet Union, giving the British a breathing spell to recoup their strength in North Africa and the eastern Mediterranean.

Operation Barbarossa: Germany Invades the Soviet Union

The eventual conquest of the Soviet Union had always been uppermost in Hitler's thoughts, despite his deceptive pact with the USSR. Even before that 1939 deal, Hitler had revealed his true intentions to a group of associates: "Everything I do is directed against Russia. If the West is too stupid and blind to understand that, I shall be forced to reach an agreement with the Russians and strike at the West. Once [the West] is defeated, [I shall] turn my concentrated forces against the Soviet Union." Conquest of the Soviet Union would bring Germany "living space" as well as vast industrial and agricultural resources. It would also eliminate any threat from Nazism's great ideological enemy. And it would afford Germany access to millions of Jews— Hitler's "blood enemy"—living in the Soviet Union. Still, the Nazi leader had hoped to subdue the British before turning to the Soviets. Failing that, he decided to invade the Soviet Union anyway.

In June 1941, the Germans launched Operation Barbarossa, sending more than three million soldiers, 3,700 tanks, and 2,500 planes against the USSR. Hitler expected to crush Soviet resistance in six weeks, well before the notorious Russian winter set in. "You only have to kick in the door, and the whole rotten structure will come crashing down," he claimed. But he also warned his generals, "The war against Russia will be . . . one of ideologies and racial differences and will have to be conducted with unprecedented, unmerciful and unrelenting harshness."

Stalin had long suspected that Hitler would someday turn against him, yet he believed that a German invasion was impossible before spring 1942, when Britain would be too crippled to constitute much of a diversion to German forces. Moreover, recent evidence suggests that Stalin himself may have planned to turn the tables on Hitler and launch his own full-scale preemptive attack on German forces in eastern Europe. In the days before the June invasion by Germany, Stalin refused to believe numerous reports from many sources that Hitler's forces were about to attack. He even ignored warnings from some of his top generals.

On the morning of June 22, the Germans launched their assault. Caught off guard, Stalin delayed his response. For a few days, he disappeared from the public eye. Finally, he urged the Soviet people to rally to "the Great Patriotic War." Not everyone rose to the challenge. Indeed, the Ukrainians and some other Soviet groups initially greeted the Germans as liberators. The German forces quickly shattered Soviet armies. On July 3, the chief of Germany's General Staff wrote in his journal, "The Russian Campaign has been won in the space of two weeks." In just the first twenty days of the campaign, 600,000 Soviet soldiers lost their lives.

Even in the face of such destruction, most Soviet peoples put up a determined resistance. The weather worked against the enemy. The September mud season slowed German troops and tanks, and the unusually harsh winter that followed caught the invaders unprepared. Nevertheless, the German war machine crunched forward. By December 1, it had come within sight of Moscow and had nearly surrounded Leningrad (see **Map 24.3**). A confident Hitler announced the imminent, permanent destruction of the USSR.

Once again, the weather intervened. The winter tightened its grip, subjecting the lightly clothed and weakly supplied Nazis to frigid temperatures. Moreover, Japan's decision not to go to war against the USSR saved the Soviets from a disastrous two-front struggle. Stalin could now move troops from the Far East to the West. The combination of punishing weather and Russian counterattacks forced the Germans to halt and in some places even retreat—but only temporarily. By then, German forces had slaughtered more than three million Soviet soldiers and captured another three million. But the Soviet forces were not yet broken.

Japan Attacks

Farther east, events were brewing that would add yet another dimension to the war. Specifically, Western imperial presence in Asia and the Pacific had frustrated Japan's dreams of expansion. The resource-poor island nation depended on foreign raw materials and markets to fuel its industrial economy. During the 1930s, the Great Depression had weakened Japan's democratic regime and made the army a more potent political as well as military force. As military men gained control of the government, Japan's foreign policy shifted to expansionism (see Global Connections). By 1939, Japan had conquered the populous coastal areas of China and pushed Chinese forces well into the interior. When the war in Europe weakened European colonial powers—which controlled much of Southeast Asia, with its wealth of essential resources such as oil, tin, and rubber—Japan joined the Rome-Berlin Axis. It quickly occupied French Indochina and threatened the Dutch East Indies. The United States responded with a total economic embargo on all exports to Japan, threatening Japan's oil supplies in particular.

Hoping that the war in Europe would induce the United States to cede dominance to the Japanese in Southeast Asia, Japan struck. On December 7, 1941, Japanese air forces surprised the American fleet anchored in Pearl Harbor, Hawaii, crippling the U.S. naval and air forces. President Franklin D. Roosevelt (1882–1945) called it "a day that will live in infamy." The United States immediately declared war on Japan, and within days Germany and Italy declared war on the United States. Several Latin American nations joined the United States in the Grand Alliance against the Axis.

The U.S. enters the war

The long-isolationist United States had an army with limited capabilities. In addition, it had sent huge quantities of arms, equipment, and food across the Atlantic in its role as "the arsenal of democracy." Roosevelt agreed with Churchill to make the war in Europe the United States' first priority, and Americans started mobilizing their country's vast resources for the fight.

Meanwhile, the Japanese conquered a vast area in Southeast Asia and the Pacific (**Map 24.4**), creating The Greater East Asia Co-Prosperity Sphere. Japan claimed to be liberating Asia from the imperial West, but it dominated the new territories through nationalist leaders ready to collaborate with Japan's occupation forces and treated the conquered peoples as inferior subjects. Scoring victory after victory, the Japanese and Germans seemed to be winning the war.

BEHIND THE LINES: THE STRUGGLE AND THE HORROR

By 1942, Hitler ruled most of continental Europe from the English Channel to the outskirts of Moscow (see **Map 24.3**). In administering his lands, he pursued two primary goals. First, he hunted for ways to keep Germany supplied with war materials and maintain the standard of living for Germans without having to call on them to make unpopular sacrifices. Second, he sought to fulfill his racist agenda. To these ends, he implemented his "New Order," a program of economic exploitation and racial imperialism in the lands that he now controlled. He used conquered peoples according to their ranking in his racial hierarchy. Those most directly related to the Nazi conception of the Aryan race, such as Scandinavians, Anglo-Saxons, and Dutch, were treated well and might be absorbed into the Nazi

Hitler's "New Order"

MAP 24.3

World War II in Europe

This map shows Hitler's empire at its height in 1942, the front lines in the following years as the Allies closed in on Germany in 1945, and the major battles of the war.

Explore the Map

1. What does this map indicate about the military problems confronting Hitler after 1942?

2. Compare the eastern, southern, and western fronts. How might the fighting have differed in these three areas? Why?

3. Locate the western, Italian, and Russian fronts in February 1945, just a few months before the end of the war. What might these troop locations suggest about spheres of influence during the postwar decades?

empire as partners with the Germans. He considered the Latin races, such as the French, inferior but tolerable as supportive cogs in the New Order. Slavs ranked toward the bottom of Hitler's hierarchy; they were to be isolated, shoved aside, treated like slaves, or killed.

The Holocaust

Lowest on Hitler's racial scale were the Jews, and they fared the worst in Hitler's scheme. Nazis herded Jews into ghettos in German, Polish, and Russian cities. For a while, the Nazis envisioned forced

The Rise of Japanese Ultranationalism

During the 1920s, Japanese liberals who supported the international system established at the end of World War I held most of the power in the island nation's government. However, ultranationalists and militarists rejected the "Western" system and argued for an expanding Japanese empire in east Asia. These opponents of the system gained increasing power, especially after the Great Depression struck in 1929 and weakened Japan's economy.

During the 1930s, as some Western nations expressed alarm over Japanese expansionist moves, Hashimoto Kingoro, a leading ultranationalist, challenged them to reexamine their thinking. Western nations, Hashimoto proclaimed, were in no position to complain about Japan's desire to take territories it needed: "[W]e may wish to ask the white race just which country it was that sent warships and troops to India, South Africa, and Australia and slaughtered innocent natives, bound their hands and feet with iron chains, lashed their backs with iron whips, proclaimed these territories as their own, and still continues to hold them to this very day?" Okawa Shumei, another leading ultranationalist, built on Hashimoto's reasoning. A "struggle between the great powers of the East and the West," Okawa claimed, "which will decide their existence, is at present, as in the past, absolutely inevitable" if a better world for Asia was to come about. In Okawa's view, Japan's proper role in this new world

was clear: "Heaven has decided on Japan as its choice for the champion of the East. Has not this been the purpose of our three thousand long years of preparation?"

Over the course of the 1930s, liberals lost ground to the ultranationalists and militarists, who increasingly took over Japan's government. In 1931, Japanese troops created an "incident" in Manchuria that ignited a war with China and led to the establishment by the Japanese of a puppet state, Manchukuo, in Manchuria. In 1937, Japan again attacked China, launching a full-scale but undeclared war against the beleaguered nation. Soon Japan had seized large areas of east and north China. In 1940, Japan allied itself with the two main ultranationalist powers in the West: Nazi Germany and Fascist Italy.

The following year, just a few months before the Japanese attack on Pearl Harbor, Japan's Ministry of Education distributed *The Way of Subjects*—required reading for all Japanese high school and university students. The pamphlet revealed the thinking behind Japanese ultranationalism. The document pointed to the harmful "influx of European and American culture into this country," by which the authors meant individualism, liberalism, and materialism. Thanks to these outside influences, "the traditional character of the country was much impaired and the virtuous habits and customs bequeathed by our ancestors were affected unfavorably." Japan's

mission, the document continued, was "the emancipation of East Asian nations." Throughout Asia, "hopes to be free of the shackles and bondage of Europe and America were ablaze."

In 1942, at the height of its power, the Japanese government created a plan for the establishment of the Greater East Asia Co-Prosperity Sphere, which echoed ultranationalist thought. The plan asserted that "the Japanese empire is the center and pioneer of Oriental moral and cultural reconstruction." Moreover, Japan's mission was "to cause East Asia to return to its original form of independence and co-prosperity by shaking off the yoke of Europe and America." By this time, Japan controlled much of east and south Asia as well as the Pacific Basin. But this year also saw the beginning of the end of Japan's power, for U.S. military might had begun turning the tide against Japan. Ultranationalist dreams and policies finally collapsed in the summer of 1945. That year, American planes dropped atomic bombs on Hiroshima and Nagasaki, defeating Japan and ending World War II.

Making Connections

1. Why might the arguments of ultranationalists have appealed to various political and military groups?

2. How were Western imperialist practices used to justify Japanese expansion?

---

emigration of Jews, perhaps to the island of Madagascar off the east coast of Africa, to solve the "Jewish problem." In 1941, such ideas ended and Hitler initiated a policy of genocide, formally adopted in a January 1942 meeting, which came to be known as the **Holocaust.** Mobile SS squads under Reinhard Heydrich (1904–1942) and Heinrich Himmler began the wholesale killing of Jews, along with Slavic prisoners of war, in Poland and Russia. Firing squads shot victims en masse. Dissatisfied with the pace of the killings, the Germans began using mobile vans that murdered people by gas. Finally, when that

MAP 24.4

World War II in the Pacific

This map shows Japan's empire at its height in 1942 and traces the course of the Allied counteroffensive that led to Japan's defeat in 1945.

Explore the Map

1. What was the extent of Japan's territorial domination at this time?

2. What problems did the Japanese face in trying to control their far-flung territories?

3. Consider the Allies' strategy in their counteroffensive against the Japanese. Why did this strategy differ from that used in Europe?

method still did not seem efficient enough, the Nazis used large gas chambers that killed thousands at a time. Heydrich, the Plenipotentiary for the Preparation of the Final Solution of the European Jewish Question, promised that this campaign—"a historic moment in the struggle against Jewry"—would be carried out "effectively but silently." Heydrich charged Adolf Eichmann (1906–1962) with managing this task.

The Nazis built six huge death camps in what had been Poland. From gathering points all over Europe, unknowing victims were crowded into cattle cars, where they soon became dehydrated, disoriented, and

terrorized; many died in transit. Upon their arrival, officials divided families, segregated people by sex, and made the first "selection." "Inside the camp, one's first view was fixed on a mountain of children's shoes," recalled a woman survivor. "To tell the truth I did not understand what that meant." Those who could not work as the Nazis wanted—therefore more women, children, and elderly—were sent to the "showers"— the Nazis' euphemism for the gas chambers. Officials especially targeted pregnant women to prevent the birth of more Jews. They sent the rest, now physically and mentally terrorized, to the work camps.

Death camps

The scale and depravity of this programmed inhumanity, torture, and death were unprecedented; thus the victims simply could not grasp what was happening until it was too late. Some Jews rebelled—in the Warsaw ghetto and the Treblinka camp, for example. They and others who fought back may have made important moral statements, but they stood no real chance against the Nazis. The masses of Jews trapped in ghettos or camps, their strength sapped by hunger and illness, had little choice. For many, the only way to maintain a shred of dignity against the degradation and death was silence. The Nazis had trapped these victims in a merciless, thoroughly organized system from which few escaped.

Struggling to survive in the camps, many people tried to help one another, though the desperate conditions at times also brought out the worst in people. In this surreal world, the Germans applied assembly-line methods to the destruction of millions of human beings. A French doctor described the killing process at the Auschwitz-Birkenau camp: Once prisoners were herded and forced into the gas chambers, "the massive oak double doors are shut. For two endless minutes one can hear banging on the walls and screams which are no longer human. . . . Five minutes later the doors are opened. The corpses, squashed together and distorted, fall out like a waterfall" (see Document 24.1). In a particularly brutal twist, the Nazis forced Jewish prisoners to carry out much of the dirty work of killing. Nazi guards subjected their captives to torture and abuse, and German doctors conducted gruesome experiments on camp prisoners.

In the end, almost all prisoners slaved in the camps on starvation rations until they died or were sent to the gas chambers when no longer useful to their captors. In Auschwitz alone, the largest of these camps, the Nazis murdered more than 12,000 people a day and more than one million Jews by the end of the war. Although Jews were the Nazis' main target, many people from non-Jewish groups—communists, gypsies, Jehovah's Witnesses, Soviet prisoners of war, Slavs, homosexuals—suffered the same fate. Moreover, the elite Nazis had other ominous plans—including an eventual genocidal "resettlement" to Siberia of more than 30 million people, mainly Slavs—if the Nazis should win the war in the East. Rudolf Höss, commander of the Auschwitz camp, would describe the order for mass killings as "something extraordinary, something monstrous. However the reasoning behind the order of this mass annihilation seemed correct to me . . . I wasted no thoughts about it." Ultimately

FIGURE 24.4 Nazi Atrocities, 1945 This grim photo taken in the Landsberg concentration camp is one of many that testify to Nazi atrocities.

these genocidal efforts took priority over even the war effort and continued right up until the last days of the war.

Figure 24.4 is a photograph taken after World War II ended. Here American officials force German civilians living near the Landsberg camp to stand witness to the Nazis' shocking atrocities. Who knew about the brutal realities of the camps during the war? The Nazis had gone to great lengths to cover up the process of killing, swearing everyone involved to secrecy and presenting more benign concentration camps outside Poland for international inspection. As reports of what really was happening filtered out, many people expressed disbelief. Atrocities on such a mass scale seemed impossible. But it had taken thousands of officials, bureaucrats, soldiers, police, and SS guards to carry out the murders. At least these thousands knew. Indeed, many concentration- and death-camp officials followed orders with enthusiasm, competing for approval from their superiors. Several large German companies, including the industrial giant I. G. Farben, benefited from contracts with the camps. Most German civilians may have been apathetic or may have chosen not to think about what was going on in the east, but information—from witnesses, from individuals indirectly involved, and by word of mouth—about the camps and massive killings was widespread. While perhaps not fully comprehended, the Final Solution had become an open secret in Germany by the end of 1942. Authorities on the outside who might have tried to help did nothing. At some point, British and American commanders probably

thinking about
DOCUMENTS

The Nazi Death Camps

In 1942, the Nazis began a new phase in their campaign to murder Jews and others. Their "final solution" took the form of death camps where Nazis could kill on a larger scale. Testimonies from witnesses paint vivid pictures of the horrors that occurred daily in these camps. The first account below is from Abraham Bomba, who in 1942 was transported with his family from a Polish ghetto to the Treblinka death camp, where his job was to cut women's hair before they were gassed. He escaped in 1943 and later described his experiences at the camp. The second account comes from a French doctor, André Lettich, whose job was to remove corpses from the crematoria at Birkenau.

1. Filling the Treblinka Gas Chambers

The gas chamber . . . was all concrete. There was no window. [It] had two doors . . . [and] the people went in to the gas chamber from the one side . . . [and] they pushed in as many as they could. It was not allowed to have the people standing up with their hands down because there was not enough room, but when the people raised their hand[s] . . . there was more room. . . . And on top of that they throw in kids, 2, 3, 4 years old. . . . The whole thing took . . . between five and seven minutes. The door opened up . . . from the other side. People working in Treblinka number two took out the corpses. Some of them dead and some of them still alive. They dragged them to the ditches . . . big ditches, and they covered them. That was the beginning of Treblinka.

2. The "Shower Room"

Until the end of January 1943, there were no crematoria in Birkenau. In the middle of a small birch forest, about two kilometres from the camp, was a peaceful looking house, where a Polish family had once lived before it had been either murdered or expelled. This cottage had been equipped as a gas chamber for a long time.

More than five hundred metres further on were two barracks: the men stood on one side, the women on the other. They were addressed in a very polite and friendly way: "You have been on a journey. You are dirty. You will take a bath. Get undressed quickly." Towels and soap were handed out, and then suddenly the brutes woke up and showed their true faces: this horde of people, these men and women were driven outside with hard blows and forced both summer and winter to go the few hundred metres to the "Shower Room." Above the entry door was the word "Shower." One could even see shower heads on the ceiling which were cemented in but never had water flowing through them.

These poor innocents were crammed together, pressed against each other. Then panic broke out, for at last they realised the fate in store for them. But blows with rifle butts and revolver shots soon restored order and finally they all entered the death chamber. The doors were shut and, ten minutes later, the temperature was high enough to facilitate the condensation of the hydrogen cyanide, for the condemned were gassed with hydrogen cyanide. This was the so-called "Zyklon B," gravel pellets saturated with twenty per cent of hydrogen cyanide which was used by the German barbarians.

Then, SS *Unterscharführer* Moll threw the gas in through a little vent. One could hear fearful screams, but a few moments later there was complete silence. Twenty to twenty-five minutes later, the doors and windows were opened to ventilate the rooms and the corpses were thrown at once into pits to be burnt. But, beforehand the dentists had searched every mouth to pull out the gold teeth. The women were also searched to see if they had not hidden jewelry in the intimate parts of their bodies, and their hair was cut off and methodically placed in sacks for industrial purposes.

SOURCES: (1) United States Holocaust Memorial Museum, "The Holocaust," in *Holocaust Encyclopedia*, www.ushmm.org/wk/index. (2) J. Noakes and G. Pridham, eds., *Nazism, 1919–1945: A Documentary Reader*, vol. 3, in *Foreign Policy, War, and Racial Extermination* (Exeter: University of Exeter Press, 1995), pp. 78–79.

Analyze the Document

1. Why did the Nazis use prisoners for these tasks?

2. How do you explain the reasons behind the procedures used in these camps?

3. What might be the significance of these actions, which occurred on such a large scale?

---

knew. While the full extent of the Holocaust may not have been clear, from almost the beginning Allied leaders had received information about the Nazi killing programs from various sources. After 1942, some Western newspapers published reports about mass murders and the death camps, though how much was widely understood or accepted before 1944 is unclear. Eventually, Jewish leaders pleaded to Allied governments to bomb the gas chambers and the railway lines leading to the death camps. But Allied officials claimed that other military targets were more important for the overall war effort.

Collaboration and Resistance

Collaborating governments often copied or cooperated with the Nazis. In some countries, such as Croatia, officials willingly rounded up Jews and carried out the killing themselves. The anti-Semitic government of Vichy France under Pétain transported thousands of Jews to Nazi death camps. In almost all conquered lands, the Nazis managed to find individuals who would collaborate with them.

However, many others resisted. The Danes saved most of the Jews living in their lands. In Italy, officials often ignored Nazi directives, despite Mussolini's alliance with Hitler. Numerous stories, such as the experience of the young Anne Frank hiding in the Netherlands, record individual heroism and tragedy. Resistance organizations rose in almost every occupied territory, particularly in France, Yugoslavia, and the Soviet Union. At great risk, men and women alike established underground networks, provided intelligence to the Allied forces, conducted guerrilla actions, aided escaping prisoners, sabotaged German military installations, and engaged Nazi forces that might have been used on the war fronts. Communists, such as those in Yugoslavia under the command of Josip Broz (Tito—see Biography), often formed the core of the most determined resistance movements. Tito's organization became one of the most effective resistance forces in Europe.

But the price of fighting back was high. The Germans infiltrated resistance groups and brutally crushed any hints of threats. Collective retribution for attacks against German leaders deterred many. In one case, the Nazis massacred 7,000 people in one town in retaliation for the killing of 10 Germans by Yugoslav partisans. In some places, such as Ukraine, Greece, and Yugoslavia, resistance groups with different political agendas fought among themselves, eroding their ability to oppose the Nazis.

Mobilizing the Home Fronts

Even more than in World War I, whole societies mobilized for the war effort in the 1940s. Governments controlled production and rationed goods. As labor shortages arose, women again assumed jobs normally reserved for men (see Document 24.2). Political leaders acquired unusual powers and discouraged dissent. Even outside the Nazi empire, some groups of citizens fell victim to the suspicion that the war engendered. In the United States, for example, government agents removed Japanese Americans living on the West Coast from their homes and businesses and placed them in camps. Propaganda on all sides painted distorted, racist pictures of the enemy and whipped up civilian support of the troops.

Britain, taking the brunt of German aggression early on, mobilized thoroughly. The government drafted men between the ages of 18 and 50 and women between 20 and 30 into military or civilian war service. Women accounted for most of the increase in Britain's labor force. The government also enlisted scientists to help break the German code and work on an atomic bomb.

The Soviet Union tried everything to brace itself against the Germans. Hundreds of thousands of Russian women served in the Soviet armed forces; millions took jobs, replacing men sent to the front. In October 1941, the Soviets managed an astounding feat: They dismantled more than five hundred factories in Moscow and elsewhere and reassembled them in the east, away from the encroaching German troops. By 1942, Soviet factories were producing far more tanks, guns, and combat airplanes than their German counterparts.

The United States, less threatened geographically by the war, mobilized unevenly; still, it boosted its wartime production by 400 percent in two years and sent large quantities of supplies to its British and Soviet allies. Germany was also slower to mobilize its citizens. In the early years, Hitler instead relied on quick victories and spoils from conquered lands to fulfill his nation's needs. Millions of conscripted foreigners and prisoners of war served as Germany's laborers. Only after 1942 did Hitler turn to full mobilization, multiplying Germany's production over the following two years despite concentrated Allied bombing.

TURNING THE TIDE OF WAR,
1942–1945

The now-global war was fought in three major theaters: the Soviet Union, the Mediterranean and western Europe, and the Pacific. The turning points in all theaters came between June and August 1942. The largest, bloodiest battles occurred in the Soviet Union and were fought by some nine million soldiers. The Germans had already conquered most of that nation's lands west of the Volga River, leaving nearly half of the Soviet people under German rule.

The Eastern Front and the Battle of Stalingrad

The Germans, refreshed and reequipped, resumed their offensive against the Soviet Union in June 1942, this time in the southern sector of the USSR. In July, one German soldier expressed confidence that "the Russian troops are completely broken," and "the Führer knows where the Russians' weak point is." The soldier recorded in his diary that he fully expected German forces to "take Stalingrad and then the war will inevitably soon be over." In early August, as German forces pushed forward, he and others anticipated the rewards of victory: "What great spaces the Soviets occupy, what rich fields there are to be had here after the war's over." By mid-August, they had reached the outskirts of Stalingrad on the Volga River. However, this soldier noted that the "doomed" Russian divisions "are continuing to resist bitterly."

BIOGRAPHY

Josip Broz (Tito)
(1892–1980)

Josip Broz was a hunted resistance leader for years. Born in Croatia in 1892 to a peasant family, the young Josip became an apprentice to a locksmith and then worked as a mechanic. In World War I, he served as a platoon leader in the Austro-Hungarian army, was severely wounded, and was taken prisoner by the Russians. Already a socialist, he joined Russia's Red Army during the revolution and civil war. He also married a Russian woman, with whom he would have a son. In 1920, he returned to Croatia, became a trade-unionist, joined the Communist Party of Yugoslavia, and soon rose to a position of leadership. Eight years later, he was arrested

Communist Leader and Yugoslav Dictator

and imprisoned for six years for his communist activity—the police had discovered bombs in his apartment. He again traveled to the Soviet Union, where he rose through the ranks as a loyal Stalinist during the purges. In 1937, he became the head of Yugoslavia's Communist Party. During his underground party work, Josip assumed the pseudonym Tito.

When Hitler invaded Yugoslavia and the Soviet Union, Tito announced, "We do not recognize the various Fascist puppet governments." He called on the Communist Party of Yugoslavia to organize the "partisans," a guerrilla resistance movement against Axis forces. **Figure 24.5** shows Tito, standing on the far right, with his staff of fellow fighters. At the same time, he entered into a virtual civil war with a competing, more conservative resistance movement. Although Tito won this struggle between resistance movements, it may have cost more lives than the battle against the Nazis. While fighting occupying forces, he organized a provisional communist government that would stand ready to take over at the end of the war. With the help of Soviet troops, Tito's forces drove the retreating Germans from Yugoslavia.

FIGURE 24.5 Tito and the Yugoslav Resistance

In 1945, Yugoslavia became a federal republic, with Tito as its leader and virtual dictator. He turned the new republic into a one-party, communist state on the model of the Soviet Union. Eventually balking at Stalin's plans to purge Yugoslav leadership and undermine his authority, Tito led Yugoslavia on a separate course after 1948. Unlike Stalin, he emphasized more relaxed, decentralized control over his nation and its economy, yet he tolerated no opposition to his rule. In the 1950s and 1960s, he became a spokesperson for nations such as Egypt, Indonesia, and India who refused to align themselves with either the United States or the Soviet Union in the Cold War. He served as president of Yugoslavia until his death in 1980.

Yugoslavia would not long survive his passing. Conflict between ethnic groups had long plagued this region of Europe. Such tensions had helped ignite World War I, had contributed to the rise of authoritarian leaders of both the Right and Left during the 1930s and 1940s, and had taken thousands of lives during the resistance struggles of World War II. Now that conflict led to the undoing of the federation. Yugoslavia broke up in 1991 in a series of bloody civil wars that would drag on for years.

Connecting People & Society

1. How did Tito rise to power?

2. How does Tito's life reveal the ties among war, ideology, and politics during this period?

3. After reading this biography, what do you think of Tito?

The Battle of Stalingrad became the greatest of the war and raged for seven months. "Not a step backward," ordered Stalin. He spared no resource, including the many women who served on the front lines as combat soldiers, tankers, and snipers. Indeed, some airforce regiments were made up entirely of women. The most revered pilot, Lily Litvak, shot down twelve German planes.

Figure 24.6 provides a sense of the battle as well as the Soviets' use of propaganda. In this staged photograph, one Russian soldier has fallen for the cause. Two others, despite the danger, heroically fight on with their rifle, machine gun, and hand grenades. The photograph avoids the reality of how brutal and ignoble much of this battle was. It also suggests that these frontline soldiers willingly sacrificed themselves for

DOCUMENT 24.2

Women Go to Work in the Factories

In World War II, the major combatants recognized that victory hinged on the ability to increase industrial production. With so many men serving in the armed forces, nations called on women to work in jobs traditionally reserved for men. In this account, Elizabeth Hawes describes her experiences in an American airplane engine plant in 1943.

Now that I've worked a few months in a plant—on the graveyard shift too—the only wonder to me is that all the women in the USA aren't storming the factory gates. I'm convinced that any healthy woman can work in a factory—and like it. My biggest regret is that I had to leave because I'd agreed to do some writing. My biggest ambition is to get back.

It was a great pleasure to me that nobody gave a darn who anyone was. . . . Of course there are little discords. The foremen and subforemen are honestly scared to death of us women. When first you arrive they look at you out of the corner of their eyes. . . . Every woman machinist has to endure sheer torture from her fellow male employees at one point in her career. . . .

The men see that now you think you're a mechanic. Some honestly don't believe the Lord ever intended women to be mechanics. Others are infuriated by your presumption that you can do their work. . . . [The women] are working for money— money to feed their kids, money to keep their homes together—so their sons and husbands can fight. . . .

I want to go back to Wright's new plant because I think the women who work in war plants, and the men who first help them and then work with them are the luckiest people in the world. There's an equality developing there unlike any I've ever seen. Joe was an Italian—Nel, a Negro— Suzy, Irish—there were Germans, Poles, Hungarians, Gentiles, Jews.

Slowly you could see there was no difference between any two of us. Gradually everybody was beginning to work as one unit. When you see something like that happening you feel you're not just doing a job to help win the war. You also have the profound pleasure of seeing the future peace being worked out before your eyes.

SOURCE: Elizabeth Hawes, "My Life on the Midnight Shift," *Woman's Home Companion* (August 1943), pp. 24, 27.

Analyze the Document

1. What impresses Hawes most about her experience as a wartime factory worker?

2. How do men react to Hawes? Why do you suppose they react as they do?

3. What do you think were the longer-term consequences of such workplace experiences for women and other groups?

---

the cause and that all Soviets should make their own sacrifices for the war effort. While the scene omits the gore of the struggle, it reveals the close quarters, amid the rubble of a ruined city, in which the soldiers had to fight.

As the Russian winter again approached, Hitler ordered his army not to retreat. That decision took a huge toll on the German army. By the end of October, the German soldier's diary entries revealed a change in his optimistic attitude: "Who would have thought three months ago that instead of the joys of victory we would have to endure such sacrifice and torture, the end of which is nowhere in sight." The Germans mounted their final assault on November 11 and penetrated to the Volga. But a stalemate ensued, dragging on until November 19, when the Russians launched their long-planned encircling offensive. Though the Russian winter loomed, Hitler ordered his forces to stand firm. That decision took a huge toll on the German army. In December, the same German soldier complained, "Everybody is racked with hunger. Frozen potatoes are the best meal." Just before his death, he wrote, "The soldiers look like corpses or lunatics, looking for something to put in their mouths. They no longer take cover from

Russian shells; they haven't the strength to walk, run away and hide."

In January 1943, the Russians finally surrounded the remainder of the 300,000-man German army, now reduced by casualties to 80,000. German Sixth Army commander General Friedrich Paulus sent a note to the German high command: "Further defense senseless. Collapse inevitable. Army requests immediate permission to surrender in order to save lives of remaining troops." Hitler replied: "Surrender is forbidden. Sixth Army will hold their positions to the last man." A few days later, the German Sixth Army surrendered.

The Soviets lost one million soldiers in the bitter struggle over Stalingrad. And Germany never recovered from the massive loss of men and material, and morale suffered during the epic seven-month battle. Over the next two and a half years, Soviet forces slowly beat back the invaders (see **Map 24.3**).

The Southern Fronts

In North Africa the German general Rommel's (1891–1944) tough Afrika Korps fought to within 65 miles of the Egyptian coastal city of Alexandria.

FIGURE 24.6 The Battle of Stalingrad, 1942 In this staged photograph that exemplifies the use of propaganda during the war, Russian soldiers pose in ways suggesting the difficulty of this deadly battle.

firestorm in the German city of Hamburg. A survivor described what happened: The sky became "absolutely hellish" in minutes. "No noise made by humans—no outcry—could be heard. It was like the end of the world." The firestorm killed 40,000 people. **Figure 24.7,** a painting by British artist Leonard Henry Rosoman, suggests what civilians faced in cities subjected to heavy bombing. On the left, buildings that have stood for decades collapse in flames. Below, two firemen, armed with only a hose, fight a conflagration that is about to engulf them. While Rosoman set this in London, which endured indiscriminate rocket attacks until the last months of the war, similar and even worse scenes took place in Hamburg and many other cities.

The Western Front

On June 6, 1944 (**D-Day**), American, British, and Canadian forces under General Dwight Eisenhower (1890–1969) finally swept across the British channel to make a run at German forces holding France. Hitler, overextended in Russia and the Mediterranean, had to defend a 3,000-mile coastline in the west. Forced to gamble on where the Allies would invade, he bet on Calais, where the English Channel was narrowest. Instead, the invasion—supported by an armada of more than 6,000 vessels and 12,000 aircraft—came on the Normandy beaches. Hitler's "Atlantic Wall" of defenders took a huge toll on the invaders. In many cases, lead companies suffered 90 percent casualties; boats and tanks were often destroyed before their troops could even fire a shot. One American soldier reported that within the first ten minutes, "every officer and sergeant of the leading company had been killed or wounded. . . . It had become a struggle for survival and rescue."

Despite these losses, the Allies established a northwestern European front. Two months later, they opened a new front in southern France. Aided by French forces and resistance fighters, the Allies pushed the Germans out of most of France before year's end. Meanwhile, Allied bombs pulverized German cities and crippled Germany's transportation network.

Under the steady onslaught, Germany began running out of oil and soldiers. Early in 1945, American and British forces at last succeeded in crossing the Rhine into Germany. | Germany defeated By that time, the Russians had swept

But in August 1942, at the Battle of El Alamein, the British forces, bolstered by supplies from the United States, held. Over the following months, British and newly arriving American forces managed to push the Germans back, and in May 1943, the cornered Afrika Korps surrendered.

| The Mediterranean

The war-weary Stalin now urged Britain and America to open up a major western front in France to take the pressure off his forces. Instead, in an effort to protect British interests in the Mediterranean without risking a battle against major German forces, the Allies attacked Italy. First, they moved from the island of Sicily up into the southern Italian mainland. In July 1943, the Italian government arrested Mussolini, and two months later Italy surrendered. However, strong German forces still held most of the country. German commandos rescued Mussolini and set him up as the head of a puppet government in the north. The Allies' progress slowed through the Italian mountains, and the rest of the Italian campaign became a long and costly effort.

Meanwhile, Allied planes rained bombs on German targets. These dangerous missions took a heavy toll on both sides. In 1943, for example, only one-third of British crews flying planes across the channel would survive their first tour of duty. In late July of that same year, systematic bombing raids by British and American air forces set off a devastating through most of eastern and southeastern Europe. Along the 1,500 miles between Stalingrad and Berlin lay the wreckage of Hitler's once-mighty war machine. **Figure 24.8,** a painting by Canadian artist Charles Fraser Comfort, reveals the fate of so many combatants toward the end of World War II. Comfort, who accompanied Canadian troops in Europe, saw firsthand the horrors of war. In this haunting image, a German soldier lies dead among barbed wire on a desolate battlefield. His ravaged remains imply that the battle is long over and that his struggle was in vain. The image echoes scenes from World War I, suggesting ways in which the two wars were tragically related.

Still, Hitler would not give up. Even in the case of Berlin, he refused to evacuate civilians from the cities, despite the deaths and hardships that would result, so that his troops would feel compelled to fight even more desperately—a tactic Stalin had already used. On April 20, 1945, Berlin civilians heard the approaching Soviet troops. "Our fate is rolling in from the east," reported one woman in her diary. "What was yesterday a distant rumble has now become a constant roar. We breathe the din; our ears are deafened to all but the heaviest guns."

Germany finally surrendered on May 8, and the war in Europe ended. In what one survivor described as "the carcass of Berlin," Hitler, his wife, Eva Braun, and several other top Nazis committed suicide. In Italy, Italian partisans had already shot Mussolini and his mistress.

The War in the Pacific

In the Pacific, the turning point of the war came in the late spring of 1942 (see **Map 24.4**). American and Australian troops stopped the Japanese army in New Guinea, and the Americans turned back Japanese naval forces in the Battle of the Coral Sea, northeast of Australia. Soon, American ships, aided by intelligence from intercepted cipher transmissions, positioned themselves off Midway Island to ambush the incoming Japanese. At first, the Japanese fared well, destroying two-thirds of the American planes. Then, aided by luck, dive-bombers from American aircraft carriers spotted four Japanese carriers with their planes being refueled and rearmed. The encounter proved a disaster for the Japanese. In just five minutes, the course of the Pacific war was reversed. Three Japanese carriers went down, followed later by the fourth. The Japanese lost the advantage permanently. The U.S. arms industry was already on its way to outproducing the Japanese and creating an overwhelmingly strong fleet. The Battle of Midway

Battle of Midway

FIGURE 24.7 Leonard Henry Rosoman, *A House Collapsing on Two Firemen, Shoe Lane, London EC4,* 1940. Civilians suffered greatly from the heavy bombing of cities during the war, as suggested by this painting.

condemned the Japanese to fight defensively for the rest of the war.

In August 1942, the Americans attacked Guadalcanal in the Solomon Islands northeast of Australia. Capitalizing on their growing naval superiority and having broken the Japanese code, the Americans conducted an island-hopping campaign toward Japan. One American Marine described the "brutal, primitive hatred" that developed between the Japanese and American soldiers in this costly campaign, which "resulted in savage, ferocious fighting with no holds barred." As the battles raged on Pacific islands, "the fierce struggle for survival . . . eroded the veneer of civilization and made savages of us all."

In October 1944, the Japanese fleet made a final, desperate effort near the Philippines, but American forces annihilated it in the Battle of Leyte Gulf. However, as the United States and its allies closed in on the Japanese home islands, the most brutal land battles of the war lay ahead: Iwo Jima and Okinawa. During these

FIGURE 24.8 Charles Fraser Comfort, *Dead German on the Hitler Line*, ca. 1944 This painting of a single German soldier's remains stands for the loss of millions during this tragic, devastating war.

battles, Japanese soldiers often fought to the death or took their own lives rather than surrender. During the battle of Okinawa, Japanese pilots volunteered to fly almost 2,000 **kamikaze** missions in which they dive-bombed their planes into Allied ships (see Document 24.3). The Allies lost dozens of ships and thousands of soldiers to these desperate tactics.

Isolated, exposed, and subjected to ceaseless air and sea attacks, Japan was doomed. In February 1945, the United States began massive bomb- | The atomic bomb | ing raids on Japan's home islands, igniting huge firestorms that destroyed vast sections of Japan's cities and killed hundreds of thousands of people. After Germany surrendered in May 1945, American and British troops rushed to the Far East. In mid-July, American and British scientists finished developing and testing the atomic bomb, a new, powerful weapon the two countries had been working on for several years. To avoid the heavy casualties that a direct assault on the Japanese home islands would cause, the United States decided to use the bomb to shock Japan into surrender—a decision that has sparked controversy ever since.

While some Japanese political leaders recognized the hopelessness of continuing the war and pressed the government to pursue a peace settlement, Japan's military leaders promised a bloody fight to the finish. The fighting on Okinawa had convinced many American soldiers that the enemy would not give up. As one survivor of that battle put it, "Japan would have to be invaded with the same gruesome prospects." At the same time, many of the scientists who developed the weapon opposed using it. So did General Dwight Eisenhower: "First, the Japanese were ready to surrender and it wasn't necessary to hit them with that awful thing. Second, I hated to see our country be the first to use such a weapon."

On August 6, 1945, a U.S. plane dropped an atomic bomb that destroyed the Japanese city of Hiroshima and some 80,000 of its inhabitants; tens of thousands more died later from the effects of radiation. One survivor, Yamaoka Michiko, described the horror: "There were people, barely breathing, trying to push their intestines back in. People with their legs wrenched off. Without heads. Or with faces burned and swollen out of shape. The scene I saw was a living hell." Three days later, a second atomic bomb demolished the industrial city of Nagasaki, killing an additional 50,000. On August 8, the Soviet Union declared war on Japan and sent troops into Manchuria. The Japanese surrendered on August 15, 1945.

DOCUMENT 24.3

"We Shall Plunge into Enemy Ships"

During the last year of the war in the Pacific, the Japanese responded to widespread losses by resorting to suicide attacks on U.S. ships. The Kamikaze Special Attack Corps carried out these attacks. Heiichi Okabe was a member of that corps, and on February 22, 1945, he wrote the following letter.

I am actually a member at last of the Kamikaze Special Attack Corps. My life will be rounded out in the next thirty days. My chance will come! Death and I are waiting. The training and practice have been rigorous, but it is worthwhile if we can die beautifully and for a cause.

I shall die watching the pathetic struggle of our nation. My life will gallop in the next few weeks as my youth and life draw to a close. . . .

The sortie has been scheduled for the next ten days. I am a human being and hope to be neither saint nor scoundrel, hero nor fool—just a human being. As one who has spent his life in wistful longing and searching, I die resignedly in the hope that my life will serve as a "human document."

The world in which I lived was too full of discord. As a community of rational human beings it should be better composed. Lacking a single great conductor, everyone lets loose with his own sound, creating dissonance where there should be melody and harmony.

We shall serve the nation gladly in its present painful struggle. We shall plunge into enemy ships cherishing the conviction that Japan has been and will be a place where only lovely homes, brave women, and beautiful friendships are allowed to exist.

What is the duty today? It is to fight.
What is the duty tomorrow? It is to win.
What is the daily duty? It is to die.

We die in battle without complaint. I wonder if others, like scientists, who pursue the war effort on their own fronts, would die as we do without complaint. Only then will the unity of Japan be such that she can have any prospect of winning the war.

SOURCE: Rihihei Inoguchi and Tadashi Nakajima, *The Divine Wind* (Annapolis, MD: United States Naval Institute, 1958), pp. 207–208.

Analyze the Document

1. How do you explain Heiichi Okabe's thoughts as expressed in this excerpt?

2. How does his "duty" compare to that of other soldiers?

3. Do you agree with his statement that he is "just a human being" and neither a hero nor a fool? Explain.

PEACE AND THE LEGACY OF WAR

In 1945, Europe lay prostrate as some 50 million refugees drifted across the land and countless people faced starvation and homelessness. Memories of lost loved ones and homes, the horrors of the concentration camps, the hardships of occupation, and the echoes of mass bombings would haunt people for the rest of their lives.

Europe in shambles

Outrage, fear, and violence continued to stalk Europe. Many resistance fighters and Soviet troops executed surrendering Nazi soldiers on the spot. Angry officials and ordinary people hunted down and punished collaborators after only summary trials. To shame women they suspected of sleeping with German soldiers, irate citizens shaved off women's hair and marched them through the streets. The Soviets, Poles, and Czechoslovakians pushed 13 million ethnic Germans out of homes in Eastern Europe toward the west. One eyewitness described how "families with children, packages, hand wheelbarrows, horse-drawn wagons, and bicycles were making their way, and were being assaulted" as they fled along the roads to Germany. Stalin's officials sent thousands of returning Soviet prisoners to forced-labor camps or to the executioner for being "contaminated" by dangerous, anti-Soviet ideas. Jews who had managed to survive often found their homes destroyed, and they still suffered from flagrant anti-Semitism.

With agricultural and nonmilitary industrial production at a fraction of their prewar levels, Western Europe looked to the United States for loans, relief, defense, and leadership. Eastern Europe, in even worse shambles, was falling under the dominance of the Soviet Union. Political leaders and diplomats involved in the peace settlement hoped this time to avoid the "mistakes" made at the close of World War I. The main challenge facing them was to find a way to deal with defeated nations without spawning new conflicts.

The Settlement

The leaders of Great Britain, the United States, and the Soviet Union shaped postwar Europe in two wartime conferences, at Teheran in December 1943 and Yalta in February 1945, and one postwar conference at Potsdam in July 1945. They agreed to accept only unconditional surrender by Germany and Japan and to require complete restructuring of the aggressors' governments. Germany, which had proved so powerful in two world wars, would be disarmed and divided. The Soviet Union, having suffered so much from Germany's massive invasion, demanded and received pledges of territories on its western border as well as reparations from Germany. To further weaken Germany and recognize the impact of the war, Poland's border with Germany was pushed westward. Finally, a **United Nations** organization was founded in 1945 by fifty-one nations to promote international peace and cooperation. **Figure 24.9,** a 1947 poster marking the second anniversary of the organization's birth, reveals the high hopes of its founders. Caring hands plant a tree of peace and union, each leaf representing the flag of a member nation. People hoped that as the "sapling" grew, new "leaves" and maturity would strengthen the young organization.

On other matters, however, discord among the wartime allies created a more ominous view of the future. The most crucial disagreements came over the fate of the Eastern European countries. Stalin argued that because the Soviet Union had endured invasions through these countries in both world wars, he needed them to serve as a buffer zone of states loyal to the USSR. The United States and Great Britain demanded complete independence and democracy for these countries. Concessions on both sides at the Yalta Conference in February 1945 left Eastern Europe vaguely democratic but "friendly" to the Soviet Union. This arrangement quickly proved unworkable. Two nations—Poland and Bulgaria—were already under communist control, and pro-Soviet "coalition governments" quickly formed in other Eastern European states.

> Discord over Eastern Europe

At the final conference, at Potsdam in July 1945 (the war ended without a formal peace treaty), Stalin had the upper hand. President Roosevelt had died. Although the American president, Harry Truman, firmly demanded free elections in all of Eastern Europe, he had been in office only three months. Churchill might have been able to exert more pressure on Stalin, but the newly elected Clement Attlee replaced him during the conference. Stalin, insisting that the Soviet Union must obtain complete security against Germany and any potential Eastern European allies, refused to budge on the issue: "A freely elected government in any of these East European countries would be anti-Soviet," he admitted, "and that we cannot allow."

U.S. leaders had trouble swallowing the reality behind Stalin's words. In fact, Eastern Europe was already behind Soviet lines and occupied by Soviet troops by war's end, just as Western Europe remained behind Anglo-American lines and within the United States' and Britain's sphere of influence. "Everyone imposes his own system as far as his armies can reach," observed Stalin privately. "It cannot be otherwise."

The Legacy of War

Human beings have waged war on each other since the beginnings of civilization. But World War II, especially when viewed in connection with its twentieth-century predecessor, World War I, shook the West and the world as nothing before.

One crucial difference stemmed from technology. Bloody battles, massacres, torture, and cruelty were not new to the twentieth century. But for the first time, combatants had developed weapons to translate these acts into tens of millions of deaths on and off the battlefields. The use of chemicals, machines, and organizations to inflict a wide range of horrors on so many people so quickly was also unprecedented.

Certainly World War I set a well-remembered precedent for the decision makers of the Second World War. The 1914–1918 conflict had become a relentless mutual slaughter with single battles costing hundreds of thousands of lives and total deaths surpassing 20 million. Those years of war also carried in their wake genocidal actions by the Turks against the Armenians and Allied blockades for months after the

FIGURE 24.9 The United Nations, 1947 This period poster by Henri Eveleigh celebrates the founding of the United Nations and conveys the hopes of its founders for peace and international cooperation.

end of the war that inflicted widespread starvation on defeated nations.

The two decades after World War I brought to power regimes in Russia, Germany, and Japan that hinted at what a second world conflict might wreak on humanity. In Russia, transformed into the Soviet Union, Stalin inflicted a terror-famine on Ukraine, which cost millions of lives, and established the system of slave-labor camps (the Gulag) that also killed and imprisoned millions more. In Germany, the rise of the Nazis to power under Adolf Hitler in 1933 soon led to concentration camps, anti-Semitic terror, and policies of euthanasia. In Japan, the initiation of war against China in 1937 resulted in what is generally called the Rape of Nanking.

The outbreak of war in Europe in 1939 led to even worse acts and consequences. Violence raged across oceans and continents. The death toll alone was staggering. More than 60 million people—some scholars argue that the actual figure might be much higher—were killed during World War II.

Even more ominous, far more civilians than soldiers died, owing in part to the tactics and weapons of modern war. The drive to inflict massive damage led to indiscriminate carpet and fire bombings. These raids not only made little distinction between military and civilian targets but literally flattened German and Japanese cities such as Dresden and Tokyo. The search for revolutionary superweapons also bore frightening fruit. The atomic bomb—the weapon that finally ended the war in the Pacific—made it all too clear that human beings now had the ability to inflict unimaginable destruction with a single blow.

Meanwhile, the 11 to 12 million deaths resulting from the Nazis' genocidal program revealed a new capacity for bureaucratized and industrialized killing. Only a relatively few individuals survived the death camps to "tell the story, to bear witness." They and the rest of humanity have had to find ways to live with the realization, in the words of the Auschwitz survivor Primo Levi, "that such a crime should exist," and that it had been "introduced irrevocably into the world of things that exist."

More broadly, terror—of combatants and civilians alike—became a standard tactic during World War II. Officially sanctioned mass rape—in particular by advancing Russian forces in retaliation against the Germans and by Japanese soldiers against the Chinese—made the experience of war all the more vicious. Rape took tragic forms. For example, some 300,000 women, most of them from Korea, were forced to serve the Japanese military as "comfort women."

After World War II, it was clear that humans had acquired the capacity to annihilate peoples and civilizations. This realization called into question some of the very developments that had most characterized the West over the previous two centuries: science (used to destroy lives), industrialization (which made the war machines possible), nationalism (which mutated into militarism), ideological beliefs (which justified everything from sacrifice to terror and genocide), and humanism (which seemed irrelevant in the face of blatant inhumanity). In the European heart of the West, many people prayed that a conflict on the scale of World War II would never strike again. But even as they hoped, tensions between two countries that had once lain at the peripheries of the West—the Soviet Union and the United States—suggested that peace might prove short-lived.

LOOKING BACK & MOVING FORWARD

Summary World War II devastated much of Europe and left scars across the globe from North Africa and the Middle East to East Asia and the Pacific. The first battles erupted in Asia when the Japanese, eager to expand their empire, invaded China. Then Nazi Germany and Fascist Italy struck in Europe. The Axis powers piled up victories until the Allies, with their superior industrial might and manpower, finally turned the tide.

The war took a staggering toll. The Nazis not only waged war against the Allies, millions of European Jews, and other "undesirable" groups but also conducted nothing less than a campaign to destroy eastern European nations. Twenty-seven million Soviets, perhaps many more, perished in the struggle. Germans treated Soviet prisoners of war savagely—shooting, working, or starving to death some two million of them. The Soviets dealt with German prisoners only marginally better. German armies had left the Soviet Union's cities in smoking ruins and ravaged its countryside. Despite aid from the United States and Great Britain, the

KEY TERMS

Popular Front, *p. 748*

Axis, *p. 749*

appeasement, *p. 750*

Munich Conference, *p. 750*

blitzkrieg, *p. 751*

Holocaust, *p. 757*

D-Day, *p. 764*

kamikaze, *p. 766*

United Nations, *p. 768*

Soviets produced 90 percent of their supplies themselves. They had turned the tide against the Germans in Europe well before the Americans and British opened a western front in France. Understandably, the Soviets maintained that they had sacrificed more than any other nation to defeat Germany.

Other countries also sustained terrible losses. Some fifteen million Chinese died. Germany gave up six million lives; Japan almost two million. Poland suffered horribly: In addition to losing hundreds of thousands of ordinary citizens, its elites were systematically rounded up and executed by both the Soviets and the Germans.

At war's end, tens of millions of Europeans had been uprooted and were homeless. Western and non-Western societies, weary and bloodied, now faced an overwhelming task: to recover from the devastation of the war and regain some sense of order. The road ahead looked hard. In Asia, rumblings of national revolutions had already begun. There, the Japanese invaders had inadvertently emboldened nationalists by demonstrating that an Asian people could defeat Western overlords. Such developments all unfolded under the shadow of a sobering new realization: Through modern warfare and new technology, human beings now had the power to obliterate the entire world.

REVIEW, ANALYZE, & CONNECT TO TODAY

REVIEW THE PREVIOUS CHAPTER

Chapter 23—"Darkening Decades"—traced the rise of fascism, the development of the Soviet Union, and the trials of nations struck by the Great Depression.

1. How might one argue that World War II stemmed directly from World War I and the Great Depression?

2. What qualities of fascism and authoritarian governments fed the forces for war in the 1930s?

ANALYZE THIS CHAPTER

Chapter 24—"Into the Fire Again"—studies the causes, course, and consequences of World War II.

1. Analyze some of the thinking behind Japanese aggression during the 1930s and 1940s.

2. How was the Holocaust connected to Hitler's Nazi ideology and the course of World War II?

3. How did the Allies turn the tide and defeat the Axis powers in World War II?

4. What problems faced negotiators trying to design a settlement at the end of World War II?

CONNECT TO TODAY

Think about how World War II was fought and what happened during the war, both on the front lines and behind the lines.

1. In a major new war, what problems might there be in maintaining a meaningful distinction between civilians and combatants?

2. In today's world, how might propaganda be used to justify war and support a major war effort?

3. What communication channels that were not available during World War II do present-day propagandists use? For what specific activities do they—or might they—use them?

BEYOND THE CLASSROOM

THE ROAD TO WAR, 1931–1939

Crozier, Andrew. *The Causes of the Second World War.* London: Blackwell, 1997. A book with good detail within a world context.

Neville, Peter. *Hitler and Appeasement: The British Attempt to Prevent the Second World War.* New York: Continuum, 2005. Defends British efforts to avoid war and places "appeasement" in a broad context.

Watt, Donald Cameron. *How War Came: The Immediate Origins of the Second World War.* London: Heinemann, 1989. A helpful coverage of events directly leading to the war.

AXIS VICTORIES, 1939–1942

Keegan, John. *The Second World War.* New York: Viking, 1990. A book that is particularly good on battles and strategy.

Weinberg, Gerhard L. *A World at Arms: A Global History of World War II.* New York: Cambridge University Press, 1994. Excellent in its global perspective and its examination of the Nazi plan for world order.

GLOBAL CONNECTIONS

Irokawa, Daikichi. *The Age of Hirohito: In Search of Modern Japan.* New York: The Free Press, 1995. A broad study that covers the topic and more.

BEHIND THE LINES: THE STRUGGLE AND THE HORROR

Fritzsche, Peter. *Life and Death in the Third Reich.* Cambridge, MA: Harvard University Press, 2008. A well-argued interpretation.

Jackson, Julian. *France: The Dark Years, 1940–1944.* New York: Oxford University Press, 2003. A fine study of collaboration and resistance in France.

Kershaw, Ian. *Hitler, the Germans, and the Final Solution.* New Haven, CT: Yale University Press, 2008. A highly respected set of essays on the topics.

TURNING THE TIDE OF WAR, 1942–1945

Beevor, Anthony. *The Fall of Berlin 1945.* New York: Penguin, 2003. An effective narrative covering the final siege against Berlin.

Frank, R. B. *Downfall: The End of the Imperial Japanese Empire.* New York: Penguin, 2001. A balanced account of the end of the war in the Pacific.

Overy, Richard. *Russia's War: A History of the Soviet War Effort, 1941–1945.* New York: Penguin, 1998. A well-written account of the war on the eastern front.

PEACE AND THE LEGACY OF WAR

Glover, Jonathan. *Humanity: A Moral History of the Twentieth Century.* New Haven, CT: Yale University Press, 2000. A superb analysis of the grave challenges from the twentieth century that combines psychological, philosophical, and historical perspectives.

Winter, Jay, and Emmanuel Sivan. *War and Remembrance in the Twentieth Century.* Cambridge: Cambridge University Press, 1999. A series of interdisciplinary essays focusing on memory and loss in twentieth-century wars.

Forming the Present

The end of World War II marked the dawn of a new era that we can best understand by widening our focus from the West to the entire world. Between 1945 and the first decade of the twenty-first century, four key developments dominated interactions among civilizations around the globe. First, peoples throughout the world increasingly believed that being modern meant becoming Westernized. Second, more and more non-Western peoples agitated to free themselves from Western imperial control. Third, contradictory political beliefs emerged that pitted democratic capitalism against Marxist communism. And, fourth, a vast movement of ideas, technologies, labor, capital, and goods across borders further blurred lines between the West and the non-Western world.

The decades after 1945 witnessed an affirmation of the civilization located in the West and uncertainty about its borders and defining characteristics. In many areas of the world, Western civilization became a model for change and modernization. Indeed, some people used the term *modernization*—for example, the spread of cutting-edge science, technology, and industry—interchangeably with *Westernization*. The West's enduring power further affirmed its standing in the world. Despite the devastation in the European heartland wrought during World War II, the West had emerged

as the globe's politically, economically, and militarily dominant player. But with Europe prostrate, the West's centers of power shifted to what once had been its peripheries—across the Atlantic to the United States and east to the Soviet Union.

At the same time, what defined the West's borders and unique characteristics became less and less clear. Great numbers of people moved in and out of the West, carrying different ways of life with them. Meanwhile, elements of Western culture—liberalism and Marxism, sneakers and hamburgers, movies and the Internet—spread into and saturated other cultures. This mingling of culture, ideas, and institutions made it difficult to discern where the West ended and other civilizations began. Nevertheless, most historians think of the West at this time as consisting of Europe and those areas (such as the Americas, Australia, and New Zealand) where Europeans arrived, adapted, dominated, and almost crushed preexisting cultures and peoples.

Outside of the West, two main struggles dominated the decades after 1945. Both involved the West in one way or another. The first struggle was for national liberation, as peoples in Africa, Asia, and elsewhere threw off their Western colonial rulers. This process sometimes required extended armed combat; other times, it took the form of a peaceful transfer of power. Most such victories left problematic legacies that would plague the freed

countries for decades. For example, many newly liberated nations in Africa and Asia would experience great difficulty achieving political stability and developing the economic means to support their populations.

The second struggle that extended beyond the West came with a battle for political power and ideological control that pitted nations headed by the United States (with its system of democratic capitalism) against those allied with the Soviet Union (which had adopted state-directed communism). This complex conflict, known as the Cold War, spread to such far-flung places as Southeast Asia, Korea, Cuba, and Angola.

Connections between the West and the rest of the world became so extensive after 1945 that many call that period the age of globalism. But in reality, waves of globalism had struck earlier. The first began in the late fifteenth century, as Western powers moved out of Europe to establish imperial or commercial links across the seas. The second wave came in the nineteenth century. In those years, industrialism and imperial ambitions pushed Western nations to increase their influence and control over much of the world. People, goods, and ideas flowed between the West and other civilizations. World War I and the economic problems of the 1920s and 1930s dampened this second age of globalism. The new age that began after World War II renewed the flood

Earth from Space
This world map view of the Earth is a composite of many different NASA satellite images.

of ideas, trade, and peoples across borders, with technology bringing hourly if not instant communications around the globe. By the end of the century, for example, goods could be designed in one country, financed internationally, produced in yet another nation, sold in faraway markets, and serviced via phones and the Internet from still different points of the globe.

The West remained at the core of this new globalism. However, other areas of the world began coming to the fore. Some in parts of Asia took over industrial production and technology first developed in the West and successfully adapted it. Others in parts of the Middle East controlled crucial,

wealth-making assets such as oil. Still others, in parts of the Islamic world, reacted in a backlash against the West. In addition to these developments, all civilizations—Western and non-Western alike—would soon face challenges they could not have imagined previously. Perhaps none were more threatening to the entire human species than the spread of nuclear arms and such dramatic environmental changes as global warming.

Thinking Globally

1. Consider the four major developments on which this essay focuses. What other developments might be added to this discussion?

2. What areas of the world are generally considered to be of the West today?

3. In the satellite image above, identify areas that border the Pacific Ocean and that might be considered part of the modernized world. Refer also to the maps of Europe and the world at the back of this book for more detail.

4. Starting from Europe, scan the rest of the world, first to the south, then the east, and finally to the west. In what ways has the West touched and affected various parts of the globe over the three ages of globalism? How might our present age of globalism resemble previous ages of globalism? How might it differ?

DON EDDY, *NEW SHOES FOR H*, 1974

In this 1974 painting, Don Eddy uses the artistic style known as photo-realism to depict
a shoe-store display in New York City. Reflected in the store window are cars, buses, a
department store sign (S. Klein), office and apartment buildings, and a pedestrian
in blue jeans—all in all, a typically vibrant street scene in a leading Western city of the era.

Superpower Struggles and Global Transformations

25

The Cold War, 1945–1980s

In 1974, a retired Frenchwoman, Françoise Giroud, contrasted her early life as a stenographer in the 1930s with the lives of young women of the 1970s. "[T]here is simply no comparison. . . . A month of paid vacation, . . . organized travel, . . . paperback books, . . . blue jeans and the T-shirts, instant mashed potatoes, the transistor, . . . the boyfriend who has a [used car], . . . and the Pill! It's not a better world; it's another world altogether." This new world that Giroud described boasted unheard-of material well-being, international peace throughout most of the West, innovative day-to-day conveniences, and striking new medical knowledge. The painting on page 774 is an apt illustration of this new age. The image reveals a wealthy, commercial society awash in consumer goods. In effect, the painting offers a view of reality from different perspectives, paralleling the efforts that many Westerners made to understand their rapidly changing world.

Yet these decades also had their dark side. Nations around the world labored to recover from the devastation of World War II. As they did so, a new menace emerged—growing tensions between the United States and the Soviet Union that for decades would overshadow international relations and everyday life. At the same time, colonial peoples took advantage of Europe's weakness and changing attitudes toward imperialism and demanded their independence in ways the West could not ignore. New nations and international organizations soon emerged throughout the world, and global interactions grew so complex that the traditional lines between Western and non-Western societies blurred more than ever.

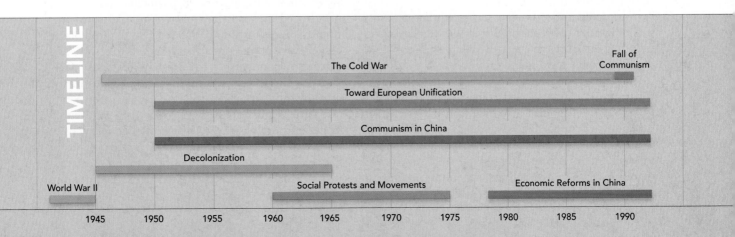

TIMELINE

World War II		Decolonization			Social Protests and Movements			Economic Reforms in China	
				The Cold War				Fall of Communism	
			Toward European Unification						
			Communism in China						
1945	1950	1955	1960	1965	1970	1975	1980	1985	1990

PREVIEW

ORIGINS OF THE COLD WAR

"At the present moment in world history nearly every nation must choose between alternative ways of life," announced U.S. president Harry Truman on March 12, 1947. Ominously, he added, "The choice is too often not a free one," referring to what he termed the "coercion and intimidation" used to force "totalitarian regimes" on the peoples of several countries. Eight months later, his secretary of state, George Marshall, pointed to the heart of the problem: "The present line of division in Europe is roughly the line upon which the Anglo-American armies coming from the west met those of the Soviet Union coming from the east. . . . Developments in the European countries to the east of that line bear the unmistakable imprint of an alien hand." According to Truman and Marshall, the "alien hand" over Eastern Europe belonged to the Soviet Union, only two years earlier an ally of the United States in World War II.

The conflict over the fate of Eastern Europe drove a sharp wedge between the World War II allies. Long-standing antagonisms and new differences soon combined to break down further any cooperation between the Western democracies and the Soviet Union. Ever since the communists had come to power in 1917, they and the capitalist democracies had viewed each other as opponents (see Chapter 23). As ideologies, communism and capitalism had always been in direct opposition. As practiced in the Soviet Union under Lenin and Stalin, the political system of communism

took a dictatorial form, in sharp contrast to the democracies of Great Britain and the United States. Hitler's invasion of the Soviet Union in World War II and the United States' entry into the war only temporarily united Great Britain, the United States, and the Soviet Union. The three powers joined as allies more in opposition to Nazi Germany than in agreement over principles or goals. Not surprisingly, when negotiations over war aims and settlement terms took place, the history of hostility, distrust, and fear between the capitalist and communist powers caused problems. After the war, when the threat of Nazi Germany no longer held the Allies together, tensions worsened.

In 1945, the U.S. cut off all aid to the USSR. The rhetoric of discord between the powers increased. The next year, Winston Churchill, speaking at a small college in Missouri, warned the world of an **Iron Curtain** descending from the Baltic to the Adriatic Seas, dividing Europe between communist East and capitalist West.

Churchill's warning proved apt. Within the next few years, Soviet-backed communist parties in Eastern Europe pushed their opponents aside and rose to power; only communist Yugoslavia and Albania would manage to follow independent courses. In Western Europe, despite the presence of popular communist parties, American-backed anticommunist politicians controlled the governments. In Greece, the two sides clashed as the British and the Americans supported the repressive anticommunist monarchy in an armed conflict against the Greek communists. The **Cold War** had begun.

The Heart of the Cold War

At the heart of the Cold War lay a troubled Germany. As **Map 25.1** indicates, the peace settlement had divided the aggressor nation into four occupation zones: American, Soviet, British, and French. The city of Berlin, in the Russian zone, was also divided into the same four sectors. Sharp disagreements soon surfaced among the occupiers. The Soviets alarmed their allies by grabbing valuable resources from Germany, including entire factories, and transporting them to the Soviet Union as reparations for war losses rather than waiting for cash payments. The Soviets also hoped to keep their old enemy Germany economically weak and fully divided. The United States and Britain, on the other hand, set out to restore and integrate economically the western sectors of Germany, seeing those regions as essential allies in the growing split with the USSR.

Matters came to a head in 1948 when the United States and Britain tried to spur economic recovery by introducing a new currency in the western zones of Germany despite Soviet opposition. Stalin countered by blockading the three western zones of Berlin. From

MAP 25.1

Europe After World War II

This map shows Europe after World War II and the dates that communists gained control of governments in Eastern Europe.

Explore the Map

1. Which territories were acquired by the Soviet Union?

2. Locate Berlin. Why was this city of such strategic, political, and symbolic importance?

3. What predicament arose for the western zones of Berlin when the Soviets cut off land traffic from the west?

4. How would you evaluate the size and potential importance of a unified Germany?

June 1948 to May 1949, the Soviets stopped all land traffic across their zone from the West to Berlin.

The Berlin blockade and the division of Germany

In response, the Western powers mounted a daring and continuous airlift that carried supplies to the city. If "Berlin falls," warned the American military commander General Lucius Clay, "western Germany will be next . . . if we withdraw, our position in Europe is threatened. . . . Communism will run rampant." The **Berlin airlift** eventually prompted the Soviet Union to back down.

In September 1949, the Western allies followed through on their plan to merge the three western zones of Germany and to create an independent West German state—the German Federal Republic. One month later, the Soviet Union established the German Democratic Republic in its eastern zone, completing the division of Germany into the capitalist West and communist East.

The Cold War spreads

Meanwhile, the Cold War chill was already spreading across the rest of Europe. In 1947, U.S. president Harry Truman (1884–1972) initiated the Truman Doctrine, a policy that offered military and economic aid to countries threatened by a communist takeover. "The peoples of a number of countries of the world have recently had totalitarian regimes forced upon them against their will," he warned. "[I]t must be the policy of the United States to support free peoples who are resisting attempted subjugation by armed minorities or by outside pressures." His immediate concern was the civil war in Greece, where local communists aided by neighboring Yugoslavia were making gains against the royalist government. His larger goal was to create a military ring of "**containment**" around the Soviet Union and its satellite states.

That same year, Truman's secretary of state, George Marshall (1880–1959), launched the **Marshall Plan,** a package of massive economic aid to European nations designed both to strengthen them and to tie them to American influence. The Soviet Union forbad Eastern European governments to accept the aid and soon established the Council for Mutual Economic Assistance (COMECON), a Soviet version of the Marshall Plan for Eastern Europe.

In 1949, the United States organized the **North Atlantic Treaty Organization (NATO),** a military alliance among the United States, Canada, and most of the nations of Western Europe against the Soviet Union. Within a few years, Greece and Turkey had joined the alliance. After West Germany signed on in 1955, the Soviet Union countered NATO by creating its own military alliance in Eastern Europe, the Warsaw Pact. Now thousands of troops in each alliance—backed by the presence and might of the two superpowers—faced each other along a line dividing Eastern and Western Europe. It had taken only a few years for each side in the Cold War to forge economic, political, and military ties among its allies and form two hostile camps (see **Map 25.2**).

The Cold War would color international relations and everyday life for more than four decades. Andrei Zhdanov (1896–1948), a powerful Soviet official, described the official Soviet view of the Cold War in 1947: U.S. goals were "domination in all countries marked out for American expansion" and "the creation in peacetime of numerous [military] bases . . . for aggressive purposes against the USSR." John Foster Dulles (1888–1959), President Dwight Eisenhower's secretary of state, presented the U.S. view in 1953: "Soviet communism . . . is the gravest threat that has ever faced . . . Western civilization, or indeed, any civilization . . . dominated by a spiritual faith." Compromise between such extreme, hostile views seemed impossible.

As Document 25.1 suggests, terror lurked just below the surface of the Cold War. By 1949, both superpowers had the atomic bomb; by 1953, the hydrogen bomb. Each

Cold War weapons

country supported growing military budgets and stockpiled huge caches of weapons, including intercontinental ballistic missiles (ICBMs) that could carry nuclear warheads. The danger rippled outward as other nations—Britain, France, India, China, Israel, and Pakistan—also developed nuclear weapons. As U.S. president John F. Kennedy (1917–1963) admitted in 1962, "The decision to use any kind of a nuclear weapon . . . presents such a risk of it getting out of control so quickly. . . ." In fact, the Cold War was fought in all ways except open military conflict between the United States and the Soviet Union. Networks of spies fanned out over the globe. Political struggles anywhere, even purely internal matters, became arenas for defining a victory or defeat in the Cold War. The competition expanded to include nonpolitical activities as well, such as space exploration and the Olympic Games.

Cold War posturing and imagery also saturated the media. In **Figure 25.1,** a 1948 poster created for the French Communist Party, atomic bombs hover over the prostrate victim, spreading death (the crosses in the background) and destruction (the burning buildings). The poster warns France against any form of alliance with Germany, which the communists claimed would amount to preparation for war against the Soviet Union. From the United States, the Voice of America radio station spread anticommunist messages throughout Europe, while the station's Soviet counterpart presented its own views. Most European governments controlled the news on their radio and television programs.

All this led to a pervasive sense of suspicion and fear. Novels, movies, and television shows featuring

thinking about
GEOGRAPHY

MAP 25.2

Europe During the Cold War

This map shows how the Cold War had divided Europe by the 1950s.

Explore the Map

1. What connections between military and economic cooperation are revealed by this map?

2. Why do you think the Soviet Union was so anxious to maintain control over its Eastern European allies?

3. Why was Turkey such an important member of NATO?

4. Notice what nations are not a part of the alliance organizations. What are the possible reasons?

spies and international intrigue proliferated. In the United States, for example, Senator Joseph McCarthy (1908–1957) led a massive name-calling campaign between 1950 and 1954 "to uncover" communists and communist sympathizers; these "fellow travelers," McCarthy claimed, had infiltrated every aspect of American life, from the armed services to Hollywood movie studios. Atomic bomb drills in American schools and bomb shelters in city basements and suburban backyards completed the picture of a Western democratic nation menaced by communism and the Soviet Union.

The Global Impact of the Cold War

The Cold War quickly spread around the globe as each side searched for allies and victories wherever they could find them (see **Map 25.3**). No area escaped from the worldwide competition, but events in Asia and Latin America especially reveal the far-reaching impact of the Cold War. In both areas, the United States forged anticommunist alliances while the Soviet Union supported communist governments and revolutionary movements. More than once, the contest fueled crises and armed conflict in these areas.

Japan had emerged from World War II defeated on sea and land, the shocked victim of history's first two atomic bombs used for military purposes. Because the United States by far had played the major role in the defeat of Japan, it refused to share the occupation and governing of the Japanese islands with its former allies. The U.S. quickly promoted political democratization and used financial aid to help Japan rebuild and conform to U.S. policies. In this way, Japan, like West Germany, would become a link in the Cold War containment "chain" that the U.S. was forging around the Soviet Union. The strategy paid off handsomely. During the 1950s and 1960s, Japan became a firm ally and used its modern industries and skilled labor to make an astounding economic recovery that surpassed even that of West Germany.

The Cold War in Asia

China, just across the Sea of Japan, moved in a different direction. The civil war between Mao Zedong's zealous Communist forces and Jiang Jieshi's

DOCUMENT 25.1

The Cold War and Nuclear Weapons

The intensity of the Cold War and the existence of nuclear weapons on both sides spread fear throughout the West during the 1950s and early 1960s. Observers debated whether nuclear weapons would deter attacks from the opposing side, whether the contestants could agree to disarm, and whether unilateral destruction of nuclear weapons made the most sense. In the following selection from a 1956 debate, Philip Toynbee of Great Britain argues for the last position.

It is obvious, surely, that this is an issue which has nothing whatever to do with party politics and nothing whatever to do with our estimations of American and Russian society. In the terrible context of nuclear war even the vital differences between Communism and Western freedom become almost unimportant. We would infinitely prefer our Western system of freedom and privacy to prevail in the world; and if we are spared we shall have an opportunity of trying to ensure that it does so. But even if it didn't prevail *mankind* would still be given the opportunity of prevailing. Mr. Kennan has said that anything would be better than a policy which led inevitably to nuclear war. But surely anything is better than a policy which allows for the *possibility* of nuclear war.

The issue has nothing do to with politics. It has little to do with causes and highmindedness. Those who have had at least a partial vision of our destruction are like people who have leant out of the window of an express train and seen that a bridge is down a little further along the line. They are urging the driver and their fellow-passengers that the train should be stopped. But the others reply, many of them from behind their newspapers, that the train can't possibly be stopped because they have important engagements in the city. As for the bridge, it may not be down after all, and even if it is the train will probably manage to jump across it somehow. Besides, it does no good to the reputation of our railways if express trains are to be halted in this way. And finally, we ought surely to be aware that there is another express train coming in the opposite direction which will certainly fall down into the river just as soon as we do.

At the very least, then, let those who wish to continue with the arms-race be prepared with competent methods of killing off their mutilated families before killing their mutilated selves. Only when we see that they have made these preparations shall we be able to believe that they have faced the implications of their policy.

SOURCE: Philip Toynbee, *The Fearful Choice* (London: Victor Gollancz, 1956), pp. 21–22.

Analyze the Document

1. What does Toynbee's argument reveal about the level of fear during the Cold War?

2. How does Toynbee justify a policy of unilateral nuclear disarmament?

3. How might his opponents have responded to this argument?

---

conservative Nationalist forces was suspended during World War II. Mao's forces waged a more incessant guerrilla warfare against the Japanese than the Nationalists did and thereby gained a growing following among the Chinese people. After the surrender of Japan in 1945, the bitter, internal struggle for control of China began anew. The United States supported the Nationalists, while ever-increasing numbers of Chinese supported the Communists. In 1949, the victorious Communists swept over the entire Chinese mainland. Jiang's Nationalists fled to the nearby island of Taiwan, where they came under the protection of the U.S. navy. Mao promptly proclaimed the People's Republic of China and joined in an alliance with the Soviet Union. With Soviet aid, he began the daunting task of industrializing and communizing China.

Less than a year later, the Cold War merged with simmering internal forces in nearby Korea to produce a major conflict that embroiled both the new Chinese communist regime and the United States. At the end of World War II, in accordance with the Yalta agreements, Soviet troops occupied Korea north of the thirty-eighth parallel, while American forces controlled the south. The Soviets and Americans had withdrawn by 1949, leaving North and South Korea as armed client states rather than a united Korean nation. The new governments of the North and South, each ruled by dictators, talked loudly of conquering each other.

The Korean War

In 1950, the Soviet-backed North Korean communists—with the approval of both Stalin and Mao—suddenly invaded U.S.-backed South Korea. The determined, well-armed North Korean communists easily defeated the South Koreans. Supported by the UN, the U.S. quickly intervened. The American and UN forces soon overcame the North Koreans, but as their troops approached the Korean-Chinese border and threatened to bomb North Korean sanctuaries in China, the Chinese entered the fray. They pushed the U.S. and UN forces back to the thirty-eighth parallel, where a stalemate developed. By the time of the armistice in 1953, the war had cost some

FIGURE 25.1 *Peace Must Be Saved,* **1948** This French propaganda poster by André Fougeron, promoted by the French Communist Party, warns of the atomic destruction that would result from a French alliance with Germany.

1.5 million casualties on each side and had left much of Korea in ruins.

These experiences with Korea and China prompted the U.S. to involve itself in nearby Vietnam, Laos, and Cambodia. The U.S. feared that the fall of one nation in that region to communism would, as with a row of dominoes, lead to the fall of other adjacent nations. "Vietnam represents the cornerstone of the Free World in Southeast Asia, the keystone to the arch, the finger in the dike," warned Senator John F. Kennedy in 1956. "Burma, Thailand, India, Japan, the Philippines, and obviously Laos and Cambodia are among those whose security would be threatened if the red tide of Communism overflowed into Vietnam. . . ."

Accordingly, the U.S. helped the French fight against Vietnamese nationalists. Vietnam had been a French colony before World War II and, under the leadership of Ho Chi Minh (1890–1969) and his Vietnamese Communist Party, had fought for its independence from France in the years after World War II. After suffering a series of defeats, France finally agreed

The Vietnam War

to withdraw in 1954. The 1954 Geneva Accords provisionally gave Ho Chi Minh's Communists control of the nation north of the seventeenth latitude and provided for elections throughout the whole country in 1956. The U.S. refused to sign the accords, and Ngo Dihn Diem (1901–1963), who took power in the south where the remnants of the old French-supported Associated State of Vietnam had fled, refused to hold the elections. The nation was divided between the North, ruled by the victorious Ho Chi Minh, and the South, under an authoritarian, anticommunist government that tried to maintain the aristocratic society of a vanishing era (see **Map 25.4**).

The unpopular regime in the South relied for its survival on the economic and political support of the United States and its allies. Military aid and armed forces soon followed, as the United States sought to increase its influence not only in South Vietnam but also in Laos and Cambodia, which had gained freedom from the French. During the mid-1960s, the U.S. sent more than 500,000 troops to Vietnam. American planes dropped more explosives there than had been used by all combatants during World War II, pummeling the tiny nation. Still, the opposing North Vietnamese—helped by material aid from the Soviet Union and China—proved skilled and tenacious fighters, and the war dragged on.

Throughout the West, the United States drew harsh criticism from antiwar demonstrators for its relentless—and apparently futile—assaults on Vietnam. **Figure 25.2,** a 1968 collage titled *Miss America,* is one example of the reproach aimed at the United States. In this disturbing image, the well-known German artist Wolf Vostell uses photo-journalism to convey his message. In the center, a National Front for the Liberation of Southern Vietnam (contemptuously called the Vietcong by its enemies) suspect in South Vietnam is being executed. At the bottom, U.S. troops loom over crumpled corpses. Above is a mutilated image of a woman. The title of the work implies a mangling of American innocence, beauty, and honor by the daily, brutal realities of Vietnam published in newspapers and beamed into televisions around the world.

The cost, futility, and unpopularity of the Vietnam War put increasing pressure on U.S. leaders to end American involvement in the conflict. In 1973, after long negotiations, the U.S. and Vietnamese forces finally signed peace agreements, and the United States withdrew its forces. The civil war in Vietnam, however, persisted for another two years before the Communists swept to victory—not only in Vietnam but also in neighboring Laos and Cambodia.

The Cold War tide shifted in Asia several times. China, which had backed the Vietnam Communists, had continued in its own direction. During the 1950s, China was engaged in trying to meet overly ambitious

NATO 1949
BELGIUM
BRITAIN
CANADA
DENMARK
W. GERMANY
GREECE
ICELAND
ITALY
LUXEMBOURG
NETHERLANDS
NORWAY
PORTUGAL
SPAIN
TURKEY
UNITED STATES

SEATO 1954
AUSTRALIA
BRITAIN
FRANCE
NEW ZEALAND
PAKISTAN
PHILIPPINES
THAILAND
UNITED STATES

WARSAW PACT 1955
BULGARIA
CZECHOSLOVAKIA
EAST GERMANY
HUNGARY
POLAND
ROMANIA
SOVIET UNION

BAGHDAD
PACT 1955
BRITAIN
IRAN
IRAQ
PAKISTAN
TURKEY

Legend:
- North Atlantic Treaty Organization (NATO)
- Warsaw Pact Nations
- Middle East Treaty (Baghdad Pact)
- Southeast Asia Treaty Organization (SEATO)
- Asian Communist Nations Considered within "Soviet Sphere of Influence"
- ✦ Conflict Areas (with date)

MAP 25.3

Cold War Alliances and Conflicts

This map shows the Cold War alliances that spread across the globe during the 1940s and 1950s and the areas where conflicts related to the Cold War broke out.

Explore the Map

1. Which countries belong to anticommunist organizations?

2. What are the geopolitical advantages and disadvantages held by each side in the Cold War?

3. What areas of conflict suggest how worldwide the Cold War was?

goals in industry and agriculture. To that end, it communized its society even more completely than had ever been attempted in the Soviet Union. In a plan called the Great Leap Forward, China's huge and burgeoning population was set to building irrigation dams and ditches, steel mills, factories, railroads, schools, and hospitals at a frenetic pace. In 1959, an alternating cycle of droughts and flooding struck, producing one of the deadliest famines in history; some 20 million Chinese may have died of starvation and malnutrition over the next three years. Overzealous local party officials provoked resentment and resistance among the already harried populace, and for years the Communist Party hierarchy was wracked by a power struggle between moderates and radicals. In 1966, Mao tried to reignite the revolutionary spirit by launching the Great Proletarian Cultural Revolution. He empowered youthful zealots to cleanse China of those who did not enthusiastically support him. Over several years, millions of people suffered humiliation or death.

China's Great Leap Forward

Mao's Cultural Revolution

At the same time, relations between China and the Soviet Union began to cool. As early as 1956, China started criticizing the USSR, which that year under Nikita Khrushchev (1894–1971) began backing away from Stalin's harshest policies. Mao denounced Moscow for softening toward the capitalistic, imperialist West and for abandoning strict Marxist-Leninist principles. In 1960, the Soviet Union began to withhold promised economic and technological aid to China. When China exploded its first nuclear device in 1964, the two communist nations moved further apart, and by 1968, they were embroiled in border disputes.

The Chinese-Soviet split

With the Soviet Union a common enemy, China and the United States tentatively looked to each other for support. During the 1970s, China normalized relations with the U.S., replaced Taiwan in the UN, and, after the death of Mao in 1976, initiated policies emphasizing economic decentralization and free-market activities. **Figure 25.3** symbolizes the new, assertive strength of communist China. In this striking photograph, a 90-foot statue of Chairman Mao Zedong towers over marchers celebrating the twenty-first anniversary of the communists' victory in China.

The Cold War soon took another turn in central Asia, where the Soviet Union became entangled in its own version of the Vietnam War. In 1979, Soviet troops intervened to support a communist coup in Afghanistan, a nation on the USSR's southern border that the Soviets considered within their own sphere

MAP 25.4

Vietnam and Southeast Asia

This map shows Vietnam and its neighbors during the 1950s, 1960s, and 1970s, when war wracked the area.

Explore the Map

1. Why might Cambodia and Laos have become involved in the conflicts?

2. Notice China to the north. Why were the U.S. bombings of Hanoi and Haiphong strategically risky?

thinking about
ART

FIGURE 25.2

Wolf Vostell, *Miss America*, 1968

In this 1968 collage, German artist Wolf Vostell conveys impressions of the war in Vietnam. A female figure suggesting a fashion model or contestant from a Miss America pageant struts provocatively, but parts of her body are blotted with red. Below, photographic images of disturbing events during the war intrude. Much of the coloring suggests not only blood but also the American flag.

Connecting Art & Society

1. Why do you think Vostell titled this work *Miss America*?

2. What might the artist have intended the viewer to understand by superimposing photos of events in Vietnam over an image of this woman?

3. Should this collage be viewed primarily as a thoughtful, realistic depiction of the war or as a piece of propaganda? Why?

FIGURE 25.3 Mao and Communist China, 1970 A statue of Mao towers over a 1970 victory parade in China, suggesting the growing strength and political will of that nation.

of influence. They promptly became locked in a ten-year war against tenacious guerrilla forces backed by the U.S. Central Intelligence Agency. In 1989 the Soviets finally withdrew, leaving Afghanistan in shambles and wracked by internal violence.

> Soviets in Afghanistan

Even the Latin American countries, far from the conflicts in Asia and long considered "friends" by the United States, got pulled into the Cold War. At the end of World War II, the governments of independent Latin American states were republics in name. In reality, however, most of them were right-wing dictatorships, representing the interests of the well-to-do bourgeoisie, the landowning classes, and the professional military. The Roman Catholic Church, which had been a powerful conservative force in this region during the nineteenth century, had grown more liberal during the twentieth century. Sometimes it even exerted its influence in social and economic reform movements. In the years following World War II, the poor in Latin America became increasingly restless. Many of them turned to communism, encouraged by the Soviet Union. The United States, on the other hand, supported the conservative governments.

> The Cold War in Latin America

Over the next four decades, the U.S. intervened in or invaded several Latin American nations to shore up conservative forces in its global struggle against communism. The Soviets, for their part, supported sympathetic revolutionary movements and regimes. Of all the Latin American countries, Cuba became the most volatile staging ground for the intensifying feud between the superpowers. In 1959, Marxist rebel leader Fidel Castro ousted the American-supported dictatorship in Cuba and launched a sweeping program of social and economic reforms. The new

> Crisis in Cuba

program included the seizure of property owned by citizens and corporations of the United States. The U.S. government promptly terminated aid to the island nation, and Castro turned to the Soviets for help. These developments threatened the Americans in two crucial ways. First, a revolutionary, left-wing regime backed heavily by the Soviet Union had suddenly gained a beachhead in Latin America—a mere 90 miles from the U.S. mainland. Second, the Americans worried that Castro's success would embolden other opposition and revolutionary movements—also typically led by Marxists—throughout Latin America. Such uprisings would lead to more Cold War victories for the communists. Three years after the Cuban revolution, the U.S. government sponsored the Bay of Pigs invasion, an ill-fated attempt by Cuban refugees to topple the Castro regime.

Tensions soon reached a new high in the Caribbean. On October 12, 1962, a U.S. spy plane discovered Soviet missiles being installed in Cuba. Privately, President Kennedy admitted: "What difference does it make? They've got enough to blow us up now anyway. . . . This is a political struggle as much as military." Although the U.S. had missiles on Russia's border in Turkey, the Americans decided that Soviet missiles in Cuba were intolerable. With the USSR's ships steaming toward the Caribbean, the U.S. Navy under orders to intercept them to prevent the arrival of more missiles in Cuba, and American forces mobilizing, people around the world braced themselves for a possible nuclear war. On October 27, the U.S. Joint Chiefs of Staff urged an all-out attack on Cuba if the Soviets did not immediately remove the missile bases. Two days later, USSR leader Nikita Khrushchev backed down, and an agreement ended the crisis.

Détente

The two superpowers would not again come so close to war with each other. Indeed, at times Cold War tensions relaxed as each side backed away from the sort of conflict that promised to devastate each nation and much of the world. Nuclear test-ban treaties in the 1960s and strategic arms limitation talks in the 1970s eased fears of confrontation. The Helsinki agreement in 1975, confirming Europe's political frontiers and recognizing certain human rights, seemed to solidify a period of **détente**—growing cooperation between Cold War adversaries. But détente went only so far. The 1980s witnessed a return to combative rhetoric and policies with the Soviet invasion of Afghanistan and the tougher anticommunist policies of the Reagan administration in the United States. By the middle of that decade, few saw any end to the Cold War.

EAST AND WEST: TWO PATHS TO RECOVERY IN EUROPE

Under the long shadow of the Cold War, Europeans again tried to return to normal life after World War II. Beyond the astounding number of deaths and widespread destruction, whole cities—such as Berlin, in the heart of Europe—had been devastated. "Nothing is left in Berlin," wrote a reporter for the *New York Herald Tribune* in 1945. "There are no homes, no shops, no transportation, no government buildings. . . . Berlin can now be regarded only as a geographical location heaped with mountainous mounds of debris." Realists declared that economic recovery alone might take twenty-five years. Others wondered whether European society would ever recover.

European nations followed two main paths toward recovery that reflected Cold War differences and the politics underlying those differences. In the Soviet Union and Eastern Europe, communist governments promised clear planning and an unquestionable sense of direction under firm party direction. In Western Europe, the capitalist democracies relied on an alliance of the free market and governmental controls to transform their societies from the wartime devastation. Each path would have its successes and problems.

Tight Control in the Soviet Union and Eastern Europe

Nowhere was the damage and upheaval from World War II worse than in the Soviet Union and Eastern Europe. Soviet citizens longed for an end to wartime deprivations and Stalin's strict controls. Eastern Europeans living along the USSR's border wondered uneasily what to expect as their governments and economies came under the rule of communist parties controlled by Moscow.

Stalin refused to relax his grip over the Soviet Union. He asserted dictatorial control, crushing the merest hint of political dissent and purging those whom he perceived as potential threats. Prisons and forced-labor camps overflowed with his victims. Nor did his economic policies—tight planning and extreme sacrifice for heavy industrialization—change. To help rebuild what the war had destroyed in the Soviet Union, Stalin drained off economic resources from the Eastern European states.

Those countries under Soviet dominance—the "satellite" states—were required to cooperate with the Soviet Union. Single-party "people's democracies" in Poland, East Germany, Czechoslovakia, Hungary, Romania, Yugoslavia, and Albania initiated Soviet-style economic planning, nationalization, collectivization of agriculture, and industrialization. Officials allowed little contact with Western Europe.

Nevertheless, Eastern Europe refused to become a mere appendage to the Soviet Union. These nations harbored strong desires for national autonomy and they often resented Soviet restrictions. Within these states, discontent also rose over the persistent shortage of consumer goods, low wages, and poor working conditions. The Soviets and their followers often had difficulty maintaining control as resistance flared into open rebellions.

Yugoslavia snapped first. The Soviet Union had a weak foothold there because the Yugoslav resistance had liberated the nation from Nazi control almost on its own. In 1948, Yugoslavia's strong and popular dictator, Tito (see Biography in Chapter 24), stood up to Stalin's threats and headed his nation on an independent course. Tito's decentralized form of communism stressed more local control and worker participation in management than the Soviet model.

In 1953, Joseph Stalin, the man who had led the USSR for a quarter-century, died. In the Soviet Union, millions mourned Stalin as the leader who had saved them from Nazism. However, some Eastern Europeans saw his death as an opportunity to step up their demands for greater independence. Workers in East Berlin initiated protests against governmental efforts to increase workloads without raising wages. Crowds soon gathered in the streets, demanding political reform and a loosening of ties to the USSR. Police and Soviet tanks promptly crushed these uprisings.

> The death of Stalin and new opportunities

In Moscow, potential successors to Stalin jockeyed for power. They quickly agreed to eliminate the dreaded head of the secret police, Lavrenti Beria (1899–1953), and restricted that organiza-tion's terrorist activities. After two years of collective leadership, Nikita Khrushchev, the son of a miner, moved up from the party bureaucracy to emerge as Stalin's successor. In a 1956 unpublished speech to startled communist leaders, Khrushchev denounced the "cult of personality" fostered by Stalin. He also accused Stalin of using "the most cruel repression, violating all norms of revolutionary legality . . . mass arrests and deportations of many thousands of people, executions without trial." Khrushchev slightly loosened government control of Soviet cultural life; authors such as Boris Pasternak (1890–1960) even managed to publish works that implied some criticism of the Soviet regime. New policies also stressed the production of consumer goods, increased housing, and better health care. Workers throughout the USSR gained more freedom to move from one job to another.

Eastern Europeans hoped that this de-Stalinization would spell a relaxation of Soviet control over their nations. In Poland, worker strikes against wage cuts expanded into demands for political change in 1956, and the Soviets threatened to intervene. Nevertheless, Poland's Communist Party elected the moderate Wladyslaw Gomulka (1905–1982) instead of the Soviet candidate. Gomulka refused to cave in to Soviet demands but promised military loyalty. A compromise left Poland within the Soviet sphere of control while enjoying some new levels of economic and cultural independence—including increased toleration of the Roman Catholic Church.

> Protests and uprisings in Eastern Europe

Next, Hungarians issued a challenging demand for independence. When Hungary's communist leaders called on troops to put down protesters in the streets, the troops refused to fire and instead switched sides. A new government under the reforming communist Imre Nagy (1896–1958) initiated major economic and political reforms that included the introduction of a multiparty system. Nagy even proposed to withdraw Hungary from the Warsaw Pact—Moscow's military alliance with its Eastern European satellites. The Hungarians had crossed the line. The Soviets sent in tanks and troops, slaughtering thousands and forcing hundreds of thousands to flee to the West. Nagy was hanged, and the lesson was made crystal clear: Cooperate with Moscow or pay the highest penalty.

In 1961, relations between East and West hit a new low. Under orders from Khrushchev, the East German government erected a 100-mile, heavily armed wall in Berlin to keep its citizens from fleeing to the West. Berlin had served as an escape route for 2.6 million people, especially professionals and the well educated who sought a higher standard of living in Western Europe. **Figure 25.4** shows a section of the **Berlin Wall** under reconstruction after it was

> The Berlin Wall

FIGURE 25.4 The Berlin Wall Workers, soldiers, and onlookers gather on both sides as the wall dividing East and West Berlin is repaired.

rammed by an East German trying to escape into West Berlin. To the left, East German workers and machines build the heavy brick barrier. In the background, a fence topped with barbed wire extends into the distance. East German soldiers, such as those on the left side of the photo, will guard the wall; they have orders to shoot anyone between the fence and the wall trying to flee to the West. To the right, West German soldiers and citizens look on. The wall graphically marked the division of Germany and symbolized the hostility between Western and Eastern Europe.

In 1964, competitors within the Communist Party's Central Committee suddenly ousted Khrushchev, who had been weakened by foreign policy embarrassments such as the Cuban missile crisis, and installed the more conservative Leonid Brezhnev (1906–1982). The new Soviet leader took a firm line in dealing with Soviet satellites in Eastern Europe. Most of these states posed no problem for him. East Germany, for example, closely followed the Soviet line while developing its industrial capacity, and it became the richest nation in Eastern Europe. Hungary remained tranquil, orienting its economy toward consumer goods, loosening state control, and introducing limited capitalistic practices at the local level.

Other satellite states caused conflict—none more than Czechoslovakia. In 1968, reformers gained control of the Czechoslovak Communist Party and replaced the country's Stalinist leader with Alexander Dubcek, who believed that communism could be made compatible with internal party democracy and personal freedom. In this **Prague Spring** uprising, the Dubcek government initiated economic decentralization, greater national independence, democratic reforms, and elimination of censorship—"socialism with a human face." The reforms gained enthusiastic support within Czechoslovakia, especially among optimistic students and intellectuals thirsting for free speech.

| The Prague Spring |

Like Hungary in 1956, Dubcek's reforms went too far for the USSR's comfort. Especially fearful that the Prague Spring could inspire similar movements throughout Eastern Europe, the Soviets sent in Warsaw Pact troops to reverse Dubcek's policies and halt Czechoslovakia's steps toward independence. **Figure 25.5** shows Soviet tanks rumbling through Prague in August 1968. Czechoslovakian citizens stand on the sidewalks watching as the tanks overwhelm any potential resistance in the streets. Fire burns in the background, adding to this image of the Soviets using brute force to compel Czechoslovakia back into line. The Czechs reacted with passive resistance; they could do little more. The Soviets removed

FIGURE 25.5 The Prague Spring, 1968 Soviet tanks roll through Prague, Czechoslovakia, crushing a 1968 reformist uprising.

Dubcek and his liberal supporters from power, and Brezhnev established his "Doctrine": Soviet intervention is justified in order to ensure the survival of socialism in another state. The conservative Brezhnev would make sure that Eastern Europe, like the Soviet Union itself, would not stray too far from the tightly controlled communist path followed since the early post–World War II years.

Parliamentary Politics and Prosperity in the Western Democracies

Western European nations proceeded on a strikingly different course to recovery, dictated by both Cold War considerations and the internal histories of those societies. In 1945, most Western European nations quickly returned to prewar democratic forms of government, and political parties leaning toward the center of the political spectrum soon gained control. In some countries, one political party dominated for long stretches of time—the Christian Democrats reigned in West Germany for two decades, for example, and in Italy for four decades following World War II. In other countries, major parties alternated in power, as the Labor and Conservative parties did in Britain. Some governments lasted only months, as happened in France, though the same group of well-known politicians usually rotated into the high offices of new governments and worked with a stable bureaucracy that carried out policy.

Initially, communist parties also gained strength after the war, especially in France and Italy. In France, elections in 1945 resulted in a sweeping victory for parties of the Left, including the communists, as well as the retirement of the conservative general Charles de Gaulle, who had set up a government in Paris in 1944. In Italy, the communists also emerged from

World War II strong. For decades, the Italian Communists would command 25 to 35 percent of the vote and win local elections. But after 1947, when the Cold War heated up, these communist parties in France, Italy, and elsewhere were systematically excluded from participation in national governments.

In the struggle to repair their broken economies, European nations benefited greatly from U.S. aid. Having emerged from the war the world's preeminent economic power, the United States pumped almost $13 billion of Marshall Plan aid into Western Europe between 1947 and 1952. More than a sense of humanity motivated the Americans. The economic aid also served U.S. Cold War interests by supporting anticommunist forces. The aid came with strings attached: international cooperation and freer trade by the recipients. By demanding these conditions, the U.S.—now producing more than half the world's industrial goods—gained unprecedented access to large European markets.

U.S. aid and economic recovery

Europeans helped themselves as well. Drawing on lessons from the Great Depression, World War II, and the British economist John Maynard Keynes, governments adopted policies to dampen recessions by deficit spending (priming the pump) and to counter inflation by tightening expenditures and interest rates. Several European states, from France to Norway, went even further by engaging in economic planning. This typically included nationalizing certain industries. In France, for example, major banking and insurance companies, coal mines, and gas and electrical utilities came under government control. In such countries, technocrats—bureaucrats with technological or scientific expertise—made economic decisions that were once the province of business owners or parliaments. Other nations avoided such extensive planning. West Germany, for example, broke up prewar corporate cartels instead and pressured labor and management to cooperate for industrial peace.

At the same time, most European nations created social programs to protect citizens from severe hardship and to promote social peace. These **welfare state** programs had roots in the late nineteenth century, when governments had begun taking responsibility for the inequities of capitalism. Concerned about declining population growth, Europeans also wanted to encourage women to have more children. In the years after World War II, many governments followed Sweden's early lead and initiated programs providing health-care benefits and family allowances as well as prenatal care, maternity benefits, child care, and nursery schooling.

The welfare state

Nowhere was the welfare state more dramatically introduced than in Britain. Having shared the toil and suffering of World War II under the effective governmental direction of the economy, British citizens believed that everyone should get a piece of the prosperity that they expected would follow the war. In 1945, they elected a Labor government under Clement Attlee (1883–1967). The new government soon nationalized about 20 percent of Britain's economy and initiated what some called "cradle-to-grave" social-welfare policies. All British citizens could now look to governmental support during times of need—whether those times involved raising children, suffering job loss or an accident, paying for adequate housing, or ensuring adequate resources for retirement. Above all, Britain's National Health Service guaranteed free medical care to all.

Scandinavian countries continued to lead, going the furthest in ensuring a decent standard of living for everyone in both good times and bad. By contrast, the Americans swam against the tide. Prosperous, with its high-spending military in close alliance with big business, the United States strenuously resisted programs smacking of socialism. Not until the 1960s did it pursue moderate social reform, such as new educational programs, low-income housing projects, and limited governmental support of medical services.

Of course, all social programs came at a price. Taxes rose, particularly for the middle and upper classes, and government bureaucracies ballooned. Moreover, critics questioned the quality of the services provided, particularly medical care. Yet once established, most social programs served enough people and gained sufficient political backing to become permanent fixtures.

The nations of Western Europe recognized that cooperation offered the best hope for competing economically in a world of superpowers. Encouraged by the Marshall Plan, these countries moved toward economic integration. In 1950, France and West Germany created the French-German Coal and Steel Authority to remove tariff barriers and manage coal and steel resources regionally. Jean Monnet (1888–1979), the architect of this organization, held high hopes: "If only the French could lose their fear of German industrial domination, then the greatest obstacle to a united Europe would be removed. . . . It could, in fact, become the germ of European unity." In 1952, the organization expanded into the European Coal and Steel Community with the addition of Italy, Belgium, Luxembourg, and the Netherlands. Five years later, these same six nations signed the Treaty of Rome establishing the **European Economic Community** (the EEC, also referred to as the Common Market). The treaty proposed to eliminate tariff barriers, cut restrictions on the flow of labor and capital, and integrate the economies of the member nations.

Beginning European economic integration

The Common Market ended tariff and immigration barriers ahead of schedule, and its member nations

DOCUMENT 25.2

DOCUMENTS

A Warning About the United States

By the mid-1960s, many Europeans sensed that the United States, although friendly, had grown overbearing in some ways. U.S. economic institutions, capital, and culture were invading Europe, even though Europe had recovered from the devastation of World War II. This sense was particularly strong in France, as evidenced by the following selection from Jean-Jacques Servan-Schreiber's The American Challenge. This widely popular book was first published in 1967.

Europeans can regain control over their destiny in this confrontation with the American challenge only by taking stock of themselves and, as we will now try to describe, by hard work and patience. What we must do is not so hard to explain, for the path of our counterattack can be clearly marked out.

1. Creation of large industrial units which are able both in size and management to compete with the American giants.

2. Carrying out "major operations" of advanced technology that will ensure an independent future for Europe.

3. At least a minimum of federal power to protect and promote European business.

4. Transforming the relationship between business, the university, and the government.

5. Broader and more intensive education for young people; specialized and continuing education for adults.

6. Finally, as the key to everything else, the liberation of imprisoned energies by a revolution in our methods of organization—a revolution to revitalize the elites and even relations between men. . . .

To build a powerful and independent Europe means strengthening the economic and political bonds of the Common Market. No single nation is strong enough to support efficient production in all areas of advanced technology, for the national framework is too narrow and cannot provide adequate markets for such products. Also, the growing diversification of these products demands a specialization that makes any attempt at national self-sufficiency virtually impossible. . . .

Our back is to the wall. We cannot have both economic self-sufficiency and economic growth. Either we build a common European industrial policy, or American industry will continue taking over the Common Market.

SOURCE: J.J. Servan-Schreiber, *The American Challenge*, trans. Ronald Steel (New York: Atheneum House, 1969), pp. 153–154, 156.

Analyze the Document

1. What does this document suggest about Europeans' perceptions of the United States?

2. How does Servan-Schreiber plan to confront the American challenge?

3. What do you think of Servan-Schreiber's ideas?

---

enjoyed increased trade, productivity, and industrial production. In 1967, the organization combined with other cooperative bodies to form the European Community (EC) to work toward even greater economic and political integration. As Document 25.2 indicates, optimistic supporters hoped that the European Community would make Western Europe an independent regional power that might economically and even politically challenge its superpower ally, the United States, as well as the opposing the Soviet bloc in Eastern Europe.

Assessing the Paths Taken

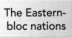

Throughout Europe, early fears about how long reconstruction would take proved unfounded (see **Figure 25.6**). The Soviet and East European economies expanded after the war, though not as rapidly as Eastern Europeans expected or hoped. The Soviets applied advanced science, technology, and engineering to establish a strong industrial

COUNTRY	1938	1953	1963	1980
Britain	181	258	330	441
France	74	98	194	362
Germany	214	224	416	747
West Germany		180	330	590
East Germany		44	86	157
Italy	46	71	150	319
Poland	19	31	66	169
Sweden	21	28	48	83
Soviet Union	152	328	760	1630

FIGURE 25.6 European Industrial Production, 1938–1980

Figures are a percentage of British industrial output in 1900.

base, support a huge military, and build large urban projects. Some Eastern European nations, such as East Germany and Czechoslovakia, also developed extensive industrial bases and even outperformed the Soviets.

Although communism stood for the end to class differences, some citizens within each nation were, in the words of British author George Orwell, "more equal" than others. Certainly the Communist Party elite and professionals enjoyed better services and a higher standard of living than everyone else. But all citizens gained access to education, free medical care, and job security under communism. Subsidies made their usually overcrowded housing inexpensive, and unemployment and abject poverty virtually disappeared.

Women participated fully in economic life in these nations, often outnumbering men in the labor force. Moreover, a majority of doctors and teachers were women. Far more women engaged in manual labor such as logging and heavy construction work than their counterparts did in the West. They also received family allowances, maternity benefits, and child-care support. Outside the higher levels of government, Soviet women gained widespread political representation in parliamentary bodies, especially in local government. Nevertheless, women's pay lagged behind men's and women usually remained responsible for traditional domestic duties.

But even with all these improvements, Eastern-bloc nations could not keep up with their citizens' growing desires for a higher standard of living and more independence. Eastern Europeans had relatively few choices in consumer goods, food, and housing. In satellite nations, longing for autonomy from the Soviet Union persisted. Within each nation, Soviet-backed regimes—for the most part dictatorships—labored under questions about their political legitimacy. For many people, a sense of isolation from the West and a stifling of free expression within their own societies dampened cultural life in those nations.

In the capitalist democracies of Western Europe, government spending and welfare-state programs, as well as U.S. aid, fueled a strong revival (see **Figure 25.6**). Europeans used this money, their growing store of new technology, and Western Europe their skilled workforce to rebuild factories and transportation networks into models of efficiency. Falling tariff barriers and a population enlarged by increased birthrates created new demand for consumer goods. Food and clothing prices declined, jobs abounded, and wages rose. By 1955, the standard of living for even those in the bottom half of society rose. In just a decade, Western Europe had recovered fully from the economic devastation of the war.

During the 1960s, some Western European nations achieved unimagined levels of prosperity. West Germany, Switzerland, and Sweden became the wealthiest nations in Europe. People in northern Italy spoke of their own "economic miracle." On the other hand, areas farther south still wedded to more traditional

agricultural economies lagged behind, and once-mighty Britain—reeling from the loss of overseas trade and investments, and hampered by the antiquated state of most of its mines and factories—suffered a relative decline.

Overall, however, Western Europe took on the look and substance of wealth. Industries such as electronics, automobiles, plastics, petroleum, prefabricated housing, and airlines flourished. Newly restored city centers attracted hordes of shoppers, suburban commuters, tourists, and pedestrians. The number of cars on Europe's streets jumped tenfold from fewer than 5 million in 1945 to over 50 million by 1970. Stores overflowed with a cornucopia of foods and clothing. Electronic gadgets—from electric can openers to hand-held audiotape players—cropped up everywhere. The proliferation of restaurants, theaters, travel, and hotels reflected the affluence and the widespread standard of a forty-hour workweek and four weeks of paid vacation each year.

The good economic news outweighed almost everything else in Western Europe, and nothing helped its politicians more, for economic growth became the key measure of political success. Moreover, as observers and visitors looked at the paths to recovery taken in Eastern and Western Europe, the West's stunning prosperity clearly contrasted with the slower growth in the East. However, Western Europe also had problems that reflected its decline from the heights of power and certainty. Not only had these nations forfeited leadership to the United States, but they lost their colonial empires as well.

THE TWILIGHT OF COLONIALISM

Even before World War II, national liberation movements around the globe had gathered momentum. When Germany defeated imperial nations such as France and the Netherlands, and Japan conquered Western holdings in Asia and the Pacific, Europe's control over its colonial territories weakened. The United States further undermined the imperial powers by pushing them to dismantle their empires at war's end. At the same time, the Soviet Union continued to spread its decades-old denunciation of Western imperialism throughout the world. In the United Nations, sentiment grew toward the view that colonial "subjugation, domination and exploitation constitutes a denial of fundamental human rights." In the colonies, people seethed with anger against the Europeans. "Leave this Europe where they are never done talking of Man, yet murder men everywhere they find them," wrote the French West Indian philosopher Frantz Fanon (1925–1961) in his widely read book *The Wretched of the Earth*. "For centuries they have stifled almost the whole of humanity. . . . Look at them today swaying between atomic and spiritual disintegration." The last emperor of Vietnam, Bao Dai, warned his French overlords about "this desire for independence which is in everyone's heart and which no human force can any longer restrain."

Despite the intensity of these sentiments, many European settlers felt they had lived in the colonies too long to cede control to the local populations. Several political leaders in Europe agreed with Winston Churchill's sentiments: "I did not become the king's first minister in order to preside over the liquidation of the British Empire." The French announced that "the attainment of 'self-government' in the colonies, even in the distant future, must be excluded." The struggle to end colonialism was on.

Revolts in Southern Asia

At the end of World War II, national liberation revolts threatened the huge British, Dutch, and French empires in southern Asia. Of the Western imperial powers, only the United States escaped direct embroilment in this revolt, by granting independence to the Philippines in 1946.

In India, the world's second most populous country, Mohandas K. Gandhi (1869–1948) led the independence movement. Educated in Great Britain, this astute middle-class Hindu used pas- sive resistance and civil disobedience rather than direct violence to pressure British officials to grant Indian independence. In 1947, Britain's Labor government finally freed India, partitioned into the separate states of India and Pakistan because of growing political divisions between Hindus and Muslims. Great Britain also relinquished Ceylon (Sri Lanka), Burma (Myanmar), and Malaya.

Independence, however, did not end problems in this troubled region. Religious and national strife soon broke out between Hindu India and Muslim Pakistan. Gandhi tried to quell the hostilities, but a fanatical Hindu nationalist assassinated him in 1948. Open war between the two states erupted in 1949 over possession of the disputed state of Kashmir. The United Nations managed to stop the shooting but failed to resolve the dispute, which would simmer for decades. This conflict, as well as border clashes with China, persuaded India to accept military aid from both the United States and the Soviet Union. India and Pakistan also faced the huge tasks of unifying their populations—divided by languages, caste, and class—and helping their millions of poverty-stricken and illiterate citizens.

In the rich and populous Dutch East Indies, nationalist leaders had established underground organizations during the wartime Japanese occupation. These leaders now stepped in and declared independence when the invaders left. The Dutch resisted fiercely for four years before yielding control. In 1949, they finally recognized the Republic of Indonesia as an independent nation.

A similar but more painful pattern emerged in France's Asian empire after the Japanese left Indochina in 1945. As we have seen (page 781), the popular Indochinese nationalists, led by Soviet-educated communist Ho Chi Minh (1890–1969), proclaimed the independent Democratic Republic of Vietnam. Heavy fighting between the French imperialists and communist nationalists ensued. In 1954, France finally admitted defeat, pulling out of Vietnam and freeing the neighboring countries of Laos and Cambodia.

Conflict in the Middle East

In the Middle East, Britain had been the dominant imperial power since World War I. However, under pressure from nationalists who had agitated for full independence since the first decades of the twentieth century, the British relaxed their control in the years before World War II. At the end of the war, British influence remained strong in several states, but only Cyprus, Palestine, and the Suez Canal were still official British possessions. Moreover, Britain was making a pronounced bid for Arab friendship and, to that end, helped to form the League of Arab States in 1945. Yet, the admission of tens of thousands of Jews into Palestine under the Balfour Declaration of 1917—a British promise to create a "national home" for Jews in Palestine—made Palestine a new trouble spot.

Palestine was the ancient home of the Jews—a people with a long history of being displaced by others. In the seventh century, the Islamic Arabs conquered Palestine and lived there until the twentieth century. In the late nineteenth century, a new movement—Zionism—emerged to restore Palestine as the national home for the Jews (see pages 637–640). During the anti-Semitic persecutions of the Hitler era, Jewish refugees poured into Palestine and bought land, enraging the dispossessed Arabs. The British were caught between their obligations to the Arab nationalists in Palestine and the Jewish settlers eager to reclaim Palestine as their homeland.

In 1948, the beleaguered British finally turned Palestine over to the United Nations. The Jews immediately proclaimed the State of Israel and accepted the boundary lines that the United Nations drew up dividing Palestine between the Jews and the Arabs. However, the League of Arab States protested this arrangement, and fighting broke out between the

Vietnam

India

Indonesia

Palestine

Israel founded

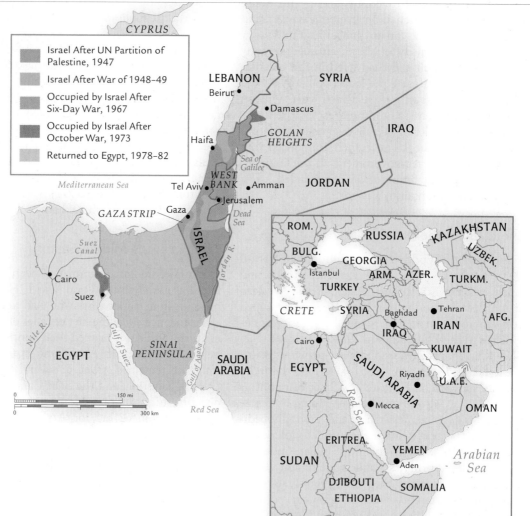

Legend:
- Israel After UN Partition of Palestine, 1947
- Israel After War of 1948–49
- Occupied by Israel After Six-Day War, 1967
- Occupied by Israel After October War, 1973
- Returned to Egypt, 1978–82

MAP 25.5

The Arab-Israeli Conflict, 1947–1982

This map shows some of the results of the various Arab-Israeli conflicts between 1947 and 1982.

Explore the Map

1. Which states in the area were most involved in these conflicts?

2. Who gained the most, and who suffered the greatest losses of territory?

3. Why were Jerusalem, the West Bank, and the Golan Heights of such importance to the parties involved?

two sides. Although outnumbered, the well-organized Jewish forces held on. After a year, the United Nations brokered a truce. During the conflict, Israel had gained some territory and had expelled more than a half-million Palestinian Arabs. Most of these refugees, not welcomed by neighboring Arab states, settled in rough camps just outside Israel's new borders. The vigorous new nation, with financial help from abroad and a social-democratic government at home, began building modern cities and a strong economy. The Arab nations, however, refused to recognize Israel, and Palestine nationalists, without a country of their own, continued to conduct border raids on the fledgling nation. Conflicts stemming from the birth of the Israeli state would drag on for decades (see **Map 25.5**).

These conflicts only compounded the broader anti-Western sentiment percolating in the region, especially in nearby Egypt, where Britain still controlled the Suez Canal. In 1952, a military coup in Egypt brought the dynamic nationalist leader Gamel Abdul Nasser (1918–1970) to power. Although Nasser kept much political power for himself, he promised parliamentary institutions, drew up a constitution guaranteeing individual rights, and distributed land to the poorer peasantry. In 1956, when the United States refused to support his plans to develop the Egyptian economy, he seized the Suez Canal. As he saw it, control of the canal would not only enrich Egypt but also symbolize Egypt's independence and Arab nationalism.

Egypt

Nasser's bold action provoked a military attack by Israel, Britain, and France. Cold War rivalries quickly came into play when the Soviet Union threatened to intervene on the side of Egypt. At this point, the United States pressured the three invading powers to retreat. Though defeated militarily, Nasser ended up a national hero and the leader of the Arab world for standing up to Israel and the Western powers. Moreover, Britain lost the canal and soon its last holdings in the Middle East, and the Soviets gained influence in the region.

When war broke out again in 1967 and 1973—between Egypt (with its Arab allies) and Israel—the Soviet Union and the United States rushed billions more dollars of arms and advisors to their respective allies. The area had become another crucible of superpower competition that would continue to generate anti-Western resentment.

Liberating Africa

As in Asia and the Middle East, movements for national liberation stirred in Africa, where France and Britain held the most territory. France faced its greatest challenge in North Africa, where the largely Islamic population seethed with nationalistic unrest. In the face of this growing force, France granted independence to Morocco and Tunisia in 1956 but drew the line at Algeria. The imperial power had held Algeria for over a century and considered it part of France rather than just a colony. In addition, more than a million French settlers lived there. They feared loss of property and reprisals from the eight million Islamic Algerians in the case of France's withdrawal. Complicating matters, the French military was determined to hold Algeria so as to repair the damage that France's reputation had sustained in Vietnam. At the same time, Arab nationalists living in Algeria believed that, with enough resolve, they just might oust the colonialist regime.

The French in North Africa

A long, bloody stalemate resulted. As one French soldier noted, "There's this staggering fact: The entire Arab population is joining the resistance against us." When the French government eventually showed a willingness to compromise, disgruntled colonial army officers threatened to overthrow the government in Paris. In 1958, as France's government teetered on the verge of collapse, retired general Charles de Gaulle was recalled to power. The World War II hero alone had the stature and legitimacy to negotiate with the forces of Arab nationalism. He granted Algeria independence in 1962 and freed almost all the other remaining French colonies.

Britain experienced similar challenges to its authority in its African colonies. The Labor government tried to prepare for the gradual freeing of British territories by sharing power with Africans in the civil service and bolstering funds for educational and economic development. The experience with Nasser in Egypt and a rebellion in Kenya from 1951 to 1956 finally persuaded the British to hasten their departure from Africa. By 1965, Britain had formally dismantled its African empire.

Britain dismantles its empire

Yet even with most imperialists gone, trouble still brewed on the African continent. Sizable white minorities living in Rhodesia and South Africa clung desperately to their power over black majorities. In Rhodesia, despite persistent guerrilla attacks by angry members of the black majority, the exclusively white regime held on until 1980. In long-independent South Africa, the prosperous white minority held fast to its power over the nonwhite majority (see Global Connections). The white minority harshly suppressed the increasingly restless black majority and enforced **apartheid** (racial segregation). This policy earned the all-white South African government decades of heated protests from nonwhites and condemnation throughout the world. Only in the 1990s would the white government under F. W. de Klerk at last allow the popular African National Congress, headed by the venerated Nelson Mandela, to assume leadership. By then, all European powers had pulled out of Africa. As **Map 25.6** shows, their departure ended Europe's domination of Africa and Asia.

Rhodesia and South Africa

Decolonization did not end Western influence in the non-Western world or bring peace and prosperity to the previously subject peoples. Newly independent nations were often left with illogical borders drawn arbitrarily by nineteenth-century European imperialists, depleted economies, and internal political divisions that drew in Cold War agents from both sides to exploit the chaos. Especially in Africa, ethnic conflict sometimes flared up into bloody civil wars, such as in Nigeria, where the Ibos in

The legacy of colonialism

Apartheid in South Africa

In 1960, the United Nations formally recognized that "the people of the world ardently desire the end of colonialism in all its manifestations." Within a few years, most of Africa would be free from white control. However, events unfolded in a strikingly different way in South Africa. Marked by its unique history, that society still labored under apartheid.

Since its virtual independence from Britain and unification in 1910, the Union of South Africa had come increasingly under the political influence of Afrikaners. These whites traced their roots back to the seventeenth century, when their Dutch ancestors had established colonies in South Africa. They were committed to ensuring their own domination over black Africans. Meanwhile, as the political winds shifted, cheap labor, cheap energy, gold, diamonds, and governmental aid fueled the country's industrialization and urbanization.

These trends culminated in 1948 with the electoral victory of the radical Afrikaner National Party. Building on established policies, the party put into practice the officially sanctioned system of apartheid (which means "separation" in Afrikaans). Through apartheid, the National Party sought to rigidly segregate people by color in order to keep nonwhites (which included blacks, Indians, and people of mixed heritage) completely subordinated to whites. Apartheid dictated where people of different groups could live, work, and go to school. It determined whom people might marry and what lavatories they could use. After 1958, Afrikaner leader Hendrik Verwoerd created "grand apartheid," which sent black South Africans to live in a patchwork of small ethnic states. He claimed that the Bible justified this policy. "We have a very fine position in South Africa; we've got

land, we've got a country and we are obliged by the love commandment to provide exactly the same to black people." However, grand apartheid kept more than 85 percent of the land in the hands of the white minority and treated blacks in white areas as foreign migrant workers.

The African National Congress (ANC), founded in 1912 by black Africans "for the purpose of creating national unity and defending our rights and privileges," actively opposed apartheid. The South African government severely repressed the ANC and other black activist groups. In 1962, government forces captured one of the ANC leaders, Nelson Mandela (1918–). At his first trial in 1963, Mandela proclaimed, "I have cherished the ideal of a democratic and free society in which all persons live together in harmony and with equal opportunities. . . . It is an ideal for which I am prepared to die." During his second trial, in 1964, Mandela cited the English Magna Carta and the American Bill of Rights in support of his cause. He also castigated the apartheid system: "The lack of human dignity experienced by Africans is the direct result of the policy of white supremacy." That year, Mandela was sentenced to life imprisonment. He soon became an internationally recognized symbol of the struggle to end apartheid; his image could be found in homes from Africa to Europe and the Americas.

For a while, repression by the white regime quelled most black protests. However, in 1976, an 18-month uprising initiated by black schoolchildren in Soweto further spread South Africa's worldwide reputation for heartless repression. In 1978, the United Nations imposed a mandatory arms embargo against South Africa in an effort to weaken the

white regime. Over the years, nation after nation cut economic ties with the country.

In 1989, National Party leader F. W. de Klerk (1936–) became president of South Africa and began dismantling apartheid. Ultimately, however many forces destroyed apartheid. Demographic trends shifted the balance of power: Though population growth tripled under apartheid, the percentage of white people declined from 21 to 14. Moreover, black African opposition movements sapped the white government's energy. International isolation also weakened the regime, and, as de Klerk explained, "the decline and collapse of Communism in Eastern Europe and Russia put a new complexion on things." In 1990, de Klerk released Mandela from jail and legalized the ANC. De Klerk, Mandela, and others created a new constitution, ending white minority rule, and in 1994, South Africa held open elections. Sally Motlana, long an ANC activist, spoke for many about her new freedom: "I never dreamt that one day I would be sitting here with other human beings and regarded as a human being. For all those years I've been made to feel that I was not part of the human race." Voters resoundingly chose Mandela, making him the first black president of South Africa. Still vital and determined despite twenty-seven years of imprisonment, the new president proclaimed his nation "free at last."

Making Connections

1. What was the nature of apartheid? What were its purposes?

2. What forces brought an end to apartheid?

3. What problems would still face South Africa after 1994?

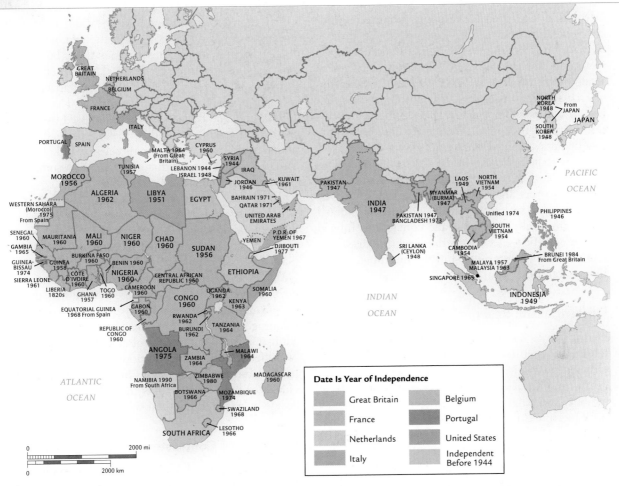

MAP 25.6

Decolonization

This map shows the colonial empires held by Western powers before World War II and the dates when the former colonies gained their independence.

Explore the Map

1. Which two nations had the most extensive colonial empires? Where were their holdings concentrated?

2. How did decolonization diminish the political reach of Europe?

3. Which former colonies became particularly volatile zones of conflict? How might that volatility have been related to decolonization?

the eastern region attempted to secede and set up the independent Republic of Biafra. Because the newly freed countries—especially in Africa—were generally left without internally generated political institutions, instability, bloodshed, and rule by military strongmen often resulted. In southern and southeastern Asia, religious and political differences broke out into wars in the years after liberation. Growing but impoverished populations lived under the threat of hunger and, in bad weather, starvation. Droughts, for example, in the huge sub-Saharan region of northern Africa during the 1970s, 1980s, and 1990s, brought famine and death to tens of thousands. Most former colonies remained "Third World" nations—relatively poor, supplying raw materials to industrialized nations and dependent on the wealthier countries' goods and aid. Interaction between Western and non-Western peoples had transformed life on both sides, and resentments nurtured by years of colonial suppression still lingered in many non-Western nations.

A SENSE OF RELATIVITY IN THOUGHT AND CULTURE

Decolonization forced Western Europeans to reevaluate themselves and their civilization. So did the rise of the United States and the Soviet Union as superpowers and the ensuing Cold War that quickly cast its shadow over the West and the world. In these decades of such accelerating change, thoughtful people struggled to understand and define their lives and the culture in which they lived. The idea of universal truths that had prevailed in earlier times gave way to a growing sense that truth was relative—to the individual, to time, and to place. Increasingly, intellectuals, scholars, and writers argued that values were defined by the cultures in which they arose, judgments stemmed from individual perceptions, and conclusions hinged on the evidence selected. In these subtle senses, the postwar decades stressed shifting meanings rather than certainties.

Existentialism: Responsibility and Despair

During the 1940s and 1950s, the philosophy of existentialism captured much attention in the West. Originating in an era marked by war, depression, mass death, and the decline of traditional standards of morality and religious beliefs, **existentialism** offered a stark interpretation of reality. France's Jean-Paul Sartre (1905–1980) (see **Figure 25.10**)

Sartre and Camus

became the most influential proponent of this body of thought. In novels, plays, and philosophical works, Sartre argued that there is no meaning to existence, no universal right or wrong. As he saw it, individuals are born and simply exist. They must make their own decisions,

define their own purpose and values, and take responsibility for their actions. "Man cannot escape from the sense of complete and profound responsibility . . . one ought always to ask oneself what would happen if everyone did as one is doing." In the end, according to Sartre, one simply dies without there being any philosophical meaning to death. The French writer Albert Camus (1913–1960) also popularized existentialism, in novels and plays such as *The Stranger* (1942) and *The Plague* (1947). He stressed the plight of the responsible individual seeking understanding and identity in an amoral, purposeless world.

The sense of despair that existentialist assumptions often engendered came forth graphically in the Theater of the Absurd, which dispensed with linear plots, definable action, and conventional

Theater of the Absurd

sets and costumes. Samuel Beckett's (1906–1989) plays are good examples of this genre. In *Waiting for Godot* (1952), two tramps wait for someone who never arrives. There is no purpose in what they do, for people in this culture no longer shared a sense of meaning. In Beckett's *Endgame* (1958), one character adrift in a world out of control describes his situation: "All life long the same questions, the same answers." In this absurd life, all responsibility rested with individuals, who had to make their own choices and decide how best to use their time on Earth.

A Culture of Contrasts and Criticism

The uncertainty and relativity implied by existentialism emerged not only in theater but also in other cultural forms. Writers, artists, and critics often disagreed with one another and with popular taste. In cinema, a stream of what critics dismissed as undistinguished movies nevertheless poured forth year after year. Yet cinema was perhaps the most original art form produced during the twentieth century. In the late 1940s and 1950s, several thoughtful movies, such as *The Bicycle Thief* by Italian filmmaker Vittorio de Sica, stressed the realistic struggles of ordinary people. During the 1960s and 1970s, the works of filmmakers such as Ingmar Bergman in Sweden, Federico Fellini and Liliana Cavani in Italy, Jean-Luc Godard in France, and Stanley Kramer in the United States exemplified the potential of cinema as a sophisticated, creative, artistic medium. These films contrasted sharply with the flashy artificiality of innumerable Hollywood movies—although many Hollywood motion pictures did feature stunning re-creations of the past, finely honed acting, and a creative mix of lighting, sound, and special effects.

Cinema

Many educators and commentators hoped that television would become a worthy cultural and educational medium as well. By the 1960s, people spent

KEY DATES

GLOBAL RELATIONS

1947	India gains independence
1948	Israel founded
1949	Indonesia gains independence
	Communist victory in China
1950–1953	Korean War
1954	France withdraws from Vietnam
1956	Egypt seizes the Suez Canal
1962	Algeria gains independence
1966	Mao's Cultural Revolution
1973	Oil crisis
1975	End of Vietnam War
1979	Invasion of Afghanistan

FIGURE 25.7 Jackson Pollock, *Convergence*, 1952
Paintings such as this work by American artist Jackson Pollock avoided realistic representations and seemed inaccessible to ordinary people.

on average fifteen to thirty hours per week watching television. To be sure, numerous situation comedies, adventure shows, dramas, and game shows celebrated the joys, anguish, and pains of everyday life—as well as violence, romance, and fantasy. Yet most television critics were disappointed. Like radio and newspapers, television crossed lines between serious news, politics, and entertainment alike. TV had an especially powerful impact on politics. Politicians sought or purchased TV exposure, shortened and simplified their messages, and cultivated an image created with the help of media and advertising professionals.

In the more traditional cultural fields, a similar pattern of conflict over new works emerged. Some of the most critically acclaimed works seemed inaccessible to ordinary people. In art, abstract expressionistic paintings, such as those created by the American artist Jackson Pollock (1912–1956), who dripped paint onto canvases, drew attention but not crowds. **Figure 25.7** is one of Pollock's best-known works. Pollock explained why he avoided realistic representations of recognizable objects: "The modern artist is living in a mechanical age and we have a mechanical means of representing objects in nature such as the camera and photograph. The modern artist . . . is working and expressing an inner world . . . expressing his feelings rather than illustrating."

Pop art, with its images of everyday objects such as hamburgers in advertisements, also gained attention but bewildered audiences. **Figure 25.8**, by the American artist Andy Warhol (1928–1987), looks like nothing more than rows of soup cans. From another perspective, however, viewers might interpret it as an image of striking, colorful unity that reproaches our commercial, prepackaged society with its standardized tastes.

Such paintings sometimes drew popular ridicule. One American newsmagazine, *Time*, called Jackson Pollock "Jack the Dripper." On one level, this popular

rejection of bold new artistic forms was nothing new. Indeed, artistic styles that were once unpopular and considered avant-garde or elite—such as nineteenth-century postimpressionism and the twentieth-century paintings of Pablo Picasso—now attracted admiring crowds.

A related, but more puzzling, pattern emerged in literature and music. For example, the "new novel," which consciously avoided clear plots and well-defined characters, gained critical acclaim but attracted little popular attention. Yet other, hard-to-categorize novels that critics praised just as heartily—for example, works by German author Günter Grass, French author Marguerite Duras, and British author Doris Lessing—won wide popularity. In music, the dissonant, atonal music of Arnold Schoenberg (1874–1951) garnered few fans compared with the hugely popular rock and roll, whereas jazz—a creation of African-American culture that emphasized sophisticated improvisation and rhythm—enjoyed a large following.

Perhaps cultural products and tastes, like the civilization they reflected, were changing too fast for most people. To be sure,

FIGURE 25.8 Andy Warhol, *One Hundred Cans*, 1962
Pop art painters such as Warhol created images filled with everyday objects that were not usually thought of as objects of art.

many Westerners worried about the speed of and the forces behind cultural changes. In Europe especially, people talked about maintaining their own cultural tastes and identities in the face of "Americanization." They complained about the Hollywood movies, blue jeans, Coca-Cola, hamburgers, and fast food that poured from the United States into Europe. They also bemoaned the drain of intellectuals and artists moving to the United States. However, they could do little about the rapid spread of ideas, tastes, talent, and culture across political boundaries. Western Europeans found themselves losing the control they once had, and even the relative stability and prosperity gained in the 1950s and 1960s came under attack.

PROTESTS, PROBLEMS, AND NEW POLITICS: THE 1960s TO THE 1980s

As the two postwar decades came to a close, the course of history in the West shifted. Events in the 1970s and 1980s unfolded in a context similar to that of the earlier decades: Cold War competition led by the United States and the USSR. Each side represented different political and economic systems that divided Europe and much of the world. Each side also marched to the beat of economic growth—more rapid in the capitalist West than the communist East. However, within this same context, economic and political trouble was afoot. During the late 1960s and early 1970s, the road to social peace grew bumpy.

A Flurry of Social Protests and Movements

During these years, the gap between the ideals and realities of democracy, equality, and prosperity became more obvious and irritating than before. In some cases, unprecedented access to education fueled a growing awareness of this gap, while in others prosperity itself gave people the confidence to demand change. Often the well-publicized efforts of one group to force change inspired similar efforts by others. Protest movements frequently began in the United States and attracted close attention throughout the West. These dissatisfied groups voiced their demands with an assertiveness that shook several Western societies and even threatened governments.

The first of the great social movements began in the United States during the 1950s. There, African Americans initiated the civil rights movement, which inspired several other protest and liberation efforts in the West. The civil rights movement stemmed from America's long failure to integrate its large black population. African-American veterans returning from World War II felt particularly

The civil rights movement

frustrated with the discrimination they again faced at home.

In 1954, the Supreme Court took a major step in the fight against discrimination by outlawing racial segregation in public schools. "Separate educational facilities are inherently unequal," the Court concluded. A year later, a quiet act by a courageous individual set a series of additional changes in motion. A black civil rights activist, Rosa Parks, took a seat in the white-only section of a bus in Montgomery, Alabama. A yearlong boycott of segregated public transportation by African Americans in Montgomery followed, the first of many mass actions throughout the United States in the 1950s and 1960s.

White resistance to the black struggle for equality flared up in the American South, and more than once the federal government had to send troops and marshals there to overcome white resistance. White opposition also mounted in the large industrial cities of the North. Many whites fled to the suburbs to avoid integration. In 1964 and 1965, Congress passed a series of civil rights acts that guaranteed voting rights for all and broadly outlawed racial discrimination. Still, the turmoil continued. Racially charged riots broke out in major cities. The violence reached a climax in 1968 following the murder of Martin Luther King, Jr. (1929–1968), the prominent African-American leader.

In the face of growing opposition and divisions within its own ranks, the civil rights movement lost steam in the 1970s, but not before inspiring other groups, such as Spanish-speaking Americans, Native Americans, young people, and women. The protests by youths became especially threatening. Like the civil rights movement, these protests began in the United States. Soon, however, they spread throughout the West.

College students, whose numbers in the West more than tripled during the 1950s and 1960s, created movements of their own. The sheer mass of this first postwar generation of students and the emergence of a separate youth culture helped give these young people an acute sense of their own power. The civil rights movement and growing opposition to the Vietnam War provided causes and experiences for many. In 1964, students at the University of California at Berkeley attacked the restrictive values, social inequities, and competitive impersonality of the university and the traditional society it represented. Students also decried racism, poverty, and the growing American participation in the Vietnam War. Sometimes the protests turned into riots when authorities used force. Similar demonstrations soon boiled up across the United States.

Student movements

In 1968, the unrest spread to the campuses and streets of capitals from Tokyo and Mexico City to

DOCUMENT 25.3

An Oxford Student Explains Revolutionary Attitudes

The period between the mid-1960s and early 1970s was marked by intense political, social, and revolutionary activism. Perhaps most striking, university students throughout the West organized radical attacks on the status quo. The following selection by Tariq Ali, a student at Oxford and a leading revolutionary socialist, demonstrates the more extreme attitudes among these activists.

What is absolutely clear is that the revolutionary movement is in a period of upswing throughout the world. The war in Vietnam, the events of May 1968 in France and the invasion of Czechoslovakia symbolize this upswing.

Vietnam is at the moment the battle-front against imperialism. France showed the extreme vulnerability of monopoly capitalism and the strength of the working class. Czechoslovakia has initiated the struggle for political revolutions in Eastern Europe and the Soviet Union itself. . . .

Those of us who form the hard core of today's new revolutionaries are still Marxists, but we abhor Stalinism; we believe in Leninism but prefer the emphasis to be upon "democracy" rather than "centralism"; we are Guevarist but can appreciate and analyse the mistakes made by Che. We are puzzled by the tendency

among many Left factions in the developed countries to devote as much time and energy to attacking each other as to attacking capitalism. The new revolutionaries fight against sectarian tendencies. And what is most important of all, we are not to be bought off by the State. WE mean business.

SOURCE: Tariq Ali, *The New Revolutionaries* (New York: William Morrow, 1969), pp. 314–315.

Analyze the Document

1. In what ways are Ali's views revolutionary?

2. What developments of the 1960s does his analysis reflect?

3. What do you think Ali means by the last sentence?

London, Amsterdam, Milan, and Berlin. Even in Eastern Europe—especially in Czechoslovakia—youthful protesters added to dissident movements demanding social change and political democratization. "We are intensely aware, in a way perhaps not possible for the older generation, that humanity stands on the edge of a new era," declared students at the University of British Columbia in Canada. Document 25.3 reveals the views of some of the radical student groups. The most dramatic confrontations took place in Paris—the Days of May uprisings. Fed up with the rigid, overcrowded university system and fearing that many would miss out on France's new prosperity after graduation, Parisian students rampaged through the streets of the French capital. Charles de Gaulle, president of France since 1958, met the demonstrators with police repression. The students then gained the support of sympathetic workers, who in turn demanded higher wages and an end to police brutality. This alliance between students and workers paralyzed France and even threatened to overturn the government. But the danger was short-lived. Agreements to raise wages appeased workers and siphoned them off from the movement, and the government once more regained control. However, the protests provoked major reforms in higher education and probably played a role in de Gaulle's resignation a year later.

Like the civil rights movement, student activism waned in the 1970s. As universities adopted reforms that met many of the protesters' demands and the

war in Vietnam came to an end, the sparks of protest faded. Among women, however, an international feminist movement was still gaining momentum.

Although feminism had a lengthy history in the West, the traditionally defined domestic role of women still had not changed much, even as late as the 1950s. In most Western nations, the dominant message from pulpits, welfare offices, doctors, and governmental officials was the same: Women should stay at home and serve as the anchor of the family, defining their social identity through their husband and focusing on raising children. But that age-old message increasingly came under attack as women gained access to higher education, experience in various protest and liberation movements, and greater awareness of the social restrictions on their lives.

The women's liberation movement

One key to this increasing awareness came from new books. In 1949, the French writer Simone de Beauvoir (1908–1986) (see Biography) published *The Second Sex*, the century's most pivotal analysis of the condition of women. In this powerful book, de Beauvoir uncovered the myths that had relegated women to second-class status relative to men. "There is an absolute human type, the masculine. . . . He is the Subject, . . . she is the Other." De Beauvoir argued that women remained in cultural and economic dependence to men and therefore did not live as free human beings. The passive role assigned to women, she explained, forced them to live according to standards set up by men. De Beauvoir recommended a difficult but rewarding role for women: a life of work, self-definition, and independence.

The Second Sex became the fundamental text for feminist movements in the 1960s. Other writers, such as the American Betty Friedan, popularized de Beauvoir's ideas and added to them. In her widely read book *The Feminine Mystique* (1963), Friedan urged women to escape the confines of home, go back to school, get new careers, and become more independent.

These ideas struck a chord, especially among many middle-class women. Increasing life expectancy and fewer children meant that more of these women than ever were living longer and devoting less of their lives to raising a family. They now had the time and resources to seek fulfillment outside the home—if they could find a way to break down traditional barriers. As more women enrolled in universities and pursued careers, discrimination against them on the job because of their gender only heightened their sense of injustice and outrage.

Starting in the late 1960s, women in several Western nations founded organizations, conducted marches, held rallies, started journals, opened feminist bookstores, and pressured officials to recognize their needs. **Figure 25.9** shows one of many demonstrations. Women—many in slacks and jeans rather than traditional dresses—along with a few supportive men march through the streets of Paris. Carrying banners, signs, and balloons, they announce their purposes—equal pay with men for equal work—and unity. In 1969, an English women's group described the essence of the women's liberation movement: "We are economically oppressed: In jobs we do full work for half pay, in the home we do unpaid work full time. We are commercially exploited by advertisements, television and the press; legally we often have only the status of children. We are brought up to feel inadequate, educated to narrower horizons than men. This is our specific oppression as women. It is as women that we are, therefore, organizing."

Such efforts inspired a barrage of specific demands, including full citizenship in the political arena, equitable wages, and access to new careers. Despite opposition from conservative and religious groups, women pushed controversial issues such as day care, maternal leave, legalized abortion, and liberalized divorce into the spotlight of public discourse. They also protested stereotypical portrayals of femininity and widespread assumptions—among women and men alike—that raised the barriers facing them. Finally, they persuaded universities to introduce women's studies programs and prompted scholars in numerous academic disciplines to include feminist perspectives in their books.

By the early 1980s, the sharp edge of women's movements had dulled, but many long-term victories were already theirs. Women had gained greater control over

FIGURE 25.9 The Women's Movement in France During the late 1960s, women in many Western nations held rallies and demonstrations such as this one in Paris.

fertility and sexuality from governments, churches, and male-dominated medical establishments. Moreover, lesbians demanded and received some recognition of their rights. As French author Monique Wittig noted in 1979, without feminism, lesbian culture and society "would still be as secret as they have always been." More women than ever flocked to universities, began careers in law, medicine, education, government, and business, and won political office. "Every girl now thinks in terms of a job. This is progress," said one Swedish vocational counselor. "They don't intend to be housewives for some future husband."

Stagnant Growth and Rising Inflation

While the protest movements inspired optimism among their proponents and anger among conservative opponents, disturbing economic developments spawned worry and doubt. A new phenomenon that became known as "stagflation"—stagnant economic growth paired with rising inflation—spread in the West. The main culprit was oil and its central role in providing cheap energy for the Western economy. During the 1950s and 1960s, Western interests had kept oil prices low by expanding production and discouraging oil-producing countries in the Middle East, Africa, and South America from presenting a united front to raise prices. The low prices encouraged many users of coal to switch to oil and helped control inflation.

In 1973, a war broke out in the Middle East between Israel and its Arab opponents. Middle Eastern oil-producing states, now organized into the Arab-dominated **Organization of Petroleum Export-ing Countries (OPEC),** began to punish the West for supporting Israel in this conflict. As they limited

The oil crisis

BIOGRAPHY

Simone de Beauvoir
(1908–1986)

Intellectual and Feminist

Simone de Beauvoir was born in 1908 to a devoutly Catholic mother and an intellectual father who practiced law. Later, after rebelling against her family's middle-class values, Simone wrote that her mother "held dear all those bourgeois, Catholic, pious, well-thinking ideas which I was learning to detest," while her father gave her "a taste for the intellectual life." World War I ruined the family financially. Realizing that she needed to support herself, de Beauvoir went to college. Reforms in 1924 gave women new access to higher education, and de Beauvoir, a brilliant student, seized the opportunity.

In 1929, while completing her degree in philosophy at the Sorbonne, Simone met and fell in love with Jean-Paul Sartre—a dazzling speaker and leader of a circle of rebellious intellectuals. "What is unique between Simone de Beauvoir and me," Sartre would later say, "is the equality of our relationship." The two vowed that "neither of us would conceal anything from the other." De Beauvoir had already concluded that "bourgeois marriage is an unnatural institution . . . that doubles one's domestic responsibilities and, indeed, all one's social chores." Neither did she want children: "I was too self-sufficient."

Through the 1930s, the couple's teaching careers in various parts of France kept them apart. De Beauvoir admitted that she and Sartre avoided getting involved in politics until 1939, when "history took hold of me and never let go thereafter." When the Germans invaded France the following year, de Beauvoir fled Paris along with thousands of others. Shortly thereafter, the Germans captured and imprisoned Sartre. Freed in 1942, he joined de Beauvoir, who had returned to Paris.

In 1944, de Beauvoir became a full-time writer. By then she had already published the successful novel *She Came to Stay* (1943), in which she discussed connections between personal life and existentialism—the philosophy she, Sartre, and their intellectual circle often discussed. Sartre had also published numerous well-received works. In 1946, the couple founded and edited the influential review *Les Temps Modernes*. Between 1946 and 1949, de Beauvoir researched and wrote her thousand-page study of women, *The Second Sex* (1949). By this time, de Beauvoir and Sartre had become France's—and perhaps the West's—leading intellectual couple (see **Figure 25.10**).

During the 1960s, de Beauvoir rejected formal participation in feminist groups, believing instead that socialism would lead women and men alike to full liberation. In the 1970s, disillusioned with socialism and impressed with the strength of the feminist movement, she changed her mind. She served as president of the French League of Women's Rights and editor of feminist journals and remained active in the feminist cause for the rest of her life.

In 1980, Sartre died. Their fifty-year relationship was not idyllic. Both had lovers, and their relationship was not equal. Much of the time, the companionship of Sartre and de Beauvoir had more of a verbal than physical intimacy. "That was why it lasted so long," said de Beauvoir just weeks before her own death in 1986.

Connecting People & Society

1. What does de Beauvoir's life reveal about the position and role of intellectuals during the twentieth century?

2. Do you think de Beauvoir should be considered one of the century's leading feminists? Explain.

3. Do you think de Beauvoir's relationship with Sartre should affect our evaluation of her as a historical figure? Why or why not?

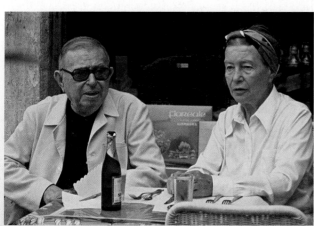

FIGURE 25.10 Jean-Paul Sartre and Simone de Beauvoir

production and increased prices, the cost of oil rose sixfold between 1973 and 1975. Prices again surged in 1979, spurring global inflation that particularly distressed the poorer nations of Asia and Africa and sent Western nations into a downward spiral of debt. Western economies, also facing disruptions in the international monetary system and growing competition from Japan, fell into recession.

In Europe and the U.S., expectations of perpetual economic growth and limitless natural resources gave way to doubt. Indeed, the very forces that had brought prosperity for some threw others out of work. For example, the increased automation of industrial plants, the substitution of oil for coal, and the growing use of computers often eliminated more jobs than they created. The "green revolution" in agriculture boosted productivity but also forced people off the land and into the urban labor market. Equally alarming, large transnational corporations cut jobs as they moved their plants to regions offering cheap labor.

All these forces worsened unemployment, which by the early 1980s hit a whopping 10 percent and higher in many Western nations. In Britain—once an economic giant—unemployment stayed at more than 12 percent year after year through the 1980s. Unions weakened, unable to protect workers in this perilous economic climate. The gap between rich and poor widened, and for many people—especially lower-wage earners—the economic good times seemed over. Least able to protect themselves were immigrant workers.

Growing unemployment

As is common during periods of economic uncertainty, wealthier nations turned against "outsiders." During the prosperity of the 1950s and 1960s, Western Europeans had opened their doors to desperate immigrants from southern Europe, Turkey, North Africa, and former colonies lured north by the promise of work. Immigrants filled the jobs that British, French, German, and Swiss workers passed over—the hardest, lowest-paid work in factories and fields, undesirable night shifts, street cleaning, and garbage collecting. Immigrant women were particularly vulnerable to exploitation in these jobs and in positions as domestics. Immigrant workers also labored under obligations to send money back home. Many, having heard myths about "lands of plenty," assumed that some day they would return home rich.

Turning against immigrants

In fact, officials often denied them social services and discouraged them from settling permanently. West Germany refused to grant citizenship to even those "immigrants" born in Germany. In the 1970s and 1980s, many governments, fearing worsening unemployment in their own countries, slammed the door shut against immigrants. The millions of foreign-born residents or "outsiders" who managed to arrive in the West increasingly suffered racial and anti-immigrant attacks.

The New Political Landscape

Reacting to social movements and uneasy about their economic fate during the 1970s and 1980s, voters throughout the West turned to political parties that they had once ignored or even disdained. Socialists, who accommodated these voters by toning down their radical message, gained the most from this new development. In 1969, the Social Democrats in West Germany won control for the first time in almost fifty years. During the 1970s, under Willy Brandt (1913–1992) and Helmut Schmidt, they eased Cold War tensions by pursuing a policy of increased diplomatic and economic relations with Eastern Europe and the Soviet Union. By the late 1970s and early 1980s, Spain, Portugal, and Greece had also elected new Socialist governments that endured and led these nations into the European Common Market. In 1981, socialists under the leadership of François Mitterrand (1916–1996) came into power in France. They nationalized industries, shortened working hours, and enacted progressive social programs. However, persisting inflation and high unemployment soon led them to reverse some of these policies.

Turning to the Left

Communist parties in Western Europe also tried to adapt to voters' demands so as to garner popularity. In Italy, Spain, and France, the communists turned to "Eurocommunism," supporting more moderate policies and vowing to cooperate with other leftist parties. They even gave up the Soviet model and its call to worldwide revolution and promised to work within Western democratic institutions and economic systems that blended free enterprise and state planning. For a while during the late 1970s and early 1980s, communists gained strength in Italy and played roles in governments in Spain and France.

Britain turned the other way. In 1979, voters handed a sweeping victory to the Conservatives and their right-wing leader, Margaret Thatcher, Britain's first female prime minister. Thatcher initiated policies to diminish state control over the economy, crush union power, and cut spending for Britain's welfare state. Some state-owned and subsidized industries were "privatized"—sold to private enterprise. Thatcher also cut taxes on the wealthy, hoping to encourage investment and a "trickling down" of wealth to the rest of British society. Bitter strikes and urban riots by workers and the unemployed decrying her hard-line policies did not dissuade her.

Turning to the Right

Across the Atlantic, Thatcher found an ideological ally in Ronald Reagan, elected president of the United States in 1980. Reagan pursued similarly conservative policies, reversing some of the liberal social policies of the 1960s, moving against unions, privatizing governmental services, cutting taxes, increasing military spending, and reviving Cold War posturing against the Soviet Union. Thatcher's and Reagan's partially successful efforts in the 1980s to limit governmental spending on social programs marked the beginning of a gentle but broad turn toward conservative politics in the West.

Despite the changes, some groups still felt left out of politics. They demanded attention, even at the price of violence. In the 1970s and 1980s, political terrorism spread across the West, conducted by groups such as the Red Brigades in Italy, the Red Army Faction in West Germany, and the Palestine Liberation Organization (PLO). Many of these groups had radical political goals. Others, such as the militant Basque separatists in Spain and the Kurdish rebels in Turkey, demanded national liberation. All desperately wanted recognition and had concluded that only assassinations, abductions, and bombings would achieve their aims.

 Terrorism

No area in Europe suffered more from terrorism than Northern Ireland. There the Roman Catholic minority struggled fiercely to gain equality with the Protestant majority. Many Roman Catholics demanded total separation from Britain and union with Ireland. The Provisional Wing of the Irish Republican Army (IRA) conducted a long campaign of terror to this end. As the Protestants fought fiercely to maintain their supremacy, violence begot even more violence.

Governments responded to terrorists, sometimes with violence and occasionally by making deals. Security measures increased, as did the presence of armed police, and occasionally governments were able to penetrate the urban anonymity of modern society to capture terrorists. For the most part, however, terrorism remained an exceptional means of protest that never gained enough support to threaten governments.

POSTINDUSTRIAL SOCIETY

The political fluctuations of the 1970s and 1980s reflected more than just economic ups and downs or politicians' efforts to garner popular support. Underlying many changes during this period was a fundamental development: The industrial societies of the West had begun transforming themselves into **postindustrial societies.** This term refers to a culmination of economic and social changes occurring in the West over several decades. Traditional manufacturing industries declined in importance as more competitive plants employing cheap labor opened outside of Europe and North America. In place of manufacturing, demand for financial, health, educational, informational, and consumer services mushroomed—all services at which the West excelled. Well-educated and handsomely paid professionals, managers, and financiers rose to prominent positions in corporations and government, joining or replacing property owners and entrepreneurs as key economic figures. The

bulk of the middle class—most of them well educated and with white-collar jobs—also grew in number and wealth. Industrial workers saw their jobs disappearing while demand for service employees expanded. Yet many of these service employees, who seemed white collar or middle class in their appearance or lifestyle, made the same income or even less than blue-collar workers. Traditional class lines were blurring.

Changing Fortunes in the Postindustrial Society

Some people gained more than others in this mobile society. The gap between rich and poor may have narrowed between the 1940s and 1960s, but that gap remained formidable and even increased in the 1970s and 1980s. Only the growing numbers of married women entering the paid workforce maintained or improved most families' standard of living after the early 1970s. Nor did overall prosperity solve problems of economic discrimination. Women generally received only two-thirds to three-fourths of men's salaries for the same work. Minority and immigrant groups still occupied the most poorly paid jobs. In many Western cities, a core of impoverished slum dwellers remained. Often without regular jobs and marked by their race or ethnic origin, they suffered the worst problems of urban life.

DEVELOPMENTS IN THE WEST

1947	Truman Doctrine
	Marshall Plan
1948	Berlin blockade begins
	NATO organized
1953	Death of Stalin
1954	Structure of DNA discovered
1955	Warsaw Pact
1956	Uprising in Hungary
1957	Common Market
1961	Berlin Wall built
1962	Cuban missile crisis
1964	Khrushchev falls from power
1968	Student uprisings
	Invasion of Czechoslovakia
1969	Americans land on the moon
1972	Britain, Ireland, Denmark join EEC
1975	Helsinki Agreement
1985	Gorbachev comes to power

KEY DATES

For most people in postindustrial societies, however, material life improved. Housing mushroomed, in France alone increasing to a half-million new units per year during the 1970s. New apartments had distinct rooms—bedroom, kitchen, living room, bathroom—and were not just for the middle class. Most homes boasted running water, indoor toilets, a bath or shower, and heating as well as an array of appliances. In the 1980s, one Italian woman reflected in amazement how her children "have grown up in a world in which washing machine, refrigerator, vacuum cleaner, and television set are taken for granted."

Daily patterns of life also changed as more and more people lived and worked in different parts of the cities and their expanding suburbs. People commuted on crowded trains or by car through traffic jams. The neighborhood cafés or pubs where people used to gather after work steadily lost customers, as did local, small stores where shoppers knew the merchants and each other. In their place, restaurants, supermarkets, and shopping malls sprang up, adding to the sense of urban anonymity.

The Baby Boom and the Booming Cities

Underlying the development of this postindustrial society were shifting populations that fueled economic growth and transformed patterns of life. Skyrocketing birthrates that had started during the war years led to the so-called **baby boom** soon after. An increase in life expectancy and the influx of immigrants added to the population growth. Europe's population, for example, increased from 264 million during the war to 320 million in the early 1970s. But the baby boom and the rapid jump in population did not last long. In the 1960s, birthrates began to decline as people returned to the long-term pattern of choosing to have fewer children. In the 1970s, these rates fell to less than half the pre–World War II figures in some areas.

Fewer of those populations lived on farms anymore. By 1955, less than a quarter of the population worked in agriculture. Over the next thirty years, that figure would fall to below 10 percent almost everywhere. Thanks to mechanization, fertilizers, pesticides, new seeds, and larger farms, dwindling numbers of farmers produced more than enough for everyone else, as well as surpluses for export. Rural economies could no longer offer employment to more than a small minority of the population. Once the heart of Western civilization, rural areas became places that city people traveled through and nostalgically imagined. Small country towns dominated by church steeples tried to stay viable by attracting tourists, people wanting second homes, or small industries looking to relocate. With the spread of highways, telephones, televisions, and computers, rural life retained only a hint of the isolation that formerly distinguished it from city life.

As they had for decades, people left rural areas and small towns in droves and headed for the cities. These migrations spread well beyond national borders. Wealthy northern European cities absorbed waves of newcomers from southern Italy, Greece, Turkey, and Africa, just as cities in North America took in Latin Americans and Asians. These immigration trends added to the traditional urban problems of congestion, overburdened transportation systems, pollution, and crime. Large parts of great cities deteriorated while the surrounding suburbs, with their own industrial plants, corporate offices, apartment complexes, and housing projects, expanded.

The Shifting Foundations of Family and Private Life

Along with this movement of people and transformation of cities, the very foundations of family and private life within postindustrial society began to shift. After the baby boom years of the 1940s and 1950s, families became smaller as people, aided by more widely available birth-control devices, chose to limit births. Families also became less stable, as married people used changing attitudes and laws concerning divorce to break apart more often. Many people decided to put off or avoid marriage altogether. Increasing numbers of single parents and same-sex partners now headed households.

The old family structure, in which the man wielded authority, weakened and began to be replaced by a sense of the family as a democratic partnership of equals. Married women streamed out of their roles as housekeepers, child rearers, and supporters of their "breadwinning" husbands. They now took paying jobs outside the home not only for the income but also for the equality and independence that paid employment offered. Especially within the middle classes, work outside the home became a sign of emancipation for women. With these changes, some homes became zones of domestic cooperation; others witnessed new battles between couples over household chores and child rearing. Overall, however, the burdens of housework and child care still rested primarily with women.

The process of raising children also changed. Children spent more years than ever in school to acquire the skills needed to excel in the competitive postindustrial society, a shift that made them financially dependent on their parents into their late teens and even early twenties. With nursery schools becoming standard, children now started school at age three rather than age six. More than ever, the socialization, training, and career choices of youths were taking place outside the home.

Within the home, an individual's private life became no longer secondary to family life. **Figure 25.11** presents the image of the small family together watching television. The television as much as the kitchen

FIGURE 25.11 Family Watching Television, 1950s
In mid-century, television viewing widely became the focal point of family gatherings and foreshadowed a continuing decline in family interactions.

Growing concern for private satisfactions became a center of nightly family gatherings. But this image may also depict a decline of family interaction. Larger apartments and houses let family members spend more time than ever in separate rooms, coming together only for meals or TV watching. Much of home life became private, with individuals spending most time apart and alone rather than joining other family members.

This growing concern for private satisfactions, which fit so well with the competitive economic individualism of postindustrial society, also played a role in the frequent separation of families. More often than ever, the ties holding marriages together began breaking apart. With love as the primary motive for marriage, the declining intensity of love that often occurs with time seemed enough to warrant divorce. As the sexual satisfaction of both partners became a core purpose of marriage, trouble in this domain also became a volatile source of discord and divorce.

Legal changes and statistics reflected these new realities. The grounds for divorce eased in most places to the point where mutual consent was enough. By the 1980s, between 25 and 50 percent of those who married would eventually get divorced. The old image of the breadwinning father, the homemaking wife, and the dependent children bonded together in a life-long relationship remained true for only a minority of the population.

The "Sexual Revolution" and the Youth Culture

Within or outside marriage, people gained new degrees of sexual freedom. Innovative methods of contraception, particularly the birth-control pill and the intrauterine device (and abortion, especially in Eastern Europe), achieved widespread acceptance in the 1960s and further separated sexual pleasure from reproduction. Manuals, sex education in schools, and the portrayal of sex in movies, books, magazines, and marketing materials became far more explicit than ever, reflecting the changing attitudes toward sex. Many conservative and religious groups strongly opposed these developments and the increase in premarital sex, though they were losing this battle by the 1970s. They also lost ground to gays, lesbians, and others who demanded respect and freedom.

Young men and women coming of age in the late 1950s and the 1960s, an era sometimes called the sexual revolution, led these widespread changes in sexual values. Their clothing—flowered shirts and beads for men, blue jeans and miniskirts for women—and long hairstyles symbolized their new sexual freedom as well as the wider challenge of their youth culture to the older generation.

Young people's taste in music and movies also announced a break between generations. In the United States, Elvis Presley led the explosion in rock and roll's popularity in the late 1950s. With his suggestive dancing, slicked-back hair, and devoted following of young, screaming fans, Presley embodied eroticism and sexual abandon. The Beatles and other popular rock groups had a similar impact. Social dancing evolved from a carefully choreographed, chaste ritual to a no-holds-barred celebration of the body and sexuality. In popular movies, brooding, sullen young actors such as James Dean and Marlon Brando portrayed rebellious youths and became icons of the expanding youth culture.

BREAKTHROUGHS IN SCIENCE

The postindustrial society and the changing patterns of urban life that characterized it owed much to the many scientific breakthroughs of the period following World War II. More than ever, science became linked to economics and the needs of large institutions—from governments and industrial corporations to universities. These links were particularly strong in "big science." Before World War II, most scientific research was carried out by individuals or small groups of scientists in a university setting. The application of their discoveries by engineers and technicians came later. After the war, funds for scientific research poured in from government and big business, forming what some called the military-industrial-university complex. With the influx of money and interest, the number of scientists jumped fivefold between 1945 and 1985, and the fields they entered divided into more and more subspecialties. Organized teams of scientists, technicians, and

The rise of big science

managers worked in large research laboratories, using expensive equipment and aiming for specific goals. The results were stunning.

From the Universe Above to the Universe Within

Cold War competition especially fueled the massive effort to put satellites and humans into space. By the 1960s, satellites spun around the earth, providing a steady stream of military surveillance, weather observations, communications, and scientific information. The "space race" between the United States and the Soviet Union climaxed with a televised walk on the moon's surface in 1969. While taking his first step, the American astronaut Neil Armstrong spoke his now-famous words: "That's one small step for man, one giant leap for mankind." **Figure 25.12** shows an American astronaut standing on the surface of the moon. One of the first things Armstrong did was to plant the U.S. flag and pose with it for a photograph. The image announced how daring and powerful the combination of government, science, and nationalism could be. Subsequent unmanned voyages carried spacecraft to planets throughout the solar system and beyond.

Government money funded other scientific and technological efforts as well. Teams of physicists used powerful particle accelerators to explore the sub-atomic world. From innovations in radar systems during World War II came microwave technology, which became central to the television and long-distance telephone industries. Work on the atomic bomb led to nuclear power plants.

Similar efforts by teams of scientists and individuals led to fundamental discoveries in fields such as genetics. In 1953, the structure of DNA, the material

FIGURE 25.12 Big Science, 1969 This photo of Americans on the moon serves to illustrate the combined power of large universities, big business, and governmental backing to carry out major scientific and technological projects.

in chromosomes that contains hereditary information, was discovered. This implied that the characteristics of all living things, including humans, could be controlled, and it opened the controversial possibility of tampering with this molecule to create new forms of life. Research into gene splitting and genetic engineering would turn this possibility into reality.

The Information Revolution

Much of the new scientific work depended on computers, which became the core of the "**information revolution.**" The computer first emerged in the 1940s as a tool for storing and manipulating information. Encouraged by business and government during the 1950s and 1960s, its scientific and economic impact widened. With miniaturization during the 1970s and 1980s, computers the size of a notebook could out-power their room-size predecessors. These new "personal computers" cropped up on desktops and in briefcases everywhere. Now most people involved in science, scholarship, and business relied on computers, and the new devices became the core of a booming, worldwide industry.

Transforming Medicine

In the decades after World War II, medicine also entered new territory—itself becoming a big business with strong links to science and economics. Long gone were the days of visits by horse-and-buggy doctors. Now most physicians saw patients in offices, clinics, and especially hospitals, which employed medical personnel working in coordinated teams with complex machines. The era of the family doctor also faded. Now patients consulted more prestigious specialists. Finally, doctors gained a new degree of power to battle medical problems. Whereas in earlier centuries physicians may have done more harm than good with their treatments, now medicine became a major lifesaver in the Western and non-Western world.

The keys to these changes were antibiotic drugs and vaccines. In the 1930s, researchers discovered that sulfa drugs could cure infectious diseases. Penicillin and other antibiotics soon followed. By the 1940s, once-fatal illnesses such as meningitis and pneumonia could be cured by antibiotic drugs. Tuberculosis, a disease so deadly that it was called the "white plague," was almost eliminated by a vaccine and antibiotics. In 1977, smallpox was literally eradicated throughout the globe. The spotlight on medicine shifted from traditional infectious diseases to cancer, heart disease, arthritis, and AIDS.

New surgical techniques also offered more hope than in previous centuries. Antibiotics let surgeons perform lung and other operations that had been too risky before because of the danger of infection. In the

1960s, open heart surgery and heart bypass operations became almost routine. Then organ replacement—first of kidneys and then even hearts—became possible. Surgery became more a process of continuous repair and replacement than cutting and removing.

Expensive new machines for diagnosis and treatment complemented all the new medical techniques. Ultrasound machines, CT scanners (which combined X rays with computer analysis), and MRI devices that used radio waves gave doctors a window into the body without having to open it up. Dialysis machines and pacemakers offered new hope to kidney and heart patients.

For those suffering from mental illnesses, effective medications emerged in the 1950s. Doctors prescribed a growing list of these psychotropic drugs for people with schizophrenic and manic-depressive conditions. Though the success of these drugs was far from complete, they contributed to the closing of many mental hospitals and asylums.

By the 1980s, medicine had become dominated by large hospitals, groups of doctors, insurance companies, and governmental agencies. Health "consumers" expected more and more from medicine—including cures for most ailments and what many saw as a right to live to retirement and a robust old age. Nations devoted more resources than ever to medicine—often more than 10 percent of the national income. Britain's minister of health once complained, "There is virtually no limit to the amount of health care an individual is capable of absorbing."

In several senses, then, the evolution of medicine since World War II reflected broader qualities of the era. Science, and especially big science, enabled doctors to expand and even revolutionize the field. Medicine also relied on the overall prosperity and governmental support of those decades, which enabled people to demand, and the health-care industry to provide, so many services. The very growth of this service industry as well as the high status and income enjoyed by its leading practitioners echoed the development of the postindustrial society, with its stress on services and technical expertise. Finally, like much else, Western medicine spilled across borders and into the non-Western world—though also in ways that highlighted the disparities of wealth between the Western and non-Western worlds and the conflicts that often arose when those different cultures met.

LOOKING BACK & MOVING FORWARD

Summary   The decades between 1945 and 1989 witnessed a quickening pace of change as more people than ever were drawn into the swirl of politics, economic development, and urban life. The Cold War, whose contours came into sharp focus after 1945, cast a pall over the entire era. Each side represented different paths to recovery after World War II and competitive ideologies that had their roots in the nineteenth century. Yet despite people's worst fears, the Cold War never ignited into an actual conflagration between the two superpowers. As we will see, it evaporated with surprising rapidity in the late 1980s.

During these decades, Western society became more technocratic, affluent, welfare oriented, and culturally open—characteristics that also had first come to light at the end of the nineteenth century. Western Europe, in particular, managed this transformation despite ceding leadership to the United States and losing its colonial empires. Although Western Europe's status in the world declined, it remained a strikingly prosperous, dynamic region.

As the final decade of the twentieth century approached, the West as a whole remained powerful and was often envied abroad. At the same time, it had become clear that the Western powers could no longer act without taking into account the concerns, power, and problems of the non-Western world. Soon, stunning developments in Eastern Europe would mark 1989 as the dawn of a new historical era.

KEY TERMS

Iron Curtain, *p. 776*

Cold War, *p. 776*

Berlin airlift, *p. 778*

containment, *p. 778*

Marshall Plan, *p. 778*

North Atlantic Treaty Organization, (NATO), *p. 778*

détente, *p. 785*

Berlin Wall, *p. 786*

Prague Spring, *p. 787*

welfare state, *p. 788*

European Economic Community, *p. 788*

apartheid, *p. 793*

decolonization, *p. 793*

existentialism, *p. 796*

Organization of Petroleum Exporting Countries (OPEC), *p. 800*

postindustrial societies, *p. 803*

baby boom, *p. 804*

information revolution, *p. 806*

REVIEW, ANALYZE, & CONNECT TO TODAY

REVIEW THE PREVIOUS CHAPTER

Chapter 24—"Into the Fire Again"—analyzed the devastating war that encompassed the world.

1. In what ways did World War II set the stage for the Cold War and the different paths followed by Western and Eastern Europe?

2. In what ways did World War II hasten decolonization in the following decades?

ANALYZE THIS CHAPTER

Chapter 25—"Superpower Struggles and Global Transformations"—traces the Cold War competition between the United States and the Soviet Union. Within this context, the recovery of the West and the end of colonialism are examined.

1. How did Cold War tensions influence international affairs in the Western and non-Western worlds?

2. In what ways did Western life during these decades represent a triumph of Western industrialization and political democracy? What sorts of problems persisted despite this triumph?

3. Compare and evaluate the two paths followed by Western and Eastern Europe during this period.

4. Evaluate the process of decolonization. What problems faced the newly independent nations of the non-Western world?

CONNECT TO TODAY

Think about the Cold War and the legacy of colonialism.

1. In what ways might international affairs in today's world reflect the end of the Cold War?

2. How might international politics in our times be different if the Cold War had *not* ended?

3. Even though colonialism has ended for the most part, how might its legacy still influence world affairs today?

BEYOND THE CLASSROOM

ORIGINS OF THE COLD WAR

Gaddis, John Lewis. *The Cold War: A New History.* New York: Penguin, 2005. An authoritative history of the Cold War.

Patterson, Thomas G. *On Every Front: The Making and Unmaking of the Cold War.* New York: W.W. Norton, 1992. Analyzes both the domestic and foreign policy aspects of the Cold War.

EAST AND WEST: TWO PATHS TO RECOVERY IN EUROPE

Judt, Tony. *Postwar: A History of Europe Since 1945.* New York: Penguin, 2005. Excellent, extensive treatment of the period, emphasizing how post–World War II Europe dealt with its own past and modernization.

Mazower, Mark. *Dark Continent: Europe's Twentieth Century.* New York: Knopf, 1999. A survey that emphasizes political developments.

THE TWILIGHT OF COLONIALISM

Ansprenger, Franz. *The Dissolution of the Colonial Empires.* London: Routledge, 1989. Stresses the legacy of inequality and cells of poverty created by imperialism but also asserts that imperialism helped to create a global economy.

Springhall, John. *Decolonization Since 1945: The Collapse of European Empires.* London: Palgrave Macmillan, 2001. A good overview with colony-by-colony coverage.

A SENSE OF RELATIVITY IN THOUGHT AND CULTURE

Maltby, R., ed. *Passing Parade: A History of Popular Culture in the Twentieth Century.* New York: New Oxford Press, 1989. Excellent in its breadth of coverage.

Stromberg, Roland N. *After Everything: Western Intellectual History Since 1945.* New York: St. Martin's Press, 1986. An excellent survey of ideas and ideology in the postwar period.

GLOBAL CONNECTIONS

Maier, Karl. *Into the House of the Ancestors: Inside the New Africa.* New York: John Wiley and Sons, 1998. A balanced and well-supported account.

PROTESTS, PROBLEMS, AND NEW POLITICS: THE 1960S TO THE 1980S

Caute, David. *The Year of the Barricades: A Journey Through 1968.* New York: Harper & Row, 1988. Examines the revolutionary upheavals in a period called "year one" of the revolution.

Lovenduski, Joni. *Women and European Politics: Contemporary Feminism and Public Policy.* Amherst: University of Massachusetts Press, 1986. Compares the movement for women's liberation in the 1960s with previous women's movements.

POSTINDUSTRIAL SOCIETY

Hoffman, Stanley, and Paschalis Kitromilides. *Culture and Society in Contemporary Europe.* London: Allen & Unwin, 1981. A wide-ranging, interpretative survey connecting cultural and social developments.

BREAKTHROUGHS IN SCIENCE

Ziman, John. *The Force of Knowledge: The Scientific Dimension of Society.* Cambridge: Cambridge University Press, 1976. A useful examination of connections between science and society during the postwar years.

CHINA, 2008

On an early morning in December 2008, the large steel mill in Baotou, China, is already in full production. The mill supports this rapidly expanding one-industry town, located just west of China's capital city, Beijing, and, along with similar cities, testifies to China's growing role as a leading industrial nation. The carbon-rich smoke pouring into the air and creating pollution that will spread east to Beijing and beyond also reveals the accelerating environmental problems—above all, global warming—facing China and the world in the twenty-first century.

Into the Twenty-First Century 26

The Present in Perspective

"The 20th century is now over." The historian John Lukacs made this announcement in a 1991 issue of the *New York Times.* By "20th century," Lukacs meant the 75-year era that began in 1914 and ended in 1989. The year 1914 marked the outbreak of World War I, which for most historians represented the beginning of the twentieth century. That conflict and World War II dominated the period. "The Russian Revolution, the atom bomb, the end of the colonial empires, the establishment of the Communist states, the emergence of the two superpowers, the division of Europe and of Germany—all of these were the consequences of the two world wars, in the shadow of which we were living, until now," wrote Lukacs. The year 1989 saw the nations of Eastern Europe break from their Soviet ties and from communism. In just two more years, the Soviet Union itself would fall apart.

Other developments, also with roots in the past, added to the sense that the world had just lived through the closing of one historical era and the opening of another. The movement toward economic integration in Western Europe, the growing strength of the newly unified Germany, and the changing position of the United States altered international relations. Beyond the West, the Pacific Rim—particularly East Asia—gained enormous economic clout. In the Islamic world, stretching from North Africa through the Middle East to Indonesia, mounting pressures posed a variety of threats to stability in those regions and beyond. From a global perspective, three regional power centers had emerged—Europe, North America, and East Asia. Almost everywhere, people, problems, cultures, and histories spilled across national borders, challenging those living in the Western and non-Western worlds to broaden their understanding of the world and their place in it.

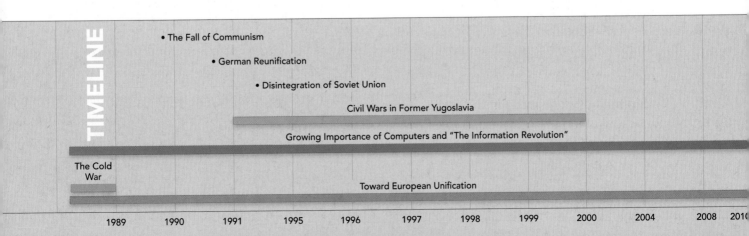

TIMELINE

- The Fall of Communism
- German Reunification
- Disintegration of Soviet Union

Civil Wars in Former Yugoslavia

Growing Importance of Computers and "The Information Revolution"

The Cold War

Toward European Unification

1989 1990 1991 1995 1996 1997 1998 1999 2000 2004 2008 2010

THE COLLAPSE OF COMMUNISM

Of all these developments, the collapse of communism in the Soviet Union and Eastern Europe arguably had the most dramatic and far-reaching global impact. In a startling public announcement early in November 1989, East Germany's communist leader succumbed to months of growing pressure and ordered the Berlin Wall, the most powerful symbol of the Cold War, torn down. **Figure 26.1** shows Germans from East and West climbing over the Berlin Wall near the Brandenburg Gate. A reporter described the scene: "Nearby, before the Brandenburg Gate . . . people climbed up onto the rim of the wall during the night of November 9 . . . taking pickaxes to it." Then the cranes and bulldozers came. "People stared unbelieving, as East German cranes lifted away the slabs of concrete. . . ." As the wall crumbled, another observer described the Berlin border crossings: "The streets were packed with people streaming past the East German border guards. . . . Cars from East Berlin slowed to a crawl alongside the crowds of West Berliners waiting just over the white stripe painted on the asphalt, cheering every car . . . handing cans of beer to the drivers." In those first heady days, millions of East Germans crossed the border, some to stay, others to return again and again "loaded down with full plastic shopping bags." The mayor of West Berlin declared, "This [is] the greatest historical event since the French Revolution."

Everywhere in Eastern Europe, communist governments were collapsing. The Soviet bloc, which had seemed so impenetrable, quickly dissolved. Soon the Soviet Union itself would break apart.

Undermining Communism in the Soviet Union

What explains this massive historical reversal? The story begins in the Soviet Union, where communist power was most firmly entrenched. During the two or three decades following World War II,

FIGURE 26.1 The Berlin Wall, November 1989
Demonstrators celebrate the fall of the Berlin Wall, which served as a barrier between Eastern and Western Europe. "In the Name of the People," written in English, credits popular will for tearing down the wall and announces the importance of the event to a watching world.

the Soviet Union, like other communist nations, enjoyed economic growth and relative prosperity (see Chapter 25). The USSR boasted impressive factories and elaborate technical projects such as dams, railway systems, military hardware, and manned rockets. Rapid industrialization, which pulled peasants and women into the urban workforce by the millions, boosted productivity.

However, during the 1970s and 1980s, central planning and collectivization—the hallmarks of the Soviet economic system—failed to match new consumer demands. Keeping up with the rapidly changing, technologically sophisticated economy of the 1970s and 1980s required flexibility, a willingness to experiment with new production methods, and local decision making—all of which the Soviet economic system lacked. Instead, economic decisions came from high officials more sensitive to political pressures than to economic realities. Central planners, pursuing out-of-date strategies or unaware of changes in grassroots needs, often ordered factories to produce goods that did not meet consumers' demands. Local plant managers, struggling to get needed materials and

> Problems with central planning

labor, suffered long delays while distant officials made decisions. Workers, their jobs guaranteed, had little incentive to work hard or even show up consistently. Similar problems plagued agriculture, where collectivization discouraged effective decision making and hard work. As the rate of economic growth declined, embarrassed Soviet planners had to import grain again and again from the capitalist West. Government leaders worried that the Soviet economy would never catch up with formidable capitalist competitors such as the United States, Germany, and Japan.

Worse, everyday dissatisfactions spread. Soviet workers had money but not the selection or quality of goods that they wanted and that they knew were available to people in the West. Instead, they regularly stood in lines for as long as two hours a day just to buy basic supplies. Even urban professionals, managers, and technicians, although relatively wealthy and well educated, experienced similar frustrations. Far too obviously, only a small corps of Communist Party officials and privileged elites enjoyed access to the most desirable goods and services in this supposedly egalitarian society, fueling resentment. For everyone else, the only alternative was the thriving, but expensive and illegal, black market. Faith in the communist system, even among members of the Communist Party, began to evaporate. "I'm not a good Party member because I don't believe in Communism . . . nor do a lot of Party members," admitted one 40-year-old Communist in 1990. "Joining the Party was for me entirely a calculated way of furthering my career."

Three pivotal developments during the late 1970s and 1980s exacerbated the problems undermining the Soviet brand of communism. First, **Growth of dissent** the spread of modern communications broke down the old Stalinist policy of enforced isolation from the rest of the world and fueled the growing dissident movement. By watching television, people saw for themselves the material wealth enjoyed by Western nations. They also perceived the swirling cultural and intellectual currents that officials tried to stifle within the Soviet Union. Yet photocopiers and computers spread information easily, making censorship difficult. Privately published manuscripts criticizing Soviet life circulated among the educated elite. The dissident movement grew, led by the Nobel Prize–winning physicist Andrey Sakharov (1921–1989) and others. Dissidents demanded more democracy, greater civil liberties, and some independence for nationalities within the Soviet Union. Although such demands earned Sakharov and others exile, the dissident movement persisted. Moreover, among many people not yet ready to join the dissident movement, the increasingly

obvious contradictions between the official party line and the harsh realities of Soviet life engendered cynicism and apathy.

Second, military and wartime expenditures increasingly burdened the Soviet economy. In the 1980s, the United States under President Ronald Reagan vigorously pursued the Cold War arms race, forcing the Soviets— **Military burdens** with their fundamentally weaker economy—to struggle to keep up. At the same time, the 1979 Soviet invasion of Afghanistan turned into a costly military quagmire. The widely condemned conflict wore on for years, straining the USSR's economy and diminishing the Soviet leadership's popularity.

Third, the quality of the Soviet leadership declined in the 1970s and 1980s. Leonid Brezhnev weakened noticeably and repeatedly fell ill in the seven years before his death in 1982. Most of his colleagues were **Declining leadership** long established in their offices. Brezhnev's immediate successors, Yuri Andropov (1982–1984) and Konstantin Chernenko (1984–1985), each died shortly after assuming office. These older men were reluctant to alter the USSR's course or to make way for a younger generation of reformers. But in 1985, a new leader—Mikhail Gorbachev—was appointed head of the Soviet Union. Just 54 years old, he had very different ideas about how the Soviet Union should operate.

Gorbachev Launches Reforms

Born into a peasant family, Mikhail Gorbachev (1931–) studied law as a youth at the University of Moscow. He moved rapidly up through the Communist Party ranks, eventually taking responsibility for agricultural policy. Charming and astute, he became a capable manipulator of people and events. Britain's prime minister, Margaret Thatcher, recognized him as a man "with whom we can do business." Gorbachev also had bold plans to lead the Soviet Union in new directions. Soon after assuming power in 1985, he replaced a third of the old party leadership with new supporters. By then, he shared the views of reformers who recognized the fundamental economic problems plaguing the Soviet Union. In his willingness to grapple with problems, Gorbachev echoed Khrushchev's attack on Stalinism some thirty years earlier. Nevertheless, he had no intention of loosening the party's hold on power.

Gorbachev embarked on a three-pronged policy: *perestroika* (restructuring), *glasnost* (openness to discussion), and disarmament. All three were intended to bring the *Perestroika* Soviet economy up to the standard of Western capitalist societies. No one—not even

Gorbachev—imagined the consequences that would flow from these daring reforms.

Perestroika involved a thorough restructuring of the Soviet economy. The program's goals included decentralizing planning, allowing market forces rather than officials to set prices, and putting control of land and agricultural practices into the hands of families and cooperatives rather than large state farms. In short, *perestroika* would create a mixed economy featuring a blend of socialist planning and a capitalist, free market. Gorbachev knew that the transformation would take time and cause short-term pain, including further shortages of consumer goods, inflation, and unemployment. To gather the political backing and the financial resources he needed to carry out the program, he initiated *glasnost* and an arms-reduction plan.

Glasnost curtailed censorship, encouraged freer discussion of everything from culture to politics, and opened the doors to the partial

| Glasnost |

democratization of the Communist Party and the Soviet political system. Officials freed dissidents such as Andrey Sakharov. Some governmental proceedings were made visible to the public and even televised. In the spring of 1989, the government held the first open elections since 1917, which resulted in the defeat of numerous communist dignitaries. Gorbachev hoped that *glasnost* would elevate his prestige internationally, win him foreign political and financial support, and inspire intellectuals and workers at home to accept his bold restructuring of the Soviet economy.

His arms-reduction plan served the same ends. In meetings with U.S. presidents almost every year between 1985 and 1991, Gorbachev

| Arms reduction |

pushed for more and more reductions in both countries' military stockpiles. These meetings bore fruit: Both the USSR and the United States agreed to limit nuclear weapons and conventional forces not only on their own soil but also in Europe. At the same time, Gorbachev tried to extract Soviet forces from the war in Afghanistan. The effort took four years, but in 1989 the last Soviet troops finally came home. These feats burnished Gorbachev's reputation at home and abroad and promised to ease the USSR's heavy burden of military expenditures.

However, implementing *perestroika* proved more difficult than Gorbachev and his supporters expected. Entrenched officials resisted the changes, as did many Soviet individuals whose jobs and incomes were threatened by economic restructuring. Gorbachev's promises also raised the Soviet people's expectations to impossible heights. Some reformers even criticized him for moving too slowly.

To complicate matters, ethnic groups and republics within the Soviet Union began agitating for national autonomy and the freedom to express their own cultural beliefs. Peoples from central Asia and Armenia to the Baltic republics had long harbored resentments against the

| Demands for autonomy |

Soviet state. Most of these republics had been forced to join the Soviet Union during the devastating civil wars of 1917–1921. When Gorbachev weakened the monopoly power of the Communist Party, he undermined the principal institution holding the multinational Soviet Union together. Emboldened by Gorbachev's promised leniency in Eastern Europe, the republics took action. The greatest threat came from elites in Latvia, Lithuania, and Estonia on the Baltic coast, who led demands for political autonomy. As tensions mounted, events in Eastern Europe took a dramatic turn, overshadowing developments in the Soviet Union.

Revolutions in Eastern Europe

Ever since coming under the USSR's control, many people living in the communist nations of Eastern Europe had yearned to reclaim their national autonomy. Moreover, economic and cultural problems similar to those undermining communism in the Soviet Union plagued these societies and their governments. Though dissent did not always result in public protests, strikes, or demonstrations, it still simmered. In 1978, the Czechoslovakian playwright Václav Havel (see Biography) mocked the words of the *Communist Manifesto*: "A spectre is haunting eastern Europe: the spectre of what in the West is called 'dissent.'" Underground publications demanding honesty and civil rights circulated through intellectual and artistic circles in Poland, Hungary, and Czechoslovakia.

Two developments in the late 1980s strained the communist regimes trying to maintain control over these satellite states. First, economic difficulties mounted as Eastern

| Economic problems |

European governments labored to keep prices artificially low. To make matters worse, foreign loans from the West to Eastern European nations such as Poland became more expensive and began drying up. When those governments finally tried to increase prices without raising wages, public opposition mushroomed. Second, Gorbachev revoked the long-standing Brezhnev Doctrine. In 1989, he made his intentions clear: "Any interference in domestic affairs and any attempts to restrict the sovereignty of states, both friends and allies or any others, are inadmissible." Gorbachev had decided

| Revoking the Brezhnev Doctrine |

to let events in Eastern Europe unfold without Soviet intervention. For reformers and dissenters, this policy was a green light to action.

Poland led the way in the rush for liberation. This nation already had a history of protest movements that made it a weak link in the Soviet chain. In 1980, shipyard workers in Gdansk struck against rising consumer-goods prices. The strikers

Poland leads

organized a noncommunist union, Solidarity, under the leadership of Lech Walesa. Support for Solidarity spread throughout the nation, forcing the government to recognize the new organization and accede to some of its demands. When the union pushed for more, resistance from Moscow and conservative elements in the Polish government stiffened. In late 1981, General Wojciech Jaruzelski, the new leader of the Polish Communist Party, declared martial law, arrested Walesa, and outlawed Solidarity.

However, the union survived these reversals. Early in 1989, with the Polish economy in crisis, negotiations began between Jaruzelski and Solidarity, still led by Walesa. The Polish Catholic Church, which had maintained a position in the nation and indeed enhanced its own prestige with the visit of Pope John Paul II in 1979, helped mediate discussions. The talks resulted in the legalization of Solidarity and, in June, new elections. Solidarity's stunning victory at the polls prompted Jaruzelski to ask the union to form a new government. A few months later, the communist leader stepped down, and the Communist Party gave up power in Poland without a fight.

Hungary soon followed suit. This satellite state already had a mixed economy, with almost one-third of its wealth coming from a private sector of small enterprises, crafts, and family agriculture. Reformers within the Hungarian Communist

Hungary

Party gained some power in 1988 and removed the old leader, János Kádár, from office. In the summer and fall of 1989, Hungary held elections, established a multiparty political system, and initiated economic reforms to open the country to private enterprise. **Figure 26.2,** a poster published by the Hungarian Democratic Forum, captures the sense of ushering out a bygone era. The poster announces the fall of communism in Hungary with the words "Comrades, It's Over," and with the depiction of the back of a departing man's head. The military hat symbolizes the confining authority of the old regime, and the wide neck perhaps represents the resentment against communist officials who had enjoyed special privileges.

Next came Czechoslovakia. In the fall of 1989, student demonstrators took to the streets demanding academic freedom and human rights. When police responded with clubs and tear gas, the demonstrators turned against them and other

The "velvet revolution" in Czechoslovakia

authorities. Workers and employers alike joined the students in the streets of Prague and in the great St. Wenceslas Square in the city center. In November, the call went out for a general strike.

FIGURE 26.2 Istvan Orosz, *Comrades, It's Over,* 1989
This poster published by the Hungarian Democratic Forum announces the fall of communism in Hungary and elsewhere in Eastern Europe.

Within a few days, the hard-line Communist government resigned. Václav Havel, the playwright and dissident leader who had been imprisoned for his views, and Alexander Dubcek, who had tried to liberalize Czechoslovakia in 1968, quickly rose to power. As in Poland and Hungary, the fall of the communist regime in Czechoslovakia was bloodless—a "velvet revolution."

In East Germany, the wealthiest and most powerful of the Eastern European states, even people who did well under communism wanted to head west by the thousands. An American woman residing in East Germany described

East Germany

the growing dissatisfaction. "Too many . . . things were wrong. . . . Too much was missing from the shops. . . . There were no spare parts to fix home appliances or cars. Assembly lines were halted for want of supplies from auxiliary plants. It was the same on building sites, and the workers stood idle and furious. What good was this kind of socialism? Why did everything work so smoothly in the Germany next door?" When Hungary opened its borders with Austria in September 1989, tens of thousands of

BIOGRAPHY

Václav Havel
(1936–)

Playwright,

Dissident,

and

Politician

In May 1989, Czechoslovakian authorities released the playwright and dissident leader Václav Havel from jail. Just seven months later, the nation elected him as its new president. The well-known American author Arthur Miller called Havel "the world's first surrealist president" in reference to his unusual literary and intellectual background. *Time* magazine described him as "the conscience of Prague." Havel referred to himself as a mere writer who lacked "any of the necessary qualities" of a politician. "I've always understood my mission to be to speak the truth about the world I live in, to bear witness to its terrors and its miseries—in other words, to warn rather than hand out prescriptions for change."

Václav was born in 1936 into a well-known, middle-class family of engineers. With the advent of the communist regime in 1948, the family lost much of their property and position. Havel thanked "the apparent disadvantage of coming from a bourgeois background and growing up in a Communist state" for enabling him to see "the world . . . as it really is."

At age 13, Havel began writing poetry and philosophy. Over the next several years, he developed an interest in the theater and started writing plays. In 1956, he met his future wife, Olga Splichalova, who would become the first person to read each of his manuscripts.

In the early 1960s, Havel wrote plays and articles while attending night classes at the Academy of Performing Arts. The boyish, blue-eyed writer often stayed up all night working or talking with friends in beer pubs. Soon he earned acclaim as one of Czechoslovakia's most successful playwrights. His best-known works included *The Garden Party, The Increased Difficulty of Concentration, The Memorandum,* and *Largo Desolato.*

Havel also acquired a reputation as a dissident in 1965 by publicly criticizing the Writers' Union for acting "as a broker between politics and literature" rather than "defending the right of literature to be literature." During the Prague Spring of 1968 (see Chapter 25), Havel published a bold article suggesting the end of single-party rule in Czechoslovakia. Warsaw Pact troops crushed that moment of liberation, and the new, repressive regime banned Havel's works.

In the 1970s, Havel helped establish an underground press that published many disapproved and hard-to-find works. He wrote several influential essays on totalitarianism and dissent, including "The Power of the Powerless." Further, he argued that the communist regime in Czechoslovakia was based on fundamental lies, though he had faith that truth could penetrate these lies. In 1977 he became a founding spokesman for Charter 77, signed by hundreds of Czechs, Slovaks, and intellectuals from other countries. The charter called for people to do

---

East Germans used that escape route to stream into the West. "They had been watching it longingly on West German television all their young lives. They knew from the commercials exactly how they would furnish their homes and make them shine."

In October 1989, antigovernment demonstrations spread throughout East Germany. People brandished signs proclaiming "We are the people." Long-suppressed criticism of the state's feared "security" forces surfaced. The hard-line communist leader was ousted from office. In November 1989, his communist successor bowed to the inevitable and ordered the Berlin Wall torn down. Joyful demonstrators celebrated for days. Soon, communists lost power, and within a year East and West Germany had reunified.

The rest of Eastern Europe also quickly followed. In Bulgaria, an internal coup deposed the Stalinist ruler. In Romania, the relatively independent but dictatorial communist leader Nicolae Ceauşescu ordered troops to fire on demonstrators, setting off a bloody revolution. His overthrow cost many lives and ended with the execution of Ceauşescu and his wife. The following year, Albania's independent but highly Stalinist regime also collapsed.

The freeing of Eastern Europe took less than a year. One after another, these nations cut the ties binding them to the USSR, enacted democratic reforms, and introduced capitalism into their economies (see **Map 26.1**). The repercussions of these events echoed throughout the Soviet Union, quickly pushing developments beyond the control of Gorbachev and his supporters.

The Soviet Union Disintegrates

The Soviet leader had managed only halting steps in his effort to restructure the Soviet economy—*perestroika.* High officials announced plans to move the economy away from central planning and then delayed the plans in the face of determined opposition by hard-liners. These officials

Problems with reform

all they could for human rights in Eastern Europe. Officials labeled the publication "reactionary," something "delivered to Western agents as instructed by anti-Communist and Zionist headquarters." Police quickly rounded up and interrogated signers.

Havel spent most of the period from 1977 to 1983 in prison for his human rights activities. Nevertheless, his wife, Olga, continued the underground publishing. Václav would later publish a book of his letters to her. Not long after his release, he reflected on his prison experience:

"[A]ll that heroic time in prison was in fact one long chain of worries, fears, and terrors . . . and despite all this, I know that, if it were necessary, I would go back to prison again. . . ."

His words were prophetic. In February 1989, Havel once more languished in a prison cell for his criticisms of the communist regime. Yet his fortunes were about to change. Not far from the walls of his prison, student demonstrators marched angrily through the city streets. A petition campaign somehow persuaded authorities to release Havel in May. He soon took up his role again as a leader of the dissidents, circulating petitions demanding democratic reforms.

In November 1989, he helped found the Civic Forum, which led the opposition movement in Czechoslovakia. Before the end of the year, the Czech parliament elected Havel president, completing his

stunning transition from prison cell to the halls of government. **Figure 26.3** shows Havel in November 1989 at Sparta Stadium in Prague toasting the resignation of the communist politburo. He was soon elected to lead Czechoslovakia's new, noncommunist government. In his 1990 New Year's address, he announced, "People, your government has returned to you!"

Through the 1990s, the people again and again reelected Havel president. Some critics saw him as too much of an intellectual. Still, he gained a worldwide reputation as a moral spokesperson for Europe who stressed "the tolerant coexistence of different cultural identities" and the "ties that link everything in this world together."

Connecting People & Society

1. Why might intellectuals such as Havel have posed a threat to Czechoslovakia's authorities?

2. How did communist authorities try to maintain power during the 1960s, 1970s, and 1980s?

3. How does Havel's life reveal the forces behind the fall of communism in Eastern Europe?

FIGURE 26.3 Václav Havel and the 1968 liberal leader Alexander Dubcek publicly celebrate the fall of Czechoslovakia's communist government.

also worried about the difficulties—including unemployment, inflation, and dislocation—that the transition would cause. Gorbachev watered down his reforms to the satisfaction of no one. The waffling and controversy only worsened the frustrations of hardliners and reformers alike. Reformers who wanted Gorbachev to move faster grew disgusted with the moderate pace of change, while the old communist guard became increasingly alienated. As the economy began to spin out of control, the Soviet leader's popularity dwindled.

Gorbachev tried pushing through promising political reforms as part of his *glasnost* policy, but, as with *perestroika*, each step taken to enact reforms opened the door further for new expressions of dissatisfaction. In 1990, he persuaded the Communist Party's Central Committee to eliminate the party's constitutional monopoly on political power. He created a new, strong presidency—an office separate from the Communist Party hierarchy. Equally daring, he called for new elections.

All these changes democratized Soviet politics and undermined the power of the Communist Party—in the process exposing the corruption of the old Soviet regime. Party members resigned in droves. These policies also facilitated the rise of Gorbachev's chief rival, Boris Yeltsin (1931–2007), the newly elected president of the Russian Republic. A charismatic, liberal reformer, Yeltsin publicly resigned from the Communist Party in July 1990. In another bold move, he declared the Russian Republic an independent state.

At the same time, movements for independence gained momentum within several ethnic groups and nationalities throughout the USSR. The Soviet Union contained more than a hundred ethnic groups, as well as some 50 million Muslims in central Asia. Many of these groups considered themselves separate nations and the Soviet Union as a collection of nations rather than a single whole. The republics of Estonia, Lithuania, and Latvia led in pressing Moscow for independence. In 1991,

Independence movements

Eastern Europe, 1989

This map shows the upheavals that toppled the communist regimes in Eastern Europe.

Explore the Map

1. How widespread were the public protests and demonstrations of the times?

2. Which Western European states had the potential to gain more influence in Eastern Europe as Soviet control over the area waned?

3. Why might several of these states have been interested in joining Western European organizations such as NATO and the European Community?

Site of Popular Demonstrations

Capital Cities

the Ukraine joined the Russian Republic in declaring itself independent. Ethnic conflict and nationalistic demands spread in the Soviet republics of Armenia, Azerbaijan, Moldova, Georgia, and elsewhere. Though Gorbachev resisted these demands and tried to quell the ethnic conflicts, the situation had gone beyond anyone's control. In the spring of 1991, he proposed a compromise: the Treaty of Union, in which all the Soviet republics would be independent but held together as a confederation.

In August 1991, with the Treaty of Union about to take effect, communist hard-liners from inside the government and the KGB tried to oust Gorbachev. Within three days, the hard-liners' ineptitude and the opposition marshaled by Russian president Yeltsin doomed the coup to failure. Indeed, Gorbachev's authority was slipping away to Yeltsin even at this moment. In late 1991, after the two leaders stripped the Communist Party of much of its power, Gorbachev resigned.

Hard-liners' coup

In the end, no one, including the once-dominant Russians, wanted to save the old Soviet Union. Gorbachev had unleashed the forces of revolution, and he—along with the USSR itself—became

revolution's victim. The long Cold War was over (see Document 26.1). In 1999, Gorbachev would look back and explain, "Communism—as the inventors of the theory imagined it—never existed anywhere. . . . What did exist was Stalinist socialism. That system had exhausted itself and was doomed to disappear." **Map 26.2** shows what became of the former Soviet Union. Most of the republics within the old structure joined the new Commonwealth of Independent States, a loose confederation. A few republics, such as the Baltic states, broke away altogether.

Life After the Collapse of Communism

After the celebrations in the former communist bloc ended, people awoke to new, dismaying realities. In his 1990 inaugural address, Václav Havel had issued a warning that applied just as much to other nations in Eastern Europe as it did to Czechoslovakia: "Our

DOCUMENT 26.1

The End of the Cold War

In 1985, Mikhail Gorbachev rose to power in the Soviet Union and initiated the major reform policies of glasnost (political and cultural openness) and perestroika (economic restructuring). Major changes within the Soviet Union, in other Eastern European countries, and in international affairs streamed from these policies. By 1991, the Soviet Union had lost control over the states of Eastern Europe and was itself disintegrating—the Cold War was over. In the following selection, historian John Lewis Gaddis analyzes the causes of the Cold War's end.

Nevertheless, the upheavals of 1989, like those of 1789, caught everyone by surprise. Historians could of course look back, after the fact, and specify causes: frustration that the temporary divisions of the World War II settlement had become the permanent divisions of the postwar era; fear of the nuclear weapons that had produced that stalemate; resentment over the failure of command economies to raise living standards; a slow shift in power from the supposedly powerful to the seemingly powerless; the unexpected emergence of *independent* standards for making moral judgments. Sensing these trends, the great actor-leaders of the 1980s had found ways to dramatize them to make the point that the Cold War need not last forever. Not even they, however, foresaw how soon and how decisively it would end.

What no one understood, at the beginning of 1989, was that the Soviet Union, its empire, its ideology—and therefore the Cold War itself—was a sandpile ready to slide. All it took to make that happen were a few more grains of sand. The people who dropped them were not in charge of superpowers or movements or religions: they were ordinary people with simple priorities who saw, seized, and sometimes stumbled into opportunities. In doing so, they caused a collapse no one could stop. Their "leaders" had little choice but to follow.

One particular leader, however, did so in a distinctive way. He ensured that the great 1989 revolution was the first one ever in which almost no blood was shed. There were no guillotines, no heads on pikes, no officially sanctioned mass murders. People did die, but in remarkably small numbers for the size and significance of what was happening. In both its ends *and* its means, then, this revolution became a triumph of hope. It did so chiefly because Mikhail Gorbachev chose not to act, but rather to be acted upon.

SOURCE: John Lewis Gaddis, *The Cold War: A New History* (New York: Penguin Press, 2005), pp. 238–239, as excerpted.

Analyze the Document

1. According to Gaddis, what are the most commonly named causes for the upheavals of 1989?

2. What does Gaddis mean that the Soviet Union was a "sandpile ready to slide" in 1989?

3. What role did Gorbachev play in the upheavals of 1989?

---

country is not flourishing. . . . Entire branches of industry are producing goods which are of no interest to anyone, while we are lacking the things we need. A state which calls itself a workers' state humiliates and exploits workers. Our obsolete economy is wasting the little energy we have available. . . . We have polluted our soil, our rivers and forests. . . ." Leaders in Eastern Europe and the former USSR faced a crucial problem: how to institute capitalism and liberal democracy in nations with little experience of either.

The economic transition proceeded quickly in Poland and Hungary, but more moderately in Bulgaria, Romania, and Albania. Almost everywhere, however, it brought **Eastern Europe** pain. When governments closed the doors of inefficient state industries or sold them, many workers lost their jobs. The removal of price controls also provoked instant inflation that especially hurt those living on fixed incomes. Some people took advantage of new opportunities that came with the transition; for example, former communist officials in particular benefited from lucrative insider deals. Several cities—such as Prague in the Czech Republic, with its domes, spires, cobblestone alleys, pubs, cafés, and secondhand bookstores—also fared well with heightened tourism. But too many people had let themselves expect more than the eradication of

FALL OF COMMUNISM

1980–1981	Solidarity union in Poland
1985	Gorbachev comes to power
1986	Chernobyl accident
1989	Soviet troops withdraw from Afghanistan
	Revolutions in Eastern Europe
1991	Disintegration of the Soviet Union
1993	Division of Czechoslovakia

KEY DATES

Population (in millions)

Russia	147.4
Ukraine	51.7
Estonia, Latvia, Lithuania	8.0
Georgia	5.5
Armenia	3.3
Turkmenistan	3.5
Moldova	4.3
Kyrgyzstan	4.3
Tajikistan	5.1
Azerbaijan	7.0
Belarus	10.2
Kazakhstan	16.5
Uzbekistan	19.9

Ethnic Groups

Russian	50.8%
Ukraine	15.4%
Other	8.2%
Kyrgyz	0.9%
Turkmen	1.0%
Lithuanian	1.1%
Moldovan	1.2%
Georgian	1.4%
Tajik	1.5%
Armenian	1.6%
Azerbaijani	2.4%
Tatar	2.4%
Kazakh	2.8%
Belarusian	3.5%
Uzbek	5.8%
Ukrainian	15.4%

RUSSIA	Republics Joining Commonwealth
GEORGIA	Not Joining

MAP 26.2

The Dissolution of the Soviet Union, 1991

This map shows the division of territory resulting from the disintegration of the former Soviet Union.

Explore the Map

1. Which states became the largest and potentially the most powerful in the former USSR?

2. Which areas had the greatest likelihood of being influenced by European states to the west, and which by Islamic states to the south?

3. Notice the ethnic divisions in the former USSR. What political and social problems did this ethnic diversity have the potential to cause after the USSR's breakup?

communism could deliver. In the face of widespread bitterness, governments struggled to gain stability and institute unpopular but apparently necessary economic policies such as closing state industries and allowing prices to rise.

In the former Soviet Union, people were unaccustomed to democratic politics, managers were unfamiliar with the market economy, and many officials resisted reform. The economy stumbled badly. Year after year, Russia's economic output decreased, as did its population. Removing price controls and privatizing industry had eliminated lines in front of stores and created economic opportunities for

The former Soviet Union

some. However, prices skyrocketed beyond the reach of average consumers, the Russian currency lost its value, and some 30 percent of the population struggled to subsist on approximately $1 per day.

The collapse of communism proved particularly stressful for Russian men. From Communist Party officials and generals to physicists and professors, men who had once enjoyed status, security, and relative wealth lost these benefits in the turmoil of the postcommunist era. Life expectancy for Russian men plummeted to fifty-eight years, a decline that was "the steepest and most severe ever documented anywhere in the world" according to one researcher. Alcoholism more than tripled in the years after the collapse.

For women, the story was different. Although many women suffered from unemployment when state industries folded, perhaps their losses were not so great and were eased by new opportunities. In any case, they seemed to manage the transition better than men, maintaining a life expectancy of seventy-three years. Indeed, a growing elite of women entered managerial positions and earned increasing salaries.

Boris Yeltsin retained a precarious hold on power as president of Russia and, despite illnesses, was reelected in 1996. But the Russian people resisted his inconsistent efforts at reform. In the parliament, with its tangled array of different political parties, fragmentation ruled. Moreover, "reformed" communists retained positions of power, as they did in Eastern European states such as Serbia, Bulgaria, and Lithuania. With control disintegrating, lawlessness—from street crime to organized crime—rapidly spread. By 1998, the fumbling Yeltsin had lost his popularity and much of his power as the Russian economy verged on collapse.

| Yeltsin's problems |

When he resigned on the last day of 1999, turning power over to Vladimir Putin, many Russians yearned for the power, order, and stability that communism had brought. While rich oligarchic figures and organized crime still sapped Russia's wealth, Putin, supported by an increasingly loyal bureaucracy and some genuine popularity, provided some functional stability and considerable respect within and outside Russia. He effectively supported Russia's evolving market economy and legal system. Although he moved against the independent media and undermined political opposition, he provided a welcome relief from Yeltsin, whose uneven and unpopular reign witnessed the collapse of basic industries and social services along with the growth of crime and widespread corruption.

In 2008, Putin gave up the presidency to his protégé, Dmitry Medvedev (1965–), and moved to the post of prime minister. By then, political stability and increasing wealth from oil and gas had propelled Russia's economy forward. While no longer a superpower, the country—described by Putin as a "managed democracy"—increasingly acted like a regional power ready to assert itself in disputes with neighbors.

Nationalism Unleashed

Despite its drawbacks, communism had provided many people with a sense of unity and security. Its fall opened a void that nationalistic sentiments rose to fill. As had often been the case in nineteenth- and twentieth-century history, nationalism provoked heated conflict along with a feeling of belonging. Ethnic and cultural struggles raged in several republics of the former Soviet Union. In Azerbaijan, the Azerbaijanis and Armenians clashed. The most violent outburst came in secessionist Chechnya, where Russians fought an unpopular war with Chechnyans demanding their independence. The indecisive two-year conflict cost some 80,000 deaths and 250,000 wounded, although the Chechnyans gained many of their goals. In 1999, another draining war broke out between Chechnyans and Russians.

In Eastern Europe also, nationalistic, ethnic, and religious rivalries opened old wounds and created new divisions. **Maps 26.3** and **26.4** reveal some of these problems. In 1993, the Slovak minority in Czechoslovakia, pushed by ambitious Slovak politicians, voted for independence. Czechoslovakia reluctantly agreed to divide itself into the Czech Republic and Slovakia. In Romania, ethnic friction between the Romanian majority and the Hungarian minority flared up.

The bloodiest conflicts broke out in Yugoslavia, where chaotic civil wars marked the disintegration of that country. **Figure 26.4,** a chart listing the many ethnic groups living in Yugoslavia, reveals the complexity of ethnic divisions in the country. In some regions, one ethnic group made up the vast majority of the population, but in other areas several ethnic groups lived as large minorities. The six republics that constituted Yugoslavia had been held together under communist rule since World War II (see **Map 26.4**). With the death of Tito in 1980 and the fall of communism in the rest of Eastern Europe in 1989, Yugoslavia began to crack. In 1991, Slovenians, angered by the refusal of the dominant Serbian communists to liberalize economic and political policies, detached themselves from Yugoslavia. Peoples in Croatia, Bosnia-Herzegovina, and Macedonia followed suit. War soon erupted between the religiously Orthodox Serbs, attempting to expand the territory they controlled, and their longtime Catholic Croatian rivals to the northwest. Trapped between the two antagonists were the mostly Muslim Bosnians and other peoples who lived as minorities in these areas.

| Civil wars in Yugoslavia |

The war for a Greater Serbia raged with appalling brutality. The worst fighting took place in Bosnia-Herzegovina. On this bloody battlefield, the Serbs initiated a policy of **ethnic cleansing,** driving Muslim Bosnians from their homes; placing them in concentration camps; and raping, murdering, and starving them. In 1992, a Serb guard at one concentration camp proudly explained, "We won't waste our bullets on them. . . . They have no roof. There is sun and rain, cold nights, and beatings two times a day. We give them no food and no water. They will starve like animals." A survivor reported seeing "corpses piled one on top of another. . . . The bodies eventually were gathered with a forklift . . . this happened almost every day." **Figure 26.5** shows some of the hastily created graves in Bosnia-Herzegovina's capital city, Sarajevo. Residents, still suffering from the ongoing struggle, search for the lost and visit the dead. Many

Capital

Former Border of Yugoslavia

Border of Bosnia-Herzegovina

Dayton Agreement Inter-entity Boundary (November 1995)

Bosnian Serb Territory, After Dayton

Croat-Muslim Federation Portion of Bosnia, After Dayton

MAPS 26.3 AND 26.4

Disintegration of Czechoslovakia and Yugoslavia, 1991–2007

These maps respectively show the division of Czechoslovakia into the Czech Republic and Slovakia and the disintegration of Yugoslavia.

Explore the Maps

1. Compare the maps. How do you explain the different paths to the breakup of these two nations?

2. Why did problems in this area of Europe lead to war at the beginning, as well as the end, of the twentieth century?

3. Why might so many people favor integrating these areas of Europe into the European Union?

---

more would be added to graves such as these during the following years.

The Bosnians, supported by aid from the Islamic world, fought back desperately for more than four years. Only a Western embargo and NATO intervention brought an uneasy end to the violence and peace accords in 1996. The conflict had killed 250,000 people, displaced three million, and left 800,000 antipersonnel mines embedded in the land. Moreover, peace still depended on the continued presence of international troops. In 1997, a NATO commander in Bosnia warned that "if we withdraw our forces, there will be slaughter in the streets" and predicted that complete recovery would take decades.

Just two years later, brutality like that unleashed in Bosnia rose in nearby Kosovo—another region within Yugoslavia. Serbians, led by President Slobodan Milosevic, met rising demands for independence from the Albanian majority in Kosovo with

ETHNIC GROUP	PERCENTAGE
Serbians	36
Croatians	20
Bosnians (Muslim)	9
Slovenes	8
Albanians	8
Macedonians	6
Montenegrins	3
Hungarians	2
Others	8

FIGURE 26.4 Ethnic Groups in Yugoslavia, 1991

overwhelming military force. Renewing the practice of ethnic cleansing, Serbian troops slaughtered thousands of Kosovar Albanians and forced hundreds of thousands to flee to neighboring states.

After diplomacy failed, NATO unleashed its military resources for the first time in its fifty-year history. Member air forces, led by the United States, opened a three-month bombing campaign on Serbian forces and on Serbia itself. Milosevic finally agreed to terms and withdrew his forces. Protected by NATO troops, the Kosovar Albanians streamed back to their badly damaged land, bringing with them few hopes for ethnic cooperation in the region. In 2000, Vojislav Kostunica defeated Milosevic in Yugoslavia's presidential election, and soon Milosevic found himself standing trial for war crimes before an international tribunal in The Hague, Netherlands.

REPERCUSSIONS AND REALIGNMENTS IN THE WEST

Repercussions from the collapse of communism spread around the world. As communism lost its credibility, nations still committed to the Soviet model, such as Cuba and North Korea, were left isolated. Capitalism gained renewed respect and even inspired awe in both the Western and non-Western worlds. For many, the collapse of communism in Eastern Europe and the USSR signified the final triumph of capitalism. With the end of the Cold War, the contours of domestic and international politics began to shift.

The United States Unchallenged and Germany Rising

With the former Soviet forces in decline and the Warsaw Pact dissolved, the United States and Germany rose in stature. The United States emerged as the world's only military superpower. It flexed its military muscle in 1991 by leading a United Nations–authorized coalition that repelled Iraq's invasion of tiny, neighboring Kuwait. In the short war, the U.S.-dominated coalition easily defeated Saddam Hussein's forces. In 2001 and 2003, it again demonstrated its military might, in Afghanistan and Iraq (see pages 828–831). The U.S. also contributed to international peacekeeping efforts by sending forces to troubled areas such as Somalia, Haiti, Bosnia, and Kosovo. Despite years of large budget deficits and apparent decline, the U.S. economy rebounded in the mid-1990s to a position of leadership that inspired envy the world over.

Germany's influence and potential also rose. In 1990, German unification confirmed Germany as a European and world economic leader—in exports, in balance of trade, and in gross domestic product. Emerging victorious from the first national elections, the former West German chancellor Helmut Kohl and his conservative Christian Democrats vowed to bring eastern Germany's economy up to the high standard enjoyed in the West. The costs of the transition

FIGURE 26.5 Civil War in Bosnia-Herzegovina The dead and the suffering from the civil war in Bosnia-Herzegovina mingle in a cemetery in January 1993.

mushroomed far beyond expectations; as state industries collapsed in the East, unemployment and the cost of welfare benefits shot up. Nevertheless, the reunified state still ranked as the top economic power in Europe. Clearly, Germany stood poised to exert new influence in Eastern Europe and the European Community.

Politics Shift to the Right

In the United States, Germany, and elsewhere in the West, politics shifted to the Right. The reasons behind this change were complex, but economic forces played a major role. Despite the continued overall prosperity enjoyed in the West, many nations suffered from high unemployment and declining growth rates during the 1980s and 1990s. In part, the free flow of trade and capital had created a new international labor market that operated outside the control of national governments and labor unions, resulting in the loss of many business opportunities and manufacturing jobs in the West. As global economic competition stiffened and nations struggled to stay in the game, many people blamed costly social programs—often supported by the political Left—for their nation's economic problems. The changes wrought by the postindustrial society, especially the shift from manufacturing to services, also weakened labor unions—the Left's traditional source of support. The previous sense that government was obligated to provide for rich and poor alike—a belief that had fueled the post–World War II welfare state—faded along with memories of those older times. Government regulation of economic affairs and the cost of social programs came under question everywhere.

Conservatives began scoring record successes at the polls. Citing the apparent triumph of capitalism, they attacked expensive programs and sometimes fanned the flames of anti-immigrant sentiments, playing on the popular perception that foreign-born newcomers took jobs. France's right-wing National Front, led by Jean-Marie LePen, attained particular prominence by blaming immigrants from North Africa and elsewhere for France's economic problems. The traditional communist parties in Western Europe declined, and socialist parties, whether in power or not, moderated their policies to shore up their popularity. In Austria, Italy, Germany, and Spain, conservative and right-wing politicians gained popularity. Even when traditional parties of the Left regained power, as they did in many countries during the late 1990s, their platforms were more muted and conservative than in the past. No other nation ventured as far down the conservative path as Great Britain and the United States. In Great Britain, the Conservatives led by Margaret Thatcher and her successor dominated throughout most of the 1980s and 1990s, cutting taxes, attacking social programs, and selling state-owned industries to private investors. When the Labor Party finally came to power in Great Britain in 1997, it pursued only mild changes. In the United States, Republicans rolled back liberal programs and Democrats scrambled to adopt more conservative platforms. The sharply conservative administration of George W. Bush came to power in 2001. Mostly in the name of economic development and the war against terrorism, it aggressively pursued many policies initiated by the Reagan administration in the 1980s, including loosening environmental protections, reducing social programs, lowering taxes in ways that favored the wealthy and corporations, increasing military spending, and cutting into the protection of civil liberties.

Questioning traditional politics

By the mid-1990s, this conservatism had merged with a broader questioning of traditional politics in the West. As anxieties over economic problems intensified and as scandals rocked governments, people voted for unknowns or stopped voting altogether. Especially in France, Italy, and Austria, candidates who voiced disenchantment with the standard politics of the Left and Right attracted popular support.

In 2008, elections swept Barack Obama into office as president of the United States. Backed by national and international popularity, as well as a more liberal administration, Obama promised to reverse some of his predecessor's conservative policies. Whether this new focus represents a broader political change in the West remains to be seen. All these shifts in domestic politics gained much attention. However, events beyond state borders would soon overshadow these internal concerns throughout the West.

Toward European Integration

The end of the Cold War may have left the United States the world's sole superpower, but it also strengthened the movement toward unity that had been unfolding in Europe since the 1950s. According to Michael Naumann, in 2002 the editor of a leading German magazine, the "huge influence of the world's single superpower, the United States, will push Europeans together." Moreover, many Europeans agreed with Michel Albert, a leading French official and industrialist, who in 1991 argued, "If the aim is to harness capitalism without impairing its efficiency, it is no longer to the nation-state that we must look, but to Europe."

In 1992, the 12 members of the European Community (EC) eliminated all major internal barriers to trade, the flow of capital, and the movement of people. That same year, the EC joined with the seven-member European Free Trade Association to form the European Economic Area, creating the world's largest trading bloc and paving the way for several new countries to seek full membership (see **Map 26.5**). Between 1999 and 2004, a number of Eastern European nations, such as Poland, the Czech Republic, Hungary, Lithuania, and Slovakia joined NATO and were accepted for membership in the European Union. Also in 1992, France and Germany formed a joint army corps, the European Corps, open to other participants in the European Union. With the Maastricht Treaty of 1992 (which changed the name of the EC to the European Union), most members of the **European Union (EU)** agreed to establish a common currency (the **Euro**) controlled by a central European bank by 1999. The plan required great economic discipline, above all controlling the large yearly budget deficits most nations ran. By 2002, people in most countries of the European Union carried Euros in their pockets, wallets, and purses.

The potential of the European Union seemed tremendous. In 2010, the twenty-seven member nations had more than 491 million inhabitants and a combined gross national product greater than that of the United States. Perhaps in response to the growing power of the European Union, the United States joined with Mexico and Canada in 1994 to create a new free-trade zone—the **North American Free Trade Agreement (NAFTA).** Not everyone embraced the idea of such alliances. Many Europeans opposed further integration, clinging to national preferences and warning against the dangers of giving up sovereignty to an international body of bureaucrats. To be sure, the European nations had great difficulty joining forces to put down the crisis in Bosnia, but their joint action as part of a NATO force to quell the violence in Kosovo in 1999 led to a vow by the leaders of fifteen European countries to make the European Union a military power for the first time. The Union adopted plans to build its own military of up to 60,000 troops. Moreover, by that same year, the European Union had opened its arms to possible membership for Turkey as

The European Union, 2010

This map shows the European Union in 2010 and identifies nations that have applied for membership.

Explore the Map

1. Notice how inclusive membership is. Which nations form the core of a potentially united Europe?

2. How economically and politically powerful might a united Europe be?

3. Why is it significant that several Eastern European nations have joined or applied for membership in this association?

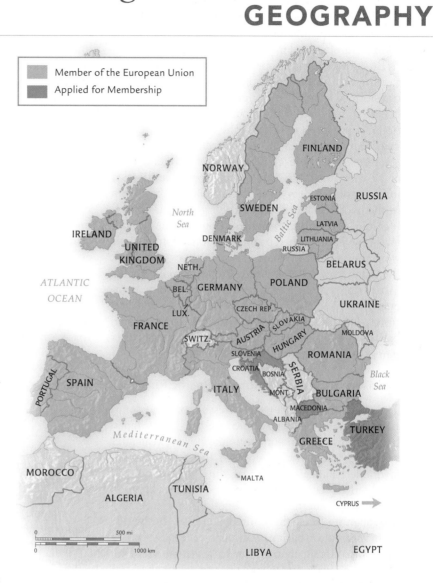

well as virtually all of central and eastern Europe. Despite many reservations, most Europeans seemed willing to cooperate. The statement by a German woman early in 2002 reflected the sense of many: "I feel German, but also European."

In 2005, French and Dutch voters rejected a newly drafted constitution designed to strengthen the European Union. This outcome signaled the voters' broad ambivalence about taking further steps toward European integration and, in particular, their concerns about welcoming the populous, Muslim, and relatively poor Turkey into the Union—as well as their worries about a potential influx of immigrants and migrant workers. However, in 2009, member states finally ratified the Lisbon Treaty designed to streamline European Union institutions.

THE WORLD AND THE WEST FROM A GLOBAL PERSPECTIVE

As they took further steps toward unity, Europeans had more in mind than competing with the United States. They also knew that they had to meet the changes sweeping through much of the Western and non-Western worlds. Since the end of colonialism, European nations could no longer rely on colonies as controllable markets. By the 1990s, all nations faced a global economy marked by the presence of multinational enterprises beyond the command of individual states. Waves of huge corporate buyouts and mergers increased this concentration of economic power. By 2000, small handfuls of these corporations controlled more than half the global market in oil, automobiles, electronics, multimedia, and personal computers. Westerners also confronted new competitors, from Latin America to East Asia, who wielded growing economic and political clout. In addition, various international agencies and organizations, such as the International Monetary Fund, the World Bank, and the World Trade Organization, wielded great economic clout over financial aid and international commerce that affected governments, corporations, and ordinary people throughout the world. Finally, the pace of global economic integration and change had quickened, complicating international business for

Globalization

everyone. Certain technological advances, above all the development of the computer, the Internet, and genetic engineering, had the potential of creating the equivalent of a third industrial revolution.

By 2000, the mushrooming use of computers and the Internet in business and commerce had already transformed many economies. Increasingly, goods could be designed in one country, financed internationally, produced overseas, sold worldwide, and serviced through phones and the Internet from numerous locations. All these changes tended to blend local and national markets into global markets and called into question the very issue of national identity. Even in the poorest nations, signs of this **globalization** proliferated. As just one example, workers in new manufacturing plants owned by multinational corporations wore the same brand-name athletic shoes and drank the same beverages as their Western counterparts. Moreover, thanks to films, television, radio, computers, cellular phones, fax machines, satellites, and travel, ideas and images flowed across international borders as easily as money, goods, and services, further blurring the distinctions between cultures.

East Asia and the Rise of the Pacific Rim

The greatest challenge to the West's economic dominance came from East Asia. Since the 1960s, Japan had grown into a major economic power. Year after year, this island nation enjoyed the world's largest favorable balance of trade. By the 1980s, it boasted the world's second-largest gross domestic product. A giant in automobile production and electronics, Japan replaced the United States as the world's topmost creditor nation. Although reversals brought Japan's economic momentum to a virtual standstill during the 1990s, and even a decline during the 2001 and 2002 world economic slowdown, the nation still led the world in per capita gross domestic product.

FIGURE 26.6 Factory Workers in China Row after row of women workers sew clothing for worldwide export.

In the 1990s, other regions on the periphery of the Pacific Ocean attracted wealthy investors with their political stability, cheap and disciplined labor force, and openness to capitalism. Multinational corporations opened offices and made investments throughout this so-called Pacific Rim. Hong Kong, Taiwan, South Korea, Malaysia, Indonesia, and Singapore all boomed, drawing manufacturing jobs away from Europe and the United States in industries such as electronics, textiles, plastics, metals, computers, automobiles, and leather goods. Visitors found thriving cities such as Kuala Lumpur in Malaysia—with the world's two tallest buildings marking its skyline and its high-rise apartment houses serviced by climate-controlled malls—"unrecognizable to anyone who knew it 30 years ago." On the outskirts of such glittering urban centers, satellite communities and industrial parks rose where jungles used to thrive. Similar developments transformed other great cities of East Asia, from Singapore and Bangkok to Jakarta and Hong Kong.

Yet no country experienced a more stunning economic transformation than China. In 1978, the successors to Mao, led by Deng Xiaoping (1904–1997), had initiated the Four Modernizations program to foster rapid economic development and greater productivity. The program departed dramatically from Mao's economic policies by decentralizing decision making and introducing a market-oriented economy into the countryside and, later, into some urban areas. By the mid-1980s, these policies had opened China to tourism and foreign investment, stimulated new economic growth, and created greater economic freedom within China. Agreements with Japan and the United States rapidly expanded trade as well. For the first time, Chinese farmers produced a surplus of food for export. In certain areas of the country, particularly the New Economic Zones in the southeast, capitalistic investments and manufacturing practices spurred high rates of growth. By the first decade of the twenty-first century, China had become the world's most important manufacturing nation and a major player in international finance. **Figure 26.6** shows one of the many new factories that fueled China's growing economic prowess. Here, women workers wearing coats in an unheated factory sew clothes that sport Western brand names and that are destined for export throughout the world.

Nevertheless, China made these economic reforms without corresponding political reforms. Whether that practice could continue was called into question in 1989, when students and intellectuals demanding political reform organized massive demonstrations in Beijing. After a brief standoff, the government, supported by China's rural population and most of the army, violently crushed the demonstrations and jailed the leaders. In the years that followed, as China's

> The economic transformation of China

leadership aged and pressures for political reform persisted, analysts watched carefully for change within the great Asian country. By the first decade of the twenty-first century, China stood as a rapidly growing economic power with tremendous political potential on the international stage.

The Challenge of Islam

Other areas of the world presented different challenges to the West. In particular, several Islamic nations in North Africa and the Middle East developed a new assertiveness and a willingness to make their dissatisfaction with Western ways known. They had long resented the former Western imperial powers' condescension toward them. The West's support of Israel only irritated an already raw nerve.

The emergence of combative leaders in states such as Libya, Syria, Iran, and Iraq—some of whom advocated Islamic or Pan-Arab unity against Israel and Western influence—stepped up tensions further. Moreover, in nations from Algeria and Turkey to Afghanistan and Pakistan, Islamic fundamentalists had gained strength. Western secular notions such as individualism, capitalism, materialism, commercialism, gender equality, and sexual freedom were flooding across airwaves and borders into the Islamic world. These notions seemed to insult and threaten fundamentalists' traditional and religious beliefs. Condemning Westernization and the secularization of life in their countries, they demanded a return to traditional symbols of their conservative views, such as the veil that they required women to wear in public. Iran's fundamentalist leader Ayatollah Ruholla Khomeini (1900–1989), who had come to power as the leader of a revolution in 1979, epitomized rejection of the West. "With the Qur'an in one hand and a gun in the other, defend your dignity and honor" against the "oppressive powers" of the West, he told his nation in 1980. He especially castigated the United States, labeling it the "great Satan" because it had supported Israel and had intervened several times in the region. Finally, many Middle Eastern Islamic states possessed the crude-oil reserves on which the West and Asia depended, and they used the precious resource to command international respect and attention. The potential of Middle Eastern states to pull Western nations into armed conflict was made all too clear in 1990 when Iraq invaded oil-rich Kuwait, prompting a UN-backed military response, in 2003 with the U.S.-led invasion of Iraq, and with the persisting violence in Afghanistan that threatened to spread into neighboring Pakistan.

International Terrorism and War

On the morning of September 11, 2001, coordinated teams of terrorists hijacked four U.S. American airliners. They slammed two of the planes into Manhattan's famed World Trade Center (Twin Towers) office buildings and a third into the Pentagon, headquarters of the U.S. Department of Defense in Washington D.C. Passengers apparently brought down the fourth plane before it could reach its target. Nearly 3,000 people lost their lives in the attacks, most of them perishing when the Twin Towers collapsed later that morning. Blame soon fell on the shoulders of a well-financed international terrorist group, **al-Qaeda,** which professed a radical version of Islamic fundamentalism, under the leadership of Osama bin Laden.

The forces behind this tragedy and the responses to it were complex, and historians can make only tentative analyses at this point. However, analysts point to the intensifying anger toward the West among radical Islamic fundamentalists as one major underlying force for the attack. Islamic fundamentalists had long lamented what they saw as the West's corruption of regimes within the Islamic world. Authoritarian governments that fundamentalists viewed as too secular and too connected to the West ruled most Islamic states. Fundamentalism found growing support among people who were outraged by this supposed perversion of Islamic law and who were enraged at the reality of masses of people living far below the wealthy elites in these countries.

Most Muslim leaders and clerics rejected violence and terrorism. But against the overwhelming military, political, and economic forces that Western nations and nonfundamentalist Islamic states could marshal, terrorism seemed a legitimate and even religiously justified way to assert some fundamentalists' point of view. For a group such as al-Qaeda, terrorism might catalyze widespread fundamentalist revolts that would bring down "corrupt" governments in the Islamic world.

A second force came in the form of the festering Israeli-Palestinian conflict. This struggle deepened Islamic fundamentalists' rage toward the West—in particular the United States. In various ways, Israel and the Arab world had been at odds since the mid-twentieth century (see Chapter 25). Moreover, Israel had long been perceived as a Western outpost in the Middle East. The close relationship between Israel and the United States encouraged that perception, and many held the United States partly responsible for the sufferings of Palestinians. For example, al-Qaeda's Osama bin Laden railed against "the crusader-Jewish alliance, led by the United States and Israel."

Israeli-Palestinian conflict

Fueled by these forces and religious enthusiasm, terrorist organizations grew in the 1980s and 1990s and adopted bolder tactics aimed at both military and civilian targets. Some of these groups gained strength and reach through financial support by wealthy

thinking about GEOGRAPHY

MAP 26.6

Israel and the Occupied Territories, 2010

This map shows Israel, the occupied territories of the West Bank, and the Gaza Strip. It also identifies areas of varying Palestinian and Israeli control, as well as Jewish-Israeli settlements.

Explore the Map

1. Identify the location of settlements and the divided areas of Palestinian and Israeli control.

2. What difficulties do Palestinians and Israelis face in trying to establish a permanent peace?

3. How might any settlement affect surrounding states with large numbers of Palestinian refugees?

patrons. The growing availability of modern communications and military technology also enhanced their power.

During the first years of the new century, tensions grew. After efforts to forge a U.S.-sponsored settlement of the Israeli-Palestinian dispute collapsed in 2000, a new, more deadly round of violence erupted between Israelis and Palestinians (see **Map 26.6**). Day after day, pictures, reports, and stories of the conflict focusing on Palestinian deaths at the hands of the Israelis spread across the Islamic world. In Israel, suicidal terrorists bombed shopping centers, restaurants, and buses. Within Palestinian areas, the death tolls from missiles, planes, and guns fired by the well-armed and trained Israeli forces rose dramatically. By 2004, much of the violence had subsided, and in 2005 Israel unilaterally withdrew from the Gaza Strip. However, in 2006 an election gave the militant Islamic organization Hamas—considered a terrorist group by many in the West—governing power in Palestine, raising tensions again. That same year, a war broke out in Lebanon between Israel and Hezbollah, a radical Islamic organization apparently backed by Iran and Syria. In 2008, Israel, citing a growing number of rocket attacks on its territory, invaded the Gaza Strip, now controlled by Hamas.

The devastating attacks of September 11, 2001, against the United States were intended to strike at symbols of U.S. "imperial" power. The United States answered the attacks by declaring war against terrorism. President George W. Bush vowed to pursue terrorists wherever they lurked in the world and punish those who harbored them. Drawing on the sympathy and support of many nations, the U.S. military launched a massive aerial assault on al-Qaeda strongholds in Afghanistan, as well as on the Taliban, the radical fundamentalist regime that ruled the mountainous nation (see **Map 26.7**).

Afghanistan had a history of strife. During the 1980s, the Afghani people had endured a long, bloody war against Soviet invaders (see pages 783–784). The impoverished, war-torn country again suffered from the turmoil following the Soviet withdrawal in the late 1980s. In the mid-1990s, the Taliban seized power in most of Afghanistan, and there al-Qaeda found a home.

War in Afghanistan

In 2001 and 2002, the U.S. military, using anti-Taliban Afghan forces for much of the campaign on the ground, crushed most of the al-Qaeda and Taliban forces harbored within Afghanistan. However, President George W. Bush declared the war on terrorism far from over, pointing to the possibility that other terrorists and regimes might acquire and wield weapons of mass destruction. He warned that other states might also feel the force of U.S. military power in the future.

MAP 26.7

The Middle East and Iraq, 2003

This map shows the Middle East, estimated oil reserves in several nations, and ethno-religious groups in Iraq at the beginning of the U.S.-led invasion in 2003.

Explore the Map

1. Why is the Middle East of such strategic importance?

2. In what ways might the war in Iraq change this region?

3. What problems loom for Iraqis who are trying to establish a stable, unified nation?

In March 2003, the United States took another step in the name of its war on terror. The U.S. military, backed by British forces and the token support of other nations, attacked Iraq. During the months leading up to the war, the Bush administration, building on fears stemming from the September 11, 2001, terrorist attacks, cited the development and existence of terrifying weapons of mass destruction (chemical, biological, and nuclear) in Iraq that threatened the United States and the whole international community. Administration officials also claimed that Iraqi leader Saddam Hussein's dictatorial regime had links with international terrorist organizations such as al-Qaeda. The United States, officials said, had a duty to rid the world of Iraq's violent, brutal regime. Under these justifications for invading Iraq lay a vision

War in Iraq

within the Bush administration of aggressively and, if necessary, single-handedly reforming oil-rich Iraq. Other authoritarian regimes in the strategic Middle East, administration officials hoped, would then transform themselves into democracies or at least reform. These new regimes would become friends of the United States and its allies as well as stable sources of oil (see **Map 26.7**).

Within weeks, U.S. and British air and ground forces overwhelmed Iraqi defenders and toppled Saddam Hussein and the Baathist Party, which had ruled Iraq with an iron fist for more than twenty years. Although President Bush declared victory in June 2003, achieving peace, stability, or international acclaim in the months that followed proved daunting. The United States, backed by Great Britain, refused to cede authority over the stabilization and rebuilding of Iraq to the United Nations. Many potential allies who had opposed the war in the first place—including France, Germany, Russia, India, Turkey, and most Arab states—refused to lend a hand under those conditions. The cost and responsibility for the process fell squarely on the shoulders of the United States and Great Britain, though other allies provided some support. Within Iraq, guerrilla and suicide attacks steadily raised the death toll into the thousands each month. Looting and sabotage further undermined efforts to establish security and promote recovery. Some of these problems are suggested by **Figure 26.7.** The photograph shows a United States Marine sitting in a schoolroom below a damaged mural of the country he and his fellow soldiers are occupying and trying to pacify. He is part of a military operation in western Iraq, which in 2005 was still a stronghold of insurgent activities. In the following two years, violent insurgent attacks increased. By 2007, Iraq seemed on the verge of civil war.

Moreover, U.S. ambitions to usher in a new, democratic government met with mounting discord among factions within Iraq. Historic rivalries between majority Arabs and minority Kurds in the north, and between the majority Shi'ites and minority Sunnis in the center and south, stymied efforts to create a new,

FIGURE 26.7 The Occupation of Iraq A United States Marine rests below a map of Iraq in an Iraqi schoolroom.

effective government (see **Map 26.7**). Finally, despite the eventual capture of Saddam Hussein in December 2003 and extensive searches, U.S. investigators could find no weapons of mass destruction or links to the sort of international terrorist organizations that carried out the September 11, 2001, plot.

Only time will enable us to make firm judgments about the U.S. actions in Iraq and the policies underlying them. However, these actions and policies may prove to have greater historical significance than the toppling of Saddam Hussein's regime. First, the Bush administration set what many critics worldwide considered dangerous precedent by initiating a **preemptive war,** based on the *assertion* that Iraq had imminent plans to attack the United States, or, even worse, a "preventive war," based on the *possibility* that Iraq might attack sometime in the distant future. In these relatively nonthreatening circumstances, such a war violated long-established rules of international relations and dashed ambitions of those hoping to strengthen international barriers to the outbreak of wars.

> Preemptive war, unilateralism, and the occupation

Second, the Bush administration not only failed to win important UN and international support for the war but also appeared to punish those who disagreed with its foreign policies—including longtime major allies such as France and Germany. Indeed, the United States seemed to discard the principles of internationalism that had informed global diplomacy since the end of World War II. In place of those principles, it appeared to favor a kind of **unilateralism** in which the world's only superpower pursued its own interests regardless of its allies' views and interests. The administration's abandonment of the Kyoto Protocol, which sought to limit global-warming emissions; its plans to develop an antiballistic missile shield and a new class of nuclear weapons; its desertion of international efforts to strengthen rules against biological weapons, land mines, and small arms; and its attacks on the International Criminal Court all added to the impression that the United States had decided to go it alone.

Third, the way the U.S. government justified its invasion of Iraq and what many in the world saw as the destructive mishandling of the occupation that followed diminished the sympathy and support for the United States that had been offered after the September 11 attacks. Moreover, the bloodshed and political turmoil that reigned in Iraq year after year during the presence of U.S.-led coalition forces served to increase the regional influence of Iran, still ruled by a fundamentalist regime that now embarked on a policy to develop its own atomic resources. These developments, along with veiled threats by the U.S. government to launch strikes against Iran, cast a darkening shadow over the Middle East.

In 2008 and 2009, some of the violence within Iraq abated. The new president of the United States,

DOCUMENT 26.2

War in Afghanistan

After the attacks of September 11, 2001, the United States, supported by several other countries to various degrees, became deeply enmeshed in Middle Eastern affairs. By 2009, the United States had been fighting in Afghanistan for eight years, and that battle threatened to spill over into Pakistan. Some observers called for greater military commitments, while others argued for withdrawal. In 2009 Barack Obama, the recently elected president of the United States, announced his decision to send a limited number of additional U.S. troops into Afghanistan. The following are selections from Obama's December 2009 speech.

I have determined that it is in our vital national interest to send an additional 30,000 U.S. troops to Afghanistan. After eighteen months, our troops will begin to come home. These are the resources that we need to seize the initiative, while building the Afghan capacity that can allow for a responsible transition of our forces out of Afghanistan.

I do not make this decision lightly. I opposed the war in Iraq precisely because I believe that we must exercise restraint in the use of military force, and always consider the long-term consequences of our actions. We have been at war for eight years, at enormous cost in lives and resources. Years of debate over Iraq and terrorism have left our unity on national security issues in tatters, and created a highly polarized and partisan backdrop for this effort. And having just experienced the worst economic crisis since the Great Depression, the American people are understandably focused on rebuilding our economy and putting people to work here at home. . . .

This is not just America's war. Since 9/11, al Qaeda's safe-havens have been the source of attacks against London and Amman and Bali. The people and governments of both Afghanistan and Pakistan are endangered. And the stakes are even higher within a nuclear-armed Pakistan, because we know that al Qaeda and other extremists seek nuclear weapons, and we have every reason to believe that they would use them.

These facts compel us to act along with our friends and allies. . . .

SOURCE: Government document in public domain.

Analyze the Document

1. How does President Obama justify a new military effort in Afghanistan?

2. Why does he want to begin to bring troops home after eighteen months?

3. What do you think led Obama to emphasize connections between national security and the economy?

Barack Obama, riding a wave of national and international popularity, signaled changes in U.S. policy in Iraq and committed to the withdrawal of U.S. forces by 2011. But already, with U.S. troops and money diverted to Iraq since 2003, violence and instability were worsening in neighboring Afghanistan, where Taliban and al-Qaeda forces had gained new life and threatened the weak central government that relied heavily on financial and military aid from the West (see Document 26.2).

Terrorism and the war in Afghanistan also had implications for neighboring Pakistan. This predominantly Muslim nation had long-simmering problems with India, a primarily Hindu country, over Kashmir. These two nations'

Crisis over Kashmir

struggle for control over Kashmir (see **Map 26.8**) had sparked armed conflict several times over previous decades. The growing threat of terrorism made the area even more volatile. In 2002, the two sides again seemed on the verge of war. This time, however, both Pakistan and India had demonstrated to each other and the world their ability to use nuclear weapons. In 2008 a terrorist organization, apparently based in Pakistan, launched a deadly suicidal attack on one of India's major cities, Mumbai, an event that again threatened peace in the region. By the next year, the ability of Pakistan's central government to exercise control over the nation was in question, especially in its northern and western lands, where openly aggressive Taliban and pro-Taliban forces had found sanctuary and were gaining strength.

In various ways that drew the attention and involvement of the West, much of the Middle East, from the eastern shores of the Mediterranean to India, suffered from instability, threats of conflict, and outbreaks of violence. The turbulence was not simply about terrorism. Rather, the roots of these problems reach far back into the twentieth century and are entwined with the legacy of the West's imperialism, periodic wars within the region, the world's growing reliance on the area's oil deposits, and complex sectarian politics within Islamic states. But to many people around the world, it seemed clear that terrorism—and the conflicts, poverty, and political tensions that fueled it as well as reactions to it—had greater global significance than ever before. The images of peace and security that many people had envisioned after the fall of communism gave way to a new sense of vulnerability in a world that seemed to be slipping out of control.

MAP 26.8

Afghanistan, Kashmir, and South-Central Asia, 2002

This map shows Afghanistan, Kashmir, and the surrounding areas in 2002.

Explore the Map

1. What difficulties might there be in controlling conflicts in these areas?

2. What is strategically significant about this region?

3. Why might the conflict over Kashmir be of such importance to India, Pakistan, and the world community?

Across Borders: Cultural Conflict and Convergence

All these developments—in the Middle East, North Africa, and East Asia—revealed the West's inextricable ties with the non-Western world. They also posed new challenges to the dominance that the West had enjoyed for so long. Perhaps most important, they

illustrated a problem that spread well beyond any one region: the chafing of local cultures against global and even national influences. On one level, globalization meant the invasion of Western culture into centuries-old but vulnerable non-Western cultural legacies. **Figure 26.8** reveals this tenuous mixture and clash of cultures in Mexico. A descendant of the Olmecs, who once dominated parts of Mexico some three thousand years ago, prepares to dance as a jaguar to bring rain. The boy's clay-covered body is being stamped with ashes by an adult using a Coca-Cola bottle—one of the most recognized symbols of Western commerce. This image was soon transmitted by a Western photographer to a magazine with circulation in the millions, perhaps encouraging Western tourists and companies to invade this traditional culture even further. On another level, nationalism and religious fundamentalism revealed a deep resistance to globalization. The struggles of minorities to retain their own sense of identity in the face of demands for national and religious conformity within their own nations reflected a parallel resistance to

> Resistance to globalization

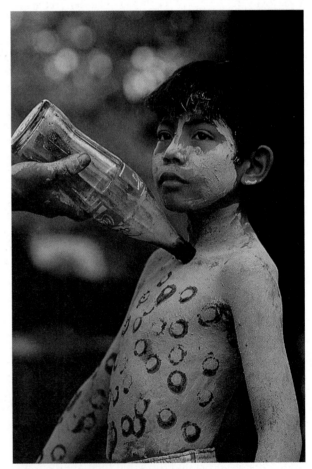

FIGURE 26.8 The Clash of Cultures   In this striking photograph, a Coca-Cola bottle is used to prepare a boy, representing the ancient Olmec civilization, to dance as a jaguar to bring rain.

outside meddling. In one terrifying variation of this pattern, in the central African state of Rwanda, ethnic Hutu extremists slaughtered more than 500,000 ethnic Tutsi during the mid-1990s; fighting and civil war plagued the area for years. Another variation of this violence occurred in the western Sudan region of Darfur, where political disputes between Arabs and non-Arab rebels arose. Between 2004 and 2006, government-backed Arab militias carried out a systematic campaign that killed 300,000 non-Arab farmers and displaced two million people. In the West and elsewhere, these multilayered resentments and struggles formed a complex backdrop for other emerging developments.

While ethnic conflict and nationalism intensified in several parts of the globe, cultural differences among Western nations and between Western and non-Western peoples also softened with an increase in international contacts. People migrated in droves to the West and other wealthy areas of the world, such as the oil-rich Middle East, and crossed countless borders in the search for work. The new immigration opened doors for many people, but it also had its dark side. The opening of frontiers within Europe during the 1990s and the desperation of millions throughout the world made the movement of people difficult to control. Illegal immigration skyrocketed to more than 10 million people a year globally. For example, immigrants from Iran, Turkey, Iraq, Pakistan, Bangladesh, Albania, and elsewhere risked dangerous boat passages and expulsion to reach places such as Italy's long, exposed southern coast. "We lived like animals. . . . If we had not brought some biscuits and water, we would have starved," said a Kurdish immigrant in 1997. Some of the thousands who crossed North American borders each year—legally and illegally—told similar stories.

Germany in particular drew people from Turkey, Yugoslavia, Italy, Eastern Europe, and Russia and attracted asylum-seekers from many other parts of the world. In 1997, almost 9 percent of Germany's population were immigrants, many of whom remained unassimilated and yet alienated from their lands of origin. One Turkish woman who worked in her father's pizzeria in Berlin described the situation: "People like me are foreigners in Turkey. . . . There you are not a real Turk, and here you are not a complete German. We are somewhere in between." Her father agreed: "Even if I had a German passport, I would still feel like a foreigner and be regarded as a foreigner."

By 2010, some 20 million Muslims lived in Western Europe, many of whom were frustrated by bleak job prospects, outraged by discrimination, and yearning for a sense of respect. A French youth of Algerian descent living in one of the rough housing projects just outside of Paris explained: "You wake up every morning looking for work. But why? There isn't any." Like millions of other Arab and African immigrants and their French-born children and grandchildren, he had not been well integrated into French society. In 2005 and 2006, groups of young immigrants displayed their frustration in riots.

During these same decades, a common popular culture, especially among the youth in American, European, and non-Western cities, spread with increasing speed across all borders. The worldwide popularity of Hollywood movies, Disney products, soccer, Nintendo computer games, hamburgers, pizza, shopping malls, noodle soup, Nike shoes, Benetton clothes, TV series, and rock and roll all reflected this standardization of cultural tastes. The spread of English as the world's second language and the beaming of television shows across borders by satellite facilitated the convergence of cultures. No medium offered more potential for this crossing of cultural lines in the future than the Internet. Instantaneous electronic communication and access to burgeoning informational, commercial, and scientific resources on the World Wide Web seemed to have dissolved time and space as well as national borders, spawning what some observers called the "global village."

Immigration

Popular culture

THE WEST AND THE WORLD

KEY DATES

FIGURE 26.9 Marco Ventura, *Mona Lisa Contemplating the Bust of Nefertiti as God Creates Order out of Chaos on a Starry Night on the Island of La Grande Jatte as the Infanta Margarita Looks On,* 1993 The artist used familiar masterpieces of Western art to suggest the blending of Western history and culture.

The easing of more traditional forms of travel also added to the meeting of cultures, particularly for middle-class tourists who journeyed throughout the world, visited museums, and absorbed at least visual images of different nations' cultural past and present. **Figure 26.9,** an illustration for the *Sophisticated Traveler* supplement to the *New York Times,* captures this sense of historical and cultural convergence. In this composite of six masterpieces of Western art, the artist makes a playful statement about the blending of Western cultures. Most of this image's components, which span three thousand years of Western history, are probably familiar to the millions of museum-going, "sophisticated" middle-class travelers for whom this magazine is intended.

Other cultural changes also set off the 1990s as unique. In the arts, what was once seen as modern in 1914 or even as late as mid-century—the glass skyscrapers and the abstract paintings of Mondrian and Pollock, for example—now seemed old and were taken for granted. Artistic and intellectual movements adopted the "postmodern" label. In the arts, followers of **postmodernism** became less concerned with austere principles. Architects, for example, rejected the pure forms and plain glass walls of the modern style in favor of buildings with elaborate shapes and ornamentation. Intellectuals and critics sympathetic to postmodernism attacked all ideologies—from liberalism to Marxism—and even the intellectual foundations of most academic disciplines as outmoded, oppressive distortions of the truth. Skeptical that

Postmodernism

objective truth was possible, they claimed that science itself was infected by the dominant values and beliefs of the culture that produced it.

Beyond Borders: Uncertainty and Opportunity in a Shrinking World

The spreading webs of communications and the goods and services radiating out from the West promised satisfactions galore for anyone who wanted to—and could afford to—participate. However, recessions during the 1980s and after 2000 reminded Westerners and non-Westerners alike that economic growth could not be taken for granted. Despite the West's overall prosperity, inflation and declining personal incomes for the bottom half of society spawned social discontent in these decades. In most of Europe, unemployment continued to hover above 10 percent and reached as high as 20 percent during the 1990s. Unions everywhere lost membership and clout, leaving more workers than ever without protection in a shifting, competitive marketplace.

In addition, with international economic ties proliferating, problems in one area of the world quickly made themselves felt in other regions. For example, the financial crisis and economic turmoil that struck Asia in 1998 spread rapidly, creating huge losses for investors and trading partners throughout the world. In 2008, another financial crisis, this time much more serious and combined with a collapse of real estate values, struck the United States. Repercussions quickly spread to Europe and around the globe, leading to what some economists have called the worst financial crisis, economic crisis, and recession since the Great Depression of the 1930s. Tens of millions of people lost their jobs, stock markets plunged, and bankruptcies felled large corporations and financial institutions. Trying to stem the losses, governments from the United States to Europe and China intervened massively in their economies.

Oil presented another long-term problem that spilled across borders in recent decades. Economic development in the West and elsewhere heightened demand for energy derived from oil and natural gas. Most Western nations consume far more oil than they produce, and nations with rising economies such as China and India want the oil-fueled wealth enjoyed in the West. In a competitive international arena, they vie for supplies from major producers such as Saudi Arabia, Iran, Iraq, Russia, Venezuela, and Nigeria. Webs of politics, arms, money, and influence surround this growing international need for oil. More insidiously, the divisions between rich and poor presented pressing across-borders dilemmas. The relatively affluent West, with its multinational corporations, could no longer ignore

Growing international economic ties

MAP 26.9

The Growth of Cities

This map shows those areas with the largest urban populations and the growth of population in the world's largest cities.

Explore the Map

1. Where has the greatest growth of large cities occurred?

2. What cities are expected to grow the most?

3. What problems might this growth in urban populations pose for the West and the world?

---

nations scourged by crushing debts, pressing economic needs, and unmet demands. The evolving global economic landscape added to the uncertainty. Despite the rise of East Asia and India, the gap between the affluent, industrialized nations of the northern latitudes and the poorer, developing nations of the south widened. Incomes in most nations in sub-Saharan Africa and Latin America actually declined from 1960s levels. In 2005, more than two billion people in the world subsisted on the equivalent of less than $1 per day.

As world population in 2010 approached seven billion—more than double that at the end of World War II—the poorer southern half of the globe carried the heaviest burden of population growth. **Figure 26.10** shows population changes for major areas of the world since 1900 and estimates population figures for the mid-twenty-first century. Europe, with declining birthrates, will experience a drop in population, while Asia and Africa will gain the most. Many Western nations—particularly the United States—have relied on immigration to bolster population figures.

The distinction between Europe and the rest of the world in population trends is also reflected in the process of urbanization (see **Map 26.9**). Although the wealthy areas of the West once experienced the most rapid urban growth, other parts of the world gained the lead during the second half of the twentieth century. Moreover, in 1950, six out of the ten largest cities were in Europe and the U.S.; by 2000, most of the world's largest cities were in the non-Western world, a trend likely to grow in the future.

Economic growth, population increases, and urbanization created alarming environmental problems in the late twentieth century (see **Map 26.10**). The earth's air, water, and seas became more and more polluted, while acid rain, caused by smoke and fumes, damaged more than one-third of Germany's remaining forests. Great rivers such as the

> Environmental costs

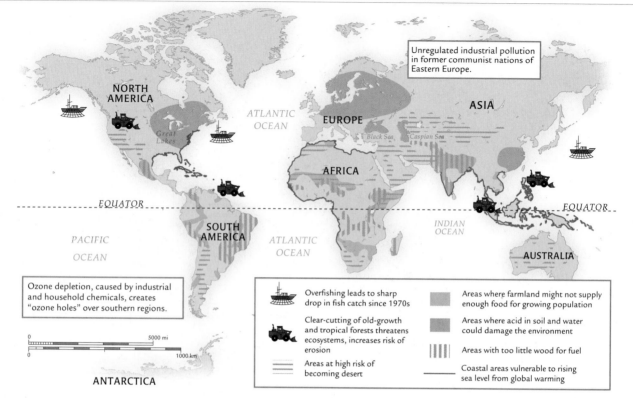

Unregulated industrial pollution in former communist nations of Eastern Europe.

Ozone depletion, caused by industrial and household chemicals, creates "ozone holes" over southern regions.

Overfishing leads to sharp drop in fish catch since 1970s	Areas where farmland might not supply enough food for growing population
Clear-cutting of old-growth and tropical forests threatens ecosystems, increases risk of erosion	Areas where acid in soil and water could damage the environment
Areas at high risk of becoming desert	Areas with too little wood for fuel
	Coastal areas vulnerable to rising sea level from global warming

MAP 26.10

Global Environmental Problems

This map focuses on various widespread environmental problems confronting the world today, most of which stem from industrialization, the exploitation of natural resources, urbanization, and population increases.

Explore the Map

1. Which areas of the world are most affected by environmental problems?

2. How interconnected are these difficulties?

3. What environmental problems are not adequately revealed by this map?

4. What steps might world leaders take to diminish the present and future impact of these problems?

MAJOR AREA	1900	1950	2000	2050
	Population (in millions)			
Asia	947	1402	3672	5428
Africa	133	221	794	2000
Europe	408	547	727	603
Latin America	74	167	579	806
North America	82	172	389	438
Oceania	6	13	31	47
World (total)	1650	2522	6192	9322

FIGURE 26.10 Population Changes Across the Twentieth and Twenty-first Centuries

Rhine and the Danube became like sewers, and waters such as the Mediterranean and Black seas were fouled by runoff from industrial sites and cities. Even the monuments of ancient Greece and Rome were rapidly deteriorating and crumbling from the onslaught of fumes and vibrations of city life. In Eastern Europe and the Soviet Union, environmental problems had been virtually ignored for decades. The collapse of communism in those areas revealed staggering environmental degradation. In many Western countries, the growing importance of Green parties pushed environmental concerns into the political spotlight.

As **Map 26.10** shows, environmental problems extended well beyond the West. Thirteen of the fifteen cities with the worst air pollution in the world were in Asia. Of the estimated 2.7 million people worldwide who died each year from illnesses caused by air pollution, the majority were Asians. Each year, Asia lost 1 percent of its forests. As humanity consumed more and more resources and disrupted the globe's natural balance, thousands of plant and animal species became extinct each year. Humanity's need for more and more energy also led many nations to rely increasingly on nuclear power. The 1986 accident at the Chernobyl plant in the Soviet Union shed new light on the potential dangers of nuclear power—the accident released two hundred times the radiation of the two bombs dropped in World War II.

Many observers believe that **global warming** has become our most threatening environmental problem. Most scientists agree that in recent decades the Earth's atmosphere has heated up at an alarming rate, in great part thanks to the heat-trapping so-called greenhouse gases, such as carbon dioxide, that have been created through the combustion of coal and petroleum products. Factories, power plants, urban growth, and gas-guzzling motor vehicles in the West and in rapidly developing nations such as China and India add to those greenhouse gases every day. According to most scientists, the warming process is probably irreversible and, unless slowed by policies that crucial nations seem unwilling to adopt, could produce dramatic climate changes, resulting in the melting of ice sheets and glaciers, coastal flooding, widening droughts, worsening hurricanes, and rapid extinction of plant and animal species by the end of this century. **Figure 26.11** shows one example of the many glaciers that have been melting throughout the world. On the top is a photograph of the Muir Glacier in Alaska taken in August 1941. On the bottom is a photograph taken from the same vantage point in August 2004. The glacier had retreated more than seven miles, allowing ocean water to fill the valley. What remained of the glacier, now in the distance, had thinned by more than 875 yards. Some experts feel that such dramatic environmental developments will diminish or destroy our ability to sustain Earth's population. Climate-induced food shortages, mass migrations, and possible pandemics could destabilize entire regions of the world. Global warming is "the single biggest challenge facing the planet, the equal in every way to the nuclear threat that transfixed us during the past half-century and a threat we haven't even begun to deal with," warned one distinguished scientist.

People have turned to science and government to solve these environmental problems, but thus far the results have been mixed at best. On the one hand, scientists and governmental officials finally recognized the severity of these problems and have begun to address them by committing more funds to

Global warming

FIGURE 26.11 Global Warming, 1941–2004 Two photographs of Muir Glacier, Alaska, in 1941 (top) and 2004 (bottom) reveal the signs of global warming.

research and coming to agreements on new regulations to minimize the damage (see Document 26.3). On the other hand, anxieties about the environment have often conflicted with a stronger desire of many people for continued economic growth. Businesses and governments, reflecting this desire, have often proved reluctant to commit to expensive environmental-protection programs.

Like the environment, health issues have also received an ambivalent response. In the last few decades of the twentieth century, many officials and commentators recognized that an aging population, particularly in the West, presented a growing health problem that would strain medical facilities and budgets, but they were unsure what to do. With certain health problems—the worldwide AIDS (acquired immune deficiency syndrome) epidemic is just one example—recognition of the dangers came too late. Even then, many efforts to address such crises proved halfhearted. Again, AIDS is an apt example. Between 1978 and 2006, 26 million people died from this disease. AIDS became the most deadly epidemic in recent global

AIDS

thinking about

ART

FIGURE 26.12

Charles Michael Helmken, *Loveaidspeople*, 1989

This poster shows two figures lovingly aiding the Christian martyr Saint Sebastian as the saint, having been wounded by many arrows, looks up desperately for help. The poster was designed to increase public awareness of AIDS and to address negative attitudes toward individuals affected by AIDS.

Connecting Art & Society

1. How do you explain the meaning of the title *Loveaidspeople*? How has the artist interpreted the title in his depiction?

2. Why might the artist have chosen to feature the Christian martyr Saint Sebastian in this poster?

3. How, as a viewer, do you interpret the details and colors in this poster?

history, yet many people initially denied its existence or criticized those who had contracted it. The AIDS poster in **Figure 26.12**, *Loveaidspeople*, uses Renaissance painter Tanzio da Varallo's painting of the Christian martyr Saint Sebastian to protest these attitudes. In this poignant image, a modern-day AIDS victim has been wounded by the "arrows" of officials and social attitudes that condemn both the third-century martyr and the twentieth-century AIDS victim as morally dirty and sinful. The poster makes an urgent plea for assistance for AIDS sufferers. After several years, some help began to arrive, but not nearly enough. In 2006, the United Nations estimated that 40 million people in the world were living with AIDS or HIV, the virus that causes AIDS. In some sub-Saharan countries of Africa, one in four adults were infected.

In the face of frightening diseases, environmental degradation, economic uncertainty, and devastating weaponry, many people looked to the new century with cynicism or dread. Some found it all too easy to imagine even the violent destruction of all life on Earth, as **Figure 26.13** suggests. This painting, by American artist Jennifer Bartlett, shows a firestorm sweeping away everything in its path. Sculptural objects are dashed to the floor between the viewer and the canvas. In a world that still had unimaginably destructive weapons of war at its fingertips, this scene may well have offered a visual warning of the potential for holocaust that hung over the West and the rest of the world as the twenty-first century began.

Perhaps in response to these anxieties, the last two decades of the twentieth century saw a renewal of religious commitment among many people. In the United States and Europe, evangelical Christianity—with its emphasis on personal salvation and spiritual experience—became the fastest-growing religious movement. In Russia, an outpouring of religious sentiment within the Orthodox Church followed the collapse of communism. Islamic | Movements of religious revival

fundamentalism, calling for a return to traditional ways and a rejection of alien ideologies, intensified in lands from West Africa to East Asia. All of these movements reflected a hunger for a sense of meaning and a clarity of values by which to live in an uncertain time.

Yet, despite these anxieties, there were also reasons to look to the coming century with hope and optimism. After all, the West had surmounted major obstacles. It had enjoyed more than sixty years of relative peace and had managed to avert the dreaded clash | Accomplishments and optimism of superpowers during the Cold War. In Eastern Europe, most nations had gained their long-sought independence with a minimum of violence. In some areas, seemingly hopeless problems

DOCUMENT 26.3

The Copenhagen Accord on Climate Change

While many scientists have long warned about the dangers of global warming, only in recent years has the international community recognized the gravity of the problem. Building on earlier conferences, the United Nations organized a major conference on climate change in Copenhagen, Denmark, late in 2009. The following are excerpts from the resulting Copenhagen Accord.

We underline that climate change is one of the greatest challenges of our time. We emphasise our strong political will to urgently combat climate change in accordance with the principle of common but differentiated responsibilities and respective capabilities. To achieve the ultimate objective of the Convention to stabilize greenhouse gas concentration in the atmosphere at a level that would prevent dangerous anthropogenic interference with the climate system, we shall, recognizing the scientific view that the increase in global temperature should be below 2 degrees Celsius, on the basis of equity and in the context of sustainable development, enhance our long-term cooperative action to combat climate change. We recognize the critical impacts of climate change and the potential impacts of response measures on countries particularly vulnerable to its adverse effects and stress the need to establish a comprehensive adaptation programme including international support. . . .

Enhanced action and international cooperation on adaptation is urgently required, . . . especially in those [countries] that are particularly vulnerable, especially least developed countries, small island developing States and Africa. We agree that developed countries shall provide adequate, predictable and sustainable financial resources, technology and capacity-building to support the implementation of adaptation action in developing countries.

SOURCE: Governmental document in public domain.

Analyze the Document

1. What goals does this agreement set?

2. In what ways, and why, does the accord make distinctions between developed and less developed countries?

3. Many observers were disappointed with the results because the accord did not mandate change. Why might some countries be unwilling to accept legally binding actions to stem global warming?

---

showed signs of being solved. For example, in Northern Ireland, Protestants and Catholics created a power-sharing government, ending a decades-long bitter conflict.

For many people around the world, the standard of living had risen to unprecedented levels. In Asia, for example, increasing prosperity had lifted some 400 million people out of abject poverty. Between 1999 and 2008, the global economy doubled. Although social equality still remained only an ideal, the Western promise of continually improving well-being for everyone seemed to hold firm. The increasing human life span and rising numbers of elderly—in part thanks to the global increase in food production and better access to health care—attested to that well-being. Moreover, many women gained access to opportunities once available only to men: By the late 1990s, roughly equal numbers of women and men in the West received higher education and pursued paying careers. Women's presence in professional life and in politics continued to grow. True, traditionalists worried about the destruction of the family as an institution, citing the growing prevalence of two-career parents, a rise in cohabitation and single motherhood, and accelerating divorce rates. Nevertheless, family structures persisted, although many of them took new forms, such as "an emotionally bound partnership."

FIGURE 26.13 Jennifer Bartlett, *Spiral: An Ordinary Evening in New Haven,* 1989 Contemporary artists have sometimes focused on the growing popular concern that all life on earth could be violently destroyed in the near future.

Continuing scientific discoveries suggested that the West and the rest of the world could look forward to dramatic developments in the future. Perhaps most

thinking about
SCIENCE & TECHNOLOGY

FIGURE 26.14 The CERN Hadron Collider

CERN

What gives matter its mass? What makes up the invisible 96 percent of the universe? These are two of the fundamental research questions being investigated by the European Organization for Nuclear Research (CERN). Located in Switzerland but spilling over the border into France, this is the world's largest particle physics laboratory. Ideas for the international organization first surfaced in the 1940s. Finally established in 1954 by eleven Western European countries, CERN now includes twenty European member states and many more observer nations. The organization employs some 8,000 scientists who split their time between the main CERN site and hundreds of universities and national laboratories in their home countries. The dual goals of projects such as those conducted by CERN are to advance knowledge and, in doing so, to set the stage for later practical applications to life.

One of CERN's best-known achievements was the invention of the World Wide Web in 1989. Originally designed to enable scientists in different institutes and universities to share information, the Web was expanded to a world audience in 1993. CERN's new, extremely expensive Large Hadron Collider, shown in **Figure 26.14,** is a current worldwide scientific cooperation project. Sixteen miles in circumference and buried 300 yards underground, the massive collider will be used to study the subatomic world and the nature of the universe in all its vastness. Computers around the world will process information from the Collider experiments, which perhaps will lead to yet-unimagined applications.

CERN represents another extension of the connections among science, universities, and governments we examined in Chapter 21, as well as the growth of big science, discussed in Chapter 25.

Connecting Science & Society

1. In what ways does CERN represent big science?

2. What are some effects that the World Wide Web has had on peoples around the world?

3. Do you think that projects as costly as those undertaken by CERN can be justified only if they lead to practical applications such as the World Wide Web? Explain.

4. How might the rise of organizations such as CERN reflect globalization?

stunning was the prospect of changes stemming from the decoding of the human genome—determining the chemical sequence of the DNA in every cell of the human body. In 2001, this costly, long-term project carried out by hundreds of scientists in six countries was completed. With this "blueprint" of human life, scientists hoped to revolutionize medicine and gain new insights into human nature. Another international organization, CERN (see Thinking About Science & Technology), has been conducting research into the nature of matter.

Overall, the West has gained a much needed appreciation of its place in the world, and human beings around the globe have new tools to understand themselves within a widening universe. Technology, trade, and instant communications provide growing opportunities for cooperation across national boundaries. As the second decade of the twenty-first century opens, life offers more options to more people than ever.

LOOKING BACK & MOVING FORWARD

Summary   In 1989, history in the West abruptly shifted course. The communist regimes in Eastern Europe fell, severing these nations' ties to the Soviet Union and sparking unprecedented political and economic reforms. Two years later, the Soviet Union itself disintegrated. The Cold War ended and along with it, a sharply defined historical era stretching back to 1914. The end of the Cold War renewed the commitment to democracy and capitalism in the West, accelerated the existing movement toward unification in Europe, and left the United States standing as the sole military superpower in the world.

But the collapse of communism did not end all the anxieties present during the Cold War era. The transition in Eastern Europe and the Soviet Union proved rocky, and Westerners realized that despite their lofty global position, they could no longer keep the rest of the world at arm's length. Indeed, the West's global status began to change, as statistics reveal. In 1950, some 30 percent of the world's population lived in Europe and North America. In 2010, that figure dropped below 15 percent. As peoples around the world interacted more and more, cultures mingled, producing both conflict and convergence; our time may mark the beginning of a new global society. The relentless human desire for limitless economic growth and material security also left its mark on the environment in ways that spread concern across national boundaries. Western civilization, so long centered on the western tip of the Eurasian continent, now seemed to be just one of many lights shining on this shrinking globe. As one era closed and another opened, great challenges faced all of humanity. Whether and how the West—and the world— would embrace these challenges remained to be seen.

KEY TERMS

perestroika,   *p. 813*

glasnost,   *p. 813*

ethnic cleansing,   *p. 821*

European Union (EU),   *p. 824*

Euro,   *p. 824*

North American Free Trade Agreement (NAFTA),   *p. 824*

globalization,   *p. 826*

al-Qaeda,   *p. 827*

preemptive war,   *p. 830*

unilateralism,   *p. 830*

postmodernism,   *p. 834*

global warming,   *p. 837*

REVIEW, ANALYZE, & CONNECT TO TODAY

REVIEW THE PREVIOUS CHAPTER

Chapter 25—"Superpower Struggles and Global Transformations"—analyzed the Cold War competition between the United States and the Soviet Union. Within the Cold War context, the recovery of the West and end of colonialism were analyzed.

1. How might you argue that developments since 1989 are not the begining of a new historical era and that, instead, they are a continuation of trends that first emerged in the post–World War II decades?

2. Do you think that the collapse of communism and the end of the Cold War should have been predictable by the early 1980s? Why?

ANALYZE THIS CHAPTER

Chapter 26—"Into the Twenty-First Century"—traces the collapse of communism and the intense interaction between the Western and non-Western worlds.

1. Analyze the consequences of the collapse of communism outside Eastern Europe and the Soviet Union.

2. In what ways has much of Europe become integrated, and what steps remain to achieve full integration?

3. What forces are pulling the world together? How do these forces compare with those dividing the world?

CONNECT TO TODAY

It is always difficult to predict the future, but history can sometimes provide grounds for reasonable guesses.

1. In the near future, what might be the consequences of continuing steps toward the unification of Europe?

2. From a historical perspective, what consequences might flow from the financial crisis and recession that began in 2008?

3. Judging from developments since 1989, which problems do you think will prove the most serious in the years to come? Why? Do you think there is good reason for optimism? Why or why not?

BEYOND THE CLASSROOM

THE COLLAPSE OF COMMUNISM

Garton Ash, Timothy. *In Europe's Name: Germany and the Divided Continent*. London: Jonathan Cape, 1993. Stresses the history of tensions between East and West Germany as background to their reunification.

Lucas, Edward. *The New Cold War: Putin's Russia and the Threat to the West*. London: Palgrave, 2008. A challenging interpretation of recent developments in Russia.

Remnick, David. *Lenin's Tomb: The Last Days of the Soviet Empire*. New York: Random House, 1994. Journalistic coverage of the final period before the collapse of the Soviet empire, stressing the role played by Yeltsin.

Service, Robert. *Russia: Experiment with a People*. Cambridge, MA: Harvard University Press, 2003. Solid, scholarly coverage of Russia from 1991 until the early 2000s.

Silber, Laura, and Allan Little. *Yugoslavia: Death of a Nation*. New York: TV Books/Penguin USA, 1996. An account of the nation's ethnic troubles.

Stokes, Gale. *The Walls Came Tumbling Down: The Collapse of Communism in Eastern Europe*. Oxford: Oxford University Press, 1993. Analyzes the decline and fall of communism in Eastern Europe between 1968 and 1991.

REPERCUSSIONS AND REALIGNMENTS IN THE WEST

Caplan, Richard, and John Feffer, eds. *Europe's New Nationalism: States and Minorities in Conflict*. New York: Oxford University Press, 1996. A collection of essays by scholars on the growth of nationalism in Europe after the collapse of communism.

Cheles, Juciano, et al., eds. *The Far Right in Western and Eastern Europe*, 2nd ed. London: Longman, 1995. A comparative study of fringe movements in these areas.

Dinan, Desmond. *Europe Recast: A History of the European Union*. New York: Lynne Rienner Publishers, 2003. A well-written overview.

THE WORLD AND THE WEST FROM A GLOBAL PERSPECTIVE

Cohen, Daniel. *Globalization and Its Enemies.* Boston: MIT Press, 2006. A brilliant discussion of the promises and problems of globalization in a broad historical context.

Friedman, Thomas L. *The Lexus and the Olive Tree.* New York: Farrar, Straus, Giroux, 1999. An engaging, boldly interpretive analysis of globalism.

Kolbert, Elizabeth. *Field Notes from a Catastrophe: Man, Nature, and Climate Change.* New York: Bloomsbury Publishing, 2006. A very well-written, well-documented account.

Mandelbaum, Michael. *The Case for Goliath: How America Acts as the World's Government in the 21st Century.* New York: Perseus, 2005. A sharp, challenging interpretation of America's changing role in world affairs.

McNeill, J.R. *Something New Under the Sun: An Environmental History of the Twentieth-Century World.* New York: W.W. Norton, 2000. An important union of historical and environmental perspectives.

Rashid, Ahmed. *Descent into Chaos: The United States and the Failure of Nation Building in Pakistan, Afghanistan, and Central Asia.* New York: Viking Penguin, 2008. A disturbing, critical interpretation.

Note to users: Terms that are foreign or difficult to pronounce are transcribed in parentheses directly after the term itself. The transcriptions are based on the rules of English spelling; that is, they are similar to the transcriptions employed in the *Webster* dictionaries. Each word's most heavily stressed syllable is marked by an acute accent.

A

Absolute monarch (máh-nark) A seventeenth- or eighteenth-century European monarch claiming complete political authority.

Absolutism (áb-suh-loo-tism) (Royal) A government in which all power is vested in the ruler.

Abstract expressionism (ex-présh-un-ism) A twentieth-century painting style infusing nonrepresentational art with strong personal feelings.

Acropolis (uh-króp-uh-liss) The hill at the center of Athens on which the magnificent temples—including the Parthenon—that made the architecture of ancient Athens famous are built.

Act of Union Formal unification of England and Scotland in 1707.

Afrikaners Afrikaans-speaking South Africans of Dutch and other European ancestry.

Age of Reason The eighteenth-century Enlightenment; sometimes includes seventeenth-century science and philosophy.

Agora In ancient Greece, the marketplace or place of public assembly.

Agricultural revolution Neolithic discovery of agriculture; agricultural transformations that began in eighteenth-century western Europe.

Ahura Mazda In Zoroastrianism, the beneficial god of light.

Ahriman In Zoroastrianism, the evil god of darkness.

Akkadian (uh-káy-dee-un) A Semitic language of a region of ancient Mesopotamia.

Albigensians (al-buh-jén-see-unz) A medieval French heretical sect that believed in two gods—an evil and a good principle—that was destroyed in a crusade in the thirteenth century; also called Cathars.

Alchemy (ál-kuh-mee) The medieval study and practice of chemistry, primarily concerned with changing metals into gold and finding a universal remedy for diseases. It was much practiced from the thirteenth to the seventeenth century.

Allies (ál-eyes) The two alliances against Germany and its partners in World War I and World War II.

Al-Qaeda A global terrorist network headed by Osama bin Laden.

Anarchists (ánn-ar-kissts) Those advocating or promoting anarchy, or an absence of government. In the late nineteenth and early twentieth centuries, anarchism arose as an ideology and movement against all governmental authority and private property.

Ancien régime (áwn-syáwn ráy-zhéem) The traditional political and social order in Europe before the French Revolution.

Antigonids (ann-tíg-un-idz) Hellenistic dynasty that ruled in Macedonia from about 300 B.C.E. to about 150 B.C.E.

Anti-Semitism (ann-tye-sém-i-tism) Prejudice against Jews.

Apartheid "Separation" in the Afrikaans language. A policy to rigidly segregate people by color in South Africa, 1948–1989.

Appeasement Attempting to satisfy potential aggressors in order to avoid war.

Aramaic (air-uh-máy-ik) A northwest Semitic language that spread throughout the region. It was the language that Jesus spoke.

Archon (áhr-kahn) A chief magistrate in ancient Athens.

Areopagus (air-ee-áh-pa-gus) A prestigious governing council of ancient Athens.

Arête (ah-ray-táy) Greek term for the valued virtues of manliness, courage, and excellence.

Arianism (áir-ee-un-ism) A fourth-century Christian heresy that taught that Jesus was not of the same substance as God the father, and thus had been created.

Assemblies, Roman Institutions in the Roman Republic that functioned as the legislative branch of government.

Assignats (ah-seen-yáh) Paper money issued in the National Assembly during the French Revolution.

Astrolabe (áss-tro-leyb) Medieval instrument used to determine the altitudes of celestial bodies.

Augury (áh-gur-ee) The art or practice of foretelling events though signs or omens.

Autocracy (au-tóc-ra-cee) Government under the rule of an authoritarian ruler.

Autocrat (áuto-crat) An authoritarian ruler.

Axis World War II alliance whose main members were Germany, Italy, and Japan.

B

Baby boom The increase in births following World War II.

Babylonian Captivity Period during the fourteenth century in which seven popes chose to reside in Avignon instead of Rome. Critics called this period the "Babylonian Captivity" of the papacy.

Bailiffs Medieval French salaried officials hired by the king to collect taxes and represent his interests.

Balance of power Distribution of power among states, or the policy of creating alliances to control powerful states.

Balkans States in the Balkan Peninsula, including Albania, Bulgaria, Greece, Romania, and Yugoslavia.

Baroque (ba-róak) An artistic style of the sixteenth and seventeenth centuries stressing rich ornamentation and dynamic movement; in music, a style marked by strict forms and elaborate ornamentation.

Bastard feudalism (feúd-a-lism) Late medieval corruption of the feudal system replacing feudal loyalty with cash payments.

Bastille (bas-téel) The royal prison symbolizing the old regime that was destroyed in the French Revolution.

Bauhaus (bóugh-house) An influential school of art emphasizing clean, functional lines founded in Germany by the architect Walter Gropius just after World War I.

Bedouin (béd-oh-in) An Arab of any of the nomadic tribes of the deserts of North Africa, Arabia, and Syria.

Berlin airlift The airborne military operation organized to supply Berlin's Western-occupied sectors during the Soviet Union's 1948 Berlin blockage.

Berlin Wall The wall erected in 1961 to divide East and West Berlin.

Bessemer (béss-uh-mer) **process** A method for removing impurities from molten iron.

Black Death Name given the epidemic that swept Europe beginning in 1348. Most historians agree that the main disease was bubonic plague, but the Black Death may have incorporated many other diseases.

Blackshirts Mussolini's black-uniformed Fascist paramilitary forces in the 1920s and 1930s.

Blitzkrieg (blíts-kreeg) "Lightning war," a rapid air and land military assault used by the Germans in World War II.

Boers (boars) Dutch settlers in south Africa.

Bolshevik (bówl-shuh-vick) "Majority faction," the Leninist wing of the Russian Marxist Party; after 1917, the Communist Party.

Bourgeoisie (boor-zhwa-zée) The middle class.

Boxers A nineteenth-century Chinese secret society that believed in the spiritual power of the martial arts and fought against Chinese Christians and foreigners in China.

Boyar A Russian noble.

Brezhnev (bréhzh-nyeff) **Doctrine** Policy that justified Soviet intervention in order to ensure the survival of socialism in another state, initiated by USSR leader Brezhnev in 1968.

Brownshirts Hitler's brown-uniformed paramilitary force in the 1920s and 1930s.

Burschenschaften (bóor-shen-sháhf-ten) Liberal nationalist German student unions during the early nineteenth century.

C

Cabinet system Government by a prime minister and heads of governmental bureaus developed by Britain during the eighteenth century.

Caesaropapism (see-zer-oh-pápe-ism) The practice of having the same person rule both the state and the church.

Cahiers (kye-yéah) Lists of public grievances sent to the French Estates General in 1789.

Caliph (káy-liff) A title meaning "successor to the Prophet" given to Muslim rulers who combined political authority with religious power.

Capitalists Those promoting an economic system characterized by freedom of the market with private and corporate ownership of the means of production and distribution that are operated for profit.

Capitularies (ka-pít-chew-làir-eez) Royal laws issued by Charlemagne and the Carolingians.

Caravel (care-uh-véll) A small, light sailing ship of the kind used by the Spanish and Portuguese in the fifteenth and sixteenth centuries.

Carbonari (car-bun-áh-ree) A secret society of revolutionaries in nineteenth-century Italy.

Cartel (car-téll) An alliance of corporations designed to control the marketplace.

Cartesian (car-tée-zhen) **dualism** A philosophy developed by René Descartes in the seventeenth century that defines two kinds of reality: the mind, or subjective thinking, and the body, or objective physical matter.

Catacombs Underground burial places. The term originally referred to the early Christian burial locations in Rome and elsewhere.

Cathars (cáth-arz) A medieval French dualist heretical sect; also called Albigensians.

Central Powers World War I alliance, primarily of Germany, Austria, and the Ottoman Empire.

Centuriate (sen-chúr-ee-ate) **Assembly** An aristocratic ruling body in ancient Rome that made the laws.

Chancellor A high-ranking official—in Germany, the prime minister.

Chartists English reformers of the 1830s and 1840s who demanded political and social rights for the lower classes.

Checks and balances A balanced division of governmental power among different institutions.

Chivalry (shív-el-ree) Code of performance and ethics for medieval knights. It can also refer to the demonstration of knightly virtues.

Christian humanists During the fifteenth and sixteenth centuries, experts in Greek, Latin, and Hebrew who studied the Bible and other Christian writings in order to understand the correct meaning of early Christian texts.

Civil Constitution of the Clergy New rules nationalizing and governing the clergy enacted during the French Revolution.

Civic humanists Those practicing a branch of humanism that promoted the value of responsible citizenship in which people work to improve their city-states.

Classical style A seventeenth- and eighteenth-century cultural style emphasizing restraint and balance, and following models from ancient Greece and Rome.

Cold War The global struggle between alliances headed by the United States and the Soviet Union during the second half of the twentieth century.

Collectivization The Soviet policy of taking agricultural lands and decisions away from individual owners and placing them in the hands of elected managers and party officials.

Comecon (cómm-ee-con) The economic organization of communist eastern European states during the Cold War.

Committee of Public Safety Ruling committee of twelve leaders during the French Revolutionary period of the Terror.

Common law Laws that arise from customary use rather than from legislation.

Common market The European Economic Community, a union of Western European nations initiated in 1957 to promote common economic policies.

Commonwealth of Independent States A loose confederation of several former republics of the disintegrated Soviet Union founded in 1991.

Commune (cómm-yune) A medieval or early modern town; a semi-independent city government or socialistic community in the nineteenth and twentieth centuries.

Communist Manifesto A short, popular treatise written by Karl Marx and Friedrich Engels in 1848 that contained the fundamentals of their "scientific socialism."

Complutensian Polyglot (comm-plue-tén-see-an pólly-glàht) **Bible** An edition of the Bible written in 1520 that had three columns that compared the Hebrew, Greek, and Latin versions.

Compurgation (comm-pur-gáy-shun) A Germanic legal oath taken by twelve men testifying to the character of the accused.

Concert of Europe The alliance of powers after 1815 created to maintain the status quo and coordinate international relations.

Conciliar (conn-síll-ee-ar) **movement** The belief that the Catholic Church should be led by councils of cardinals rather than popes.

Concordat (conn-córe-dat) A formal agreement, especially between the pope and a government, for the regulation of church affairs.

condottieri (conn-duh-tyáy-ree) From the fourteenth to the sixteenth century, captains of bands of mercenary soldiers, influential in Renaissance Italy.

Congress of Vienna The peace conference held between 1814 and 1815 in Vienna after the defeat of Napoleon.

Conquistadors (conn-kéy-stah-doors) Spanish adventurers in the sixteenth century who went to South and Central America to conquer indigenous peoples and claim their lands.

Conservatism An ideology stressing order and traditional values.

Constitutionalism The idea that political authority rests in written law, not in the person of an absolute monarch.

Constitutional monarchy Government in which the monarch's powers are limited by a set of fundamental laws.

Consuls (cónn-sul) The appointed chief executive officers of the Roman Republic.

Containment The Cold War strategy of the United States to limit the expansion and influence of the Soviet Union.

Continental System Napoleon's policy of preventing trade between continental Europe and Great Britain.

Contra posto (cón-tra páh-sto) A stance of the human body in which one leg bears weight, while the other is relaxed. Also known as counterpoise, it was popular in Renaissance sculpture.

Copernican (co-pér-nick-an) **revolution** The change from an earth-centered to a sun-centered universe initiated by Copernicus in the sixteenth century.

Corinthian order One of three architectural systems developed by the Greeks to decorate their buildings. The Corinthian order is marked by the capitals of columns decorated with acanthus leaves.

Corn Laws British laws that imposed tariffs on grain imports.

Corporate state Mussolini's economic and political machinery to manage the Italian economy and settle issues between labor and management.

Corsair A swift pirate ship.

Cossacks The "free warriors" of southern Russia, noted as cavalrymen.

Cottage industry Handicraft manufacturing usually organized by merchants and performed by rural people in their cottages.

Coup d'état (coo-day-táh) A sudden taking of power that violates constitutional forms by a group of persons in authority.

Creoles (crée-ohlz) People of European descent born in the West Indies or Spanish America, often of mixed ancestry.

Crusades From the late eleventh century through the thirteenth century, Europeans sent a number of military operations to take the Holy Land (Jerusalem and its surrounding territory) from the Muslims. These military ventures in the name of Christendom are collectively called the Crusades.

Cult of sensibility The eighteenth-century emphasis on emotion and nature forwarded by several European artists and authors.

Cuneiform (cue-née-uh-form) A writing system using wedge-shaped characters developed in ancient Mesopotamia.

Curia Regis (kóo-ree-uh régg-ees) A medieval king's advisory body made up of his major vassals.

Cynicism (sín-uh-sism) A Hellenistic philosophy that locates the search for virtue in an utter indifference to worldly needs.

Cyrillic (suh-ríll-ik) **alphabet** An old Slavic alphabet presently used in modified form for Russian and other languages.

D

Dada (dáh-dah) An early twentieth-century artistic movement that attacked traditional cultural styles and stressed the absence of purpose in life.

Dauphin (dough-fán) Heir to the French throne. The title was used from 1349 to 1830.

D-Day The day of the Allied invasion of Normandy in World War II—June 6, 1944.

Decembrists (dee-sém-brists) Russian army officers who briefly rebelled against Tsar Nicholas I in December 1925.

Decolonization The loss of colonies by imperial powers during the years following World War II.

Declaration of the Rights of Man and Citizen France's revolutionary 1789 declaration of rights stressing liberty, equality, and fraternity.

Deductive reasoning Deriving conclusions that logically flow from a premise, reasoning from basic or known truths.

Deism (dée-iz-um) Belief in a God who created the universe and its natural laws but does not intervene further; gained popularity during the Enlightenment.

Demotic A form of ancient Egyptian writing used for ordinary life. A simplified form of hieratic script.

Détente (day-táhnt) The period of relative cooperation between Cold War adversaries during the 1960s and 1970s.

Devotio moderno (day-vóh-tee-oh moh-dáir-noh) A medieval religious movement that emphasized internal spirituality over ritual practices.

Diaspora The dispersion of the Jews after the Babylonian conquest in the sixth century B.C.E. The term comes from the Greek word meaning "to scatter."

Diet The general legislative assembly of certain countries, such as Poland.

Directory The relatively conservative government during the last years of the French Revolution before Napoleon gained power.

Division of labor The division of work in the modern process of industrial production into separate tasks.

Doge (dóhj) The chief magistrate of the Republic of Venice during the Middle Ages and Renaissance.

Domesday (dóomz-day) **Book** A record of all the property and holdings in England, commissioned by William the Conqueror in 1066 so that he could determine the extent of his lands and wealth.

Doric order One of three architectural systems developed by the Greeks to decorate their buildings. The Doric order may be recognized by its columns, which include a wide shaft with a plain capital on the top.

Drachma (dróck-mah) Hellenistic coin containing either 4.3 grams (Alexander's) or 3.5 grams (Egypt's) of silver.

Dreyfus (dry'-fuss) **affair** The political upheaval in France accompanying the unjust 1894 conviction of Jewish army officer Alfred Dreyfus as a German spy that marked the importance of anti-Semitism in France.

Dual Monarchy The Austro-Hungarian Empire; the Habsburg monarchy after the 1867 reform that granted Hungary equality with Austria.

Il Duce (ill dóoch-ay) "The Leader," Mussolini's title as head of the Italian Fascist Party.

Duma Russia's legislative assembly in the years prior to 1917.

E

Ecclesia (ek-cláy-zee-uh) The popular assembly in ancient Athens made up of all male citizens over 18.

Edict of Nantes (náwnt) Edict issued by French king Henry IV in 1598 granting rights to Protestants, later revoked by Louis XIV.

Émigrés (em-ee-gráy) People, mostly aristocrats, who fled France during the French Revolution.

Emir (em-éar) A Muslim ruler, prince, or military commander.

Empirical method The use of observation and experiments based on sensory evidence to come to ideas or conclusions about nature.

Ems (Em's) **Dispatch** Telegram from Prussia's head of state to the French government, edited by Bismarck to look like an insult, that helped cause the Franco-Prussian War.

Enclosure Combining separate parcels of farmland and enclosing them with fences and walls to create large farms or pastures that produced for commerce.

encomienda (en-koh-mee-én-da) A form of economic and social organization established in sixteenth-century Spanish settlements in South and Central America. The encomienda system consisted of a royal grant that allowed Spanish settlers to compel indigenous peoples to work for them. In return, Spanish overseers were to look after their workers' welfare and encourage their conversion to Christianity. In reality, it was a brutal system of enforced labor.

Enlightened absolutism (áb-suh-loo-tism) Rule by a strong, "enlightened" ruler applying Enlightenment ideas to government.

Enlightenment An eighteenth-century cultural movement based on the ideas of the Scientific Revolution and that supported the notion that human reason should determine understanding of the world and the rules of social life.

Entente Cordiale (on-táhnt core-dee-áhl) The series of understandings, or agreements, between France and Britain that led to their alliance in World War I.

Entrepreneur (on-truh-pren-óor) A person who organizes and operates business ventures, especially in commerce and industry.

Epic (épp-ik) A long narrative poem celebrating episodes of a people's heroic tradition.

Epicureanism (epp-uh-cúre-ee-an-ism) A Hellenistic philosophy that held that the goal of life should be to live a life of pleasure regulated by moderation.

Equestrians (ee-quést-ree-ans) A social class in ancient Rome who had enough money to begin to challenge the power of the patricians.

Essenes (Ess-éenz) Members of a Jewish sect of ascetics from the second century B.C.E. to the second century C.E.

Estates Representative assemblies, typically made up of either the clergy, the nobility, the commoners, or all three meeting separately.

Estates General The legislature of France from the Middle Ages to 1789. Each of the three Estates—clergy, nobility, and bourgeoisie—sent representatives.

Ethnic cleansing The policy of brutally driving an ethnic group from their homes and from a certain territory, particularly prominent during the civil wars in the Balkans during the 1990s.

Eugenics (you-génn-iks) The study of hereditary improvement.

Euro (yóu-roe) The common currency of many European states, established in 1999.

Eurocommunism The policy of Western European Communist parties of supporting moderate policies and cooperating with other Leftist parties during the 1970s and 1980s.

European Economic Community The E.E.C., or Common Market, founded in 1957 to eliminate tariff barriers and begin to integrate the economies of western European nations.

European Union (EU) The community of European nations that continued to take steps toward the full economic union of much of Europe during the late twentieth century.

Evolution Darwin's theory of biological development through adaptation.

Existentialism (ekk-siss-ténn-sha-lism) A twentieth-century philosophy asserting that individuals are responsible for their own values and meanings in an indifferent universe.

Expressionism A late-nineteenth- and early-twentieth-century artistic style that emphasized the objective expression of inner experience through the use of conventional characters and symbols.

F

Fabian (fáy-bee-an) **Society** A late-nineteenth-century group of British intellectuals that advocated the adoption of socialist policies through politics rather than revolution.

Factory system Many workers producing goods in a repetitive series of steps and specialized tasks using powerful machines.

Falange (fa-láhn-hey) A Spanish fascist party that supported Francisco Franco during the Spanish civil war.

Fascism (fáh-shism) A philosophy or system of government that advocates a dictatorship of the extreme right together with an ideology of belligerent nationalism.

Fealty (fée-al-tee) In the feudal system, a promise made by vassals and lords to do no harm to each other.

Federates In the late Roman Empire, treaties established with many Gothic tribes allowed these tribes to settle within the Empire. The tribes then became "federates," or allies of Rome.

Fibula (pl. fibulae) An ornamented clasp or brooch, favored by the ancient Germanic tribes to hold their great cloaks closed.

Fief (feef) In the feudal system, the portion—usually land—given by lords to vassals to provide for their maintenance in return for their service.

Five-Year Plan The rapid, massive industrialization of the nation under the direction of the state initiated in the Soviet Union in the late 1920s.

Forum The central public place in ancient Rome which served as a meeting place, marketplace, law court, and political arena.

Fourteen Points U.S. President Wilson's plan to settle World War I and guarantee the peace.

Frankfurt Assembly Convention of liberals and nationalists from several German states that met in 1848 to try to form a unified government for Germany.

Free companies Mercenary soldiers in the Middle Ages and Renaissance who would fight for whoever paid them. They were called "free" to distinguish them from warriors who were bound by feudal ties to a lord.

Free Corps (core) Post–World War I German right-wing paramilitary groups made up mostly of veterans.

Free trade International trade of goods without tariffs, or customs duties.

Fresco A technique of painting on the plaster surface of a wall or ceiling while it is still damp so that the colors become fused with the plaster as it dries, making the image part of the building's surface.

Fronde (frawnd) Mid-seventeenth-century upheavals in France that threatened the royal government.

Fundamentalists Those who believe in an extremely conservative interpretation of a religion.

G

Galley A large medieval ship propelled by sails and oars.

General will Rousseau's notion that rules governing society should be based on the best conscience of the people.

Gentry People of "good birth" and superior social position.

Geocentric Earth-centered.

Gerousia (gay-róo-see-uh) Ruling body in ancient Sparta made up of male citizens over age 60.

Gestapo (guh-stóp-po) Nazi secret police in Hitler's Germany.

Girondins (zhee-roan-dán) Moderate political faction among leaders of the French Revolution.

Glasnost (gláz-nost) Soviet leader Gorbachev's policy of political and cultural openness in the 1980s.

Globalization Twentieth-century tendency for cultural and historical development to become increasingly worldwide in scope.

Global warming The heating of the earth's atmosphere in recent decades, caused in part by the buildup of carbon dioxide and other "greenhouse gases" produced by burning fossil fuels.

Glorious Revolution In 1688, English Parliament offered the crown of England to the Protestant William of Orange and his wife Mary, replacing James II. This change in rule was accomplished peacefully and clarified the precedent that England was a constitutional monarchy with power resting in Parliament.

Gosplan The Soviet State Planning Commission, charged with achieving ambitious economic goals.

Gothic (góth-ik) A style of architecture, usually associated with churches, that originated in France and flourished from the twelfth to the sixteenth century. Gothic architecture is identified by pointed arches, ribbed vaults, stained-glass windows, and flying buttresses.

Grand tour An educational travel taken by the wealthy to certain cities and sites, particularly during the seventeenth and eighteenth centuries.

Great Chain of Being A traditional Western-Christian vision of the hierarchical order of the universe.

Great Depression The global economic depression of the 1930s.

Great fear Panic caused by rumors that bands of brigands were on the loose in the French countryside during the summer of 1789.

Great Purges The long period of Communist Party purges in the Soviet Union during the 1930s, marked by terror, house arrests, show-trials, torture, imprisonments, and executions.

Great Reforms Reforms instituted by Russia's tsar Alexander II in 1861 that included freeing Russia's serfs.

Great Schism (skíz-um) Period in the late Middle Ages from 1378 to 1417 when there were two (and at times three) rival popes.

Greek fire A Byzantine naval weapon made of combustible oil that was launched with a catapult or pumped through tubes to set fire to enemy ships.

Guild An association of persons of the same trade united for the furtherance of some purpose.

Guillotine (ghée-oh-teen) A device for executing the condemned used during the French Revolution.

H

Hacienda (ha-see-én-da) Large landed estates in Spanish America that replaced encomiendas as the dominant economic and social structure.

Haj (hodge) The Muslim annual pilgrimage to Mecca, Medina, and other holy sites.

Hasidim (hah-see-déem) Sect of Jewish mystics founded in Poland in the eighteenth century in opposition to the formalistic Judaism and ritual laxity of the period.

Heliocentric (hee-lee-oh-sén-trick) Pertaining to the theory that the sun is the center of the universe.

Hellenes (Héll-eenz) The name ancient Greeks assigned to themselves, based on their belief that they were descended from a mythical King Hellen.

Hellenistic Of or related to the period between the fourth century B.C.E. and the first century B.C.E.

Helot (héll-ots) A serf in ancient Sparta.

Heresy A religious belief that is considered wrong by orthodox church leaders.

Hermetic doctrine Notion popular in the sixteenth and seventeenth centuries that all matter contains the divine spirit.

Hieratic (high-rát-ick) A form of ancient Egyptian writing consisting of abridged forms of hieroglyphics, used by the priests in keeping records.

Hieroglyph (high-roe-gliff) A picture or symbol used in the ancient Egyptian writing system—means "sacred writing."

Hijra (hídge-rah) (also *Hegira*) Muhammad's flight from Mecca to Medina in 622 B.C.E.

Holocaust (hóll-o-cost) The extermination of some six million Jews by the Nazis during World War II.

Holy Alliance Alliance of Russia, Austria, and Prussia to safeguard the principles of Christianity and maintain the international status quo after the Napoleonic Wars.

Homeopathy (home-ee-áh-pa-thee) Medical treatment emphasizing the use of herbal drugs and natural remedies.

Hoplites (hóp-lights) Ancient Greek infantrymen equipped with large round shields and long thrusting spears.

Hubris Excessive pride, which for the ancient Greeks brought punishment from the gods.

Huguenots (húgh-guh-nots) French Protestants of the sixteenth, seventeenth, and eighteenth centuries.

Humanists Students of an intellectual movement based on a deep study of classical culture and an emphasis on the humanities (literature, history, and philosophy) as a means for self-improvement.

Hundred Years' War A series of wars between England and France from 1337 to 1453. France won and England lost its lands in France, thus centralizing and solidifying French power.

I

Icon (éye-con) A sacred image of Jesus, Mary, or the saints that early Christians believed contained religious power.

Iconoclasm (eye-cónn-o-claz-um) A term literally meaning "icon breaking" that refers to an eighth-century religious controversy in Byzantium that argued that people should not venerate icons.

Ideogram (eye-dée-o-gram) A hieroglyph symbol expressing an abstract idea associated with the object it portrays.

Ideograph A written symbol that represents an idea instead of expressing the sound of a word.

Ideology (eye-dee-áh-lo-gee) A set of beliefs about the world and how it should be, often formalized into a political, social, or cultural theory.

Imam Muslim spiritual leader, believed by Shi'ites to be a spiritual descendant of Muhammad who should also be a temporal leader.

Imperialism The policy of extending a nation's authority by territorial acquisition or by the establishment of economic and political control over other nations or peoples.

Impressionism A nineteenth-century school of painting originating in France that emphasized capturing on canvas light as the eye sees it.

Indo-European Belonging to or constituting a family of languages that includes the Germanic, Celtic, Italic, Baltic, Slavic, Greek, Armenian, Iranian, and Indic groups.

Inductive reasoning Drawing general conclusions from particular concrete observations.

Indulgence A certificate issued by the papacy that gave people atonement for their sins and reduced their time in purgatory. Usually indulgences were issued for performing a pious act, but during the Reformation, critics accused the popes of selling indulgences to raise money.

Industrial revolution The rapid emergence of modern industrial production during the late eighteenth and nineteenth centuries.

Information revolution A rapid increase in the ability to store and manipulate information accompanying the development of computers during the second half of the twentieth century.

Inquisition A religious court established in the thirteenth century designed to root out heresy by questioning and torture.

Intendant (ann-tawn-dáunt) A French official sent by the royal government to assert the will of the monarch.

Internationalism The principle of cooperation among nations for their common good.

Ionia (eye-ówn-ee-uh) Ancient district in what is now Turkey that comprised the central portion of the west coast of Asia Minor, together with the adjacent islands.

Ionic order One of three architectural systems developed by the Greeks to decorate their buildings. The Ionic order may be recognized by its columns, which are taller and thinner than the Doric columns and capped with scroll-shaped capitals.

Iron Curtain The dividing line between Eastern and Western Europe during the Cold War.

Islamic fundamentalism A movement within Islam calling for a return to traditional ways and a rejection of alien ideologies that gained strength during the second half of the twentieth century.

J

Jacobins (jáck-o-bins) A radical political organization or club during the French Revolution.

Jacquerie (zhak-rée) The name given to the peasant revolt in France during the fourteenth century.

Jansenism A religious movement among French Catholics stressing the emotional experience of religious belief.

Jesuits (jéh-zu-it) Members of the Catholic religious order the Society of Jesus, founded by Ignatius Loyola in 1534.

Jihad (jée-hod) Islamic holy war in which believers feel they have the authority to fight to defend the faith.

Joint-stock company A business firm that is owned by stockholders who may sell or transfer their shares individually.

Journeyman A worker in a craft who has served his or her apprenticeship.

Joust A medieval contest in which two mounted knights combat with lances.

Junkers (yóong-kers) Prussian aristocracy.

Justification by faith The belief that faith alone—not good works—is needed for salvation. This belief lies at the heart of Protestantism.

K

Kamikaze (kah-mih-káh-zee) Usually refers to suicidal attacks on Allied ships by Japanese pilots during World War II.

Kore (kóh-ray) (pl. *korai*) Greek word for maiden that refers to an ancient Greek statue of a standing female, usually clothed.

Kouros (kóo-ross) (pl. *kouroi*) Greek word for a young man that refers to an ancient Greek statue of a standing nude young man.

Kristallnacht (kriss-táhl-nahkt) The "night of the broken glass"—a Nazi attack on German Jewish homes and businesses in 1938.

Kulak (kóo-lock) A relatively wealthy Russian peasant labeled by Stalin during the period of collectivization as a "class enemy."

Kulturkampf (kool-tóur-kahmpf) Bismarck's fight against the Catholic Church in Germany during the 1870s.

L

Laissez-faire (léss-say-fair) "Hands-off." An economic doctrine opposing governmental regulation of most economic affairs.

Laudanum (láud-a-numb) Opium dissolved in alcohol, used as a medicine in the eighteenth and nineteenth centuries.

League of Nations A post–World War I association of countries to deal with international tensions and conflicts.

Lebensraum (láy-benz-rowm) "Living space." Hitler's policy of expanding his empire to the east to gain more land for Germans.

Legume (lég-yoom) A pod, such as that of a pea or bean, used as food.

Levée en masse (le-váy awn máhss) General call-up of all men, women, and children to serve the nation during the French Revolution.

Levellers Revolutionaries who tried to "level" the social hierarchy during the English civil war.

Liberalism A nineteenth- and twentieth-century ideology supporting individualism, political freedom, constitutional government, and (in the nineteenth century) laissez-faire economic policies.

Liege (léezh) **lord** In the feudal system, a lord who has many vassals, but owes allegiance to no one.

Linear perspective An artistic technique used to represent three-dimensional space convincingly on a flat surface.

Lollards Followers of the English church reformer John Wycliffe who were found heretical.

Long March An arduous Chinese communist retreat from south China to north China in 1934 and 1935.

Luddism The smashing of machines that took jobs away from workers in the first half of the nineteenth century.

M

Ma'at (máh-aht) An Egyptian spiritual precept that conveyed the idea of truth and justice, or, as the Egyptians put it, right order and harmony.

Maccabean (mack-uh-bée-en) **Revolt** Successful Jewish revolt led by Judas Maccabeus in the mid-second century B.C.E. against Hellenistic Seleucid rulers.

Madrigal Musical composition set to a short poem usually about love, written for several voices. Common in Renaissance music.

Magi (máyj-eye) Ancient Persian astrologers or "wise men."

Maginot (máh-zhin-oh) **Line** A string of defensive fortresses on the French/German border that France began building in the late 1920s.

Magna Carta The Great Charter that English barons forced King John of England to sign in 1215 that guaranteed certain rights to the English people. Seen as one of the bases for constitutional law.

Marshall Plan A package of massive economic aid to European nations offered in 1947 to strengthen them and tie them to American influence.

Marxism A variety of socialism propounded by Karl Marx stressing economic determinism and class struggle—"scientific socialism."

Megalith An archaeological term for a stone of great size used in ancient monuments.

Meiji (máy-jee) **Restoration** The reorganizing of Japanese society along modern Western lines; initiated in 1868.

Mendicant orders Members of a religious order, such as the Dominicans or Franciscans, who wandered from city to city begging for alms rather than residing in a monastery.

Mercantilism (mírr-kan-till-ism) Early modern governmental economic policies seeking to control and develop the national economy and bring wealth into the national treasury.

Mercator projection (mer-káy-ter) A method of making maps in which the earth's surface is shown as a rectangle with Europe at the center, causing distortion toward the poles.

Mesolithic Of or pertaining to the period of human culture from about 15,000 years ago to about 7000 B.C.E. characterized by complex stone tools and greater social organization. "Middle Stone Age."

Methodism A Protestant sect founded in the eighteenth century that emphasized piety and emotional worship.

Metics (métt-iks) Foreign residents of Athens.

Miasma (my-ázz-ma) Fumes from waste and marshes blamed for carrying diseases during the eighteenth and the first half of the nineteenth centuries.

Middle Passage The long sea voyage between the African coast and the Americas endured by newly captured slaves.

Minoan (mínn-oh-an) A civilization that lived on the island of Crete from 2800 to 1450 B.C.E.

Mir (mere) Russian village commune.

Missi dominici (mée-see do-min-ée-kee) Royal officials under Charlemagne who traveled around the country to enforce the king's laws.

Mithraism (míth-ra-ism) A Hellenistic mystery religion that appealed to soldiers and involved the worship of the god Mithra.

Mughals (móe-gulls) Islamic rulers of much of India in the sixteenth, seventeenth, and eighteenth centuries.

Munich Conference The 1938 conference where Britain and France attempted to appease Hitler by allowing him to dismantle Czechoslovakia.

Mycenean (my-sen-ée-an) A civilization on the Greek peninsula that reached its high point between 1400 and 1200 B.C.E.

Mystery religions Ancient religions that encouraged believers to cultivate a deep connection with their deity. Initiates swore not to reveal the insights they had gained during rites and ceremonies; the shroud of secrecy resulted in the name "mystery" religions.

N

Napoleonic (na-po-lee-ón-ik) **Code** The legal code introduced in France by Napoleon Bonaparte.

Nationalism A nineteenth- and twentieth-century ideology stressing the importance of national identity and the nation-state.

Natural law Understandable, rational laws of nature that apply to the physical and human world.

Nazi Party Hitler's German National Socialist Party.

Neolithic (nee-oh-líth-ik) Of or denoting a period of human culture beginning around 7000 B.C.E. in the Middle East and later elsewhere, characterized by the invention of farming and the making of technically advanced stone implements. "New Stone Age."

Neoplatonism (nee-oh-pláy-ton-ism) Views based on the ideas of Plato that one should search beyond appearances for true knowledge; stressed abstract reasoning.

New Economic Policy (NEP) Lenin's compromise economic and social policy for the USSR during the 1920s.

New imperialism The second wave of Western imperialism, particularly between 1880 and 1914.

Night of August 4 Surrender of most privileges by the French aristocracy at a meeting held on August 1, 1789.

Nominalism (nóm-in-al-ism) A popular late medieval philosophy based on the doctrine that the universal, or general, has no objective existence or validity, being merely a name expressing the qualities of various objects resembling one another in certain respects. Also called New Nominalism.

North American Free Trade Agreement (NAFTA) The 1994 agreement between the United States, Mexico, and Canada to create a free trade zone.

North Atlantic Treaty Organization (NATO) A military alliance against the Soviet Union initiated in 1949.

Nuremberg Laws Hitler's anti-Jewish laws of 1935.

O

Ockham's razor A principle that states that between alternative explanations for the same phenomenon, the simplest is always to be preferred.

October Revolution The 1917 Bolshevik revolt and seizure of power in Russia.

Old Regime (re-zhéem) European society before the French Revolution.

Oligarchy (áh-luh-gar-kee) Rule by a small group or by a particular social class—often wealthy middle classes, as in ancient Greek or medieval European cities.

Operation Barbarossa (bar-bar-óh-ssa) The German invasion of the USSR during World War II.

Optimates (ahp-tuh-máht-ays) The nobility of the Roman Empire. Also refers to the political party that supported the nobility. Contrast with the *populares*.

Ordeal An ancient form of trial in which the accused was exposed to physical dangers that were presumed to be harmless if the accused was innocent. Ordeals might include grasping hot pokers, trial by battle, immersion in water, and other similar challenges.

Organization of Petroleum Exporting Countries (OPEC) An Arab-dominated organization of Middle Eastern oil-producing states that became effective during and after the 1970s.

Ostracism (áhs-tra-sism) A political technique of ancient Greece by which people believed to be threats to the city-state were chosen for exile by popular vote.

P

Paleolithic (pay-lee-oh-líth-ik) Of or pertaining to the period of human culture beginning with the earliest chipped stone tools, about 750,000 years ago, until the beginning of the Mesolithic, about 15,000 years ago. "Old Stone Age."

Pantheon (pán-thee-on) A great temple in Rome built in 27 B.C.E. and dedicated to all the gods. In 609 C.E., it was rededicated as a Christian church called Santa Maria Rotunda.

Paris Commune The revolutionary government of the city of Paris, first in the 1790s and then in 1871.

Parlement (parl-máwn) A French court of law during the Old Regime.

Parliament Britain's legislature, including the House of Commons and House of Lords.

Parthenon (párth-uh-non) A famous Doric temple of Athena on the Acropolis in ancient Athens.

Patricians The ancient Roman aristocracy who populated the Senate and were particularly powerful during the Republic.

Pax Romana ("pocks" or "packs" row-máhn-ah) Literally, "Roman Peace." Two hundred years of relative, internal peace within the Roman Empire beginning with the rule of Caesar Augustus.

Peace of Paris The 1919 peace settlement after World War I.

Peers Members of the House of Lords in England.

Perestroika (pair-ess-trói-ka) Gorbachev's policy of "restructuring" the Soviet economy during the 1980s.

Petrine (pée-tryn) **doctrine** The belief that the popes, bishops of Rome, should lead the church because they are the successors of Peter, who many claim was the first bishop of Rome.

Phalanstery (fa-láns-ter-ee) The model commune envisioned by the French utopian socialist Fourier.

Phalanx (fáy-langks) An ancient Greek formation of foot soldiers carrying overlapping shields and long spears.

Pharaoh The title of the rulers of ancient Egypt. Also refers to the household and administration of the rulers.

Pharisees (fáir-uh-sees) Members of an ancient Jewish sect that rigidly observed purity laws, including dietary rules. They also believed in the resurrection of the just and the existence of angels.

Philosophes (fee-low-zóff) Leading French intellectuals of the Enlightenment.

Phonogram A character or symbol used to represent a speech sound used in ancient writing.

Physiocrats (fízz-ee-oh-crats) Eighteenth-century French economic thinkers who stressed the importance of agriculture and favored free trade.

Pictogram A picture representing an idea used in ancient writing.

Pietism (píe-uh-tism) An eighteenth-century Protestant movement stressing an emotional commitment to religion.

Plebeians (pleb-ée-an) The members of the urban lower classes in ancient Rome.

Plebiscite (pléb-uh-sight) A direct vote that allows the people to either accept or reject a proposed measure.

Pogrom ('puh-grúhm'; also 'póe-grom') An organized persecution or massacre of Jews, especially in eastern Europe.

Polis (póe-liss) (pl. *poleis* [póe-lease]) An ancient Greek city-state.

Poor Laws Eighteenth- and nineteenth-century British laws enacted to deal with the poor.

Populares (pop-you-lahr-ays) In Roman history, the political party of the common people. Also refers to the people themselves. Contrast with the *optimates*.

Popular Front The political partnership of parties of the Left, particularly in France and Spain, during the 1930s.

positivism A mid-nineteenth-century theory of sociology holding that scientific investigation could discover useful fundamental truths about humans and their societies.

Postindustrial societies Late-twentieth-century societies that moved from manufacturing to services led by professionals, managers, and financiers.

Postmodernism A late-twentieth-century approach to the arts stressing relativism and multiple interpretations.

Pragmatic Sanction The international agreement secured by the Habsburg emperor in the 1730s to ensure that his daughter would succeed him without question.

Prague Spring The brief period of democratic reforms and cultural freedom in Czechoslovakia during 1968.

Predestination Doctrine claiming that since God is all-knowing and all-powerful, he must know in advance who is saved or damned. Therefore, the salvation of any individual is predetermined. This doctrine is emphasized by Calvinists.

Preemptive War War initiated by one side on the justification that another side was on the verge of attack.

Prefect Powerful agents of the central government stationed in France's departments.

Preventive war War initiated by one side on the justification that another side might attack sometime in the future.

Principate (prínce-a-pate) The governmental system of the Roman Empire founded by Octavian (also known as Caesar Augustus).

Privateer An armed private vessel commissioned by a government to attack enemy ships.

Protestant Of or pertaining to any branch of the Christian church excluding Roman Catholicism and Eastern Orthodox.

Psychoanalysis Pioneered by Sigmund Freud, a method of investigating human psychological development and treating emotional disorders.

Ptolemaic (ptah-luh-máy-ik) **system** The traditional medieval earth-centered universe and system of planetary movements.

Ptolemies (ptáh-luh-meez) Hellenistic dynasty that ruled in Egypt from about 300 B.C.E. to about 30 B.C.E.

Purgatory In Roman Catholic theology, a state or place in which those who have died in the grace of God expiate their sins by suffering before they can enter heaven.

Purge Expelling or executing political party members suspected of inefficiency or opposition to party policy.

Puritans In the sixteenth and seventeenth centuries, those who wanted to reform the Church of England by removing all elaborate ceremonies and forms. Many Puritans faced persecution and were forced to flee to the American colonies.

Q

Quadrant An instrument for taking altitude of heavenly bodies.

Quadrivium (quad-rív-ee-um) The medieval school curriculum that studied arithmetic, music, geometry, and astronomy after completion of the trivium.

Quadruple (quad-róo-pull) **Alliance** Alliance of Austria, Prussia, Russia, and France in the years after the Napoleonic Wars to maintain the status quo.

Quietism (quíet-ism) A movement among seventeenth-century Spanish Catholics that emphasized the emotional experience of religious belief.

Qur'an (also Koran) The Muslim holy book recorded in the early seventh century by the prophet Muhammad.

R

Racism Belief that racial differences are important and that some races are superior to others.

Raison d'état (ráy-zawn day-táh) "Reason of state." An eighteenth- and nineteenth-century principle justifying arbitrary or aggressive international behavior.

Rationalism The belief that, through reason, humans can understand the world and solve problems.

Realism A medieval Platonist philosophy that believed that the individual objects we perceive are not real, but merely reflections of universal ideas existing in the mind of God. In the nineteenth century, this referred to a cultural style rejecting romanticism and attempting to examine society as it is.

Realpolitik (ray-áhl-po-lee-teek) The pragmatic politics of power; often a self-interested foreign policy associated with Bismarck.

Redshirts Garibaldi's troops used in the unification of Italy.

Reform Bill of 1832 English electoral reform extending the vote to the middle classes of the new industrial cities.

Reichstag (ríkes-tahg) German legislative assembly.

Reign of Terror The violent period of the French Revolution between 1792 and 1794.

Relativity Einstein's theory that all aspects of the physical universe must be defined in relative terms.

Relics In the Roman Catholic and Greek Orthodox churches, valued remnants of saints or other religious figures. Relics usually are parts of bodies but may also include objects that had touched sacred bodies or that were associated with Jesus or Mary, such as remnants of the True Cross.

Renaissance Literally, "rebirth." The term was coined in Italy in the early fourteenth century to refer to the rebirth of the appreciation of classical (Greek and Roman) literature and values. It also refers to the culture that was born in Italy during that century that ultimately spread throughout Europe.

Resistance movements Underground opposition to occupation forces, especially to German troops in conquered European countries during World War II.

Restoration The conservative regimes in power after the defeat of Napoleon in 1815 that hoped to hold back the forces of change or even turn back the clock to prerevolutionary days.

Risorgimento (ree-sor-jee-mén-toe) A nineteenth-century Italian unification movement.

Rococo (roe-coe-cóe) A style of art developed from the baroque that originated in France during the eighteenth century that emphasized elaborate designs to produce a delicate effect.

Romanesque (Roman-ésk) A style of architecture usually associated with churches built in the eleventh and twelfth centuries and that was inspired by Roman architectural features. Romanesque buildings were massive, with round arches, barrel vaulted ceilings, and dark interiors.

Romanticism A cultural ideology during the first half of the nineteenth century stressing feeling over reason.

Rosetta Stone A tablet of black basalt found in 1799 at Rosetta, Egypt, that contains parallel inscriptions in Greek, ancient Egyptian demotic script, and hieroglyphic characters. The stone provided the key to deciphering ancient Egyptian writing.

Rostra The speaker's platform in the Forum of ancient Rome.

Roundheads Members or supporters of the Parliamentary or Puritan party in England during the English civil war (1642).

Royal absolutism The seventeenth- and eighteenth-century system of elevated royal authority.

S

Sacraments In Christianity, rites that were to bring the individual grace or closeness to God. In Roman Catholicism and Greek Orthodoxy there are seven sacraments: baptism, confirmation, the Eucharist, penance, extreme unction, holy orders, and matrimony. Protestants in general acknowledge only two sacraments: baptism and the Lord's Supper.

Sadducees (sád-juh-sees) Members of an ancient Jewish sect that emphasized worship at the Temple in Jerusalem. They rejected new ideas such as resurrection, insisting on only those ideas that could be found in the Torah.

Saga A medieval Scandinavian story of battles, customs, and legends, narrated in prose and generally telling the traditional history of an important Norse family.

Salon (suh-láhn) Seventeenth- and eighteenth-century social and cultural gatherings of members of the upper and middle classes.

Sans-culottes (sawn-key-lóht) Working-class people of Paris during the French Revolution.

Sarcophagus (sar-kóff-a-gus) A stone coffin.

Satellite states Eastern European states under the control of the Soviet Union during the Cold War.

Satrap (sát-trap) An ancient Persian governor in charge of provinces called "satrapies."

Schlieffen (shléaf-en) **Plan** German military strategy in World War I that called for a holding action against Russia while German forces moved through Belgium to knock out France.

Scholasticism The dominant medieval philosophical and theological movement that applied logic from Aristotle to help understand God's plan. It also refers to the desire to join faith with reason.

Scientific Revolution The new sixteenth- and seventeenth-century methods of investigation and discoveries about nature based on observation and reason rather than tradition and authority.

Scutage (skyóot-ij) Medieval payment in lieu of military service.

Seleucids (se-lóo-sids) Hellenistic dynasty that ruled in Asia from about 300 B.C.E. to about 64 B.C.E.

Semitic (sem-ít-ik) Of or pertaining to any of a group of Caucasoid peoples, chiefly Jews and Arabs, of the eastern Mediterranean area.

Senate, Roman The deliberative body and influential governing council of Rome during the Republic and Empire. Composed of ex-magistrates with lifetime membership, the Senate did not legislate, but conducted foreign policy and warfare and authorized public expenditures.

Septuagint (sep-tu-eh-jint) A Greek translation of the Hebrew scriptures (the Old Testament), so named because it was said to be the work of 72 Palestinian Jews in the third century B.C.E., who completed the work in seventy days.

Serfs Medieval peasants who were personally free, but bound to the land. They owed labor obligations as well as fees.

Shi'ite (shée-ite) **Muslims** Those who accepted only the descendants of 'Ali, Muhammad's son-in-law, as the true rulers. It was not the majority party in Islam but did prevail in some of the Muslim countries.

Shire An English county.

Sinn Fein (shín féign) "Ourselves Alone." An extremist twentieth-century Irish nationalist organization.

Skepticism (skép-ti-cism) The systematic doubting of accepted authorities—especially religious authorities.

Second Reich (rike) German regime founded in 1871 and lasting until the end of World War I.

Sepoy (sée-poy) **Mutiny** The 1857 uprising of Indians against British rule.

Social Darwinism The effort to apply Darwin's biological ideas to social ideas stressing competition and "survival of the fittest."

Socialists Those promoting or practicing the nineteenth- and twentieth-century ideology of socialism, stressing cooperation, community, and public ownership of the means of production.

Socratic method The method of arriving at truth by questioning and disputation.

Solidarity A Polish noncommunist union that became the core of resistance to the communist regime during the 1980s.

Sophists (sóff-ists) Fifth-century B.C.E. Greek philosophers who were condemned for using tricky logic to prove that all things are relative and success alone is important.

Sovereignty (sóv-rin-tee) The source of authority exercised by a state; complete independence and self-government.

Soviet A workers' council during the 1905 and 1917 Russian revolutions and part of the structure of government in the Soviet Union.

SS The Schutzstaffel, Hitler's elite party troops of the 1930s and 1940s.

Stadholder (stáhd-holder) A governor of provinces in the Dutch United Provinces.

Statutory law Laws established by a king or legislative body. Contrast with common law.

Stoicism (stów-i-cism) A Hellenistic philosophy that advocated detachment from the material world and an indifference to pain.

Strategoi (stra-táy-goy) Generals in ancient Athens who eventually took a great deal of political power.

Struggle of the Orders The political strife between patrician and plebeian Romans beginning in the fifth century B.C.E. The plebeians gradually won political rights as a result of the struggle.

Sturm und drang (shtúrm unt dráhng) "Storm and stress." A literary movement in late eighteenth-century Germany.

Sumptuary (súmp-chew-air-ee) **laws** Laws restricting or regulating extravagance (for example, in food or dress), often used to maintain separation of social classes.

Sunna (sóon-a) A collection of sayings and traditions of the prophet Muhammad that delineates the customs adhered to by Muslims.

Supply and demand Adam Smith's liberal economic doctrine that demand for goods and services will stimulate production (supply) in a free-market system.

Surrealism (sur-rée-a-lism) A twentieth-century literary and artistic style stressing images from the unconscious mind.

Symphony A long sonata for orchestra.

Syncretism (sín-cre-tism) The attempt or tendency to combine or reconcile differing beliefs, as in philosophy or religion.

Syndicalism (sín-di-cal-ism) A late-nineteenth-century anarchist ideology envisioning labor unions as the center of a free and just society.

T

Taliban The strict, fundamentalist Islamic regime that ruled most of Afghanistan from 1996 to 2001.

Tennis Court Oath Oath taken by members of the French Estates General not to dissolve until they had created a constitution for France.

Tetradrachma (tet-ra-drák-ma) Hellenistic coin worth four drachmas.

Tetrarchy (tét-rar-key) The governmental system of the Roman Empire founded by Diocletian that divided the empire into four administrative units.

Theocracy (thee-áh-kruh-see) Government by priests claiming to rule by divine authority.

Theme A division for the purpose of provincial administration in the Byzantine Empire.

Thermidorian (ther-mi-dór-ee-an) **Reaction** The overthrow of Robespierre and the radicals in July 1794, during the French Revolution.

Third Estate Commoners, or all people except the nobility and clergy, in early modern European society.

Third French Republic The republican government established in 1871 and lasting until Germany's defeat of France in 1940.

Torah (tór-uh) The first five books of the Jewish sacred scriptures, comprising Genesis, Exodus, Leviticus, Numbers, and Deuteronomy.

Tories A conservative British political party during the eighteenth and nineteenth centuries.

Totalitarianism A twentieth-century form of authoritarian government using force, technology, and bureaucracy to effect rule by a single party and controlling most aspects of the lives of the population.

Total war A form of warfare in which all the forces and segments of society are mobilized for a long, all-out struggle.

Transubstantiation (trán-sub-stan-chee-áy-shun) In the Roman Catholic and Greek Orthodox churches, the belief that the bread and wine of the Eucharist were transformed into the actual body and blood of Christ.

Trench warfare An almost stagnant form of defensive warfare fought from trenches.

Triangular trade Trade pattern between European nations and their colonies by which European manufactured goods were traded for raw materials (such as agricultural products) from the Americas or slaves from Africa.

Tribune An official of ancient Rome chosen by the common people to protect their rights.

Triple Alliance Alliance of Germany, Austria-Hungary, and Italy in the years before World War I.

Triumvirate (try-úm-vir-ate) A group of three men sharing civil authority, as in ancient Rome.

Trivium (trív-ee-um) The basic medieval curriculum that studied grammar, rhetoric, and logic; after completion, students could proceed to the quadrivium.

Troubadour (tróo-buh-door) Poets from the late twelfth and early thirteenth centuries who wrote love poems, meant to be sung to music, that reflected the new sensibility of courtly love, which claimed that lovers were ennobled.

Truman Doctrine U.S. policy initiated in 1947 that offered military and economic aid to countries threatened by a communist takeover with the intention of creating a military ring of containment around the Soviet Union and its satellite states.

Tsar The emperor of Russia.

Twelve Tables According to ancient Roman tradition, popular pressure in the fifth century B.C.E. led to the writing down of traditional laws to put an end to patrician monopoly of the laws. The resulting compilation—the Twelve Tables—was seen as the starting point for the tradition of Roman law.

U

Ultra-royalism The nineteenth-century belief in rule by a monarch and that everything about the French Revolution and Enlightenment was contrary to religion, order, and civilization.

Unconscious According to Freud, that part of the mind of which we are not aware; home of basic drives.

Unilateralism Actions or policies taken by one nation in its own interests regardless of the views and interests of its allies.

United Nations (UN) An international organization founded in 1945 to promote peace and cooperation.

Universal A metaphysical entity that does not change, but that describes particular things on earth—for example, "justice" or "beauty." Explained by the ancient Greeks and examined by subsequent philosophers. (Also called "forms" or "ideas.")

Utilitarianism (you-till-a-táre-ee-an-ism) A nineteenth-century liberal philosophy that evaluated institutions on the basis of social usefulness to achieve "the greatest happiness of the greatest number."

Utopian (you-tópe-ee-an) **socialism** A form of early nineteenth-century socialism urging cooperation and communes rather than competition and individualism.

V

Vassal In the feudal system, a noble who binds himself to his lord in return for maintenance.

Versailles (ver-sígh) **treaty** Peace treaty between the Allies and Germany following World War I.

Victorian Referring to the period of Queen Victoria's reign in Britain, 1837–1901.

Vulgate (vúll-gate) A version of the Latin Bible, primarily translated from Hebrew and Greek by Jerome.

W

Wahhabism (wuh-háh-biz-uhm) An Islamic reform movement founded in the eighteenth century that stressed a strict, literal interpretation of the Qur'an.

War guilt clause Article 231 of the Treaty of Versailles that places all blame on Germany for causing World War I.

Warsaw Pact A military alliance in Eastern Europe controlled by the Soviet Union and initiated in 1955.

Waterloo Site in Belgium of a decisive defeat of Napoleon in 1815.

Weimar (wy'e-mar) **Republic** The liberal German government established at the end of World War I and destroyed by Hitler in the 1930s.

Welfare state Governmental programs to protect citizens from severe economic hardships and to provide basic social needs.

Wergeld (véhr-gelt) In Germanic law, the relative price of individuals that established the fee for compensation in case of injury.

Whigs A British political party during the eighteenth and nineteenth centuries.

Witan The ancient Anglo-Saxon men who participated in the Witenagemot.

Witenagemot (wí-ten-uh-guh-mote) Ancient Anglo-Saxon assembly of nobles.

Z

Zealots (zéll-ets) An ancient Jewish sect arising in Palestine in about 6 C.E. that militantly opposed Roman rule and desired to establish an independent Jewish state. The sect was wiped out when the Romans destroyed Jerusalem in 70 C.E.

Zemstva (zémst-fah) Municipal councils established in Russia in the second half of the nineteenth century.

Ziggurat (zíg-gur-raht) A pyramid-shaped Mesopotamian temple.

Zionism A late-nineteenth- and twentieth-century Jewish nationalist movement to create an independent state for Jews in Palestine.

Zollverein (tsóll-ver-rhine) Nineteenth-century German customs union headed by Prussia.

Zoroastrianism (zorro-áss-tree-an-ism) An ancient Persian religion that had a belief in two gods: a god of light named Ahura Mazda and an evil god named Ahriman.

PHOTOS

Erich Lessing/Art Resource, NY; p. 532T: The Granger Collection; p. 536: Erich Lessing/Art Resource, NY; p. 539: The Granger Collection; p. 541: Erich Lessing/Art Resource, NY.

Chapter 17

p. 546: Lady Lever Art Gallery, National Museums Liverpool/Bridgeman Art Library; p. 549: The Royal Collection © 2003, Her Majesty Queen Elizabeth II; p. 553: Science Museum, London, UK/Bridgeman Art Library; p. 554: Musée des arts et métiers—CNAM, Paris/Photo: P. Faligot, Seventh Square; p. 556: New Walk Museum, Leicester City Museum Service, UK/Bridgeman Art Library; p. 557: Guildhall Library, Corporation of London, UK/Bridgeman Art Library; p. 561: General Research Division/Print Collection/Science, Industry & Business Library. New York Public Library/Art Resource; p. 563: Trade Union Congress, London, UK/Bridgeman Art Library; p. 566: The New York Public Library/Art Resource, NY; p. 568: Naudet, Caroline. *Voyage Et Conduite D'Un Moribund Pour L'autre Monde.* 1988-102-116. Philadelphia Museum of Art: The William H. Helfand Collection, 1988; p. 570: *Merrymakers*, 1870. Carolus-Duran. Founders Society Purchase, Acc. # 80.37. Robert H. Tannahill Foundation Fund. Photograph © 1989 The Detroit Institute of Arts/Bridgeman Art Library; p. 573: Courtesy of Cadbury Ltd.

Chapter 18

p. 576: Erich Lessing/Art Resource, NY; p. 579: AKG Images, London; p. 585: The British Library/HIP/Art Resource; p. 588: Bildarchiv Preussischer Kulturbesitz/Art Resource, NY; p. 589B: Bildarchiv Preussischer Kulturbesitz/Art Resource, NY; p. 589T: Yale Center for British Art, Paul Mellon Collection, USA/Bridgeman Art Library; p. 593: The Granger Collection; p. 594: Musée des Beaux-Arts, Bordeaux, France/Bridgeman-Giraudon/Art Resource, NY; p. 595: Chateaux de Versailles et de Trianon, Versailles, France/Bridgeman-Giraudon/Art Resource, NY; p. 599: Musée du Petit Palais, Paris, France/Bridgeman-Giraudon/Art Resource, NY; p. 603: The Louvre Museum, Paris, France/Bridgeman-Giraudon/Art Resource, NY; p. 604: Hamburger Kunsthalle, Hamburg, Germany/Bridgeman Art Library.

Chapter 19

p. 608: Bildarchiv Preussischer Kulturbesitz/Art Resource, NY; p. 613: Culver Pictures, Inc.; p. 617: Bildarchiv Preussischer Kulturbesitz/Art Resource; p. 618B: The Bridgeman Art Library; p. 618T: Image copyright © The Metropolitan Museum of Art/Art Resource, NY; p. 621: Staedtische Kunsthalle, Mannheim, Germany/Erich Lessing/Art Resource, NY; p. 623: National Army Museum, London/The Bridgeman Art Library; p. 624L: The Granger Collection; p. 624R: Sovfoto.

Chapter 20

p. 628: Bildarchiv Preussischer Kulturbesitz/Art Resource, NY; p. 631: Private Collection/Photo © Christie's Images/Bridgeman Art Library; p. 632: Eugene Appert/Hulton/Getty Images; p. 634: Musée d'Orsay, Paris, France/Erich Lessing/Art Resource, NY; p. 636: Branger/Roger Viollet/Getty Images; p. 638: Gift of the Estate of Rose Mintz. The Jewish Museum, New York, NY, USA. Photo by Richard Goodbody, Inc./Art Resource, NY; p. 640: Culver Pictures, Inc.; p. 641: Royal Museum of Fine Arts, Antwerp. Image courtesy of Reproductiefonds Vlaamse Musea NV/Lukas Art in Flanders; p. 643: Mary Evans Picture Library; p. 651: Hulton/Archive/Getty Images; p. 654: Marine Corps Historical Society; p. 655: Keystone-Mast Collection (14757)/California Museum of Photography, University of California at Riverside.

Chapter 21

p. 658: Harrogate Museums and Art Gallery, North Yorkshire, UK/Bridgeman Art Library; p. 660: ullstein bild/The Granger Collection; p. 662: Tallandier; p. 665: Archives Charmet/The Bridgeman Art Library; p. 667B: Archives Charmet/The Bridgeman Art Library; p. 667T: Cadbury Ltd; p. 668: Frederic, Leon (1856–1940) © ARS, NY. *The Ages of the Worker*, triptych. Oil on canvas, 1895–97. Musee d'Orsay, Paris, France Musée d'Orsay/Reunion des Musées Nationaux/Art Resource, NY; p. 670: Magyar Nemzeti Gallery Budapest/Gianni Dagli Orti/The Art Archive; p. 673: Musée d'Orsay, Paris, France/Réunion des Musées Nationaux/Erich Lessing/Art Resource, NY; p. 675: Public Domain; p. 676: The Granger Collection, NY; p. 679: Allgemeines Krankenhaus (General Hospital), Vienna, Austria/Erich Lessing/Art Resource, NY; p. 680: Bildarchiv Preussischer Kulturbesitz/Art Resource, NY; p. 681: Musée d'Orsay, Paris, France/Réunion des Musées Nationaux/Erich Lessing/Art Resource, NY; p. 683: National Gallery of Art, Washington/The Art Archive; p. 685B: Munch, Edvard (1863–1944) *The Scream*. 1893 (Tempera and pastels on cardboard, 91 × 73.5 cm.) © Copyright ARS, NY. National Gallery, Oslo, Norway. Erich Lessing/Art Resource, NY; p. 685T: *Christ's Triumphant Entry into Brussels*, 1888 (oil on canvas), Ensor, James (1860–1949)/J. Paul Getty Museum, Los Angeles, USA. © ARS, NY. © DACS/Lauros/Giraudon/© 2010. ARS, NY/SABAM, Brussels/The Bridgeman Art Library.

Chapter 22

p. 690: Dix, Otto (1891–1969) *The War.* Triptych, oil on wood, 1929–32. © 2010. ARS, NY/VG Bild-Kunst, Bonn. Staatliche Kunstsammlungen, Dresden, Germany. Erich Lessing/Art Resource, NY; p. 695: Meidner, Ludwig (1884–1966) *Apocalyptic Landscape*, 1913. Painting, Oil on canvas, 37 1/2 × 31 5/8 in. (95.25 × 80.33 cm). Gift of Clifford Odets (60.65.1b). Los Angeles County Museum of Art, Los Angeles, CA. © Ludwig Meidner-Archiv, Jüdisches Museum der Stadt Frankfurt am Main. Digital Image © 2009 Museum Associates/LACMA/Art Resource, NY; p. 696: Corbis; p. 699: Roger Viollet/Getty Images; p. 700: Mary Evans/Robert Hunt Collection/The Image Works; p. 701: Imperial War Museum, London; p. 703: Imperial War Museum, London; p. 704: Mary Evans Picture Library; p. 707: Memorial depicting the artist and her husband mourning their dead son, Peter Kollwitz, dedicated in 1931 (stone), Kollwitz, Kathe Schmidt (1867–1945)/Vladslo German Military Cemetery, Vladslo, Ypres, Belgium © 2010. ARS, NY/VG Bild-Kunst, Bonn. © Paul Maeyaert/© 2010. ARS, NY./VG Bild-Kunst, Bonn./The Bridgeman Art Library; p. 708: Bettmann/Corbis; p. 713: Scala/White Images/Art Resource, NY; p. 714: Sovfoto; p. 716: © DACS/Archives Charmet/The Bridgeman Art Library.

Chapter 23

p. 720: *Pillars of Society*. 1926. Grosz, George (1893–1959) Oil on canvas, 200,0 × 108,0 cm. © Estate of George Grosz/Licensed by VAGA, New York, NY. Stuetzen der Gesellschaft. Inv.: NG 4/58. Photo: Joerg P. Anders. Nationalgalerie, Staatliche Museen zu Berlin, Berlin, Germany. Bildarchiv Preussischer Kulturbesitz/Art Resource, NY. © Estate of George Grosz/Licensed by VAGA, New York, NY; p. 724: AKG Images, London; p. 726: Dix, Otto (1891–1969) © 2010. ARS, NY/VG Bild-Kunst, *Bonn. Grosstadt—Big town*, tryptich, left wing. 1927/28, wood, distemper 181 × 101 cm. Inv. 0-1890. Kunstmuseum, Stuttgart, Germany. Erich Lessing/Art Resource, NY; p. 727: UFA/The Kobal Collection; p. 728: Michael Nicholson/Corbis; p. 729: Mansell/Time Life Pictures/Getty Images; p. 731: AP Images; p. 734: Fotomas/Bridgeman Art Library; p. 736: RUSU 2225, Poster Collection, Hoover Institution Archives; p. 737: Isaac Soyer, *Employment Agency*, 1937. Oil on canvas. 34 1/4 × 45 in. (87 × 114.3 cm.) Whitney Museum of American Art, New York; purchase. 37.44; p. 741: Heinrich Hoffmann/Timepix/Time Life Pictures/Getty Images; p. 742: Nussbaum, Felix (1904–1944) *Self-portrait with Jewish Identity Card.* 1943. Oil on canvas, 56 × 49 cm. © 2010. ARS, NY/VG Bild-Kunst, Bonn. Bildarchiv Preussischer Kulturbesitz/Art Resource, NY.

Chapter 24

p. 746: Strempel, Horst (1904–1975) © 2010. ARS, NY/VG Bild-Kunst, Bonn. *Night Over Germany*. 1945. Oil on canvas. Inv. A III 257. Photo: Joerg P. Anders. Nationalgalerie, Staatliche Museen, Berlin, Germany. Bildarchiv Preussischer Kulturbesitz/Art Resource, NY; p. 750: Picasso, Pablo (1881–1973) *Guernica*. 1937. © ARS, NY. Oil on canvas, 350 × 782 cm. Museo Nacional Centro de Arte Reina Sofia,

Madrid, Spain. John Bigelow Taylor/Art Resource, NY; p. 753: Bettmann/Corbis; p. 754: Imperial War Museum, London. IWM ART LD 2750; p. 759: AP Images; p. 762: Bettmann/Corbis; p. 764: Archive Photos/Hulton Archive/Getty Images; p. 765: Imperial War Museum/The Art Archive; p. 766: Canadian War Museum, Ottawa, Canada/Bridgeman Art Library; p. 768: Archives Charmet/The Bridgeman Art Library; p. 772–773: KATIA CHRISTODOULOU/Corbis; p. 773: NASA/Corbis.

Chapter 25

p. 774: Don Eddy (American, b.1944). *New Shoes for H*, 1973–74. Acrylic on canvas; 111.7 × 121.9 cm. © The Cleveland Museum of Art, Purchased with a grant from the National Endowment for the Arts and matched by gifts from members of The Cleveland Society for Contemporary Art, 1974.53.; p. 781: © DACS/Roger Perrin/The Bridgeman Art Library; p. 784L: Museum Ludwig/Rheinisches Bildarchiv; p. 784R: Goksin Sipahiouglu/Sipa Press; p. 786: Bettmann/Corbis; p. 787: Joseph Koudelka/Magnum Photos; p. 797B: © 2003 Andy Warhol Foundation for the Visual Arts/ARS, NY/TM Licensed by Campbell's Soup Co. All rights reserved. Albright-Knox Art Gallery, Buffalo, New York, Gift of Seymour H. Knox, Jr., 1963/Art Resource, NY; p. 797T: Pollock, Jackson (1912–1956) © ARS, NY.*Convergence*. 1952. Oil on canvas, framed: 95 1/4 × 157 1/8 × 2 7/8" (241.935 × 399.0975 × 7.3025); support: 93 1/2 × 155" (237.49 x 393.7 cm.). Gift of Seymour H. Knox, Jr., 1956. Albright-Knox Art Gallery, Buffalo, New York. Albright-Knox Art Gallery/Art Resource, NY; p. 800: Georges Pierre/Corbis SYGMA; p. 801: Gianni Giansanti/Sygma/Corbis; p. 805: Lambert Studios/Hulton Archive/Archive Photos/Getty Images; p. 806: NASA.

Chapter 26

p. 810: Ryan Pyle/Corbis; p. 812: © Régis Bossu/Corbis Sygma; p. 815: Musee d'Histoire Contemporaine, BCIC, Universite de Paris, France; p. 817: Peter Turnley/Corbis; p. 823: Antoine Gyori/Sygma/Corbis; p. 826: China Photos/Getty Images; p. 830: Jehad Nga/Corbis; p. 832: Kenneth Garrett/National Geographic Image Collection/Getty Images; p. 834: Marco Ventura; p. 837B: Bruce F. Molnia/USGS; p. 837T: William O. Field; p. 838: Courtesy of the National Library of Medicine; p. 839: Jennifer Bartlett. *Spiral: An Ordinary Evening in New Haven*, 1989. Painting: oil on canvas, tables: painted wood and steel, cones: break formed hot rolled welded steel painting: 108" × 192", tables: 30" × 32"× 35", 39"× 41" × 35" cones: 20" × 30 " × 21", © J. Bartlett. Private Collection, Greenwich, CT. Courtesy of the Paula Cooper Gallery, NY; p. 840: Valerio Mezzanotti/The New York Times/Redux.

TEXT CREDITS

Chapter 1

From the Revised Standard Version of the Bible, copyright © 1946, 1952, and 1971 the National Council of the Churches of Christ in the USA. Used by permission. All rights reserved.

From THE HISTORIES by Herodotus, translated by Aubrey de Selincourt, revised with introductory matter and notes by John Marincola (Penguin Classics 1954, Second revised edition 1996). Translation copyright 1954 by Aubrey de Selincourt. This revised edition copyright © John Marincola, 1996. Used by permission of Peguin Group UK.

Chapter 2

Excerpt from OEDIPUS REX OF SOPHOCLES: AN ENGLISH VERSION by Dudley Fitts and Robert Fitzgerald, copyright 1949 by Harcourt, Inc., and reviewed 1977 by Cornelia Fitts and Robert Fitzgerald, reprinted by permission of the publisher.

Reprinted by permission of the publishers and the Trustees of the Loeb Classical Library from DIODORUS SICULUS: LIBRARY OF HISTORY, VOLUME IX, BOOKS XVIII-XIX.65, translated by Russel M. Greer, Cambridge, Mass.: Harvard University Press, Copyright © 1947 by the President and Fellows of Harvard College. The Loeb Classical Library® is a registered trademark of the President and Fellows of Harvard College.

Chapter 5

Naphtali Lewis and Meyer Reinhold, Roman Civilization: Sourcebook II: The Empire. Reprinted by permission of Columbia University Press.

Aurelius Victor, Lives of the Emperors, in Naphtali Lewis and Meyer Reinhold, Roman Civilization: Sourcebook II: The Empire. Reprinted by permission of Columbia University Press.

Chapter 6

Islam: From the Prophet Muhammad to the Capture of Constantinople, Volume 2: Religion and Society. Ed. Bernard Lewis, NY: Oxford University Press, 1987. Used by permission of Oxford University Press.

Chapter 8

Guibert de Nogent. The Autobiography of Guibert, Abbot of Nogent-Sous-Coucy. Translated by C.C. Swinton Bland (London: George Routledge & Sons, Ltd. And E.P. Dutton & Co., New York, 1926), p. 32.

Chapter 11

Used by permission of Elisabeth M. Wengler. From VAN VOORST. Readings in Christianity, 1E. © 1997 Wadsworth, a part of Cengage

Learning, Inc. Reproduced by permission. www.cengage.com/permissions.

Chapter 13

J.B. Bossuet, Politics Drawn from the Very Words of Holy Scritpure, 1709 in Brian Tierney and Joan Scott, Western Societies: A Documentary History, Vol II, McGraw-Hill, 1984, pp. 11–13. Used by permission of The McGraw-Hill Companies, Inc.

Chapter 14

Jean Antoine Nicholas Caritat Marquis de Condorcet, Sketch for a Historical Picture on the Progress of the Human Mind, tr. June Barraclough, Weidenfeld and Nicolson (Orion Books), 1955, pp. 236–237, 244.

Chapter 22

Frank A. Golder, DOCUMENTS OF RUSSIAN HISTORY 1914–1917, Peter Smith Publisher, Inc., Goucester, MA 1964. Reprinted by permission of Peter Smith Publisher, Inc.

"Does It Matter", from COLLECTED POEMS OF SIEGRRIED SASSOON by Siegfried Sassoon, copyright 1918, 1920 by E.P. Dutton. Copyright 1936, 1946, 1947, 1948 by Siegfried Sassoon. Used by permission of Viking Penguin, a division of Penguin Group (USA) Inc.; Copyright Siegfried Sassoon by kind permission of the Estate of George Sassoon.

Chapter 23

Adolf Hitler, The Speeches of Adolf Hitler, vol. 1, trans. and ed. by Norman Baynes, Oxford University Press, 1942, pp. 72–73.

Excerpt from page 123 from THE EDUCATION OF A TRUE BELIEVER by LEV KOPELEV and TRANSLAGED BY GARY KERN. English translation copyright © 1980 by Harper & Row, Publishers, Inc. Reprinted by permission of HarperCollins Publishers.

Chapter 24

Reproduced by permission of The United States Holocaust Memorial Museum.

Reprinted, by permission, from Capt. Rikihei Inoguchi and Cdr. Tadashi Nakajima with Roger Pineau, The Divine Wind: Japan's Kamikaze Force in World War II (Annapolis, Md: Naval Institute Press, © 1958).

Chapter 25

Philip Toynbee, The Fearful Choice, Victor Gollancz, Ltd., 1956. Used by permission of Victor Gollancz, Ltd., a division of The Orion Publishing Group.

THE AMERICAN CHALLENGE by Jean Jacques Servan-Schreiber. English Translation copyright © 1968 by Atheneum House. Originally published in French as Le Defi Americain Copyright © 1967 by Editions Denoel. Reprinted by permission of Georges Borchardt, Inc., for Editions Denoel.

D

goats, 17
Gobineau, Comte de, 637
"God is dead,» 684
Godard, Jean-Luc, 796
Gods on the Parthenon, ca. 440 B.C.E., 64
Goebbels, Joseph, 740–742
Goethe, Johann Wolfgang von, 503, 584, 742
  Faust, 586
  The Sorrows of the Young Werther, 586
Gold Coast, 723
golden mean, 69, 150
Goldsmith, Oliver: "The Deserted Village," 562
Goliath, 329–330
Gompers, Samuel, 634
Gomulka, Wladyslaw, 786
Gorbachev, Mikhail, 813–814, 816–818
Gospel of Matthew, manuscript illustration from, ca. 700, 218
Gosplan, 734
Gothic architecture, 250–251, 251, 264, 586
Gouges, Olympe de: Declaration of the Rights of Women, 521, 529
Goya, Francisco de
  The Executions of the Third of May, 1808, 541
GPS. See global positioning system
Gracchi, Reforms of, 129–131
grain dole, 131
grain imports, to Soviet Union, 813
Granada, 264, 362
Grand Alliance, 425
Grand National Consolidated Trades Union, 563
grand tour, 505–507
Grands et Petits Voyages, 405
Grass, Günter, 797
Great Britain. See also Parliament of Great Britain
  Bill of Rights of, 442
  China and, 550
  colonies in Americas, 491–492
  colonies in India, 494–495, 723
  colonies in South Africa, 646, 793
  commercial vigor of, 549–550
  Commonwealth, 1649–1660, 439
  democracy in, 630–631
  dissolution of monastic communities in England, 358
  Egypt under control of, 646
  Empire of, 723
  England, eighteenth century, 551
  English Civil War, 1642–1649, 436–439, 437
  in Entente Cordiale, 692
  Hundred Years' War, 289–294, 291
  independence of India from, 791
  Industrial Revolution in, 546–558
  liberalism in, 630–631
  medieval England, tenth through fourteenth centuries, 263
  National Health Service of, 788
  in nineteenth century, 578–579, 593–594, 596–597
  overseas expansion of, 540
  Pax Britannica (Britain's peace), 650
  plague in, 441
  railroads in, 555–557
  Reform Bill of 1832, 596
  Renaissance in, 337–339
  Restoration, 1660–1688, 440–441
  taxes in, 635
  in Triple Entente, 692
  as United Kingdom, 594
  Victorian Britain, 666
  Wars of the Roses, 294, 338, 358
  welfare state in, 788
  Women's Suffrage Movement in, 1914, 640
  in World War I, 694–696, 698–706, 708–709
  in World War II, 747, 750–754, 761, 764, 766–768
Great Chain of Being, 416

Great Colonial Rivalry, 488–495
Great Continental Express, 556
Great Council, 261–262, 319
Great Depression, 736–739, 755, 757, 788, 834
"Great Hunger," 561
Great Lakes, 393
Great Leap Forward, 783
Great Mother, 158
"Great Patriotic War," 755
Great Purges, 736
Great Pyramid of Giza, 19, 174
Great Pyramid of Khufu, 19
"Great Reforms" of Alexander II, 623–624, 633
Great Schism, 1378–1417, 287–289, 288, 321, 360
"Great War." See World War I
"Greater East Asia Co-Prosperity Sphere," 755
Greater Serbia, 821
Greece. See also Hellenistic Age
  civil war in, 778
  Ottoman Empire and, 594–595
  war for independence, 594–595
  in World War II, 754
Greece, classical, 40–75, 43. See also Hellenistic Age
  Architectural Orders of, 62, 62
  bisexuality in, 54
  city-states of, 51–61
  classical age of, 479–336 B.C.E., 61–64
  colonies of, 500 B.C.E., 46–47, 47, 58
  conquest of by Rome (republic), 123
  Dark Ages of, 46, 48
  democracy in, 53–57, 60–62, 68–69, 71
  emotional life in, 54
  heroes of, 42–46, 95
  heroic values of, 46–51
  individualism in, 48, 71, 73
  key dates, 70
  literature of, 42, 46–48, 61, 64–65, 312
  mathematics of, 50–51
  medicine in, 70–71
  mercenary armies in, 71–72
  music of, 48, 50
  Olympic Games of, 58, 58, 67
  Peloponnesian War and, 64–71, 66, 79
  Persian Wars and, 58–61, 59
  philosophy of, 41, 51, 53, 61, 68–71
  poetry of, 46, 54, 58
  poleis of, 51–61
  politics in, 52–53, 69, 71
  prostitution in, 53–54
  religion in, 48, 48–49, 49, 51
  science in, 49–51, 50
  sculpture in, 48, 48, 63
  slavery in, 53–54, 57
  theater in, 64
  timeline for, 41
  women in, 53, 57
  writing in, 46
Greek Comedy, fourth century B.C.E., 70
Greek Fire, 194, 195
Greek language, 89, 91, 119, 126, 177, 195, 350
Greek peninsula, 42–44, 43
"Green Armies," 732
"green revolution," in agriculture, 802
greenhouse gas concentration, 839
Greenland, 175, 232
Gregory II, Pope, 196
Gregory of Tours, 186
Gregory the Great, Pope, 187–189, 217
Gregory VII, Pope, 267
Gregory XI, Pope, 287, 287
grenades, 709
Greuze, Jean-Baptiste: The Father's Curse, ca. 1778, 504, 505
Grimm, Friedrich, 472
Grimm fairy tales, 589
Grimmelshausen, John von, 343
Gropius, Walter, 727

Grosseteste, Robert, 258
Grosz, George: The Pillars of Society, 720
Guadalcanal, 765
Guarino da Verona, 313
Guérin, Pierre-Narcisse: Henri Duverger, earl of the Rochejaquelein, 1817, 527
Guerre, Martin, 347–348, 367, 375
Guevara, Che, 799
Guibert of Nogent, 253
guilds, 247–248, 313, 404, 502, 562
Guise family, 367
Guizot, François, 599
Gulag, 769
gunpowder, 290, 338, 345–347, 346, 369, 385, 394
"gunpowder plot," 435
guns, 300, 345, 407
Gupta dynasty, 39
Gustavus Adolphus, 369–371, 431
Gutenberg, Johannes, 316
Guthrum, 219
gymnasia, 92, 98

H

Habsburg dynasty, 266–267, 344, 349, 369, 427–429, 483–485, 600, 621
Habsburg-Valois Wars, 345, 349, 358, 360
haciendas, 396
Hadrian, 143, 147
Hadrian's Wall, 38, 147–148, 148, 153
Hadron Collider, 840
Hagia Sophia (Holy Wisdom), 537, 189, 190
Haiti, 531, 532, 537, 823
Haj, 199
Halley's comet, 261, 333
hallucinogens, 376
Hamas, 828
Hamburg firestorm, 764
Hammurabi, 13, 33
Han dynasty, 38, 145, 174
Han Wudi, 145
Handel, George Frideric, 505
Handwriting, Early Medieval, 225, 226
Hannibal Barca, 120–123
Hanoverian dynasty, 443–444, 490
Hanseatic cities, 642
Hanseatic League, 250
Hanukkah, 96
happiness, 474, 509
  of family life, 98, 666, 670–671
  Freud and, 684
Harald Sigurdson of Norway, 231–233
Harappa, 38
hard times, 664
Hardenberg, Baron, 578
Hargreaves, James, 553
Harmhab, 25
Harold Godwinson, 261
Harold Hardradi, 261
harpsichord, 333
Harter, William, 561
Harun al-Rashid, 208, 223–224
Harvey, William, 458
Hasan, 204
hashish, 673
Hasidic Judaism, 508, 638
Hastings, Battle of, 261
Hathaway, Anne, 339
Hatshepsut, 22–25, 25
Hauser, Heinrich, 737
Haussmann, Georges, 620, 664
Havel, Václav, 814–819, 817
  The Garden Party, 816
  Increased Difficulty of Concentration, 816
  Largo Desolato, 816
  The Memorandum, 816
  "The Power of the Powerless," 816
Hawes, Elizabeth, 763

Mun, Thomas: "*Discourse on England's Treasure by Foreign Trade*", 402
Munch, Edvard: *The Scream*, 685, *685*
Munich Conference, 747, 750
Munkacsy, Mihaly: *Paris Interior*, *670*
music
    baroque, 504
    of classical Greece, 48, 50
    of early Middle Ages, 223–224
    in Europe, eighteenth century, 504–506
    of Hellenistic Age, 91–93
    Phrygian modes of, 50
    of Renaissance, 331–333
    of romanticism, 587
    in Western society, 1850–1914, 686
musical notation, 223
Muslim societies, 197–209, *205*, 827. *See also*
        Ottoman Empire
    Africa and, 200, 202
    architecture in, 209
    banking techniques of, 201
    education in, 206–207
    equality in, 204
    as heirs to Hellenistic learning, 206–208
    hospitals in, 207
    literature of, 201, 208
    maritime raiders from, 228, *230*
    mathematics in, 207–208
    medicine in, 206–207
    philosophy in, 206–207, 209
    pilgrimages in, 199, 201
    reconquest of Muslim lands in Spain, 255,
        263–264, 276, 362
    science in, 206
    in Spain, 199, 203, *204*, *205*, 249
    women in, 202–203
Mussolini, Benito, 729, *731*, 731–732, 749, 754, 761
    downfall and death of, 764–765
    Roman Catholic Church and, 731
mutual aid societies, 562
Mycenaean civilization, 45–46
    trade in, 45
myrrh, 202
mystery religions, 157–158
    afterlife in, 100
    fresco, first century C.E., *158*
mysticism, 255, 257, 287, 349, 364–365, 586, 713

N

NAFTA. *See* North American Free Trade
        Agreement
Nagasaki, 757
Nagy, Imre, 786
Nain, Louis le: *The Cart*, 416, *417*
Nanking, 748, 769
Naples, 318–321, 335, 421, 564, 579, 593, 611
Napoleon III, 602, 611, 615, 620–621, 631, 664
Napoleonic Code of 1804, 535, 537, 539–540, 570
Napoleonic wars
    Austrian Empire and, 533, 536–537, 542
    Prussia and, 537, 542–543
    Russia and, 537, 542, 680
Nasser, Gamel Abdul, 793
nasturtium, 239
National Assembly of France, 519–522, 524, 620
National Convention, 525–526, 528, 530–531, 533
National Fascist Party, 731
National Front for the Liberation of Southern
        Vietnam, 781
National Order of Merit, 623
National Trades Union, 563
National Trades Union Congress, 634
National Union of Women's Suffrage
        Societies, 640
nationalism, 583–586, 588, 608–627
    Austrian Empire and, 618–619
    in Austro-Hungarian Empire, 633

authoritarian, 620
Balkan, 618–619
birth control and, 672
cultural, 584
economic, 403
fascism and, 730
in France, 619–621
imperialism and, 642–643
Japanese ultranationalism, 757
liberalism and, 603
Nationalist forces in China, 780
in Poland, 596
Roman Catholic Church and, 632
romanticism and, 588–589, 595
in Russia, 621–624
ultranationalism, 634, 637
in Yugoslavia, 821–832
nationalization
    of industry, 785, 788, 802
    of land in Russian Revolution, 716
    of Roman Catholic Church in France, 523
nation-states, building, 610
Native Americans, 174–175
NATO. *See* North Atlantic Treaty Organization
natural history, 69
Natural History of Brazil, 409
natural selection, 674, 677
naturalism, 679–681
Nauder, Caroline: *Journey of a Dying Man to the
        Other World*, 568, *568*
Naumann, Michael, 824
Navajo people, 391
Navarre, 263
Navigation Acts, 441
navigation instruments, 384
Nazi Art Council, 741
Nazi Germany (Third Reich), 657, 745, 771
    Afrika Korps of, 754, 763–764
    death camps of, 758–760
    decadence in, 742
    family life in, 741
    German Expansion, 1936–1939, *752*
    invasion of Denmark, 753
    invasion of France, 753
    invasion of Norway, 753
    invasion of Poland, 747–748, 750
    invasion of Soviet Union, 754–755
    Jews in, 739–740, 742, 747, 757, 759–760, 769
    Nazi-Soviet nonaggression pact, 750
    as police state, 741
    in World War II, 749–757, 759–769
Nazi Labor Front, 743
Nazism (National Socialism), 738–743
    collaboration with, 760–761
    growth of, 739
    Nazi Atrocities, 1945, 759
    youth organizations of, 741
Ndebele, 655
Near East, ancient, ca. 1450 B.C.E., *21*
Nebuchadrezzar, 33, 50
Necker, Jacques, 519
Nefertiti, *23*, 23–24
Neferure, 24
Nehru, Jawaharlal, 723
Nelson, Admiral, 533, 537
neoclassical style, 504
Neolithic period, 6–8, 391
    agriculture 0f, 6–8
Neoplatonism, 157, 168, 315, 453–454
NEP. *See* New Economic Policy
nepotism, 321, 322
Nero, 143, 163, 202
Nerva, 143
nervous breakdowns, 691
Netherlands
    in 1792, *534*
    Belgium and, 596
    "Council of Blood," 367–368

expansion by, 389
in Protestant Reformation, 344, 357, 367–369
as republic, 444–447
shipbuilding in, 445
South African colonies of, 389
Spanish Netherlands, 1609, *444*
tulip industry in, 402
unified, 578
War of Devolution in, 425
neutrality, 696, 731
New Comedy, 98
New Economic Policy (NEP), 732–733
"New Economic Zones," 826
New England, 436
New Guinea, 765
New Harmony, Indiana, 590
new imperialism, *629*, 642–656
New Kingdom, of Egypt, 22–24
New Model Army, 436
"new money," 433–434, 560, 662, 665
new nominalism, 294
New Plants and Animals, *407*
New Spain. *See* Mexico
New Stone Age. *See* Neolithic period
New York (city), 441
New York stock market crash, 737, 739
New Zealand, 641, 655, 701
Newcomen, Thomas, 554
Newton, Isaac, 443, 457, 462–463, *464*
    Opticks, 457
    Principia (*The Mathematical Principles of Natural
        Knowledge*), 457, 466
Newtonianism for Women, 463
Ngo Dihn Diem, 781
Nicaea, 167, 289
Nicene Creed, 167
Nicephorus, 223
Nicholas I, Tsar, 593, 601, 603
Nicholas II, Pope, 267
Nicholas II, Tsar, 638, 701, 710, 712–714, 717
Nietzsche, Friedrich, 684, 727
Nigeria, 723, 793
"Night of the Long Knives," 740
Nightingale, Florence, 622–623, *623*, 671
    Notes on Nursing, 623
Nika riot, 189
Nike (victory), 2002, *40*
Nike (Winged Victory), ca. 190 B.C.E., *90*
Nikitenko, Aleksandr, 625
Nikolayev, Leonid, 736
Nile, Battle of the, 533
Nile River, 15–17, 19, 21–22, 25, 158
Nîmes, 127
Niña, 386
Ninety-Five Theses, 351
Ninos, 98
Nitocris, 20
nitrous oxide, 568
Nivelle, General, 699
Noah, 198
Nobili, Roberto de, 400
nobility, 235, 238–239
    feudal obligations of warriors, 236–238
    loss of respect for, 433–434
    marriages of, 239
    Noble Couple Hunting, *261*
The Noble and the Peasant, Seventeenth
        Century, *418*
Noble Couple Hunting, *261*
A Noble's Estate in Russia, 1861, *624*
Nogarola, Isotta, 313
nominalism, 294
nonconformists, 435–436
Norman conquest, 261–262
Normandy, 262, 265
North America
    1755 and 1763, *497*
    national unity in, 617–618

North American Free Trade Agreement (NAFTA), 824
North Atlantic Treaty Organization (NATO), 778, 782, 822–824
North German Confederation, 614
North Korea, 780–781, 823
North Sea, 229
North Star, 384
A Northern Factory, 618
Northumbria, 215
Norway, 268, 753
novels
    in Enlightenment, 465, 473
    in Europe, eighteenth century, 503
    in Hellenistic Age, 98
    in Industrial Revolution, 569, 571
November revolution, 716
Novgorod, 299
Nubia, 17, 20–21, 31, 86, 92
nuclear weapons, 780, 814, 830
numerology, 461
Numidia, 122, 130
Nur Jahan, 432
Nuremberg, 741
Nuremberg Laws, 742
nursing, 622–623, 679
Nussbaum, Felix: Self-Portrait with Jewish Identity Card, 742, 742–743
nutrition, 239, 245

O

Obama, Barack, 824, 831
obituaries, Egyptian, 16
Ockham's razor, 294
Octavia, 139
Octavian. See Augustus Caesar
Odovacar, 183, 185
Oedipus, 64–65
oil prices, 800–802, 834
Okabe, Heiichi, 767
Okinawa, 765–766
Olaf Sigurdson, 233
Old and New Means of Warfare, 701
Old Kingdom, of Egypt, 15–20
Old Market Woman, third or second century B.C.E., 76
Old Regime, 1715–1789, 478–513
    timeline for, 479
Old Stone Age. See Paleolithic period
Old Testament, 162
oligarchy, 53, 71, 318, 444, 821
olive trees, 53
Olives, Mount of, 164
Olmec civilization, in Mexico, 832
Olympias, 79
Olympic Games, 58, 58, 67, 669, 778
Omdurman, Battle of, 645
"Open Door" policy, 653
opium, 207, 566, 652, 673
Opium Wars, in China, 651–652
optimates, 129–131, 133
optimism, 673–679, 681–686, 838–839
oracles, 49, 49
Orange Free State, 648
orator addressing the Roman people, 106
ordeal, 214–215
Order of the Dragon, 304
orderly universe, 51, 224
organ replacement, 807
Organization of Petroleum Exporting Countries (OPEC), 800–801
organized crime, 821
Origen, 582
Orlando, Vittorio, 706, 708
Orleanist dynasty, 632
Orléans, 292
Orosz, Istvan: Comrades, It's Over, 815, 815

Ortega y Gasset, José: Revolt of the Masses, 728
Orthodox Church, 196–197, 288, 303, 838
    Russian, 303, 431, 593
Orwell, George, 790
Oseberg Viking Ship, 231
Osiris, 15, 23, 100, 101, 157–158
ostracism, 57
ostracon, 57
Ostrogoths, 178, 182, 185–186, 191
Oswald, King, 242
Otto I, 266
Ottoman Empire
    in 1526, 345
    Austrian Empire and, 427–429
    in Crimean War, 610
    decline of, 482, 620
    Greece and, 594–595
    independence movements in, 618–619
    in late Middle Ages, 300–304, 301
    Russia and, 431, 482, 621
    trade and, 385
    Western Europe and, 344
    in World War I, 692–693, 701, 705, 708, 718
    Yemen and, 203
Ottonian dynasty, 266
overspending, 403–404
Owen, Robert, 590
Owen, Wilfred, 691, 699, 705, 709
oxen, 234, 499
Oxford University, 338

P

Pacific rim, 826–827
pacifists, 355, 696
"Pact of Steel," 749
Paganini, Niccolò, 587
pagans, 165, 182, 184, 188, 197, 217, 222
Paine, Thomas, 468, 524
Pakistan, 791, 833
Palatine Hill, 117
Paleolithic period, 4–7
    agriculture of, 6–7
    sculpture of, 5
    trade in, 5
Palestine, 96, 158–160, 165, 638, 723, 791–793
    Israeli-Palestinian conflict, 827–828
Palestine Liberation Organization (PLO), 803
Palmares, 399
Panama, 387, 391
Panama Canal, 645, 661
Pan-Arab unity, 827
Panathenaic festival, 56
pandemics, 153, 282–283, 837
Pan-German Association, 637
Pankhurst, Emmeline, 640, 640
Pantheon, 125 C.E., 127, 128, 328
Paolo di Giovanni Fei: Catherine of Siena, ca. 1447, 287, 287
papal curia, 268
papal infallibility, 632–633
Papal States, 186, 267–276, 321–323, 593, 611
Papal Supremacy, ca. 1007, 188
Papen, Franz von, 740
papyrus, 18, 98
Paracelsus, 458
Paradise, 295
parchment, 98, 225, 314
Paris, 252, 471, 664. See also French Revolution
Paris Commune, 525–526, 528, 631–632, 632
A Paris Department Store, 662
Paris Peace Conference, 611
parish priests, 166, 218, 226
parishes, 166, 223, 226, 232
Parks, Rosa, 798
Parlement of Paris, 265, 289
parlements, 488–490, 516–518

Parliament of Great Britain, 261–263
    Charles I and, 436
    key dates, 262
    "Long Parliament," 436
    "Model Parliament," 263
    politics in, 490–491
    Rump Parliament, 438–439
Parthenon, 63, 63, 64
Pascal, Blaise, 451
Passchendaele offensive, 699
Pasternak, Boris, 786
Pasteur, Louis, 678
Patel, Pierre, the Elder: View of Versailles, 1668, 423
patriarchs, 196, 303
patricians, 110–111
Patrick, Saint, 188
patriotism, 630
patronage, 315, 420, 423, 443, 491
patrons, 94, 111–112, 313–316, 321–322, 504
Paul, 161–163, 166, 419
Paullus Fabius Maximus, 140
Paulus, Friedrich, 763
Pausanias, 80
Pavlov, Ivan, 676–677
Pax Britannica (Britain's peace), 650
Pax Romana, 27 B.C.E. to 180 C.E., 138–148
"pay-bringers," 53
Peace Must Be Saved, 1948, 781
Peace of Amiens, 536
Peace of Augsburg, 354–355, 357, 369
Peace of Bretigny, 290
"Peace of God," 259
Peace of Nijmegen, 425
Peace of Utrecht, 425, 480
Peace of Westphalia, 368, 371
Pearl Harbor attack, by Japan, 755, 757
Pearson, Karl: National Life from the Standpoint of Science, 645
peasants
    Peasants in a Russian Village, 624
    Peasants' Revolt, 1381, 286
    revolt in French Revolution, 520–521
    revolt in late Middle Ages, 285–286
    revolt in Protestant Reformation, 353–354
peat, 416
Pedro Berruguete: Federico da Montefeltro and his son Guidobaldo, ca. 1476, 308
Peel, Robert, 565
peers, 433
Peloponnesian League, 65, 68
Peloponnesian War, 431–404 B.C.E., 64–71, 66, 79
penance, 351
penicillin, 407, 806
penology, 469
Pentagon, 827
Pentarchs, 196
pentathlon, 58
"people of the Book," 200
People's Charter, 597–598
People's Republic of China, 780
The People's Will, 633
Pepi II, 20
Pepin the Short, 185–186, 233
Pepys, Samuel, 440, 442–443, 443, 446
perestroika ("restructuring"), 813–814, 816–817, 819
Pergamum, 94, 95, 98, 101, 123
Pericles, 56–57, 62, 66
Periodic Table, 676
Perry, Matthew, 654
Persepolis, 34, 82
Persian Empire, 30, 33–36, 49
    ca. 500 B.C.E., 34
    Byzantine Empire and, 191–192, 197, 199, 201
    conquest by Alexander the Great, 80
    mercenary soldiers in, 71–72, 80
    religion in, 35–36
    Royal Road of, 34, 34